Twentieth-Century
Literary Criticism

Guide to Gale Literary Criticism Series

When you need to review criticism of literary works, these are the Gale series to use:

If the author's death date is:	You should turn to:
After Dec. 31, 1959 (or author is still living)	***CONTEMPORARY LITERARY CRITICISM*** for example: Jorge Luis Borges, Anthony Burgess, William Faulkner, Mary Gordon, Ernest Hemingway, Iris Murdoch
1900 through 1959	***TWENTIETH-CENTURY LITERARY CRITICISM*** for example: Willa Cather, F. Scott Fitzgerald, Henry James, Mark Twain, Virginia Woolf
1800 through 1899	***NINETEENTH-CENTURY LITERATURE CRITICISM*** for example: Fedor Dostoevski, Nathaniel Hawthorne, George Sand, William Wordsworth
1400 through 1799	***LITERATURE CRITICISM FROM 1400 TO 1800 (excluding Shakespeare)*** for example: Anne Bradstreet, Daniel Defoe, Alexander Pope, François Rabelais, Jonathan Swift, Phillis Wheatley ***SHAKESPEAREAN CRITICISM*** Shakespeare's plays and poetry
Antiquity through 1399	***CLASSICAL AND MEDIEVAL LITERATURE CRITICISM*** for example: Dante, Homer, Plato, Sophocles, Vergil, the Beowulf Poet

---

Gale also publishes related criticism series:

CHILDREN'S LITERATURE REVIEW

This series covers authors of all eras who write for the preschool through high school audience.

SHORT STORY CRITICISM

This series covers the major short fiction writers of all nationalities and periods of literary history.

ISSN 0276-8178

R

Volume 31

Twentieth-Century Literary Criticism

**Excerpts from Criticism of the
Works of Novelists, Poets, Playwrights,
Short Story Writers, and Other Creative Writers
Who Died between 1900 and 1960,
from the First Published Critical Appraisals
to Current Evaluations**

**Paula Kepos
Dennis Poupard
Editors**

**Marie Lazzari
Thomas Ligotti
Joann Prosyniuk
Associate Editors**

Gale Research Inc.
Book Tower • Detroit, Michigan 48226

Library of Congress Catalog Card Number 76-46132
ISBN 0-8103-2413-X
ISSN 0276-8178

Printed in the United States of America

Contents

Preface

It is impossible to overvalue the importance of literature in the intellectual, emotional, and spiritual evolution of humanity. Literature is that which both lifts us out of everyday life and helps us to better understand it. Through the fictive lives of such characters as Anna Karenina, Jay Gatsby, or Leopold Bloom, our perceptions of the human condition are enlarged, and we are enriched.

Literary criticism can also give us insight into the human condition, as well as into the specific moral and intellectual atmosphere of an era, for the criteria by which a work of art is judged reflect contemporary philosophical and social attitudes. Literary criticism takes many forms: the traditional essay, the book or play review, even the parodic poem. Criticism can also be of several types: normative, descriptive, interpretive, textual, appreciative, generic. Collectively, the range of critical response helps us to understand a work of art, an author, an era.

Scope of the Series

Twentieth-Century Literary Criticism (TCLC) is designed to serve as an introduction for the student of twentieth-century literature to the authors of the period 1900 to 1960 and to the most significant commentators on these authors. The great poets, novelists, short story writers, playwrights, and philosophers of this period are by far the most popular writers for study in high school and college literature courses. Since a vast amount of relevant critical material confronts the student, *TCLC* presents significant passages from the most important published criticism to aid students in the location and selection of commentaries on authors who died between 1900 and 1960.

The need for *TCLC* was suggested by the usefulness of the Gale series *Contemporary Literary Criticism (CLC)*, which excerpts criticism on current writing. Because of the difference in time span under consideration (*CLC* considers authors who were still living after 1959), there is no duplication of material between *CLC* and *TCLC*. For further information about *CLC* and Gale's other criticism series, users should consult the Guide to Gale Literary Criticism Series preceding the title page in this volume.

Each volume of *TCLC* is carefully compiled to include authors who represent a variety of genres and nationalities and who are currently regarded as the most important writers of this era. In addition to major authors, *TCLC* also presents criticism on lesser-known writers whose significant contributions to literary history are important to the study of twentieth-century literature.

Each author entry in *TCLC* is intended to provide an overview of major criticism on an author. Therefore, the editors include fifteen to twenty authors in each 600-page volume (compared with approximately thirty-five authors in a *CLC* volume of similar size) so that more attention may be given to an author. Each author entry represents a historical survey of the critical response to that author's work: some early criticism is presented to indicate initial reactions, later criticism is selected to represent any rise or decline in the author's reputation, and current retrospective analyses provide students with a modern view. The length of an author entry is intended to reflect the amount of critical attention the author has received from critics writing in English, and from foreign criticism in translation. Critical articles and books that have not been translated into English are excluded. Every attempt has been made to identify and include excerpts from the seminal essays on each author's work.

An author may appear more than once in the series because of the great quantity of critical material available, or because of a resurgence of criticism generated by events such as an author's centennial or anniversary celebration, the republication or posthumous publication of an author's works, or the publication of a newly translated work. Generally, a few author entries in each volume of *TCLC* feature criticism on single works by major authors who have appeared previously in the series. Only those individual works that have been the subjects of vast amounts of criticism and are widely studied in literature classes are selected for this in-depth treatment. George Orwell's *Animal Farm* and Willa Cather's *My Ántonia* are examples of such entries in *TCLC*, Volume 31.

Organization of the Book

An author entry consists of the following elements: author heading, biographical and critical introduction, list of principal works, excerpts of criticism (each preceded by explanatory notes and followed by a bibliographic citation), and an additional bibliography for further reading.

- The *author heading* consists of the author's full name, followed by birth and death dates. The unbracketed portion of the name denotes the form under which the author most commonly wrote. If an author wrote consistently under a pseudonym, the pseudonym will be listed in the author heading and the real name given in parentheses on the first line of the biographical and critical introduction. Also located at the beginning of the introduction to the author entry are any name variations under which an author wrote, including transliterated forms for authors whose languages use nonroman alphabets. Uncertainty as to a birth or death date is indicated by a question mark.

- The *biographical and critical introduction* contains background information designed to introduce the reader to an author and to the critical debate surrounding his or her work. References are provided to past volumes of *TCLC* and to other biographical and critical reference series published by Gale, including *Children's Literature Review, Contemporary Authors, Dictionary of Literary Biography*, and *Something about the Author*.

- Most *TCLC* entries include *portraits* of the author. Many entries also contain illustrations of materials pertinent to an author's career, including manuscript pages, title pages, dust jackets, letters, or representations of important people, places, and events in an author's life.

- The *list of principal works* is chronological by date of first book publication and identifies the genre of each work. In the case of foreign authors with both foreign-language publications and English translations, the title and date of the first English-language edition are given in brackets. Unless otherwise indicated, dramas are dated by first performance, not first publication.

- *Criticism* is arranged chronologically in each author entry to provide a perspective on changes in critical evaluation over the years. All titles by the author featured in the critical entry are printed in boldface type to enable the user to easily locate discussion of particular works. Also for purposes of easier identification, the critic's name and the publication date of the essay are given at the beginning of each piece of criticism. Unsigned criticism is preceded by the title of the journal in which it appeared. When an anonymous essay is later attributed to a critic, the critic's name appears in brackets at the beginning of the excerpt and in the bibliographic citation. Many critical entries in *TCLC* also contain translated material to aid users. Unless otherwise noted, translations within brackets are by the editors; translations within parentheses or continuous with the text are by the author of the excerpt. Publication information (such as publisher names and book prices) and parenthetical numerical references (such as footnotes or page and line references to specific editions of works) have been deleted at the editors' discretion to provide smoother reading of the text.

- Critical essays are prefaced by *explanatory notes* as an additional aid to students using *TCLC*. The explanatory notes provide several types of useful information, including the reputation of a critic, the importance of a work of criticism, the specific type of criticism (biographical, psychoanalytic, structuralist, etc.), a synopsis of the criticism, and the growth of critical controversy or changes in critical trends regarding an author's work. In some cases, these notes cross-reference the work of critics who discuss each other's commentary.

- A complete *bibliographic citation* designed to facilitate location of the original essay or book by the interested reader follows each piece of criticism.

- The *additional bibliography* appearing at the end of each author entry suggests further reading on the author. In some cases it includes essays for which the editors could not obtain reprint rights.

An acknowledgments section lists the copyright holders who have granted us permission to reprint material in this volume of *TCLC*. It does not, however, list every book or periodical reprinted or consulted in the preparation of the volume.

Cumulative Indexes

Each volume of *TCLC* includes a cumulative index listing all the authors who have appeared in *Contemporary Literary Criticism, Twentieth-Century Literary Criticism, Nineteenth-Century Literature Criticism, Literature Criticism from 1400 to 1800, Classical and Medieval Literature Criticism*, and *Short Story Criticism*, along with cross-references to the Gale series *Children's Literature Review, Authors in the News, Contemporary Authors, Contemporary Authors Autobiography Series, Dictionary of Literary Biography, Concise Dictionary of American Literary Biography, Something about the Author, Something about the Author Autobiography Series*, and *Yesterday's Authors of Books for Children*. Readers will welcome this cumulated author index as a useful tool for locating an author within the various series. The index, which lists birth and death dates, is particularly valuable for those authors who are identified with a certain period but whose death date causes them to be placed in another, or for those authors whose careers span two periods. For example, F. Scott Fitzgerald is found in *TCLC*, yet a writer often associated with him, Ernest Hemingway, is found in *CLC*.

Each volume of *TCLC* also includes a cumulative nationality index, in which authors' names are arranged alphabetically under their respective nationalities.

Title Index

An important feature of *TCLC* is a cumulative index to titles, an alphabetical listing of the literary works discussed in the series since its inception. Each title listing includes the corresponding volume and page numbers where criticism may be located. Foreign language titles that have been translated are followed by the titles of the translations—for example, *Voina i mir (War and Peace)*. Page numbers following these translated titles refer to all pages on which any form of the titles, either foreign language or translated, appear. Titles of novels, dramas, nonfiction books, and poetry, short story, or essay collections are printed in italics, while all individual poems, short stories, and essays are printed in roman type within quotation marks. In cases where the same title is used by different authors, the author's surname is given in parentheses after the title, e.g., *Collected Poems* (Housman) and *Collected Poems* (Yeats).

Acknowledgments

No work of this scope can be accomplished without the cooperation of many people. The editors especially wish to thank the copyright holders of the excerpted criticism included in this volume, the permissions managers of many book and magazine publishing companies for assisting us in securing reprint rights, and Anthony Bogucki for assistance with copyright research. We are also grateful to the staffs of the Detroit Public Library, the Library of Congress, the University of Detroit Library, the University of Michigan Library, and the Wayne State University Library for making their resources available to us.

Suggestions Are Welcome

In response to suggestions, several features have been added to *TCLC* since the series began, including explanatory notes to excerpted criticism, a cumulative author index listing authors in all Gale literary criticism series, entries devoted to criticism on a single work by a major author, more extensive illustrations, and a title index listing all literary works discussed in the series since its inception.

Readers who wish to suggest authors to appear in future volumes, or who have other suggestions, are cordially invited to write the editors.

Authors to Be Featured in Forthcoming Volumes

Henri Bergson (French philosopher)—One of the most influential philosophers of the twentieth century, Bergson is renowned for his opposition to the dominant materialist thought of his time and for his creation of theories that emphasize the supremacy and independence of suprarational consciousness.

Edgar Rice Burroughs (American novelist)—Burroughs was a science fiction writer who is best known as the creator of Tarzan. His *Tarzan of the Apes* and its numerous sequels have sold over thirty-five million copies in fifty-six languages, making Burroughs one of the most popular authors in the world.

Samuel Butler (English novelist and essayist)—Butler is best known for *The Way of All Flesh*, an autobiographical novel that is both a classic account of the conflict between father and son and an indictment of Victorian society.

Stephen Crane (American novelist and short story writer) Crane was one of the foremost realistic writers in American literature. *TCLC* will devote an entry to his masterpiece, *The Red Badge of Courage*, in which he depicted the psychological complexities of fear and courage in battle.

Theodore Dreiser (American novelist)—A prominent American exponent of literary Naturalism and one of America's foremost novelists, Dreiser was the author of works commended for their powerful characterizations and strong ideological convictions.

James George Frazer (Scottish anthropologist)—A social anthropologist who spent a lifetime examining and attempting to explain the primitive bases of human social behavior, Frazer is often linked with Charles Darwin, Karl Marx, Sigmund Freud, and Albert Einstein as central to the shaping the modern consciousness. He is best known as the author of *The Golden Bough*, a massive anthropological study that had a particular influence on the development of twentieth-century literature.

Thomas Hardy (English novelist)—Considered one of the greatest novelists in the English language, Hardy is best known for his portrayal of characters who are subject to social and psychological forces beyond their control. *TCLC* will devote an entry to *The Mayor of Casterbridge*, a tragedy of psychological determinism in which Hardy introduced his belief that "character is fate."

William James (American philosopher and psychologist)—One of the most influential figures in modern Western philosophy, James was the founder of Pragmatism, a philosophy that rejected abstract models of reality in an attempt to explain life as it is actually experienced.

Nikos Kazantzakis (Greek novelist)—Kazantzakis was the author of works embodying Nietzschean and Bergsonian philosophical ideas in vividly portrayed characters, the most famous of which was the protagonist of *Zorba the Greek*.

D. H. Lawrence (English novelist)–Controversial during his lifetime for the explicit sexuality of his works, today Lawrence is considered one of the most important novelists of the twentieth century for his innovative explorations of human psychology. *TCLC* will devote an entry to his highly esteemed novel *Women in Love*, which is often identified as the fullest exposition of Lawrence's complex personal mythology.

Thomas Mann (German novelist)—Mann is credited with reclaiming for the German novel an international stature it had not enjoyed since the time of the Romantics. *TCLC* will devote an entry to his novel *Buddenbrooks*, a masterpiece of Realism which depicts the rise and fall of a wealthy Hanseatic family.

Arthur Wing Pinero (English dramatist)—Once the most popular playwright in England, Pinero is remembered today for his topical "problem plays," which brought dramatic realism to the English stage, and for his well-crafted, highly successful farces.

Marcel Proust (French novelist)—Proust's multivolume *A la recherche du temps perdu (Remembrance of Things Past)* is among literature's works of highest genius. Combining a social historian's chronicle of turn-of-the-century Paris society, a philosopher's reflections on the nature of time and consciousness, and a psychologist's insight into a tangled network of personalities, the novel is acclaimed for conveying a profound view of all human existence.

Joseph Roth (Austrian novelist)—A chronicler of the last years of the Austro-Hungarian Empire, Roth is best known for his novels *Radetzky March, Job,* and *Flight without End*.

Italo Svevo (Italian novelist)—Svevo's ironic portrayals of the moral life of the bourgeoisie, which characteristically demonstrate the influence of the psychoanalytic theories of Sigmund Freud, earned him a reputation as the father of the modern Italian novel.

Mark Twain (American novelist)—Considered the father of modern American literature, Twain combined moral and social satire, adventure, and frontier humor to create such perenially popular books as *The Adventures of Tom Sawyer, The Adventures of Huckleberry Finn,* and *A Connecticut Yankee in King Arthur's Court*.

Additional Authors to Appear
in Future Volumes

Abbey, Henry 1842-1911
Abercrombie, Lascelles 1881-1938
Adamic, Louis 1898-1951
Ade, George 1866-1944
Agustini, Delmira 1886-1914
Akers, Elizabeth Chase 1832-1911
Aldrich, Thomas Bailey 1836-1907
Aliyu, Dan Sidi 1902-1920
Allen, Hervey 1889-1949
Archer, William 1856-1924
Arlen, Michael 1895-1956
Austin, Alfred 1835-1913
Bahr, Hermann 1863-1934
Bailey, Philip James 1816-1902
Barbour, Ralph Henry 1870-1944
Benjamin, Walter 1892-1940
Bennett, James Gordon, Jr. 1841-1918
Berdyaev, Nikolai Aleksandrovich 1874-1948
Beresford, J(ohn) D(avys) 1873-1947
Binyon, Laurence 1869-1943
Bishop, John Peale 1892-1944
Blake, Lillie Devereux 1835-1913
Blest Gana, Alberto 1830-1920
Blum, Léon 1872-1950
Bodenheim, Maxwell 1892-1954
Bowen, Marjorie 1886-1952
Byrne, Donn 1889-1928
Caine, Hall 1853-1931
Cannan, Gilbert 1884-1955
Carducci, Giosuè 1835-1907
Carswell, Catherine 1879-1946
Churchill, Winston 1871-1947
Corelli, Marie 1855-1924
Croce, Benedetto 1866-1952
Crofts, Freeman Wills 1879-1957
Cruze, James (Jens Cruz Bosen) 1884-1942
Curros, Enríquez Manuel 1851-1908
Dall, Caroline Wells (Healy) 1822-1912
Daudet, Léon 1867-1942
Delafield, E.M. (Edme Elizabeth Monica de la Pasture) 1890-1943
Deneson, Jacob 1836-1919
Diego, José de 1866-1918
Douglas, (George) Norman 1868-1952
Douglas, Lloyd C(assel) 1877-1951
Dovzhenko, Alexander 1894-1956
Drinkwater, John 1882-1937
Durkheim, Émile 1858-1917
Duun, Olav 1876-1939
Eaton, Walter Prichard 1878-1957
Eggleston, Edward 1837-1902
Erskine, John 1879-1951
Fadeyev, Alexander 1901-1956
Ferland, Albert 1872-1943

Field, Rachel 1894-1924
Flecker, James Elroy 1884-1915
Fletcher, John Gould 1886-1950
Fogazzaro, Antonio 1842-1911
Francos, Karl Emil 1848-1904
Frank, Bruno 1886-1945
Frazer, (Sir) George 1854-1941
Freud, Sigmund 1853-1939
Fröding, Gustaf 1860-1911
Fuller, Henry Blake 1857-1929
Futabatei Shimei 1864-1909
Gamboa, Federico 1864-1939
Glaspell, Susan 1876-1948
Glyn, Elinor 1864-1943
Golding, Louis 1895-1958
Gould, Gerald 1885-1936
Guest, Edgar 1881-1959
Gumilyov, Nikolay 1886-1921
Gyulai, Pal 1826-1909
Hale, Edward Everett 1822-1909
Hansen, Martin 1909-1955
Hernández, Miguel 1910-1942
Hewlett, Maurice 1861-1923
Heyward, DuBose 1885-1940
Hope, Anthony 1863-1933
Ilyas, Abu Shabaka 1903-1947
Imbs, Bravig 1904-1946
Ivanov, Vyacheslav Ivanovich 1866-1949
James, Will 1892-1942
Jammes, Francis 1868-1938
Johnson, Fenton 1888-1958
Johnston, Mary 1870-1936
Jorgensen, Johannes 1866-1956
King, Grace 1851-1932
Kirby, William 1817-1906
Kline, Otis Albert 1891-1946
Kohut, Adolph 1848-1916
Kuzmin, Mikhail Alexseyevich 1875-1936
Lamm, Martin 1880-1950
Leipoldt, C. Louis 1880-1947
Lima, Jorge De 1895-1953
Locke, Alain 1886-1954
López Portillo y Rojas, José 1850-1903
Louys, Pierre 1870-1925
Lucas, E(dward) V(errall) 1868-1938
Lyall, Edna 1857-1903
Machar, Josef Svatopluk 1864-1945
Maragall, Joan 1860-1911
Marais, Eugene 1871-1936
Masaryk, Tomas 1850-1939
Mayor, Flora Macdonald 1872-1932
McClellan, George Marion 1860-1934
Mirbeau, Octave 1850-1917
Mistral, Frédéric 1830-1914

Monro, Harold 1879-1932
Moore, Thomas Sturge 1870-1944
Móricz, Zsigmond 1879-1942
Morley, Christopher 1890-1957
Morley, S. Griswold 1883-1948
Murray, (George) Gilbert 1866-1957
Nansen, Peter 1861-1918
Nobre, Antonio 1867-1900
O'Dowd, Bernard 1866-1959
Ophuls, Max 1902-1957
Orczy, Baroness 1865-1947
Oskison, John M. 1874-1947
Ostaijen, Paul van 1896-1928
Owen, Seaman 1861-1936
Page, Thomas Nelson 1853-1922
Parrington, Vernon L. 1871-1929
Paterson, Andrew Barton 1864-1941
Peck, George W. 1840-1916
Phillips, Ulrich B. 1877-1934
Pinero, Arthur Wing 1855-1934
Powys, T. F. 1875-1953
Prévost, Marcel 1862-1941
Quiller-Couch, Arthur 1863-1944
Ramos, Graciliano 1892-1953
Randall, James G. 1881-1953
Rappoport, Solomon 1863-1944
Read, Opie 1852-1939
Reisen (Reizen), Abraham 1875-1953
Remington, Frederic 1861-1909
Reyes, Alfonso 1889-1959
Riley, James Whitcomb 1849-1916
Rinehart, Mary Roberts 1876-1958
Ring, Max 1817-1901
Rivera, José Eustasio 1889-1928
Rozanov, Vasily Vasilyevich 1856-1919
Saar, Ferdinand von 1833-1906
Sabatini, Rafael 1875-1950
Sakutaro, Hagiwara 1886-1942
Sanborn, Franklin Benjamin 1831-1917
Sánchez, Florencio 1875-1910
Santayana, George 1863-1952
Sardou, Victorien 1831-1908
Schickele, René 1885-1940
Seabrook, William 1886-1945
Shestov, Lev 1866-1938
Shiels, George 1886-1949
Singer, Israel Joshua 1893-1944
Solovyov, Vladimir 1853-1900
Sorel, Georges 1847-1922
Spector, Mordechai 1859-1922
Squire, J(ohn) C(ollings) 1884-1958
Stavenhagen, Fritz 1876-1906
Stockton, Frank R. 1834-1902
Subrahmanya Bharati, C. 1882-1921
Sylva, Carmen 1843-1916
Talvik, Heiti 1904-1947?

Taneda Santoka 1882-1940
Thoma, Ludwig 1867-1927
Tomlinson, Henry Major 1873-1958
Totovents, Vahan 1889-1937
Tuchmann, Jules 1830-1901
Turner, W(alter) J(ames) R(edfern) 1889-1946
Upward, Allen 1863-1926
Vachell, Horace Annesley 1861-1955

Van Dyke, Henry 1852-1933
Villaespesa, Francisco 1877-1936
Wallace, Edgar 1874-1932
Wallace, Lewis 1827-1905
Walsh, Ernest 1895-1926
Webster, Jean 1876-1916
Whitlock, Brand 1869-1927
Wilson, Harry Leon 1867-1939

Wolf, Emma 1865-1932
Wood, Clement 1888-1950
Wren, P(ercival) C(hristopher) 1885-1941
Yonge, Charlotte Mary 1823-1901
Yosano Akiko 1878-1942
Zecca, Ferdinand 1864-1947
Zeromski, Stefan 1864-1925

Readers are cordially invited to suggest additional authors to the editors.

Mikhail (Petrovich) Artsybashev

1878-1927

(Also transliterated as Artsuibashev, Artzibashef, Artzibasheff, Artzibashev, Artzybashef, and Artzybashev) Russian novelist, dramatist, short story writer, and essayist.

Artsybashev is chiefly remembered as the author of *Sanin (Sanine)*, an immensely popular novel of its time that detailed the sensual exploits of an unapologetic egoist. Extremely rebellious and nihilistic in spirit, Artsybashev was preoccupied with sex and death and with the stultification of the free expression of individual will by social conventions. In all of his works, society crumbles as its members succumb to despair and suicide; only Sanine, through his unabashed individualism and sensuality, avoids the spiritual malaise suffered by Artsybashev's other characters. However, in his later works, Artsybashev even doubts the viability of his own creed of anarchism as a response to the human condition and ultimately concedes the utter futility of being.

The only son of small landowners, Artsybashev was born in the Kharkov region of southern Russia. He was extremely unhappy in school, the brutal discipline of which he later described in his first short story, "Pasha Tumanov." He demonstrated an early aptitude for painting, and his father, a retired army officer who wanted his son to pursue a military career, reluctantly allowed him to study art. While attending art school, Artsybashev began writing, at first experimenting primarily with poetry. In 1898 he provoked a bitter feud with his father by marrying a woman of a slightly lower social class, and thereafter his father refused to support him financially. When Artsybashev left a year later to study at the Imperial Academy of fine arts, he earned money by drawing cartoons and writing articles for local newspapers. During the unsuccessful Revolution of 1905, which Artsybashev supported, he wrote several short stories that recorded some of the bloodiest and most dramatic events of the uprising. In 1907, the publication of *Sanine* brought Artsybashev immediate fame and inspired numerous imitations as well as *Sanine* cults which many young people organized in order to give expression to their defiance of tradition and restraint. Translated into every major European language, the novel was widely censored for its promotion of unrestrained sexuality and rebellion against authority. His next novel, *U posledney cherty (Breaking Point)*, was similarly rebellious in tone, and after its publication in 1912 Artsybashev was imprisoned for several months as an enemy of the czarist government, an experience that further confirmed his nihilistic and anarchistic beliefs. At this time, Artsybashev began writing dramas as well as fiction and soon began to publish *Svoboda*, a weekly magazine which became a vehicle for his opinions. The paper was suppressed after the outbreak of World War I, but was revived after the Bolshevik Revolution in 1917. Because of his anarchistic beliefs, Artsybashev soon became estranged from the Bolsheviks and was persecuted by them: *Svoboda* was again suppressed, he was imprisoned several times, and his books were placed on the "forbidden list." In 1923, Artsybashev left Russia for Poland, where he published bitter invectives against the Bolsheviks. He died of tuberculosis in Warsaw in 1927.

Sanine, Artsybashev's most widely read work, was a succès de scandale that glorified the defiant egoism of its eponymous protagonist. Rejecting the authority of society to limit his behavior, Sanine believes that only through self-willed activity, and not socially induced passivity, can life be lived to the fullest. Nicholas Luker wrote that "Sanin embodies Artsybashev's advocacy of the natural life free of moral and social constraints," and that the dominance that Sanine exerts over all of the other characters attests to the efficacy of his worldview. Sanine regards those who are constrained by society as vulgar and stupid, and the numerous suicides at the end of the novel as evidence that their social order is crumbling. While the novel was widely denounced as pornographic, some critics defended the artistic merit and philosophical sophistication of the work, and many have viewed Sanine as a literary descendant of German philosopher Friedrich Nietzsche's *Übermensch* ("superman") because of his unapologetic self-assertion. However, Artsybashev disavowed this comparison and instead pointed to the influence of Max Stirner, a nineteenth-century philosopher who argued that the suppression of human will by civilization and government subverted the natural expression of life. Early commentary on *Sanine* often discussed the work in relation to contemporary politics: Gilbert Cannan wrote in his preface to the first English translation that the novel "was written in the despair which seized the Intelligentsia of Russia after the last abortive revolution" in 1905. However, Artsybashev contended that the novel was written in 1903, but because of its controversial nature was withheld from publication until 1907; thus, later critics argued that interpreting the novel as a reaction to the failed Revolution of 1905 overestimates the social purpose of the book. Sanine, although openly defiant of all authority, has no interest in revolution nor in joining with others to achieve social change; he looks upon the submission of others to authority only as a sign of their own weakness.

While *Sanine* is in part an apology for the uncompromising pursuit of pleasure, *Breaking Point* emphasizes the bankruptcy of sensuality as a way of life. Sanine is never bored by his pursuit of pleasure; Dchenev, the central character in *Breaking Point*, becomes satiated and no longer interested in self-assertion. James Huneker, who described *Breaking Point* as "the most poignant and intolerable book I ever read," called Artsybashev "a prophet of pessimism." Death and suffering pervade the novel, a fact which has led many critics to compare it to the works of Fyodor Dostoevsky. However, whereas Dostoevsky saw suffering as a vehicle for redemption, Artsybashev recognized only the universality and inescapability of suffering. He concluded that the only response to endless and meaningless suffering is suicide, reflecting a pure intellectual nihilism that is the major theme of the novel. Artsybashev's dramas, like his novels, deal explicitly with sex and relations between men and women. They focus on what the author saw as the inevitable unhappiness of marriage, an institution that inhibits the natural desires of its participants. In his plays, Artsybashev continued to express the "anarchical individualism" that is the hallmark of his fiction.

Early critical reaction to Artsybashev's works concentrated on his frank treatment of sexuality and unabashed sensuality. Many critics dismissed *Sanine* as prurient; D. S. Mirsky, who called it "the Bible of every schoolboy and schoolgirl in Russia," maintained that it "contributed to [the] moral deterioration of Russian society, especially of provincial schoolgirls." Other critics, however, lauded Artsybashev for his daring frankness and found literary value in his works, praising their philosophical depth and artistic candor. Later critics, accustomed to what seemed at the time sensational excesses, have recognized the value in Artsybashev's articulation of the moral, social, and intellectual turmoil of his age.

PRINCIPAL WORKS

Sanin   (novel)   1907
   [*Sanine*, 1915]
U posledney cherty   (novel)   1912
   [*Breaking Point*, 1915]
Revnost   (drama)   1913
   [*Jealousy*, 1923]
Vragi   (drama)   1913
   [*Enemies*, 1927]
Zakon dikarya   (drama)   1913
   [*The Law of the Savage*, 1923]
The Millionaire   (short stories)   1915
Voyna   (drama)   1915
   [*War*, 1915]
Tales of the Revolution   (short stories)   1917
*Dikie   (novel)   1923
   [*The Savage*, 1924]
Zapisky pisatelya   (essays)   1925

*This work was written during 1917 and 1918.

WILLIAM LYON PHELPS   (essay date 1911)

[*An American critic and educator, Phelps was for over forty years a lecturer on English literature at Yale. His early study* The Beginning of the English Romantic Movement *(1893) is still considered an important work and his* Essays on Russian Novelists *(1911) was one of the first influential studies in English of the Russian Realists. From 1922 until his death in 1943 he wrote a regular column for* Scribner's Magazine *and a nationally syndicated newspaper column. During this period, his criticism became less scholarly and more journalistic. In the following excerpt, he discusses the major themes of* Sanine.]

Not the greatest, but the most sensational, novel published in Russia during the last five years is *Sanin,* by Artsybashev. It is not sensational in the incidents, though two men commit suicide, and two girls are ruined; it is sensational in its ideas. To make a sensation in contemporary Russian literature is an achievement, where pathology is now rampant. But Artsybashev accomplished it, and his novel made a tremendous noise, the echoes of which quickly were heard all over curious and eclectic Germany, and have even stirred Paris. Since the failure of the Revolution, there has been a marked revolt in Russia against three great ideas that have at different times dominated Russian literature: the quiet pessimism of Turgenev, the Christian non-resistance religion of Tolstoi, and the familiar Russian type of will-less philosophy. Even before the Revolution Gorki had expressed the spirit of revolt; but his position,

extreme as it appears to an Anglo-Saxon, has been left far behind by Artsybashev, who, with the genuine Russian love of the *reductio ad absurdum,* has reached the farthest limits of moral anarchy in the creation of his hero Sanin.

In an admirable article in the *Westminster Gazette,* for 14 May 1910, by the accomplished scholar and critic, Mr. R. C. Long, called "The Literature of Self-assertion," we obtain a strong smell of the hell-broth now boiling in Russian literature. . . .

> Russia always had her literature of adventure, and Russian novels of manners and of psychology became known to Westerners merely because they were the best, and by no means because they were the only books that appeared. The popular taste was formerly met with naïve and outrageous "lubotchniya"-books. The new craze for "Nat Pinkerton and Sherlock Holmes" stories is something quite different. It foreshadows a complete change in the psychosis of the Russian reader, the decay of the literature of passivity, and the rise of a new literature of action and physical revolt. The literature of passivity reached its height with the *(sic)* Chekhov. The best representative of the transition from Chekhov to the new literature of self-assertion is Maxim Gorki's friend, Leonid Andreev. . . .
>
> These have got clear away from the humble, ineffectual individual, "crushed by life." Full of learned philosophies from Max Stirner and Nietzsche, they preach, in Stirner's words, "the absolute independence of the individual, master of himself, and of all things." "The death of Everyday-ism," the "resurrection of myth," "orgiasm," "mystical Anarchism," and "universalist individualism" are some of the shibboleths of these new writers, who are mostly very young, very clever, and profoundly convinced that they are even cleverer than they are.
>
> Anarchism, posing as self-assertion, is the note in most recent Russian literature, as, indeed, it is in Russian life.

The most powerful among this school of writers, and the only one who can perhaps be called a man of genius, is Michael Artsybashev. He came honestly by his hot, impulsive temperament, being, like Gogol, a man of the South. (pp. 248-50)

Sanin appeared at the psychological moment, late in the year 1907. The Revolution was a failure, and it being impossible to fight the government or to obtain political liberty, people in Russia of all classes were ready for a revolt against moral law, the religion of self-denial, and all the conventions established by society, education, and the church. At this moment of general desperation and smouldering rage, appeared a work written with great power and great art, deifying the natural instincts of man, incarnating the spirit of liberty in a hero who despises all so-called morality as absurd tyranny. It was a bold attempt to marshal the animal instincts of humanity, terrifically strong as they are even in the best citizens, against every moral and prudential restraint. The effect of the book will probably not last very long,—already it has been called an ephemeral sensation,—but it was immediate and tremendous. It was especially powerful among university students and high school boys and girls—the "Sanin-morals" of undergraduates were alluded to in a speech in the Duma.

But although the book was published at the psychological moment, it was written with no reference to any post-revolution spirit. For Artsybashev composed his novel in 1903, when he was twenty-four years old. He tried in vain to induce publishers to print it, and fortunately for him, was obliged to wait until 1907, when the time happened to be exactly ripe.

The novel has been allowed to circulate in Russia, because it shows absolutely no sympathy with the Revolution or with the spirit of political liberty. Men who waste their time in the discussion of political rights or in the endeavour to obtain them are ridiculed by Sanin. The *summum bonum* [''supreme good''] is personal, individual happiness, the complete gratification of desire. Thus, those who are working for the enfranchisement of the Russian people, for relief from the bureaucracy, and for more political independence, not only have no sympathy with the book—they hate it, because it treats their efforts with contempt. Some of them have gone so far as to express the belief that the author is in a conspiracy with the government to bring ridicule on their cause, and to defeat their ever living hopes of better days. However this may be, *Sanin* is not in the least a politically revolutionary book, and critics of that school see no real talent or literary power in its pages.

But, sinister and damnable as its tendency is, the novel is written with extraordinary skill, and Artsybashev is a man to be reckoned with. The style has that simplicity and directness so characteristic of Russian realism, and the characters are by no means sign-posts of various opinions; they are living and breathing human beings. I am sorry that such a book as *Sanin* has ever been written; but it cannot be black-balled from the republic of letters.

It is possible that it is a florescence not merely of the author's genius, but of his sickness. The glorification of Sanin's bodily strength, of Karsavina's female voluptuousness, and the loud call to physical joy which rings through the work may be an emanation of tuberculosis as well as that of healthy mental conviction. Shut out from active happiness, Artsybashev may have taken this method of vicarious delight.

The bitterness of his own enforced resignation of active happiness and the terror inspired by his own disease are incarnated in a decidedly interesting character, Semionov, who, although still able to walk about when we first see him, is dying of consumption. He has none of the hopefulness and cheerfulness so often symptomatic of that malady; he is peevish, irritable, and at times enraged by contact with his healthy friends. After a frightful attack of coughing, he says:

> I often think that soon I shall be lying in complete darkness. You understand, with my nose fallen in and my limbs decayed. And above me, where you are on the earth, everything will go on, exactly as it does now, while I still am permitted to see it. You will be living then, you will look at this very moon, you will breathe, you will pass over my grave; perhaps you will stop there a moment and despatch some necessity. And I shall lie and become rotten.

His death at the hospital in the night, with his friends looking on, is powerfully and minutely described. The fat, stupid priest goes through the last ceremonies, and is dully amazed at the contempt he receives from Sanin.

Sanin's beautiful sister Lyda is ruined by a worthless but entirely conventional officer. Her remorse on finding that she is with child is perfectly natural, but is ridiculed by her brother, who saves her from suicide. He is not in the least ashamed of her conduct, and tells her she has no reason for loss of pride; indeed, he does not think of blaming the officer. He is ready to commit incest with his sister, whose physical charm appeals to him; but she is not sufficiently emancipated for that, so he

advises her to get married with a friend who loves her, before the child is born. This is finally satisfactorily arranged. Later, Sanin, not because he disapproves of the libertine officer's affair with his sister, but because he regards the officer as a blockhead, treats him with scant courtesy; and the officer, hidebound by convention, sees no way out but a challenge to a duel. The scene when the two brother officers bring the formal challenge to Sanin is the only scene in the novel marked by genuine humour, and is also the only scene where we are in complete sympathy with the hero. One of the delegates has all the stiff courtesy and ridiculous formality which he regards as entirely consistent with his errand; the other is a big, blundering fellow, who has previously announced himself as a disciple of Tolstoi. To Sanin's philosophy of life, duelling is as absurd as religion, morality, or any other stupid conventionality; and his cold, ruthless logic makes short work of the polite phrases of the two ambassadors. Both are amazed at his positive refusal to fight, and hardly know which way to turn; the disciple of Tolstoi splutters with rage because Sanin shows up his inconsistency with his creed; both try to treat him like an outcast, but make very little progress. Sanin informs them that he will not fight a duel, because he does not wish to take the officer's life, and because he does not care to risk his own; but that if the officer attempts any physical attack upon him in the street, he will thrash him on the spot. Enraged and bewildered by Sanin's unconventional method of dealing with the difficulty, the discomfited emissaries withdraw. Later, the challenger meets Sanin in the street, and goaded to frenzy by his calm and contemptuous stare, strikes him with a whip; he immediately receives in the face a terrible blow from his adversary's fist, delivered with all his colossal strength. A friend carries him to his lodgings, and there he commits suicide. From the conventional point of view, this was the only course left to him.

In direct contrast to most Russian novels, the man here is endowed with limitless power of will, and the women characterised by weakness. The four women in the story, Sanin's sister Lyda, the pretty school-teacher Karsavina, Jurii's sister, engaged to a young scientist, who during the engagement cordially invites her brother to accompany him to a house of ill-fame, and the mother of Sanin, are all thoroughly conventional, and are meant to be. They are living under what Sanin regards as the tyranny of social convention. He treats his mother's shocked amazement with brutal scorn; he ridicules Lyda's shame at being *enceinte* [''pregnant'']; he seduces Karsavina, at the very time when she is in love with Jurii, and reasons with cold patience against her subsequent remorse. It is clear that Artsybashev believes that for some time to come women will not accept the gospel of uncompromising egoism.

The most interesting character in the book, apart from the hero, is Jurii, who might easily have been a protagonist in one of Turgenev's tragedies. He is the typical Russian, the highly educated young man with a diseased will. He is characterised by that indecision which has been the bane of so many Russians. All through the book he seeks in vain for some philosophy of life, some guiding principle. He has abandoned faith in religion, his former enthusiasm for political freedom has cooled, but he simply cannot live without some leading Idea. He is an acute sufferer from that mental sickness diagnosed by nearly all writers of Russia. He envies and at the same time despises Sanin for his cheerful energy. Finally, unable to escape from the perplexities of his own thinking, he commits suicide. His friends stand about his grave at the funeral, and one of them foolishly asks Sanin to make some appropriate remarks. Sanin, who always says exactly what he thinks, and abhors all forms of hypocrisy, delivers the following funeral oration—heartily endorsed by the reader—in one sentence: "The world has now one blockhead the less." The horror-stricken consternation of his friends fills Sanin with such scorn that he leaves the town, and we last see him in an open field in the country, giving a glad shout of recognition to the dawn.

The motto that Artsybashev has placed at the beginning of the novel is taken from Ecclesiastes vii. 29: "God hath made man upright: but they have sought out many inventions." This same text was used by Kipling as the title of one of his books, but used naturally in a quite different way. The Devil has here cited Scripture for his purpose. The hero of the novel is an absolutely sincere, frank, and courageous *Advocatus Diaboli*. He is invariably calm and collected; he never loses his temper in an argument; he questions the most fundamental beliefs and principles with remorseless logic. Two of his friends are arguing about Christianity; "at least," says one, "you will not deny that its influence has been good." "I don't deny that," says the other. Then Sanin remarks quietly, "But I deny it!" and he adds, with a calmness provoking to the two disputants, "Christianity has played an abominable rôle in history, and the name of Jesus Christ will for some time yet oppress humanity like a curse."

Sanin insists that it is not necessary to have any theory of life, or to be guided by any principle; that God may exist or He may not; He does not at any rate bother about us. The real rational life of man should be exactly like a bird. He should be controlled wholly by the desire of the moment. The bird wishes to alight on a branch, and so he alights; then he wishes to fly, so he flies. That is rational, declares Sanin; that is the way men and women should live, without principles, without plans, and without regrets. Drunkenness and adultery are nothing to be ashamed of, nor in any sense to be called degrading. Nothing that gives pleasure can ever be degrading. The love of strong drink and the lust for woman are not sins; in fact, there is no such thing as sin. These passions are manly and natural, and what is natural cannot be wrong. There is in Sanin's doctrine something of Nietzsche and more of Rousseau.

Sanin himself is not at all a contemptible character. He is not argumentative except when dragged into an argument; he does not attempt to convert others to his views. He has the inner light which we more often associate with Christian faith. In the midst of his troubled and self-tortured comrades, Sanin stands like a pillar, calm, unshakable. He has found absolute peace, absolute harmony with life. He thinks, talks, and acts exactly as he chooses, without any regard whatever to the convenience or happiness of any one else. There is something refreshing about this perfectly healthy, clear-eyed, quiet, composed, resolute man—whose way of life is utterly unaffected by public opinion, who simply does not care a straw for anything or anybody but himself. Thus he recognises his natural foe in Christianity, in the person of Jesus Christ, and in His Russian interpreter, Leo Tolstoi. For if Christianity teaches anything, it teaches that man must live contrary to his natural instincts. The endeavour of all so-called "new religions" is rootless, because it is an attempt to adapt Christianity to modern human convenience. Much better is Sanin's way: he sees clearly that no adaptation is possible, and logically fights Christianity as the implacable enemy of the natural man. (pp. 251-60)

William Lyon Phelps, "Artsybashev," *in his* Essays on Russian Novelists, *The Macmillan Company, 1911, pp. 248-61.*

JAMES HUNEKER   (essay date 1915)

[Huneker was an American musician and critic. As a critic, he concentrated on discovering the best of European music and literature and introducing them to the American public. Huneker was an early advocate of impressionism in literary criticism and, as such, his writings in this genre were characteristically subjective and marked by his often contagious enthusiasms, love for the voluptuous and eloquent prose style. Huneker's critical ideas strongly influenced many young writers of the twenties. In the following excerpt, he surveys Artsybashev's works, focusing on Sanine *and* Breaking Point.]

Little more than a decade has passed since the appearance of a young man named Michael Artzibashef who, without any preliminary blaring of trumpets, has taken the centre of the stage and still holds it. He is as Slavic as Dostoievsky, more pessimistic than Tolstoy, though not the supreme artist that was Turgenev. Of Gogol's overwhelming humour he has not a trace; instead, a corroding irony which eats into the very vitals of faith in all things human. Gorky, despite his "bitter" nickname, is an incorrigible optimist compared with Artzibashef. One sports with Nietzsche, the other not only swears by Max Stirner, but some of his characters are Stirnerism incarnate. His chosen field in society is the portrayal of the middle-class and proletarian. (pp. 34-5)

His first successful tale was **"Ivan Lande."** It brought him recognition. This was in 1904. But the year before he had finished *Sanine,* his masterpiece, though it did not see publication till 1908. This was three years after the revolution of 1905, so that those critics were astray who spoke of the book as a naturally pessimistic reaction from the fruitless uprising. Pessimism was born in the bones of the author and he needed no external stimulus to provoke such a realistic study as *Sanine.* Whether he is happier, healthier, whether he has married and raised a family, we know not. Personal as his stories are said to be, their art renders them objective.

The world over *Sanine* has been translated. It is a significant book, and incorporates the aspirations of many young men and women in the Russian Empire. It was not printed at first because of the censorship, and in Germany it had to battle for its life.

It is not only written from the standpoint of a professed immoralist, but the Russian censor declared it pernicious because of its "defamation of youth," its suicidal doctrine, its depressing atmosphere. The sex element, too, has aroused indignant protests from the clergy, from the press, from society itself.

In reply to his critics Artzibashef has denied libelling the younger generation. *"Sanine,"* he says, "is the apology for individualism: the hero of the novel is a type. In its pure form this type is still new and rare, but its spirit is in every frank, bold, and strong representative of the new Russia." And then he adds his own protest against the imitators of *Sanine,* who "flooded the literary world with pornographic writings." Now, whatever else it may be, *Sanine* is not pornographic, though I shall not pretend to say that its influence has been harmless. We should not forget *Werther* and the trail of sentimental suicides that followed its publication. But *Sanine* is fashioned of sterner stuff than Goethe's romance, and if it be "dangerous," then all the better.

Test all things, and remember that living itself is a dangerous affair. Never has the world needed precepts of daring, courage, individualism more than in this age of cowardly self-seeking, and the sleek promises of altruism and its soulless well-being. *Sanine* is a call to arms for individualists. And recall the Russian saying: Self-conceit is the salt of life.

That Artzibashef denies the influence of Nietzsche while admitting his indebtedness to Nietzsche's forerunner, Max Stirner, need not particularly concern us. There are evidences scattered throughout the pages of *Sanine* that prove a close study of Nietzsche and his idealistic superman. Artist as is Artzibashef, he has densely spun into the fabric of his work the ideas that control his characters, and whether these ideas are called moral or immoral does not matter. The chief thing is whether they are propulsive forces in the destiny of his puppets.

That he paints directly from life is evident: he tells us that in him is the débris of a painter compelled by poverty to relinquish his ambitions because he had not money enough to buy paper, pencil, colour. Such a realistic brush has seldom been wielded as the brush of Artzibashef. I may make one exception, that of J.-K. Huysmans. The Frenchman is the greater artist, the greater master of his material, and, as Havelock Ellis puts it, the master of "the intensest vision of the modern world"; but Huysmans lacks the all-embracing sympathy, the tremulous pity, the love of suffering mankind that distinguishes the young Russian novelist, a love that is blended with an appalling distrust, nay, hatred of life. Both men prefer the sordid, disagreeable, even the vilest aspects of life.

The general ideas of Artzibashef are few and profound. The leading motive of his symphony is as old as Ecclesiastes: "The thing that hath been, it is that which shall be." It is not original, this theme, and it is as eternal as mediocrity; but it has been orchestrated anew by Artzibashef, who, like his fellow countrymen, Tschaikovsky and Moussorgsky, contrives to reveal to us, if no hidden angles of the truth, at least its illusion in terms of terror, anguish, and deadly nausea produced by mere existence. With such poisoned roots Artzibashef's tree of life must soon be blasted. His intellectual indifferentism to all that constitutes the solace and bravery of our daily experience is almost pathological. The aura of sadism hovers about some of his men. After reading Artzibashef you wonder that the question, "Is life worth living?" will ever be answered in the affirmative among these humans, who, as old Homer says, hasten hellward from their birth.

The corollary to this leading motive is the absolute futility of action. A paralysis of the will overtakes his characters, the penalty of their torturing introspection. It was Turgenev, in an essay on Hamlet, who declared that the Russian character is composed of Hamlet-like traits. Man is the only animal that cannot live in the present; a Norwegian philosopher, Sören Kierkegaard, has said that he lives forward, thinks backward; he aspires to the future. An idealist, even when close to the gorilla, is doomed to disillusionment. He discounts to-morrow.

Russian youth has not always the courage of its chimera, though it fraternises with the phantasmagoria of its soul. Its Golden Street soon becomes choked with fog. The political and social conditions of the country must stifle individualism, else why should Artzibashef write with such savage intensity? His pen is the pendulum that has swung away from the sentimental brotherhood of man as exemplified in Dostoievsky, and from the religious mania of Tolstoy to the opposite extreme, individual anarchy. Where there is repression there is rebellion. Max Stirner represents the individualism which found its vent in the Prussia of 1848; Nietzsche the reaction from the Prussia of 1870; Artzibashef forestalled the result of the 1905 insurrection in Russia.

His prophetic soul needed no proof; he knew that his people, the students and intellectuals, would be crushed. The desire of the clod for the cloud was extinguished. Happiness is an eternal hoax. Only children believe in life. The last call of the devil's dinner-bell has sounded. In the scenery of the sky there is only mirage. The moonlit air is a ruse of that wily old serpent, nature, to arouse romance in the breast of youth and urge a repetition of the life processes. We graze Schopenhauer, overhear Leopardi, but the Preacher has the mightiest voice. Naturally, the novelist says none of these things outright. The phrases are mine, but he points the moral in a way that is all his own.

What, then, is the remedy for the ills of this life? Is its misery irremediable? Why must mankind go on living if the burden is so great? Even with wealth comes ennui or disease, and no matter how brilliant we may live, we must all die alone. Pascal said this better. In several of his death-bed scenes the dying men of Artzibashef curse their parents, mock at religion, and— here is a novel nuance—abuse their intellectual leaders. Semenow the student, who appears in several of the stories, abuses Marx and Nietzsche. Of what use are these thinkers to a man about to depart from the world? It is the revolt of stark humanity from the illusions of brotherly love, from the chiefest illusion—self.

Artzibashef offers no magic draft of oblivion to his sufferers. With a vivid style that recalls the Tolstoy of *The Death of Ivan Illitch* he shows us old and young wrestling with the destroyer, their souls emptied of all earthly hopes save one. Shall I live? Not God's will be done, not the roseate dream of a future life, only—why must I die? though the poor devil is submerged in the very swamp of life. But life, life, even a horrible hell for eternity, rather than annihilation! In the portrayal of these damned creatures Artzibashef is elemental. He recalls both Dante and Dostoievsky.

He has told us that he owes much to Tolstoy (also to Goethe, Hugo, Dostoievsky, and much to Tchekov), but his characters are usually failures when following the tenets of Tolstoy, the great moralist and expounder of "non-resistance." He simply explodes the torpedo of truth under the ark of socialism. This may be noted in **"Ivan Lande"**—now in the English volume entitled *The Millionaire*—where we see step by step the decadence of a beautiful soul obsessed by the love of his fellows.

It is in the key of Tolstoy, but the moral is startling. Not thus can you save your soul. Max Stirner is to the fore. Don't turn your other cheek if one has been smitten, but smite the smiter, and heartily. However, naught avails, you must die, and die like a dog, a star, or a flower. Better universal suicide. Success comes only to the unfortunate. And so we swing back to Eduard von Hartmann, who, in his philosophy of the unconscious, counsels the same thing. (A ferocious advocate of pessimism and a disciple of Arthur Schopenhauer, by name Maïnlander, preached world destruction through race suicide.)

But all these pessimists seem well fed and happy when compared to the nihilists of Artzibashef. He portrays every stage of disillusionment with a glacial calmness. Not even annihilation is worth the trouble of a despairing gesture. Cui bono? Revolutionist or royalist—your career is, if you but dare break the conspiracy of silence—a burden or a sorrow. Happiness is only a word. Love a brief sensation. Death a certainty. For such nihilism we must go to the jungles of Asia, where in a life-long silence, some fanatic fatidically stares at his navel, the circular symbol of eternity.

But if there is no philosophical balm in Gilead, there is the world of the five senses, and a glorious world it may prove if you have only the health, courage, and contempt for the Chinese wall with which man has surrounded his instincts. There are no laws, except to be broken, no conventions that cannot be shattered. There is the blue sky, brother, and the air on the heath, brother! Drop the impedimenta and lead a free, roving life. How the world would wag without work no one tells us. Not didactic, the novelist disdains to draw a moral.

There is much Stirner, some Nietzsche in Sanine, who is a handsome young chap, a giant, and a "blond barbarian." It is the story of the return of the native to his home in a small town. He finds his mother as he left her, older, but as narrow as ever, and his sister Lydia, one of the most charming girls in Russian fiction. Sanine is surprised to note her development. He admires her—too much so for our Western taste. However, there is something monstrous in the moral and mental make-up of this hero, who is no hero. He may be a type, but I don't believe in types; there are only humans. His motto might be: What's the difference? He is passive, not with the fatalism of Oblomov, Gontcharov's hero; not with the apathy of Charles Bovary, or the timid passivity of Frederic Moreau; he displays an indifference to the trivial things of life that makes him seem an idler on the scene.

When the time arrives for action he is no skulker. His sister has been ruined by a frivolous officer in garrison, and she attempts suicide. Her brother rescues her, not heroically, but philosophically, and shows her the folly of believing in words. Ruined! Very well, marry and forget! However, he drives the officer to suicide by publicly disgracing him. He refuses a duel, punches his head, and the silly soldier with his silly code of honour blows out his brains. A passive rôle is Sanine's in the composition of this elaborate canvas, the surface simplicity of which deceives us as to its polyphonic complexity. He remains in the background while about him play the little destinies of little souls. Yet he is always the fulcrum for a climax. I have not yet made up my mind whether Sanine is a great man or a thorough scoundrel. Perhaps both.

A temperamental and imaginative writer is Artzibashef. I first read him (1911) in French, the translation of Jacques Povolozky, and his style recalled, at times, that of Turgenev, possibly because of the language. In the German translation he is not so appealing; again perhaps because of the difference in the tongues. As I can't read Russian, I am forced to fall back on translations, and they seldom give an idea of personal rhythm, unless it be a Turgenev translating into Russian the *Three Tales* of his friend Flaubert.

Nevertheless, through the veil of a foreign speech the genius of Artzibashef shines like a crimson sun in a mist. Of course, we miss the caressing cadence and rich sonorousness of the organ-toned Russian language. The English versions are excellent, though, naturally enough, occasionally chastened and abbreviated. I must protest here against the omission of a chapter in *Breaking Point* which is a key to the ending of the book. I mean the chapter in which is related the reason why the wealthy drunkard goes to the monastery, there to end his days. Years ago Mr. Howells said that we could never write of America as Dostoievsky did of Russia, and it was true enough at the time; nor, would we ever tolerate the nudities of certain Gallic novelists. Well, we have, and I am fain to believe that

the tragic issues of American life should be given fuller expression, and with the same sincerity as Artzibashef's, whose strength is his sincerity, whose sincerity is a form of his genius.

The very air of America makes for optimism; our land of milk and honey may never produce such prophets of pessimism as Artzibashef, unless conditions change. But the lesson for our novelists is the courageous manner—and artistic, too—with which the Russian pursues the naked soul of mankind and dissects it. He notes, being a psychologist as well as a painter, the exquisite recoil of the cerebral cells upon themselves which we call consciousness. Profoundly human in his sympathies, without being in the least sentimental, he paints full-length portraits of men and women with a flowing brush and a fine sense of character values. But he will never bend the bow of Balzac.

Vladimir Sanine is not his only successful portrait. In the book there are several persons: the disgraced student Yourii, who is self-complacent to the point of morbidity; his lovely sister, and her betrothed. The officers are excellently delineated and differentiated, while the girls, Sina Karsavina and her friend the teacher, are extremely attractive.

Karsavina is a veracious personality. The poor little homeless Hebrew who desires light on the mystery of life could not be bettered by Dostoievsky; for that matter Artzibashef is partially indebted to Dostoievsky for certain traits of Ivan Lande—who is evidently patterned from Prince Myshkin in *The Idiot*. Wherever Sanine passes, trouble follows. He is looked on as possessing the devil's eye, yet he does little but lounge about, drink hard, and make love to pretty girls. But as he goes he snuffs out ideals like candles.

As Artzibashef is a born story-teller, it must not be supposed that the book is unrelieved in its gloom. There are plenty of gay episodes, sensational, even shocking; a picnic, a shooting-party, and pastorals done in a way which would have extorted the admiration of Turgenev. Thomas Hardy has done no better in his peasant life. There are various gatherings, chiefly convivial, a meeting of would-be intellectuals for self-improvement—related with blasting irony—and drinking festivals which are masterly in their sense of reality; add to these pages of nature descriptions, landscapes, pictures of the earth in all seasons and guises, revealing a passionate love of the soil which is truly Russian. You fairly smell the frosty air of his Winter days.

Little cause for astonishment that *Sanine* at its appearance provoked as much controversy, as much admiration and hatred as did *Fathers and Sons* of Turgenev. Vladimir Sanine is not as powerful as Bazarov the anarchist, but he is a pendant, he is an anarch of the new order, neither a propagandist by the act, but a philosophical anarch who lazily mutters: "Let the world wag; I don't care so that it minds its own business and lets me alone." With few exceptions most latter-day fiction is thin, papery, artificial, compared with Artzibashef's rich, red-blooded genius.

I have devoted so much attention to *Sanine* that little space is left for the other books, though they are all significant. *Revolutionary Tales* contains a strong companion picture to *Sanine,* the portrait of the metal-worker Schevyrjov, who is a revolutionist in the literal sense. His hunted life and death arouse a terrific impression. The end is almost operatic. A captivating little working girl figures in one episode. It may be remarked in passing that Artzibashef does not paint for our delectation the dear dead drabs of yesteryear, nor yet the girl of the street who heroically brings bread to her starving family (as does Sonia in *Crime and Punishment*). Few outcasts of this sort are to be found in his pages, and those few are unflinchingly etched, as, for example, the ladies in **"The Millionaire."**

This story, which is affiliated in ideas with *Sanine,* is Tolstoyian in the main issue, yet disconcertingly different in its interpretation. Wealth, too, may become an incitement to self-slaughter from sheer disgust. The story of Pasha Tumanow is autobiographical, and registers his hatred of the Russian grammar schools where suicides among the scholars are anything but infrequent. **"Morning Shadows"** relates the adventures of several young people who go to Petrograd to seek fame, but with tragic conclusions. The two girl students end badly, one a suicide, the other a prisoner of the police as an anarchist caught red-handed. A stupefying narrative in its horrid realism and sympathetic handling. The doctor gives us a picture of a pogrom in a tiny Russian province town. You simply shudder at the details of the wretched Jews shot down, ripped open, maltreated, and driven into the wilderness. It is a time for tears; though I cannot quite believe in this doctor, who, while not a Jew, so sympathises with them that he lets die the Chief of Police that ordered the massacre. Another story of similar intensity, called **"Nina"** in the English translation, fills us with wonder that such outrages can go unpunished. (pp. 35-48)

Perhaps the most touching story in *Revolutionary Tales* is **"The Blood Stain,"** confessedly beloved by its author. Again we are confronted by the uselessness of all attempts to right injustice. Might is right, ever was, ever will be. Again the victims of lying propagandists and the cruel law lie "on stretchers, with white eyes staring upward. In these eyes there was a look, a sad, questioning look of horror and despair." Always despair, in life or death, is the portion of these poor. (p. 49)

Without suggesting a rigid schematology, there is a composition plan in his larger work that may be detected if the reader is not confused by the elliptical patterns and the massive mounds of minor details in his novel *Breaking Point.* The canvas is large and crowded, the motivation subtly managed. As is the case with his novels, the drama plays in a provincial town, this time on the steppes, where the inhabitants would certainly commit suicide if the place were half as dreary as depicted. Some of them do so, and you are reminded of that curious, nervous disease, indigenous to Siberia, named by psychiatrists "myriachit," or the epidemic of imitation. A man, a sinister rascal, Naumow, preaches the greyness and folly of living, and this "Naumowism" sets by the ears three or four impressionable young men who make their exit with a bare bodkin or its equivalent. Naumow recalls a character in *The Possessed,* also the sinister hero of *The Synagogue of Satan* by the dramatic Polish writer Stanislaw Przybyszewski. To give us a central point the "chorus" of the novel is a little student who resembles a goldfinch, and has a birdlike way of piping about matters philosophical.

There are oceans of talk throughout the novels, talks about death. Really, you wonder how the Russians contrive to live at all till you meet them and discover what normal people they are. (It should not be forgotten that art must contain as an element of success a slight deformation of facts.) The student watches the comedy and tragedy of the town, his brain flaming with noble ideas for the regeneration of mankind! Alas! Naumow bids him reflect on the uselessness of suffering from self-privation so that some proletarian family may eat roast larks in the thirtieth century. Eventually he succumbs to the contagion of resemblance, takes to drink, and hangs himself to a

nail in the wall, his torn gum shoes, clinging to his feet, faithful to the last—they, Dickens-like, are shown from the start.

There is a nihilistic doctor—the most viable character of all about whose head hovers the aura of apoplexy—a particularly fascinating actress, an interesting consumptive, two wretched girls betrayed by a young painter (a Sanine type, *i. e.,* Max Stirnerism in action), while the officers of the garrison and club life are cunningly pictured. A wealthy manufacturer, with the hallmarks of Mr. Rogozhin in Dostoievsky's *The Idiot,* makes an awful noise till he luckily vanishes in a monastery. Suicide, rapine, disorder, drunkenness, and boredom permeate nearly every page. *Breaking Point* is the most poignant and intolerable book I ever read. It is the prose complement of Tschaikovsky's so-called "Suicide Symphony." Browning is reversed. Here the devil is in heaven. All's wrong in the world! Yet it compels reflection and rereading. Why?

Because, like all of his writings, it is inevitable, and granting the exaggeration inherent in the nature of the subject, it is lifelike, though its philosophy is dangerously depressing. The little city of the steppes is the cemetery of the Seven Sorrows. However, in it, as in *Sanine,* there is many an oasis of consolation where sanity and cheerfulness and normal humans may be enjoyed. But I am loath to believe that young Russia, Holy Russia, as the mystagogues call her, has lost her central grip on the things that most count; above all, on religious faith. Then needs must she pray as prayed Des Esseintes in Huysmans's novel *A Rebours:* "Take pity, O Lord, on the Christian who doubts, on the sceptic who desires to believe, on the convict of life who embarks alone, in the night, beneath a sky no longer lit by the consoling beacons of ancient faith." (pp. 49-52)

> *James Huneker, "Artzibashef," in his* Unicorns,
> *Charles Scribner's Sons, 1917, pp. 49-52.*

THE NEW YORK TIMES BOOK REVIEW   (essay date 1915)

[*In the following excerpt, the reviewer discusses* Breaking Point.]

Mr. James Huneker has characterized *Breaking Point* as "the most poignant and intolerable book I ever read" [see excerpt above]. Considering the extent of the adventures of Mr. Huneker's soul among masterpieces—and others—this is a broad indictment, but it is none too broad. The mature reader of the book gets the same sort of impression from it that filled him when at 14 he sat flat on the library floor and fed upon the play of *Titus Andronicus,* too glutted with horrors to know or care that the foot curled under him was asleep or that the edge of the bookcase was cutting into his oblivious back. This while reading. At the end of the book and after a pause for meditation and a mental calculation that out of the fifteen or so characters seven deliberately kill themselves, three die natural deaths of detailed ghastliness, and that every woman in the book, except one who is dying of consumption when it opens, is seduced during the course of the story, one finds it as hard to take it seriously as one does a bad dream recalled at noonday.

Yet *Breaking Point* possesses significance, both in itself and as marking a stage in its author's development. For Artzibasheff is a man of extraordinary power, and the direction which it takes is a matter of no small importance to the world.

One of the most interesting things about *Breaking Point* is the offhand fashion in which it confounds the critics, admiring and otherwise, who have read *Sanine* and made up their minds firmly about its author. In that book Artzibasheff was the Russian moralist par excellence, preaching the dogma of unmorality; a devil's advocate; a formidable opponent of Tolstoy, arguing against his doctrines of charity and non-resistance in Tolstoy's own best manner. *Sanine* brought the superman down from the realms of the abstract to everyday life; it was the bible of ruthless individualism.

But in *Breaking Point* the bubble the individualist blows is pricked; the weak point in *Sanine* is located, emphasized, one might say danced upon, if any act so gay could possibly be associated with a book so grim. Pleasure is a good, acknowledged, but it is not an endless good. There lies the trouble. As long as we could see Sanine proceeding from one conquest to another and never wearying of conquest, drinking champagne and vodka continuously en route without acquiring cirrhosis of the liver—in brief, eating his cake and having his cake—the doctrine of ruthless individualism had charms. But alas! In *Breaking Point* we learn that this, too, is vanity. At the turn of every lane satiety lurks.

Dchenieff, the artist, whom all women love and who loves the woman in all women, is Sanine carried to a logical conclusion. He has been called a weaker Sanine, but his weakness is only the normal reaction of his environment, the return of his own deeds upon himself, which the hero of the earlier book lacked. His logical conclusion is suicide, the only resource of a soul emptied of belief in a world peopled with ghosts.

Breaking Point, though frequently intolerable, though its heaped-up tragedy sometimes comes dangerously near producing the recoil into comedy in the mind of the reader which naturally follows an exaggerated gloom, remains a far deeper and richer work than *Sanine,* and one of the most remarkable produced in any country in many years. There is no use in trying to reconcile it with any of our accepted theories. It stands as possibly the strongest exposition of pure intellectual nihilism known to modern readers. Political nihilism known to modern readers. Political nihilism is brushed aside, and the measure of the author's contempt for Socialists is found in the fact that Dchenieff, the haunted sensualist, on the last terrible night of his life, is brought so low as to envy them:

> My God, how I envy these dull Socialists who believe in their program and are firmly convinced that they only live in order to provide everybody with a fowl in their soup in the forty-second century! But there is nothing in my soul—do you understand?—nothing!

Individualism, the doctrine of the superman, breaks down not only because of intrinsic weakness, but because, in the relation of the sexes, where individualism is most useful and precious to a man, woman is not only never individualistic enough herself, but cannot understand the quality in him. Which leads to many of the embarrassments and most of the tragedies of life, a fact emphasized more strongly in *Breaking Point* than in any other book we can think of.

Many of the incidents in Artzibasheff's novel are so needlessly horrifying to our Western taste that we involuntarily cry out against him for leading us from Gogol's spacious highway into his blind alley, among the carcasses of worn-out pleasures and the shards of shattered ideals. But even at its worst the alley does not wind aimlessly, nor, wholly without purpose, clutter itself with garbage. Here and there it touches most unexpectedly Dostoevski's path among the stars. Dostoevski, like Tolstoy, preached redemption through suffering. Without pain no man progresses, only through anguish does he see God. As to

the suffering, and even as to its purpose, Artzibasheff agrees with him perfectly:

> Suffering is the cause of progress. Give us happiness and we shall stand still. . . . The whole history of the world is one uninterrupted stream of sorrow, pain, hate, and all that is dark in human imagination. That is the life of man.

Then, without warning, the path dips away again:

> But why shall man go on suffering forever? It's high time people understood that they have no right to condemn the endless generations of the future to the same sufferings that millions of those who have gone before have already lived through.

In other words, though progress is the reward of pain, the game is not worth the candle.

Upon the premise of the universality of suffering, the usefulness of suffering, even a certain curious and to us morbid and inverted delight that grows out of suffering, Artzibasheff and Dostoevski stand hand in hand. But one sees a goal, the other sees none. To both, humanity is eternally martyred by fire; but to the one humanity will emerge pure gold, tried by the furnace; the other believes that its dreams and aspirations and desires will sink to crumbling ash. And since in the fullness of time the ash will cover all, why linger dying in a dying world? Suicide is the only way out, annihilation the only refuge; to Artzibasheff tradition means so little that it apparently has never occurred to him to fear that in the final sleep dreams may come. Yet his skepticism is so great that it embraces even itself. Naumoff, the exponent of the cult of the bare bodkin, is a megalomaniac, half fanatic, half fraud, who himself finds too much joy in preaching self-destruction to destroy himself, and we are left gazing into the void without the assurance that even that is safe from the touch of Artzibasheff's corroding irony.

"A Renaissance of Russian Realism," in The New York Times Book Review, *October 24, 1915, p. 408.*

PRINCE D. S. MIRSKY   (essay date 1926)

[Mirsky was a Russian prince who fled his country after the Bolshevik Revolution and settled in London. While in England, he wrote two important histories of Russian literature, Contemporary Russian Literature *(1926) and* A History of Russian Literature *(1927). In 1932, having reconciled himself to the Soviet regime, Mirsky returned to the USSR. He continued to write literary criticism, but his work eventually ran afoul of Soviet censors and he was exiled to Siberia. He disappeared in 1937. In the following excerpt, he notes that, for Artsybashev, the only realities are sex and death.]*

Soon after the First Revolution, Andreev's popularity was almost eclipsed by the great vogue of the author of *Sanin,* Michael Petrovich Artsybashev. Born in 1878, Artsybashev made his first appearance in literature in 1902. In 1904 he attracted attention and roused hopes by **"The Death of Lande,"** the story of a life of quest followed by a tragically meaningless death. In 1905-1906 he pleased the Radical public by a series of stories of the Revolution. But the Revolution was defeated, the intoxication passed, and a wave of disillusionment in public ideals swept the *intelligentsia.* Personal enjoyment and freedom from morality became the order of the day, and sexual licence, often on a definitely pathological foundation, spread like an epidemic. This epidemic was both reflected and further favoured by Artsybashev's famous novel which appeared in 1907.

Its success was instant and tremendous. The old-fashioned critics cried out against its immorality, and the modernists pointed out the absence in it of all literary merit. But it was a sensation and everyone had to read it. It became for a few years the Bible of every schoolboy and schoolgirl in Russia. It would be wrong to suppose that Artsybashev consciously sought either to corrupt schoolgirls or to gain money by pandering to animal instincts—Russian literature has never been openly meretricious; and he had from the very beginning shown symptoms of that Andreevian nihilism which was the brand-mark of the generation. Still, the effect was certainly serious, and the author of *Sanin* cannot be exculpated from having contributed to that moral deterioration of Russian society, especially of provincial schoolgirls. The didactic character of Russian literature (or at least the didactic spirit in which it had always been approached) was the cause of the strangely serious reception given to *Sanin*—it was not read as light literature, but as a revelation and a doctrine. The book is indeed didactic; it is a heavy, professorial sermon on the text: Be true to yourselves and follow your natural inclinations. These inclinations, Artsybashev preaches, can all be reduced to a carnal desire for the other sex—that man is good who obeys them, and that man bad who tries to hoodwink them. There is no such thing as love—it is a mere invention of artificial culture—the only reality is desire. Artsybashev's preaching proceeds direct from Tolstoy, only it is Tolstoy the other way round, and Tolstoy without genius. But the common ground is unmistakable—it is contempt for human conventions and culture, and the negation of all but the primitive realities. As literature *Sanin* is very mediocre. It is long, tedious, overloaded with "philosophical" conversations. Artsybashev avoids the modernist pitfalls of Andreev, but his psychology is puerile: it can all be reduced to one pattern, borrowed from Tolstoy; he (or she) thought he wished this and that, but in reality he only wished quite another thing—that is, to quell his sexual desire, which is the only human reality.

The other reality of Artsybashev's world is death; and to death is devoted his second big novel, *At the Brink* (in the English translation, *Breaking Point*). It is all heavily didactic—its subject is an epidemic of suicides in a provincial town, which destroyed all its intellectual élite. All Artsybashev's stories, long or short, are stories with a purpose, and the purpose is always to show the inanity of human life, the unreality of artificial civilization, and the reality of only two things—sex and death. In long stories and in little parable-like sketches, it is always the same over again. With painstaking and conscientious monotony, the sermon is hammered into the reader—as long as he agrees to submit to this dreary lecturing.

After *At the Brink*, Artsybashev devoted himself to the stage. His plays (*Jealousy, War,* etc.) are also purpose plays; and the "message" is always the same. They are constructed with simple straightforwardness, and this is not out of place in the drama. It is precisely owing to this organizing force of the "purpose" that they have, unlike most Russian plays, a genuine dramatic skeleton. They are quite actable, and with good actors have had deserved successes.

The Bolsheviks treated Artsybashev very harshly, and included *Sanin* and other of his works in their index of forbidden books, and finally expelled him from Russia (in 1923). So it is not surprising that he has adopted a very intransigent anti-Bolshevik attitude. He has devoted himself to political journalism in the Russian press of Warsaw. His reputation in Russia (including emigrated Russia) has suffered a complete eclipse. It is significant that *Sanin* has not been reprinted even outside of

Russia. At present no one regards him as a significant writer, but only as a curious and, on the whole, regrettable episode in the history of Russian literature. (pp. 139-41)

Prince D. S. Mirsky, "Artsybashev," in his Contemporary Russian Literature: 1881-1925, *Alfred A. Knopf, 1926, pp. 139-41.*

FRANK W. CHANDLER   (essay date 1931)

[*Chandler was an American critic whose primary area of interest was modern drama. In the following excerpt, he examines the major themes of Artsybashev's drama.*]

The quiet and refined naturalism of Chekhov which displays the crushing of the individual by his environment is not likely to satisfy the self-assertive. For such, Mikhail Petrovich Artzybashev, following the sensational naturalism of Strindberg, provides more thrilling entertainment. A great-grandson of Kosciusko, he was born in 1878 and won fame in fiction by his daring novel *Sanine.* For the stage he has written a few plays of careful structure ringing the changes upon disordered love. Passion he exhibits as the only occupation of woman and the most interesting concern of man. To give free play to instinct he declares to be our duty. Although he distinguishes between physical and spiritual attractions, it is clear that the former are for him dominant. So he depicts what Granville Barker has called "this barnyard world of sex." A cynic in the drama *Jealousy* remarks of his own intrigue that it involves "a concert of amorous tom cats." The same cynic affirms that men foolishly continue to look for Lauras and Beatrices, failing to understand that these ideal ladies never existed except in the minds of their self-deluded lovers. "Not only could a woman never be a Laura;" he remarks, "she could never even invent one," adding that: "When a man and a woman love, we say, 'She gives herself to him'; but that is a pious fraud. The right expression would be, 'She's caught him.'" In illustration of this concept of the seductive and pursuing female, Artzybashev here depicts a wife who strives to fascinate every man she meets, from youthful student to elderly physician and imperious prince. In the last act, however, she is strangled by her jealous husband, warned by a friend of her perfidy and infuriated when she taunts him with the fact that the suspected prince has not been her only lover.

More artistic because more subtle than *Jealousy* is Artzybashev's *Enemies.* Here, without a suicide or a murder to punctuate the play, there is a more elaborate analysis of the difficulties that attend marriage. An elderly professor resents his wife's devotion to housekeeping and her meddling with his studies. Yet, when she dies, he finds himself lonely and conscience-stricken. "I gave her too little care," he says; "I thought only of myself. . . . I imagined that she was in my way, that she was spoiling my life, that she was not worthy of me. . . . I flattered myself that with another wife I might have been different." Now he perceives that, "Nothing is more precious than love, and that there is no punishment more painful than fruitless regret and a tardy repentance." The unhappy marriages of his daughter and his son, added to his own, make the play. The son, a composer deficient in vitality, is wed to a woman who requires it and for that reason takes an officer of the guards, though she recognizes him to be a fool. "Our intimacy shames me like a slap in the face," she admits; "yet while it lasts it makes me forget everything. . . . I have no self-control left, no self-respect."

The professor's daughter suffers because her husband, a physician, insisting that man can love more than one woman at a time, acts upon his theory. "Why must one love necessarily destroy another?" he asks. "We can love both music and painting, Pushkin and Lermontov, the beauty of nature and the beauty of the human body." For her such amorous catholicity is less possible. "I love my love in you," she tells him. "A woman can never forget her first love, while a man rarely even remembers his." To the dashing girl that he has taken for second companion the husband says, "Can't you understand that we can love two, that there is no fraud, nothing low, nothing vile in such a love?" On her declaring that she cannot understand, he retorts, "No woman can, but every man will understand me; it's our nature." The wife in this case, like the husband in the former, forgives. "I shall forget what has happened," she says; "I shall love you again." But there is a telltale gleam in her husband's eyes. Can he forget the other woman? A rude old army physician, father of this other, stands as spokesman for Artzybashev's biological theory of love. Karnovich, too, has had his experience with matrimony, and when a lady prays for a good spring rain which will bring everything out of the ground, he exclaims: "God forbid! I have two wives resting there." He holds that a happy marriage is impossible because the interests of men and women are bound to clash. The man who marries can never again feel alone. "Take two of the greatest of friends and put them into one cell," says Karnovich; "they will begin to hate each other. Life together is only possible when there are constant and mutual sacrifices. But where there are sacrifices there can be no happiness." He believes that the soul is but the product of a complicated chemical process, and the purpose of existence is a new product. Love is dependent upon the glands as laughter upon a contraction of the muscles of the throat. Men for him are naturally polygamous. He warns his daughter that: "Every man, including the saintliest of saints, is absolutely capable of loving a thousand women. . . . Woman dreams of some individual, while man dreams of the sex."

In *The Law of the Savage,* these ideas are repeated by a Freudian, who believes that the soul feeds on love, that a man who loves but one woman is either a phenomenon or a cripple. "No matter how strongly a man's love may center on one woman," says Vorosov, "he cannot help feeling attracted when youth and beauty pass his way. He may fight against his instinct; he may crush it. But no such repression goes unpunished." According to the new ethics, repression rather than transgression deserves reproof. The story of the play illustrates the author's conception of the forces that rule humanity, his folk being savages in fine clothes. The central figure is a libertine lawyer, who, like Sanine, is a Nietzschean individualist. As a guest in the house of his friend, he makes love to the friend's wife, with whom he has earlier had an intrigue. Then, though beloved by his own wife, he captures the heart of her younger sister, whom he advises that instinct should be her guide. Discovered by the first lady while embracing the second, he is exposed to his wife, to whom his best excuse for loving her sister lies in the fact that this sister resembles her as she was in days gone by. The outraged wife proceeds to seek revenge by giving herself to a lover, but repents, and tells him that she still loves her Boris. Yet, when the latter appears, she avows her disloyalty in order to wound him. He flies into a rage, arranges to duel with his rival, and then, as his wife kneels to beg his forgiveness, kicks her full in the chest. Such is Artzybashev's application of the double standard. This bounder of a husband, who admits that he has betrayed Zina at every opportunity without any feeling of guilt, makes her the victim of his jealous

rage after a single offence on her part. In the last act, though admitting that he has long lived a life of lies, he explains: "I am as you made me and as environment moulded me. I cannot be different, nor do I wish to be. I am a child of my age. I have no faith in anything, and I ask only one thing of life—pleasure, variety." For the law of the duel he would substitute the law of the savage; so, instead of waiting for the signal to fire, he shoots down his rival without allowing him a chance to shoot back in fair play. "This is murder!" cries one of the seconds. "What have you done?" And Boris replies coldly, "What you have seen," and stalks out.

In a later play, *War,* Artzybashev exhibits the life of a family as affected by the great conflict, considering specifically the effect upon women of the loss or maiming of their lovers and husbands. The central figure is a milder matron of Ephesus, devoted to her lord so long as he is whole and sound, able to excite and respond to her passion; yet, during his absence at the front, succumbing in thought to a former admirer, and, upon his return as a cripple, falling into the admirer's embrace. A second woman in the play, when she learns that her lover has died on the field of honor, gives herself to his consumptive rival who has slyly induced the other to enlist. For women the half-living, according to Artzybashev, are better than those who live no longer, just as the strong and the well are better than the maimed. In such matters women, like men, must obey the Life Force. Artzybashev defines his self-assertive doctrine as anarchic individualism. Thus, in his plays there sounds a new note, not only an appeal to sensation, but a challenge to the will. They may mark, as has been alleged, the liberation of the Russian drama from monologue and philosophical discussion, but they exhibit so drastic an individualism that they have fallen under the ban of the Communist régime. Moreover, they are naturalistic, whereas the Communists have turned from the art which transcribes reality to that which suggests meanings through symbols. (pp. 94-8)

Frank W. Chandler, "The Little Eccentrics: Artzybashev, Sologub, Evreinov," in his Modern Continental Playwrights, *Harper & Brothers, 1931, pp. 94-110.*

MARC SLONIM (essay date 1953)

[*Slonim was a Russian-born American critic who wrote extensively on Russian literature. In the following excerpt, he assesses Artzybashev's literary importance.*]

In his first stories, which he began publishing in 1901, Artzybashev was under the double influence of Tolstoy and Dostoevsky. The hero of his **"Lande's Death,"** in reality a popular version of Prince Myshkin (*The Idiot*), is a non-resister to evil and rejects physical love. Later, however, Artzybashev concentrated precisely on the portrayal of sex and violence: his story of the high-school student who murders his headmaster (**"Pasha Tumanov"**) and particularly his tales of the revolutionary period depicting punitive expeditions, mass executions, bloodshed, and death throes are not devoid of a certain gruesome power. They all imply that man is by nature a scoundrel, that life has no meaning, while culture is merely a blind for unspeakable instincts. Sanin, the hero of Artzybashev's most important novel, repeats these statements and also expresses his contempt for any code of morality. His philosophy is quite simple: "I do what I want to do and can do"; man should be as free as a bird; he has the right to enjoy love-making without fear or scruples—and the liberation of his body is one of the great tasks of modern times. As a novel of "sexual emancipation" *Sanin* fits into the general anti-puritanical and erotic trend of twentieth-century European literature, but its hero belongs to a Russian environment. His theory and practice of sexual freedom, which are described with naturalistic details, are offered to the reader as an answer to all questions concerning life.

Just as half a century before Chernyshevsky had portrayed Rachmetov (in *What Is To Be Done*) as a model man of his generation, so Artzybashev presented Sanin. Those who saw in the much discussed novel only suggestive scenes, shocking their morality or titillating their senses, were mistaken: it was, as is usual in Russia, a book with a message, and Sanin slept with all his mistresses to prove a thesis rather than to obey a natural urge. Artzybashev preached physiological gratification as a credo, and the influence of his novel was amazingly extensive and completely disproportionate to its limited intrinsic value. It expressed the mentality of bourgeois youth who sought to forget the unpleasant experiences of an abortive revolution and needed new idols to worship; it also challenged the customary restraint of Russian writers in matters of sex. The realistic school of the nineteenth century had avoided any direct description of physical passion. This tradition was broken by the Decadents and Symbolists, and Artzybashev reflected the new spirit.

Liberation through the assertion of the flesh, however, did not make Sanin very happy. The kind of love he advocated brought but momentary relief: *amor furor brevis* ["brief passionate love"]. Artzybashev's eroticism, like that of most of his contemporaries, had pessimistic overtones and seemed more like an outlet than like self-affirmation. The heroes of his next novel, *At the Brink,* oscillate between sexual desire and the death instinct, and seven of them commit suicide; this lengthy, utterly gloomy work of decay and annihilation goes on and on in endless conversations and stops only because most of its protagonists are dead. Artzybashev's plays were also despondent and negativistic (*The Law of the Savage, Jealousy, War*). On the whole, Artzybashev's characters were schematic and artificial; they did not live but presented evidence and made declarations of faith or disbelief. Although, as a writer, Artzybashev had some dramatic qualities and knew how to build suspense in a thrilling plot, his success was not due to any enduring literary assets. His naturalism was crude, and his ideas imitative or superficial. He emigrated in 1923 and died four years later in Poland. By that time it had become obvious that the work of this second-rate writer offered merely historical interest: he represented and reflected the era of reaction on the eve of World War I. (pp. 165-67)

> *Marc Slonim, "1905 and Its Aftermath," in his* Modern Russian Literature: From Chekhov to the Present, *Oxford University Press, 1953, pp. 153-83.*

CHARLES I. GLICKSBERG   (essay date 1975)

[*An American critic and educator, Glicksberg has written widely on American literature. In the following excerpt, he explores the themes of nihilism and suicide in* Breaking Point.]

Michael Artzybashef, the Russian novelist, works in the pessimistic tradition exemplified by Andreyev; he depicts the various strategies, all of them useless, that men adopt when their faith in life is shattered. Artzybashef articulates a nihilism more uncompromising than that of Andreyev. Whereas in *Sanine* he glorified the life of instinct and seemed to support the Nietz-

schean conception of love and sex, in his more representative, though less popular novel *Breaking Point,* he takes for his theme the omnipotence of death and seems to preach the desirability of universal suicide. What saves this work from sheer melodrama is the use of ironic counterpoint in highlighting the absurdity of rushing to meet the fate of death that everyone fears.

Artzybashef's suicidal pessimism is altogether different in tone and content from the tragic pessimism of Dostoevski. Artzybashef rejects the Christian doctrine in its entirety. The blend of Schopenhauer and Nietzsche yields a nihilism that finds suicide the only "logical" way out, even though this solution is full of absurd contradictions. But *Breaking Point* is, like *The Possessed,* the classic novel of the absurd. Cornet Krause, methodical in his reasoning, a fanatic in his reliance on logic, his intellect ever active while his heart remains underdeveloped, is a twentieth-century version of Kirillov, but he differs from Kirillov in that he possesses none of his ecstatic mysticism and is not motivated by his sacrificial craving to liberate mankind from the bugaboo of death. Cornet Krause suffers from acedia: the curse of indifference. Cherishing no illusions, drained of hope, infernally bored, he broods constantly on the idea of taking his own life. He is determined to carry out this project without fuss or fanfare. Artzybashef describes how this character is held back by an incomprehensible impulse, a blind, irrational clinging to life; he cannot shoot himself in the dark, when he is alone in his room, and he decides to do it in the company of others at the club, where nothing will distract him from acting out his fixed purpose.

He is confirmed in his decision by the rabid spouting of the engineer, Naumoff, who proclaims the salvationary doctrine of universal suicide. The latter argues that life is a cruel farce, full of misery and suffering; freedom from all this can be achieved by the extinction of the race of man. A minor epidemic of suicides breaks out in this provincial town. Naumoff is not the direct instigating cause; he is merely the catalytic agent. The opposition to Naumoffism is represented by Tchish, a student who supports himself by giving lessons. He had been arrested and imprisoned for his revolutionary activities, but he still believes ardently in a glorious future for mankind to be ushered in by Communism. In the meantime, however, he, too, is a victim of boredom; he is poor and lives as a lodger in a widow's boarding house. Finally, after his "fall," he comes to realize that his dazzling vision of a utopian future is a pipe dream. After succumbing, while drunk, to "the charms" of the fat, sensual widow, he hangs himself.

There is no touch of comic relief, no glimmer of hope or humor, in this depressing picture of life in Russia before the October Revolution. Love is presented as a biological trap. The local Don Juan, Dchenieff, an artist, after ruining a number of women, perceives at last the emptiness and futility of his life, and shoots himself. Lisa, one of his conquests, drowns herself. Ryskoff, a poor clerk without talent who nourishes pathetic dreams of becoming a professional writer, hangs himself. Nelly, another of Dchenieff's victims, tries to take her own life. Trenieff, after being drawn again into one of his chronic quarrels with his wife, cuts his throat.

This bald summary omits the number of cases Artzybashef piles up of various characters stricken with some incurable disease. We witness the death of a child and the inconsolable grief of the parents. Professor Ivan Rasumovski is dying and knows the end is near; in his state of terror he turns to prayer but immediately before his death he lapses into silence and then laughs aloud with satanic strangeness. Eugenia Samoilovna, formerly an actress, is dying of tuberculosis. Dr. Arnoldi, who inwardly despairs of life, is moved by deep compassion for all those who suffer, but there is nothing he can do.

It is difficult to determine Artzybashef's intention in all this. He is responsible, of course, for the composition as a whole: the selection of naturalistic details, the grim scenes delineated of disease and death, the wave of suicides, the brooding atmosphere of boredom and wretched despair. He evidently considers life an incomprehensible and futile affair, but he is able to distance his material sufficiently to make us realize the ridiculousness of such a conclusion. He shows that Naumoff, for all his impassioned evangelism, is loath to take his own life: he is buoyed up by an inflated sense of his own importance as a prophet of doom. What drives him to choose this path, to preach this grotesque message of redemption by means of universal suicide, is his overweening egotism. Yet there can be little doubt that Artzybashef sympathizes with a character like Krause and the miserably disillusioned Tchish. He exposes the folly of all ideals directed toward the achievement of a paradisal future. Life is the fatal sickness from which these cruelly afflicted creatures will never recover. Death is the trap sooner or later sprung, from which there is no possibility of escape.

It is perhaps Dr. Arnoldi who sums up most closely the author's position. He is surprised at nothing; he seeks to ease the pain of life in others, whereas he himself has died within. He goes through the monotonous ritual of living: he drinks, visits his patients, spends time at the club, but he sees no meaning in any of his actions. He has died spiritually long ago. He feels there is no point in his committing suicide. He has no answer for the questions the principal characters in the novel ask him in their anguish. His reply is that he does not know. As far as he is concerned, there are no solutions. Dr. Arnoldi's humanity, his unfailing compassion, his readiness to do whatever he can to help others—all this offsets his nihilistic conviction and makes him the most lovable character in the story.

The action of the novel, however, is so constructed as to confirm and reinforce the pervasive philosophy of nihilism. Death represents the nadir of futility; the sooner it is made welcome the better. That is how some of these Russian characters plan to revenge themselves upon life: they will commit suicide when they finally realize that there is no reason for going on living and every reason for bringing this hideous mummery to an end. The instinctive clinging to life, the superstitious dread of what might lie beyond, these obstacles must be overcome. We observe how a few of the suicides *reason* their way to death; before they take the irretrievable step they must make certain that their logic is foolproof.

Situated in the Steppes, this God-forsaken town, which forms the fitting background of the plot, accentuates the atmosphere of oppressive tedium. Everything about the place is "as formless and insignificant as a heap of ashes before the wind scatters them." The dismal images used to describe the hamlet stress the point that here, in this desolate region of Russia, terrible thoughts are being born, thoughts that will later shake the town to its depths, compelling the inhabitants to confront the idiotic specter of death.

Artzybashef foreshadows the nature of the catastrophe that is to occur, a catastrophe precipitated by the new engineer Naumoff, but the author insists that the trouble could not rightly be attributed to a human agency; his declared belief is "that the human will is incapable of changing in any minute detail what Life has ordained. Sooner or later it must lead to one inevitable end." Artzybashef uncovers the determinism that shapes the course of events, humdrum and trivial as they may seem, and brings them to a disastrous end. The dreary round of existence, however, gives no indication that there is anything brewing that will cause a violent break in the unvarying routine, just as a healthy man suspects naught of the germ of a fatal disease that has insidiously lodged itself inside his body and is beginning to undermine it. Tchish, for example, is enraged by the apathy induced by his environment, but his rage is pointless. "He understood as well as anyone the complicated web of fatality that enmeshes people even in such remote places." And yet he clings all the more fervently to his revolutionary, utopian expectations. He prides himself in particular on not being one of those who believe that the game of life is not worth playing. Artzybashef analyzes the specious content of the romantic faith he embraces.

> He believed that only the life of yesterday and to-day, and perhaps of to-morrow also, presented such a chaotic, aimless outlook. After that a mighty wave would come, sweeping away all that was old and dirty and bringing with it a harmonious, mathematically regulated happiness, in which he, the young exiled student, that paltry mortal creature, should have his share, his value and his duty.

The phrase *a mathematically regulated happiness* registers the controlling mood of deflationary mockery. Bitter irony is present, too, when Tchish, in his discussion with such fanatical pessimists as Cornet Krause and Naumoff, defends his philosophy of strenuous social optimism.

Tchish and Dr. Arnoldi form an excellent study in contrasts: one enthusiastic and idealistic, and the other sunk in indifference, aware that the struggle for existence is basically the same everywhere. He knows that everyone is fated to die, and that no one is happy. A change of government, technological innovations, the conquest of the air by the wings of man—all this will make no difference in the human condition. Tchish, for his part, believes in the greatness of humanity. He looks upon the vicissitudes of history, the creative efforts made by artists, the works of philosophers, the battles fought in the arena of politics, as integral parts of a Promethean epic to conquer Nature and arrive at the Truth. Nevertheless, Tchish, despite his bravely affirmed utopian hopes, suffers from painful seizures of depression, when everything around him seems drab and uninteresting. The old doctor, on the other hand, doggedly pursues "an aimless path, without reason and without joy." He has seen too many people die to be stirred by desire or moved by regret. When the dying ask him what is the use of all this human suffering, his invariable reply is: "I don't know." Death at least grants the victim release from the bed of pain, a way out of the biological trap, but he cannot say why human beings must be tortured before the blessed peace of death descends upon them. Gazing upon his patient, the battered wreck of this once brilliant professor, who is fighting against the terrible realization that his life is over, Dr. Arnoldi saw

> how unmeaning were the dreams of man's immortality, as humanity, death's prey, vainly tried to picture them. It was as though he saw some absurd, crude picture, painted upon a curtain by a dilettante, hiding the black emptiness beyond. . . . What were they, God, heaven, the cosmos? . . . a little heap of decaying bones, a light flickering out, and nothing more. One might argue about religion and believe in

immortality as long as the intellect could work and the body enjoy life to the full, but now, when all might see how man turned to a dying animal, an idiot, a mass of crumbling bones and failing organs, these ideas seemed as ludicrous as old-wives' tales of demons and fairies.

For these characters in *Breaking Point,* whether they seek relief in wine and sex and pleasure or fall into indifference and take their own life, there is no Dostoevskian crisis of conversion, no theophany, no promise, however ambiguous, of redemption. Death is the common sordid end, that is all. Nothing more remains to be said. Words are of no avail, faith is illusion, pity a vain indulgence. Yet life goes on steadily and renews itself as if in fulfillment of some great purpose. Though *Breaking Point* contains some lively scenes of love-making and merry-making, these are but pathetic, ineffectual distractions; the primary theme drives home the lesson that death reduces all human pride and ambition to nothingness. Children are born in pain, and all for what? That in time, as Dr. Arnoldi sees it, the next generation "too should be crushed by the wheels of fate." Death is inescapable; one may fend it off today, only to be forced to face its terrors on the morrow. Though Dr. Arnoldi is, like Dr. Rieux in *The Plague,* a man who has lost his faith in God, he is no secular saint fighting to the last ditch against the tyrannical power of death. He would gladly have sacrificed his own life if by so doing he could have helped to cure the sick.

> And had he known who was guilty of this mass of useless agony, the old doctor would have gone up to him with fearless, open countenance, and cursed him— nor feared pain, death, or the last judgment. . . . So full of pity and bitterness was this man's weary soul.
>
> But he knew that help was impossible and that neither entreaty nor arguments would ever make reply.

In a sense it is merciful that the sick child he is attempting to save will perish before learning the fear of death or experiencing a strong attachment "to this beloved or accursed existence."

The most gripping parts of the novel confront the problem of suicide. Cornet Krause, the Mephistophelean persona, seeks to find a valid justification for suicide, whereas Naumoff, the egregious believer in salvation through universal death, keeps harping on his mythomania. The latter insists there is no necessity that binds the individual to life. Tchish continues to uphold the ethic of striving. He tells Krause: "You can propound any theories you like about the futility of life, and I shall always say that they are the outcome of your own slackness and nothing else. Damn it all, life never promised you anything. It was left you to make what you pleased of it." Man can choose his own weapons in his battle with Nature and thus be able to conquer it. The main thing is not to lose heart and cry aloud but to keep up the struggle. The world is not a lazar-house; there are man-made evils to be eradicated, freedom to be won, art to be created, scientific advances to be made. Krause, the skeptic, is not in the least impressed by these humanistic arguments. Suppose, he asks, he cares naught for progress but prefers to cast away the privilege of life? Is he to be accounted a criminal? He is not at all interested in promoting the happiness of mankind. Such an attitude brings Tchish up short.

> To a certain extent he was convinced that it was everyone's duty to believe in something, that phrases like: "A person who believes in nothing, who only thinks of himself," were insults. . . . He could not

imagine how anybody could help trying to clear himself from this imputation.

He cannot understand how Krause is capable of advancing, with apparent conviction, precisely such irresponsible and "insane" views. Enraged, Tchish accuses him of being dead, a living corpse, and cries out that such people ought to be killed. "If you believe in nothing, and have no use for humanity, if your soul is a blank and your life is uninteresting, then be good enough to put a bullet through your head. . . ." Krause replies by asking calmly how Tchish can tell whether that is not what he intends to do.

Tchish must contend with another formidable adversary, Naumoff, who attacks his condemnation of suicide as an act of moral cowardice. Fanatically the engineer argues that

> every death is monstrous, though it were a thousand times a law of nature. Death is an act of violence against the race, and only suicide is free. You can't say it's natural if I want to live and have to die, but still less can you say it's unnatural if I die of my own free will as soon as there is nothing left for me to live for, simply because I don't want to live any longer.

Tchish concedes that suicide is understandable if one has no desire to go on living, but what seems to him positively morbid is that death should be painted in glowing colors. "I am convinced that it would never occur to anyone who was not ill, mad, or had gone off the tracks in some way, to send a bullet through his head, or crawl into the noose, the devil only knowing why." But Naumoff sticks grimly to his Schopenhauerian thesis that life is incurably unhappy; it is irrational and unnatural for humanity not to realize that death is their best remedy. He can comprehend the fear of death but not the will to live.

Naumoff is bent on exploding the pernicious myth of happiness. Life consists of suffering, sorrow, conflict, pain. Why must this demented martyrdom be allowed to go on forever? He does not deny the titanic strength of the incomprehensible will to live, but it is this very instinct that must be suppressed. He will point the way. When Tchish retorts that human nature will frustrate his mad plan of universal suicide, Naumoff maintains that since everything in Nature dies, a time will come when people will grow tired of living and regard death as a blessed deliverance. The men who had in the past been hailed as benefactors of the race were really its enemies, for they perpetuated a lie, a harmful illusion, thus exposing men to more and more senseless suffering.

The debate over the justification of suicide is continued at the picnic. Naumoff holds the floor, asserting that it is sheer folly to die for a cause. Nothing on earth can bring man the gift of happiness. Since death always waits in the offing, no revolution can do any good. Even if men were allowed to live forever, they would be horribly bored and beg for the boon of death. The best thing, he concludes, is to die. That brings life at last to an end. But first people must be shown "that they have no right to protract the senseless comedy."

That is the theme reiterated with gloomy, unsparing emphasis: there is no possibility of happiness, but death, fortunately, terminates the misery of man. All things come to that at last. When Dr. Arnoldi is at the cemetery where the professor and the actress lie buried, he thinks to himself that Naumoff is right. "Every human thought and action can have only one end . . . death." Even Tchish suffers recurrently from doubts about the future. He tries to whip his ebbing enthusiasm for the social ideal, but he knows that by the time it is achieved, if it is ever achieved, he will be dead and utterly forgotten, and what will it avail him then?

Krause is the absurd hero who plans to commit suicide, but he must first make sure of his ground; he tests the logic of the engineer's argument. If Naumoff lives on while preaching that life is meaningless and that death is to be deliberately chosen, then why should others not follow his example? Naumoff retorts that his theory is stronger than himself. He refuses to make his exit from the earthly scene until he has done everything possible to spread his gospel. He does not hate his own life, he hates life in general. He is even prepared to kill in support of his theory. It is his unshakable faith in death as salvation that gives him the right to kill. He has abandoned all ideas of progress, sacrifice, revolution, the emancipation of the proletariat from bondage. It is under the banner of death that he fights against life. Though he is but an infinitesimal speck of energy in the universe, he has to affirm his individuality "so that I could oppose it to the whole universe, to the universal will, God . . . or whatever else there may be." Krause, who is a more complex if less articulate person than Naumoff, makes the point that Naumoff does not actually believe in his theory but clings to it out of an overweening ambition. He challenges Naumoff to prove his sincerity by immediately approving of Krause's suicide. Krause raises his revolver but he does not shoot himself—not this time.

Though Krause has not pulled the trigger, Naumoff is convinced that he will surely kill himself later on, perhaps this very night. He hates the man because he has disclosed the truth about his own conflicting motives. There were two beings in Naumoff: "one believed in his theory with a fanatic's obstinacy, desiring annihilation and death; the other feared them, choked with detestation and vented his own cowardice and despair on everyone else." He is consumed by a maniacal self-love. Artzybashef unmasks his devouring egotism. Krause, on the other hand, struggles with himself as he tries to summon up the strength to act on his fixed beliefs. Joy and sorrow, love and hate, everything, he feels, "is useless. It is futile to begin a new day, to dress, to eat and drink, to speak, to think. Not that he was tired of it all . . . no, it is merely that it is so pointless." He holds the pistol in the darkness of his room; one impulse from his finger and it will be all over, he will know Death, but he cannot act; he is filled with an indefinable dread.

Instinct is stronger than the force of logic; the living draw back in horror from the final step. The conscious will gives way before this nameless fear, and this, Krause perceived, betrayed some serious flaw in his chain of reasoning. "It must mean that his life was precious to him . . . this empty, unessential life was, in spite of its proved absurdity, dearer to him than his inmost self, which clung grovelling to the life that had cursed it." He would have to consider the case for suicide all over again, he would have to marshall his forces anew. Life and death, he muses, are intertwined. "Nothing can sever life from death. Death conquers and vanishes in the victory, and the dread of death exists only as long as life lasts!" Resolved to overcome this indwelling terror, he makes up his mind to commit suicide not in darkness, which reinforces his terror, but in public.

Then comes the riotous scene at the club. Trenieff, the officer who will later slash his own throat, twits Krause on his suicidal obsession. Krause, in full dress, wearing a resplendent uni-

form, announces that he intends to shoot himself, at once. The others imagine he is joking, but Krause never jests. Rising to his full height, he declares that his action is of no special importance; he wants to take his own life at the most ridiculous moment so as to rob the deed of any special significance. There is, he assures his audience, nothing heroic or tragic about his gesture. The truth is he cannot go on living.

> To me life is not a tragedy, nor a horror, nor a senseless episode, but merely uninteresting. Nature and beauty are so trivial, one gets so tired of them . . . love is so petty . . . humanity—simply foolish. The mysteries of the universe are impenetrable, and even should one fathom them it would be just as dull as before. Everything is as uninteresting as what we know already. In eternity there is nothing either small or large, and therefore even a match is a mystery and a miracle . . . but we know the match and it is uninteresting. And it's the same with everything. In the same way God would be tedious if we could see Him. Why have a God at all? It's superfluous.

Then he says goodbye and before anyone can prevent him he puts the barrel of his pistol into his mouth and pulls the trigger.

His suicide is indirectly responsible for a wave of suicides in the town. The officers who knew him well recall his oddities of behavior, especially his remark that life and everything connected with it is loathsome. The revolver shot that Krause fired shatters the accustomed and reassuring routine of life. Now the presence of death overshadows everyone's consciousness. Those who frequent the club cannot believe in the reality of what has taken place. Naumoff denies that he is responsible for Krause's death on the ground that "nobody can force a man to believe that he must die if he wants to live . . . no persuasion and no theories can accomplish that." He regrets nothing that he has said or done. Once more he announces that happiness is impossible and nonexistent. He repeats the old familiar arguments. What is the good of life? Why live if all that life brings is sorrow? What good are the gods man invented or the lofty ideals he professes to believe in or the opiate dream of everlasting bliss in heaven? What is the value of this mythical posthumous reward if existence on earth is so full of misery? God, if He exists, cannot be forgiven for imposing this terrible burden of suffering on mankind. If he [Naumoff] drove Krause to his self-inflicted death, then that is entirely to his credit. "And I'd drive the whole world to it, if I could . . . with the greatest pleasure."

Even Tchish is affected by this suicide. Ryskoff, the clerk, has been converted to Naumoff's view of things; he is sick of life. Tchish attempts to argue him out of his suicidal mood. Why should Ryskoff allow himself to become infected by the present morbid intellectual atmosphere? Society will soon recover from this craze of Naumoffism. The future belongs to the people, the golden age will soon dawn. Ryskoff, thrilled by the thought that in taking his own life he will become, like Krause, a tragic figure, one who nobly despises life, goes home and hangs himself.

The sudden wave of suicides stirs the town to its depths, especially the death of this nonentity of a clerk. Many feared "that this one impetus would shatter the majestic fabric of centuries and cause them to fling away their lives in masses." Only Dr. Arnoldi is unsurprised and unmoved. It was as if he had expected nothing else. If he does not kill himself it is because, as he says, he has been dead for a long time. And Tchish, despite his brave affirmation of faith in the future of humanity, comes to a point where he can no longer endure his wretched existence. He believes that he "believes in something, suffers for something, and is full of zeal for the cause. . . . He does not himself know in what, but he believes! Full of grief, full of tormenting agonies he believes without hope!" He tries hard to persuade himself that life is noble and beautiful, but he realizes that all this means absolutely nothing to him; he has been an utter failure; he can no longer fool himself with vainglorious dreams, and so he hangs himself.

Like Dostoevski, Artzybashef reveals that the Nemesis of the nihilist is that he can give himself to no project, at least not for long. Whatever work he sets his hand to, whatever cause he supports, sooner or later seems foolish and futile. He is the man devoid of faith, but life without some kind of faith is insupportable, and therefore he acts on his own negative faith— he takes his own life. Nothing, not even life, is sacred. The nihilist as suicide achieves nothing. His death leaves the universe of the absurd intact, unchanged, and unchallenged. (pp. 103-15)

> *Charles I. Glicksberg, "Nihilism and Suicide," in his* The Literature of Nihilism, *Bucknell University Press, 1975, pp. 95-115.*

NICHOLAS LUKER   (essay date 1980)

[In the following excerpt, Luker examines the major themes and techniques of Sanine.*]*

> The author of *Sanin* cannot be exculpated from having contributed to [the] moral deterioration of Russian society, especially of provincial schoolgirls. [D. S. Mirsky, *Contemporary Russian Literature;* see excerpt dated 1926.]

During the first decade of this century Russian prose underwent a brief but vigorous revival, and by the outbreak of the First World War it had become immensely rich and varied. Gorky, Andreyev and Bunin—to mention only three writers active during those years—have long been familiar to Western readers, yet the author responsible for what was probably the greatest literary sensation of that decade is now virtually forgotten both in Russia and the West, and has received practically no detailed critical attention for the last seventy years.

When Mikhail Artsybashev's novel *Sanin* appeared in 1907 it enjoyed a *succès de scandale* comparable with that surrounding the publication of Lawrence's *Lady Chatterley's Lover* almost half a century later. While in general terms the work was regarded as highly suggestive, certain passages in it were considered downright pornographic. Publishers in several countries were not slow in responding to popular demand for what they believed was titillating reading, with the result that translations of the novel appeared with indecent haste in France, Germany (an edition of 100,000 copies), Italy, Denmark, Bulgaria, Hungary and even Japan. The affront to public morality seen in the work and the corrupting effect that it was said to have on the young gave rise to a number of court cases, not only in Russia but also in Germany, Austria and Hungary.

Needless to say, it was the novel's allegedly sensational aspects, not its literary or philosophical qualities, which attracted such avid attention and provoked such indignant comment. Though some voices were raised in its defence, the general attitude of "respectable" Russian society towards the work was hostile, an attitude summed up by the remark quoted above made by the well-known literary historian Prince Mirsky. "I may, however, without exaggeration assert," wrote Artsy-bashev many years later, "that no one in Russia took the trouble really to fathom the ideas of the novel. The eulogies and the condemnations are equally one-sided."

This article attempts partly to redress the critical balance in favour of *Sanin* by evaluating the work and by showing that, contrary to the general view, it examines issues other than sex and physicality. Like several of his literary contemporaries, Artsybashev is a much-underestimated writer, and *Sanin,* arguably his most significant work, should not be summarily dismissed as "a curious and . . . regrettable episode in the history of Russian literature" [Mirsky].

When placing *Sanin* in its political and social context in the early 1900s, one is confronted at the outset by a problem of chronology. If we are to believe Artsybashev's assertion that he wrote the novel in 1903, we must reject the standard critical assumption that it reflects the Russian intelligentsia's disenchantment with public ideals after the failure of the 1905 Revolution and that it expresses the extreme sexual freedom which became fashionable as a result before the end of that decade. Artsybashev thus became the victim of socio-political circumstance, for when the novel was published in 1907 it was automatically seen as exemplifying a social phenomenon of the time, whereas in reality its author had never intended any such thing. "*Sanin* made its appearance five years too late," Artsybashev explained. "This was very much against it: at the time of its appearance literature had been flooded by streams of pornographic and even homosexual works, and my novel was liable to be judged with these." From 1907 onwards, however, Artsybashev's name became inextricably linked with *Sanin* and with all that it was said to be, and the inordinate scandal surrounding the work did permanent damage to his literary reputation. Without ever having read him, many students of Russian literature today are convinced that Artsybashev is little more than a talented pornographer.

The novel is set in a provincial town in the south of Russia, a setting which figures in several of Artsybashev's earlier works and is probably based on the remote and undistinguished Akhtyrka in Kharkov Province where he was born. It examines the effect produced by Vladimir Sanin on his family and their acquaintances when he returns home after an absence of several years. Those years, Artsybashev tells us in his opening sentence, constitute the crucial formative period of human life, and they are years which the young hero has spent away from his family, unschooled and free. Sanin stays about five months (late spring to early autumn) at home, and during this time acts as a catalyst both upon the people and their relationships around him. He saves his sister Lida from committing suicide because she is pregnant; arranges her marriage to Novikov, a local doctor who is passionately in love with her; publicly humiliates Zarudin, the army officer who seduced her, by striking him a terrible blow in the face; and then virtually rapes Karsavina, an attractive young schoolmistress. Shortly after this, Sanin suddenly catches a train and vanishes into the limbo from which he first so unaccountably sprang.

Between the episodes of the hero's arrival and departure, however, we find much more than the succession of sensational scenes which the above outline suggests. As Artsybashev said, it was precisely here that his imitators went wrong. Without grasping what he had wanted to say, they hurried to turn the novel's success "to their own advantage . . . by flooding the literary world with pornographic, wantonly obscene writings, thus degrading in the readers' [sic] eyes what I wished to express in *Sanin*." Sanin's behaviour is designed to demonstrate Artsybashev's conviction that man is no longer true to his essential self and that he has become constrained by empty conventions and false priorities, a conviction neatly expressed by the epigraph to the novel taken from the book of Ecclesiastes: *"Lo, this only have I found, that God hath made man upright; but they have sought out many inventions."*

The structure of *Sanin* suggests that Artsybashev is concerned to tell a good story as well as to present a philosophy. Events in the novel occur for the most part in chronological order, but, given the many different character groupings (Lida-Zarudin; Lida-Novikov; Lyalya-Ryazantsev; Karsavina-Svarozhich) together with the relations between them and Sanin's involvement with them all, Artsybashev is faced with the task of maintaining narrative momentum in several directions at the same time. Moreover, the fact that Sanin is frequently the most important character in a scene and that the author is interested primarily in his reactions to the other characters does not always help to keep secondary issues in focus. On three significant occasions, however, Artsybashev uses a "flashback" technique which allows us a glimpse of significant events in the novel and at the same time serves to tighten up the various strands of the plot. The first is in Chapter XI, after Semenov's death of consumption in the preceding chapter, and describes the sick man's state of mind as far back as the onset of his illness. With an increasing sense of approaching doom Artsybashev takes us from Semenov's occasional recollections that his death is inevitable to his last moments of conscious life in the hospital, when both the women's weeping and the priest's blessing seem absurdly irrelevant. Aware now as we are of the manner of Semenov's decline and death, we are more able to judge the effect they have had upon Svarozhich, whose own obsession with mortality was fuelled by Semenov's gloomy words to him in Chapter IV. The second flashback comes rather later, in Chapter XXIII, and is less dramatic. It shows Sanin bringing Novikov to see Lida after the doctor has learnt the truth about Lida's affair with Zarudin. Sanin urges the nervous Novikov to go out into the garden where Lida is waiting, an episode which enables us to see Lida's state of mind in more detail: her fear and shame, and her desire for Novikov's forgiveness and love. The brevity of the third flashback, in Chapter XXVII, reflects the increasing momentum of events to be detected as the novel draws to its close. (Tension in the work begins to mount from Chapter XVI onwards, in which Lida tells Zarudin she is pregnant). This third example occurs during the visit made by Zarudin and Voloshin to the Sanin home and, like its predecessor, it offers another glimpse of Lida's state of mind. As she appears in the doorway (just after Sanin has told the unwelcome guests to leave), Artsybashev takes us back to her renewed thoughts of suicide in her humiliation at the visit. But, after regaining her composure in the quiet garden, she returns bravely to the house to face her seducer. Not only do such episodes enable Artsybashev to vary the pace of his narrative (Lida's appearance after the third example serves to defuse the dangerous situation created by Sanin's rudeness to Zarudin); they also supply us with vital background information which the scene before us cannot provide.

Another, more obvious, structural device is apparent elsewhere in the novel. In order to bring Sanin into situations where his behaviour can be demonstrated or his views expressed, Artsybashev resorts to the use of coincidence. It is by chance, for example, that Sanin appears on the river bank to save Lida from drowning herself, a coincidence which then allows him to explain to her at length why her intention was wrong; by chance Ivanov and he glimpse Karsavina swimming naked in the river, a sequence that not only anticipates Sanin's later urge to possess her but also reveals him as a supremely physical creature at one with the whole of creation; and it is by chance that Sanin meets the small boy bringing the message for Karsavina, a situation which enables him to accompany the girl on her walk back to town and leads swiftly to their intimacy in the river scene. There are other occasions on which Sanin appears quite unexpectedly and adds a new dimension to the situation concerned. He comes with the priest and psalm-reader to the dying Semenov's bedside, and Ryazantsev is astonished to find him at the peasant's camp-fire after his nocturnal hunting expedition with Svarozhich. Occasionally the unpredictable nature of Sanin's movements is disconcerting to those around him, especially if it reminds them of their own inadequacies. Thus later in Chapter XIII Sanin can be heard laughing with the gay peasant girls in the darkness beyond the firelight, "a few paces away and not at all where Yuri had thought he was. . . ."

Who, then, it must be asked, *is* Sanin? The answer is that we do not really know. So scant is the information supplied by Artsybashev about his hero that it is hard to believe in his existence outside the novel. Of his past we learn little more than that he has travelled about Russia, suffered privation, and taken part in revolutionary activity. He became bored by the latter, however, and now rejects it, just as he rejects religion. And yet, despite his youth, Sanin possesses a maturity and poise that seem to derive from close experience of a much wider world than the provincial town to which he belongs. As for his physical reality within the novel, however, we can be in no doubt, for Artsybashev's repeated mention of Sanin's prominent muscles, powerful shoulders, and calm, faintly mocking eyes lends his hero a positive presence designed to remind us that actually and figuratively this is a giant among pygmies. Sanin is first and foremost a mouthpiece for the author's views, a preceptive, didactic figure who at times considers it his duty to become involved in the lives of his fellow-men and to demonstrate his *Weltanschauung* in his dealings with them. Forceful though he may be, it must be said that he asserts himself only when the occasion demands it: when he detects injustice, falsehood or cruelty, or when he feels that his own inviolable self is threatened. Thus the blow which he deals Zarudin is struck primarily in self-defence, not in revenge for his sister's shame at the officer's hands and still less out of a sense of wounded pride.

The assumption that Sanin is a direct descendant of Nietzsche's *Übermensch* [superman] is an easy one to make and has unfortunately become virtually automatic in much of what little criticism of Artsybashev exists. It would, however, seem to be erroneous. How, Artsybashev once asked, could Nietzsche ever have influenced him, for he confessed that he had never read him properly. "This brilliant thinker," he went on, "is out of sympathy with me, both in his ideas and in the bombastic form of his works, and I have never got beyond the beginnings of his books." As if to underline his rejection of the German's philosophy, as early as Chapter III Artsybashev has Sanin idly open a copy of *Also sprach Zarathustra* (which he has found in Lida's room) while lying in bed. But after the first few pages he becomes annoyed and bored, spits in disgust, flings the book aside, and falls instantly asleep. "The bombastic images did not touch his soul," Artsybashev explains. The real lessons offered by life, he implies, are worth infinitely more than the theoretical ones to be found in books.

To whom does Sanin owe his ideas, if it is not to Nietzsche? A telling clue is to be found in two remarks made by Artsybashev, firstly that the 1905 Revolution "long distracted me from what I consider 'mine'—the preaching of anarchical individuality," and secondly, after denying Nietzsche's influence, that "Max Stirner is to me much nearer and more comprehensible." Max Stirner (pseudonym of Johann Kaspar Schmidt, 1806-1856) is a little-known individualist anarchist philosopher and author of *Der Einzige und Sein Eigentum (The Ego and His Own)* (1844), a book which attracted the attention of several Russian writers around the turn of the century, notably Artsybashev's contemporary and acquaintance, Alexander Kuprin.

Stirner's work turns on the contrast between the ancient and the modern world, and shows that modern man no longer knows how to live in the natural world of the present. Whilst, as Feuerbach maintained, "to the ancients the world was a truth," Christianity has deprived modern man of his forefathers' awareness of reality by directing his attention inwards, to his own self, his own mind. Stirner states the contrast thus: "All wisdom of the ancients is the science of the world, all wisdom of the moderns is the science of God." Theology and Christianity rose from the spirit and have left their proponents ill-equipped for life amid the reality of the present. "The man who still faces the world *armed*," writes Stirner, "is the ancient, the *heathen;* the man who has come to be led by nothing but . . . his fellow-feeling, his *spirit,* is the modern, the Christian." Stirner believes that because the life of modern man is "occupation with the spiritual—*thinking*," he is ruled by abstract notions such as law, morality, property and the State, which derive chiefly from Christian ethics. But if man supplants Christianity with supreme love of his own unique self—"Nothing is more to me than myself!"—then such notions become irrelevant. Stirner's self-conscious egoist, his self-willed man, denies, like Feuerbach, any being higher than himself—"Man is to man the supreme being"—and sees himself as the God of all that lives in a world in which "God has had to give place . . . to Man."

Taken to its ultimate conclusion, the development of his egoism by Stirner's individual anarchist leads to dissolution of the State and to the union of free men. General liberty can come about only when tyranny is met with the concerted opposition of intelligent human beings who refuse to submit to its domination. Herein lies an essential difference between Stirner and Nietzsche, and in his introduction to Stirner's work J. L. Walker has summed up that difference:

> Stirner loved liberty for himself . . . and he had no lust of power. Democracy to him was sham liberty, egoism the genuine liberty.
>
> Nietzsche, on the contrary, pours out his contempt upon democracy because it is not aristocratic. He is predatory to the point of demanding that those who must succumb to feline rapacity shall be taught to submit with resignation.
>
> Stirner shows that men make their tyrants as they make their gods, and his purpose is to unmake tyrants.
>
> Nietzsche dearly loves a tyrant.

The echoes of Stirner's philosophy in Sanin's words and behaviour are clear, though Artsybashev seems to have introduced a pessimistic note of his own. There is nothing essentially *good* in life, Sanin asserts, for the world of nature is as bad as the world of men. A human being's role in life is purely passive, and his death is just as necessary to the process of existence as his life. But while man is alive he must live life to the full

and not allow it to be a torment. If Stirner believes that life is full of pleasure ("living is . . . in enjoyment"), then Sanin advises us to live like carefree birds and take all that life has to offer. To enjoy life to the full, Sanin needs above all to satisfy his natural desires. If man suppresses those desires, he believes, then he destroys himself.

A significant point on which Stirner and Artsybashev differ, however, is the relationship between the individual and the society to which he belongs. For his part, Stirner wishes to unite with intelligent fellow-egoists so as to destroy the State and form in its place a *Union of Egoists*. Sanin, however, has no illusions about his fellow-men. How vulgar and stupid they are, he thinks, and how much horror there is in human life! Man is lord of the earth, and yet he suffers continually and goes in fear of his own shadow. Man is vile by nature, he declares, and we should expect nothing good from him, for then the evil that he does us will cause us neither trouble nor grief. Nothing is further from Sanin's mind than to associate with other human beings for revolutionary purposes, since he considers his fellow-men contemptible. Just as he asks nothing from life, so he needs nothing from them—"I live alone. . . ."

It is, however, for Christianity that Sanin reserves his most mordant criticism, and his words develop Stirner's point that the doctrine has left its adherents ill-equipped for real life. He denies that Christianity has had a beneficial effect on mankind, for its emphasis on humility and submission took away men's urge to fight, with the result that the underprivileged and dispossessed (epitomised by the three peasants Sanin meets in the closing chapter) failed to rise up and destroy the established order holding them in subjection. Christ's name is an everlasting curse on mankind, Sanin declares, for his doctrine destroyed the passionate freedom and beauty of life, replacing it only by tedious duty and a senseless dream of happiness in the distant future. Christianity, he concludes, has done absolutely nothing to make the improvement of man's lot any easier. While pious platitudes go on being mouthed about love of one's neighbour and the desirability of humanitarianism, genuine change still comes about only through bloodshed and revolution.

In view of Stirner's thesis that modern man is preoccupied by *"thinking,"* it is interesting to note that Sanin excepts literature from his general contempt for intellectual activity. Shortly after denying the beneficial influence of Christianity, he asserts that genuine literature "reshapes the whole of life and passing from one generation to the next, enters into the very blood of mankind." If literature were to be destroyed, he adds, then life itself would lose much of its colour and gradually fade. It is the craft of writing, Artsybashev infers, that possesses the potential to ameliorate the human condition, not Christianity which, far from gladdening our lives, has inflicted untold suffering on mankind.

Sanin's total participation in life as he sees it is emphasised by his intensely physical response to the natural world of which he feels so much a part. There are three occasions on which this organic bond is strikingly demonstrated. The first is in Chapter XXXV, when Sanin and Ivanov go out of town on a hot summer's day. From the pair's barefoot walk along a warm, sandy road to their naked dance on the lush, sunlit grass, the episode pulses with primitive, quasi-pagan *joie de vivre*. But the climax of the scene is the invigorating storm, during which Sanin tries to outshout the claps of thunder. Filled with ecstasy by the noise, he feels strength flooding his body, and throwing up his arms, cries out to the echoing sky. On the second occasion, in Chapter XXIX, Sanin's response is the direct result of intense sexual experience. After his passionate intimacy with the beautiful Karsavina, the hero rows out into the river and gives a great shout of animal joy which is answered by both the forest and the mist of dawn. Finally, the closing lines of the novel remind us once again of Sanin's conscious oneness with the whole of creation, as with a loud cry he strides powerfully off into the immensity of steppe towards the rising sun. Sanin, then, is a supremely physical creature who revels in the vigour and immediacy of the natural world. But not only does *he* respond to that world; it also seems to acknowledge the importance of his place in it by responding to *him*. As early as Chapter I, after his hero has flung a thick branch into the river, Artsybashev tells us that the sedge on the bank "bowed to Sanin, as though greeting him as its own."

If Sanin embodies Artsybashev's advocacy of the natural life free of moral and social constraints, then the alternative and unnatural way of being is demonstrated by the technology student Yuri Svarozhich, who serves as a foil to the hero. Sanin and he thus represent what Artsybashev saw as the positive and negative polarities operative among the Russian intelligentsia around the turn of the century, a neat contrast affirmed by the fact that both characters have their disciples: Sanin is followed by the teacher, Ivanov, and Yuri by the student, Shafrov. Whereas Sanin's behaviour testifies to the joy of being alive in a world brimming with physical promise, Yuri's reflects the profoundly life-denying pessimism that sapped the creative strength of so many members of his generation. Not for nothing does his sister Lyalya refer to him early in the novel as a "knight of the sorrowful countenance." Though formerly active in revolutionary circles (he has spent six months in prison and has been exiled from Moscow under police surveillance), Yuri is now a man with few convictions and even less drive. His capacity for effective action is crippled by morbid introspection of truly Dostoevskian proportions. Excessively cerebral and filled with maudlin self-pity, he regards his life as "exceptionally unsuccessful" and himself as "exceptionally unhappy." Obsessed by thoughts of the essential futility of all human endeavour—an obsession reinforced by his frequent reading and occasional masochistic imitation of Ecclesiastes—he experiments with guns and toys with the idea of suicide. The death of Semenov early in the novel only confirms his belief that the black void of oblivion nullifies whatever efforts man may make during his lifetime. Though the two suicides which precede his own are more explicable in terms of the psychological condition of the victims concerned, Yuri's death by his own hand is still inevitable. Convinced that an inexorable fate is pursuing him and that his life is irrevocably gone, he allows himself to become persuaded by the deaths of others into believing that suicide is the only escape for him too. In Chapter IX Artsybashev lays the first clue to Yuri's eventual fate when Dubova asks him whether he has ever thought of committing suicide. And then, rather later, in Chapter XXXIII, Yuri for some reason asks Ryazantsev what gun Zarudin used to shoot himself: "With a Browning?" From then on it is merely a question of time. From the conviction that death is better than the sad old age which awaits him, Yuri moves on to reflect how fine it would be if someone were to kill him. Prompted by Lyalya's unwittingly apposite remark "You're burying your own youth," he takes the final step and pulls the trigger himself.

It is in Chapter XXXVIII, well before Yuri's suicide, that Sanin pronounces his verdict on Yuri and his kind, and at the same time explains his credo. The chapter is thus crucial to an un-

derstanding of Artsybashev's philosophy. Significantly, Sanin's words are addressed to Karsavina, with whom Yuri has failed sexually in the immediately preceding chapter and whom Sanin, by contrast, is masterfully to possess only a few minutes later. Significantly, too, Sanin's opinion of Yuri is expressed against a backcloth of immense natural beauty (the peaceful, moonlit river), which implicitly affirms once more the hero's kinship with the physical world and quietly confirms the accuracy of his judgement.

Sanin explains that Yuri is a latter-day last of the Mohicans, the final representative of the second and conscious phase of human development (the first was instinctive and brutish), a phase characterised by the reappraisal of all man's feelings, needs and desires. Yuri, he goes on, has no real life as such, for everything he does is subject to endless questionings and doubts as to whether his actions are good or bad. He takes this agonised self-scrutiny to ludicrous lengths: "When he joins the party, he wonders whether it isn't beneath his dignity to stand alongside other people, whereas when he leaves the party he is tormented by the thought that it might be degrading to stand aside from the general movement!" There is, therefore, nothing exclusive or noble about this man who is organically dissatisfied with life; instead he is simply pitiful and wretched. No man can be "above life," Sanin declares, for he himself is only a minute part of it. The reasons for Yuri's dissatisfaction lie only within himself: "He simply cannot or dare not take from life's riches as much as he really needs." For his part, Sanin continues, he is always dreaming of "a joyous time . . . when nothing will stand between man and his happiness, and when man will give himself freely and without fear to all the pleasures available to him." But this will not mean a return to barbarity, he explains, for mankind has not lived in vain; it is gradually "evolving new conditions of existence in which there will be no place for either bestiality or asceticism. . . ." As for love, he concludes, that imposes obligations on man only because of the jealousy it arouses, a feeling which is born of slavery. "People should enjoy love without fear or constraint. . . . And if they can do so, then even the forms which love takes will be extended to become an infinite series of chance meetings, unexpected encounters and coincidences."

All this, however, is for Karsavina's benefit, and after Yuri's suicide Sanin is very much less kind. When asked by Shafrov to make a speech over Yuri's grave, he declares loudly that there is now one fool less on earth. Yuri lived stupidly, tormented himself over trivia, and died an idiotic death. Such is Artsybashev's judgement on the bloodless intellectuals of his time who lost faith in the possibility of social change in Russia and who failed to find the alternative which he now advocates—supremely individual egoism and the enjoyment of life in all its manifestations.

If Svarozhich is shackled by excessive introspection, then the Jew Soloveichik is burdened by the hereditary pacifism of his race, a crippling legacy which leaves him unable to cope with the difficulties presented by life. Though far less intellectualised than those of Svarozhich, his weaknesses put Soloveichik in the same broad psychological category, and he serves as a partial pendant to the more complex student. Both men feel that they are superfluous in the society of their time, and both escape their inner doubts in self-destruction. Ironically as careworn as his namesake ("little nightingale") is carefree, the ingratiating, nervous Soloveichik is an undeveloped but interesting character through whom Artsybashev intends a critique of the Tolstoyan doctrine of non-resistance to evil.

The issue of the individual's response to violence and evil is raised by Sanin's physical reaction to Zarudin in Chapter XXX. When Sanin hits Zarudin in self-defence, Soloveichik bursts into tears at the sight of the officer crawling on all fours and spitting blood. His cry to Sanin of "Why . . . Why?" is echoed immediately by Yuri's exclamation "How vile!" Just two chapters later and during the same evening, Sanin visits Soloveichik at his deserted mill and explains why he met violence with violence. Whilst acknowledging that he had effectively destroyed Zarudin, Sanin protests that he had no choice in the circumstances and adds that his conscience is therefore clear. When Soloveichik suggests that it would have been better for Sanin to suffer Zarudin's blow without retaliation, Sanin replies that moral victory does not lie in proffering the other cheek on each and every occasion but in being right *vis-à-vis* one's conscience. What follows reveals why Sanin holds such a view and at the same time sheds more light on his philosophy. When Soloveichik asks him whether he has always been so calm and self-assured, Sanin reveals that he was once prey to all kinds of doubt and seriously dreamed of the ideal of a truly Christian existence. He then talks at length about his former fellow-student, Ivan Lande, and explains why he no longer subscribes to the Christian doctrine of passive resistance to violence and evil. Lande was a Christian to the depths of his being, and so completely was Sanin under his influence that when once struck by a fellow-student, he did not retaliate. As a result, however, Sanin conceived a bitter hatred for his attacker—not because he had been struck by him but because by refusing to fight back he had given his adversary immense pleasure. After a time, though, Sanin saw the hypocrisy of his position, ceased to pride himself on his false moral victory, and at the first opportunity beat his enemy senseless. It was then that he realised Lande's life was essentially unhappy, and he broke inwardly with him. As he sees it now, Lande's happiness consisted in uncomplainingly accepting all unhappiness, while life's richness lay in denying himself all the riches that life had to offer. He was thus no more than "a voluntary beggar and dreamer, who lived for something about which he knew nothing whatsoever. . . ." Lande was valuable purely in himself, Sanin believes, and with his death his worth simply ceased to exist. It is fruitless to attempt to emulate him, he concludes, for men such as Lande are born, not made; in the same way Christ was a fine human being, while the Christians who followed him were insignificant creatures.

Although Artsybashev's attention in **Sanin** is focused chiefly on young representatives of the civilian middle class, intellectuals and otherwise, he is also at pains to examine members of the army. His portrayal of the military, brief though it is, continues a literary tradition established by several of his predecessors in the nineteenth century, notably Tolstoy (*Sebastopol Stories* and *The Raid*) and Garshin (*From the Memoirs of Private Ivanov* and *Four Days*). As a result of Russia's military involvement in the Far East around the turn of the century and her humiliating defeat in the war with Japan in 1905, the tradition received fresh impetus. Grave public concern about the military as a select and virtually autonomous caste in Russian society found particular reflection in Kurpin's novel *The Duel* of 1905, which caused a furore by its revelation of the hypocrisy and cruelty that bedevilled the Tsarist army. More specifically, Artsybashev's treatment of the subject of duelling as Zarudin agonises over the fact that Sanin will not fight him in the traditional way, echoes a topical concern of the mid-1890s, for 1894 saw the introduction of official regulations authorising duelling between officers in certain circumstances.

Unlike Tolstoy and Garshin, however, and anticipating Kuprin, Artsybashev shows the army in peace not war, placing his soldiers in a remote and drab provincial environment. Despite its limited nature, his portrayal is most unflattering. The military are arrogant and vain, believe that distinction and honour are their sole prerogatives, and hold ordinary mortals in supreme contempt. Moreover,—and this is Artsybashev's chief criticism—they consider themselves eminently desirable to women, whom they regard as no more than vehicles for sexual gratification. As though we needed further proof of it, the latter point is forcibly demonstrated in Chapter XXVII when Zarudin's essential animality is aroused by the prurience of the debauched Voloshin. But the episode also shows how different Zarudin and Sanin are in the sexual sense, for however desirous of women Sanin may be, he is never lascivious. (Taking this difference further, it is interesting to compare Zarudin's response to Lida with Sanin's response to Karsavina after their respective intimacies. Of the two, it is Sanin—the alleged sensual villain of Artsybashev's piece—who is sincerely grateful to his mate for a unique experience that has brought him incomparable joy.)

Deeply humiliated by Sanin's disfiguring blow, Zarudin comes face to face with himself for the first and only time in his life. Through the confrontation Artsybashev not only reveals the officer's utter solitude now that his military honour is forever tarnished, but also points to the spiritual bankruptcy of army existence. Never, Zarudin feels, will he be a free man again, a state symbolised by his recollection of a fly dragging a trail of thick spittle across the floor, its wings and legs smeared with fatal slime. But then his abject shame brings him a sudden and totally novel lucidity, as he sees that the reason for his present suffering is that he has never been truly free, never been able to call life truly his own. Recalling his heartless rejection of Lida during her final visit, he sees that she must have been suffering even more than he is now, and wonders whether his present pain might atone for the past. But in his heart he knows she will never return. Suddenly he realises that in his life, which is now gone forever, there was nothing beautiful or fine at all; instead it was all "confused, foul and stupid." To live again, he thinks, he must renounce his former way of life and become a completely different man. But the glimmer of hope dies even as it is born. The mark left on Zarudin by the army is there for life, and it is the impossibility of ever obliterating it that makes his death inevitable.

Just as Sanin pronounces his verdict on Svarozhich as a type, so he utters his opinion of Zarudin. Here it is Soloveichik who is the listener, and he hears from Sanin what amounts to a summary denunciation of army life: "People learn how to kill other people and how to cherish their own bodies, yet completely fail to understand what they are doing and why. . . . They are madmen, idiots!" The law of army life, he declares, demands vengeance whatever the cost, so the outcome of his collision with Zarudin was a foregone conclusion. When shortly afterwards Sanin sees Zarudin's orderly running by in panic and guesses that the officer has shot himself, his response anticipates the words he is to speak over Yuri's grave later in the novel: "One more, one less—what does it matter?" As Artsybashev sees it, soldier and intellectual have led equally incomplete existences, for both have failed to discover their essential selves and to exploit the boundless potential inherent in life.

The rash of suicides towards the end of the novel—all of them committed by members of the younger generation—suggests that the social fabric is unstable if not crumbling. Though each of the suicides (officer, student and Jew) occurs for different reasons, the victim in each case represents a significant element in Russian society around the turn of the century. The army enables the autocratic apparatus to maintain the status quo; the student body traditionally questions or even threatens it; and the Jew is the standard whipping-boy for public discontent, as demonstrated by the pogroms which swept Russia in the late 1800s and early 1900s. As Artsybashev shows, the character representing each of these social elements finds his life wanting. Zarudin comes to see military existence as an empty falsity, Svarozhich fails to secure in his revolutionary activities a lasting *raison d'être*, and Soloveichik finds his continual suffering and lack of purpose intolerable. At the same time these three deaths raise the question of whether other members of the same generation may find solutions to their problems before it is too late. But Artsybashev implies that they will not. Even those who do not kill themselves out of despair are either afflicted by consumption or are so steeped in mediocrity that their lives hold little promise. Nor, it should be noted, does the elder generation escape unscathed from the epidemic of destruction, for Yuri's father, a retired colonel, has a stroke when his son commits suicide. If even the revolutionary way— for so long the cherished hope of Russian intellectuals—has proved non-viable (Sanin himself has rejected it too), then what way of being is left? Stirner offers an answer. His self-willed man believed that only his own self lay at the centre of all things: "*I* am everything to myself and I do everything *on my account.*" This is the new *raison d'être* which Artsybashev offers to a generation lost in the wilderness of introspection and doubt—egoistic concern with one's own uniquely individual self.

What *Sanin* loses in ponderously didactic monologues uttered by its hero, it gains in masterfully evocative descriptions of natural settings. Nature is a constant presence in the work, serving to remind us of the primacy of organic life and of the myriad living things that contribute to it. Artsybashev's use of changes of season emphasises the cyclical pattern of life and death in the natural world and enables him subtly to vary the atmosphere of the novel, passing from warm promise through heady intoxication to chill disillusionment. Beginning with the sunlit vivification of late spring, the work takes us through the sultry heat of high summer to the cold winds and leaden skies of early autumn. Not only does the natural world passively reflect a character's mood (this is especially true of the melancholy Yuri); it also actively responds to it, as we have seen with Sanin.

The pictorial quality of so many of Artsybashev's natural scenes is a reflection of his experience as an art student at Kharkhov before he took up literature. Though his style is often formless and occasionally tiresome, his acuity of vision and sensitivity to colour are remarkable. "I love colours more than words," he once wrote. If any colour predominates in the work, it is green, the natural colour not only of the plant world but also of many creatures that inhabit it, creatures such as the "supple, grass-green" lizard which slips across the hero's path. Green is emphasised again and again in descriptions of the Sanins' long garden that runs down to the river, a place of elemental vegetable profusion where countless leaves and branches produce infinite variations of dappled, greenish shadow. It is in this garden that Sanin spends his first full day after coming home, declining to uproot the tall weeds as his mother suggests for, as he tells her, "I love every kind of greenery." And it is through this same garden with its bare trees and cold earth—

a garden where so much has happened during the novel but which "nobody needed any more now"—that he walks to the station at the close. Significantly, green is absent from this final description, for the garden is now devoid of life.

Yellow and gold occur frequently too. When used in a positive sense, they usually describe the life-giving sunlight with which Sanin is so often associated. Elsewhere, though, yellow is highly suggestive of death and decay, processes which in Artsybashev's world are as important as life. Thus the glove which Lida drops into the river as she is about to commit suicide is light yellow. (It grows dark with water and, twisting as though in symbolic agony, sinks slowly into the greenish-black depths.) The motif of yellow leaves becomes hauntingly insistent towards the end of the novel, as autumn draws on and Yuri becomes increasingly preoccupied by thoughts of death. So ubiquitous are these leaves that attempting to avoid them is as futile as trying to avoid one's own dissolution, and their countless multitudes presage the bodily decay which so horrifies Yuri whenever he thinks of it. Yellow leaves carpet the ground as he walks through the garden for the last time; yellow leaves float in the bucket of water carried past him by the coachman; and yellow leaves seem to press heavily on his forehead and then envelop him completely as he lies dying under the oak— the only tree in the garden that is still green and that symbolises the precious life now ebbing from him.

Black is more often than not a negative, even sinister colour, exemplified by the slippery black snake which sets the dead leaves rustling as it crosses Sanin's path in the cemetery shortly after Yuri's burial. The old mill where the sad Soloveichik lives is a "vast, black building with . . . narrow, coffin-like outhouses" under an ominous black sky. But it is in connection with the doomed Semenov that black is particularly emphasised. The movement of his arm resembles the flapping wing of "some black bird of prey"; he imagines death as a "vast, round, completely black abyss"; the flies soundlessly circling the lamps above his hospital bed are a sinister black colour; and, as death finally overtakes him, he sinks into "rolling waves of black mist." Elsewhere Artsybashev uses black with white to create a visual effect of stark simplicity. A striking example is the study of Soloveichik's face not long before he hangs himself: "It was quite dark, and in the gloom his face seemed as white as that of a corpse, while his eyes looked like empty, black sockets." The same contrastive technique is used in very different circumstances as Sanin gazes at Karsavina's "white face with its black eyebrows" while they are in the boat.

Not only does Artsybashev use single colours to great effect— he refers, for example, to the "red, white and green flowers" entwined around the dead Yuri's face—but he also demonstrates a painter's eye for the play of light and shade. Nearing death, Semenov becomes afraid to look into the darkness and starts sleeping with the lamp on; en route to the hospital he glimpses lights burning in the windows of houses and at the same time sees the dark trees racing past his carriage. In the river scene in Chapter XXXVIII the "dark blue moon" shining in a "dark blue sky" shimmers on the bright, smooth water, picking out Karsavina in her startlingly white blouse and transforming her into an alluring creature of fantasy for Sanin. By contrast, after their love-making in the boat, the tonality of the natural setting shows a rapid change: as river and fields are wreathed in the white mist of dawn, the moon shines "indistinct and pale, like an apparition fading at the break of day." Occasionally, Artsybashev also displays an artist's sensitivity for combinations of colours that are delicately suggestive. In the closing lines of Chapter XLII, for example, he describes the "golden garden," the "greenish—light blue autumn sky" reflected in the river, and the distant fields "silvered with gossamer."

What contributes most, however, to the atmosphere of sadness that pervades the closing chapters of the novel is Artsybashev's unerring eye for scenes which evoke melancholy and nostalgia. His delicate touch is apparent, for example, in the description of the cemetery after Yuri's burial. The trees are sprinkled with the "gold and red rain" of their dying foliage, white crosses stand beside black or grey marble headstones and gilt ornamental railings, while among the silent graves it seems as though "someone sad has been walking . . . and grieving without hope or tears." Autumn is here, too, in all her sombre glory, for the cold, yellowing earth is covered by a thick carpet of yellow leaves which the wind has piled up on the paths so that it looks as if "streams of yellow are flowing throughout the cemetery." But the picture in Chapter XLIII of the drunken old chorister Piotr Ilyich walking among the deserted summer residences *(dachas)* is a descriptive *tour de force* without parallel in the novel. Here the exquisite but fleeting beauty of autumn evokes a subtle mood of quiet resignation. The fences are hung with garlands of red hops, the tracery of thinning branches stands golden against the sky, and the flower beds lie bare save for coldly beautiful asters, while lingering like a late bird in the deserted avenues can be glimpsed the solitary figure of a woman, sadly pensive and strangely beautiful. And over the empty houses and dying gardens hangs the stillness of locked windows and doors, the all-embracing, mysterious stillness of autumn.

Artsybashev's descriptive skill should not, however, blind us to the fact that *Sanin* is essentially a *roman à thèse* ["thesis novel"] in the best traditions of Russian literature. He himself considered it "neither a novel of ethics nor a libel on the younger generation," but an "apology for individualism." "The hero of the novel is a type," he went on. "In its pure form this type is still new and rare, but its spirit is in every frank, bold and strong representative of the new Russia." Sanin's rarity as a type is emphasised by his sudden departure at the close of the novel. By the end of his brief stay in the town he is thoroughly bored, for though the people around him seemed interesting enough at the beginning, they have all failed to come up to his expectations. Even his sister Lida, he thinks, in whose fall he saw such poetic passion and strength, might have done better to drown herself after all.

How marked has Sanin's effect been on this provincial town whose anonymity implies that it is typical of the whole of Russia and perhaps, too, of the world at large? He has been the indirect cause of Zarudin's suicide; he has agreed with Soloveichik's conviction that the Jew can serve no useful purpose among his fellow-men, so prompting him to hang himself; and by making spontaneous, passionate love to Karsavina he has implicitly passed sentence on the vacillating, introspective Yuri. The closing pages of the novel reveal what Artsybashev believes about his fellow-human beings. Just as in life, so in the town a small minority of people—Karsavina and Lida among them—possess the capacity to be true to themselves for a time. But none of them can be so for good, because like the vast majority they eventually succumb to the flabby mediocrity of their convention-bound lives. Even Sanin's faithful disciple Ivanov lacks the strength or vision to break with his monotonous existence, and as the hero's train disappears into the

darkness, he wanders despondently off towards the tavern, accompanied by the "tall, pale spectre of his long, colourless life." Sanin's ideological and social exclusiveness at the close is underlined by the hostility shown towards him by his herd-like contemporaries after Yuri's funeral. Led by Shafrov, Yuri's former follower, they are angry with him for having spoken the truth not only about Yuri but also about the generation to which he belonged—their own.

In the social sense Artsybashev's conclusion is decidedly pessimistic. However great Sanin's desire to propagandise his fellow-men in the ways of true being, his words have no more than a temporary effect on them, and to a man they fail to emulate him. He thus remains forever apart from them, convinced that he is infinitely above them. Their society is as constrictive and loathsome to him as the cramped and airless railway carriage, and he opts out of it without a moment's hesitation. Artsybashev's extraordinarily vigorous hero who leaps off the moving train into unashamedly splendid isolation in the closing lines of the novel is a descendant of Stirner's "king of the world," a defiantly egoistic God-man who acknowledges no authority save his own unique will and who sets above all else in life the desire to win himself a place in the sun. (pp. 58-78)

> *Nicholas Luker, "Artsybashev's 'Sanin': A Reappraisal," in* Renaissance and Modern Studies, *Vol. XXIV, 1980, pp. 58-78.*

ADDITIONAL BIBLIOGRAPHY

Boyd, Ernest. Preface to *Sanine*, by Michael Petrovich Artzibashev, pp. v-ix. New York: The Viking Press, 1926.
    Defends *Sanine* against critics who found it pornographic and vulgar.

Boynton, H. W. "Varieties of Realism." *The Nation* 101, No. 2624 (14 October 1915): 461-62.
    Calls *Breaking Point* "a disheartening example of that frantic and unfruitful pessimism to which the Russian realist has so often descended. This nightmare of lust and despair and death is the more dreadful because of the intellectual energy relentlessly devoted to its weaving."

Brewster, Dorothy. "The Old and the New." *The Nation* 118, No. 8056 (30 January 1924): 119-20.
    Criticizes the views on marriage and sexual relationships expressed in *Jealousy, Enemies*, and *The Law of the Savage*.

Dana, H. W. L. "Russia." In *A History of Modern Drama*, edited by Barrett H. Clark and George Freedley, pp. 370-481. New York: D. Appleton-Century Co., 1947.
    Explores the major themes of *Sanine* and of Artsybashev's plays.

Eagle, Solomon [pseudonym of J. C. Squire]. "A Picture of Chaos." In his *Books in General, second series*, pp. 81-5. New York: Alfred A. Knopf, 1920.
    Claims that *Sanine* is worth studying because "it discusses 'sex-problems' with unusual honesty. . . . It gives a vivid picture, within certain limitations, of Russian life. . . . And it reflects the welter of thoughts and aspirations which are common to the whole contemporary Western world."

Hackett, Francis. "A Free Man." *The New Republic* I, No. 13 (30 January 1915): 27-8.
    Explicates *Sanine*, calling it "a novel of Russians confused about their ideals and themselves, but most of all confused about sex. The only one who is not confused is the man who understands his own desires, Sanin."

Luker, Nicholas. "A Vegetarian's Nightmare: Artsybashev's 'Krov'."
The New Zealand Slavonic Journal (1985): 89-104.
    Explicates Artsybashev's 1903 short story "Krov" in an attempt
    to demonstrate that Artsybashev was not exclusively concerned
    with sex and death.

"Recent Russian Tales by Sologub and Artzibashef." *The New York
Times Book Review* (1 July 1917): 249.
    Lauds the stories collected in *Tales of the Revolution* and notes
    that they possess an interest beyond works of fiction because of
    what they reveal about the Russian mind.

"Rattling Russian Chains." *The New York Times Book Review* (25
May 1924): 9.
    Calls *The Savage* "a very terrible and very powerful novel, whose
    absolute honesty is its justification."

Olgin, Moissaye J. "M. P. Artzybashev." In his *A Guide to Russian
Literature: 1820-1917*, pp. 265-69. New York: Harcourt, Brace and
Howe, 1920.

    Surveys Artsybashev's works in the context of Russian literature
    and outlines their reception by Russian critics.

Pachmuss, Temira. "Mikhail Artsybashev in the Criticism of Zinaida
Gippius." *The Slavonic and East European Review* XLIV, No. 102
(January 1966): 76-87.
    Analyzes Gippius's criticism of Artsybashev's works. Pachmuss
    calls *Sanine* "a crude advocacy of individualism and a rather bold
    treatment of sexual themes" and describes Gippius's objections
    to Artsybashev's style and themes.

Palmer, Cleveland. "Russia's Latest Novelist." *The Bookman* XLI,
No. 2 (April 1915): 135-38.
    Praises the "liberal and generous spirit" of *Sanine*.

Zavalishin, Vyacheslav. "Gorki and the Realists." In his *Early Soviet
Writers*, pp. 61-7. New York: Frederick A. Praeger, 1958.
    Maintains that Artsybashev's works, although characterized by
    "a racy, ostentatious sexiness which robs them of esthetic value,"
    are undervalued by critics, and that his novella *The Dikii Family*
    is "one of the gems of postrevolutionary Russian literature."

Willa Cather

1873-1947

The following entry presents criticism of Cather's novel *My Ántonia*. For a discussion of Cather's complete career, see *TCLC*, Volumes 1 and 11.

My Ántonia is often considered the best of Cather's twelve novels and the work in which she most effectively communicated her transcendent vision of American pioneers. In creating this portrait of a Czech immigrant and the rural values she embodies, Cather used symbols, images, and allusions to link the heroism and vitality of her central character, Ántonia Shimerda, with the universal physical and spiritual drives that have permitted humanity to flourish. The skill with which she did so has greatly contributed to Cather's reputation as one of the outstanding prose stylists of the twentieth century, while her sophisticated treatment of her subject matter has led critics to identify *My Ántonia* as a classic work of American literature.

Following the publication of her third novel, *The Song of the Lark,* in 1915, Cather suffered a series of personal losses that changed her life and influenced the tone of *My Ántonia*. Between 1900 and 1906, Cather had lived and worked in the home of her closest friend, Isabelle McClung, and after moving to New York in 1906, she continued to regard the McClungs' stately, serene residence as her home. Moreover, Cather gradually came to view the McClungs' house as her retreat from the world and returned there as often as her many literary activities permitted. However, after McClung's father died in November of 1915, the remaining family members were unwilling to maintain the large estate, and the house was closed. The loss of a man she had come to regard as a friend and the place she had considered her refuge saddened Cather, but these losses were followed by a more devastating blow: early in 1916 McClung, who had been Cather's constant companion—possibly her lover—for over a decade, married a concert violinist named Jan Hambourg. Although the Hambourgs planned to settle in New York, thus enabling Cather to visit often, she believed that her relationship with Isabelle had been destroyed, and her anguish over the situation temporarily deprived her of the desire to write.

In an attempt to alleviate her sadness, Cather traveled to New Mexico and Wyoming during the summer of 1916. While the ultimate product of this trip was a narrative of the Southwest in her later novel *The Professor's House*, the immediate result was a renewal of her enthusiasm for a novel she had conceived before her departure, which was to be based on the life of a woman Cather had known since childhood, Annie Sadilek. Returning to New York on Thanksgiving Day, she immediately began work. Elizabeth Singer Sergeant, a close friend of Cather, has recorded an incident that provides some insight into Cather's aspirations for the novel during the early stages of composition: one afternoon during the winter of 1917, Cather visited Sergeant's apartment and, noticing an antique apothecary jar on the floor, placed it in the center of an otherwise empty table. "I want my new heroine to be like this," she is reported to have said, "like a rare object in the middle of a table, which one may examine from all sides. I want her to stand out—like this—because she *is* the story." Cather continued to work on *My Ántonia* throughout the remainder of 1917 and much of

1918, continuing to make revisions in the text until a few weeks before the publication of the novel in the autumn of 1918.

In a recent biography of Cather, James Woodress noted that "in one sense Cather had been preparing to write *My Ántonia* for a third of a century," having known and admired Annie Sadilek for that length of time. Cather was particularly impressed with Sadilek's ability to endure adversity and still retain her enjoyment of life; in 1921 she told a reviewer that Sadilek was "one of the truest artists [she] ever knew in the keenness and sensitiveness of her enjoyment, in her love of people and in her willingness to take pains." These qualities are embodied in the title character of *My Ántonia* and are revealed by means of a complex narrative structure. In the introduction to the novel, an unnamed narrator, ostensibly Cather herself, tells of meeting an old friend, Jim Burden, who has written a memoir of a girl both knew during their childhood. The narrator of the introduction agrees to read Burden's manuscript, which then forms the body of the novel. In Book I, Burden describes his initial encounter with the Shimerda family, his friendship with fourteen-year-old Ántonia, and her father's suicide. Book II follows both Burden and Ántonia in their move to the town of Black Hawk, Ántonia having left her family to work for the Burdens' neighbors, the Harlings. Ántonia is absent from Book III, in which Burden goes to the state university, and she is featured only indirectly in Book IV, with Burden learning of her scandalous love affair and illegitimate child from a neighbor. She reappears only in the final section of the novel, when Burden visits the farm where she and her husband are raising their large family.

On the most basic level, *My Ántonia* is a celebration of the Nebraska pioneer as exemplified by Ántonia; her love for the landscape, her undaunted cheerfulness, and her resiliency are all representative of what Cather considered the pioneer spirit at its best. By surrounding Ántonia with symbols of fecundity, Cather gives her a mythical quality which, according to Woodress, marks her as "both the Madonna of the wheat fields and the symbol of the American westering myth." A number of critics, most notably John H. Randall III, have also observed in the novel allusions and images relating to natural cycles, noting that such elements significantly strengthen Cather's portrayal of the struggles and victories of human existence. However, contemporary critics assert that upon reexamination of more subtle levels of operation, *My Ántonia* emerges as a much less affirmative statement than was originally thought. One of the first of these darker meanings to be noticed was the elegiac tone of the novel, introduced in the Vergilian epigraph: "Optima dies . . . prima fugit" ("The best days are the first to flee"). As she wrote *My Ántonia*, Cather was acutely aware that the way of life she was documenting had begun to vanish, and her reluctant awareness of this fact was underscored by her personal losses. Her sense of nostalgia was markedly increased by her dislike for the twentieth century, which she regarded as an era of soulless materialism. Critics agree that this melancholy sentiment informs *My Ántonia*. Woodress has discussed the novel as a pastoral elegy in which the recurring epigraph serves as the primary leitmotif, while Lois Feger has observed that the images death, darkness, cold, and the setting sun within the text, by their sheer preponderance, "carry thematic significance far beyond their literal function."

Another negative aspect of *My Ántonia* that has been the subject of much critical discussion in recent decades is the complete absence of mutually satisfactory sexual relationships in the novel. In particular, critics have focused on the asexual relationship between Burden and Ántonia. While admitting that Cather's avowed impatience with the limitations imposed by men upon women in the nineteenth century led to a consistently negative portrayal of male-female relationships in her fiction, many commentators nevertheless consider such portrayals reflections of Cather's more basic and unacknowledged ambivalence toward heterosexuality. One of the earliest comments on this aspect of *My Ántonia* came in 1953 from Cather biographer E. K. Brown, who observed that between Burden and Ántonia "there is an emptiness where the strongest emotion might have been expected to gather." Brown suggested that this apparent incongruity was the result of an inherent weakness in Jim Burden as a literary device, explaining that in seeking to create in her narrator both a sympathetic participant in Ántonia's life and an objective observer, Cather had set a goal that was impossible to achieve. However, Blanche Gelfant later suggested that Burden's lack of sexual initiative is indicative of Cather's own repressed fear of adult heterosexuality, noting the grim images surrounding the few explicitly sexual encounters in the novel, and subsequent analyses have often discussed Burden as a manifestation of Cather's homosexual persona.

In an early review of Cather's novel, Randolph Bourne asserted that with *My Ántonia* Cather had "taken herself out of the rank of provincial writers and given us something we can fairly class

with the modern literary art the world over that is earnestly and richly interpreting the spirit of youth." Later assessments of the novel have only increased critical appreciation for the artistry and sophistication of Cather's masterpiece. While some believe that Gelfant and others have overemphasized the "aberrant" qualities of this novel in recent years, commentators nevertheless agree that, in addition to its value as an excellently wrought narrative of pioneer life, *My Ántonia* exhibits the thematic complexity common to all great works of literature and thus constitutes a major achievement in American letters.

(See also *Contemporary Authors*, Vol. 104; *Something about the Author*, Vol. 30; *Dictionary of Literary Biography*, Vol. 9: *American Novelists, 1910-1945*; Vol. 54: *American Poets, 1880-1945*; *Dictionary of Literary Biography Documentary Series*, Vol. 1; and *Short Story Criticism*, Vol. 2.)

RANDOLPH BOURNE (essay date 1918)

[*An American essayist who wrote during the early years of the twentieth century, Bourne is recognized as one of the most astute critics of American life and letters of his era. During his short life, he contributed numerous articles to national magazines and became known as a champion of progressive education and pacifism, as well as a fierce opponent of sentimentality in literature. Bourne was on the original staff of the* New Republic *and was also a contributing editor of the* Dial *and the* Seven Arts, *until the latter was officially suppressed during the First World War for its pacifist position. In a tribute published in the* New Republic, *Floyd Dell listed the characteristics of Bourne's mind as "restless and relentless curiosity, undeterred by sentiment and never recoiling in cynicism; the mood of perpetual inquiry, and the courage to go down unfamiliar ways in search of truth." In the following review of* My Ántonia, *Bourne notes the superiority of Cather's novel over similar works.*]

Willa Cather has already shown herself an artist in that beautiful story of Nebraska immigrant life, *O Pioneers!* Her digression into *The Song of the Lark* took her into a field that neither her style nor her enthusiasm really fitted her for. Now in *My Ántonia* she has returned to the Nebraska countryside with an enriched feeling and an even more golden charm of style. Here at last is an American novel, redolent of the Western prairie, that our most irritated and exacting preconceptions can be content with. . . . [Miss Cather is] of the brevity school, and beside William Allen White's swollen bulk she makes you realize anew how much art is suggestion and not transcription. One sentence from Miss Cather's pages is more vivid than paragraphs of Mr. White's stale brightness of conversation. The reflections she does not make upon her characters are more convincing than all his moralizing. Her purpose is neither to illustrate eternal truths nor to set before us the crowded gallery of a whole society. Yet in these simple pictures of the struggling pioneer life, of the comfortable middle classes of the bleak little towns, there is an understanding of what these people have to contend with and grope for that goes to the very heart of their lives.

Miss Cather convinces because she knows her story and carries it along with the surest touch. It has all the artistic simplicity of material that has been patiently shaped until everything irrelevant has been scraped away. The story has a flawless tone of candor, a naive charm, that seems quite artless until we realize that no spontaneous narrative could possibly have the clean pertinence and grace which this story has. It would be cluttered, as Mr. White's [*Heart of a Fool*] is cluttered; it would have uneven streaks of self-consciousness, as most of the younger novelists' work, done impromptu with a mistaken ideal of "saturation," is both cluttered and self-conscious. But Miss Cather's even novel has that serenity of the story that is telling itself, of people who are living through their own spontaneous charm.

The story purports to be the memories of a successful man as he looks back over his boyhood on the Nebraska farm and in the little town. Of that boyhood Ántonia was the imaginative center, the little Bohemian immigrant, his playmate and wistful sweetheart. His vision is romantic, but no more romantic than anyone would be towards so free and warm and glorious a girl. He goes to the University, and it is only twenty years later that he hears the story of her pathetic love and desertion, and her marriage to a simple Bohemian farmer, strong and good like herself.

> She was a battered woman now, not a lovely girl; but she still had that something which fires the imagination, could still stop one's breath for a moment by a look or gesture that somehow revealed the meaning in common things. She had only to stand in the orchard, to put her hand on a little crab tree and look up at the apples, to make you feel the goodness of planting and tending and harvesting at last. All the strong things of her heart came out in her body, that had been so tireless in serving generous emotions. It was no wonder that her sons stood tall and straight. She was a rich mine of life, like the founders of early races.

My Ántonia has the indestructible fragrance of youth: the prairie girls and the dances; the softly alluring Lena, who so unaccountably fails to go wrong; the rich flowered prairie, with its drowsy heats and stinging colds. . . . [This] story lives with the hopefulness of the West. It is poignant and beautiful, but it is not sad. Miss Cather, I think, in this book has taken herself out of the rank of provincial writers and given us something we can fairly class with the modern literary art the world over that is earnestly and richly interpreting the spirit of youth. In her work the stiff moral molds are fortunately broken, and she writes what we can wholly understand. (p. 557)

> *Randolph Bourne, "Morals and Art from the West,"*
> *in* The Dial *Vol. LXV, No. 779, December 14, 1918,*
> *pp. 556-57.*

H. L. MENCKEN (essay date 1920)

[*From the era of World War I until the early years of the Great Depression, Mencken was one of the most influential figures in American letters. His strongly individualistic, irreverent outlook on life and his vigorous, invective-charged writing style helped establish the iconoclastic spirit of the Jazz Age and significantly shaped the direction of American literature. As a social and literary critic—the roles for which he is best known—Mencken was the scourge of evangelical Christanity, public service organizations, literary censorship, boosterism, provincialism, democracy, all advocates of personal or social improvement, and every other facet of American life that he perceived as humbug. In his literary criticism, Mencken encouraged American writers to shun the anglophilic, moralistic bent of the nineteenth century and to practice realism, an artistic call-to-arms that is most fully developed in his essay "Puritanism as a Literary Force," one of the seminal essays in modern literary criticism. A man who was widely renowned or feared during his lifetime as a would-be destroyer of established American values, Mencken once wrote: "All of my work, barring a few obvious burlesques, is based upon three*

fundamental ideas. 1. That knowledge is better than ignorance; 2. That it is better to tell the truth than to lie; and 3. That it is better to be free than to be a slave." In the following excerpt, he discusses the rapid development of Cather's literary talents, noting that My Ántonia *represents "the best piece of fiction ever done by a woman in America."*]

Four or five years ago, though she already had a couple of good books behind her, Willa Cather was scarcely heard of. When she was mentioned at all, it was as a talented but rather inconsequential imitator of Mrs. Wharton. But today even campus-pump critics are more or less aware of her, and one hears no more gabble about imitations. The plain fact is that she is now discovered to be a novelist of original methods and quite extraordinary capacities—penetrating and accurate in observation, delicate in feeling, brilliant and charming in manner, and full of a high sense of the dignity and importance of her work. Bit by bit, patiently and laboriously, she has mastered the trade of the novelist; in each succeeding book she has shown an unmistakable advance. Now, at last, she has arrived at such a command of all the complex devices and expedients of her art that the use she makes of them is quite concealed. Her style has lost self-consciousness; her grasp of form has become instinctive; her drama is firmly rooted in a sound psychology; her people relate themselves logically to the great race masses that they are parts of. In brief, she knows her business thoroughly, and so one gets out of reading her, not only the facile joy that goes with every good story, but also the vastly higher pleasure that is called forth by first-rate craftsmanship.

I know of no novel that makes the remote folk of the western farmlands more real than *My Ántonia* makes them, and I know of none that makes them seem better worth knowing. Beneath the tawdry surface of Middle Western barbarism—so suggestive, in more than one way, of the vast, impenetrable barbarism of Russia—she discovers human beings bravely embattled against fate and the gods, and into her picture of their dull, endless struggle she gets a spirit that is genuinely heroic, and a pathos that is genuinely moving. It is not as they see themselves that she depicts them, but as they actually are. And to representation she adds something more—something that is quite beyond the reach, and even beyond the comprehension of the average novelist. Her poor peasants are not simply anonymous and negligible hinds, flung by fortune into lonely, inhospitable wilds. They become symbolical, as, say, Robinson Crusoe is symbolical, or Faust, or Lord Jim. They are actors in a play that is far larger than the scene swept by their own pitiful suffering and aspiration. They are actors in the grand farce that is the tragedy of man.

Setting aside certain early experiments in both prose and verse, Miss Cather began with *Alexander's Bridge* in 1912. The book strongly suggested the method and materials of Mrs. Wharton, and so it was inevitable, perhaps, that the author should be plastered with the Wharton label. I myself, asslike, helped to slap it on—though with prudent reservations, now comforting to contemplate. The defect of the story was one of locale and people: somehow one got the feeling that the author was dealing with both at second-hand, that she knew her characters a bit less intimately than she should have known them. This defect, I venture to guess, did not escape her own eye. At all events, she abandoned New England in her next novel for the Middle West, and particularly for the Middle West of the great immigrations—a region nearer at hand, and infinitely better comprehended. The result was *O Pioneers,* a book of very fine achievement and of even finer promise. Then came *The Song of the Lark*—still more competent, more searching and con-

vincing, better in every way. And then, after three years, came
My Ántonia, and a sudden leap forward. Here, at last, an
absolutely sound technique began to show itself. Here was a
novel planned with the utmost skill, and executed in truly
admirable fashion. Here, unless I err gravely, was the best
piece of fiction ever done by a woman in America.

I once protested to Miss Cather that her novels came too far
apart—that the reading public, constantly under a pressure of
new work, had too much chance to forget her. She was greatly
astonished. "How could I do any more?" she asked. "I work
all the time. It takes three years to write a novel." The saying
somehow clings to me. There is a profound criticism of criticism in it. It throws a bright light upon the difference between
such a work as *My Ántonia* and such a work as—... But I
have wars enough. (pp. 29-31)

H. L. Mencken, "Willa Cather," in The Borzoi 1920,
edited by Alfred A. Knopf, 1920, pp. 28-31.

REGIS MICHAUD (essay date 1928)

[*In the following excerpt, Michaud praises Cather's sympathetic
yet realistic treatment of Nebraska pioneers in* My Ántonia.]

My Ántonia is what is called in America an "immigrant" novel.
Immigration has given to America a new exotic background,
and a new source of local color. In *My Ántonia* Willa Cather
studies the immigrants with her usual sympathy. Ántonia is a
portrait drawn from within. Her self-abnegation is rare. A hard
worker, devoted to children, betrayed yet ever faithful, she is
a new edition of Flaubert's "Simple Heart." She is the incarnation of the motherly feeling. The sites of the Far West,
the rustic rites of the seasons form the background of this canvas
painted with the simplicity and the forcefulness of a master.

It is difficult to find in *My Ántonia* passages for an anthology.
Everything in it holds together. The tale is unfolded, "not as
a thing of which one thinks, but as conscience itself," slowly,
in sheer duration. *My Ántonia* is a little epic, the "Evangeline"
of the Far West. Here is a description of a Nebraska hamlet.
It tells a lot as to the nostalgia of its inhabitants. It is Jim, the
hero of the story, who is speaking:

> In the evening I used to prowl about, hunting for
> diversion. There lay the familiar streets, frozen with
> snow or liquid mud. They led to the houses of good
> people who were putting the babies to bed, or simply
> sitting still before the parlor stove, digesting their
> supper. Black Hawk had two saloons. One of them
> was admitted, even by the church people, to be as
> respectable as a saloon could be. Handsome Anton
> Jelinek, who had rented his homestead and come to
> town, was the proprietor. In his saloon there were
> long tables where the Bohemian and German farmers
> could eat the lunches they brought from home while
> they drank their beer. Jelinek kept rye bread on hand,
> and smoked fish and strong imported cheeses to please
> the foreign palate. I liked to drop into his bar-room
> and listen to the talk. But one day he overtook me
> on the street and clapped me on the shoulder.

> "Jim," he said, "I am good friends with you and I
> always like to see you. But you know how the church
> people think about saloons. Your grandpa has always
> treated me fine, and I don't like to have you come
> into my place, because I know he don't like it, and
> it puts me in bad with him."

> So I was shut out of that.

Black Hawk is about as dead as Gopher Prairie or Winesburg,
Ohio. Poor Jim! There are very few distractions in this far
Western village. There is the druggist across his ice-cream and
soda counter, the tobacconist and the old German who stuffs
birds, both of them great gossips. The great thrill is going to
see the night train fly by at the depot. At the telegraph office,
the idle clerk comforts himself in pinning on the wall portraits
of actors and actresses which he procured with cigarette pre-
miums. Then there is the station master who tries to forget the
death of his twins by fishing and writing letters to obtain a
change of residence:

> "These," says Jim "were the distractions I had to
> choose from. There were no other lights burning
> downtown after nine o'clock. On starlight nights I
> used to pace up and down those long, cold streets,
> scowling at the little, sleeping houses on either side,
> with their storm-windows and covered back porches.
> They were flimsy shelters, most of them poorly built
> of light wood, with spindle porch-posts horribly mu-
> tilated by the turning-lathe.

> "Yet for all their frailness, how much jealousy and
> envy and unhappiness some of them managed to con-
> tain! The life that went on in them seemed to be made
> up of evasions and negations; shifts to save cooking,
> to save washing and cleaning, devices to propitiate
> the tongue of gossip. This guarded mode of existence
> was like living under a tyranny. People's speech,
> their voices, their very glances, became furtive and
> repressed. Every individual taste, every natural ap-
> petite, was bridled by caution. The people asleep in
> those houses, I thought, tried to live like mice in their
> own kitchens; to make no noise, to leave no trace,
> to slip over the surface of things in the dark. The
> growing piles of ashes and cinders in the back yards
> were the only evidence that the wasteful, consuming
> process of life went on at all. On Tuesday nights the
> Owl Club danced; then there was a little stir in the
> streets, and here and there one could see a lighted
> window until midnight. But the next night all was
> dark again."

(pp. 241-43)

The art of Miss Cather shows itself in these sketches of nature
faithfully and minutely observed, but pervaded too with a sympathetic emotion. She herself has given us the key of her art,
in an article which she wrote when *The Professor's House* was
published. Her ideal in writing, she tells us, would be to have
people and things posing before her as they would for painters
of still life, like Rembrandt or Chardin, omitting nothing from
the background up to the surface. This "still-life" painting is
the most correct definition of Miss Cather's art. Her ambition
is to treat style as secondary in respect to the characters. She
wants to omit what is only picturesque in order to let people
tell their own story, without any comment on her part. She
takes a green vase and a yellow orange and puts them side by
side on a table. She carefully avoids interfering and relies
entirely on the objects thus placed to produce an artistic effect.
Let her make the reader *see* the green vase beside the orange.
Nothing else matters. She would like to have the style fused
so completely with the object that the reader would not even
suspect the former's existence. The people for whom she writes
are those whose chief interest is in the vase and the orange as
such, and in the way each lends its color to the other.

Here is an original programme of static and intimate realism
based upon a scrupulous reproduction of the object, a realism

which could not exist without this gift of sympathetic intuition (the Germans call it *Einfühlung*) characteristic of Miss Willa Cather. (pp. 245-46)

Régis Michaud, "Reinforcements: Willa Cather, Zona Gale, Floyd Dell, Joseph Hergesheimer, Waldo Frank," in his The American Novel To-Day: A Social and Psychological Study, *1928. Reprint by Kennikat Press, 1967, pp. 238-56.*

RENE RAPIN   (essay date 1930)

[*In the following excerpt, Rapin contends that* My Ántonia *is inferior to Cather's two previous novels,* O Pioneers! *and* The Song of the Lark.]

[*My Ántonia*] has been extravagantly praised, H. L. Mencken calling it the best novel by an American woman [see excerpt dated 1920]. Latrobe Carroll (writing, it is true, in 1921, when neither *One of Ours, The Professor's House,* nor *Death Comes for the Archbishop* were in existence) proclaimed it Willa Cather's most powerful work. The truth is that *My Ántonia,* though a lifelike portrait of a pioneer girl and, in its first part at least, a striking collection of vignettes, is inferior to *O Pioneers* in warmth of passion, to *The Song of the Lark* in variety and scope of interest, and has the defects in structure of both.

Like them it begins well, one hundred and fifty pages evoking in strong, direct prose the difficulties and joys of pioneer days, more particularly as exemplified in the fortunes of the Shimerdas, a family of Bohemian settlers newly arrived in Nebraska. The elder generation (melancholy Mr. Shimerda, sour grumbling Mrs. Shimerda) never get used to the incredibly primitive conditions in the new country. Their children, on the contrary, that is, first and foremost, Ántonia, take to the new land with the greater adaptability of their age, and fall to the tremendous task of making it habitable and fruitful with almost superhuman doggedness. In these pages (Book I, "The Shimerdas" of *My Ántonia*) Willa Cather reaches (though she does not surpass) the high level of the first part of *O Pioneers.* With Ántonia we roam the boundless prairie, lost in the tall "shaggy red grass . . . , the color of wine stains"; we drift along the "dewy, heavy-odored cornfields"; perched "on the slanting roof of the chicken-house" we watch, on summer nights, the lightning break "in great zigzags across the heavens," or "hear the felty beat of the raindrops on the soft dust of the farmyard." We visit Ántonia in the Shimerdas' hovel of a sod-house, Mr. Shimerda's dignified presence giving us a glimpse of an older, mellower, soberer world, the mysterious, almost mythical world over the seas. With Ántonia we call at Russian Peter and Pavel's, in open-mouth wonder watch Russian Peter eating melons uncountable, the juice trickling from his greedy mouth "down on to his curly beard." On winter nights, while drifts accumulate outside and the world is a blur of spilling snow, snugly sitting round the old stove in the Burdens' basement kitchen, with Ántonia we listen to wonderful stories—stories of "gray wolves and bears in the Rockies, wildcats and panthers in the Virginia mountains," and, best of all, the terrible, fascinating story of the bride thrown over to the wolves by Russian Peter and Pavel.

The pages have the freshness, vitality and beauty of the country and the days they recreate. Yet it is chiefly through Ántonia that they live, Ántonia, an eager, passionate bit of womankind, strong as an ox and as stubborn, tenacious and ambitious, generous and impulsive, a tall sturdy girl, a future mother of generations.

A peasant Thea, her deep-rooted virtues can only blossom out in the country, on the big flat wind-swept tableland where there is space around her, room for her to play unconstrained and free and write upon the horizon the great simple gestures of man wringing his bread from the earth. In the town, where Parts II and III of the book soon take her, Ántonia is under a cloud, we lose sight of her in the crowd of chattering servant girls of which she is now part. For some two hundred pages (Book II, "The Hired Girls," Book III, "Lena Lingard," Book IV, "The Pioneer Woman's Story") we see but little of her, until, towards the end of the book, we meet her once more, the mother of almost a dozen children, "a battered woman now," but intensely alive as ever.

A strong personality is Ántonia, a strong personality yet, like Thea Kronborg, a very simple one, and so, for all her strength—strength of physique, strength of character, strongly-defined idiosyncrasies—only in her own natural habitat can she hold our attention and capture our emotion. Willa Cather knew it. No sooner does she take Ántonia to the town, a small town in the prairie, than she tries to focus the reader's attention on Ántonia's friends, the other hired girls. The attempt is a vain one. We cannot forget Ántonia, and the book has become out of focus for the sake of two hundred dull pages concerning secondary characters whom we care little about. How could Willa Cather fail to see that with Ántonia's personality and Ántonia's conquest of the soil, her whole book stood and fell?

Her old enemy, sentimentality, her new friend, realism, here combined to blind her.

Sentimentality, Willa Cather had subdued without crushing it quite. But little apparent in *O Pioneers,* in *The Song of the Lark* with Fred Ottenburg it raised its triumphant head again. But how did it creep into *My Ántonia*? Ántonia stood firm and sturdy, of the earth earthy, proof against the monster's touch. There was no weak spot in her. There was one in her creator. When Willa Cather, having written her first one hundred pages, looked upon her work and found it good, the tempter rose at her shoulder and whispered: "A brave, hardy creature this, but what about feminine charm?" Willa Cather resumed her work, and this is the picture she painted—Ántonia doing a man's work, breaking sod with the oxen, growing coarser every day:

> Her outgrown cotton dress switched about her calves, over the boot-tops. She kept her sleeves rolled up all day, and her arms and throat were burned as brown as a sailor's. Her neck came up strongly out of her shoulders, like the bole of a tree out of the turf.

High time Ántonia remembered she is but fifteen, and a woman! And accordingly, thirty pages only further on, Ántonia dons a cook's apron at the Harlings in Black Hawk—a more feminine occupation that, the tempter ingratiatingly observes! And a pretty picture she makes, standing before a mixing-bowl in her tidy apron . . . But where is the *real* Ántonia?

Perhaps I have exaggerated the part which affection for her heroine had in inducing Willa Cather to take Ántonia to the town. Yet who will say that sentimentality had no part in the sudden decision that took Ántonia from the plough? A sentimentality against which Willa Cather was all the less on her guard as it probably came to her dressed in the garb of that very realism, that same close adherence to her own experience which, in *O Pioneers,* had saved her from both unreality and sentimentality. Realism, Willa Cather had not experienced yet, is a double-edged tool. A necessity in a novel which purports to represent a country and people which have played an important part in the writer's life, it should yet be kept a servant. Did Willa Cather sufficiently realize that realism and truth are not interchangeable terms? Patiently following Ántonia Shimerda's actual progress from care-free little girl to plodding farm-hand, from farm-hand to hired girl, and hired girl to wife and mother, Willa Cather neglected her artist's privilege, and duty, to excise, condense, select. The woman in her could care for Ántonia the hired girl as much as for Ántonia the farm girl; the artist should have seen that only the latter mattered, that the cook's apron hid where the farmer's masculine garb revealed the essential, the deeper Ántonia . . .

In *O Pioneers,* and still more in *The Song of the Lark,* Willa Cather while controlling imagination by experience had kept experience subservient to passion, the latter book indeed deserving to be called, in Stuart Sherman's eloquent words, ''Miss Cather's most intimate book—the book which she has most enriched with the poetry and wisdom and passion of her experience, and made spacious with the height and the depth of her desire.'' Where *The Song of the Lark* soared, *My Ántonia* kept close to the solid earth, which gave it its strength, preserved it from its predecessor's worst failure, yet left it, artistically, an inferior book, one that, however rich with experience, has not been made spacious with desire. (pp. 47-51)

René Rapin, in his Willa Cather, *Robert M. McBride & Company, 1930, 115 p.*

E. K. BROWN (essay date 1953)

[*Brown was a Canadian critic and educator. Chief among his works is the critical survey* On Canadian Poetry *(1943), in which Brown traces the development of Canadian poetry from its preconfederation era to the notable achievements of its three major figures, Archibald Lampman, Duncan Campbell Scott, and E. J. Pratt. Brown was also the author of the first major critical biography of Cather, and in the following excerpt from that work, he notes the interpretive implications of Cather's use of Jim Burden as her narrator.*]

[Willa Cather] always showed impatience at the complaint that *My Ántonia* is not precisely a novel. Why should it be? She had never said it was. In this book she was gathering her memories of some persons and places very dear to her, and as she was a writer of stories, the memories had taken a narrative form. Besides, in the very curious preface she had given notice of what the book would be like. This introduction, like so many of her writings, opens on a scene in a train to the west of Chicago. She is talking, she says, with Jim Burden, whom she had known when she was a girl, and who is now the legal counsel for a Western railway. They both live in New York, but she rarely sees him, for she dislikes his wife. Mrs. Burden, who is not aboard the train, is given a full page: she is a superficial, spoiled, restless woman, who has her own money and lives her own life. The failure of Jim Burden's marriage has not injured his character: he remains what he always was, romantic in disposition, in love with the Western country, as impressionable as a boy. They talk of the early days in Nebraska, and find they ''kept returning to a central figure, a Bohemian girl, whom we had known long ago and whom both of us admired. More than any other person we remembered, this girl seemed to mean to us the country, the conditions, the whole adventure of our childhood.'' Willa Cather says she had the feeling that Jim Burden could tell the story of Ántonia better than she could: ''he had had opportunities that I, as a little girl who watched her come and go, had not.'' It was agreed that both would record their memories of Ántonia; but

when in the course of the next winter Jim Burden called at her apartment with his manuscript complete, she had not gone beyond a few straggling notes. Jim was taken aback at the mention of notes for what was to be not a created fiction but a record of fact and impression. ''I didn't arrange or rearrange,'' he says, ''I simply wrote down what of herself and myself and other people Ántonia's name recalls to me. I suppose it hasn't any form. It hasn't any title either.'' Then across the cover of the manuscript he wrote ''Ántonia,'' prefixing in a moment ''another word, making it 'My Ántonia.' '' When she read his memoir she was so pleased, Willa Cather says, that she did not write hers, and it is his she presents.

This is the substance of the preface in the early editions. Willa Cather was never happy about it; she had found it, unlike the rest of the book, a labor to write. For the reissue of 1926 she revised it in important ways. The agreement that both she and Jim would record their memories of Ántonia is removed; and instead of Jim's undertaking to write because of his talk with her, he has been at work on his manuscript long before the meeting in the train. By these changes the effect is, I believe, improved. Jim's concern with Ántonia seems more profound when the decision to record his memories stems not from a meeting with a professional writer but from his own inward impulse. The agreement had, besides, the defect of starting in the reader's mind a question that could do the book no good—

MY ÁNTONIA

BY

WILLA S. CATHER

Author of

THE SONG OF THE LARK, O PIONEERS! *etc*

OF all the remarkable women that Miss Cather has created no other is so appealing as Ántonia, all impulsive youth and careless courage. Miss Cather has the rare quality of being able to put into her books the flame and driving force of unconquerable youth.

MY ÁNTONIA is a love story, brimming with human appeal, and a very distinguished piece of writing.

WE unreservedly recommend it to all lovers of good stories and to those who appreciate the very best in fiction.

Houghton Mifflin Company

Dust jacket for My Ántonia. *Reprinted courtesy of Houghton Mifflin Company.*

whether in fact it would not have been better told by another woman. . . . Most of the satirical account of Mrs. Burden was removed, though enough was left to establish the failure of Jim's marriage. The excision at this point is also a gain: for the earlier text left one wondering whether Jim was not ignominiously weak in continuing to lend himself to the purposes of such a creature. Unless Jim can satisfy the reader that his impressions and judgments about women are sound, his value as an appreciative recorder of Ántonia is threatened. What was important in the original preface remains: that the book is to be taken as the work of an unprofessional writer; of a man who had left the Divide, Red Cloud, the West, but kept his attachment to all three; of a man whose personal life in later years has been frustrated and who has judged the phase to which Ántonia belonged to have been the high water-mark of the whole.

It could do the book no good, I suggest, for the reader to ponder whether it might not have been better told by a woman. The new preface does not raise the question; but readers are likely to raise it for themselves before the book ends. A young man who feels that a young woman is the most important thing in his life might be expected to fall in love with her. Jim is curious about Ántonia, interested in her, charmed by her, but he does not fall in love with her; nor when in later years he visits her at her farm (as Willa Cather visited the original of the character), does he have any feeling that he ought to have married her, though he does say that when he was a young boy he had been unconsciously in love with her. At the very center of his relation with Ántonia there is an emptiness where the strongest emotion might have been expected to gather. A comment on *My Ántonia* that Willa Cather made in an interview she gave in Lincoln a few years after the book came out shows that in her use of Jim as narrator she had been trying to achieve two effects that were not really compatible: Jim was to be fascinated by Ántonia as only a man could be, and yet he was to remain a detached observer, appreciative but inactive, rather than take a part in her life.

Jim's failure to take a part in Ántonia's life is made conspicuous by one of the main social themes in the book. In *O Pioneers!* as in **"The Bohemian Girl,"** people of old American stock had no roles; apart from the Scandinavians and Bohemians the only other racial group to appear (in "The White Mulberry Tree" section of *O Pioneers!*) was the French. In *The Song of the Lark* individuals of old American stock had important roles even in the early Western chapters, but they appeared as individuals; there was no study of a family of old American stock, nothing to approach the account, so tenderly discerning, of the old German couple with whom Wunsch, the music teacher, lived. In *My Ántonia* Willa Cather is deeply concerned with the relations between the families of old American stock and the families of the immigrants from Europe. The reader is constantly required to make comparisons, and to perceive superiorities in the immigrants. At no point are the comparisons more pointed, the superiorities more conspicuous, than when the Scandinavian girls like Lena Lingard and the Bohemians like Ántonia are set beside the girls of old American stock who have grown up not on the Divide but within the rigid code of the leading families in town. For the young man in one of those families who has marriage in his mind, the choice is between life and death. Sylvester Lovett, the son of a local bank president, appears in the book for a moment to make his choice. He has danced with Lena Lingard, taken her driving, and shown the world that he is infatuated; but marry her he will not, he chooses a well-to-do widow much older than him-self. Jim Burden had hoped that Lovett would marry Lena; if he had done so, Jim thinks the "foreign girls" would all have taken higher places in the town's scale of values. When Lovett did not, Jim burned to find some way of manifesting his contempt for the white-handed high-collared young man.

Jim too had his chance to marry Lena and did not take it. Lena is the most beautiful, the most innocently sensuous of all the women in Willa Cather's works. The portrait of Lena has a merciful softness as if the novelist's critical power were deliberately withheld except for an occasional touch of humorous realism. Lena is never a rival for the central place in the book—she has not Ántonia's force or her insight, she is never so much alive. At times she is a foil: her fairness against Ántonia's sparkling nervous dark beauty, her slowness and quietness against Antonia's vivacity. It is easy to understand how in her rosy semi-naked beauty she became so constant a figure in Jim's adolescent dreams. Despite her richness in what a younger generation than Willa Cather's calls "sex appeal," her hold on Jim never becomes firm. She and Jim were attracted to each other early in the book; but it is only after he has gone to Lincoln as an undergraduate and Lena as a dressmaker that he singles her out. In his own town he did not have the daring. Just as Sylvester Lovett had found her a girl who could really dance, Jim finds her a girl who can really respond to the theater. Their relation is one of the most beautiful elements in the book, with the charm of an idyll (it is intertwined with his study of the *Georgics*), of a sharing of youth rather than a relation between two personalities. Jim is no better than the Sylvester Lovett he had so despised. When his favorite instructor warns him he should part from his "beautiful Norwegian," who is "quite irresponsible," he does so without even an appearance of struggle. I seem to hear the creaking of the novelist's machinery as the idyll ends and Jim retreats so easily into the status of a detached observer. What is excellent in *My Ántonia* does not depend on a masculine narrator. It inheres in the material itself and in the appreciation of it, which might have been just as sensitive, just as various, if Willa Cather had presented this story omnisciently—as Miss Jewett counseled earlier—as she had presented Alexandra Bergson's, or if she had made herself a part of the structure.

The beauty of the book was at once apprehended by W. C. Brownell in a letter (still unpublished) to one of Willa Cather's associates at *McClure's*, Viola Roseboro'.

> I feel somehow [he wrote] as if the proper epithets to characterize the book were something "up," almost physically floating above the material, as it were. I don't mind being incoherent, if I convey my notion in the least by my flounderings. Arnold, on Homer, talks about Homer not (like a Dutch painter) "sinking with his subject." This has that air. But would it be too much to say it *lifts* the subject somehow—not, of course, by treating it idealistically, since it is one of the most notable instances I know of the contrary—but by a sort of continuous and sustained respect for the material: a sort of "what God hath made call thou not common" implication, putting Nature for God, of course. . . . At first I thought it was casual and episodical (though *so* well written, so simple, so obviously saying all it felt and with such ease) and though large minded and as unmeretricious as salt itslf, still rather a desultory document of Western civilization. But ere long it differentiated itself imperceptibly and subtly into a picture crowded with real people, made somehow real, given souls, by—well, by what? I don't know. I don't remember any art more essentially elusive.

Where so penetrating a critic as Brownell was aware of floundering, and pronounced an author's art "essentially elusive," one hesitates to offer clarifications. I believe that something can be said of the means that have given this book its effect of "almost physicaly floating above the material." The elements that weigh a book down scarcely exist here. In *My Ántonia* there is no massive central trunk such as the development of Thea Kronborg, phase by phase, provided for *The Song of the Lark*. In *My Ántonia,* instead, there is a gallery of pictures. For a while, as happened to Brownell, the pictures seem to be hung in a casual and episodical fashion; before long they affect one as illuminating one another and contributing to a general tone. They have been painted and arranged so that one may apprehend the values in that old Nebraska world, gone forever before the book was written.

The epigraph and the comment upon it taken together are a sufficient clue to the method of the book. The epigraph, from the third *Georgic*, runs: "*Optima dies . . . prima fugit.*" Jim was preparing this part of the poem and translating this passage as "the best days are the first to flee," when Lena Lingard made her first visit to him at Lincoln. When she had gone, "it came over me, as it had never done before, the relation between girls like those [Lena, Ántonia, and their friends] and the poetry of Virgil. If there were no girls like them in the world, there would be no poetry." His old dream of Lena returned to him awake, and "it floated before me on the page like a picture, and underneath it stood the mournful line: '*Optima dies . . . prima fugit.*' "

Everything in the book is there to convey a feeling, not to tell a story, not to establish a social philosophy, not even to animate a group of characters. The feeling attaches to persons, places, moments: if one were to pin it in a phrase it might be called a mournful appreciation of "the precious, the incommunicable past"—those are the last words in the book. Earlier Jim Burden has voiced the feeling in the remark: "Some memories are realities, and are better than anything that can ever happen to one again."

This feeling attaches itself above all to Ántonia. She is the person whose inner strength enables her to live the enviable life. At the foot of Willa Cather's scale, as usual, are people who live in the town or on the Divide and make nothing of the opportunity. These are the narrow money-minded people like Wick Cutter and Ántonia's brother Ambrosch. Then come the people who must go away to achieve a life. They are much more important to the book; Jim Burden and Lena Lingard are among them. Their lives will not bear comparison with Ántonia's. Jim has become wealthy and "important"; but he is childless and has no attachments to any person or any place except what he preserves of the Nebraska past. Lena has been successful—and her friend Tiny Soderball, another girl from the Divide, has had almost unbelievable success; but their lives in San Francisco are solitary and rootless. Ántonia has remained on the Divide; she had found a good husband, who has fragrant memories of Prague and Vienna, of music and song; she has a dozen children, all of them delightful; the farm is big and fertile; and Ántonia has given it some of the amenities that would have pleased her fastidious father—orchards and hedges and a grape arbor. She had worked herself and worn herself to accomplish her life, but if she was "battered" she was not "diminished." In middle life, when she makes her last appearance, her hair is grizzled and most of her teeth have gone; but she "was still there in the full vigour of her personality." Looking at her, one feels that is how one should have lived—if one could. (pp. 199-207)

E. K. Brown, in his Willa Cather: A Critical Biography, *Alfred A. Knopf, 1953, 351 p.*

JAMES E. MILLER, JR.   (essay date 1958)

[*An American critic, Miller has written and edited studies of numerous literary figures, including Henry James, J. D. Salinger, and F. Scott Fitzgerald. In the following essay, he suggests that the structural unity of* My Ántonia *rests in Cather's use of recurrent images of natural cycles.*]

Critics of Willa Cather have long been confronted with the baffling persistence in popularity of a novel apparently defective in structure. *My Ántonia* may well turn out to be Willa Cather's most fondly remembered and best loved novel, while the perfectly shaped, brilliantly executed *A Lost Lady* continues unread. It does seem strange that one who wanted to unclutter the novel by throwing the furniture out the window should have bungled so badly the structure of one of her most important works.

René Rapin blames Cather for transplanting Ántonia from the country to Black Hawk: "only in her own natural habitat can she hold our attention and capture our emotion." And Rapin censures Cather severely for losing sight of Ántonia completely in the closing books of the novel [see excerpt dated 1930]. David Daiches discovers the source of the defect in Cather's point of view. The "narrator's sensibility," he says, "takes control; and this raises problems which Willa Cather is never quite able to solve" [see *TCLC*, Vol. 1, p. 158]. Like Daiches, E. K. Brown is disturbed by the disappearance of Ántonia for pages at a time, and says in the novel's defense: "Everything in the book is there to convey a feeling, not to tell a story, not to establish a social philosophy, not even to animate a group of characters" [see excerpt dated 1953].

Most critics, like Brown, have felt the unified emotional impact of *My Ántonia* and have grappled with the puzzling problem of the book's actual lack of consistent central action or unbroken character portrayal. It is indeed a fine creative achievement to give the effect of unity when there apparently is none, and there are those who would claim that the nature of Cather's accomplishment is beyond the critic's understanding, an inscrutable mystery of the artist's miraculous creative process.

The action in *My Ántonia* is episodic, lacks focus and abounds in irrelevancies (consider the inserted wolf-story of Pavel and Peter, for example). Indeed, there is in the novel no plot in the accepted sense of the word. And further, there is not, as there usually is in the plotless story, a character who remains consistently on stage to dominate the obscurely related events. In the second and third books, entitled respectively "The Hired Girls" and "Lena Lingard," Ántonia fades gradually but completely from view, and the reader becomes engrossed, finally, in the excitingly sensual but abortive relationship of the narrator, Jim Burden, and the voluptuous hired girl turned seamstress, Lena Lingard.

But there is that quality of evoked feeling which penetrates the pages of the book, inhering even in the scenes omitting Ántonia, and which gathers finally to a profound and singular focus which constitutes the emotional unity of the book. We sense what we cannot detect—structural elements subtly at work reinforcing and sharpening the aroused feeling.

Jim Burden's assertion in the "Introduction" that he supposes the manuscript he has written "hasn't any form" should not deceive the reader too readily. He also states of Ántonia, "I simply wrote down pretty much all that her name recalls to me." If these confessions reveal that neither action nor character gives unity to the novel, they also suggest, indirectly, that a feeling—the emotion attached to Ántonia's name—informs the novel structurally. When Jim Burden, dissatisfied with "Ántonia" as his title, prefixes the "My," he is informing the reader in advance that the book is *not* about the real Ántonia, but rather about Ántonia as personal and poignant symbol. For Jim, Ántonia becomes symbolic of the undeviating cyclic nature of all life: Ántonia is the insistent reminder that it is the tragic nature of time to bring life to fruition through hardship and struggle only to precipitate the decline and, ultimately, death, but not without first making significant provision for new life to follow, flower and fall. The poignancy lies in the inability of the frail human being to rescue and retain any stage, no matter how beautiful or blissful, of his precious cycle. When Jim Burden asserts at the close of *My Ántonia* that he and Ántonia "possess" the "incommunicable past," he does not convince even himself. It is precisely this emotional conviction that neither they nor anyone else can possess the past, that the past is absolutely and irrevocably "incommunicable" even to those who lived it—which constitutes the novel's unity.

The "feeling" of *My Ántonia* is not the divorced and remote and discomforting "feeling" of the author, nor the displayed or dramatized "feeling" of a character, but the evoked feeling of the reader. And the element in the novel which produces and controls this feeling exists in the sensibility of the narrator, Jim Burden. It is in the drama of his awakening consciousness, of his growing awareness, that the emotional structure of the novel may be discovered.

It is Jim Burden's sensibility which imposes form on *My Ántonia* and, by that form, shapes in the reader a sharpened awareness of cyclic fate that is the human destiny. The sense of cyclic fate finds expression first in an obsessive engagement with the colorful, somber and varied seasons of the year, next in an unfolding realization of the immutable and successive phases of human life, and, finally, in an engrossing but bewildering encounter with the hierarchic stages of civilization, from the primitive culture to the sophisticated.

"The Shimerdas," the first book of *My Ántonia,* introduces from the start the drama of time in the vivid accounts of the shifting seasons. The book encompasses one year, beginning with the arrival in Autumn of the Shimerdas and Jim Burden on the endless Nebraska prairie, portraying the terrible struggle for mere existence in the bleakness of the plains' Winter, dramatizing the return of life with the arrival of Spring, and concluding with the promise of rich harvest in the intense heat of the prairie's Summer. This is Jim Burden's remembered year, and it is his obsession with the cycle of time that has caused him to recall Ántonia in a setting of the changing seasons.

Almost every detail in "The Shimerdas" is calculated to shrink the significance of the human drama in contrast with the drama of the seasons, the drama of nature, the drama of the land and sky. The struggle becomes, then, not merely a struggle for a minimum subsistence from the stubborn, foreign soil, but also even more a struggle to re-create and assert existence in a seemingly hostile or indifferent land. No doubt all of the Nebraska pioneers experienced Jim Burden's sensation on arriving on the prairie: "Between that earth and that sky I felt erased, blotted out."

The drama of "The Shimerdas" is the drama of the human being at the mercy of the cyclic nature of the universe. The "glorious autumn" of their arrival on the treeless prairie contributes to that acute sense that "the world was left behind" and that they "had got over the edge of it." The autumn is not the autumn of bountiful nature but the autumn of vast distances and approaching death. The descent of the winter snows heightens the vast primitive beauty of the undisturbed plains: "The sky was brilliantly blue, and the sunlight on the glittering white stretches of prairie was almost blinding." But even innate to the sharp-colored beauty is an apparent hostility. The whiteness not only blinds but brings in its wake despair and death. When, after the first primitive struggle is over, Ántonia cries out to Jim in the midst of summer, "I wish my papa live to see this summer. I wish no winter ever come again," she displays intuitive insight into the relation of her father's suicide to the cosmic order of time which decrees that the death of winter must unfailingly follow the ripening autumn.

Like autumn, spring when it comes to the prairie is not so much manifest in visible nature as it is a hovering presence compellingly alive and dominant: "There was only—spring itself; the throb of it, the light restlessness, the vital essence of it everywhere: in the sky, in the swift clouds, in the pale sunshine, and in the warm, high wind." It is only with the arrival of spring, at its appointed time, that the Shimerdas and the Burdens, Ántonia and Jim, can emerge from the enforced retreat of winter to look forward to some benevolence from the enduring land. But as the winter shaped, and even took, the life of the prairie pioneer, so the spring imposes a cruelly exacting ritual of tilling and tending the virgin land. Life is hard and the soil close and unyielding without its due. And the "breathless, brilliant heat " of summer, when it descends with fiery fury on the empty lands, brings with its devastation also fertility: "The burning sun of those few weeks, with occasional rains at night, secured the corn."

Throughout the first book of *My Ántonia,* it is the world of nature rather than the human world which dominates, and even the human beings tend to identify themselves with the things of the land. One of Jim Burden's first vivid sensations in the new land is in his grandmother's garden: "I was something that lay under the sun and felt it, like the pumpkins, and I did not want to be anything more. I was entirely happy." During their first year on the prairie the rotation of the decreed seasons imposes a primitive existence not far different from that of the plains' animals, and impresses on the pioneers a keenly felt truth: "In a new country a body feels friendly to the animals." If in the garden Jim imagined himself a pumpkin, there were other times when he and the rest felt a sympathetic resemblance to the gopher, in their intimate dependence on the land for sustenance and home. At the end of this first year's struggle with the land, Ántonia emerges with an essential and profound wisdom that only the cyclic seasons in their cruelty and their beneficence could bestow. She reveals to Jim, "Things . . . will be hard for us."

As Ántonia and Jim are shaped and "created" by the successive seasons, so their lives in turn are cycles of a larger order in time, and shape and create the nation. It is in the dramatization of Ántonia from the girlhood of the opening pages through her physical flowering in the middle books to, finally, her reproduction of the race in a flock of fine boys in the final pages of the book that her life is represented, like the year with its seasons, as a cycle complete in its stages of birth, growth, fruition and decline. Although Ántonia's life represents a greater cycle than that of the year, the pattern remains the same in both. The year, of course, is merely a term for the designation of a unit of time, and its resemblance to the life-cycle suggests that life, too, is a physical representation of time.

As the seasons of fall, winter, spring and summer impose a structure on the first book of Willa Cather's novel, the successive stages of Ántonia's life assist in imposing a structure on the total work. We may trace these stages through the various books into which the novel is subdivided. Some critics have called Ántonia an earth goddess. She is a re-creation of an archetypal pattern—woman as the embodiment of self-assured if not self-contained physical fertility which insures the endurance of the race. Ántonia never despairs, not even in the first book of the novel in which the hostility of the first prairie winter deprives her of her father; but throughout she works and lives with an innate dignity which springs from her intuitive knowledge of her appointed function in the continuation of the species. Even in the second book, called "The Hired Girls," Antonia feels no sense of an enforced inferiority but rather a supreme reliance on the hidden resources bestowed upon her by the hard physical struggles of her past.

As Ántonia stands out sharply in the first book, in the second she merges with many "hired girls" in Black Hawk who are of her kind, and in the third, called "Lena Lingard," she does not even appear except as a remembered presence in the talks about the past between Lena and Jim Burden in Lincoln. In these conversations there is a foreshadowing of Ántonia's fate which is the subject of the fourth book, entitled "The Pioneer Woman's Story." If in Book I Ántonia represents the eternal endurance under supreme hardship of woman appointed propagator of the race, and in Book II she represents the overflowing liveliness and energetic abundance of physical woman come to the flower, in Books III and IV she symbolizes the calm and faithful endurance of woman eternally wronged. In Ántonia's fierce love for her fatherless child exists the full explanation of mankind's continuing to be. But Willa Cather insists on Ántonia's appearing in a double role, not only as woman wronged, but also as woman fulfilled in her destiny. In the last book of the novel, "Cuzak's Boys," Ántonia is glimpsed in her declining years surrounded by the "explosive life" of her many children. When Jim Burden sees her after the absence of all those years, he recognizes in her the persistence of that quality he had sensed when they roamed the prairie as boy and girl: "She was there, in the full vigour of her personality, battered but not diminished, looking at me, speaking to me in the husky, breathy voice I remembered so well."

In the closing books of *My Ántonia* ("The Pioneer Woman's Story" and "Cuzak's Boys"), Ántonia emerges as vividly as she did in the first. For an explanation of the fading of Ántonia in Books II and III ("The Hired Girls" and "Lena Lingard"), we must turn to a third principle of structure operating in the book, another cycle greater in scope than either a year or a life. For a foreshadowing of this cycle we may turn to Frederick Jackson Turner and his famous essay, "The Significance of the Frontier in American History." Turner asserted, in the late nineteenth century, that the distinguishing feature of America's development was the cyclic character of the movement westward, conquering over and over again a new wilderness. There was, Turner said, "a recurrence of the process of evolution in each western area reached in the process of expansion."

My Ántonia exemplifies superbly Turner's concept of the recurring cultural evolution on the frontier. There is first of all the migration from the East, in the case of the Shimerdas from Czechoslovakia, in Jim Burden's case from Virginia, both lands of a high cultural level. In the West these comparatively sophisticated people are compelled literally to begin over again, on a primitive level, shedding their cultural attainment like an animal its skin, and, like animals, doing battle with the land and the elements for the meanest food and shelter.

The books of *My Ántonia* reflect the varying stages of this evolutionary process in cultural development. On this level of structure, not the seasons of the year, nor the phases of Ántonia's life, but the successive cultural plateaus of the nation operate as ordering elements in the novel. And it is on this level of significance and in the dramatization of this epic archetypal cycle of the country that justification for those sections of the book, so frequently condemned because they lose focus on Ántonia, may be found.

In the first book, "The Shimerdas," the newly arrived pioneers from the East discover nothing but their strength and the prairie's stubborn soil out of which to create for themselves a new world in their own image. In this primitive struggle with the prairie, on a level with the struggle of prehistoric man in the dawn of time, some lose their lives, some their spirit, and all lose that overlay of softening civilization which they brought from the East. There is not only the primitive struggle but these pioneers became primitive men in the harshness of the struggle. Ántonia's father, sad for the old country, dies; and Ántonia takes a man's place behind the plow. On the prairie the elements, the sky and the land impose a communal democracy in all of the meager human institutions.

"The Hired Girls," the second book of *My Ántonia,* portrays a higher stage in the cultural evolution of the frontier: the small town comes to the wilderness. If Jim Burden discovers his own hidden courage and becomes a man in the snake-killing incident of Book I, in Book II he discovers the genuine complexity of adulthood, especially in a social context which the bare prairie does not afford. Jim is puzzled by the stratification of society in Black Hawk, a stratification that could not exist on the virgin prairie, and which does not tally with Jim's moral judgment: the "hired girls" are for Jim the most interesting, the most exciting and the liveliest of all possible companions, far superior to the dull conformists of the town. It is the strong lure of the hired girls, however, which precipitates Jim's first crucial decision: in spite of the strong spiritual and physical attraction of these girls, Jim turns to the study which will prepare him for college and which, in Black Hawk, culminates in the triumph of his high school commencement oration. Already there has come to the frontier prairie that element whose absence caused Ántonia's father to despair. After Ántonia has heard Jim's speech, she tells him: "there was something in your speech that made me think so about my papa." In her instinctive way Ántonia dimly understands her father's sacrifice of his life and Jim's yearning for higher intellectual achievement, even though her own destiny, centered in the physical reproduction of the race, may be and is to be fulfilled on the innocent and unsophisticated prairie.

Jim's discoveries, both intellectual and emotional of Book II, are continued and intensified in the next book, "Lena Lingard." Lincoln, Nebraska, is as far above Black Hawk culturally as Black Hawk is above the empty, untouched prairie, and though the university has the limitations imposed by the isolation of the plains, there is "an atmosphere of endeavour, of expectancy and bright hopefulness" which prevails. It is Jim's good fortune to develop a close association with Gaston Cleric, the intellectually alive and intense head of the Latin

Department, who introduces Jim to the exciting world of ideas. Jim discovers that "when one first enters that world everything else fades for a time, and all that went before is as if it had not been." But the climax of Jim's awakening is a realization of the persistence of the past: "Yet I found curious survivals; some of the figures of my old life seemed to be waiting for me in the new." Jim's awareness of the crucial impingement of his prairie heritage on his involvement in a received culture seems an instinctive artistic confirmation of Turner's frontier thesis.

Culture does come to the Nebraska prairie, not only in the form of a world of ideas via Gaston Cleric, but also in the form of music and theater. The nature of the curious impact is revealed brilliantly when Jim describes his and Lena's reaction to the traveling "Camille": "A couple of jackrabbits, run in off the prairie, could not have been more innocent of what awaited them." Throughout Book III of the novel, there is a delightful rediscovery by the children of the pioneer generation of a cultural world forsaken by their parents for the hard and isolated life of the prairie. But the pioneer values of freshness and courage and integrity—and many more—survive and condition the responses.

Lincoln, Nebraska, though it offers much, offers a mere token of what waits in the rich and glittering East. Lured on by bright dreams of intellectual achievement, Jim Burden follows Gaston Cleric to Harvard, which, in the book's developing hierarchy, is to Lincoln as Lincoln is to Black Hawk and Black Hawk to the barren prairie. But with the dramatization of three stages of civilization as it comes to the wilderness, and with the suggestion of the future destiny by the "invocation" of "ancient" Harvard and by the suggestion of greater cultural riches farther East, Willa Cather shifts the focus from the dream of the nation and, indeed, of civilization, back to Ántonia of the prairies. The novel has, in a sense, come full circle when Jim, in the last book, finds himself in the midst of that very culture the nostalgic remembrance of which drove Ántonia's father to despair: "Once when I was abroad I went into Bohemia, and from Prague I sent Ántonia some photographs of her native village." By this casual visit, the return to the point of origin, the cycle of cultural movement is symbolically completed. And when the sophisticated, world-traveled, perhaps even world-weary, Jim Burden returns to the prairie scenes of his boyhood and discovers Ántonia and her houseful of boys, he discovers at the same time the enduring quality of those values not dependent on cultural level, but accessible on the untutored prairies. Ántonia, "in the full vigour of her personality, battered but not diminished," not only endures but achieves an emotionally and physically fulfilled life. Her boys are her triumphant creative achievement.

My Ántonia closes with the dominant image of the circle, a significant reminder of the general movement of all the structural elements in the book. After his visit with Ántonia, Jim confesses, "I had the sense of coming home to myself, and of having found out what a little circle man's experience is." This vivid image reinforces the cyclic theme which pervades the book: the cycle of the seasons of the year, the cycle of the stages of human life, the cycle of the cultural phases of civilization. *My Ántonia* is, then, ultimately about time, about the inexorable movement of future into present, of present into past. Against the backdrop of this epic drama of the repetitive movement of time, man poignantly plays out his role. Ántonia, when she cries out to Jim, "I wish no winter ever come again," more nearly expresses the essence of the book's theme than

does Jim when he asserts at the end, "whatever we had missed, we possessed together the precious, the incommunicable past." *Optima dies . . . prima fugit,* translated by Jim as "the best days are the first to flee," stands as the book's epigraph. This intensely felt awareness of the past *as past* is the emotional heart of the novel, and is evoked and sustained by the book's several levels of structure and their involvement with the revolving cycles of time. (pp. 476-84)

> James E. Miller, Jr., " 'My Ántonia': A Frontier Drama of Time," in American Quarterly, Vol. X, No. 4, Winter, 1958, pp. 476-84.

JOHN H. RANDALL III   (essay date 1960)

[*In the following excerpt, Randall examines agricultural imagery in* My Ántonia.]

My Ántonia is the most famous of Willa Cather's prairie novels and is generally considered to be her best. It contains the fullest celebration ever to come from her pen of country life as opposed to the life of the cities, for the book is one long paean of praise to the joys of rural living and shows her a passionate advocate of the virtues of a settled agricultural existence. In *My Ántonia* the rural-urban conflict hardly seems to exist. The characters pass from farm to town or city and back again without feeling any incompatibility between value systems; instead they manage to extract the maximum of joy from each. But it is always the country to which they return; Ántonia permanently after a brief sojourn in Black Hawk (Red Cloud) and Denver, and the narrator Jim Burden periodically whenever he can get away from his job in a large Eastern city. Native born or immigrant, all the good characters in the book sooner or later yield to the spell of the land, and there is no doubt in the author's mind as to whether country or city is the real America. (p. 105)

If one of the main themes of *My Ántonia* is the superiority of the countryside and the excellence of rural life, the chief image that Willa Cather uses to express that excellence is . . . that of the garden of the world. It is in fact the basic metaphor of the whole book; everything in the novel leads up to the final section in which Ántonia has become the mistress of a large and fertile farm.

The garden image is present in the minds of both Willa Cather and some of her characters. Not the least of Grandfather Burden's insights is his ability to understand the larger meaning of the enterprise in which he and his neighbors are engaged. To the hundreds of thousands of toiling individuals who settled the West it must have seemed that each of them was seeking solely to improve his own lot, but according to the thinking of the time they were actually fulfilling a much larger destiny. The settlement of America was considered to be a part of a divine plan. When the great basin of the Mississippi Valley was completely populated, it was to become not only an earthly paradise for the inhabitants, who would thus live in a latter-day Garden of Eden, but also the whole earth's granary; by means of its immense fertility it would feed the people of Europe and Asia as well. Willa Cather had hinted at this in *O Pioneers!*; in *My Ántonia* she makes it quite explicit:

> July came on with the breathless, brilliant heat which makes the plains of Kansas and Nebraska the best corn country in the world. It seemed as if we could hear the corn growing in the night; under the stars one caught a faint crackling in the dewy, heavy-odored cornfields where the feathered stalks stood so juicy and green. If all the great plain from the Mis-

souri to the Rocky Mountains had been under glass, and the heat regulated by a thermometer, it could not have been better for the yellow tassels that were ripening and fertilizing each other day by day. The cornfields were far apart in those times, with miles of wild grazing land between. It took a clear, meditative eye like my grandfather's to foresee that they would enlarge and multiply until they would be, not the Shimerdas' cornfields, or Mr. Bushy's but the world's cornfields; that their yield would be one of the great economic facts, like the wheat crop of Russia, which underlie all the activities of men, in peace or war.

This is one way in which Willa Cather adjusts Nebraska to the macrocosm and gives local happenings a cosmic importance.

But it is not merely the garden that Willa Cather is celebrating in *My Ántonia*; it is a garden with people living in it, and the people form one of those tightly knit Willa Cather families. The ultimate achievement of Willa Cather's heroine in *My Ántonia* is the setting up of a family. The whole drive of her nature is toward this; we could have guessed it from the description of the basic likeness between Ántonia and her town employer, Mrs. Harling:

> They loved children and animals and music, and rough play and digging in the earth. They liked to prepare rich, hearty food and to see people eat it; to make up soft white beds and to see youngsters asleep in them.

Ántonia makes two attempts at marriage and the founding of a family: the first is unsuccessful but the second succeeds. . . . Jim Burden does not witness the events leading up to it, since after graduation from college he has moved east permanently, but he does hear that another Bohemian has married her, that they are poor, and that they have a large family. He does not come back to visit his home town for nearly twenty years, and when he does he is afraid to visit Ántonia. "In the course of twenty crowded years one parts with many illusions," he says. "I did not wish to lose the early ones. Some memories are realities, and are better than anything that can ever happen to one again." In such brief passages as this he lets the reader know that he has become disappointed in life, that he has been beaten in the things that really count. But his dread turns out to be needless, for Ántonia when he sees her is not a disappointment to him; she has become old and battered, but her vitality is undiminished. She is surrounded by a large happy brood of eleven children, all of whom either come tumbling around him in curiosity to see the man their mother has talked so much about, or else are attractively shy. Ántonia's fecundity is a sign of vitality and success, and the nicest compliment she can pay to some friends of their youth, the three Bohemian Marys, is that they are now married and have large families of their own. The lack of offspring, on the other hand, she regards as a sign of failure. Significantly enough, when she hears that Jim Burden has no children she becomes embarrassed, and tries to shift the conversation to a more neutral subject.

The relation between the various members of this large and happy family are of intense interest to Jim, who feels that he himself has failed at human relations. He observes that there is a kind of physical harmony between them, and that they are not afraid to touch each other. They take great pride in each other, and particularly in their wonderful mother. He describes the attitude of husband and wife toward each other as being "easy friendliness touched with humor." Father Cuzak in par-

ticular seems to express his affection for his family by finding them highly amusing: "He thought they were nice, and he thought they were funny, evidently." It is clear that love is the tie that binds them all together, and that they are very happy in one another's affection. And yet there is some slight suggestion of tension between Cuzak, the city-bred man, and Ántonia, the country girl. In the struggle between the sexes envisaged by Willa Cather, Ántonia seems to have gotten the upper hand:

> I could see the little chap, sitting here every evening by the windmill, nursing his pipe and listening to the silence; the wheeze of the pump, the grunting of the pigs, an occasional squeaking when the hens were disturbed by a rat. It did rather seem to me that Cuzak had been made the instrument of Ántonia's special mission. This was a fine life, certainly, but it wasn't the kind of life he had wanted to live. I wondered whether the life that was right for one was ever right for two!

This last comment brings into question the entire feasibility of a city-country union. Willa Cather seems to have doubts as to whether the two modes of life can ever be rendered compatible. In addition, it also recalls her distrust of marriage in general. The marriage of the Cuzaks is as idyllic a union as she was ever to portray in any of her novels, and yet even here there is the suggestion not only of female dominance but of marriage as being inevitably frustrating.

The human fertility of the Cuzak homestead is matched by the fertility of the soil. The years of backbreaking labor spent tending the crops has at last yielded a rich fruit. Ántonia is especially proud of her orchard, which has been planted in the painstaking way that orchards are in Willa Cather's novels: every tree had to be watered by hand after a hard day's labor in the fields. The result is a yearly apple crop that far surpasses that of any of their neighbors. At the center of all this fertility is a symbol of civilization. Years before, Ántonia had told Jim she was homesick for the garden behind her father's house in Bohemia which had had a table and green benches in it where they could entertain their friends and talk about such things as music and woods and God and when they were young. This garden image seems to stand in her mind for exactly the right relation between human beings and the nature in which they are placed, a nature modified and well stocked with benches so that civilized people need not get their clothes dirty when they discuss philosophical problems and wish to sit down. Now Ántonia leads Jim to the center of her orchard, and there he finds a grape arbor with seats along the sides and a warped plank table. She has reproduced in the middle of her ideal farm her own idea of the civilized garden. Jim's detailed description of it enhances its importance:

> We sat down and watched them. Ántonia leaned her elbows on the table. There was the deepest peace in the orchard. It was surrounded by a triple enclosure; the wire fence, then the hedge of thorny locusts, then the mulberry hedge which kept out the hot winds of summer and held fast to the protecting snows of winter. The hedges were so tall that we could see nothing but the blue sky above them, neither the barn roof nor the windmill. The afternoon sun poured down on us through the drying grape leaves. The orchard seemed full of sun, like a cup, and we could smell the ripe apples on the trees. The crabs hung on the branches as thick as beads on a string, purple-red, with a thin, silvery glaze over them. Some hens and ducks had crept through the hedge and were pecking at the fallen apples. The drakes were handsome fel-

lows, with pinkish gray bodies, their heads and necks covered with iridescent green feathers which grew close and full, changing to blue like a peacock's neck. Ántonia said they always reminded her of soldiers— some uniform she had seen in the old country, when she was a child.

This passage contains a cluster of images, all of which contribute to the agricultural image used also in *O Pioneers!*, that of the garden of the world. Several ideas are at work here. First, there is the idea that at the center of all this fertility of farm and family is a place of quietness, a place which contains the deepest peace which human beings can know. The still center is protected from the outside world by a triple barrier which excludes not only strangers (the wire fence) but also extremes of heat and cold, with their connotation of everything else which man finds unpleasant. But aside from shutting out, it also shuts in; it confines the inhabitants of the garden so they cannot tell what is going on in the outside world; they can't even see their farm or windmill, the symbols of the way in which they earn their living. Thus the garden becomes another of those images of sanctuary and retreat which we have seen as giving so important a clue to Willa Cather's attitude toward life. The orchard resembles a cornucopia; it is full like a cup, and the fragrance of its fruit hangs over it. The concept of plenitude finds further development in the idea of roundness, when the crab apples on the trees are compared with beads on a string. Finally Ántonia's comparison between the iridescent shimmeringness on the necks of her ducks and the uniforms of soldiers she had seen as a child in Bohemia suggest that the aesthetic response to life has been carried from Europe to America, but instead of being aroused by an artificial and destructive product of civilization, it is now tamed and rendered beneficent by being brought closer to nature, and is simulated by such a harmless and thoroughly natural creature as a barnyard fowl.

In the middle of this earthly paradise stands its Eve, the now victorious Ántonia. She has triumphed over adversity and over nature; she has wrestled with life and imposed an order on it, her order, just as she has imposed order on the wilderness of Nebraska by converting part of it into a fruitful farm with a garden at its center. In her double role as founder of a prosperous farm and progenitor of a thriving family she becomes the very symbol of fertility, and reminds us of Demeter or Ceres of old, the ancients' goddess of agriculture. Willa Cather herself points up the comparison, and it is of value to her to do this, for she makes an earth-goddess of Ántonia; the mortal who struggles with the adverse powers of nature and conquers them becomes the type of all successful human endeavor and passes over into the realm of myth. (pp. 138-43)

And what becomes of the other protagonist in the story, Jim Burden? When he revisits his past by returning to Black Hawk, it gives him no clue to his identity or to the meaning of life such as he has found in the Cuzak farm. He is not able to build on his past as Ántonia is on hers:

My day in Black Hawk was disappointing. Most of my old friends were dead or had moved away. Strange children, who meant nothing to me, were playing in the Harlings' big yard when I passed; the mountain ash had been cut down, and only a sprouting stump was left of the tall Lombardy poplar that used to guard the gate. I hurried on.

The town no longer means anything to him, although the country still does. It has changed too much; the children and the trees are gone. The town families he had known had had no roots, since the community in which they lived had given them none, and so they had passed on to other places. But there are parts of the country that haven't changed at all. Jim takes a long walk out of town and stumbles upon an old road, the first road built from Black Hawk to the north, in fact the very same road over which Ántonia and he had traveled on the first night of their arrival in the Midwest. The road becomes a symbol of the unchanging quality of the countryside, and carries him back to the region of childhood memories:

I had only to close my eyes to hear the rumbling of the wagons in the dark, and to be again overcome by that obliterating strangeness. The feelings of that night were so near that I could reach out and touch them with my hand. I had the sense of coming home to myself, and of having found out what a little circle man's experience is.

The wheel has come full circle, and the same road which had first brought him to Black Hawk now carries him away from an unsatisfying present and into a nostalgically remembered past. Nothing could illustrate better than this final contrast between the Cuzak farm and Black Hawk the difference between country and town, Ántonia and Jim, the yea-saying and nay-saying attitudes toward life. Both had been set down in the Middle West without any previous training which would help them, both had once literally traveled down the same road, but their circumstances and temperaments were different. Ántonia now prefers the country because it gives her a greater chance to fulfill herself; Jim because it has changed less than the city and because it is linked with the past, to which he turns because it is all he has. . . . (pp. 143-44)

In the largest sense the structure of *My Ántonia* is based on the vegetation myth. The core of this age-old mystery . . . is the taking of the cycle of the seasons as the pattern for all recurrent rhythmical processes in nature, including human death and birth. It regards birth as rebirth and holds that, although death is inevitable, every person is "born again" through his children; the individual dies but the community lives on. *My Ántonia* is about this mystery of death and birth. Mr. Shimerda dies in the dead of winter, and when Ántonia is reborn as the head of a group of her own she is described in terms of the sensuous summer imagery of the garden of the world. In a sense when Mr. Shimerda dies, a good part of his daughter dies too; all her more civilized attributes wither away. She gives up her fine manners and becomes coarse and crude like her brother Ambrosch. She is reborn to civilization when she goes to town to live and relearns nice ways of doing things from the Harlings. Finally, after learning all she has to learn, she is ready to take her place in society by starting a family of her own and is reborn once again into the human community.

If we compare the two prairie novels in terms of their use of vegetation myth, we find that *O Pioneers!* deals with the death of nature and *My Ántonia* with its rebirth. *O Pioneers!* presents fertility of the soil and sterility in human beings; *My Ántonia* shows fertility of both the soil and human beings. Thus, in a profound sense *My Ántonia* is the most affirmative book Willa Cather ever wrote. Perhaps that is why it was her favorite.

But . . . Willa Cather could not face certain facts of human experience—as, in *My Ántonia,* the problem of apparently motiveless evil involved in Larry Donovan's seduction and abandonment of Ántonia. It is also true that in her work as a whole she could not accept the emotional profundity of the vegetation myth as for the most part she did in this novel. In brief, she could accept fertility in crops more easily than in human beings, the reason being her fear of physical passion and the depen-

Cather in 1901 or 1902.

dence upon others which it entails. This is evident even in *My Ántonia,* which of all her novels most celebrates fecundity. As far as the reader is concerned, Ántonia's family is produced ready-made. Never once is a pregnancy or birth directly presented in Willa Cather's novels; what we do see is the corn growing. This implies that she only half understood the vegetation myth; she understood the cycle of the seasons but did not understand its application to the life of human beings and to their recurrent crises of birth, love, and death. She substituted in its stead, as we . . . see in her later novels, an almost Platonic belief in essences, and the desire to freeze the world in the grip of form once the ideal is achieved. (pp. 148-49)

> *John H. Randall III, in his* The Landscape and the Looking Glass: Willa Cather's Search for Value, *Houghton Mifflin Company, 1960, 425 p.*

ROBERT E. SCHOLES   (essay date 1962)

[*Scholes is an American scholar and critic who has written widely on postmodernist fiction. He is also the author of two highly esteemed introductions to contemporary critical thought,* Structuralism and Literature *(1974) and* Semiotics and Interpretation *(1982). In the following essay, Scholes discusses* My Ántonia *as an example of the myth of the American Adam: an individual with the vast potential in a new land to create a new history for humankind.*]

R.W.B. Lewis in *The American Adam* has suggested that the "most fruitful" ideas circulating in nineteenth-century America were embodied in the image of "the authentic American as a figure of heroic innocence and vast potentialities, poised at the start of a new history." The currency of this image, according to Mr. Lewis, dates from the close of the War of 1812, and is prominent in the writings of both philosophers and journalists in pre-Civil War America. Mr. Lewis is relatively successful in demonstrating that men like Emerson, Thoreau, Holmes, Lowell and the elder Henry James were concerned with this vision of the new American man; but he is much less convincing when he attempts to show that their novelist contemporaries relied on this same notion in their works. He is put to such shifts as considering the *last* novel of Hawthorne and of Melville, rather than their *best* in his attempt to illustrate the ubiquity of the Adamic idea.

The great fruition in fiction of the theme of the heroic innocent in conflict with society actually occurred in the latter part of the nineteenth century and the early part of the twentieth. Whether this theme was really important in the works of Melville and Hawthorne, and whether novelists will find it stimulating or useful in the future are two questions beyond the scope of the present inquiry (though I suspect the answer to both should be negative). It is nevertheless interesting to note that the American Innocent was a major preoccupation of American novelists from James and Howells down to Willa Cather and F. Scott Fitzgerald. And it may be useful to examine exactly how one novelist, Willa Cather, made use of the Adamic myth in her fullest treatment of it: *My Ántonia*.

As Mr. Lewis distills it, the myth of Adam in America is that of an "individual emancipated from history, happily bereft of ancestry, untouched and undefiled by the usual inheritances of family and race; an individual standing alone, self-propelling, ready to confront whatever awaited him with the aid of his own unique and inherent resources." This Adamic person is "thrust into an actual world and an actual age," and, in the fully developed myth, undergoes a "fall": suffers "the necessary transforming shocks and sufferings, the experiments and errors . . . through which maturity and identity may be arrived at." Mr. Lewis is a bit mysterious about what he means by "identity," but self-knowledge or self-discovery are probably safe, if not totally accurate, substitutes.

The two central figures in *My Ántonia* are, in different senses, Innocents. Jim Burden, bereft of both his parents within a year, is removed from the warm and comfortable Virginia of his early days and thrust into the strange and frightening world of Nebraska. As he bumps along on the wagon ride to his new home, he feels that he has left even the spirits of his dead parents behind him:

> The wagon jolted on, carrying me I know not whither. I don't think I was homesick. If we never arrived anywhere, it did not matter. Between that earth and that sky I felt erased, blotted out. I did not say my prayers that night: here, I felt, what would be would be.

Ántonia Shimerda, though also a young, innocent creature in a raw country, is not bereft of the past as Jim Burden is. Ántonia's Bohemian ancestry is a part of her and exerts a decided influence on her present and future. We are reminded of this past constantly: by the observations of Otto Fuchs on the relationship of Austrians and Bohemians in the old country; and especially by the Catholic religion of the Bohemians, which is their strongest link with the past, and which serves to bind them together and to separate them from the Protestant society of their adopted land. But, most important, Ántonia herself cherishes her connection with the past. When Jim asks if she remembers the little town of her birth, she replies,

> "Jim . . . if I was put down there in the middle of the night, I could find my way all over that little town; and along the river where my grandmother lived. My feet remember all the little paths through the woods, and where the big roots stick out to trip you. I ain't never forgot my own country."

But despite the importance of the past for Ántonia, she and the other hired girls are figures of heroic and vital innocence, associated with nature and the soil. Like Lena Lingard, they all "waked fresh with the world every day." They are unused to the ways of society, and Ántonia, especially, is too trusting. Lena tells Jim that Ántonia "won't hear a word against [Larry Donovan]. She's so sort of innocent." The struggle of the "hired girls" with society is one of the important themes of the novel. Jim Burden remarks that

> the country girls were considered a menace to the social order. Their beauty shone out too boldly against a conventional background. But anxious mothers need have felt no alarm. They mistook the mettle of their sons. The respect for respectability was stronger than any desire in Black Hawk youth.

This struggle of the country girls with the city is a very perplexing one, in which apparent victory and apparent defeat are both apt to prove evanescent in time. Lena Lingard and Tiny Soderball become successful, triumphing even in the metropolis of San Francisco, while Ántonia becomes the foolish victim of her love for a conniving railroad conductor. But Lena and Tiny succeed only in becoming more like the society from which they had been ostracized, while Ántonia, and the other country girls who stay on the land, ultimately change the structure of society itself. Jim Burden remarks,

> I always knew I should live long enough to see my country girls come into their own, and I have. Today the best that a harassed Black Hawk merchant can hope for is to sell provisions and farm machinery and automobiles to the rich farms where that first crop of stalwart Bohemian and Scandinavian girls are now the mistresses.

Jim Burden, like Lena and Tiny, has made his success in the city and on the city's terms. From the narrator of the introductory chapter we learn that Jim's personal life, his marriage, has not been a success though his legal work flourishes. Jim's failure to find happiness or satisfaction in his career and in the city, constitutes for him the "fall" into self-knowledge which is characteristic of the Adamic hero. It is Jim's recognition of his own fall that makes him superior to Lena and Tiny, and enables him to live vicariously through Ántonia and her children.

Antonia's seduction is a more clear-cut "fall" than Jim's unhappiness, and her subsequent self-knowledge is more strikingly evidenced. When Jim meets Ántonia after she has had her illegitimate child, he notices "a new kind of strength in the gravity of her face." At this meeting she asks Jim whether he has learned to like big cities, adding that she would die of lonesomeness in such a place. "I like to be where I know every stack and tree, and where all the ground is friendly," she says; and after they part Jim feels "the old pull of the earth, the solemn magic that comes out of those fields at night-fall," and he wishes he could be a little boy again, and that his way would end there.

When Jim revisits Ántonia and her thriving family, she has in some ways relapsed toward the past. " 'I've forgot my English so.' " She says, " 'I don't often talk it any more. I tell the children I used to speak it real well.' She said they all spoke Bohemian at home. The little ones could not speak English at all—didn't learn it until they went to school." But her children, her involvement in life, makes her concerned for the future. She has lived "much and hard," reflects Jim as they meet, but "she was there, in the full vigor of her personality, battered but not diminished, looking at me, speaking to me in the husky, breathy voice I remembered so well." Jim, however, is not recognized by Ántonia at first, even though he has "kept so young." He is less battered, perhaps, but he is more diminished.

So it is that Ántonia, who is always conscious of the past, is nevertheless free of it, and capable of concern for the future. And her past is not merely that of a generation or so. Jim observes, "She lent herself to immemorial human attitudes which we recognize by instinct as universal and true. . . . It was no wonder that her sons stood tall and straight. She was a rich mine of life, like the founders of early races." Whereas Jim, who has no such connection with the past, who came to Nebraska without a family and rode on a wagon into a new life which he felt was beyond even the attention of God, is still bound by the recent past, by what has happened to him in his own youth, and he lives in both the present and the future only vicariously through the plans and lives of others. He reflects, "In the course of twenty crowded years one parts with many illusions. I did not wish to lose the early ones. Some memories are realities, and are better than anything that can happen to one again." Jim is haunted by the past, by the sense that, in the phrase of Virgil which is the novel's epigraph, *Optima dies . . . prima fugit.* When he contemplates in the closing lines of his narrative the road on which he had entered his new life as a boy, he reconsiders his whole existence:

> I had the sense of coming home to myself, and of having found out what a little circle man's experience is. For Ántonia and for me, this had been the road of Destiny; had taken us to those early accidents of fortune which predetermined for us all that we can ever be. Now I understood that the same road was to bring us together again. Whatever we had missed, we possessed together the precious, the incommunicable past.

Ántonia's life is not tragic. She is neither defeated nor destroyed by life, not even diminished. Yet the distinguishing characteristic of this novel is its elegiac tone; the eternal note of sadness pervades especially the closing passages of the book. The direct cause of this element of sadness is the nostalgia of Jim Burden, through which the story of Ántonia filters down to the reader. But behind Jim Burden's nostalgia, and merged with it, is the nostalgia of Willa Cather herself.

There is a suggestion in this novel and in the earlier *O Pioneers!* that the younger brothers and the sisters of this splendid generation of pioneer women will not be their equals. Emil Bergson—the youth in *O Pioneers!* for whom his older sister Alexandra labors and plans—attends the university, escapes from the plough, only to ruin several lives through his adulterous love. And in *My Ántonia* there is the suggestion that the coming generations will be less heroic and more ordinary than the present breed. Jim Burden at one point muses on this problem, thinking of the hired girls in Black Hawk:

> Those girls had grown up in the first bitter-hard times, and had got little schooling themselves. But the

younger brothers and sisters, for whom they made such sacrifices and who have had "advantages," never seem to me, when I meet them now, half as interesting or as well educated. The older girls, who helped to break up the wild sod, learned so much from life, from poverty, from their mothers and grandmothers; they had all, like Ántonia, been early awakened and made observant by coming at a tender age from an old country to a new.

The circumstances which formed Ántonia will not be repeated; the future will be in the hands of a diminished race. It is the feeling which haunts Willa Cather's novel. Ántonia looks to the future of her children, but Jim Burden knows that the future will be at best a poor imitation of the past. Ántonia's life is a triumph of innocence and vitality over hardship and evil. But Willa Cather does not celebrate this triumph; rather, she intones an elegy over the dying myth of the heroic Innocent, over the days that are no more. (pp. 24-9)

Robert E. Scholes, "Hope and Memory in 'My Án-tonia'," in Shenandoah, Vol. 14, No. 1, Autumn, 1962, pp. 24-9.

SISTER PETER DAMIAN CHARLES, O.P. (essay date 1967)

[*In the following excerpt, Charles utilizes the Freudian concepts of Eros (light) and Thanatos (dark) to analyze Cather's characterization of Jim Burden. Freud considered the essential dynamic of the human personality to be the conflict between the drive toward Eros, or affirmation of life, and the desire for extinction, which he termed Thanatos; as a result, he viewed all human behavior as a manifestation of one of these conflicting urges. Below, Charles regards Ántonia as a symbol of Eros, while her father represents Thanatos, and contends that Burden's attitudes toward these two characters reveal the nature of his personality.*]

The power and vigour of the heroine of Willa Cather's novel *My Ántonia* cannot be denied, nor can the persistent perfection of the author's style; yet every serious critic of the work faces the problem of the structural significance of the narrator, Jim Burden. David Daiches believes that Jim's position in the book "raises problems which Willa Cather is never able to solve" [see *TCLC,* Vol. 1, p. 158], while E. K. Brown, in his generally perceptive study, admits bafflement in the matter of Jim's relationship with Ántonia, and finally concludes, "What is excellent in *My Ántonia* does not depend on a masculine narrator. It inheres in the material itself. . . ." [see excerpt dated 1953]. James E. Miller [see excerpt dated 1958] sees Jim as structurally essential to the story, but only insofar as the narrator elucidates Professor Miller's thesis: "the cyclic fate of human destiny"—a conclusion that seems to narrow unduly the broad impact of Miss Cather's rich and complex vision as embodied in Ántonia. Though John H. Randall [see excerpt dated 1960] recognizes the importance of Jim as narrator, his solution to the problem in a consideration of the work as "the story of parallel lives" does not do justice to the integrity of the novel as a whole. I suggest, however, that the key to the book's structure—and theme as well—lies in a careful examination of the Thanatos-natures of two important characters: Jim Burden, the narrator, and Mr. Shimerda, Ántonia's father. Their union of spirit creates, as it were, a single dark shadow which emphasizes the brilliance of Ántonia's life-force. A study of this "shadow" will, I believe, ultimately illuminate the work as a whole.

The first hint of "darkness" in the work occurs early, in the melancholy line of the epigraph: "*Optima dies . . . prima fugit;*

the best days are the first to flee," taken from Virgil's *Georgics.* The ephemeral nature of time itself is evoked here, and a glance at the line in context merely strengthens the sense of sadness, for Virgil continues, "Disease and old age come on, and work; / the ruthless grasp of death ensnares us all!" This emotional penumbra, one discovers in the "Introduction," has been cast over the book by the narrator, Jim Burden, a disappointed, romantic lawyer, whose imagination has recently been fired to artistic heat by a renewal of friendship with a childhood neighbor, Ántonia Shimerda. The book, Jim warns the reader through the author, is simply an attempt to record "pretty much all that her name recalls to me." And what does Ántonia's name recall? The author insists that to Jim and her, Ántonia means "the country, the conditions, the whole adventure of childhood"; in other words, the "best days" and all the resonances those words carry. That the name of his heroine has for the narrator a special, personal meaning is clear when he shows satisfaction with his title only after having affixed the other word, making it "My Ántonia." The brooding, elegiac tone, then, generated by the epigraph, and the authorial explanation of the novel's inception, provide the initial suggestions of the darkness that heighten the radiance of Ántonia's portrait.

In the first part of Book I, "The Shimerdas," Jim retrospectively establishes himself as a romantic, imaginative, sensitive ten year-old, who sets out to "try his fortunes in a new world," following "into the empty darkness" the same country road that Ántonia and her family travel in the wagon ahead of him. His thoughts turn easily and naturally to death even as they thrill to life, for as the wagon jolts away from the train station in Black Hawk, Jim has the feeling "that the world was left behind, that we had got over the edge of it, and were outside man's jurisdiction." In this wilderness he feels not homesick, but "erased, blotted out." Later, exploring the farm with his grandmother as guide, Jim plunges beyond the normal boy-child curiosity about the plant and animal life of the prairies to a kind of supernatural perception of Nature in the earth, of its surging, powerful growth, "as if the shaggy grass were a sort of loose hide, and underneath it herds of wild buffalo were galloping, galloping. . . ." Jim's desire to "walk straight on through the red grass and over the edge of the world" achieves a more direct expression as a death-wish when the maturer Jim Burden comments authorially, "Perhaps we feel like that when we die and become a part of something entire, whether it is sun and air, or goodness and knowledge. At any rate, that is happiness; to be dissolved into something complete and great. When it comes to one, it comes as naturally as sleep." It is in terms of death, too, that Jim sees the time of day which is to him most beautiful—sunset. As he describes the glorious fall afternoons of that first year on the Nebraska plains, he reveals an almost religious reverence for the close of day:

> As far as we could see, the miles of copper-red grass were drenched in sunlight that was stronger and fiercer than at any other time of the day. The blond cornfields were red gold, the haystacks turned rosy and threw long shadows. The whole prairie was like the bush that burned with fire and was not consumed. That hour always had the exultation of victory, of triumphant ending, like a hero's death—heroes who died young and gloriously. It was a sudden transfiguration, a lifting-up of day.

Undoubtedly this penchant, manifested so early, for discerning and aggrandizing a brilliance so soon to be engulfed in darkness has its significance for the rationale of the novel as a whole.

The fact, too, that many key scenes in the work are pictured in the glow of the setting sun discloses lawyer Jim Burden's affinity for viewing *as passing* or even *as having passed,* the "best days." For him, indeed, the sinking sun affords symbolic illumination for his own "golden age."

In Chapter III when Jim introduces the Shimerda family, he again betrays his tendency to see light in reference to dark, for he focusses his attention primarily on Ántonia and her father, almost symbolic representations of the light and the dark sides of life, Eros and Thanatos. Out of the darkness of their wretched dug-out home step both these figures, yet how differently they face the prairie world! Ántonia's youthful innocence manifests itself in her spontaneously hopeful acceptance of the Burdens as neighbors. Even her physical presence shows an openness to life and love. Her eyes, "big and warm and full of life, like the sun shining on brown pools in the wood," hint of her Eros-nature, just as do her rich, dark, glowing skin and curly, wild-looking hair. Her actions, too, convey this affirmative spirit as she grasps Jim's hand and races off with him and Yulka toward Squaw Creek, where she seems to revel in the bracing prairie winds and the rugged natural beauties at the ravine's edge. Jim notes Ántonia's eagerness to learn "a score of words" in their brief time together the first afternoon, and he is non-plussed by her reckless extravagance in wishing to reward with a little silver ring his modest attempt to teach her a few English phrases. Finally, he records the vivacious Ántonia's quick and loving response to her frail father's call. Mr. Shimerda, on the other hand, emerges from the dark "hole" an old, weak man whose tall, thin frame seems but loaned to the prairie world. His eyes are melancholy and deeply set, and his face looks "like ashes—like something from which all the warmth and light had died out." Though his manner is dignified and his dress meticulous, these very marks of natural aristocracy forecast his doom. Jim includes Otto Fuchs' comments about him: ". . . the father . . . knew nothing about farming. He was a weaver by trade; had always been a skilled workman on tapestries and upholstery materials . . . He had brought his fiddle with him, which wouldn't be much use here. . . ." Indeed, Mr. Shimerda appears to be an artist-figure shadowed by death, a Thanatos-character in every detail.

In the closing scene of the chapter, as Ántonia runs with characteristic vibrancy to answer her father's mournful call, Jim recounts the first step toward his own unique relationship with Mr. Shimerda. "When I came up," he tells the reader, "he touched my shoulder and looked searchingly down into my face for several seconds. I became somewhat embarrassed, for I was used to being taken for granted by my elders." There is something solemn, almost sacred, about the old man's action, that carries with it adumbrations of an "ordination" to sonship, or a ratification of some spiritual bond. This idea is further reinforced when Mr. Shimerda, in his "sacramental" fashion—for his words were few—shows Jim the English-Bohemian dictionary, places the book in Grandmother Burden's hands, and concludes his plea with the earnest words, "Te-e-ach, te-e-ach my Ántonia!" Into this brief entreaty is condensed all that Mr. Shimerda cannot say: the book, as symbol of all civilized influences, he places in the care of Jim and his grandmother, to be given by them to "My Ántonia," the flesh-and-blood embodiment of all he hopes for in the "new" world, and all he held precious in the old. His use of the endearing epithet here does indeed enrich the connotations of Jim's choice of the novel's title just as the whole scene adds weight to the meaning of the boy's name.

As Jim's friendship with Ántonia grows in the days that follow, so too grows his understanding of her father. The two children witness his comradeship with Pavel and Peter, but they see also his increasing torpor. Of all the family, only Ántonia, Jim informs the reader, can draw from her father "a wintry flicker of a smile"; only her loving spirit can interest him in the future: it is to Ántonia that he promises the winter hat made of rabbit skins. But Jim, too, significantly, shares Mr. Shimerda's concern at this time, and proof of this interest occurs when Jim and Ántonia meet the old man one evening at sunset as he returns from hunting, "dragging his feet along as if he had no purpose." While Ántonia arouses her weary father's spirit by showing him the green, faintly chirping insect that she had carried to him unharmed in her hair under the kerchief, Jim picks up the old man's heavy gun. Noting this, Mr. Shimerda turns upon Jim "his far-away look that always made [him] feel as if [he] were down at the bottom of a well" and speaks to him "kindly and gravely." Ántonia's translation of her father's words reveals another step in the boy's relationship with Mr. Shimerda: when he is a "big boy," Jim is to have the gun for his own—this symbol of paternal protectiveness, of reward for service rendered, of Old-World craftsmanship and largesse. With boy-like relief, Jim records, "I was glad that this project was one of futurity," and it was, in truth, to be many years before he was to assume responsibility for Ántonia and all that she represented in the old man's eyes. That this gun was never to get to Jim, that it was to be the instrument of Mr. Shimerda's self-destruction, is, of course, important. The old man's tragic failure lay in the fact that he could not reconcile his European heritage with the prairie world; he could not transplant the Muse from his native Bohemia to the Nebraska plain; whereas Jim was, through knowing Ántonia, to accomplish an analogous feat. (pp. 91-6)

Book II of the novel, "The Hired Girls," chronicles one of the major hardships which immigrant girls like Ántonia had to overcome—their inferior social position despite their rich European heritage and their natural beauty and vigor. The Burdens are, in a sense, responsible for this phase of Ántonia's life, for Grandmother Burden sought, by interesting the Harlings in employing her, to rescue Ántonia from the wretched life imposed on her by her brother Ambrosch. Telling the Harlings of her, Mrs. Burden recalls, " 'When she first came to this country . . . and had that genteel old man to watch over her, she was as pretty a girl as I ever saw. But, dear me, what a life she's led, out in the fields with those rough threshers. Things would have been very different with poor Ántonia if her father had lived'." After Ántonia comes "into service" at the Harlings, Jim's pride in her harmony with her cultured mistress is unmistakable, and under Mrs. Harling's guidance, he sees her growing into a fulfilled young woman. Describing their vigorous characters, he says:

> They had strong, independent natures, both of them. They knew what they liked, and were not always trying to imitate other people. They loved children and animals and music, and rough play and digging in the earth. They liked to prepare rich, hearty food and to see people eat it; to make up soft white beds and to see youngsters asleep in them. They ridiculed conceited people and were quick to help unfortunate ones. Deep down in each of them there was a kind of hearty joviality, a relish of life, not over-delicate, but very invigorating. I never tried to define it, but I was distinctly conscious of it.

But with the advent of Vanni's dancing pavilion in Black Hawk, Ántonia reveals other characteristics, irresponsibility and recklessness—qualities of an uncontrolled love of life—which grow also, and soon result in her dismissal from the Harling home. Mrs. Harling and Frances, attempting to reason with her, only draw forth the response, " 'My own father couldn't make me stop'," emphasizing the extent to which Ántonia is committed to her own independence. Her subsequent employment in the Cutter household, the transfer from a house of love to a house of hate, from a warm family to a spiteful childless couple, works subtle changes upon Ántonia's generous spirit, and Jim soon finds that "she seemed to care about nothing but picnics and parties and having a good time." Points of contact between him and Ántonia become more and more tenuous.

The dance floor does provide a frequent meeting-place for them, however, and Jim is mindful of her father's musical legacy to her as he remarks Ántonia's "spring and variety" in dance rhythm: "If, instead of going to the end of the railroad, old Mr. Shimerda had stayed in New York and picked up a living with his fiddle, how different Ántonia's life might have been." How different indeed. This comment leads Jim to make his first mention of Larry Donovan, who was to prove another great hardship for Ántonia, and to explain indirectly his own failure to avert this catastrophe which he clearly foresaw. Jim's love for Ántonia (and hers for him) is undoubtedly deep; yet it is a love that has been marked and set apart by the spiritual relationship that Jim has contracted with Mr. Shimerda. When Jim endeavors to show his love for Ántonia in what he considers a normal way—a passionate kiss—she is horrified: " 'Why, Jim! You know you ain't right to kiss me like that.' " And his reply that Lena Lingard, of whom he is not half so fond, accepts such kisses, infuriates Ántonia into a sisterly rebuke: " 'If she's up to any of her nonsense with you, I'll scratch her eyes out. . . . You can like me all you want to, but if I see you hanging around with Lena much, I'll go to your grandmother, as sure as your name's Jim Burden!' " Jim's reaction to this heated threat is not a lover's sulk but a brother's pride: "I was so proud of her that I carried my head high as I emerged from the dark cedars. . . . Her warm, sweet face, her kind arms, and the true heart in her; she was, oh, she was still my Ántonia!" With Mr. Shimerda's meaningful epithet on his lips, Jim tells how his love overflowed into the dreams of happy moments on the farm with Ántonia. Yet never was she to acquire any sexual importance for him—even in a dream world. Though his conscious self might so desire such a relationship, his unconscious ego was distinctly aware of far deeper ties between them.

In the months that follow, with Mr. and Mrs. Burden's discovery of Jim's "dance hall" activities and their open disapproval, the boy becomes more and more lonely and withdrawn from the life of the town. This alienation, however, provides him with time to delve into the knowledge of the past, and he spends his evenings "reading Latin that was not in our high school course." The fruits of this study, as well as the results of his perceptive probings into the small-town values, appear in the commencement address which, in his own opinion, was "very good" for "it stated with fervour a great many things I'd lately discovered." Mrs. Harling's pleasure with his efforts gratifies him immensely, but it is Ántonia's response that senses the truest depths and touches Jim most profoundly. Waiting with the rest of the "hired girls" a block or so from the Opera House where the graduation ceremony had taken place, Ántonia bursts forth from the shadows with her sincere praise, " 'Oh, Jim, it was splendid!' " And then she adds, " 'Oh, I just sat there and wished my papa could hear you! Jim . . . there was something in your speech that made me think so much about my

papa!' " Jim acknowledges the mysterious kinship with the words, " 'I thought of your papa when I wrote my speech, Tony. . . . I dedicated it to him'."

Jim's first small success in bringing the Muse into his own country—the task that Mr. Shimerda would have understood so well—is rewarded by Ántonia's love and tears. Despite their differences of temperament, of occupation, of attitudes (with Tony's periods of reckless selfishness), the firm bond of deep unity between them still remains Ántonia's dead father. Another such moment of union occurs during the mid-summer picnic with the "hired girls" when Jim discovers Ántonia crying as she sits under the flowering elder trees along the bank of the river. The delicate odor, she explains, reminds her of her father's garden where took place the "beautiful talk" of " 'music, and the woods, and . . . God, and when they were young'." Jim comforts her by telling of his mystical experience with her father's soul that day many years ago, and of his certainty that her father's spirit has found rest in his own country. Ántonia accepts his word as if it were that of her father himself. Calmed and reassured, Ántonia tells Jim the story of her parents' marriage, the heroic generosity and uprightness of heart that prompted her father to marry Mrs. Shimerda despite parental and fraternal disapproval. Their union, Ántonia implies, had been one of justice rather than love, perhaps partially accounting for Mr. Shimerda's orientation toward death. Association with her father's sensitive nature, even through memories, brings a renewal within her of all the fine qualities of her strong Eros-nature, and Jim feels her to be once more "exactly like the little girl who used to come to our house with Mr. Shimerda."

Still under the spell of the two Thanatos-characters, Ántonia begs Jim to tell the other girls the story of Coronado and his search for the Seven Golden Cities. That the great explorer had traveled along the very river they were overlooking was an idea that thrilled the imagination of Ántonia as it did that of Jim and Charley Harling. When the group discusses the Spanish explorer, the question of his last years comes up, and Jim can only tell them, "the schoolbooks said 'he died in the wilderness, of a broken heart'." Ántonia's sad comment, " 'More than him has done that,' " brings Mr. Shimerda's frail westering spirit within the same tradition as that of the mighty Spaniard whose final desires too were unfulfilled. Looking back on this scene, Jim remembered it in the golden glow of the setting sun: the *"optima dies"* when the symbol of pioneer vision—the plow—lay magnified within the circle of the dying disk. Though there were such moments in the past—even in his own past—in Jim's somber view, the darkness that spread over the earth and the plow's "sinking to its own littleness somewhere on the prairie" seems more truly to characterize reality.

The last scene in Book II fittingly occurs in the blackened world of the Cutters, the place in which Ántonia had allowed herself to dwell, in spite of the heritage of her artist-father and the feelings of his legatee, Jim Burden. Here, as the father would have wished, Jim takes the "burden" (at Grandmother's suggestion), and protects Ántonia from a disgraceful fall such as Mrs. Harling had warned her against. But his heroism does not fill him with pride. Unlike the snake incident when he and Ántonia were children, this contact with evil in Ántonia's behalf fills him with revulsion. He records this reaction clearly: "I heard Ántonia sobbing outside my door, but I asked grandmother to send her away. I felt that I never wanted to see her again. I hated her almost as much as I hated Cutter." Ántonia's growing deviation from the path of her true development as an Eros-nature hurts Jim as it would have hurt her father, and Jim's perceptive soul recoils from the "disgustingness" of the whole affair. It is with this dim view of Ántonia's full life-force that Jim leaves Black Hawk for Lincoln and the university.

Although Book III, "Lena Lingard," does not contain a single reference to Mr. Shimerda, it is important in tracing Jim Burden's kinship with the death-haunted old man. The two years at Lincoln do much to strengthen the work Jim began under Mr. Shimerda's aegis when he gave the commencement address as he finished high school, and Jim looks back to this time of continued mental awakening as "one of the happiest in my life." Jim's kinship with Mr. Shimerda was built on their recognition in each other of a keen sense of culture, of the truly valuable things in life, be they of art or of nature, and the young man spends his Lincoln days formulating more precisely basic notions concerning art and nature and their mutual relationship. Earnestly studying the classics, Jim discovers that the past has for him, as it had for Mr. Shimerda, an irresistible pull, but he also concludes:

> I knew that I should never be a scholar. I could never lose myself for long among impersonal things. Mental excitement was apt to send me with a rush back to my own naked land and the figures scattered upon it. While I was in the very act of yearning toward new forms . . . my mind plunged away from me, and I suddenly found myself thinking of the places and people of my own infinitesimal past. They stood out strengthened and simplified now, like the image of the plough against the sun. They were all I had for an answer to the new appeal.

For this reason Jim responds with empathy to Virgil's hope "at once bold and devoutly humble, that he might bring the Muse . . . not to the capital . . . but to his own little 'country'; to his father's fields, 'sloping down to the river and to the old beech trees with broken tops'." Old Mr. Shimerda, frustrated in his artistic questings, would have understood this; perhaps this was why Jim was so sure, and hastened to confirm Ántonia's hesitant hope that her father's spirit was "at home" in his own country at last. The same kindred spirit prompts Jim's reflections on Virgil's line, "The best days are the first to flee," and allows him the moment of illumination after Lena's departure, the inspiration which was to be ultimately responsible for his own "Georgics," his *My Ántonia:* "It came over me, as it had never done before, the relation between girls like those [the "hired girls"] and the poetry of Virgil. If there were no girls like them in the world, there would be no poetry. I understood that clearly for the first time. This revelation seemed to me inestimably precious. I clung to it as if it might suddenly vanish."

This section of the novel also marks the beginning of Jim's sharp deviation from the road that he, Ántonia, and the Shimerda family traveled down together nearly ten years before. Simultaneously it records his first real shirking of the "burden" of care for Ántonia that Mr. Shimerda silently imposed upon him so long ago. When Lena first visits Jim in Lincoln, he inquires after his old friend. Reminded of her love ("she's always bragging about you") and informed of her "foolishness" over Larry Donovan, Jim remarks paternally, " 'I think I'd better go home and look after Ántonia'," but he does not. The very months—March through June—that Jim spends "drifting," indulging his romantic nature by gazing long hours at Lena's warm, earthy beauty, and attending with her shows like Dumas' *Camille,* full of the "spirit of 1840, which had

sighed so much," are the months that Ántonia lives, at first joyfully, then with more and more misgiving, in Denver, at the mercy of Larry Donovan. Betrayed by her own positive nature ("if she once likes people, she won't hear anything against them," she returns to Black Hawk, "crushed and quiet," while Jim, rescued by Gaston Cleric, settles down to the grind again once he reaches Boston and Harvard. Just as old Mr. Shimerda had deserted his beloved daughter because he could not reconcile his dreams of a happy past in Bohemia with the cold reality of a Nebraska winter, so Jim too leaves her defenseless, preferring a dream of romance with Lena to the hard reality of Tony's danger.

Book IV of the novel, "The Pioneer Woman's Story," gives an account of Jim's return to Black Hawk at the age of twenty-one before entering Harvard Law School, and the gradual transformation of his disappointment in Ántonia into a realization of her solid worth. Ántonia's plight as an unwed mother has earned for her the title "Poor Ántonia," an expression which tortures Jim by its contrast in meaning to the plentitude of his own designation of her as "My Ántonia." Bitterly dissatisfied with her, he comments, "I tried to shut Ántonia out of my mind. . . . I could not forgive her for becoming an object of pity. . . ." But Jim's dark view is somewhat mitigated when, visiting the photographer's shop, he sees displayed in a great gilt frame a picture of Tony's baby. The young mother's strength and pride of spirit shine through the action, and Jim leaves the shop feeling that he must see his old friend again. Before actually facing her, however, he hears the story of her "disgrace" from Mrs. Steavens, the widow who had moved into the old Burden homestead near the Shimerda farm. As if the possession of the home initiated her into the circle of 'My Ántonia's' protectors, Mrs. Steavens had taken over the "burden" of caring for the young girl and appreciating her true worth throughout the period of preparation for her marriage as well as the time of her return, preceding the child's birth. The widow tells Jim of Ántonia's departure for Denver: " 'She laughed kind of flighty like and whispered, "Goodbye, dear house!" and then ran out to the wagon. I expect she meant that for you and your grandmother, as much as for me, so I'm particular to tell you. This house had always been a refuge to her'." And later, recounting her sad conversation with Ántonia about Larry's desertion, Mrs. Steavens adopts the familiar epithet that means so much to Mr. Shimerda and Jim: " 'My Ántonia, that had so much good in her, had come home disgraced'."

The next day, seeking out Ántonia in the fields, Jim is made conscious of that good as her warm hand clasped his: " '. . . there was a new kind of strength in the gravity of her face, and her colour still gave her that look of deep-seated health and ardour." Instinctively the two old friends walk toward "that unploughed patch at the crossing of the roads as the fittest place to talk to each other." Shadowed by Mr. Shimerda's grave, and faced with the full force of Ántonia's goodness, Jim pours out the story of the past few years. When he tells Ántonia of his decision to work in New York, she responds with immediate understanding, once more linking him with her dead father: " 'But that don't mean I'll lose you. Look at my papa here; he's been dead all these years, and yet he is more real to me than almost anybody else. He never goes out of my life. I talk to him and consult him all the time. The older I grow, the better I know him and the more I understand him'." And Jim's admission of her place in his life intensifies their solidarity:

"Do you know, Ántonia, since I've been away, I think of you more often than of anyone else in this part of the world. I'd have liked to have you for a sweetheart, or a wife, or my mother or my sister—anything that a woman can be to a man. The idea of you is a part of my mind; you influence my likes and dislikes, all my tastes, hundreds of times when I don't realize it. You really are a part of me."

Walking home in the golden glow of the sunset, Ántonia questions, " 'You'll always remember me when you think about old times, won't you?' " and the very scene itself is her answer. Ántonia is indeed a part of Jim's "golden age," his *"optima dies,"* the force whose life and love work upon him the old magic, pulling him back to the past, to his boyhood, to the earth. Holding her hands over his heart, he strains through the darkness to glimpse her face, "the closest, realest face, under all the shadows of women's faces, at the very bottom of his memory." His promise to return provokes Ántonia's firm answer, which emphasizes the strong spiritual bond between them, " 'But even if you don't, you're here, like my father, so I won't be lonesome'." Turning to leave her, Jim is indeed alone, but he is back on the "familiar road."

It is twenty years before Jim finally returns to Black Hawk to see Ántonia, now a happy mother of a large brood of children, and he entitles the section which records his experience "Cuzak's Boys," giving prominence to the male line through which Ántonia's vibrant spirit is to extend throughout the land. The title also betrays a kind of "hyper-consciousness" of his own inadequacy as a "founder of races," of his own personal *Weltschmerz* despite his success as a lawyer. This spirit is manifested early in the section when Jim explains to the reader his reasons for putting off a visit to Ántonia: "I did not want to find her aged and broken; I really dreaded it. In the course of twenty crowded years one parts with many illusions. I did not wish to lose the early ones. Some memories are realities, and are better than anything that can ever happen to one again." The sight of Ántonia in "the full vigour of her personality, battered but not diminished" appears the more brilliant against the dark background of Jim's disillusionment.

Indeed, Jim articulates this difference in words evocative of the sun image so personally meaningful when he compares Ántonia to the many women of his own milieu: "I know so many women who have kept all the things that she had lost, but whose inner glow was faded. Whatever else was gone, Ántonia had not lost the fire of life." Her teeming fruitfulness, imaged so aptly as Jim describes her children bursting forth from the fruit cellar as a "veritable explosion of life out of the dark cave into the sunlight," is an overt commentary on the barrenness of his own home with a wife who "has her own fortune and lives her own life" ("Introduction"). Jim's interest in all Cuzak's boys, his delight in the companionship of Ambrosch and Anton in the fields, his willingness to spend the night in the hayloft with Leo and Ambrosch, his promise to take Rudolph and Ambrosch hunting on the Niobrara—all evidence the frustrations of his own paternity. His admitted curiosity about the state of the relationship between Ántonia and Cuzak—what it "had become or remained"—shows his cynicism of the possibility of complete accord in marriage. Even when he finds them "to be on terms of easy friendliness, touched with humour," he cannot refrain from the final judgment, "It did rather seem to me that Cuzak had been made the instrument of Ántonia's special mission. . . . I wondered whether the life that was right for one was ever right for two."

Jim's world-travels, it appears, though they have contributed to his artistic experiences, have not supplemented substantially his belief in basic human values. These, he finds, are rooted and grounded in the past. The return to Ántonia, to his own land, brings Jim also back to the "old road" that he and Ántonia had traveled that first night when they got off the train at Black Hawk. To Jim, sitting in the slanting rays of the sinking orb, contemplating that half-hidden stretch of original road, comes the sensation of "coming home to himself, and of having found out what a little circle man's experience is." This discovery signals for Jim, the world-weary traveler, a re-assessment of the "best days," a paradoxical re-creation of that which he and Ántonia possess together, "the precious, the incommunicable past."

Thus the novel comes full circle, not only in its symbolic representation as the road with which the story opened reappears before Jim's eyes at its close, but also as the situation which provoked the novel's publication—Jim's giving the "thing about Ántonia" to the author, as related in the "Introduction"—meets the event which precipitated his reminiscences—his final return to Ántonia and his inspiration by her Eros-spirit. In addition, the Eros-Thanatos polarities which produce the novel manifest their intricate workings when one considers the inner story of Ántonia's powerful, affirmative nature encircled by the dark frame of Jim's Thanatos-character, united with that of her father, which presents Ántonia's life and love in the golden glow of the past, as a memory which is a reality "better than anything that can ever happen to one again." A further dimension of the Eros-Thanatos complexity appears in the final fulfillment of Jim as "poet" of the "patria," the essentially Thanatos-figure whose sublimation of failure in his personal life effects his triumph as an artist. Only by the sensitive registering and ordering of his memories of "the best days" does he create the Ántonia who embodies that ideal vision of both Mr. Shimerda and himself, the Ántonia who possesses "that something which fires the imagination" making of his own story—and Miss Cather's book—a flaming, forceful assertion of all that is universal and true. (pp. 99-108)

Sister Peter Damian Charles, O.P., " 'My Ántonia': A Dark Dimension," in Western American Literature, *Vol. II, No. 2, August, 1967, pp. 91-108.*

TERENCE MARTIN (essay date 1969)

[*In the following excerpt, Martin attempts to explain what critics have described as structural ambiguities in* My Ántonia *by viewing the essential action of the novel as the resolution of Jim Burden's personal conflicts.*]

From the time of the composition of *My Ántonia,* the role of Jim Burden has invited attention. Perhaps feeling the need to define that role more specifically, Willa Cather revised the preface of the novel for the reissue of 1926, making changes that altered Jim Burden's relation to the story he tells. In the 1918 preface, for example, Jim agrees to record his memories of Ántonia, which he has not thought of doing before; in the second preface, however, he is already at work on the manuscript before the meeting and conversation that supposedly take place with Willa Cather on the train. Such a change implies that something private and personal has been at work in the mind of Jim Burden, that the manuscript has taken initial shape because of an inner need to articulate the meaning of a valued, ultimately treasured, memory. Willa Cather has amended her first (prefatory) thoughts by bringing her narrator closer emotionally to the substance of the narrative.

Readers have continued to assess the role of Jim Burden because of its relevance to the structure of the novel as a whole. David Daiches, for example, believes that "the narrator's development goes on side by side with Ántonia's" and finds the symbolism uncertain at the conclusion: "The final suggestion that this is the story of Jim and Ántonia and their relation is not really borne out by the story as it has developed. It begins as that, but later the strands separate until we have three main themes all going—the history of Ántonia, the history of Jim, and scenes of Nebraska life." The result, Daiches feels, and no mean achievement, is "a flawed novel full of life and interest and possessing a powerful emotional rhythm in spite of its imperfect structural pattern" [see *TCLC*, Vol. 1, p. 158]. E. K. Brown [see excerpt dated 1953] sees a potential problem in the choice of a man as narrator: Jim Burden "was to be fascinated by Ántonia as only a man could be, and yet he was to remain a detached observer, appreciative but inactive, rather than take a part in her life." The consequence of Willa Cather's effort to achieve these two not fully compatible effects is an emptiness "at the very center" of Jim's relation to Ántonia, "where the strongest emotion might have been expected to gather." Stressing the function of the narrator, James E. Miller, Jr., believes that the "emotional structure of the novel may be discovered" in the drama of Jim Burden's "awakening consciousness," which "shapes in the reader a sharpened awareness of cyclic fate that is the human destiny" [see excerpt dated 1958]. John H. Randall, III, in his impressive study of Willa Cather, would seem to agree with the implications of some of the previous arguments when he says that Jim Burden is more than "a first-person onlooker who is relating someone else's story" [see excerpt dated 1960]. Randall develops the idea of a double protagonist, part Ántonia, who faces the future, part Jim Burden, who faces the past. Together, Jim and Ántonia make a complete, albeit "Janus-faced," personality.

If structural coherence is to be found in **My Ántonia,** the character of Jim Burden seems necessarily to be involved. As the story of Ántonia, the novel is quite rightly found inadequate; and even as the story of Ántonia and Jim Burden, the narrative strands, as Mr. Daiches indicates, tend to separate. For it is the story of Jim's Ántonia, and the meaning and implications of that term must somehow subsume the various elements of the novel. As I see it, the substance and quality of the narrative itself—at once evolving toward and conditioned by the image of Jim's Ántonia—provide a principle of unity that takes the special form of a drama of memory. (pp. 304-05)

The pace and emphases of the narrative in **My Ántonia** come of course from Jim Burden. As we know, the point of view is retrospective, and despite his disclaimer in the preface, Jim has both the perspective and the inclination to shape his material with care. Accordingly, Book One has a definite pattern, that of the seasons: beginning with the autumn of his arrival, Jim takes us through the year to the fullness and heat of the following summer. Moreover, he portrays himself predominantly in terms of his reactions to the seasons during his first year on the prairie. The first section of the novel thus operates as a kind of rehearsal for nostalgia. For this year lives at the center of Jim's memory, never to be relived, never to be forgotten. It has for him an idyllic quality, a quality of tenderly remembered freedom and happiness resulting from his surrender to the forces of nature with which everyone else must contend. On the night of his arrival in Nebraska, we recall, Jim adopts

Cather in 1912.

an attitude of resignation: "here . . . what would be would be." The next day in his grandmother's garden he relaxes against a "warm yellow pumpkin," crumbles earth in his fingers, and watches and listens to nature. "Nothing happened," he says. "I did not expect anything to happen. I was something that lay under the sun and felt it, like the pumpkins, and I did not want to be anything more. I was entirely happy." He thinks of death (his parents, we remember, have recently died) and wonders if death makes us "a part of something entire." "At any rate," he concludes, "that is happiness; to be dissolved into something complete and great."

Jim Burden, in short, makes an immediate surrender to nature in this garden with its ripe pumpkins. And his feeling of immersion in nature has a significant and permanent effect upon him, for he never loses his ability to appreciate the prairie in a personal way or his need to find happiness amid the ripeness and fulfillment of life. Though he must tell us of human hardship, Jim reveals his sense of rapture as he recalls and describes the seasons. "All the years that have passed," he says, "have not dimmed my memory of that first glorious autumn." The new country lay open before him, leading him to celebrate the splendor of the prairie in the last hour of the afternoon:

> All those fall afternoons were the same, but I never
> got used to them. As far as we could see, the miles
> of copper-red grass were drenched in sunlight that

was stronger and fiercer than at any other time of the day. The blond cornfields were red gold, the haystacks turned rosy and threw long shadows. The whole prairie was like the bush that burned with fire and was not consumed. That hour always had the exultation of victory, of triumphant ending, like a hero's death—heroes who died young and gloriously. It was a sudden transfiguration, a lifting-up of day.

Jim's tone is reverential, replete with wonder, the product of a deep respect for the prairie and for the sunlight that brings it to ripeness.

Winter becomes primarily a time of taking refuge. Snow disguises the prairie with an insidious mask of white, leaving one, as Jim says later, with "a hunger for color." He is convinced that "man's strongest antagonist is the cold," though, in the security of his grandmother's basement kitchen, which "seemed heavenly safe and warm in those days," he can hardly experience its bitterness in the manner of the Shimerdas, who have only one overcoat among them and takes turns wearing it for warmth. On cold nights, he recalls, the cry of coyotes "used to remind the boys of wonderful animal stories." A sense of adventure pervades Jim's life: by comparison, the life represented in books seems prosaic: the Swiss family Robinson, for example, "had no advantage over us in the way of an adventurous life"—and, later, Robinson Crusoe's life on the island "seemed dull compared with ours." If winter means taking refuge, it also satisfies the needs of Jim's young imagination and contributes the memory of adventure, a feeling of hardship happily domesticated by the company, the kitchen, and the stove "that fed us and warmed us and kept us cheerful."

Spring with the reawakening of the prairie and summer with its sense of fruition complete the cycle of the seasons. The pervasive lightness of spring delights Jim: "If I had been tossed down blindfold on that red prairie, I should have known that it was spring." And July brings the "breathless, brilliant heat which makes the prairies of Kansas and Nebraska the best corn country in the world. It seemed as if we could hear the corn growing in the night; under the stars one caught a faint crackling in the dewy, heavy-odored cornfields where the feathered stalk stood so juicy and green." These are to become the world's cornfields, Jim sees in retrospect; their yield will underlie "all the activities of men in peace or war."

A sense of happiness remembered pervades Book One, softening and mellowing the harsher outlines of the story Jim Burden has to tell. We are never really on the prairie with Jim, nor does he try to bring us there. Rather, he preserves his retrospective point of view and tells us what it was like for him on the prairie. "I used to love to drift along the pale-yellow cornfield," he says; and (as we have seen) "All the years that have passed have not dimmed my memory of that first glorious autumn"; and, again, though she is four years his senior and they have arrived on the prairie at the same time, Ántonia "had come to us a child, and now she was a tall, strong young girl." Such statements, and numerous devices of style throughout the novel, make a point of narrative distance and deliver the story to us in an envelope of memory. The style, that is to say, makes a deliberate—and almost total—sacrifice of immediacy in favor of the afterglow of remembrance. Even the scenes of violence are kept at a distance by having someone else tell them to Jim Burden; indeed, they are not so much scenes as inset stories, twice removed from the reader. Pavel's story of the wolves in Russia, Ántonia's story of the tramp who jumped into the threshing machine, the story of Wick Cutter's death (told by one of Ántonia's children)—

all these contain a terror and a violence that is subdued by having them related to Jim as part of his story to us. In a similar indirect way we learn of Mr. Shimerda's death and of the seduction of Ántonia by Larry Donovan (whom we never meet). Only when Jim kills the snake, thus, in a sense, making the prairie safe for Ántonia, and when for Ántonia's sake he decoys himself in Wick Cutter's bedroom, are terror and violence (and in the latter case a mixture of comedy) brought close; and, in keeping with the retrospective point of view, these episodes, too, come to us through the spectrum of Jim's memory.

Defining the mode of Jim Burden's relation to his narrative leads us to see the special character of the novel itself and to judge it on its own terms rather than on any we might inadvertently bring to it. The statement of one critic that "something precious went into American fiction with the story of Ántonia Shimerda" is meant as a tribute to Willa Cather's novel; but it seems to me a misdirected tribute. For the novel does not present the *story* of Ántonia; it does, I believe, present a drama of memory by means of which Jim Burden tells us how he has come to see Ántonia as the epitome of all he has valued. At the time he writes, Jim Burden has made sense of his experience on the prairie, has seen the meaning it has and will have in his life. The early sections of *My Ántonia* present in retrospect the substance of meaning, conditioned throughout by Jim's assurance of that meaning. The latter sections justify his right to remember the prairie in the joyous manner of his youth. And the process of justification involves, most importantly, the image of Ántonia. This image acquires symbolic significance for Jim; embodying and justifying his memories, it validates nostalgia by giving his feeling for the past a meaning in the present.

By common consent, the "I" of the preface is taken to be Willa Cather. In the preface we learn that both to Jim Burden and Willa Cather, Ántonia, "more than any other person we remembered, . . . seemed to mean . . . the country, the conditions, the whole adventure of our childhood." Miss Cather says that she had lost sight of Ántonia, but that Jim "had found her again after long years." The preface thus establishes a relation between Jim Burden and Willa Cather outside the narrative that is important to the relationship of Jim and Ántonia within the narrative. Jim Burden becomes the imaginative instrument by means of which Willa Cather reacquaints herself with Ántonia: "He made me see her again, feel her presence, revived all my old affection for her." Her narrator, in short, serves Miss Cather as the vehicle for her own quest for meaning and value; his success measures her success; his symbol becomes her symbol; for his Ántonia is the Ántonia she has created for him.

If Jim Burden is to be made more than a heuristic phantom of the imagination, however, he must be given some kind of autonomy as a fictional character. Some drama, however quiet it may appear in retrospect, must play itself out in his life; some resolution must come inherently from the narrative. If we are to have a drama of memory, Jim's memory must somehow be challenged before it is vindicated in and by the image of Ántonia. The offstage challenges, those involved, for example, when Jim explains his twenty-year absence from the Nebraska prairie by saying "life intervened," afford little but material for conjecture and inference. The onstage challenge, however, affording material for analysis, enters Jim's room in Lincoln in Book Three in the very pretty form of Lena Lingard.

Lena Lingard first appears as one of the hired girls in Book Two, along with Tiny Soderball, lesser characters such as the

Bohemian Marys and the Danish laundry girls, and, of course, Ántonia, who has come to Black Hawk to work for the Harlings. The move to Black Hawk does take Ántonia away from the prairie and tend to merge her importance with that of a group of girls. But by placing Ántonia and Lena Lingard together, as friends, Willa Cather can begin to suggest the different roles each of them will play in the life of Jim Burden. Moreover, Black Hawk provides a canvas on which Miss Cather can portray social consciousness and burgeoning social change in the Nebraska of this time. Despite the domestic vitality of the Harling family, readily available for Jim Burden (now living next door with his grandparents) to draw on, Black Hawk seems increasingly dull to Jim during his high-school years. Small and very proper, the town makes life for young men an initiation into monotony. Except, of course, for the presence of the hired girls. These young women, all of foreign families, bring vivacity to Black Hawk; light-hearted, gay, and unpretentious, at the dances they are in great demand. More often than not, however, the proper young men must meet them surreptitiously, for the hired girls enjoy a lower social status than do the girls of the older American families in the town. Remarking on the social distinction, Jim Burden says that

> the daughters of Black Hawk merchants had a confident, uninquiring belief that they were 'refined,' and that the country girls, who 'worked out,' were not. The American farmers in our county were quite as hard-pressed as their neighbors from other countries. All alike had come to Nebraska with little capital and no knowledge of the soil they must subdue. All had borrowed money on their land. But no matter in what straits the Pennsylvanian or Virginian found himself, he would not let his daughters go out into service. Unless his girls could teach a country school, they sat home in poverty.

Kept from teaching by their inadequate knowledge of English, yet determined to help their families out of debt, the hired girls took domestic or similar employment. Some remained serious and discreet, says Jim, others did not. But all sent home money to help pay "for ploughs and reapers, brood-sows, or steers to fatten." Jim frankly admires such family solidarity, as a result of which the foreign families in the county were "the first to become prosperous." Today, he says, former hired girls are "managing big farms of their own; their children are better off than the children of the town women they used to serve." Pleased with their success, Jim feels paternal toward the entire group of girls and applauds the social change which accompanies their prosperity.

A single generation serves to bring about the kind of change Jim describes. In the Black Hawk of his youth, however, "the country girls were considered a menace to the social order." And surely none of them represented more of a menace than Lena Lingard. Demure, soft, and attractive, Lena radiates sexual charm without guile or effort. Before Jim has finished high school, both the married Ole Benson and the proper young bachelor Sylvestor Lovett have become driven, obsessed men because of her. Later in Lincoln, her landlord, Colonel Raleigh, and the Polish violin teacher, Mr. Ordinski, are entranced by Lena and suspicious of Jim on her account. A blonde, Norwegian, Nebraskan Circe, Lena is a temptress who "gave her heart away when she felt like it," as Jim says, but "kept her head for business." If she does not literally turn her admirers into swine, she cannot prevent their appetites from giving them at times hardly less graceful postures. When dancing, says Jim, Lena moved "without exertion rather indolently." If her part-

ner spoke to her, she would smile, but rarely answer. "The music seemed to put her into a soft, waking dream, and her violet-colored eyes looked sleepily and confidingly at one from under her long lashes. . . . To dance 'Home, Sweet Home' with Lena was like coming in with the tide. She danced every dance like a waltz, and it was always the same waltz—the waltz of coming home to something, of inevitable, fated return."

This is the Lena Lingard who walks into Jim's room in Lincoln, who dominates Book Three and seems very close to taking command of the novel. Like Ántonia, she has come from off the prairie; like Ántonia, too, she is generous and forthright. But unlike Ántonia, she makes a success of herself in business, as a fashion designer, first in Lincoln, later in San Francisco. And unlike Ántonia, she is determined not to marry, not to have a family. Lena's unconscious power to distract a man from whatever he may or should be doing exerts its influence on Jim during his final year at the University of Nebraska. He begins to drift, as he says, to neglect academic life, to live from day to day languidly in love with Lena. His mentor, Gaston Cleric, tells him to "quit school and go to work, or change your college and begin again in earnest. You won't recover yourself while you are playing about with this handsome Norwegian." To Gaston Cleric, Lena seems "perfectly irresponsible." In the light of her successful career, the judgment seems only partially valid. But Cleric is near the mark; Lena induces irresponsibility in the men who know her. And Jim is coming to know her well.

No overt antagonism exists between Lena and Ántonia, who are friends with a great deal in common. Yet Ántonia warns Jim in good-natured seriousness not to see too much of Lena; and when Ántonia discovers the manner in which Jim kisses Lena, she exclaims, "If she's up to any of her nonsense with you, I'll scratch her eyes out." Jim's dreams suggest the different roles the girls have in his life. At times he dreams of Ántonia and himself, "sliding down strawstacks as we used to do; climbing up the yellow mountains over and over, and slipping down the smooth sides into soft piles of chaff." He has also a recurrent dream of Lena coming toward him barefoot across a field, "in a short skirt, with a curved reaping-hook in her hand." "She was flushed like the dawn," he continues, "with a kind of luminous rosiness all about her. She sat down beside me, turned to me with a soft sigh and said, 'Now they are all gone, and I can kiss you as much as I like'." Jim says, "I used to wish I could have this flattering dream about Ántonia, but I never did."

Jim's dream of Ántonia, we note, is based on the memory of shared childhood experiences, its sexual significance sublimated in terms of youthful fun and adventure. In Black Hawk, Ántonia has forbidden Jim to kiss her as he apparently kisses Lena, thereby rejecting his tentative gesture toward a relationship of adolescent sexuality. If he is to dream of Ántonia, he must put her in a context of their youth. His dream of Lena, however, more frankly sexual (with the reaping-hook suggestive of such things as fulfillment, castration, and the negation of time), has no context; it can take place only because "they are all gone." Jim's wish that he could have such a dream about Ántonia is part of his larger desire to have some definite, some formal relationship with her. As he says to her later, "I'd have liked to have you for a sweetheart, or a wife, or my mother or my sister—anything that a woman can be to a man." With Lena he drifts into a hedonistic relationship which carries with it the peril of irresponsibility. Somehow Lena always seemed fresh, new, like the dawn: "she wakened fresh with the world everyday," Jim says, and it was easy to "sit idle all through a Sunday morning and look at her." (Ántonia, of course, would be worshipping, not being worshipped, on a Sunday morning.) Like all enchantresses, Lena inspires a chronic forgetfulness. In an ultimate dramatic sense she would be fatal to memory. Consequently, she stands opposed to Ántonia, who will come to bear and to justify the burden of Jim's memory.

The structure of the narrative in Book Three suggests the charm that Lena exercises on Jim. Her entrance into his room, we recall, interrupts his study of Virgil. After she leaves, Jim thinks of all the country girls of Black Hawk and sees a relation between them and the poetry of Virgil: "If there were no girls like them in the world, there would be no poetry. I understood that clearly, for the first time. This revelation seemed to me inestimably precious. I clung to it as if it might suddenly vanish." The country girls are the raw material of poetry; and Jim feels that without them there can be no valid life of the mind. But when he sits down to his lesson for the following day, his newly acquired insight into the relation of "life" and "art" yields up his old dream of Lena, "like the memory of an actual experience." "It floated before me on the page like a picture," he recalls, "and underneath it stood the mournful line: '*Optima dies . . . prima fugit*'—the best days are the first to flee." Since this quotation from the *Georgics* serves as the epigraph of the novel, one has here, I believe, a sense of being close to the emotional center of Jim Burden's narrative. And yet Lena, not Ántonia, inspires the melancholy reflection. In the light of Jim's return to the prairie in Book Four, and, especially, in Book Five, one must conclude that, however tender, this is an unproductive nostalgia, an indulgence in romantic melancholy. Jim's dream of Lena only *seems* "like the memory of an actual experience." And the reality of memory rather than the artificiality of dream will finally serve him as a basis for happiness. Ultimately, the epigraph of the novel comes, as it must, to have fuller and deeper reference to the memory of Ántonia than to the dream of Lena.

Lena Lingard, it is important to see, retards the drama of memory. She represents in the novel not so much an anti-theme as a highly diversionary course of inaction. Promising repose, a blissful release from time, she can be identified by Jim with nothing but herself—which is to say that she does not, as does Ántonia, lend herself "to immemorial human attitudes which we recognize by instinct as universal and true."

Returning to Black Hawk after an absence of two years, Jim is "bitterly disappointed" that Ántonia, betrayed by Larry Donovan, has become "an object of pity," whereas Lena commands wide respect. Having gone to school to Lena, Jim has little immediate sympathy for one who cannot give her heart and keep her head for business. But he responds once again to the country, and its changes seem to him "beautiful and harmonious": "it was like watching the growth of a great man or a great idea." He goes to his old house on the prairie to hear about Ántonia from the Widow Steavens, sleeps in his old room, and confronts his only source of disappointment when he meets Ántonia working in the fields. While they talk, near Mr. Shimerda's grave, he perceives a "new kind of strength in the gravity of [her] face" and confesses that the idea of her is part of his mind. His old feeling for the earth returns, and he wishes he "could be a little boy again." Committed to his early definition of happiness, and thus to the idea of the prairie, and thus to that of Ántonia, he looks hard at her face, which, as he says, "I meant always to carry with me; the closest

realest face, under all the shadows of women's faces, at the very bottom of my memory." The drama of memory has been resolved; Jim's memories will take form around the image of Ántonia.

Having placed so much value on a single memory, Jim feels both impelled and afraid to test its validity by a return to the prairie after an absence of many years. Throughout these years he has apparently maintained a kind of inner life; the image of Ántonia, suggesting youth and early happiness, has hardened into a reality which he fears to see shattered. But his visit to the Cuzaks in Book Five vindicates and fulfills the memory of he has treasured. "Ántonia had always been one to leave images in the mind that did not fade—that grew stronger with time," he says; "in my mind there was a succession of such pictures." To indicate the value of the past to her, Ántonia produces for him her collection of photographs—of Jim, Jake Marpole, Otto Fuchs, the Harlings, even of Lena Lingard—as part of her family's heritage. Together they look through these photographs of old times, but in such a rich, lively context of the present, with children of all sizes laughing and crowding around to show that they, too, know of the early days, that past and present tend to merge in a dynamic new image of happiness that makes the future possible. Amid Ántonia's large family Jim feels like a boy again, but—and this I feel measures the final success of his return—he does not *wish* that he were a boy again, as he did in Book Four. He has no more need to cling to the past, for the past has been transfigured like the autumn prairie of old. He has "not been mistaken" about Ántonia: "She was a rich mine of life, like the founders of early races." "She had only to stand in the orchard, to put her hand on a little crab tree and look up at the apples, to make you feel the goodness of planting and tending and harvesting at last." The somewhat contrived scene of Ántonia's children scrambling and tumbling up out of their new fruit cave, "a veritable explosion of life out of the dark cave into the sunlight" which makes Jim dizzy for a moment, proclaims the relationship between Ántonia and the prairie: both have yielded life in abundance; both have prevailed.

The unity of *My Ántonia* thus derives, I believe, from a drama of memory fulfilled in the present. Clearly the novel does not give us the story of Ántonia's life nor that of Jim's. Rather, it brings us to see the meaning of Ántonia to a man whose happiest days have been those of his youth, who, in the apotheosis of Book Five, becomes reconciled to the present because of the enduring value of the past, even as he comes to possess that past anew because of the promise and vitality of the present. Jim's image of Ántonia has proved fruitful; his drama of memory is not only resolved but fulfilled. He has attained a sense of meaning in his narrative by confronting in retrospect the elements of his early world: from Jim we have learned of the land, the various people who work the land, and the change which the passing of a generation brings about; from Jim, too, we have had the portrait of the Shimerdas and that of Lena Lingard; and from Jim we have the triumphant image of Ántonia, "battered but not diminished," as his personal symbol of the value of human experience. The elements of the novel cohere in Jim Burden's drama of memory. And in Jim's Ántonia they are all subsumed. (pp. 306-11)

Terence Martin, "The Drama of Memory in 'My Ántonia'," in PMLA, Vol. 84, No. 2, March, 1969, pp. 304-11.

BLANCHE H. GELFANT (essay date 1971)

[*In the following excerpt, Gelfant suggests that Jim Burden's portrait of Ántonia is distorted by his own, and Cather's, fear of adult heterosexual relations. Gelfant's argument has been disputed by John J. Murphy, who contends that the barriers which separate Jim and Ántonia are social rather than sexual; for Murphy's comments, see the excerpt dated 1973.]*

Our persistent misreading of Willa Cather's *My Ántonia* rises from a belief that Jim Burden is a reliable narrator. Because we trust his unequivocal narrative manner, we see the novel as a splendid celebration of American frontier life. This is the view reiterated in a current critique of *My Ántonia* [see excerpt by Terence Martin dated 1969] and in a recent comprehensive study of Cather's work: "*My Ántonia* shows fertility of both the soil and human beings. Thus, in a profound sense *My Ántonia* is the most affirmative book Willa Cather ever wrote. Perhaps that is why it was her favorite" [see excerpt by John H. Randall III dated 1960]. Critics also elect it *their* favorite Cather novel: however, they regret its inconclusive structure, as did Cather when she declared it fragmented and unsatisfactory in form. David Daiches's complaint of twenty years ago prevails: that the work is "flawed" by "irrelevant" episodes and material of "uncertain" meaning [see *TCLC*, Vol. 1, p. 158]. Both critical positions—that *My Ántonia* is a glorious celebration of American life and a defective work of art—must be reversed once we challenge Jim Burden's vision of the past. I believe we have reason to do so, particularly now, when we are making many reversals in our thinking. As soon as we question Jim's seemingly explicit statements, we see beyond them myriad confusions which can be resolved only by a totally new reading. This would impel us to reexamine Jim's testimony, to discover him a more disingenuous and self-deluded narrator than we supposed. Once we redefine his role, *My Ántonia* begins to resonate to new and rather shocking meanings which implicate us all. We may lose our chief affirmative novel, only to find one far more exciting—complex, subtle, aberrant.

Jim Burden belongs to a remarkable gallery of characters for whom Cather consistently invalidates sex. Her priests, pioneers, and artists invest all energy elsewhere. Her idealistic young men die prematurely; her bachelors, children, and old folk remain "neutral" observers. Since she wrote within a prohibitive genteel tradition, this reluctance to portray sexuality is hardly surprising. What should intrigue us is the strange involuted nature of her avoidance. She masks sexual ambivalence by certainty of manner, and displays sexual disturbance, even the macabre, with peculiar insouciance. Though the tenor of her writing is normality, normal sex stands barred from her fictional world. Her characters avoid sexual union with significant and sometimes bizarre ingenuity, or achieve it only in dreams. Alexandra Bergson, the heroine of *O Pioneers!*, finds in recurrent reveries the strong transporting arms of a lover; and Jim Burden in *My Ántonia* allows a half-nude woman to smother him with kisses only in unguarded moments of fantasy. Their dreams suggest the typical solipsism of Cather's heroes, who yield to a lover when they are most solitary, most inverted, encaptured by their own imaginations. As Alexandra dispels such reveries by a brisk cold shower, their inferential meaning becomes almost comically clear. Whenever sex enters the real world (as for Emil and Marie in *O Pioneers!*), it becomes destructive, leading almost axiomatically to death. No wonder, then, that Cather's heroes have a strong intuitive aversion to sex which they reveal furtively through enigmatic gestures. In *A Lost Lady*, when young Niel Herbert, who idealizes the Forrester's sexless marriage, discovers Mrs. Forrester's love affair, he vents his infantile jealousy and rage the only way he can—symbolically. While the lovers are on the phone, he takes

his "big shears" and cuts the wires, ostensibly to prevent gossip, but also to sever a relationship he cannot abide. Ingenious in rationalizing their actions, Cather's heroes do not entirely conceal an underlying fear of physical love; and the connection between love and death, long undiscerned in Cather's work, can be seen as its inextricable motif. Even in her first novel, *Alexander's Bridge*, the hero's gratuitous death—generally thought to flaw the work—fulfills the inherent thematic demand to show physical passion as disastrous. Here, as in *O Pioneers!*, a later work, illicitness is merely a distracting irrelevance which helps conceal the fear of sexuality in all relationships. *O Pioneers!* reduces the interval between love and death until they almost coincide. At three o'clock, Emil races "like an arrow shot from the bow" to Marie; for the first time they make love; by evening, they are dead, murdered by the half-demented husband.

In *My Ántonia*, Jim Burden grows up with an intuitive fear of sex, never acknowledged, and in fact, denied: yet it is a determining force in his story. By deflecting attention from himself to Ántonia, of whom he can speak with utter assurance, he manages to conceal his muddied sexual attitudes. His narrative voice, reinforced by Cather's, emerges firm and certain; and it convinces. We tend to believe with Jim that his authoritative recitation of childhood memories validates the past and gives meaning to the present even though his mature years stream before him emptied of love, intimacy, and purpose. Memory transports him to richer and happier days spent with Ántonia, the young Bohemian girl who signifies "*the country, the conditions, the whole adventure of . . . childhood.*" Because a changing landscape brilliantly illumines his childhood—with copper-red prairies transformed to rich wheatfields and corn—his personal story seems to epitomize this larger historical drama. Jim uses the coincidence of his life-span with a historical era to imply that as the country changed and grew, so did he, and moreover, as his memoirs contained historical facts, so did they hold the truth about himself. Critics support Jim's bid for validity, pointing out that "*My Ántonia* exemplifies superbly [Frederick Jackson] Turner's concept of the recurring cultural evolution on the frontier" [see excerpt by James E. Miller dated 1958].

Jim's account of both history and himself seems to me disingenuous, indeed, suspect; yet it is for this very reason highly pertinent to an understanding of our own uses of the past. In the introduction, Jim presents his memoirs as a spontaneous expression—unselected, unarranged, and uncontrolled by ulterior purpose: "*From time to time I've been writing down what I remember . . . about Ántonia. . . . I didn't take time to arrange it; I simply wrote down pretty much all that her name recalls to me. I suppose it hasn't any form, . . . any title, either.*" Obviously, Jim's memory cannot be as autonomous or disinterested as he implies. His plastic powers reshape his experience, selecting and omitting in response to unconscious desires and the will. Ultimately, Jim forgets as much as he remembers, as his mind sifts through the years to retrieve what he most needs—a purified past in which he can find safety from sex and disorder. Of "a romantic disposition," Jim substitutes wish for reality in celebrating the past. His flight from sexuality parallels a flight from historical truth, and in this respect, he becomes an emblematic American figure, like Jay Gatsby and Clyde Griffiths. Jim romanticizes the American past as Gatsby romanticizes love, and Clyde money. Affirming the common, the prototypical, American dream of fruition, all three, ironically, are devastated—Gatsby and Clyde die violently, while Jim succumbs to immobilizing regressive needs.

Their relationship to the dream they could not survive must strike us oddly, for we have reversed their situation by surviving to see the dream shattered and the Golden Age of American history impugned. Out of the past that Jim idealized comes our present stunning disorder, though Jim would deny such continuity, as Cather did. Her much-quoted statement that the world *broke* in 1922 reveals historical blindness mistaken for acuity. She denied that "the beautiful past" transmitted the crassness, disorder, and violence which "ruined" the present for her and drove her to hermitic withdrawal. She blamed villainous men, such as Ivy Peters in *A Lost Lady,* for the decline of a heroic age. Like her, Jim Burden warded off broad historical insight. His mythopoeic memory patterned the past into an affecting creation story, with Ántonia a central fertility figure, "a rich mine of life, like the founders of early races." Jim, however, stalks through his myth a wasteland figure who finds in the present nothing to compensate him for the loss of the past, and in the outer world nothing to violate the inner sanctum of memory. "Some memories are realities, are better than anything that can ever happen to one again"—Jim's nostalgic conclusion rationalizes his inanition. He remains finally fixated on the past, returning to the vast and ineffaceable image that dominates his memoirs—the Nebraska prairie yielding to railroad and plough. Since this is an impersonal image of the growth of a nation, and yet it seems so personally crucial to Jim, we must be alerted to the special significance it holds for him. At the very beginning of the novel, we are told that Jim *"loves with a personal passion the great country through which his railway runs."* The symbolism of the railroad penetrating virgin fields is such an embarrassingly obvious example of emotional displacement, it seems extraordinary that it has been so long unnoted. Like Captain Forrester, the unsexed husband of *A Lost Lady,* Jim sublimates by traversing the country, laying it open by rail; and because he sees the land grow fertile and the people prosper, he believes his story to be a celebration.

But neither history's purely material achievement, nor Cather's aesthetic conquest of childhood material, can rightfully give Jim Burden personal cause to celebrate. Retrospection, a superbly creative act for Cather, becomes for Jim a negative gesture. His recapitulation of the past seems to me a final surrender to sexual fears. He was afraid of growing up, afraid of women, afraid of the nexus of love and death. He could love only that which time had made safe and irrefragable—his memories. They revolve not, as he says, about the image of Ántonia, but about himself as a child. When he finds love, it seems to him the safest kind—the narcissistic love of the man for himself as a boy. Such love is not unique to Jim Burden. It obsesses many Cather protagonists from early novels to late: from Bartley Alexander in *Alexander's Bridge* to Godfrey St. Peter in *The Professor's House.* Narcissism focuses Cather's vision of life. She valued above all the inviolability of the self. Romantically, she saw in the child the original and real self; and in her novels she created adult characters who sought a seemingly impossible reunion with this authentic being—who were willing to die if only they could reach somehow back to childhood. Regression becomes thus an equivocal moral victory in which the self defies change and establishes its immutability. But regression is also a sign of defeat. *My Ántonia,* superficially so simple and clear a novel, resonates to themes of ultimate importance—the theme of identity, of its relationship to time, and of its contest with death. All these are subsumed in the more immediate issue of physical love. Reinterpreted along these lines, *My Ántonia* emerges as a brilliantly tortuous novel, its statements working contrapuntally against its meanings, its apparently random vignettes falling together to form a pattern of sexual aversion into which each detail fits—even the reaping-hook of Jim's dream:

> One dream I dreamed a great many times, and it was always the same. I was in a harvest-field full of shocks, and I was lying against one of them. Lena Lingard came across the stubble barefoot, in a short skirt, with a curved reaping-hook in her hand, and she was flushed like the dawn, with a kind of luminous rosiness all about her. She sat down beside me, turned to me with a soft sigh and said, "Now they are all gone, and I can kiss you as much as I like."

In Jim's dream of Lena, desire and fear clearly contend with one another. With the dreamer's infallibility, Jim contains his ambivalence in a surreal image of Aurora and the Grim Reaper as one. This collaged figure of Lena advances against an ordinary but ominous landscape. Background and forefigure first contrast and then coalesce in meaning. Lena's voluptuous aspects—her luminous glow of sexual arousal, her flesh bared by a short skirt, her soft sighs and kisses—are displayed against shocks and stubbles, a barren field when the reaping-hook has done its work. This landscape of harvest and desolation is not unfamiliar; nor is the apparitional woman who moves across it, sighing and making soft moan; nor the supine young man whom she kisses and transports. It is the archetypal landscape of ballad, myth, and drama, setting for *la belle dame sans merci* who enchants and satisfies, but then lulls and destroys. She comes, as Lena does, when the male is alone and unguarded. "Now they are all gone," Lena whispers, meaning Ántonia, his threshold guardian. Keeping parental watch, Ántonia limits Jim's boundaries ("You know you ain't right to kiss me like that") and attempts to bar him from the dark unexplored country beyond boyhood with threats ("If I see you hanging around with Lena much, I'll go tell your grandmother"). Jim has the insight to reply, "You'll always treat me like a kid"; but his dream of past childhood games with Ántonia suggests that the prospect of perpetual play attracts him, offering release from anxiety. Already in search of safety, he looks to childhood, for adolescence confronts him with the possibility of danger in women. Characteristically, his statement that he will prove himself unafraid belies the drift of his unconscious feelings. His dream of Lena and the reaping-hook depicts his ambivalence toward the cycle of growth, maturation, and death. The wheat ripens to be cut; maturity invites death. (pp. 60-6)

To say that Jim Burden expresses castration fears would provide a facile conclusion: and indeed his memoirs multiply images of sharp instruments and painful cutting. The curved reaping-hook in Lena Lingard's hands centralizes an overall pattern that includes Peter's clasp-knife with which he cuts all his melons; Crazy Mary's corn-knife (she "made us feel how sharp her blade was, showing us very graphically just what she meant to do to Lena"); the suicidal tramp "cut to pieces" in the threshing machine; and wicked Wick *Cut*ter's sexual assault. When Lena, the essence of sex, appears suddenly in Black Hawk, she seems to precipitate a series of violent recollections. First Jim remembers Crazy Mary's pursuit of Lena with her sharpened corn-knife. Then Ántonia recalls the story of the crazy tramp in details which seem to me unconsciously reverberating Jim's dream. Like Jim, Ántonia is relaxed and leaning against a strawstack; similarly, she sees a figure approach "across the stubble"—significantly, his first words portend death. Offering to "cut bands," within minutes he throws himself into the threshing machine and is "cut to pieces." In his pockets the threshers find only ''an old penknife'' and the ''wish-bone of a chicken.'' Jim follows his anecdote with a vignette of Blind d'Arnault, a black musician who, as we shall see, represents emasculation; Jim tells how children used to tease the little blind boy and try ''to get his chicken-bone away.'' Such details, I think, should not be considered fortuitous or irrelevant; and critics who have persisted in overlooking them should note that they are stubbornly there, and in patterned sequence.

I do not wish to make a case history of Jim Burden or a psychological document of *My Ántonia,* but to uncover an elusive underlying theme—one that informs the fragmentary parts of the novel and illuminates the obsession controlling Cather's art. For like most novelists, Cather writes out of an obsessive concern to which her art gives various and varied expression. In *My Ántonia,* her consummate work, that obsession has its most private as well as its most widely shared meanings. At the same time that the novel is highly autobiographical, it is representatively American in its material, mood, and unconscious uses of the past. In it, as in other novels, we can discover that Cather's obsession had to do with the assertion of self. This is the preoccupation of her protagonists who in their various ways seek to assert their identity, in defiance, if necessary, of others, of convention, of nature, of life itself. Biographers imply that Cather's life represented a consistent pursuit of autonomy, essential, she believed, to her survival as an artist. Undoubtedly, she was right; had she given herself to marriage and children, assuming she could, she might have sacrificed her chance to write. Clearly, she identified writing with masculinity, though which of the two constituted her fundamental drive is a matter of psychological dynamics we can never really decide. Like Ántonia, she displayed strong masculine traits, though she loved also feminine frilleries and the art of cuisine. All accounts of her refer to her ''masculine personality''—her mannish dress, her deep voice, her energetic stride; and even as a child she affected boyish clothes and cropped hair. Too numerous to document, such references are a running motif throughout the accounts of Mildred Bennet, Elizabeth Sergeant, and E. K. Brown. Their significance is complex and perhaps inescapable, but whatever else they mean, they surely demonstrate Cather's self-assertion; she would create her own role in life, and if being a woman meant sacrificing her art, then she would lead a private and inviolate life in defiance of convention.

Her image of inviolability was the *child.* She sought quaintly, perhaps foolishly, to refract this image through her person when she wore a schoolgirl costume. The Steichen photograph of her in middy blouse is a familiar frontispiece to volumes of her work; and she has been described as characteristically ''at the typewriter, dressed in a childlike costume, a middy blouse with navy bands and tie and a duck skirt.'' In life, she tried to hold on to childhood through dress; in art, through a recurrent cycle of childhood, maturity, and childhood again: the return effected usually through memory. Sometimes the regressive pattern signalized a longing for death, as in *The Professor's House* and *Death Comes for the Archbishop;* always it revealed a quest for reunion with an original authentic self. In *My Ántonia,* the prologue introduces Ántonia and the motif of childhood simultaneously, for her name is linked with ''*the country, the conditions, the whole adventure of . . . childhood.*'' The memoirs proper open with the children's journey into pristine country where men are childlike or project into life characters of the child's imagination: like Jake who ''might have stepped out of the pages of 'Jesse James.''' The years of maturity comprise merely an interim period—and in fact, are hardly

dealt with. For Jim, as for Cather, the real meaning of time is cyclical, its purpose to effect a return to the beginning. Once Jim finds again ''the first road'' he traveled as a wondering child, his story ends. Hardly discernible, this road returns him to Ántonia, and through her, to his real goal, the enduring though elusive image of his original self which Cather represents by his childhood shadow. Walking to Ántonia's house with her boys—feeling himself almost a boy again—Jim merges with his shadow, the visible elongation of self. At last, his narcissistic dream comes to fulfillment: ''It seemed, after all, so natural to be walking along a barbed-wire fence beside the sunset, toward a red pond, and to see my shadow moving along at my right, over the close-cropped grass.'' Just as the magnified shadow of plow against sky—a blazing key image— projects his romantic notion of the West, so ''two long shadows [that] flitted before or followed after'' symbolize his ideal of perennial children running through, imaged against, and made one with the prairie grass.

Jim's return ''home'' has him planning a future with Cuzak's boys that will recapitulate the past: once more he will sleep in haylofts, hunt ''up the Niobrara,'' and travel the ''Bad Lands.'' Play reenters as his serious concern, not the sexual play of imminent manhood, but regressive child's play. In a remarkable statement, Jim says: ''There were enough Cuzaks to play with for a long while yet. Even after the boys grew up, there would always be Cuzak himself!'' A current article on *My Ántonia* [see Martin excerpt above] misreads this conclusion: ''[though] Jim feels like a boy again . . . he does not *wish* that he were a boy again. . . . He has no more need to cling to the past, for the past has been transfigured like the autumn prairie of old.'' Such reasoning falls in naively with Jim's self-deception, that the transformation of the land to country somehow validates his personal life. Jim's need to reenter childhood never relents, becomes even more urgent as he feels adult life vacuous. The years have not enriched him, except with a wealth of memories—''images in the mind that did not fade—that grew stronger with time.'' Most precious in his treasury of remembered images is that of a boy of ten crossing the prairie under ''the complete dome of heaven'' and finding sublimity in the union of self with earth and sky. An unforgettable consummation, never matched by physical union, he seeks to recreate it through memory. Jim's ineffable desire for a child more alive to him than his immediate being vibrates to a pathetic sense of loss. I believe that we may find this irretrievable boy in a photograph of young *Willie Cather,* another child who took life from imagination and desire. (pp. 75-8)

This Romantic mystique of childhood illuminates the fear of sex in Cather's world. Sex unites one with another. Its ultimate threat is loss of self. In Cather's construct, naively and of course falsely, the child is asexual, his love inverted, his identity thus intact. Only Ántonia manages to grow older and retain her original integrity. Like Tom Outland, her affinity is for the earth. She ''belongs'' to the farm, is one with the trees, the flowers, the rye and wheat she plants. Though she marries, Cuzak is only ''the instrument of Ántonia's special mission.'' Through him she finds a self-fulfillment that excludes him. Through her, Jim hopes to be restored to himself.

The supreme value Jim and other Cather characters attribute to ''old friendships'' reflects a concern with self. Old friends know the child immanent in the man. Only they can have communion without causing self-estrangement, can marry ''safely.'' They share ''the precious, the incommunicable past''—as Jim says in his famous final words. But to keep the past so precious, they must romanticize it; and to validate childhood, they must let memory filter its experiences through the screen of nostalgia. Critics have wondered whether Jim Burden is finally the most suitable narrator for *My Ántonia.* I submit that Cather's choice is utterly strategic. For Jim, better than any other character, could control his memories, since only he knows of but does not experience the suffering and violence inherent in his story. And ultimately, he is not dealing with a story as such, but with residual "images in the mind." *My Ántonia* is a magnificent and warped testimony to the mind's image-making power, an implicit commentary on how that creative power serves the mind's need to ignore and deny whatever is reprehensible in whatever one loves. Cather's friend and biographer said of her, "There was so much she did not want to see and saw not." We must say the same of Jim Burden, who held painful and violent aspects of early American life at safe distance, where finally he could not see them.

Jim's vignette of Blind d'Arnault, the black piano player who entertains at Black Hawk, is paradigmatic of his way of viewing the past. Its factual scaffolding (whether Cather's prototype was Blind Boone, Blind Tom, or a "composite of Negro musicians") seems to me less important than its tone. I find the vignette a work of unconscious irony as Jim paints d'Arnault's portrait but meanwhile delineates himself. The motif of blindness compounds the irony. D'Arnault's is physical, as though it is merely futile for him to see a world he cannot enter. Jim's is moral: an unawareness of his stereotyped, condescending, and ultimately invidious vision. Here, in his description of the black man, son of a slave, Jim's emblematic significance emerges as shamefully he speaks for himself, for Cather, and for most of us:

> [His voice] was the soft, amiable Negro voice, like those I remembered from early childhood, with the note of docile subservience in it. He had the Negro head, too; almost no head at all, nothing behind the ears but the folds of neck under close-cropped wool. He would have been repulsive if his face had not been so kindly and happy. It was the happiest face I had seen since I left Virginia.

Soft, amiable, docile, subservient, kindly, happy—Jim's image, as usual, projects his wish-fulfillment; his diction suggests an unconscious assuagement of anxiety, also. His phrase of astounding insult and innocence—"almost no head at all"—assures him that the black man should not frighten, being an incomplete creature, possessed, as we would like to believe, of instinct and rhythm, but deprived of intellect. Jim's final hyperbole registers his fear of this alien black face saved from repulsiveness only by a toothy servile smile (it might someday lose). To attenuate his portrait of d'Arnault, Jim introduced innuendoes of sexual incompetence. He recognizes d'Arnault's sensuality but impugns it by his image of sublimation: "all the agreeable sensations possible to creatures of flesh and blood were heaped up on those black-and-white keys, and he [was] gloating over them and trickling them through his yellow fingers." Jim's genteel opening phrase connotes male sexuality, which he must sublimate, displace from the man to the music, reduce to a *trickle.* D'Arnault "looks like some glistening African god of pleasure, full of strong, savage blood"; but superimposed is our familiar Uncle Tom "all grinning," "bowing to everyone, docile and happy."

Similarly, consider Jim's entrancing image of the four Danish girls who stand all day in the laundry ironing the townspeople's clothes. How charming they are: flushed and happy; how fatherly the laundryman offering water—no swollen ankles; no

boredom or rancor; no exploitation: a cameo image from "the beautiful past." Peter and Pavel, dreadful to any ordinary mind for their murderous deed, ostracized by everyone, now disease-ridden and mindless, are to Jim picturesque outcasts: Pavel spitting blood; Peter spitting seeds as he desperately eats all his melons after kissing his cow goodbye, the only creature for him to love. And Mr. Shimerda's suicide. Jim reconciles himself to the horror of the mutilated body frozen in its own blood by imagining the spirit released and homeward bound to its beloved Bohemia. Only the evocative beauty of Cather's language—and the inevitable validation as childhood memory—can romanticize this sordid death and the squalor in which it takes place. Violence is as much the essence of prairie life as the growth of the wheat and blossoming of the corn. Violence appears suddenly and inexplicably, like the suicidal tramp. But Jim gives violence a cameo quality. He has the insistent need—and the strategy—to turn away from the very material he presents. He can forget the reaping-hook and reshape his dream. And as the novel reveals him doing this, it reveals our common usage of the past as a romance and refuge from the present. *My Ántonia* engraves a view of the past which is at best partial; at worst, blind. But our present is continuous with the whole past, as it was, despite Jim Burden's attempt to deny this, and despite Cather's "sad little refrain": "Our present is ruined—but we had a beautiful past." Beautiful to one who recreated it so; who desperately needed it so; who would deny the violence and the destructive attitudes toward race and sex immortalized in his very denial. We, however, have as desperate a need for clarity of vision as Jim had for nostalgia; and we must begin to look at *My Ántonia,* long considered a representatively American novel, not only for its beauty of art and for its affirmation of history, but also, and instructively, for its negations and evasions. Much as we would like to ignore them, for they bring painful confrontations, we must see what they would show us about ourselves—how we betray our past when we forget its most disquieting realities; how we begin to redeem it when we remember. (pp. 79-82)

Blanche H. Gelfant, "The Forgotten Reaping-Hook: Sex in 'My Ántonia'," in American Literature, *Vol. XLIII, No. 1, March, 1971, pp. 60-82.*

WILLIAM J. STUCKEY (essay date 1972)

[*Stuckey is an American critic and editor. In the following excerpt, he discusses the importance of Jim Burden's nostalgic idealization of Ántonia in interpreting the central message of* My Ántonia.]

Critics who are most committed to defending Willa Cather's integrity as an artist seem to have developed a talent for talking about *My Ántonia* out of both sides of their mouths. For though Miss Cather's admirers have found much to praise in the individual parts of this book, they have turned up a fairly large number of serious flaws as well. It is generally acknowledged, for example, that the book is very loosely organized, that many incidents have no apparent function in the novel, and that though it is supposed to be about Ántonia, most of the five books that make up the novel are about the narrator, Jim Burden. Even more damaging has been the critics' admission that, in spite of Jim Burden's assertion that he would have liked to have had Ántonia for a wife, there is little in the novel to support this. Indeed, one critic has said that there is an emotional emptiness in Jim and Ántonia's relationship.

The conclusion of *My Ántonia* has also given some critics pause, for although it is this section that does most to create the beautiful symbolic Ántonia, there is the feeling among some readers that this is a tacked-on happy ending and, further, that the method of creating this beauty is not altogether honest. Instead of pursuing the implications of their insights, however—by asking how these flaws may be squared with the rest of the novel—critics have either set them aside or found a means of explaining them away. And so, the general impression one gets from reading Miss Cather's critics is that *My Ántonia* is a beautiful book celebrating agrarian values, but that it is not one that will bear much looking into.

This attitude is hardly a compliment either to Willa Cather or to *My Ántonia,* for though it may help preserve the popular view that *My Ántonia* is an inspired novel about a vital, dynamic earth mother living on the Nebraska frontier, it keeps us from exploring the contradictions beneath the surface story. And surely, unless those contradictions are faced, we cannot say with much conviction what this novel actually is about.

One way to square these contradictions with the surface events of the story is to see that though *My Ántonia* is ostensibly about Ántonia, actually, technically, it is about what Ántonia *comes to mean* to Jim Burden.

This is not a trivial distinction, as I shall try to show, for though there is much in the novel that cannot be fully brought into a single design, much of it can be seen as a consistently playing down, even a denying of what Ántonia is, and a playing up of what Jim Burden is finally able to make her into. And so it might be said that *My Ántonia* is not so much the story of Ántonia's agrarian success, as it is Jim Burden's success in converting her into a symbol of a way of life that he approves of. This is not to say, of course, that the details of Ántonia's life are not an important part of Jim's story. They are. But they are also the raw materials from which Jim Burden is able to select those things that can be made to fit *his* picture of Ántonia. In the process, some of this raw material has to be suppressed. And it is this suppression, particularly in the conclusion, that strikes some readers as dishonest. But if one sees how this suppression follows logically from what has gone before, then it will seem no more or less dishonest than the rest of the book.

The general pattern of Jim Burden's success comes from his desire to convert Ántonia into a beautiful image of agrarian life and Ántonia's resistance to that conversion—a pattern that might be sketched somewhat as follows: at first Jim is attracted to Ántonia's warmth and vitality, but at the same time repelled by the grosser aspects of her behaviour; later, while still drawn to her, he is further repelled by her growing crudeness and, still later, by the way she is attracted to other men. It is not masculine jealousy that Jim appears to feel, but some deep sense of outrage and frustration. He likes Ántonia and wants to approve of her, but her manners and her animal vitality prevent him from doing so. As a consequence, Jim's relationship with Ántonia shifts back and forth between liking and disgust.

The high point of Jim's disgust comes after a fight between Jim and Wick Cutter, a would-be seducer of Ántonia. After the fight, Jim says that he hates Ántonia and that he never wants to see her again. Shortly thereafter (and apparently without being reconciled with her), Jim goes away to the University at Lincoln. There, from reading Vergil, he comes to understand that without vital, earthy girls (like Ántonia, though he does not specifically name her) there would be no poetry. This insight appears to be a turning point in Jim's relationship with

Ántonia, for when he goes home and discovers that she has been seduced by a cheap ladies' man named Larry Donovan and has borne his child, he is not shocked or disgusted. Instead, he is able to think of Ántonia in a wholly idealized way. When he goes East to Harvard Law School, he carries with him a warm and happy image of his childhood friend.

In the concluding section of the novel, Jim rounds out his beautiful portrait of Ántonia. He has returned to Nebraska after an absence of twenty years and has found in Ántonia's life nothing to shock or dismay him. Indeed, he is able to see in her and in the beautiful family and the fine orchard and fertile farm she has created a symbol for the source of civilization itself.

The pattern I have described starts at the beginning of the novel, shortly after Jim and Ántonia meet. Jim, of course, does not know Ántonia very well and is not as deeply attracted to her as he is later to become, but he "snuggles" down with her in the prairie grass and admires the beauty of the landscape. He thinks Ántonia "quick and very eager" and remarks that it was "wonderfully pleasant" there with the blue sky over them and the gold tree in front. Then Ántonia spoils the beauty of the occasion by making a gesture that Jim regards as too familiar. She offers him "a little chased silver ring she wore on her middle finger. When she coaxed and insisted" that he take it, Jim "repulsed her quite sternly." He remarks, "I didn't want her ring, and I felt there was something reckless and extravagant about her wishing to give it away to a boy she had never seen before." These are to be Ántonia's most exasperating qualities—her extravagant vitality and her improper behaviour, for the early Jim can be wholly content with her only when her vitality is checked by what he sees as appropriate formal gestures.

The same problem occurs again in the "rattlesnake incident," except that instead of being overly friendly, Ántonia is now being overly oppressive. Just previous to this incident, Ántonia has been "taking a superior tone" with Jim and he resents it. It is not that he wants Ántonia's affection. What he wants is for her to behave toward him the way a girl should behave toward a boy. The encounter with the snake, which Jim kills, terrifies Ántonia, and Jim's bravery in killing it chastens her into paying him the deference he feels is his due. "She liked me better from that time on, and she never took a supercilious air with me again. I had killed a big snake—I was now a big fellow." This incident is handled rather lightly and Jim's wish to be treated as a "big fellow" is no doubt humorously meant. Still, it is significant that Jim's dissatisfaction, here again, is due to Ántonia's refusal to take what he regards as a proper attitude toward him. And, also significant, she pleases him only when she expresses that attitude.

There is in the novel, as I have said, a good deal that cannot be assimilated to this pattern. Our concern, however, is with Jim the image-maker, not with Ántonia, the raw material on which the image draws. Still, the things that Jim chooses to tell about his grandparents and about their home, about the town of Black Hawk and the townspeople, and especially what he says about Ántonia's family, fall more fully into place when one sees how they are related to this pursuit of a forced image of excellence. Take, for example, the way Jim creates for us an image of his grandparents. There are a number of characters in the book that are treated with astringent realism, but the Burdens are handled as gently as if they were two valuable old woodcuts. They are homely, to be sure, for they are country people, but they are spotlessly beautiful. Their manners and dress, the way they treat Jim and the hired hands, their relations with their neighbors, the way the conduct their household—all possess a kind of aloof serenity. The Burden grandparents, it seems, have achieved a perfection of form that Jim wants Ántonia to have.

Jim's trouble lies, of course, in his initial failure to see that Ántonia will not be able to learn that form from his grandparents. But then Jim is not concerned with reasons. He merely sees how imperfect Ántonia and her family are and he displays their imperfections with harsh clarity. The Shimerdas are pictured by Jim as dirty, disorganized, inept, and ill-mannered. Whereas the Burden grandparents never exhibit any unattractive emotions, the Shimerdas appear to do nothing but quarrel, whine, steal, and beg. Only Mr. Shimerda, the Austrian violinist, keeps up an attractive exterior and significantly is the only one among the Shimerdas who deeply appreciates the Burdens' good manners. Indeed, he finds their well-ordered house a civilized refuge in an otherwise savage world. When Mr. Shimerda takes his life, Jim has the feeling that the old violinist's soul visits the Burdens' house before departing for the next world. Jim thinks that had Mr. Shimerda been able to live in the Burdens' house, ''this terrible thing would never have happened.''

As Jim gets to know Ántonia better, his difficulty with her reduces to the unpleasant fact that she prefers to be more like her family than like his. That is why Jim grows angry with Ántonia when she takes her family's side in a fight with one of the Burdens' hired hands, and that is why he is so repelled by her when she imitates her brother's crude table manners. It does not occur to Jim to admire Ántonia's loyalty to her family or to see that table manners are not a reliable indication of human worth. Here again, what is important to Jim is how Ántonia behaves and, at this point in the novel, he cannot accept her behaviour.

Essentially the same thing is brought out, but in a positive manner, on the one occasion in the early part of the book when Ántonia deeply pleases Jim. A number of things have happened just before this to make Jim vow he will never be friends with the Shimerdas again, but then Ántonia (unaccountably) comes to work for Jim's grandmother and now that Ántonia is under the Burdens' roof Jim is delighted with her. ''We were glad to have her in the house,'' Jim says. ''She was so gay and responsive that one did not mind her heavy, running step, or her clattery way with pans.'' And Ántonia pleases Jim by expressing her liking for the Burden household. ''I like your grandmother,'' she tells him, ''and all things here.'' Jim comes back, ''Why aren't you always nice like this, Tony?''

If Tony had remained in the Burden household or, later, had stayed in the cultivated Harling household (where she continues to be a ''nice'' motherly hired girl), Jim might have been able to keep her high in his estimation, but Ántonia's old wilfulness reasserts itself along with her animal vitality. She insists on going to the notorious Saturday night tent dances and this indecorous behaviour causes her to lose her position with the Harlings. Perversely, it seems to Jim, Ántonia goes to work for Wick Cutter, an infamous woman chaser. Mrs. Harling predicts that Ántonia will ''have a fling'' at the Cutters that she ''won't get up from in a hurry.'' As it turns out, Ántonia does have her fling, but it is Jim who has trouble getting up. In an attempt to protect Ántonia's honor from Wick Cutter, he gets his eye blackened and his lip cut. This experience deeply depresses him. He says that he hates Ántonia for having let him in ''for all of this disgustingness.''

Cather and S. S. McClure in 1944. From The Voyage Perilous: Willa Cather's Romanticism, *by Susan J. Rosowski. University of Nebraska Press, 1986.*

This incident perhaps more than any other one gives us an important insight into Jim's attachment to Ántonia. His interest is not the conventionally romantic one that some readers have tried to find (and which Miss Cather to some extent encourages). Jim does not love Ántonia as a man would. His feeling for her is that of a child who ''hero-worships'' an older person. He wants to admire and look up to Ántonia and, of course, he is inevitably disappointed. It never occurs to Jim to question his demands on Ántonia. He is too preoccupied with his ideal of her.

The solution for getting Ántonia permanently enshrined in Jim's admiration is not directly presented in the novel. Jim simply goes off to the university at Lincoln, acquires a certain distance from her, along with an insight by way of Vergil into the poetic worth of primitive women, which hardly prepares us for his ability to accept so readily behaviour from Ántonia (her ''elopement'' with Larry Donovan and the illegitimate baby) that would have shocked him earlier. But the problem for the skeptical reader is that Jim does not really accept what Ántonia has done. He avoids it or, more accurately, his author arranges matters so that none of the potentially unpleasant details are allowed to get through to Jim. He learns of Ántonia's affair indirectly, and through a woman who likes Ántonia very much and who therefore puts her situation in an attractive light. His only contacts with Ántonia's baby, moreover, are in a photographer's studio where he notices a picture of it (''one of those depressing 'crayon enlargements' often seen in farmhouse parlours''), and, later, when given a quick look by Ántonia's sister. Then when Jim sees Ántonia again, he sees her alone, out-of-doors, under a beautiful sky and against a backdrop of trees and shocks of wheat. Ántonia almost spoils the beauty of this meeting by talking about her little girl, but Jim, who perhaps is clinging fast to his revelation from Vergil, quickly lifts the conversation to a higher plane. ''Do you know,

Ántonia,'' he says, ''since I've been away, I think of you more
often than of anyone else in this part of the world. I'd have
liked to have you for a sweetheart, or a wife, or my mother
or my sister—anything that a woman can be to a man. The
idea of you is part of my mind. . . . You really are a part of
me.''

Jim has at last succeeded in getting Ántonia detached from the
disappointing realities of her life and converted into a beautiful
picture he can carry East with him when he goes off to Harvard.

It takes twenty years for the full idealization of Ántonia to take
place. And during that time she has had the opportunity not
only to increase in her ability to reflect Jim's ideal, but to take
on the ability to reflect the timeless pattern of civilization as
well. She is married now, the mother of eleven children, the
mistress of a fertile farm and a well-ordered household. She
can no longer spoil Jim's ideal of her, for she is, from Jim's
point of view, a completed, a finished person. And he is only
a visitor in her house, a status that gives him the distance and
detachment necessary to his idealization. Gone are both the
appearance and the necessity for seeing anything unpleasant in
Ántonia's life; instead are manifestations of the rural virtues
that Jim associates with his grandparents and their beautifully
managed old farm; cleanliness, order, decorum. The only vestige of the Shimerda household is, happily, the violin that once
belonged to Ántonia's unhappy father, which two of Ántonia's
children play, with less than moderate success. For it is not
the fine arts that Ántonia comes to symbolize for Jim Burden,
but the domestic ones. He is able to see her permanently at
last, as the maker of formal gestures which, he says, ''we
recognize by instinct as universal and true.''

From the standpoint of ordinary human behaviour, Jim Burden's interest in Ántonia is unconvincing. This is implied in
E. K. Brown's suggestion that Miss Cather might better have
employed a feminine point of view. Perhaps. But this is like
saying she might better have given us a different Ántonia. We
have no way of knowing what Ántonia might have been (or,
indeed, whether she would have been) had Miss Cather chosen
to create her from a different point of view. All we have is
what we have been given. Nor need we believe that Jim Burden
is a real man in order to accept the fact that Miss Cather used
him to create *her* Ántonia. Jim Burden, convincing or not, is
the special consciousness out of which Ántonia has been brought
before us and we cannot separate the two.

Most writers, whether deliberately or not, try to keep the special
consciousness out of which a novel comes from showing—
perhaps because the process of writing fiction is an evasion as
well as an affirmation. In *My Ántonia* Miss Cather did something most unusual. She not only allowed this special consciousness to show; she put it in the forefront of her story and,
whether she meant to or not, made it the chief focus of attention. She did that, I believe, out of psychological as well as
artistic necessity.

We can, perhaps, see better why Jim Burden is necessary if
we compare him with a similar but significantly different narrator—Nick Carraway of the *Great Gatsby*. Nick Carraway
and Jim Burden are, in a sense, narrative devices for making
''objective'' a special kind of romantic sensibility. Both novels
include a heroine who is the embodiment of that sensibility—
Daisy Buchanan and Ántonia Shimerda—and both are made
to reveal their romantic significance through the subjective
response of a character who may also be said to have ''created''
them. But there is an important difference between Fitzgerald's

treatment and Willa Cather's. Fitzgerald has two narrators, one
romantic, one realistic. Gatsby, the romantic, creates Daisy
romantically. Nick, the realist, communicates Gatsby's romantic creation and supplies, along with it, a realistic portrait
of Daisy. We are not meant to share Gatsby's vision of Daisy,
but rather to understand it and to admire the vitality and the
sense of wonder that such a vision implies. Miss Cather, on
the other hand, combines in one character, Jim Burden, romantic vision and realistic skepticism. Burden tries to make
us see Ántonia (and her unpleasant family) in an unillusioned
way, but he also wants to make us accept certain illusions
about Ántonia as well. Jim's problem (which is also Miss
Cather's) is that he cannot get Ántonia into romantic focus
until he is far enough away to keep from seeing the things that
make her seem unromantic. An essential difference, then, between these two novels is that Fitzgerald, while technically
writing ''objectively'' about a romantic vision, still keeps that
vision mysterious; whereas Miss Cather, who wishes to give
direct expression to that vision, shows us much about her heroine that is unromantic. This is, in part, a failure of technique.

A failure of technique in a writer of Willa Cather's talent is
more than a technical failure, of course. It is a failure of sensibility as well. For what is significant about Jim Burden is
not that he is a clumsy device the reader must somehow see
around, but that Miss Cather chose to use him in the first place
and that she kept on using him even when it must have been
apparent that he was not working. But technique, if I may shift
the perspective somewhat, is often the result of compromise
between what the writer wishes to say and what, given the
material he has to work with and the nature of his sensibility,
he is able to write. In this sense, the point of view from which
a novel is told is the writer himself, or as much of him as we
can ever know.

Willa Cather, when pressed by critics who complained that *My
Ántonia* was not a novel, maintained that it was not intended
as such. It was, she said, simply about people she had once
known. Technical failures cannot be so easily explained away.
My Ántonia, though evidently based on the facts of Willa Cather's life, obviously is fiction. Still, it is more autobiographical
than Willa Cather's other fiction, not just because it closely
follows those facts (often in a pointless way) but because it
reveals a side of her that does not show itself so visibly in her
other novels. Jim Burden is, in an important sense, Willa Cather,
and *My Ántonia* demonstrates the way Miss Cather's imagination set about converting the raw materials of experience into
art. For her, the creation of fiction was not the striking of a
balance between personal feeling and the facts of experience
(or, as T. S. Eliot has said, of intensifying the world to fit
one's feelings). For Miss Cather, it was the imposing of her
strong and intensely personal feelings upon a sometimes intractable world. The much admired image of the ''plough against
the sun,'' for example, illustrates specifically the way her imagination worked. The plough that Jim and the hired girls see
magnified into heroic size against the setting sun can stand as
a symbol for the real world; the sun, for the writer's vision
which lifts up that world and intensifies it to match the writer's
feelings. This imaginative process, however, is partly a romantic heightening, partly a matter of excluding what is ugly
or extraneous.

The extent to which this process was a characteristic of Willa
Cather's mind is revealed in a remark made by Elizabeth Shep-
ley Sergeant, a friend of hers. ''There was so much that Willa
Cather did not want to see and saw not,'' but ''what she did

see she had selected instinctively and in that instinctual sharing of it she gave it a sort of halo of brightness.'' Willa Cather, her friend makes clear, did not want to see unpleasant things in places or in people she liked, and she was not able to see anything to admire in what she disapproved of. When she wrote, she was capable of being mercilessly realistic about what she despised. What she loved, she had to beautify. That is what great art meant to Willa Cather: making things beautiful.

Willa Cather's talent for beautifying worked best when it was called upon to deal with things remote, with landscapes, village streets, houses, groups of people, or single persons detached from relationships with others and caught in a characteristic attitude. It was the surface of life and isolated moments of exalted emotion that gave Willa Cather her most satisfying clues to the meaning of experience. Jim Burden's problem with Ántonia was Willa Cather's problem as well, possibly because Ántonia was based upon someone in her own past whom she had known too personally to romanticize completely. It was only when, like Jim Burden, she had put time and distance between her and her past, after having lived long enough in Pittsburgh and, later in New York, that she could see it in the beautiful way her imagination required.

It is commonly said that in turning away from stories about artists and New England aristocrats, which had preoccupied her in earlier years, and directing her attention to the Nebraska frontier on which she had grown up, Willa Cather was heeding the advice of Sarah Orne Jewett to deal with the life in her own particular corner of the world. But Miss Cather's imaginative return to Nebraska was as much an escape as it was a return, for the failures and defeats, the emotional sterility of pioneer life that she had depicted with such bitterness in her earliest fiction, are not really faced in *My Ántonia*. It is simply there, in inert passages of unassimilated realism (the story of Pavel and Peter, Mr. Shimerda's suicide, the death of the tramp who flings himself into a harvesting machine), preserved like a fly in the amber of Willa Cather's mellifluous prose. Had she really gone home again, had she come to grips with what it was in frontier culture (and perhaps in herself) that destroyed sensitive people or turned them into sterile dilettantes, *My Ántonia* might have been a moving tragedy rather than a potential tragedy with a tacked-on happy ending.

However aware Willa Cather may have been of the tragic implications of her material, she was not capable of writing that kind of book. Her method was to reject failure by rejecting life and by finding in the past, her own and later—in works like *Death Comes for the Archbishop* and *Shadows on the Rock*—in the remoter lives of historical personages, materials out of which she could construct beautiful images of life. *My Ántonia* to some extent escapes the deadly beautifying process. There is in it still a sense of life but it is life struggling to resist the embalming of art.

The story of Jim Burden's struggle and final success with Ántonia is, then, the story of an artist who triumphs over life by converting it into an art object. This, of course, is what all artists do, but Miss Cather has taken it a step farther; she has put the artistic process into the center of her story. A novelist like Fitzgerald or Hemingway or Henry James (to name a writer Miss Cather is said most to resemble) uses art to catch the very feel of life itself. At the end of novels like *The Great Gatsby, A Farewell to Arms,* and *The Portrait of a Lady* (a James novel that illustrates, I believe, how little of the essential James is in Willa Cather) there is a final opening out of the fictional

world into the world of reality. Gatsby is delivered from his cocoon of illusion into the frighteningly real world of men. Frederic Henry walks out of romance into the cold and sobering rain, and Isabel Archer is at last made to see the ugly truth her romantic imagination had concealed from her. These conclusions, of course, are still fictions, but the intent one senses behind them is to make them resemble the world of actual experience.

The intent one senses behind the conclusion of *My Ántonia,* on the contrary, is to lift Ántonia out of her ''real'' world into a world of changeless art. The Ántonia of the final pages of this novel—the vital, irrepressible Ántonia—has become at last the beautiful tomb of Jim Burden's past. (pp. 473-82)

> *William J. Stuckey, '' 'My Ántonia': A Rose for Miss Cather,''* in *Studies in the Novel, Vol. IV, No. 3, Fall, 1972, pp. 473-83.*

JOHN J. MURPHY   (essay date 1973)

[*In the following excerpt, Murphy refutes Blanche H. Gelfant's conclusion that Jim Burden's failure to become sexually involved with Ántonia is a reflection of Cather's own homosexuality. Murphy argues instead that Burden was prevented by social prejudice from forming such a liaison. For Gelfant's comments, see the excerpt dated 1971.*]

Blanche H. Gelfant's recent article, ''The Forgotten Reaping Hook: Sex in *My Ántonia*,'' indicates an unfortunate trend in Cather criticism in which the novelist's fiction is confused with her life in order to destroy her traditional, healthy image. For example, John H. Randall in his consideration of *My Ántonia* confuses Willa Cather with Jim Burden to prove that the novel implies Cather's fear of life, of explosive, spontaneous affections and her distrust of marriage. (The confusion of Cather with the narrator is so extensive that at one point Randall, in referring to Jake and Otto, writes, ''Willa Cather says of them, 'Jake and Otto served us to the last, etc.''') Another indication of this trend is the article on *The Professor's House* by James Schroeter, who interprets the characterization of Louie Marsellus as an expression of the novelist's jealousy of Jan Hambourg, the husband of her Pittsburgh roommate, Isabelle McClung. Gelfant's criticism is in this vein. Her worthy attempts to establish Jim as the central concern of the novel, analyze his relationship to Ántonia and to Lena, come to grips with Pavel's story, the snake episode, the Cutter affair, the coming of Blind d'Arnault and the performance of *Camille* in Lincoln are marred by undue reliance on the Cather biography. Her critical basis becomes Cather's avoidance of normal sex and too close identification with her narrator: ''*My Ántonia* emerges as a brilliantly tortuous novel, its statements working contrapuntally against its meanings, its apparently random vignettes falling together to form a pattern of sexual aversion into which each detail fits.''

While all three critics can be charged with ruining a good thing in their handling of Cather's fiction, the two critics of *My Ántonia* at least manage to point us in a meaningful direction regarding that novel. Randall implies and Gelfant states that Jim Burden is of primary concern in any critical effort; he is ''a more disingenuous and self-deluded narrator than we supposed.'' In attempting, however distortingly, to come to grips with the seemingly disparate episodes of *My Ántonia* mentioned above, Gelfant has come a long way from the earlier consideration by David Daiches, who concluded that in these episodes ''Willa Cather occasionally lost sight of her main theme.''

Gelfant must be credited with having focused on the two aspects of primary critical concern: one, the characterization of Jim, his inconsistencies, his relationship to Ántonia and Lena; two, the integration of the episodes through a common theme.

Jim's failure to actively participate in Ántonia's life, to fall in love and marry her, has always been a problem for critics of *My Ántonia*. E. K. Brown detected that at the center of Jim's relationship with Ántonia there is "an emptiness where the strongest emotion might have been expected to gather" [see excerpt dated 1953]. Brown also found some fault in Jim's not taking his chance to marry Lena, but he attributed this and the other failure to the "creaking of the novelists' machinery" rather than to the aversion to sex theme which has since become fashionable. Factors other than that of sexual abnormality, yet deeper than mechanics, frustrate the Jim-Ántonia relationship. Jim is three years younger than Ántonia, a significant difference in age in the decade of his closest relationship to her, between his tenth and seventeenth years. Throughout most of the relationship Jim is regarded by Ántonia as a child. She reveals this toward the end of the novel when, referring to the Harling children and Jim, she declares, "I loved you children almost as much as I loved my own." The social aspect of the novel also contributes to the distance between Jim and Ántonia. Jim is of old American stock, from a class which considers foreigners like Ántonia "ignorant people who couldn't speak English." These social distinctions become obvious in "The Hired Girls" section of the novel. They are as thematically important in *My Ántonia* as they are in *Main Street*, where Swedes and Norwegians are good for making a profit from and begrudgingly allowed the status of hired help. If there is irony in Cather's novel, it is in Jim's analysis of class distinctions in the light of his own blindness regarding himself; if there is anything that defeats Cather's West it is the emergence of classes and the materialistic struggle accompanying it.

The lyricism of "The Shimerdas" section of *My Ántonia* is due in part to the sublimation of class sense during the heroic struggle with Nature. As Miller points out [see excerpt dated 1958], cultural development—class sense as well as artistic achievement—was minimized in the West as "comparatively sophisticated people [were] compelled literally to begin over again, on a primitive level, shedding their cultural attainment like an animal its skin, and, like animals, doing battle with the land and the elements for the meanest food and shelter." There is more equality, more democracy, if more savagery, manifest during this stage. While we are never allowed to forget the social superiority of the Burdens over the Shimerdas, Grandmother and Grandfather Burden's sense of Christian duty toward the unfortunate family minimizes the class separation. A suggestion of equality is achieved in Chapter 18, when Jake, the Burden hired hand, fights Ambrosch over a horse collar and Ántonia hotly declares her independence from the Burdens: "I never like you no more Jake and Jim Burden. . . . No friends any more!"

Fortunately, it is a friendlier equality that dominates the Jim-Ántonia relationship in this section. The discovery of the wonders of the new country do much to make these pages memorable; memorable also is the struggle with Nature. An aspect of this struggle is dramatized in the snake episode, in which man combats the beast for survival. Although this is reduced to a mock adventure, it looks forward to a more noteworthy struggle with the beast in the story of the wolves. Peter and Pavel were reduced to savagery in this episode, which, while it took place in a far-off land, epitomizes the shedding of

civilization now occurring on the Nebraska plains. The Russians' story contains another aspect of the reduction to primitivism evident in this section, the struggle with cold. This struggle commences in the marvelous episode where Ántonia rescues a half frozen insect from the grass and places it in her hair, is developed in the story of the wolves, and reaches a ghastly climax in the discovery of the frozen body of Mr. Shimerda. The outcome of this struggle with the cold is not primarily savagery, however, but a sense of brotherhood. After Mr. Shimerda's suicide the pioneers become more talkative: "It releases speech in the people who hear about it, thus unites the living into a closer knit group than they had formed before. Since their talk is mostly about the deaths of others they have known or heard about, it serves to tighten the organic bonds of the little frontier community."

"The Hired Girls" section depicts social fragmentation rather than the tightening of the organic bonds of the frontier. A dubious but higher stage in the cultural evolution of the frontier is portrayed; the small town comes to the wilderness and in it there is a stratification of society largely suppressed on the virgin prairie. This change is not abrupt. Indications of social fragmentation come to the surface at various points in "The Shimerdas" section. From the very beginning Jake warns Jim that foreigners are disease ridden. Later on Mrs. Burden throws away Mrs. Shimerda's gift of mushrooms as unfit to eat. Near the end of this first section Otto tells Jim not to expect much from a Czech. Social prejudice and class pride appear most significantly after Mr. Shimerda takes his life. Neither the Catholics nor the Norwegians will allow Shimerda's body to be buried in their cemeteries. Grandmother Burden reveals her own class feeling in her indignation at these refusals: "If these foreigners are so clannish . . . we'll have to have an American graveyard that will be more liberal-minded."

Black Hawk is "American" but hardly liberal-minded. The Bohemians, the Norwegians, the Danes, etc. are considered inferior by the so-called respectable classes. The foreign girls who are hired out are "considered a menace to the social order." Embittered by class consciousness, Jim insists that the hired girls are superior to the daughters of Pennsylvania and Virginia immigrants. (pp. 149-53)

Black Hawk class consciousness has its effect on the relationship of Jim and Ántonia. Jim reveals himself as one of the respectable young men who will risk nothing more than general disapproval for the excitement of a waltz with the hired girls. He fails to recognize the similarity between himself and Sylvester Lovett, who after his fling with Lena, a girl of "inferior" class, protected himself from her by running away with an acceptable widow six years older than himself. An irate Jim concludes that anxious mothers of Black Hawk "need have felt no alarm. They mistook the mettle of their sons, for respectability was stronger than any desire in Black Hawk youth." When Jim agrees to give up dancing with the hired girls to satisfy his grandparents he is doing no less than bowing to respectability. Perhaps his irritation with Black Hawk is in part self-condemnation. Antonia is certainly conscious of her social position, which, when added to her natural maternalism and age, causes her to reject Jim's advances. She wants Jim to have the schooling she is not able to have; she sets her heart on his becoming a doctor. Her aspirations for Jim are far above any she would entertain for a member of her own class. All this must be considered when she warns Jim against his passionate advance: "You know you ain't right to kiss me like that. I'll tell your grandmother on you." She would also protect

Jim from the advances of Lena, whom she considers a threat to the aspirations of his class: "If she's up to any of her nonsense with you, I'll scratch her eyes out. . . . You are going away to school and make something of yourself. I'm just awful proud of you. You won't go and get mixed up with the Swedes, will you?" It can be argued that Jim is hardly sexually aggressive, but it must also be recognized that Ántonia gives him no encouragement. The social structure more than any other factor defeats a normal male-female relationship; it also encourages Jim to make a symbol out of the woman he never possesses.

Jim's symbol-making ability is the result of the cultural evolution of the frontier. The cultural evolution contains two elements: class consciousness and artistic achievement. In Cather's system of values, the former is an evil and the latter a good. The development of art, especially the performing arts, on the prairie is an important aspect of *My Ántonia.* The harmonica, which provides musical expression during the first days of prairie life, gives way to the piano in "The Hired Girls" section, first the Harling piano and then the playing of Blind d'Arnault. The dance is also introduced in this section. Music develops in direct opposition to class consciousness. Richard Giannone has noted that the Shimerda violin, which was silenced during the first section of the novel, is played again in the last. When Jim submits to his grandparents' wishes to stop going to dances with the hired girls, he turns to literature: "I sat at home with the old people in the evenings now, reading Latin that was not in our high-school course." Through the classics, especially Virgil, Jim is able to bridge imaginatively the distance society has opened up between himself and Ántonia and, at the same time, escape self-condemnation for his own inability to bridge realistically that distance.

As a real person, Ántonia now begins to retreat from Jim. This becomes obvious as he makes his way to the picnic with the hired girls. He sees Ántonia seated alone under the pagoda-like elders. She is becoming for him the symbol of his first experience in the new country. (There is an element of narcissism in this, evident, perhaps, when he admits being reluctant to leave the green enclosure in which he dries himself after a swim.) By making Ántonia the romantic image of his own initiation into the prairie country, he can possess her without crossing class lines. The Cutter episode represents a challenge to this romancing, however. As in the snake episode, which it parallels, Ántonia is the damsel in distress and Jim comes to her aid. The results are different, however. Jim's relationship with Ántonia was simple when he "rescued" her from the sluggish snake; his feelings are ambivalent when he "rescues" her from the wiles of Wick Cutter. Because Ántonia is the object of Cutter's desire and because her social class makes her vulnerable, the reality Jim has tried to sublimate in his romantic image comes back to him in a flash. His reaction is harsh: "I felt that I never wanted to see her again. I hated her almost as much as I hated Cutter. She had let me in for all this disgustingness."

Jim's relationship with Lena Lingard represents another challenge to his image of Ántonia. Lena reflects Jim's retreat from reality and invades the romantic realm in which Ántonia has become enshrined. This is obvious during the above-mentioned picnic scene when Lena interrupts Jim's tête-a-tête with Ántonia and demolishes their flowery pagoda. Lena, through her acceptance of the class structure and her determination to rise in it by leaving the farm and not marrying or having a family, exposes both the worldliness and unnaturalness of Jim's po-

sition. This "violation" of Nature is suggested in Jim's dream of Lena carrying a reaping hook and emerging from a field of stubble. The Lincoln setting of the "Lena Lingard" section has an unreality appropriate to the Jim-Lena relationship; it is dominated by music, poetry and especially the theatre. Thrilled now by make-believe people and situations rather than by Nature, Jim has changed the position he had in the first section, where, as Martin has noted [see excerpt dated 1969], he surrendered to Nature among the ripe pumpkins in his grandmother's garden. Jim and Lena can play at make-believe for only a brief time, however. Any permanent relationship between them would challenge Lena's vows against marriage and family and also the privileges cherished by Jim's social class. They renounce each other for the sake of worldly position in a scene as indirect as the artificial world they inhabit. During a performance of *Camille* they give vent to their feelings of parting; the actual parting is a rather pallid affair sometime later, after which Jim continues his studies at Harvard and Lena goes on to become a successful dressmaker in San Francisco.

Having survived the threat of Lena, Jim's Lincoln experiences only strengthen the romance of his lost childhood and Ántonia. They become one in his mind. The "My" with which Jim prefixed "Ántonia," when he supposedly gave the manuscript to Willa Cather, pertains to Book IV, "The Pioneer Woman's Story," and Book V, "Cuzak's Boys." Jim's imaginative powers are indeed formidable when, after she has borne her child, he meets Ántonia in the fields at sunset. The beauty of this scene obscures the extent to which Jim has lost touch with reality. He tells Ántonia, "I'd have liked to have you for a sweetheart, or a wife, or my mother or my sister—anything that a woman can be to a man. The idea of you is a part of my mind. . . . You really are a part of me." Jim has become so self-centered that he feels no embarrassment in his use of the past tense to an abandoned young woman no longer significantly different from him in age.

My Ántonia is a hauntingly sad testimony to the unfulfilled potential of Jim Burden and the American West. The image of the plough, briefly magnified into epic proportions by the setting sun, symbolizes the short-lived potential of the early years, a potential destroyed by social habit and small-minded, materialistic values. (pp. 153-56)

> *John J. Murphy, "The Respectable Romantic and the Unwed Mother: Class Consciousness in 'My Ántonia'," in* Colby Library Quarterly, *Series X, No. 3, September, 1973, pp. 149-56.*

PHILIP GERBER (essay date 1975)

[*Gerber is an American critic and the author of studies of Willa Cather and Theodore Dreiser. In the following excerpt, he examines Cather's attitude toward the heroine of* My Ántonia.]

Superficially the story of Ántonia Shimerda seems cut from a quite different piece of cloth than its predecessors. A Bohemian girl, she is trapped in the worst possible conditions on the Nebraska Divide: indentured to a town family, uneducated, bereft of special talents, so trusting as to be easy prey to a glib scoundrel. Yet maintaining a steel-like equanimity, she becomes a farmer's wife, mother to a houseful of happy children. Hers is the rarest of Cather's lives—a joyous one.

For Ántonia, no iron bridges span obedient rivers, no spread of prairie transforms into pasture and cornfield, and no audiences pay homage to a perfect aria. The professional career underlying previous stories is entirely removed, allowing Cather to show "just the other side of the rug, the pattern that is supposed not to count in a story." Celebration of professional fulfillment broadens to a struggle for personal identity. Ántonia's instinct plunges her always into life's mainstream, disregarding money, position, possessions, or career. To live merely for the rich experience of living itself is the "career" she labors at with as much diligence as Kronborg ever practiced her scales. One thinks of Thoreau withdrawing to Walden purposely to confront life, drive it into a corner, and derive its essential quality—all to determine whether it be mean or fine and finally to be able to say that he had lived. So armed with a fierce necessity to breathe and act, Ántonia rises relatively unscathed from ordeals that might ruin a lesser spirit. Lacking any "talent," she possesses the gift of a warm heart, a buoyant sense of humor, and an infinite capacity for enthusiasm.

This pursuit of life—not to achieve any lofty aim but merely to go with the tides, to exist fully, passionately—was foreign to Cather's nature. But the more she came to understand the toll exacted by a career, the more attractive seemed the life given over wholly to immediate experiences, and the more she came to admire—almost to envy—those equipped to approach their lives in this seemingly easy fashion. Cather could never truly comprehend such persons, the Ántonias of the world. The Thea Kronborgs, the Alexandra Bergsons she knew intimately, for they were so nearly surrogates for herself. In contrast, Ántonia Shimerda required not analysis but worship. She was to be marveled at, something like a Sequoia that stands forever in contradiction of all one's experience.

Thus Cather needed to contemplate her heroine from a safe distance in order to protect herself (as author) from an involvement so intimate that it might reveal her inability to project the girl's personality firsthand. When Cather was writing *The Song of the Lark,* her delight at and fascination with the creative process had allowed her to crawl temporarily inside the skin of another individual. But this was not possible with Ántonia; she and the Bohemian girl had too little in common. Cather's solution was to tell the story through the viewpoint of a relatively detached narrator. It was a relatively common device, much used by Henry James, that Cather's knowledge of painters and their methods would seem to have suggested. Elizabeth Sergeant remembers a discussion of artistic form and technique that occurred in the spring of 1916, when Willa Cather was beginning *My Ántonia.* Cather learned forward suddenly, took a Sicilian apothecary jar filled with orange-brown flowers, and placed it alone on an antique table. For a moment she might have been a painter setting up a still-life arrangement. "I want my new heroine to be like this," she said, "like a rare object in the middle of a table, which one may examine from all sides. I want her to stand out—like this—because she *is* the story."

The narrator whom Cather selected, Jim Burden, allows for Ántonia to be examined in this manner and the various "sides" from which she is seen correspond to the different ages at which Jim knows (of) her—as a child, as an adolescent, as a maiden in full bloom, and finally as a mature woman. Because Jim Burden himself grows older as the story progresses and because his experiences alter him as Ántonia's experiences alter her, each successive view or "side" from which she is observed is more complex and more interesting. At the same time, the adoption of Jim's point-of-view not only explains but actually mandates the episodic structure of the novel. In the introductory chapter Jim is shown as he emphasizes the personal nature of his memoir: "He . . . wrote on the pinkish face of the portfolio the word, 'Ántonia.' he frowned at this a moment, then prefixed another word, making it 'My Ántonia.' That seemed to satisfy him." The most effective way for Jim to create the really strong impressions that will make the manuscript-Ántonia *his* and not another's is to see or hear of her at widely scattered but fairly regular intervals—above all at moments of significance in her life. This, of course, is the manner in which the novel proceeds.

Even though Sarah Orne Jewett had warned Cather about the risks involved in using a masculine viewpoint in fiction, Cather felt that in this case nothing but a male narrator would suffice, hazardous as the experiment might be and artificial as it might appear if she failed. Her decision to use Jim Burden was not happenstance but, on the contrary, carefully reasoned out. Ántonia was to be created from a group of real-life models, and since the most interesting things about these women had been told to Cather by men, she felt that logically Ántonia's story should be presented through the memory of a man. Because the novel was to be a story of feeling, rather than a flurry of plot and action, Jim Burden would tell it in the first person; thus would the emotions involved be best expressed. To establish the nostalgic mood that would color the novel, Cather borrowed from Russian and French literature the device by which an author (unnamed, but clearly Cather herself) meets the narrator (Jim Burden) on a transcontinental train: the pair reminisce about a person (the Bohemian girl) they both knew as children, an experience that triggers the narrator's written account—the remainder of the book.

Cather's introduction was calculated to serve a further purpose: that of establishing about Jim Burden certain important facts that affect the story he tells. A mature man of the world, he is able now to evaluate Ántonia's worth more fully than he could at an earlier, less experienced age. Because he is childless and unhappy in his marriage, he tends to look backward rather than forward; therefore, his dwelling with such concentration and sympathy upon his early, happy years—and the Bohemian girl who influenced them—is made more plausible. Finally, Cather felt that the struggle she had gone through in order to ghostwrite S. S. McClure's autobiography, and the resounding success she had made of it, had equipped her to handle a masculine viewpoint convincingly. She felt she had been able to "become" Mr. McClure because she knew him so thoroughly; she was positive that in *My Ántonia* she could achieve the same success with Jim Burden because (although she declined to name a specific individual) she intended to base her narrator on a man she knew fully as well as she knew McClure.

In its elementals Ántonia's story tallies with the novels preceding it: a young person's struggle, obstacles to be surmounted, contrasts sharpening the central actor's achievement. But, the world of art aside, Ántonia surpasses previous Cather protagonists in maintaining an integrated personality. It is for her to avoid Thea's dry preoccupation, Alexandra's sense of confinement, and Bartley Alexander's dread that middle age will be a dark cloud blotting the sun from his universe. One need not search outside the novel for comparisons, however, for a contrast with the conventional success story is built into the fabric of *My Ántonia* itself. Jim Burden, in his forties, is a member of an important New York legal firm, is instrumental in the progress of a great railway, and is married to a handsome woman of social prominence. But the reader knows him to be far from fulfilled; his childlessness and marital estrangement dampen his spirits, and his greatest thrill seems to derive from opportunities to sponsor others' dreams, now that his own are over. By contrast, Ántonia in her middle years shines "in the full vigour of her personality, battered but not diminished." She is at the close of the novel fully as life loving as she was when, an immigrant girl of fourteen and bright as a new dollar, she rode the Burlington into the Nebraska plains.

Her secret is enthusiasm—to retain a child's delight in existence. Her effervescence contrasts with the aridity of lives around her. The tone is set when in the opening pages of the novel, Jim Burden thinks of Ántonia and her difference from his "unimpressionable" wife, so "tempermentally incapable of enthusiasm." Set down on the raw Divide, where Ántonia's great desire to learn alerts her to every aspect of the wild land, she contrasts with her own depressive father, who is Cather's last fiction. rendering of the Sadilek suicide that never loosed its grip on her imagination. In Black Hawk, town girls are but pale tintypes beside the living, breathing vigor of the immigrant girls, of whom Ántonia is the prime representative. Eventually, those daughters of merchants and tradesmen—trapped in their mystique of "refinement," corseted literally and figuratively by the demands of convention and reared with blind trust in their natural superiority—provide too simple a contrast; and the phenomenon of Ántonia must be presented within her own small circle. For she is not wholly typical; Tiny Soderball, to cite one instance, who becomes the greatest worldly success among the immigrant group, dwindles into "a thin, hard-faced woman, very well dressed, very reserved in manner. . . . like someone in whom the faculty of becoming interested is worn out." Ántonia is cut from sturdier goods; she wears well, showing her quality even when threadbare.

In her struggle to tame life, Ántonia gropes; fumbling repeatedly, she runs a zigzag path but makes relentless progress. If ever there were a true-born victim of circumstance, it should be she: a stranger, unacclimated to frontier life, unable to speak the lingua franca, socially outcast, with a defeated dreamer for a father, a harridan for a mother, a sullen lout for a brother. But Ántonia transcends every disadvantage and does so without soiling herself. Every day she runs barefoot to the Burden home to pick up a few English phrases. No corner of the plains is exempt from her inquiring eye. She is no scholar, of course, for there is no time for school: "I ain't got time to learn," she tells Jim; "I can work like mans now. My mother can't say no more how Ambrosch do all and nobody to help him. I can work as much as him. School is all right for little boys. I help make this land one good farm."

Lacking the resources of an Alexandra, she cannot erect a farming empire; instead, yielding to inevitable conditions, she goes to town as hired girl to the Harlings, where she is exposed to new ways and put in touch for the first time with civilized refinements. She throws herself into those aspects of social life open to Bohemian girls, but she keeps her individuality intact by refusing to drop the new friends made in the "dancing school" tent, even when refusal to conform threatens to cost her the household post on which she exists. When at last Ántonia is betrayed in the only way she could be, self-blinded to the hypocrisy of the railroader who seduces her, this betrayal and the child she bears leave her self-esteem unscarred. Eventually, with the man meant to be the "instrument of her special mission," she mothers her large family, giving herself without reservation to the renewal of life. Those close to Ántonia see her life as ideal. To Cather she is cause for celebration; she justifies the human race.

To what extent the story of Ántonia Shimerda fits into the characteristic pattern of "artist's youth" is a question answered by Cather herself, and in the simplest manner. Of the painter, writer, sculptor, singer there is no question; but in the new dimension Cather includes as artists "the German housewife who sets before her family on Thanksgiving Day a perfectly roasted goose" and "the farmer who goes out in the morning to harness his team, and pauses to admire the sunrise." Ántonia's function is to epitomize this group: "One of the people who interested me most as a child was the Bohemian hired girl of one of our neighbors, who was so good to me. She was one of the truest artists I ever knew in the keenness and sensitiveness of her enjoyment, in her love of people and in her willingness to take pains." After celebrating the ultimate professional achievement—a portrait of success exceeding Thea Kronborg's is inconceivable—Cather caps her theme of youthful struggle with the saga of this hired girl's personal triumph. The entire story is a paean, and no Cather heroine evokes such admiration as this Bohemian girl who is so warmly eulogized as the novel ends:

> She lent herself to immemorial human attitudes which we recognize by instinct as universal and true. . . . She was a battered woman now, not a lively girl; but she still had that something which fires the imagination, could still stop one's breath for a moment by a look or gesture that somehow revealed the meaning in common things. She had only to stand in the orchard, to put her hand on a little crab tree and look up at the apples, to make you feel the goodness of planting and tending and harvesting at last. All the strong things of her heart came out in her body, that had been so tireless in serving generous emotions.
>
> It was no wonder that her sons stood tall and straight. She was a rich mine of life, like the founders of early races.

(pp. 87-92)

Philip Gerber, in his Willa Cather, *Twayne Publishers, 1975, 187 p.*

DEBORAH G. LAMBERT   (essay date 1982)

[*In the following excerpt, Lambert offers a feminist interpretation of* My Ántonia, *arguing that Ántonia's apparent triumph over adversity in fact represents the neutralization of what Cather perceived as her threateningly promiscuous nature.*]

My Ántonia, Willa Cather's celebration of the American frontier experience, is marred by many strange flaws and omissions. It is, for instance, difficult to determine who is the novel's central character. If it is Ántonia, as we might reasonably assume, why does she entirely disappear for two of the novel's five books? If, on the other hand, we decide that Jim Burden, the narrator, is the central figure, we find that the novel explores neither his consciousness nor his development. Similarly, although the narrator overtly claims that the relationship between Ántonia and Jim is the heart of the matter, their friendship actually fades soon after childhood: between these two characters there is only, as E. K. Brown said, "an emptiness where the strongest emotion might have been expected to gather" [see excerpt dated 1953]. Other inconsistencies and contradictions pervade the text—Cather's ambivalent treatment of Lena Lingard and Tiny Soderball, for example—and all are in some way related to sex roles and to sexuality.

This emphasis is not surprising: as a writer who was also a woman, Willa Cather faced the difficulties that confronted, and still do confront, accomplished and ambitious women. As a professional writer, Cather began, after a certain point in her career, to see the world and other women, including her own female characters, from a male point of view. Further, Cather was a lesbian who could not, or did not, acknowledge her homosexuality and who, in her fiction, transformed her emotional life and experiences into acceptable, heterosexual forms and guises. In her society it was difficult to be a woman and achieve professionally, and she could certainly not be a woman who loved women; she responded by denying, on the one hand, her womanhood and, on the other, her lesbianism. These painful denials are manifest in her fiction. After certain early work, in which she created strong and achieving women, like herself, she abandoned her female characters to the most conventional and traditional roles; analogously, she began to deny or distort the sexuality of her principal characters. *My Ántonia,* written at a time of great stress in her life, is a crucial and revealing work, for in it we can discern the consequences of Cather's dilemma as a lesbian writer in a patriarchal society. (pp. 676-77)

Cather never adequately dealt with her homosexuality in her fiction. In two early novels, the question of sexuality is peripheral: *Alexander's Bridge* and *The Song of the Lark* concern the integration of identity, and the expression of sexuality is limited and unobtrusive. Yet Cather began to approach the issue of homosexuality obliquely in subsequent novels. Many, although not all, of the later novels include homosexual relationships concealed in heterosexual guises. Joanna Russ points out that these disguised relationships are characterized by an irrational, hopeless quality and by the fact that the male member of the couple, who is also the central consciousness of the novel, is unconvincingly male—is, in fact, female and a lesbian. The relationships of Claude and Enid in *One of Ours* and Niel and Marian Forrester in *A Lost Lady* are cases in point. In *O Pioneers!,* the novel which preceded *My Ántonia,* the love story of Alexandra's brother Emil and Marie, is also such a transposed relationship: to consider its treatment is to notice, from another perspective, the significant changes that occurred in Cather's writing at the time of *My Ántonia.*

In the subplot of Emil and Marie's love, which unexpectedly dominates the second half of *O Pioneers!,* Cather implies the immense dangers of homosexual love. The deaths of Emil and Marie at the moment of sexual consummation suggest more than a prohibition against adultery: their story expresses both a fantasy of sexual fulfillment and the certainty that death is the retribution for this sort of passion. Seeing the story of Emil and Marie in this way, as the disguised expression of another kind of passion, becomes increasingly plausible when one examines Emil's character and behavior and observes that he is male in name only; moreover, it offers a convincing explanation for the sudden and shocking intrusion of violence in this otherwise uniformly elegiac novel. But what is most important here is that Alexandra, Cather's hero, is not destroyed by the consequences of Emil's passion; instead, passion vicariously satisfied, Alexandra retreats to the safety of heterosexual marriage. Thus the fantasy of homosexuality, and the fear of it, are encapsulated and controlled, only slightly distorting the narrative structure. Three years later, Cather's fear is pervasive and dominates the development of *My Ántonia,* so that the narrative structure itself becomes a defense against erotic expression.

The original of Ántonia was Annie Sadilek Pavelka, a Bohemian woman whom Cather had loved and admired from childhood, and with whom she maintained a lifelong, affectionate friendship. In 1921, after completion of the novel, Cather wrote of her feeling for Annie and her decision to use the male point of view:

> Of the people who interested me most as a child was the Bohemian hired girl of one of our neighbors, who was so good to me. . . . Annie fascinated me and I always had it in mind to write a story about her. . . . Finally, I concluded that I would write from the point of view of the detached observer, because that was what I had always been. Then I noticed that much of what I knew about Annie came from the talks I had with young men. She had a fascination for them, and they used to be with her whenever they could. They had to manage it on the sly, because she was only a hired girl. But they respected her, and she meant a good deal to some of them. So I decided to make my observer a young man.

Here Cather suggests the long genesis of this tale and, significantly, her own replication of the "male" response to Annie, reflected in the language of the passage: "Annie fascinated me"/"She had a fascination for them." The fascination here seems to imply not only a romantic and sexual attraction, but also horror at the attraction. Cather suggests that the young men's response to Ántonia is ambivalent because Annie is forbidden; she is a hired girl, with all of that phrase's various suggestions, and so they see her "on the sly." For Cather that fascination is more complex. Identifying with the young men in their forbidden response to Annie, her impulse is that of the lesbian. Yet, when she wrote the novel and transposed to Jim her own strong attraction to Annie/Ántonia, she also transposed her restrictions on its erotic content. Although she adopts the male persona, she cannot allow him full expression of her feelings. Thus, what would seem to be Jim's legitimate response to Ántonia is prohibited and omitted: its homosexual threat is, evidently, too great, and so we find at the heart of the novel that emptiness noted by Brown.

The avoidance of sexuality (which does not extend beyond the Jim-Ántonia relationship, however) must be seen in connection with [Isabelle] McClung's desertion of Cather, which occurred after she had composed the first two or three chapters of *My Ántonia.* During this time of grieving, she seemed not to trust herself to write of her own experience of love and sex. For the Cather persona and the beloved woman are not only separated: both are actually denied sexuality, although sexuality arises in distorted, grotesque forms throughout the novel.

During the writing of *My Ántonia,* Cather's grief coincided with the already great burden of anxiety of the woman who is a writer. After this time, her heroic stance in her fiction could not continue, and she abandons the creation of strong fictional women. In *My Ántonia* she denies Jim's erotic impulses and Ántonia's sexuality as well; and she retreats into the safety of convention by ensconcing Ántonia in marriage and rendering her apotheosis as earth mother. She abandons Ántonia's selfhood along with her sexuality: as Mrs. Cuzak, Ántonia is "a battered woman," and a "rich mine of life, like the founders of early races." Interestingly, critics have recognized the absence of sexuality in Jim, although not in Ántonia, and focus their analyses on the male in the case, as though the novel had been written about a male character by a male author—or, as if the male experience were always central.

The most complex and instructive of the psychological analyses of Jim is by Blanche Gelfant [see excerpt dated 1971], who sees Jim as a young man whose adolescence "confronts him with the possibility of danger in women." He cannot accept the "nexus of love and death," and so retreats to perpetual boyhood. Noting many of the novel's ambiguous elements, Gelfant assumes that male fragility and male fear of womanhood is the crux of the problem. In her view, Jim is the protagonist and Ántonia is his guide: she is responsible for his failed initiation and, later, for his sexual humiliation and confusion. Gelfant's analysis assumes traditional sex roles as normative: Jim's experience is central and Ántonia's is the subordinate, supporting role in his adventure. Yet, to understand the ambiguity in this, and perhaps in other texts by women writers, requires the reversal of such assumptions. If we assume the centrality of Ántonia and her development in the novel, we can observe the stages by which Cather reduces her to an utterly conventional and asexual character.

In childhood, Ántonia is established as the novel's center of energy and vitality. As a girl she is "bright as a new dollar" with skin "a glow of rich, dark colour" and hair that is "curly and wild-looking." She is always in motion: holding out a hand to Jim as she runs up a hill, chattering in Czech and broken English, asking rapid questions, struggling to become at home in a new environment. Wanting to learn everything, Ántonia also has "opinions about everything." Never indolent like Lena Lingard, or passive like her sister Yulka, or stolid like the Bohemian girls, Ántonia is "breathless and excited," generous, interested, and affectionate. By the end of her childhood, however, intimations of her future social roles appear.

When Ántonia reaches puberty, Cather carefully establishes her subordinate status in relation to three males, and these relationships make an interesting comparison with Alexandra's and Thea's. First, Ántonia's brutal brother, Ambrosch, is established as the head of the house and the "important person in the family." Then Jim records his need to relegate Ántonia to secondary status and receive deference, since "I was a boy and she was a girl," and in the farcical, pseudo-sexual snake-killing episode, he believes he accomplishes his goal. In fact, he and Ántonia enact a nearly parodic ritual of male and female behavior: in his fear, he turns on her with anger; she cries and apologizes for her screams, despite the fact that they may have saved his life; and she ultimately placates him with flattery. Forced to leave school, she soon relinquishes all personal goals in favor of serving others. No longer resentful or competitive, she is "fairly panting with eagerness to please" young Charley Harling, the son of her employers: "She loved to put up lunches for him when he went hunting, to mend his ball-gloves and sew buttons on his shooting coat, baked the kind of nut-cake he liked, and fed his setter dog when he was away on trips with his father." Cather's protagonist has been reduced to secondary status, as Alexandra and Thea were not: having challenged our expectations in earlier works, Cather retreats in this novel to the depiction of stereotypical patterns.

The second book of *My Ántonia,* with its insinuative title "The Hired Girls," dramatizes the emergence of Ántonia's intense sexuality and its catastrophic effects on her world. Now a beautiful adolescent woman, Ántonia is "lovely to see, with her eyes shining and her lips always a little parted when she danced. That constant dark colour in her cheeks never changed." Like flies the men begin to circle around her—the iceman, the delivery boys, the young farmers from the divide; and her employer, Mr. Harling, a demanding, intimidating, patriarch insists that she give up the dances where she attracts so much attention. When she refuses, he banishes her from his family. Next becoming the object of her new employer's lust, Ántonia loses Jim's affection and, by the end of the summer, has embarked on a disastrous affair with the railroad conductor, Donovan. Ántonia's sexuality is so powerful, in Cather's portrayal, that it destroys her oldest and best friendships and thrusts her entirely out of the social world of the novel.

Jim's intense anger at Ántonia once again reveals his fear, this time a fear of her sexuality that is almost horror. When Cutter attempts to rape her, Jim, the actual victim of the assault, returns battered to his grandmother's house. He then blames Ántonia and her sexuality for Cutter's lust, and recoils from her: "I heard Ántonia sobbing outside my door, but I asked grandmother to send her away. I felt I never wanted to see her again. I hated her almost as much as I hated Cutter. She had let me in for all this disgustingness." This eruption of sexuality marks the climax, almost the end, of the friendship between Ántonia and Jim, and after this, Ántonia is virtually banished from the novel.

At this point, Cather, evidently retreating from the sexual issue, broadens the novel's thematic focus. Jim and Ántonia do not meet again for two years, and all of Book III is devoted to Jim's frivolous, romanticized affair with Lena Lingard, with which he and the reader are diverted. Moreover, the events of Ántonia's life—her affair with Donovan, her pregnancy, her return home, the birth of her daughter—are kept at great narrative distance. Two years after the fact, a neighbor describes these events to Jim as she has seen them, or read about them in letters. Yet, as though banishing Ántonia and distracting Jim were not sufficient, her sexuality is diminished and then, finally, destroyed. After a punitive pregnancy and the requisite abandonment by her lover, she never again appears in sexual bloom. The metaphoric comparisons that surround her become sexually neutral, at best. In one example her neck is compared to "the bole of a tree," and her beauty is cloaked: "After the winter began she wore a man's long overcoat and boots and a man's felt hat with a wide brim." Her father's clothes, like Mr. Harling's ultimatum, seem well designed to keep Ántonia's sexuality under wraps.

After a two-year separation, during which Ántonia returns to her brother's farm, bears her child, and takes up her life of field work, Jim and Ántonia meet briefly. Dream-like and remote, their meeting is replete with nostalgia not readily accounted for by events; as Jim says, "We met like people in the old song, in silence, if not in tears." Inappropriately, though in a speech of great feeling, Ántonia compares her feeling for Jim to her memory of her father, who is lost to her for reasons that the text does provide:

> ". . . you are going away from us for good. . . .But that don't mean I'll lose you. Look at my papa here, he's been dead all these years, and yet he is more real to me than almost anybody else. He never goes out of my life."

Jim's response expresses similar nostalgia and an amorphous yearning:

> ". . . since I've been away, I think of you more often than of anyone else in this part of the world. I'd have liked to have you for a sweetheart, or a wife, or my mother, or my grandmother, or my sister—anything that a woman can be to a man. . . . You really are a part of me."

The seductive note of sentiment may blind us as readers to the fact that Jim might offer to marry Ántonia and instead abandons her to a life of hardship on her brother's farm with an empty, and ultimately broken promise to return soon. Cather forcibly separates Jim and Ántonia because of no logic given in the text; we have to assume that her own emotional dilemma affected the narrative and to look for the reasons within Cather herself.

Following this encounter is a twenty-year hiatus: when Jim and Ántonia finally meet again, the tensions that have lain behind the novel are resolved. Ántonia, now devoid of sexual appeal, no longer presents any threat. In addition, she has been reduced to a figure of the greatest conventionality: she has become the stereotypical earth mother. Bearing no resemblance to Cather's early female heroes, she is honored by Jim and celebrated by Cather as the mother of sons. By the novel's conclusion, Cather has capitulated to a version of that syndrome in which the unusual, achieving woman recommends to other women as their privilege and destiny that which she herself avoided. While recognizing the conflict that issues in such self-betrayal, one also notes the irony of Cather's glorification of Ántonia.

Autonomy and unconventional destiny are available only to the subordinate characters, Lena Lingard and Tiny Soderball, two of the hired girls. Lena, having seen too much of marriage, child-bearing and poverty, has established a successful dress-making business and, despite her sensuous beauty, refrained from marriage. Her companion, Tiny, made her fortune in the Klondike before settling down in San Francisco. They lived in a mutually beneficial, supportive relationship: "Tiny audits Lena's accounts occasionally and invests her money for her; and Lena, apparently, takes care that Tiny doesn't grow too miserly," Jim tells us. Both Lena and Tiny are independent and unconventional; Lena particularly understands and values the single self. In a revealing detail, she instructs her brother to buy handkerchiefs for their mother with an embroidered "B" for her given name, "Berthe," rather than with an "M" for mother. Lena, who describes marriage as "being under somebody's thumb," says, "It will please her for you to think about her name. Nobody ever calls her by it now." Although relegated to subordinate roles, these women are initially presented favorably; but, by the end of the novel, Cather simultaneously praises Ántonia's role as mother and demeans the value of their independent lives.

In her concluding gesture, Cather offers a final obeisance to convention. Her description of Lena and Tiny undercuts their achievement and portrays them as stereotypical "old maids" who have paid for their refusal of their "natural" function. Thus, Tiny has become a "thin, hard-faced woman, very well dressed, very reserved" and something of a miser; she says "frankly that nothing interested her much now but making money." Moreover, Tiny has suffered the "mutilation" of her "pretty little feet"—the price of her unnatural success in the Klondike. Though a little more subtly, Lena is similarly disfigured, physically distorted by her emotional aberration. Jim presents her as crude and overblown in a final snapshot: "A comely woman, a trifle too plump, in a hat a trifle too large. . . ." So it is, too, with their friendship. Jim's barren account stresses unpleasantness about clothes and money and implies that an edge of bitterness has appeared. So much for female independence and success; so much for bonds between women. Cather, through Jim's account of them, has denigrated Tiny and Lena and their considerable achievement. In betraying these characters, versions of herself, Cather reveals the extent of her self-division.

Equally revealing is the transformation of Ántonia in the concluding segment. Now forty-four, she is the mother of eleven children, a grandmother without her former beauty. So changed is she that Jim at first fails to recognize her. She is "grizzled," "flat-chested," "toothless," and "battered," consumed by her life of child-bearing and field work. The archetypal mother, Ántonia now signifies nourishment, protection, fertility, growth, and abundance: energy in service to the patriarchy, producing not "Ántonia's children" but "Cuzak's boys" (despite the fact that five of the children mentioned—Nina, Yulka, Martha, Anna, and Lucie—are girls). Like Cather's chapter title, Jim recognizes only the male children in his fantasy of eternal boyhood adventure, forgetting that in an earlier, less conventional and more androgynous world, his companion had been a girl—Ántonia herself.

Now Ántonia is glorified as a mythic source of life. Not only the progenitor of a large, vigorous family, she is also the source of the fertility and energy that have transformed the barren Nebraska prairie into a rich and fruitful garden. From her fruit cellar cavern pour forth into the light ten tumbling children—and the earth's abundance as well. In the images of this conclusion, she, no longer a woman, becomes Nature, a cornucopia, a "mine of life." Representing for Jim "immemorial human attitudes" which "fire the imagination," she becomes an idea and disappears under a symbolic weight, leaving for his friends and companions her highly individualized male children.

The conclusion of *My Ántonia* has usually been read as a triumph of the pioneer woman: Ántonia has achieved victory over her own hard early life and over the forces of Nature which made an immense struggle of farm life in Nebraska. But in fact, as we have seen, Cather and her narrator celebrate one of our most familiar stereotypes, one that distorts and reduces the lives of women. The image of the earth mother, with its implicit denial of Ántonia's individual identity, mystifies motherhood and nurturing while falsely promising fulfillment. Here Cather has found the means to glorify and dispose of Ántonia simultaneously, and she has done so in a way that is consonant with our stereotypical views and with her own psychological exigencies. The image of Ántonia that Cather gives us at the novel's conclusion is one that satisfies our national longings as well: coming to us from an age which gave us Mother's Day, it is hardly surprising that *My Ántonia* has lived on as a celebration of the pioneer woman's triumph and as a paean to the fecundity of the American woman and American land.

Cather's career illustrates the strain that women writers have endured and to which many besides Cather have succumbed. In order to create independent and heroic women, women who are like herself, the woman writer must avoid male identification, the likelihood of which is enhanced by being a writer who is unmarried, childless, and a lesbian. In the case of *My Ántonia,* Cather had to contend not only with the anxiety of creating a strong woman character, but also with the fear of a homosexual attraction to Annie/Ántonia. The novel's defensive narrative structure, the absence of thematic and structural unity that readers have noted, these are the results of such anxieties. Yet, because it has been difficult for readers to recognize the betrayal of female independence and female sexuality in fiction—their absence is customary—it has also been difficult to penetrate the ambiguities of *My Ántonia,* a crucial novel in Cather's long writing career. (pp. 681-90)

Deborah G. Lambert, "The Defeat of a Hero: Autonomy and Sexuality in 'My Ántonia'," in American Literature, *Vol. 53, No. 4, January, 1982, pp. 676-90.*

SUSAN J. ROSOWSKI (essay date 1986)

[*An American critic, Rosowski is the author of* The Voyage Perilous: Willa Cather's Romanticism, *in which she examines the nature of Cather's Romantic attitudes. In the following excerpt from that work, Rosowski discusses elements of romanticism in* My Ántonia.]

In her early essays and short stories [Willa Cather] . . . told of imaginatively fusing two worlds—that of ideas and that of experience, of the general and the particular. She allegorically described the need to do so in *Alexander's Bridge*, then focused sequentially on each world, in *O Pioneers!* so celebrating the idea that she seemed to leave physical realities behind, and in *The Song of the Lark* so involved with particulars that they sometimes seem all there is. In *My Ántonia* she put the two together. The result was the single work that would insure Cather's place in literature.

One sign of Cather's achievement is that *My Ántonia* defies analysis, a quality critics often note when beginning a discussion of it. In 1918 W. C. Brownell said he did not "mind being incoherent" in writing of Cather's new book if he could "convey his notion in the least by [his] flounderings," compared its air to that of Homer, who lifted his subject "somehow," then concluded, "I don't know any art more essentially elusive." Half a century later James Woodress wrote of the same quality in different terms [see Additional Bibliography]. *My Ántonia* has passion, and though "one knows when he is in the presence of it, . . . the identification of it is somewhat intuitive. . . . it is difficult to explain." More specific readings differ dramatically—David Stouck interprets it as a pastoral [see Additional Bibliography] and Paul A. Olson as an epic [see Additional Bibliography]; James E. Miller, Jr., as a commentary on the American dream [see Additional Bibliography] and Blanche H. Gelfant as a drama of distorted sexuality [see excerpt dated 1971]—until one wonders how a single work can mean so many things to so many people. Yet the greatness of the book lies in precisely this capacity. With *My Ántonia* Cather introduced into American fiction what Wordsworth had introduced to English poetry a century earlier—the continuously changing work.

By creating a narrator, Jim Burden, to recall Ántonia, a girl he knew while growing up in Nebraska, Cather for the first time in a novel used the narrative structure ideally suited to the romantic. She made the reacting mind a structural feature of her book. She then provided what E. K. Brown called a "very curious preface," in which she instructed her reader about what was to follow. In that preface Cather anticipated major questions raised by critics. Is *My Ántonia* about Jim or about Antonia? The question assumes mutually exclusive alternatives Cather rejected. Jim originally titled his story simply "Ántonia," then frowned, added "my," and seemed satisfied. As his title indicates, *My Ántonia* is about neither Jim nor Ántonia per se, but how the two, mind and object, come together, so "this girl seemed to mean to us the country, the conditions, the whole adventure of our childhood."

Is it a novel, and has it any form? The impetus for Jim's story was his desire to recollect his emotions, so that he might understand the pattern that emerges from them. To speak Ántonia's name "was to call up pictures of people and places, to set a quiet drama going in one's brain," and in writing, Jim was true to his experience of remembering. He didn't make notes, didn't arrange or rearrange, but "simply wrote down what of herself and myself and other people Ántonia's name recalls to me." Thus his story is not structured by situation, as novels usually are, but by one person's feelings, in the manner of a lyric. Its meaning is as personal as its form; Jim specifies that his story won't be his reader's. When he presents

his manuscript to Cather (and implicitly to each reader), he asks, "Now what about yours?" then cautions, "Don't let it influence your own story." This is a book, then, that hasn't a settled form, but instead that sets in motion an ever-changing, expanding process of symbolic experience, "a quiet drama" in the mind of each reader.

That is not to say *My Ántonia* is formless. From the apparently episodic looseness of Jim's recollections emerges the classic romantic pattern of a dialectic between subject and object, momentarily resolved as a symbol. It consists of two major movements, followed by fusion: first, awakening to experience (Part I) and moving outward by its physicality (Part II), then awakening to ideas (Part III) and returning by them (Part IV); finally, fusing the two as symbol (Part V). By turning back upon itself, the pattern forms circles of expanding meaning. As Jim returned to scenes of his childhood, so the story returns the reader to the beginning, to recognize as symbols particulars once seen discretely. This is precisely the process Jim articulates at the conclusion (a misnomer, for here there is no conclusion; meaning is open-ended and ongoing), when he walks again along the first road over which he and Ántonia came together and realizes that man's experience is "a little circle."

That circle begins in and returns to childhood, "the fair seed-time" of the soul. Part I, "The Shimerdas," tells of a child's awakening to nature. When he came to Nebraska as a ten-year-old orphan, Jim Burden felt he had entered a prairie that at night seemed the void predating creation. Awakening the next morning, Jim found himself in the beginning of a new world. It was a pastoral, Edenic world, in which his grandmother's garden seemed nature's womb. There Jim was warmed by the earth, nourished by fruit within arm's reach, entertained by acrobatic feats of giant grasshoppers, and comforted by the wind humming a tune. His was the unconscious sensation of "something that lay under the sun and felt it, like the pumpkins, and . . . [he] did not want to be anything more." As if one with the mother who holds him within her body, he feels the happiness of being "dissolved into something complete and great."

The scene anticipates point of view throughout this section, in which Cather describes geographical and imaginative expanses from carefully defined vantage points, usually nestled within the earth. Jim is characteristically stationary, securely protected within a bed of one kind or another—a womblike garden, a prairie nest, a hay bed in Peter's wagon, his own bed beside the open window, even his grandmother's kitchen, "tucked away so snugly underground." And Ántonia too is associated with a bed within the earth, dug into the wall of her family's cave and "warm like the badger hole."

Stationary themselves, Jim and Ántonia are witness to the miraculous activity of nature. From it flowers grow as big as trees and cottonwoods shimmer with colors of a fairy tale; from it too come animal forms, astonishing in their variety. When Jim watched the Shimerdas emerge from a hole in the bank, it was as if the earth was giving birth to life itself. First appeared a woman with "an alert and lively" face and "a sharp chin and shrewd little eyes," then a girl of fourteen with eyes "full of light, like the sun shining on brown pools in the wood" and wild-looking brown hair. Following them came a foxlike son of nineteen, with sly, suspicious little hazel eyes, which "fairly snapped at the food" Jim's grandmother brought, and following him a little sister, mild, fair, obedient. From behind the barn appeared another Shimerda son, unexpectedly with webbed hands and the speech of a rooster. Finally, most surprising of all, the father emerges, neatly dressed in a vest and a silk scarf, carefully crossed and held by a red coral pin. When he bends over Mrs. Burden's hand, he could be greeting her in the most formal of drawing rooms rather than on a wild prairie in an unsettled land. (pp. 75-8)

In *My Ántonia* particulars anchor the story, keeping it from floating away from this world. On their way to meet their new Bohemian neighbors, the Burdens pass through a natural paradise with sunflowers making a gold ribbon across the prairie and one of the horses munching blossoms as he walked, "the flowers nodding in time to his bites." The scene could easily seem a fantasy, yet the Burdens carry with them "some loaves of Saturday's bread, a jar of butter, and several pumpkin pies," and the everyday reality of the supplies, listed and identified by historical reality (the bread was baked on Saturday), keeps the scene within the here and now. The Shimerdas' dough has the fairy-tale mystery of a witch's brew, yet it is mixed "in an old tin peck-measure that Krajiek had used about the barn," and a storybook storm, when snow "simply spilled out of heaven, like thousands of feather-beds being emptied," takes place on January twentieth, Jim Burden's eleventh birthday.

Thus the ideal and the real, the general and the particular, are fused by the synthetic power of the imagination, especially strong in childhood. The ten-year-old Jim Burden sees his grandparents' hired men as Arctic explorers, his grandfather as a biblical prophet or an Arabian sheik, and their lives in Nebraska as more adventurous than those of characters in *The Swiss Family Robinson* and *Robinson Crusoe*. When transformed by the imagination, nature, like the Burdens' Christmas tree, is "the talking tree of the fairy tale; legends and stories nestled like birds in its branches."

From the beginning Ántonia embodies these connections; she is a coming together of man and nature, a mediator between them. Her wild-looking hair, her eyes like the sun shining on brown pools, her spontaneity, make her seem nature's child, able to direct Jim's awakening to beauty. Her first act with him is to take his hand and lead him into the prairie, not stopping "until the ground itself stopped—fell away before us so abruptly that the next step would have been out into the tree-tops"; then from a nest in the long prairie grass, she points to the sky. As she will later stand in an orchard and reach out to a fruit tree or look up at the apples, so she here draws Jim toward the horizon, where this world stops and another begins—the bourne of heaven. She brings the Old World into the New (when an insect's song reminds her of Old Hata, the beggar woman in her childhood Bohemian village comes close to the Nebraska prairie), and she changes hardship into joy (when she tells of it, a hole dug into the wall of a primitive cave becomes a warm burrow, and a frightening encounter with a rattlesnake becomes a heroic adventure).

Nature fosters "alike by beauty and fear"—Wordsworth's words might have been Cather's description of the childhood section of *My Ántonia,* in which she included as an undercurrent to joy reverberations of loss and death. Two black shadows flit before or follow the children, Mrs. Burden's garden conceals a snake, Mr. Shimerda's smile suggests profound sadness, and the fullness of autumn's beauty contains "a shiver of coming winter in the air." This darker reality is conveyed especially by the story of Peter and Pavel, so powerful it is often the single episode people remember years after first reading *My Ántonia*. The story is simple. Returning home over snow, a wedding party is overtaken by wolves, and to lighten their load Pavel throws the groom and bride from his sledge. Even in the barest outline it is a powerful incident, for as the snake in Mrs. Shimerda's garden represents the oldest Evil, so the story does our most basic fears. Cather intensifies its effect in the telling.

As the context for Pavel's story Cather establishes the vastness of a wilderness, the darkness of night, and especially, the emptiness of silence. No one talks during the ride to Peter and Pavel's house; there, Pavel is asleep, awakening only to tell his story, then returning to sleep; following the tale Ántonia and Jim scarcely breathe. As is life within a wilderness or light within darkness, sound which breaks silence is dramatic; it is a principle Cather uses throughout this episode. Pavel begins his story in a whisper which grows to a raging cry, cut short by convulsive coughing, then by sleep. Ántonia's translation to Jim similarly builds from the merriment of the wedding guests to the shrieks of people and screams of horses attacked by wolves, then stops short, for Pavel could remember nothing of throwing over the bride and groom. When this silence too is broken by another sound, the reader expects still other wolves to be pursuing the last members of the wedding party, then realizes these are monastery bells in Peter and Pavel's village calling people to early prayer. Like the knocking on the gate in *Macbeth*, the bells signal a more profound horror than any thus far realized—a reentry of the ordinary world from which Peter and Pavel will henceforth be outcasts.

Repetition evokes the sense of ongoing truth. Three times friends journey home together, and three times the tale is told. Peter, Mr. Shimerda, Ántonia, and Jim travel by wagon to Peter and Pavel's house, where they hear of other friends traveling by sledge to their village; afterwards, they return by wagon to the Shimerda farm. Similarly, Pavel first tells his story in Russian; Ántonia repeats it in English; then Jim and Ántonia tell it to one another. Russian merges with English; cries of coyotes are answered by a man, and both echo those of wolves; screams of horses and of people combine; the moans of the wind seem spirits to be admitted, answered by a dying man soon to be among them. Different voices combine to tell a truth so profound all of nature speaks of it, the tragedy of life in a wilderness.

The idea appears in various forms throughout this first section: during that first hard winter the Shimerdas faced starvation. Pavel died of consumption, Peter lost his land, and Ántonia's father committed suicide. Indeed, the childhood scenes contain such hardships that one wonders how a mood of joy survives. Again, Pavel's story suggests an explanation. Jim recalled that "for Ántonia and me, the story of the wedding party was never at an end. We did not tell Pavel's secret to anyone, but guarded it jealousy—as if the wolves of the Ukraine had gathered that night long ago, and the wedding party been sacrificed, to give us a painful and peculiar pleasure." This is the egocentricity of childhood, and it proves a saving protection.

Like Wordsworth, Cather recognized that nature ministers to the child, not literally, of course, but psychologically. Rowing late at night in a stolen boat and suddenly seeing the mountain uprear its head, the boy Wordsworth felt as if it were rising in response to him; in his recollection of the episode he is truthful to the childhood perception rather than to his adult understanding of the facts. Similarly, Cather presents a child's view of the outside world as if it existed for him. The wind hummed to Jim, a small frail insect sang for Ántonia, and people, like characters from a fairy tale, appear to tell their tales, then disappear. Not surprisingly, to Jim Russia seems as remote as the North Pole, and the personal lives of Peter and Pavel, strange men with unpronounceable names, are obscured in the distant realm of adulthood.

Through it all there is a child's belief that things will always be this way, made poignant by adult awareness of change. This is, after all, the middle-aged Jim Burden's recollection of his childhood, a retrospective Cather recalls by phrases repeated so often they become motifs—"I still remember," "they are with me still," and "I can see them now." Tension between innocence and experience increases with changes in Ántonia. By the end of their first year in Nebraska, Ántonia has left the security of childhood to work the land; she aches with exhaustion and, realizing other hardships lie ahead, wishes winter would not return. Meanwhile Jim, only eleven, is still reassured by the notion that it "will be summer a long while yet."

"When boys and girls are growing up, life can't stand still. . . . they have to grow up, whether they will or no." In recognition that Jim was getting older and needed to attend school in town, the Burdens moved from their homestead to Black Hawk, a small prairie town halfway between the country and the city, wilderness and civilization. Ántonia followed them, to work as a hired girl for the Burdens' neighbors, the Harlings. The move signals the transition from childhood to adolescence, from receptivity to irrepressible energy. In Black Hawk the beauty of the immigrant girls suddenly shines forth, stunning within the narrow confines of a small community, and the energy of boys and girls alike spills over.

Music announces the change in mood. In the childhood scenes music provided an elegiac background: an insect singing before winter, Mr. Shimerda removing his violin from its box but never playing it, Fuchs singing a hymn while making a coffin and the community singing another by Mr. Shimerda's grave. In Part II, "The Hired Girls," the people are eased from the harsh struggle of those first years, and they burst into song. Jim Burden is drawn to his neighbors' home by the notes which filter from it: there everyone plays the piano, Ántonia hums as she works, children sing, and Mrs. Harling conducts them all. As Jim recalled, "Every Saturday night was like a party." With Mrs. Harling at the piano it seems inevitable that they begin to dance, Frances teaching the younger children.

From the Harlings the dancers begin a procession which wends its way through Black Hawk. They go next to Mrs. Gardner's hotel, where the tempo changes dramatically. When Mrs. Gardner is out of town one Saturday, her carefully ordered establishment erupts into revelry, inspired again by a piano player—no longer the motherly Mrs. Harling but Blind d'Arnault. Looking "like some glistening African god of pleasure, full of strong, savage blood," d'Arnault played barbarously, wonderfully, awakening in his listeners their own savage blood, which erupts in a wild, frenzied dancing that he will not allow them to stop. Like him, they are blind to the consequences.

When the setting again changes, so does the mood. Three Italians come to Black Hawk and look over the children, then set up a dancing pavilion that is "very much like a merry-go-round tent, with open sides and gay flags flying from the poles." From it come siren sounds to which the youth are irresistibly drawn: "First the deep purring of Mr. Vannis's harp came in silvery ripples through the blackness of the dusty-smelling night; then the violins fell in—one of them was almost like a flute. They called so archly, so seductively, that our feet hurried toward the tent of themselves." Upon hearing the music, Ántonia would hurry with her work at the Harlings, drop-

ping and breaking dishes in her excitement, and "if she hadn't time to dress, she merely flung off her apron and shot out the kitchen door. . . . the moment the lighted tent came into view she would break into a run, like a boy." Energy until now barely contained spills over in animal heat. The iceman, delivery boys, young farmers, all come tramping through the Harlings' yard, and "a crisis was inevitable." Told to cease attending the dances or to leave the Harlings' employ, Ántonia moves into household of the notoriously dissolute Wick Cutter.

Still, the dancers do not stop. When the Vannises dismantle their tent and move away, the same people who attended it go to the Fireman's Hall Saturday dances. And as Ántonia earlier had broken from the Harlings, so now Jim breaks out, crawling from his grandparents' window on Saturday nights, kissing Ántonia as he has no right to do, and dreaming Lena Lingard turns to him saying, "Now they are all gone, and I can kiss you as much as I like."

Two concluding episodes present two aspects of this energy, one pointing back, the other forward. In the first Jim and the hired girls return to the prairie for a picnic, feeling the idyllic contentment of childhood one last time. They play a game, then sit talking; it is one of the few scenes in this section in which they are physically still. The scene ends with one of the most famous images in Cather's writing, that of the plow momentarily transformed into heroic size by the blood-red energy of the sun, then fading into littleness. This is the passion of imaginative perception. The second episode points ahead ominously, to the dark side of passion that degenerates into debauchery. At Wick Cutter's, Ántonia is in danger of rape; and sleeping in her place, Jim is attacked. He emerges bruised and bitter, as if he had fallen and been trampled upon by the bacchanalian parade in which he had been dancing.

Having followed physicality to its darkest extreme, Jim turns away from it altogether. He moves from Black Hawk to Lincoln, where, at the university, he awakens to a world of ideas. Part III, "Lena Lingard," is complementary to Part I, "The Shimerdas": the two sections present two awakenings to two worlds, one of nature, the other of ideas. In this second awakening Jim again feels happiness so complete that it momentarily erases his past, for "when one first enters that world [of ideas] everything else fades for a time, and all that went before is as if it had not been." Indeed, Jim jealously protects his new life from his former one, shutting his window when the prairie wind blows through it and begrudging "the room that Jake and Otto and Russian Peter took up in my memory, which I wanted to crowd with other things." Not only Ántonia but nature itself seems remote; this is a time of interiors, and appropriately, it is set within Jim's rooms, Lena Lingard's workrooms, the theater.

Yet memories are there. As when he opened his window the earthy smell of the prairie outside wafted through, so "whenever my consciousness was quickened, all those early friends were quickened with it, and in some strange way they accompanied me through all my new experiences." When Lena Lingard quietly but inevitably reenters Jim's life, she seems the physical form of the early memories accompanying him. And drawing upon those memories, Jim grasps the idea that great art arises from particulars: "If there were no girls like them in the world, there would be no poetry."

During this period, however, Jim is far detached from those particulars in his own life. His first year at the university is as idyllic as was his first year in Nebraska—and as suspended from reality. Because Jim is totally absorbed in the mental world opening to him, his early friends are real only as ideas he holds within himself, "so much alive" *in* him that he "scarcely stopped to wonder whether they were alive anywhere else." As Ántonia and Jim had once played in nature, so now Lena and Jim play with ideas; as innocence once protected Ántonia and Jim from suffering pains, so it now protects Lena and Jim from seeing reality. When they attend *Camille,* they are as innocent as "a couple of jack-rabbits, run in off the prairie," of what awaits them. And they are open to experience as only children can be. The curtain rises upon a brilliant world they have never before imagined, and they enter it so completely that they leave the real world behind. Dumas's lines alone are enough to convey the idea of tragic love, an "idea . . . that no circumstances can frustrate," not an old, lame, stiff actress playing Marguerite or a disproportionately young, perplexed fellow playing her Armand, not faults in staging or weaknesses of the orchestra.

For a while Jim and Lena, luxuriating in newly discovered roles, are as oblivious to circumstances in their own lives as they had been to those in *Camille.* But when the school year comes to an end so does their pastoral interlude. Gaston Cleric is offered a position at Harvard, and he proposes that Jim follow him in the fall. The return is comically abrupt. Jim goes to Lena with the rather self-serving but noble resolution that he has been standing in her way, "that if she had not me to play with, she would probably marry and secure her future," only to learn that she has no intention of marrying him or anyone else.

Thus closes Jim's chapter with Lena, and one of Cather's most interesting characters recedes from view. By temporarily moving Ántonia to the background of the narrative and the recesses of Jim's memory, Cather releases Jim to revel in ideas. Appropriately, he does so with Lena, the idea of sexuality without its threatening reality. She is sensuously beautiful, and not surprisingly, men cluster about her: in Black Hawk Ole Bensen, Sylvester Lovett, and Jim Burden; in Lincoln the Polish violin-teacher Ordensky, old Colonel Raleigh, and (again) Jim Burden. What is striking is the contrast between these men paying the court to Lena and those clustering about Ántonia in Black Hawk. The courtship of Lena is conducted languidly, devoid of animal vitality, by old men and boys to whom she appeals because she knows they are only playing at love. Nobody needed to have worried about Ole Bensen, she recognized, because he simply liked to sit and look at her; similarly, she allows the old men of Lincoln to court her, for "it makes them feel important to think they're in love with somebody." Implicitly she has a similar bemused affection for the schoolboy Jim Burden.

Even while Jim is most detached from Ántonia, however, the memory of her remains, awaiting a return. Part IV, "The Pioneer Woman's Story," tells of beginning that return. Ántonia has continued to live her own life, following Larry Donovan to Denver, becoming pregnant, and returning alone and unmarried to give birth to a daughter. Bitterly disappointed in her, Jim has tried to shut her out of his mind until, seeing a crayon enlargement of her daughter displayed prominently in a Black Hawk photographer's window, he feels he must see her again. He goes first to the Widow Steavens, the Shimerdas' neighbor who assisted Ántonia in the preparations for her marriage and in the delivery of her baby; from her, Jim learns Ántonia's story. Only then does he go to the Shimerdas' homestead, where he sees Ántonia. Their brief meeting builds to

Jim's declaration of faith: "Do you know, Ántonia, since I've been away, I think of you more often than of anyone else in this part of the world. I'd have liked to have you for a sweetheart, or a wife, or my mother or my sister—anything that a woman can be to a man. The idea of you is a part of my mind; you influence my likes and dislikes, all my tastes, hundreds of times when I don't realize it. You really are a part of me."

The moment is important in Jim's imaginative return, as interesting for what it does not include as for what it does. Jim here affirms his idea of Ántonia as archetypal woman—that much is clear: he sees her face "under all the shadows of women's faces, at the very bottom of my memory." But this is *his* idea only, and when he imagines linking that idea to the real world, he rather indiscriminately wishes she could be whatever a woman can be to a man—sweetheart, wife, mother, sister—apparently it doesn't matter. There is strikingly little of Ántonia in this meeting; the scene is almost wholly centered upon Jim, with only perfunctory references to Ántonia's life or child. Because he has not yet grasped her particularity, he is as yet unable to conceive of Ántonia as apart from him; and without the yoking of the idea with the particular that enables the romantic to unite subject and object in symbolic perception, Jim's return is incomplete.

Part V, "Cuzak's Boys," is the closing of the circle. Allegiance to his idea has kept Jim away from Ántonia for twenty years, for he has heard that she had married an unsuccessful man and lived a hard life. Perhaps it was cowardice, he recalled, but "I did not want to find her aged and broken; I really dreaded it. In the course of twenty crowded years one parts with many illusions. I did not wish to lose the early ones. Some memories are realities, and are better than anything that can ever happen to one again." Again, Lena Lingard acts as an intermediary. As she had appeared in Jim's student rooms and brought with her memories of his past, so years later she gives Jim a cheerful account of Ántonia and urges him to see her.

When the middle-aged Jim returns to the scenes of his childhood, it is to fuse the idea and the particular by seeing what Coleridge called "the universality in the individual, or the individuality itself." First Jim sees Ántonia in all her physical reality, an aging woman with grizzled hair, missing teeth, and hands hardened from work; then he realizes the timeless truth that resides within that reality. For the first time it is her identity rather than his idea of her that he affirms.

As if "experience . . . repeated in a finer tone," scenes from childhood recur, metamorphosed. Jim enters by wagon (then as a boy, now as an adult) and looks about a kitchen (then Jim's grandmother's sunny one, now Ántonia's); Jim at first sees Ántonia and especially her eyes (then of a girl, now a woman), and they talk alone on the prairie (then a wild spot, now planted with an orchard); Jim witnesses an unexpected explosion of life from the earth (then the Shimerdas' cave, now Ántonia's fruit cellar), and he lies down in nature, feeling great contentment (then in the garden, now a hayloft). Even the most apparently ordinary detail resonates with childhood memories: Ántonia's white cats sunning among yellow pumpkins echo Jim's first morning in his grandmother's garden, sunning himself among other pumpkins.

With each scene there is the familiarity of recognition coupled with an explosion of meaning, as the particular is fused with an idea and experienced as a symbol. This is the return of the romantic sensibility, now refined and able to understand the emotional pattern that emerges from the experience:

Ántonia had always been one to leave images in the mind that did not fade—that grew stronger with time. In my memory there was a succession of such pictures, fixed there like the old wood cuts of one's first primer: Ántonia kicking her bare legs against the sides of my pony when we came home in triumph with our snake; Ántonia in her black shawl and fur cap, as she stood by her father's grave in the snow-storm; Ántonia coming in with her work-team along the evening skyline. She lent herself to immemorial human attitudes which we recognize by instinct as universal and true. I had not been mistaken. She was a battered woman now, not a lovely girl; but she still had that something which fires the imagination, could still stop one's breath for a moment by a look or gesture that somehow revealed the meaning in common things. She had only to stand in the orchard, to put her hand on a little crab tree and look up at the apples, to make you feel the goodness of planting and tending and harvesting at last. All the strong things of her heart came out in her body, that had been so tireless in serving generous emotions.

It was no wonder that her sons stood tall and straight. She was a rich mine of life, like the founders of early races.

Here is the peace of resolution. When Jim leaves the Cuzak farm, he feels a sense of loss, yet reassures himself with the possibility of return. Ántonia—and her children after her—will endure, and the memories of her are "spots of time" by which he can renew himself.

The overall pattern of *My Ántonia,* with its separation, resolution, and return to separation, is familiar to readers of romantic literature: one need think only of Wordsworth's "Tintern Abbey," Coleridge's conversation poems, and Keats's odes. Like her predecessors in romanticism, Cather uses that pattern to write of the individual imagination perceiving the world symbolically. Unlike them, however, she uses gender assumptions to heighten tension between her subject and object. As her early essays make clear, Cather was acutely aware that our culture assigns to men the position of subject and to women that of object, and she incorporates those assumptions into her novel. Jim Burden expresses conventionally male attitudes: he assumes the subject position, moves outward, engages in change and progress, and writes possessively about *his* Ántonia as the archetypal woman who provides an anchorage for his travels and a muse for his imagination. Through Jim, Cather presents myths of male transcendence, of man as a liberating hero, romantic lover, and creative genius; of women to be rescued, loved, and transformed into art. In Ántonia, however, Cather contradicts these assumptions by creating a woman who works out her individual destiny in defiance of her narrator's expectations.

My Ántonia is Jim's account of all that Ántonia means to him, or more precisely, of his youthful attempt to *make* her "anything that a woman can be to a man." By his account Ántonia seeks primarily to nurture by giving—to give her ring to the ten-year-old Jim and to admire his exploits, to give her love to Larry Donovan, and to give to her children a better chance than she had. As important, she makes no demands upon the world or upon others in it. Even after becoming pregnant, Ántonia does not press Larry Donovan to marry her, for "I thought if he saw how well I could do for him, he'd want to stay with me." Her husband, Cuzak, affirms "she is a good wife for a poor man" because "she don't ask me no questions." Ántonia offers unconditional love; both her strength and her weakness are that she could never believe harm of anyone she loved. Through her love, Ántonia, like the orchard she tends, offers "the deepest peace" of escape from worldly demands. To Jim, Ántonia is a wellspring for male activity in the larger world. On a physical level she bears sons. Jim titles his final chapter "Cuzak's Boys," and he concludes, "It was no wonder that her sons stood tall and straight." On a spiritual level she is a muse to Jim, for she "had that something which fires the imagination."

At the same time that Cather uses Jim to present "the collective myths" about women, she builds tension against his account. There emerges a certain ruthlessness about Jim's affection for Ántonia that belies his stated affection for her. His love, unlike hers, is conditional. He is proud of Ántonia when he believes her to be "like Snow-white, in the fairy tale"; he turns from her when she asserts her individuality. He resents her protecting manner toward him, is angered over her masculine ways when she works the farm, is bitter when she "throws herself away on . . . a cheap sort of fellow" and, once pregnant, falls from social favor. Jim's allegiance is consistently to his ideas; when they conflict with reality, he denies the reality.

The world and the people in it just as consistently belie the myths Jim attempts to impose upon them. Otto Fuchs is not a Jesse James desperado but a warmhearted ranchhand; Lena Lingard is not a wild seductress but a strong-minded girl who becomes an independent businesswoman; Jim himself is not the adventurer, the lover, or the poet he pretends to be. By contrasting the boast and the deed, Cather suggests comic, self-serving, and ineffectual dimensions of male gallantry. Picturing himself as a dragon slayer, Jim kills an old, lazy rattlesnake. Drafted by his grandmother into service as Ántonia's rescuer, Jim sleeps at the Cutters, saving Ántonia from rape but feeling something close to hatred of her for embarrassing him. Resolving to "go home and look after Ántonia," Jim returns to her only twenty years later, after being assured that he will not have to part with his illusions. Finally, Ántonia and Lena, the objects of Jim's benevolence, react to his promise with smiles and "frank amusement." They get on with their lives basically independently from men, whether by design, as when Lena resolves that she will never marry, or by necessity, as when Ántonia proceeds to rear her daughter alone.

Tension against Jim's account increases as his narrative role changes. In the initial sections Cather presented Ántonia through Jim's point of view. Jim measured Ántonia against his idea of women, approving of her when she assumed a role he expected of her. But in Book IV, "The Pioneer Woman's Story," Cather moved Jim aside, to the position of tale recorder, and made the midwife who attended Ántonia the tale teller. The Widow Steavens provides a woman's account of a woman's experience, and with it a significant change in tone toward Ántonia. She relates her story with understanding and sympathy rather than with Jim's shocked and bitter insistence that Ántonia play her part in his myth.

By Part V, Jim and Ántonia have reversed roles. Jim began the novel as the story teller in several senses, telling the account he titles *my* Ántonia, and also telling it in terms of stories he has read or heard—*The Life of Jesse James, Robinson Crusoe, Camille,* the *Georgics.* But the child Jim grew into a man who followed the most conventional pattern for success: he left the farm to move to town, then attended the university, studied law at Harvard, married well, and joined a large corporation. In the process, his personal identity seems to have faded. Ántonia, who began the novel as a character rendered by Jim, in the fifth section breaks through myths Jim had imposed upon her and emerges powerfully as herself. With her children around her, she is the center of "the family legend," to whom her children look "for stories and entertainment." Ántonia's stories, unlike Jim's, are not from literature. They are instead domestic ones drawn from life, "about the calf that broke its leg, or how Yulka saved her little turkeys from drowning . . . or about old Christmases and weddings in Bohemia."

As Jim leaves the Cuzak farm in the last paragraphs, Ántonia recedes into the background. One of a group standing by the windmill, she is waving her apron, as countless women have said goodbye to countless men. Returning to the larger male world, Jim spends a disappointing day in Black Hawk, talking idly with an old lawyer there. Finally, he walks outside of town to the unploughed prairie that remains from early times. There Jim's mind "was full of pleasant things," for he intended "to play" with Cuzak's boys and, after the boys are grown, "to tramp along a few miles of lighted streets with Cuzak." But these plans seems curiously empty, irrelevant to the center of life represented by the female world of Ántonia. The early male myths of adventure have led to pointless wandering and lonely exile, and the women, originally assigned roles of passivity, have become the vital sources of meaning. (pp. 78-91)

Susan J. Rosowski, in her The Voyage Perilous: Willa Cather's Romanticism, *University of Nebraska Press, 1986, 284 p.*

JAMES WOODRESS   (essay date 1987)

[*Woodress is an American critic and the author of two biographies of Cather,* Willa Cather: Her Life and Art *(1970) and* Willa Cather: A Literary Life *(1987). In the following excerpt from the latter, he provides an assessment of* My Ántonia.]

Few novels are likely to be read longer than *My Ántonia.* In it character, theme, setting, myth, and incident are combined into a narrative of great emotional power. The prose is limpid, evocative, the product of Cather's nearly three decades of learning to master her instrument. For many readers it is her greatest work. She knew she had done well with this book and told Carrie Sherwood in 1938 that "the best thing I've done is *My Ántonia.* I feel I've made a contribution to American letters with that book." On other occasions she gave this precedence to *Death Comes for the Archbishop.* In 1943 [Ferris] Greenslet wrote her that *My Ántonia* was a novel to cherish. It had sold twenty-five hundred copies in the previous year, and he didn't think there was another novel published a quarter of a century before that had continued to do so well. These were all copies in the regular hardcover edition, and this in the middle of the war. Through the years the novel has always sold steadily and never has been out of print.

Everything went right in this work—a great concept executed with consummate artistry—and it goes well beyond any of her first three novels. While Alexandra Bergson is the strong, intelligent tamer of the wild land, Thea Kronborg with the godlike name the climber of Olympus, Ántonia Shimerda is the mother of races. She is the most heroic figure of all, both the Madonna of the Wheat Fields and the symbol of the American westering myth. Although there are somber tones in her story, it ends on an affirmative note. The suicide of her father, the hard toil on the prairie farm, the desertion by her lover—these things have receded into the past by the final chapter, and what remains at the end is the indelible picture of Ántonia and her children: "It was no wonder that her sons stood tall and straight.

She was a rich mine of life, like the founders of early races." Even after several readings one cannot finish this novel without being moved.

Cather managed to avoid the pitfalls inherent in her narrative method. Jim Burden as an unreliable narrator, childless, unhappily married to a promoter of avant garde causes, a man who jots down at random his memories of his youth, could have produced a story excessively sentimental; but he did not. There is the aura of nostalgia frequently found in Cather's fiction, but the sentiment does not become sentimentality. Cather escapes this by her usual juxtaposition of contrasts; in this case good and evil are alternated. Jim Burden's golden memories are constantly being interrupted by the sterner realities. The idyl of Jim's boyhood is punctuated by the rattlesnake episode, the suicide of Ántonia's father, the deviltries of Wick Cutter, the meanness of Ántonia's older brother, the horrible story of Pavel and Peter, and Ántonia's seduction. The cruel and ugly scenes and characters balance nicely the pleasant memories: the wonderful first autumn, the happy Christmas scene, Mrs. Harling's music, the picnic, the exhilarating talk of Gaston Cleric, the final visit to Ántonia's farm.

One of the remarkable aspects of this novel is its appeal to unsophisticated and sophisticated readers alike. The college freshman who has read very little is just as captivated by *My Ántonia* as his English professor who has read everything from *Beowulf* to Thomas Kennerly Wolfe. The freshman finds a simple, human story dealing with genuine people facing recognizable problems. He can relate to it; he is touched by the real feeling evoked; he can read it without a dictionary or recourse to someone else's notes or annotations. The professor finds in the novel, besides a moving story, a richness of allusion, myth, and symbol presented by one of the great stylists of this century. This wide appeal results from Cather's blending together her native experience and her wide knowledge of European literature and culture. Her memories of Nebraska give her novel color, romance, emotional content; her general culture supplies texture, profundity, intellectual content. Together they make a literary classic.

The reader who plunges into Sinclair Lewis, for example, is likely to hit his head on the bottom, but in Cather there is no danger. He can dive as deep as he wishes and stay down as long as he can. The reader who plunges into the Thomas Wolfe of *Look Homeward, Angel* is swamped by the astonishing vitality of his work but dismayed, as Lionel Trilling puts it, by "the disproportion between the energy of his utterance and his power of mind." It is the intellection coming from European culture that gives one room to swim in Cather's fiction. She did not write intellectual novels, but there is substance in them to nourish the mind, subtly mixed with emotion and feeling. The affective content derives from her prairie youth and what she liked to call "the gift of sympathy." These two kinds of experience are of the body and the mind: friendships with people like Ántonia in post-frontier Nebraska and travel through Europe and books from Homer to Housman. Cather's roots in the soil of Webster County were deep and well-watered; her knowledge and use of Old World culture was substantial and pervading. The warp and woof of her work is native American, but threads of European culture are woven into the fabric.

From the very opening of the novel Jim Burden evokes the land as Cather remembered it when she was a child in Catherton: "As I looked about me I felt that the grass was the country; as the water is the sea. The red of the grass made all the great prairie the colour of wine stains, or of certain seaweeds when they are first washed up. And there was so much motion in it; the whole country seemed, somehow to be running.'' And later: ''I felt motion in the landscape; in the fresh, easy-blowing morning wind, and in the earth itself, as if the shaggy grass were a sort of loose hide, and underneath it herds of wild buffalo were galloping, galloping.'' When Jim later lies in his grandmother's garden under a warm autumn sun, he listens to the wind, feels the warm earth under him, watches the insects: ''I kept as still as I could. Nothing happened. I did not expect anything to happen. I was something that lay under the sun and felt it, like the pumpkins, and I did not want to be anything more. I was entirely happy. Perhaps we feel like that when we die and become a part of something entire, whether it is sun and air, or goodness and knowledge. At any rate, that is happiness; to be dissolved into something complete and great.''

Soon Jim and his grandparents drive over to meet the Shimerdas, their new neighbors, who live in a sod house like badgers in a hole. ''I saw a door and a window sunk deep in the drawbank. The door stood open, and a woman and a girl of fourteen ran out and looked up at us hopefully.'' This is Ántonia. Her eyes were ''big and warm and full of light, like the sun shining on brown pools in the wood. Her skin was brown, too, and in her cheeks she had a glow of rich, dark colour. Her brown hair was curly and wild-looking.'' From this first memory comes a lasting relationship that Jim later sums up: ''The idea of you is part of my mind; you influence my likes and dislikes, all my tastes, hundreds of times when I don't realize it. You really are a part of me.'' Then at the end of the novel, for Jim as well as for Cather, the experience of knowing the fictional and the real Ántonia produces the realization that ''whatever we had missed, we possessed together the previous, the incommunicable past.''

Underlying this affecting story of human friendship is the use of myth and symbol to give the novel universality. This dimension of Cather's art seems more intuitive than deliberate, the result of her assimilation of literary tradition and western culture; but whether it is conscious or instinctive, it adds unobtrusively significance to the narrative. Cather mythologizes American experience in creating Ántonia as an embodiment of the westward movement, the pioneer woman, the symbol of the frontier. Her life is emblematic of the breaking of the sod, the cultivation of the wilderness, the migration of peoples from the Old World to the New. Cather did it earlier in Alexandra's epic struggle to tame the wild land. In *My Ántonia* the symbol comes into sharp focus in the picnic scene. Jim and the hired girls with their picnic baskets meet on the banks of the river outside of Black Hawk. After the meal and a good bit of talk about the girls' immigrant experiences and their families, Jim tells about a Nebraska farmer who found a Spanish stirrup when he was plowing. He tells the girls about Coronado's adventures in the New World and speculates that Coronado must have explored their region in his search for the Seven Golden Cities. Jim concludes his story with the statement from his school textbook that Coronado ''died in the wilderness, of a broken heart,'' a highly colored account of a much more prosaic history. To this tale Ántonia rejoins: ''More than him has done that,'' and the girls murmur assent. This conversation is followed by a remarkable scene:

> Presently we saw a curious thing: There were no clouds, the sun was going down in a limpid, gold-washed sky. Just as the lower edge of the red disk rested on the high fields against the horizon, a great black figure suddenly appeared on the face of the

> sun. We sprang to our feet, straining our eyes toward it. In a moment we realized what it was. On some upland farm, a plough had been left standing in the field. The sun was sinking just behind it. Magnified across the distance by the horizontal light, it stood out against the sun, was exactly contained within the circle of the disk; the handles, the tongue, the share—black against the molten red. There it was, heroic in size, a picture writing on the sun.

As a symbol of the Westward Movement, the plow against the sun appropriately stands for the farming frontier, which had followed the earlier frontiers of the trapper and the miner; and its use here reinforces meaning.

An even more impressive use of myth and symbol occurs in the final book in which Jim Burden returns twenty years later to visit Ántonia. She and her children show Jim their fruit cave, which is a cornucopia of the earth's bounty. They go down into the earth where Jim sees shelf upon shelf of preserved fruit and barrels of pickles. After inspecting the contents of the cave: ''We turned to leave the cave; Ántonia and I went up the stairs first, and the children waited. We were standing outside talking, when they all came running up the steps together, big and little, tow head and gold heads and brown, and flashing little naked legs; a veritable explosion of life out of the dark cave into the sunlight. It made me dizzy for a moment.''

The description here has the same effect on the reader, and in this picture of the explosion of life out of the dark womb, myth and symbol again add meaning. This scene climaxes a modern enactment of the ancient Eleusian Mysteries that celebrated the earth's fertility two thousand years before Christ. It is so thoroughly domesticated in the Nebraska landscape, however, that no one need bother about its link to ancient rites, but the image of Ántonia as earth goddess certainly makes a subliminal impact on the reader. In *My Ántonia* Cather has succeeded not only in giving significance to the American westering experience, but she also has tied her story to man's primitive relationship with the earth. This scene resonates in the mind long after one has closed the book. Again the polarity in Cather between primitivism and civilization adds tension to her fiction.

There are two other examples worth noting of general culture and reading that reinforce meaning. In an early scene when Jim and Ántonia are roaming the countryside during their first idyllic autumn, they come to a prairie dog town. Jim kills an enormous rattlesnake that he finds sunning itself amid the burrows. This episode serves nicely as an exciting bit of action and also as a rite of passage for Jim, but it is equally clear from the text that Cather is linking it to myth. Jim's summary reference to himself as a dragon-slayer and the snake as ''the ancient, eldest Evil'' make a subtle connection between American frontier experience and its cultural antecedents—all the literary examples as well as the visual representations of dragon slayers. Pictures of St. George and the dragon, besides depicting a knight impaling a dragon on his lance, always show an adoring maiden watching the slaying, and in this scene on the Nebraska prairie there are both ingredients. After Jim finishes off the rattler with a spade, Ántonia says in her broken English: ''You is just like big mans.'' When the hero returns to his admiring people in triumph, Cather adds a neat touch of twentieth-century irony. She has Jim reflect that his dragon was old, lazy, well-fed, and an easy mark for a ten-year-old St. George.

The other exhibit is a scene in Lincoln when Jim is squiring Lena about the state capital. He takes her to a performance of

Camille, a second-rate production by a mediocre road company, but both Jim and Lena are thrilled by the romantic drama as it unfolds accompanied by incidental music from Verdi's version of the same play, *La Traviata.* In this episode literary allusion reinforces events taking place in the novel. The renunciation of love for duty to family, central to the action of the play, is about to be enacted in the parting of Jim and Lena. Gaston Cleric, Jim's professor, plays the same role in the novel as the elder Duval in the play. He calls on Jim to follow his destiny to Harvard and to stop "playing about with this handsome Norwegian." For contemporary readers who had seen Dumas' play on the stage or later generations who remember Greta Garbo's film version or know Verdi's opera, this scene adds significance to the story.

Cather's thorough grounding in Latin also gives depth to her narrative. As Jim studies the classics under Gaston Cleric, he develops a passion for Virgil, whose *Georgics* he is studying one night in his room. His book is open to the passage: *"Optima dies . . . prima fugit"* ("the best days are the first to flee"). Jim reflects on the dying Virgil at Brindisi, who must have remembered his youth in his native Mantua. Jim too has left his native Black Hawk, Ántonia, and his grandparents. His destiny will take him East and turn him into a corporation lawyer. The theme from Virgil supplies a leitmotif for this elegiac narrative. Cather also quotes another line from Virgil: *"Primus ego in patriam mecum . . . deducam Musas"* ("I shall be the first to bring the Muse into my country"), which has a parallel contemporary meaning. Cleric has explained to his class that Virgil meant by *patria* the region along the Mincio River where he had been born, not all of Italy. The reader realizes that what Virgil did for his native place, Cather also was doing for Nebraska—putting it on the literary map.

The strong classical influence on Cather's work affected *My Ántonia* in another significant way. To tell her story, she employed the pastoral mode, a manner of expression that "counters the failures of the present by moving back into the past." Even in her early fiction and poetry she sometimes adopted the pastoral tone of retrospection and elegy in an effort to recapture the past. She was drawn to the classic Arcadian theme of a Golden Age, a grander, more perfect time gone by, and it suited her personality. It also provided a very appropriate method for writing a drama of memory and gave her imagination full scope to fashion a story intensely subjective. The autobiographical form that she selected was well adapted both to the Arcadian theme and to her own romantic art. It wasn't different from the strategies Wordsworth had used in "Tintern Abbey" and "The Prelude."

The human impulse to remember the past as somehow better than the present, the days of one's youth as happier than the years of adulthood, has a wide appeal. In point of fact, childhood is often unhappy, beset with problems of poverty, broken homes, painful psychological adjustments, but the yearning for the innocence of childhood is undeniably attractive. Cather's youthful nonconformity, sexual ambivalence, and community disapproval kept her own early years from being an unalloyed idyll, but the pastoral ideal always fired her imagination. The tension in the pastoral mode between the desire to return to the past and the knowledge that one cannot go back gives Cather's fiction a dramatic quality, but the conflict can never be resolved. Her life itself had this tension, and *My Ántonia* comes at a point in her career when the past began to seem more attractive than the present. As she was writing this novel during the First World War, her mind began to turn backwards

more and more. Personal problems from within and the devastation of Europe from without accentuated her growing nostalgia. She told [Elizabeth] Sergeant after the war broke out: "Our present is ruined—but we had a beautiful past."

Related to the backward-looking pastoral mode is the yearning for the pre-puberty years of sexual innocence. Cather always regarded the days when she played with her brothers, unconscious of sexual difference, as times of golden memory. Her narrator-persona Jim Burden shares this feeling in his reconstruction of his idyllic months of childhood with Ántonia. His adult life, however, is impoverished by Cather's adult bias against romantic love. Her greatest failing as an artist is her inability to depict heterosexual adult relationships affirmatively. As a celibate writer herself, she gives Jim her own aversion to sex, and when he finishes law school and seeks a wife, she gives him a frigid, unhappy marriage. In compensation, however, he is able to evoke in his memoir a happily married Ántonia, who is one of the memorable characters in American literature.

Jim's aversion to sex is developed early in the novel, first symbolically by the rattlesnake episode and then by the attempted rape scene. When Jim kills the snake, an obvious sex symbol, he is sickened by the experience, but he fights with a fury as he slashes at the reptile with his spade. Later when he is past puberty and getting ready to go to college, Ántonia fears Wick Cutter's lechery and arranges for Jim to sleep in her bed one night while Mrs. Cutter is out of town. Cutter sneaks into the bedroom planning to rape Ántonia, finds Jim and a furious struggle ensues. Jim runs home through the streets in his night shirt bleeding from the fight and utterly repelled by the experience. As humorous as the reader might find the episode, Jim feels defiled and hates Ántonia for getting him into this predicament.

During the same period in Jim's life his sexual awakening takes place, but Cather allows it to happen only in his mind. He dreams that he is in a harvest field when Lena, now a woman of great physical attraction, comes towards him with a reaping hook in her hand, sits beside him and says: "Now . . . I can kiss you as much as I like." Later in Lincoln Jim carries on an apparently sexless affair with Lena, who is not interested in any permanent emotional attachment to a man. The lovemaking in that part of the novel takes place on stage when Jim and Lena go to see *Camille.* Jim then goes to Harvard and after he finishes law school remains in the East.

In the final book when Jim returns to visit Ántonia twenty years later, she is a mother figure, and he recaptures his lost youth in his relationship with her children. He finds warmth and happiness in her kitchen, as he once did in his grandmother's; he finds peace in her garden; he sleeps in the barn with the boys. Memories of his childhood friends return in the names Ántonia has given her children. Although he had dreaded going back, fearing that he would find Ántonia aged and broken, he need not have worried. He does not have to abandon his feeling that "some memories are realities, and are better than anything that can ever happen to one again." (pp. 293-300)

James Woodress, in his Willa Cather: A Literary Life, *University of Nebraska Press, 1987, 583 p.*

ADDITIONAL BIBLIOGRAPHY

Bloom, Edward A. and Bloom, Lillian D. *Willa Cather's Gift of Sympathy*. Carbondale: Southern Illinois University Press, 1962, 260 p.
  Study of Cather's "principal thematic concerns and . . . the narrative techniques which she employed in their development."

Boynton, H. W. "All Sorts." *Bookman* 48 (December 1918): 495.
  Laudatory review of *My Ántonia*.

Fairbanks, Carol. *Prairie Women: Images in American and Canadian Fiction*. New Haven, Conn.: Yale University Press, 1986, 300 p.
  Study which makes frequent reference to Cather's portrayals of pioneer women, including those in *My Ántonia*.

Fryer, Judith. "Book III: Willa Cather." In her *Felicitous Space: The Imaginative Structures of Edith Wharton and Willa Cather*, pp. 203-342. Chapel Hill: University of North Carolina Press, 1986.
  Discusses the importance of setting in Cather's fiction.

Giannone, Richard. *"My Ántonia."* In his *Music in Willa Cather's Fiction*, pp. 107-23. Lincoln: University of Nebraska Press, 1968.
  Discusses the role of music in *My Ántonia*, contending that in Cather's characterizations, "musical spirit connotes a constructive view of life."

Harris, Richard C. "Jim Burden, Willa Cather, and the Introductions to *My Ántonia*." *Willa Cather Pioneer Memorial Newsletter* XXX, No. 3 (Summer 1986): 33-4.
  Compares the original and revised versions of the introduction to *My Ántonia*, concluding that "significant emotional and psychological changes that had occurred in Willa Cather herself between 1918 and 1926 seem to manifest themselves in the two descriptions of Jim Burden."

Havighurst, Walter. Introduction to *My Ántonia*, by Willa Cather, pp. v-xvi. Boston: Houghton Mifflin, 1949.
  Provides background information concerning pioneer life and Cather's early experiences.

Helmick, Evelyn. "The Mysteries of Ántonia." *Midwest Quarterly* XVII, No. 2 (Winter 1976): 173-85.
  Compares Jim Burden's reverence for Ántonia to a classical fertility ritual known as the Eleusinian Mysteries.

McFarland, Dorothy Tuck. *"My Ántonia."* In her *Willa Cather*, pp. 39-50. New York: Frederick Ungar, 1972.
  Discusses the primary elements of the novel.

Miller, James E., Jr. "*My Ántonia* and the American Dream." *Prairie Schooner* XLVIII, No. 2 (Summer 1974): 112-23.
  Suggests that the power and importance of *My Ántonia* seem disproportionate to its actual merits as a novel, and that the discrepancy may be due to its evocative portrayal of a quintessentially American experience.

O'Brien, Sharon. *Willa Cather: The Emerging Voice*. New York: Oxford University Press, 1987, 464 p.
  Biography which focuses on Cather's life prior to 1915, on the various stages of her gender confusion, and on her search for a personal narrative voice.

Olson, Paul A. "The Epic and Great Plains Literature: Rølvaag, Cather, and Neihardt." *Prairie Schooner* 55, Nos. 1 & 2 (Spring-Summer 1981): 263-85.
  Examines *My Ántonia* as an example of the "plains epic" mode in American literature.

Romines, Ann. "After the Christmas Tree: Willa Cather and Domestic Ritual." *American Literature* 60, No. 1 (March 1988): 61-82.
  Contends that "Cather's handling of [domestic] ritual . . . changed tellingly during her most productive years," reflecting her "increased awareness of 'women's culture' and the domestic rituals in which it is enacted."

Rose, Phyllis. "Modernism: The Case of Willa Cather." In *Modernism Reconsidered*, edited by Robert Kiely, pp. 123-45. Cambridge: Harvard University Press, 1983.
  Links Cather's narrative techniques with those of Modernist authors Virginia Woolf and James Joyce.

Shaw, Patrick W. "*My Ántonia*: Emergence and Authorial Revelations." *American Literature* 56, No. 4 (December 1984): 527-40.
  Suggests that Cather used a non-linear temporal structure in *My Ántonia* because of her desire to overcome "the complexes that first create and then feed upon guilt and repression," reflecting her deep-seated fear of adult sexuality.

Slote, Bernice and Faulkner, Virginia, eds. *The Art of Willa Cather*. Lincoln: University of Nebraska Press, 1974, 267 p.
  Collection of essays on various aspects of Cather's fiction by noted Cather scholars.

Stouck, David. "Pastoral." In his *Willa Cather's Imagination*, pp. 35-72. Lincoln: University of Nebraska Press, 1975.
  Suggests that "the imaginative tension in *My Ántonia* is perhaps best described as a creative opposition between the novel's content and its form. As the narrator . . . tells his life story revolving around the Bohemian immigrant girl . . . , he attempts to shape a happy and secure world out of the past by romanticizing disturbing and unpleasant memories. Yet the novel's form . . . invalidates the narrator's emotional quest, for the passing of time continuously moves the narrator away from the happy point of childhood and brings . . . the tragic realization that the past can never be recaptured."

Wagenknecht, Edward. "Willa Cather and the Lovely Past." In his *Cavalcade of the American Novel*, pp. 319-38. New York: Henry Holt and Co., 1952.
  Overview of Cather's writings in which Wagenknecht suggests that her range and depth as an author are much greater than is generally acknowledged.

Watkins, Floyd C. "*My Ántonia*: Still, All Day Long, Nebraska." In his *In Time and Place: Some Origins of American Fiction*, pp. 73-101. Athens: University of Georgia Press, 1977.
  Discusses *My Ántonia* as a pioneer novel, noting that Cather's "materials in the composition of this book are rich but limited in scope."

Woodress, James. *Willa Cather: Her Life and Art*. New York: Pegasus, 1970, 288 p.
  The first of Woodress's two critical biographies of Cather. For the second, see the excerpt dated 1987.

Anton (Pavlovich) Chekhov

1860-1904

(Also transliterated as Chekov, Tchehov, Tchehoff, Tchekhof, Tchekhov, Čexov, Čekov, Čecov, Čechov, Chekhoff, and Chehov; also wrote under the pseudonym Antosha Chekhonte) Russian dramatist, short story writer, and novelist.

The following entry presents criticism of Chekhov's dramas. For a discussion of Chekhov's complete career, see *TCLC*, Volumes 3 and 10.

Chekhov is the most significant Russian author of the literary generation to succeed Leo Tolstoy and Fyodor Dostoevsky. Preeminent for his stylistic innovations in both fictional and dramatic forms, he is also revered for his depth of insight into the human condition. While Chekhov's most characteristic writings began in extremely personal feelings and observations, their ultimate form was one of supreme emotional balance and stylistic control. It is precisely this detached, rational artfulness that distinguishes his work from the confessional abandons of Dostoevsky or the psychological fantasies of Nikolai Gogol. This artistic control made Chekhov one of the masters of the modern short story and the modern drama.

Chekhov's grandfather was a serf who bought his freedom, and his father was the owner of a small grocery business in Taganrog, the village where Chekhov was born. When the family business went bankrupt in 1876, the Chekhovs, without Anton, moved to Moscow to escape creditors; Anton remained in Taganrog until 1879 in order to complete his education and earn a scholarship to Moscow University. There he studied medicine and, after graduating in 1884, went into practice. By this time he was publishing sketches, mostly humorous, in popular magazines. Chekhov did this to support his family, and although he wrote literally hundreds of these pieces, he did not take them very seriously. In 1885, however, Chekhov moved to St. Petersburg and became friends with A. S. Suvorin, editor of the journal *Novoe vremja*, who encouraged the young writer to develop his obvious gifts. At this time, and for several years afterward, Chekhov's writings were profoundly influenced by Tolstoy's ideas on ascetic morality and nonresistance to evil. But after Chekhov visited the penal settlement on the island of Sakhalin, which he would make the subject of a humanitarian study, he rejected Tolstoy's moral code as an insufficient answer to human suffering. It was in the late 1880s that Chekhov began to produce what are regarded as his mature works in the short story form. While he was also engaged in writing plays during this period, his first major work as a dramatist was not produced until 1896, when the Moscow Art Theater staged *Chayka (The Seagull)*. The same company also presented the first performances of *Dyadya Vanya (Uncle Vanya), Tri sestry (The Three Sisters),* and *Vishnevy sad (The Cherry Orchard)*. In 1901 Chekhov married Olga Knipper, an actress with the Moscow Art Theater. Because of his worsening tuberculosis, from which he had suffered since 1884, Chekhov was forced to spend a great deal of time in European health resorts and was often separated from his wife, who was frequently performing in Moscow. He died in a Black Forest spa in 1904.

Chekhov's three periods in the short story genre—early sketches, stories influenced by Tolstoy, and later stories—comprise the

major stages of his fiction. The early sketches display many of the traits of popular fiction: swift development of action, superficial yet vivid characterization, and surprise endings. But while many of these pieces were written as humor, they also contain qualities that led Maxim Gorky to call them "tragic humor." Gorky wrote of Chekhov: "One has only to read his 'humorous' stories with attention to see what a lot of cruel and disgusting things, behind the humorous words and situations, had been observed by the author with sorrow and were concealed by him." Chekhov's Tolstoyan period was influenced primarily by the older writer's ideas on sexual abstinence, devotion to the plight of others, strict antimaterialism, and nonresistance to the natural evil of the temporal world. During this period Chekhov believed that literature had the power to effect positive change in the world and that it was obliged to critique the lives of its readers. In consequence, stories like "Niscij" ("The Beggar") were written to convey a message, though this message is nonetheless delivered with the subtle artistry and restraint Chekhov cultivated throughout his career. This second period of Chekhov's fiction includes many features characteristic of all his works. "Step" ("The Steppe"), which was the author's first story to appear in a serious literary journal, substitutes for the mechanical tensions of plot a tightly-strung network of images, character portraits, and dense actionless scenes of commonplace tedium. Rather than detracting from reader involvement, these qualities contribute to an overall effect of tense realism which serves its author's private vision of art and morality, a vision that led Chekhov to focus on the tragedies of everyday existence and portray them in a sympathetic yet unsentimental manner. In the final period of his fiction, Chekhov rejected and attacked his former master's ideas. "Duel" ("The Duel") critically examines the antisexuality message of Tolstoy's *Kreutzer Sonata*, and "Moya zhizn" ("My Life") elaborates on the adverse effects in general of the Tolstoyan dogma. In "Palata nomer 6" ("Ward Number 6"), a story of madness and misery, Chekhov opposed the doctrine of nonresistance to evil by depicting the downfall of one of its proponents. This is considered the period of Chekhov's full genius in the short story form, the era in which his art and insight achieved the level that placed him among the greatest figures in modern literature.

Chekhov's interest and participation in the theater had its origins in his schooldays at Taganrog, when he acted and wrote for the local playhouse. His first serious effort in drama was written during his residence in Moscow. This work, *Pyesa bez nazvaniya (That Worthless Fellow Platonov)*, initiated the first of two major periods of the author's dramatic writings. The works of this first dramatic period are characterized by the theatrical conventions and subject matter of the times. *Platonov*, a long and somewhat declamatory social drama, features a leading character whose reformist ideals are negated by the indifference of others and by his own ineffectuality. Chekhov's next drama, *Ivanov*, is less bulky and more realistic than its predecessor, though critics still view it as a theatrically exaggerated and traditional period piece. Written during the Tolstoyan phase of Chekhov's works, *Leshy (The Wood Demon)* was his first attempt at the artistic realism fully achieved only in his later dramas. This didactic morality play on the theme of vice and virtue is criticized for the same dramatic faults as the other works of this period.

The dramas of Chekhov's second period constitute his major work in the theater. These plays are primarily noted for their technique of "indirect action," a method whereby violent or intensely dramatic events are not shown on stage but occur during the intervals of the action as seen by the audience. The main action, then, is made up of conversations alluding to the unseen moments in the characters' lives. In this way Chekhov was able to study and convey more precisely the effects of crucial events on a character's personality. The first drama done in this manner was *The Seagull*. Written seven years after *The Wood Demon*, *The Seagull* was a complete failure in its opening performance at St. Petersburg. Two years later, however, it was produced successfully in Moscow under the direction of Constantin Stanislavsky, who emphasized, some critics say overemphasized, the more dismal aspects of Chekhov's "art of melancholy." Critics attribute the artistic success of *The Seagull* to a subtle interweaving of theme and character. The resulting scenario is one in which viewed action is reduced to a minimum and in which nuances of pacing and mood become paramount to the full realization of dramatic tension.

In *The Seagull* and the dramas that followed—*Uncle Vanya*, *The Three Sisters*, and *The Cherry Orchard*—the mood and meaning hovers somewhere between the tragic and the comic. *Uncle Vanya*, a revised version of *The Wood Demon*, stresses the influence of economic and social conditions on everyday life and the inability of people to change. *The Three Sisters* is the closest to tragedy among Chekhov's dramas, the play which most heavily contributes to his reputation as a portrayer of

futile existences and a forerunner of the modernist tradition of the absurd. Controversy has arisen over the interpretation of Chekhov's last play, *The Cherry Orchard*, which he subtitled "A Comedy," genuinely intending it to be viewed as such. Often perceived as a nostalgic parable on the passing of an older order in Russian history, this late work displays one of Chekhov's most important themes: the triumph of ignorance and vulgarity over the fragile traditions of elegance and nobility. Yet Chekhov was unhappy with the Moscow Art Theater's original production of *The Cherry Orchard*, which stressed, as many critics have, the pathos of the characters' situation. Dorothy Sayers, commenting on the inescapable humor of the play, wrote that "the whole tragedy of futility is that it never succeeds in achieving tragedy. In its blackest moments it is inevitably doomed to the comic gesture." Chekhov masterfully depicted the "ordinary drabness" of life, bringing to the stage a realism that eschewed the epic scale of traditional drama and a model of dramaturgy that demonstrated previously unrealized possibilities for the stage. Francis Fergusson wrote, "If Chekhov drastically reduced the dramatic art, he did so in full consciousness, and in obedience both to artistic scruples and to a strict sense of reality. He reduced the dramatic art to its ancient root, from which new growths are possible."

In comparison with the work of other great Russian authors, in particular the variety and vaulting ideological proportions of Tolstoy, Chekhov's stories and dramas are more uniform in mood and narrower in scope, frequently illustrating situations of hardship, boredom, and mundane suffering. The view of Chekhov as an utter pessimist, however, has always met with opposition, especially from those Soviet critics who see him as a chronicler of the degenerating land-owner classes during an era of imminent revolution. The exact relationship between Chekhov and his work has been a matter of interest for critics, and an attempt is often made to isolate the somber spirit of the stories and plays from the personal philosophy of their author. Critics such as Ronald Hingley have attempted to modify the view of a pessimistic Chekhov, while at the same time avoiding the equally erroneous image of an optimistic one. In either case, Chekhov's prominent stature in world literature is not a consequence of his philosophy or worldview as much as it is based on fiction and dramas executed with a phenomenal artistry which permanently altered the literary standards for these genres.

(See also *Short Story Criticism*, Vol. 2 and *Contemporary Authors*, Vol. 104.)

PRINCIPAL WORKS

Pyostrye rasskazy (short stories) 1886
Ivanov (drama) 1887
   [*Ivanoff* published in *Plays*, 1912]
Nevinnye rechi (short stories) 1887
V sumerkakh (short stories) 1887
Leshy (drama) 1889
   [*The Wood Demon*, 1926]
Rasskazy (short stories) 1889
Chayka (drama) 1896
   [*The Seagull* published in *Plays*, 1912]
*Dyadya Vanya (drama) 1899
   [*Uncle Vanya* published in *Plays*, 1912]
Chekhov: Polnoe sobranie sochinenii (short stories and dramas) 1900-04
Tri sestry (drama) 1901
   [*The Three Sisters*, 1922]

The Black Monk, and Other Stories   (short stories)   1903
Vishnevy sad   (drama)   1904
    [*The Cherry Garden*, 1908; also published as *The Cherry
    Orchard*, 1912]
The Kiss, and Other Stories   (short stories)   1908
Plays   (dramas)   1912
The Darling, and Other Stories   (short stories)   1916
The Duel, and Other Stories   (short stories)   1916
The Lady with the Dog, and Other Stories   (short stories)
    1917
The Party, and Other Stories   (short stories)   1917
The Wife, and Other Stories   (short stories)   1918
The Witch, and Other Stories   (short stories)   1918
The Bishop, and Other Stories   (short stories)   1919
The Chorus Girl, and Other Stories   (short stories)   1920
The Letters of Anton Chekhov   (letters)   1920
The Horse-Stealers, and Other Stories   (short stories)
    1921
The Schoolmaster, and Other Stories   (short stories)   1921
The Schoolmistress, and Other Stories   (short stories)
    1921
The Cook's Wedding, and Other Stories   (short stories)
    1922
Love, and Other Stories   (short stories)   1922
***Pyesa bez nazvaniya*   (drama)   [first publication] 1923
    [*That Worthless Fellow Platonov*, 1930]
Polnoe sobranie sochinenii i pisem A. P. Chekhova
    (dramas, short stories, notebooks, diaries, and letters)
    1944-51
The Oxford Chekhov. 9 vols.   (short stories and dramas)
    1964-80

*This work is a revision of the earlier *Leshy*.

**This work was written in 1881.

EMMA GOLDMAN   (essay date 1914)

[*Goldman was a Russian-born American libertarian and anarchist
who rose to fame in the United States and Europe during the
opening decades of the twentieth century. A proponent of free
speech, birth control, and other individual freedoms, she addressed these issues and the need for sweeping economic, political, and social revolution in numerous speeches and articles. In
the following excerpt from her book* The Social Significance of
Modern Drama, *she examines* The Seagull *and* The Cherry Orchard.]

When Anton Tchekhof first came to the fore, no less an authority than Tolstoy said: "Russia has given birth to another
Turgenev." The estimate was not overdrawn. Tchekhof was
indeed a modern Turgenev. Perhaps not as universal, because
Turgenev, having lived in western Europe, in close contact
with conditions outside of Russia, dealt with more variegated
aspects of life. But as a creative artist Tchekhof is fitted to
take his place with Turgenev.

Tchekhof is preëminently the master of short stories. Within
the limits of a few pages he paints the drama of human life
with its manifold tragic and comic colors, in its most intimate
reflex upon the characters who pass through the panorama. He
has been called a pessimist. As if one could miss the sun
without feeling the torture of utter darkness!

Tchekhof wrote during the gloomiest period of Russian life,
at a time when the reaction had drowned the revolution in the
blood of the young generation,—when the Tsar had choked
the very breath out of young Russia. The intellectuals were
deprived of every outlet: all the social channels were closed to
them, and they found themselves without hope or faith, not
having yet learned to make common cause with the people.

Tchekhof could not escape the atmosphere which darkened the
horizon of almost the whole of Russia. It was because he so
intensely felt its oppressive weight that he longed for air, for
light, for new and vital ideas. To awaken the same yearning
and faith in others, he had to picture life as it was, in all its
wretchedness and horror.

This he did in *The Seagull*, while in *The Cherry Orchard* he
holds out the hope of a new and brighter day.

In *The Seagull* the young artist, *Constantine Treplef*, seeks new
forms, new modes of expression. He is tired of the old academic
ways, the beaten track; he is disgusted with the endless imitative methods, no one apparently capable of an original thought.

Constantine has written a play; the principal part is to be acted
by *Nina*, a beautiful girl with whom *Constantine* is in love.
He arranges the first performance to take place on the occasion
of his mother's vacation in the country.

She herself—known as *Mme. Arcadina*—is a famous actress
of the old school. She knows how to show off her charms to
advantage, to parade her beautiful gowns, to faint and die
gracefully before the footlights; but she does not know how to
live her part on the stage. *Mme. Arcadina* is the type of artist
who lacks all conception of the relation between art and life.
Barren of vision and empty of heart, her only criterion is public
approval and material success. Needless to say, she cannot
understand her son. She considers him decadent, a foolish rebel
who wants to undermine the settled canons of dramatic art.
Constantine sums up his mother's personality in the following
manner:

> TREPLEF. She is a psychological curiosity, is my
> mother. A clever and gifted woman, who can cry
> over a novel, will reel you off all Nekrassov's poems
> by heart, and is the perfection of a sick nurse; but
> venture to praise Eleonora Duse before her! Oho! ho!
> You must praise nobody but her, write about her,
> shout about her, and go into ecstasies over her won-
> derful performance in *La Dame aux Camélias*, or
> *The Fumes of Life;* but as she cannot have these
> intoxicating pleasures down here in the country, she's
> bored and gets spiteful. . . . She loves the stage; she
> thinks that she is advancing the cause of humanity
> and her sacred art; but I regard the stage of to-day
> as mere routine and prejudice. When the curtain goes
> up and the gifted beings, the high priests of the sacred
> art, appear by electric light, in a room with three
> sides to it, representing how people eat, drink, love,
> walk and wear their jackets; when they strive to squeeze
> out a moral from the flat, vulgar pictures and the
> flat, vulgar phrases, a little tiny moral, easy to com-
> prehend and handy for home consumption, when in
> a thousand variations they offer me always the same
> thing over and over and over again—then I take to
> my heels and run, as Maupassant ran from the Eiffel
> Tower, which crushed his brain by its overwhelming
> vulgarity. . . . We must have new formulae. That's
> what we want. And if there are none, then it's better
> to have nothing at all.

With *Mme. Arcadina* is her lover, *Trigorin,* a successful writer. When he began his literary career, he possessed originality and strength. But gradually writing became a habit: the publishers constantly demand new books, and he supplies them.

Oh, the slavery of being an "arrived" artist, forging new chains for oneself with every "best seller"! Such is the position of *Trigorin:* he hates his work as the worst drudgery. Exhausted of ideas, all life and human relations serve him only as material for copy.

Nina, innocent of the ways of the world and saturated with the false romanticism of *Trigorin's* works, does not see the man but the celebrated artist. She is carried away by his fame and stirred by his presence; an infatuation with him quickly replaces her affection for *Constantine.* To her *Trigorin* embodies her dream of a brilliant and interesting life.

> NINA. How I envy you, if you but knew it! How different are the lots of different people! Some can hardly drag on their tedious, insignificant existence; they are all alike, all miserable; others, like you, for instance—you are one in a million—are blessed with a brilliant, interesting life, all full of meaning. . . . You are happy. . . . What a delightful life yours is!

> TRIGORIN. What is there so fine about it? Day and night I am obsessed by the same persistent thought; I must write, I must write, I must write. . . . No sooner have I finished one story than I am somehow compelled to write another, then a third, and after the third a fourth. . . . I have no rest for myself; I feel that I am devouring my own life. . . . I've never satisfied *myself.* . . . I have the feeling for nature; it wakes a passion in me, an irresistible desire to write. But I am something more than a landscape painter; I'm a citizen as well; I love my country, I love the people; I feel that if I am a writer I am bound to speak of the people, of its suffering, of its future, to speak of science, of the rights of man, etc., etc.; and I speak about it all, volubly, and am attacked angrily in return by everyone; I dart from side to side like a fox run down by hounds; I see that life and science fly farther and farther ahead of me, and I fall farther and farther behind, like the countryman running after the train; and in the end I feel that the only thing I can write of is the landscape, and in everything else I am untrue to life, false to the very marrow of my bones.

Constantine realizes that *Nina* is slipping away from him. The situation is aggravated by the constant friction with his mother and his despair at the lack of encouragement for his art. In a fit of despondency he attempts suicide, but without success. His mother, although nursing him back to health, is infuriated at her son's "foolishness," his inability to adapt himself to conditions, his impractical ideas. She decides to leave, accompanied by *Trigorin.* On the day of their departure *Nina* and *Trigorin* meet once more. The girl tells him of her ambition to become an actress, and, encouraged by him, follows him to the city.

Two years later *Mme. Arcadina,* still full of her idle triumphs, returns to her estate. *Trigorin* is again with her still haunted by the need of copy.

Constantine has in the interim matured considerably. Although he has made himself heard as a writer, he nevertheless feels that life to-day has no place for such as he: that sincerity in art is not wanted. His mother is with him, but she only serves

to emphasize the flatness of his surroundings. He loves her, but her ways jar him and drive him into seclusion.

Nina, too, has returned to her native place, broken in body and spirit. Partly because of the memory of her past affection for *Constantine,* and mainly because she learns of *Trigorin's* presence, she is drawn to the place where two years before she had dreamed of the beauty of an artistic career. The cruel struggle for recognition, the bitter disappointment in her relation with *Trigorin,* the care of a child and poor health have combined to change the romantic child into a sad woman.

Constantine still loves her. He pleads with her to go away with him, to begin a new life. But it is too late. The lure of the footlights is beckoning to *Nina;* she returns to the stage. *Constantine,* unable to stand the loneliness of his life and the mercenary demands upon his art, kills himself.

To the Anglo-Saxon mind such an ending is pessimism,—defeat. Often, however, apparent defeat is in reality the truest success. For is not success, as commonly understood, but too frequently bought at the expense of character and idealism?

The Seagull is not defeat. As long as there is still such material in society as the Constantines—men and women who would rather die than compromise with the sordidness of life—there is hope for humanity. If the Constantines perish, it is the social fault,—our indifference to, and lack of appreciation of, the real values that alone advance the fuller and more complete life of the race.

The Cherry Orchard is Tchekhof's prophetic song. In this play he depicts three stages of social development and their reflex in literature.

Mme. Ranevsky, the owner of the cherry orchard, an estate celebrated far and wide for its beauty and historic traditions, is deeply attached to the family place. She loves it for its romanticism: nightingales sing in the orchard, accompanying the wooing of lovers. She is devoted to it because of the memory of her ancestors and because of the many tender ties which bind her to the orchard. The same feeling and reverence is entertained by her brother *Leonid Gayef.* They are expressed in the *Ode to an Old Family Cupboard:*

> GAYEF. Beloved and venerable cupboard; honor and glory to your existence, which for more than a hundred years has been directed to the noble ideals of justice and virtue. Your silent summons to profitable labor has never weakened in all these hundred years. You have upheld the courage of succeeding generations of human kind: you have upheld faith in a better future and cherished in us ideals of goodness and social consciousness.

But the social consciousness of *Gayef* and of his sister is of a paternal nature: the attitude of the aristocracy toward its serfs. It is a paternalism that takes no account of the freedom and happiness of the people,—the romanticism of a dying class.

Mme. Ranevsky is impoverished. The cherry orchard is heavily mortgaged and as romance and sentiment cannot liquidate debts, the beautiful estate falls into the cruel hands of commercialism.

The merchant *Yermolai Lopakhin* buys the place. He is in ecstasy over his newly acquired possession. He the owner—he who had risen from the serfs of the former master of the orchard!

> LOPAKHIN. Just think of it! The cherry orchard is mine! Mine! Tell me that I'm drunk; tell me that I'm off my head; tell me that it's all a dream!. . . If only

my father and my grandfather could rise from their graves and see the whole affair, how their Yermolai, their bogged and ignorant Yermolai, who used to run about barefooted in the winter, how this same Yermolai had bought a property that hasn't its equal for beauty anywhere in the whole world! I have bought the property where my father and my grandfather were slaves, where they weren't even allowed into the kitchen.

A new epoch begins in the cherry orchard. On the ruins of romanticism and aristocratic ease there rises commercialism, its iron hand yoking nature, devastating her beauty, and robbing her of all radiance.

With the greed of rich returns, *Lopakhin* cries, "Lay the ax to the cherry orchard, come and see the trees fall down! We'll fill the place with villas."

Materialism reigns supreme; it lords the orchard with mighty hand, and in the frenzy of its triumph believes itself in control of the bodies and souls of men. But in the madness of conquest it has discounted a stubborn obstacle—the spirit of idealism. It is symbolized in *Peter Trophimof,* "the perpetual student," and *Anya,* the young daughter of *Mme. Ranevsky.* The "wonderful achievements" of the materialistic age do not enthuse them; they have emancipated themselves from the Lopakhin idol as well as from their aristocratic traditions.

> ANYA. Why is it that I no longer love the cherry orchard as I did? I used to love it so tenderly; I thought there was no better place on earth than our garden.
>
> TROPHIMOF. All Russia is our garden. The earth is great and beautiful; it is full of wonderful places. Think, Anya, your grandfather, your great-grandfather and all your ancestors were serf-owners, owners of living souls. Do not human spirits look out at you from every tree in the orchard, from every leaf and every stem? Do you not hear human voices?. . . Oh! it is terrible. Your orchard frightens me. When I walk through it in the evening or at night, the rugged bark on the trees glows with a dim light, and the cherry trees seem to see all that happened a hundred and two hundred years ago in painful and oppressive dreams. Well, well, we have fallen at least two hundred years beyond the times. We have achieved nothing at all as yet; we have not made up our minds how we stand with the past; we only philosophize, complain of boredom, or drink vodka. It is so plain that, before we can live in the present, we must first redeem the past, and have done with it.
>
> ANYA. The house we live in has long since ceased to be our house; I shall go away.
>
> TROPHIMOF. If you have the household keys, throw them in the well and go away. Be free, be free as the wind. . . . I am hungry as the winter; I am sick, anxious, poor as a beggar. Fate has tossed me hither and thither; I have been everywhere, everywhere. But everywhere I have been, every minute, day and night, my soul has been full of mysterious anticipations. I feel the approach of happiness, Anya; I see it coming . . . it is coming towards us, nearer and nearer; I can hear the sound of its footsteps. . . . And if we do not see it, if we do not know it, what does it matter? Others will see it.

The new generation, on the threshold of the new epoch, hears the approaching footsteps of the Future. And even if the Anyas and Trophimofs of to-day will not see it, others will.

It was not given to Anton Tchekhof to see it with his bodily eyes. But his prophetic vision beheld the coming of the New Day, and with powerful pen he proclaimed it, that others might see it. Far from being a pessimist, as charged by unintelligent critics, his faith was strong in the possibilities of liberty.

This is the inspiring message of *The Cherry Orchard.* (pp. 283-93)

Emma Goldman, "Anton Tchekhof," in her The Social Significance of the Modern Drama, *Richard G. Badger, 1914, pp. 283-93.*

STORM JAMESON   (essay date 1920)

[*Jameson is one of England's leading writers of the "family chronicle" novel, in the tradition of John Galsworthy and Arnold Bennett. A prolific author with liberal sympathies, she is frequently concerned, in her literary criticism as in her novels, with the changes in Western mores occasioned by World War I. In the following excerpt, Jameson discusses what she considers flaws in Chekhov's drama.*]

The drama of Anton Tchekhov is concerned, not with the facts of everyday life, but with life itself, its value and its meaning. Whereas Tolstoy and Gorki sought the meaning in an ideal of life that a social revolution might accomplish, Tchekhov reached deeper, to question the value of life, to criticise its forms. In this, his dramatic ideal differs from that of the drama of ideas. Mr Shaw, master of that form, criticises not life, but manners: the drama of ideas, as a whole, criticises conditions: its value is, in consequence, constantly decreasing. Its present importance, being a question of a knowledge of conditions, is limited by the quality of the intellect behind it as much as by the quality of dramatic art in its expression. At best, it is not reality but a phase of reality. The drama of Tchekhov is the only modern realism that has attempted a vision of reality. For reality is not a matter of facts: it is a matter of artistic conception. In the strictest sense of the term, art creates life. Life is an artist's vision of it. For this purpose, intellect is not sufficient. Beyond intellect, greater than intellect, it needs the supreme creative activity that makes order in the disorder confronting an untutored vision of life, that is compelled to interpret what it sees, because mastery and interpretation are the first necessity of its existence. Ibsen had such a power: he interpreted the life of small towns in the light of humanity. Alone of those who have succeeded him in the way of realism, Tchekhov has the same creative need. In his plays of the Russian "intellectuals" he sought to express the rhythm of life. His men and women are types of humanity, questioning, enduring, rarely mastering life. They hope or despair, but always life itself is the measure of their being. They reject the ease of mental and spiritual sloth. They know that to strive is to suffer, and that it is better to suffer than not to strive and not to understand. (pp. 245-46)

Further, Tchekhov had a rare understanding of the relation of life and art. He saw life in the average realist drama a mean and narrow thing; and knew that its debasement implied the debasement of art. For the artist creates life, and the forms of life, and if the thing he creates be weak and valueless, his art and the forms of his art are like unto it. Even so, the form of the modern suburban drama befits the value of its content: it is poor-spirited, it means nothing to humanity, it steals and defaces life. Against the paltry conception and worse execution of this late realism, Tchekhov flung an artist's scorn of incompetence. Treplieff protests in *The Seagull.* "The theatre is merely the vehicle of convention and prejudice. When the curtain rises on that little three-walled room, when those mighty geniuses, those high priests of art, show us people in the act of eating, drinking, loving, walking, and wearing their coats, and attempt to extract a moral fit for household use, from their insipid talk; when playwrights give us under a thousand different guises the same, same, same old stuff, then I must needs run from it, as Maupassant ran from the Eiffel Tower that was about to crush him by its vulgarity.'' Tchekhov's own drama attempts a new form: it is hardly successful, and in consequence his new conception of life hardly realised. But the vision is there, and the movement of life: to be ignored or understood, and once understood to be for ever held.

At best, the distinction of Tolstoi's peasants and Gorki's outcasts is the distinction of a dream and a spirit that come from the dramatist himself. In themselves, they have no more value for drama than the maundering peasants and cursing outcasts of the average hovel and doss-house play. Tchekhov, artist where Tolstoi and Gorki were merely idealists, knew that distinctive characters are the first necessity of a great play. The people of his drama come from the educated classes of the provinces; they have intellect, and artistic capacity or imaginative charm. Their ideas are in advance of the civilization of Europe; their capacity for feeling and understanding is at once the promise of strength and a threat of weakness. Tchekhov wrote during the worst years of the nineteenth century, when their life was incredibly hopeless. Enslaved by the slavery of a lower class, they could do nothing to lift themselves or the people. The death of Alexander II ended a period of high hope and activity. The glorious movement of young people, the effort of the ''intellectuals'' to put their knowledge at the service of a revolution, were crushed out. The eighties were a horrible chaos of despair and treachery. The intellectuals were driven back on themselves, and the aimless monotony of the life in this old Russia—''The people here do no more than eat, drink, sleep, and die. Others are born who eat, drink, and sleep in their turn; and lest boredom should destroy them altogether, they seek change in scandal, vodka, cards, and intrigue. . . . Wives are unfaithful to their husbands and the husbands lie and pretend they have seen nothing. The vulgar tradition descends upon the children, clouding their minds until the spark of divinity within them is extinguished, and they grow up to be just such pitiable, trivial, commonplace corpses as their fathers and mothers were before them. Shame upon such a life!''

Tchekhov's drama is a cry from the heart of their despair. The younger men came from college to their estates, hopes and ideals high, determined to lift the misery of the people by their own efforts. For a time they struggled, then slowly the apathy and meanness of the life round them choked strength and energy out of them. Opposition might have saved them: indifference gave them despair and weakness. They lost faith in themselves, finally in their ideals. After that, only the terrible weariness of eternal card-parties, the feeble desire for life and the bitter realisation of impotence. Listen to Ivanoff,—

> I was young once: I have been eager and sincere and intelligent. I have loved and hated and believed as no one else has. I have worked and hoped and tilted against windmills with the strength of ten—not sparing my strength, not knowing what life was. I shouldered a load that broke my back. I drank, I worked, I excited myself, my energy knew no bounds. Tell me, could I have done otherwise? There are so few of us, and so much to do, so much to do! And see how cruelly fate has avenged herself on me, who fought with her so bravely! I am a broken man. I am old at thirty. I have submitted myself to old age.

> With a heavy head and a sluggish mind, weary, used up, discouraged, without faith or love, or an object in life, I wander like a shadow among other men, not knowing why I am alive or what it is that I want. Love seems to me to be folly, caressses false. I see no sense in working or playing, and all passionate speeches seem insipid and tiresome. So I carry my sadness with me wherever I go; a cold weariness, a discontent, a horror of life. Before you stands a man who at thirty-five is disillusioned, wearied by fruitless effort, burning with shame, and mocking at his own weakness.

Failure as Ivanoff is, he has rebelled. That is his distinction and his profound interest. It is the interest and distinction of all Tchekhov's characters. They have failed: but they were worth saving, and have spent their strength in the vain effort.

This protest and continual struggle is the spirit that informs Tchekhov's vision of life. His dramatic method suggests it very incompletely. The atmosphere of the plays is perfect in their sense of despair and futile effort. Their technique is new: the characters wander across the stage in the inconsequent fashion of life, talking perpetually. They are constantly interrupted and drift away, but the talk goes on. It is excellent; the distinctive speech of cultured, thoughtful people. Gradually a vision of them shapes itself from their conversation, intimate, of intense interest. Beyond them a vision of life unrolls from their words and slow self-revelation. Behind the individual man is humanity and the vision of humanity. The past conditions him, the future calls him: his present mastery or submission to the past are making the years to come. Strife is born of this ceaseless need of the future to free itself from the past. Life *is* this continued struggle, its confusion given coherence and value by an understanding of its eternal creative need. Only in this effort towards the highest ideal he knows may a man solve the problem of life. Himself, his use of his inheritance, determine his future and the future of humanity. Then what is failure, provided the protest has been made in all the strength of will and action? Some such vision is the significance of all Tchekhov's plays. There is *The Seagull.* Here the mediocre art that imitates life is opposed to the activity of the creative mind. The egoism of success, the life that sponges on life, the discipline of pain are here, in the selfishness of Arkadina, famous actress, the weak mischief wrought by Trigorin, and the final victory of Nina. And above the waste of fine lives and brave effort is the sense of a triumphant activity that creates new forms in destroying old. The artist dies, but life and art, the spirit of life, change and are re-created without end.

The characters of *The Seagull,* as of all the plays, elude our grasp. A subtle weakness, which is half want of technical skill, half a distrust of life, destroys their complete reality. In their fragmentary talk the rhythm of their lives and of all life is but half-articulate. Take *Uncle Vanya.* It is another story of lost effort. For years Sonia, daughter of Serebrakoff, and Voitski, her uncle, have toiled on her father's estate, wasting youth and strength to keep up his position as Professor. He is utterly selfish, taking their slavery as his right, wearing out Helena, his second wife, with his ceaseless demands. When it is too late, Voitski sees the uselessness of the sacrifice and tries to shoot himself. He is prevented, and an agony of shame is added to his misery. When Helena and her husband come to the estate, her beauty destroys Sonia's poor dream of happiness. And with their return to St Petersburg, the terrible despair of disillusion falls on the two left behind. They turn again to the weary slavery of the past; and Sonia's resignation is almost intolerably sad.

We shall live, Uncle Vanya. We shall live through the long procession of days before us; we shall patiently bear the trials that fate imposes on us; we shall work for others without rest, both now and when we are old; and when our last hour comes, we shall meet it humbly, and there beyond the grave we shall say that we have suffered and wept, that our life was bitter, and God will have pity on us. . . . We shall rest—we shall rest.

The terrible waste of life is in this play, and the loneliness in which the souls of all men move, and the deathless courage of the spirit of man. But it is ill-realised. Throughout, the words are uneasy in their sense of so much unsaid. It is as though the characters struggled to free themselves from the sound of their speech; for a moment they come to the verge of clear revelation, and in a moment slip back into the shadows. Their intense anxiety to be clear deepens the sense of effort; they are near and unapproachable. Tchekhov's is the imagination of an artist; his craftsmanship never comparable with that of dramatists far less important.

This, their technical weakness, is the first reason for the comparative failure of his plays. The second is a weakness of spirit. Tchekhov's need to solve the problem of life carried him further than the same need carried Tolstoi and Gorki. They were satisfied with their answers. Tchekhov is not: he is wise enough to know that there is no answer; artist enough to accept the truth and attempt to subdue it to the forms of art, but the disillusion that follows on such knowledge demands supreme strength. Tchekhov's art, exhausted by its struggle with life, by the weight of the despair and misery it shouldered, has no such supreme power. The creative genius that makes the greatness of his drama wearies itself against a distrust of life. The result is a want of dramatic grasp, the passing weakness of doubt, the perpetual weakness of divided effort. In *The Three Sisters,* when the hope that flamed so swiftly has sunk down in the darkness, Irina cries through her anguish. "There will come a time when everybody will know why, for what purpose there is all this suffering, and there will be no more mysteries. . . ." But Tchekhov does not himself believe this. His faith is a desperate shrinking from unfaith, his hope rooted in utter hopelessness.

The Cherry Orchard is the only play that suggests the coming of new life into the exhausted provinces. It is also the least convincing in its faith, the clearest in its disillusion. Lophakhin alone has any power to shape his future or see the possibility of change; and he mistrusts and is almost ashamed of himself. Beyond the hope and effort of youth, the dramatist sees the inevitable failure, the decay of life even now in the germ. Some one speaks of the great misfortune. "What great misfortune?" "The Liberation." The old life is incapable of change, the new hurries on, hopeful because it is ignorant. In no other play is Tchekhov so hopeless, so unable to see beyond disillusion to the last undying reality.

Nevertheless, he has seen. He knows that life itself is perpetual discontent, with no peace attainable. The value of his drama lies in the courage with which, for the most part, it faces and masters disillusion. Its broken rhythm holds the meaning of life: effort, new life, decay, and fresh creative effort. With that, an undertsanding that art suffers as life is degraded, that the creative activity constantly changing life must shatter the old forms of art to find expression for the new spirit. Because he had the vision, and because he protested, in the distinction of his characters and speech, in his drama's unresting note of revolt against surrender to worn-out forms of life and art,

Tchekhov is a great artist. He is not a great dramatist, but his plays, faulty as they are, lie on the threshold of the future. (pp. 246-53)

Storm Jameson, "The Drama of Italy and Spain," in her Modern Drama in Europe, W. Collins Sons & Co. Ltd., 1920, pp. 221-70.

PETER M. BITSILLI (essay date 1942)

[*Bitsilli was a Bulgarian critic and educator. In the following excerpt, he argues that Chekhov's plays do not conform to the conventional requirements for dramatic production, which accounts for the difficulties in staging them successfully, and observes that these works more closely resemble fiction narratives than dramas.*]

The most knowledgeable critic of Chekhov's drama, S. Balukhaty, has convincingly shown the many innovations in Chekhov's drama and has subtly analyzed those devices whereby the playwright renders on stage life as it really is. Already during his lifetime Chekhov was duly credited for the contributions he made to the theater. Chekhov's name, as we know, was linked with the Moscow Art Theater, whose directions shared his aspirations for the drama.

It was primarily the performance of Chekhov's plays at the Art Theater that established a new era in the history of Russian theater. It is puzzling, therefore, that despite Chekhov's close association with Stanislavsky and Nemirovich-Danchenko, and despite their efforts to understand the spirit of Chekhov's art, their production of his last play, *The Cherry Orchard,* in which his dramatic intentions were fully realized, left Chekhov profoundly dissatisfied. He wrote to his wife:

> Nemirovich and Alekseev (Stanislavsky) positively fail to see what I wrote in my play, and I am ready to wager that neither of them has read it carefully even once.

Compare this to what he said to E. P. Karpov:

> Is this really my *Cherry Orchard?.* . . Are these really my types?. . . With the exception of two or three in the cast, none of this is mine. . . . I write of life. . . . It is a gray, everyday life . . . but not this tedious whining. . . . They make of me either a crybaby or simply a dull writer.

Evidently Chekhov was displeased with Stanislavsky's efforts to emphasize the emotional tone of the play. Stanislavsky strove to realize this tone (as is clear from his director's remarks in the text of *The Seagull*) by providing elaborate comments on gesticulation, mimicry and details which would add brilliance, clarity and concreteness to the images. This is precisely what Meyerhold criticized.

> In Meyerhold's opinion [writes S. Balukhaty] the use of images which are impressionistically scattered onto a canvas makes up the basic characteristic of Chekhov's dramatic style; it provides the director with material suitable for filling out the characters into bright, defined figures (types). Hence, the characteristic enthusiasm of directors for details which distract from the picture as a whole.

He then quotes Meyerhold's letter to Chekhov about the staging of *The Cherry Orchard:*

> Your play is abstract, like a Chaikovsky symphony. The director, first of all, ought to sense it with his ear. In the third act, unnoticed by anyone, against

the background of stupid patter, Horror enters—it is just this "patter" which should be heard: "The cherry orchard is sold." Dancing. "Sold." And so on until the end.

Meyerhold considered Chekhov a symbolist and thought that his plays should be staged symbolically, not realistically (as in the Art Theater). In a way he was right. He may have understood Chekhov more profoundly than Chekhov himself.

Every work of art, like every person, has petty traits which at first glance may seem insignificant; they are, in fact, very characteristic—like birth marks—and the coincidences to be found are very revealing. In **The Cherry Orchard** we find a twice-repeated stage direction:

> They all sit, deep in thought. It is quiet. Only Firs' muttering is audible. Suddenly a distant sound is heard, as if coming from the sky, the sound of a breaking string, mournfully dying away.

Consider the end of the play:

> A protracted sound is heard, as if coming from the sky, the sound of a breaking string, mournfully dying away.

Evidently Blok found something in this stage direction which had an innate appeal; he used it in "The Song of Destiny" ["Pesnya sud'by"]:

> At this moment a sound is carried from the plain—tender, soft, musical: as if a crow cawed or someone touched a taut string.

I will cite one other parallel, from **"Three Years"**:

> Yartsev drove on farther to his place. . . . He dozed off, swaying in his seat and thinking about the play. Suddenly he thought he heard a fearsome noise, a clanking, and shouting in some strange tongue, which might have been Kalmuck; he saw a village overcome by flames, and neighboring forests, covered with hoar frost, and light pink from the fire could be seen all around in the distance . . . ; some kind of savage people, on horseback and on foot, swept through the village, both men and horses just as crimson as the fire's glow in the sky.
>
> "The Polovtsy," thought Yartsev.
>
> One of them—an old man with a fearsome, bloody face, covered with burns—was tying a young girl with a pale, Russian face to his saddle. The old man was shouting wildly about something, and the girl gazed sadly, thoughtfully. . . .

How much this excerpt shares with sections from Blok's cycle, "Homeland" ["Rodina"]! They have in common not only themes, but more importantly, tone and coloring. Symbolists recognized their predecessor in the later Chekhov. Interestingly, Chekhov himself advised Suvorin to produce Maeterlinck's plays and wrote that "were [he] the director of [Suvorin's] theater, then . . . he would have made it decadent in two years. . . . Perhaps the theater would seem strange, but, nevertheless, it would have its own physiognomy."

A similarity to the Symbolists notwithstanding, there is no doubt that Chekhov was adamant on the subject of truthfulness and naturalness in art—i.e., the correspondence of art with everyday reality. He would have been horrified had **The Cherry Orchard** or **The Seagull** been produced as was the *The Puppet Show* [*Balaganchik*] or *The Unknown Lady* [*Neznakomka*], or produced as Treplev had wanted to stage his "mystery play." And to a degree he would have been right. Chekhov stood

midway between realism and symbolism. Only from a pseudo-historical, doctrinaire point of view would it be possible to regard *ipso facto* the phenomena of a transitional period as imperfect. We have seen that in his best works Chekhov developed his own form wholly appropriate to their idea and content. He was able to attain complete artistic perfection by merging "genre" and "landscape" into one; he did not frame characters with setting, but showed both people and setting as a manifestation of a single life.

It is evident that his dramatic works do not succeed in this respect. Otherwise, how can one explain the failure of his plays on the stage? S. Balukhaty is correct in saying that Chekhov the dramatist remained true to himself; in the drama he struggled with various traditions and aspired to overcome all sorts of conventions. We concede that he found new means to express that same vision of life in the drama which is reflected in his narrative works. His plays do not divide characters into "major" and "minor figures"; they lack the traditional "intrigue" which begins with a "conflict" and ends with a "resolution." His task here, as in his stories, is to show in one segment of time—however incidental or trivial it may be—all life as a single process, having neither beginning nor end. But S. Balukhaty has not given sufficient attention to Chekhov's frequent lack of consistency in his struggle with scenic traditions and dramatic conventions. Above all, he has not considered the significance of the many incongruities which Chekhov let slip by; the mere fact of these inconsistencies is extremely important.

I will discuss some of the most significant examples. Let me first consider the final scene of **The Wood Demon** [*Leshii*], (in which there happens to be a "resolution"). More important than the fact of a denouement is that of all the possible resolutions, Chekhov chose the most stereotyped: the "kind old man" "arranges"—moreover quite unexpectedly—the "happiness" of two young couples. In the third act of **Uncle Vanya** [*Dyadya Vanya*] Astrov and Elena Andreevna are embracing and do not notice when Voinitsky appears on stage. S. Balukhaty mentions the interesting fact that Chekhov himself seems to parody this banal device in Act Four of the same play. As he is saying good-bye to Elena Andreevna, Astrov tells her: "As long as there is no one here, let me kiss you before Uncle Vanya comes in with his bouquet." The same shortcoming occurs in **The Cherry Orchard**. Anya appears on stage, unnoticed by Gaev and Varya, and overhears what Gaev is saying about her mother; this is a hackneyed device of old-fashioned drama.

The farther Chekhov progressed in this artistic development, the more subtly, the more carefully and the more diversely did he reveal the traits of a given personality, and the qualities which characterized him as a "type"—be he a representative of a certain social milieu, an historical moment, or an expression of some idea or human psychic feature. We find this in **The Three Sisters**, when Soleny continually takes out a bottle of perfume and sprinkles it on himself; this oft-repeated action ultimately becomes boring and irritating. It is nothing more than an unsuccessful method of deprecating this pseudo-Lermontovian character.

There is an analogous example of deprecation in **Uncle Vanya**. I have in mind Astrov. His prototype, Khrushchov in **The Wood Demon**, still fits into the hero mold: he is a positive type. Linked to Khrushchov is Fedor Ivanych who is "dissolute" and abuses the traits of his own "generous nature." Thus, in **Uncle Vanya**, a reworking of **The Wood Demon**, Chekhov has created an amalgam of Khrushchov and Fedor Ivanych. Like Khrushchov, Astrov utters the same noble speeches, imbued with lofty ideas, and without warning he sometimes repeats the cynical verbal pranks of Fedor Ivanych. That, however, does not make him more real or more ordinary. This process of character "fabrication" provides evidence against Chekhov the dramatist; it shows that Chekhov's creativity was on the wane when he began to write for the theater.

I would point out, moreover, that Chekhov is far from being consistent in his attempt to replace stage "types" with real people. Epikhodov in **The Cherry Orchard** and the kind old nurse in **Uncle Vanya** are more clearly pure "types" than people.

My purpose in mentioning such evidence will become apparent if we consider the above relationship to a striking feature common to all Chekhov's plays. Chekhov continually strove for maximum verisimilitude and fought against anything which rang of falseness; ultimately he accomplished this in his stories. The characters in his plays, however, indulge in melodramatic outpouring of feelings, they argue emotionally about topics from "progressive articles," using a "literary" language full of complex sentences which people would ordinarily never use in conversation. This lack of verisimilitude is even more striking and shocking when his characters suddenly switch to everyday, conversational language. In view of this, one might be convinced that Chekhov was betrayed by his artistic powers when he began writing drama. It prompts one to think that in a certain respect people (like Tolstoy, for example) were correct in thinking that drama was something alien to Chekhov.

How can we explain this? I think it may be that the inner form of the drama was utterly incongruous with his vision of life. Every drama, whether it be "classical," "realistic," or "symbolic," is composed of action which occurs *hic et nunc* ["here and now"] in the present, in the literal meaning of the word. Whether the characters are "classical heroes" or "comic types," embodying some human "passion," "virtue" or "vice," or whether, as in "realistic" drama, they represent certain aspects of "everyday reality" or of social mores, or finally, whether they personify certain intelligible quantities as in "symbolic" drama—regardless of the extent to which they are endowed with ordinary human characteristics—they are still pure monads. In drama everyday life is shown statically and not dynamically, from the point of view of being, not of becoming; true, it is shown as a struggle, as a series of external or internal conflicts, but these conflicts are revealed outside of real time. No matter how boldly dramatists of the Augustan Age in England and elsewhere in the nineteenth century violated the principle of "unity of time," which confined the action to a twenty-four hour period (conventionally regarded as "present" time), dramatic action was, nevertheless, perceived as occurring in the "extended present." The reason is that the *dramatis personae*—despite the complexity of their characters, revealed in different ways in different "scenes" ("acts")—are shown statically and not dynamically; the conflict, intrigue and resolution are all separate moments of a comprehensible existence and not of an evolutionary process.

The design of Chekhov's drama is of a wholly different nature. The monads, who reveal themselves as much by their actions as in their speeches, are replaced in the plays by people transplanted from his stories. As in the stories, they are shown "flashing by," emerging from the past and ready at any moment to be submerged into the past. In his stories Chekhov comes to the aid of his characters as well as of his readers; he remembers and reflects along with them and for them; he combines his "genre" with his "landscape" into a single whole, and his characters are no more than symbols, merely elements of one poetic image. On stage they are unwittingly forced to become somewhat independent—and here they prove to be helpless; they remain the same patients, and not agents, not *dramatis personae*.

It is significant that Chekhov went to great lengths, even here, to "help" his characters. I have in mind certain stage directions in **The Cherry Orchard**, which have already been pointed out by S. Balukhaty:

> A room *which to this day is called the nursery.* . . . Dawn is breaking, and the sun will soon be up. It is already May . . . , *but it is cold everywhere*, and there is a morning frost.

> An open field. A small tumble-down old church, *long since abandoned* . . . , large stones that *apparently once were* tombstones. . . . There is a row of telegraph poles in the distance, and far, far away on the horizon one can make out the faint outlines of a city, *which is only visible in very fine, clear weather.*

Or about Anna we read: "Her calm mood returned."

The underscored phrases are clearly intended for a reader, rather than for a director. It is as if Chekhov occasionally forgot that he was writing for the stage. Certain contemporary critics had good cause to remark that his plays were more suited for reading than for staging. If we delete all these stage directions (and there are many), the total effect is diminished. It is simply not possible to show these directions on stage. Such details attest that Chekhov did not achieve complete mastery of the inner form of the drama. It is no accident that his best play in this respect, **The Cherry Orchard,** more closely resembles the short story or novella than any of his other plays. We have already mentioned that Chekhov was particularly dissatisfied with its staging; the Moscow Art Theater was not responsible for this failure, however, but Chekhov himself.

We can best explain Chekhov's theater by contrasting it to Gogol's. The *dramatis personae* in *The Inspector General* [*Revizor*] and *The Marriage* [*Zhenit'ba*] essentially are deprived of character too, but in a completely different sense. Chekhov's *dramatis personae* lack character because they do not possess enough will power to realize their desires. Gogol's figures, by contrast, lack character because in general they have no personal desires. For example, when Khlestakov first appears on stage, basically he wants one thing only—to eat. Gogol's characters have an almost animal relationship to life; they react spontaneously to outside stimuli, especially to anything which might for some reason inspire fear. We find only one such character in Chekhov—"The Man in a Case." Like animals, because of their complete emotional and spiritual void, they easily submit to "training" and can be filled with any content one wishes. Unbeknownst even to himself, Khlestakov suddenly becomes an imposter and an extortionist, automatically playing and then gradually assuming the role which has been imposed on him by the provincial officials. The same thing occurs in *The Marriage;* all the major characters seem possessed by something. They submit to external suggestion: for example, when Kochkarev plays with Agafya Tikhonovna or Podkolesin as if they were puppets; or they submit to a kind of auto-suggestion, as in the case of Kochkarev who does not understand what forces him to try so hard:

> Why the devil . . . am I worrying about him. . .? Goodness only knows why! You just ask a man sometimes why he does a thing.

They are playthings in the hands of destiny: "It's true enough that you can't escape your destiny," says Agafya Tikhonovna. Even when Podkolesin flees his bride, this still does not reveal his character as one which is totally incapable of an independent decision. He submits to a kind of automatism—like a cat which jumps out of an open window because it is open.

Gogolian comedy is, so to speak, ancient tragedy turned inside out. Its senselessness defines its polar relationship to tragedy. As in Chekhov the "zero" resolution, based on the motif of escape, corresponds to the tragic resolution which gives rise to a feeling of catharsis. The difference between the drama of these two authors is that in Gogol the characters, although drawn by destiny into a "weaving" of circumstances and subject to suggestion, nevertheless act, becoming involved in the most varied comic situations; moreover, they themselves create these situations. Thus, the outer form of Gogol's comedy is consistent with the inner form. Gogol's comedies demand staging, in contrast to Chekhov's, which seem more like a sketch for a story.

The fact is that Chekhov, unlike Gogol, is a realist. He depicted living people, however characterless they were. They are characterless because they are weakwilled, indecisive and lack confidence and not simply because they lack personality as do Gogol's *dramatis personae*. The latter can put on any mask, "mug," and become any *persona*—in the sense in which the term was used in ancient drama. This is precisely the reason why Chekhov's people are unsuited for the theater. (pp. 115-23)

> *Peter M. Bitsilli, in his* Chekhov's Art: A Stylistic Analysis, *translated by Toby W. Clyman and Edwina Jannie Cruise, Ardis, 1983, 194 p.*

ALLARDYCE NICOLL   (essay date 1949)

[Called "one of the masters of dramatic research," Nicoll is best known as a theater historian whose works have proven invaluable to students and educators. Nicoll's World Drama from Aeschylus to Anouilh *(1949) is considered one of his most important works; theater critic John Gassner has stated that it is "unquestionably the most thorough (study) of its kind in the English language (and) our best reference book on the world's dramatic literature." Another of his ambitious theater studies is the six-volume* A History of English Drama, 1660-1900 *(1952-59), which has been highly praised for its perceptive commentaries on drama from the Restoration to the close of the nineteenth century. Nicoll was also a popular lecturer on Shakespearean drama and the author of several studies on William Shakespeare's works. In addition, he was the longtime editor of* Shakespeare Survey, *an annual publication of Shakespearean scholarship. In the following excerpt, he surveys Chekhov's dramatic works.]*

For the first years of his dramatic career Chekhov restricted himself to the one-act play form, gaining mastery of situation and of character by means of short sketches of life. His first composition was a sketch, or "dramatic study," entitled *Na bolshoi doroge* (*On the High Road;* written in 1884, but for a time denied theatrical representation because of the opposition of the censorship). There is no plot here, just a picture of a number of ill-assorted characters lodged temporarily in a roadside inn. There are touches of laughter, but the atmosphere in general is one of gloom. Quiet, resigned acceptance of life's despairs is the mood of *Lebedinaia pesnia* (*Swan-Song,* 1889), in which an aging comic actor, left alone on the stage of a small theatre, dreams of his past life, of the visions that once were his, and of the reality before him.

This sadness, generally induced by contemplation of life's failures, is an inherent part of Chekhov's being, yet his real strength comes from his mastery of laughter. In one of his earliest sketches, *Medved* (*The Bear,* 1888), an irate young landowner calls on a neighbour lady to demand repayment of a debt: there is a violent quarrel between them, yet before the half-hour's action is over they have become engaged. Here the spirit of Musset is being transformed into Russian terms. *Predlozhenie* (*The Marriage Proposal*, 1889) shows a timorous young suitor calling on the lady of his choice and becoming so involved in an acrimonious debate concerning the ownership of some worthless land as almost to wreck his hopes—and the girl's. For *Svadba* (*The Wedding,* 1890) Chekhov takes as setting a bridal feast, and derives much merriment from the contrasting characters introduced—particularly from those of a retired naval captain who is mightily aggrieved because, snobbishly, he is being introduced to the company as a general and a nobleman, and of a self-effacing clerk who, himself wishing to have been the bridegroom, seeks to pacify his anger by pretending that after all her family is vulgar and ignorant. *Zhubilei* (*The Anniversary*, 1892) is a hilarious study of the celebrations attendant upon the fiftieth anniversary of the founding of a bank—celebrations considerably interrupted by the love-affairs of the bank manager. Laughter too predominates in *Tragik ponevole* (*A Tragedian in Spite of Himself*, 1893), where the wretched husband Tolkachov, burdened with commissions imposed upon him by members of his family comfortably established in a country cottage, seeks sympathy from his friend Murashkin. After listening to the tale of woe Murashkin adds a commission of his own, and the sketch ends with poor Tolkachov madly losing his temper, attacking his friend, and crying out hysterically for blood.

An appreciation of these one-act pieces is absolutely essential for an understanding of Chekhov's full-length plays. While it is true that some of these latter works end with suicide and that all introduce an atmosphere of darkness, it would seem that a true interpretation of their spirit demands a full acceptance of the humorous qualities inherent in their being. There is nothing here of the gloomy pessimism characteristic of Hauptmann's *Before Sunrise*, nothing of the frenzied self-centredness of Strindberg's work. A deep understanding of human souls is Chekhov's prime quality, and, together with that, an ability to view life ironically. He is deeply moved as he contemplates his scenes, yet no bitterness, no fervent anger, stirs his being.

In 1887 he first tried his hand at the composition of a long play, and succeeded in turning out what must be regarded, in every respect, as a failure. *Ivanov* nowhere reveals Chekhov's genuine spirit. Unsuited to the expression of his genius is this story of a spineless man who marries a Jewess, finds his love for her depart, and falls in love with a neighbour's daughter. The wife, he knows, is dying of consumption, and in one terrible scene, when she upbraids him for his intrigue, he flings the knowledge of her close-approaching death in her face. Shortly after this she departs from life: Ivanov, though racked by conscience, plans to go ahead with a second marriage, but when the doctor declares he will publicly expose him he seeks release in suicide.

Except for the fact that Ivanov himself is akin to other characters in the later plays who fail in their adjustment to life, this drama has but little in common with Chekhov's masterpieces. It aims at creating a tragic impression, and for that his powers were eminently unsuited.

His first true triumph came with *Chaika (The Seagull),* unsuccessfully produced in 1896, and two years later destined to become the primal glory of the Moscow Art Theatre. *Ivanov* had been constructed more or less along traditional lines, and all stress was laid on one central figure. In *The Seagull,* Chekhov abandoned the traditional formulas and set himself to depict a group rather than an individual. To narrate the plot of such a work is almost impossible, so closely intertwined are the characters with one another. Four persons in particular concern us—the successful actress Irina Arkadina, who, despite her reputation, is obsessed by fears of becoming too old for the stage; her son, Konstantin Treplev, gifted with literary powers, yet submerged by the dominant personality of his mother; Trigorin, a fashionable and successful novelist, conscious of the fact that for all his esteem his genius is not of the highest; and Nina, a young idealistic girl who dreams of a great theatrical career. These are the central figures, but even these four cannot be considered in isolation as a group, for their lives are intimately associated with, and illuminated by, other characters—Irina's good-humoured, slightly soured brother, Piotr Nikolaevich Sorin; his steward, Ilia Shamraev; his wife, Polina Andreevna, and daughter, Masha; the doctor, Evgeni Dorn; and the schoolmaster, Semion Medvedenko. All these persons Chekhov has wrought into a harmonious whole, while apparently allowing his action to drift and even to stagnate.

This play too ends with suicide (Treplev's), but it cannot be styled a tragedy. Throughout its length, despite the many soul sorrows that are revealed by the various persons in the action, ironic laughter is rippling: it was, indeed, Chekhov's unique discovery that the spirit of high comedy could be evoked by means of effects which in the hands of another author might have led only to the tragic or the melodramatic. "Why do you always wear black?" asks Medvedenko of Masha at the very beginning of the play, but the reference to her black dress is not, as one might have thought, a symbolic introduction to a tragic theme. Her reply—"I am in mourning for my life. I am unhappy"—at once reveals to us the mood in which we are to accept the following scenes. This is serious, but somehow not tragically serious. Medvedenko is a sorry creature, and so is Masha; when, however, the two start to argue fitfully on which is the more miserable, while each, despite the fact that they are conversing, remains inwardly intent on his or her own thoughts, the mood evoked is an ironically comic one. . . . (pp. 682-85)

The quality that is in *The Seagull* also renders this play essentially poetic. Here is life apparently depicted with an utterly naturalistic pen, and yet the impression we have in our minds is entirely imaginative. Partly this comes from the way in which unobtrusively Chekhov weaves symbol into reality. . . . Partly it comes from the sharp juxtaposition of different thoughts uttered by two or more characters as each remains involved in his own meditations: the effect occasionally is akin to the juxtaposition of images in a passage of lyrical poetry: it is as though the imaginative quality of a Hamlet soliloquy were orchestrated for a quartette; it is as though Hamlet and many Hamlets, their tongues incapable of fully expressing their thoughts, were desperately trying to make others listen, without anyone to heed them or to understand.

How difficult was the task that Chekhov had set himself is revealed in his next play, *Diadia Vania (Uncle Vania,* 1899). Already in 1888 he had tried his hand at dealing with the theme here presented, in his *Leshii (The Wood Demon).* The character of Professor Serebriakov is common to both plays, and Uncle Vanya appears in the former as Uncle George, killing himself at the end of the third act. There is, however, in *The Wood Demon* a jangling of notes, a lack of a central tune, and it is easy to see why Chekhov himself was dissatisfied with it. Even in the rewriting, or rather re-creation, *Uncle Vanya* may be regarded as less powerful than *The Seagull.*

The central figure here is the retired and widowed Professor Serebriakov, who lives on his small estate with his daughter, Sofia, and his brother-in-law, Ivan Petrovich Voinitski, known as Uncle Vanya. Into this circle the Professor brings a young wife, a woman of twenty-seven, Elena Andreievna. With her Vanya falls in love, and at the same time the man whom Sofia loves, Dr Astrov, is also attracted by her. Serebriakov is a pompous, fussy egoist; Vanya is a man who has sacrificed everything for his dead sister's estate, which he manages; Sofia is a woman, unattractive, to whom the joys of life have been denied; Astrov is a strange mixture of the cynic and the idealist, a drunkard who yet has a great vision of afforestation designed to change Russia's climate and better her peoples; Elena is a woman who, after marrying the Professor, discovers that she does not love him and yet is resolved to remain faithful to him. When Vanya learns that Serebriakov intends to sell the estate to which he himself has given his whole life he tries, unsuccessfully, to shoot him, and in the last act we are back, as it were, at the beginning. Vanya and Sofia are left alone; the vision that was Elena has gone; for Vanya there may be release in carrying on the work that no longer gives him satisfaction, for Sofia there is hope only of happiness in a life other than this:

> We shall go on living, Uncle Vanya. We shall live on through a great, great line of days, of long evenings; we shall patiently endure the trials our fate brings us; we shall toil for others, now and when we are old, without rest; and when our time comes we shall die submissively, and there beyond the grave we shall say that we have suffered, that we have wept, that our lives were bitter, and God will take pity upon us, and I and you, uncle, dear uncle, shall see a life that is luminous, beautiful, splendid. . . . In your life you have not known any joy, but wait, Uncle Vanya, wait. . . . We shall have rest.

After this exploration of the human soul Chekhov had acquired sufficient power to create his two outstanding final dramas—*Tri sestri (The Three Sisters,* 1901) and *Vishnevii sad (The Cherry Orchard,* 1904). Here the plots are even less firm and at the same time, paradoxically, more complex. All that *The Three Sisters* has to tell is the story of Olga, Masha, and Irina, three sisters living in a small provincial town and ever dreaming of escaping to the joys of Moscow life. In the action of the play we see nothing more than the slow, gradual fracturing of these dreams. What is remarkable in this play is the quality—still more marked in *The Cherry Orchard*—of a strange mood born out of nostalgia for the lovely things of life that are passing and of some dim hope of future happiness. Men and women are at odds here, with one another, with themselves, with their circumstances. Colonel Vershinin, whose own life is a failure, considers the problems of existence: "Well, I don't know," he says:

> It seems to me that everything on this earth must change little by little, that it's actually changing as we look at it. In two hundred years, three hundred, maybe a thousand years—how long doesn't matter— a new, happy life will arise. We shan't be able to share in that life, of course, but we are living for it now, we're working for it, yes, suffering for it: we

are creating it—and in this one effort is the reason
for our existence and, if you like, our happiness.

And, as if in comment, comes the stage-direction—"Masha
laughs softly." "What is it?" she is asked. "I don't know,"
she replies. "I've been laughing all day." The close of the
play is in keeping with this tone.

Finally comes *The Cherry Orchard,* in which Chekhov finds
complete mastery of his medium. The last scene shows the old
Firs left alone in a dark and shuttered house, there presumably
to die: throughout the course of the action a sad, nostalgic
sorrow prevails for the beautiful things that are being sacrificed.
"My dear, my tender, beautiful orchard!" sighs Lubov as she
leaves. "My life, my youth, my happiness, good-bye!. . . Good-
bye!" But before that the student has been speaking to Anya:

> All Russia is our orchard. The land is great and beau-
> tiful, there are many wondrous places in it. *(A pause)*
> Think, Anya: your grandfather, your great-grand-
> father and all your ancestors were owners of serfs,
> holders of living souls—and can you fail to see some-
> thing human looking at you from every cherry in the
> orchard, from every leaf, from every stem? Don't
> you hear voices there?. . . Oh, your orchard is fear-
> some and frightening; and when in the evening or at
> night you walk through it, then the old bark on the
> trees glows dimly and the old cherry-trees seem to
> be dreaming of all that was a hundred, two hundred
> years ago, and their visions weigh them down. Well,
> then, we have remained for at least two hundred
> years, it means nothing to us, we don't realize our
> relationship to the past—we can only philosophize,
> complain of boredom or drink vodka. And yet it's
> so clear: in order to begin to live in the present we
> must first pay for the past, make our peace with the
> past, and that payment can be made only through
> suffering, through extraordinary, uninterrupted
> toil. . . . I feel that happiness is coming, Anya, I see
> it already.

Not that such a speech by Trofimov makes *The Cherry Orchard*
into a thesis play. There is nothing intellectual and rational
here: all is imaginative and emotional. As the characters are
seated outside by the bank of a river, "suddenly a distant sound
is heard as from the sky, the sound of a breaking harp string,
sadly dying away." "What's that?" asks Lubov, the graciously
useless owner of the orchard. "I don't know," replies the
wealthy peasant Lopakhin. "A bucket's fallen down a shaft
somewhere far off. It's certainly far off." "Or perhaps it's
some bird . . . like a heron," hazards the drifting intellectual
Gaev. "Or an owl," adds Trofimov satirically. Lubov shud-
ders: "It's unpleasant, somehow," she remarks, and there is
a pause. Then the old Firs speaks, he who had been a slave in
the days before the emancipation of the serfs: "Before the
misfortune the same thing happened. An owl screamed and the
samovar simmered without stopping." "Before what misfortune?" Gaev asks, and the old man's answer comes from the
depth of memory—"Before the Emancipation."

In this drama, where tears are blended with laughter, hope with
despair, Chekhov carries to the farthest limit his peculiar power
of suggesting the inner loneliness of his characters. Each one
speaks for himself, and there is no one to listen. The talk drifts
on, thoughts welling up from within the breasts of these waifs,
tossed on the air and vanishing like bubbles. We know these
people as we do not know even the strongly delineated types
created by Ibsen, for Chekhov's art is a poetic art where implications and associative values fire the creative process in
our own minds.

It has taken many years for Chekhov's peculiar artistry to win
general acceptance, but that acceptance has now come, and
the success which has attended the many productions of his
dramas during recent years seems to indicate that he possesses
that almost indefinable quality which alone can win universal
and enduring life in the theatre. His world is in truth far farther
removed from that of London and New York than the pro-
vincial-city flavour set as a background to most of Ibsen's
plays, and one might well have thought that things so strange
could never have been successful outside of Russia. The fact
is, however, that, whenever produced, *The Cherry Orchard*
and *The Seagull* have demonstrated their power of making a
direct appeal in spite of the strangeness of their atmosphere:
by some magic, the precise operation of which baffles our
intelligence, Chekhov has been able to invest the particular
with universal attributes, so that even when his delicately poised
dialogue suffers inevitable coarsening in being transformed into
another tongue the play of his creative imagination still casts
a warm glow over his characters. Although his dramatic work
falls quantitatively far below that of Ibsen, of Strindberg or of
Hauptmann, perhaps future historians of the theatre, surveying
the fortunes of the stage at the turn of the century, may decide
that so far as quality is concerned no other author can vie with
him: his subtlety is supreme. (pp. 686-89)

> Allardyce Nicoll, "The Extension of the Realistic,"
> in his World Drama: From Aeschylus to Anouilh,
> George G. Harrap & Company Ltd., 1949, pp.
> 682-718.

VLADIMIR YERMILOV   (essay date 1956?)

*[Yermilov is a Russian critic and educator who has written several
books on Chekhov. In the following excerpt, he analyzes* Uncle
Vanya.]

The theme of *Uncle Vanya* is the life of "little men" with its
hidden sufferings and self-effacing toil for the happiness of
others; in fact, it is the theme of beauty wasted in vain.

From the memoirs of Nadezhda Konstantinovna Krupskaya,
Lenin's wife, we learn that Lenin had a very high opinion of
this play.

After seeing *Uncle Vanya* produced by the Art Theatre in October 1899, after its successful tour of the provinces, Gorky
wrote to Chekhov:

"Since you say you do not want to write for the theatre I feel
I ought to let you know what people of discernment think of
your plays. They say, among other things, that *Uncle Vanya*
and *The Seagull* represent a new kind of dramatic art, in which
realism is raised to the level of inspired, deeply thought-out
symbolism. And in my opinion this is quite true. As I watched
your play I thought of life being sacrificed to an idol, of the
invasion of the wretched life of man by beauty, and of many
other fundamental things. Other plays do not lead one away
from everyday reality to the sphere of philosophy, as yours
do. . . ."

Chekhov indicates by the very title of the play the simplicity
and workaday ordinariness both of his characters and their
sufferings.

Uncle Vanya and his niece, Sonya, have toiled all their life
on behalf of another's happiness: they work for the material
well-being of Sonya's father, Professor Serebryakov, whom
they have taught themselves to regard as a great scholar, gifted

and advanced. Professor Serebryakov, now retired, is married for the second time to a young and beautiful woman. His first wife, Sonya's mother and Uncle Vanya's sister, has long been dead.

The estate which Uncle Vanya and Sonya managed had belonged to Sonya's mother. Sonya was now its sole owner, Uncle Vanya having relinquished his share in the legacy in favour of his beloved sister, thanks to which sacrifice, their father had been able to buy landed property. But he had paid nothing like the whole sum, and it was deeply encumbered with debt. Uncle Vanya toiled to pay off these debts and set the estate in order. For twenty-five years he had worked "like the most diligent bailiff," receiving a wretched salary from Serebryakov, to whom he sent the entire profits yielded by the estate, so that the professor could write his scientific papers and deliver himself of his University lectures in peace. Uncle Vanya and Sonya seldom left the estate, went without sufficient food, oblivious to everything but their solicitude for the professor. Not once had the idea that the estate, both morally and legally, belonged to *them* and not to Serebryakov, entered into their minds; they had voluntarily taken up the role of unmurmuring, selfless servants of their "idol." The dullness of daily practical cares, the nights spent in copying out papers or translating books for the Professor, their utter renunciation of all personal pleasures, the wretched salary received by Uncle Vanya from Serebryakov—all this was sanctified in the eyes of Uncle Vanya and Sonya by their lofty purpose. They were inspired by the thought that in serving a scientist they served science, civilizaton, progress—in a word, the ruling principle. The professor was a "being of the sublime order" in their eyes.

Uncle Vanya is forty-seven, and a pauper. He has never known either rest or enjoyment.

And now that the best years of his life have already gone, his eyes are opened to the terrible truth. He sees that he has given up his best years, his youth, his entire self, to the service of a worthless being. He realizes that his former god is nothing but a pompous mediocrity, chock-full of pretensions and self-importance, "a dryasdust, a learned fossil." All this was seen with especial clarity when Serebryakov retired—"not a soul in the world has ever heard of him, he is utterly unknown; this means that for the last twenty-five years he has been occupying someone else's place." For twenty-five years he has been lecturing on art without understanding a thing about art, chewing the cud of other men's thought; for twenty-five years Uncle Vanya has been toiling in order to keep Professor Serebryakov in another man's place. Serebryakov, spoilt by easy success in his career, by the love of women, by the fact that Uncle Vanya and Sonya worked for him, is callous and selfish. During all these twenty-five years he never once so much as thanked Uncle Vanya, nor thought of raising his wretched salary by a single farthing.

And now he has come with his beautiful wife to settle down on the estate for good, for he has retired and cannot afford to live in the capital.

His arrival breaks up the accustomed routine of work on the estate. The Professor torments everyone with his whims, his gout, his callous selfishness. No one around him is allowed to think of anything but his welfare.

Uncle Vanya is in the painful situation of one who is driven to admit, on the threshold of old age, that he has lived in vain. If he had not sacrificed all his strength and talents to the serving of an "idol" he might have done useful work and himself gained the gratitude of men. He might have been happy, have loved and been loved!

Thus begins Uncle Vanya's tragically delayed "rebellion." He seems to clamour for the restoring of his ruined life. He falls in love with the Professor's wife. For the first time in his life he begins to drink. He is oppressed by the thought that all is lost, his life ruined.

And the Professor contributes the last straw. He summons the household for a solemn conference and lays before them his latest project: to sell the estate so that, on the sum realized, he can live in the capital. He cannot stand country life, he is accustomed to the bustle of the city.

Uncle Vanya is astounded. It is not enough apparently that he had given up all his money, his very life to Serebryakov. Now, just when he is beginning to get old, he and Sonya, in gratitude for all they have done, are to be turned out of their home to shift for themselves.

Uncle Vanya's rebellion reaches its climax.

"You have ruined my life!" he shouts at Serebryakov. "I have never lived! Never! Thanks to you I destroyed, laid waste the best years of my life! You are my worst enemy!"

For all reply, the Professor flings in his face the word: "Nonentity!"

"My life has been wasted!" exclaims Uncle Vanya in despair. "I am gifted, clever, daring. . . . If I had had a normal life, I might have turned out a Schopenhauer, or a Dostoyevsky. . . . Oh, I don't know what I'm saying! I'm going mad. . . ."

Uncle Vanya's words about the possibilities in his turning out a great man do not evoke an incredulous smile. During the three acts in which we have learned to know him, we have felt his intelligence, his ability to make sacrifices on behalf of what he considered the ruling principle in the name of science, progress and reason, regarding Serebryakov as the torch-bearer of these ideals. Familiar with Chekhov's characters, we are not surprised to discover once more *a great little man.*

Uncle Vanya's "rebellion" ends in his shooting at Serebryakov. After this climax, Uncle Vanya thinks of committing suicide, but, influenced by the affectionate and gentle Sonya, he returns to his work—work that will benefit Serebryakov.

After all that has happened, the Professor and his wife cannot go on living on the estate. They leave, not for the metropolis, it is true, but for Kharkov. A reconciliation of a sort is brought about, and Uncle Vanya tells Serebryakov that all will go on as formerly. The retired Professor will, as usual, receive all the profits.

Such is the story of a life given up to an "idol." Gorky was perfectly right when he discovered a symbolic meaning underlying it. How many such Uncle Vanyas, unassuming toilers, always in the background, have given their best for the sake of making some nonentity happy, of serving some false idol, convinced they were serving the "ruling principle," deceived by life! The spiritual beauty, the faith, the purity that have been spent in vain! (pp. 349-53)

Whole life-stories pass before us in Chekhov's plays. The past, present and future of his characters, the development of their destinies and individualities, rise before us as in a novel. We ourselves can form in our imagination a perfectly clear artistic image of Vanya Voinitsky when he was a whole-hearted, straightforward, single-minded, serious and dreamy youth, an "idealist," as they used to say in those days. All the romantic aspirations of youth, all the yearnings after ideals and self-sacrifice of this young man had been centred on Professor Serebryakov, whom he regarded through the eyes of his sister, a poetically-minded girl who had reverently devoted her youth and purity to Serebryakov. The family have made a cult of Serebryakov. The years pass on the peaceful estate, years completely given up to the cult of the "great scientist," till the rapid development of events is unfolded in the play. And with the same clarity with which we see Voinitsky's past and present, we can imagine his wretched future, his old age, no longer gilded by dreams, illusion, or anything else.

A contemporary critic remarked that in "*Uncle Vanya* we have a symbol of the whole province, placing all its hopes in Professor Serebryakov, who turns out to be a learned fossil, a nonentity, battening on the province, smugly confident that he is its spiritual leader, its pride and hope, the only guarantee of a better life in store for it."

The character of Professor Serebryakov affords copious material for generalization. In him are debunked the idols of the intelligentsia of those times, the liberal "leaders of opinion," learned fossils, dry-as-dust, estranged from true Russian life, infatuated with themselves, scornful of ordinary people like Astrov and Voinitsky, dogmatic, convinced of their own high position as the Elect, as brilliant personalities raised high above the "crowd."

The exposure of the appalling futility of serving the Elect, this typically Chekhov theme, is penetratingly and powerfully treated in *Uncle Vanya.* Even Uncle Vanya's rebellion is futile, for it is directed against a single individual, the same in whose service he has expended all his energies.

The theme of the fading, perishing beauty of life is the leitmotif of the play. All the chief *dramatis personae* are involved in it.

What is true beauty, and what is false beauty?

We know that in the opinion of Chekhov, as expressed through his characters, only work, creative work, is capable of creating human beauty.

No one before Gorky in world literature has ever been so much the inspired poet of work as Chekhov was. All his writings compose a song, now joyous, now sad, of work. To him work was the basis of all that was human, of all morals and aesthetics, and the theme of work was always bound up for him and his characters with the dream of free, creative toil. It will be remembered how Irina, the youngest of the three sisters, yearned for such work, and how life destroyed her dream. "'Work without poetry, work without thoughts," she complains.

The poetry of work and the longing for such poetry—therein lies the secret charm of Chekhov's men and women.

All those Abogins, Princesses and such like, lack the true inner beauty, precisely because they are strangers to work, are hostile to the idea of work.

Here is what Uncle Vanya's friend, Dr. Astrov, says about Yelena Andreyevna, Serebryakov's wife:

> Everything about a human being should be beautiful: his face, his clothes, his soul, his mind. She is beautiful, there is no gainsaying that, but—she does nothing but eat, sleep, walk about, charm us all with her beauty. She has no duties, others work for her . . .

you know this is true. And a life of idleness cannot be a pure life.

And it is Astrov himself, strongly attracted by Yelena Andreyevna, who says this, that same Astrov, who, like so many other Chekhov characters, sets such a high value on beauty. "There is one thing that can still move me," he says, in explanation of his feeling for Yelena Andreyevna, "and that is beauty. I cannot be indifferent to it." And yet he senses something about her beauty which is offensive to his conception of beauty. He sees something impure in it. "I feel that if she cared to Yelena Andreyevna could turn my head in a single day. . . . But that's not real love, you know, not a lasting attachment. . . ."

False, impure beauty is incapable of inspiring deep human feeling.

Only that which serves creative effort is beautiful. Passionately enamoured of the loveliness of his native land, of its woods and orchards, and distressed by the rapacious way in which the forests were being felled, Astrov says:

> I could understand it if, in place of these forests, high roads and railways were laid out, or factories and schools built—the people would then gain health, wealth and knowledge, but we see nothing of the sort! Everywhere swamps and mosquitoes, impassable roads, poverty, typhus, diphtheria, fires. . . . Almost everything has been destroyed, and nothing has been put up in its place.

Astrov grieves over the destruction of the beauty of the world, the beauty of human beings. He breaks off in the middle of an impassioned speech in which he tries to express his thoughts to Yelena Andreyevna, and says coldly: "But I can see by your face that I'm boring you."

A beautiful woman, she is incapable of feeling any interest in the theme nearest to Astrov, that of beauty of life. What, then, is her beauty? It is not quite the same as the parasitical beauty of the various Abogins and Princesses. Yelena Andreyevna is profoundly unhappy herself, she made a mistake when she gave up her youth to Professor Serebryakov, moved not by spontaneous love or passion, but influenced by a purely intellectual feeling for one she believed to be a great and gifted scholar. Her life, too, has been swallowed up in the service of her idol. However that may be, she is perishing from boredom and spiritual vacuity, and, unable to create, can only destroy. Her very beauty becomes a travesty of true human beauty. That is why there is such an unmistakable tinge of cynicism and disrespect in the way Astrov makes love to her. If she and her husband had not gone away, there would undoubtedly have been an affair between her and Astrov, which would have left Astrov with nothing but a sense of devastation and futility.

> "Yes, go," he tells her. *(Thoughtfully.)* "You seem to be a good kind of person, and yet there is something unaccountable in your whole being. You came here, you and your husband, and all those who had been working, busying themselves with getting things done, were obliged to leave their activities and devote themselves all the summer to your husband's gout, and to you. The two of you seem to have infected us all with your idleness. I let myself be carried away, did nothing for a whole month, and all the time people fell ill, and the peasants let the cattle run into my woods and thickets. . . . And so, wherever you and your husband go, you bring destruction with you . . . and I am sure, if you had stayed for good, the devastation would have been immense."

Estranged from work and creative effort, and therefore gradually becoming estranged from life itself, herself a wreck and the cause of devastation in others, Yelena Andreyevna, without realizing it, ruins everything beautiful, great, human which comes her way. She is a bird of prey without knowing it. She it is who destroys the friendship which might have blossomed into love between Astrov and Sonya.

Astrov is a creative man on a big scale. Yelena Andreyevna justly estimates him in talking about him to Sonya:

> But, my dear, he's a genius! And do you know what that means? It means courage, a free mind, wide scope. . . . No sooner does he plant a tree than he begins thinking of how it will all be in a thousand years, and dreaming of the millennium. . . . It's true he drinks and is sometimes rude—but what of it? Just think of the life this doctor leads! Impassable mud on the roads, frost and blizzards, tremendous distances, the people coarse and half-savage, poverty and sickness all round—a man who has to work and struggle every day of his life in such circumstances cannot be expected always to be clean and sober by the age of forty. . . .

Astrov loves life; like all Chekhov's favourite characters he strains towards the future, longs to catch a glimpse of its face, to divine the aspect of the native land and mankind beneath the rays of the morrow's happiness.

> "As for my own personal life," he tells Sonya, "I swear there is absolutely nothing good to be said about it. When you are going through the woods on a dark night, and there's a light far ahead, you don't feel tired, you know, you don't notice it's dark, or that the twigs are scratching your face. . . . I work, as you know, like no one else in our district, life deals me constant blows, sometimes my sufferings are almost more than I can bear, and there is no light ahead. I expect nothing for myself. . . ."

And yet there was a bright spot in his life: his friendship with Sonya and Uncle Vanya.

Sonya is in love with Astrov.

If it had not been for the incursion of Yelena Andreyevna into their life, he might have married Sonya. At any rate, he would not have had to give up her friendship.

But Yelena Andreyevna must needs, "from sympathy," help the shy Sonya, and takes upon herself to speak to Astrov and find out if he loves Sonya. If he does not, so she reasons, let him stop his visits—it will be better for Sonya. Sonya hesitates: is the interview necessary, after all? For if he were to say "no," it would mean the end of all hope, and the end of their friendship, too. Would it not be better to leave herself at least hope? Astrov is the only bright spot in her life, so full of toil and care, the light seen in the distance in the dark, dark forest. . . .

She agrees, however, under the influence of Yelena Andreyevna, to allow her to speak to him.

Now why should Yelena Andreyevna want this conversation? The reason, though she may not be fully aware of it, is quite obvious: she is attracted by Astrov herself. The subtle, intelligent Astrov divines this.

> ASTROV. There's just one thing I cannot understand: What made you start this interrogation? (*Looking her straight in the eyes and shaking his finger at her.*) You're very deep, you know.

YELENA ANDREYEVNA. What do you mean?

ASTROV (*laughs*). Oh, you're very deep. Say Sonya suffers, I can readily believe that, but why this interrogation?. . . Now, don't look at me like that, sweet bird of prey. . . .

Yes, she is a bird of prey, she has stolen Sonya's happiness by forcing Astrov to admit he does not love Sonya.

It was the very essence of the relations between Astrov and Sonya that they could not and should not be defined as yet. Yelena Andreyevna felt this and achieved "clarity," thereby spoiling all.

But though she destroyed another person's happiness, she could not create either her own or Astrov's. She wrecks other people's lives just as senselessly and aimlessly as she drags her empty beauty, which is incapable of contributing to happiness, through life. Soulless, uninspired, unlovely beauty!

The leit-motif of the play—the destruction of beauty—reappears in many variations. Astrov himself, grieving over the wrecking of the beauty of life, is an image of wasted beauty.

Sonya begs him to give up vodka. "It does not suit you at all! You are so smart, your voice is so gentle. . . . I would say more—of all the people I know, you are the most exquisite. Why do you want to be like ordinary people who drink and play cards? Don't be, I implore you! You are always saying that people don't create anything, and only destroy what has been sent them from above. Why, why then must you destroy yourself?"

But the beauty of Astrov, his inner and outward harmony, are destroyed by life itself. In the final scene he says to Uncle Vanya:

> We're in a hopeless plight, you and I. . . . Those who live a hundred, or two hundred years after us, and who will despise us for having lived our lives so stupidly, with such lack of taste, may perhaps find a way to be happy themselves, but we. . . . That's it, friend. There used to be two decent intellectuals in our district—you and I. But in the short space of ten years a despicable philistine life has dragged us into itself; it has poisoned our blood with its rancid fumes, and we have become as vulgar as the rest. . . .

Much too severe a sentence. Neither Astrov nor Uncle Vanya had become philistines, living a complacent despicable life. But they have no beacon, they are faced by a great blank. We discern the traits of degeneration in Astrov. There are certain signs of decay about him. Alas, Astrov is not mistaken in the diagnosis of his state. It really was a hopeless one. It could not be otherwise with a man who despised half-measures and philistinism, and was yet far from that revolutionary movement of the working class developing more and more in the nineties. Astrov, like his friend Voinitsky, was incapable of consoling himself with some trifling "saving" idea, with "small deeds," rosy illusions; nor could he acquire a lofty purpose in life, being too far removed from those who were waging the struggle for the purpose so dear to him—a rational, pure, just way of life. The tragedy of this Chekhov character was deepened by his political indifference, his limitations as an intellectual.

There is no doubt that Astrov would have preserved both his personality and his dream, and would have been able to cope with the vicissitudes of life, if he had been warmed by the consciousness that his modest labour was part of the general plan of reorganization, the re-creation of life. But he lacks this consciousness.

Serebryakov and Yelena Andreyevna take their departure. Astrov goes away, out of Sonya's life for ever. Uncle Vanya and Sonya are alone again. But a cardinal change has taken place in their life. Hope has gone out of it for ever.

> "Well, it can't be helped, we must live," says Sonya. "We will go on living, Uncle Vanya. There is an endless procession of days, of long, long evenings before us, we will bear patiently all the trials fate sends us; we will work for others, now and when we are old, never resting, and when our hour comes, we will die without a murmur, and there, beyond the grave, we shall tell them that we suffered, that we wept, that we went through great bitterness, and God will have mercy on us, and you and I, dearest Uncle, will know a beautiful, bright, exquisite life. . . . We will rest! We will hear the angels singing, we will see the sky studded with diamonds, we will see all the world's evil, all our sufferings drowned in a mercy filling the whole universe. . . . *(Wiping his eyes with her handkerchief.)* Poor Uncle Vanya, you're crying. . . . *(Speaking through her tears.)* You have never known joy, but wait, Uncle Vanya, you just wait. . . . We will rest. . . . *(Throwing her arms round him.)* We will rest!"

In the final scene of *Uncle Vanya* Chekhov managed to give expression to that beauty of human grief, which, as he said, "people will not soon learn to understand, still less to describe, and which, probably, can only be conveyed by music."

It would certainly be erroneous to think that Chekhov, with his hostility to religious emotions of any sort, sought comfort for his heroes in religion. But there was nothing else for Sonya to cling to, nothing with which she could try to comfort Uncle Vanya. And this makes the hopelessness of the dream of peace and joy for herself and Uncle Vanya all the more vivid. The wisdom of such a conclusion lies in the fact that the "bright, beautiful, exquisite" life referred to was exactly the life deserved by Sonya, Uncle Vanya, Astrov, and all the "little people," the toilers devoting their whole lives to the happiness of others. . . .

And soaring above the hopeless life of these little, unimportant people, above the dark, cruel forces of destruction, is Chekhov's dream of life in the future, when everything about a human being would be beautiful! As always with Chekhov, the conception of beauty is blended with that of truth and creative effort: the aesthetic principle is merged with the ethical. Truth and work, those are the foundations, the ever-flowing sources of beauty. Life ought to be such as not to destroy the beauty of these great little individualities, not to allow the spiritual strength, the self-sacrifice, the selfless toil to be wasted in serving false gods, life in which it would be no longer the Serebryakovs who set the fashion, but the Astrovs, Uncle Vanyas and Sonyas, adorning their native land with free, creative work.

Astrov's words that "everything about a human being should be beautiful: his face, his clothes, his soul, his mind," this formula of the indivisible unity of beauty and truth, were found in the notebook in which the heroic Komsomol girl Zoya Kosmodemyanskaya, barbarously tortured and hung by the German fascists, wrote down her most cherished maxims. (pp. 354-63)

Vladimir Yermilov, in his Anton Pavlovich Chekhov: 1860-1904, *translated by Ivy Litvinov, Foreign Languages Publishing House, 1956?, 415 p.*

ROBERT LOUIS JACKSON (essay date 1967)

[*Jackson is an American critic who specializes in Russian literature. In the following excerpt, he examines the major themes and techniques of* The Seagull.]

Art is at the center of *The Seagull.* Four characters in the play are actresses or writers. Everybody talks about art. Everybody embodies or lives out a concept of art. The problem of talent—what it takes and means to become an artist—is a fundamental theme of the play. Illusion and reality, dream and fulfillment in art and life constitute the innermost concern of the author. Finally, art in its most basic form as myth gives expression to the underlying dramatic conflicts and realities in the play: the myth of creation, the Oedipal syndrome and the metaphor of the journey.

In his myth-play in Act I of Chekhov's *The Seagull* the young writer Konstantin Gavrilovich Treplev pictures a bleak future for the world: thousands of centuries have passed and all life has vanished. The bodies of living beings have long ago crumbled into dust, and eternal matter has turned them into stone, water, and clouds; their souls have merged into one. A doleful moon vainly sheds light on this desolation. And desolation it is: "Cold, cold, cold. Empty, empty, empty. Terrible, terrible, terrible."

Konstantin's play itself, as commentators on *The Seagull* have observed, is also terrible. It is a concoction of melodramatic posturing and mannered symbolism. Yet—though bad art—it is, paradoxically, full of Chekhov's art. The action, the character-symbols and portents—all the devices which fail so miserably in Konstantin's play taken by itself and which seem merely a Chekhovian parody of a "decadent" theatrical style—have a distinctly allegorical character in the context of the larger play, *The Seagull.* Just as in Shakespeare's *Hamlet,* so in *The Seagull,* the play within the play reaches out into the psychological drama. But while the import of Hamlet's theatrical is immediately evident, both before and after the performance, the significance of Konstantin's play is only fully apparent by the end of *The Seagull.* Chekhov's use of Konstantin's play is crucial to his whole development of the character of Konstantin and to the expression of some of the central ideas of *The Seagull.* A discussion of Chekhov's play, then, may properly begin with an analysis of the play within the play.

"Cold, cold, cold. Empty, empty, empty. Terrible, terrible, terrible."

The state of Konstantin's world of tomorrow, unpromising as it appears at first glance, is not entirely without hope. On closer investigation it becomes apparent that Konstantin is dramatizing in mythopoetic language a physical world that is delicately poised between death and life, between sterility and creation, between the negative force of the "father of eternal matter, the devil," and the beneficent, life-stimulating power of "spirit." We have here, essentially, a dramatization of unliberated life and creation; and, it is further apparent, this is also a crucial self-dramatization. The author Konstantin not only projects a vision of a universe in biological limbo; he, or his alter ego, also inhabits it. But what is not quite clear or established is the poet-narrator's exact status in this created legend.

At the end of the first half of his soliloquy—after referring to the merging of the souls into one—the poet identifies himself directly with the force of spirit and creation which continues to inhabit the universe.

The universal world soul—that's me, me. In me there is the soul of Alexander the Great, and of Caesar, and of Shakespeare, and of Napoleon, and of the last worm. In me the consciousness of people is united with the instincts of animals, and I remember everything, everything, everything, and I experience anew every life in myself.

This is the high point of the soliloquy. His self-centered exaltation is not without a sort of naïve charm. The poet completely identifies himself with his muse. And this muse is ascendant.

But at this point—and we are now halfway through Konstantin's play—the "marsh fires" (will-o'-the-wisp) appear. (The reader will recall that Konstantin's mother, the actress Irina Nikolaevna Arkadina, exclaims at this juncture: "This is something decadent"—to which Konstantin replies with a pleading "Mama!") The marsh fires, it is evident, take on the character of some kind of robot creature-symbols which have depressing import to the poet. Indeed, their appearance, signals the collapse of his poetic ego: the "universal soul" metamorphoses into a petty anthropomorphic soul. "I am alone. Once in a hundred years I open my lips to speak and my voice echoes gloomily in this emptiness, and nobody hears me." The pale fires, born from the rotten bog, wander mindlessly and without will or beat of life, toward the dawn. Fearing that life will awaken in them, the poet tells us, the "father of eternal matter, the devil" keeps the atoms in these fires on constant flux. "Only spirit remains constant and unchangeable in the universe." But now spirit seems to be keeping very much to itself. The poet, plainly, is abandoned by his muse.

Like a prisoner thrown into an empty, deep well. I do not know where I am or what awaits me. One

thing, however, is not concealed from me: in stubborn, savage struggle with the devil, with the element of material forces, I am destined to conquer, and then matter and spirit will unite in a beautiful harmony and the kingdom of the world will is to arrive.

Konstantin's play gives expression to the *pro* and *contra* in his nature. It dramatizes his creative yearnings, the flight of his poetic muse, but in the final analysis it is paradigmatic of the downward spiral of a hopelessly crippled creative spirit. "There's something in it," Dr. Dorn observes after seeing Konstantin's play, something "fresh, naïve." The play, indeed, partakes of poetry, as the audience realizes in Act IV when the young actress Nina Mikhailovna Zarechnaya recites again the opening lines from Konstantin's youthful work. But apart from revealing a propensity for abstractions and symbols ("not a single character that's alive," Trigorin later observes of Konstantin's writings in general), the play discloses Konstantin's tendency toward grandiose dreams and impetuous challenges, on the one hand, and passive retreats and sterile reconciliations on the other. The movement of the play—all appearances to the contrary—is precipitous from self-exaltation to a depressed posture of defeat. Here in his well the poet prophesies "stubborn, savage struggle with the devil" and eventual victory. But this is empty prophecy: the well is dry. The poet himself is inwardly aware of the emptiness of his prophecy, of the utopian character of his mythic dream of "beautiful harmony" and of a "kingdom of world will." He resolves the contradiction between the reality of his nature (his weakness of will, his impotence) and his fantastic dream in the manner of a familiar Chekhovian type.

But all this will only take place when, little by little, through long, long series of millennia, both the moon,

Chekhov reading The Seagull *to the directors and actors of the Moscow Art Theater, 1898.*

and the bright Sirius, and the earth will turn into
dust. And until then, horror, horror.

The "horror" here is, in a sense, an intuition: the self's fore-
reading of its own tragic emptiness.

It may be argued that our analysis of the inner direction of
Konstantin's play—the view that it moves toward compromise
and defeat—must be permanently flawed by the fact that we
are analyzing an incomplete drama: the play within the play,
as we know, is cut short by a flurry of argument between
mother and son. There is no question that the outcome of the
poet-narrator's struggle with the "devil" cannot be deduced
with complete certainty from Konstantin's text alone, just as
it is impossible at the outset of *The Seagull* clearly to anticipate
the denouement of Konstantin's struggle to become a mature
artist. Both destinies are to a large extent "open." But in the
action that brings Konstantin's play to an end Chekhov subtly
prefigures the sad fate of Konstantin and, at the same time,
indicates the inner direction of Konstantin's play, that is, discloses that *conclusion* which is embryonic in the play's development. This action is so ordinary and so distracting as to
conceal its profound meaning. We have in mind Konstantin's
altercation with his mother.

This altercation is the momentary point of intersection of two
lines: the line of the poet-narrator's struggle with the "devil"
in the play within the play, and the line of Konstantin's permanent psychological duel with his mother. The duel—one
marked throughout *The Seagull* by alternating acts of hostility,
magnanimity, and submission—forms a real-life prologue to
Konstantin's play; it bisects the play at its halfway point (the
appearance of the bog fires and the deflation of poetic ego—
the painful exchange between mother and son); finally, it is
the immediate cause of the play's ending. "My mighty opponent, the devil, is now approaching," the poet declares. "I
see his fearful, crimson eyes. . . ." At this point Konstantin's
own mighty antagonist, his mother, once and for all shatters
his magic lantern with some disruptive, sarcastic comments on
the play. Put out by this cruel teasing, Konstantin declares:
"The play is finished! Enough! Curtain!" And in a childish
fit he retires from the scene. His retreat, of course, constitutes
an ironic commentary upon the bold resolve of his fictional
alter ego. In the context of Chekhov's subtle juxtaposition and
interplay of real and fictional lines in the episode of the play
within the play, we recognize that Konstantin's announcement,
"the play is finished," anticipates the abortive ending of his
life drama; it constitutes a dramatic rehearsal for the ending of
The Seagull.

The negative attitude of Madame Arkadina toward her son—
unfavorable circumstances, indeed, for the artistic as well as
psychological development of Konstantin's personality—cannot be underestimated in any evaluation of his personal tragedy.
But in the final analysis it is Konstantin himself who chooses
to ring down the curtain on his own life, as he does on his
own play. We may note in passing, here, that Konstantin's
impulsive retreat before his mother's jibes contrast pointedly
with Nina's efforts, in the midst of the quarrel, to continue the
play. Konstantin's behavior in this episode, then, reveals fundamental character weaknesses which will manifest themselves
in his life at large. Konstantin's confrontation with his mother
is of a very petty nature. Yet as Chekhov once observed: "Let
everything on the stage be just as complex and at the same
time just as simple as in life. People dine, merely dine, but at
that moment their happiness is being made or their life is being
smashed." So, also, here—in an ordinary quarrel, in a single

moment, Chekhov discloses the compound character and fate
of his hero.

Konstantin created for himself in his play a legend not too
different in character from the typical fairy tale, with its demons, its embattled and enchanted knights, and its golden
kingdoms at the end of the trail. As in a fairy tale, so in
Konstantin's legend we are in a world of magic, of the supernatural. The hero in this legend, plainly, finds himself imprisoned by some evil force (the devil). But how will he get
out? In stubborn, savage struggle, he declares, "I am destined
to conquer" *(mne suzhdeno pobedit')*. The passive structuring
of this thought is revealing. Who has destined this victory?
What fairy of fate, what magic is going to liberate the hero
from his dry prison-well? The appeal here on the part of the
poet to a force, fate *(sud'ba)*, outside of self points to the tragic
flaw in Konstantin, this modern pseudo-tragic hero of *The
Seagull:* his refusal to recognize his essential freedom and to
accept the responsibility that it implies.

Chekhov alludes to this refusal at the very outset of the play
when Konstantin casually tries his fortune by an age-old means:
"(Picking petals from a flower) She loves me, loves me not,
loves me, loves me not, loves me, loves me not. (Laughs.)
You see, my mother doesn't love me. You can say that again!"
A search for authority, for a decision-maker outside of oneself,
of course, is characteristic of all immaturity. The young actress
Nina also reveals a penchant for fortune-telling: "Even or odd,"
she asks Trigorin at the beginning of Act III. "No," Nina
sighs, "I have only one pea in my hand. I was trying my
fortune: should I become an actress or not? I wish somebody
would advise me." Trigorin's reply—and we have no difficulty
recognizing Chekhov in these words—is that "in this sort of
thing nobody can give advice." We are free. Nina must accept
her freedom: the choice must be one's own. "No general ethics
can show you what is to be done," Sartre wrote in *L'existen-
tialisme est un humanisme* in connection with another case of
decision-making. "There are no omens in the world." This is
a painful lesson that many of Chekhov's heroes experience. It
is of the essence of Chekhov's conception of Nina that she
ultimately accepts a world without omens, that, in a very real
sense, she takes her fate into her own hands. "Boris Alek-
seevich," she exclaims to Trigorin at the end of Act III, "I
have made an irrevocable decision; the die is cast; I am going
on the stage. Tomorrow I will not be here any longer; I am
leaving my father, abandoning everything; I am beginning a
new life." Nothing is fated, nothing postponed here; a choice
is arrived at lucidly. If anything Nina's decision constitutes a
challenge to fate, to the force of circumstances (her family
life) which is so hostile to her choice of an artistic career. "The
main thing is to give a new turn to life," Sasha tells Nadya
in Chekhov's last story, **"The Betrothed."** And Nadya leaves
her provincial town, breaks out of the rut. The tragic consequences of this kind of challenge to fate are part of the story
of Nina in *The Seagull.* But it is tragedy in which the consequences are surmounted and a new vision attained.

Chekhov sees in the individual's attitude toward "fate"—whether
expressed in discussion or in casual or unconscious acts—a
measure of the individual's own capacity to respond to the sum
total of forces acting upon him, to necessity, to the *given* in
life. (pp. 99-104)

Those characters in Chekhov who accept the notion of fate, of
a force acting independently and capriciously outside of human
will, seem to bear within themselves the element of defeat.
The fatalistic philosophy of Tusenbach, so poignantly ex-

pressed in Act II of *The Three Sisters,* is an ingredient of his tragic fate. "The die is cast," he exclaims in connection with his decision to retire from the army. But his decision to take charge of his life comes too late. This amiable but weak man is the victim, quite ironically, of the meaningless universe that he posits as a philosopher. His would-be partner in life, Irina, also relates passively to life; like Konstantin Treplev in *The Seagull,* she reveals the character of her world view in her casual play with cards: "It's coming out right, the patience, I see. We shall be in Moscow." Fate, chance, luck, of course, is not going to bring the sisters to Moscow, any more than Charlotta Ivanovna's tricks (in *The Cherry Orchard*) will save the orchard. Chance is never productive, creative in the world of Chekhov. On the contrary. When the owners of the cherry orchard renounce their option to decide upon the fate of the estate, when they renounce their freedom actively to participate in their own fate, the estate and their lives are ceded both literally and symbolically to the caprice of chance—the auction block. We discern in the magician Charlotta Ivanovna a symbol of that haphazard universe for which Lyubov Andreevna Ranevskaya and her brother opt (the scattering of money, the game of billiards are symbolic). It is the merchant Lopakhin—no relier on chance or the help of others, but a man who lifts himself by his own bootstraps—who takes fate into his own hands and who triumphs.

The objective passiveness of the three sisters in fact leaves everything open to counter-productive chance: their weak brother *gambles* away their money; his wife, Natasha, and her lover Protopopov, untroubled by any fate or a sense of the meaninglessness of life, reap the benefits of this play with the wheel of fortune. "It's all the same," mutters the defunct doctor Chebutykin throughout the tragic Act IV of *The Three Sisters.* But whatever meaninglessness, chaos, or nonsense exists in the world outside of Chebutykin's will, he generously contributes to it through his own action or inaction. He himself, in his renunciation of knowledge, his philosophy of nonexistence, his bankruptcy as a doctor, and his indifference to the fate of Tusenbach (and therefore, for all practical purposes, to the fate of Irina), is the agent of blind, accidental fate. The life of Tusenbach and the half-happiness of Irina are sacrificed to Solyony's bullet of chance. "He was sentimental," Dostoevsky observed of Fyodor Karamazov, "he was evil and sentimental." These words might have been applied by a sterner Chekhov to Chebutykin.

Chebutykin's refrain, "it's all the same," is juxtaposed at the end of the play with the theme of knowledge, of knowing. "If we only knew, if we only knew!" Olga exclaims. "A man must be a believer or must seek some belief," Masha says in the same play, otherwise life is empty, empty. . . . Either he knows what he's living for, or it's all nonsense." Whether or not Chekhov believed that absolute insight into the meaning and purpose of life was attainable, he did believe that a creative life had to be based upon a striving for that knowledge. Happiness or despair, truth or void, lie not outside man, not in Moscow or in the falling snow, but in man, in his choices, and in his attitude toward the world about him. "I am destined to conquer," Konstantin's protagonist declares. We are not *a priori* destined for anything—is Chekhov's reply in *The Seagull.* Nor is the universe *a priori* a meaningful one. Man creates meaning, he gives embodiment to his "history," his destiny. His first step, everywhere, must be to recognize his fate in himself, his past in his present, and so come to grips with the only real *given* in history: man. This step Konstantin Gavrilovich Treplev is incapable of making.

"I love you just as tenderly and devotedly as in childhood," Konstantin tells his mother. "Except for you there's nobody left me now." The neurotic deadlock that constitutes his relation with his mother remains unbroken from the beginning to the end of *The Seagull.* "Can you imagine anything more hopeless than my position in her house?" he asks his uncle Sorin, in Act I. But, unlike Nina, who wrenches herself free from the stifling confines of her family, Konstantin chooses to remain with his dilemma. His last words, in Act IV, after Nina runs out of the house and out of his world once and for all, point to his peculiar oedipal paralysis. "It would be too bad if anybody met her in the garden and then told Mama. That might upset Mama."

Konstantin cannot leave the illusory "magic lake"; he cannot step out of the magic circle of his love-hate relationship with his mother; he cannot cease being a child. He finds himself surrounded by successful people whom he despises and who, so he believes, despise him as the son of a "burgher of Kiev." Certainly imagination, as much as reality, feeds his hypersensitivity. "*It seemed to me* that with their glances they measured my insignificance, *I guessed* their thoughts and suffered from humiliation" (italics mine—R.L.J.). He has contempt for the stale, though glamorous theatrical world of his mother. He is convinced that "new forms are necessary"; yet it is characteristic of his frayed and offended ego that he is equally convinced that "if we don't get them then nothing is necessary." Maupassant, he observes, "ran away from the Eiffel Tower which oppressed him with its vulgarity." But Konstantin himself does not run away from the vulgarity of his world: he stays with it, sinks ever more deeply into it, with his rankling ambition and sniveling self-depreciation, his wounded pride and peevish vanity.

He clearly seeks a kind of surrogate-mother in Nina. Yet the tragedy of his emotional quest is not that he seeks warmth and affection, love, but that this love becomes a kind of *sine qua non* for any sustained interest and progress in art. As he broods over the "failure" of his play (significantly this is his own judgment), he complains to Nina about her coldness. "Your coldness is terrible, unbelievable, it's as though I woke up and looked out and saw this lake suddenly dried up or sunk into the earth." And later, embracing his mother after his quarrel with her, he exclaims: "If you only knew! I have lost everything. She does not love me, I can no longer write, all my hopes have been smashed."

"Love," Chekhov jotted down in his notebook, "is either the remnant of something long past which is dying out but was once tremendous, or it is a part of something which in the future will develop into something tremendous; at the present time, however, it doesn't satisfy, offers far less than one expects." "If you fear loneliness, then don't marry," reads another note. In his well-known letter to his brother Nikolai in March 1886, in which he defines a cultured person, Chekhov remarks that if the cultured person possesses talent he respects it, he sacrifices "peace, women, wine, vanity to it." The creative personality does not passively subject itself to the love relationship. Love alone, Chekhov suggests in *The Seagull,* does not provide a firm foundation for a creative life. The tragedy of Masha in *The Seagull* is that, unlike Nina, she desires nothing but love.

Chekhov, however, does not adopt a monastic attitude toward the love relationship. Nina, in her final talk with Konstantin, indicates her readiness to plunge back again into the maelstrom of life. She says of Trigorin at this point: "I love him. I love him even more than before. 'An idea for a short story.' I love, I love passionately, I love to desperation.'' This is active love: love that is combined with a readiness to face life; it may not carry Nina to Arcadia, but it is love without illusions, love which seeks to envelop and not to be enveloped in warm self-oblivion.

Konstantin, on the other hand, seeks to be enveloped in love. He is ''cold'' and desires warmth: he yearns for the waters of the womb. Psychologically, he finds himself trapped in the ''oedipal situation.'' But if he is trapped, he has nonetheless, like Oedipus or Hamlet, the option of self-discovery in art or action. This option he rejects, for he lacks the courage to face himself, his talent. The self-knowledge that he attains in the end is too incomplete and too incidental to his real condition to grant him any tragic stature. Like so many Chekhovian heroes, his tragedy consists in his inability to rise to the level of tragedy. He is far from being a Hamlet. And for all the noise of his departure from this world, the real truth is that he leaves this life—to borrow the words from T. S. Eliot—''not with a bang but a whimper.''

The real knowledge of self, the blinding vision, the tragic perception, on the other hand, is granted to Nina. Her drama in its painful dialectic is symbolized in the complex image of the seagull; in its living and dead incarnations this image enters her being as a *pro* and *contra*. ''I'm a seagull. No, that's not it. I'm an actress.'' In her anguished outpouring to Konstantin in Act IV she speaks of her growing spiritual strength. ''Now I know, I understand, Kostya, that in our work—it makes no difference whether we are on the stage or writing—the main thing is not fame, not glory, not what I dreamed of, but the ability to endure. Be able to bear your cross and have faith. I have faith and it doesn't hurt me so much, and when I think about my calling, I do not fear life.''

Just before the performance of Konstantin's play, Medvedenko matter-of-factly observes that Nina ''will do the acting, while the play is written by Konstantin Gavrilovich.'' It is, indeed, Nina who *acts* in Konstantin's play and in the broader drama of life, who summons the will to confront the devil in ''stubborn, savage struggle,'' who emerges in *The Seagull* as the embodiment of Konstantin's ''world soul.''

The myth of Plato's ''cave'' and its inhabitants may or may not have been a conscious allegorical point of reference for Chekhov when he wrote *The Seagull,* especially its last act. But the fundamental elements of this myth nonetheless inform Chekhov's play (as they do Gorky's later play, *The Lower Depths*) on its deepest level of meaning—that level in art where character and idea merge with archetypal pattern and source. The central problem here is unquestionably that of illusion and reality and man's necessary movement from the former to the latter; the relevant metaphor, appearing in art and epic, is the *journey*. It is Nina, like Plato's wanderer, who leaves the magic world of illusions to make the difficult journey—the Platonic ''steep and rugged ascent''—to reality, to knowledge, to quintessential meaning; while it is Konstantin who chooses to remain forever secure in his world of shadows, illusions, and disembodied forms. ''You have found your road,'' he declares to Nina in Act IV, ''you know where you are going, but I am still moving in a chaos of dreams and images, not knowing for what or for whom this is necessary. I do not have faith and do not know where my calling lies.''

Two worlds are juxtaposed in the last act of *The Seagull* (as they are in the first scenes of *Hamlet*): the inner, comfortable world of warmth and the outer world of dark, threatening reality. ''Evening. A single lamp with a shade is lighted. Semidarkness. The sound from the outside of trees and rustling and the wind howling in the chimney. The night watchman is knocking.'' Outside, behind the glass door to the terrace which faces the audience, the garden is dark. Nina, like the wanderer in Plato's myth who revisits his den of old, returns to her native nest. She observes: ''It's warm, nice here,'' and again: ''It's nice here, warm, comfortable. Do you hear—the wind outside? Turgenev says somewhere: 'Happy is he who in such a night sits under the roof of a house, who has a warm spot.' I'm a seagull. No, that's not it. Where was I? Yes, Turgenev. 'And God help all homeless wanderers.''' And Nina, in her tears of pain and anguish, tears evoked by the contrast of past and present, recalls her ''clear, warm, joyful, pure life,'' her naïve dreams of fame, and her dreamlike love. But Konstantin misunderstands Nina's feelings. He begins to speak—trying to pick up the threads of the past, to reweave the old pattern; he reaffirms his love for her. Nina is brought up with a start. ''Why does he talk that way, why does he talk that way?'' The question is a pertinent one. Konstantin answers the question. ''I am alone, not warmed by anybody's affection, I am cold, as in a cave, and no matter what I write it's dry, harsh, and gloomy. Stay here, Nina, I beg of you, or let me go away with you. (Nina quickly puts on her hat and cape.)''

Why is Nina in such haste to leave? Socrates, discussing the return of the wanderer to the cave, observes that the wanderer would find it easier ''to endure anything, rather than think as they do [in the cave] and live after their manner.'' Men in the cave would say of the wanderer, according to Socrates, that ''up he went and down he came without his eyes; and that it was better not even to think of ascending.'' But for the wanderer—''he would rather suffer anything than entertain these false notions and live in this miserable manner.'' It is in these terms that we can understand Konstantin's view of Nina as a failure (his story of Nina's two years away from home) and Nina's attitude toward his appeal to remain with him. There can be no return to the innocence and illusions of the past. Nina's reply to Konstantin's plea is replete with real and symbolic meaning. ''My horses are standing at the gate. Don't see me off. I'll make it by myself. (Through her tears) Give me some water.'' Nina dashes into the play on a horse—''A red sky, the moon is already rising, and I raced the horse, I raced it.'' Nina's horse—Pegasus, winged horse of inspiration—stands ready to carry her away. Brutal reality (''we have both been drawn into the maelstrom'') is preferable to Konstantin's sterile cave. ''Give me some water.'' Nina's request for water—over and above its perfectly ordinary meaning—takes on special poetic significance in the context of the rich water imagery in *The Seagull* (Nina's name, Zarechnaya—''beyond or across the river,'' the ''magic lake''). Water is creation, life. Konstantin offers Nina some water to drink. Yet in the arid world that he still inhabits there is none of the water for which Nina craves and upon which art and life flourish. The ''magic lake'' toward which Nina once had been drawn ''like a seagull'' has vanished. All that is left is a cold cave, a dry lake, an empty well.

The personal tragedy of Konstantin is that he chose not to make the journey of his life; overwhelmed by his character, he remained forever in the shadow of his fear of life. The triumph of Nina is her free choice of the journey, her willingness, finally, to *endure*. One may say, of course, that this is a very narrow, precarious triumph. And so it is. But Chekhov, like Dostoevsky, was a realist where man is concerned. He knew that the only triumph that counts is the precarious one, the one, in short, that is organically fused with tragic knowledge and experience.

The painful relinquishment of golden childhood and the dream of innocence before the bitter necessity of knowing reality—this is the poignant and tragic side of Nina Zarechnaya's journey into life. Art, or, at least, "pure art" with its efflorescence of beauty, is somehow permanently linked with that dream of innocence. In this sense Nina's awakening in real life reenacts the tragedy of the fall. Yet it is clear that Chekhov does not envisage the renunciation of art or illusion (in the deepest creative sense) in the journey to reality. In the lucid confrontation with reality—the "paradox of the fortunate fall"—lies all realistic hope, the hope once again of reappropriating the dream. (pp. 105-11)

> Robert Louis Jackson, "Chekhov's 'Seagull': The Empty Well, the Dry Lake, and the Cold Cave," in Chekhov: A Collection of Critical Essays, *edited by Robert Louis Jackson, Prentice-Hall, Inc., 1967, pp. 99-111.*

RANDALL JARRELL (publication date 1969)

[*Jarrell was an American poet, critic, novelist, and translator whose extensive knowledge of American history, world literature, and the experience of war informed many of his works, including his best known poem, "The Death of the Ball Turrett Gunner." In the following excerpt, he discusses the themes and structure of* The Three Sisters *and gives an act-by-act analysis of the play.*]

In a sense **The Three Sisters** needs criticism less than almost any play I can think of. It is so marvelously organized, made, realized, that reading it or seeing it many times to be thoroughly acquainted with it is all one needs. In it Chekhov gives us a cluster of attitudes about values—happiness, marriage, work, duty, beauty, cultivation, the past, the present, the future—and shows us how these are meaningful or meaningless to people. Values are presented to us through opposed opinions, opposed lives; at different ages in life with different emotions; and finally, on different levels.

Take the ways, for instance, that marriage is presented: so obviously, so tenuously, so alternatively. All the marriages we see are disasters; but Vershinin's goes wrong for different reasons than Andrei's, and Andrei's goes wrong for different reasons than Masha's. Still, Chekhov can lump them into one generalization that we accept when Vershinin says, "Why is a Russian always sick and tired of his wife . . . and his wife and children always sick and tired of him?" Then he uses a generalization from particular experience when he has Andrei tell us, "People shouldn't get married. They shouldn't because it's boring." These are bold truths. And yet, surrounded by bad models (and in Kulygin's case, involved in one), Olga remains convincingly dedicated to marriage as an ideal—woman's role, woman's duty. And Kulygin never loses his faith in its value as a value, or as an "institution" to belong to for its own sake, and continues to encourage the single ones to marry.

"Love and Marriage" is a little ballet for Irina and Tuzenbach of coming together and parting, of going separate ways yet looking over shoulders. First they are on the same side about love. Both of them idealize it and want it, but while his dream of love is Irina, hers is Moscow where she'll meet "the real one." Later, when she gives up her dream, they come together on the marriage level (long enough to be engaged) but not at the love level. Theirs is a poignant pas de deux when, first,

Irina truthfully declares it is not in her power to love this homely man and, after that, Tuzenbach's own sensitive drawing back from marriage on those terms. Both of them achieve their maximum substance as human beings at this moment. When he says to her, "There isn't anything in my life terrible enough to frighten me, only that lost key . . ." (the key to Irina's love), and when he puts love ahead of the imminent duel, Tuzenback is ennobled. The ambiguities here make it possible for us to wonder whether the marriage would really have gone ahead the next day if he had not been killed, whether the "dead tree" allusion of Tuzenbach's meant he *knew* (by willing it) that he was going to die. (pp. 103-04)

There is a real geometry to **The Three Sisters**. It has an ideological, character, and chain-of-events organization that develops with an inevitableness akin to Greek tragedy. After making his logical skeleton Chekhov invents and *invents* plausible disguises that keep the play from having the Ibsen-well-made surface and the symbols from having the Ibsen starkness. Indeed, having so many symbols and leitmotivs prevents the most important of any of them from sticking out or being too differentiated from the rest of the surface. While the underlying organization is extremely plain, parallel, and symmetrical, it is masked by a "spot-surface" or expressed in terms of these "spots" themselves.

A visual counterpart of this very method uncannily exists in the work of the painter Vuillard. In certain of his indoor and outdoor scenes of French domestic life, the foundation areas on the canvas are made less emphatic by the swarms of particles that mottle the walls with rose-printed paper, the rugs with swirls, the lawns with pools of sun and shade. From such variation and variegation comes his cohesion. Vuillard commingles plaids and dappled things as non sequitur as the jottings in Chebutykin's notebook. He alludes to a mysterious darkness by leaving a door ajar. He baffles the viewer by a woman's ear glowing red. What does she hear? In the same way, Masha's eccentric line "By the curved seastrand a green oak stands / A chain of gold upon it . . ." baffles us. What *does* it mean?

These Vuillard "spots" are found in bizarre, grotesque, homey touches in a speech, a mannerism, a trait, an incident that add up to several dozen possibly. Solyony, Chebutykin, Kulygin, Natasha, and Ferapont are covered with them; Olga and Irina and Vershinin scarcely have any; with Masha and Tuzenbach they are used sparingly but memorably. Chekhov made such imaginative and original use of the indeterminacy principle on the microscopic level (the opposite of Ibsen) while maintaining on the macroscopic level firm causality. The more his themes and characters were contradictory, inconsistent, and ambiguous, the more the play got a feeling of the randomness and personalness of real life. (pp. 105-06)

In a certain sense **The Three Sisters** is as well-made as an Ibsen play in that everything is related to everything else, except that Chekhov relates things in a musical way, or in a realistic-causal, rather than geometrical-rhetorical-causal, way. The repeated use of Wagnerian leitmotivs occurs not only for characters but for themes, ideology, and morality. Diffusing the themes required more concentration, he wrote in letters when he was working on **The Three Sisters,** than for any other play. He perfected it to relax the essential structural framework the play is built on. In the exchange of themes, overly defined edges of characterization and situation are blurred and, to him, more realistic. In particular, Chebutykin's "What's the difference?" is his own special leitmotiv that, however, is borrowed by nearly everyone at sometime or other, just as themes of fatigue, happiness, boredom, etc., are shared.

Loneliness (hardly a value or a philosophy) becomes a sort of ghost that haunts Andrei all the time, Irina until she gets older, and Solyony under cover of his Lermontov personality. (pp. 110-11)

[Chekhov] keeps us conscious of the loneliness underneath the general animation. At the birthday party in Act I, there is Vershinin's line about the gloomy-looking bridge in Moscow where the water under it could be heard: "It makes a lonely man feel sad." Later on we hear again when Chebutykin tells Andrei about being unmarried, even if marriage is boring: "But the loneliness! You can philosophize as much as you please, but loneliness is a terrible thing, Andrei. . . ." With the "good-bye trees" and "good-bye echo" and the embraces, tears, *au revoir*'s and farewells, loneliness has built up like entropy as the good social group—that partly kept people from being lonely—has been broken into by the inferior outside world. The organized enclave of Act I, after being invaded by the relatively unorganized environment, loses its own organization like a physical system and runs down to almost nothing . . . Andrei.

The musical side of Russian life, and Chekhov, comes into the play in every act: Masha whistles, the carnival people play off-stage, Chebutykin sings nervously after the duel. Specifically, Act I opens with Olga remembering the band's funeral march after the father's death and Act IV ends with the band playing a march as the brigade leaves and Olga has her last, summarizing speech. The "yoo-hoos" beforehand have imparted a faintly musical nostalgia to the scene, too. In Acts I and II there are guitar and piano and singing. "My New Porch" is a song everyone knows like "Old MacDonald Had a Farm," so that when Tuzenbach starts it off, even lonely Andrei and old Chebutykin can carry it along. Masha and Vershinin's duet becomes a witty—but entirely different—parallel of this formula. The camaraderie at the bottom of the first is countered with the romantic insinuation of the second. "Unto love all ages bow, its pangs are blest . . ." leaves nothing in doubt, and when Masha sings a refrain of this and Vershinin adds another, they make a musical declaration of love. This is an excellent preparation for Act III when, after Masha's love confession, it would have been awkward for Vershinin and her to appear together on stage. Their intimacy is even strengthened, in our minds, by his off-stage song to Masha which she hears, comprehends, and answers in song before leaving the stage to join him.

There was always a piano in Chekhov's house, and having someone play helped him to write when he got stuck. Rhythms came naturally to him, and just as he has varied them in the lines of *The Three Sisters*—from the shortest (sounds, single words) to the arias and big set speeches—similarly there is a rhythmic pattern like that on a railway platform where all the people know each other and little groups leave, say good-bye, meet.

To me, Davchenko's comment on the lack of spontaneity of this play is really a tribute to its extraordinary solidity of construction. How frail, spontaneously lyric, and farcical *The Cherry Orchard* is in comparison. Chekhov said of it, "I call it a comedy." It was the work of a dying man who had strength to write only a few lines a day, whereas *The Three Sisters: A Drama in Four Acts* is his crowning work. It is the culmination of his whole writing life. *Uncle Vanya* is the nearest thing, but

nothing equally long (none of the short novels) is as good as *The Three Sisters.* (pp. 111-13)

Taking place at noon on a spring day before the first leaves come out, Act I is one of beginnings. Irina, the young girl whose birthday it is, is beginning her new year quite recovered from the death in the family and filled with happiness at the expectations of going back to Moscow soon. We see Baron Tuzenbach's beginning declarations of love for her. We see a friendship beginning in the meeting of Colonel Vershinin and the social group who, as Moscow speaking to Moscow, are immediately at ease with each other and like each other at once. With Masha's "I'm staying to lunch," we have the first intimation of her love affair with Vershinin. While there is mention made that their brother Andrei is beginning studies in Moscow to be a professor, he has actually begun—by his proposal of marriage that day to Natasha, "one of the local girls"—something quite different.

In this act occurs the establishment of a social situation that's mostly very pleasant; mostly there are happy expectations, mostly they are friendly and well-off. The Prozorovs and their extensions—Anfisa and Ferapont, the family servants; Chebutykin, the longtime family friend; Vershinin and the young officers who knew the family or of it—*all* make a little, foreign, cultivated, highly organized cell inside a provincial, crude city. The family is a father-organization that has lost its father. General Prozorov represented the days when they were governed, had their life and ideals prescribed for them, and revolt, or breaking free for a little space, was their only necessity. His censorship they obeyed, or fooled. With it gone they can say anything; but in this terrible freedom the vacancy of grown-ups who governed them has to be filled by themselves, the new grown-ups. They had a paradise in which they had only to follow the rules. Now they have to make the rules they follow—and they long to be in that earlier existence with Father. Moscow is their past, but just as definitely it is their future.

They are surviving partly happily, partly unhappily, in the midst of their uncultivated environment when the only son, who is the family's weakest element, introduces into it a powerful representative of the environment who manages to dominate him completely and, in the long run, to drive out the other members of the father-group. In the affectionate joking and teasing of part of the family by the rest are the first hints of anything troubling underneath the pleasant surface, and then we begin to see that Irina *is* partly troubled by life, that Masha is very much so, and that Olga is extreme and psychosomatic.

After Act I's spring, noon, Act II is between 8 and 9:30 at night in cold winter weather with the wind howling in the chimney. Act II begins with the continuation of the proposal: Here Natasha and Andrei are after a year or so of marriage, and the directness of their condition has a slap-in-the-face force. Here, also, is the continuation of Vershinin and Masha, of the "happiness" and "future" and meaning of life. The Andrei-Ferapont relationship is now fixed so that change can be indicated by change in it, i.e., Andrei's demanding to be called "your honor." There is a continuation of Tuzenbach's work-longing; with Irina there is the first dissatisfaction with her work. Act II is preparation for a party as is Act I, but a much more troubled preparation, which, when in full swing of beginning, is canceled out by Natasha (the provincial city element inside the little foreign cell, itself inside the provincial city), the element that's begun to destroy, grows and grows, and finally does destroy.

At the start of tea with singing, the litle group is almost as pleasant as in the first act, but now needs the drunkenness, obliviousness, as in Act I it didn't. Being undermined by Natasha, the group continues more hectically with drinking and quarreling, and comes to nothing in a dreadfully anticlimactic, damped-out way. Solyony's declaration of love to Irina is unpleasant nothing to Irina, and results in unpleasant nothing to Solyony. The threat about successful rivals brings out in the open the unpleasantness toward Tuzenbach and Irina that finally kills Tuzenbach. Olga's exhaustion leads her straight to bed. The exhausted Kulygin doesn't get his evening in congenial company, and won't accompany Vershinin who (still tealess) has had nothing to eat all day, has to go out all alone. The act ends with most of them, and the carnival people, frustrated in some way; all, except Natasha, who gets her troika ride with Protopopov. Her temporary driving away of most of the family in Act II is foreshadowing what will happen permanently later. The stage is empty at the last with Irina alone, saying yearningly, "To Moscow! To Moscow! To Moscow!"

Just as the two preceding acts, [Act III] is a large *social* thing (Act I birthday dinner and Act II Mardi Gras preparations that are canceled). Act III is carried along by the arrangements necessitated by a social disaster, the fire in the town. The whole household is either taking part or avoiding taking part in it. We hardly notice what time of year it is. Under such unusual circumstances the unusual can be said or asked, and the extraordinary truth about most of the characters comes out at this extraordinary time.

With all the climaxes in Act III: Olga and Natasha's quarrel, Chebutykin's and Masha's confessions, Andrei's exposure, and Irina's breaking down, the first announcement is made of the brigade's leaving which will result in the departure of Vershinin and the military attachments of the Prozorovs.

The spring and birth beginnings of Act I have proceeded to the fall's prelude to winter, with the swans and geese flying south, departures, death, and conclusions.

The enclave's allies are leaving, the last remnants of the father-organization are gone. Natasha has complete victory in the house. Irina and Olga have been driven out, and Masha no longer enters the house. Natasha has all the rooms she wants, she can chop the trees down, and she has Protopopov there every day. Natasha, by being introduced into the family-society of *The Three Sisters,* destroys it, just as Yelena's introduction into the family-society in *Uncle Vanya* disrupts it. But Yelena leaves, and that society reforms and tries to go on as before. Natasha has broken to pieces the Prozorov society whose fragments go on as best they can.

What to make of a diminished thing, how to get partial satisfaction, get along, make life on a lower level of expectation? They now regard this existence as necessary, their fate, their lot (like growing old) rather than as something escapable (like leaving for Moscow). Not living in Moscow is accepted.

Olga does this with her impersonal schoolwork and being headmistress. No further mention of headaches and tiredness from her.

Irina plans to be satisfied without love, but with work away from home, and with marriage to a good man whom she doesn't love. This makes her feel happily anticipating again. When Tuzenbach is killed, the marriage part is removed, but she still sticks to the work ideal. Masha, after the partial satisfaction of the love affair with Vershinin, has to settle for continuing life without him but with Kulygin.

Chebutykin leaves for retirement, and Andrei surrenders in complete, abjectly nervous defeat.

In Act I Olga has the first lines and she recalled the band playing at the father's funeral. In Act IV Olga has the last lines to speak, and the band music accompanies her. As *The Three Sisters* ends, Olga puts her arms around the other two and makes a long speech that sums up her sisters' last words and one half of the play itself: the half that is about the meaning of life. She ends this speech by repeating the two Russian words that in an entirely literal translation would be *If knew, If knew!* and that in ordinary American English are *If only we knew, if only we knew!* Chebutykin once more sings his nonsensical little song and then says twice over the two Russian words that have ended three out of four of his last speeches, words which sum up the meaningless, senseless, hopeless half of life. "What's the difference?" Olga repeats, "If only we knew, if only we knew," and the play is over. (pp. 156-60)

Randall Jarrell, "Chekhov and the Play" and "The Acts," in The Three Sisters *by Anton Chekhov, edited and translated by Randall Jarrell, The Macmillan Company, 1969, pp. 103-13, 156-60.*

J. L. STYAN (essay date 1971)

[*Styan is an English critic and educator who has written extensively on the theater. In the following excerpt, he comments on the major themes and techniques of* The Cherry Orchard.]

Chekhov's advances in craftsmanship in *The Cherry Orchard* suggest a complete confidence in what he was doing at the last. One might point to the progress of the setting of the play from act to act, moving from the house out to the estate itself (almost, indeed, to the town beyond) and back to the house again; and, within the house, from the most intimately evocative room, the nursery, to more public rooms, and back again to the nursery. Parallel with these visual changes, Chekhov makes a more thematic use of the weather and the seasons, passing from the chill of spring with its promise of warmth to the chill of autumn with its threat of winter. In this, the lyricism of *The Seagull* returns to Chekhov's dramatic writing. The growth of the year from May to October is precisely indicated, and the cycle of the cherry trees, from their blossoming to their fruiting and their destruction, matches the cycle of joy and grief, hope and despair, within the family. As in *Three Sisters,* time and change, and their effects wrought on a representative group of people, are the subject of the play. But in feeling for this, Chekhov knows that the realism of the chosen convention can dangerously narrow his meaning until it seems too particular and finally irrelevant. He thus works hard to ensure that his play projects a universal image, giving his audience some sense that this microcosm of the cherry orchard family stands, by breadth of allusion and a seemingly inexhaustible patterning of characters, for a wider orchard beyond.

The cherry orchard is a particular place and yet it is more. It represents an inextricable tangle of sentiments, which together comprise a way of life and an attitude to life. By the persistent feelings shown towards it, at one extreme by old Firs, the house-serf for whom the family is his whole existence, and at another by Trofimov, the intellectual for whom it is the image of repression and slavery; by Lopahin, the businessman and spokesman for hard economic facts, the one who thinks of it primarily as a means to wiser investment, and by Mme Ranevsky, who sees in it her childhood happiness and her former innocence, who sees it as the embodiment of her best values— by these and many other contradictions, an audience finds that the orchard grows from a painted backcloth to an ambiguous, living, poetic symbol of human life, *any* human life, in a state of change.

Inseparable from these patterns are those into which the cherry orchard characters are woven by their brilliant selection. Chekhov claimed that his cast for the play was small, but in performance they seem curiously to proliferate. Offstage characters increase the complexity, like the lover in Paris, the Countess in Yaroslavl, Pishtchik's daughter Dashenka, Lyubov's drowned son Grisha. But the true reason for this sense of proliferation is because the same dozen players, each supplied with a character of three-dimensional individuality in Chekhov's impressive way, are encouraged to group and regroup themselves in our minds. He had always been meticulous in delineating the social background to his situation. Now he plans the play's context as a living environment. What is "a cross-section of society?" It may be a division by birth and class, by wealth, by age, by sex, by aspirations and moral values. Chekhov divides the people of the cherry orchard in a variety of ways, so that the orchard and its sale take on a different meaning for each group.

By birth and class, we see the members of the land-owning upper middle class, Mme Ranevsky, Gaev, Anya and, accordingly, the foster-daughter Varya, slipping from their security: we are made to feel what it is like to be uprooted. Lopahin, Epihodov, Yasha and Dunyasha, the servants and former peasants, are straining, comically it may be, to achieve a new social status. For some, Charlotta, Trofimov and Pishtchik for much of the play, their future security is in doubt. Forty years after the Emancipation, each character is still making a personal adjustment to the social upheaval according to age, sex or rank, and according to his lights. As a group, the cherry orchard people demonstrate the transition between the old and the new, bringing life to Chekhov's idea of an evolving social structure. The passing of time is thus represented *socially*. The three classes on the stage, owners, dependents and the new independents like Lopahin, are a social microcosm at a given point in time, so that any shift in the pattern of dependence forces an audience to acknowledge the reality of social time.

From economic considerations, the one-time wealthy landowners, Mme Ranevsky, Gaev and Pishtchik, are in great distress. The responsibile ones, Lopahin, Charlotta and Varya, are intimately concerned: to those who must battle the real world, money matters. However, the new generation, Trofimov and Anya, are largely indifferent, and the servants are unaffected. But money is the least of it.

By age, those of middle years who live in and for the past, like Mme Ranevsky and Gaev, the sale of the orchard is a blow striking at their very souls. For Anya, Trofimov, Dunyasha and Yasha, the young who, naturally, live for the future, the event is an opportunity for enterprise of one kind or another, self-interested or altruistic as the case may be. For those who are neither young nor old, for Varya, Lopahin and Charlotta, those concerned with the pressing problems of the present, the auction is an urgent call for decisions and practical measures. Firs, aged eighty-seven, is beyond time. *The Cherry Orchard* is thus, in part, a "generations" play, marking the conflict between the old and the young, the substance of a thousand dramatic themes. To watch the interactions of the four age-groups is to watch the cycle of life itself. Time will be alive on the stage, and the characters will seem human milestones.

By sex, the departure from the orchard means an assessment of marital needs and opportunities, and the spinsters, Charlotta, Varya and Dunyasha, are troubled in varying degrees. But Pishtchik, Lopahin and Yasha, because of other pressures, fail to respond. While Anya and Trofimov claim idealistically to be "above love," at least for the time being, Mme Ranevsky is thrown back on her other resource, her Paris lover; as instinct or impulse brought her back to the orchard, so one or other drives her back to Paris. Only Firs has arrived at that time of life when nothing, neither status, money, past nor future, can affect him any more. With exquisite irony, it is he whose neglect by the family in the last act passes the final comment on them all.

This is not the best place to indicate the echoes and parallels and parodies built into this restless group of people: these are better observed as the action of the play proceeds. Mme Ranevsky finds her counterpart in the feckless optimist Pishtchik, the neighbouring landowner. Epihodov the clerk counters Pishtchik's trust in fate with an equally pessimistic fatalism. While Epihodov declares that he has resigned himself to his position, Yasha, who aspires to higher things than the life of a servant, is treading on necks as he climbs. When Gaev finds Yasha, a servant, playing his own aristocratic game of billiards, the valet's impertinence measures his master's own precarious status. Gaev, sucking his caramels, will, in spite of his disclaimers, never do a day's useful work, and Chekhov sets this weakness against the practical energies of Lopahin. And Lopahin against Trofimov. And Trofimov against Mme Ranevsky. *La ronde* continues ceaselessly.

Patterns of characters, then, make patterns of dramatic emphasis, and this "plotless" play is one with *too many* plots, however fragmentary, to permit analysis finally to untangle all its threads. In *Three Sisters,* Chekhov traced the passing of the months and years from scene to scene, and we watched the visible transformation of the people of the play. In *The Cherry Orchard,* time past, present and future are at the last all one, the play's last act an integrated moment of revelation. We know the orchard must go, just as surely as the curtain must fall, and in Act IV Chekhov counts out the minutes, as in the first three acts he counted out the days to the sale. As the minutes pass, we scrutinize the whole family. Every exchange, between Lopahin and Trofimov on their futures, between Mme Ranevsky and Pishtchik on the vagaries of fate, between Varya and Lopahin in their abortive proposal scene, refocuses the image of the play. When Varya seems to strike Lopahin with a stick, the notions both of differences in class and of sexual need are by one gesture violently yoked together, simultaneously reintroduced to contradict one another. When Trofimov refuses Lopahin's generous offer of a loan, the student's youth and idealism are in pathetic contrast with Lopahin's maturity and common sense. When Mme Ranevsky gives away her purse to the peasants at her door (her name "Lyuba" means "love"), we see in the gesture her failure to be realistic about her financial circumstances as well as her paternalistic affection for all the orchard stood for in the past. One incident comprehends and generates the next, endlessly, and the last act is a masterpiece of compact concentration.

"The entire play is so simple, so wholly real, but to such a point purified of everything superfluous and enveloped in such a lyrical quality, that it seems to me to be a symbolic poem."

Chekhov and his wife, Olga Knipper.

So wrote Nemirovich-Danchenko, early recognizing the gratifying contradiction that a play can be naturalistic and poetic at the same time. *The Cherry Orchard* has the poetic strength of simplicity. The interweaving in the play, the relationships between one generation and another, between master and servant, between the love-lorn and the less concerned, with the ebb and flow of such relationships, are the source of *poetic* energy in the play. But the subtle shifts across the social fabric are also the source of the play's *comic* energy, compelling its audience to remain both alert and amused as it watches. In *The Cherry Orchard,* Chekhov consummated his life's work with a *poetic comedy* of exquisite balance. (pp. 240-44)

> *J. L. Styan, in his* Chekhov in Performance: A Commentary on the Major Plays, *Cambridge at the University Press, 1971, 341 p.*

JEAN-PIERRE BARRICELLI   (essay date 1977)

[*Barricelli is an American critic, translator, and poet. In the following essay, he explores the significance of the snapping string in* The Cherry Orchard.]

To the author of *The Cherry Orchard,* to be a member of the human race meant to be a confused victim of oppositions or paradoxes, of counterpoints. For this reason, paradox is inherent in Chekhov's concept of dramaturgy, and something provoking bewilderment does not necessarily constitute an extraneous element in a play. A case in point is the unexpected and vaguely disconcerting sound of a snapping string that is heard in the distance and from the sky twice in *The Cherry Orchard,* once toward the end of Act II, and again at the conclusion of the fourth and final act. Critical bewilderment before the sound has persisted since the first rehearsals in Moscow, attended by the author during December and January of 1903-4. To our way of thinking, the two counterpoising soundings, symmetrically placed, are central to the play: to its structure and symbolism and therefore to its innermost meaning. More than a psychological device for the audience, the double sounding is a substantive and structural device embedded deep in its heart, though all too often it has not been considered in this light. J. L. Styan declares correctly that "To interpret that sound is to interpret the play," although his interpretation follows that of many others who simply relate the sound to the passing of time, to the demise of the old social order, and the ushering in of a new one. H. Pitcher contends that by it Che-

khov did not intend "one specific meaning," and F. Fergusson hears it as a "sharp, almost warning signal," but nothing more. And C. B. Timmer, in an otherwise enlightening article on Chekhov's use of the bizarre, the grotesque, and the absurd—that is, in an article which, by drawing careful distinctions among these aspects of his art, would seem, therefore, to lend itself somewhere to a consideration of the weird, bizarre, and potentially absurd sound—makes no mention of it.

As might be expected, Soviet criticism, which eschews the exploration of metaphysical or symbolical forms that are not directly related to "social realism" and that may in fact controvert its goals, engages in no discussion of the meaning of the snapping string. Vsevolod Meyerkhol'd once came close when in criticizing Stanislavskiy's interpretation he sought the key to the play in its acoustics and inner rhythm (comparing it to a symphony of Chaykovskiy!), and concluded that the producer "must first of all understand it with his hearing." Clearly for Chekhov words are not the best vehicle to express thoughts and feelings. But more recently, Georgiy Berdnikov, who speaks of "devices" as coordinated with the characters, of "pauses" as revealing their inner substance, and of "sounds" as adding to the lyrical idea of the play, is silent on how this special sound may reveal the inner substance of *The Cherry Orchard.* Aleksandr Revyakin merely calls our attention to how the generally sad mood "finds correspondence in the words of Lopakhin, in the melancholy song of Yepikhodov, and is diffused in the sounds of a breaking string," though a few pages later he returns to the sound, suggesting that it has "an especially large, realistico-symbolic meaning"—but only, again, because it "announces a coming catastrophe." Again, no attempt is made to come to grips with the actual sound of the snapping string, which, in this nonformalistic body of criticism, is totally ignored. Abram Derman, whose chapters on "The Structural Elements in Chekhov's Poetics" or "The Poetry of Chekhov's Creativeness" would otherwise be likely places for such a discussion, overlooks it, as do Korney Chukovskiy and Vladimir Yermilov. One of the most striking omissions occurs in Sergey Balukhatyy's study of Chekhov as a dramatist, where a whole chapter is devoted to *The Cherry Orchard* with no mention of the sound despite an important comparison between Act II and Act IV. And we are not farther advanced in our inquiry by consulting the works of Aleksandr Roskin or Vasiliy Golubkov.

Maurice Valency, in his fine study of Chekhov's plays, despite its revealing title (*The Breaking String*) as well as its concluding chapter called "The Sound of the Breaking String," accepts the sound metaphorically, but does not explore its more intitmate meanings, either contextually or intextually. While he recognizes that "*The Cherry Orchard* centers upon the sound of the breaking string," he prefers to leave it shrouded in mystery: "The sound of the breaking string remains mysterious, but it has finality. The symbol is broad; it would be folly to try to assign to it a more precise meaning than the author chose to give it. But its quality is unequivocal. Whatever of sadness remains unexpressed in *The Cherry Orchard,* this sound expresses." And later, following up the observation that the sound is heard when the young people, Varya, Anya, and Trofimov find the aging Gayev's lyrical tribute to nature unbearable and force him to silence, Valency explains the metaphor in terms of a generation gap: "The golden string that connected man with his father on earth and his father in heaven, the age-old bond that tied the present to the past, was not to be broken lightly. When at last it snapped, the result . . . was both world-shaking and soul-shaking." While Pitcher finds the interpretation forced, we might nonetheless admit to the logic of its spirit. In any event, no further sense is made of the mysterious occurrence.

To be sure, the sound bespeaks a mood (and as such should not be explained with specifics), what Mirsky would call one of Chekhov's "purely atmospheric creations." For, as the critic remarks, in Chekhov, where no one person seems to listen to his neighbor, there is not straight line but a series of moods. It was reported by Stanislavskiy that during the December rehearsals, one of the actors casually made an imitative sound with his lips of the kind the author had described, and Chekhov turned to him exclaiming: "That's just what we want!" Yet, because of its highly unusual quality—even for Chekhov—Styan believes that he took "an extraordinary risk" in introducing it in Act II, and Mirsky goes even further: ". . . in his search for suggestive poetry he sometimes overstepped the limits of good taste—. . . for instance, the bursting of a string in *The Cherry Orchard*. . . ."

The implication here is that, while Chekhov's world is filled with noises, they are not necessarily stage noises, and that in *The Cherry Orchard* he planned something much out of the ordinary. The apocalyptic sound, as Mirsky describes it, is not typical of Chekhov. It is different from the guitar string which snaps in a dark room in the story **"The Dream Fiancée."** It is even different from the *"Takh! t! t! t!"* that reverberates across the steppes' thin air in **"Happiness"**: it may be equally mysterious and receive a similar explanation ("It must have been a bucket falling in a mine shaft," says Panteley, unperturbed, just as in *The Cherry Orchard* Lopakhin attempts to identify the sound the same way), but it is nowhere near as "apocalyptic," and furthermore it sounds only once. The episode recalls the passage in **"A Rolling Stone,"** of the same year, where the hero falls to the bottom of a mine when the chain holding his bucket snaps. Hence Hingley's comment about the extraordinary sound which baffles stage directors: "One remarkable sound effect has caused some embarrassment to producers, and illustrates the production of *nastroenie* on a more surrealist level. . . . The play does not make it entirely clear how this noise is supposed to have originated, but Chekhov certainly regarded it as important in evoking the right sort of mood in his audience."

If the engimatic sound stands out, however, it does so because it does more than provoke the "right sort of mood." Chekhov was too precise and self-conscious an artist to allow a gratuitous or solely mood-setting, isolated incident to enter his work. As we know, he insisted that all specifics in his plays be executed down to the last particular, but, by the same token, not overexecuted. The Chekhovian pattern of understatement obtained even in expressing the significant detail. He used all sound effects in his stage directions with great subtlety, and did not fill his plays with mysterious happenings which require a spectator to turn detective. There are no "secret connotations which must be pieced together like a jigsaw puzzle." The sound in *The Cherry Orchard* cannot be said even to fit the musical dimensions of the play; it may be "a musical sound in its way, but contrasting so strangely with the thoroughly familiar sounds of Yepikhodov's guitar" or the Jewish orchestra that it commands direct attention. The simple fact that Trofimov and Gayev *hear* it suggests that the incident is woven firmly into the fabric of the play. That Chekhov wanted his characters to take note of the sound is best suggested by his change of setting from a river to a chapel, as if to allow the greater quiet to bring out better the distant vibrations: "In the second act I have substi-

tuted the river with an old chapel and a well. It is quieter so." Furthermore, Chekhov's direction or description concerning the sound is expressed verbatim both times it is heard—as sure an indication of the importance he placed on it as we might wish to have. So if *ultimately* it is a mere sound effect, *intimately* it has much to say.

The most important thing it has to say, regardless of Chekhov's own paradoxical assertions about his plays being comedies and not tragedies (another counterpoint!), is that the play is not an "undramatic drama" (as Mirsky likes to call Chekhov's dramas) but indeed a tragic drama. It is not a cheerful message the story conveys; yet, strange as it may sound, an optimistic interpretation is not uncommon. For there are those like Yermilov who in good Soviet fashion see the play's ending as bright, as introducing a new, powerful, and decisive force in society, the Russian working class, and who accordingly entitles his chapter on *The Cherry Orchard:* "Welcome, New Life." To put an end to the past: this is the emotional significance of the play. "Laughter, gay and unrestrained, penetrates every situation in the play. . . . Karl Marx expressed a profound thought when he called laughter a way of 'bidding farewell' to the old, exhausted forms of life." Similarly, outside the Soviet periphery, Sophie Lafitte, while recognizing that the basic theme of Chekhov is the "contrast affirmation of inner solitude," insists that at the end of *The Cherry Orchard* (and *Uncle Vanya*!) there "bursts the hope of a better future, of happiness which is not only possible, but certain, though still far off." Pitcher, more cautiously and neutrally, sees no *real* pessimistic or tragic implications.

We believe the opposite, however, and concur with Aimée Alexandre: "*The Cherry Orchard* is the drama of death, the disappearance of a past with all that it contained that was good and bad, with all the nostalgia it will create, with all the sadness over the passage of time." The important concept is the "drama of death," and the snapping string is the surrealistic symbol relating to it, reminiscent of the final snipping of the thread by Atropos. It provides a mood not just of "wonder" but of "regret," stressing nostalgically "time past and time passing" rather than "bidding farewell" to them with "bursts of hope" for time future. Let us not forget, among other indications, that at the end Mme. Ranevskaya and Gayev—not villains in any way—sob in each other's arms, according to the stage directions, *"in despair"* (*v otchayanii*) that the family is dispersed, and that the final posture and situation of good Firs *does* remind us of death. It should not be surprising that, running down the aisle during a rehearsal, Chekhov had insisted that the sound be made "more painful" or dolorous (*zhlobnye*). Therefore, many critics and directors have indeed associated the sound with death, generally relating it, like Styan and Valency, to the death of values and way of life of the older Russian society of the Ranevskayas and Gayevs, symbolized by the cherry orchard—nostalgically "a sort of requiem for the 'unhappy and disjointed' lives of [Chekhov's] characters." But in doing so, they have indicated at best only *what* the sound seems to signify, and if its meaning is tragic, we must still be able to say *how* it got to have this meaning, and *how* it reveals it structurally within the play. Given the dissension over the optimism or pessimism of the message, we should look for clues to validate the latter interpretation *inside* the play, for the former interpretation is little more than a superimposition.

To begin with, and with no intention of detracting from its arcane quality, the background of the snapping string must be sought in folklore. The sound establishes the folklore element inside the play. This possibility is hinted when Mme. Ranevskaya refers to the sound as "ill-omened" (ominous or foreboding: *neschastnyy*). Perhaps this is what led a German critic to claim that it is used "as a symbol for the end of the aristocracy's splendor, as a ghostly omen" (*Menetekel*). There can be no question that Chekhov used the motif in its most widespread folklore application concerning unhappiness associated with the end of life. Its homeopathic aspects appear all over Western and Central Europe, Western Slavic countries included. Though one cannot yet locate immediate evidence of the motif's presence in Russia itself, folklorists find it legitimate (and logical) to suppose its existence in Russian folklore because it is well known, for example, in Slovak folklore which in turn shows frequent links with Russian popular traditions. And Chekhov, being well acquainted with Eastern Slavic folk traditions, was undoubtedly familiar with this motif.

In folklore, a player may leave his instrument behind as a "life token," an extension of himself, and if during his absence a string breaks, this is considered an evil portent. The chord that snaps involves the idea of a separable soul. One may come upon several such examples of a breaking string: "If a string of an instrument breaks for no special reason, then there will soon be a wedding, or, according to a more widespread superstition, one must expect a death." With reference to *The Cherry Orchard*, it is clearly the more common belief, the *Todesfall*, that draws our attention. A typical illustration of the "snapping-chord-of-death" motif is the story of the Swiss fiddler:

> A fiddler living in the wilds of Elvig used to visit his loved one, who used his fiddle, twice a week in the Balmen Lötschenpass. She always knew exactly at what time he would walk into her house. Suddenly a chord of another violin snapped. "Oh Lord," cried she, "now something unfortunate has happened to my beloved," and correctly, at that exact moment he had been struck dead.

Again, there is the story from Syra of Strong Hans, who could not be made to do anything except play the zither, and who sallied forth one day to fight the ogre (who had ravished the king's daughter), telling his mother: "If you see that the strings of my zither are broken, then come and seek me [for I shall be dead]." Folktales such as these form the tradition underlying the question of how the breaking string got to mean what it means in Chekhov's play.

How this sound reveals its meaning structurally in the play is a question which leads us to the heart of Chekhov's art in *The Cherry Orchard*, the art of counterpoint. Its ingredients combine in a pattern of oppositions, establishing architectural and conceptual relationships, expressively balanced, while retaining a clear individuality of their own at all times. Fundamental are the images of the owl and heron, not only because they appear in the very center of the play (end of Act II) and just before the first instance of the snapping string, but also because of their symbolic significance juxtaposing life and death, the drama's main counterpoint. Furthermore, a number of ancillary contrapuntal motifs come forth in the same scene. Yepikhodov has just crossed the stage, playing his guitar:

> GAYEV. Ladies and gentlemen, the sun has set.
>
> TROFIMOV. Yes.
>
> GAYEV. (*in a low voice, declaiming as it were*) Oh, Nature, wondrous Nature, you shine with eternal radiance, beautiful and indifferent! You, whom we call

our mother, unite within yourself life and death! You animate and destroy!

> VARYA. (*pleadingly*) Uncle dear!
>
> TROFIMOV. You'd better bank the yellow ball in the side pocket.
>
> GAYEV. I'm silent, I'm silent. . . .
>
> *All sit plunged in thought. Stillness reigns. Only Firs's muttering is audible. Suddenly a distant sound is heard, coming from the sky as it were, the sound of a snapping string, mournfully dying away.*
>
> MME. RANEVSKAYA. What was that?
>
> LOPAKHIN. I don't know. Somewhere far away, in the pits, a bucket's broken loose; but somewhere very far away.
>
> GAYEV. Or it might be some sort of bird, perhaps a heron.
>
> TROFIMOV. Or an owl. . . .
>
> MME. RANEVSKAYA. (*shudders*) It's weird, somehow. (*Pause*)
>
> FIRS. Before the calamity the same thing happened— the owl screeched, and the samovar hummed all the time.
>
> GAYEV. Before what calamity?
>
> FIRS. Before the Freedom. (*Pause*)
>
> MME. RANEVSKAYA. Come, my dear friends, let's be going. It's getting dark. . . .

Then the poor stranger appears, in a shabby white cap, begs thirty kopecks, and Mme. Ranevskaya, who has no silver in her purse, gives him a gold piece (to Varya's annoyed astonishment).

The break in silence, like the quiet tranquility of the old world that comes to an end, is anticipated by Gayev's words concerning the animating and destructive manner of nature, and what he exclaims literally about life and death is balanced and restated symbolically after the break in silence by the heron and the owl—the former alluded to by Gayev himself, who dreams of his tranquil, older world continuing, and the latter by the representative of the younger generation, Trofimov, who wants its demise (and who strangely, and ironically, it might appear, seems to hoot at the very end of the play, over Anya's happy calls, while the older people leave and the orchard starts falling: "Aoooo" [*Au!*]). In folk literature, the hooting of an owl represents a bad omen, while hearing the heron's cry represents a good one. In the Egyptian systems of hieroglyphs, the owl symbolizes "death, night, cold and passivity" and also pertains to the realm of the dead sun (a sun that has set), and not surprisingly Virgil speaks of the owl's mournful strain when Dido longs for death. Similarly, among the Egyptians, the heron (together with the stork and ibis) symbolized morning and the generation of life, and Homer has Athene send a heron to Odysseus and Diomedes as they set out on a perilous mission, in order to insure their success.

Old Firs had heard an owl years before, while the graciously living society kept minding its cup of tea, after which the bad portent became reality: the emancipation of the serfs in 1861, serfs who became the Lopakhins of the next generation, the one that buys and axes the orchards.

Once the heron-owl pattern is set, the rest of the counterpoint falls into place, and we come to realize that hearing the sound of the snapping string twice underscores the structure. An expressive series of sometimes obvious but more often subtle oppositions between death and life forces makes up this dialectic, as it were, which creates a tension throughout the play, and how the tension is resolved—the chord snaps—can only invite a pessimistic interpretation. But this becomes clear only at the end, because before that the dialectic operates ambiguously on an optical and phonic as well as on an actional and perceptional level.

On the optical level, we note that, as the tombstones of Act II counterpoise the chapel, so do the telephone poles the cherry orchard. The industrial and the natural, the city and the meadow, the skeletal and the rounded, termination and hope, face each other in precarious balance. In addition, the death instruments, the gun Sharlotta carries and the revolver Yepikhodov reveals, act to counterpoise the musical instruments as well as the expressed desires for continued life or the rays of hope emanating from the many telegrams, torn up or not, Mme. Ranevskaya receives every day from that "savage" who needs her and whom she loves in Paris. Yepikhodov's query, "Should I live or should I shoot myself . . .?" creates more tensions than the words by themselves seem to betray, as does his ominous remark, "Now I know what to do with my revolver," followed by his reassured walking off playing his guitar. In effect, his query does not differ from his double-edged, symbolic observations at the beginning of the play that while "there's a frost this morning—ten degrees below—. . . yet the cherries are all in bloom" (and at the end: "It's devilishly cold here . . . yet it's still and sunny as though it were summer"), or from Mme. Ranevskaya's romantic attempt to poison herself in Paris coupled ambivalently with her sudden magnetic attraction for life in Russia. Even the stage directions, as N. A. Nilsson points out, are composed of "wholly opposing parts" ("cheerfully through tears [*radostno skvoz' slezy*]," as an example; the non sequiturs too [Varya's and Anya's in Act I] amount to "oppositions"). Almost everything we see, from tombstones to guitars, exists in dialectical relationship with other objects. And observations and events follow the same pattern.

The optical level of interpretation is intensified by Chekhov's insistence on the use of the color white. White pervades the play, not merely as a refraction of the heron, but as a veritable tonality struck about a dozen and a half times during the drama: one of Mme. Ranevskaya's two rooms is white, Firs wears a white waistcoat and puts on white gloves, Sharlotta appears in a tightly laced white dress, Mme. Ranevskaya imagines her mother "all in white" in the orchard, and even Pishchik discovers white clay on his land. Furthermore, the orchard, as Gayev describes it, "is all white," and Mme. Ranevskaya laughs with joy at its being "all, all white!" while she visualizes her mother in it in the form of "a little white tree, leaning over." Then she underscores: "What an amazing orchard! White masses of blossom. . . ." Chekhov's intent is clear from his correspondence: in his mind, even Lopakhin has a white waistcoat, and "in Act One cherry trees can be seen in bloom through the windows, the whole orchard is a mass of whites. And ladies in white dresses." Hardly any other color is mentioned in the play.

Inside and outside Western folk tradition, white has symbolized the positive and timeless. It is considered purified yellow; it is the hope of life. By the same token, yellow is considered impure white, or life in a state of decay, or, at least, of imperfection. One is reminded of Balzac's character Poiret, in *Old Goriot*, whose white ivory cane handle has turned yellow with age and use, or of the aged countess' yellow gown in Pushkin's *The Queen of Spades*. The figurative meaning of yellow as a color given in Ozhegov's dictionary includes the notions of conciliation, reform, and betrayal of the interests of the working class (used contemptuously). One should not overlook, then, Gayev's many, although eccentric, references to the "yellow ball" bank shot in the side pocket, for through his very eccentricity Gayev tacitly suggests that he realizes, at least subconsciously, what is happening to Russia. Despite his white waistcoat, suggesting the higher-class status he has now attained, Lopakhin still wears "yellow shoes," almost as if to suggest his peasant stock. Thus, the mood of counterpoising oppositions is enforced, shaping the play with tensions as it develops, and guiding it to its final expression of the snapping string.

Actional and perceptional levels of interpretation corroborate the optical. In a spatial context, the counterpoint between Mme. Ranevskaya's kissing her "darling bookcase" or Gayev's tearful and impassioned encomium to it on the one hand, and the epidemic of knocking over furniture accidentally or breaking belongings on the other, is quite obvious. Lack of control over the physical world symptomizes the collapse of the spiritual. The spatial context is corroborated in turn by the temporal: in Act I, Mme. Ranevskaya says of Varya what she will also say of Lopakhin, that she is "the same as ever," which at different times is what Yasha says of Gayev and Varya of her mother, like a variation of Lopakhin's phrase to Gayev: "You're as splendid as ever." The phrases "You haven't changed a bit" and "just the same as ever" take on the qualities of a leitmotif by the end of the first act. They imply a desire to hang on to the status quo, to have it continue as splendidly as before, to prolong the "whiteness." But as the play wears on and, let us say, the heron turns owl, we hear the opposite theme sounded, that of change: "How you've aged," exclaims Mme. Ranevskaya to Firs, the way Varya laments to Petya: "How old you look!" Together, the spatial and the temporal dimensions produce a counterpoint of their own: that of the wishful, dreamy, and passive world of the status quo which Mme. Ranevskaya, Gayev, Firs, and Dunyasha live in, epitomized by the latter's remark: "I am daydreaming"; and that of the realistic, pragmatic, and materialistic world of change which Anya and Trofimov look to, or the mercantile logic of Lopakhin prepares. Says Lopakhin: "I'm always handling money. . . . Sometimes I lie awake at night, I think. . . ."

The most encompassing counterpoint, of course, operates on the phonic level, and it climaxes with the sound of the snapping string. The meaning of *The Cherry Orchard* is rooted in a kind of recondite music, or unmusic, contrasting intensely with the clumsiness of the characters or their inability to harmonize (*neskladnyy*), and is expressed on the surface in many ways—the distant sound of a shepherd's piping and the allusion to bells in Act I, the guitar (confused with a mandolin) and the band (four violins, a double bass, and a flute) in Acts II and III, the waltz and the frequent mention of the musicians in Act III, and Yasha's and Sharlotta's humming in Act IV. In point of fact, however, all this music leads to naught; it represents little more than an attempt by the characters to impose happiness artificially—again, to retain the "whiteness." It echoes in an empty shell of vapid desire. The pessimism could not ring more poignantly. For in *The Cherry Orchard* the music, like the whiteness, ultimately becomes an illusion, a pathological form of wishful thinking. These two would-be positive forces resemble the orchard itself—an illusion of a past life that the protagonists perceive more easily than the audience, which sees more poplars and telephone poles through the set windows than anything else. Symbolically, the sprightly sound of a band's music yields to the dull, unmusical clicking of billiard balls—all of which lends significance to the double innuendo that people are like the balls on a billiard table, knocked about in a series of banked shots before being pocketed away, and that they are made to act like melancholy puppets on a string, dancing ritually as if in a state of benumbed dream, not knowing the reason for what they do. This is the forlorn state of those who can say soulfully with Pishchik: "Everything in this world comes to an end."

Out of a simple pair of bird images, then, Chekhov cross-weaves a network of motifs which culminates in the final counterpoint: the sounds of the snapping string and of the felling ax. That both are related intrinsically, and gloomily, is certain from Chekhov's description of them: both ring indentically: mournfully and sadly (*grustno, pechal'nyy*). The first instance of the snapping string in the middle of the performance is not accompanied by the thuds of axes against trees, for at this point, like the characters, we do not know whether it is a heron or an owl that we have heard. In the reverberation there is hope rather than finality: at least there is questioning. Life and death hang in the balance, so the counterpoint may continue: the cherry orchard may still not be sold to strangers and leveled for commercial purposes. But the first sounding leads to the second, as if answering the question with death. "A feeling of emptiness" takes over, and in the shell of the house the tunes have vanished, leaving nothing but the faint echoes of humming voices. Since the string's sound and the ax's thud become synonymous (as if the ax had struck the string and broken it), it becomes painfully clear that a breaking string is after all a broken string. Here it does sound with finality, and here the counterpoint ends. This is not a case of "emotional distancing," as has been claimed. *The Cherry Orchard* is written in an emotional key, deeper or more overt, perhaps, than we are used to in Chekhov, and the emotional experience finds its objective correlative in sounds. And the experience is far from optimistic: that the white illusion of life is finally crushed by the axed trees, just as the musical illusion of happiness is finally destroyed, as in the ending of folktales, by the snapped string—all this bespeaks a pessimistic message, a "drama of death." The ending is tragic:

> FIRS: . . . Life has gone by as if I had never lived. (*Lies down*) I'll lie down a while. . . . There's no strength left in you, old fellow; nothing is left, nothing. Ah, you addlehead! (*Lies motionless. A distant sound is heard coming from the sky as it were, the sound of a snapping string mournfully dying away. All is still again, and nothing is heard but the strokes of the ax against a tree far away in the orchard.*)

In every other full-length play, Chekhov made a pistol shot dominate the climax. He was well aware that *The Cherry Orchard* represented a departure from this practice: ". . . there's something new about it . . . there's not a single pistol shot in the whole play." But the snapping string is a pistol shot of a different order of magnitude: rather than limit itself immediately and primarily to the physical world, it reverberates throughout the world of the spirit, regardless of whether mortals can make sense out of it. It has contrapuntal associations which the other Chekhov "sounds" do not have, and because of its distant origin in folklore, uniting the light and dark of creation, one could say, its vibrations can be overpowering. Perhaps Chekhov was aware of this potentially deafening resonance when he tried to tone down the enthusiasm for sound effects

of his directors, who were trying hard to make acoustic sense out of the enigmatic sound. Chekhov naturally spoke in terms of a simple sound effect, which, after all, is all the snapping string is when it comes to producing the play: "Tell Nemirovich that the sound in Acts Two and Four of *The Cherry Orchard* must be shorter, a lot shorter, and must be felt as coming from a great distance. What a lot of fuss about nothing—not being able to cope with a trifle like this, a mere noise, although it's so clearly described in the play." For us, however, this trifle, or mere noise, well illustrates what Thomas Mann said of Chekhov: that he was one of those major writers who could embrace the fullness of life in a simple incident. (pp. 111-23)

> *Jean-Pierre Barricelli, "Counterpoint of the Snapping String: Chekhov's 'The Cherry Orchard'," in* Chekhov's Great Plays: A Critical Anthology, *edited by Jean-Pierre Barricelli, New York University Press, 1981, pp. 111-28.*

IRINA KIRK (essay date 1981)

[*Kirk is a Chinese-born American critic and educator. In the following excerpt, she evaluates Chekhov's early dramas.*]

Chekhov wrote his first plays at the age of eighteen, but all that survived of those efforts are the titles: a drama *Without Fathers,* a comedy *Laugh It Off If You Can,* and a one-act comedy *Diamond Cuts Diamond.* (These titles are mentioned by Chekhov's eldest brother, Aleksandr, in a letter of October 14, 1878.) The manuscript of the earliest preserved play by Chekhov was discovered after his death and published in 1923. Because of the missing title page it was published as *A Play without a Title,* but later it was named *Platonov* after the play's main character. Although the manuscript is undated there is evidence that the play was written in 1881, since Chekhov's brother Mikhail refers to it in his introduction to the second volume of Chekhov's letters. Apparently Chekhov took this play to the then-famous actress Mariya Yermolova with hopes that it would be performed at the Maly Theatre, and its rejection caused him great disappointment.

The play lacks artistic merit. It is too long, melodramatic, and as Mikhail wrote, "unwieldly," but it does offer interesting material for a study tracing some of Chekhov's themes and characters to their original sources. It is also significant as Chekhov's first effort to portray those sociological problems and conflicts that resulted from the emancipation of the serfs in the last two decades of the nineteenth century.

As in any period of transition there was uncertainty and confusion among the land-owning class, and many felt a helpless frustration at their inability to cope with change. Platonov, formerly a rich landowner and now a village teacher, is, in the words of one of the characters, "an admirable representative of our modern uncertainty."

To escape his frustration, Platonov involves himself with different women. Married to Sasha, a pious and innocent woman, he is having an affair with Anna, a general's widow. On discovering this, Sasha throws herself under a train, but is saved by the horse thief Osip. In the third act, she finds out that her worthless husband has also been trying to revive his old love for Sonya, who viewed him in her student days as a second Byron.

Sonya decides to "save" Platonov, and she offers him a new, meaningful life with her: "I'll make a worker out of you. We'll be decent people, Mikhail. We shall eat our own bread. We shall live by the sweat of our brows. We shall have calloused hands. I shall work, Mikhail.'' Platonov agrees to this scheme without much conviction or enthusiasm, but just as he prepares to leave, he is summoned to court ''in the case of an assault committed upon the person of Mariya Grekhova daughter of Councellor of State.'' The summons does not deter Platonov, but at this point he finds it convenient to spend two weeks with Anna, prior to leaving with Sonya forever.

The last act is filled with every theatrical cliché and melodramatic device possible. Sasha poisons herself with matches, Sonya throws herself on her knees in the presence of Anna and begs Platonov to leave with her, and Mariya Grekhova comes in to announce that she is withdrawing her summons and that she too loves Platonov.

Exasperated, Platonov vows to revenge himself on all these loving women: ''They all love me. When I get well I'll corrupt you. Before I used to say nice things to them, but now I'm corrupting them all.'' Sonya relieves him from the necessity of fulfilling such an ambitious vow by shooting Platonov with a pistol and wounding him fatally. The play ends with a lament of Colonel Triletsky, Sasha's father: ''The Lord has forsaken us. For our sins. For my sins. Why did you sin, you old jester? Killed God's own creatures, drank, swore, condemned people. . . . The Lord couldn't put up with it any more and struck you down.''

Such lamentations were not part of Chekhov's later art, but the spiritual bankruptcy, the destructive forces of ennui, and the idea that work is man's salvation were to become some of his recurring themes. The figure of a bored, impoverished landowner unable to revive his youthful ideals and resentful of any efforts to save him appears again in Chekhov's next play, *Ivanov.*

It is apparent that Chekhov himself rejected *Platonov* so completely that he considered *Ivanov* his first play. In a letter to his brother Aleksandr in October of 1887 Chekhov said, ''It is the first time I have written a play, ergo, mistakes are unavoidable. The plot is complicatd and not stupid. I end each act like a short story. All the acts run on peacefully and quietly, but at the end I give the spectator a punch in the face. My entire energy is concentrated on a few really powerful and striking scenes; but the bridges joining them are insignificant, dull, and trite. Nevertheless, I am pleased, for however bad the play may be, I have I think, created a type of literary significance.''

The type Chekhov created was not new in Russian literature. Aside from the fact that Ivanov was a reworked version of Platonov, he was similar to many so-called superfluous men who dominated Russian novels since the early nineteenth century. Behind his melancholy, boredom, and cosmic fatigue stood his idealistic past, where his powers were directed toward passionate speeches about progress, human rights, and agricultural improvements. It is the discrepancy between what he had dreamed he would become and what he actually did become that lies at the source of his illness. As a part of his rebelliousness and youthful dreams, Ivanov married a Jewish girl, Sarah, who gave up her inheritance and her faith to become his wife. As the play opens, Sarah is suffering from tuberculosis, Ivanov's lands are mortgaged to Lebedev, and he himself is about to become involved with Sasha, a young and idealistic daughter of Lebedev who is bent on saving Ivanov. Chekhov said of Sasha, ''She is the type of female whom the males do not conquer by the brightness of their feathers, their fawning or their bravery, but by their complaints, their whining, their failures. She is a woman who loves a man at the moment of his downfall. The moment Ivanov loses heart, the girl is at his side. That was what she was waiting for. . . . She is not in love with Ivanov but with that task of hers.''

Ivanov's relationship to his wife is seen and evaluated by different people: by common gossipers (act 2), by Dr. Lvov, by Sarah, and by Ivanov himself. The issue becomes a catalyst that reveals the degree of honesty each character has toward himself and others.

According to gossip, Ivanov is a murderer, a blood sucker, and a thief: an opinion that is a crude distortion of the truth. Dr. Lvov pronounces a similar judgment on Ivanov. Unlike the gossips, Lvov is motivated by sincere honesty and by a genuine concern for Sarah's health. Dr. Lvov correctly sees that Ivanov's lack of reaction to the fact that his wife is dying and his behavior with Sasha are largely responsible for Anna's death. Still, he fails to take into account Ivanov's idealistic past and his present ennui. Chekhov writes of the doctor: ''He belongs to the type of honest, straightforward, excitable, but also narrow-minded and plain-spoken man.'' As the count says of Lvov, he is ''like a parrot who thinks of himself as a second Dobrolyubov.'' His role is thus a caricature of the liberal *narodnichestvo* (populism) dramas popular at the time.

Ivanov's reaction to Dr. Lvov is indicative of his attitude toward himself. Ivanov is not intentionally evil, but he feels himself powerless to resolve all the contradictions and complexities of his weak nature. Thus he admonishes Dr. Lvov for his harsh judgment, which is lacking in depth and perception:

> No, doctor. We all have too many wheels and gears for us to be judged by first impressions or by a few external traits. I don't know you, you don't know me, and we don't know ourselves. Isn't it possible to be a good doctor—and at the same time not understand people? You'll have to admit that, unless you're blind.

Although Ivanov does not fully accept Lvov's definition of him, he realizes that he alone is responsible for his life. Still he cannot reconcile himself to his present ennui:

> I can stand all these things! Anxiety, depression, bankruptcy, the loss of my wife, premature old age, loneliness, but I just can't bear the contempt I have for myself. The shame that I, a strong, healthy man, have somehow become a kind of Hamlet, a Manfred, just about kills me! Oh, I know there are fools who are flattered when you call them a Hamlet, but to me it's an insult! It wounds my pride, I'm oppressed with shame, and I suffer. . . .

Ivanov agrees with the doctor that his passivity is the indirect cause of both his wife's death and of his financial problem.

The dramatic action of this play is developed in accordance with the painful self-revelation which in the end drives Ivanov to suicide. Ivanov's psyche is revealed through his own remarks about himself, his gestures, his reactions, and the pauses in his speech.

Each act places an emphasis on Ivanov's estrangement from his surroundings. This is frequently comic, as in the contrast between Ivanov and Borkin, but it is just as often tragic. The comic episodes balance the tragic ones and serve as parodies, reflecting as if in a distorted mirror the plight of the main character. Both Count Shabelsky, Ivanov's uncle, and Lebedev, chairman of the County Council, speak of their idealistic past with humor, yet Ivanov cannot feel indifferent to what he has become, and hence he suffers. Ivanov's relationship with Sasha is parodied by Shabelsky's vacillating intention to marry the rich young widow Babakina. Just like Ivanov, the count reasserts his honesty at the end of the play, telling Babakina he hates her. However, Ivanov must pay a tragic price to extricate himself from his marriage to Sasha. Lvov's aggressive honesty is a parody of what Berdnikov calls Ivanov's "subjective honesty." Although the doctor acts honorably, Ivanov's passive honesty enables him to judge himself and others with more insight than Lvov.

Chekhov wrote to Suvorin about *Ivanov* on January 7, 1889: "In the conception of Ivanov I hit approximately on the dot, but the performance is not worth a damn. I should have waited." Chekhov's conception was to portray the "superfluous man" of the 1880s in all of his psychological complexity, but he had not yet mastered the dramatic subtleties of characterization. The excess of monologues and self-explanatory speeches in *Ivanov* kept it well within the bounds of the traditional theater, while Chekhov was striving to achieve something new. In a letter of October 10-12 to his brother Aleksandr he says of *Ivanov,* "Korsh hasn't found a single mistake or fault in it so far as stage technique is concerned which proves how good and sensible my critics are." Korsh hadn't found a mistake because *Ivanov* conformed to the requirements of the conventional play.

Ivanov is certainly a vast improvement over *Platonov.* It is much more concise, and Chekhov realized the importance of ending each act definitely. At the end of the first act Sarah leaves her house to follow Ivanov, and at the end of the second act she appears at the very moment of Sasha's and Ivanov's kiss. The third act ends with Ivanov's rebuke to Sarah that she will soon die, and the fourth act with his suicide.

Chekhov failed to make an original creation out of a character that had become stock in Russian literature. As Suvorin said, "Ivanov was a ready-made man." Chekhov denied the charge and replied that Ivanov was not static because he was "ready-made" but because the author's hands were unskillful. Chekhov obviously tried to portray the inner emotional life of his hero, but didn't know how to do it except with worn-out devices.

While Chekhov was writing *The Wood Demon* he was at the same time at work on **"A Boring Story."** However, whereas **"A Boring Story"** displays all the control of an admirable craftsman, *The Wood Demon* confirms Chekhov's own suspicion that he was not yet a playwright. When the play was passed by the censor in October, 1889, it was rejected by the Literary-Theatrical Committee of St. Petersburg, among whose members was Grigorovich. Lensky, an actor of the Moscow Maly Theatre for whose benefit night the play was submitted, wrote Chekhov two weeks later, "Write stories. You are too scornful of the stage and the dramatic form. You respect these things too little to write plays." Nemirovich-Danchenko was more charitable and more perceptive. He wrote, "You ignore too many of the requirements of the stage, but I have not observed that you scorn them; simply, rather, that you don't know what they are."

In December, Chekhov finally sold the play to the private Abramov Theatre in Moscow, and it was presented on the Moscow stage on December 27th. The criticism of the play was singularly severe. The kindest review came from a mag-

azine *The Actor,* No. 6, 1890 which said, "Chekhov's talent, without a doubt, is above the play he wrote, and the play's strange qualities are explained, probably, by the speed of the work and a sad delusion regarding inescapable qualities of every dramatic work." Chekhov added his personal criticism of *The Wood Demon,* which had also failed his own artistic expectations. In a letter to Urusov, literary critic and chairman of a drama society, he stated, "I cannot publish [*The Wood Demon*]. I . . . am trying to forget it." (The play was in fact later revised and staged as *Uncle Vanya.*).

Chekhov did succeed in removing the conventional plot from *The Wood Demon,* but he had not yet mastered the technique of portraying inner psychological action. The play is too mechanical, undisciplined, and verbose. The inner psychological moments which in later plays would be depicted by a suggestive line of speech or a mere gesture, are expressed in loud monologues or bathetic dialogues. The play is also undermined by unconvincing coincidences and melodramatic situations. Letters and diaries serve to communicate information in a contrived manner, characters appear on stage at the proper moments as if by chance, and in Act Four a fire is created to get Khrushchev off stage. The play ends with the clown Dyadin's remark which ironically defines not only his own absurdity but also the play's: "That is delightful—Just delightful."

The theme and characterization are developed in accordance with the love relationships in the play. Serebryakov, an old and insufferable professor, is married to a very young and beautiful woman, Elena. The stupid boor Orlovsky and the Byronic rake Fedor both crudely attempt to seduce Elena, but receive only moral lectures for their pains.

Chekhov was obviously under the influence of Tolstoi's teachings at this time. The passive but virtuous Elena delivers speeches on the sanctity of marriage, purity, loyalty, and self-sacrifice. Although Elena is unjustly maligned throughout the play she is inwardly sustained by her false belief that she is the paragon of Russian womanhood:

> Oh, to be free as a bird, to fly away from all your drowsy faces and your monotonous mumblings and forget that you've even existed at all! Oh, to forget oneself and what one is. . . . But I am a coward; I am afraid, and tortured by my conscience. I know that if I were to be unfaithful, every other wife would do the same thing and leave her husband, too. But then God would punish me. If it weren't for my conscience, I'd show you how free my life could be.

There is another love triangle between the profesor's spoiled daughter Sonya, the idealistic "wood demon" Dr. Khrushchev, and the scoundrel Zheltukhin. Khrushchev eventually proposes to Sonya, who accepts his offer, at which point she too starts mouthing Tolstoian precepts: "There is no evil without some good in it. Our sorrow has taught me that we must forget our own happiness and think only of the happiness of others. Our lives should be a continual act of self-sacrifice. . . ."

All the characters are united by the thematic leitmotif of their wasted lives, and by their attempt to delude themselves with rationalizing philosophy. The "wood demon" Khrushchev sums up the lives of everyone in the play as follows:

> We say that we are serving humanity, but at the same time we inhumanly destroy one another. For instance, did you or I do anything to save George? Where's your wife, whom we all insulted? Where's your peace of mind, where's your daughter's peace of mind?

Everything's been destroyed, ruined. You call me a Wood Demon, but there's a demon in all of you. You're all wandering lost in a dark forest, you're all groping to find a way in life. We know just enough and feel just enough to ruin our own lives and the lives of others.

Voinitsky has sacrificed his entire identity to Serebryakov, whom he has worshipped as a great genius for years, only to discover his mistake when it is too late. Serebryakov, whose entire youth was devoted to work, tries desperately to achieve happiness as an old man by exercising the power of his position, but he only succeeds in destroying those around him. Elena is proud of her "virtue," but she is a failure in her inability to love anyone and quite rightly defines herself as a "worthless, empty and quite pathetic woman." Fedor and Zheltukhin are leading senseless lives, and justifying themselves with cynicisms modeled after Lermontov's Byronic hero Pechorin.

Though *The Wood Demon* was a failure in terms of its artistry, its conception of form revealed the trend toward dramas of "inner action" which was to become fully actualized in Chekhov's later plays. *Uncle Vanya,* which was modeled after *The Wood Demon,* will give the most concrete example for studying the development of Chekhov's technique from banal melodrama to masterful dramatic art. (pp. 126-33)

> *Irina Kirk, in her* Anton Chekhov, *Twayne Publishers, 1981, 165 p.*

ADDITIONAL BIBLIOGRAPHY

Beckerman, Bernard. "The Artifice of 'Reality' in Chekhov and Pinter." *Modern Drama* XXI, No. 2 (June 1978): 153-61.
  Explains how Chekhov creates a sense of dramatic "reality" in terms distinct from those of conventionally naturalistic theater.

Bill, Valentine Tschebotarioff. *Chekhov: The Silent Voice of Freedom.* New York: Philosophical Library, 1987, 277 p.
  Argues that the primary goal of Chekhov's work was "to light the path of the human individual toward freedom."

Bristow, Eugene K., ed. *Anton Chekhov's Plays.* New York: W. W. Norton & Company, 1977, 412 p.
  Contains translations of Chekhov's major dramas and fifteen critical essays on Chekhov, his dramaturgy, the Russia of his day, and his literary legacy.

Brooks, Cleanth and Heilman, Robert B. "Notes on *The Sea Gull.*" In their *Understanding Drama: Twelve Plays,* pp. 490-502. New York: Holt, Rinehart and Winston, 1948.
  Points out several conflicts in *The Seagull,* briefly discusses the themes of love, art, and tradition, and describes Chekhov's attitude towards his characters as "esthetic distance," which accounts for the fusion of tragedy and comedy in his plays.

Bruford, W. H. *Chekhov and His Russia: A Sociological Study.* London: Kegan Paul, Trench, Trubner & Co., 1947, 233 p.
  Analyzes the view of Russian society conveyed by Chekhov's work.

Bunin, Ivan. "Chekhov." *Atlantic Monthly* 188, No. 1 (July 1951): 59-63.
  Memories of the Russian novelist Bunin concerning his friendship with Chekhov.

Clyman, Toby, ed. *A Chekhov Companion.* Westport, Conn.: Greenwood Press, 1985, 347 p.
  Collection of seventeen essays on various aspects of Chekhov's works.

Corrigan, Robert W. "The Plays of Chekhov." In *The Context and Craft of Drama: Critical Essays on the Nature of Drama and Theatre,* edited by Robert W. Corrigan and James L. Rosenberg, pp. 139-67. San Francisco: Chandler Publishing Company, 1964.
  Discusses the major themes and techniques of Chekhov's dramas.

Debreczeny, Paul, and Eeckman, Thomas, eds. *Chekhov's Art of Writing: A Collection of Critical Essays.* Columbus: Slavica Publishers, 1977, 199 p.
  Essays from a predominantly formalist-structuralist critical perspective.

Deer, Irving. "Speech as Action in Chekhov's *The Cherry Orchard.*" *Educational Theatre Journal* X, No. 1 (March 1958): 30-4.
  Argues that the apparent formlessness of dialogue in Chekhov's plays actually reflects the inner conflicts of the characters which are integral to the outward conflicts of the plays.

Emeljanow, Victor, ed. *Chekhov: The Critical Heritage.* London: Routledge & Kegan Paul, 1981, 471 p.
  Collection of short reviews of Chekhov's works from the time of their first appearance through 1945.

Epstein, Joseph. "Chekhov's Lost Souls." *The New Criterion* 4, No. 9 (May 1986): pp. 13-24.
  General assessment of Chekhov's life and works, arguing that his chief themes, "helplessness, hopelessness, misunderstanding, and defeat," make him the first serious writer to express the malaise of modernity.

Erlick, Victor, ed. "Chekhov and West European Drama." *Yearbook of Comparative and General Literature* 12 (1963): 56-60.
  Remarks by several critics on the relationship between Chekhov and Western literature.

Gassner, John. "Chekhov and the Sublimation of Realism." In his *Masters of the Drama,* pp. 508-25. New York: Dover Publications, 1954.
  Surveys Chekhov's development as a dramatist, calling him the Sophocles of modern Europe.

Gottlieb, Vera. *Chekhov and the Vaudeville: A Study of Chekhov's One-Act Plays.* Cambridge: Cambridge University Press, 1982, 224 p.
  Studies Chekhov's earliest dramatic efforts, tracing the development of themes and techniques that appear in his later plays.

Hahn, Beverly. *Chekhov: A Study of the Major Stories and Plays.* Cambridge: Cambridge University Press, 1977, 350 p.
  Sees Chekhov's work as highly psychological and claims he is "a more positive writer than even his strongest supporters often contend."

Hingley, Ronald. *A New Life of Chekhov.* New York: Alfred A. Knopf, 1976, 352 p.
  Much significant documentary material used which became available since publication of Hingley's *Chekhov: A Biographical and Critical Study* [see *TCLC,* Vol. 3].

Koteliansky, S. S., ed. *Anton Tchekhov: Literary and Theatrical Reminiscences.* New York: Benjamin Blom, 1965, 249 p.
  Collection of personal essays on Chekhov and his works. This volume also includes excerpts from Chekhov's diary and several previously unpublished stories and dramas.

Kropotkin, P. "A. P. Tchéhoff." In his *Russian Literature,* pp. 308-17. New York: Benjamin Blom, 1905.
  Comments on Chekhov's works, noting his ability to unveil in only a few pages "a world of aimless philistine life."

Latham, Jacqueline E.M. "*The Cherry Orchard* as Comedy." *Educational Theatre Journal* X, No. 1 (March 1958): 21-9.
  Demonstrates that, despite overtones of pathos and tragedy, *The Cherry Orchard* is essentially a comedy.

Lavrin, Janko. "The Dramatic Art of Chekhov." In his *The Dramatic Art of Chekhov,* pp. 174-91. London: Sylvan Press, 1948.
  Analyzes the spirit and general character of Chekhov's work, attributing its greatness to "the skill with which he proved that

the very drabness of life can be turned into great and significant art."

MacCarthy, Desmond. "A Master of Natural Dialogue." In his *Theatre*, pp. 21-7. London: MacGibbon and Kee, 1954.
Discusses several of Chekhov's major themes and techniques.

Melchinger, Siegfried. *Anton Chekhov*, translated by Edith Tarcov. New York: Frederick Ungar Publishing Co., 1972, 184 p.
Detailed study of how Chekhov's plays should be produced in order to best convey the author's intentions.

Meyerhold, Vsévolod. "The Naturalistic Theatre and the Theatre of Mood." In his *Meyerhold on Theatre*, translated and edited by Edward Braun, pp. 23-34. New York: Hill and Wang, 1969.
Comments on the original Moscow Art Theater productions of Chekhov's plays, noting that *The Seagull* and *Uncle Vanya* were great successes because the actors captured the rhythm of language which was "the secret of Chekhov's mood."

Nemirovitch-Dantchenko, Vladimir. "Chapter One." In his *My Life in the Russian Theatre*, translated by John Cournos, pp. 3-23. New York: Theatre Arts Books, 1968.
A cofounder and director of the Moscow Art Theatre discusses several aspects of the first successful production of *The Seagull*.

Persky, Serge. "Anton Tchekoff." In his *Contemporary Russian Novelists*, pp. 40-75. Translated by Frederick Eisemann. Boston: John W. Luce and Company, 1913.
Describes the major themes of many of Chekhov's stories and dramas.

Slonim, Marc. "The Beginnings of the Moscow Art Theater." In his *Russian Theater: From the Empire to the Soviets*, pp. 100-32. Cleveland: The World Publishing Co., 1961.
Plot outlines and theatrical history of the major dramas.

Speirs, Logan. "Chekhov: The Plays." In his *Tolstoy and Chekhov*, pp. 185-223. Cambridge: Cambridge University Press, 1971.
Sees the major similarity between Tolstoy and Chekhov in their realistic re-creation in literature of the world around them, and their major difference in their divergent philosophical outlooks, Tolstoy's that of dogmatic religiosity and Chekhov's that of agnostic materialism.

Styan, J. L. "Naturalistic Shading." In his *The Dark Comedy: The Development of Modern Comic Tragedy*, pp. 53-112. Cambridge: Cambridge University Press, 1968.
Traces the development of Chekhov's dramatic technique and analyzes Act IV of *The Cherry Orchard*.

Trilling, Lionel. "Commentary on *The Three Sisters*." In his *The Experience of Literature*, pp. 250-55. New York: Doubleday & Company, 1967.
Attempts to reconcile his description of *The Three Sisters* as "one of the saddest works in all literature" with Chekhov's view that it was a "gay comedy, almost a farce."

Tulloch, John. *Chekhov: A Structuralist Study*. New York: Barnes and Noble, 1980, 225 p.
Study of the thematic structure of Chekhov's works, with chapters devoted to *The Three Sisters* and *The Cherry Orchard*.

Williams, Raymond. "A Generation of Masters: Anton Chekhov." In his *Drama: From Ibsen to Brecht*, pp. 101-11. New York: Oxford University Press, 1969.
Argues that Chekhov created a new dramatic form that rejected naturalistic theatrical conventions.

Young, Stark. "Gulls and Chekhov." *Theatre Arts Monthly* XXII, No. 10 (October 1938): 737-42.
Criticizes and corrects some English translations of *The Seagull*. The critic also attempts to remedy Chekhov's widespread image as an artist of gloom and morbidity.

————. "The Sea Gull." In his *Immortal Shadows*, pp. 200-05. New York: Charles Scribner's Sons, 1948.
Notes that English-language translators of Chekhov's dramas tend to make his simple, natural language more complicated and formal.

Ralph Connor

1860-1937

(Pseudonym of Charles William Gordon) Canadian novelist, short story writer, and autobiographer.

A popular novelist in the early twentieth century, Connor combined realistic descriptions of life in the Canadian wilderness with moralistic story lines dramatizing the struggle of good against evil. His novels captured and mythologized the Canadian West, introducing character types that later became common in Canadian literature. Though by contemporary standards Connor's work appears simplistic and melodramatic, he helped to shape a uniquely Canadian mythos and national spirit.

Connor was born Charles William Gordon in Glengarry County, Ontario. His father was a Presbyterian minister who had immigrated from Scotland to Canada in the mid-nineteenth century; his mother, a native of New England, was a former philosophy teacher. Gordon studied at Knox Theological College in Toronto, the University of Toronto, and Edinburgh University, earning Doctor of Divinity and Doctor of Literature degrees. In the early 1890s he spent several years as a frontier missionary among lumbermen and miners in the Rocky Mountains, an experience that gave him the background for his novels of the Canadian Northwest. Gordon left missionary work in 1894 to become pastor of St. Stephen's Church in Winnipeg. A few years later he discussed with a friend, the Reverend James A. MacDonald, the possibility of writing some stories about his missionary work for the *Westminster,* a Presbyterian newspaper edited by MacDonald. The stories Gordon sent were surprisingly exciting and filled with action, and MacDonald immediately decided to print them. Gordon had chosen "Cannor" as a pseudonym composed of the first three letters of "Canada" and of "Northwest Territory," but MacDonald altered the construction to a less odd-sounding surname and added a given name, publishing the stories under the name "Ralph Connor."

In 1898 Connor's series of *Westminster* stories were collected and published as his first novel, *Black Rock.* The novel sold well in Canada, and pirated editions gained recognition for Connor in the United States, paving the way for the success of his second novel, *The Sky Pilot.* Connor continued writing novels as often as his duties as a minister allowed, although he encountered difficulties in meeting publishing schedules and frequently had to be brought to Chicago or New York in order to finish a manuscript. Within two decades from the publication of *Black Rock,* Connor became nationally known as both a writer and a church figure. He left active pastoral duty in order to devote himself more completely to the church as a whole and to the service of his country, acting as Moderator of the General Assembly of the Presbyterian Church in Canada, as a member of the Dominion Labour Board, and, during World War I, as a chaplain in the Forty-Third Cameron Highlanders, a volunteer regiment from Winnipeg. Throughout his career Connor worked for the cause of ecumenicity among Canadian churches, and in 1925 the Presbyterian, Methodist, and Congregational churches of Canada merged to form the United Church of Canada. Connor continued to write until his death in 1937.

Connor always considered himself more a preacher than a writer, and his novels reflect his intense concern with religious values. He saw life as a great struggle between good and evil, and the plots of his novels tend to resolve into situations in which evil characters are pitted against good ones and are either overcome or reformed in the end. While some critics consider Connor's moralism a grave defect in his writing, others consider this objection merely the result of modern critical prejudice, noting that Connor's earlier and more overtly moralistic novels are more successful than his later works, in which Connor self-consciously attempted to write in a more artistic and less didactic fashion. The chief interest in Connor's novels, however, is his vivid portrayal of the rugged beauty of life in the Canadian Rocky Mountains, as well as of life in other sections of Canada, particularly Glengarry County, where he grew up. Connor was the first to exploit the literary possibilities of the Canadian wilderness, and his portrayals of Canadian lumbermen, miners, and other common figures of the Northwest Territory were copied by later authors and became stock types in Canadian fiction. Critics agree that Connor's mythologizing of the Canadian wilderness captured the Canadian imagination and helped to form a Canadian national identity in the early twentieth century.

(See also *Contemporary Authors,* Vol. 109.)

PRINCIPAL WORKS

Black Rock   (novel)   1898
The Sky Pilot   (novel)   1899
The Man from Glengarry   (novel)   1901
Glengarry School Days   (novel)   1902
The Prospector   (novel)   1904
The Doctor   (novel)   1906
The Foreigner   (novel)   1909; also published as *The Settler,* 1909
Corporal Cameron of the North West Mounted Police (novel)   1912
The Patrol of the Sun Dance Trail   (novel)   1914
The Major   (novel)   1917
The Sky Pilot in No Man's Land   (novel)   1919
To Him That Hath   (novel)   1921
The Gaspards of Pine Croft   (novel)   1923
Treading the Winepress   (novel)   1925
The Friendly Four, and Other Stories   (short stories)   1926
The Runner   (novel)   1929
The Rock and the River   (novel)   1931
The Arm of Gold   (novel)   1932
The Girl from Glengarry   (novel)   1933
Torches through the Bush   (novel)   1934
The Rebel Loyalist   (novel)   1935
The Gay Crusader   (novel)   1936
He Dwelt among Us   (novel)   1936
Postscript to Adventure [as Charles W. Gordon] (autobiography)   1938

GEORGE ADAM SMITH   (essay date 1900)

[*In the following introduction to* Black Rock, *Smith praises the artistry and moralism of Connor's work.*]

I think I have met ''Ralph Connor.'' Indeed, I am sure I have—once in a canoe on the Red River, once on the Assinaboine, and twice or thrice on the prairies to the West. That was not the name he gave me, but, if I am right, it covers one of the most honest and genial of the strong characters that are fighting the devil and doing good work for men all over the world. He has seen with his own eyes the life which he describes in [*Black Rock*], and has himself, for some years of hard and lonely toil, assisted in the good influences which he traces among its wild and often hopeless conditions. He writes with the freshness and accuracy of an eye-witness, with the style (as I think his readers will allow) of a real artist, and with the tenderness and hopefulness of a man not only of faith but of experience, who has seen in fulfillment the ideals for which he lives.

The life to which he takes us, though far off and very strange to our tame minds, is the life of our brothers. Into the Northwest of Canada the young men of Great Britain and Ireland have been pouring (I was told), sometimes at the rate of 48,000 a year. Our brothers who left home yesterday—our hearts cannot but follow them. With these pages Ralph Connor enables our eyes and our minds to follow, too; nor do I think there is any one who shall read this book and not find also that his conscience is quickened. There is a warfare appointed unto man upon earth, and its struggles are nowhere more intense, nor the victories of the strong, nor the succors brought to the fallen, more heroic, than on the fields described in this volume. (pp. v-vi)

George Adam Smith, in an introduction to Black Rock: A Tale of the Selkirks *by Ralph Connor, Fleming H. Revell Company, 1900, pp. v-vi.*

GRANT OVERTON   (essay date 1923)

[*Overton was an American novelist and critic. In the following excerpt he extols Connor's work, writing in the Glengarry dialect of some of Connor's characters.*]

I'll not have to be telling you what it was in *Black Rock* won so many readers for Ralph Connor. Humour and pathos are bound up in the lives the young minister of St. Stephen's was writing about; ye could lay hold quickly of his sympathy for those men who were in some ways as helpless as bairns and were half-brutalised by their work and surroundings. It's the effect they have on each other, too. Them picking up *Black Rock* to read were struck with something fresh and wild and clean, withal. They sensed a tenderness about the feeling of the story, like heather softening the bare hillside, and more than a morsel of the everlasting hope in which men endure hard and lonely toils. The same held true of the books that followed *Black Rock*; for there had to be other books. Ye mind *The Sky Pilot* and *The Man From Glengarry* and *The Foreigner* and *Corporal Cameron* and *The Patrol of the Sun Dance Trail.* Take *The Foreigner.* On the edge of Winnipeg, Charles Gordon found a settlement of Slavs—Ruthenians, Russians, Galicians and who not. They lived in a grim little collection of huts, a dozen in a room, all huddled up, drinking and dirty and violent; and on them was still the shadow of tyrannies in the Old Country. Drinking and dirty and violent with a violence dark and beautiful, Charles Gordon found them. Aye, he found the huts and the men, and Ralph Connor that was in him found a story. Ralph Connor took the splendid young heart in Kalmar, the son of a nihilist, and brought it to fight its way out of the ruck of aliens and make for the new country beyond the Saskatchewan, where there is prairie and where the lakes lie on the surface of the prairie like jewels on a woman's breasts. Then, in *Corporal Cameron,* was Connoring the first grand tale of the North-West Mounted Police, by a man who kenned them, as followers in his tracks scarce can be said to. A richt fine love story is this of the lad who was born in a Scottish glen and came to ride out in the Canadian blizzards; it's furthered in *The Patrol of the Sun Dance Trail,* which makes use of the half-breed and Indian rebellion of Louis Riel. But there's a muckle I love in the book besides the adventure—Cameron and his gold-haired, plucky wife and the hesitant wonder of the first fine feeling of the lover. It fashes me how a man says what's down in the hearts of such a many other men and women. Give me to understand how it's done! (pp. 182-84)

The Major and *The Sky Pilot in No Man's Land* are books ye'll verra well recollect; likewise the novel of twa years back, *To Him That Hath.* Since ye hanna read it, it's the new novel from the pen of Ralph Connor, I'll just speak a word of to ye. He calls it *The Gaspards of Pine Croft* and explains it is ''a romance of the Windermere Valley.'' A story of the life and moulding of Paul Gaspard, it is. Here's a mon with two powerful strains mixed and fighting for mastery of him. From his mither, Paul inherits a rare sense of the presence of God; his father gifted him with a fine artist sense, and a bounding spirit, a passion for life to the full. The clash of the two men in the boy grows with him to manhood, so that after the death of his mither he stands between two women, who beckon different ways. Then when a great decision is put before him the mon takes upon himself a burden and a responsibility that test him body and soul. 'Tis a life and death struggle set in the grand country Ralph Connor makes his own. There's the valley of the Windermere before you with the Gaspard ranch, Pine Croft, flanked on one side by a great bend of the Columbia River and on the other by a mountain wall of virgin forest. In this mysterious wilderness, the figures of Indians do come and go, touching the lives of the white people with disaster, with dread—with an unco beauty as well. (pp. 186-87)

> *Grant Overton, "The Man Called Ralph Connor,"*
> *in his* American Nights Entertainment, *D. Appleton*
> *& Co., 1923, pp. 178-88.*

DONALD G. FRENCH (essay date 1930)

[*In the following excerpt, French groups Connor's novels according to their settings and evaluates his abilities as a novelist.*]

Ralph Connor's novels fall into several groups. **Black Rock** and **The Sky Pilot** are tales of the Rocky Mountain foothills, telling of the wild life of the West and of the work of the missionary. **The Man from Glengarry** and **Glengarry School Days** deal with the life of the author's boyhood days in Eastern Ontario. **The Prospector** and **The Doctor** combine East and West by following their leading characters through the University of Toronto and transferring them to Western Canada. **The Foreigner** has a Manitoba setting and concerns itself with the problem of the assimilation of the foreigner. **Corporal Cameron** and **The Patrol of the Sun Dance Trail** carry a young Scot to Canada and through the ranks of the Mounted Police. The Great War gave material for **The Major** and **The Sky Pilot in No Man's Land**; labor troubles for **To Him That Hath**; while in **The Gaspards of Pine Croft,** the author reverted to a setting not so far from that of his first novel, but produced a story more emotional and psychological in nature than his others.

The circulation of Ralph Connor's novels has been phenomenal and has reached somewhere between two and a half and three millions, yet his reputation is not that of a literary artist. His stories carry the reader because of action, incident, and tense emotional situations. They have always an underlying ethical and spiritual significance and they promulgate a belief in the presence of some redeeming feature in every human being, and so continue to touch the responsive chord in the heart of a common humanity. It is sometimes the insistence of this thesis that causes the author to develop his characters with a lack of consistency.

It is generally agreed that none of Ralph Connor's later works come up to the standard of **Black Rock** or **The Sky Pilot** in consistency of characterization, in spontaneity, and in unity of total effect. Indeed **The Sky Pilot** is the most artistically finished of all his works because of the natural coherence of its parts in their development of the central theme. Dramatic power he has to a marked degree, so far as the presentation of individual scenes is concerned, such as the fight in the lumber camp, the horse race, the barn-raising, and many other thrilling episodes; but his grasp of dramatic values is not broad enough to escape melodrama. The constructive dramatic instinct which weaves each separate incident into a chain of cause and effect dependent upon the character and motives of the leading personages of the story is often little in evidence. Whole chapters might be lifted bodily from some of these novels without interfering with the thread of the story.

His imagination is reproductive rather than creatively constructive. The stories of the foothills are built upon his own mis-

sionary experiences at Banff and elsewhere; the Glengarry tales deal with his schoolboy experiences and his knowledge of the rough life of the lumber woods and the drive; the stories of East and West are also drawn from his own experiences in college and in the missionary field. The result of his method is that his characters tend to become types, and though fairly individual and distinctive they incline to act mechanically and without sufficient inherent motivation.

Three great ideas run concurrently through nearly all Ralph Connor's work—the nobility of sacrifice, the power of sympathy, and the widespread influence of a strong personality. In all his stories he shows the leading characters doing noble work as the result of self-sacrifice and self-denial, reaching the heart of all classes of people by a spontaneous but unobtrusive sympathy, and radiating a personal influence over all those with whom they come in contact. (pp. 77-8)

> *Donald G. French, "Who's Who in Canadian Literature: Ralph Connor," in* The Canadian Bookman,
> *Vol. XII, No. 4, April, 1930, pp. 77-9.*

F. W. WATT (essay date 1959)

[*In the following excerpt, Watt discusses Connor's portrayal of the Canadian West.*]

The world of Ralph Connor, in so far as it existed at all, lasted for only a short period. It was already passing as he wrote about it. And indeed, he was well aware of this, for he set himself in part the task of recording it before it was entirely lost. Why, it might be asked, did he choose for his subject what nineteenth century Canadian novelists preferred to ignore for that very reason, the changing immediate scene? The answer is, I believe, that he saw what other novelists failed to realise; that the present moment, with all its novelty and its fluidity, is significant only in so far as it reveals an old, stable, enduring subject, man's essential nature and condition, and he felt the transient life of the West to be especially illuminating in this respect. Like James Joyce, Connor saw himself as writing a chapter in the moral history of his country, and the fact that his best novels can still catch at our attention despite their radical faults suggests to me that he sometimes came close to succeeding.

In the opening pages of that first novel **Black Rock,** the narrator Ralph Connor is led far away from the familiar East, from the "cosmopolitan and kindly city" of Toronto, into a primitive lumber camp six miles from the mining village of Black Rock in the heart of the Selkirks. Connor is a photographic observer, and we get details of the camp which make the then original setting vivid. The loggers are a tough, colourful, uncouth bunch— Connor nicely catches their mixture of dialects and accents— but they meet their match on Christmas Eve when the hero of the tale appears, the Presbyterian minister Mr. Craig, and proceeds to Christianize, willy-nilly, their rollicking pagan festival. The key-note of the book, and indeed of much of the later Connor, is struck when Craig, by telling the meaning of the Christmas story in the most informal of sermons, captures his reluctant audience, and especially the oldest, hardest, fiercest sinner of them all: "Old man Nelson held his eye steadily on the minister," Connor says. "Only once before had I seen that look on a human face. A young fellow had broken through the ice on the river at home, and as the black water was dragging his fingers one by one from the slippery edges, there came over his face that same look. I used to wake up for many a night after in a sweat of horror, seeing the white face with its parting lips and its piteous, dumb appeal, and the black water slowly sucking it down.'' Connor narrates as at first hand the long, violent, brutal and not entirely successful struggle of the powers for good, lined up with Craig, to save souls like Nelson's from their black waters of damnation, against the powers of evil, the bootlegger and gambler Slavin and his gang of rough-necks. The tale is full of action, from the vivid knock-down-drag-out fight between the Drys and the Wets, to the colourful race of four-horse combinations, in which the loggers' team edges out the citizens' and the miners' in a wild finish; but the theme of conversion and re-birth underlies it all.

The novels that followed in the next decade largely develop and vary the **Black Rock** formula. It had proved a sudden and unexpected success. There were, aside from the large official issue, eleven pirated editions of that first book. The Rev. Charles W. Gordon had become the famous novelist Ralph Connor overnight, and he worked his vein thoroughly. Take a wild, barbaric setting away from the civilized gentility of the East; fill it with a crowd of virile, bold, lusty, profane, hard-fighting and hard-living men, often with pasts to live down, who are exploiting the unrestrained individuality of frontier life to the full; introduce morality and religion, usually in the form of a Presbyterian minister who fights bravely against great odds to save the souls of the indifferent and hostile sinners; add a touch of romance, a virtuous maiden, wife or mother to soften and uplift the harder hearts; mix up the moral and physical battles, letting the blood flow freely, and bring off victory for the forces of good; cap it with conversion and salvation for the evil as well. All this Connor did with considerable technical fluency, and a clever manipulation of tensions and contrasts and the simpler dramatic devices that appeal immediately to our feelings. The mild, gentle, boyish Sky Pilot, humble, aware of his own inadequacies as a man of God, shatters the cynical, callous indifference of the Albertan cowboys by his enthusiasm and his innocence. The Glengarry war-horse Macdonald, recently converted, endures the cruellest goadings of his enemies rather than forget the Lord's message, ''Vengeance is *Mine*.''

Individual scenes of dramatic power and photographic vividness stand out in each novel, as for example the funeral procession in *The Man from Glengarry*: at night by the light of cedar bark torches the body of young Cameron is carried home to his waiting parents, and when the bearers arrive the father silences the mother's terrible scream of grief, recalling her to her duty—''Whisht, Janet, woman! . . . Your son is at the door.'' Every novel has its special locality to exploit (the Selkirks, the foothill country, the Ottawa river, the Crow's Nest Pass, and that boyhood home described so lovingly in *Glengarry School Days*); there are many special customs or colourful local activities to describe: maple-sugaring, a stump-pulling bee, a house-raising, a wake, a harvesting contest, and so on. The informative scope is panoramic (Connor's regions include almost the entire breadth of Canada), and sometimes we are shown striking scenes and experiences once common enough in this country but long since forgotten. *The Foreigner,* for example, describes the sordid shack-life of Russian immigrants in Winnipeg in the early 1900's; to find any other writer who dares deal with such material we have to turn to the sociologists, or rather to their only equivalent at that time, men like J. S. Woodsworth whose *My Neighbour* and other books angrily drew attention to the same situation. Throughout Connor's novels we get a sense of teeming vitality and an endless reservoir of varied experiences and exciting adventure. It is not surprising that the rough-riding Teddy Roosevelt and Ralph Connor were mutual admirers.

Through all the novels too runs a rich vein of humour. The vivid McGill-Toronto rugby match which is described at the beginning of *The Prospector* gains a dimension by the presence there of the pious little old Scots widow, Mrs. Macgregor, for whom the players' violence is nothing compared to the clan-wars she has known in the Old Country; who turns out to be an expert in the subtleties of the game; and who sends her giant of a son ''Shock'' into the scrimmage with the admonition, ''Run away Hamish, and be careful of the laddies.'' The sentimentality of the Sky Pilot's funeral is cut astringently by the description of another funeral procession which ends in an unseemly race between the sleigh bearing the corpse and the two carrying the mourners and the pallbearers respectively. Afterwards, the corpse-driver, having won the race to the burial-ground, ''fairly distributed the blame,'' as Connor tells us: '' 'For his part,' he said, 'he knew he hadn't ought to make no corp get any such move on, but he wasn't goin' to see that there corp take second place at his own funeral. Not if he could help it. And as for the others, he thought that the pall-bearers had a blanked sight more to do with the plantin' than them giddy mourners'.''

But humour is after all not an added feature, an occasional ornament of the sugar-coating to Connor's writing; it is an aspect of his essential good-will, high-spirits, tolerance, or to choose the best word—charity. There is a love of action, of experience, and of people of all kinds and classes running through much that Connor has written that makes far better Canadian writers seem by comparison a little cold, narrow, priggish, snobbish, or dessicated in their orientation to their own lives and towards their fellows.

The chief reason for the large sale of Connor's earlier books was no doubt their timeliness. By the late 1890's all eyes were on the West. The flood of immigrants from the East and from abroad so long expected was at last flowing strongly. What was the new land they were going to really like? Was it as thrilling as the reports claimed? Connor provided answers, and exciting ones at that. The country west of the Great Lakes was vast, infinitely rich in potential. If at times the latter part of *The Man from Glengarry* now reads to us like propaganda for the Canadian Pacific Railway, it is more likely that many of its first readers were deeply stirred by the vision of the ''empire of the Canadian West'' that it tries to project before our eyes. And it was the existence of real opportunities, not merely enthusiasm, that peopled Connor's novels with men on the make, young Scots from Glengarry or immigrant Slavs, rising in spectacular fashion from ignorance or poverty to power, importance and the life of wealth and refinement. The West, indeed, was a world on the make.

Naturally there was less time for some of the subtleties, even religious subtleties, of more settled communities, and human beings were likely to appear in their simplest, clearest outlines. The God of Connor's West is of an appropriate nature, generous minded, not too concerned with the letter (too little the theologian to satisfy Calvin, surely), sympathetic to the spirit in unlikely places, ready to have His work done by whoever will put a hand to it. Presbyterian ministers, saintly widows, Catholic priests, rough-mannered miners or lumbermen may equally enter into and even (at a pinch) conduct religious services. The people tend to be a little larger than life as the Easterner knows it. The men are tall, broad-shouldered, immensely strong, hardy, brave and tender-hearted. There are of course cads as well as

Christian gentlemen (a distinction in nature, not social class), but the most vicious of villains are redeemable despite their terrible cruelty and wickedness; they repent movingly. The women are pure and modest and maidenly and beautiful. Nothing quite equals in the power for good "the sweet uplift of a good woman's face" (in those days no other uplift would have crossed a gentleman's mind). Their voices have such a sweet, thrilling tone that the savage breast is soothed with a single song; their eyes plumb the depths of a man's heart and see what really lies there, or glow luminously with a warmth of simple love, or fill with tender tears, or disappear modestly from the too frank gaze of admirers. What mothers they make, and what wives! Timid and gentle, but brave as lions in the cause of virtue.

As the novels proceed we become aware that we are in the presence of a full-blown myth of the West, not merely a feeling of jingoistic patriotism or a sense of vast resources just being realized. When one of the characters in *The Foreigner* exclaims, "It is a wonderful country, Canada," she has something else in mind, for she says: "How wonderful the power of this country of yours *to transform men!*" In *The Prospector* Connor may be giving us an account of his own evolving experience when he describes the impact of the West on Shock, the book's hero:

> He was making the discovery that climate changes the complexion, not only of men, but of habits of thoughts and action. As Shock was finding his way to new adjustments and new standards he was incidentally finding his way into a new feeling of brotherhood as well. The lines of cleavage which had hitherto determined his interests and affinities were being obliterated. The fictitious and accidental were fading out under this new atmosphere, and the great lines of sheer humanity were coming to stand out with startling clearness. Up to this time creed and class had largely determined both his interest and his responsibility, but now, apart from class and creed, men became interesting, and for men he began to feel responsibility. He realized as never before that a man was the great asset of the universe—not his clothes, material, social or religious.

This is a somewhat startling position for a budding young Presbyterian minister to have reached (such is Shock) and for Connor it is an expression of a genuine break-through from the excessive refinement and gentility which swaddled many Victorian Canadians. The West had become a mythical land, a place where such revelations were forced upon one. Men went there to escape the old life and in search of a new life, and there the faith in conversion and re-birth took on a new meaning. It was a place where biblical parables easily merged with actuality. The Rev. Craig telling the story of the Prodigal Son's home-coming to his congregation of western fugitives and exiles (who listen like so many distraught Dean Moriaritys) concludes: "There you are, men, every man of you, somewhere *on the road*. Some of you are too lazy, and some of you haven't enough yet of the far country to come back . . . Men, you all want to go back home." This is a world seen through Christian eyes, where all endeavour, temptation, success, failure and hope is translatable into terms of heroic Christian struggle.

No one would think of Connor's portrayal of the West as realistic any longer. Far from it. Too often he stepped from actuality into far-fetched success stories or melodramatic love fantasies. But many of his distortions are of another kind, the result of his endeavour to see religious meaning in the drama of western life. It is for this reason that Connor stands above

his contemporary Canadian novelists, and because he dared to write about things that really mattered—the state of his characters' morals and of their souls, not merely the historical past or the surfaces of contemporary life. In this way he often escaped the incredible triviality of so many of the other western writers, Nellie McClung, Stringer and Stead for example, and there is often a touch of grandeur in what he was trying to do. Moreover it is not because Connor was a preacher first and an artist second that he failed. Distinctions of this sort are based on a modern notion with which many great writers would have little patience. In fact one could argue that Connor failed because he did not take his role of preacher earnestly and profoundly enough, but gave it up at times for a feeble and debased notion of "novelist." For not being a good or a passionate enough preacher we must blame him; for his conception of the novelist we must blame his readers, his critics, his society as well. They wanted and expected romantic nonsense, and too often he willingly provided it. It is interesting to notice in this respect that the later novels, in which Connor is very rarely the preacher, are his most unconvincing and trivial.

For the writer of realistic fiction the chief challenge is to project an image of life which is both consistent and deeply problematical. Connor came within hairsbreadth of a solution in his conception of the West. Here was an arena where the ancient battle was actually being fought out daily (or so it seemed to him) between good and evil, Christian and Hopeful and Mr. Valiant-for-truth against the forces of Appolyon and the temptations of Vanity Fair. Connor only regretted that his palette did not contain sharp enough whites and blacks to show the intensity of that conflict, in which the costs at stake were (to him the only ones that really mattered) the salvation or damnation of human souls. He tried to see life everywhere in the same thrilling terms. But, as I have said, Connor could never sustain a level of consistency for long. His realism had a disconcerting way of shifting abruptly into romantic fantasy and back again, like those incongruous mixtures of photography and cartooning perpetrated by Walt Disney. No doubt the life of the West failed Connor as much as Connor failed the West; it could scarcely avoid the descent to the ordinary and humdrum, losing its angels and its devils. (pp. 29-36)

F. W. Watt, "Western Myth: The World of Ralph Connor," in Canadian Literature, *No. 1, Summer, 1959, pp. 26-36.*

EDWARD McCOURT   (essay date 1970)

[*McCourt is an Irish-born Canadian novelist, biographer, juvenilia and travel writer, and critic. In the following excerpt, he argues that the strengths of Connor's novels derive from the sincerely held moral and spiritual values on which they are based.*]

It is easy now to understand why Ralph Connor enjoyed such popularity at the turn of the century. In books like *Black Rock, The Sky Pilot, The Prospector* and *The Doctor* he wrote of a locale which was in itself of absorbing interest to the ordinary Easterner or Old Country man. For the Canadian West was the last great frontier of the New World, an Empire within an Empire already absorbing immigrants at the rate of nearly fifty thousand a year and calling for more. It was a land of promise, a land of romance—by 1900 the tradition of the North-West Mounted Police had been firmly established—a land where it was possible, if need be, to forget the past and begin again. Unlike the northern frontier of today, which has not excited comparable interest, the West of fifty years ago was readily accessible and invited settlement. It was almost instinctive for the man seeking an opportunity to create a home for himself and his family to turn his thoughts and eventually his face west. And in the pages of *The Sky Pilot* and *Black Rock* and *The Prospector* he found much to encourage his dream.

For Ralph Connor, writing with the authority of a veteran western missionary, painted the West as the land of beginning again. The mining camps of British Columbia and the ranches of the foothills he peopled with many types, which tend to fall into two general categories, heroes and villains. The heroes behave in traditional fashion; so, up to a point, do the rogues and outcasts. But the evil-doers are seldom in the end destroyed; rather through the power of God they are transformed into repentant and respectable citizens. Such transformation is not always a deliberate sentimentalizing of character. For it was Ralph Connor's earnest conviction that in every man there is some element of good, some claim to God-hood which the right environment may bring into the light. So it is that he sees the West as a land where there is hope for even the weakest of the misfits of an older society. Nor is it altogether true to say that the kind of hope which Ralph Connor creates is a spurious one, born of false optimism and wishful thinking. It stems from passionate conviction which has its origin in temperament and its confirmation in experience. As missionary and clergyman he had seen, not once but many times, the startling regenerative effort of religious conversion. Men, he knew, could be changed. And the West, free from the restraints and conventions of an older society—simpler, more wholesome—provided the ideal environment for the change. By temperament sanguine, Ralph Connor found it easy to imagine the kind of transformation he had seen taking place in individuals being extended, under appropriate conditions, to entire groups. Hence the mass reforms and conversions which are a characteristic feature of several of his novels. No doubt the readers of an earlier day, to whom the West was a young and enchanted land, were readily persuaded that in the loneliness of the great open spaces a man found it easy to come to grips with his God.

The sincere faith with which Ralph Connor illustrates his doctrine of regeneration is reflected in his characters. They are extreme simplifications of good and evil, but there is nothing to show that the author is himself aware of the simplification. To the contrary he believes in his characters implicitly because in his own life he tended to see people in strong blacks and whites and outlines larger than human. His autobiography, *Postscript to Adventure*, overflows with superlatives. His father (the Rev. Alexander Murray of the Glengarry stories) "was indeed a great preacher. Not one of all the great preachers I have known could thrill my soul as could my father when I was a little lad." His brother Gilbert was a man "of magnificent physique and invincible pluck . . . strong, cool, quick, with a courage that nothing could daunt." Among his friends and fellow ministers not one was commonplace. Dr. Henry Drummond "had an amazing power to draw the best out of you. What a hero! He died like one. What a saint! He lived like one." And in the personality of the Rev. Dr. James Robertson, for twenty years superintendent of missions for the Presbyterian Church in the West "were to be found the qualities of a statesman—vision, organizing ability, power to inspire heroic deeds, selfless devotion to his country, a courage that never faltered and a persistence that never swerved from the line of duty."

It was inevitable that the combination of *naïveté* and hero-worship so apparent in these sketches of the people of Ralph Connor's real world should contribute to the creation of fictitious characters in whom there should be no shadings, no delicate nuances. But it must not be forgotten that they were given to the public at a time when the traditional conception of the frontiersman as a simple-hearted rugged individualist was still strong; and the average reader no doubt found, in Ralph Connor's missionaries and doctors and prospectors and outlaws-with-hearts-in-the-right-place, confirmation of his vague romantic notions. It is true that one querulous critic protested his inability to believe in a hero like Shock MacGregor of *The Prospector,* who was "an Apollo, a John Wesley and a Livingstone all in one." But such objections were rare. Ralph Connor's enthusiasm for his own characters was contagious. He himself knew and believed in Barney Boyle and the Sky Pilot and Corporal Cameron and Shock MacGregor; and his readers found it easy to share his conviction.

The women of Ralph Connor's novels are even more limited in range than the men. The men at least fall into two broad divisions—good and bad. But Ralph Connor created no "bad" women. One suspects that he found it hard to acknowledge the fact of their existence. And yet his stereotyped heroines, like so many of his heroes, carry a kind of conviction because their creator never doubts their reality. To him Mrs. Mavor of *Black Rock,* Lady Charlotte Ashley of *The Sky Pilot,* and Mrs. Murray of the Glengarry books are living persons because they are idealizations of his own mother. Ralph Connor never wrote his mother's formal biography; instead, he introduced her in fictitious guise into nearly every novel he wrote. Of the passionate sincerity of his devotion to her memory there can be no question. And the devotion was not misdirected. There is evidence to suggest that Mary Robertson was as remarkable a woman as Barrie's Margaret Ogilvy. Certainly she made it impossible for her son to think evil of any woman. And because so many of his characters are idealized projections of Mary Robertson he is sometimes able, through his own passionate belief in their reality, to persuade the reader that such women actually exist in the flesh.

When Ralph Connor tried to create a feminine character who was a departure from the type which early became conventional with him the results were usually unfortunate. Mandy Haley, the heroine of *Corporal Cameron,* is at first appearance a far cry from the traditional heroine of the author's earlier novels. She is a slatternly Ontario farm girl, ignorant, stupid, vaguely heartsick for the better things of life. The reader's—and Cameron's—first glimpse of her is unpleasant but convincing:

> Turning, he saw a girl of about seventeen, with little grace and less beauty, but strongly and stoutly built, and with a good-natured if somewhat stupid and heavy face. Her hair was dun in colour, coarse in texture, and done up loosely and carelessly in two heavy braids, arranged about her head in such a manner as to permit stray wisps of hair to escape about her face and neck. She was dressed in a loose pink wrapper, all too plainly of home manufacture, gathered in at the waist, and successfully obliterating any lines that might indicate the existence of any grace of form, and sadly spotted and stained with grease and dirt. Her stout red arms ended in thick and redder hands, decked with an array of black-rimmed nails.

Her character is in keeping with her appearance. She is good-natured, slow-witted, with no apparent interests beyond the narrow confines of her physical existence. But because, portrayed realistically, Mandy no doubt offended his conception of true womanhood, the author is unable to resist sentimentalizing his creation. Through the inspiring influence of love Mandy is transformed in body, soul and intellect. When, nearly two years after he has left the farm, Cameron again sees her—

> Before his eyes there floated an illusive vision of masses of fluffy golden hair above a face of radiant purity, of deft fingers moving in swift and sure precision . . . of two round capable arms whose lines suggested strength and beauty, of a firm-knit, pliant body that moved with an easy sinuous grace, of eyes— but at the eyes he paused, forgetting all else, till, recalling himself, he began again, striving to catch and hold that radiant, bewildering elusive vision. That was a sufficiently maddening process, but to relate that vision of radiant efficiency, strength and grace to the one he carried of the farmer's daughter with her dun-coloured straggling hair, her muddy complexion, her stupid face, her clumsy, grimy hands and heavy feet, her sloppy figure, was quite impossible. After long and strenuous attempts he gave up the struggle.

So, unfortunately, must the reader. This is the kind of fantastic implausibility which outrages the intelligence of even the most uncritical romanticist. But, at least, acquaintance with Mandy is sure proof of Ralph Connor's wisdom in adhering to the type which he drew with love and conviction. The re-emergence in novel after novel of the woman cast in the mould of Mary Robertson suggests Ralph Connor's creative limitations; but it also suggests a recognition of those limitations which—Browning to the contrary—is the beginning of wisdom.

Perhaps the most obvious explanation of Ralph Connor's popularity with readers not primarily interested in the Western frontier is to be found in his strong dramatic sense. That sense operated within the strict limits of the physical. A Highlandman by inheritance, Ralph Connor loved conflict. As a small boy he listened with rapt attention to stories of the wild Glengarry men of old and found in them inspiration and material for many of the dramatic incidents of his novels. "The tales of the fierce old days survived down into my times," he says, "stirring my youthful heart with profound regret that deeds so heroically splendid should all be bad. For in spite of the Great Revival we were of the same race, with the ancient lust of battle in our blood." It is not surprising, in the light of this confession, to find that Ralph Connor tends to see life in terms of conflict on a simple level of physical strife. For the Hamlet-like struggles of the human spirit within itself he cares little. Good and evil are represented in his books by hero and villain: the hero beats the villain to a pulp and the villain as often as not benefits by his beating and reforms. Even the simplest and most prosaic physical operation—the raising of a barn, the binding of a grain-field—he turns into a primitive battle in which Right and Justice invariably triumph.

Nor can it be denied that Ralph Connor describes this kind of simple, elemental conflict—hero against villain or against the forces of nature—with a fine dramatic intensity. Even a turnip-hoeing competition becomes an heroic struggle demanding epic phraseology for its description; and he must indeed be a hardened reader who follows unmoved the progress of twelve-year-old Tim Healey, Cameron's protégé, as he forges ahead of Perkins (an unpleasant person who deserves a taking-down) to win the unofficial county turnip-hoeing championship.

And surely nowhere else in literature, except possibly in *Tom Brown's Schooldays*, are there such football games as in the pages of Ralph Connor. The match between Varsity and McGill, described in the second chapter of *The Prospector,* is a classic

of its kind; although some readers may prefer the brief paragraph in *Postscript to Adventure* which describes the actual game on which the fictitious account is based:

> The story of the football match in Ralph Connor's *Prospector* gives a true picture of a terrific struggle, not with McGill, however, but with a band of savage Irishmen from Ottawa College who played to win regardless of rules and regulations and reckless of life and limb, their own or the enemy's. In spite of their unscrupulous tactics, they were a great football team. It was a joy to meet them on the field, a glorious triumph to defeat them, and no shame to be beaten by them.

The effectiveness of a description of athletic competition is in part dependent on the sincerity of the author. Certainly Ralph Connor never saw a football game as a rather ridiculous exercise in which two teams of young men spend a futile afternoon pushing each other about a field while endeavouring to carry a ball across a white line. A football game was to him a stern test not only of a man's physical, but also of his moral, attributes. Thus when Cameron, the Scottish full-back, through a moment's fatal hesitation loses the game for his country to Wales, he is guilty not merely of bad football but of a moral lapse as serious in its way as Lord Jim's desertion of his ship, and equally demanding of a great act of atonement. And since it is human to enjoy physical combat so long as one is not personally involved, it is easy to understand Ralph Connor's appeal to the kind of audience which today gets its vicarious thrills from telecast showings of mayhem on the ice in the Maple Leaf Gardens.

Finally, in the sum of things which help to account for Ralph Connor's early reputation, the patriotic element in his work cannot be ignored. He was not a jingo patriot in the conventional sense, but his novels do express a serene confidence in the ability of the Briton—and particularly the North Briton— to bear the White Man's Burden in the new land of the West and to extend his control over the lesser breeds without the law in a manner beneficial to both ruler and ruled. He acknowledges that in the Canadian West the Indian has not always been fairly dealt with, but he clearly feels that occasional injustice and exploitation are more than compensated for by the protection which the Empire extends to even the humblest of its subjects. Nor does he seem aware of the ironic paradox implicit in much of his work, that the greatest menace from which the Indian must be protected is the white man. When the outlaw Raven, a cultured Old Country black sheep, risks his freedom and perhaps his life in order to help frustrate a rising of the Blackfeet in support of Riel, he speaks for his creator when he says that he is "not quite prepared to hand over this country to a lot of bally half-breeds and savages." In thus helping to maintain the supremacy of the white man he presumably makes atonement for a number of venial sins, including whisky-running and murder. Ralph Connor was a humanitarian, a man who despised cruelty and oppression in every form. In an age when, as Lytton Strachey has it, imperialism was a faith as well as a business, his confidence in the generally beneficent nature of the white man's rule was no doubt reassuring to his readers in Eastern Canada and the Old Country.

It was inevitable that Ralph Connor should be the victim of a reaction as disproportionate as the enthusiasm which had greeted his books at the beginning of the century. The reaction was intensified by the spiritual depression which followed the First World War. In the decade of the twenties, the decade of Hemingway and T. S. Eliot and the Lost Generation, there was no place for the optimism and serene faith of a naive prairie missionary. Ralph Connor's autobiography, *Postscript to Adventure,* published in 1938, attracted little attention. Its readers were the men of a former generation, and they read it in the hope of re-kindling emotions which had been dead for many years.

It is natural that the reader who knew and loved Ralph Connor long ago, and who now seeks to appraise him with some objectivity, must hesitate to take down from their shelves the worn volumes in their characteristic black-lettered red binding to read again tales which half a century ago were, to the adolescent at least, just as thrilling as *Treasure Island* and *King Solomon's Mines* and much more real. Such hesitation is justified. For many of the great reading experiences of a man's life, and especially those of boyhood, are so by happy accident—because a particular book and a particular mood or age are, for the time of reading, in absolute harmony. But because such harmony can be rarely, if ever, achieved more than once it is always dangerous to re-read books which were a peculiar treasure in childhood. So it is that the mature reader must feel that *Corporal Cameron* and *The Patrol of the Sun Dance Trail* belong in the catalogue of books to be remembered fondly and left undisturbed on their shelves.

Assuredly a re-reading of Ralph Connor calls to our attention a score of obvious and distressing faults. There is, above all, his agonizing sentimentality. Like Dickens he at times ceases to be a rational being who brings the steadying light of intelligence to bear on all that he writes. Instead he from time to time abandons himself to a shameless wallowing in emotion. Few of his deathbed scenes can be read without a sense of the most acute embarrassment. It is in such scenes that Ralph Connor—in spite of the evidence of his own tears—is open to a charge that cannot often be laid against him, that of insincerity. The danger inherent in this kind of writing, in which the author abandons himself to the control of his emotions, has been pointed out most explicitly by Joseph Conrad:

> In order to move others deeply we must deliberately allow ourselves to be carried away beyond the bounds of our normal sensibility, innocently enough, perhaps, and of necessity, like an actor who raises his voice on the stage above the pitch of natural conversation—but still we have to do that. And surely this is no great sin. But the danger lies in the writer becoming the victim of his own exaggeration, losing the exact notion of sincerity, and in the end coming to despise truth itself as something too cold, too blunt for his purpose—as, in fact, not good enough for his insistent emotion. From laughter and tears the descent is easy to snivelling and giggles.

Ralph Connor's sentimentality is not, unfortunately, confined to individual scenes; it tends to permeate all his work. It expresses itself, for instance, in the ease with which he assumes the innate goodness of man and the ultimate working out of all things on earth for the best. To a generation to whom Buchenwald and Hiroshima and the gas-chambers of Oswiecim and Birkenau are monstrous facts, the devil in man is at least as obvious as the god. Yet it is possible that some readers may find in Ralph Connor the vision of the prophet. Says Old Man Nelson, a typical *Black Rock* down-and-out, to Mr. Craig, the minister, who is calling on him to follow Christ, "If this is no good it's hell for me." And the minister replies, "If it's no good it's hell for all of us."

Paradoxically, Ralph Connor's limitations are sometimes responsible for his best writing. He lacked inventive power, or at least patience to create fictitious incidents. Instead he relied for his material almost entirely upon incidents drawn from his own rich and crowded experience, and on characters whom he had known in life. *Glengarry School Days* is a dramatized account of his own boyhood. *The Sky Pilot* and *Black Rock* and *The Prospector* are founded on his experiences as missionary in the foothills. "I knew the country. I had ridden the ranges. I had pushed through the mountain passes. I had swum my broncos across its rivers. I had met the men—Hi Kendal and Bronco Bill and the rest were friends of mine." His best minor characters are undoubtedly these friends of his. Hi Kendal and Bronco Bill, the cowpunchers who provide most of the comedy relief in *The Sky Pilot,* are no doubt over-simplified, but Ralph Connor succeeds in making the reader feel their *naïveté,* their childlike wonder in the presence of anything outside the scope of their immediate environment. Bill's interpretation of Biblical narrative in terms of his own life is rendered with skill and insight. Thus Saint Paul, "the little chap who got mixed up in a riot and stood off a whole gang of thieves and cut-throats," is, in Bill's eyes, a stout-hearted Westerner involved in a saloon brawl who conducts himself in a manner worthy of the traditions of the frontier. It is, too, an accurate reflection of Bill's character that when an agnostic challenges his unquestioning acceptance of the Biblical story, Bill retorts by giving his tormentor a sound thrashing. Unfortunately the reader is left with the impression that Ralph Connor, too, considers the clenched fist the best of all possible replies to the doubter.

So long as Ralph Connor is content to deal with the simplified types whom he knew well in life his characters have some reality. Occasionally, too, he achieves an effective imitation of a type made familiar to him through his reading of Dickens. Mr. Rae, the family solicitor in *Corporal Cameron,* is an eccentric, tagged, like Uriah Heep, by a physical peculiarity:

> An amazing smile was Mr. Rae's; amazing both in the suddenness of its appearing and the suddenness of its vanishing. Upon a face of supernatural gravity, without warning, without beginning, the smile, broad, full and effulgent, was instantaneously present. Then equally without warning and without fading the smile ceased to be. Under its effulgence the observer unfamiliar with Mr. Rae's smile was moved to a responsive geniality of expression, but in the full tide of the emotion he found himself suddenly regarding a face of such preternatural gravity as rebuked the very possibility or suggestion of geniality. Before the smile Mr. Rae's face was like a house, with the shutters up and the family plunged in gloom. When the smile broke forth every shutter was flung wide to the pouring sunlight, and every window full of flowers and laughing children. Then instantly and without warning the house was blank, lifeless and shuttered once more, leaving you helplessly apologetic that you had ever been guilty of associating anything but death and gloom with its appearance.

But most of Ralph Connor's imitations of literary types are not so inoffensive as Mr. Rae. He wrote at his best when he drew his stories and characters from his own experience, at his worst when he was self-consciously the man of letters. *The Doctor* is an unhappy example of a novel written in accordance with what the author seems to have thought was the mode of the hour. The story begins in a manner familiar to the reader of the earlier Connor. The hero, Barney Boyle, is a rugged Ontario farm boy haunted by the dream of becoming a great surgeon.

The heroine, Margaret Robertson, is in the traditional mould, the author even going so far this time as to give her his mother's maiden name. The early chapters contain typical accounts of a barn-raising and a grain-binding competition, both described with characteristic lavish use of superlatives. But a new note is struck with the introduction of the *femme fatale* in the form of the beautiful, talented school-ma'am, Iola Lane. Iola is sensuous, passionate, and spiritual. Barney falls in love with her; and expresses his love in a manner which seems to be typical at one time or another of nearly all Ralph Connor heroes, through his fists. He hears Iola's name being lightly bandied at a Medical Association dinner and rises to her defence. The ensuing slaughter is awful to behold. Having literally wiped the floor with the besmirchers of Iola's name, Barney rages up and down in a fury that intimidates—as well it might—an entire roomful of besotted medical men:

> He walked up and down before the group which stood huddled in the corner in abject terror, more like a wild beast than a man. ''You're not fit to live! You're beasts of prey! No decent girl is safe from you!'' His voice rose loud and thin and harsh. He was fast losing hold of himself. His ghastly face, bloody and horribly disfigured, made an appalling setting for his blazing eyes. Nearer and nearer the crowd he walked, gnashing and grinding his teeth till the foam fell from his lips. The wild fury of his Highland ancestors was turning him into a wild beast with a wild beast's lust for blood. Further and further back cowered the group without a word, so utterly panic-stricken were they.

It would seem that absurdity could go no further. But the scene in which Barney chastises the entire Medical Society is almost tolerable by comparison with the one in which he resists Iola's seductive wiles and refuses to take advantage of her willingness to surrender herself to him.

In fairness to Ralph Connor it must be pointed out that he seldom exceeded the limitations which his lack of creative power imposed upon him. The secret of his success lay partly in the fact that—in the early years at least—he did not consider himself a novelist at all, and hence did not dissipate his powers in attempted inventions for which he had neither liking nor talent. It was only after he had become conscious of his position as a man of letters and tried to live up to it that he perpetrated the kind of absurdity in which *The Doctor* abounds.

Just as his best characters are simplifications of people whom he knew in real life, so his most exciting bits of descriptive writing are drawn from personal experience. The description of frontier funeral mores in *The Sky Pilot* is one of the best things in our Western literature. It deserves to be quoted in full:

> In the old times a funeral was regarded in the Swan Creek country as a kind of solemn festivity. In those days, for the most part, men died in their boots and were planted with much honour and libation. There was often neither coffin nor shroud, and in the far West many a poor fellow lies as he fell, wrapped in his own or his comrade's blanket.
>
> It was the manager of the XL Company's ranch who introduced crepe. The occasion was the funeral of one of the ranch cowboys, killed by his bronco, but when the pall-bearers and mourners appeared with bands and streamers of crepe, this was voted by the majority as ''too gay.'' That circumstance alone was sufficient to render the funeral famous, but it was remembered, too, as having shocked the proprieties in another and more serious manner. No one would

> be so narrow-minded as to object to the custom of the return procession falling into a series of horse-races of the wildest description, and ending up at Latour's in a general riot. But to race with the corpse was considered bad form. The ''corpse-driver,'' as he was called, could hardly be blamed on this occasion. His acknowledged place was at the head of the procession, and it was a point of honor that that place should be retained. The fault lay clearly with the driver of the XL ranch sleigh, containing the mourners (an innovation, by the way), who felt aggrieved that Hi Kendal, driving the Ashley team with the pall-bearers (another innovation), should be given the place of honour next the corpse. The XL driver wanted to know, in the name of all that was black and blue, what the Ashley ranch had to do with the funeral? Whose was the corpse anyway? Didn't it belong to the XL ranch? Hi, on the other hand, contended that the corpse was in charge of the pall-bearers. ''It was their duty to see it right to the grave, and if they were not on hand, how was it goin' to get there? They didn't expect it would git up and get there by itself, did they? He didn't want no blanked mourners foolin' round that corp till it was properly planted; after that they might git in their work.'' But the XL driver could not accept this view, and at the first opportunity slipped past Hi and his pall-bearers and took the place next the sleigh that carried the coffin. Hi might have borne the affront and loss of position with even mind, but the jeering remarks of the mourners as they slid past triumphantly could not be endured, and the next moment the three teams were abreast in a race for dear life. The corpse-driver, having the advantage of the beaten track, soon left the other two behind running neck and neck for second place, which was captured finally by Hi and maintained to the graveside, in spite of many attempts on the part of the XL's. The whole proceeding, however, was considered quite improper, and at Latour's, that night, after full and bibulous discussion, it was agreed that the corpse-driver fairly distributed the blame. ''For his part,'' he said, ''he knew he hadn't ought to make no corp git any such move on, but he wasn't goin' to see that there corp take second place at his own funeral. Not if he could help it. And as for the others, he thought that the pall-bearers had a blanked sight more to do with the plantin' than them giddy mourners.''

We can only regret that there is so little of this kind of writing in Ralph Connor. By comparison, the conventional sentimental account of the burial of the Pilot is made all the more unpalatable to the present-day reader.

Ralph Connor's descriptions of landscape are commonplace and without flavour. It is impossible to claim for him the discerning eye or sensitive imagination. His descriptive passages are neither photographic, in the sense that they record precisely the physical details of a scene, nor suggestive in that they give sentience to the inanimate. He sketches his Western pictures in vague generalities that with a little transposing could be adapted to suit any foothills landscape, as in the following characteristic passage:

> What a morning it was! How beautiful our world seemed! About us rolled the round-topped, velvet hills, brown or yellow or faintly green, spreading out behind us to the broad prairie, and before, clambering up to meet the purple bases of the great mountains that lay their mighty strength along the horizon and thrust up white, sunlit peaks into the blue sky. On the hillsides and down in the sheltering hollows we could see the bunches of cattle and horses feeding

upon the rich grasses. High above, the sky, cloudless and blue, arched its kindly roof from prairie to mountain peaks and over all, above, below, upon prairie, hillsides and mountains, the sun poured his floods of radiant yellow light.

As we followed the trail that wound up and into the heart of these rounded hills and ever nearer to the purple mountains, the morning breeze swept down to meet us, bearing a thousand scents, and filling us with its own fresh life. One can know the quickening joyousness of these Foothill breezes only after he has drunk with wide-open mouth, deep and full of them.

There is a suggestion, certainly, of spaciousness and colour here, but nothing more. The landscape lacks individuality; and nowhere in this passage is there a phrase—as there must be in great descriptive writing—which suggests that the author was looking at the scene through his own eyes and recording what was visible to him alone.

If we agree with Virginia Woolf that the business of the novelist is to create character, then Ralph Connor is not a novelist; if we agree with Arnold Bennett that the business of the novelist is to tell the truth in the form of fiction, then Ralph Connor is not a novelist; if we agree that the novelist's only obligation is to tell a good story, then Ralph Connor is not a novelist, for his books lack unity and tend to resolve themselves into a series of episodes loosely strung together. In a way, his popularity in his own time seems to have been as much a matter of shrewdness as of talent: he was sufficiently alert to see the value of material which had hitherto been neglected, and the human interest appeal of types hitherto largely unrecorded— the Mountie, the missionary, the remittance-man, the oldtimer. He had a keen eye for the obvious in character, situation and landscape, and the ability to record it in generalities comprehensible and agreeable to the ordinary reader. Finally, the emphasis on the Christian way of life so characteristic of all that he wrote, gave many readers the satisfying feeling that in addition to enjoying themselves they were experiencing genuine spiritual uplift. Ralph Connor was himself fully aware of the effect of this strong religious sentiment which pervades his books. He says:

Another cause of the phenomenal editions of these Ralph Connor books, and a very influential cause, was the fact that though in fiction form they possess a definitely religious motif. Religion is here set forth in its true light as a synonym of all that is virile, straight, honourable and withal tender and gentle in true men and women. And it was this religious motif that startled that vast host of religious folk who up to this time had regarded novel-reading as a doubtful indulgence for Christian people. I have received hundreds of letters expressing gratitude for a novel that presented a quality of religious life that "red-blooded" men could read and enjoy.

But for none of these reasons is Ralph Connor likely to be read today or in the future. The Mountie has become a stock character of Canadian and American popular fiction. His habitat, the West, is no longer a land of romance because it is the last frontier, the last frontier having shifted a thousand miles north. Nor—although it is still true that the student on a mission-field who can play baseball or run a fast hundred yards is more likely to have a full church than one whose interests are less "red-blooded"—is Christianity of the muscular variety as popular nowadays as it was fifty years ago. And even a generation brought up on soap operas is likely to find Ralph Connor's sentimentality out of date, just as his Doctor, Barney Boyle,

lacks the glamour interest of the Caseys and Kildares and Corwins who weekly display their professional and other talents on TV.

And yet, one hardly dares predict oblivion for *The Sky Pilot.* Paradoxically the secret of Ralph Connor's astonishing vitality may lie in the fact that he was a novelist second, a man with a message first. Like the preacher of all ages he tells a tale to point a moral. Nor is the practise always artistically indefensible as *The Pardoner's Tale* bears witness. What Ralph Connor's son, King Gordon, has finely said of his preaching, is in part true of his books. "The secret of his power lay in his awareness of the tremendous mission of the church in desperate times and in the imaginative qualities of heart and mind which may well be the very essence of the life of the spirit."

And even those who deny everything that Ralph Connor preached, who detest his crudities and flinch from his breaches of good taste, who deride the simplicity of his character and the genial optimism of his faith, must recognize that intense spiritual awareness, which, however distorted in the presentation, gives his novels a passionate sincerity rare in Canadian literature. Whatever Ralph Connor's faults—and they are legion—it must be said of him as he said of his own Sky Pilot, that he had a true man's heart and a great purpose in it. (pp. 26-41)

> *Edward McCourt, "Sky Pilot," in his* The Canadian West in Fiction, *revised edition, The Ryerson Press, 1970, pp. 24-41.*

LEE [BRISCOE] THOMPSON AND JOHN H. THOMPSON (essay date 1972)

[In the following excerpt, the critics discuss Connor's portrayal of Canadian national identity.]

Beginning in 1898 with *Black Rock* and concluding thirty-eight years later with *The Gay Crusader,* Connor expounded a philosophy of confident Canadianism admirably suited to the aggressive young nation which looked forward into the Twentieth Century, a century her Prime Minister had promised was hers alone. The situations and characters of Connor's novels reflected and reinforced the intellectual assumptions that underlay this conviction of their country's unique destiny. Whether they lived in the newly-opening West, rural Ontario, Nova Scotia, or Lower Canada during the early Nineteenth Century, Connor's heroes and heroines were, to use his own words, "good, clean young Canadians, worthy in body, mind, and spirit of the new nation that was coming into being in the minds of the Canadian people." This new national spirit is the real hero of a Ralph Connor novel, and when Kalman Kalmar protects his mine from the wily Rosenblatt or Corporal Cameron rejects his dissolute past for the wholesome life of a Mounted Policeman, the triumph belongs to Canada as much as to the individuals concerned.

What then were the elements which Connor identified as part of this "spirit of the new nation"? Although he insisted upon the uniqueness of Canada's collective personality, Connor never failed to acknowledge that his newborn Canadian owed much to British parentage. Connor's Canadians frequently express their admiration for the Empire. Barry Dunbar of *The Sky Pilot in No Man's Land* dies defending it in the Great War, and a host of other Connor characters enlist for active service and make "the supreme sacrifice". But the loyalty of Connor's Canada is that of a grown son to his revered parent, founded on filial piety but tempered with a strong sense of independence. As J. H. Gilchrist, M.P. for Wolf Willow, Sask., says in his Dominion Day address in *The Major,* Canadians "belong to a great world Empire. This connection we value and mean to cherish, but our Imperial relations do not in the slightest degree infringe upon our liberties. The Government of Canada is autonomous."

After making clear their political and constitutional independence, Connor's Canadians were able to draw on the rich resources of the British heritage. To Connor, the most important of Britain's contributions was an intangible quality which he invariably referred to as "the British sense of fair play". By this he meant a peculiar combination of justice and humanity which characterized both Britain's dealings with the world and her citizens' contact with individuals of different nationality. In *The Gay Crusader,* for example, Harry Dymont criticizes "a base dog of an American reporter" for his anti-Semitism, and expresses pride in his inherited freedom from such prejudice with the comment that Canadians as Britishers are "religion and colour blind" since their Empire citizenship makes them "the only world citizens among the nations". When a heckler interrupts an evangelical meeting in *The Major,* the speaker has only to "appeal to the audience for British fair play" to gain a hearing for his unpopular point of view.

Another British trait which Connor's Canadians espouse wholeheartedly is a respect for legitimate authority and a recognition of the need for law and order within society. This they accept whether their society is the rugged mining camp of *The Prospector* or the industrial town of *To Him That Hath.* Newcomers to Canada, from the United States as well as Europe, are quickly taught that they must accept the social restraints upon violence in their new country. Idaho Jack, the American professional gambler in *Black Rock,* is shocked to discover that he is not allowed to keep his revolver on the card table while he is playing, but soon conforms when confronted with Mounted Police Constable Jackson. In *The Foreigner,* the Galician immigrant who tries to decapitate Jack French with a stake is told firmly that "his people must learn to fight without club or knife", since in Canada it will "land them in prison or on the gallows".

This did not mean that Connor's Canada was pacifistic or nonviolent. His characters are offered numerous opportunities to prove their manhood in clean, face-to-face competition, which might take place on the football field, in the hockey arena, or in the boxing ring. The important thing is that such confrontations have to be on equal terms, without resort to trickery or unfair advantage. The attitudes which guarantee such fair encounters have, in Connor's view, profound implications not only for Canada's character and development, but also for the condition of world history and harmony. Comparing the wildness of the American West with the law-abiding nature of its Canadian counterpart, he makes bold to place the hope of world peace in the lap of "Canadian civilisation", speaking of "not in the West alone, but throughout the whole Dominion, a mighty force for reverence of law, for orderly government and for national righteousness, whose world influence it would be difficult to overvalue."

But despite his reverence for these facets of the British tradition, Connor finds much to criticize in Great Britain. Especially obnoxious to Connor is the stratified society of the mother country, which he has Sybil Waring-Gaunt of *The Major* denounce as a system of "hideous inequalities, injustices, and foolish class distinctions". Connor makes it plain that this "caste law" must not be transplanted in the new land, and his

characters loudly affirm that "in Canada social distinctions are based more upon worth than upon wealth, more upon industry and ability than upon blue blood."

To make more explicit the fact that the Canadian is not simply an Englishman in North America, Connor introduces English characters designed to produce derision or disgust in his readers. Silly, bumbling misfits, they speak with affected "rawther" accents and attempt to perpetuate in Canada an antiquated and undemocratic class structure. In *The Runner,* the Honourable Eustace Burton is identified by his limp handshake and by "his supercilious indifference to all things and persons colonial". The inept Edgar Penny of *The Foreigner* who "cawn't go a step farther in this beastly cold" has to be rescued by young Canadian Kalman Kalmar, while "Lily" Laughton of *Corporal Cameron* expresses disgust when he discovers that Canadian farmers are not "gentlemen" but actually work "with the plough and hoe, and that sort of thing". In *The Sky Pilot in No Man's Land* Canadian chaplain Barry Dunbar encounters an even more vicious form of English arrogance among his fellow officers. Col. Leighton, his regimental commander, is "a sporting man, of easy morality, fond of his glass and of good living", a teller of off-colour jokes in the officers' mess, and Captain Hopeman, who laughs at these stories, displays the "bored and supercilious air" of a "typical young English public school boy". The other end of the English social ladder produces an equally debased product, as is exemplified by Joe Wigglesworth, the constantly dissatisfied workman of *To Him That Hath,* who loudly demands his "rights as an H'Englishman", but becomes craven and obsequious in the presence of his employer.

Another attribute which many of Connor's English characters share is their inability to succeed in the new land. Captain Hopeman fails as a rancher, Edgar Penny as a personal secretary, Eustace Burton as an Indian administrator, and Joe Wigglesworth as a rabble rouser. All tend to blame this failure on Canada, "this Gawd forsaken country", but the reader quickly realizes that the flaws belong not to the adopted land but to the Englishmen themselves. In direct competition with a Canadian, an Englishman cannot hope for success, whether the field is business, athletics, or romance. One of Connor's favourite symbolic struggles occurs when Englishman and Canadian compete for the hand of the same girl. Faced with such a choice, the Connor heroine is swept away by the vigour and manliness of her Canadian suitor, leaving the aristocratic Englishman to accept his defeat "with the cool steadiness with which men of his race have been wont to meet shattering disaster."

Just as Connor accepts or rejects various aspects of the British tradition, so he turns an ambivalent eye toward the United States as a formative influence on the Canadian character. Connor finds much to admire in America, and avoids the anti-American excesses of nineteenth-century Canada. In the two novels which he devotes to the War of 1812, *The Runner* and *The Rock and the River,* Connor is careful to have his characters point out that "all Americans are not our enemies, the best Americans are our friends and are opposed to this foolish War." In novels set during the First World War he makes apologetic comments about America's three-year neutrality. In *Treading the Winepress,* for example, young Americans like Dale and Diana Farrer are "horribly mortified that America has not come in yet" and do their bit by enlisting in a British ambulance unit.

Connor discovered in the United States some of those qualities he found lacking in Great Britain. In *The Rock and the River* a young New Yorker, Madeleine Van Rancken, chides class-conscious Lower Canadians and tells them that in her country their "Member of Congress sells tapes and needles, can't speak decent English, and yet dines at [her] father's table." Connor also admires America's ability to assimilate successive waves of European immigration into a common Americanism, and hopes that Canada might adopt some of her techniques. In *The Major* he has Monteith describe in glowing terms the Oath of Allegiance Ceremony at a school in Oregon:

> I watched those kids with their foreign faces, foreign speech—you ought to hear them read—Great Scott, you'd have to guess at the language. Then came this flag-saluting business. A kid with Yiddish written all over his face was chosen to carry in the flag, attended by a bodyguard for the colours, and believe me they appeared as proud as Punch of the honour. They placed the flag in position, sang a hymn, had a prayer, then every kid at a signal shot out his right hand toward the flag held aloft by the Yiddish colour bearer and pledged himself, heart, and soul, and body, to his flag and to his country. The ceremony closed with the singing of the national hymn, mighty poor poetry and mighty hard to sing, but do you know listening to those kids and watching their foreign faces I found myself with tears in my eyes and swallowing like a darn fool. Ever since that day I believe in flag-flapping.

Also deserving of praise is American enterprise and initiative, and as far as Connor's Canadians are concerned, the United States is a prime source of potential immigrants.

But just as Britain cannot be an entirely satisfactory model for the emergent Canada, so the U.S. fails in several important respects. First and foremost of these is the American penchant for lawlessness and undisciplined behaviour. "Red Rory" Fraser makes this clear in *The Rock and the River* when he attributes American failure in the War of 1812 to a lack of discipline and an unwillingness to accept discipline. René LaFlamme of *The Runner* blames Indian dislike of Americans on the allegation that "the Americans have broken their treaties and are stealing their land from them." Connor's autobiography underlies this theme of a violent and lawless United States. To him the American frontier was "a 'Wild West', the stamping ground of the 'gunman' and the 'Vigilance Committee'," as opposed to its more law-abiding and temperate Canadian equivalent.

In Connor's later novels, there is also a suggestion that American excess has corrupted American enterprise to produce a crass materialism. The nation, like the rich Americans in *The Arm of Gold,* has forgotten the Lord's Second Commandment, and has created in the United States an aristocracy of wealth equally as artificial as the British aristocracy based on birth. Thus, "The Inmans had lots of money, but nothing else—neither education nor breeding." Patty Olivant, the young American of *Treading the Winepress,* goes so far as to reject her countrymen as hopelessly lost to the material. She tells a fellow American that she is "a little sick of a lot of them. They've got all the things that money can buy. Their houses are so crowded with things gathered from all over the world that there isn't room to live in them. And they're so busy rushing about from one house to another, and from one rout to another, that they've got to spend half their time in sanatariums, resting up for the next fight." For Connor's Canadian,

then, the American dream must be as incomplete an identity as the British tradition.

Canada to Connor is more than a halfway house, suspended between the old and new worlds. In one of his rare forays into symbolism, he demonstrates his deeply held conviction that a Canadian identity transcends the simple combination of American and British contributions. The opening chapters of *The Rock and the River* focus upon a horse race between "Black Duke", a stallion bred in England and trained in the United States, and "Vitesse", a mare bred and trained in Canada like her master, "Red Rory" Fraser. The symbolic significance of this confrontation develops throughout the first seven chapters of the novel, and culminates in the eighth in which Rory and Vitesse gain a dramatic victory for Canada and Canadianism.

It is symbolic too that the race in which Vitesse bests Black Duke takes place in midwinter on the frozen St. Lawrence River, for it is in Canada's northern environment that Connor finds the catalysts capable of assisting the transformation of varied ingredients into a *tertium aliquid* ["a third something"], that new and unique force which is the Canadian identity.

In isolating the land as the crucial factor in the Canadian identity, we come to the core of Connor's thesis, of his vision, and of his art. Looking back over his career and attempting to account for the phenomenal success of his books, Connor attributed their popularity to three things. The feature which, although probably most important to him personally, he was obliged by honesty to stress least, was what we would call the "muscular Christianity" of his message. The second source of success Connor saw as the sensitivity of his artist's eye, the verisimilitude which brought his narratives to life for the reader. It is certainly in this area that scholars tend to find his major literary and historical merit. Not so with the author himself. It is extremely significant that Connor chooses as the greatest reason for his triumph the power of Canada's story and Canada itself. As he explains in his autobiography, "[I] gave an authentic picture of life in the great and wonderful new country in Western Canada." That the artist was, like Plato's Ion, a mere tool of a higher force, is evidenced by Connor's third-person remark that "Of all men, the most surprised at this reception of his books was Ralph Connor himself. He had not the slightest ambition to be a writer. He made little effort after polished literary style. Things just came to him and he put them down." The impact of the land and its development on Connor's mind was so substantial that he felt it actually took over and managed the creative process for him. And we may deduce from the popularity of the novels that the readers participated fully in that process.

In making his case for the dramatic power of the Canadian landscape, Connor had to overcome common misconceptions about the Canadian wilderness. The contemptuous reference of an American to Canada in *The Runner* says it best. Canada is dismissed as "a strip of frozen country, fit only for Indians and trappers." But in Connor's hands, a "typical Canadian winter day" boasts "brilliant sunshine, clear, mildly frosty air, and over all the trees, fields, and houses a dazzling, diamond-sewn mantle of new-fallen snow." The immense and undeniable physical beauty of Canada, from Bras D'Or to the Pacific, is spread lavishly over the pages of a Connor novel and soon assumes the importance of a major, almost *the* major, character.

Having established the majesty of the Canadian landscape generally, Connor moves on to the contention that the rural Canadian scene is superior to the urban one. Evelyn Neeves of *Torches Through the Bush* is pitied for her urban dwelling; "Poor child . . . She has never known anything but the society life of Montreal." The wealthy, but soul-poor, New Yorkers learn rural virtues and values at the gentle hands of the intuitively noble Cape Breton folk in *The Arm of Gold*. Hope of *The Runner* obeys the myth of the land in instinctively preferring the Canadian countryside to the city's stuffiness and sidewalks. Jack Maitland of *To Him That Hath* teaches the mill hands "clean and vigorous outdoor sports" so that they will not be corrupted by "lounging in pool rooms" in town. Again and again Connor plays upon the northern myth as he lays the groundwork for his final position, that it is the peculiar catalytic properties of *Western* Canada which bring the Canadian identity to fruition. The emerging West is what Connor knew best, and it provides the setting for his most eloquent work.

The Foreigner contains what is probably Connor's finest and most exhilarating statement on the development and the destiny of the Canadian spirit. In his preface, he proclaims that "In Western Canada there is to be seen today that most fascinating of all human phenomena, the making of a nation. Out of breeds diverse in traditions, in ideals, in speech, and in manner of life, Saxon and Slav, Teuton, Celt and Gaul, one people is being made. The blood strains of great races will mingle in the blood of a race greater than the greatest of them all." Any rural Canadian area may contribute to a morally upright world, but the arena for the fusion of disparates into "the Entity of our Canadian national life" must be the Canadian West. There, inspired by natural splendours, challenged by natural barriers, tested in the crucible of a stern but redemptive environment, "we fuse into a people whose strength will endure the slow shock of time for the honour of our name, for the good of mankind, and for the glory of Almighty God."

Connor's conviction that the West was the exclusive cradle of the new Canadian race surfaces repeatedly. Corporal Cameron of the North West Mounted Police flees a drinking problem in Scotland and comes to Canada in search of grace and fulfillment. In the materialistic culture of Eastern Canada he finds new world rudeness and treachery combined with old world autocracy; his subsequent attempt to find himself in rural Ontario reveals its limited financial, social, cultural, and spiritual horizons. He must eventually go all the way to Western Canada to realize his dreams. The West brings out his true worth; together with his brothers in fortitude and trial, "rank comes to mean little and manhood much."

Lest we miss this crucial point, Connor reiterates the situation in other novels. The young minister of *The Prospector* can make the breakthrough from the "fictitious and accidental" to the "great lines of sheer humanity" only in the crystal clear atmosphere of the Prairies. Similarly the Company of Noble Seven in *The Sky Pilot,* "freed from the restraints of custom and surrounding, soon shed all that was superficial in their make-up and stood forth in the naked simplicity of their native manhood."

When a man is stripped down to his pure Canadian skin, what is revealed? Nothing but goodness, replies the idealistic Connor. The true Westerner is "a high-class chap" who makes people "proud to be a Canadian". He and his good works upon the Prairies represent "what [is] best and most characteristic in Canadian civilisation." He is inordinately sensitive: "There is no man living so quick to feel your mood, and so ready to adapt himself to it, as is the true Westerner." He is

innately chivalrous: "No men are so truly gentle as are the Westerners in the presence of a good woman." Westerners have common sense and right values: "They were evidently of all classes and ranks originally, but now, and in this country of real measurements, they ranked simply according to the 'man' in them." The Westerner's relationship with the land that makes him what he is is as basic and deep as the one with men: given the chance to return to Eastern cities and a life of comfort and wealth, he is invariably "too truly Western to imagine that any inducements the East could offer could compensate for his loss of the West."

So it goes with myriad other adjectives. The quintessential Canadian, nurtured in the Great Canadian West, exhibits "courage, faith, and self-denial", a good heart, competence, enterprise, a respect for law and the individual, and frequently a deep gratitude to the land that has made him a man. If the "true Westerner"—the new Canadian—is larger than life, it is because of the metamorphosis he has undergone in the presence of the Canadian West. There are undoubtedly renegades and derelicts impervious to the redemptive powers of the land but Connor weeds out these unfortunate exceptions with the use of the phrase "*true* Westerners". As in all mythologies, reality may not impinge too fully upon the dimensions of a vision.

Like any other single definition of a Canadian character which claims universality, Connor's Canadian identity is foredoomed. By presupposing one common Canadian type, Connor fails to acknowledge the possibility of cultural diversity. To him all Canadians, exposed to similar traditions and environment, could effortlessly be induced to conform to one standard national pattern. Connor makes this clear in *The Foreigner* which, despite the critics' claims for *The Man from Glengarry,* is probably his most important novel. It concerns Kalman Kalmar, of unspecified Eastern European origin, who is undergoing the process of Canadianization which of course takes place in the West. From the British tradition Kalmar is taught respect for law and order and fair play, and from the North American he learns to reject the artificial class distinctions of Europe. The book's climax occurs when he rescues Marjorie, the heroine, from a blinding blizzard and in the process discovers a rich deposit of coal. Invigorated by the spirit of the new land, Kalman is able to exploit his discovery, become wealthy, and eventually make Marjorie his wife. It is at that moment that his Canadianization is complete, and he becomes to Marjorie "my foreigner, my *Canadian* foreigner".

Few Canadians would have found fault with Connor's opinion that the European immigrant had to be forced to abandon his foreignness and be assimilated. Connor's all-encompassing Canadianism provided an excellent intellectual framework for a small nation faced with more than a million newcomers in the short space of fifteen years. Connor's version of the Canadian identity failed not because of these newest Canadians, but because of a group of Canadians who pre-dated the British tradition by a century and a half. French Canada simply defied Connor's model.

With few exceptions Connor's French-Canadian characters are cast in one-dimensional supporting roles as hewers of wood, drawers of water, or devoted servants. Joe Perrotte in *To Him That Hath,* Alphonse la Roque in *Glengarry School Days,* or Joe Gagneau in *The Major,* all display what Connor called the "patient endurance of grinding toil characteristic of the French-Canadian habitant." Connor never missed an opportunity to phrase a conversation in dialect, and often accomplished this with skill, but his French Canadians are straight from the pages of William Henry Drummond. "You be my boss, I be your man—what you call slave. I work for not'ing, me," says LeNoir to Macdonald in *The Man from Glengarry.* "I'm ver' bad man me. I lak to know how you do dat—what you say—forgive. You show me how," LeNoir continues, reinforcing the unequal relationship which always exists between Connor's French and English characters.

In two of Connor's novels, the hero is of mixed French-English parentage, but in both cases it is the English strain which predominates. Whether one has a French father, as in the case of René LaFlamme of *The Runner,* or a French mother, like "Red Rory" Fraser of *The Rock and the River,* one lives his life in the dominant English-speaking milieu, and is careful not to "speak and act like a habitant, full of whiskey blanc." Both René and Rory stand apart from the common habitants, who we learn are simple souls who "must be humoured like children". When Rory Fraser tries to convince the residents of a seigneury to help with fortifications during the War of 1812, he has first to win their attention with talk of horse-racing and the good life they will enjoy in Quebec, and then invoke the aid of the curé before the men can be persuaded to do their duty.

Connor was never definite about the French Canadian's place in his grand design. In *The Rock and the River* he tries to suggest assimilation as an eventual goal, with education as the means to its achievement. Rory tells his young cousin Alain McNab, also of mixed parentage, not to waste his time on a French classical education, but to begin the study of mathematics. He further counsels Alain to speak English at every possible opportunity. But Connor did realize that educative assimilation would be difficult, since many French Canadians were like Joe Gagneau in that they "no lak dat school", preferring instead the open fields and forests. Connor never found a satisfactory answer to the French-Canadian question, and for this reason never advanced beyond commonplace English stereotypes in his evaluation of French contributions to the Canadian character. Like many of his readers, however, Connor died long before the Quiet Revolution could have forced him to alter his interpretation.

As with most novelists who enjoy spectacular success, Connor was irrevocably a man of his time. Connor struck a responsive chord during the first decades of this century because he described the new Canada of popular imagination, a Canada neither British nor American, peopled by "a race greater than the greatest of them all". But this vision was never transformed into reality. In Connor's novels Kalman Kalmar and René LaFlamme eagerly sacrificed their language and heritage to become part of this new race, but their real life counterparts displayed considerable reluctance when invited to enter the melting pot. During the twenties and thirties the image of a universal identity was abandoned for a recognition of the pluralism which marked Canadian society. The favourite metaphor for this pluralism became the mosaic, bound together by what W. L. Morton has described as a "unity admitting of a thousand diversities".

As both European immigrants and French Canadians demonstrated their determination to maintain their cultural distinctiveness, the flaws in Connor's monothematic definition became more noticeable. The fading popularity of his novels serves as a barometer of the acceptability of that definition. During the 1920s, Connor seemed to lose rapport with his readers, and he gradually became a frequent choice on Christmas shopping lists for nephews and grandchildren. As his version of the Canadian identity became less realistic, Connor lost that robust certainty which had so distinguished his earlier writings. To an audience which no longer shared his underlying assumptions, Connor's literary deficiencies became painfully evident. By the time of his death in 1937, the novelist who had chatted with statesmen, been the making of at least one publishing house, and painted a national portrait, was in irreversible decline. (pp. 160-69)

> *Lee [Briscoe] Thompson and John H. Thompson, "Ralph Connor and the Canadian Identity," in* Queen's Quarterly, *Vol. LXXIX, No. 2, Summer, 1972, pp. 159-70.*

ADDITIONAL BIBLIOGRAPHY

Bassett, Isabel. "The Transformation of Imperialism: Connor to MacLennan." *Journal of Canadian Fiction* 2, No. 1 (Winter 1973): 58-62.
  Compares Canadian novels that glorify war, such as Connor's *The Major,* with others written later that condemn war.

Review of *The Foreigner,* by Ralph Connor. *The Canadian Magazine* XXXIV, No. 4 (February 1910): 390-93.
  Commends Connor for his accuracy in depicting the Canadian Northwest and his sincerity in the moral and spiritual values he advocates.

Doran, George H. "A Modern Apostle." In his *Chronicles of Barabbas, 1884-1934,* pp. 200-06. New York: Harcourt, Brace and Co., 1935.
  Biographical sketch of Connor by an admiring friend.

Gordon, J. King. Introduction to *Postscript to Adventure: The Autobiography of Ralph Connor,* by Charles W. Gordon, pp. v-xiv. New York: Farrar & Rinehart, 1938.
  Reminiscence by Connor's son.

Marble, Annie Russell. "History and Romance." In her *A Study of the Modern Novel: British and American since 1900,* pp. 3-41. New York and London: D. Appleton and Co., 1928.
  Includes a brief biographical sketch of Connor.

Pringle, Ian. "The Gaelic Substratum in the English of Glengarry County and Its Reflection in the Novels of Ralph Connor." *The Canadian Journal of Linguistics* 26, No. 1 (Spring 1981): 126-40.
  Analyzes Connor's reproduction of the dialect spoken in Glengarry County, Ontario, in his four novels set in that county.

Rhonenizer, V. B. "Other Novelists, Historical and Regional." In his *A Handbook of Canadian Literature,* pp. 95-102. Ottawa, Canada: Graphic Publishers Ltd., 1930.
  Includes a biographical sketch and a favorable mention of Connor's historical novel *The Runner.*

R[obins], J. D. Review of *The Runner,* by Ralph Connor. *The Canadian Forum* X, No. 115 (April 1930): 260.
  Dismisses *The Runner* as "a very careless novel," observing that its "disregard of form and style, and the Hentyesque unconvincingness of its superman hero prevent it from being a good story for adults while the mawkishness of its love story takes it out of the class of boys' books."

Vicente Huidobro

1893-1948

Chilean poet, novelist, essayist, and dramatist.

Huidobro was one of the most influential Spanish-language poets of the twentieth century. As the leading proponent of *Creacionismo* ("Creationism"), he was part of the literary avant-garde that challenged the conventions and traditions of literature. Creationism was based on the idea that a poet must no longer merely imitate nature by using images of the real world, but must create a new world by inventing wholly original images that go beyond the confines of ordinary experience. Huidobro wrote: "We must release our infinite, our eternal side. We must liberate our powers. Those who cannot accomplish this release will remain in the realm of ephemeral things; their works will be but for a day." To this end, he produced a variety of experimental works in both poetry and prose, including the cinematic novels *Mío Cid Campeador (Portrait of a Paladin)* and *Cagliostro (The Mirror of a Mage)*. Huidobro's innovations and experiments with new modes of expression and his enthusiastic defense of his poetic theories provoked controversy among his literary peers and in many circles inspired a reevaluation of the function of literature.

Huidobro was the son of one of the wealthiest families in Chile. His mother, a writer who used the pseudonym "Monna Lisa," encouraged her son's interest in literature. Educated in Catholic schools, Huidobro experienced at an early age a spiritual crisis which led him to reject Christianity. He was critical of his Jesuit teachers and later wrote that he was expelled from school for defending in class the merits of the Naturalist author Emile Zola. In 1911 Huidobro published his first book of poetry, *Ecos del alma,* and soon after he founded *Musa joven,* the first of many journals that he published. Interested in finding new methods of poetic expression, Huidobro moved to Paris in 1916 to associate himself with the leading artists and writers of the French avant-garde, including Jean Arp, Juan Gris, Pablo Picasso, and Jean Cocteau, and worked on the Cubist literary journal *Nord-Sud* with Pierre Reverdy. Huidobro published further collections of poetry, and his writings on Creationism established him as one of the leaders of the avant-garde in Europe.

Huidobro believed that controversy was a dynamic part of literary development, and he was an ardent polemicist who became embroiled in many disputes. Not content with his role as a member of the avant-garde, he wanted to be at the center of it. One contemporary wrote that he had "an ego that dims the brilliance of his enormous talent." The most serious and damaging dispute was with Reverdy, who accused Huidobro of imitating him and of falsifying the date of *El espejo de agua,* Huidobro's first truly Creationist work. Huidobro never had the opportunity to publish his vitriolic defense, and the originality of his works remained in question throughout his lifetime. Another literary dispute in which Huidobro involved himself was incited by the advent of Dada and Surrealism. Observing that interest in Cubism and Creationism had waned as the avant-garde experimented with Dada and Surrealism, Huidobro published an attack on these artistic movements in his 1925 collection of essays, *Manifestes.* Huidobro objected not so much to the literary results of Surrealism and Dada, but to their

methods of production. He asserted that reliance on automatic writing and chance associations, techniques fostered by Surrealism and Dada, repudiates the creative role of the poet and "cheapens poetry by opening it up to everybody like a simple after-dinner game." However, Huidobro could not revive interest in his theories and, realizing his isolation, turned his passion from literary polemics to politics. He returned to Chile and unsuccessfully ran for president as the nominee of the Chilean Youth Party. In the latter half of the 1920s, Huidobro wrote his first novel, *Portrait of a Paladin,* and worked on his two most important poems, *Altazor o el viaje en paracaídos* and *Temblor de cielo,* both of which attracted little attention when first published. Huidobro continued his political involvement, joining the Communist party and working to establish a Popular Front government in Chile. He went to Spain in 1936 to fight for the Republic, but when its defeat became apparent he returned to Chile and continued to write. In 1944 he went to France as a war correspondent and received a serious head wound. He later boasted of his wartime experience, saying that he had been with the army that captured Adolf Hitler's Berchtesgaden retreat and that he had taken Hitler's personal telephone. In his later years, Huidobro served as a mentor for many of Chile's young poets (with the notable exception of Pablo Neruda, who engaged in a bitter feud with Huidobro). He died in 1948 from a stroke that was partially caused by his war injury.

Huidobro's poetic career may be divided into three main periods. During the first period, lasting from 1911 to 1916, he displayed a mastery of traditional poetic techniques and at the same time a restless striving for novelty. During his second phase as a poet, from 1916 to 1925, Huidobro developed Creationism. Huidobro's Creationist writings commonly juxtaposed unrelated ideas and images which, through the "magnetic words of poetry," are transformed into lyric metaphors that have a new existence independent from the world of everyday experience. For example, in "Moi flamfolle" ("My Flashfool"), Huidobro wrote: "The puppets that hang / from the rays of the stars / are spiders." Huidobro also used unorthodox typography in an attempt to create "word-paintings" that conveyed meaning through their design as well as through their content. Throughout the 1920s, however, even as Huidobro was publicly advocating Creationism as the newest and best type of poetry, his own work was already progressing beyond it. In the third and final period of his career, Huidobro published two longer poems, *Temblor de cielo* and *Altazor,* the latter of which is considered his greatest work. The exact relationship of *Altazor* to Huidobro's theory of Creationism is disputed by critics. Some maintain that it is the ultimate expression of Creationism. Nancy B. Mandlove, for instance, perceived *Altazor* as an attempt to make the poem "a mirror of Creation itself," using "language that reaches beyond ordinary verbal and logical connections to create new meanings from the word as the only reality, in and of itself." Other critics, however, argue that *Altazor* is an anti-Creationist poem that expresses, as Merlin H. Forster wrote, "the impossibility of transforming language into the vital and expressive 'magnetic words' of poetry" of Creationism. René de Costa has argued that the seven cantos of *Altazor* represent a trajectory from order to disorder, from intelligibility to incoherence, contending that Huidobro's search for a meaning in life was unsuccessful. This disintegration of meaning is exemplified by cantos three through seven of the poem, which de Costa describes as "a trek through the blind alleys of linguistic experimentation, a literary 'quest' in which the speaker wrestles with one new combinatory device after another, leaving each behind when its limitation becomes apparent." In the final canto, poetry is reduced to sounds devoid of meaning which, de Costa argues, demonstrates Huidobro's artistic passage "from the celestial poetics of the avant-garde to a concern with the emptiness of the world in which one must live and die."

Huidobro's preoccupation with innovation extended to other literary genres as well. He achieved popular success through his novels *Portrait of a Paladin* and *The Mirror of a Mage,* both of which were conceived as the bases for films and are commonly called "novel-films" due to their reliance on cinematic devices. In *Portrait of a Paladin,* Huidobro updated the story of *El Cid,* playfully "improving" upon original materials and including many slightly altered borrowings from familiar literary sources. He also tinkered with conventions of literary realism by reminding the reader that it is he who is writing what is being read and that the novel is an artistic retelling of something that has already happened. Intrigued by the way film represented motion, time, and space, Huidobro incorporated into the novel a number of cinematic conventions, including scenes of daring heroics reminiscent of the film exploits of Douglas Fairbanks (to whom the book is dedicated), cliff-hanging rescue situations, and a variety of special visual effects, such as close-up, gradual dissolve, and superimposition. *The Mirror of a Mage,* the story of an eighteenth-century necromancer, similarly evinces the influence of cinema, with its fast-paced plot, rapid characterization, and visually oriented

style and language. These innovations of the novel complemented Huidobro's relentless experimentation with poetry and further established his place as the leading Latin-American avant-garde writer of his day.

PRINCIPAL WORKS

Ecos del alma   (poetry)   1911
Canciones en la noche   (poetry)   1913
La gruta del silencio   (poetry)   1913
Las pagodas ocultas   (essays and prose poems)   1914
Pasando y pasando   (essays)   1914
Adán   (poetry)   1916
El espejo de agua   (poetry)   1916
Horizon carré   (poetry)   1917
Ecuatorial   (poetry)   1918
Hallali   (poetry)   1918
Poemas árticos   (poetry)   1918
     [*Arctic Poems,* 1974]
Tour Eiffel   (poetry)   1918
Saisons choisies   (poetry and essays)   1921
Finis Britannia   (essay)   1923
Automne régulier   (poetry)   1925
Manifestes   (essays)   1925
Tout à coup   (poetry)   1925
Vientos contrarios   (essays)   1926
Mío Cid Campeador   (novel)   1929
     [*Portrait of a Paladin,* 1931]
Altazor o el viaje en paracaídos   (poetry)   1931
Temblor de cielo   (prose poem)   1931
Gilles de Raíz   (drama)   1932
Cagliostro   (novel)   1934
     [*The Mirror of a Mage,* 1931]
En la luna   (drama)   1934
Papá o el diario de Alicia Mir   (novel)   1934
La próxima   (essay)   1934
Tres novelas ejemplares [with Hans Arp]   (novels)   1935
Sátiro o el poder de las palabras   (novel)   1939
El ciudadaño del olvido   (poetry)   1941
Ver y palpar   (poetry)   1941
Ultimos poemas   (poetry)   1948
Obras completas   (poetry, novels, and essays)   1976
The Selected Poetry of Vicente Huidobro   (poetry)   1981

*This work was first published in English translation.

VICENTE HUIDOBRO   (essay date 1925)

[*In the following selection from* Manifestes, *Huidobro states his poetic principles.*]

No true road, and a poetry skeptical of itself.

And then? The search goes on.

In scattered tremblings my nerves without guitar, without qualms, the thing thus conceived far from the poem, to steal snow from the pole and the pipe from the sailor.

A few days later I figured out the pole was a pearl for my tie.

And the Explorers?

They became poets and sang upright on the spilled waves.

And the Poets?

They became explorers and looked for crystal in the throats of nightingales.

That is why Poet equals Globe-trotter without active profession, and Globe-trotter equals Poet without passive profession.

Especially necessary to sing or simply speak without mandatory double meaning, but a few disciplined waves.

No fictive heights, only the true which is organic. Leave the sky to astronomers, cells to cytologists.

The poet is not always a telescope able to change into its opposite, and if a star slides up to the eye through the hollow of the tube, it's not like an elevator, but a magic lens.

No machine or modernity for its own sake. No gulf-stream or cocktail, because gulf-stream and cocktail have become more machine than a locomotive or a deep sea diver, and more modern than New York and catalogues.

Milan . . . naive city, exhausted virgin of the Alps, virgin still.

AND THE GREAT DANGER TO THE POEM IS THE PO-ETIC

So I say let's look elsewhere, far from machine and dawn, as far from New York as from Byzantium.

Don't add poetry to what has it already without you. Honey poured on honey, it's sickening.

Let factory smoke and the handkerchiefs of farewell dry in the sun.

Put your shoes in the moonlight and we'll talk of it later, and especially, don't forget that Vesuvius, inspite of futurism, is all full of Gounod.

And the unexpected?

Doubtless it could be a thing presenting itself with the impartiality of an unwilled gesture born of change, but it is too close to instinct and even more animal than human.

Chance is fine when you're dealt five aces or at least four queens. Otherwise, forget it.

No poem drawn from lots. No one shoots craps on the poet's table.

And if the best poem is made in the throat, it is because the throat is dead center between heart and head.

Make poetry, but don't drape it around things. Invent it.

The poet must no longer be an instrument of nature, but he will make nature his instrument. That's the whole difference with the old schools.

And now a new fact is brought to you, completely simple in its essence, independent of any other external phenomena: a human creation, very pure and polished by the brain with an oyster's patience.

Is it a poem, or something else?

It hardly matters.

It hardly matters that the creature be boy or girl, or that it be lawyer, engineer, or biologist, provided that it be.

It lives and it disturbs, even crouched calmly in its depth.

It is not perhaps the ordinary poem, but nevertheless it is.

Thus: first effect of the poem, transfiguration of our daily Christ, innocent upheaval, eyes wide open to the flowing edge of words, brain descends to the chest and heart rises to head, all the while remaining heart and head with their essential faculties: at last, total revolution. Earth turns backwards, sun rises in the West.

Where are you?

Where am I?

The cardinal points are lost in the shuffle like the four aces in a deck of cards.

Later, you love or you reject, but illusion sat in comfortable chairs, boredom moved at a good clip, and the heart spilled its vial of unconscious odors.

(Love or rejection have no importance for the true poet, for he knows that the world moves from right to left and men from left to right. It's the law of equilibrium.)

And then, it is my hand that has guided you, that has shown you willed landscapes and that has caused a brook to be born from an almond tree without giving it a lance prick in the ribs.

And when the camels of your imagination tried to scatter, I stopped them cold, faster than a thief in the desert.

No idle promenades!

The stock market or life.

There, it's clear, it's clean. No private interpretation.

The market doesn't mean the heart, nor life the eyes.

The market is the market and life is life.

Each line of the poem is the point of an angle that is closing, not the meeting of an angle opening to every wind.

The poem, such as it is presented here, is not realistic, but human.

It is not realistic, but it becomes reality.

Cosmic reality with the right atmosphere and clearly it contains earth and water, just as earth and water embrace all disciplines that honor each other.

You must not look through these poems for a memory of things seen, nor the possibility of seeing other things.

A poem is a poem, just as an orange is an orange, and not an apple.

You will not find things that already existed nor come into direct contact with objects of the external world.

The poet will no longer imitate nature, for he doesn't allow himself the right to plagiarize God.

You will find what you have never seen before: the poem. A creation of man.

And of all human forces, that which interests us the most, is the creative force. (pp. 76-8)

Vicente Huidobro, "Manifesto Perhaps," translated by Geoffrey Young, in The Selected Poetry of Vicente Huidobro, *edited by David M. Guss, translated by David M. Guss and others, New Directions, 1981, pp. 76-8.*

ANGEL FLORES (essay date 1931)

[*Flores is a Puerto Rican critic and translator who has written extensively on Spanish and Latin American literature. In the following essay, he reviews* The Mirror of a Mage.]

Huidobro left Chile in 1916. Like most South Americans, he had two fatherlands: his own, and France. When he settled in war-hysteric Paris he had not accomplished much; he was just a sweet-singing nightingale of the Ruben Dario family. An anachronistic gulf separated the honeyed bard from the embittered capital. Nobody seemed to care about pale princesses, dying swans, and faded roses in a season when grenades and bombs had become so persistently eloquent and convincing. Nevertheless, Huidobro insisted on making history. He began to study the poets of the hour. Soon he discovered Pierre Reverdy. His liking became decidedly exasperating—but how he hated to have to imitate Reverdy! Under the circumstances, the only plausible thing for him to do was to prove that he had anticipated and influenced Reverdy. And so he published, duly ante-dated, a plaquette containing six poems. A "humorous" scandal followed, punctuated by manifestoes, little-magazines squabbles, challenges, duels.

Thus, during the exciting days of cubistic gestures, Huidobro made his entrance into contemporary literature under the double appellation of "Fool" and "Master." Even now, after the truth about the Huidobro versus Reverdy case has been thoroughly cleared, one can not help admiring the Chilean's clever publicity stunt. His *reclame* put him on the literary map, and when he went for a rest to quiet Madrid, he met many good poets willing to call him "Master." Thus, if he failed to be accepted as the founder of French "creationism" he became at least the undisputed founder of Spanish "ultraism," and even today his poems and pupils' exercises can be placed next to Cummings's tulips and chimneys.

Recently Huidobro has turned to prose fiction. In his *Portrait of a Paladin,* dedicated to Douglas Fairbanks, he so modernized and jazzed the legend of the Cid that Humbert Wolfe ticklishly and praisingly classified it as "a delicious rhodomontade." Today with *The Mirror of a Mage,* fragmentarily published in advanced reviews in 1921-22, one feels that Huidobro has brilliantly succeeded in finding both a subject and a valid application of his literary method.

The Mirror of a Mage is a "visual" novel about Cagliostro. Imagine a mixture of *Vathek* and *Trilby,* a romantic wind fraught with weirdness and incantatory grace, savagely illumined by supernatural flashes and cinema transitions! Huidobro presents a powerful magician, initiated in and conversant with the mysteries of life and death. His miraculous hands cure the sick and resurrect the dead, his magnetising eyes change the flight of pigeons and stop runaway horses. From his laboratory he controls the France of Louis XVI, re-ordering at his will the course of history and the laws of Nature. But at last the heart of a woman becomes his Waterloo. His magic virtue may regulate the heart's metronome, the nature of its tempo and sound, but not its innermost essence.

To narrate Cagliostro's adventures, to express all these miracles and shifting moods, Huidobro has had to recur to the technique of motion pictures and to his early creationist-ultraist vocabulary. The modern reader finds himself at home with a novel absolutely free from the well-known trappings and tricks of the old story-tellers. Here the words dance in a new atmosphere, in a refreshing forest of bristling symbols. Cagliostro makes his entrance in a tempest, "between two thunderclaps," his coach "cleaving through the rain as if through cane-fields in the great plains of the tropics," the headlights "swaying from side to side like a drunkard singing his way over the horizon." The reader is cautioned to step aside a pace or two lest he be bespattered by the wheels of mystery. And from then on, the story begins to tremble as if under the iron shoes of galloping stallions.

Huidobro's utterance is singular, novel, scandalously modern. To illustrate fully its countless facets one would have to quote the entire volume. Yet, it is not all a matter of phraseology. The reader himself is constantly forced into the story, cordially invited to collaborate with the author. For instance, when the heroine appears, Huidobro does not burn the precious-to-all-novelists handful of adjectival fireworks. He only says: "Reader, think of the most beautiful woman you have ever seen, and then apply her beauty to Lorenza. So you and I may both spare ourselves a long description." Similarly, when the accidented hour of climaxes comes, one is pushed through a wise short-cut: "It was a solemn night, a night which seemed to know its own importance in history. (Reader, take any novel, and read in it the description of any night in which a grave happening is about to take place. Then resume this page.)" Huidobro is always on the qui vive, avoiding used cliches, ready to destroy meaningless platitudes: "The pigeon sped away like an arrow—or, rather, it would have sped like an arrow, were it not that this simile has been overdone."

The modern reader exhausted by the all-too-popular, drawn-out introspective novels of the day, should turn immediately to this brief masterpiece, comparable to a stimulating cordial were it not that its sparkling quality reminds one, rather, of an exquisite, jubilant sauterne.

> *Angel Flores, "A High-Speed Cagliostro," in* New York Herald Tribune Books, *November 29, 1931, p. 17.*

BETTY DRURY (essay date 1932)

[*In the following essay, Drury reviews* Portrait of a Paladin.]

The Cid Campeador thunders again through this break-neck chronicle that would make an excellent scenario for some Douglas Fairbanks—to whom, by the way, [*Portrait of a Paladin*] is dedicated. Now it is a question whether the great warrior were not better left to the tender mercies of legend—whether national heroes, like saints and martyrs, should not be seen dimly through the haze of Valhalla to be appreciated. Señor Huidobro's evident glee at the resuscitation of a superman is easily understood, but a measure of suspicion exists that the Cid, hearty figure, ferocious beard and all, was dragged down from his pedestal to make a movie holiday.

Vicente Huidobro, the Chilean poet who makes Paris his literary headquarters, and claims for himself the inception of the school of poetry known as "creationist," has produced an unusual but by no means remarkable portrait of the Spanish hero. He writes a vigorous electric prose—to judge by Mr. Wells's translation—and avails himself frequently of current idiom to secure vitality. "Rodrigo had the power of forty horses, 40 horsepower, and they called him Rodrigo Diaz de Vivar." A wealth of language was squandered on this biography, and the most quotidian ideas are apt to come wrapped up in the cellophane of lyrical prose. As Señor Huidobro tosses a flock of figures from his pen and indulges gloriously in pleonastic flights, he manages that there be no trace of stiffness in his style, but, on the contrary, an extreme and disarming relaxation. His characterizations are graceful: "Jimena half-closed her eyes of the Middle Ages." "Vivar dreamed battles, slept among swords. Epic was tangled in the hair of the sleeping children." "The wind of dawn arose. The sky was luminous with rays of violet, electric with rays beyond the range of vision." At times he exults in Rabelaisian extravagances, as in the passage dealing with the Cid's childhood: "His lungs were so capacious that every time he breathed, he drew in half the oxygen in the world." Fanciful lines chronicle the mythological attributes of Rodrigo's steed: "There, on the topmost arch of story, Babieca stamps, rears on her hind legs to nibble a star."

His style is so fortunate that it is regrettable that he did not pull his story together. The truth of the matter is that he has combined too much material for the good of his plot; the legend of the Cid is a jointed one, and the seams are apt to show. Furthermore, since the climax occurs early in the book, shortly after the slaying of Jimena's father, the account of campaigning and exile which follows seems overlong.

Señor Huidobro has taken liberties with the tradition which states that the Cid's daughters married the infantes of Carrión and were shamefully mistreated at Corpes. He has greatly expanded the love interest which was added to the legend by Guillén de Castro, a contemporary of Lope de Vega, in his drama *Las Mocedades del Cid,* and ignored the conflict between love and duty developed by Corneille.

Now the absence of psychological struggle detracts from the gravity of the work. The substitution of a series of romantic interludes—Rodrigo playing Ring-around-a-Rosy with Jimena, Rodrigo climbing to his sweetheart's balcony, Rodrigo rescuing Jimena from the flames—is so much Hollywood small change.

The characterizations are adequate. Jimena is the perfect type of wife and mother, and the Cid strides through the narrative with all the subtlety of a gridiron hero. Some day somebody is going to forget the qualities which make Rodrigo Diaz such a pious Aeneas and turn out a rip-snorting novel that will show him up for the brutal and crafty old Ulysses he was.

> Betty Drury, *"The Cid Campeador in Modern Dress,"* in The New York Times Book Review, *March 13, 1932, p. 6.*

HENRY ALFRED HOLMES (essay date 1942)

[*Holmes was an American critic and translator. In the following excerpt, he surveys Huidobro's career.*]

Because of his acumen, which is not inconsiderable; or perhaps because of the facility with which such literary novelties as *el creacionismo* were propagated in the fifteen years from 1915 to 1930; or, what is still more probable, because of [his] entrance on the stage of letters at this time and at Paris, [Huidobro] found a cordial welcome for his message of "Creationism." This welcome has run the gamut from well-founded appreciative criticism like that of Cansinos-Assens to delirious paragraphs like those of the Spanish critic Pedro Sains Rodríguez and the Mexican Germán List Arzumbide.

Said Cansinos-Assens: "The biggest event of the literary year 1918 now closing, has been the visit of the Chilean poet Vicente Huidobro to Madrid. In Paris Huidobro has fathered 'Creationism' with another unique poet, Pierre Reverdy. The young-

est poets have flocked to him. They had a flair for the new day that was dawning in his poems. He has jarred more than one writer wide awake. I myself have listened to him as he preached his gospel and have been privileged to see the rejuvenating effect even on the youngest in the poetic succession." (*La nueva literatura,* III.)

Said Sains Rodríguez: "The intellectual 'meridians' pass through certain men's heads, not through spots on the globe. Today our spiritual meridian passes through the brain of Huidobro." (In *Presentacions,* Barcelona, 1932.)

And List Arzumbide: "This poet is no longer Latin America's property—the universe has taken him away from us. His very name now implies a new life. His coming on the stage is an augury—it implies the immense role of the true poetry." (In *Presentaciones,* Barcelona, 1932.)

Huidobro says that it was after his lecture at Buenos Aires in 1916 that he was baptized with the name of "Creationist," for having said that the first duty of the poet is to create; the second, to create; and the third, likewise, to create. However, he had been uttering this for several years in Chile, and the writer has been told by eyewitnesses of his beginnings that it is rather difficult to conceive the regard, verging on adulation, which some of the younger intellectuals of Santiago had for him even then. He is still acclaimed by the youthful Chilean intelligentsia, though the acclaim is now divided between him and Neruda.

In *La gruta del silencio* he does not versify: he writes an apparent prose with peculiar rhythms rather than cadences. In his poem *Adán* (1916) he is more daring than the *Surréalistes.* He varies at will the number of syllables in his verses; his rhymes are unique. He is already with this sixth (?) volume, well along in his curious method of humanizing things; of making the abstract concrete and the concrete abstract; of changing the "value" usually attributed to things, in order to make them poetic in the realm of art; and of dropping anecdotes and descriptions, and "making the poem whole," its emotional appeal deriving from the creative power alone.

The years passed in Paris, with their wartime poignancies, their stimulating associations, especially his friendship with Apollinaire, and their literary lance-breakings with Futurists and Surrealists. Huidobro saw naught to be ashamed of in his own tenets, and he deepened and regularized them, finding bases for his convictions in Hegel and Schleiermacher. The acknowledged spokesman of a "school," reputable author of numerous "advanced" works, he published his *Création pure* in good orthodox Latin Quarter fashion (1921). In this brilliant and suggestive preface to *Saisons choisies,* the psychological basis for *creacionismo* and its rules of technique and style are discussed in pages which throw off, as a matter of course, such scintillations as "L'homme ne cherche plus à imiter la Nature dans ses apparances, mais à faire comme elle en l'imitant dans le fond de ses lois constructives." ("Man no longer strives to imitate Nature in her mere outward aspect, but to act like her, imitating the essence of her creative principles.")

Let it not be imagined that the Chilean was merely a *polemista* ["polemicist"]. His *Hallali* in French, published in 1917, drew from Guillaume Apollinaire the encomium, "It is a distinct find; it is the best poem published in these wartimes." Then too the material that was later to be integrated in his *Temblor de cielo* was gradually taking shape in the poet's mind; in fact, some of it was taken by him to Spain in 1919 and originated a most lively discussion among those privileged to hear it.

Automne régulier (1925) incorporated not only the final portion of *Saisons choisies*, but also other poems of the 1921 period. While *Manifestes* (1925) is somewhat too obviously the proclamation of a *jefe de escuela* ["school principal"], a volume published in the following year, *Vientos contrarios*, covers a wide range of essay topics—unevenly, to be sure, but with all the suggestiveness that one associates with the pen of Huidobro.

The year 1929 marks a "divide" in his production. *Mío Cid Campeador* is the first of a series of novelized biographies in which the whimsical genius of the Chilean has gleamed with renewed brilliancy. While it is asserted that his poems have been translated into eleven different languages, English-speaking readers will find a special interest in the fact that this book and *Cagliostro* (French version,1931; Spanish version, 1934) have been translated into English by Warre B. Wells and published in both London and New York. Yet this chronicle form is not sufficient for all his amazing activity: he essays the dramatized biography, in French, with *Gilles de Raiz* (1932)! Moreover, the experiments in Ultraistic verse continue with *Temblor de cielo* and *Altazor*. This period is thus seen to be the logical extension and expansion of the *Nord-Sud* or *Espejo de agua* (1916) tendencies. There is sufficient energy to move the London *Times* Literary Supplement to say of *Cagliostro:* "This book must be taken more seriously than it is by its author"; and the review *Comedia* of Paris to adjudge it "a little masterpiece."

Most daring of all these works is *Altazor*. Its seven cantos challenge all the accepted doctrines of the past: philosophers, prophets, and poets are called upon to bring the Creationist order into being—"there is no time to lose." It is a soul-shaking new universe which "Altazor" or Huidobro or any other soul evolves with such lucubrations; but the comforting feeling of familiarity is anathema in this case. The reader may judge for himself how far he wishes to accompany Huidobro in the venture, as he reads the selection from Canto III.

Huidobro's daring inventiveness achieves new impossibles in *Altazor* and *La próxima*; it almost falls, but not quite, into reprehensible *enfantillages* in the drama *Gilles de Raiz:*

> THE BISHOP. Have you made a pact with the devil?
>
> GILLES. Isn't it rather the devil who probably made a pact with me?
>
> BISHOP. You have profaned the temples.
>
> GILLES. The temples have profaned me.

In *Papá: El diario de Alicia Mir:*

> Mamma says that Papa's friends are a lot of crazy people, and Papa says her friends are a collection of idiots.
>
> She says: "Your friends come from the madhouse."
>
> He retorts: "Yours come from the asylum."
>
> Papa: "I prefer to go through life surrounded by friends whose eyes are starting from their sockets, rather than by those who are always drooling."
>
> Mamma: "Your crazy friends are here, get ready the strait-jackets."
>
> Papa: "My lady's reception is over. Just as soon as they've gone, we must wipe the drool up from the floor."

There are, however, in *Papá*, as in every work of Huidobro, no matter how the author may seem to outrage the conventionalities of letters, many appealing and persuasive passages on art, on morals, and on social phenomena. *El Sátiro* (1939), as its publishers point out, is the story of an introvert, whose many-phased misanthropy is all the more arresting because his nature is hypersensitive. Losing contact with reality, he fancies he hears society's accusing voices, and he is driven to demonstrate that the accusation was just.

Thus startling and shocking, Huidobro is nevertheless forever "arriving," and coming before us with that which commands a hearing. His work was foreordained to be experimental and progressive. In his very progress, therefore, are the tokens of large success. He will always be a "Creationist," but less than anyone else would he hesitate to throw away the term if he thought he could serve his literary gods better by abandoning it in favor of some other.

Here we may profitably recapitulate the various phases of this Creationist career.

I. The Chilean, to 1916. "Bursting his bonds."

II. The European, especially the Parisian stimulation, 1916-1920. Association, or rivalry, with outstanding Ultraist authors.

III. Founding and progress of the Creationist "School," 1921-1932.

IV. The Satiric, 1933—. Again in Santiago, Chile.

"Conspicuous among the Creationist poets are Pablo de Roka and Angel Cruchaga Santa María of Chile; César Vallejo of Peru; Juan Larrea and Gerardo Diego, of Spain; Jorge Luis Borges of Argentina and Alberto Hidalgo of Peru, pursuing paths fairly parallel to Huidobro's," and the same could be said of the Frenchmen Pierre Reverdy and Jean Cocteau as long as their comradeship with Huidobro endured.

What is Creationism? "It means in effect a shift in the application of the poet's creativeness from phrases, pictures, and concepts, to a world or worlds beyond our humdrum accepted world. Huidobro says (*Temblor de cielo*, Prologue): 'When the poet reaches the last boundary (of imagination), the usual chain of phenomena loses its logic, and on the farther side, *where the poet's realm begins* (italics mine), the chain is forged anew, with a new logic. Poetry is thus seen to defy reason, for it is the only Reason.'"

In setting forth his principles, Huidobro found illuminating the following words of the Symbolist poet and dramatist St.-Pol Roux:

"Art is now going to establish original countries where time will be told by a poet's heartbeats, where the atmosphere will be the result of his fluid, where the forces will be the muscles of his energy, and the poet will people these lands with the spontaneous population of his own types."

The founder of Creationism continues: "Anyone who cannot understand the mystic drama which makes colleagues of the *thing* and the *word*; or, if you will, of the brain of man and the world without, will hardly appreciate Creationism."

We close with some representative sayings of Huidobro.

"Poetry is the revelation of oneself. This comes out of the contact of a special individual (the poet) with nature. Poetry is the spark that flashes out of this contact."

''The poet is the man who is conscious of himself in the great Being; who hails the universe saying, I belong to you because you belong to me.''

''Poets are not called on to make beauty. It is theirs to make man.''

''We must release our infinite, our eternal side. We must liberate our powers. Those who cannot accomplish this release will remain in the realm of ephemeral things; their works will be but for a day.''

''The poet is the man who breaks through limitations. At each instant he hears the echo of his footsteps in eternity.'' (pp. 159-64)

Henry Alfred Holmes, "Vicente Huidobro," in his Contemporary Spanish Americans, *F. S. Crofts & Co., 1942, pp. 158-71.*

FREDERICK S. STIMSON (essay date 1970)

[*In the following excerpt, Stimson discusses the three periods of Huidobro's poetic development.*]

It should be noted that although Huidobro is commonly associated with Creationism, he did not always follow that movement. As a matter of fact, three fairly distinct periods are evident in his poetry. Of the four collections of his first period, the Chilean period lasting until his trip to Paris in 1916, two, *Ecos del alma* and *Las pagodas ocultas,* are basically romantic in tone. For instance, in . . . **"La muerte del poeta"** of the former collection, he is seen to consider himself a typical romantic hero, misunderstood and persecuted by society. Of these early, juvenile poems Bary writes: ''Since he was very young he adopted the romantic idea of the poet as a hero, as a lone champion of the ideal; and later he comes to identify the poet . . . with the sorrowing Christ.'' . . .

The other two collections of his first period, *La gruta del silencio* and *Canciones en la noche,* are more Modernist in tone, but romantic preoccupations continue. Romantic themes, like *mal de siècle* and death, reappear in **"La balada triste del largo camino"** and other works of *La gruta del silencio.* The poet's suffering for his art, another romantic attitude, is found in the two versions of **"Coloquio espiritual."** . . . (p. 101)

At this point in his career, Huidobro's versification was still relatively traditional. **"La balada triste,"** for instance, contains lines of twelve syllables, with only a few of eleven, thirteen, and fourteen. He made use of assonance and even consonance; both are found in **"El poema para mi hija."** Bary observes that ''For Huidobro, the word 'rhythm' seems to have meant the succession of stresses within the verses, the number of syllables in the verses, and the number of verses in the stanza. For stanzas, he prefers the quatrain, which at times alternates with couplets and groups of five verses. The total effect is that of a traditional regularity, with infrequent small variations.''

Beginning as a romantic, Huidobro soon embraced Modernism. For a time he combined the two tendencies. Dominant in *Canciones en la noche* is the theme, both romantic and Modernist, of the unavoidable melancholy which a poet must suffer— *hamletismo,* as it has been called. **"Estas trovas"** contains a reference to the late romantic Peninsular poet, Gustavo Adolfo Bécquer, but essentially it is Modernist, even to the point of incorporating the color blue. With the repeated rhyming of *mente* [''mind''] and mention of violins, *languidez* [''languor''], *ensueños* [''dreams''], *murmuro* [''murmur''], and

so forth, a musical, dreamy effect, reminiscent of Claude Debussy's mood music, is attained. (p. 102)

With frequent references to sensory matters, exotic colors, perfumes, flowers, and hard and rare objects and stones, the Modernist style is evident also in poems like **"Balada para el Marqués de Bradomín." "Salomé"** . . . is especially Parnassian. (pp. 102-03)

Perhaps the most Parnassian of all is **"Nipona,"** with references to turquoise, onyx, and especially the Oriental world, the favorite source of inspiration for the Cuban Modernist, Julián del Casal. In addition, this poem is distinguished by unusual typography. . . . **"Nipona,"** like **"La capilla aldeana"** and **"Japonerías del estío,"** is printed so that the poem's outline resembles the outline of the poem's subject—in the manner of Guillaume Apollinaire's *Calligrammes.* Perhaps here at last is the beginning of Huidobro's Creationism. (p. 103)

Huidobro is most famous, of course, for his second period, the Creationist-Cubist period in Paris, beginning roughly with the publication in 1917 of *Horizon carré* and ending about 1925. The Cubist style of *Nord-Sud* and Pierre Reverdy is more than evident in this first Parisian collection. The calligram technique has been carried to an extreme. In poems such as **"Tormenta," "Año nuevo," "Paisaje," "Mañana,"** as they are entitled in their Spanish versions, words and fantastic metaphors are printed in almost every possible direction on the page. **"Fin"** illustrates the technique of printing words vertically at the side of the poem; like the Cubist painters, Cubist poets wanted the object to be seen simultaneously at various angles. The tendency to use capital letters for emphasis is found here, too, as in the. . .last part of **"Tam."** (pp. 103-04)

One of the best-known poems of this collection, **"Cowboy,"** the last part of which follows, gives a very curious and original impression of the United States.

> *New York*
> > *a pocos kilómetros*
>
> *En los rascacielos*
> *Los ascensores suben como termómetros*
>
> *Y cerca del Niágara*
> > *que apagó mi pipa*
> *Miro las estrellas salpicadas*
>
> *El Cow-Boy*
> > *sobre una cuerda de violín*
> *Atraviesa el Ohio.*
>
> [''New York
> > a few kilometers
>
> In the skyscrapers
> The elevators rise like thermometers
>
> And near Niagara
> > which has put out my pipe
> I watch the spattered stars
>
> The Cow Boy
> > on a violin string
> Crosses the Ohio''
> > (Translation by David M. Guss)]

Bary believes that in this poem Huidobro came close to achieving his goal. Although the rhythm and typography are Reverdy's, this ''moving picture'' (and movies fascinated the poets of Apollinaire's school) is Huidobro's—because of its ''light fantasy, humor and 'created' images.'' Upon creating this very personal cowboy, ''Huidobro gives the best explanation possible of his intentions, as announced in the preliminary note of *Horizon carré.*'' There the poet wrote that he wanted to ''create a poem by borrowing from life its motifs and by transforming them, so as to give them a new and independent life.''

Although Huidobro spoke disparagingly of Futurism, in poems like **''Aeroplano''** machines and mechanisms of the modern world constitute the main motifs. . . . (pp. 104-05)

In 1918 Huidobro published in Madrid *El espejo de agua,* the collection which he maintained had seen a first printing in Buenos Aires two years earlier. Its outstanding work is . . . **''Arte poética,''** considered one of his major manifestoes of the theory of Creationism. The same year and in the same city he published another important collection, *Ecuatorial.* In the long poem giving the title to this book, he sang of Futurist motifs, such as trains, telegraph wires, and . . . the ''divine airplane.'' But more conventional and romantic motifs from his first period, such as birds, especially swallows and gulls, appear frequently, too. . . .

Three more Cubist collections appeared in Madrid that same year of 1918, *Poemas árticos, Tour Eiffel,* and *Hallali.* The Cubist style, characterized by vivid, unexpected, and wild metaphors, by lack of punctuation, and by startling typographical effects, is to be found throughout the first book. On the other hand, rather romantic and old-fashioned motifs, such as birds, the sea, and sailors, make their appearance, as in the well-known poem **''Bay Rum.''** . . . (p. 105)

Some of the themes are romantic, too. In **''Marino''** Huidobro's belief in the heroic and divine qualities of a poet is implied. In **''Exprés''** he attributes to human beings cosmic proportions and powers. Thus endowed, a poet can cause almost anything to happen in nature and is immortal, ideas present in the last part of **''Vermouth.''** . . .

One of Huidobro's favorite, recurring symbols is tobacco. Gloria Videla tries to explain his use of this and other small objects as follows: ''Man and the small beings which surround him (birds, objects of daily life, above all, cigars) become huge and, reversely, the cosmos becomes human and small.'' The following lines from **''Exprés''** may illustrate her interpretation.

> *Aspirar el aroma del Monte Rosa*
> *Trenzar las canas errantes del Monte Blanco*
> *y sobre el Zenit del Monte Cenis*
> *Encender en el sol muriente*
> *El último cigarro.*
>
> [''To breathe the perfume of Mount Rose
> To braid the flowing hair of Mont Blanc
> And then on top Mount Summit
> To light the last cigar
> In the dying sun''
>
> (Translation by David M. Guss)]

Of **''Exprés,''** with its list of European cities and world rivers, Silva Castro writes that it is definitely ''anecdotal,'' and **''Alerta,''** concerning the First World War, is certainly ''narration,'' not ''creation.'' Thus this critic believes that more often than not Huidobro failed to carry out his credo and to practice what he preached.

Humorous, frivolous elements, such as a musical scale and wild typography, characterize the book-length poem *Torre de Eiffel,* first written in French *(Tour Eiffel.)* (p. 106)

Silva Castro points out that here again Huidobro ''sings and does not create.'' Parts are descriptive, and some metaphors

are not unexpected nor original. He concludes that many of Huidobro's poems consist of ''vulgarities, small, unfinished judgements, very brief, short-winded explanations, and gratuitous inferences'' and that the poet's only originality lies in his mishapen forms.

In the last of the four Madrid collections, *Hallali* (*Halalí*), Cubist calligrams and Futurist machines and instruments of war recur throughout. Many poems, however, such as **''Las ciudades,''** **''La trinchera,''** and **''El cementerio de los soldados,''** as they are entitled in the Spanish version, are concerned not with a new, created world, but with this one and with World War I.

Huidobro's third period witnessed a return to the descriptive and anecdotal and to the romanticism which, according to some critics, was basically inherent in him. This period is considered to have begun about 1925, yet, as already noted, romantic elements are found as early as 1918, interspersed with the Creationist ones in the Madrid publications.

In the collection *Automne régulier* (*Otoño regular*) of 1925 there is a return to the romantic theme of melancholy, especially in connection with the passing of the seasons and the inexorability of time. Symbols are also of the romantic type. In **''Hiver à boire,''** a title usually kept in French, a bird again symbolizes the poet's grief. Other favorite motifs from the past, such as the sea, are to be found in poems like **''Marinera.''** Certain poems reflect Huidobro's desire to return to the more conventional versification of his early period. More traditional rhyme, cadence, and stanza structure, and longer verses appear.

Probably the outstanding example of Huidobro's tendencies in the third period is *Altazor* (1931), not exactly a narrative work, but one concerned with an external event, the First World War. In this long poem much is made of the windmill, another favored motif—perhaps favored because of its soaring, airy quality, reminiscent of that associated with birds, ships, and airplanes. Although partially romantic, *Altazor* nonetheless contains some of Huidobro's most far-fetched metaphors and most daring experiments with neologisms and alliteration, in the manner of Mariano Brull's *jitanjáfora.* Onomatopoetic effects are attained, as in the following well-known lines, with fanciful plays on the names of birds, especially *golondrina.*

> *Ya viene viene la golondrina*
> *Ya viene viene la golonfina*
> *Ya viene la golontrina*
> *Ya viene la goloncima*
> *Viene la golonchina*
> *Viene la golonclima*
> *Ya viene la golonrima*
> *Ya viene la golonrisa*
> *La golonniña*
> *La golongira*
> *La golonlira*
> *La golonbrisa*
> *La golonchilla*
> *Ya viene la golondía*
>
> [''Here alights alights the hirondelle
> Here alights alights the clearondelle
> Here alights the trillondelle
> Here alights the hillondelle
> Alights the chippondelle
> Alights the whiffondelle
> Here alights the chirpondelle
> Here alights the cheerondelle
> The girlondelle
> The whirlondelle
> The lyrondelle

The chillondelle
The shrillondelle
Here alights the hironday"
                    (Translation by Eliot Weinberger)]

Later collections, such as *Ver y palpar* (1941), are also romantic. Despite fantastic metaphors, **"Ronda de la vida riendo,"** for instance, is romantic in its protest against modern life filled with "terrifying speed." Many poems of *El ciudadano del olvido* (1941), such as **"Tiempo de espera,"** are romantic in their note of melancholy and hopelessness, a note especially evident in the following stanza.

> *Pasan los días*
> *Las piedras lloran con sus huesos azules*
> *Pero no se abre la puerta*
> *No se descubre la caída de la noche*

> ["The days pass
> The stones weep with their blue bones
> But the door doesn't open
> The fall of night is not revealed"
>   (Translation by David M. Guss)]

In subsequent publications Huidobro showed an inclination to become interested in the poet rather than in poetry, that is, in man, rather than art, perhaps in humanism rather than pure aestheticism. In one of his late manifestoes, *Total,* he appeared to be trying to resurrect a type of Renaissance figure: "But we need a fearless man. We want a broad, synthetic spirit, a total man, a man who reflects our entire epoch."

It is difficult to summarize and assess Huidobro's contributions, but certainly he deserves considerable credit along various lines. With respect to European literature, it may be noted that he was a colorful figure who helped immeasurably to publicize in France and elsewhere a relatively neglected poetry, that of Spanish America. And he has been one of the few Spanish Americans to contribute to the development of French letters, especially French Cubism, as well as Hispanic.

With respect to Spanish literature, it must be admitted that in Madrid he helped to encourage Peninsular poets to open their doors to outside influences, especially to the experiments being carried on in Paris. And certainly he helped to force the entire Hispanic world to accept Vanguard poetry, as Darío had forced the acceptance of Modernism. Cansinos-Asséns wrote: "Because if Rubén finished romanticism, Huidobro revealed the senescence of the Modernist cycle. . . . Huidobro's arrival spread all the wrinkles of decrepitude over the masked countenance of the nineties. Everything became terribly old upon contact with the immature youth of his poems."

In assessing Huidobro's contribution to literature, many conclude that as a poet he was less than second-rate; few, however, deny the historical importance of his manifestoes, such as **"Non serviam,"** *Horizon carré,* **"Arte poética,"** **"La creación pura,"** and *Manifestes.* Of course these were needed to explain his own poetry, as one doubting Thomas wryly notes: "Huidobro's poetry required explanation, and he did not refuse to give it." Huidobro should be remembered, too, for his efforts in other genres, such as the drama and novel. If hard put to find any really praiseworthy elements in his work, one may at least credit him for being highly original most of the time. (pp. 107-09)

> *Frederick S. Stimson, "Vanguardismo (World War I to World War II)," in his* The New Schools of Spanish American Poetry, *University of North Carolina, Department of Romance Languages, 1970, pp. 59-179.*

Huidobro with his wife and children, 1916. From Vicente Huidobro: The Careers of a Poet, *by René de Costa. Clarendon Press, 1984. Reprinted by permission of Oxford University Press.*

MERLIN H. FORSTER   (essay date 1970)

[*Forster is an American critic who specializes in Latin American literature. In the following excerpt, he examines the major themes, structure, and techniques of* Altazor.]

The Chilean poet, novelist, and theoretician Vicente Huidobro has been one of the most disputed figures in Spanish-American literature of the 20th century. Critical opinion, much of it impressionistic and highly emotional, varies widely and in general has a primary focus in *creacionista* theory rather than in Huidobro's own creative work. Arturo Torres Ríoseco's terse judgment has been a very influential negative evaluation: "In speaking of Spanish-American poetry, one cannot avoid mentioning Vicente Huidobro, poetically a third-rate talent, but at the same time a writer who has achieved wide notoriety for his literary manifestoes. . . . He gave expression to poetical theories which attracted wide attention, but his creative work was not able to maintain his reputation." This comment, originally made in 1942, is a point of departure for Raúl Silva Castro's blistering review article on *Poesía y prosa,* the 1957 anthology of Huidobro's work published by Aguilar. . . . At the opposite pole is Antonio de Undurraga's prolix essay on Huidobro and creationism which occupies the first 186 pages of the already mentioned *Poesía y prosa.* Undurraga not only sees Huidobro as the brightest star in the poetical firmament, but in addition feels himself called upon to champion Huidobro's primacy in the development of *creacionismo.*

There are several important contributions to the criticism of Huidobro's work that stand at various points between these two extremes. Guillermo de Torre's extensive contributions to the history of the vanguardist movements and their important figures, among them Huidobro and creationism, are landmarks in the criticism of this period, but are inevitably biased by Torre's own participation in many of the events he considers. The works of Cedomil Goic and David Bary are without doubt the most balanced and detailed critical studies on Huidobro. Even here, however, the approach is through creationist theory, and Huidobro's poetic production is measured according to the enunciated theoretical rules. My basic position . . . is to assert that Huidobro's own poetry is of much greater value than has been generally admitted heretofore, and that it is more than a sterile illustration of a previous theoretical elaboration. Specifically, through examination of Huidobro's most important single work, I shall attempt to show that his poetic practice often measures up to or even exceeds in importance his much more frequently discussed poetic theory.

Altazor, o viaje en paracaídas, Huidobro's longest and most complex single poetic text, was published for the first time in Madrid in 1931. Critical attention given to the poem since that time has been contradictory. For example, Goic observes: "*Altazor* es la obra más notable del creacionismo. . . ." ["*Altazor* is the most notable work of creationism. . . ."] In contrast, Bary strongly represents the opposite view in his well-argued article: "El poema significa el fin de la época creacionista. Hasta podría afirmarse que es el poema anticreacionista por excelencia." ["The poem signifies the end of the creationist era. One could even assert that it is the anti-creationist poem *par excellence.*"] Again, my intent is to set aside the external materials of creationism, and to attempt an internal analysis of theme, structure, and technique as the basis for re-evaluation.

The poem is organized in seven cantos of varying length (plus a curious, fairy-tale-like preface), and is a complex interweaving of several thematic threads of varying size and importance. The fundamental theme which shapes the poem is the impossibility of transforming language into the vital and expressive "magnéticas palabras" ["magnetic words"] of poetry, and with some temporary suspensions the direction of this theme is downward. The image of a fall through space implied in the full title of the poem is used constantly in the development of this main theme: a fall from coherence to incoherence, from life to death, from verbal question to inarticulate wail. This idea gives strength and direction to the whole poetic structure and forms as well a center around which secondary themes can be placed. For example, the obsessive striving to discover the absolute parameters of poetic expression brings with it an insistent probing into the metaphysical meanings of life, death, and eternity. . . . (pp. 297-99)

Also strongly visible as a secondary theme, particularly in Canto I, is an apocalyptic, prophetic view of the world and of contemporary society. In addition, a double personification Altazor-Vicente Huidobro appears constantly through the poem and makes possible the interweaving of several other sub-themes: *anguish and fear . . . ; duality and ambiguity . . . ; the revolutionary and contradictory strength of the poet . . . ;* [and] *death in life or life toward death. . . .* (pp. 299-300)

The structure and technique of the poem show the same complexity found in the thematic patterning. The seven cantos, of widely differing length, tone, and tempo, carry along the fluctuating but constantly descending theme line as would the movements of a major musical composition. Canto I, for example, can be seen as the rather rapidly paced theme-presentation section on which the entire poem is based. The longest

of the seven, occupying seventeen and one-half pages in the *Obras completas* text, it is circuitous and at times even overlapping in the presentation of theme and sub-themes. There is considerable variation in length, and the tone is first anguished, then angry, then prophetic, then tragic, and so on around and around in continually widening and descending circles.

Canto II represents a complete change of pace. It is a four and one-half page contemplative *andante* ["rambling"] which checks for a moment the movement of the previous canto while the poet meditates on the grace and mystery of woman, perhaps seeing in her the elusiveness of the muse for whose touch he so ardently strives. . . . (p. 300)

Canto III approximates in length the preceding section, but again represents a radical change in tempo and tone. Beginning with twenty rhymed couplets of various conventional line lengths, the canto then moves furiously toward a violent denial of the expressiveness of "poetic language." . . . (p. 301)

There follows an open-ended series of interconnected similes. . . . The series has the dual purpose of ridiculing decrepit poetic expression and of illustrating the brilliant skill of the new poet-juggler "jugando con magnéticas palabras" ["playing with magnetic words"]. The canto closes with a pyrotechnic image depicting the cataclismic destruction of conventional language, which Huidobro calls, "El simple sport de los vocablos" ["The simple sport of words"], in order to allow the dramatic reordering which will mark the "new poetry":

> Saltan chispas del choque y mientras más violento
> Más grande es la explosión
> Pasión del juego en el espacio
> Sin alas de luna y pretensión
>
> Combate singular entre el pecho y el cielo
> Total desprendimiento al fin de voz de carne
> Eco de luz que sangra aire sobre el aire
>
> Después nada nada
> Rumor aliento de frase sin palabra
>
> ["Sparks leap from the collision and then more violent
> More enormous the explosion
> Passion of the game in space
> Without moon-wings and pretense
> Single combat between chest and sky
> Total dissolution at last of the voice from flesh
> Echo of light that bleeds air over the air
>
> Then nothing nothing
> Spirit whisper of the wordless phrase"
>   (Translation by Eliot Weinberger)]

Following this sky-rocket burst, Canto IV opens on a note of urgency, "No hay tiempo que perder" ["There's no time to lose"], a line which is repeated often in the eight and one-half pages that the canto occupies. With a tempo somewhat less rapid than the furious pace of Canto III, the view taken is panoramic and multiple. . . . In this canto a disintegration of traditional word shapes becomes evident, as can be seen in the well-known "golondrina" passage:

> Al horitaña de la montazonte
> La violondrina y el goloncelo
> Descolgada esta mañana de la lunala
> Se acerca a todo galope
> Y viene viene la golondrina
> Ya viene viene la golonfina
> Ya viene la golontrina
> Ya viene la goloncima
> Viene la golonchina
> Viene la golonclima

Ya viene la golonrima
Ya viene la golonrisa
La golonniña
La golongira

["At the horitain of the mountizon
The violondelle and the hironcello
Slipping down this morning from a lunawing
It hurries near
Here alights alights the hirondelle
Here alights alights the clearondelle
Here alights the trillondelle
Here alights the hillondelle
Alights the chippondelle
Alights the whiffondelle
Here alights the chirpondelle
Here alights the cheerondelle
The girlondelle
The whirlondelle"

(Translation by Eliot Weinberger)]

Another example of this technique is the following passage in which the musical scale is embedded in a series of created words:

Pero el cielo prefiere el rodoñol
Su niño querido el rorreñol
Su flor de alegría el romiñol
Su piel de lágrima el rofañol
Su garganta nocturna el rosolñol
El rolañol
El rosiñol

["But the sky prefers the nighdongale
Its favorite sun the nighrengale
Su flor de alegría el romiñol
Su piel de lágrima el rofañol
Su garganta nocturna el rosolñol
El rolañol
El rosiñol"

(Translation by Eliot Weinberger)]

Both these passages, as well as several others in the canto, seem to be a first attempt at the restructuring of language and thereby the rebuilding of the world suggested at the end of Canto III. The attempt is not entirely successful, and there is a strong sense of anguished failure in these closing lines:

En cruz
       en luz
La tierra y su cielo
El cielo y su tierra
Selva noche
Y río día por el universo
El pájaro tralalí canta en las ramas de mi cerebro
Porque encontró la clave del eterfinifrete
Rotundo como el unipacio y el espaverso
Uiu uiui
Tralalí tralalá
Aia ai ai aaia i i

["In height
       In light
Earth and its sky
Sky and its earth
Forest night
River day through the universe
The bird tralalee sings in the branches of my brain
For I've found the key to the infiniternity
Round as the unimos and the cosverse
Ooheeoo ooheeoohee
Tralalee tralala
Aheeaah ahee ahee aaaheeah ee ee"

(Translation by Eliot Weinberger)]

Canto V occupies fifteen and one-half pages of text (only two pages less than the long initial canto) and with its somewhat ponderous searching and unhurried pace suspends for a time the urgent motion of the preceding section. The first line of the canto suggests a questioning and probing of conventional time and space: "Aquí comienza el campo inexplorado" ["Here begins the unexplored ground"]. The verbal experimentation begun in Canto IV is carried further, and becomes a functional part of this search. The most striking example of this technique, though not the most successful, is a curious grinding, almost kaleidoscopic image which begins as follows:

Jugamos fuera del tiempo
Y juega con nosotros el molino de viento
Molino de viento
Molino de aliento
Molino de cuento
Molino de intento
Molino de aumento
Molino de ungüento
Molino de sustento
Molino de tormento

["We play outside time
And the windmill plays with us
Mill of wind
Mill of breath
Mill of story
Mill of purpose
Mill of growth
Mill of ointment
Mill of food
Mill of torture"

(Translation by Stephen Fredman)]

These lines are followed by four pages of variations on the pattern, and while one is willing to admit that the constant rotation of the windmill may be a reminder of the inexorable movement of time, the space occupied by this single revolving image appears excessive. . . . The canto ends with another glimpse of the presence that pervades the whole poem:

En el instante en que huyen los ocasos a través de las llanuras
El cielo está esperando un aeroplano
Y yo oigo la risa de los muertos debajo de la tierra

["At the moment when the sunsets flee across the plains
The sky is looking for an aeroplane
And I hear the laughter of the dead beneath the earth"

(Translation by Stephen Fredman)]

Canto VI, four and one-half pages in length, approximates the size of Cantos II and III. Here again the pace changes, and the pulsing of short, almost stacatto lines pierces the slow-moving plateau established in Canto V. Meaningful expression and life as well dissolve among the crystaline shapes of the natural world, and there remain only unconnected flashes conveying the same anguish and fear which have been visible throughout the poem. . . . The verbal plays, seeming now obsessive and sterile, continue. At times they are echoes of previous cantos. . . . At other times they are sequences which heighten a sense of advanced decomposition:

Lento
    nube
        Ala ola ole ala Aladino
El ladino Aladino Al ladino dino la
Cristal nube

["Slow
    cloud
        Ala ola ole ala Aladino
El ladino Aladino Al ladino dino la
Crystal cloud"

(Translation by Stephen Fredman)]

This canto, tottering precariously on the edge of intelligibility, makes the final plunge of the next canto not at all unexpected.

Canto VII occupies less than two pages of text, and is by far the shortest of all the divisions of the poem. It opens with an anguished moan reminiscent of the final lines of Canto IV and continues with the "Tralalí" sequence woven at times into other cantos. We soon become aware that the poet has finally passed the point of no return—all is sound alone, with no conventional meaning whatsoever. Many segments seem to bear some resemblance to conventional words, but not enough to produce even a flash of intelligibility:

> Montresol y mandotrina
> Ai ai
> > Montesur en lasurido
> > Montesol
> Lusponsedo solinario
> Aururaro ulisamento lalilá
> Ylarca murllonía
> Hormajauma marijauda
> Mitradente
> Mitrapausa
> Mitralonga
> Mitrisola
> > matriola
> Olamina olasica lalilá
> Isonauta

The moan which opens the canto appears in fragmentary form throughout and becomes the closing three lines both of the canto and of the poem, a strident and sub-verbal cry of despair: "Io ia / i i i o / Ai a i ai a i i i o ia." This canto becomes, then, the final plunge into the yawning pit of non-expression and death. Here is the moment of fall, of dissolution, of non-being toward which the poem has moved inexorably in spite of the poet's every effort to reverse the course of events.

My discussion of *Altazor* as a poetic entity brings me now to the point of evaluation. To begin with, the entire poem might easily be taken as indeed Silva Castro and others have done, as an unstructured and overly complicated mass with no esthetic value. However, the present examination of theme, structure and techniques leads, I believe, to a much more positive conclusion: *Altazor* as a work of art rises far above that negative assessment. The poem is long, and at times overly diffuse, but its rich thematic texture and its intricate formal structure create their own unity and strength. Verbal patterning is complex and at times ostentatious, but with some few exceptions these unusual sequences are organic to thematic or structural development.

There is one more vexing problem. Does the poem succeed in establishing what John Ciardi has called the "sympathetic contract," or is there only a sensation of deception and sterility? Is the reader drawn into the development, movement, and emotion of the poem, or is he left as a passive spectator, contemplating a *tour de force* but without being moved by what he sees? David Bary seems to take the latter position with his suggestion that the poem should be considered as a parody: "Huidobro . . . finge traducir algo que no ha experimentado. Observamos en *Altazor* una especie de 'divina parodia' del verbo creador que el poeta anhelaba sin creer en él." ["Huidobro . . . feigns changing something that he has not tried. We observe in *Altazor* a type of 'divine parody' of the creative word that the poet craves without believing in it."] My reading suggests the opposite point of view. Huidobro is able to establish an emotional bond with me, and I see *Altazor* in all its consciously brilliant verbosity and symphonic structure as a

moving expression of the anguished artist-man coming to grips with the ultimate and insoluble problems of his existence. Huidobro convinces me that he is a serious and able practitioner of the art as well as the theory of poetry. (pp. 301-07)

> Merlin H. Forster, "Vicente Huidobro's 'Altazor': A Re-evaluation," in Kentucky Romance Quarterly, Vol. XVII, No. 4, 1970, pp. 297-307.

RENÉ DE COSTA (essay date 1975)

[*De Costa is an American critic who has written several books on Huidobro. In the following excerpt, he examines the influence of Huidobro's poetry and literary theories on the development of Spanish American literature.*]

Huidobro's role in the development of the new poetry in Spanish America is seminal. A Spanish American residing in Paris during the twenties, he served as a kind of esthetic liaison between the New World and the Old. Formed in Santiago de Chile, in the refined esthetic tradition of Hispanic Modernism, he participated in his generation's almost epochal urge to renovate poetic diction. Arriving in France in the middle of the First World War, he was immediately integrated into the cultural milieu of the Parisian avant-garde and was thus among the first of that generation of New World artists who participated directly in the renovation of European literature. Huidobro did not simply elaborate new techniques; he became a champion of the new esthetic: its herald and spokesman for Spain and Spanish America, for the generation of Borges and Hidalgo. The Peruvian poet acknowledged as much in January of 1926 when he wrote to Huidobro soliciting his collaboration in the *Indice de la nueva poesía americana:*

> Deseo que Ud. escriba un capítulo del prólogo. Por su obra personal primero, por los discípulos que ha hecho y luego por lo que significa dentro de la lírica española como solución de una época literaria.

> ("I would like you to write a chapter of the prologue. For your own work first, for the disciples you have made, and finally, for what you represent in Hispanic poetry as the outcome of a literary epoch.")

For his many trips between Europe and America, between Paris, Buenos Aires, New York, Santiago and Madrid, Huidobro had come to be considered a kind of traveling salesman of the avant-garde, an "agente viajero de la poesia." For Hidalgo he was the "solución" ["answer"] of an epoch, a culture hero who had led the transition from the old to the new. We do not know Huidobro's personal response to Hidalgo's request, but we do know what he contributed for the prologue: a Spanish version of his 1924 **"Manifeste peut-être"** prefaced by a dedicatory epigraph in which he assigns himself a Promethean role:

> A los verdaderos poetas, fuertes y puros, a todos los espíritus jóvenes, ajenos aa bajas pasiones, que no han olvidado que fue mi mano la que arrojó las semillas.

> ("To the true poets, strong and pure, to all the young in spirit, alien to base passions, who have not forgotten that it was my hand that sowed the seeds.")

That Hidalgo published this Olympian dedication is itself indicative of Huidobro's truly seminal function in the development of the Spanish American avant-garde. (pp. 21-2)

So it is not inaccurate to say, as did Huidobro, that he did indeed sow the seeds of the new tendency in literature. Nor is it unfair to ask just what were these seeds for which the conditions seemed so fertile.

The seeds were those of Creationism. Neither a school nor a literary movement, Creationism is a personal esthetic elaborated by Huidobro which shares certain principles of French Cubism and Anglo-American Imagism. Chief among these is the notion that the poet is first and foremost a creator, a "pequeño dios," a little god, in the words of Huidobro. The idea is not especially new. Aristotle, making a distinction between poetry and history in the *Poetics,* reserved for the poet the privilege of invention. And Huidobro, like other writers of the avant-garde, recognized the traditional, almost classic goal of the creative endeavor; yet his practice was not traditional, it was radically different. Different in its use of language. Different in its construction of the image. Different in its theme and subject. In Spanish America these differences spelled an end to the era of art for art's sake and with it the refined pantheism of the hypersensitive artist. The end of the poetry of exteriorization; in Huidobro's words, the end of *"esa poesía de buey rumiante y de abuela satisfecha,"* the poetry of mooing cows and contented grandmothers. Gone were the standard themes of poetry: love, death, anguish and ecstasy. Abolished too, in this new scheme, was the metaphysical attitude of the poet-philosopher and the provincialism of a New World poetry which had too long sought to justify itself in the exaltation of the autochthonous. Such a tabula rasa was needed for the creation of a new poetry based not on the principle of mimesis, of imitation, but on the principle of creation, of imaginative invention. The new poetry was to be decidedly intellectual, oriented towards the mind and not the senses, and based not on theme but on imagery. As Borges said in his prefatory remarks to the *Indice de la nueva poesía americana:* "La imagen es, hoy por hoy, nuestro universal santo y seña" ["Today the image is our universal password"]. The cult of the image was a constant in the new poetry, and in Spanish America it was Vicente Huidobro who first diffused the idea of the totally created image, the startling metaphor. Creationism, like its counterpart in literary Cubism, maintained that the effectiveness and strength of an image derive from the dissimilarity of the terms which it forcefully brings together. The Creationist image is based on the principle of juxtaposition. A convenient example is found in the title of Huidobro's first book of poems in French, *Horizon carré.* Here, two terms, each quite ordinary, are combined in such a way as to present as a linguistic possibility for the reader's imagination what experience dictates to be impossible in the real world: the squaring of the horizon. In this way the poet does not copy reality; he makes real what never existed before. Huidobro explained this concept in an essay on **"Le Créationnisme":**

> Je vous dirai ce que j'entends par poème créé. C'est un poème dans lequel chaque partie constitutive et tout l'ensemble présente un fait nouveau, indépendant du monde externe détaché de toute réalité autre que lui-même, car il prend sa place dans le monde comme un phénomène particulier à part et différent des autres phénomènes. Ce poème est une chose qui ne peut pas exister ailleurs que dans la tête du poète. . . .
>
> Lorsque j'ecris "L'oiseau niché sur l'arc-en-ciel" je vous presente un phénomène nouveau, une chose que vous n'avez jamais vue, que vous ne verrez jamais et que pourtant on voudrait bien voir. Un poète doit dire ces choses qui sans lui ne seraient jamais dites.
>
> ("I will tell you what I mean by a created poem. It is a poem in which each constituent part, and in which

all the parts together, present something new, something independent of the external world, separate from any other reality that is not its own, since it takes its place in the world as a unique phenomenon separate and distinct from other phenomena. Such a poem is something that can exist only in the mind of the poet. . . . When I write "The bird nestled in the rainbow" I present you with something new, something you have never seen before, that you never will see, but that you would very much like to see. A poet must say those things that would never be said without him.")

Here we can appreciate the importance placed on perception. The new poem is designed not as a record of hypersensitive insights, but as an intellectual creation. As a result, the active participation of the reader is required to imaginatively complete the linguistic creation constituted by the poem. Poetry is thus not about something; it is itself an esthetic happening. In the anthology this idea became a command: "Haced la poesía, pero no la pongáis en torno de las cosas. Inventadla" ["Make poetry, but don't make it about things. Invent it"].

The diffusion of these ideas and the compositions which embodied them in the *Indice de la nueva poesía americana* radically transformed the literature of Spanish America, giving rise to a New Poetry and eventually a New Novel. Poetry was creation, the creation through language of the extraordinary, the marvelous:

> El poeta no debe ser el instrumento de la Naturaleza, sino convertir a la Naturaleza en su instrumento. He ahi toda la diferencia con las viejas escuelas. Y he aquí ahora que él os trae un hecho neuvo, simple en su esencia, independiente de todo otro fenómeno externo, una creación humana, muy pura y trabajada por el cerebro con una paciencia de ostra. Es un poema u otra cosa? Poco importa.
>
> ("The poet should not be the instrument of Nature, but rather make Nature his instrument. This is all the difference with the old schools. And now the poet brings us something new, simple in its essence, independent of every other external phenomenon, a human creation, very pure and elaborated by the mind with the patience of an oyster. Is it a poem or is it something else? It doesn't matter.")

Another generation would apply these same principles of literary creation to narrative prose and create the "Nueva Novela" ["New Novel"]. Abandoning the traditional mimetic function of novelistic realism, and substituting a kind of magic realism, "lo real maravilloso," the New Novelist seems almost laconically to narrate the extraordinary in a matter-of-fact tone and style. Here too, Huidobro—and Borges—led the way; the Chilean with his "cuentos diminutos" (mini-stories), the Argentine with his famous "ficciones" ["fictions"].

While the *Indice de la nueva poesía americana* was prepared by one generation under the tutelage of another, it also served to launch the next generation of new poetry: the generation of Pablo Neruda. Portions of *Tentativa del hombre infinito,* Neruda's first hermetic work, were included in the anthology and mark the twenty-two year old poet's first recognition outside Chile. Thus we see a pattern: Huidobro as the herald of the avant-garde in the New World; Borges and Hidalgo at the head of the first generation of Spanish American writers to go beyond a decadent estheticism and the provincialism of creole cultural values; Neruda as the originator of a new poetic language, the discoverer of the creative possibilities of ordinary speech. These are achievements that were not lost, for the *Indice de la nueva poesía americana* both recognized and furthered a tradition of innovation in Spanish American poetry. (pp. 22-4)

René de Costa, *"Huidobro and the New Poetry of Spanish America,"* in Chicago Review, *Vol. 27, No. 2, Autumn, 1975, pp. 20-5.*

DAVID M. GUSS (essay date 1976)

[*In the following excerpt, Guss examines Huidobro's views on the cultural role of the poet and on the nature of the poetic process.*]

While many North American readers are by now familiar with the dark earth of Vallejo and the passionate seas of Neruda, the aerial world of their most important contemporary remains little known in this country. And yet in Latin America it was Vicente Huidobro who opened the doors and retuned the lyre. It was Huidobro who "made rivers run where none had been before." Latin American poets know this. Octavio Paz calls Huidobro the "magnificent bird" and writes: "He is everywhere and nowhere. He is the invisible oxygen of our poetry." Huidobro knew this too. He wrote about himself: "At seventeen, I told myself, 'I must become the first poet of America.' Soon, after just a few years, I thought: 'I must become the first poet of my language.' Then, as time went on, my ambitions rose and I told myself: 'I must become the first poet of my age.'" As to the fulfillment of this prophecy, Huidobro had no doubts. In a 1938 interview he said: "Modern poetry begins with me." And then finally: "I am poetry!"

The "I" is a mythic one, a part of the heroic persona which Huidobro assumed for himself. As in Whitman, it is a "self" transcending the ego, a public *mythos* evolving into commentary on the printed word. The *mythos* created by Huidobro is a complex one. It is both trickster and shaman, both clown and clairvoyant. It is "the one who sees himself working and laughs at the other face to face."

Many have claimed that it is the fantastic legend of Huidobro that has obscured the appreciation of his poetry, and it is true that scandals and public controversy attracted as much attention to him as did the publication of his many books of poems, novels, plays, and essays. And so, perhaps it is only today—more than thirty years after the poet's death—that we can start to read his work without the distraction of the literary and political feuds with which it was initially received. And yet, the Huidobro legend is as important a part of Huidobro's work as was Rimbaud's flight to Africa or Duchamp's silence, for Huidobro saw himself as the total poet on the "ultimate frontier" of consciousness—the "demigod" on the epic quest for the infinite. (pp. x-xi)

> I'm the mad cosmic
> Stones plants mountains
> Greet me Bees rats
> Lions and eagles
> Stars twilights dawns
> Rivers and jungles all ask me
> What's new How you doing?
> And while stars and waves have something to say
> It's through my mouth they'll say it

(Altazor, Canto I)

This is the poet summoning his spirits in the same way a shaman would. For Huidobro, poetry is just this invocation: a magic rite whereby "man puts himself in contact with the Universe, discovers its sense of unity, turns himself into a small God, and makes his cosmos." The poet is once again "maker," and

"Creationism" is meant in the most literal sense of the word: the creation of "new worlds that never existed before, that only the poet can discover." The discovery is of the "inner word—the magic one." Huidobro claimed that the inspiration for his poetic theories came from the words of an Aymara Indian poet who said: "The poet is a God. Don't sing about rain, poet. Make it rain!" The poet was to be a sorcerer of language, endowed with the supernatural powers to create "separate realities":

> We've accepted, without greater thought, the fact that there can be no other realities beyond those surrounding us, and we haven't believed that we, too, can create realities in a world of our own, in a world awaiting its own flora and fauna. Flora and fauna which only the poet can create, through that special gift which Mother Nature has given him and him alone.

The poet was to be the new culture hero—a Prometheus who would not only create "new worlds" but also new and "liberated" humans through the reenactment of the primordial "heavenly crime," the theft of fire from the gods. It is in the word that this fire becomes manifest and it is through the word that the individual realizes the possibility of liberation—the possibility of ecstasy and of the infinite. Like Prometheus, Huidobro too creates his new human "looking into the stars." To read one of his poems is to pass through the sky. It is to pass through a landscape filled with planets and birds, with feathers, comets and angels, with the beating wings of the poet in flight, the poet on his epic voyage.

> The hero is an unrealized God, or rather the concept of God, our desire for God. Our desire for the absolute made flesh.

Huidobro—not unlike Rimbaud whom he greatly admired—attempted to become this new culture hero through both his poetry and the *mythos* he surrounded it with. He claimed to be the last living descendant of the Cid and actually rewrote the great adventurer's history in ***Mío Cid Campeador***. He wrote too of Columbus, Napoleon, Cagliostro, Don Juan, and Joan of Arc, believing himself to be their heir in the greatest quest of all—that of the infinite and the new language which would liberate it.

Finally, he created Altazor, the personification of the Promethean hero:

> The double of myself
> The one who sees himself working and laughs at the other face
>   to face
> The one who fell from the heights of his star
> And travelled for twenty-five years
> Loaded with the parachutes of his own prejudices
> I am Altazor of the infinite desire
> Of the hunger eternal and unsatisfied
> With flesh tilled by the plows of grief
> How can I rest with unknown worlds inside?

Altazor is Huidobro's great epic and one of the most important poems in the Spanish language. It is, as the Chilean poet Enrique Lihn has written, Huidobro's "Song of Myself." Through Cubist objectivism, Huidobro had been liberated from the breast-beating sentimentality which had come to weigh down so much of Latin American and Spanish literature. Through a reordering of the image and a reorganization of the line, he had been able to create startling and beautiful "new worlds," worlds where the "emotion is born from the creative strength alone." In *Poemas árticos,* he had written:

> With a shout I made a mountain rise
> And now we do a new dance around it

But the mountain was not high enough. A more total vision was still required. The poet and the word were still "moored." His last two books in French, *Automne Régulier* and *Tout à coup* are filled with foretellings of the eruption about to take place, foretellings of the "universe coming loose." And so, as if to reject the world that had shaped his poetry so thoroughly, he gave up its language and returned to Spanish. The Cubist tradition which had once freed him had by now become constrictive. Nonreferential poetry, calligrams, mixed typography, lack of punctuation, imagery that "unglued the moon" had all been revolutionary, but in the end, were not enough to achieve the language of power and revelation which Huidobro ultimately sought.

It is in *Altazor* that Huidobro achieved his true poetry of "transubstantiation." It is here that he becomes the true visionary poet "measuring the infinite step by step." Here is "the unexplored ground" and the word made flesh. Here is the world recreated through the word, and language recreated through the ecstatic vision of the poet. And here is the poet in flight, the poet "in parachutes": the poet "falling to the very bottom of himself" "to break all the chains."

Altazor, subtitled *The Parachute Voyage,* was begun in 1919 and published in Madrid in 1931. The first edition ran 111 pages and included a preface and seven cantos. In it, the poet continues the journey begun in *Poemas articos* and *Ecuatorial.* Language and the word itself are systematically reconstructed. The process is careful and clear, the poet's voyage fastidiously described. The voyage, once again, the ultimate Creationist one from "man-mirror to man-God." In the middle of the poem sits the windmill, physical presence of the transformation of consciousness and language. It is through this mill—the ancient symbol of Cervantes—that all language (and prejudice) must pass to be ground and recreated: "And wheat comes and goes, from earth to heaven."

The mill becomes a mantra. "The poet goes into a trance of communication with the universe" and the universe speaks through him. . . . Poet becomes creation itself, bursting through the "last horizon," past death, with the "keys to the infinite" gripped tightly in his hand.

Altazor ends with the scream of the poet in full flight—consciousness hurtling at the speed of light. The final canto is untranslatable. The roots of some of the words can be traced but they are predominantly the vocables of revelation.

Altazor is Huidobro's most famous work, but it is only a stop on the long journey from *Ecos del Alma* to *Ultimos poemas.* To read through this great body of work is to witness a poet giving birth to himself. Inside the avant-garde artist who talks of "pure poetry" is the one forever moving inward, the one "tapping his own roots." Inside the ever present metaphor of outer exploration and the exhortations of "ONWARD" is the "endless traveller" on the road to the inner world. "The one with flesh falling off on all sides." The one peeling off mask after mask. The one "in other objects." The animist, looking for God in trees and waves. The "magician" imploring us to fly with him. The "antipoet" giving us a new language. The one of the endless hunger "to be the first free man, the first to break all the chains." (pp. xvii-xxi)

David M. Guss, "Introduction: Poetry Is a Heavenly Crime," in The Selected Poetry of Vicente Huidobro, *edited by David M. Guss, translated by David M. Guss and others, New Directions, 1981, pp. x-xxi.*

CECIL G. WOOD   (essay date 1978)

[*In the following excerpt, Wood analyzes the philosophical background of Creationism.*]

A close examination of the early poetry of Vicente Huidobro reveals a preoccupation with certain problems that recur with increasing intensity throughout his subsequent work. These problems originate from, and can be defined basically in terms of an existential situation which developed from the spiritual crisis occasioned by the poet's early rejection of Christianity. The sense of the absurdity of his existence and the fear of the constant threat of death which resulted, produced in him a series of concerns. First, in the absence of the Christian ethic, Huidobro is anxious to find a substitute that will give new meaning to life. Second, since the absurdity of the existential situation is closely related to the threat of death, he sees the need to unravel its mystery as a precondition to providing a solution to his problems. Third, he is preoccupied by the desire to experience the infinite, and since there is no hope for this in a life beyond, he wishes, at least, a momentary experience of it here on earth in order to offset the certainty of total oblivion which death presents.These are the preoccupations that motivate Huidobro's search. Their expression in his poetry is of special significance in determining the new attitude that will eventually develop into a particular *Weltanschauung.*

Examples of his sense of the absurdity of existence can be found in his early collection *La gruta del silencio.* In the poem **"La balada triste del camino largo,"** for example, where Huidobro is sympathizing with poets who are suffering the ill effects of their Bohemian way of life, he includes himself among these life-weary wanderers. His existence, like theirs, is one of boredom, solitude, and emptiness, and can be compared to that of an orphan without a guardian. . . . (pp. 8-9)

The theme of the search for the meaning to life is clearly defined in the poem **"El viejecito del barrio,"** where Huidobro portrays the familiar figure of the old man whose life has been completely wasted in efforts to find solace for his grief. For this old man who had vainly sought action in war to relieve the boredom and anguish of his existence, the only solution left was to turn to drink. But for Huidobro, this would not have been satisfactory. (pp. 9-10)

[A] reference taken from *Las pagodas ocultas* will suffice to show Huidobro's expression of his preoccupations at this early stage of his writing. The reference comes from **"El paseo de los amigos,"** where the poet, after describing the similarity in the existential condition of his kindred spirits ("El primer amante," "El amigo artista," "El amigo doloroso," "El amigo solitario" ["'The first lover,' 'The artistic friend,' 'The sorrowful friend,' 'The solitary friend'"]), terminates the group of poems with the question, "Pero ¿cuándo dejaremos de ansiar eternamente?" ["But when will we stop this eternal worrying?"]

The poet's anxieties and his desire to find meaning to life as expressed in the above references are not entirely restricted to the poetic "yo" ["I"] and are therefore susceptible to interpretation beyond the purely personal. In fact, the broadening of his interest to focus on his fellow man is revealed in the activities of his early youth. Henry Alfred Holmes testifies to this fact in terms of Huidobro's stance when he writes, "He [Huidobro] tells with delight of anarchistic attitudes akin to Bolshevism which were prevalent in those *liceo* ["high school"] coteries long before Bolshevism had made headway in Russia." In Huidobro's poetry also, as early as *Las pagodas ocultas,* we find some indication of the broadening perspectives of his human concern. In **"Primera invitación a los amigos,"** the poet calls on his friends to traverse the paths of night in search of a solution to the metaphysical problems that were plaguing mankind. Another example comes in the poem **"Lo que pudo no ser,"** where Huidobro discourses on the happiness brought him by his daughter and on the possibility of not having been able to enjoy it had she not been born. He suggests a broader application of these reflections when, in the final question, he wonders about those people who have been denied the happiness he had enjoyed; those who, in one way or another, have been denied life. (pp. 10-12)

However, it is only with the publication of *Adán* in 1916 that the poet clearly outlines the problems confronting him—seen in the poetic as well as in the broader human context—and the means he will adopt to find a solution to them. From this point in his poetic production, Huidobro's literary preoccupations and the concern he expresses for human problems grow with increasing intensity. They reveal themselves, for example, in the poems contained in *Poemas árticos,* in *Ecuatorial,* in his masterpiece *Altazor,* and perhaps most effectively in *Temblor de cielo* where the two aspects of *creacionismo* as we will define it are most admirably combined. The poet's genuine interest in achieving his goal is evident as late as **"Voz de esperanza,"** one of his *Ultimos poemas,* in which he calls for the removal of those who inhibit man's ability to create and thus fulfil himself. He then offers his entire being in total support of the claim for the restoration of man's rights. (p. 12)

While Huidobro's endeavor may seem familiar in its idealistic intentions, it is certainly unusual in the execution. He approaches the problem from what can be termed a phenomenological perspective. Poetic expression within the Hispanic context had been quite naturally influenced by Western and especially Christian philosophical thought. Since this provided the basis for the associative and imagistic power of the language, it was necessary to destroy this base if the creation of a new medium of poetic expression were to be considered at all possible. Phenomena normally used in poetry with their accumulated connotations and associations would have to be reduced and conceived of in their basic and originary state— mainly visual and auditory—before they could be used in the formation of this novel medium. The means by which Huidobro proposed to achieve this goal was furnished by *creacionismo*— a twofold concept which he elaborated.

First, as the development of a new kind of poetic expression, *creacionismo* would be essentially different from the existing one in its content and associations. This difference would be realized by adopting, initially, a new concept of the Word— the Word as the essence of all life, the very mystery of creation. This new concept of the Word would lead to the revelation of hidden resources whose discovery and use were essential to the development of the new system the poet had envisaged. He writes in *La poesía,* one of his theoretical manifestoes, "Aparte de la significación gramatical del lenguaje, hay otra, una significación mágica, que es la única que nos interesa" ["Apart from the grammatical meaning of language, there is another, a magical meaning, that is the only one that interests us"].

Until now, Huidobro suggests, poets have only used language in its capacity to name objects from the world of Nature, but without removing the quality of denominator from the medium employed. In *La creación pura,* he had classified such usage as "Arte inferior al medio" *(Arte reproductivo)* ["'Art inferior to the medium' *(Reproductive Art)*"], and its logical development as "Arte en armonía con el medio" *(Arte de adaptación)* ["'Art in harmony with the medium' *(Adaptive Art)*"]. With the elaboration of *creacionismo* he is proposing a new kind of art which he sees as the absolute in the new use of language. It is "Arte superior al medio" *(Arte creativo)* ["'Art superior to the medium' *(Creative Art)*"], and to achieve it he sets out the basic prerequisite in the following words taken from *La poesía:* "En todas las cosas hay una palabra interna, una palabra latente y que está debajo de la palabra que las designa. Esa es la palabra que debe descubrir el poeta." ["In everything there is an inner word, a latent word that is underneath the word that designates it. That is the word that the poet must discover.'"] This "inner word"—divested of all its customary associations, pure in its virgin form—will be transformed by the new technique to produce a poetry which, according to Huidobro, is the language of Creation.

Secondly, *creacionismo* can be seen as the use of this language of Creation, with the Word at its center, to bring new worlds into being. The satisfaction derived from these creative endeavors will enable the poet to transcend the spiritual anguish and suffering which seem to be an inalienable part of his destiny. But for Huidobro's goal to be complete, ordinary man had to be able to make use of the new language to aid in the solution of those problems which, for him as well, seem eternal. (pp. 13-15)

The entire concept and the resulting elaboration of it in poetic form are to be seen strictly in terms of an artistic reality as opposed to an objective one. The failure to conceive of Huidobro's effort in this way has been a stumbling block to many who have unsuccessfully attempted an interpretation of his poetry. The misconception of the poet's aim is to be found especially among those who claim that he has failed in the execution of the poetic as well as the conceptual goals he had set for himself. Huidobro is fully aware of the pitfalls and inconsistencies of literary criticism, and in the elaboration of the manifestoes which help to elucidate his poetic theory, he is careful to clarify, at great length, the need for the distinction between artistic and objective reality. (p. 18)

The possibility of achieving the ability to create one's own world, parallel to and independent of that of Nature, could only result from a previous and thorough grasp of the difference between the two realities. (p. 19)

Creacionismo is not just another of those "isms" that flourished fleetingly during the first decades of the twentieth century. Neither is it merely a different poetic theory whose *raison d'être* lay in the desire to substitute a reasoned approach to the writing of poetry with one which claimed to be essentially a-rational or "surrealist." More than these, it represents a search for the absolute in poetry in the original sense, where poetry is taken to mean—as it did in the Greek—creation, production. *Creacionismo* is also a search for the absolute, in a broader sense, that is systematically carried on throughout the poet's career. In this context, it is the means by which Huidobro, and hopefully mankind in general, will be able to make use of the Word to forge new worlds in an "ocio lúdico" ["playful idleness"] that will enable them to transcend the existential problems which are an obstacle to a fulfilled life on earth. (p. 20)

Cecil G. Wood, in his The Creacionismo of Vicente Huidobro, *York Press, 1978, 300 p.*

NANCY B. MANDLOVE   (essay date 1979)

[*In the following excerpt, Mandlove studies how Huidobro used traditional nature symbols in an artistic schema intended to transcend nature.*]

Vicente Huidobro, Chilean poet and major proponent of the theory of Creationism, states in his poetic manifesto, **"Non serviam,"** that the poet should not affect a slavish imitation of nature, but should attempt to imitate nature only in her most basic function—that of creation. "I need not be your slave, Mother Nature; I will be your master. You will make use of me; that is fine. I do not want to avoid that, nor can I; but I will also make use of you. I will have my trees that will not be like yours; I will have my mountains, my rivers and my seas, I will have my sky and my stars."

Huidobro imitates nature's most fundamental characteristic—creation—in an attempt to transcend the limitations that nature imposes on man. The poet re-creates the world of nature through language in an effort to go beyond ordinary reality into the realm of the Absolute. Common natural objects and events are transformed through the poetic imagination and acquire new and often startling properties: wounds that bleed birds, children with wings, fermented stars, people who flower or do not flower. In individual poems, the result of Huidobro's re-creation of nature is often very surrealistic and frequently hermetic. A cowboy on a winged horse crosses the Ohio on a violin string; the poet makes a necklace of the Amazon, the Thames and the Rhine.

The key to Huidobro's surrealistic imagery, however, lies in the fact that while objects of nature are endowed with new and fantastic characteristics, the poet's world is based almost entirely on the use of traditional symbolic concepts associated with nature imagery. Individual poems often appear to be composed of images "out of Spiritus Mundi," the subconscious or some private mythology due to the context in which such symbolic elements occur. A study of the whole body of Huidobro's poetry however, reveals a very definite pattern of traditionally symbolic associations.

The poet's search for the Absolute and his inevitable disillusionment and failure to attain the ideal world are the central thematic concerns in Huidobro's work. The form of the Absolute varies. Time, love, beauty, poetry and peace are all common themes, but in each case the ultimate aim of the poet lies "allá lejos," far, far away. The realm of the Absolute, the world of ultimate reality lies beyond man's reach and is always represented by the traditional concept of the heavens. The sky and celestial bodies are concrete representations of Huidobro's ideal. Thus, on those rare occasions when events in the ordinary world approach those of the ideal world, heaven and earth come together and man is, at least momentarily, in touch with the stars. Such is the case in **"Halalí,"** a poem celebrating the end of the First World War and the restoration of peace.

> Y cuando llegue la noche
> Las estrellas caerán sobre la muchedumbre
>
> Y después
> En la cumbre de la torre Eiffel
> Yo enciendo mi cigarro
>   Para los astros en peligro

> Allá lejos
>
>   En los extramuros del mundo
>   Alguien canta un himno de triunfo.
>
> (And when night comes
> The stars will fall over the crowd
>
> And afterwards
> At the top of the Eiffel Tower
> I light my cigar
>   For the stars in danger
>
> Far, far away
>
>   Beyond the walls of the world
>   Someone sings a hymn of triumph.)

When the war ends and the long awaited first night of peace arrives, man's world is in harmony with the universe and the earth is touched by a shower of stars. The poet ascends to the top of his man-made world, the top of the Eiffel Tower, where the tiny light of his cigar joins that of the falling stars and the music of the spheres echoes over the world.

More often however, the shining light of the infinite, ideal world remains beyond man's reach and serves only as a hope, a reminder of the remote possibility of identification with a transcendent world. The stars are often obscured by clouds or extinguished by events which cut off all hope of attaining the Absolute. Thus in **"Halalí"** before peace comes and the stars are not only visible but tangible, the heavens are obscured by the smoke and black clouds of war. The soldiers themselves are dressed in blue clouds. . . . The displacement which occurs in this image, transferring the clouds from the heavens to men, indicates that their existence is ephemeral, fragile and that their vision of the stars, of the ideal world is hopelessly obscured by the conflict in which they are engaged. The earth runs with the blood of those who seek peace and harmony.

> Se ve sangrando en tierra
> Al aviador que azota su cabeza contra una estrella
> apagada.
>
> (One sees blood turn to earth
> From the aviator who hits his head on a
> burned out star.)

In the midst of war the pursuit of the Absolute, of peace and harmony, is futile. The star of hope is unattainable and does not exist for the soldier. The ascent toward the ideal leads not to harmony with the celestial world, but to death and destruction. Again in **"Gare,"** a poem about soldiers departing for war, the loss of the star indicates the loss of the possibility of attaining the ideal, transcendent world. The soldiers disembark from the troop train and begin to seek their way in the night. "Y en todos los caminos se ha perdido una estrella" ("And on all the paths a star has been lost"). The loss of the star is an indication that each of these soldiers has lost the possibility of escaping the bonds of ordinary and in this case, horrifying reality to attain to the realm of the stars, beyond man.

Just as it is the traditional concept of the heavens that represents Huidobro's ideal world, it is conventional imagery of the sea of life that indicates the world below the stars, the sphere of man. The sea is represented as the vast, uncharted realm of possibilities, the ocean waves as unlimited experience. In **"Balandro"** (**"Boat"**) the poet equates his life with a small boat.

> Como un balandro joven
> Crucé muchas tormentas
> Entre canciones marineras.

(Like a young boat
I crossed many storms
Amidst songs of the sea.)

Again in **"Exprés"** Huidobro uses the common metaphor of life as a journey.

Buen viaje

Un poco lejos
Termina la Tierra

Pasan los ríos bajo las barcas

La vida ha de pasar.

(Bon voyage

A little farther off
The Earth ends

Rivers pass under the boats

Life must go on)

Huidobro views man's condition in life as a threatening thing which prevents him from achieving the glory of the infinite. Altazor, the symbolic bird of Huidobro's longest poem, returning to earth, finds that he is threatened by the sea of life and hopelessly far from the stars of the infinite. (pp. 107-10)

The sea is filled with waves of experience. Generally they are negative experiences, such as failure and defeat. Huidobro employs the word *olas* (waves) in many poems, accompanied by various adjectives: black waves, concave waves, forgotten waves, wasted waves, inverted waves and common waves.

Among the waves of experience, shipwrecks are common symbols of man's failure. In **"Astro"** (**"Star"**) where the poet is seeking the creation of poetry, it eludes him and sinks into oblivion. (p. 110)

Thus far we have been concerned with Huidobro's symbolic representation of the world of the Absolute, which remains in the heights outside of human time and space, and man's world below. There must be a symbolic link between the two if man is to attempt to rise above his earthly level. Huidobro uses imagery of birds and song to extend himself into the infinite. The themes of poet, song and the bird are inextricably interwoven throughout the poetry. The bird with its wings and song is capable of soaring from earth up toward the Absolute. The song of the bird and the song of the poet are comparable in that respect. However, the upward movement is not always successful and often failure to find the Absolute is symbolized by the death of the bird, loss of its wings or its falling back to earth. The bird, as a link between the temporal and eternal, is identified with perfection, beauty and happiness. It is also associated with death, as attempts to reach the absolute are perilous and frequently futile.

In **"Cow-boy"** one finds the association of the bird and perfection.

SU POTRO HERRADO CON ALAS
JAMAS HA TENIDO UN DESPERFECTO.

(HIS HORSE SHOD WITH WINGS
HAS NEVER HAD AN IMPERFECTION.)

At the end of the war, "Cantará un pájaro sobre el arco de triunfo" ("A bird will sing on the arch of triumph"). Altazor, the cosmic bird of the long poem by the same name, symbolic both of the poet and of a Christ-like saviour, takes his name from *alta* (high) and *azor* (hawk) and alternately soars toward

the realm of the poet's longing or falls hopelessly back into the world.

The feathers and wings of birds are often attributed to people and objects to symbolize their desire to rise above their condition, but usually their wings are incapable of lifting them above the sphere of temporality. In **"Gare,"** the poem quoted above, the loss of wings adds another dimension to the loss of the star.

En las espaldas de un mutilado
Las dos pequñas alas se han plegado.

(On the shoulders of a cripple
The two little wings have folded.)

The image of the cripple evokes the horror of war and the possibility of death or injury. But it is the addition of the tiny, withered wings that indicates not only the possible physical danger, but the loss of the means of transcendence. The horror of war clips man's wings and keeps him chained to the reality of earthly existence.

In **"Ecuatorial"** a young girl gives up hope of being free from the mortal when she leaves behind her wings.

Una muchacha enferma
Dejando sus dos alas a la puerta
Entraba al sanatorio.

(A sick child
Leaving her two wings at the door
Entered the sanitarium.)

"Cruz" (**"Cross"**) describes a bird or hope destroyed from too much preoccupation with life.

Mi cruz sin alas iba en mi pecho
Y no ha querido nunca cerrar los ojos

Un pájaro se quema en el Ocaso

Cuantas cosas hemos olvidado

Mirando hacia la vida.

(My cross without wings was carried in my chest
And it has never wanted to close its eyes.

A bird catches fire in the West

How many things we have forgotten

Looking toward life.)

The death of the bird is linked with traditional imagery of death—autumn, winter, snow, the setting of the sun, silence and falling. The successful ascension of the bird is set in an atmosphere of light, spring and song.

The relationship between the poet and the bird lies in the song or the poem. The poet's wings are his song which carries him toward the infinite. Occasionally the throat of the poet is endowed with feathers and his body with wings, thus intertwining the bird and the poet as instruments for achieving the Absolute.

Huidobro often expands the metaphor of the song to include other types of musical imagery. The poem or song is not only apparent in the melody of the bird, but is converted into violin notes, harp strings and guitar music. When the poet is in harmony with the universe, the musical imagery contributes to his joy, as in **"Cow-boy,"** a fanciful, humorous poem.

El Cow-boy
    sobre una cuerda de violín
Atraviesa el Ohio.

(The Cow-boy
on a violin string
Crosses the Ohio.)

In contrast, when the poet is overcome by disillusionment, his ability to sing or make music disappears.

Sobre el cañon
Un ruiseñor cantaba
yo he perdido mi violín.

(On the cannon
A nightingale was singing
I have lost my violin)

Huidobro's poetic world represents a concentration of the universe. The poet's aspirations, frustrations, disillusionment with life and the means by which he hopes to achieve the Absolute are symbolically interwoven so that often he depicts the whole of the universe in only a few lines.

Isolated images taken from Huidobro's poetry reveal the use of traditional symbolism. However, the poetry remains unique due to the context in which the symbolic figures are found. Recognition of Huidobro's use of the consistent pattern of traditional nature symbolism provides the reader a means of initial identification with the poet's world. Separated from the often startling contexts in which they appear, natural images become conventional symbols. The celestial world represents the Absolute and the sea of life, man's world. The two realms are symbolically linked by flight or ascension in the form of bird or song. Through common symbolic association it is then possible to follow Huidobro in his flights of fantasy and his re-creation of the world and to extract meaning from the surrealistic images resulting from the use of traditional symbols in unconventional contexts. While it may not always be possible to account for every image in a given poem, recognition of the basic pattern does provide a key to many poems which might otherwise be less accessible. In **"Mares árticos" ("Arctic Seas")** for example, the pattern described above allows the reader to make connections which are not explicitly expressed in the poem between one image and another and to identify a central theme which might not be apparent without reference to the pattern.

Los mares árticos
Colgados del ocaso

Entre las nubes se quema un pájaro

Día a día
Las plumas iban cayendo
Sobre las tejas de todos los tejados

Quién ha desarrollado el arco-iris

Ya no hay descanso

Blando de alas
Era mi lecho

Sobre los mares árticos

Busco la alondra que voló de mi pecho.

(The arctic seas
Suspended from the sunset

Among the clouds a bird is on fire

Day by day
the feathers kept on falling
On the tiles of all the roofs

Who has unfurled the rainbow

There is no longer any rest

Soft with wings
was my bed

On the arctic seas

I seek the lark that flew from my chest)

The first three lines of the poem are a direct reflection of the pattern described above. The arctic seas (the world of man) cold and fraught with danger are suspended from the celestial world represented by the brilliance of the setting sun. The bird, symbolic link between the two worlds and emissary of the poet's longing, catches fire as, lost in the clouds, it approaches the realm of the Absolute. Attempts to attain the unattainable through symbolic flight or through the poet's song are doomed to failure. The feathers of the bird fall once again to earth and there, as remnants of the transcendent voyage, they support the poet through the sea of life. Although doomed to failure, there is no rest from the search and the poet continues to seek out the bird, the song of his soul on its impossible voyage.

Huidobro has been criticized for not adhering to his own creationist manifesto, for not creating the kind of new realities he has stated that he will create. While it may be true that he does not "make it rain" in the poem or "make roses grow" on paper as he advocates in his **"Arte poética,"** it is also true that

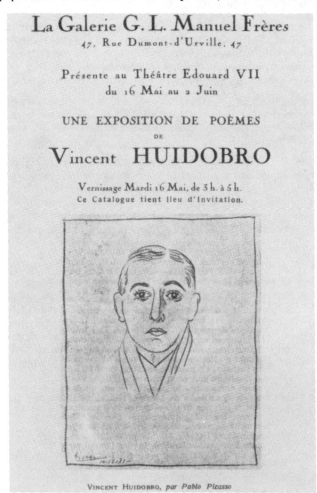

Catalogue of the painted-poem exhibition. From Vicente Huidobro: The Careers of a Poet, *by René de Costa. Clarendon Press, 1984. Reprinted by permission of Oxford University Press.*

the aspect of Huidobro's poetry that is not new, his underlying reliance on traditional symbolism, is what makes his work accessible to the reader. Huidobro's work thus has a universal dimension which differentiates it from the very private worlds of some experimental poets of that period. At the same time, Huidobro does indeed create new and exciting images which evoke unique perceptions of reality through the incorporation of traditional symbolism into unconventional contexts. (pp. 111-15)

Nancy B. Mandlove, "Burning Wings and Wounded Stars: Creation and Re-creation in the Poetic World of Vicente Huidobro," in Perspectives on Contemporary Literature, *Vol. 5, 1979, pp. 107-15.*

SAUL YURKIEVICH (essay date 1981)

[*Yurkievich is an Argentine critic and poet. In the following essay, he traces the development of Huidobro's poetry.*]

Vicente Huidobro was, in every sense, the freest of poets: a liberating force for whom total freedom meant abolishing all empirical, rhetorical and imaginative restrictions on the autonomy of the poem. Such a radical challenging of literary precept implied not only a new esthetic order, but a new mental order as well: an expressive leap into an unexpanded consciousness of the world and our modes of perceiving it and representing it. The preachings and practices of the avant-garde had made the leap possible and it was fulfilled, in gesture and utterance, in *Altazor,* where the disruption of language through metaphorical transposition severs the last bonds of rational usage and referentiality in order to recover the fullness of the word in all its hidden potential.

Starting with *Pasando y pasando (Passing Along,* 1914), Huidobro proclaimed his zeal for novelty, his revolt against routine and cliché (against the aesthetic of the library and the museum). His poet was the detector of the unexpected; an admirer of the majesty of modern machinery; a literary engine himself, thrilling to the call of heights and depths and aspiring to the poem that would glide like the shadow of a bird over water. He promoted the art of suggestion, of the shortcut: an elusive and allusive art independent of plot or description, undulant of phrase and open to the sudden surprise. Distrustful at first of Futurism's aggressive worship of modernity, he nevertheless agreed with Marinetti's defense of free verse and revolutionary renewal: principles he attempted to put into practice in *Adán (Adam,* 1916), where he reenacted the creation myth from the primeval nebula to the engendering of the first man and woman in our ancestral Eden. Possessor of the primordial word, Adam baptizes the newborn universe; he is the first Creationist poet, battling the "organ-grinding" monotony of traditional metrics with free-flowing internal rhythms responsive to the all-encompassing vision rather than to the rules of prosody.

By then Huidobro had announced his scorn for "manicured language," for the "poetic poetry" of the "poetic poet" who polishes without creating anything radically new, imitating Nature in her external manifestations rather than her generating power. The guiding principles of the new poetics had been foreshadowed in the Modernista movement—Huidobro's point of departure; but the first theoretical exposition of Creationism, the manifesto **"Non serviam"** (**"I Will Not Serve"**), and its first practical (if still timid) application, the poems of *El espejo de agua (Mirror of Water),* both date from the period 1914-16. As the point of access to all mystery, poetry is capable of transcending antinomies, of going beyond the compartmental-

izations of the empirical world. The poet perceives the hidden signs, the obscure links that unite the most distant things; he hears things calling for the words that name them. His dazzling images reveal unsuspected identities that he invents through convergences of parallel times and spaces that create new facts. The created poem, as a purely textual entity, a fact or event not verifiable beyond itself, has the same ontological status as any other external object. The poet is a demigod who shapes an independent reality. Such is the platform from which Creationism was launched on its ascending orbit from *El espejo de agua* to *Altazor.*

In *El espejo de agua*—nine poems later translated into French and incorporated with ideographic effects in *Horizon carré (Square Horizon)*—there is still a gap between intention, as enunciated epigrammatically in the first poem, **"Arte poética"**: "Let the verse be like a key / that opens a thousand doors" or the emblematic "Let everything the eyes may see created be," and its realization in the remaining eight poems, which break only mildly with traditional poetic form. They are impressionistic poems, softened into fluid lines and blurred contours: a constant vibration in search of subtle harmonies. The world, in these poems, becomes a vast echo chamber, at once expansive and accessible to the imagination capable of abolishing distances and bringing everything into unexpected correspondence. The sensory immediacy negates time and space as it delights in capturing the most fleeting impulses at the point where the undefined borders on the inexpressible. There is a structural loosening that avoids isometry and fixed principles of numerical organization. The arrangement of variable stanzas and verses, scattered lines and isolated words that hang weightless and unvoiced, is as lax as the rhythmic pace. The dominant effect, which amounts to a definition of Huidobro's poetry, is that of a string of evanescent images in loose juxtaposition, unattached to particular meanings and devoid of all emphasis, as if floating in a dream. Allowing himself to be carried along in a current of fantasy unencumbered by realistic expectations, Huidobro raises free association to a level unknown until then in the poetry of the Spanish language.

During the years of the European avant-garde, Huidobro's nebulous fusion of meaning and form, while retaining its aqueous, dream-like quality and sense of disembodied flight from static reality, attached itself to the symbols of modernity. This is particularly true of his prolific writings between 1917 and 1918, when he settled in Paris, in close contact with the inventors of modern art (writers like Apollinaire, Max Jacob, Pierre Reverdy, Tristan Tzara, André Breton; painters and sculptors like Picasso, Gris, Arp, Lipschitz, Delaunay). *Horizon carré, Tour Eiffel, Hallali, Ecuatorial (Equatorial)* and *Poemas árticos (Arctic Poems),* all written in those years, are the result of his fruitful and often quarrelsome interaction with such groups as the Cubists and Dadaists. Like Apollinaire, the model of the avant-garde poet, Huidobro wanted to ally (to alloy) magic and mechanics. And so, the free-floating fantasy took on the syncopated stridency of the urban Babel: the electrified swarm of metropolitan life spreading its mass turbulence across the planet in fleets of packet boats and express trains and the flying machines that shared the air waves with the flashing words of radiotelegraphy.

Huidobro adapted his poetic techniques to the whirl of random, fleeting sensations that characterize contemporary life—the clashing juxtapositions produced by rapid changes in technology and in urban environment and by the consumer culture itself with its incessant demand for new products, new inventions. Perception, which previously had always reflected relatively stable points of reference, suddenly became multifocal, protean, equivocal. Reality was now refracted into a multitude of unstable, fragmentary sensations. To adequately reflect the dynamism of this profusion of perpetually changing phenomena, art had to become as multivalent and multivoiced as reality itself. To reflect the arbitrary, absurd juxtapositions produced in the flux of random events, Huidobro adopted a kind of cinematic montage that allowed him constant changes of focus, framing and perspective. Just as painting in this period attempted to infuse space with temporal dynamism, poetic temporality attempted to conquer graphic space: Huidobro broke with traditional typographical alignment; words were upended, slanted, stairstepped, merged, or scattered across the page like stars in a galaxy. Reading became more complex as the poem's organization increasingly depended on a response to both verbal and spatial cues. The esthetics of dissonance led naturally to the collage or mosaic of disparate fragments confronting one another in perfect, irreconcilable contradictions.

Paradigm of the machine age, *Ecuatorial* was the most successful achievement of this period of avant-garde furor and fervor. It had all the hallmarks of modernity: obsession with technology, the "swing" of the big city, and the dizzying perspectives of a rapidly shrinking planet; and a whole spectrum of literary innovations—free verse, typographical experimentation, elimination of punctuation, time-space inversions, kaleidoscopic montage, disconcerting nonsequiturs, disruptive humor and metaphorical transfigurations that reestablished the primacy of fantasy over so-called reality.

Huidobro recorded the dissolution of the twilight world of traditional humanism—anthropocentric, geocentric, theocentric—destroyed at its foundation by the technological revolution and by a war that announced, catastrophically, the birth of the machine age. Between *Ecuatorial* and *Altazor,* the stable, dependable, redundant vision of the world became unstable, dubious, unpredictable. A new sense of history had begun to emerge, based on notions of change, crisis and collapse. Poetry had to find its bearings in an atmosphere of fragmentation and incoherence.

The problem, at this point, was to recapture the magic of an art denied its cathartic force and referential imagery and therefore, perhaps, also its Adamic powers and privileges. The solution was to open the poem, wherever possible, to the lyrical levitation that provides escape and evasion from loss and trauma into dream, play, humor and mystery.

The ultimate in linguistic inversions and metaphorical transpositions was *Altazor,* which clearly exceeded the limits of rational expression to make way for the inexpressible. In *Altazor,* Huidobro broke through the last mental boundaries in a total subversion not only of referential, syntactic, lexical, and even phonetic systems, but of meaning itself.

Although beyond language, the multiple voice that is the real subject of *Altazor,* drawn from the common source of all language at the pre-verbal stage of maximum potential, pervades the entire discourse like a steady murmur that never quite articulates its message: an entropic presence that dissolves poetic structures, revealing, through the violation of the linguistic code, the power of that vast excess of being that cannot be reduced to a system of signs. When it prevails, all divisions will cease, the schism that isolates subjectivity will disappear and all fragmentation will be resolved in a return to the wholeness of the origin of being. The destructuring devices, including

the famous "short-circuited sentences and grammatical catastrophes," are intended to derail discourse by calling attention to the discrepancies that exist between subject, language and the world. Language is thus compelled to represent a coherence deeper than the superficial coherence of conventional forms of expression. With the signifiers semanticized and the signified somatized, the divisive categories simply cease to exist and we move inward to the core of pure sound, where time and space are reunited in the vocal rhythms of an oral Eden restored to its fluid state by a tongue calling back to its origins. (pp. 26-7)

> *Saul Yurkievich, "A Tongue Calling Inward," translated by Felix Aub, in* Review: Latin American Literature and Arts, *No. 30, September/December, 1981, pp. 26-7.*

RENÉ DE COSTA   (essay date 1984)

[In the following excerpt, de Costa analyzes the major themes and techniques of Mío Cid Campeador *and* Cagliostro.]

Even before [Huidobro's] involvement in politics, he was seeking a wider public through the mass-oriented art of the cinema. An entertainment column in *Paris-Journal* (20 April 1923) reveals that Huidobro, "one of the luminaries of literary Cubism, is secretly at work on a film that will revolutionize viewing habits." A decade later, trying to revolutionize political habits, he would turn to the stage and the novel: 1934, along with *En la luna,* would see the publication of *La próxima,* a prescient prose narrative whose subject was the next world war. While Huidobro's career as a film-maker was cut short by the emergence of the "talkies" and his political novel just as quickly outdated by the thrust of history, true popular success came to him when his efforts at novel and film were combined, creating, almost by accident, a filmic novel; what he himself called a "novela-film."

In this somewhat hybrid genre he produced two masterworks: *Cagliostro* (1934) and *Mío Cid Campeador* (1929). Both, like *En la luna,* are conceived as entertainments: one updates the story of the medieval hero of Castille; while the other deals with the larger-than-life adventures of an eighteenth-century mesmerizer. In both cases Huidobro borrowed freely from a variety of sources and made up the rest. The idea was not to tell an original story, but to retell the familiar in an original way. A kind of *re-escritura* ["rewriting"].

The impetus to do a novel probably came from Joseph Delteil, a now-forgotten French novelist who was all the rage back in the 1920s. The fact is that when Huidobro returned to Paris in 1928, Delteil's *Jeanne d'Arc* (1925) had already gone through several editions and was still a runaway best-seller. Lives of other heroes were soon to follow (*La Fayette,* 1928; *Napoléon,* 1929). Essentially, Delteil brought these figures back to life by retelling their stories with the metaphoric verve of the avant-garde. Huidobro, ever the competitor, was anxious to try his hand at such a novel, but in Spanish (Delteil was his friend), and with the even more extravagant culture heroes of that world. What is more, the year before, in 1927, he had met Douglas Fairbanks and was encouraged to do a filmscript with a swashbuckling hero. Not surprisingly, Huidobro in 1928 is writing to his friend Larrea, then in Madrid, asking for books on the Cid and Cortés.

Yet, there was perhaps another, more personal factor motivating his final choice of subject: a romantic attachment to a young woman named Ximena, a circumstance which must have prompted him to see himself as being somehow connected to the Cid. To this end, he consulted experts in heraldry (one of Huidobro's ancestors, the first Marqués de Casa Real, had actually come from Burgos), and at one point he even wrote to Menéndez Pidal seeking to connect the Cid's line of descent with his own.

Whether actually believing himself a descendant, or simply feigning belief, the result was the same: an impishly arrogant present-day narrator, anachronistically at ease with the past. Regarding the ''Afrenta de corpes'' incident in the medieval poem, Huidobro has this to say: ''I just can't see my grandfather the Cid allowing my aunt Mary and my grandmother Christine being thrashed without eating their husbands alive. This incident never occurred. I swear it. If it had we would know about it in the family, and then you would see how I would have made mincemeat out of such scoundrels in these pages.''

This glib self-confidence is part of what makes Huidobro's novel so unique, permitting the author to ''improve'' upon his source materials at will; and, in so doing, to surpass his literary models. While Delteil had breathed new life into Joan of Arc by retelling her legend in contemporary language, Huidobro decided to carry the process much further, updating not only the *Cantar* [Spanish epic poem] but also the manner of its formation. For example, the circumstances casting the Cid as something of an outlaw are conveyed through a use of anachronism that borders on the ludicrous: the *jongleurs* of yesteryear as newsboys hawking an ''extra'' in today's Madrid. Thus, when the news of Count Lozano's murder breaks, the narrator is able to conjure up a scene like the following:

> The cafés in the Puerta del Sol are literally filled with people. Not even a pin can get inside (unless it is a tie-pin, pocketed by a pickpocket). The evening papers hit the streets with their huge headlines, those headlines that devour everything around them, that swallow up people, cars, houses and tramways. Those enormous headlines dominate all, with newsboys shouting:
>
> COUNT LOZANO MURDERED MONTES D'OCA SEIZED CRISIS BETWEEN KING AND POPE
>
> Suspicions of guilt in the murder of Count Lozano today centre upon Rodrigo Díaz de Vivar. The alleged assassin is said to have fled from his house, with a band of relatives and friends, seeking asylum elsewhere.
>
> The Count's body was horribly mutilated, one hand having been cut off. According to the police, bruises on the body indicate that the murderer repeatedly kicked the victim after he had fallen to the ground.
>
> Oh, how deplorable!
>
> Fortunately though, back in those crude times, there were no newspapers, nor even cafés in the Puerta del Sol. The earth, spinning in its chaos, rotates on the daily news of banal hearsay. In the old days it rolled out on its elliptic orbit a poem that is now legend. Let's return to those days. But first let's shake out the dust, for Rodrigo kicked up a lot of it when he and his men took flight.

The aside to the reader, although a borrowing from the rhetoric of radio drama, bears a functional comparison to the formulaic modes of address found in the *Cantar* where the narrator clues the public to what it is about to hear, reminding the listener that he is present at a narration about something that has already happened and that is being artistically retold. Huidobro too

feels the need to frequently remind the reader that *Mío Cid Campeador* is a retelling, *his* retelling. The literary convention informing this work is not unlike that of Huidobro's poetry at its most inventive level: whatever is said is real, or at least functions as though it were. The threshold connecting words with the reality they can evoke is regularly crossed, often flamboyantly. Thus, following a particularly emotional moment for Ximena when tears well up in her eyes, the narrator informs us that one of those tears he has just described, ''trembles briefly before falling into the novel and I am helpless to stop it from rolling across this page.''

Huidobro never lets the reader forget that it is he who is writing what is being read and that he feels no constraints whatsoever on his imagination, especially when it comes to altering history so as to make it more entertaining. Sometimes though he makes imaginative use (and abuse) of historical fact for the same purpose. At one point, after detailing the preparatory manœuvres for what is to be a decisive battle between the Cid and his arch-enemy García-Ordóñez, an unexpected twist is given to the narration when it turns out that the battle cannot take place as anticipated. A small fact of history thwarts Huidobro's plans:

> The hour of justice is near. All of Spain eagerly awaits this moment. The Chronicle fixes its anxious eyes upon it; the Legend rises to attention. Oh, with what gusto are we going to witness and describe the battle in which the Cid will once more pluck the beard of his mortal enemy!
>
> Unfortunately, we cannot describe the battle: that scheming García-Ordóñez has tricked us. He went off with his troops; he retreated without even getting near the site where the Cid was waiting for him.
>
> In vain my pen had been rinsed in rose-water getting ready to give a few good pricks to that miserable Count, take him prisoner and rub his face in a manure-heap. But he doesn't show. There is no sign of the Count at all. He leaves me with my pen in my hand, he snatches the honey right out of my mouth, he robs me of the joy of vengeance.
>
> So, you don't dare to show your face? Alright; you'll be exposed as a coward, a vile and insidious schemer. Here I pillory you before the world, I run you through on this page, and I myself pluck your beard. You swine!

Playfulness of this sort within a text is one of the mainstays of children's literature, and so it is not surprising that Isabel Shepard, an enterprising author of children's books, wrote to Huidobro proposing an abridged edition of his *Mío Cid Campeador*. He was of course delighted at the prospect of reaching those ''virginal minds.''

In *Altazor* (1931) he would portray himself as an anti-poet, ''a savage who was parachuted one morning into the landscaped garden of literary precepts''; here, in his first novel, the pose is similarly irreverent: an anti-novelist gleefully trampling on the conventions of literary realism. Writing this highly personal account of the Cid some eight hundred years after the fact, Huidobro has occasion to mock traditional authorial modes of ''seeing'' into the past. In one scene, in which Ximena is described as either embroidering or spinning (''bordando o hilando''), Huidobro blurts out that ''at this distance, at the distance of all these years, I really can't make out if she is spinning or embroidering; she is working at something though.'' (pp. 120-24)

The literary tradition of the Cid is always present; sometimes the allusion is to the *Cantar,* at other times to the *Romancero* or any of the many rewrites they have spawned. In a whimsical reversal of chronology, Huidobro has the hero operate with an awareness that he is the source of this long tradition and must therefore live up to it. Early in the novel, there is a childhood contest over who can leap farthest. When the turn comes to Huidobro's Cid, the young man "thinks first of the *Cantar,* then he thinks of the *Romancero* and the epic, of Guillén de Castro, of Corneille, and of me; gathering his strength, he leaps."

Other works of literature also weigh heavily in the novel, complementing those on the Cid. While the telescope scene alludes rather indirectly to the famous opening of Clarin's *La Regenta,* other allusions are more explicit. Valle Inclán for example: when an old hag appears at a window, "en una ventana asoma la nariz de alcuza una vieja de Valle" ["in a window an old Valle hag stuck out her oil-can nose"]. Even the *Quijote* is present when the Cid, faced with a field of windmills, "feels some crazy urge to spur his horse on, to attack them with his lance, riveting them to the sky. But he holds himself back and I hear him exclaim—'Let's leave that to someone else.'"

Tradition is an important informing principle in just about every work of literature, with the author usually writing against it or within it. Huidobro, though, does things somewhat differently. A good portion of his novel consists of slightly altered borrowings from familiar sources. Not plagiarisms as someone has recently suggested, but artful remakes. The *Romancero,* itself a compendium of remakes, is present on practically every page. When Huidobro calls attention to such an obvious source it is often with a humorous intent. In one of the central chapters, the Infanta de Zamora becomes so enraged at the sight of the Cid at her palace gates, that she spews out a *romance* ("Afuera, afuera Rodrigo"), inadvertently "forgetting its assonant rhyme scheme." (pp. 124-25)

It is [Huidobro's] dynamically inventive use of language, forging a new myth out of the old, that makes this book of fifty years ago seem so alive today, pertinent to the experimentalism of what has come to be called the New Novel. Alejo Carpentier, dean of Latin America's "new novelists," recognized as much when he reviewed *Mío Cid Campeador* back at the time of its original publication: "Huidobro has given us a mythic biography of the Cid that will forever fix the hero in our minds— how could History ever pretend to have more authority than the Novel?" What most delighted Carpentier, and was largely responsible for Huidobro's success as a modern mythmaker, was the novel's highly charged language; *Mío Cid Campeador* is the novel of a poet, an avant-garde poet. In his fertile imagination, the most prosaic scene can lead into the most extravagant scenario. Simply paying homage to Babieca (the Cid's horse), the narrator can get carried away:

> Babieca would make any poet soar higher than Pegasus. She hears me and stamps her hoof. She is pleased with me. I thank you Babieca.
>
> There, at the extreme edge of fable, Babieca prances, she rears up on her hind legs in order to nibble on a star; she lifts up her tail and breaks wind on History, letting cascade a stream of golden verses, and in a bound she is galloping off to the other side of the world.

Sometimes though, this overwriting gets out of hand and the author must be restrained. On one occasion, the Cid himself steps into the novel to straighten things out. The poet, waxing eloquent over Ximena's beauty—her long neck, her lily-white skin, her coral lips—heaps up literary clichés, making her into a goddess; the ghost of the Cid then appears at this writing-table: "Poet, you are dead wrong. Ximena was not Greek, she was Spanish (. . .). If you want to make things up about me, I don't care; but I can't allow you to lie like this about Ximena. She had a wonderful [Spanish] body, broad hips and big breasts, without any of that business of amphoras and marble."

Mío Cid Campeador was Huidobro's first novel, and it shows him at his most playful. Using and abusing the conventions of the serious novel of his time, he succeeds in creating a work that is highly original and broadly entertaining. Although avant-garde, it is still accessible to the common reader. The reason for this is less ideological than circumstantial: Huidobro originally wrote the novel to serve as the basis for a film. The cinema is the most popular of the arts, the spectacle appealing to almost everyone. Paradoxically however, the most cinematic portions of the text are those which are least appealing today: scenes of individual derring-do originally conceived for the likes of a Douglas Fairbanks, great battles laid out along the epic lines of D. W. Griffith, cliffhanging rescue situations, and a variety of special visual effects. Some of the visual effects became a problematic concern for the author because the publisher decided to bring out a deluxe edition with illustrations. Their correspondence on this gives us an inside view into Huidobro's thinking with regard to the functioning of his text.

Having decided to fill in where the *Cantar* was blank, with the birth, childhood, and adolescence of the Cid, Huidobro not only lengthened the story considerably, but also created some special difficulties for himself. How does one portray a hero in diapers? Huidobro's Cid, born with an awareness of his epic obligations, simply refuses to be diapered, letting out a universe-piercing wail:

> At that moment an enormous storm shakes the firmament, making the air shudder and shattering all the windows in heaven. A blinding flash of lightning shoots across the sky writing in billboard-size letters:

In correcting the page-proofs, Huidobro objected to the line-drawing for this chapter. In his view, the artist had stolen the thunder from his text: "There is one sketch that must be corrected. It's the one on page twenty-five which shows the newborn Cid. The word Campeador that falls from the sky must be erased because it completely destroys the ending of the chapter and kills the surprise I had planned for the reader. This should be easy to fix up: just leave the lightning bolt without the word inside."

Despite Huidobro's cavilling, the visual qualities of the novel were really interpreted quite well by Ontañón, a Spanish set-designer who did the illustrations (thirty-one line-drawings and seven in colour). Nor did its filmic qualities go unnoticed by critics in Spain. Fernando Mantilla, reviewing the novel for the cinema section of *Atlántico* magazine, called for it to be made into a movie right away: "The novel is better than Douglas Fairbanks deserves. It should go to launch a new star . . . in a Spanish superproduction. The Cid, with his powerful lance could ride through our borders and Babieca's hooves could bring to the talkies an as yet unheard success among the sounds of the silver screen." The review is so gushy that it could have been ghosted by Huidobro himself. Publicity is but another dimension of art, and not the least creative. We know for certain that he did coach the publisher on promotion:

> For bookstore placards and newspaper ads you might want to use something like this:
>
> HERE THE CID IS REBORN
> AND THE GREATEST EPIC OF HIS PEOPLE.
>
> But if you prefer to use the inflated style of Yankee books, we might as well go all out and simply announce:
>
> THE BOOK OF TODAY . . .
> AND OF THE CENTURY.
>
> Although one should be modest, it doesn't really affect me since all this is just a question of commercial puffery (and only the two of us are in on the secret).

Modesty notwithstanding and all secrets aside, the book was a great success in Spain. So much so that it was quickly translated and published in England under the title *Portrait of a Paladin*; and so successful was it there that the translator (Warre B. Wells) obtained contract for other, unpublished manuscripts from Huidobro.

It was in this roundabout way that *Cagliostro* came into print in English several years before being published in Spanish. When the original finally did appear, in 1934, it was billed as a "novela-film." The novel did in fact have its beginnings as a filmscript, a scenario for a silent movie. It will be recalled that in April of 1923 *Paris-Journal* reported Huidobro to be at work on a Cubist film that was to "revolutionize viewing habits." Yet another newspaper, a month later, contained further details on the project: "Vicente Huidobro, the pure poet of *Horizon carré* and *Tour Eiffel,* has completed the scenario of a film *Cagliostro,* in which the specifically cinegraphic action is 'visualized' with an acute sense of optic rhythm." The film must have already been shot, for among Huidobro's papers there is a memo in which the writer and director jointly declare their dissatisfaction with the "découpage" ["cutting"].

This film of 1923, to my knowledge, was not released nor have any copies survived. The script however did resurface in 1927, when it won a prize in New York from the League for Better Pictures. The *New York Times* for 23 July 1927, under the heading "Chilean Gets Film Prize," reports the following: "Vicente Huidobro, young Chilean poet and novelist, was announced yesterday as the winner of a $10,000 prize offered by the League for Better Pictures for the book of the year having the best possibilities for moving-picture adaptation. The book, still in script form in the hands of Paris publishers, is called *Cagliostro* and is based upon the life of the eighteenth-century necromancer and popular mystic." *Cagliostro* was truly ill-fated. The book that was so promising in July was outmoded just a few months later when, in October of 1927, Warner Brothers released *The Jazz Singer*, the talking picture that turned the film world upside down. Especially the New York film world, bumping it off to Hollywood. Huidobro's *Cagliostro* was left behind, an instant relic of the past; it was written in the language of the silent film.

By design its imagery was created in the film tradition of the great German silents of the 1920s, the Expressionist-Cubist world of the studio-filmed horror tale. Even the classics of the genre, such as *The Cabinet of Dr. Caligari* and *Nosferatu,* are gimmicky films by today's standards, their horrific impact the result of a deliberate unnaturalness. Still-shots, painted sets, stilted acting, and Gothic subtitling were all systematically used to create the illusion of an otherworldly reality. And Huidobro's novel, concerned with the exploits of an eighteenth-century master of the black arts, was equally contrived so as to make the greatest use of the possibilities of the genre. Accordingly, scenes of levitation, spatial projection, hypnotism, and black magic abound.

Huidobro's interest in film was not unique. Like other writers of the avant-garde, he was intrigued by this modern form of illusion that relates motion, time, and space in a new kind of composition. In fact, as early as 1916, there is a poem in *El espejo de agua* whose subject is the magic of the Newsreel:

> El sueño de Jacob se ha realizado
> Un ojo se abre frente al espejo
> Y las gentes que bajan a la tela
> Arrojaron su carne como un abrigo viejo.
>
> La película mil novecientos dieciséis
> Sale de una caja.
>
> La guerra europea
>
> Llueve sobre los espectadores. . . .

(Jacob's dream has been realized / An eye opens in front of the mirror / And the people who come on screen shed their skin like an old overcoat / The movie 1916 / Comes out of the box / The European War / Rains down over the viewers . . .)

The jumpy discontinuity of the poem is not unlike that of the early one-reelers, whose compressed treatment of time derived from the sequential montage of separately filmed scenes. It should be remembered that the rise of literary Cubism is intertwined with the development of film as an art form, and that both rely on essentially similar compositional techniques: montage and cutting. Montage is metaphor. Even the theory is the same. The most effective metaphor, according to Reverdy, the principal theoretician of Cubist poetry, was that produced by the juxtaposition of "distant realities"; similarly, the most effective montage, according to Eisenstein, the principal theoretician of the silent film, was that produced by the "collision" of conflicting shots. In both cases the result was the same: a new and dynamic reality created by the unexpected association forced to take place in the mind of the reader, or viewer.

There were important differences however. Film was public and narrative, while poetry was personal and lyrical. One was commercially oriented toward a mass audience and the other was the artistic property of an élite. Huidobro in the 1920s was searching for a wider public. Unable to bring out a film, he was forced to settle with bringing film to the novel. In this regard, the preface to the English-language edition of *Cagliostro* contains an important statement:

> As for the form of this book, I have only to say that this is what may be called a visual novel, with a technique influenced by the cinematograph. I believe that the public of today, which has acquired the cinema habit, may be interested in a novel in which the author has deliberately chosen words of a visual character and events that are best suited to comprehension through the eyes (. . .). Character drawing today has to be more synthetic, more compact, than it was before. Action cannot be slow. Events have to move more rapidly. Otherwise the public is bored.

Huidobro was concerned with the cinema's influence on the novel. Contemporary criticism looks at the problem from the other end, focusing on the literary properties of cinema: the director as author, the film as narrative, even the camera as pen. Obviously, things were not always this way. For Huidobro exactly the reverse was true. For him, the cinema was the new art form, hence his effort to bring out a novel utilizing the procedures of film for readers who had picked up the "cinema habit." The informing principles of *Cagliostro,* as outlined in the 1931 preface, were four; they refer to plot, character, style, and language. Essentially, the plot is to be fast-paced since the reader habituated to film will not tolerate much descriptive exposition. Characterization likewise is to be rapid, "four strokes of the brush," Huidobro says, "and a living being is painted." Furthermore, the style is to be visual, that best suited "to comprehension through the eyes." And, finally, the language is to be of a "visual character." An examination of *Cagliostro* in the light of these principles of composition should permit us to appreciate the uniqueness of Huidobro's literary hybrid, the "novela-film."

With regard to plot and character, history tells us that Cagliostro was a famous Italian adventurer, magician, alchemist, and protagonist of many scandals in Europe during the late eighteenth century, the age of the Enlightenment. Huidobro focuses on his adventures in France on the eve of the French Revolution. When the reader first "sees" the protagonist he is disembarking from a carriage in the dead of night. Draped with a cape only his eyes are visible. The narrator rhetorically draws our attention to those eyes:

> The strange door of the strange coach creaked as it slowly opened, and a man, wrapped in a cape that left nothing visible save his eyes, protruded his head from the night within the coach into the night outside to find out what was going on.
>
> Did you see those eyes? Those eyes phosphorescent as the streams that run through mines of mercury; those eyes suddenly enriched the night, they are the only light emerging from the depths of his existence. Take a good look at them, for they are the centre of my story.

This kind of rhetorical persuasion, with direct authorial intrusion, might seem a bit overwrought to readers accustomed to the objectivity of the modern novel, but in the convention of the visual language of the silent film the eyes told all. There was a kind of filmic physiognomy, whereby the facial features of an individual were supposed to reveal qualities of mind and character: the shifty eyes of the untrustworthy, the flashing eyes of the lover, and here the phosphorescent eyes of the mesmerizer, Cagliostro. Other characters in the novel are typed with equal rapidity. So rapidly, in fact, that the narrator on occasion avoids all description and asks the reader to fill in with a familiar stereotype. For example, when Lorenza, Cagliostro's mistress and medium appears for the first time she is described in this way: "She is beautiful, a brunette with great dark eyes full of light and grace. (Reader, just think of the most beautiful woman you ever saw and apply her beauty to Lorenza; that way you'll save me and yourself a lengthy description)." Such descriptive shorthand takes advantage of the avant-garde's rediscovery of the expressive power of cliché when transferred to a new context.

As for plot, it is so slickly contrived for special effects that it is almost impossible to summarize. Suffice it to say that Cagliostro is a magician, so all sorts of tricks and magic effects come into play. At the outset he is seen arriving in France, putting his occult powers to good use, raising the dead, healing the sick, and so forth. His fame soon spreads and he is asked to perform before the court of Louis XVI. This gives rise to a flash forward, a vision of the guillotine, with powdered heads tumbling to the ground. The plot, although streamlined, is not without complications: the prefect of police, for example, is determined to put Cagliostro away for practising black magic; certain of the rich and powerful want him to use his power to their advantage; while others, more scientific-minded, like Rousseau, Marat, and Sade, seek to persuade him to establish a secret sect (this permits a flashback as Cagliostro recounts for them his own initiation into the occult). And as though all this were not enough, everything functions contrapuntally, balanced out by the conflicting forces of love and greed, good and evil. In tune with the moralizing stance of American movies, Huidobro's Cagliostro has a tragic flaw: driven by ambition and bloated with his own importance, he abuses his power, utilizing it for personal gain. Good can then struggle with evil, and Marcival, a rival magician, steps in to undo Cagliostro's magic. Lorenza, medium (and lover), apprised of Cagliostro's wrongdoing, kills herself. Only then does he realize the error of his ways (and his true love for her), but it is too late of course, and the novel ends with his going off into the darkness from whence he came, carrying the limp cadaver of Lorenza. Before leaving though, he dutifully sets fire to his laboratory and library, salvaging two potions: one marked life, the other death. Supposedly, he will try to revive Lorenza and true love will triumph; or, failing at that, he will join her in death:

> Cagliostro appears in the doorway, bearing in his arms the body of Lorenza. He goes down the steps and gets into his coach. The coach starts off at a trot, pulled by the horses of history. Behind him the house is burning. Huge flames gobble up everything and a dark cloud rises up into the sky. In front of him, a long road leads off into the horizon. The carriage reaches the end of the road. In the distance its rear-window winks like an almond-shaped eye. A cloud sinks slowly to the ground. The great mage is lost to the eyes of the world behind that mysterious cloud.

* * * * * * * * *

> What happened afterwards? Where did he find refuge? Was he able to conquer death? Does he still live somewhere with his beloved?

THE END

The rhetorical finale, holding out the possibility of the hero's return, is styled to read like the closing titles of a serial.

While rapid characterization and a fast-moving plot were once the qualities that made *Cagliostro* a prizewinner, of more enduring value has been its cinematic texture: fifty years later the novel still reads like a movie. It was Huidobro's original intention to organize the action around what was best suited to "comprehension through the eyes," and to this end he sometimes used even the most restrictive of filmlike procedures. Perspective, for example: fixed for the movie-house spectator it is fixed for the reader of the novel, as though the camera-eye recording the action were also fixed:

> Cagliostro appears on the path leading toward his coach. As he approaches, he gets incredibly bigger. He arrives, boards, and the coach sets off at a gallop. At the end of the road, when it is very far away, nothing can be seen of it except the little rear-window, almond-shaped, like a smiling eye between heaven and earth. Then a cloud, fulfilling its mission drops to the ground so as to hide everything from the curious eyes of men.

The scene closes with a standard cinematic device: the gradual dissolve. Corresponding to a fade-out, in which the last frames go out of focus, is the dark cloud dropping to the ground. The novel, it will be recalled, ends with a similar cloud blacking out everything.

The reader is always aware of the text's visual dimension. To get at the contents of a purloined letter, Cagliostro does not break it open, but resorts to Lorenza, his paramour and medium. Huidobro makes this rather simple act of clairvoyance visually spectacular through a quick-paced sequence involving close-up, dissolve, and superimposition:

> Cagliostro examines the letter. He holds it up to the light, then he places it on Lorenza's forehead, commanding her.
>
> —Read this message to me!
>
> Lorenza's head grows in size before our eyes, blown up by our common curiosity. Her brow dissolves and in its place appears the letter so that its text can be plainly read:
>
> "To M. Sardines, Paris Police: In accordance with your wishes, I have taken certain steps. . . ."
>
> The letter thus read, thanks to the special vision of Lorenza, her head returns to its normal size, scaled down five times.

As in film montage, separate image sequences are joined together so as to create a single narrative flow. A flow, needless to repeat, specifically designed for "comprehension through the eyes."

But a novel's imagery is generated by words, and comprehension, however oriented, necessarily begins at the lexical level. Hence Huidobro's concern with "words of a visual character." The highly stylized language of the novel, and its visual impact, is enhanced for the reader through a clever set of framing devices. The front matter alerts us to the idea that reading *Cagliostro* may be an unusual experience: following the subtitle "novela-film," there is a prefatory page with a discursive aside:

FROM AUTHOR TO READER

> Let the reader suppose that he has not bought a book in a bookstore, but rather a ticket to the movies. So, reader, you are not coming out of a store but going into a theatre. You take a seat. Some music is being played that gets on your nerves. It is so ridiculous. Yet it must be so to please the crowd. The orchestra stops. The curtain goes up; or, rather, the curtains part and there appears on the screen:

CAGLIOSTRO
by
Vicente Huidobro

> After the credits there is a brief. . . .

And on the very next page the "film" begins, prefaced in turn by some frames of high-sounding historical summary:

PREFACE

> Towards the end of the reign of Louis XV, there sprang up all over France and most of Europe many secret sects, whose activities, although ignored by the masses, had an enormous impact on the events of the time.

> How many events whose origins we ignore were perhaps hatched underground by these persecuted souls over the half-light of a candle!

> These sects had their beginnings in the mysterious Orient; the power of the occult sciences concerned the greatest minds of the West who feverishly studied Alchemy, Magic and the secrets of the Kabala, drawn by the beauty of this arcane knowledge.

> Among the adepts there were some who had truly extraordinary power.

> Admission to these sects entailed oaths of secrecy. Woe to him who violated this trust!

This highly stylized opening, with its ominous clue as to what is to follow, is in the best tradition of the early cinema. Once the narrative begins, the film has supposedly begun to roll and the novel's language changes accordingly. Rolling forth from every sentence on every page there is a most extravagant series of visual metaphors which "collide" and run into one another sparking a sense of the visual. By way of illustration there follows a passage from the beginning of chapter one:

> An eighteenth-century storm broke that night over Alsace, over Alsace so blond from her turning leaves and her lovely daughters ['la dulce Alsacia rubia a causa de sus hojas y sus hijas']. Great clouds, black and bulging like seals' bellies, swam in the wet winds toward the west. From time to time a well-aimed lightning bolt made the warm blood of a pierced cloud drip over our stricken panorama. It was a night for the hammering of counterfeit coins and the galloping of History's wolves. To the reader's right there is rain and the source of the storm; to his left, forests and hills. The magnificent forest moans like an organ or a sea-cave as the wind passes through, it moans as though all the world's children were calling for their mother. This page I am now writing is crossed by a trail of mud, the muck and mire of legend. At the end of the road there suddenly appear two lanterns balancing themselves like a drunkard singing to the horizon. A coach, of strange shape and colour, advances toward the reader, the heavy thud of the horses' hooves making the whole novel shake. The coach is coming right at us, it is just a few feet from our eyes. The rain beats meanly down upon the driver. All my readers, men and women, must now step back a pace or two so as not to be spattered by the wheels of this strange vehicle as it passes by.

And so the action goes, careening from page to page. Scenes common to the movies of the time are transformed into the boldest of verbal images. The reader-spectator is thus made to "see" things that, although impossible to occur in reality, became possible to present visually through the cinematic art of illusion. For example, Cagliostro makes flowers bloom in midwinter with the "magnetic heat" of his hands (a standard film trick created by shooting separate frames of film over a long period of time). In another scene Cagliostro's spirit takes leave of his body in the middle of a Paris seance so that he can slip off to snow-stricken Russia to save a maiden whose runaway coach is nearing a precipice (a trick achieved by superimposition, exposing the film twice).

The novel, like the movies it emulates, was conceived as an entertainment. Huidobro, ever the performer, was prepared to go to any lengths to make his fictional construct engaging. And, just as in *Mío Cid Campeador* he posed as a descendant of the hero, in order to promote this novel he prepared a preface with the unlikely title "I was Cagliostro." Evidently intended for the English language edition, this preface was never used; probably because it was so patently preposterous. Here too, he has the protagonist step in, correcting the author where necessary:

> I am sure the magician came in the night to read the day's work, and to approve or disapprove when my fancy led me too far astray. In reality the magician did not come, but quit my own body and divested himself powerfully. If it were not him, it was surely a kindred spirit of his. One morning I found a line written on the back of my manuscript. This line read: "False and without grace," referring to a passage in the work. The writing was not mine, and certain experts that I consulted declared, after having compared the lines, that it was that of Cagliostro, the type of each letter being exactly his. I have kept this page and it is at the disposition of those who wish to be convinced of the truth herein set down. The life of Cagliostro is a novel, or a marvellous film. It is not for this reason that I call this work a film-novel, but because it is written as if it were a film. I wished the scenes to unfold themselves to the reader as the scenes in a moving picture. I have selected the most visual words, I have tried to give the characters the greatest possible amount of life without the aid of long commentaries, or heavy descriptions, as on the screen. I have followed a movie technique throughout, because I believe the picture-going public of today cannot only understand it, but would prefer novels of this kind. And so I present you with my old life, made flesh and blood and dressed in the linen of the screen.

The mixed metaphor which closes this aborted project for a preface synthesizes better than any words of mine the exact nature of Huidobro's attempt to create a filmic novel, as well as his success in doing so. (pp. 125-36)

> *René de Costa, in his* Vicente Huidobro: The Careers of a Poet, *Oxford at the Clarendon Press, 1984, 186 p.*

ANNA BALAKIAN   (essay date 1986)

[*Balakian is a critic of French literature who has written extensively on writers of the Symbolist, Surrealist, and Dadaist movements. In the following excerpt, she comments on Huidobro's poetic themes and techniques.*]

The poetry of Rimbaud and Mallarmé was [Huidobro's] literary matrix. There was also a strong philosophical factor in his development, namely the impact of Hegel and Heidegger. This double affiliation is evident in all of Huidobro's poetry. Like a Hispanic Victor Hugo, he provides such a prolific body of poetry as well as prose that the choice of references here becomes strictly eclectic, as one selects significant pieces in what is, not surprisingly, an uneven work.

I am particularly drawn to his *El espejo de agua,* which marks a distinct break with his earlier symbolist-oriented poetry. Like the titles of Reverdy, those of Huidobro had intricate connotations in their apparent simplicity. The objective realities do not seem too distant here: mirror, of course, has had from time immemorial metaphoric affiliations with water. So here we see two reflecting agents juxtaposed. But is reflection a *state* or a visionary agent? Are we involved with a new kind of mirror? The very first poem, entitled **"Arte poetica,"** initiates the animistic intimacy of the indeterminate "also." . . . The referential discontinuity is accompanied . . . by clear delineation of

objects, be they man-made or natural: "Que el verso sea como une llave / Que abra mil puertas" (Let poetry be like a key / Opening a thousand doors). But *llave* ["key"] also means *faucet,* which brings us back to water, although on the rational level suggesting that poetry may be a key to open many doors is more acceptable. But in the wider circumference of double connotation the poem touches the broad notion of unlocking restrained energies, thus manifesting the process of poetic creativity. "Inventa mundos nuevos y cuida tu palabra" (Invent new worlds and watch your word). Obviously this is not to be a subconscious or intuitive pouring out of words if the poet is to mind his words, but a process strictly under control. We are reminded of Reverdy's "Art begins where chance ends." This advice is reinforced later in the poem by the simple statement that true vigor resides in the *head.* And when he concludes that everything under the sun lives for us, this is not to be taken for a spiritual anthropocentrism. To live for us really means to him: to be at our disposal. He had heard an indigenous poet say: "Don't sing of the rain, poet, make it rain." Rain is a result; *making it rain* is a creative process. In line with this image, Huidobro says in his **"Arte poetica":** "Por que cantais la rosa, oh Poetas! / Hacedla florecer en el poema!" Why sing of the rose, make it flower! Everything is there, in other words, not to be admired but to be manipulated because the poet, that agent of manipulation, is, as the final line of the poem tells us, "a small god."

In the second poem, having the same title as the collective work, **"El espejo de agua,"** the transformational capacity we guessed in the title, "the mirror," makes of it a river, then a watery globe, a fishbowl where all the swans drown, and as we go from one image to the next we notice that the orb, which also means globe, becomes more than a reflecting object; it causes an active assault on the swan-poetics of symbolism.

Mi espejo, corriente por las noches,	(My mirror, flowing through the night,
Se hace arroyo y se aleja de mi cuarto.	Has become a brook streaming out of my room.
Mi espejo, más profundo que el orbe	My mirror, deeper than the globe
Donde todos los cisnes se ahogaron.	Where all the swans drown.)

In *Poemas árticos,* where the contamination of cubism becomes evident, we can find two kinds of poems; on the one hand the passive juxtaposition of objects (what painters call nature-morte) and others more relevant to the pattern here described: images in movement, displaying the process of creation rather than the crystallization of the art process. This effect is produced, for instance, in a poem called **"Marino,"** where the sailor demonstrates godlike activities in concordance with the image of a bird about to soar in initial flight. The creations are a series of displacements not of vision but of human and cosmic phenomena; it is indeed a broader extension of the "making roses" proposed in his **"Arte poetica."** An ancient mariner (Huidobro was familiar with English romanticism) intrudes upon the cosmography and disturbs the temporal structure of the earth as well:

Hice correr ríos que nunca han existido	(I made rivers run Where none had been before
De un grito elevé una montaño	With a shout I made a mountain rise
Y en torno bailamos una nueva danza	And now we do a new dance around it. . . .
Y enseñé a cantar un pájaro de nieve	And I taught a snowbird how to sing

Marchemos sobre los meses
   desatados
Soy el viejo marino que cose
   los
horizontes cortados

Let us depart upon the floating
   months
I am the old sailor
Who mends torn horizons.)

Like Victor Hugo's *La Légende des siècles,* Huidobro's *Adán* and *Altazor* encompass the first and last man. Although in *Altazor* there are many references to God and to Satan, these are not personal identifications of divinity; rather, they embody the powers of generation and destruction. The sense of apocalypse that has been associated in this poem with modern tendencies toward deconstruction can only result from a partial reading of the poem. The devastation is described only to give the god-poet an opportunity to rethink the universe. The seismograph has taken note of his birth. The sun is born in his right eye and sets in his left eye, meditates Altazor, and he suggests that if God exists at all it is thanks to the poet. This echoes what he had earlier questioned in *Adán:* whether the poem exists because of the water perceived, or the water exists because the poet has perceived it. He wonders: "Si tu agua forma el canto / O si tu canto forma el agua" ["If your water forms the song / Or if your song forms the water"].

Independent in his breathing and in his nourishment, the new god-poet knows it is late: "there is no time to lose," "no hay tiempo que perder" becomes a refrain in canto 4 of *Altazor.* His last image is that of a mill, but a mill reaching out eventually to constellations; distant realities again combined, the earth-power creating energy and by extension nourishment, and the cosmic power providing another form of energy, i.e., luminosity.

The epic poems of Huidobro rise to an ecstatic pitch at which the aesthetic experience of creativity becomes a substitute for religious communion. The line between the messiah and the antichrist of magic, as he describes himself in *Altazor,* grows very faint. (pp. 118-21)

> *Anna Balakian, "A Triptych of Modernism: Reverdy, Huidobro, and Ball," in* Modernism: Challenges and Perspectives, *edited by Monique Chefdor, Ricardo Quinones, and Albert Wachtel, University of Illinois Press, 1986, pp. 111-27.*

ADDITIONAL BIBLIOGRAPHY

Dowling, Lee H. "Metalanguage in Huidobro's *Altazor.*" *Language and Style* XV, No. 4 (Fall 1982): 253-66.
    Closely examines the linguistic innovations in *Altazor.*

Francis, Claude. "Vicente Huidobro: Image as Magic." *Papers on Language and Literature* 12, No. 3 (Summer 1976): 311-20.
    Compares the similarities between Huidobro's theory of creationism, Carlos Castaneda's studies of the teachings of Don Juan, and the philosophy of Jean Paul Sartre.

Holmes, Henry Alfred. "The Creationism of Vicente Huidobro." *The Spanish Review* 1, No. 1 (March 1934): 9-16.
    Briefly discusses Huidobro's career and explains the basic tenets of Creationism.

———. *Vicente Huidobro and Creationism.* New York: Institute of French Studies, 1934, 71 p.
    Examines Huidobro's life and career, focusing on his role in the development of Creationism and his influence on other writers. Holmes concludes that "Huidobro is distinctly a great force among the poetic personalities of the age, for in the primary meaning of the word, none could be more truly a *poet* (from the Greek *poieo,* I create) than he."

Mandlove, Nancy B. "At the Outer Limits of Language: Mallarmé's *Un coup de dés* and Huidobro's *Altazor.*" *Studies in 20th Century Literature* 8, No.2 (Spring 1984): 163-83.
    Describes the similarities between *Altazor* and Stéphane Mallarmé's *Un coup de dés,* noting that both works "are based on the same archetypal and linguistic patterns" and that both try to make the poem "a mirror of Creation itself."

Osgood, Eugenia V. "Two Journeys to the End of Night: Tzara's *L'homme approximatif* and Vicente Huidobro's *Altazor.*" *Dada Surrealism,* No. 4 (1974): 57-61.
    Compares the major themes of Tristan Tzara's *L'homme approximatif* and *Altazor,* describing them as morality plays that "go beyond adherence to any school and become personal and moving testimonies to their authors' concern with the universal."

Rutter, Frank P. "Vicente Huidobro and Futurism: Convergences and Divergences (1917-1918)." *Bulletin of Hispanic Studies* LVIII, No. 1 (January 1981): 55-72.
    Examines the impact of Futurism on the poetry that Huidobro wrote in 1917-18.

Wood, Cecil G. "The Development of *Creacionismo:* A Study of Four Early Poems of Vicente Huidobro." *Hispania* 61, No. 1 (March 1978): 5-13.
    Discusses the development of Huidobro's poetic theories as they are demonstrated in four of his earliest poems: "La capilla aldeana," "Montonía odiosa de las tardes nubladas," "La alcoba," and "Los estanques nocturnos."

(Mary) Jane Mander

1877-1949

(Also wrote under the pseudonym Manda Lloyd) New Zealand novelist, journalist, essayist, and critic.

Mander is best remembered for her four novels set in New Zealand: *The Story of a New Zealand River, The Passionate Puritan, The Strange Attraction,* and *Allen Adair.* These works offer vivid, evocative depictions of New Zealand life, portraying characteristic New Zealanders and their occupations rather than the transplanted Britishers or New Zealand natives copying English society that were common to earlier New Zealand fiction. Mander is also credited with introducing into her country's literature a hitherto unaccustomed frankness in dealing with sexual situations.

Mander was the eldest of five children born to Janet and Francis Mander in Auckland. Because of her father's work as a lumberman, her early years were spent moving frequently between remote outposts and often into the sparsely populated bush country. As a result of these frequent relocations ("as many as twenty-nine in a few years," Mander told an interviewer), she was only able to attend four or five widely scattered years of school. When Mander was fifteen her family was living in a region of the Kaipara district that had no high school. She began teaching primary school there while studying privately with the school's headmaster, completing her high school education within a year. Mander's father eventually became the owner of a successful lumber mill, and in 1900 the family finally settled at a permanent home in the large North Auckland town of Whangarei. Francis Mander was elected to Parliament, where he sat for the next twenty years, and bought a newspaper, the *Northern Advocate,* where Jane Mander worked from 1902 through 1906 as a reporter. The family's comfortable financial situation enabled Mander to travel to Australia in 1907 and 1910; in 1912, at the age of thirty-five, she left New Zealand to study at the Columbia University School of Journalism in New York.

Mander excelled in her classes at Columbia while working steadily on the manuscript of a novel about her homeland in her spare time. After several years in New York she became involved in the women's suffrage movement and was soon much in demand as a public speaker representing a country where women had had the vote for more than twenty years. She eventually abandoned her studies and worked at a series of jobs while seeking publication for her first novel, *The Story of a New Zealand River.* Published in 1920, the book received favorable reviews in the United States and England, and while living in New York Mander wrote and published two more novels with New Zealand settings, *The Passionate Puritan* and *The Strange Attraction.* In 1923 she moved to London. During the next ten years she published three more novels, *Allen Adair, The Beseiging City,* and *Pins and Pinnacles,* and sent columns on art, literature, and current events to New Zealand periodicals. Mander returned to New Zealand in 1932 after her mother's death and managed her father's household until his death in 1942. During the last seventeen years of her life, she published little outside of local magazines and newspapers; however, she became a source of guidance for young New Zealand

writers, whom she supplied with editorial and often material aid. She died in 1949.

Mander's first four novels—*The Story of a New Zealand River, The Passionate Puritan, The Strange Attraction,* and *Allen Adair*—were set in her homeland, and each featured characters involved in such typical New Zealand occupations as bushfelling, kauri milling, and gumdigging, as well as the less exotic professions of journalism and schoolteaching, which were among the few open to women. Mander's protagonists are frequently women supporting themselves, and her interest in women's employment was central to her own life: she had earned her own living at a time when it was uncommon for New Zealand women to do so, and her independent, self-supporting female protagonists are considered by critics to be partial portraits of Mander herself. *The Story of a New Zealand River* began her record of the New Zealand frontier experience that she had directly observed from childhood, and the three novels that followed it each dealt similarly with a different phase of New Zealand settlement. These early works also contain attacks on the Puritanism, conformity, and snobbery that Mander portrayed as an ingrained part of nascent New Zealand society. Mander's novels of New Zealand life were for the most part well received. Although almost all critics praised her descriptions of characteristic New Zealand locales and industries and her skill in depicting characters, New Zealand commentators and reviewers were quick to criticize Mander's outspoken frankness on sexual matters. According to biographer Dorothea Turner, the overwhelmingly negative reception of her novels in her homeland was a shaping force on Mander's career. After her first three novels were each criticized in turn for focusing on sexual relationships, Mander wrote her fourth novel, *Allen Adair,* specifically to counter such criticism, describing the book as "guaranteed to shock not even my mother." Nevertheless, this novel too was criticized in New Zealand for radical ideas about marriage and sexuality, although it received the usual commendations for its characterizations and beautifully described New Zealand landscapes. Some critics speculate that it may have been the continued rejection of her works in her own country that led Mander to set her last two novels in other locales: *The Besieging City* in New York and *Pins and Pinnacles* in London. Generally dismissed as inferior to her New Zealand novels, these works have received little attention, although Turner has commented that they add to Mander's gallery of carefully drawn characters, in particular strong-minded, independent women.

Mander contributed significantly to the development of New Zealand literature by introducing more sophisticated subject matter, as well as through her intense nationalism at a time when British traditions figured prominently in New Zealand society, arts, and letters. Mander's novels were among the earliest fictional works set in New Zealand that were published and read in the United States and England. In introducing the customs, occupations, and scenery of her country to a wide readership, Mander played a part in inspiring critical and popular interest in New Zealand literature.

PRINCIPAL WORKS

The Story of a New Zealand River   (novel)   1920
The Passionate Puritan   (novel)   1921
The Strange Attraction   (novel)   1922
Allen Adair   (novel)   1925
The Besieging City   (novel)   1926
Pins and Pinnacles   (novel)   1928

THE TIMES LITERARY SUPPLEMENT   (essay date 1920)

[*In the following excerpt, an anonymous reviewer praises* The Story of a New Zealand River.]

[*The Story of a New Zealand River*] gives us a new and not insignificant paragraph in the history of the impact of ideas. The main subject of the story is an Englishwoman married to an Australian pioneer in an undeveloped part of New Zealand; and her difficulties in the fresh environment occupy much of the book. But the authoress is too subtle a writer to confine herself to one flat contrast between the mental attitudes of the old and new worlds. Alice, brought up among inhibitions and conventions, finds them perpetuated in an exaggerated form in the Auckland boarding-houses; and, besides the conflict between culture on the one hand and vitality on the other which the book portrays, there is the opposition between Alice's traditional beliefs and the "modern" opinions which reach her—partly through the agency of Shaw and Wells from England, and partly from America. The authoress has a real ability to describe character and differences of outlook; but she does not

allow the plot to become lost in disquisitions. The book would have been more emphatic if it could have been shortened, but in its present form it is a patient study of one example of the immemorial clash between impulse and convention. The authoress never exactly hits the bull's-eye, but she is always on the target.

A review of "The Story of a New Zealand River,"
in The Times Literary Supplement, *No. 961, June 17, 1920, p. 385.*

KATHERINE MANSFIELD   (essay date 1920)

[*Mansfield, a New Zealand-born English short story writer and novelist, was an important pioneer in stream-of-consciousness literature. She was among the earliest English writers whose fiction depended upon incident rather than plot, a development that significantly influenced the modern short story. Throughout 1919 and 1920 Mansfield wrote a weekly book-review column in the* Athenaeum. *In the following excerpt from a 1920 review in which she discusses* A Child of the Alps *by Margaret Symonds and Mander's* Story of a New Zealand River, *Mansfield criticizes the latter as an overlong novel that is only occasionally enlivened by passages of skilled writing.*]

A Child of the Alps and **The Story of a New Zealand River** are two first novels which convey the impression that their authors were by no means sensible to the idea that there might be danger in the leisurely style. Miss Margaret Symonds, in particular, writes with a strange confidence; she has the reader's attention caught and thrilled by her artless tale of the "strange child" Linda. (p. 227)

The case of Miss Jane Mander is very different. Her **Story of a New Zealand River,** which takes four hundred and thirty-two pages of small type to tell, has none of Miss Symonds' sophistication, or European atmosphere. The scene is laid in the back blocks of New Zealand, and, as is almost invariably the case with novels that have a colonial setting, in spite of the fact that there is frequent allusion to the magnificent scenery, it profiteth us nothing. "Stiff laurel-like puriris stood beside the drooping lace fringe of the lacy rimu; hard blackish kahikateas brooded over the oak-like ti-toki with its lovely scarlet berry." What picture can that possibly convey to an English reader? What emotion can it produce? But that brings us to the fact that Miss Jane Mander is immensely hampered in her writing by her adherence to the old unnecessary technical devices—they are no more—with which she imagines it necessary to support her story. If one has the patience to persevere with her novel there is under all the false wrappings, the root of something very fresh and sturdy. She lacks confidence and the courage of her opinions; like the wavering, fearful heroine, she leans too hard on England. There are moments when we catch a bewilderingly vivid glimpse of what she really felt and knew about the small settlement of people in the lumber-camp, but we suspect that these are moments when she is off her guard. Then her real talent flashes out; her characters move quickly, almost violently; we are suddenly conscious what an agony, what an anguish it was to Bruce when he felt one of his drunken fits coming on; or The Boss reveals his extraordinary simplicity when he tells his wife he thought she'd been unfaithful to him for years.

But these serve nothing but to increase our impatience with Miss Mander. Why is her book not half as long, twice as honest? What right has she to bore her readers if she is capable of interesting them? It would be easy to toss **The Story of a New Zealand River** aside and treat it as another unsuccessful novel, but we have been seeking for pearls in such a prodigious number of new books that we are forced to the conclusion that it is useless to dismiss any that contain something that might one day turn into a pearl. (pp. 228-29)

Katherine Mansfield, in a review of "The Story of a New Zealand River," in her Novels and Novelists, *edited by J. Middleton Murry, Alfred A. Knopf, 1930, pp. 227-29.*

THE NEW REPUBLIC   (essay date 1920)

[*In the following excerpt, the reviewer praises the characterization and plot in* The Story of a New Zealand River *but suggests that the novel's theme is insufficient for its length.*]

The spiritual struggle that makes up the major theme of *The Story of a New Zealand River* defeats its own purpose by its meticulous regard for endless analysis. It was evidently Jane Mander's conviction (doggedly adhered to) that by elaborating every incident and bringing to the fore every facet of a complex situation that extends over a number of years the interest of the reader would be heightened and better retained. Instead of this, the reader becomes wearied.

The theme of this book is good but it is not good enough for 430 pages of closely printed matter. Even the sense of reality that the author had undoubtedly captured and the consistency of her character-drawing become tiresome after a time. A novel that moved more readily, that had been shaken down to lesser space, would have proved more compelling.

Of the characters that create *The Story of a New Zealand River,* which, by the way, is an extremely bad title, nothing but praise may be given. They display an inordinate amount of careful study of human nature, moving and thinking with the absolute reality of rounded figures.

The central idea itself is excellent. Alice Roland, gentle, super-refined, quite Victorian in her mental attitudes, finds the primitive uncouthness of her settlement home in New Zealand hardly reassuring or conducive to happiness. She instinctively revolts against the bareness of things, the lack of comforts, the free and easy life. Proud and distant where men are concerned she is especially so toward David Bruce, who happens to be the only cultured man at the lumber-camp.

Immediately this is postulated the reader knows that a love affair is imminent between the two. So the triangle begins, Tom Roland, the husband, crude and unthinking; Alice, the wife, gentle and absurdly conservative, and David, apparently the only normal person of the three. Those same conventions loom greatly in Alice's mind and although love is acknowledged that is as far as it goes.

With the growth of her daughter, Asia, a new and entirely alien mental outlook is forced upon Alice. Asia goes to the man she loves although he is married, and goes without any hesitation. That her child should do this while for years she has crushed her passion within her is a source of torture for Alice. Her spiritual viewpoint has bound and gagged her all her life; it has denied her happiness.

Only in the sunset of life after her husband is providentially killed in an accident does Alice go to David. Two great attitudes toward a mighty problem are presented here and it may be inferred that the author approves of Asia's choice.

The great care expended upon the character-drawing of Alice Roland is remarkable. Stroke after careful stroke completes a personage not especially complex but yet difficult of full portraiture. One hardly feels sympathetic toward her; she arouses impatience but she must be pitied. David Bruce, except that he is somewhat idealized and suggestive of the stage hero at times, is consistently developed and Tom Roland, who also is heroized a bit at the end, is painted with due regard for his complexities. But it is Asia that the reader remembers; she is the sanest and simplest of them all.

H. S. G., in a review of "The Story of a New Zealand River," in The New Republic, *Vol. XXIII, No. 294, July 21, 1920, p. 234.*

THE NEW YORK TIMES BOOK REVIEW   (essay date 1921)

[*In the following excerpt, a reviewer of* The Passionate Puritan *praises Mander's skill in depicting New Zealand settings as well as in portraying the interaction between the novel's main characters.*]

Jane Mander comes from New Zealand and she writes about that most interesting country with the surety of thorough knowledge and with the insight of the born story teller who knows that human drama in richest quantity is always to be found where mankind strips itself of conventions and measures its forces with those of nature. Last year her first novel, *The Story of a New Zealand River,* proved her to be a writer of unusual and striking quality who could identify her people and their drama with their surroundings so completely and weave the two together so deftly as to make age-old human passions take on new freshness and interest because of the novelty and the beauty of their background. We Americans have been interested in New Zealand chiefly as a country of what was, a few years ago, rather daring industrial and social adventure. For a dozen years in that long-ago time before the war it was the custom to refer to it as "the social experiment station of the world." A few American travelers discovered it to be also a country of rare scenic beauty, a wonderful tourist playground, but Miss Mander shows the little Dominion to us now as a country rich in fictional material, dowered by nature with scenic backgrounds of surpassing loveliness and fascination and peopled by men and women of varied and interesting types, where personality is prone to make its own way regardless of conventions, and problems of life and conduct take on new shapes and colors.

This new story from Miss Mander's pen [*The Passionate Puritan*], is a tale of the working out of two personalities under their reciprocal influence upon each other and under the influence of their surroundings. It is scened, as was her previous novel, in the northern part of the North Island of New Zealand, in the timber land where lumbering operations are going on in the mighty forests of the magnificent kauri pine. Therefore, in both stories, the surroundings correspond somewhat to those primitive frontier conditions in our own country which we have always believed ought to be productive of great fiction but which, with the exception of Cooper's romances, have yielded scarcely any of consequence. But Miss Mander has several possibilities in her favor which she has utilized cleverly and with striking effect. For she has in her frontier conditions the precious element of striking contrasts which were almost wholly absent with us even up to the time when our frontier disappeared before the onward rush of civilization. The globe-trotting Englishman with his tradition of culture penetrates to all parts of the colonies and, as one of the characters in **The Passionate Puritan** remarks, "You can meet an Oxford accent all the way from a gumhut to a university." Sometimes he is a drunken derelict, and a down-and-outer of the saddest sort may prove to be a scion of nobility who will unexpectedly reveal the manners and the speech of breeding and education. What we have always called "the frontier" the New Zealanders call "the bush," which means the virgin forest, and "the back-blocks," which means a region into which civilization has penetrated with its first outposts and where it is making the first effort to conquer the wild, whether by farming or lumbering or mining. But for a generation and more these back-blocks—and there began to be backblocks in New Zealand only two generations ago—have felt the breath of modern intellectual inquiry and demand, quest and progress. And this intellectual stir, bound to be brought into almost every remote corner by some person newly come from the outer world, by books and magazines and papers, produces still another contrast, another possibility of clash of motive and character. Such contrasts and clashes were not possible in the time of our own frontier days, for several reasons.

Both these opportunities for contrast Miss Mander has used in her novels with an understanding of their value and a skill in utilizing them which add greatly to the interest of the stories. In **The Passionate Puritan** a clever and attractive young woman, whose mind is foursquare and open to all the intellectual winds that blow, and whose temperament is quickly responsive, goes from Auckland—Auckland which Kipling sang as "last, loneliest and loveliest" of the cities of the empire—as a school teacher in a newly-organized school in a tiny settlement of the lumber region.... The story is mainly concerned with the reactions of this very attractive young woman to the scenic surroundings, the activities of the place, the varied experiences which befall her as an important citizen, and especially to the influence which Arthur Devereux, wandering young Englishman of leisure and culture, and husband of a superfluous wife somewhere back in England, soon begins to cast upon her. Their attraction for each other and their intellectual and temperamental pleasure in each other's society carry them along to the point where the absent wife must be considered, and where the girl must consider not only her feeling for him but also her attitude toward his tendency, which she discovers and holds up to him with scorn and anger, to indulge in casual and irresponsible love affairs with as little concern about them afterward as an alley cat feels for its amorous adventures. Something within her, complicated of many elements, curbs her Old Adam's willingness to become another of his adventures and enables her, a "puritan" still, though a "passionate" one, to discipline both herself and him and hold matters with a hand more or less steady until she regains her trust in him and the future opens before them.

The girl's struggle with herself and her controversy with her lover, which she carries on with an open mind and with willingness to face all the facts of life, are portrayed with dramatic touches, with knowledge of the innermost recesses of the human heart and with a rapid evolution that keeps it always interesting. The spirit of comedy, moreover, hovers over it constantly. There is interplay of influence between the two characters that adds much to the interest and the reader watches the glimpses of Devereux's development from the time he asks himself, with anticipatory relish, "Is she that kind?" until he drinks his toast "To monogamy, and may it be as interesting as it ought to be," with almost as much curiosity as to its

outcome the struggle of the girl, portrayed much more intimately, arouses.

But the love story, while it furnishes the chief personal thread of the novel, is only one of its several claims upon the reader's attention. The minor characters, of whom there are many, all show striking freshness and vitality in their presentation, even when the reader gets but a glimpse. The author always senses the essential, the outstanding in character, and with a sweeping stroke or two of a colorful brush sets the individual before you, very much alive. There are variety and contrast among these few people of the tiny milling settlement, from Jack Ridgefield, the young boss, silent, capable, forceful, whom the heroine and her lover nickname as "the eye of God," because he is always where he is needed, to Mrs. Bill Hardy and her unassorted brood of nobody knew how many fathers. And, colorful and characteristic touch in a New Zealand novel, there is Mana, the handsome and cultured Maori woman with her tasteful home and her intellectual tastes hidden away on a little farm nearby, where the heroine finds understanding and companionship. The reader is likely to find as perplexing as does the heroine Mana's point of view with regard to sexual morality, but the author has indicated with skill the typical, bred-in-the-bone, Polynesian conception of the inconsequentialness of sexual relations. The heroine is interested and amused, and equally so is the reader, by the social grades and barriers, the social relaxations and experiments of the community, about which Miss Mander makes many pithy comments.

The American reader will get from both these novels not a little illumination on a subject which to him is always a bit puzzling, because it offers so many apparent contradictions—the attitude of the Australasian colonial toward the mother country. Perhaps one should say the attitude of the New Zealander, for there is observable a subtle but distinct change in that attitude when one crosses the Tasman Sea and lands in Australia. But Miss Mander, in her two novels, partly by her own interpretative comments, but mainly by her characters themselves, throws interesting rays of light on every phase of that attitude as it manifests itself in New Zealand. The variety of that feeling, which is likely to run the whole gamut from devoted love to scorn and derision in any single individual, is one of the unique and fascinating characteristics of the island Dominion and Miss Mander gives it accurate and delightful embodiment. At its base is a filial devotion which leads the New Zealander, even though he may be of the second generation born on the islands and may never have been off them, to speak always of England as "home" and always to write "Home," when he means England, with a capital letter, although he is likely the next moment to launch into scathing criticism of England's social, political and industrial shortcomings. Miss Mander puts a little of that basic feeling into these eloquent words:

> No Englishman is capable of feeling for London that concentrated reverence and yearning that comes to the dreaming colonist on a New Zealand hilltop or an Australian plain. To most of them London has the painful lure of the unattainable—the mournfulness of saying year after year, "Perhaps I can manage it next," and of fearing the while that it won't be managed. But the illusion is hugged and fed and never allowed to die. There is always the prospect that something may happen and one may get there at last.... No one can tell you what it means to him. It is just London, sung from the tongue, with a comprehensive smile and something indefinable in the eyes.

Both New Zealand and Australia have furnished literature by native writers worthy of attention by American readers, and there ought to be much interest here, much more than there ever has been, in Australasian books. Several novels have come in recent years from that region as excellent as Miss Mander's two stories of New Zealand life—books that are written with skill and understanding, that tell fascinating stories and are vivid with native color, that deal with a life and a people nearer to us in spirit, in conditions, in background and in feeling than are novels from England.

"New Zealand in Fiction and Reality," in The New York Times Book Review, *June 12, 1921, p. 15.*

THE NEW YORK TIMES BOOK REVIEW   (essay date 1922)

[*In the following excerpt, the reviewer commends the vividly portrayed New Zealand settings of Mander's first three novels and comments on the interesting depiction of feminist issues in* The Strange Attraction.]

It adds much to the pleasure afforded by a good story to find it scened in some strange, far land against whose unfamiliar background is shown the same human nature with which the reader is so well acquainted in his own vicinity. And when that scene has the wild loveliness of antipodean New Zealand and is depicted with such a sure, intimate and skillful touch as Miss Mander possesses, the background can furnish—although the proportion depends much on the temperament of the reader—an important part of the satisfaction to be found in the book. Miss Mander's stories, however, are intrinsically very interesting, notwithstanding the amount of allure she can put into their setting. [*The Strange Attraction*] is her third novel since she came to New York and made her bid for the favor of the American public with her first book, *The Story of a New Zealand River,* some four or five years ago. This was followed last year by *The Passionate Puritan,* also scened in the back country of New Zealand.

The action of this new novel takes place in a little coast town at the mouth of a river in the northern part of the North Island, not far from Auckland. Further north are the kauri forests, port of missing men whom life has shipwrecked and their relatives have lost. But they merely show faintly in the background of the tale as a source of mystery and romance. The story itself is very much alive and in touch with life and the present. As always in Miss Mander's fiction, the spirit of the modern woman in revolt glows through it like a continuous flash of lightning. It is interesting to see the same spirit flaming up on that far New Zealand shore that long ago began to create unrest among American women and marched militantly on toward freedom in England. Miss Mander has caught the essential essence of the spirit and its revolt, which is more than can be said of some of the American and British novelists who have tried to picture it in words. Her Valerie Carr is a woman who might belong in any English-speaking country and is representative of the longing to achieve freedom from conventional and stifling and useless bonds. She belongs to a family of aristocratic lineage who are leaders of the most exclusive society in Auckland, where her father is the leading lawyer. But she wants none of their diversions of society and bridge and husband hunting. Instead, she is determined to set forth on her responsibility, to achieve financial independence, to investigate life, to see the world. When the reader meets her on the first page of the story she is taking her first steps toward all this free and glorious future, having got the position of assistant on a tri-weekly paper

in the little coast town of 2,000 inhabitants. When the young man who is the editor and manager of the paper—he is the son of the Bishop of Auckland—hopes on her arrival that she will like it she tells him, "I don't care a cuss if I don't. I shall stay till I've got all I can out of it."

Miss Mander has succeeded in making the reader feel the superb vitality of this girl. Her self-centredness, her ruthlessness, her determination to express herself in life, her crudity, her attractiveness, her warmly human qualities, are all made evident in her own actions and speech. She is not only the essence of woman in revolt everywhere, she is also herself, a clearly conceived and vividly realized personality, and she is also, in addition, definitely a product of her own distant land. So complete and so alive is she that almost any novelist might be proud to have created her. The other women in the story are the merest casual shadows, but it has several men and each of them definitely stands out, a personality in his own right. The story is largely concerned with Valerie's love for one of them, a writer of Australasian fame, and with how their romance fares. The author has the instinct for good story telling and she offers in this book a story rather better and decidedly better told than she gave in her previous books. She is making good with the promise held out in her earlier work.

"'A Strange Attraction'," in The New York Times Book Review, *October 29, 1922, p. 12.*

J. C. REID   (essay date 1946)

[*Reid is a New Zealand critic, biographer, and poet who has edited several anthologies of New Zealand prose. In the following excerpt from his* Creative Writing in New Zealand: A Brief Critical History, *he discusses Mander's four novels with New Zealand settings as products of the newly liberalized literary climate that followed World War I, focusing on the strengths and weaknesses of* The Story of a New Zealand River.]

The effect of the 1914-18 war in producing cynicism and exclusive scepticism in writing was not immediately apparent in New Zealand, although it contributed its part to the radicalism of several later writers. The war left its mark in two other directions, however; first, in an intensification of the writers' sense of New Zealand, with some relaxing of self-consciousness. Possibly New Zealand's awareness of her nationhood as a result of her worthy contribution to the war-effort was a strong factor in this process. In any case, New Zealand themes and settings were used with greater freedom, but with more poise and assurance than before.

The second result, in line with world-wide tendencies, was that the attitude to moral codes was weakened and radical ideas on sex and politics became more evident. These came, as most things come, a little late to New Zealand, since Shaw and Wells had been pounding at the bastions of conventional morality for many years. With the influx of "modern" views, a great deal of the earlier priggishness and naïveté disappeared from New Zealand fiction. In the same process, while nobody went so far as some English writers, many important restraints vanished also, resulting in, among other things, the sensationalism of Jean Devanny and the adolescent naughtiness of parts of Robin Hyde's novels.

Liberal views of this kind showed themselves strikingly in women, who predominated in fiction in the early twenties. The first of these was Jane Mander who, between 1920 and 1925, wrote four novels with New Zealand settings, *The Story of a New Zealand River, The Passionate Puritan, The Strange At-*

traction and *Allen Adair. The Story of a New Zealand River* is one of the most widely-read of all New Zealand novels. If it is, however, as Alan Mulgan says it is, "considered by some to be the best New Zealand novel" [see Mulgan entry in Additional Bibliography], it does not say a great deal for New Zealand fiction.

The title suggests that the book is an imitation of Olive Schreiner's *Story of an African Farm,* and this is borne out by the common "feminist" mood of both novels, and the similarity between the sexual morality and the agnosticism preached in their pages. In Jane Mander's novel, the ideas on the emancipation of women, on freer relations between the sexes and all the "reforms" of the "advanced" thinkers find expression in the education of the sensitive, inhibited Alice Roland by her modern daughter, Asia, and the inevitable remittance man, David Bruce.

This kind of thing is typical:

> My dear, do you really believe that a girl is branded in some mysterious way if she has relations with a man on the prehistoric side of the marriage ceremony? Do you think the failure to repeat a few words alters cells?
>
> It alters minds, David.
>
> Oh, no. It's the attitude of other people towards your action that affects your mind when it is affected. There is nothing in the action itself that does it.

It is not surprising that the book was received with considerable indignation on its first publication, although (*O tempora, o mores!*) it seems to have provoked no such reaction when reissued in 1938. The novel has some merit. Many of the characters are vividly realized. But its chief quality is the picture it conveys of life in the timber-milling settlements of the Kaipara district. Like Satchell's books, it has a definite sense of place; there is the feeling of North Auckland in it.

In her other novels as well, Jane Mander related her plots intimately to aspects of the New Zealand setting. Apart from this, her work exhibits many crudities. In *The Story of a New Zealand River* there is a banal plot, thinly drawn out, and a conventional solution in which a superfluous husband is removed by a fatal accident. The dialogue is sometimes on the level of a cheap romance, and, despite some insight into human nature, the emotional situations are often improbable. Altogether, whatever its merits, *The Story of a New Zealand River* is just the kind of book that helps to create the widespread prejudice against most women novelists.

But Jane Mander's novels do show a certain level of taste and intelligence, and make some claim to be regarded as serious works. (pp. 52-3)

> *J. C. Reid, "Fiction to the Present Day," in his* Creative Writing in New Zealand: A Brief Critical History, *Whitcombe and Tombs Limited, 1946, pp. 49-66.*

ALAN MULGAN (essay date 1962)

[Mulgan was a New Zealand novelist and critic. In the following excerpt from his Great Days in New Zealand Writing, *he pronounces* The Story of a New Zealand River *important for its introduction of realism in style and subject matter to New Zealand fiction.]*

[*The Story of a New Zealand River*], took the New Zealand novel into fresh ground, the realities of life. Probably the adjective most frequently applied to it has been "sophisticated." Applied to fiction, the terms "sophisticated" and "sophistication" mean degrees of realism in dealing with sex. In this respect *The Story of a New Zealand River* was very sophisticated for its time (published in 1920) though today it might be considered quite average. The book is about life in the timber industry on the Kaipara Harbour, in North Auckland. Opposite, on the other side of the island, is Whangarei, the chief town of Northland. With the reservation that the Mander family moved about a lot—twenty-nine times in a few years, Jane Mander said in an interview—Whangerei can be said to have been Jane's home town. *The Story of a New Zealand River* was written in the tower of the Manders's big house Pukenui, which stands on the high bank of the Whangarei River above the town. But the book shocked Whangarei, as it did many people elsewhere. At the Whangarei Public Library it was put on the "discretionary shelf", in the librarian's office, to be given to people of suitable maturity and signed for.

It was certainly strong meat in those days. Marital and extra-marital relations are an integral part of the story. From the memorable opening, where David Bruce meets Alice Roland and her children to row them down the river on the Kaipara to their new home, a very remarkable romance begins which is not resolved till the end of the long book, years later. Bruce is a young doctor in the general employment of Tom Roland, timber miller, and becomes his partner. Tom has married Alice, a destitute widow with one child, partly out of pity, partly for social reasons. Alice bears more children to her husband, whom she does not love, and pregnancy is mentioned as a matter of course. As the only doctor available, David has to attend Alice in her first confinement. Tom is notoriously promiscuous. Arriving at womanhood, the lively and intelligent eldest daughter, who has been supposed to be an unsophisticated country child, reveals in comment how much experience can be picked in such a home in a backblocks timber village. "Why don't our parents realise that we children have eyes to see and ears to hear?"

New Zealand inherited the Puritan tradition, which included a taboo on sex discussions. One may surmise that for many readers the seriousness with which Jane Mander treated the theme was not sufficient to break down the old barrier. She poses the question how much the moral law and the conventions should weigh in sex decisions, as these considerations affect the destiny of her diverse characters.

But no more of this just now. The success of the novel has *not* depended on sexual problems. It is also an epic story of a long dramatic and at times tragic development in North Auckland—the cutting out of the kauri [New Zealand pine]. Like William Satchell's classic, *The Land of the Lost,* it breathes the spirit of the North. In this case the scene is the bush and its waters, and the material theme is the energy with which living nature was despoiled. The time is the turn of the century, when the wasteful treatment of the kauri forest and its fire risk were in blast. (pp. 84-5)

[In the novel] Tom Roland pits himself against nature and all the other hazards of the timber-getting business. He is driven near to bankruptcy, but he wins. Jane Mander knew this kind of struggle well, as she knew the whole setting. Her father, Frank Mander, spent years at it in the North. "He built and organised timber mills," she told her interviewer. "As soon as one was up, he went off to another spot, taking his family with him." For twenty years Mander was member of Parliament for Marsden, a local electorate, and after that he was in the Legislative Council. So Jane saw life in the primitive. She met many unusual types and learned to live without luxury of any kind. It should be added that she was a much-travelled woman, with wide experience of the world. She was associate editor of a paper in Whangarei, went to Australia, studied at Columbia University, New York, lived in that city for some years, and was a reader for publishers in London. She wrote other novels but none had the success of *The Story of a New Zealand River.*

With such experiences, Jane would not find it difficult to describe realistically Tom's gang of men; "old men and young men; men of finished and unassuming blackguardism, and crude youngsters swaggering with first knowledge. . . . English university men bunked next to the colonial-born sons of pioneer traders. The men who still got literary reviews and scented letters read side by side with those who revelled in Deadwood Dicks and got no letters at all." The one thing the motley group would not stand and could detect instantly was "side." Tom Roland, vital, thrusting, and capable, was a real king of his realm. Careless and insensitive in his home, so that he meant little or nothing to his children, loose in his morals, Tom was liked by all his workers. "He worked with them. He ate with them. He swore with them. He was extraordinarily fair with them. He had a way all his own of being familiar, and yet, at the same time, commanding their respect." Once when there was no money to pay wages, the men worked on without. When at the end of the story he was accidentally killed in the tide of the prosperity he had built up, the whole district mourned him.

Jane Mander also takes a look at the gumdigger, and a sombre picture she paints of what to her, as to Satchell, is the land of the lost. The most poignant scene in the book is the visit of the eldest Roland girl and her Australian lover to a lonely gumdigger dying of tuberculosis in a hut made of sacking on a tea-tree frame, a common kind of dwelling. The man dies as Asia tends him. "These gum-fields are the saddest places in the world," declares Asia.

One difference between Satchell and Jane Mander is in dialogue. Satchell used the stilted speech that was conventional in much Victorian fiction. Jane Mander did much to set New Zealand fiction on the road of naturalism in talk. The main human drama of the novel is long, complex and tense. Jane Mander set herself a formidable task in depicting the domestic triangle of Alice, the highly conventional, Puritan-minded immigrant, unfitted for grappling with the roughnesses of life; Tom Roland, the coarse-grained and straying husband; the cultivated, understanding young doctor, friend of both. Jane loaded the dice against herself by giving Alice a secret, which has strengthened her resistance to change, but is not revealed till near the end. David has his secret too, and is liable to bouts of drinking. There is a conspicuous irony in the situation. David is free in his ideas about love. He considers that men and women have the right to live together without marriage if they are sincere in pursuit of happiness. Ultimately he advises Asia, the daughter, to this effect when she falls in love with a married man. Yet, through a long lapse of time, though he and Alice, thrown closely together, are strongly attracted to each other, David keeps his emotions in check. His sense of honour in a position of trust holds him back. When at length there is a confession of feeling in Alice's presence, Tom expresses astonishment that the two have *not* been lovers. What else could

he suppose he asks. That is what men do. When David explodes in wrath at the imputation, Tom splutters out that he had failed to win his wife's love; he owed David a good deal, and thought he could do him a good turn by leaving it open to him to take Alice! Tom has the grace to end up his defence by bursting into sobs. The friendship and partnership between the two remain unbroken. It is an extraordinary scene, but credible.

Alice is an unsympathetic character. Many readers must have wished to shake the snobbishness and general malady of reserve out of her. We know her type of Briton—though it is less frequently met with now—who regards the "worker" as a class apart, and shows it. When Alice first meets David, she takes him for this, and is distant to him, though he is helping her. I should have thought four years in New Zealand would have smoothed away some of this exclusiveness. Besides, we are told her father was a Presbyterian. If he were a Scot, his daughter would not have been like that. Bruce does his best to break down what Jane calls an aloofness from anything she does not like, amounting to mania. We do get glimpses but not enough, of the attractiveness attributed to her. A foil to the unsure self-consciousness of Alice is the old English lady, Mrs Brayton, who has made a beautiful home in this wilderness. Paying a first call in silk gown and and carrying a card case, Mrs Brayton may seem a figure of fun, but her type is also established in our society. Many a cultivated Englishwoman has made a happy home in the New Zealand countryside because she has been brought up to feel that she is never "lost," intellectually or socially. Such people make the best of the new world while retaining and diffusing the charm and experience of the old. (pp. 87-9)

The logging accident by which Alice and David are freed may seem contrived, but so are many such untyings of knots in novels, not excluding the great. It happens in the course of Tom's work, and his recklessness and self-sacrifice are in character. *The Story of a New Zealand River* is a notable mark in the development of New Zealand novel—notable for its wider and more realistic concept of life, its character-drawing, its presentation of the New Zealand scene, and the freer style in the writing. (p. 89)

Alan Mulgan, "The Story of a New Zealand River," in his Great Days in New Zealand Writing, A. H. & A. W. Reed, 1962, pp. 84-9.

DOROTHEA TURNER (essay date 1972)

[*Turner is a New Zealand critic. In the following excerpt from her critical biography* Jane Mander, *she surveys public and critical reaction to Mander's novels, focusing on the response to her work in New Zealand.*]

[Jane Mander] had no writing of relevance to offer publicly until her first—and best—novel, when she was forty-three. (p. 130)

Overseas reviews of *The River* were encouraging; critics noted the strengths as well as the stumblings; in the United States and Australia they were openly pleased to read about a little-known country. The *New York Times,* the *New Republic,* and the *Sydney Mail* featured it; the *San Francisco Bulletin,* the *Boston Transcript,* and Katherine Mansfield in the *Athenaeum* [see excerpt dated 1920] considered it at length.

New Zealand newspapers for the most part swept it under the carpet, having no precedents for judging local literature. The *New Zealand Herald,* the Auckland morning paper, in 350 words under a very small heading wrote sensibly enough: "What matters most—whether or not one accepts Miss Mander's challenge—is that this is a real novel, written of a real New Zealand, which can enter the lists in any large reading town of the world and command attention." The reservation is unstressed: "It is a weakness, one thinks, that a girl of eighteen should solve her love problem as she does—the standard of decision is too early for good public morality." The *Dominion*, a Wellington newspaper, in brief but quite enthusiastic treatment gently sounded the notes that were to prevail for the decade: "The author . . . by the way is the daughter of a much-respected member of the New Zealand Parliament. . . . Her novel comes under the category of 'sex-problem' fiction."

In Whangarei, the home town, *The River* went on the Public Library's discretionary list, to be lent only to approved adults who made special application; it stayed on the "Reserved" shelf in the librarian's private room with *Tess of the d'Urbervilles* and *The Water Gypsies*. In Port Albert a subscriber took it upon herself to withdraw it as unfit, present residents skeptically recall. Other northerners testify that the book was kept from them as youngsters, to be handed over when they were "old enough." But the north had the peculiar and personal difficulty of its respect for the Mander family; embarrassment was in the air, and it was too decent to want to draw in the young. The northern "censorship" was a special case.

Most well-read youngsters of the day grew up without hearing of *The River* simply because New Zealand literature was outside consideration. University entrance scholarships, even degrees in English, went through in that decade without reference to New Zealand books. The few who were conscious of a need for their own regional literature were still too few to be effective; the forces against a book did not have to be strong to finish it. Between distaste and indifference—in proportions impossible now to determine—*The River* was lost.

The unspoken difficulty was that Jane Mander had written a story in which the reading public might see parallels between the principals and her family. Knowing as a novelist that the family setting had been only a starting point for her imagination, she did not foresee the literal identifications New Zealand readers would make—a habit of theirs which was to hound succeeding novelists into putting fictitious names to the towns of their stories and into other furtive devices. As late as 1961 the *New Zealand Listener* was forced by a naïve correspondent into editorial defense of writers:

> People often dislike a story and write to say what they think is wrong with it. At such times we are always interested to notice how many readers want to discuss stories as if they were factual narratives. . . . Our pragmatic temper reveals itself in a reluctance to make any concession to fancy. Artistic effect, which must be the writer's aim, is disregarded. Writers are judged, again and again, on questions of fact which for them are of secondary importance or barely relevant.

That some of the facts of *The River* were literally true naturally confused unsophisticated readers and played into the hands of the unsympathetic. The place names were all real: Kaiwaka showed on the map; Point Curtis was a tiny headland with wharf and pub—just as in the book—in use for those few years of milling. Therefore Tom Roland must be Frank Mander; it was not too implausible that Asia was Jane Mander, and how much of the rest might not be "true"? Looking at the story this way we can see how dreadful the implications could be.

If there had been any previous experience of the impact of a realistic novel about a small New Zealand area, Jane Mander could have seen how it might be construed and given camouflage. If she had stayed in her own country to write, she must have been aware of how it would read there—so much so that the book would probably not have amounted to anything. We owe its creative strength to the freedom New York gave her to be a novelist. But if the result was to bring soreness where she hoped it would be only the cause of pride, the wound, in the long run, may have been greatest of all to herself. If her innocent spontaneity had misfired, could she allow it to recharge itself?

We do not know how soon repercussions reached the author. Mails were slow; it took about a month each way for letters, longer for parcels of books. New Zealand booksellers tended to wait for the English edition (which was some months later in this case) and to "wait and see" on principle before ordering a book with a New Zealand setting. Knowledge of the reception would creep in slowly; the second novel was almost certainly in the press and the third one at least drafted before Jane Mander would have a real idea of the reckoning in New Zealand.

Reviews of *The Passionate Puritan* the next year ranged from a full page in the *New York Times Book Review* [see excerpt dated 1921], attractively though incongruously illustrated with photos of Milford Sound and of Rotorua Maoris dancing to welcome the Prince of Wales, to three inches of admonition in the *New Zealand Herald*, ending: "Has not the sex problem become somewhat of an obsession with many modern novelists? Jane Mander's description of the bush fire and of the men who fought it, is fine. This kind of thing we really look for in New Zealand fiction." The Wellington morning paper said reasonably enough that it was not up to her previous book and concluded, six inches later: "It is a pity Miss Mander does not give us a story of New Zealand country life, which would be free from the sex problem motif which has been over-prominent in the present story and its predecessor." She was now doomed in New Zealand by being named as a sex-problem specialist. The word "sex" was itself to be avoided in conversation; classrooms of teen-aged girls would blush if it turned up in a botany lesson, and teachers went to much trouble to avoid it.

When *The Strange Attraction* arrived the next year, reviewers consolidated the old positions: the Americans found points to criticize in the writing but were pleased to read about a strange place; the British took the writing seriously, for better or worse, but were unenthusiastic about the setting; New Zealand reviewers kept to morality:

> One can have nothing but the highest praise for the use she makes of the inanimate material she has at her disposal. The *Post's* London correspondent regrets the combination of what one may call the "sex" novel and the New Zealand bush country as unnecessary and misleading. (*Evening Post*, Wellington.)

> It is a great pity that Miss Jane Mander, the New Zealand novelist whose first story, *The New Zealand River,* was so well reviewed both in London and New York, should continue to be so obsessed by sex problems. (The *Dominion*, Wellington.)

> It is somewhat unfortunate that Miss Mander's heroine is so determined to confuse the "freedom" of woman with a much older profession. Nor is it complimentary to the New Zealand girl, that what other readers may be led into thinking is a typical Aucklander, should punctuate her conversation with "Hell," should drink beer (though Miss Mander carefully terms

it "ale") in the dining room of a rough country hotel, not because she particularly likes it, one feels sure, but merely to emphasise her distinction from what she would call "wowsers"—in short, an out-and-out pose! This Remuera girl (why this hit at Remuera in particular?). . . . (*New Zealand Herald.*)

The *Auckland Star,* quite out of step, found enough good for a kindly column and a half. But if a novel is reckoned to have undesirable aspects, its innocuous pages will not save it; and once again the author was evilly served by the dustjacket—still to be seen with the Alexander Turnbull Library's copy—which even overseas reviewers castigated for its lurid and repellent blonde. Jane Mander replied at last, in a letter from London to the *Auckland Star:*

> As you were interested enough to publish the most impersonal review I have yet seen from the New Zealand Press of my third novel, and one that gave unusually representative quotations, I ask space to reply through your columns to some of the remarks of my New Zealand critics.
>
> I really cannot understand why some of them call me sex-obsessed. Am I being compared out there with the publications of the Religious Tract Society? If I am being compared, as I should be, with the modern novel writers on this side of the world, that term cannot truthfully be applied to me. As a matter of fact I'm not half sexy enough for hundreds of thousands of readers here. The people who read my books here read them for the New Zealand colour, and certainly not for the sex element. I can think of only one review I have seen in the Old World that used the term in connection with my work. . . .

It is ironically true that her books are "not half sexy enough" for popularity in that their love interest is inherently unmoving, being mind-dominated and calculating sometimes to the point of incredibility; because of the strongly supporting social context of these affairs, readers can suppress some of their impatience with the love interest per se. Professional reviewers of the Old World were not likely to confuse theme and treatment, but in New Zealand they pounced on the word, as censors do. "I'm going to keep on believing," Jane Mander continued, "that my native land is producing about the same number of intelligent adults per thousand of the population as any other British country. It is unfortunate that the general newspaper has to be run for the average person, but at least the average person need not be misinformed."

> I have been accused of putting into my third book characters who are "unrepresentative" of the community in which they are placed. Now a writer who is trying to be an artist, as I sincerely am, has nothing whatever to do with being a tourist agent, or a photographer, or a historian, or a compiler of community statistics. The question for critics is, not did two such people as Valerie Carr and Dane Barrington ever actually live in Dargaville, but might they have lived there? And the answer is that exceptional people may be found anywhere. And even if it has to be a question of fact, anyone who ever lived in the North of New Zealand for many years, as I did, must have been struck over and over again, by finding the most unlikely people in out-of-the-way places. If there was one thing significant about our North it was just that. I could not begin to put into books all the "unrepresentative" people we came across in the bushes, about the gumfields, and in the small towns. . . .
>
> But I can assure my critics I am not "hitting" at anything. . . . Nobody knows better than I that I have

> a lot to learn, and . . . that to be an artist one must not be petty. . . . Nobody who reads my books here will suppose that Dargaville is any different from the countless small towns all over the world, or that the fashionable suburb of Remuera is any worse than any other fashionable suburb simply because my unconventional character came out of it. Really we writers are not taken as literally as all that.
>
> And, furthermore, I am not trying to shock anybody. I am writing to please myself, without any thought as to whether I am pleasing or annoying or shocking anybody else. If an artist stops to consider any section of his public, or what his friends would like, or what his publisher would like, or anything at all but that inner light inside himself, he ceases to be an artist and becomes a purveyor of goods. Unfortunately there are too many purveyors of goods trying to masquerade as artists in the world today. I am simply trying to be honest and to be loyal to my own experience.

Eighteen months later the *London Mercury* carried a brief survey of New Zealand literature from Alan Mulgan in Auckland with this conclusion:

> New Zealand literature, however, cannot live wholly in the past. The work of the living proceeds, amid many difficulties; Miss Mander has written three novels of New Zealand life and is writing a fourth. She announces, however, that if she does not get more encouragement from her own country, she will write no more about it. In some candid counsel to New Zealanders who aspire to London success, she says . . . that although she is supposed to have had a considerable literary success in England and America, and has enjoyed a good Press, she is today hundreds of pounds to the bad. . . . Perhaps Miss Rosemary Rees, whose *Heather of the South* has been running serially in New Zealand, will be more successful financially. This is a more conventional and less ambitious novel than those of Miss Mander, and has that pleasantness of romance and unclouded happiness of ending (besides some excellent local colour) which the average New Zealander, not differing in this respect from other British publics, prefers.

Jane Mander's "candid counsel" had been a column in New Zealand papers urging young artists to stay away from London unless they had a safe occupation or money to fall back on; unembittered as always, and conceding that writers are better off than painters or musicians, she lays it down in terms of rent and royalties what "considerable success" such as hers adds up to. "Then, on the colonial sale, we writers get threepence a copy. Calculate again how many copies we must sell to our sceptical or admiring compatriots before we make £10 out of those who should be proud to shake us by the hand." Printings of her novels had been up to two thousand copies in America and England; she can scarcely have made £10 out of any of them in New Zealand. The unprovocative *Allen Adair* in 1925 did little for her. Two or three approved writers of "pleasantness" continued to flourish, and in 1926 Jean Devanny's first novel, *The Butcher Shop,* offered a formula for successful unpleasantness. This book gallops along with a violent sensuality which can still strike one as wilfully outrageous. The New Zealand board of censors banned it; the author reported her publishers delighted with its sales which reached fifteen thousand.

The only readers Jane Mander and Jean Devanny have in common are those who set themselves to read New Zealand fiction right through, but these authors shared the experience of testing local reaction to the idea that life in their country was less smooth than the carefully protected public image of it. The unsmiling belief in placid progress would admit no eccentricity, somber or gay. Confused and humbled by the depression of the 1930's, New Zealanders came at last to countenance various versions of their society—with protective gasps at first—but by the 1960's open to the implications of Janet Frame, Sylvia Ashton-Warner, and Ian Cross. New Zealand novels have in fact run ahead of the prediction made by Robin Hyde (who hailed Jane Mander as a "modern") that "they won't be surface compilations of the cheerful commonplaces of life."

> I venture to make this prophecy. The best New Zealand literary work written in the next fifty years will bear the stamp of oddity. This is because, whether you like it or not, New Zealand is an extremely odd place, and the tenement of moody spirits. Look out for them when they get going.

The New Zealand Jane Mander returned to in 1932 knew vaguely that she had been controversial but would have been hard put to it to say what she had written. The novels were not in evidence; the legend itself was already distorted: a long survey of New Zealand literature in *The Bookman* in February, 1930, said that "receiving scant support from her own people, she left for America with the avowed intention of writing no more of New Zealand. With her departure it may be said that there

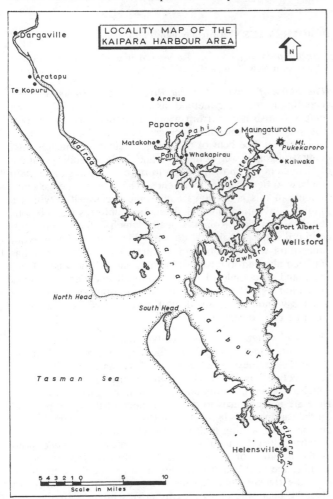

New Zealand's Kaipara Harbour area. Reprinted by permission of Auckland University Press.

are none now writing novels of New Zealand life." Her presence in Auckland possibly aroused some interest in her books, but the country's changing temper probably had more to do with it; neither trend can have seemed very marked to the aging and unproductive author, and the major improvement in the country's disposition—an almost explosive movement toward liberation, diversity, and identity—began later, about the year of her death. By 1938 there was just enough persistent demand for *The River* to embolden her to arrange its reissue by other publishers, one of them in New Zealand.

Reviewing was now in the hands of professional writers: Frank Sargeson in the *Auckland Star*, and, in the South, C. R. Allen in the *Otago Daily Times* and M. H. Holcroft in the Christchurch *Press* all had space for proper appraisal. By 1960 another edition was needed, and here the State Literary Fund came forward to bridge the gap between high publishing costs and small population. It was on most college reading lists by this time, quite widely known and oddly at ease among recent novels; only the dates and an occasional long memory drew attention to the solitariness of its first appearance. *The River* had become the book against which phases of New Zealand's literary awareness could be measured.

The old attitude and the new met for one more duel in the *New Zealand Listener* in 1955, when a correspondent complained about the Gillespie Radio Portrait:

> Miss Mander appears to have been a forthright woman, but the world is full of forthright women and unfortunately full also of women, who, thinking they have a greater brain than their sisters, write books. If the BBC made programmes on every woman who had written a few books and acted the suffragette they would be overloaded with dull features.
>
> . . . If we have had no geniuses in the arts I can't see that it matters very much: there are plenty of international ones to go round. In our isolation, Mr. Gillespie could bring the rest of the world closer by compiling programmes on some of the truly great artists.
>
> It seems a pity we have to call Miss Mander "one of our most important writers" because it only shows our poor source of selection. She is not an important writer, but if she really is one of *our* most important then we should keep it quiet and certainly not broadcast the fact. Why don't we face it? We've never had anyone of real literary worth (I can hear the roar), but after all Miss Mansfield only reads well if one hasn't read Tchekov. . . .

In an editorial, "Who Was Jane Mander?", the journal answered that she "was indeed forthright; more important she was honest about herself as well as other people, and she would never have pretended that she had any claims to genius. . . . But she was one of the first New Zealanders to write novels with a genuine flavour of life in this country. . . . and people who were not young in those days may scarcely imagine the bareness of the literary scene. . . . Moreover Jane Mander's personal story exemplified the struggle of all our writers: the turbulent youth and the frustration, the travels abroad, the attempt to establish an imaginative hold upon a country in which not enough people have lived and died. . . ." The editor continues:

> A national literature, modest though it may be, has functions and values which cannot be supplied from outside; and these are not weakened or destroyed because better books have been published elsewhere.

Books that are written here are helping us to strengthen our foothold on two islands in the Pacific; they are products of an experience which cannot be complete until it has been lived again in the imagination.

Two attitudes stand in the way: an uncritical enthusiasm which inflates New Zealand writing beyond its true worth, and a sweeping denigration. Between these extremes is, of course, the placid indifference of the multitude, but writers are, or should be, used to it and need not be dismayed. The extremes of opinion are dangerous, not because they silence writers or lift them to a spurious reputation, but because they interfere with critical standards. No attempt has been made to exalt Jane Mander beyond her real achievement. . . . She has been introduced to a new generation of New Zealanders because, apart from her work as a writer, she was an extremely interesting person whose friends remember her with affection and respect. She influenced many people, including younger writers; and her imprint on New Zealand letters, although not deep, is firm and clear. Detraction cannot harm her; but it can harm the rest of us, much more than some of us may realise, if we allow it to pass unchallenged.

"Uncritical enthusiasm" has been a minor problem compared with the more prevalent "sweeping denigration"—an attitude in which critics have often seemed primarily concerned to demonstrate their own acquaintance with "the truly great." When desire for a regional literature came to be felt, some New Zealand critics were guilty of applying yet another pressure: instead of fostering numbers for safety they tended, like ambitious parents of only children, to look for "the great New Zealand novel" from any writer who dared humbly to exist. Most of these obstructions have been dispersed during the 1960's as the thoroughly diverse talents of a number of new novelists have taught the country to rely on a literature rather than on a few named books.

Though technically clumsy compared with some of the moderns, Jane Mander would seem to have gained more than she has lost by becoming part of a concourse. It is one that sees no need to repudiate her; all that is lost is her isolation and her compatriots' naïveté. She is due for rehearing—one might better say that she is overdue for a hearing, as the first one was lost in irrelevancies—and it will be interesting to see what comes of it. Broad popularity is unlikely: she lacks magic, and the rough surface of her style deters the casual or self-indulgent reader. To judge, though, by the respect of younger writers and serious students one might predict the widening of an audience sophisticated enough to cut through the blemishes to the dynamic integrity of her central achievement.

One can see her taking a possibly mistaken direction in her later novels, driven as she was to try various ways of becoming a full-time novelist. Yet the significance of her life may lie most of all in her quite extraordinary grasp of what professionalism implied. Until the last two decades in New Zealand, practitioners in all the arts have had their wry amusement from the dictionary definitions which relate profession to livelihood; in a society offering neither the economy, the framework, the encouragement, nor the competition productive of standards, artists have drawn on their own very solitary resolves first to formulate their aim and then to reach it by spare-time application. It has meant withdrawal—often unrespected and misunderstood—from an otherwise pleasant and friendly society.

Jane Mander took overseas a firm resolve and a practiced capacity for abstention. As Sargeson wrote: "The novelist's craft is surely a strange one: most New Zealanders, I should say, can readily imagine their doing much more exciting things in New York and London than sitting down and re-creating on paper the kauri forests and tidal rivers of North Auckland. Not so Miss Mander, and anyone who visits the North will recognise how close to reality her scenes are. It is this solid realism which is Miss Mander's greatest strength as a writer." New York did indeed give her a thoroughly good time which her popularity and enterprise could have extended indefinitely. In an intense act of will she excluded New York and denied her other talents, keeping the way clear for the facts of New Zealand to creep in upon her again. She was quite mistimed for her own happiness as a professional New Zealand novelist. "My whole life has been lived round the motiv . . . too late" she wrote in her **"Preface to Reminiscences."** By present reckoning she was at least thirty years too soon for the appreciation and moral support her writing merited. From yet another viewpoint, her books might be seen as justly timed—as the leading obituary said: "Even a competent novel is a sort of miracle when it comes, unannounced and lonely, to a country with a weak literary tradition." It was a comfortless destiny, perhaps, but one she can be imagined volunteering for if it had to be undertaken by someone. (pp. 130-40)

Dorothea Turner, in her Jane Mander, *Twayne Publishers, 1972, 164 p.*

DOROTHEA TURNER   (essay date 1976)

[*In the following excerpt, Turner provides an analysis of* The Story of a New Zealand River.]

[**The Story of a New Zealand River**] is constructed entirely according to the stage method, as were most of the nineteenth century British novels from which it plainly derives. In form it is very much what the average reader of the day was accustomed to. The bent of the author's talent accentuates this, being strongest in well edited dialogue, in the episodic grouping of characters, in knowing when to raise and lower the curtain and how to tie in all the loose ends. The contrivance we sense in some of this is not too troublesome because it is within a familiar convention to which the author conforms with obvious delight. Even Tom Roland's death, which is far too conveniently timed for probability, does not disconcert us because our concern for what shall become of him after the story's end has not been allowed to develop; he has changed the whole landscape and so completed his life, himself unchanged. Tom is the author's most vivid creation; at no point could the novel manage without him, nor does it try to; he is dismissed only when he can be spared.

The novel's literary style is as conventional as the management of its plot, seldom rising above the derivative and predictable. "A stiff wordiness which none the less can be the vehicle of deep feeling" is David Hall's apt description of the writing which is indeed ungainly and quite uninviting to most readers. Here are no sentences to dwell on, none of the quiet pleasure for the ear one finds in Satchell or Robin Hyde. The descriptive and narrative writing is at its best when it is functional, terse and dry; when it is required to dress up for romantic occasions or the beauties of nature, it awkwardly overdresses. In describing the visible and tangible, in either people or things, it has little finesse, though when set to exploring the processes of mind, heart and motive it can move with authoritative precision. The very nature of the style conveys something of the quality of the life described which was harsh, exposed, vigorous, improvisatory and earnest. The dialogue, at its best, is in almost another class of writing, being rich in aural discrimination, variety and fidelity to character; it is even at times a major index of personality, the speech style of each of the principals being quite distinct. This is perhaps the novel's most surprising achievement, that it should excel in verbal nuances in a country so belated in its attention to them.

The River's blemishes and inequalities are easily listed, but its substance continues to hold us. It resembles those people of whom we say that they have good bones, implying that unblessed by the glamour of prettiness they have what may serve them better in the long run. The book's total personality is indeed substantive, multidimensional, sculptural. To earlier readers this was often a difficulty in that certain aspects were uncongenial and these could seem to protrude, blocking the view of the rest. Some readers were worried by an indoor drama with sex problems interrupting the bustle and swagger of a bushfelling story; others were disturbed by the free-ranging conversations about religion, or the personal decisions made according to a standard (as one reviewer put it) "too early for good public morality"; others again were confused by the need to distinguish the story's creative truth from the literal truth of people and places still within living memory. After half a century all this has receded into perspective; the shapes and angles, the light, shade and balance are clearly discernible.

Even so, one can approach the novel from only one direction at a time and in any one reading, particularly the first, some continuous line must be found through the story. Alice is inevitably the central line in that what happens to her most engages our concern; if she cannot change or let herself be changed it can go well for none of them. Many see her as an unsympathetic character; even her physical beauty does not come through and may need to be supplied by our own knowledge of that fineness of feature and colouring which some young Scotswomen have and hold through vicissitudes of health and mood. Alice is there for our use, with no obligation to enchant or to endear herself; we are committed to her as to a difficult relative. She is a complex of qualities, some dormant, some over-developed, which are so arranged that we are forced through her to question the very nature of virtue, and to question it in ways so relevant to our New Zealand background that we can see her as a cultural symbol. Moreover she has the capacity for growth. David and Mrs. Brayton do not change throughout the story; each keeps to an already settled style and each speaks like a guru from infinite experience. Tom Roland, the only New Zealander before us, ends as he begins, an unreflective mixture of shrewdness and innocence, high courage and paternalism. Asia's development is natural to her age. But the fact that an adult should be brought from self-torturing formality to humanity and liberation of feeling is given enough consequence to become the central curve of the structure. The slowness of the change, Alice's obduracy and embarrassments, make the change plausible. Because the others must conspire to help her, turning every circumstance to this end, they are forced into explicitness about her and about themselves in relation to her. They become the author's allies in exposition.

Little happens of which Alice is not the centre, even when she is physically absent, as in Asia's farewell visit to Mrs. Brayton. The house she lives in with its own development from unfinished shack to over-decorated comfort has a curiously focal place in the story; the dwelling does much to establish the prevailing viewpoint which is of Alice indoors, looking out. Any précis we might make of the book would be busy with coming and going and strenuous outdoor activity, all of which is of course there. Yet after the initial scenes of movement—the journey up the river, the visit to Mrs. Brayton, the picnic at the tree-felling site—the author contracts the setting to intensify the study of Alice, expanding it again only in Book IV with the entry of the two Australians. The central chapters, covering about ten years, are the long winter of Alice's life; she must make what she can of herself within the domestic confines; others leave home for a while, or they go out for news, and we find ourselves waiting with her. There is "stage method" here, moving beyond tidiness of plot and timing . . . into an approach to the techniques of intimate theatre in that the physical aspects of movement and events remain for the most part off stage, their consequences being left to be developed in front of the audience.

The illusion of intimate theatre is strengthened by the author keeping us aware, as a playwright must, of how the cast stand in relation to one another, even those who are not at the moment in the centre of action; the novel is rich in cross-currents which both engage and satisfy our speculations. The mastery with which the complex human material is handled, a mastery Jane Mander never again achieved on this scale, gives us a sense of being present at a production. Yet any attempt to dramatise the story shows at once how far it is from being a play, the extent of the dialogue being less than the impression it leaves. The authorial voice does in fact convey most of the unfolding of motive and character, in a tone both omniscient and intimate; through it we overhear unspoken thoughts, the dialogues of the minds. The voice is more intimate with some characters than with others, being most at home in Alice's mind, very close to Asia's and at ease in David's. With Tom it is cool and distant; any justice done him is at the prompting of the other characters; he comes and goes, as if of his own volition, under an independent spotlight. On *The River* one might build the hypothesis that the author is naturally closer to her female characters and that a known campaigner for women's suffrage might lean towards the woman's viewpoint—only to have it shot down by *Allen Adair* where the narrative voice speaks on a man's behalf with such intimacy and partisanship that reviewers have convicted Jane Mander of unfairness to his wife. The differential treatment is rather a technique for giving prominence to characters whose way of life has far-reaching implications. Though she had too much ability to resort to stereotypes, and indeed had grown up where people were so few that she continued to see human beings as unique and irreplaceable, she put forward some quite ordinary people as key figures whom our society must understand for its salvation.

Alice must be accepted as an ancestor by any Pakeha family of a few decades' residence in New Zealand. We look to *The River* to throw light on our puritan origins and the equally troublesome current revolt against them. The novel holds and convinces because it is primarily about the beliefs and emotions of very credible people. Its documentary aspects are now secondary, though they kept the book afloat during the years of indifference and may even have been the decisive factor with the first publisher. The author herself, having wisely decided to write first of the people and places she had known when young, could scarcely avoid the commitment to a documentary novel. This is how she had lived. Her talents and even her ambitions were probably stronger for other types of fiction; given another society she might have been able to close the windows on the struggle against external nature and keep to the turbulence of the human spirit. As it was, to have avoided the documentary which enveloped the lives of the people she understood best would have been artificial.

The main requirement of a documentary is that the received impression should be faithful to the reality. Here she has never been faulted; men who worked in the bush and gumfields have spoken of her as of an equal. Her family's continued involvement kept bush, mills and gumfields in the table talk, even after she grew up and they lived in town. She made many occasions for visiting field camps, going from Whangarei to check her memory of Kaipara bush-felling practices when she was drafting her first novel. Local legend has it that she embarrassed them all by coming closer than a lady should to the falling trees and the men's language. She had the advantage also of taking very seriously any person's occupation, caring about accuracy as to its special demands on skill, time and character, whether it was gum-spearing in the Kaipara or political journalism in Greenwich Village. Vocations she had not observed closely she left unchronicled. On the other hand she would rearrange a district's population and topography, putting a mill and a village at Pukekaroro and enough water in the Otamatea for logging ships to come right up; in other novels she moved schools and gumfields around, and once an electoral boundary. Though an excellent history student she fiercely deplored the idea that fiction was accountable to historians; the line she drew between what could be manipulated and what should not makes sense in terms of the novel's conventions.

Timber milling was transient in any area, the men and their equipment moving on after a few years; the mill village could be a separate, self-absorbed microcosm, having little household interchange with the permanent settlers, either Pakeha or Maori. White settlers are on the very perimeter of *The River:* the shadowy Harold Brayton and the little group on the wharf, the women looking as if "they had been stretched out and dried on crosses in the sun, and then dropped suddenly and left to curl up and contract." Maoris for the most part had made their own separate settlements; David, as a doctor who goes everywhere, rows ashore at one on the first day and "Maori children on the beach ran up to him, and women, brilliant spots of colour, waved their hands at him from the fields." There is no longer the same involvement that there was for early missionaries or traders; it was a period of quiescence and separation, nearly half a century after the Treaty of Waitangi. Jane Mander has often been reproached for excluding Maoris, as greater novelists have been for excluding what no doubt ought to have been in the minds of their characters but was not. Her own knowledge of the race was another story, never fully written but hinted at in *The Passionate Puritan* where a Maori character is given a position comparable to Mrs. Brayton's in *The River.* To have imported Maoris into the consciousness of Alice or Mrs. Brayton would have been as insincere as are the objects embellished with cave drawings manufactured nowadays for tourists. *The River* gives us a painfully credible picture of British immigrants more interested in themselves and in one another than in the native born, brown or white.

Vestiges of the story's literal truth are a few piles of the Pukekaroro logging tramway still standing on the beach below the site of Tom Roland's house. As one drives south towards Kaiwaka these can be seen from Highway 1, a road with such vistas of the East Coast that it seems incredible that this piece of tide has crawled in from the much more distant West Coast. Seeing the river at this point and envisaging the long journey in from the south west with which the novel opens, one can begin to grasp the settlement's isolation in the 1880's.

These tributaries of the Kaipara Harbour are a hybrid of sea and stream, unrelated to the South Island's seasonal rivers or to the steady flow of the Waikato and Wanganui. What water the hills give the Kaipara is seen at low-tide hours, running meagrely through mudflats; twice a day the sea moves in to surround the mangroves, lapping the jetties and lifting the stranded boats. People could navigate freely around high tide; for the rest they might have to sit it out where they happened to be. It was not dangerous travel compared with that on most New Zealand waterways—merely frustrating. David Bruce was justified in opening the story with an oath; if Alice had been a few minutes later they would all have had to wait till next day. Jane Mander's father took as the theme of his maiden speech in Parliament the interminable delays of wind and tide in an area not yet provided with road or rail. Yet in their ordinary lives they might not see the open sea which was many tortuous bends away: though it controlled their daily timetables, they received its commands, as they received the consuming ideas which reached them from abroad, at some distance from the source.

The river of this story has none of the inexorability of a one-way current; the tide which cuts the lifeline twice daily restores it as often. It is a pulse, offering renewal after every withdrawal. Renewal and the possibility of a second chance are not what Alice can easily understand; these she must learn. People may go but they can come back; one may hurt them but there are ways of putting that right. Just as she fails to grasp the demands of the first day's outgoing tide, so she is unhopeful of ever being at ease with David after her initial misjudgment of him; again and again she makes mistakes with David and Asia, grieves for her actions' finality, only to find that these two do come forward again, giving her another chance. She wastes time and we suffer with her. David has learned to submit to the ebb and flow of life. Asia, born hopeful, lives within the pulse.

Is Asia then symbolically a gift from the sea, like the Asia of *Prometheus Unbound* a regenerative spirit, daughter of the Oceanides? In all six novels this is the only character to whom the author has given a name at all peculiar. It is scarcely credible that Alice, in her circumstances, would have given the child a conspicuous, fanciful name, much less a pagan one. She was no solo parent of the brave new world, flying a romantic flag; on the contrary she was secret and ashamed. One can only assume that the author has named the girl over the mother's head, making to readers a direct signal which should not be disregarded, however reprehensible technically such a gesture may be. She may even have had her dry amusement over her young heroine's waterborne entrances and exits and in particular over the late solo entry where she sails in like an apparition upon the two Australians. To these young men, on their next meeting, "she looked like the Greek spirit incarnate." All this is surmise, but Shelley's doctrine encompasses Jane Mander's in its belief that Utopia is possible here on earth; the barrier for Christians was the concept of sin and of man as a fallen being which postponed Utopia to the hereafter. At the very heart of *The River* lies Asia's cry: "Sin—sin—the word that has hypnotised the world."

Though the novelist left no record of a debt to Shelley, she named two other philosophers who had left their mark on *The River.* Looking at the book again in her sixties she wrote to a friend, "too much of reading Shaw and Nietzsche." Shaw's impress is very clear: he asked and answered many relevant questions and he encouraged her love of dialectics. David Bruce often sounds like Shaw himself speaking. Jane Mander also said, "Parts of it read as if I'd been trying to show off—and perhaps I was." Shaw's stimulus often affected people this way and it is on those clever, up-to-the-minute, hortatory passages where she seeks to impress that the dust has settled, as it has on Shaw's writings. She was with him in opening her mind to all knowledge in the search for human perfectibility, perhaps with more optimism: Shaw's beliefs appear often as an act of desperation at the unthinkable alternatives, such as Darwinism and its "chapter of accidents . . . When its whole significance dawns on you, your heart sinks into a heap of sand within you." Both the Shaw and Mander doctrines have an anthropocentric view of the universe, a legacy of Christian theology. In *The River* nature is secularised, it exists for man's use, replenishment and occasional wonder rather than in its own right; and the central concerns of life, as well as the human race's future prospects, are seen as being negotiable within the realm of human relationships. These philosophies are less comprehensive than Shelley's as an answer either to Darwinism or to the questions raised by modern scientists of the biosphere. But it is just because the prevailing religions and philosophies were inadequate guidance for the people who changed the New Zealand landscape that Jane Mander's documentary is a faithful record of more than the mechanics of their operations; it reveals, sometimes unconsciously and in a way still painfully relevant, the disastrously simple conception of progress which has underlain the attack on the country's natural resources.

Nietzsche's effect, though less patent than Shaw's, may have been more dynamic in that his writing goes beyond the cerebral, invading the whole being; even his aphorisms are powerful talismans. His is a complex gospel from which people have uplifted what suited them, but he was urgently on the same search: to find a new image of man which would give him a sense of his essential dignity, now that the ancient theological picture had gone. He deplored the concept of sin and retribution, saw no virtue in resignation, martyrdom or other meek and propitiatory attitudes. Alice has in her so much of what Shaw and Nietzsche deplored that these two may be credited with helping to define her portrait and to sharpen the issue between the negative and positive aspects of goodness which is a preoccupation of *The River*—if help were needed. Jane Mander is too close to the truth of New Zealand society to be greatly indebted to any perceptions beyond her own; to encounter philosophies codifying those very problems which to her had been personal might affect her less with a sense of revelation than with the more stimulating shock of recognition.

The River can be seen as a quest for a new ethic outside Christian theology and entrenched privilege, but not excluding anything of value which may be contributed by individuals with those backgrounds. Indeed exclusiveness cannot be afforded because in such a small, interdependent microcosm everyone must be provided for, nobody can dodge the issues by escaping to the company of those who think like him and nobody can be spared. The first lesson is, as Mrs. Brayton says to Alice: "What does anything matter in a place like this except that we be human?" Other distinctions soon enter. Mrs. Brayton asks Alice whether she is a "churchwoman." "To Mrs. Brayton there was only one 'Church'." She is relieved to find that Alice is a Presbyterian, not a Wesleyan. "It's a state church anyway, and they do educate their parsons." Mrs. Brayton, we suspect, is one who cleaves to her church's aesthetics as much as to its doctrines; she is quite at ease with all kinds of ideas and with David Bruce who, when asked by Alice, "Mr. Bruce, how do you get on without God?" replies "'Well, as you see,' . . .

stretching his feet comfortably towards the fire." Mrs. Brayton is later bored with a young curate whom the author describes as not having been in New Zealand "long enough to realise that in that radical country church membership did not constitute an entree to exclusiveness, and that in the remote districts of the northern bushes it was not regarded as important." Jane Mander was of Noncomformist parents to whom the explicit unsectarianism of the Albertland Settlement was congenial; she had grown up in an atmosphere of doctrinal give and take among spirited individuals and could plausibly people her childhood environment with such characters as would share her adult concerns. She had emerged too independent in spirit ever to need the support of countering dogmas or binding causes in her emancipation; like Shaw she remained a free explorer of fundamentals.

It is notable how little *The River* contains of evil in its darker aspects. The principals are all moral beings who take full responsibility for themselves and suffer deeply when defeated in the battleground of their own minds. David and Mrs. Brayton, as well as Alice, are haunted by past mistakes made unthinkingly in pride or greed; David even flies from his past into bouts of drinking. Dark thoughts surface in Alice and David when Tom attempts suicide by poison and it is in their power to let him die; but they are all incapable of deliberate harm or of nurturing malevolence. The search for right and wrong takes place on a level of morality where answers are less obvious: given goodwill and rectitude, what prevents the happiness of a vivid, dignified and fulfilled life? Rebirth or regeneration the new world might offer; for what would this opportunity be used? To this end the characters are scrutinised, their beliefs and experience sifted and tested, to see what should go into the making of Asia who is to be the herald of the new.

The fact that Alice was not married to Asia's father is more relevant to the girl's strategic placing in the story and to what she may symbolise than to the plot. As an explanation of Alice's repressions and fears it is scarcely necessary; thousands of women of unblemished conduct spent their lives in those days in just such a state of neurosis. Indeed Alice is so archetypal in her attitudes that her upbringing alone could have been left to account for them. Nor does it add anything to her reasons for marrying Tom Roland; had she been in truth a widow she might well have felt forlorn enough to decide similarly. The ways in which a shy middle-class woman might support herself in New Zealand then were almost as few and as poorly paid as those open to Jane Eyre.

Asia's illegitimacy serves rather to set her apart from the rest of the family. Her superior qualities are enhanced by Alice's inability to talk about the father or to make real any background which might account for them. Many a young girl daydreams for herself a mysterious, unknown father, being unable to relate her sense of sublimity and uniqueness to the man she has always known. In *The Godwits Fly* one of the children goes so far as to insist to her father that she is not his; her real father was someone in Johannesburg, a gentleman. "Her Johannesburg gentleman gave her a curious exemption from family troubles. "I'm not yours," she reminded John gravely; and he left her alone." A novelist wishing to endow a young woman permanently with the kind of significance a girl imagines transiently for herself might well see the solution in taking the unknown father dream and positing it as fact. Where a character is a symbolic figure with oracular and messianic overtones, as Asia is in some of her aspects, mystery should surround the origins. Prophets cannot be launched successfully with the normal complement of relatives and the genetic father is the one who can most conveniently be left outside the picture, unspecified, for imaginations to work on.

Though by no means so complex as her mother, Asia has a multiplicity of functions as the representative of ideas and attitudes. As the only child given prominence in the story, and later as its only young woman, she is the medium for everything the author wishes to put to us about the child's view of life and about the future of the world as the young see it. In a first novel, long in the writing, there were many points to be made; we can see Asia as overendowed. Yet reason tells us that a girl in such an underpopulated microcosm would, if she had the ability, expand to fill the unclaimed roles. The circumstances themselves enforced all-round capability; education was a matter of chance, depending on whether the available adults had time, books and ideas. With David, Mrs. Brayton and her mother on hand and others to talk to around the bay, Asia is fortunate. Modern education has so bemused us with schools, peer groups and social promotion that we can forget the flowerings possible in opposite circumstances. Asia is not presented as in any way deprived; she stands for the author's belief in these early, isolated places, and in the colonial opportunity itself. (pp. 3-11)

Asia is also, of course, the fictional self, one of its five variations around which the author built novels, *Allen Adair* being the only one without her. In the other novels, the fictional selves are introduced as adults; they at once dominate the scene. Outside *The Passionate Puritan,* where a nimble-witted Englishman manages to disconcert the heroine more than once, even to tame her, no characters are built up with sufficient body to keep these young women in their place. Only in *The River* is there an adequate range of ages, a natural balance of old and young; elsewhere the search for freedom becomes a chimerical and often strident tussle against the state of things in general. When people become irritated with Jane Mander it is usually on account of her heroines. As Asia grows up the author comes close to letting her exasperate us. Asia grows overfond of being listened to and of manoeuvring for positions where she will be seen as wonderful; there is, for instance, her visit with Allen Ross to the gumfield, an episode which would have been better left as stark realism but which becomes, for her sake, a melodramatic interpolation ending with a love scene. We may agree that Asia is usually in the right, but we are glad when both David and Alice manage to confound her, though we have to admit that she takes setbacks graciously.

We forgive her much because she has wholly engaged our affections as a child; she is a superb little girl, her response to any situation just what we would hope a child's could be. Her conversations are a realistic mixture of shrewdness and innocence; in her questions on life and religion she speaks for thousands who wondered but had not the nerve to ask. The questions do more than illuminate her thought processes: they are a spotlight on the elders' way of confronting issues. David and Mrs. Brayton, who are smooth and practised with new ideas, try to be undogmatically honest. Alice fights with her back to the wall, like many others of her troubled generation, attacked by new questions before the authorities have issued the new answers.

Asia comes before us so vividly in the early scenes that it is a surprise to find Alice quietly dominating the book. Was the author also surprised? At what point did she realise that this had to be? Novelists make discoveries as they write and Jane Mander, on her own admission, was one whose characters

could run away with her. One expects that *The River* will be Asia's story and that as the girl grows up the mother will recede, as mothers do. Yet the contrary comes about, and it is the bond between mother and daughter, already firm when the story opens, which keeps our interest, overshadowing what develops between Alice and David and between Asia and Allen.

The explanation of Alice is in Asia's search for fulfilment and the need to personify the opposing forces which can be seen here as gentility, possessiveness and fear. Alice's gentility is thrust at us many times in the early chapters, never more emphatically than when she tells David she prefers to teach Asia at home, just reading and music; he prescribes geography, arithmetic and so forth. Alice, as a Scot, might have been granted a more creditable attitude on this; but she is a musician, and there is nothing like executant music for so engaging the mental and emotional powers that other ideas remain unformulated or naive. Many a shrewd ruler, public or private, has seen music as an innocuous safety-valve, the only permissible art for people who must be kept under; the visual arts are dangerous, literature is dynamite. By confining Alice's interests to music the author helps establish her as the quiescent puritan woman, liable to circumscribe daughters similarly with the best of intentions.

In the argument about Asia's education it is Alice who is on trial, not the question of whether girls should study. That had been settled in the year of the author's birth, about a decade before these scenes at Pukekaroro, by the Education Act which made primary schooling obligatory for all children; if girls went to free state schools they learned alongside their brothers, although well-to-do parents could make other arrangements if they preferred. In the same year, 1877, the daughter of the Baptist minister of Kaipara's Albertland Settlement had become the first woman graduate in the British Empire by studying unopposed at Auckland University College; many other girls were moving in the same direction through state secondary schools. Jane Mander grew up knowing these opportunities to be there; circumstances kept them out of her reach for a long time, but in the end she arrived at an overseas university subsidised by her almost unschooled father. When anything beyond lack of means kept a girl from a liberal education, only the parents were answerable. (Tom Roland's attitude is illuminating: the younger girls become schoolteachers, he having decided that "they would have to earn their own living and be useful, whether he could afford to keep them or not.") In the New Zealand context, where options freely existed and were taken up by some, the issue can be seen to have moved from that of feminism, in which rights must be argued on principle, to a position where acceptance or rejection of opportunity could be used as a guide in defining people. The author could move beyond causes, which are doom to a novel anyway, to the fruitful area of class discrimination.

The origins of New Zealand, and of Northland in particular, explain some of her advanced assumptions. In certain streams of British society girls were given the best education the family could manage: daughters of Quaker and Unitarian communities were notably cared for, as were those of many clergy in many denominations, besides the daughters of some scholars and of the unafraid stratum of the upper class. Nineteenth century Britons were overwhelmingly colonialist towards their wives and daughters, as towards other races, if one broadly defines colonialism as the refusal to share what one values most with the people in one's power, as the assumption of the right to live by a double standard. But there were minorities who were different, through belief or temperament; some of these had long experience of being underprivileged, excluded. Such elements surfaced strongly enough in New Zealand to determine the shape of education and of much else. In Jane Mander's environment many privileges still strong in Britain had quite surely gone, including of course the dominance of the Established Church. The author came in at the point where the technical barriers to freedom were down; she stood in the detritus of old battles, confronted with the peace-time problem of re-educating human nature.

Alice's difficulties are due only in part to her temperament; some judgment, we feel, is being made of her class. The social and mental confidence of David and Mrs. Brayton, characteristic of their class, is beyond her, as is Asia's straightforward adventurousness. In Alice's conversations with David and Mrs. Brayton, with pertinent help from the child Asia, Jane Mander appears to search for new class definitions for the unfixed local society, even for a new hierarchy. As convinced as any other New Zealander that British heritage was the best in the world, she was prepared nevertheless to decide for herself who were Britain's élite, having known immigrants of all types at close range from childhood.

Our compassion for Alice, often at odds with irritation, is won by her circumstances which are grim enough in the early years to be just cause for fears sharper than her moral and religious ones. Even happiness in marriage could not have guarded her wholly from loneliness, and from childbirth poorly supported. For daily exhaustion there was the ubiquitous Kaipara mud to be handwashed from clothes and bodies, and meals to be cooked from crude supplies on crude stoves in a makeshift house. The author drives these points in with oblique little strokes on her way to something else as, for instance, when she describes the family's arrival at Pukekaroro: "Immediately after the evening meal, to Alice's dismay, they began to weather-board the kitchen." Alice belongs, with Marion Adair, Lady Barker and Edith Searle Grossman's Adelaide, to that company of pioneering women to whom the life had less to offer than it did to their men. The woman's greater suffering was intrinsic, scarcely to be ameliorated by any feminist prescription of emancipation; indeed prosperity and technology could do more for her. The changes prescribed for Alice, and for Marion, are ones of personality and of outlook; towards their practical difficulties the author is if anything too bracing.

When prosperity brings Alice a little leisure and choice, Jane Mander is ready with the question she was always waiting to ask, of communities or individuals: one works as long and as hard as need be at pioneering, but what comes next? In the later chapters hints of overt feminism ruffle the surface as Asia tries to educate her mother "in the direction of modernism." Here one might surmise that the author was unsettled by the current struggle in New York where she was attending a university which allowed women very limited entry, and where she was helping her friends, unsuccessfully, to claim the right to vote which in New Zealand had been waiting for her as she grew up. But the solution for Alice is allowed to remain consistent with her nature; she is a dependent figure and Asia must settle for effecting such changes as will help make her happy as a womanly woman. Apart from a few impatient lapses, essential to the realism of the picture, Asia deals as she would be dealt with, succeeding in loving and admiring a nature the opposite of her own, and hoping for equal charity from her mother because freedom without loving approval is barren.

Behind the prominent mother and daughter theme lies the enigmatic theme of Asia's paternity. Her genetic father is an unknown figure; Tom Roland, her stepfather, provides materially for her; paternal affection and advice come from David Bruce. Tom has his moments of affability with Asia when she amuses him and towards a stepchild more might not be expected of him; but his welcome, or lack of it, to his own babies in the first chapter and his subsequent detachment from them make a chilling picture of his role as a father. The young, it would seem, are the woman's affair. He is far from being a cold man; towards the community and his employees he is strongly paternal. Tom is obsessed by work, justifiably he might think, because many depend on him; with his household he restricts himself to the role of provider, a second-best which Alice accepts and builds on: "She knew now that he was a power in the land. He would make money, and perhaps he really meant to do his best for her and the children. She determined that she would try to think better of him." Here in the making is that polarisation of the functions of mother and father which has become the malady of our society and the despair of its therapists.

Allen Adair contains another version of this theme in a couple quite different from the Rolands, analogous rather to the Bennets of *Pride and Prejudice*. Allen is gentle, unambitious and better educated than his wife; he stakes some claim to the company of their first child, weakly allows himself to be dispossessed, consoles himself with books and male company and finishes an outsider to his children's concerns. Mr. Bennet is censured for letting his daughters down by his detachment; his distaste for their mother's silliness is seen as no excuse for sidestepping paternal duties. The author of *Allen Adair* goes no further than to see Allen as failing to try to enlarge his wife's mind; Allen has time and some inclination to be an all-round father but there is obviously no supporting convention to give him courage to strive for the role.

In the Pukekaroro household David, as adopted uncle, supplies the cultural side of fatherhood; he hands on to Asia what he can of the race's accumulated wisdom, all with the persuasive assumption that there is time in everyone's life for this; he undertakes affectionate and moral responsibility for her. David and many others like him were immigrants; the type did not renew itself as the imports dwindled. The paternal functions David represents were taken over later by mothers, so far as was in their power; the domestic transmission of religion and legend, books and the arts became a sex-linked inheritance to a degree which tended to brand these subjects as feminine. Fathers developed along Tom Roland's lines: busy, pragmatic, justified by the work ethic and by their promotion of the family's material prosperity. They had the resource of strong male friendships—as Tom with David, Allen with Dick Rossiter—and the comradeship of the place of work and the clubs and the pubs which could have no counterpart in most women's lives. If the home seemed wanting, discontented, surely that could be put right if there was more money, a faith the wives were tempted into accepting; it could be easier to pursue jointly a material goal than to halt, discuss, maybe criticise, and then try to work out a new formula. Had Jane Mander been writing of the settlers of the era another pattern might have emerged. Farming, being a family enterprise, does not encourage the father's detachment; prosperity, even survival, depends on his attentive fostering of the young; whatever limitation they suffer, they are together. Tom Roland, who goes out to work and stays out, is the prototype of modern urban man who, now required to be both David and Tom for his family's well-being, finds he has built up neither the personal resources nor the social structure for expanding the inherited role.

Jane Mander set herself a technical problem when she embarked on an intricate social study of men and women so oppressed by elementary labour as those in *The River*. Unremitting work is a leveller, removing variety from the novelist's material, limiting the choice people have in their personal development. Part of the author's solution here is to select wisely from the diversity of material natural in a group of fairly recent immigrants and to make emphatic use of the diversity. She keeps us aware that even in the gumfield, where men live with the lowly uniformity of ants, any accent or background can be encountered. The principals are a credibly haphazard set of individuals, retaining life styles developed elsewhere. David, though run off his feet, is always ready to burst into practised eloquence. Alice is never too oppressed to explore, as her religion has taught her to, the moral implications of conduct. Mrs. Brayton, a shrewdly selected extra, maintains an upper class English household; and when the story needs young men for Asia they drift in readymade from Sydney. Some of them may feel that life has treated them oddly, setting them down here, but this need not seriously diminish them, any more than malnutrition alters the bone structure of a grown person. They keep some hold on what they are used to enjoying, on social intercourse and the sharing of ideas.

But it is the strategically placed Mrs. Brayton who supplies most of the force which binds together a cast who might otherwise tend to stray around the landscape, dispersed by the exigencies of their lives and their inability to understand one another. As it is, the author can muster them into Mrs. Brayton's co-ordinating presence, and into a household where servants light fires and bring in meals, and children and wet oilskins are cared for out of sight. The respite is used for uninterrupted conversation. Immensely conscious of class structure, the old lady is subtle in her placing of people. Sure enough of herself to be bold in her apparent inconsistencies, she is the perfect foil to Alice who can work only by rules whose origin and relevance she does not always understand. The power and charm of this woman and her hilltop setting are developed at length in the third chapter; thereafter she remains an eminence, a point of referral both in overt crisis and in soliloquy. Mrs. Brayton is the mentor and arbiter in whose sight the other characters most wish to stand well; we feel that the author, too, is laying every case before her. When she dies, two thirds of the way through the book, "To Alice, Bruce and Asia some virtue had gone out of the place never to return." Some virtue goes out of the book itself at this point; Mrs. Brayton has had the power to make the rest of the cast synthesise their thoughts and edit themselves for the reader.

Mrs. Brayton is Jane Mander's homage to England, the symbol of what she most loved in its character and culture. The manner of portrayal illustrates the author's practice of putting forward her characters without antecedents, leaving them to be judged by the way they comport themselves in the new situation; she is continually searching for that cultural essence of a person which will survive transplantation and isolation. This habit of thought may be a necessary part of a novelist's equipment but it has been unusual, until perhaps recently, in New Zealand's assessment of arrivals from Britain. With less native shrewdness than Huck Finn, our society has let the magic phrases "well connected" or "of good family" serve for discrimination. Jane Mander's peculiar upbringing perhaps accounted for the analytical precision of her social awareness. People of all types came to join her father's camps and mills, travelling light and often in poor shape; prediction of their potential could be more than a game. She learned about British society through studying its separate particles out of their context and under a bright light. At the time of writing she knew no more of England itself than she had seen from a London boardinghouse during a month mainly occupied in visiting four publishers and thirteen performances by Nijinksy.

A few years of everyday journalism preceded this first novel but no short stories, nothing to indicate to the author how her creative writing might be received. *The River* has a splendid innocence. As awareness came, Jane Mander altered her focus on New Zealand; the towns and their values began to impinge unhappily on the consciousness of her books; the northern outposts became a refuge for the individual rather than a hopeful social beginning. The genteel, conforming, life-denying traits, curable in Alice, grew to be intractable and pervasive; society itself became the adversary. *The River,* arising entirely from its author's own choice of disciplines, is distinct from her other novels. This adds to its isolation in our history where it was, as M. H. Holcroft said, a sort of miracle in that it came "unannounced and lonely, to a country with a weak literary tradition." (pp. 12-18)

Fresh from reading *The Strange Attraction,* his review of which the *Triad* carried a few days later, Frank Morton went on to instance Jane Mander:

> Today she is making such a success in one literary form—the novel—as no other New Zealand woman has achieved. It is a flaw in her work that she is a trifle inclined to—say, épater les bourgeois—and snap at the queer little harmless, cramping things in the New Zealand country that exasperated her as a young girl. We all become gentler as we grow older. Miss Mander makes progress and will write a very fine novel yet if God spares her.

Gentler *Allen Adair,* her next book, certainly was, and though not as fine a novel as might have been hoped for, it is not the vehicle of exasperation and desire to shock as is *The Strange Attraction* in which we can read a retort to New Zealand's distaste for *The River.* Yet Morton's juxtaposition of the genteel convention and the desire to shock is the essence of a problem which troubles even *The River:* that a writer may be led into confusing outspokenness with honesty. This was most liable to happen during the transition between nineteenth and twentieth century thought. On the one hand were Ibsen, Shaw, Nietzsche, Freud and many others inviting the interested to cultivate "a modern intellect," as Mrs. Brayton put it, to re-think, to take a few lids off and let in cleansing winds; on the other hand were those who hugged rules and beliefs more tightly the more they were threatened. In the New Zealand towns where Jane Mander had lived as a young adult the "distinctive spirits" she claimed always to have found were a minority; there was no real insulation from the majority viewpoint. In such a situation a person whose first efforts at honesty are met with outrage tends to remember the outrage; some of the energy which should go into the search for truth is diverted into mere lack of reticence; outspokenness comes to be seen as a medicine to be administered for others' good. At the same time those who are trying to break from the genteel convention have so little experience in discussing taboo subjects that what they say can sound crude. It seems strange, after all that has happened in fiction in the last 50 years, still to find indelicacy in Jane Mander's writing; yet in her dealings between man and woman, particularly where physical intimacy is at issue, her touch is often discordant. *The River* is patchy in this respect; the startling honesty of the scene between David, Alice and Tom in chapter XXX is in contrast to the awkward discussion of their unsolved relationships in the following pages. None of the personal themes of this novel were ones which could have been talked over openly in current New Zealand society, where duty and loyalty forbade discussion, or even recognition, of the more intimate strains of family life. An author with this background had to discover for herself not only the right tone of voice but also the very phraseology. If Jane Mander was sometimes confused, and her solutions infelicitous to the present viewpoint, her achievement was nevertheless extraordinary. (pp. 18-19)

> *Dorothea Turner, "The Story of a New Zealand River: Perceptions and Prophecies in an Unfixed Society," in* Critical Essays on the New Zealand Novel, *edited by Cherry Hankin, Heinemann Educational Books, New Zealand, 1976, pp. 1-23.*

ADDITIONAL BIBLIOGRAPHY

McCormick, E. H. "Years of Prosperity." In his *New Zealand Literature: A Survey*, pp. 82-107. London: Oxford University Press, 1959.
    Discusses the documentary value of Mander's novels of New Zealand life and her contributions to "a freer and healthier tone" in New Zealand literature.

Mulgan, Alan. "An Historical Survey." In his *Literature and Authorship in New Zealand*, pp. 7-39. London: George Allen & Unwin, 1943.
    Finds that Mander's fiction, like that of Katherine Mansfield, "helped to make New Zealand letters more sophisticated."

Sternberg, Freda. "Jane Mander." *The Bookman* (London) LXV, No. 390 (March 1924): 296-97.
    Biographical sketch by an interviewer who discussed Mander's childhood and career with her on her arrival in England.

Stevens, Joan. "The Forerunners (1910-1939)." In her *The New Zealand Novel: 1860-1960*, pp. 35-49. Wellington, New Zealand: A. H. & A. W. Reed, 1961.
    Mentions Mander's four novels with New Zealand settings, calling *The Story of a New Zealand River* "well above any New Zealand novel published up to 1920."

"Life in Old New Zealand." *The Times Literary Supplement*, No. 3757 (8 March 1974): 237-38.
    Notes the "modern" aspect of *Allen Adair*, which deals frankly with sexual relationships despite the fact that it was written, in part, to put an end to criticism of sexual emphasis in Mander's first three novels.

Turner, Dorothea. Introduction to *Allen Adair*, by Jane Mander, pp. ix-xviii. Auckland: Auckland University Press, 1971.
    Analysis of *Allen Adair* as a conscious attempt on Mander's part to write a book with authentic New Zealand settings and characters that would not offend New Zealanders as her first three novels had.

Kálmán Mikszáth

1847-1910

(Also wrote under the pseudonyms Kákay Aranyos, Scarron, and others) Hungarian novelist, short story writer, and journalist.

Mikszáth was a prominent Hungarian short story writer, novelist, and political commentator during the late nineteenth and early twentieth centuries. Described by critics as "the Hungarian Mark Twain," he is best known for lighthearted, anecdotal narratives satirizing the social and political institutions of his day. Mikszáth's works earned him wide popular and critical acclaim during his lifetime and posthumous recognition as the most important Hungarian fiction writer of the period.

Mikszáth was born in 1847 in the village of Szklabonya in Nográd County, near the Czechoslovakian border of Hungary. Although his family was of modest means—his father worked as an innkeeper and, occasionally, as a butcher—it counted among its ancestors members of the Lutheran landed gentry. According to biographers, Mikszáth was a sickly child whose father hired local storytellers to entertain him whenever he was confined to bed; in this way, he gained an extensive knowledge of regional folklore. After completing his secondary education at schools in Rimaszombat and Selmecbanya, Mikszáth studied law at the University of Budapest. While still at the university, he published his first essays, and began to seriously consider becoming a writer. Mikszáth left the university without taking his examinations; thereafter he worked for two years as a jurist for the chief administrative officer of Nográd County, then as a journalist and apprentice lawyer, while writing fiction in his spare time. In 1873 he married Ilona Mauks, the daughter of his former employer, despite her father's objection that Mikszáth would not be able to support a wife on a writer's income. Mikszáth indeed earned very little at this time, and his first book of short stories, whose publication he financed himself in 1874, proved a failure. A year later his wife became ill and returned to her father's home to convalesce; Mikszáth, unwilling to earn his living by means other than writing, yet wishing to spare his wife further hardship, persuaded her to divorce him.

Beginning in 1878, Mikszáth began to gain recognition for his articles and editorials written for a daily paper in Szged. Returning to Budapest, he worked first as an assistant editor of *Ország-Világ*, then as editor and staff writer with *Pesti-Hírlap*, and soon developed a following for his witty, satirical writings about Parliamentary activities and other political matters. While exposing what he considered to be examples of corruption and injustice, Mikszáth always tempered his indictments with humor and an apparent willingness to forgive the transgressions described. Gradually, he became one of the most popular and respected political commentators in Hungary. During this time Mikszáth, who had formerly sympathized with the progressive Independence Party, switched his allegiance to the more conservative Liberal Party, becoming good friends with its leader, Kálmán Tisza. His success as a journalist was paralleled by equal good fortune in his literary endeavors. Two collections of his short stories, *A tót atyafiak* and *A jó palócok*, published in 1881 and 1882, were warmly received by both critics and the public. Confident in his newfound fame and financial sol-

vency, he began to court his former wife, eventually persuading her to marry him again.

Throughout the remainder of his career Mikszáth wrote prolifically, with continued success. He was appointed to several prestigious literary societies and received many other honors, including acceptance into the Hungarian Academy. His work as a journalist brought him considerable political power as well as popular acclaim, and in 1892 he was elected Parliamentary representative of Fogaras, an area in southeastern Transylvania. He continued to serve as a member of Parliament, and to write, for the rest of his life. In 1908, the government changed the name of his birthplace to Mikszáthfalva in his honor, and presented him with a gift of an estate that had belonged to his ancestors. He died in 1910, several days after festivities were held to celebrate his fortieth year as a professional writer.

Commentators have divided Mikszáth's career as a fiction writer into three periods: a romantic period, characterized by idyllic representations of childhood, romantic love, and fabulistic evocations of peasant life; an ironic period, characterized by cynical yet good-humored portrayals of humanity's baser instincts; and a realistic period, characterized by increasingly pessimistic depictions of social and political life. The works of Mikszáth's first period include numerous children's stories; highly praised for their affectionate portrayals of children, many of these have become classics of Hungarian children's literature. The short stories and novels of Mikszáth's second, ironic, period are much like his political writings, describing the failings he found in his society yet never offering outright condemnation or advocating reform. The theme of greed, recurrent in his fiction, is exemplified in the story ''A gavallerok,'' about the inhabitants of a small town whose odd predilection for acting out elaborate charades designed to gratify their desire to be rich baffles an out-of-town observer. Mikszáth also explored the shortcomings he found in society through the theme of the conflict between the ideal and reality. For example, in ''Gallamb a kalitkaban,'' which consists of two variations on a single story line, Mikszáth portrayed two cultivated gentlemen proving their friendship for one another through a series of noble, self-sacrificing gestures and two politicians engaged in ruthless attempts to do each other in.

Many of Mikszáth's other novels and short stories of this period contrast the delusions of misconceptions of his characters with the truth, which is ironically evident both to readers and to the story's narrator. The protagonist of one early novel, *Beszterce ostroma* (*The Siege of Beszterce*), is an eccentric nobleman who, oblivious to the realities of modern Hungary, insists on behaving like a feudal lord. A comic treatment of a similar theme is *Új Zrínyiáz*, about a sixteenth century warrior hero who, resurrected in the present day, creates havoc by applying battlefield methods to his new career as a bank manager. Mikszáth's best-known novel, *Szent Péter esernyöje* (*St. Peter's Umbrella*) concerns an old umbrella mistakenly regarded as evidence of a miracle by the inhabitants of a village. While Mikszáth emphasized the comic absurdity of the situations he depicted, he also usually chose to elicit the reader's sympathy for his hapless protagonists.

The fiction of Mikszáth's final period increasingly reflected his distress at the unsavory dealings he witnessed in politics, the problems brought about by the inequities of the class system, and the deteriorating state of the nation, both domestically and in its international position. In his last works, he evokes situations of inhumanity, suffering, and amorality. The hero of *Különös házasság* (*A Strange Marriage*) is forced to marry the pregnant mistress of a local priest, and must spend the rest of his life struggling to escape the match in order to be reunited with the woman he truly loves. In *A Noszty fiú esete Tóth Marival*, an unscrupulous nobleman schemes to replenish his family fortune by seducing an heiress. Commentators regard the last novel Mikszáth completed before his death, *A fekete város*, as his bleakest in outlook. It concerns a pair of young lovers whose happiness is destroyed by a senseless and violent political feud.

During his lifetime, Mikszáth's fiction was overshadowed by that of his popular contemporary Mór Jókai; today, however, his works are the subject of increasing interest both within and without Hungary. As Joseph Remenyi has written: ''In comparison with the common run of Hungarian novelists and storywriters, Mikszáth is exceptional indeed, and it is fair to say that his literary importance transcends the political and cultural boundaries of his native land.''

PRINCIPAL WORKS

Elbeszélések. 2 vols.   (short stories)   1874
A tót atyafiak   (short stories)   1881
A jó palócok   (short stories)   1882
*Nemzetes uraimék: Mácsik, a nagyerejü   (novel)   1884

****Szent Péter esernyöje*   (novel)   1895
   [*St. Peter's Umbrella*, 1900]
Beszterce ostroma: Egy különc ember története   (novel)
   1896
   [*The Siege of Beszterce*, 1982]
Prakovszky, a siket kovács   (novel)   1897
   [*Prakovszky, the Deaf Blacksmith*, 1962]
Új Zrínyiász: Társadalmi és politikai szatirikus rajz   (novel)
   1898
Különös házasság. 2 vols.   (novel)   1901
   [*A Strange Marriage*, 1964]
A szelistyei asszonyok   (novel)   1901
Akli Miklós cs. kir. udv. mulattató   (novel)   1903
A vén gazember   (novel)   1906
Jókai Mór élete és kora. 2 vols.   (novel)   1907
A Noszty fiú esete Tóth Marival. 3 vols.   (novel)   1908
Két Választás Magyarországon   (novel)   1910
A fekete város. 3 vols.   (novel)   1911

*This work was originally published in serial form under the title *Mácsik, a nagyerejü* in 1882 and 1883.

**This work was originally published in the journal *Uj Idök* in 1895.

WILLIAM MORTON PAYNE   (essay date 1901)

[*An American critic, Payne served as literary editor for several publications during the late nineteenth and early twentieth centuries, notably the influential journal the* Dial. *In the following excerpt, he favorably reviews the first English edition of* St. Peter's Umbrella.]

[*St. Peter's Umbrella*] is a quaint, whimsical narrative of life in a Slovak village, with much folk-lore and local coloring, rich in a shrewd sort of philosophy, and brightened by flashes of the most unexpected yet unmistakable humor. The story itself is of the slightest, and there is little attempt at serious characterization, but upon the thread of his invention the author has strung such a succession of pretty pictures and witty remarks that the interest is not allowed to flag for a moment. We feel that a real treasure has been unearthed for us by the translator of this delightful book. (p. 139)

> *William Morton Payne, in a review of ''St. Peter's Umbrella,'' in* The Dial, *Vol. XXXI, No. 365, September 1, 1901, p. 139.*

JOSEPH REMENYI   (essay date 1949)

[*Remenyi was a Hungarian-born American man of letters who was widely regarded as the literary spokesman for America's Hungarian community during the first half of the twentieth century. His novels, short stories, and poetry often depict Hungarian-American life, and his numerous translations and critical essays have been instrumental in introducing modern Hungarian literature to American readers. In the following excerpt, he discusses Mikszáth's career, focusing on his role as a satirist and commentator on Hungarian society.*]

In the late nineteenth and early twentieth centuries in Hungarian literature, an era of optical illusions and wasted lives, the works of Kálmán Mikszáth represented an outlet for socially significant, humorous and satirical energies. Mikszáth was not only accepted, but acclaimed by the Hungarian ruling classes. In their estimation no apparent damage had been done to their social status by his novels, stories and sketches. Although he saw how badly things were going, and though his level-headed judgement was immune to self-deception, he identified himself with his own social stratum, which was that of the gentry. Richard Chase's criterion of "ordealist criticism," that is, "being interested in the suffering and failure of the artist and his estrangement from society," could not be applied to the life and works of the Hungarian humorist, although it would be applicable to several of his contemporaries. Mikszáth was not an "accursed" creator or a spiritual exile. His political alignment with the Liberal Party (really a conservative party) proved his "social dependability," and as he could use his pen for the political objectives of the ruling classes, obviously his political writings did not serve to undermine their faith in the continuation of their power. Objectively evaluated, Mikszáth seemed like a literary showpiece of a fading social system. Stories were woven around his figure which portrayed him as a benevolent cynic, rather than a social critic. Both traits were characteristic of him. He followed the code of his class, yet he was also conscious of their "pride-before-fall" psychology. When new horizons seemed to be opening up, he recognized them, but—in his imaginative writings as well as in his political causerie—he was quite careful not to offend the conventions of his class, even when he could not resist or avoid the indirect method of criticism. In recent years, however, an attempt has been made to re-evaluate Mikszáth by accentuating his condemnation of the deformities and incompetence of the Hungarian upper classes.

Mikszáth, sometimes called the Hungarian Mark Twain, lacked the disposition of a crusading knight; at the same time, like his American colleague, he sensed the thwarting elements of his surroundings, and again, like Mark Twain, he had the faculty of considering the plight of mankind as congenital, but also as the result of the increased callousness of human life. Basically he had little confidence in man although he enjoyed gazing at things through rose-tinted glasses, especially when he wrote about children. He was always conscious of man's predatory behavior; that is to say, he remained close to the ground of empirical truth. The world of the Hungarian gentry, middle class and peasantry—the world of Palóc and Slovak peasants—the historical past and contemporary politics (he was a member of the Hungarian Parliament and on intimate terms with the Tisza family, the leaders of the Liberal Party), were shown in a light in which adaptation to the superficialities, bizarreness or vanity of life seemed necessary in order to overcome the tension of the human struggle.

In the works of Mikszáth it is the artificial peculiarity of the individual or a form of social conduct in discord with a person's natural rhythm that provokes a humorous or satirical reaction. Dominated by this point of view, the "gay-hearted" author could not escape the temptation of pessimism; his humor is tragicomic, actuated by a desire to comprehend destiny through laughter. He manifests good sense in the description of witless or Don Quixotean characters who never feel failure while they live in their imaginary universe; with gusto he relates the Sancho Panza attributes of petty schemers or dull people who plod along well-established lines. He does this with a straightforward or oblique technique, or with anecdotal authenticity, which was his way of having justice meted out to those who maintained that a wrong has to be made right, but who as a rule had neither the patience nor the moral outlook necessary for the application of this principle.

There is a story told by Mikszáth to the effect that a newspaper publisher justified the small print of poems by saying that his small advertisements were printed in similar letters and he received money for them. This story does not typify Mikszáth's sense of humor, but it implies a kind of satirical wit related to his views about a rapidly growing avaricious civilization. By nature Mikszáth was a provincial. He never liked Budapest, and when the Hungarian capital became his permanent home, its "urbane" pattern disturbed and annoyed him. At the turn of the century in Budapest, as in eighteenth-century London, the meeting place of authors and "wits" was the coffeehouse. Mikszáth had very little use for it. He preferred the "casino," the meeting place of the gentry. He abhorred the utilitarian devices of a modern community, for he saw in them a distortion of progress, the thread of human action which "devitalized" the country gentleman and the common people. On the other hand, his humor was such that it made him critical (in the midst of laudatory words) of the protagonists of socially immobile and intellectually impassive provincialism. But in his "criticism" he never overlooked the fact that the social and spiritual archaisms of the small town or village were more relevant to his nature than the unscrupulous attitudes of a metropolitan city. He was not an angry man, as he was too conscious of human foibles; neither was he a passionately subjective individual, as he was too conscious of the contradictions that determine the temper or are determined by the temper of human beings. His writings, even in their derogatory intent, seem to say that nothing matters but life's hybrid reality. And while "his humor gains in depth and charm from his power of detecting the attractive and poetical in the simplest circumstances of life," in essence his worldview is "complete disillusionment." There are Swiftian elements in Mikszáth's works.

How can one harmonize these conflicting views in Mikszáth's thinking? It seems that while his rationalizing intelligence negated the purpose of life, his imagination subordinated his negating attitude to a smiling or laughing view which enabled him to treat his subject matter in a manner preserving the humorous substance of the character or the situation. His primary aim was not to depict social evils, but to portray individuals in their Hungarian setting. His aristocrats, landed gentry, county officials, politicians, teachers, merchants, money lenders, tavern proprietors, artisans, clergymen, students, gypsies, grafters, drunkards, pranksters, nimble-tongued good-for-nothings, tricky simpletons, thrifty, shrewd or phlegmatic peasants and shepherds were representative of a society in which it seemed impossible to persuade people to mend their ways. Mikszáth was aware of the impending collapse of the ruling classes, but whatever opinion he formed of the approaching social change, it was not said with the doomsday voice of an hysterically prophetic preacher. There was neither "heroism" in Mikszáth's Hungarian *Götterdämmerung,* nor "whimper" as suggested in T. S. Eliot's "The Hollow Men"; rather a jocose, sometimes clowning, despair-hiding spirit, the admission of a fruitless effort to change things. Mikszáth's women characters—as naive, fragile, coy or inexperienced as the women characters of Turgenev, but less poetical and rarely intensely in love, or clumsy, awkward, heavy-set females, housewives, ladies, flighty or flirting creatures—are of minor interest compared with their male counterparts. Evidently Mikszáth ignored the "complexities" of feminine psychology. He reconciled extremes and oddities through analogies drawn from reality, without being consistently realistic. Like Gogol—in spite of his realism—he preferred to exaggerate. The words allegedly uttered by the Russian writer before his death, "I shall laugh with bitter laughter," echo in the Hungarian author.

In Mikszáth's early stories (published in two volumes in 1874 and attracting small attention) one notices the influence of Mór Jókai, the widely-read Hungarian romanticist. Later he was somewhat influenced by the pseudo-realistic sketches of Zsolt Beőthy, who, by the way, is chiefly known as a literary historian. One appreciates Mikszáth's admiration for Charles Dickens and Alphonse Daudet, especially when one reads his juvenile stories, which are among the most beautiful products of Hungarian letters, and which place him among the foremost writers in any language. *Tündérvilág* (*Fairyland*), a book of inferior artistic quality but of enchanting spirit, appeared in 1875.

After having developed his own manner of writing, based on inventiveness and observation, mixing innocent humor with mocking irony, Mikszáth measured all things within the boundaries of a world in which life revolved around unfulfilled hopes, illusions and twisted or selfish actions. No wonder that it was written of him that "his characters seem like wounded souls, who pass through various stages from the normal to the abnormal; externally they seem healthy, but their souls surrender to a powerful force, and they cease to be their own masters." This too was written of him: "Many of his stories seem like folk-ballads in prose." Another view: "Through Mikszáth's writings money became the driving motive of many characters in Hungarian literature. In this respect he is as much of an innovator as Balzac is in French fiction." These statements show how far critics agreed and disagreed in their estimate of his fundamental characteristics, yet in each instance evaluation is related to the paramount features of his art and psychology. (pp. 214-17)

In a discussion of Mikszáth it seems unfair to dismiss his minor writings, notwithstanding their artistic shortcomings. Mikszáth knew how to create a farcical situation or to portray three, sometimes only two, dimensional characters in a fashion which, on the surface, seemed to have a purely entertaining purpose. To be sure, many of his stories and sketches have ephemeral significance; they are narrative projections of whims or moods, starting with the assumption that the reader wishes to be amused, startled and stimulated. However, in those works which are truly expressive of his exceptional ability, he analyzed the deeper levels of human nature; though he was inclined to describe details profusely in a "talking" manner, as if speaking to a neighbor who enjoyed listening, in his best works one recognizes the eminence of a creative writer. One must take note of the public he wrote for; it would have been too much to ask of him to neglect the extra-esthetic elements which affected the artistic validity of some of his writings. He never succumbed to plebeian taste, and there is no flagrant violation—at least not in a broader sense—of the sincerity of his creative procedure. He did not promulgate any abstract theories of his own; consequently, in an effort to be truthful, despite an occasionally deliberate catering to public taste, he has not betrayed his organic relationship to narrative art. Too often he lacked self-restraint and did not know when to stop. He seldom took the trouble to revise his works. No critic could have dissuaded Mikszáth from his method of writing. As a narrator, he would have felt paralyzed if he had had to write in a Flaubertian manner; of course, it is a matter of conjecture whether his art would have improved by following certain esthetic canons. He believed that a story should be well told and sustain the reader's interest. To make of him an "esthetically representative writer" would be like trying to perform a Henry Jamesian operation on Mark Twain.

Mikszáth achieved distinction in both genres of narrative art, in the short story and the novel. Coincidence and well motivated psychology play identical parts in the development of plot and in the delineation of characters. As a short-story writer, Mikszáth knew how to focus attention on a revealing situation or action; and despite a somewhat loosely constructed presentation, one feels the unity of atmosphere, the interrelationship of movement. Some of his stories seem like vignettes, others lack brevity; then he wrote stories in which the maximum of interest is achieved through the writer's power—independently of technical finesse—to create "the illusion of small things being great and great things small."

One hesitates to make a selection of Mikszáth's best stories, but the following ought to be mentioned: **"Pipacsok a buzában"** (**"Poppies among the Wheat"**), **"Galamb a kalitkában"** (**"Pigeon in the Cage"**), *Prakovszky, a siket kovács* (*Prakovszky, the Deaf Smithy*), **"A kis csizmák"** (**"The Little Boots"**), **"A Lohinai fű"** (**"The Grass in Lohina"**), **"Az öregek"** (**"Old Folks"**), **"A gavallérok"** (**"The Cavaliers"**). As his stories are marked by simplicity and ingenuity, in praising them the critic's evaluation is naturally an expression of inherent attitude about simplicity and ingenuity. Generally these tales are humorous and the characters are rarely complicated. Their interest in money to pay off debts or other "pressing obligations" suggests the inevitable ludicrousness or pathos of materialistic necessity; their interest in "influence" or "prestige" is the face-saving means of those whose sentimental or pragmatic vanity is a prerogative of their "social position." Faced with the responsibility of making a decision, some characters show weak willpower; others know how to foil their foes; some are doubting Thomases or full of petty spite; but they are human, all too human, and all seem gathered under the traditional roof of Hungarian social history. Several stories have roots in age-old tales. For example, the plot of **"Galamb a kalitkában"** is traceable to János Haller's seventeenth-century Transylvanian *Hármas história* (*Threefold History*), the material of which is derived from foreign sources. In some of the stories sorrow brings understanding to seemingly unsolvable problems. The stories hold up well in re-reading; their incongruities and incompatibilities provide amusement for many present-day readers, regardless of how much they are hypnotized by the complexities of modern narrative art.

Mikszáth's children-stories are among the most admirable works of Hungarian literature. **"A piros harangok"** (**"The Red Bells"**), **"A ló, bárányka és a nyúl"** (**"The Horse, the Lamb and the Rabbit"**), **"A zöld légy és a sárga mókus"** (**"The Green Fly and the Yellow Squirrel"**) are charming and deeply moving expressions of a tender heart. Tears and chuckles mingle when one reads Mikszáth's juvenile tales. Their plots develop from a profound understanding of the nature of childhood; their tone is appropriate, the emotional impact is great, the portrayal of the pathetic disparity between children and adults is convincing. In these stories there seems a physical and spiritual awareness of the joys and anxieties of children, and while the pattern is not varied, the effect of irony (so frequent in his other works) is determined by the incapacity of grown-ups to comprehend children rather than by the situation of the children themselves. This Hungarian author, who constantly recognized the parody of human ideals and rejected the idea that the stupid, hypocritical, or monstrous actions of men are intricate or mystifying, appears to be trying to counteract the weakness and futility of human fate with the image of youthful guilelessness. Guided by intuition and affection, almost as a revenge against the "happy-ending" anticipations of intellectually or ethically immature adults, in his children-stories he restricted the comic content of life to the minimum. Of his works written for juvenile readers, *A két koldusdiák (The Two Mendicant Students)* attained popular success.

In his novels—perhaps because of their larger scope—Mikszáth turned more to "problems" than in his short stories. However, in his novels too the onlooker is predominant, and the author does not offer solutions. Often the behavior of his characters changes from pathos to bathos. Their views and actions seem an anticlimax of real or assumed nobility or of other self-deceiving attributes of human nature; at times they are absurd while realizing an appetite for life which leads to fatal cosmic indigestion. Some of the characters are crude, others are cruel; some are fools in their good intentions, others have merely foolish intentions without the redeeming feature of goodness; some are deluded by self-importance, others aimless or useless permutations of the norms of a seemingly permanent social order. Their *noblesse oblige* as a postulate of their social standing, or their attitude of *nobile officium* as a sign of their "selfless" service to their political or social obligations, really is an indirect condemnation of their own existence. While Mikszáth recognized their trite characteristics and is effective in his ironic portrayal, one also senses his sympathy for his social equals. They were "within his social set," and while in terms of creative and impartial psychology they represented a fantastic caricature of the Hungarian social pageant, he could not but see in their instincts and chivalrous manners or mannerisms the tragic aspects of a comedy in which he, too, by his very position in Hungarian public life and by tradition, was involved. He could not transform them, as he could not transform himself. In some of his novels, preoccupied with an imaginative horizon rather than with observations, his yearnings for pastoral and other simple scenes neutralized or silenced his satirical realism. As mentioned above, the ruling classes of Hungary—except for a few discerning people—did not feel that any apparent damage had been done to the stability of their social status by Mikszáth. This was unfortunate, as it might have stirred their conscience, but it is also possible that this would have been vain expectation, and it is also possible that Mikszáth himself preferred their conception of his "gentlemanliness" to that of a "social critic." Furthermore, his skepticism interfered with the view that his works represented the influence of imaginative literature on political and social reforms.

Mikszáth started to write novels after he achieved fame as a writer of short stories. His first novel, *Szent Péter esernyője (Saint Peter's Umbrella)* appeared in 1895, and was dramatized in 1907. It is one of his most delightful works. It has the simplicity of a fable, the device of an utterly unsophisticated narrative, and is based on the assumption that readers are interested in the uncovering of emotional secrets. The plot relates the story of a certain Pál Gregorics, who has hidden in an umbrella stick the will which contained the inheritance of his son. After years the son, in search of the will, reaches a small Slovak village where, instead of finding the will, he finds love in the heart of Veronika, the sister of the village priest. The symbol of the umbrella—the umbrella is presupposedly a gift from Saint Peter—has all the implications of a legend. It brought happiness to people—for example the village priest, his sister, the young man and others—and while the author follows the convention of Hungarian fables, his artistic performance justifies faith in his creative originality. Mikszáth's second novel, *Beszterce ostroma (The Siege of Beszterce)*, also published in 1895, is the story of a nobleman who wishes to live and act

in the nineteenth century with all the privileges of a feudal lord. Although the story ends with the aristocrat's suicide, it is humorous in many parts. The central figure, who is close to madness, never learns the lesson of anachronistic behavior. The various characters, including a young woman with whom the nobleman falls in love, are well drawn. There are hilarious and excellent scenes in the novel, but all the pages are not the work of an accomplished novelist. It is interesting to observe the writer's attitude about the unrealistic psychology of his "hero." By portraying the impulses that govern him, by using an ingenious method for the portrayal of his farfetched and silly views, by undressing, so to say, his obsessions, Mikszáth speaks with the voice of a critic and judge regarding that social class of Hungary, the life of which was related to the past, a past dead long ago.

In manner and spirit Mikszáth's next novels showed an increased social orientation. *A fekete város (The Black City)*—chronologically his last work, since it appeared in 1910, the year of his death—concerns early eighteenth-century Hungary, the *Kuruc* era. The compositional defects of the novel are obvious; the author concentrated on historical authenticity at the expense of artistry. What the novel signifies in a sociological sense is the conflict between the well entrenched forces of the gentry, represented by Pál Görgey, a high public official in county Szepes, and the ascending middle class, represented by Antal Fabricius, a judge in the city of Lőcse. A tragic love-plot intensifies the story.

In Mikszáth's earlier novels, *Uj Zrinyiász (New Zrinyiad)*, published in 1898, and *A Noszty fiú esete Tóth Marival (The Case of the Noszty Boy with Mary Toth)*, published in 1908, social criticism is more pointed. Nonetheless, in these novels too Mikszáth is primarily a storyteller; he fails, when he endeavors to be didactic. In *Uj Zrinyiász,* Miklós Zrinyi, the hero of Szigetvár, a brave fighter against the Turks in the sixteenth century, rises from his grave to find himself in the nineteenth-century business environment of Budapest. Despite his adaptability (he becomes a bank-director), he is an alien in this world. The novel is a sarcastic picture of plutocratic and political forces, of talkative modern lawmakers and other leaders. Fiction has always been a good medium for the travesty of historical an psychological contradictions; in Mikszáth's novel one is somewhat reminded of Mark Twain's *A Connecticut Yankee in King Arthur's Court*. Both novels reveal the incongruities of ancestral and timely standards or lack of standards. *A Noszty fiú esete Tóth Marival . . .* is the story of a young gentleman in need of money. He plans to marry Mary Tóth, the daughter of Mihály Tóth, a man of the people, who accumulated his fortune in America. The scheme of the "mesalliance" fails, as the father of the girl sees through the young man. Here we have the portrayal of the degenerated gentry and the "kulak" type of Hungarian society. The writing is verbose, the psychology of eccentricities is overdeveloped, the action is filled out with needless digressions; nevertheless, as the interpretation of a dying social order the novel is an example of Mikszáth's satirical bent.

Other novels and stories could be mentioned to illustrate Mikszáth's approach to his task as a storyteller and as an indirect critic of Hungarian society. His major and minor figures alike represent either the irrepressible imagination of a resourceful fabulist, or a social comedy in which stiltedness is mistaken for dignity, a blend of lies with a sense of decorum as a norm of respectability, a violation of the natural rhythm of organic sincerity as a sign of legitimate superiority. But it should be repeated that with all his ability to ridicule, in his innermost self the author was not separated from his surroundings. His artistic detachment, notwithstanding his class-consciousness, was stronger than his belief that through creative writing one could transmit to the world principles which, by being recognized as truthful, would be put into action. In the final analysis, Mikszáth cultivated a stoic attitude which—while not divorced from reality—opposed the righteousness of reformers. He certainly was not a militant social critic.

Mikszáth's political sketches, such as **"Apróságok a házból"** (**"Trifles from the Parliament"**), **"Ujabb fény és árnyképek"** (**"Newer Shades and Shadows"**), **"Katánghy levelei"** (**"Katánghy's Letters"**), show to what extent he specialized in the "fragmentary" existence of political moguls and nonentities. He well knew that much of politics is but gesticulation with a "civic minded" vocabulary. With a tendency to discern grimace behind the "lofty" physiognomy or speeches of a politician, he consistently indicated his poor faith in human reliability. Yet he was not hostile to his parliamentary colleagues. His sketches convey the innocence of diabolical helplessness regarding the elimination of those factors which make of some people politicians and induce others to flatter or to fear them.

Mikszáth's *Jókai Mór élete és kora* (*The Life and Epoch of Mór Jókai*), is a sympathetic presentation, in two volumes, of the Hungarian romanticist's literary and social significance. *Az én kortársaim* (*My Contemporaries*)—also in two volumes—is a vivid record of Hungarian public life, gathered from the experiences of the writer throughout a number of years. He edited a literary almanac, and he is also the author of stories in verse which, however, have very little literary merit.

Contrary to a widespread opinion, Kálmán Mikszáth is not only "entertaining," but he bears comparison with truly great writers. No doubt, he rose to prominence because of his storytelling qualities and his anecdotal technique. It is true that his works contain a set pattern; the focal point seems at times an imaginatively imparted triviality; in many of his stories it appears doubtful that he had any other intent but the offering of momentary pleasure. It is also true, as one of his critics said, that "he tried to please the ruling classes." But this same critic stated that "Mikszáth's works perpetuate a vanished world," and other critics speak about his "classical virtues as a prose writer, his humor, his narrative felicity, his knowledge of human nature." The fact is that Mikszáth had an acute sense of reality, sometimes founded on worthy motives. Even in his "light moments" he was motivated not by destructive cynicism, but a grotesque sense of humor combined with a sense of proportion about the proportionless phenomena of human life. When Boccaccio was asked why he wrote the *Decameron,* he replied that he had stories to tell and he enjoyed telling them. This surely was a good reason. Maupassant might have given a similar answer. In the case of Mikszáth, such motives should be attached to the creation of his tales.

But it is logical to ascribe values to Mikszáth's works which transcend their purely entertaining features. While he did not produce characters from all walks of life, and while he catered to his own class, he had firm control over the characters he portrayed. When in the mood, he revealed an independence of his social and political backers and exposed their fallacies. And as Boccaccio and Maupassant showed qualities of creativeness which, when properly examined, have depth (sometimes merely the depth of surface) not to be ignored, so Mikszáth turned out novels and stories which distinguished him from "pastime" writers. He represents the spirit of a Hungarian era in which

writing on the wall was not taken seriously by most members of his class. To the gentry, life meant fun, wine, women, gay parties, gypsy music, card playing, fierce class-pride and an attitude which may be summed up in this phrase: "Let the devil take care of the future." Mikszáth had too much insight into human nature to be fooled by such mental blindness and willful wrongheadedness. Yes, he amused his own class, but it was like amusing a dying host, who has amassed a wealth of memories without the strength to create new, worthwhile experiences. The author knew his social and literary position in this frame of Hungarian society. He knew that his class was death-bound, and that nothing could revive its instinct for self-preservation; its existence could be only prolonged. At the same time the idyllic, harmless or cunning life of shepherds and peasants, their ability to commune with nature, seemed to justify a smiling approach to their simple problems. Like Čekhov in Russian literature, Mikszáth in Hungarian literature performed an artistic and social service in the portrayal of the unstable characters of a dying class and in the portrayal of the more or less nameless destiny of peasants. In comparison with the common run of Hungarian novelists and storywriters, Mikszáth is exceptional indeed, and it is fair to say that his literary importance transcends the political and cultural boundaries of his native land. (pp. 218-25)

Joseph Remenyi, "Kálmán Mikszáth (1847-1910),"
in The American Slavic and East European Review,
Vol. VIII, No. 3, 1949, pp. 214-25.

THE TIMES LITERARY SUPPLEMENT   (essay date 1962)

[*In the following review of the revised English edition of* St. Peter's Umbrella, *the critic discusses Mikszáth's stature in Hungarian letters and characterizes his writing.*]

Hungary has produced three or four poets who must rank among the world's greatest. If her prose-writers have not reached such Olympian heights, they certainly include a number of remarkable artists. The nineteenth century was the great era of Hungarian literature and its latter half was dominated by two giants— by international standards perhaps moderately sized giants. Kálmán Mikszáth (1847-1910) was overshadowed in his lifetime by Mór Jókai, a Hungarian literary cousin of Walter Scott and Alexandre Dumas, a prodigious story-teller, a man of vivid, poetic imagination but a poor creator of character. Mikszáth played second fiddle to Jókai and was regarded as a pleasant, likable and amusing writer, who, however, was not to be taken too seriously. Time has corrected this view. Today Mikszáth outshines Jókai and has proved greater than his rival. Jókai today is mostly read by children and adolescents; Mikszáth, however, is enjoying a well-deserved renaissance: he reads, indeed, as fresh, as delightful and amusing as he did sixty-two years ago when [*St. Peter's Umbrella*] was first published in England.

St. Peter's Umbrella is the story of a young priest, János Bélyi, and his younger sister, Veronica. Father Bélyi is a parish priest at Glogova, a god-forsaken, poverty-stricken but light-hearted Slovak village, at the time of writing under the Hungarian crown. The story centres on an old, tattered, threadbare umbrella. This was found placed over the baby Veronica as she lay during a storm in a basket outside the church while her brother, forgetful of the world, was praying inside. The umbrella saved the little girl's life and the villagers decided that a miracle had occurred. It was, they said, St. Peter himself who had placed the protective umbrella over the child. Indeed, a few of them had actually seen a vague figure, reminiscent of St. Peter. The old umbrella becomes an object of veneration until it disappears. It turns out that a large fortune had been hidden in its handle and the rest of the story is the search for the umbrella which turns up in the end and brings happiness to Veronica and her fiancé.

Mikszáth—a Hungarian Mark Twain, if we must find a parallel—was perhaps the greatest artist of the anecdote. Some writers write with their eyes—wrote Antal Szerb, the literary historian—others with their ears: Mikszáth wrote with his mouth. Every line of his is as lively and intimate as a story told by a great *raconteur*. He lifts the humble anecdote to great literary heights, his humour and charm, his gusto and love of people are heart-warming.

But Mikszáth was much more than a purveyor of anecdotes. He was a shrewd and occasionally outraged critic of society: he saw clearly the inhuman poverty of the Glogova peasant as well as the irresponsibility and stupidity of the gentry. But he could not sustain his anger. He described what he saw, then shrugged his shoulders and washed his hands, as though saying: such is the world, not very pretty perhaps but no one will ever change it. Poverty is not funny but one can tell a most entertaining story even about poor Slovak peasants. And that is exactly what he did in this minor masterpiece.

"Such Is the World," in The Times Literary Supplement, *No. 3171, December 7, 1962, p. 949.*

R. B. C. (essay date 1966)

[*In the following excerpt, the critic comments on Mikszáth's literary achievement and his style.*]

Because of his immense output, the [Hungarian] literary field was for many years dominated by Mór Jókai (1825-1904), a romantic novelist with close affinities to Sir Walter Scott, Jules Verne, and Alexandre Dumas. His vivid narrative imagination was such that, during his lifetime, he completely overshadowed his contemporaries, even despite the fact that his novels show an almost total absence of characterization. Among those whose achievements were never fully recognized while Jókai was flooding the market was Kálmán Mikszáth. Today, however, it is accepted that Mikszáth's talents were of a far higher order than Jókai's, and that it was he who raised Hungarian prose writing to a new level, so marking the transition between the nineteenth and twentieth centuries. (p. 8)

The influences of his childhood, the countryside in which he grew up—very like that which forms the background to *St. Peter's Umbrella*—and his early knowledge and love of the rich folk culture he found around him, all played a major part in Mikszáth's artistic development. As he himself said in later life: "I learnt to tell a story not from the writers of novels but from the Hungarian peasants." It is in his ability to fuse colloquial speech and the telling of anecdote into a work of art, in his skill in reflecting the realities of daily life in a way that both delights and amuses the reader, that raises Mikszáth to a position of eminence not only in Hungarian but also in European literature. That his works also reflect the social criticism of a liberal politician is equally true, but having made his point—the disgrace of poverty or the fecklessness of the gentry—he does not labour it. To amuse the reader is his prime purpose; focusing attention on the evils of the world is done by implication. (p. 9)

R. B. C., in an introduction to St. Peter's Umbrella *by Kálmán Mikszáth, translated by B. W. Worswick, The Folio Society, 1966, pp. 7-9.*

STEVEN C. SCHEER (essay date 1977)

[*A Hungarian-born American critic and educator, Scheer is the author of the biographical and critical study* Kálmán Mikszáth. *In the following excerpt from that work, he discusses the stages of Mikszáth's literary development, critical views of the contrasting Romantic and Realist elements in his writings, his use of metafiction, and his place in literary history.*]

Attempts by Mikszáth's critics to differentiate sharply between the various stages of Mikszáth's development are almost always disappointing. They seem to create the Mikszáth whose stages they thus categorize. One recent attempt, for example, insists that the early Mikszáth, as exemplified by the stories of *A tót atyafiak* (*Our Slovak Kinfolk*) and *A jó Palócok*, (*The Good Palóc People*) is idyllic. In these stories Mikszáth idealizes the folk. In this early period, as many of his critics have noted, the adult Mikszáth recreates his own childhood impressions of the peasantry, impressions at once idealized and authentic. Mikszáth's second stage is said to be permeated by an overriding sense of irony. The best work of his ironic period includes such novels as *Beszterce ostroma* (*The Siege of Beszterce*) or *Új Zrinyiász* (*New Zrinyiad*). These works are heavy with dramatic irony, with the difference between what the characters think and experience and what the narrator (and along with the narrator, the reader) sees and knows. In these novels romantic characters are pitted against a real world, but not necessarily with negative results as far as the attitude of the reader is concerned. More often than not, from the reader's point of view, the loser is not the romantic but the real, and therein, I think, lies the real irony of these works. The third stage is said to be Mikszáth's Realistic stage. The great novels of Mikszáth's final period, *Különös házasság* (*Strange Marriage*), *A Noszty fiú esete Tóth Marival* (*The Noszty Boy's Affair with Mari Tóth*), and *A fekete város* (*The Black City*), are said to be Realistic because they are more critical of the society of the present as well as of the past than any of his previous novels. . . . [But] these distinct stages are not as sharply differentiated as the particular Mikszáth critic in question seems to imply. Rather than distinct stages, they represent different degrees or emphases of the same basic mode of perception. The idyllic is predominant in the early Mikszáth, while the ironic dominates the middle and the Realistic the late. But all of these different degrees or emphases are present throughout, from beginning to end. (pp. 21-2)

One of the most conspicuous characteristics of Mikszáth's writings (whether his stories or novels are lifted from the world of his contemporaries or from that of the historic past makes little difference here) is the mixture of Romanticism and Realism they tolerate. . . . [The] conflict between the Romantic and the Realistic in Mikszáth is not a simple matter. At times the Romantic is clearly allowed to triumph over the Realistic, whereas at other times the latter is clearly victorious. Each case has a meaning of its own. This question, then, is at once technical and thematic. On the technical side it is not at all clear whether Mikszáth is primarily a Romanticist or a Realist, whereas on the thematic side it is usually clear as to when the Romantic or when the Realistic view of life is preferred or preferable. Since Mikszáth conceived of literature as a realm where justice and goodness triumph—that is, as a kind of antidote to life—, it would seem safe to say that he was essentially a Romanticist. Since, however, he also saw that Romantic illusions or delusions are detrimental to happiness (as witness his many eccentrics who are defined by such illusions, delusions, or obsessions), it would also seem safe to say that he was essentially a Realist. (pp. 25-8)

The specter of the Realistic Mikszáth has been one of the most persistent and problematic issues haunting Mikszáth criticism almost from the time of the first critical response to his work. The problem is intensified by the fact that Mikszáth himself seems to have flirted with the Realism (though not with the Naturalism) that came to dominate the international literary scene toward the end of the nineteenth century.

One of the first signs of Mikszáth's awareness of certain Realistic doctrines comes with his emphasis on "observation" at the expense of "fantasy" in **Galamb a kalitkában.**" As the original subtitle of this story indicates, the two narratives that comprise it are meant, among other things, to distinguish the Realistic and the Romantic precisely on the basis that the first is the product of the observer's eye while the second is the offspring of the teller's imagination. But . . . the tongue-in-cheek authorial quarrels with projected or implied readers render Mikszáth's stance with respect to the two modes ultimately indeterminate.

The "Preface" to the 1889 *Almanach* is much more helpful in this regard in that here Mikszáth speaks in a straightforward manner of a "healthy realism" clearly in the making which manifests itself by virtue of the fact that a "writer is inspired by what he has seen rather than by what he has read." This pronouncement is certainly in accord with one of the most clearly formulated tenets of Realism recorded as early as 1826 by an anonymous French critic who states that the new "literary doctrine" attempts a "faithful imitation not of the masterworks of art but of the originals offered by nature." Mikszáth's pronouncement also implies that its author would be in wholehearted agreement with the notion that Realism involves a desire to abandon the metaphysics of Romantic Idealism on the basis that "reality [should] be viewed as something immediately at hand, common to ordinary human experience, and open to observation."

Unfortunately, however, this probable agreement between Mikszáth and certain tenets of Realism cannot be taken for granted because Mikszáth himself seems to contradict it. In his "Preface" to the 1910 *Almanach,* written in praise of the educational value of fairy tales, Mikszáth speaks of "fantasy" as God's special gift to mankind. Another passage that modifies Mikszáth's supposed insistence on "observation" can be found in his "Epilogue" to *Jókai Mór élete és kora* (*The Life and Times of Mór Jókai*) where he claims to have sought not the "inert truth of a photograph, but the truth of the artist."

By itself this is, of course, not in contradiction to any Realistic tenet; but . . . Mikszáth's artistic truth is intricately and inseparably connected with his poetic vision of life. This vision, in turn, frequently pits the Romantic against the Realistic where the first is almost always associated with what is beautiful or desirable in life while the second is usually characterized by what is materialistic, selfish, or downright spineless. And whether the Romantic wins (as it does in *Szent Péter esernyöje* and *Különös házasság*) or loses (as it does, partly, in *Beszterce ostroma* and, completely, in *A fekete város*), the reader's sympathies are unquestionably enlisted on its side.

Evidence to the contrary notwithstanding, most of Mikszáth's critics seem obsessed with the idea of his Realism. For ex-

ample, István Király, the author of the last full-length monograph to appear on Mikszáth to date, insists time and again that Mikszáth is either a Realist or moving toward Realism. He sees a significant and proportionate relationship between Mikszáth's changing political affiliations and his ever more Realistic criticism of the society of his age. According to Király, the more Mikszáth sees the corruption and the decadence of the once worthwhile Liberal Party, the more he moves away from Romanticism and the more he moves toward Realism.

The implication in this, as well as the implication in other, similar statements, is that an author's Realism has less to do with his characteristic modes of perception than with his characteristic attitude about what is perceived. In other words, the form (which in Mikszáth is almost never Realistic) is conveniently overlooked when it comes to the content or matter (which is frequently Realistic, that is, which is frequently critical of the way things are in Mikszáth's age). In the final analysis, however, Király can do no more than claim that "for Mikszáth realism did not mean a stubborn adherence to external, surface reality, but the creative imagination's careful liberation of the spirit of observed phenomena," and that the purpose of this "liberation" is to "reveal the internal, essential truth" of things and events.

István Sötér also sees Mikszáth's Realism in terms of his changing political attitudes. In an essay on *Beszterce ostroma* he argues that prior to the writing of this novel Mikszáth is still the victim of his own illusions about the historic role of the nobility, and that in this particular novel we are the witnesses of a process of disillusionment which is, at the same time, a "strengthening" of Mikszáth's move toward Realism. This, however, does not stop Sötér from seeing that the novel is composed of "contradictory elements," and that the scenes that take place inside the Pongrácz castle are not as Realistic as those that take place outside it.

Writing about Mikszáth's poetics, Béla Illés, a more recent critic, states pointblank that Mikszáth "demanded that writers present a *true* picture of life and *true* portraits of man," that he himself dismissed idealized heroes but without accepting or advocating the other extreme, the extreme of "clinical studies" of despicable characters, for these are no more "true of the *whole* of life" than are the former. Overlooking the fact that many of Mikszáth's characters *are* highly idealized (this is especially true of his heroines), and even characters such as Mihály Tóth in such otherwise Realistic novels as *Noszty fiú,* Illés simply reaches the rather tame conclusion that in the final analysis Mikszáth "favors" and "recommends" Realism.

Two important essays appearing in the early 1960's take a much more sophisticated and tenable stance with respect to the whole question of Mikszáth's Realism. The first of these conceives of the whole question as a series of "problems" peculiar to Mikszáth, while the second places the word *Realism* in quotation marks in its title, thereby indicating that the Realism in question is fraught with difficulties.

The first of these essays, Barta's, is an excellent and intelligent study of various "Mikszáth problems," and foremost among these is the problem of Mikszáth's Realism. This essay reopens a whole series of questions treated by Mikszáth's earliest critics . . . , namely, the relationship between folk and fairy tales and Mikszáth's Romantic vision of life, and the role of the "live" narrator assumed by most of Mikszáth's projected storytellers. Barta emphasizes the fact that in Mikszáth's novels the narrative voice plays a more prominent role (that it is more an integral part of the novels' overall effect on the reader) than in most novels that emphasize action or character, and that the narrator's apparent artlessness hides an artistic pose of the highest order. Because Mikszáth's readers are charmed, ultimately, by the author's own personality as it manifests itself in various and sundry narrative poses, the world presented by Mikszáth's novels takes on an authenticity and credibility that is the direct result of the underlying personality implied by their narrators.

But, Barta adds, this should not stop the reader from seeing that Mikszáth's novels are full of well-known (and frequently outmoded) conventions, and that this is true of such late novels as *Noszty fiú* where the heroine's disguising herself as a serving girl or the fortune hunter's disguising himself as a hunter can be seen as shopworn examples of certain traditional conventions. Barta concludes that Mikszáth is a "romantic realist."

Mezei's essay, which is a direct response to Barta's, speaks of the various "Mikszáths" as in some sense the creations of Mikszáth's various critics. Apparently somewhat unhappy with Barta's conclusion, Mezei attempts to place the Hungarian "realism" of the latter half of the nineteenth century in a historical perspective. He speaks of the end-of-the-century tendency to romanticize everyday life and the world of politics, and he concludes that the Realism of the age is at best a "medley" composed of elements from fairy tales and pictures of life as life is actually lived.

In the end, Mezei sees Mikszáth's entire career as an uninterrupted struggle for the establishing of a "national" prose, as an attempt to "find the novel in the land of anecdotes." It is for this reason that in Mikszáth's works "motives as well as problems recur," and it is for this reason that the Mikszáthian world is ultimately accumulative in its effects. Mezei's conclusion is that Mikszáth's "'humorous' works are born, as it were, against his own tendency to be well disposed toward report and naturalistic objectivity." (pp. 137-40)

There is a sense in which Mikszáth's Realism is clearly a critical fiction, that is, there is a sense in which the critic's wishes to see Mikszáth as a "Great Realist" are imposed upon his works. Such critics as Király, Sőtér, or Illés, for example, write almost as though they were determined to make Mikszáth the author of their own idea of Realism. Barta and Mezei, on the other hand, seem bent on making the whole issue seem more complicated and consequently more accurate than that (and rightly so), but they are still unwilling to relinquish the spccter of Rcalism that clcarly should not haunt Mikszáth.

Notwithstanding a few isolated and, ultimately, halfhearted pronouncements made in favor of certain Realistic tenets, Mikszáth's practice . . . is decidedly unrealistic. But saying this is still saying something very problematic. I do not wish to imply that Mikszáth is anti-Realistic (though at times he is clearly anti-Romantic), for this would be false. At the same time it would be also false, or at least highly misleading, to imply that Mikszáth's world is not a frequently accurate representation of the world of late nineteenth- and early twentieth-century Hungary. Paradoxically this is most true, perhaps, of his most self-conscious and metafictional novel, *Két választás Magyarországon.* This raises a whole new question concerning the relationship between the fictive and the real, and of Mikszáth's implicit (and at times explicit) response to this question.

In speaking of "A gavallérok," Aladár Schöpflin—one of Mikszáth's earliest critics—mentions the fact that "Mikszáth loves characters whose lives are based on a lie in such a way that the lie emerges as their subjective truth." Later Schöpflin goes on to make a statement that surprisingly anticipates much later fiction and much relatively recent criticism: "When lies thus become an important ingredient in human life, the distinction between a truth and a lie, between what is real and what is imagined, itself becomes faint . . . [and this may give rise to the question that] if what is but the offspring of imagination can thus become true, is not what we take to be reality in general itself but the offspring of imagination?"

There can be no doubt of the fact that Mikszáth's works abound in characters who live in fictions of their own making. But these characters do not fit into a single category. Count Pongrácz in *Beszterce ostroma,* for example, cannot be said to be the mere victim of his own imagination. On the surface he seems to be unaware of the difference between the age he is actually living in and the age he thinks he is living in. On a deeper level, however, it is clear that Pongrácz's choice of a quasimedieval world is based on his implicit recognition that the modern world is not an adequate stage for his life. The characters who hire a troupe of actors to represent the "delegation from Beszterce" explicitly recognize that Pongrácz's life is an implicitly theatrical performance, a quasiartistic attempt to control reality.

The clash between different versions of reality is in fact familiar in many of Mikszáth's novels. The legend created by the old umbrella in *Szent Péter esernyöje* is explicitly shown to be a lie, but the "legend" is nevertheless more real than the simple reality which underlies it. In *Akli Miklós,* on the other hand, the "legend" of the hero's treachery is also a lie, but here it is the "truth" which is more real (and more "legendary") that captures the reader's sympathies. Sometimes the clash between different versions of reality is playful, as it is in *A szelistyei asszonyok* where the King's theatrical performance belies the truth in the same way in which the Transylvanian delegation's performance implies a truth that is in reality a lie. There are times, however, when the clash is irresolvable, as in *Uj Zrinyiász* where the heroes of old remain incompatible with the modern ideas of and about the old.

But the Mikszáthian world of various characters, or classes, or whole societies living in fictions of their own conscious or subconscious making, is not exhausted by the characters, or classes, or societies themselves. The narrative voice bringing these various configurations of illusions intended to be mistaken for realities together with the various instances of self-delusions, makes itself felt at all times. The notion that "everyone sees with his own eyes, and judges and constructs according to his own mind" is at once a clue and the interpretation of the clue.

In the long run, the subjective truth of a character is not only true for that character, it is also true for the reader. This is so because all truth is, in a sense, subjective. Where there is an identity between a subjective truth and the subjective interpretation that produces it, there is always a "good" character. The characters in "A gavallérok" or Pongrácz in *Beszterce ostroma* belong to this category. Where, however, there is a discrepancy between a subjective truth and the subjective interpretation that produces it, there is always an "evil" character. Akli's enemies, the Döry witnesses in *Különös házasság* and the Noszty clan in *Noszty fiú* all belong to this category.

Mikszáth's works, then, are conventional fictions about nonconventional fictions. They are in short artistic truths about the truths of life itself where the truths of life itself are themselves "made up," as it were, in a way not unlike the way in which the novelist's truths are also made up. What Mikszáth's works constantly imply (sometimes explicitly and sometimes implicitly) is that the difference between fact and fiction is not the difference between truth and falsehood, but the difference between the merely existent and the significantly human. This seems to lead to the apparent paradox that everything significantly human is a fiction; and so, for Mikszáth, it is.

But this does not mean that there are no distinctions between truth and falsehood. There are in Mikszáth true fictions, such as those of **"A gavallérok"** or of Pongrácz in *Beszterce ostroma,* and false fictions, such as those of Katánghy in *Két választás Magyarországon* or of the Noszty clan in *Noszty fiú.* In Mikszáth the reader seldom encounters a fiction that is neither true nor false in this sense. Görgei's suspicion [in *A fekete város*] that his real daughter is dead and that the girl supposedly his daughter is not really his is an example of this. Whereas most perpetrators of false fictions deliberately intend to deceive—that is, they deliberately intend their fictions to be mistaken for realities—, and whereas most perpetrators of true fictions are more or less self-conscious victims of their own wishful thinking, Görgei is simply the victim of man's fiction-making power. He is not deliberately abusing this power; he is merely unaware of its operation. For lack of a better term, this unawareness of the operation of man's fiction-making power may be called "total fiction."

These three subdivisions under the general heading of fiction, that is, true fiction, false fiction, and total fiction, are in some form or another constantly present in metafiction. According to a recent critic the "hallmark" of all metafiction is a "keen perception of paradox in the relationship between fiction and reality. . . . If human reality is itself a dizzying kaleidoscope of individually improvised fictions . . . a novel is a fiction at a second remove, a manifest fabrication about fabrications."

This is most evidently true of *Két választás Magyarországon.* In that novel false fictions, the fictions of Katánghy and his kind, are clearly contrasted with true fiction, the fiction perpetrated by "Mikszáth" in the very act of writing the book, while total fiction applies to the characters within the novel who are duped by the various false fictions perpetrated by Katánghy or others. Here the reader is unquestionably in a privileged position. He sees what most of the characters in the book do not see, namely that Katánghy's fictions are false, but he also sees something else, namely that "Mikszáth" is writing a true fiction. From the reader's point of view, then, the difference between Mikszáth's novel and a historical work dealing with the same period would amount to a difference best summarized by the following: history is factual fiction; fiction, afactual history. It should be kept in mind that a distinction such as this is manifestly implicit in Mikszáth's work.

In the tongue-in-cheek "Preface" to the 1900 *Almanach,* Mikszáth explicitly addresses himself to this precise relationship between the fictive and the real. **"Képzeletbeli miniszterek"** (**"Imaginary Ministers"**) takes up the playful contrast between the realm of the novelist and that of the journalist. The difference between the two is that while the novelist "works for immortality, the journalist works for tomorrow." Mikszáth's subject matter in the "Preface," however, is not so much about the difference between these two realms, but about the difficulty of keeping them distinct. In order to accomplish the "impossible" feat of keeping these two "imaginary realms" separate, Mikszáth claims to require the services of two "imaginary ministers," one from each. These two ministers, how-

ever, are not always capable of keeping their respective realms from encroaching upon one another's territories. In fact, one or the other will at times deliberately create trouble for "Mikszáth" by giving the wrong kind of advice.

One such instance involves a story during the composition of which one of Mikszáth's imaginary ministers prompts the author to insert "a real name" in his fictitious text. Since the character bearing the real name is given an imaginary ring of great value, a member of the family pays a visit to Mikszáth soon after the publication of the story. This "relative" claims that other members of the family charge him with having unlawfully appropriated the valuable ring mentioned in the story. The "relative" requests that Mikszáth write a retraction of the entire episode. When Mikszáth responds that this will not be necessary since the story in question is "'not history,'" since the ring is "'imaginary,'" and since the whole episode is presented in such a way that it cannot possibly "'be taken seriously,'" the complainer's simple response is to say that "'that is all the more reason for my relatives to believe it completely.'"

Because of this "unpleasant" episode, Mikszáth calls upon his imaginary ministers and lays down the following law: "in novels no fictitious things shall be attached to real persons" and "in newspapers no real persons shall be given fictitious attributes." But the attempt to abide by this law proves futile, for soon a politician mentioned in a newspaper article complains about a fictitious attribute *he* gives himself.

This tongue-in-cheek piece about imaginary ministers is Mikszáth's testimony that there are good reasons why the realm of the real and that of the fictitious are difficult to keep apart. Rather than speak of unrealistic "form" and Realistic or occasionally anti-Romantic "matter" or "content," it would behoove Mikszáth critics to speak of the world of his novels as making constantly implied distinctions between fiction as afactual history and accounts of real life (private or public) as factual fictions. The Realistic thrust, with the occasional utilization of certain tenets peculiar to late nineteenth-century Realism, of many of his works then would no longer demand that he be viewed as a "great Realist." And this would also make adequate room for the Romantic thrust more predominantly present in Mikszáth's work.

The term "romantic realist" is, in this sense, not misapplied, but perhaps "fabulator" would do better service here. Metafiction, or fiction about fiction, is of course the mode par excellence of the Mikszáthian fabulator. His afactual histories bear a significant relationship to the factual fictions of real life in that they are the fabulous displacements of the ways in which real life itself is consciously or subconsciously invented by those who actively or passively participate in it. All of Mikszáth's works seem, in short, to "demonstrate the necessity of making up 'fictions' if we are to understand and explain our own experience."

But, as with all metafiction (and particularly so with Mikszáth's), the self-consciousness of fiction becomes an antidote for the unself-consciousness both possible and unfortunately frequent in real life. Self-consciousness is, after all, a form of self-knowledge, and self-reference is a form of self-scrutiny. Without these instances of awareness, the self runs the risk of totally eclipsing itself in unrecognized fictions of its own making. Mikszáthian self-consciousness is, in the final analysis, a constant warning to the reader: *de te fabula.* From Mikszáth's point of view, however, this Horatian admonition should be revised to: *actus fabulae fingendae de te,* for it is the act of making fables itself that concerns the reader.

No matter how eminent, there is a sense in which a Hungarian writer has no place in world literature. The school of thought that looks upon world literature from the point of view of Goethe tends to include in it the literatures of the major languages of the Western world, or, better, the literatures of the major nations. According to this school of thought almost nothing written outside of Russia, Germany, France, Italy, Spain, England, and the United States has a secure place in world literature.

There is, however, another school of thought usually, though not exclusively, advocated by the scholars of those nations that have been omitted by the above. In this sense world literature is, as the name implies, the literature of the world. It therefore seems advisable to speak of Mikszáth as having a place not so much in world literature as in the world *of* literature. Here he occupies an undeniably eminent position.

According to his life and times, Mikszáth's creative career falls roughly into the age of rising Realism and Naturalism on the one hand, and the coming of psychological and perspectival modernity on the other. He has, of course, more in common with Nikolai Gogol, Thomas Hardy, and Mark Twain than with Balzac, Emile Zola, or Theodore Dreiser. In **"Legkedvesebb könyveim"** (**"My Favorite Books"**), Mikszáth mentions that his immediate teachers included such foreign authors as Charles Dickens, Thomas Macaulay, and Thomas Carlyle. Among Dickens's novels *David Copperfield* seems to have left the greatest impression on Mikszáth. According to his own testimony, upon finishing that particular book he abstained from writing for a "period of three years" for fear of unfavorable "comparison." In this same piece Mikszáth acknowledges that his "simplicity of style" was directly influenced by the works of Macauley and Carlyle (sic). He also speaks here of a belated acquaintance with Dostoevsky, which came unfortunately at a time when its potential influence was no longer a possibility. "I was an old tree by this time," he tells us, "too old to grow in a different direction." Among Hungarian writers, Mikszáth was most manifestly influenced by Jókai, the "Great Romanticist," under whose shadow he came to prominence and whose reputation he was not able to eclipse until after Jókai's death in 1904.

Notwithstanding his reputation, partially self-generated, that he was a jovial and artless storyteller, Mikszáth was a deeply learned man. He read a great deal and at times he seems to have read relatively indiscriminately. A careful examination of his work, particularly of his quasihistorical novels, shows a great deal of research, though this research is never pedantic (except at times as a parody of pedanticism). Once an idea suggested by history becomes thematically significant, Mikszáth usually abstains from further research. Historic truth, in other words, takes second place to artistic validity. This is most manifestly true of such masterpieces as *Különös házasság, Noszty fiú,* and *A fekete város.*

His own influence on his followers is perhaps less evident than the influence he himself received. I am, of course, not speaking here of his conscious imitators. Nevertheless, without his deintoxication of Romanticism such of his followers as Gyula Krúdy, Ferenc Herczeg, and (above all) Zsigmond Móricz would not have had an easy time overcoming the necessary obstacles that could well have impeded their own development.

In the final analysis, however, Mikszáth's place in the world of literature is more important than either the immediate influences upon him or his own immediate influence upon his followers. In his work there is a strange mixture of eighteenth-century self-consciousness an early twentieth-century modernity. Were it not for the at times uncompromisingly doctrinaire insistence upon "social realism" in post-World War II Hungary, Mikszáth's continued influence would have necessarily produced unique native offshoots of such recent developments as the French *nouveau roman.* The quasisolipsistic self-consciousness of a Nabokov or a John Fowles or a John Barth could have also found a more fertile ground in present-day Hungary as a direct result of the heretofore neglected metafictional significance of Mikszáth's work. As it is, his vision of life combined with his particular embodiment of that vision is still awaiting a potential influence in a hopefully more open and more tolerant future. His works are there, and they speak a language of their own, and that language happens to be one of the major languages in the world of literature. (pp. 140-49)

> *Steven C. Scheer, in his* Kálmán Mikszáth, *Twayne Publishers, 1977, 161 p.*

ADDITIONAL BIBLIOGRAPHY

Conroy, Jack. "A Hungarian Novel." *American Book Collector* 16, No. 1 (September 1965): 6.
> Review of *A Strange Marriage.* Conroy notes that Mikszáth's "keen observation, unaffected liberalism and wit are again well displayed in this novel."

"Eastern Europe Speaking English." *Times Literary Supplement* (21 January 1965): 52.
> Brief, favorable review of *A Strange Marriage.*

Review of *St. Peter's Umbrella. Nation* 71 (22 November 1900): 409-10.
> Calls *St. Peter's Umbrella* a "refreshingly crisp and amusing romance," praising Mikszáth's "knack at portraits (many of them curios for the English reader), his unquenchable feeling for the absurd, his unsentimental pathos, his unexpectedness of device, his resilient manner."

George Orwell

1903-1950

(Pseudonym of Eric Arthur Blair) English novelist, essayist, critic, and journalist.

The following entry presents criticism of Orwell's novel *Animal Farm* (1945). For discussion of Orwell's complete career, see *TCLC*, Volumes 2 and 6; for discussion of the novel *Nineteen Eighty-Four,* see *TCLC*, Volume 15.

Orwell is significant for his unwavering commitment, both as an individual and as an artist, to personal freedom and social justice, and *Animal Farm* is the first and arguably the finest example of the fusion of artistic and political purpose in his writing. This deceptively simple animal fable about a barnyard revolt satirizes the consequences of the Russian Revolution, while also suggesting reasons for the universal failure of most revolutionary ideals. Orwell's skill in creating a narrative that functions on several levels is almost unanimously applauded, and most negative assessments of the novel, both upon its first publication in 1945 and in the decades since, have criticized Orwell's political opinions and not his crafting of the narrative, which is generally regarded as a masterpiece of English prose. Orwell's ability to perceive the social effects of political theories inspired Irving Howe to call him "the greatest moral force in English letters during the past several decades."

Orwell's commitment to justice and freedom led him to travel to Barcelona in December 1936 to investigate and write about the causes and progress of the Spanish Civil War. He almost immediately joined a militia unit and fought with the Republicans. After being wounded, Orwell returned to England and wrote *Homage to Catalonia,* an account that depicts the absurdities of warfare, the duplicity of every political ideology, and the essential decency of ordinary people caught up in events beyond their control. In his 1946 essay "Why I Write," Orwell stated that "every line of serious work that I have written since 1936 has been written, directly or indirectly, *against* totalitarianism and *for* democratic Socialism, as I understand it." He went on to say that "*Animal Farm* was the first book in which I tried, with full consciousness of what I was doing, to fuse political purpose and artistic purpose into one whole," and most critics agree that he succeeded admirably.

The search for a publisher for *Animal Farm* took eighteen months, for the novel was rejected by numerous publishing firms on the grounds that it was too harsh a criticism of the Soviet Union, then a British ally. One publisher said that it was too negative in its outlook, failing to affirm any point of view, while an American publisher turned it down because animal stories were not popular in the United States. Once the novel appeared, however, it was an immediate success, garnering enthusiastic reviews and selling out its first edition in a matter of months. It has since sold over nine million copies in dozens of languages, and together with *Nineteen Eighty-Four* remains Orwell's best-known and most widely read work.

Nothing in Orwell's career indicated that his desire to write politically committed literature that was "also an aesthetic experience" would find expression in a skillfully executed animal fable. *Animal Farm* has been described by J. R. Hammond, for example, as "totally different in style and conception

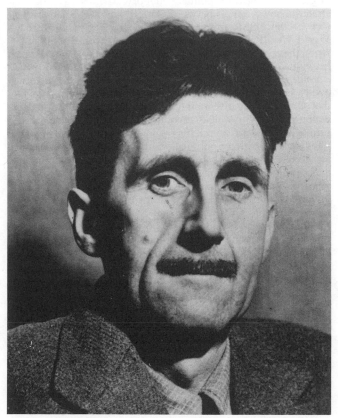

from anything Orwell had previously written," and by Laurence Brander as "a sport, out of [Orwell's] usual way; and yet more effective in the crusade to which he was dedicated than anything else he wrote." *Animal Farm* does represent a radical departure from the documentaries, essays, and novels that Orwell wrote in the 1930s; however, many commentators have noted that Orwell was undoubtedly aware that the genre of the beast fable was uniquely suited to his own purposes of social and political satire. Traditionally in such fables, each animal represents not only itself—and in the finest examples of the genre the animal characters are always recognizable as animals—but also a single aspect of human nature which the author has fixed upon for comment, thus avoiding the psychological complications inherent in presenting fully developed human characters. As George Woodcock has noted, "A fable drives home its satiric intent by presenting a simplification of complex happenings of life." The conventions of the animal fable enabled Orwell to examine simply and directly the multifarious moral decisions made within a political system. According to Rama Rani Lall: "Animal allegory prescribes two levels of perception which interact to purvey the irony in comparison and contrast. In *Animal Farm* the animals are consistently animals and Orwell keeps the reader conscious simultaneously of the human traits satirized and of the animals as animals. He has successfully played upon the two levels of perception, making us feel that his animals are really animals and are yet as human as ourselves. Though he has couched his criticism in the simplest of terms, it is convincing because of the realistic pictures of animal life.''

Although Orwell intended *Animal Farm* to depict the inevitable course of all revolutions, the Soviet Union was the primary target of the novel's pointed allegory. Critics have demonstrated many parallels between Orwell's narrative and the history of the USSR from the time of the Revolution through World War II. Commentators hostile to Orwell's political position have endeavored to demonstrate that the novel is an inadequate treatment of extremely complicated issues, or that *Animal Farm* does not contain exact parallels to the historical events being satirized and is therefore invalid. Others maintain that Orwell's negative opinions about human nature and the development of political revolutions rendered *Animal Farm* primarily an expression of his own pessimism and thus without relevance to social or political reality. Nevertheless, most critics concur that the basic plot of the novel closely parallels events in the Soviet Union. Snowball and Napoleon, the pigs who formulate the animals' revolutionary principles and who govern the farm following the overthrow of the human masters, represent Leon Trotsky and Josef Stalin, even to Snowball's eventual ouster by Napoleon, who subsequently rewrites the history of the revolution to make Snowball appear to be a villain collaborating with the humans who are constantly scheming to retake the farm. The pig Squealer represents the official Soviet news agency *Pravda;* his persuasive oratory convinces the animals that with pigs in charge conditions are better than ever, when in fact they are worse. The simple and hardworking carthorses and the anonymous sheep stand for whole classes of people whose uncomprehending complicity aids the tyrants who pervert revolutionary ideals of equality to establish themselves as the new ruling elite.

The most common critical approach to *Animal Farm* acknowledges that, while Orwell's specific political purpose was to show that the Soviet Union was not fulfilling the promise of socialism, the novel was also intended as an illustration of the inherent dangers of all totalitarian systems. One of the novel's primary themes is the inevitable failure of the egalitarian ideals that first encourage revolt against an established order. According to Orwell, the violence necessary to overthrow one system and establish another carries over into the new regime and leads to abuses of power on the part of the new leaders, who seek to retain their hold. Cyril Connolly writes that "the commandments of the Animal Revolution, such as 'no animal shall kill another animal' or 'all animals are equal' can perhaps never be achieved by a revolutionary seizure of power, but only by the spiritual operation of reason or moral philosophy in the animal heart.'' Many critics maintain that long after historical awareness of the Russian Revolution as the main target of Orwell's satire fades, the novel will retain its powerful appeal because of its universally applicable message about the dangers of totalitarian rule.

Orwell's prose style, especially in his essays, has become a model for students of writing because of its precision, clarity, and vividness. Indeed, many of his essays, which combine observation and reminiscence with literary and social criticism, are considered modern masterpieces. Orwell's fiction, however, has not been as highly praised: with the exception of *Animal Farm*, critics commonly cite weaknesses in description, plot, or characterization, or a tendency toward overt didacticism, as flaws of Orwell's novels. Many commentators contend

that in *Animal Farm* Orwell achieved his ideal of prose "like a window pane'' through which the reader can examine a topic without encountering an obtrusive authorial presence. The animal fable form eliminated the need for Orwell to intrude with his own comments: any moral is implicit in the fable and stands on its own.

Many ideas from Orwell's fiction have become a part of the modern imagination. Richard I. Smyer has said that "Orwell belongs to that small group of twentieth-century writers whose fictional works have influenced the thinking of readers who are only slightly interested in imaginative literature.'' The seventh commandment of Animalism, and its final perversion— "All animals are equal, but some animals are more equal than others''—is perhaps as widely familiar as the catchphrases from *Nineteen Eighty-Four* that have become part of the mass consciousness of the late twentieth century.

(See also *Contemporary Authors,* Vol. 104; *Dictionary of Literary Biography,* Vol. 15: *British Novelists, 1930-1959;* and *Something about the Author,* Vol. 29.)

CYRIL CONNOLLY   (essay date 1945)

[*Connolly was an English novelist and critic who reviewed books for the* New Statesman, *the* Observer, *and the* Sunday Times *from 1927 until his death in 1974. Considered a remarkably hard-to-please critic, he was the founding editor of the respected literary monthly* Horizon *(1939-1950). In the following essay, Connolly considers* Animal Farm *a "beautifully worked out'' allegory of the Russian Revolution that is valuable for its skilled writing as well as for its debatable political component.*]

Mr. Orwell is a revolutionary who is in love with 1910. This ambivalence constitutes his strength and his weakness. Never before has a progressive political thinker been so handicapped by nostalgia for the Edwardian shabby-genteel or the underdog. It is this political sentimentality which from the literary point of view is his most valid emotion. *Animal Farm* proves it, for it truly is a fairy story told by a great lover of liberty and a great lover of animals. The farm is real, the animals are moving. At the same time it is a devastating attack on Stalin and his "betrayal'' of the Russian revolution, as seen by another revolutionary. The allegory between the animals and the fate of their revolution (they drive out the human beings and plan a Utopia entrusted to the leadership of the pigs—Napoleon-Stalin, Snowball-Trotsky—with the dogs as police, the sheep as yes-men, the two cart-horses, Boxer and Clover, as the noble hard-working proletariat), and the Russian experiment is beautifully worked out, perhaps the most felicitous moment being when the animal "saboteurs'' are executed for some of the very crimes of the Russian trials, such as the sheep who confessed to having "urinated in the drinking pool'' or the goose which kept back six ears of corn and ate them in the night. The fairy tale ends with the complete victory of Napoleon and the pigs, who rule Animal Farm, with a worse tyranny and a far greater efficiency than its late human owner, the dissolute Mr. Jones.

Politically one might make to Mr. Orwell the same objections as to Mr. Koestler for his essay on Russia in *The Yogi and the Commissar*—both allow their personal bitterness about the betrayed revolution to prejudice their attitude to the facts. But it is arguable that every revolution is "betrayed'' because the violence necessary to achieve it is bound to generate an admiration for violence, which leads to the abuse of power. A revolution is the forcible removal of an obsolete and inefficient ruling-class by a vigorous and efficient one which replaces it for as long as its vitality will allow. The commandments of the Animal Revolution, such as "no animal shall kill any other animal" or "all animals are equal" can perhaps never be achieved by a revolutionary seizure of power but only by the spiritual operation of reason or moral philosophy in the animal heart. If we look at Russia without the particular bitterness of the disappointed revolutionary we see that it is an immensely powerful managerial despotism—far more powerful than its Czarist predecessor—where, on the whole, despite a police system which we should find intolerable, the masses are happy, and where great strides in material progress have been made (i.e. independence of women, equality of sexes, autonomy of racial and cultural minorities, utilization of science to improve the standard of living, religious toleration, etc.). If Stalin and his regime were not loved as well as feared the Animal Farm which comprises the greatest land-mass of the world would not have united to roll back the most efficient invading army which the world has ever known—and if in truth Stalin is loved then he and his regime cannot be quite what they appear to Mr. Orwell (indeed Napoleon's final brutality to Boxer—if Boxer symbolises the proletariat—is not paralleled by any incident in Stalin's career, unless the Scorched Earth policy is indicated). But it is unfair to harp on these considerations. *Animal Farm* is one of the most enjoyable books since the war, it is deliciously written, with something of the feeling, the penetration and the verbal economy of Orwell's master, Swift. It deserves a wide sale and a lengthy discussion. Apart from the pleasure it has given me to read, I welcome it for three reasons, because it breaks down some of the artificial reserve with which Russia is written about, or not written about, . . . because it restores the allegorical pamphlet to its rightful place as a literary force, and lastly because it proves that Mr. Orwell has not been entirely seduced away by the opinion-airing attractions of weekly journalism from his true vocation, which is to write books. (pp. 215-16)

Cyril Connolly, in a review of "Animal Farm," in *Horizon, London, Vol. XII, No. 69, September, 1945, pp. 215-16.*

GEORGE SOULE   (essay date 1946)

[*Soule was an American educator, editor, and critic. In the following excerpt from an early review of* Animal Farm, *he contends that the work fails as an allegory because the satire is too dependent upon reader identification of characters and events within the novel with historic counterparts whose roles often correspond imprecisely.*]

George Orwell in his critical writings shows imagination and taste; his wit is both edged and human. Few writers of any period have been able to use the English language so simply and accurately to say what they mean, and at the same time to mean something. The news that he had written a satirical allegory, telling the story of a revolution by farm animals against their cruel and dissolute master, and of their subsequent fortunes, was like the smell of a roast from a kitchen ruled by a good cook, near the end of a hungry morning. The further news that this book had been chosen and was being pushed by the Book of the Month Club, though it occasioned surprise, was pleasant because it seemed to herald one of those instances

when unusual talent of the sort rarely popular receives recognition and a great tangible reward.

There are times when a reviewer is happy to report that a book is bad because it fulfills his hope that the author will expose himself in a way that permits a long deserved castigation. This is not one of them. I was expecting that Orwell would again give pleasure and that his satire of the sort of thing which democrats deplore in the Soviet Union would be keen and cleansing. Instead, the book puzzled and saddened me. It seemed on the whole dull. The allegory turned out to be a creaking machine for saying in a clumsy way things have been said better directly. And many of the things said are not instantly recognized as the essence of truth, but are of the sort which start endless and boring controversy.

Orwell does know his farm animals and gives them vivid personalities. Many will recognize Benjamin, the donkey who never commits himself, never hurries and thinks that in the end nothing much matters. Mollie the saddle horse, who wanders from the puritanical path of the revolution to seek ribbons for her mane, the cat who never does any work, the hens who sabotage by laying their eggs in the rafters, Clover and Boxer, the powerful, trusting and honest draught horses, are all real enough. But these spontaneous creatures seem in action like circus animals performing mechanically to the crack of the story-teller's whip.

Part of the trouble lies in the fact that the story is too close to recent historical events without being close enough. Major, the aged pig who on his deathbed tells the animals of their oppression and prophesies revolution, must be Karl Marx. His two followers who lead the revolution, Napoleon and Snowball, are then readily identified as Lenin and Trotsky. This identification turns out to be correct in the case of Snowball, but the reader soon begins to puzzle over the fact that Napoleon disapproves the project of building a windmill—an obvious symbol for electrification and industrialization—whereas this was Lenin's program. The puzzlement is increased when Napoleon chases out Snowball as a traitor; it was Stalin who did this.

And so it goes through incident after incident. The young dogs are alone selected for schooling; later they appear as the secret police. Is this a picture of Soviet education? The pigs not only keep the best food for themselves, but also become drunkards, taking over the pasture reserved for retirement of the superannuated in order to raise the necessary barley. Of course prohibition was abolished early in the revolution, but have the leaders drunk too much and has social insurance been abolished? There is a pathetic incident when Boxer, the sturdy and loyal old work horse, is sent off to be slaughtered and turned into dog food and bone meal, under the pretext that he is being hospitalized. Just what part of Soviet history corresponds to this?

Nobody would suppose that good allegory is literally accurate, but when the reader is continually led to wonder who is who and what aspect of reality is being satirized, he is prevented either from enjoying the story as a story or from valuing it as a comment. Masters like Swift and Anatole France, with whom Orwell is compared in the blurbs, were not guilty of this fault. They told good stories, the interest of which did not lie wholly in their caricature. And their satire, however barbed, was not dependent on identification of historical personages or specific events.

The thoughtful reader must be further disturbed by the lack of clarity in the main intention of the author. Obviously he is convinced that the animals had just cause for revolt and that for a time their condition was improved under the new regime. But they are betrayed by their scoundrelly, piggish leaders. In the end, the pigs become indistinguishable from the men who run the other nearby farms; they walk on two legs, have double and triple chins, wear clothes and carry whips. Animal Farm reverts to the old Manor Farm in both name and reality.

No doubt this is what George Orwell thinks has happened in Russia. But if he wants to tell us why it happened, he has failed. Does he mean to say that not these pigs, but Snowball, should have been on top? Or that all the animals should have been merged in a common primitive communism without leaders or organization? Or that it was a mistake to try to industralize, because pastoral simplicity is the condition of equality and cooperation? Or that, as in the old saw criticizing socialism, the possibility of a better society is a pipe-dream, because if property were distributed equally, the more clever and selfish would soon get a larger share and things would go on as of old? Though I am sure he did not intend this moral, the chances are that a sample poll of the book-club readers in the United States would indicate that a large majority think so and will heartily approve the book on that account.

There is no question that Orwell hates tyranny, sycophancy, deceitful propaganda, sheeplike acceptance of empty political formulas. His exposures of these detestable vices constitutes the best passages in the book. There have been plenty of such abuses in Russia. They also crop up in other places. It is difficult to believe that they determined the whole issue of the Russian revolution, or that Russia is now just like every other nation. No doubt in some respects she is worse than most; in other respects she may be better.

It seems to me that the failure of this book (commerically it is already assured of tremendous success) arises from the fact that the satire deals not with something the author has experienced, but rather with stereotyped ideas about a country which he probably does not know very well. The plan for the allegory, which must have seemed a good one when he first thought of it, became mechanical in execution. It almost appears as if he had lost his zest before he got very far with the writing. He should try again, and this time on something nearer home. (pp. 266-67)

> *George Soule, "Orwell's Fables," in* The New Republic, *Vol. 115, No. 9, September 2, 1946, pp. 266-67.*

ADAM DE HEGEDUS (essay date 1946)

[*In the following early review of* Animal Farm, *de Hegedus notes the applicability of Orwell's satire to the Soviet system and maintains that the novel has lasting value as a parable with universal dimensions.*]

It was not a far-fetched comparison which at the time [*Animal Farm*] was published in England, likened it to *Gulliver's Travels* or rather to its chapter which is devoted to the country of the Houyhnhnms and deals with Gulliver's adventures in the realm of the horses.

On the other hand, many readers of this book would be unable to get away from *Animal Farm*'s great relevance to contemporary Russia and might think it is nothing beyond a very brilliant and very cruel satire on the communist experiment.

The temptations to regard it purely and simply as a short and brilliant *roman á clef* are very great indeed. The reader experiences a little thrill in discovering famous characters in cruel disguises. The old boar who tells the animals at Manor Farm of his dream of a happy future world in which they will not be exploited and slaughtered by Man is surely Lenin. Boxer, the strong, kind, slow-witted horse, who is heroic in an emergency, easy to mislead and fundamentally decent is obviously the Common Man who is getting more and more frightened of the century which Mr. Henry Wallace dedicated to him. In Napoleon the Machiavellian pig it is very difficult not to see Stalin, whereas Snowball the dreamer pig, who is expelled from Animal Farm and provides an excellent scapegoat for the future failures of the experiment is Trotsky. And who can be the rest of the pigs, who had helped to transform Manor Farm into "Animal Farm" under the war-cry, "Two legs bad, four legs good" and who enjoy special privileges for their leadership? They are surely members of the Communist Party.

In any case the revolution succeeds in the name of *all animals are equal,* but soon enough there are quarrels between the two pig-leaders: Snowball the dreamer and Napoleon the realist. Snowball is driven out.

Now, Snowball during the revolution had been awarded the decoration of "Animal Hero First Class" and his expulsion causes great surprise, though the sheep and the hens quickly learn that Snowball was a traitor and the decoration had been awarded by mistake. And so the story continues, about as one would expect. Finally "Animal Farm" adopts a new slogan: *all animals are equal but some animals are more equal than the rest.*

Animal Farm, however, is deeper and larger than this, in the same way as Swift's Gulliver is of a more permanent significance than just being an attack on the Tory Party in eighteenth century England. It has implications—and they are many— which are older and more universal than the past and present of the Union of Soviet Socialist Republics. It gives a splendid illumination of Acton's immortal thesis according to which power corrupts and absolute power corrupts absolutely. It also supplies a very simple, very clear and to my mind a very adequate statement on man's craving for the absolute, which is the most powerful basis of nationalism: the most important, most real and most threatening political problem of our time, which an orthodox Marxist can never see in its true proportion. He still maintains that the economic problem is more important than the political problem and that the two—the twin problems of our century—cannot be separated from each other. Orwell knows that this is not the case and that the economic problem is the lesser of the two, though being "nearer the camera" it most of the time appears to be out of correct proportion. He also knows that a man who loves his country unreasonably in as many words issues an invitation to any ruling oligarchy to be exploited and trampled upon.

> The revolution goes wrong at Animal Farm, the old doctrines, the shining words of the Constitution which were painted on the barn door are perverted, yet the animals never gave up hope.
>
> More, they never lost, even for an instant, their sense of honor and privilege in being members of Animal Farm. They were still the only farm in the whole country—in all England!—owned and operated by animals. Not one of them, not even the youngest, not even the newcomers who had been brought from farms ten or twenty miles away, ever ceased to marvel at that. And when they heard the gun booming

and saw the green flag fluttering at the masthead, their hearts swelled with imperishable pride, and the talk turned always towards the old heroic days, the expulsion of Jones, the writing of the Seven Commandments, the great battles in which the human invaders had been defeated. None of the old dreams had been abandoned. The Republic of the Animals which Major had foretold, when the green fields of England should be untrodden by human feet, was still believed in. Some day it was coming: it might not be soon, it might not be within the lifetime of any animal now living, but still it was coming. . . .

Passages like these seem to contain a good deal of survival value for *Animal Farm.* Because it is a parable, it escapes the great pitfall of reportage and documentary writing which by their very natures leave their material without significance. Orwell, however, is an artist, who knows precisely how effective it can be not to say explicitly what he means, and this little tale of a hundred and twenty odd pages has more explosive energy and actuality than a five hundred page carefully documented report on Russia. More than that: it is poetry, which is the type of journalism ''that stays news.''

Orwell is not angry with Russia, or with any other country, because that country ''turned Socialist.'' On the contrary he is angry with Russia because Russia does not believe in a classless and democratic society. His anger and frustration are those of the man who—like himself—in spite of his social origin and upbringing, had for months been dishwasher and a Down and Out In Paris And London and who—like himself—went to fight for democratic Spain in an anti-Stalin loyalist battalion. In short, Orwell is angry with Russia because Russia is *not* socialist. (pp. 528-30)

> Adam de Hegedus, in a review of ''Animal Farm,'' in The Commonweal, *Vol. XLIV, No. 22, September 13, 1946, pp. 528-30.*

GEORGE ORWELL   (essay date 1947)

[*In 1947 Orwell wrote a preface for the Ukrainian edition of* Animal Farm. *His original text has been lost, and the following excerpt is taken from a retranslation into English of the Ukrainian version. In it, Orwell explains the genesis of* Animal Farm *and his intentions in writing the novel.*]

On my return from Spain I thought of exposing the Soviet myth in a story that could be easily understood by almost anyone and which could be easily translated into other languages. However the actual details of the story did not come to me for some time until one day (I was then living in a small village) I saw a little boy, perhaps ten years old, driving a huge cart-horse along a narrow path, whipping it whenever it tried to turn. It struck me that if only such animals became aware of their strength we should have no power over them, and that men exploit animals in much the same way as the rich exploit the proletariat.

I proceeded to analyse Marx's theory from the animals' point of view. To them it was clear that the concept of a class struggle between humans were pure illusion, since whenever it was necessary to exploit animals, all humans united against them: the true struggle is between animals and humans. From this point of departure, it was not difficult to elaborate the story. I did not write it out till 1943, for I was always engaged on other work which gave me no time; and in the end, I included some events, for example the Teheran Conference, which were taking place while I was writing. Thus the main outlines of

the story were in my mind over a period of six years before it was actually written.

I do not wish to comment on the work; if it does not speak for itself it is a failure. But I should like to emphasise two points: first, that although the various episodes are taken from the actual history of the Russian Revolution, they are dealt with schematically and their chronological order is changed; this was necessary for the symmetry of the story. The second point has been missed by most critics, possibly because I did not emphasise its sufficiently. A number of readers may finish the book with the impression that it ends in the complete reconciliation of the pigs and the humans. That was not my intention; on the contrary I meant it to end on a loud note of discord, for I wrote it immediately after the Teheran Conference which everybody thought had established the best possible relations between the USSR and the West. I personally did not believe that such good relations would last long; and, as events have shown, I wasn't far wrong. . . . (pp. 405-06)

> George Orwell, *''Preface to the Ukrainian Edition of 'Animal Farm','' in his* The Collected Essays, Journalism and Letters of George Orwell: As I Please, 1943-1945, *Vol. III, edited by Sonia Orwell and Ian Angus, Harcourt Brace Jovanovich, 1968, pp. 402-06.*

LAURENCE BRANDER   (essay date 1954)

[*In the following synopsis of* Animal Farm, *Brander characterizes the novel as unique among Orwell's works in its carefully structured form as well as its ''gay and droll'' narrative style, which masks the stark satire of the novel. Brander commends the great artistry and imagination that Orwell displayed in* Animal Farm *and contends that Orwell poses questions about the nature of revolution and democracy without offering conclusions.*]

Animal Farm is one of those apparently chance pieces a prose writer throws off, which immediately becomes more popular than his more ambitious writings. A sport, out of his usual way; and yet more effective in the crusade to which he was dedicated than anything else he wrote.

For once, the gaiety in his nature had completely taken charge. He was writing about animals, whom he loved. He had had a rest of nearly three years from serious writing. He wrote with zest, and although humour rarely travels across national boundaries, his enjoyment has been shared everywhere. Humour travels most easily in peasant portraiture, as in *The Good Soldier Schweik* and *Don Camillo*; and in animal stories. Not many books have been translated into so many languages so successfully and so quickly as *Animal Farm.*

It was conceived and ''sweated over'' between November 1943 and February 1944. The worst of the war was over and its outcome assured; it was possible to write again. Orwell never stampeded with the herd, so while everyone around him was praising Russian victories, he wrote a little story to remind people what Stalinism was really like. It was his most effective sermon; many preachers are most successful with the adults during the children's sermon.

The theme is closely connected, therefore, with *Homage to Catalonia* and *1984,* and no doubt the moment of its conception decided its form. It was no time to preach overtly against Russian political methods. It was not the moment for a didactic novel. But a slip of a story, gay and droll in the tradition of animal stories, was just the thing. The story goes along so gaily, and yet the stark satire is always there like a skull behind an innocent smiling face. The animal characters fit cunningly to their human counterparts. There is a mocking similarity between what the pigs say and what politicians say. And there is such stupidity and perfidiousness in all the humans do; as if, judged by decent animal standards, we are very poor creatures indeed. It is the Houyhnhnm theme of Swift repeated. *Animal Farm* has the Swiftian indictment of the offending race of humankind.

The style, like the form, is unique in Orwell's work. He had been a master of the descriptive way of writing from the beginning, from the opening words of *Down and Out,* but he had never before achieved pure narrative. In *Animal Farm,* from the start, we feel the special power of the storyteller. The animals expel the farmer and his men and take over the farm. The farmer tries to come back but is driven away. The other farmers do not interfere because they look forward to taking the farm over cheaply when the animals have ruined it. The animals, led by the pigs, do not make a mess of it, and the farm is well enough run for the authorities to leave it alone. Eventually, the pigs turn out to be harder slave-drivers than men, so in the end the neighbouring farmers make friends with the pigs and admit that they have much to learn from the labour conditions on Animal Farm.

There is no looseness anywhere in the structure. The story is rounded, the end joining the beginning. The opening speech of the old boar, Major, is answered at the end in the words of Mr. Pilkington and Napoleon. The various levels of satire are similarly rounded, so that the story and all its implications form circles each in its own plane.

The convention of writing animal stories is as old as Æsop in European literature and has been used in England from Chaucer's time. Every animal corresponds to a human type, and though there were many animals in the Ark, there are still human types to place against them. Orwell restates the convention right at the beginning, in the meeting of the animals:

> At one end of the big barn, on a sort of raised platform, Major was already ensconced on his bed of straw, under a lantern which hung from a beam. He was twelve years old and had lately grown rather stout, but he was still a majestic-looking pig, with a wise and benevolent appearance in spite of the fact that his tushes had never been cut. Before long the other animals began to arrive and make themselves comfortable after their different fashions. First came the three dogs, Bluebell, Jessie, and Pitcher, and then the pigs who settled down in the straw immediately in front of the platform. The hens perched themselves on the window-sills, the pigeons fluttered up to the rafters, the sheep and cows lay down behind the pigs and began to chew the cud. The two cart-horses, Boxer and Clover, came in together, walking very slowly and setting down their vast hairy hoofs with great care lest there should be some small animal concealed in the straw. . . .
>
> The two horses had just laid down when a brood of ducklings, which had lost their mother, filed into the barn, cheeping feebly and wandering from side to side to find some place where they would not be trodden on. Clover made a sort of wall round them with her great foreleg, and the ducklings nestled down inside it and promptly fell asleep. . . . Last of all came the cat, who looked round, as usual, for the warmest place, and finally squeezed herself in between Boxer and Clover; there she purred contentedly throughout Major's speech without listening to a word of what he was saying.

It is an enchanting description. There is the bustle and excitement of assembly, just as in Chaucer's *Parlement of Foules*:

> And that so huge a noyse gan they make
> That erthe, and eyr, and tre, and every lake
> So full was, that unethe was there space
> For me to stonde, so full was all the place.

There is the pleasure of watching each animal comporting itself according to its nature. The animal kingdom at once becomes a reflection of human society.

The scene is a parody of a successful meeting of the political opposition. Get the people together with some bait. Turn on the orator to bemuse them, and send them away feeling happy and satisfied, but with the seeds of revolt planted where you want them. The best thing in the parody is the mockery of the egotistical gravity of political rabble-rousers:

> I feel it my duty to pass on to you such political wisdom as I have acquired. I have had a long life. I have had much time for thought as I lay alone in my stall, and I think I may say that I understand the nature of life on this earth as well as any animal now living.

Three days later, Major dies and the spotlight falls upon two younger boars, Napoleon and Snowball, the Stalin and Trotsky of the story. Napoleon was "not much of a talker" but had "a reputation for getting his own way." Snowball was intellectually quicker, but "was not considered to have the same depth of character." (Part of the fun of the animal story is the enormous gravity of the author's approach to his characters.) Snowball obviously has much more brains than Napoleon. It is Snowball who paints the seven commandments against the end wall of the barn, and when it comes to the battle for Manor Farm, and Jones the farmer tries to recover his property, it is Snowball who has prepared and drilled the animals for the expected attack. It is Snowball who leads them and Snowball who is wounded. In the whole episode, Napoleon is never mentioned.

As the community develops, it is observed that Snowball inspired the "Animal Committees," while Napoleon took no interest in such things. Snowball "formed the Egg Production Committee for the hens, the Clean Tails League for the Cows . . . the Whiter Wool Movement for the sheep. . . ." This is the sort of exuberant invention of absurd trivialities that Swift enjoyed in Gulliver. Napoleon, meanwhile, said that "the education of the young was more important than anything that could be done for those who were already grown up." Snowball had altruism, the essential social virtue; Napoleon had a lust for power, and intended to get it by making the animals "less conscious," and that was all he meant by educating the young. Eventually Napoleon wins by his education of a litter of young hounds, who attack Snowball after his eloquent exposition of the windmill scheme, and chase him out of the farm. At his best moment, just when his altruistic plans for giving warmth, food and comfort to all the animals are completed and ready to be carried out, Snowball's brutal rival strikes. It is the same sort of dramatic timing that we shall find in *1984,* an ironic twist to the satire.

After that, the Snowball theme is the denigration of the fallen hero. The animals are all greatly upset by the incident, and Napoleon's young lieutenant, Squealer, works hard to make them less conscious of what has happened:

> "He fought bravely at the Battle of the Cowshed," said somebody.

"Bravery is not enough," said Squealer. "Loyalty and obedience are more important. And as to the Battle of the Cowshed, I believe the time will come when we shall find that Snowball's part in it was much exaggerated. Discipline, comrades, iron discipline! That is the watchword for today. One false step, and our enemies would be upon us. Surely, comrades, you do not want Jones back?"

"Discipline!" the invariable cry of the political gangsters who are destroying freedom and truth. That is the first step in the legend that Snowball is the source of evil. The legend grows step by step with the building up of Napoleon as the leader who thought of everything and is the father of the farm. The windmill was of course really Napoleon's own idea, and Snowball had stolen the plans from among Napoleon's papers. When the windmill falls down at the first puff with wind, Napoleon himself comes forth and snuffs around till he smells Snowball. "'Comrades,' he said quietly, 'do you know who is responsible for this? Do you know the enemy who has come in the night and overthrown our windmill? SNOWBALL!' he suddenly roared in a voice of thunder."

Next spring, it was discovered that Snowball "stole the corn, he upset the milk-pails, he broke the eggs, he trampled the seed-beds, he gnawed the bark off the fruit-trees." A typical touch of hypnosis is supplied when "the cows declared unanimously that Snowball crept into their stalls and milked them in their sleep." Napoleon orders a full investigation, and Squealer is able to tell the animals that "'Snowball was in league with Jones from the very start! He was Jones's secret agent all the time. It has all been proved in documents which he left behind him and which we have only just discovered.'" The authentic note this, and it is heard again when Boxer argues that Snowball was once a good comrade: "'Our leader, Comrade Napoleon,' announced Squealer, speaking very slowly, and firmly, 'has stated categorically—categorically, comrade—that Snowball was Jones's agent from the very beginning.'"

Boxer was too simple to be safe. So the dogs are set on him, but he kicks them aside and releases the one he traps under his vast hoof only on Napoleon's orders. At the trial, the confessions of the animals are invariably of complicity with Snowball. Later it is discovered that far from being the hero of the Battle of the Cowshed, Snowball was censured for showing cowardice. At all these stages the simple animals are very much perplexed. Eventually it is shown (by the discovery of further documents) that Snowball fought on Jones's side at the Battle of the Cowshed. The animals are perplexed at each stage of this long denigration, but they are tired, overworked and underfed and do not remember clearly and the lies are so persuasively put across that at every stage they believe.

This parable of human perplexity in the face of contemporary propaganda methods is told with great skill. It is one of Orwell's most effective treatments of the problem which had focused his attention since his experiences in Spain.

Squealer is the modern propagandist, the P.R.O. [public relations officer] who explains away the worst with the best of spurious reasons. He is a familiar type, with: "very round cheeks, twinkling eyes, nimble movements, and a shrill voice. He was a brilliant talker, and when he was arguing some difficult point he had a way of skipping from side to side and whisking his tail which was somehow very persuasive. The others said of Squealer that he could turn black into white."

He was the mouthpiece of the pigs, the new class who were elbowing their way into power by the methods Orwell marks in an essay on James Burnham: "All talk about democracy, liberty, equality, fraternity, all revolutionary movements, all visions of Utopia, or 'the classless society,' or 'the Kingdom of Heaven on Earth,' are humbug (not necessarily conscious humbug) covering the ambitions of some new class which is elbowing its way into power."

In contrast to Squealer is Moses, the tame raven, who specialized in the kingdom of heaven, but not on earth. Moses disappeared completely for years when the animals took over. It was only when the pigs were in complete control and had turned themselves into an aristocracy at the expense of the lean and hungry animals that Moses returns. His tales of Sugar Candy Mountain, where "it was Sunday seven days a week, clover was in season all the year round, and lump sugar and linseed oil grew on the hedges," are useful again, and in no way threaten the power of the pigs.

Moses has his allowance of a gill of beer a day from the pigs and he does no work. Squealer works hard all the time. He represents the organized lying practised in totalitarian states, which, Orwell says in **"The Prevention of Literature"**: "is not, as is sometimes claimed, a temporary expedient of the same nature as military deception. It is something integral to totalitarianism, something that would still continue even if concentration camps and secret police forces had ceased to be necessary."

Squealer comes into his own when Snowball is expelled, after making his name on the milk-and-apple question. All supplies had been reserved for the pigs, and there is some grumbling: "Many of us actually dislike milk and apples. I dislike them myself. Our sole object in taking these things is to preserve our health." Needless to say, for the purpose of keeping Jones away.

At the moment of Snowball's expulsion, when Napoleon takes over the leadership, Squealer is at his best: "'Comrades,' he said, 'I trust that every animal here appreciates the sacrifice that Comrade Napoleon has made in taking this extra labour upon himself. Do not imagine, comrades, that leadership is a pleasure!'"

When there is any fighting, Squealer is unaccountably absent. His time comes afterwards, when the victory has to be celebrated.

> "What victory?" said Boxer. . . .
>
> "Have we not driven the enemy off our soil? . . .".
>
> "Then we have won back what we had before," said Boxer.
>
> "That is our victory," said Squealer.

A few mornings after that conversation, all the pigs are suffering from a dreadful hangover. It is the drollest incident in the book, and like everything else has its satirical implications.

> It was nearly nine o'clock when Squealer made his appearance walking slowly and dejectedly, his eyes dull, his tail hanging limply behind him, and with every appearance of being seriously ill. He called the animals together and told them that he had a terrible piece of news to impart. Comrade Napoleon was dying!
>
> A cry of lamentation went up. Straw was laid down outside the doors of the farmhouse, and the animals walked on tiptoe.

The next bulletin was that Comrade Napoleon had pronounced a solemn decree as his last act on earth: "the drinking of alcohol was to be punished by death." Within a couple of days the pigs are busily studying books on brewing and distilling.

Squealer is central. He keeps the animals quiet. He puts their minds at rest. He has the air of a beneficent being, sent to make animals happy. He is the agency by which they become "less conscious."

Napoleon develops in personality. He takes on the character of the legendary Leader more and more. He becomes progressively remote. From the beginning he is quite different from Snowball and Squealer. He has none of their mercurial qualities; he is no talker. In the range of porcine character—which would seem to be as great as the human range—he is at the other extreme: a saturnine, cunning pig. A deep pig, with a persistent way of getting what he wants. He is by far the strongest character on the farm. Just as Benjamin, the donkey, has the clearest idea of things, and Boxer, the cart-horse, is the strongest physically.

Boxer's simplicity of character is sentimental comedy of the purest kind. It is the story of the great big good-natured person who thinks harm of nobody, believes all is for the best, so everybody should work as hard as possible and then a little harder still. He is so simple that he does not see his questions are dangerous, and when the pigs make an effort to eliminate him—which is quite hopeless because of his great strength—he never understands what has happened. In the tiny Orwell gallery of pleasant characters, Boxer is the favourite. He is the expression of Orwell's liberal belief in the people: "one sees only the struggle of the gradually awakening common people against the lords of property and their hired liars. . .". He is the great big gentle peasant, the finest flower of the good earth; and he has the usual reward. When at last he collapses from overwork, the pigs pretend to send him to hospital, and sell him to the knacker. It is the only time that Benjamin, the donkey, forsakes cynicism for action. He attempts a rescue, but too late. With the money they get from the knacker, the pigs buy another case of whisky and hold a Boxer memorial dinner.

Squealer is able to give a complete narrative of Boxer's last moments in hospital and is able to quote his last words: "Long live Animal Farm! Long live Comrade Napoleon! Napoleon is always right." Fortunately, too, he is able to refute the ridiculous rumour that Boxer was sent to the knacker. "The animals were enormously relieved to hear this."

The last stage of the story comes with the legend on the end of the barn which has replaced the seven commandments. None of the animals ever detected that only four of them were commandments and the others were statements of belief. None, except probably Benjamin, who gave no sign, ever quite realized how they were modified. One by one they had been broken down and now they had all disappeared and in their place stood the legend: "All animals are equal but some are more equal than others." The significance of this expunging of the law is explained in Orwell's essay on *Gulliver's Travels,* where he says:

> In a Society in which there is no law, and in theory no compulsion, the only arbiter of behaviour is public opinion. But public opinion, because of the tremendous urge to conformity in gregarious animals, is less tolerant than any system of law.

Squealer arranged public opinion. The pigs were now walking on two legs and wearing clothing. Soon they were indistinguishable from the other farmers, except only in their superior discipline over their workers. Mr Pilkington, proposing the toast of "Animal Farm" at the dinner which the pigs gave to their neighbours, put it very well: ". . . a discipline and an orderliness which should be an example to all farmers everywhere. He believed that he was right in saying that the lower animals on Animal Farm did more work and received less food than any animals in the county."

Was it wonderful that when the poor animals gazed in they "looked from pig to man, and from man to pig, and from pig to man again; but already it was impossible to say which was which"?

The question one poses at the end of this fairy story is whether Orwell had given up hope that mankind would ever find decent government. It is very difficult here, as in *1984,* to decide. He had said in his essay on Swift that: "Of course, no honest person claims that happiness is *now* a normal condition among adult human beings; but perhaps it *could* be made normal, and it is upon this question that all serious political controversy really turns."

Essentially, *Animal Farm* is an anatomy of the development of the totalitarian State: "In each great revolutionary struggle

Cover of the second Russian edition of Animal Farm. *George Orwell Archive, University College London.*

the masses are led on by vague dreams of human brotherhood, and then, when the new ruling class is well established in power, they are thrust back into servitude.'' (*Second Thoughts on James Burnham*.)

It is a comment on all revolution: ''History consists of a series of swindles, in which the masses are first lured into revolt by the promise of Utopia, and then, when they have done their job, enslaved over again by new masters.'' (Same essay.)

Nothing is more obvious than where Orwell's sympathies lay. But whether he hoped that the common man could learn to find rulers is not clear. In *Animal Farm* he is an artist, posing great questions imaginatively; not a preacher, proclaiming a revelation. (pp. 171-82)

> Laurence Brander, in his George Orwell, *Longmans, Green and Co., 1954, 212 p.*

CHRISTOPHER HOLLIS   (essay date 1956)

[*Hollis is an English journalist and critic. In the following excerpt, he maintains that the primary thesis of* Animal Farm *is ''that power inevitably corrupts and that revolutions therefore inevitably fail of their purpose.'' Hollis contends, however, that* Animal Farm *succeeds as an animal fable despite the fact that the form is usually employed to convey an optimistic message or moral, which Orwell's tale does not.*]

The story of *Animal Farm* is so familiar that it hardly needs detailed recapitulation. An old boar, of the name of Major, on the brink of death summons to the barn all the animals on the farm of a broken-down drunkard, called Jones, and gives to them his farewell message—the result of his long meditation on life. It is that the enemy of all animals is Man. Man lives by exploiting his animals. The animals produce their food of one sort or another, but they are not allowed to draw for themselves any benefit from their increased production. Man seizes it all for his own need, allows to the animals only sufficient to keep them alive and able to work, cynically and ruthlessly exploits them in their lives and as cynically and ruthlessly destroys them as soon as their days of work are done. Let the animals rise up, expel the enemy Man and run the farm as a co-operative farm of animals in the animals' own interest.

Three days later Major dies, but he has left behind him his message of revolt. The animals are, it is true, not as yet clear how to carry into practice this gospel of revolt. They meet and sing together their new hymn ''Beasts of England.'' An unpremeditated accident eventually brings on the revolt. One midsummer eve Jones gets drunk in the neighbouring village of Wilmington. The hired men milk the cows, and then go off for a day's rabbiting, leaving the animals unfed. In the afternoon, when the animals can stand their hunger no longer, one of the cows breaks in the door of the store-shed with her horn and all the animals rush in and start helping themselves from the bin. Jones wakes up from his drunken slumber. He and the men rush out with whips in their hands and start laying about them. Though there had been no plan of resistance, the animals turn on Jones and the men, attack them and, before they know where they are, have driven them helter-skelter from the farm.

Thus the animals established themselves with unexpected ease as the masters of the farm. It is Orwell's humour to show no great difficulty in the task in which they had expected their main difficulty—in the seizure of power—but enormous and finally fatal difficulty—in the task which they had hardly expected to present a problem at all—in the exercise of power

when seized. With the death of Major the leadership of the animals falls into the hands of the two leading pigs, Snowball and Napoleon—for Orwell throughout represents the pigs as far more intelligent than any of the other animals. Of these he explains with delicious mock solemnity that Napoleon was ''not much of a talker'' but had ''a reputation for getting his own way.'' Snowball was quicker, but ''was not considered to have the same depth of character.'' There is a full and vivid portrait gallery of other animals of which the most notable are Boxer, the good, stupid, unsuspicious horse, of immense physical strength, to whose unquestioning mind the remedy for all problems was to work harder—Squealer, another pig, who was, as it were, the P.R.O. [public relations officer] to Napoleon— Benjamin, the donkey, the only cynic among the animals, who knows that life has always been hard, believes that it always will be hard and is sceptical of all promises of improvement, and Moses, the raven, who does no work but continually tells to the other animals his tale of the Sugar Candy Mountains above the sky where ''it was Sunday seven days a week, clover was in season all the year round and lump-sugar and linseed oil grew on the hedges.''

In the early days of Animal Farm the animals have to prepare themselves for the inevitable counter-attack when Jones and his fellow men will attempt to recapture the farm. The rivalry between Snowball and Napoleon is becoming increasingly evident and they differ and quarrel on every point of policy, but in face of the threat of Man's attack they do not dare to let things come to an open breach. Then in October Jones attacks and, owing to the heroism and strategy of Snowball, he is driven off in rout at the Battle of the Cowshed.

After the defeat of Jones there is no longer any reason why Snowball and Napoleon should preserve even an appearance of amity. The fundamental difference between them is that Snowball thinks that the animals should ''send out more pigeons and stir up rebellion among the animals on other farms,'' while Napoleon thinks that ''what the animals must do was to produce firearms and train themselves to the use of them.'' They also differ over Snowball's ambition to build a windmill to which Napoleon is opposed.

Napoleon bides his time. He has made himself the master of a litter of young puppies which he is secretly training up as his gendarmerie. Then when the day comes, he suddenly introduces these dogs, as they have by then become, into the assembly and lets them loose on Snowball, whom they chase from the farm. It is then that the pace of the degradation increases. More and more Napoleon and the pigs who are faithful to him seize for themselves almost all the food of the farm. The other animals are forced down to a standard of living lower than that which they had in Jones's time. They have to work harder. Whenever anything goes wrong on the farm, the fault is ascribed to Snowball, who is supposed to be lurking in a near-by farm and making nocturnal raids into Animal Farm. He was, the animals are told, in league with Jones from the first. Documents had proved it. The history of Animal Farm is unblushingly falsified. The animals are told, first, that Snowball's part in the Battle of the Cowshed was greatly exaggerated, then that he had in fact fought in it on Jones's side. The windmill is built, but the animals are now told that it was Napoleon who was in favour of it all along and Snowball who was against it. To all complaints that the animals may make at their hard lot the invariable and crushing reply is, ''Do you want Jones back?'' They must put up with all hardships as the only alternative to this more awful fate.

In the original constitution the animals had sworn to have no dealings with Man, but the next summer Napoleon announces the new policy by which the Farm is to trade with neighbouring men in order to obtain certain essential materials of life. The trade is of course to be kept entirely in Napoleon's own hands. No other animals than he are to have any contact with the surrounding men. Then he moves into Jones's house and establishes it as his palace. He lives a life increasingly remote from the other animals by whom he is rarely seen. In the autumn a storm blows down the windmill, but of course it is explained that its destruction is not at all due to defects in building but to the sabotage of Snowball. The winter is a hard one and there is a situation bordering on rebellion—particularly among the hens who object to the seizure of their eggs for the purpose of trade with men. Napoleon deals with it in characteristically unhesitating and terrible fashion.

> The four pigs waited, trembling, with guilt written on every line of their countenances. Napoleon now called upon them to confess their crimes. They were the same four pigs as had protested when Napoleon abolished the Sunday Meetings. Without any further prompting they confessed that they had been secretly in touch with Snowball ever since his expulsion, that they had collaborated with him in destroying the windmill and that they had entered into an agreement with him to hand over Animal Farm to Mr. Frederick. They added that Snowball had privately admitted to them that he had been Jones' secret agent for years past. When they had finished their confession, the dogs promptly tore their throats out, and in a terrible voice Napoleon demanded whether any other animal had anything to confess.
>
> The three hens who had been the ringleaders in the attempted rebellion over the eggs now came forward and stated that Snowball had appeared to them in a dream and incited them to disobey Napoleon's orders. They, too, were slaughtered. Then a goose came forward and confessed to having secreted six ears of corn during the last year's harvest and eaten them in the night. Then a sheep confessed to having urinated in the drinking pool, urged to do this, so she said, by Snowball—and two other sheep confessed to having murdered an old ram, an especially devoted follower of Napoleon, by chasing him round and round a bonfire when he was suffering from a cough. They were all slain on the spot. And so the tale of confessions and executions went on, until there was a pile of corpses lying before Napoleon's feet and the air was heavy with the smell of blood, which had been unknown there since the expulsion of Jones.

After that the old song "Beasts of England" is suppressed, and there is substituted for it Minimus's new song,

> Animal Farm, Animal Farm,
> Never through me shalt thou come to harm.

One after another the commandments on which Animal Farm was built are found to have been secretly altered. For "No animal shall kill another animal," the animals now find the commandment to read, "No animal shall kill another animal without cause." "No animal shall sleep in a bed" is now "No animal shall sleep in a bed with sheets." It had been Napoleon's plan to sell a load of timber to their neighbouring human farmer, Frederick, with the money for which he will buy machinery for the windmill. The timber is delivered and five-pound notes are paid to the animals in exchange. It is only when through their agent the animals attempt to use the five-pound notes for purchases that they find that Frederick has cheated them and

that the notes are forgeries. Napoleon attempts to enlist the alliance of the animals' other neighbour, Pilkington, against Frederick, but Pilkington is unsympathetic. "Serves you right," he says. The humans determine on a second attack on Animal Farm. They come this time armed with guns. They destroy the windmill but are driven off in a second defeat.

It is a few days later that the pigs discover a case of whiskey in Jones's cellar, and it is, naturally enough, at the same time that the commandment "No animal shall drink alcohol" is found now to read "No animal shall drink alcohol to excess."

All comes to a climax when the faithful Boxer one day falls down between the shafts and is no longer strong enough to work. Under the pretence that they are sending him to the vet to be cured, the pigs sell him to a knacker, tell the other animals that he has died at the vet's, in spite of having received every attention, and that his last words were "Forward, Comrades!! Forward in the name of Rebellion! Long live Animal Farm! Long live Comrade Napoleon! Napoleon is always right!" With the money that they have received from Boxer's carcass the pigs buy a case of whiskey and hold a banquet in Jones's house.

The great mark of Animal Farm had been its hostility to everything that went on two legs. "Four legs good, two legs bad" had been the continual bleat of the sheep and four legs had been the great mark of animalism, of animal solidarity. But now the pigs set themselves to learning how to walk on two legs. The motto of the Farm is changed into "All animals are equal, but some animals are more equal than others," and one day the pigs emerge from Jones's house walking on two legs and with whips in their hands. They take out subscriptions to *John Bull, Tit-Bits* and the *Daily Mirror*. The obedient sheep, trained in secret by Squealer, change their bleat of "Four legs good, two legs bad" into "Four legs good, two legs better."

After their second defeat in the Battle of the Windmill the neighbouring men had given up all hope of defeating and destroying the animals, nor indeed once the pigs had shown themselves as ready to impose discipline on their animals as was any human farmer, was there any longer any need, from their point of view, for them to do so. A policy of peaceful co-existence in every way suited them better. Parties of men used to come on visits to the farm and were taken round on conducted tours. At last there comes the night of the great banquet of alliance between the human Pilkington and Napoleon. The animals, looking in through the windows, see pigs and men sitting together and hear the exchange of congratulatory speeches. Mr. Pilkington "believed that he was right in saying that the lower animals on Animal Farm did more work and received less food than any animals in the county. . . . If you have your lower animals to contend with, we have our lower classes." As the celebrations proceed, the pigs, the animals notice, come to look more and more like men and the men more and more like pigs. "The creatures outside looked from pig to man and from man to pig, and from pig to man again, but already it was impossible to say which was which." But assimilation cannot bring harmony. They fall to playing cards, and the banquet breaks up into chaos as Mr. Pilkington and Napoleon each play the ace of spades simultaneously.

The interpretation of the fable is plain enough. Major, Napoleon, Snowball—Lenin, Stalin and Trotsky—Pilkington and Frederick, the two groups of non-Communist powers—the Marxian thesis, as expounded by Major, that society is divided into exploiters and exploited and that all the exploited need to do is to rise up, to expel the exploiters and seize the "surplus

value'' which the exploiters have previously annexed to themselves—the Actonian thesis that power corrupts and the Burn-
hamian thesis that the leaders of the exploited, having used the
rhetoric of equality to get rid of the old exploiters, established
in their place not a classless society but themselves as a new
governing class—the greed and unprincipled opportunism of
the non-Communist states, which are ready enough to overthrow the Communists by force so long as they imagine that
their overthrow will be easy but begin to talk of peace when
they find the task difficult and when they think that they can
use the Communists to satisfy their greed—the dishonour among
total thugs, as a result of which, though greed may make
original ideology irrelevant, turning pigs into men and men
into pigs, the thugs fall out among themselves, as the Nazis
and the Communists fell out, not through difference of ideology
but because in a society of utter baseness and insincerity there
is no motive of confidence. The interpretation is so plain that
no serious critic can dispute it. Those Russian critics who have
professed to see in it merely a general satire on bureaucracy
without any special reference to any particular country can
hardly be taken seriously.

Yet even a total acceptance of Orwell's political opinions would
not in itself make *Animal Farm* a great work of art. The world
is full of animal fables in which this or that country is symbolized by this or that animal, and very tedious affairs the
greater number of them are—and that, irrespective of whether
we agree or disagree with their opinions. To be a great book,
a book of animal fables requires literary greatness as well as
a good cause. Such greatness *Animal Farm* surely possesses.
As Orwell fairly claimed, *Animal Farm* ''was the first book
in which I tried, with full consciousness of what I was doing,
to fuse political purpose and artistic purpose into one whole''—
and he succeeded.

The problems that are set by this peculiar form of art, which
makes animals behave like human beings, are clear. The writer
must throughout be successful in preserving a delicate and
whimsical balance. As Johnson truly says in his criticism of
Dryden's *Hind and the Panther,* there is an initial absurdity in
making animals discuss complicated intellectual problems—
the nature of the Church's authority in Dryden's case, the
communist ideology in Orwell's. The absurdity can only be
saved from ridicule if the author is able to couch his argument
in very simple terms and to draw his illustrations from the facts
of animal life. In this Orwell is as successful as he could be—
a great deal more successful incidentally than Dryden, who in
the excitement of the argument often forgets that it is animals
who are supposed to be putting it forward. The practical difficulties of the conceit must either be ignored or apparently
solved in some simple and striking—if possible, amusing—
fashion. Since obviously they could not in reality be solved at
all, the author merely makes himself ridiculous if he allows
himself to get bogged down in tedious and detailed explanations
which at the end of all cannot in the nature of things explain
anything. Thus Orwell is quite right merely to ignore the difficulties of language, to assume that the animals can communicate with one another by speech—or to assume that the
new ordinance which forbids any animal to take another animal's life could be applied with only the comparatively mild
consequence of gradual increase in animal population. He is
justified in telling us the stories of the two attacks by men for
the recapture of the Farm but in refusing to spoil his story by
allowing the men to take the full measures which obviously
men would take if they found themselves in such an impossible
situation. The means by which the animals rout the men are

inevitably signally unconvincing if we are to consider them
seriously at all. It would as obviously be ridiculous to delay
for pages to describe how animals build windmills or how they
write up commandments on a wall. It heightens the comedy
to give a passing sentence of description to their hauling the
stone up a hill so that it may be broken into manageable frac-
tions when it falls over the precipice, or to Squealer, climbing
a ladder to paint up his message.

The animal fable, if it is to succeed at all, ought clearly to
carry with it a gay and light-hearted message. It must be full
of comedy and laughter. The form is too far removed from
reality to tolerate sustained bitterness. Both Chaucer and La
Fontaine discovered this in their times, and the trouble with
Orwell was that the lesson which he wished to teach was not
ultimately a gay lesson. It was not the lesson that mankind had
its foibles and its follies but that all would be well in the end.
It was more nearly a lesson of despair—the lesson that anarchy
was intolerable, that mankind could not be ruled without en-
trusting power somewhere or other and, to whomsoever power
was entrusted, it was almost certain to be abused. For power
was itself corrupting. But it was Orwell's twisted triumph that
in the relief of the months immediately after the war mankind
was probably not prepared to take such dark medicine if it had
been offered to it undiluted. It accepted it because it came in
this gay and coloured and fanciful form.

The film version gives to *Animal Farm* a happy ending. The
animals all the world over, hearing how Napoleon has betrayed
the animal cause, rise up against him at the end and in a second
revolution expel him. After this second revolution, we are left
to believe, a rule of freedom and equality is established and
survives. But of course this ending makes nonsense of the
whole thesis. It was the Orwellian thesis, right or wrong, that
power inevitably corrupts and that revolutions therefore inevitably fail of their purpose. The new masters are necessarily
corrupted by their new power. The second revolution would
necessarily have failed of its purpose just as the first had failed.
It would merely have set up a second vicious circle.

Animal Farm possesses two essential qualities of a successful
animal fable. On the one hand the author of such a fable must
have the Swift-like capacity of ascribing with solemn face to
the animals idiotic but easily recognized human qualities, deck-
ing them out in aptly changed phraseology to suit the animal
life—ascribe the quality and then pass quickly on before the
reader has begun to find the point overlaboured. This Orwell
has to perfection. Thus:

> Snowball also busied himself with organizing the
> other animals into what he called Animal Commit-
> tees. He was indefatigable at this. He formed the Egg
> Production Committee for the hens, the Clean Tails
> League for the cows, the Wild Comrades' Re-edu-
> cation Committee (the object of which was to tame
> the cats and rabbits), the Whiter Wool Movement for
> the sheep, and various others, besides instituting classes
> in reading and writing. On the whole these projects
> were a failure. The attempt to tame the wild creatures,
> for instance, broke down almost immediately. They
> continued to behave very much as before and, when
> treated with generosity, simply took advantage of it.
> The cat joined the Re-education Committee and was
> very active in it for some days. She was seen one
> day sitting on a roof talking to some sparrows who
> were just out of reach. She was telling them that all
> animals were now comrades and that any sparrow

who chose could come and perch on her paw; but the sparrows kept their distance.

(pp. 140-48)

But what is also essential—and this is often overlooked—is that the writer should have himself a genuine love of animals—should be able to create here and there, in the midst of all his absurdity, scenes of animal life, in themselves realistic and lovable. In that Chaucer, the first and greatest of Orwell's masters in this form of art, pre-eminently excelled. It was in that that Orwell himself excelled. He had always been himself a lover of animals, intimate with their ways. "Most of the good memories of my childhood, and up to the age of about twenty," he wrote in *Such, Such Were the Joys*, "are in some way connected with animals," and it was the work with animals which attracted him in maturer years to agricultural life. There is a real poetic quality, mixed whimsically in with absurdity, in his picture of the first meeting of the animals in the barn with which the book opens. (pp. 148-49)

As I say, there is no difficulty in interpreting the symbolism of the story. But it is not quite so certain what is the total moral that we are supposed to draw from it. Is it that there is some special evil and fraud in Communism which makes it inevitable that all communist movements will turn only into a new and worse tyranny? or is it rather that power is in itself, to whatever ideology it may nominally be allied, inevitably corrupting? that all promises of equality and liberty will prove inevitably to be deceptions? and that history does not, and cannot, consist of anything other than the overthrow of old tyrants in order that new tyrants may be put in their place? It is obvious that the second alternative was much more natural to Orwell's mind than the first and that Conservatives who hailed *Animal Farm* as an attack simply on Communism interpreted it too narrowly and too much to suit their own convenience. Orwell's whole record from Spanish days onwards shows his impartial hatred of all tyrannies and of all totalitarian claims, and as a matter of history, it was against what he thought of as a fascist tyranny that he first enlisted to fight. In *Animal Farm* itself we must not be diverted by the satire on the animals from noticing how utterly worthless are without exception the parts played by men, who represent the conservative principle. He complained of Mr. Rayner Heppenstall's radio version of it for "casting a sop to those stinking Catholics." There is no hint of a suggestion that Jones, a drunken brute, who was letting the farm down, did not deserve all that he got. The parts that he displayed both when he had the farm and after he lost it were alike discreditable. His men were no better. When Jones was away drunk they took advantage of his absence not to feed the animals. The two neighbouring farmers—Pilkington, "an easy-going gentleman farmer who spent most of his time in fishing or hunting according to the season"—and Frederick "a tough, shrewd man, perpetually involved in lawsuits and with a name for driving hard bargains"—are equally worthless. Their sole motive is greed. They are willing to destroy the animals, if possible, and, if it is not possible, to make out of them what they can, and they are incapable of honouring their bargains. The lesson of *Animal Farm* is clearly not merely the corrupting effect of power when exercised by Communists, but the corrupting effect of power when exercised by anybody. As for the Communists being worse than other people—clearly, rightly or wrongly, Orwell did not think that Communists were worse than Fascists. By Fascists he really meant Nazis, for he never bothered much about Mussolini one way or the other and, although in Catalonia he called the followers of Franco Fascists, he specifically recognized that they were something dif-

ferent. But Fascists, if Fascists means Nazis, he thought to be worse than Communists. It was of no great moment what were the nominal creeds either of the one party or the other, for absolute power tends to corrupt absolutely, and the totalitarian is in practice, whatever he may profess, solely concerned with maintaining and extending his power. It is power politics and nothing but power politics.

But was there then no remedy and no hope? There was certainly no hope in anything like the modern circumstances of life that we should see anything of the nature of free and equal society. From time to time Orwell expresses a hope that we may be moving "eventually" to such a consummation, but with no great confidence and for no very clear reason. "Of course no honest person claims that happiness is *now* a normal condition among adult human beings," he writes, "but perhaps it *could* be made normal, and it is upon this question that all serious political controversy really turns." All the evidence is, he admits, that we are moving away from it. All that we can really say is that time has a certain mollifying influence and that, though all governments are tyrannies, old tyrannies are less ruthless than new. The rule of law is a great deal better than the rule of public opinion or of an arbitrary tyrant. "In a society in which there is no law, and in theory no compulsion, the only arbiter of behaviour is public opinion. But public opinion, because of the tremendous urge to conformity in gregarious animals, is less tolerant than any system of law." Therefore it might appear that the conclusion that ought to follow is that no régime would be very good but that the least bad would be a moderate conservative régime—a régime which preserved the traditional structure of society and at the same time preserved the liberal principles so that those parts of it that in the development of events showed signs of collapse might be at necessity modified—indeed something of the nature of what we in the West call free institutions. The clean choice of Socialist theory between production for profit and production for social use, which Orwell had himself to some extent offered in **"England, Your England,"** belongs to the lecture room rather than to real life. In the real world of the years after 1945, with the Socialists leaving so many industries under private enterprise and the Conservatives leaving so many industries nationalized, nationalization was clearly a matter of the balance of advantage and disadvantage in each particular case rather than of absolute good and evil. It was not a stark choice of one sort of society against another sort. The policy which Orwell believed that Dickens recommended to the nineteenth century should, it would seem on this argument, be the sort of policy which he should recommend to the twentieth century.

I should myself be prepared to argue that this was the conclusion which Orwell ought to have drawn from his own writings in general and from *Animal Farm* in particular. But it must be admitted that it was not a conclusion which Orwell ever did explicitly draw. As a reporter of fact Mr. Brander is substantially accurate when he writes, "Orwell wrote very little about the Church in his criticism of society. He classed it with Conservatism as no longer serious enough to be considered." Orwell's complaint was not so much against an ideal philosophy of Conservatism, for which, when he found it, he had a reasonable respect, as against those who called themselves Conservatives and had captured the Conservative machine. His complaint against them was that they were at once too arrogant and too compromising. They were too arrogant in so far as they tended to claim their privileges as something which they had deserved and to arrogate to themselves the airs of superior people. These very claims obscured the true case for Conservatism which was that society had to be arranged, that there was little reason to think that it would ever be arranged ideally well, that it was fatally easy for men to fritter away all their energies in agitation and scheming for its rearrangement and that therefore there was always something to be said, within limits, for accepting society broadly as it is and getting on with the business of living. It may very well turn out that there would be more liberty that way than down a more revolutionary, more ideally perfectionist, road—and liberty was what really mattered. Even in his most revolutionary moods—as in "England, Your England"—he was, if we analyse his argument, primarily concerned with the proclamation of a libertarian and egalitarian purpose. Once the purpose was proclaimed he was quite content in practice to let things move forward at a slow and conservative pace. Willing to impose drastic sufferings upon himself, he never, save in moments of special exaltation, imagined that it would be possible to impose such drastic sufferings on society at large and to preserve freedom.

But a more important complaint against the Conservatives was that they were too compromising. While the case for Conservatism was that it stood for traditional ways and ancient liberties against the menace of the new philosophies, the Conservatives in practice, he complained, had shown themselves always only too ready to do a deal with the new philosophies and "the stream-lined men," as Pilkington did his deal with Napoleon, as soon as the "stream-lined men" had shown themselves to be in the least tough and strong. They did a deal with the Fascists before the war and with the Communists in the Anglo-Russian alliance during the war. Orwell despaired of the Conservatives because the Conservatives despaired of Conservatism. They were without principle. (pp. 150-53)

> *Christopher Hollis, in his* A Study of George Orwell: The Man and His Works, *Henry Regnery Company, 1956, 212 p.*

A. E. DYSON (essay date 1965)

[*Dyson is an English literary critic who has explained that while he formerly adhered to an ideology of "liberal humanism," he has for some time considered himself a "traditionalist" and a Christian. "Literature is a celebration," Dyson has stated. "Almost everything that makes life rich was said or written or created by people who are no longer living; almost all the color and joy came from religious men." In the following excerpt, Dyson discusses* Animal Farm *as the expression of Orwell's conviction that the high ideals professed by those seeking political power are never realized after they have attained it.*]

[A] few words about *Animal Farm.* Though based on the Russian Revolution and its aftermath, this grim little parable is by no means about Russia alone. Orwell is concerned to show how revolutionary ideals of justice, equality and fraternity always shatter in the event. The ironic reversals in *Animal Farm* could be fairly closely related to real events since the work was written (this is not the least of their effectiveness) as well as to the events on which they were based.

The charting of disillusionment is not new to our political scene. Shakespeare in *Julius Caesar*, Hobbes in *Leviathan*, Milton and the Romantic Poets, have all had their say. What *is* new about our modern disillusionment is its scale. More insistently than ever before, revolutionaries have proclaimed the liberation of the common man; more ironically than ever before, the common man has had to pay for revolution with his liberty, his happiness and sometimes his life.

But Orwell was never himself committed to revolutionary hopes, as the left-wing poets of the '30s were, and his charting of disenchantment was to this degree less extreme. He fought in Spain, but with grave doubts about his own side, which events did everything to confirm. His critique of revolution is basically simple, and embodies the same doubts about human nature which made benevolent paternalism more realistic for him, perhaps, than the ideal of a People's Republic. *Animal Farm* offers insights which were later spelt out, more abstractly, in the Black Book of *1984*. There always have been three classes of society, and there always will be. These are the high, the middle and the low. The war between the classes is necessary, and in normal circumstances could never have an end. The basic political reality is a struggle for power, and the basic reality of power is the ambition and self-aggrandisement of the few at the expense of the many. In this battle, ideals of justice, liberty and brotherhood are so many counters, which the various parties at different times find useful. The middle class is especially adroit in its use of them when it needs to enlist the superior numbers of the lower class in what is essentially its private cause. These ideals are emotionally explosive for two main reasons. The first is that they receive lip-service from most of us, so that politicians are enabled to manipulate the worst in us by way of what we are accustomed to regard as the best. The second is that a handful of idealists really do believe them, and those who do (such as Boxer in *Animal Farm*, or Shakespeare's Brutus) become enormously helpful by reason of their prestige. The politicians who use such slogans are, however, motivated by conscious cynicism of the deepest kind. It is a cynicism more realistic, if less amiable, than the hopes of the men whom they dupe.

In this broad approach to his theme, Orwell agrees with Bertrand Russell in taking the lowest possible view of politicians. He sees them not as ordinary men caught up in events too big for them, and forced against their will into evil moulds, but as depraved men, who have been drawn to politics in the first place by the corrupting search for power. "Sensible men do not have power," he once wrote, and the obverse of this is that the men who do have power are evil, since "sensible" in this context is a moral term. It is interesting to notice that Orwell agrees with most revolutionaries in his estimate of the men who are actually ruling us, but differs sharply in his assessment of what will happen when they are swept away. The new masters will not be saviours, restoring to us a primitive freedom. On the contrary, they will be oppressors in their turn, resembling their predecessors in ambition and cruelty, and differing only in the extremes to which these motives will lead them when stability and tradition have been removed.

Orwell's heart is with the political idealists, but his head gives its verdict the other way. In *Animal Farm* the rise of the pigs to power is presented as inevitable. Our sense of inevitability is mediated through the pervasive irony, which uses a tone of almost bedtime cosiness to unfold the horrors of the tale. We observe the pigs coming into the ascendancy almost at once, as they persuade their fellow animals through a characteristic interplay of idealism and fear. When the machinery of naked power passes into their hands, idealism is totally replaced by fear. We are shown the ensuing power struggle among the pigs at the top, with the emergence of the more evil of the two to supreme power. Events continue to unfold with something of the unassailable logic of a dream. The defeated pig is transformed into an enemy, who can both canalise hatred and justify oppression. The ruling pig is apotheosised into human semblance, and ends in alliance with the hated humans who were originally deposed. These events are intensified by our sense that human nature itself is on trial. If we detect some inevitability in the progress of events, Orwell relies on no dialectic of history to sustain this, but only on his profoundly depressing assessment of political power. The whole range of contributory causes unfolds as we watch—the cruel intelligence of the pigs, the brutality (so easily harnessed) of the dogs, the casual selfishness of the cat, the vanity of the donkey, the heroic stupidity of Boxer, the moronic stupidity of the numerically preponderating sheep. Even when writing *The Road to Wigan Pier,* Orwell had been sufficiently sickened by his experience of imperialism to record: "At that time failure seemed to me the only virtue." In *Animal Farm,* the only virtue is Boxer's failure: yet can a man at once so decent and dynamic as Orwell rest in perceptions such as these? (pp. 206-08)

> A. E. Dyson, "Orwell: Irony as Prophecy," in his *The Crazy Fabric: Essays in Irony, Macmillan and Co. Ltd.,* 1965, pp. 197-219.

STEPHEN GREENBLATT   (essay date 1965)

[*In the following excerpt, Greenblatt interprets* Animal Farm *as an expression of Orwell's loss of faith in the efficacy of democratic socialism after his experiences in the Spanish Civil War and subsequent political events of the 1930s and 1940s. Greenblatt demonstrates why he considers some differing interpretations of the novel to be incorrect, and concludes that* Animal Farm *retains its power as a satire because its major concern is not with a retelling of the Russian Revolution, but with "the essential horror of the human condition."*]

Throughout Orwell's early novels, journals, and essays, democratic socialism existed as a sustaining vision that kept the author from total despair of the human condition, but Orwell's bitter experience in the Spanish Civil War and the shock of the Nazi-Soviet pact signaled the breakdown of this last hope and the beginning of the mental and emotional state out of which grew *Animal Farm* and *1984.* The political disappointments of the late '30s and '40s did not in themselves, however, disillusion Orwell—they simply brought to the surface themes and tensions present in his work from the beginning. . . . [The] socialism Orwell believed in was not a hardheaded, "realistic" approach to society and politics but a rather sentimental, utopian vision of the world as a "raft sailing through space, with, potentially, plenty of provisions for everybody," provided men, who, after all, are basically decent, would simply use common sense and not be greedy. Such naïve beliefs could only survive while Orwell was preoccupied with his attacks on the British Raj, the artist in society, or the capitalist system. The moment events compelled him to turn his critical eye on the myth of socialism and the "dictatorship of the proletariat," he discerned fundamental lies and corruption. Orwell, in his last years, was a man who experienced daily the disintegration of the beliefs of a lifetime, who watched in horror while his entire life work was robbed of meaning.

The first of his great cries of despair was *Animal Farm,* a satirical beast fable which, curiously enough, has been heralded as Orwell's lightest, gayest work. Laurence Brander, in his biography of Orwell [see excerpt dated 1954] paints a charming but wholly inaccurate picture of *Animal Farm,* presenting it as "one of those apparently chance pieces a prose writer throws off . . . a sport out of his usual way," supposedly written by Orwell in a state where "the gaiety in his nature had completely taken charge . . . writing about animals, whom he loved." The surface gaiety, the seeming good humor and casualness, the

light, bantering tone are, of course, part of the convention of beast fables, and *Animal Farm* would be a very bad tale indeed if it did not employ these devices. But it is a remarkable achievement precisely because Orwell uses the apparently frivolous form of the animal tale to convey with immense power his profoundly bitter message. Critics like Laurence Brander and Tom Hopkinson who marvel at Orwell's "admirable good humour and detachment" miss, I think, the whole point of the piece they praise. *Animal Farm* does indeed contain much gaiety and humor, but even in the most comic moments there is a disturbing element of cruelty or fear that taints the reader's hearty laughter. While Snowball, one of the leaders of the revolution of farm animals against their master, is organizing "the Egg Production Committee for the hens, the Clean Tails League for the cows, the Wild Comrades' Re-education Committee . . . , the Whiter Wool Movement for the sheep," Napoleon, the sinister pig tyrant, is carefully educating the dogs for his own evil purposes. Similarly, the "confessions" forced from the animals in Napoleon's great purges are very funny, but when the dogs tear the throats out of the "guilty" parties and leave a pile of corpses at the tyrant's feet, the scene ceases to amuse. Orwell's technique is similar to [a device used by Evelyn] Waugh, who relates ghastly events in a comic setting.

Another critical mistake in appraising *Animal Farm* is made, I believe, by critics like Christopher Hollis who talk of the overriding importance of the author's love of animals [see excerpt dated 1956] and fail to understand that Orwell in *Animal Farm* loves animals only as much or as little as he loves human beings. To claim that he hates the pigs because they represent human tyrants and sympathizes with the horses because they are dumb animals is absurd. Nor is it necessary, as Hollis believes, that the truly successful animal fable carry with it "a gay and light-hearted message." Indeed, the very idea of representing human traits in animals is rather pessimistic. What is essential to the success of the satirical beast fable, as Ellen Douglass Leyburn observes, is the author's "power to keep his reader conscious simultaneously of the human traits satirized and of the animals as animals" [see Additional Bibliography]. The storyteller must never allow the animals to be simply beasts, in which case the piece becomes a nonsatirical children's story, or to be merely transparent symbols, in which case the piece becomes a dull sermon. Orwell proved, in *Animal Farm,* his remarkable ability to maintain this delicate, satiric balance.

The beast fable, an ancient satiric technique in which the characteristic poses of human vice and folly are embodied in animals, is, as Kernan points out, "an unrealistic, expressionistic device" [Alvin Kernan, *Modern Satire,* 1962] which stands in bold contrast with Orwell's previous realistic manner. But the seeds for *Animal Farm* are present in the earlier works, not only in the metaphors likening men to beasts but, more important, in Orwell's whole attitude toward society, which he sees as an aggregation of certain classes or types. The types change somewhat in appearance according to the setting—from the snobbish pukka sahibs, corrupt officials, and miserable natives of *Burmese Days* to the obnoxious nouveaux riches, greedy restaurateurs, and overworked plongeurs of *Down and Out in Paris and London,* but there remains the basic notion that men naturally divide themselves into a limited number of groups, which can be isolated and characterized by the astute observer. This notion is given dramatic reality in *Animal Farm,* where societal types are presented in the various kinds of farm animals—pigs for exploiters, horses for laborers, dogs for police, sheep for blind followers, etc. The beast fable need not convey an optimistic moral, but it cannot portray complex individuals, and thus it can never sustain the burden of tragedy. The characters of a satirical animal story may be sly, vicious, cynical, pathetic, lovable, or intelligent, but they can only be seen as members of large social groups and not as individuals.

Animal Farm has been interpreted most frequently as a clever satire on the betrayal of the Russian Revolution and the rise of Stalin. Richard Rees comments that "the struggle of the farm animals, having driven out their human exploiter, to create a free and equal community takes the form of a most ingeniously worked-out recapitulation of the history of Soviet Russia from 1917 up to the Teheran Conference [see Additional Bibliography]. And indeed, despite Soviet critics who claim to see only a general satire on bureaucracy in *Animal Farm,* the political allegory is inevitable. Inspired by the prophetic deathbed vision of Old Major, a prize Middle White boar, the maltreated animals of Manor Farm successfully revolt against Mr. Jones, their bad farmer, and found their own utopian community, Animal Farm. The control of the revolution falls naturally upon the pigs, particularly upon Napoleon, "a large, rather fierce-looking Berkshire boar, not much of a talker, but with a reputation for getting his own way," and on Snowball, "a more vivacious pig than Napoleon, quicker in speech and more inventive, but . . . not considered to have the same depth of character." Under their clever leadership and with the help of the indefatigable cart horses Boxer and Clover, the animals manage to repulse the attacks of their rapacious human neighbors, Mr. Pilkington and Mr. Frederick. With the farm secured from invasion and the Seven Commandments of Animalism painted on the end wall of the big barn, the revolution seems complete; but as the community develops, it is plain that there are graver dangers than invasion. The pigs at once decide that milk and apples are essential to their well being. Squealer, Napoleon's lieutenant and the ablest talker, explains the appropriation:

> "Comrades!" he cried. "You do not imagine, I hope, that we pigs are doing this in a spirit of selfishness and privilege? Many of us actually dislike milk and apples. . . . Our sole object in taking these things is to preserve our health. Milk and apples (this has been proven by Science, comrades) contain substances absolutely necessary to the well-being of a pig. . . . We pigs are brainworkers. . . . Day and night we are watching over your welfare. It is for *your* sake that we drink that milk and eat those apples. Do you know what would happen if we pigs failed in our duty? Jones would come back!"

A growing rivalry between Snowball and Napoleon is decisively decided by Napoleon's vicious hounds, who drive Snowball off the farm. Laurence Brander sees Snowball as a symbol of "altruism, the essential social virtue" and his expulsion as the defeat of "his altruistic laws for giving warmth, food and comfort to all the animals." This is very touching, but unfortunately there is no indication that Snowball is any less corrupt or power-mad than Napoleon. Indeed, it is remarked, concerning the appropriation of the milk and apples, that "All the pigs were in full agreement on this point, even Snowball and Napoleon." The remainder of *Animal Farm* is a chronicle of the consolidation of Napoleon's power through clever politics, propaganda, and terror. Dissenters are ruthlessly murdered, and when Boxer can no longer work, he is sold to the knacker. One by one, the Commandments of Animalism are perverted or eliminated, until all that is left is:

ALL ANIMALS ARE EQUAL
BUT SOME ANIMALS ARE MORE EQUAL THAN OTHERS.

After that, it does not seem strange when the pigs live in Jones' house, walk on two legs, carry whips, wear human clothes, take out subscriptions to *John Bull, Tit-Bits,* and the *Daily Mirror,* and invite their human neighbors over for a friendly game of cards. The game ends in a violent argument when Napoleon and Pilkington play an ace of spades simultaneously, but for the animals there is no real quarrel. "The creatures outside looked from pig to man, and from man to pig, and from pig to man again; but already it was impossible to say which was which."

The interpretation of *Animal Farm* in terms of Soviet history (Major, Napoleon, Snowball represent Lenin, Stalin, Trotsky) has been made many times and shall not be pursued further here. It is amusing, however, that many of the Western critics who astutely observe the barbs aimed at Russia fail completely to grasp Orwell's judgment of the West. After all, the pigs do not turn into alien monsters; they come to resemble those bitter rivals Mr. Pilkington and Mr. Frederick, who represent the Nazis and the Capitalists. All three major "powers" are despicable tyrannies, and the failure of the revolution is not seen in terms of ideology at all, but as a realization of Lord Acton's thesis, "Power tends to corrupt; absolute power corrupts absolutely." The initial spark of a revolution, the original intention of a constitution may have been an ideal of the good life, but the result is always the same—tyranny. Communism is no more or less evil than Fascism or Capitalism—they are all illusions which are inevitably used by the pigs as a means of satisfying their greed and their lust for power. Religion, too, is merely a toy of the oppressors and a device to divert the minds of the sufferers. Moses, the tame raven who is always croaking about the sweet, eternal life in Sugarcandy Mountain, flies after the deposed Farmer Jones, only to return when Napoleon has established his tyranny.

Animal Farm remains powerful satire even as the specific historical events it mocked recede into the past, because the book's major concern is not with these incidents but with the essential horror of the human condition. There have been, are, and always will be pigs in every society, Orwell states, and they will always grab power. Even more cruel is the conclusion that *everyone* in the society, wittingly or unwittingly, contributes to the pigs' tyranny. Boxer, the noblest (though not the wisest) animal on the farm, devotes his unceasing labor to the pigs, who, as has been noted, send him to the knacker when he has outlived his usefulness. There is real pathos as the sound of Boxer's hoofs drumming weakly on the back of the horse slaughterer's van grows fainter and dies away, and the reader senses that in that dying sound is the dying hope of humanity. But Orwell does not allow the mood of oppressive sadness to overwhelm the satire, and Squealer, "lifting his trotter and wiping away a tear," hastens to announce that, after receiving every attention a horse could have, Boxer died in his hospital bed, with the words "Napoleon is always right" on his withered lips. Frederick R. Karl, in *The Contemporary English Novel,* believes that *Animal Farm* fails as successful satire "by virtue of its predictablity" [see Additional Bibliography], but this terrifying predictability of the fate of all revolutions is just the point Orwell is trying to make. The grotesque end of the fable is not meant to shock the reader—indeed, chance and surprise are banished entirely from Orwell's world. The horror of both *Animal Farm* and the later *1984* is precisely the cold, orderly, predictable process by which decency, happiness, and hope are systematically and ruthlessly crushed. (pp. 59-66)

Stephen Greenblatt, "George Orwell," in his Three Modern Satirists: Waugh, Orwell, and Huxley, *Yale University Press, 1965, pp. 35-74.*

Title page of the 1954 edition of Animal Farm, *illustrated by Joy Batchelor and John Halas. Secker and Warburg, 1954. Reproduced by permission of Martin Secker & Warburg Limited.*

GEORGE WOODCOCK   (essay date 1966)

[Woodcock is a Canadian educator, editor, and critic best known for his biographies of George Orwell and Thomas Merton. He also founded Canada's most important literary journal, Canadian Literature, *and has written extensively on the literature of Canada. In the following excerpt, Woodcock contends that* Animal Farm *was the first work of Orwell's political and artistic maturity, marked by the concision of form and language that characterizes his later works. In using animal protagonists, Woodcock contends, Orwell avoided psychological complexity and was able to present a political theme simply and clearly: that all tyrannies are similar, and similarly detrimental to those living under them.]*

For more than six years, from the end of 1938 to early 1945, Orwell published neither fiction nor any important autobiographical writing, and even in terms of actual work there was a gap of more than four years between the termination of **Coming Up for Air** early in 1939 and the commmencement of **Animal Farm** some time in 1943. Yet these were not wasted years for him, even as a writer. Nearly half the pieces in his **Collected Essays** were first published between 1939 and 1943, and almost all the others in this rather massive volume appeared between 1944 and 1947. To these eight busy years, in other words, belongs virtually all the critical writing Orwell considered important enough to preserve, plus a great many political essays and three polemical pamphlets (**The Lion and the Uni-**

corn in 1941, **James Burnham and the Managerial Revolution** in 1946, and **The English People** in 1947), plus the scores of uncollected articles and reviews which appeared in the *Tribune, Partisan Review, Observer, Manchester Evening News* (for which he did a weekly book column for two or three years) and a dozen small journals and little magazines. All this he did, it must be remembered, while he was still working either at the BBC or editorially at the *Tribune* and while he was allowing at least part of his spare time to be consumed by a series of "causes" from the Home Guard to the Freedom Defense Committee. His life was also expanding in other ways, for it was during this period that he ceased to be a real solitary, and though he never became a truly gregarious man, at least he now felt himself accepted on his own terms and built up that extraordinary variety of friendships which mellowed his final years. All these forms of action seemed to stimulate each other, and doubtless they were all stimulated by the atmosphere of the time, for the war years and the period immediately after peace, up to about the time when Orwell left for the Hebrides, were much more lively from a literary and a political point of view than the period from 1948 or 1949 down to the present.

In the case of Orwell it was not merely that he worked with immense energy and produced a great quantity of writings of various kinds. There was an extraordinary change in quality, which had been foreshadowed by **Homage to Catalonia,** also the product of a period of life in a peculiarly stimulating atmosphere. Orwell's expository writing became steadily clearer and more flexible, and his critical powers, first demonstrated impressively in the long 1939 essay on Charles Dickens, were inspired and informed by an awareness which he would call political, but which—seen in the perspective of the years—seems rather to have been moral in essence. Orwell was always a moralist, even at Eton if one is to accept Cyril Connolly's account of him in *Enemies of Promise,* and when he acquired political opinions they merely channeled his moralism, but by no means tamed it. The test always came when political expediency or party interests clashed with his ideas of what might be true or decent; most often—and always in his later years—it was party interest that he let go in favor of decency.

The influence of this moral-political awareness can be seen not merely in an increased sensitivity to the social and ethical dimensions of a book or a situation he might be discussing, but also in the directness of writing it began to foster, even when he turned back again near the end of the war from essays to fiction. He tried to write, as he put it, "less picturesquely and more exactly." And he gave a more definitely political character than before to the theme of caste and alienation which re-emerges, in varying forms, in all his late works, beginning with *Animal Farm.*

"*Animal Farm,*" said Orwell in 1947, "was the first book in which I tried, with full consciousness of what I was doing, to fuse political purpose and artistic purpose in one whole." He succeeded admirably, and produced a book so clear in intent and writing that the critic is usually rather nonplussed as to what he should say about it; all is so magnificently there, and the only thing that really needs to be done is to place this crystalline little book into its proper setting.

Conciseness of form and simplicity of language are the qualities which immediately strike one on opening *Animal Farm* after having read Orwell's earlier works of fiction. The fable is about a third the length of *Keep the Aspidistra Flying,* though the events of which it tells are much more complicated, and it is written in a bare English, uncluttered by metaphor, which contrasts strongly with both the elaborately literary diction of *Burmese Days* and the racy but sometimes over-rich narrative style of *Coming Up for Air.*

> Mr. Jones, of the Manor Farm, had locked the hen-houses for the night, but was too drunk to remember to shut the popholes. With the ring of light from his lantern dancing from side to side, he lurched across the yard, kicked off his boots at the back door, drew himself a last glass of beer from the barrel in the scullery, and made his way up to bed, where Mrs. Jones was already snoring.

So it begins, and so it continues to the end, direct, exact and sharply concrete, letting events make their own impacts and stimulating the creation of mental pictures, so that one remembers the book as a series of lively visual images held together by a membrane of almost transparent prose.

There was no doubt in Orwell's mind about his intention in writing *Animal Farm.* He felt that the English in 1943 were allowing their admiration for the military heroism of the Russians to blind them to the faults of the Communist regime, and he also believed that the Communists were using their position as unofficial representatives of Russia in England to prevent the truth from being known, as they had done in Spain. *Animal Farm* was meant to set his compatriots thinking again.

At that time Orwell was fascinated by the craft of pamphleteering, which had something of a wartime vogue among British writers, so that not only likely people, such as Orwell, Read and Spender, produced pamphlets, but even unlikely people such as Forster, Eliot and Henry Miller. Besides the three unimpressive and not very successful pamphlets which he himself wrote in the 1940's, Orwell edited with Reginald Reynolds an anthology of classic pamphlets from the past, entitled *British Pamphleteers;* he believed that a revival of pamphleteering was possible and desirable. In a pamphlet one could state a case simply and concisely, and it would stand on its own feet as no article in a periodical could ever do. But pamphleteering in fact never took on that new lease of life in the postwar years which Orwell had anticipated; this was due partly to lack of interest among the booksellers and partly to the devitalization of British politics after 1945.

Yet *Animal Farm,* which was really a pamphlet in fictional form, did succeed, because it created within the dimension of a fable a perfect and self-consistent microcosm. There was nothing very original about the basic idea of a community of animals acting like men, which had been used about fifteen hundred years before by the anonymous Indian author of that extraordinary collection of political fables, the *Panchatantra.* But, like the author of the *Panchatantra,* Orwell gave his work freshness by inducing that peculiar blend of humor, incongruity and apparent candor which creates in the reader a willingness to suspend disbelief and to transfer himself in mind into the changed dimensions of a world where the pursuits of men can be seen dispassionately because it is animals which are following them.

Orwell liked animals, though he detested the sentimental British animal cult. In his world picture animals, children, oppressed people stood on one side, and the oppressors, whether they were farmers, schoolteachers, sahibs or party bosses, on the other. In *Burmese Days* . . . the relationship of Asians to animals is quite clear, and later on in *Nineteen Eighty-Four* there were to be several identifications of proles with animals. "Proles and animals are free," runs one of the Party slogans, and O'Brien, Winston Smith's tormentor, voices the dogma of the Inner Party when he says that "the proletarians . . . are helpless, like the animals. Humanity is the Party. The others are outside—irrelevant." On the other hand, for Winston in his rebellion, an inestimable power seems to lie in "the animal instinct . . . that was the force that would tear the Party to pieces."

In *Animal Farm* it is the outsiders, the helpless ones, who rise in rebellion and destroy the power of the oppressors, personified in the drunken Mr. Jones. The idea of class division which in earlier books comes very near to the conception of two nations, rich and poor, is here modified to suggest two kinds—men and animals. "All men are enemies. All animals are comrades," says the prophetic old boar Major in his great oration shortly before the uprising.

The original division between man and animal corresponds to the old social division between hereditary upper and lower castes or classes which Orwell represented in his earlier works. But his experiences in Spain had led him to delve into the history of the development of power structures during revolutions, and on this subject he was now as knowledgeable as anyone outside the ranks of specialist historians. He had learned that social caste could be replaced by political caste, and *Animal Farm* is a study in fable form of this process at work in a minuscule world which we can observe as closely as a community of ants under the glass lid of a formicarium.

The history of the revolution betrayed in the animal world is based, therefore, partly on what Orwell had seen of the Communist usurpation of power in Spain and partly on what he had read of the Russian Revolution and its abortion by the Bolsheviks. But his anticommunism does not mean that he is on the side of the traditional ruling class, represented by men. On the contrary, when the animals originally rise in revolt against the tyrannical Farmer Jones, he wins our sympathies for them, and we remain on their side throughout their subsequent struggles with humanity, accepting the fact that no matter what the pigs may do, no animal wants to be ruled again by Farmer Jones or his kind.

Yet from the very first day of insurrection it is evident that a new elite is replacing the vanished human rulers—the elite of the pigs, who are the equivalent of the Party. Immediately they arrogate privileges to themselves—first a monopoly of milk, then of apples. They become supervisors, while the other animals, with the sole exception of that arch anticollectivist, the cat, do the work. The pigs, it should be noted, are united when it is a question of defending their rights as an elite against the other animals. Orwell had no intention of making *Animal Farm* an apology for Trotskyism, as he make quite clear in a conversation which Julian Symons recorded:

> And just in case I had any illusions about his attitude, he pointed out that Trotsky-Snowball was potentially as big a villain as Stalin-Napoleon, although he was Napoleon's victim. The first note of corruption was struck, he said, when the pigs secretly had the cows' milk added to their own mash, and Snowball consented to this first act of inequality.

The struggle between Snowball and Napoleon is in fact a struggle within the party 'elite whose final result, whichever had won, would have been the increased consolidation and centralization of power in the hands of the pigs. This is what happens when Napoleon outmaneuvers Snowball and immediately after his expulsion initiates the career of purges, atrocities and deepening tyranny that reproduces in minuscule the history of the Russian Revolution from 1917 to the 1940's.

At no point in *Animal Farm* does Orwell shift his side. Though it is a third-person story, as all fables are, the point of view of the reader is always nearest to that of the unprivileged animals, and perhaps nearest of all to that of Benjamin, the sad and cynical old donkey who sides with no factions and always says that "life would go on as it had always gone on—that is, badly." Yet despite his exposure of the mounting iniquities committed by the pig elite, Orwell never falls into the error of suggesting that the farmers are any better. On the contrary, there is really nothing to choose, and the book ends in that fantastic scene in which the pigs entertain the neighboring farmers in a social gathering, and the other animals, looking in, see a quarrel break out over cheating at cards.

> Twelve voices were shouting in anger, and they were all alike. No question, now, what had happened to the faces of the pigs. The creatures outside looked from pig to man, and from man to pig, and from pig to man again; but already it was impossible to say which was which.

In other words, old and new tyrannies belong to the same family; authoritarian governments, whether they are based on the codes of old social castes or on the rules of new political elites, are basically similar and present similar dangers to hu-

man welfare and to liberty. For the interests of oppressors are identical; as Mr. Pilkington jests at a more peaceful stage in the banquet, "If you have your lower animals to contend with, we have our lower classes!"

By transferring the problems of caste division outside a human setting, Orwell was able in *Animal Farm* to avoid the psychological complications inevitable in a novel, and thus to present his theme as a clear and simple political truth. In the process he left out one element which occurs in all his other works of fiction, the individual rebel caught in the machinery of the caste system. Not until he wrote *Nineteen Eighty-Four* did he elaborate the rebel's role in an *Animal Farm* carried to its monstrously logical conclusion. (pp. 190-98)

> *George Woodcock, in his* The Crystal Spirit: A Study of George Orwell, *Little, Brown and Company, 1966, 366 p.*

KEITH ALLDRITT   (essay date 1969)

[*Alldritt is an English critic and novelist. In the following excerpt, he considers* Animal Farm *an oversimplified and unsuccessful attempt to portray the complexities of a society in revolution.*]

Orwell became famous with the publication of *Animal Farm* in 1945. Upon this book, together with *Nineteen Eighty-Four* and the essays, his reputation continues chiefly to rest. Today it is very difficult to share the admiration with which *Animal Farm* was received when it first appeared. All the comparisons with *Gulliver's Travels* and *Candide* that are to be found in the contemporary reviews must now seem, twenty years on, extremely damaging to Orwell's book. And only when we recall that its publication coincided with the beginning of the Cold War does its instant success become understandable. Certainly as a mocking allegory of the first thirty years or so of the Russian revolution it is a work of considerable poise, a poise that derives from Orwell's long nurtured cynicism about communism, which had resisted the indulgent attitude to Russia born of the war-time alliance as much as it had resisted the fashionable communism of literary and intellectual circles during the thirties. But for the reader of today it is this very poise which makes the book trivial. The allegory is too pat, the confidence of the narrator (the confidence of one telling a nursery tale) too secure. Orwell's "fairy story" is only a clever form for expressing a set of opinions that have been held so long that they no longer admit the complexity of the experience they claim to explain.

The story of the humanised beasts of *Animal Farm* treats of events that are in many ways similar to those in which Orwell himself had participated in Spain. As in *Homage to Catalonia,* we have an account of a revolution created by a community undergoing persecution and deprivation. But idealism and communal energy and purpose do not long endure, we are told again, and the selfish and the unscrupulous take over the revolution and recreate the same sort of class system and exploitation which the revolution had overthrown. It is a measure of the poverty of *Animal Farm* that it does little more than rehearse these "points." In *Homage to Catalonia* such conclusions were merely one part of an intense and movingly evoked experience. But in *Animal Farm* they form the totality of what the book has to offer us. We may perhaps derive some pleasure from elucidating the allegory. We may identify old Major, the aged porker who has the dream and who provides the ideological impulse to the revolution, as Karl Marx, and we may recognise the quarrel between Napoleon and Snowball as representing the rift between Stalin and Trotsky. And we may like to find the allegorical counterparts of the treason trials, the emergence of the Soviet secret police, the drive for technological achievement, the perversion of the ideals of the revolution and the misuse of propaganda. Nevertheless, if there is any pleasure in making such discoveries, it is hardly a literary pleasure. Indeed, in specifically literary terms, there is only one aspect of the book that continues to interest us and that is its form, and the particular tone of voice which this form enjoins upon the author. And the form is noteworthy not because of any particular distinction which it involves for the book, but rather because it is Orwell's first renewed effort to solve the problem of form in prose fiction which had been abandoned since the writing of *Coming Up For Air.*

Animal Farm is subtitled "A Fairy Story." Since the book does not tell of fairies, nor yet of the magical, this description seems hardly appropriate. Still it does suggest one intention of the book, which is to tell a story directly and simply. In this respect Orwell's purpose is a characteristic one, namely the vigorous sweeping aside of jargon, cant and hypocrisy and the presenting of issues clearly and intelligibly. But this sort of intention always has its attendant dangers and in the telling of his fairy story Orwell has succumbed to them. His account of revolution is greatly oversimplified; it is too obvious, too facile, too easy. For whatever we may think of the Russian revolution or, for that matter of any revolution, we cannot but be aware that the crises of a society are much more complex than Orwell is here able to suggest. And the feelings about revolution which the book elicits are as unsophisticated as the narrative itself. Take, for instance, the emotional climax of the book which comes when Boxer, the loyal and hard-working but unintelligent work horse, emblematic of "the common people," is sold to the knackers by the pig-commissars when he becomes too ill to work any more. The feelings of simple compassion and absolutely righteous indignation which this incident is calculated to evoke may be tolerable in a nursery tale that has no pretentions to being anything other than a nursery tale. But in one which lays claim to offer the adult intelligence some feeling for the realities of modern social and political life, they cannot, because of their crudity and sentimentality, merit serious attention. At the cost of this sort of oversimplification the sustained poise of the narrative is purchased. Clearly Orwell enjoys the easy confidence to which the position of a teller of nursery tales entitles him. The avuncular security and the poker-faced humour bestowed by the conventions of the form solve completely the difficult problem of the author-reader relationship which in the past had proved so troublesome. But in order to enjoy writing in this way, Orwell has made himself oblivious of the complexity of the experience with which his story purports to deal. He has here found a form which is easy and pleasing to him, but which is a means for turning away from the disturbing complexities of experience rather than for confronting them. It allows only of simple ideas, easy responses and obvious conclusions.

This particular form of the nursery story has been borrowed from that cosy world prior to the first World War upon which . . . Orwell was so ready to dwell. *Animal Farm* especially reminds us of Kipling's stories for children. The laws of the revolution that are painted on the wall of the cowshed and chanted by the animals clearly owe something to "The Law of the Jungle" in Kipling's *Second Jungle Book.* Indeed the central device of *Animal Farm,* the convention of humanised animals, may also derive most immediately from Kipling's *Jungle Book.* And Orwell's narrative tone is obviously modelled on that of the

Just So Stories. And of course there is the Dickensian element, that traditional element which endures beneath the experimentalism in every one of Orwell's novels and shows the strength of the premodern and the unmodern in his literary sensibility. The humour of the book, when it is not "just so" humour, is Dickensian, achieved by the use of "the unnecessary detail" which Orwell in his critical essay had identified and given examples of and relished as "the unmistakable mark of Dickens's writing." For instance, an important stage in Comrade Napoleon's gradual abandonment of the principles of animalism occurs when he sits down at table to eat. But in relating this, Orwell tells just a little bit more; he "always ate," he tells us, "from the crown Derby dinner service which had been in the glass cupboard in the drawing room." This comic surface of the prose is the major effect of *Animal Farm.* The book is, in fact, a piece of literary self-indulgence. As a writer Orwell has here taken refuge in a simple, comfortable Edwardian form which allows him a perspective upon the modern world and a relationship with his reader which, however relaxed they may be, are neither engaging nor illuminating. (pp. 147-50)

> *Keith Alldritt, in his* The Making of George Orwell: An Essay in Literary History, *Edward Arnold, 1969, 181 p.*

ROBERT A. LEE (essay date 1969)

[*In the following excerpt, Lee finds wider implications in* Animal Farm *than those of a simple allegory of the Russian Revolution or of the failure of all revolutionary ideals. According to Lee,* Animal Farm *illustrates Orwell's conviction that in the twentieth century the human condition is one of very little personal freedom. Lee discusses several of the animal characters as representative of an aspect of human nature that undermines the possibility of an equitable political and social system.*]

In **"Why I Write"** (1947), Orwell remarked that "*Animal Farm* was the first book in which I tried, with full consciousness of what I was doing, to fuse political purpose and artistic purpose into one whole." Orwell's political purposes, though varied, had been consistently present to that point in his career; however, their infusion into his novels had been the obstacle he had to overcome to achieve fully realized and coherent art. The polemicist and essayist, concerned with political problems, causes, and effects, found the form of art difficult. And the struggle for appropriate form had become more crucial following Spain, as *Coming Up For Air* witnesses. For Orwell, politics had been a *sine qua non*; the common constituents of imaginative writing—character, image, narrative—were for him obstructions rather than guideposts. He is thinking of *Burmese Days,* for example, when he says that it is "invariably where I lacked a *political* purpose that I wrote lifeless books and was betrayed into purple passages, sentences without meaning, decorative adjectives and humbug generally." Yet we also know that Orwell's impulses were toward "artistic purpose." Furthermore, his intention in the last years of his life was purportedly "to make a complete break from his former polemical, propagandist, way of writing and to concentrate on the treatment of human relationships" [Tom Hopkinson, *George Orwell,* 1962]. Despite Hopkinson's notion of a "complete break"—obviously, given *Animal Farm* and *1984,* Orwell never denied politics completely—some purposes of the essayist never left him. But Orwell had come to realize that the stance of the polemicist, never long hidden even in his self-termed "naturalistic" novels, must be abandoned. And no form suited the abandonment of this role better than the beast fable: Not only was the narrator, the potential polemicist, gone, but the demands of the appropriate conventions provided an impersonality and distance which created art, not journalism.

That the beast fable was a natural choice for Orwell is borne out by John Wain [in his *Essays on Literature and Ideas*, 1963]. *Animal Farm* is

> . . . so remarkably similar in its tone, and in the balanced fairness of its judgments, to the critical essays as to be, almost, seen as one of them. It is, after all, a fable, and a fable is closer to criticism than to fiction in the full imaginative sense.

Yet this is surely not the whole truth. Imagination must be given a more important role than Wain is willing to ascribe to it; and the underlying requirements of this form seem to me to run exactly contrary to "balanced fairness," indeed one of the consistent aspects in Orwell's essays. The essential characteristic of the beast fable is irony: The form provides for the writer "the power to keep his reader conscious simultaneously of the human traits satirized and of the animals as animals" [Ellen Douglass Leyburn, Additional Bibliography]. It demands of the reader a constant awareness of the double vision: Animal allegory prescribes two levels of perception which interact to purvey the irony in comparisons and contrasts. Orwell's essays are ironic only when they verge on fiction, as in the near-tales **"A Hanging"** and **"Shooting an Elephant."** In the kind of essays Wain has in mind, Orwell is honest and straightforward; the tone is that of the open, forthright speaker.

The use of this form provided an approach to art that Orwell clearly needed, one that differed from the conventional socially oriented novels he had been writing where he had fallen into pitfalls he now was recognizing. The need Orwell felt to criticize and attack social evils could now be subsumed into an artistic mode which by its very nature provided contrast and hence criticism. Paradoxically, the loss of a putative narrator and the gain of impersonalness that Orwell found in this form allow for a more intense criticism of social injustice and inequity than he had managed in his novels. The beast fable is in many ways the ideal form in which to articulate attack. The presence of beasts provides a ready-made vehicle for the tenor of the hatred in this essentially metaphorical mode. The correlation of a man, or a class of men, as swine or sheep allows savage hatred on the subnarrative level and concurrently provides the coolness of impersonalness in the facade of the narrative. As I. A. Richards says of the properly functioning metaphor [in *The Philosophy of Rhetoric* (1936)], the vehicle should not be "a mere embellishment of a tenor which is otherwise unchanged but the vehicle and tenor in co-operation give a meaning of more varied powers than can be ascribed to either."

Whatever Orwell gained artistically with *Animal Farm* was matched by the popular success the book enjoyed. It was the first of his books to achieve substantial commercial success, was a Book-of-the-Month Club selection in the United States, had a large sale, and was translated into many languages. Perhaps for the first time in his life, Orwell was moderately well off. The economic prosperity the book brought him was paralleled by critical accolades, and to this day *Animal Farm* is of all his works the most consistently praised. A judgment such as that of Frederick Karl, who finds the book a failure because of the "predictability" of the satire, is rare [see Additional Bibliography]. The consensus of approval is represented by a spectrum of praise that ranges from Tom Hopkinson's pronouncements that not only is it "by far Orwell's finest book," but it is one of only two present-day books so good that before it "the critic abdicates," to Sir Richard Rees's only slightly less enthusiastic encomium that the book is a "little masterpiece" in form and style.

Because *Animal Farm* is so different from anything else that Orwell wrote, it is difficult to assess it in relation to his other works. It deserves much praise simply for succeeding despite the problems that this form and Orwell's particular use of it contain. I am thinking of the dangers of allegory in general and of the specific political allegory that informs *Animal Farm*. The principal danger of allegory in fiction is artificiality: The secondary level may demand such precise equivalents that it comes to dominate the tale, with the result that the primary narrative loses its pretense of reality and spontaneity. I think it is clear that this does not happen in *Animal Farm*. The allegory of the Russian Revolution and subsequent events is probably only noticeable to the eye which has been made aware of it.

Briefly, the narrative sets up equivalents with the history of political action in Russia from roughly 1917 to the Second World War. Major and Snowball are Lenin and Trotsky; Napoleon is Stalin; and the warring farms and farmers around Manor Farm naturally come to stand for Germany (Frederick) and the Allies (Pilkington). Certain events in the story are said to represent events of history: The timber deal, in which Frederick later reneges on the animals, is of course the short-lived Russo-German alliance of 1939; the card game at the end of the book is supposed to represent the Teheran Conference following the war. The correlations are more elaborate than this, and while there are some inconsistencies in the precise political allegory it is notable that one need pay little heed to this to understand the book in its full political significance. Instead of being just an allegory of twentieth-century Russian politics, *Animal Farm* is more meaningfully an anatomy of all political revolutions. As A. E. Dyson says, *Animal Farm* "is by no means about Russia alone. Orwell is concerned to show how revolutionary ideals of justice, equality and fraternity always shatter in the event" [see excerpt dated 1965]. I would submit that the implications of this little book are wider yet: It is not merely that revolutions are self-destructive—Orwell also is painting a grim picture of the human condition in the political twentieth century, a time which he has come to believe marks the end of the very concepts of human freedom.

Nevertheless, the book starts with a relatively light tone. Mr. Jones—the commonplace name serves to diminish the importance of the human being in the story, yet gives a universal, "Everyman" quality—remembers to lock the henhouses for the night, but he is "too drunk to remember to shut the popholes." The picture of the drunken farmer, drinking his last glass of beer for the night and lurching up to bed while the animals come alive in the barn, reminds us of the cartoons (and Orwell's interest in the popular arts is surely at play here) and is primarily low keyed; at the same time, however, we note the irresponsibility of the farmer, neglecting—and endangering—those in his care. Later Jones will neglect to milk the cows, biologically a more serious omission; later yet, the pigs will also forget the milking, an ironic parallel that reveals the subsequent corruption of the revolution at the same time as it makes the pigs like humans—at that stage of the revolution a heinous sin. Nonetheless, the meeting of the animals while the humans sleep, though latently serious, forms a picture which is primarily whimsical. The description of the animals gathering for the meeting reveals the essential technique of the beast fable: Our concurrent awareness of both human and animal qualities and the several ironies which this perspective creates.

> The two cart-horses, Boxer and Clover, came in together, walking very slowly and setting down their vast hairy hoofs with great care lest there should be some small animal concealed in the straw. Clover was a stout motherly mare approaching middle life, who had never quite got her figure back after her fourth foal. Boxer was an enormous beast, nearly eighteen hands high, and as strong as any two ordinary horses put together. A white stripe down his nose gave him a somewhat stupid appearance, and in fact he was not of first-rate intelligence, but he was universally respected for his steadiness of character and tremendous powers of work.

The contrast between the strength of the horses and the fragility of the smaller, hidden animals places the scene unmistakably in the beast world; at the same time, the description of Clover's failure to get back her figure, a phrase Orwell surely chose for its commonplace, cliche quality, is representative of radical human nature. The menagerie, in fact, demonstrates a spectrum of human qualities and types, from the pigs, who take up the front seats in the audience, to Benjamin the donkey, the cynic of the farm, and to Mollie, the white mare, vain and foolish. These introductory descriptions are woven into the structure of the plot: For her vanity, Mollie will ultimately be excluded from the farm; in his cynicism, Benjamin will come to see but be incapable of changing the reality of the revolution; and the pigs will come to occupy not only the front but the total of the farm.

The awareness of simultaneous levels of animal and human existence is nicely maintained by Orwell in all the story's aspects. Major's speech, describing his dream in which man has disappeared from the earth and is replaced by animals, is at once a logical demonstration of wish fulfillment in the dream at a bestial level and a gospel of economic revolution easily understandable at the human level. ("Man is the only creature that consumes without producing" is, of course, an ironic variation of Marxian anticapitalism.) Orwell reinforces this irony by having Major's speech full of biological analogies: "The life of an animal is misery and slavery: that is the plain truth. But is this simply part of the order of nature? Is it because this land of ours is so poor that it cannot afford a decent life to those who dwell upon it?" We slide back and forth between reading this as Marxian dogma, excoriating capitalism and calling for a proletarian revolution, and reading it in terms of the mistreated animals—and we are reminded of the irresponsibility of Farmer Jones.

Moreover, there is the possibility of a fourth kind of irony: In his reading of *1984* [in *Politics and the Novel* (1957)] Irving Howe remarks that Emmanuel Goldstein's book, *The Theory and Practice of Oligarchical Collectivism,* imitates Trotsky's style in "his fondness for using scientific references in non-scientific contexts." Although there is a slightly different usage here, the employment of biological language in a political context is obviously related. We begin to be aware of the complexity of this seemingly simple little book. It is not simple political allegory, but neither is it merely classical satire built on multiple or "receding planes." The various levels interact thematically: Animals are like humans; humans are, pejoratively, only like animals; human politics are really no more profound than natural biology.

The book is also constructed on a circular basis. Major's speech builds to the rhetorical climax of "All animals are comrades," which apothegm is immediately punctuated by the dogs' pursuit of some rats that they see. A vote is taken and the rats become "comrades," followed by the animals banding together against their common enemy, man, under the aegis of the motto, "All animals are equal." The remainder of the book will be a series of dramatic repudiations of these mottoes, a return to the tyranny and irresponsibility of the beginning. The only change will be in the identity of the masters, and, ironically, even that will be only partially changed.

At the opening of the second chapter Major dies, the prophet who articulated the revolutionary ideals and in whose name they will be carried out—and perverted. Snowball and Napoleon, two pigs, assume the leadership of the rebellion, aided by their public-relations man, Squealer. And these three codify the ideals of Major into Animalism, "a complete system of thought." But Animalism, obviously analogous to communism, is significantly instituted without any plan. The rebellion occurs spontaneously: Once again Jones neglects to feed the animals, who break into the barn for food when "they could stand it no longer." Jones and his hired man come in and the animals, "with one accord, though nothing of the kind had been planned beforehand," attack the men and chase them off the farm. "And so almost before they knew what was happening, the Rebellion had been successfully carried through: Jones was expelled, and the Manor Farm was theirs." Orwell stresses the spontaneity of the Rebellion to make clear that the social revolution *per se* is not the object of his satire. He emphasizes that no matter how bad things become for the animals later—and they do become bad—the animals "were far better off than they had been in the days of Jones." Though this fact will itself have to be qualified, there is a justness in the statement. Not only does the revolution's spontaneity diminish the importance of Napoleon and Snowball's plotting—and thus provide a dramatic irony about their supposed accomplishments—but the motive, hunger, justifies the revolution more basically and irrefutably than the soundest of political theories. The revolution sprung, not from theory, but from real, natural need. No matter how corrupt the ideals of the revolution become, Orwell never questions the validity of the uprising: The target here is not social—and socialistic—revolution, contrary to the many who simply want to see the book as a satire of communism, but rather the target is the inability of humans to live within a community of ideals.

The inevitable corruption of the revolution is presaged immediately. The animals have driven out their former masters.

> For the first few minutes the animals could hardly believe in their good fortune. Their first act was to gallop in a body right round the boundaries of the farm, as though to make quite sure that no human being was hiding anywhere upon it; then they raced back to the farm buildings to wipe out the last traces of Jones's hated reign. The harness-room at the end of the stables was broken open; the bits, the nose-rings, the dog-chains, the cruel knives with which Mr. Jones had been used to castrate the pigs and lambs, were all flung down the well. The reins, the halters, the blinkers, the degrading nosebags, were thrown on to the rubbish fire which was burning in the yard. So were the whips. All the animals capered with joy when they saw the whips going up in flames.

The reaction is understandable; but the description of the inevitable and immediate violence that seems to follow all revolutions foreshadows that this revolution will suffer the common fate of its genre: reactionary cruelty, the search for the scapegoat, the perversion of the ideals of the revolution, and the counter-revolution. Thus, the good intentions of the animals are immediately endangered when it is learned that the pigs "had taught themselves to read and write from an old spelling book which had belonged to Mr. Jones's children" [the critic adds in a footnote that "it is noteworthy that these children never appear in the book: They obviously would enjoy a natural sympathy that would be contrary to the antipathy the humans receive in the fable"]. The pigs' reading ability is a valuable skill for the animals, one which is necessary to run a farm, even for animals. But it is also patently a human attribute, and one which already violates one of Major's cardinal tenets: "Remember also that in fighting against Man, we must not come to resemble him."

If seeds of destruction are immediately present, the positive aspects of the rebellion achieve their high peak with the codification of the "unalterable law by which all the animals on Animal Farm must live for ever after," the Seven Commandments.

1. Whatever goes upon two legs is an enemy.
2. Whatever goes upon four legs, or has wings, is a friend.
3. No animal shall wear clothes.
4. No animal shall sleep in a bed.
5. No animal shall drink alcohol.
6. No animal shall kill any other animal.
7. All animals are equal.

This "unalterable law" provides the major structural basis for the rest of the fable. From this point on the plot reveals a gradual alteration of these commandments, ending in the well-known contradiction that epitomizes the new nature of the farm at the end of the book. But here, Orwell's technique is of immediate irony: The animals are watching the commandments being painted on the barn when the cows begin to low, needing to be milked. They are milked, and the milk is placed in front of the animals, at which many "looked with considerable interest." But Napoleon, "placing himself in front of the buckets," will not even mix it with the hens' mash, as "Jones used sometimes to," and it disappears, eventually into Napoleon's own mash. Selfishness is the note on which the chapter concludes, following the spontaneous and successful take-over of the farm and the articulation of unselfish ideals by which all the animals are to live.

The next concern on Animal Farm is to get the hay in, and we see further spoiling of the revolution's ideals as the pigs supervise rather than work. From the beginning, all animals are *not* equal. But one must be careful. In light of what is to happen, it is easy to see that the pigs' managerial role is further foreshadowing of the ultimate perversion of the seventh commandment, but this does not mean that the revolution is therefore wrong, or that Orwell thinks that all revolutions are inevitably self-corrupting. Both farms and revolutions need leaders, managers; and, for all their evil, the pigs are the most capable animals on the farm. Orwell may be suggesting—and this would be far more profound—that capable people are inevitably evil; or, conversely, that evil people are inevitably the most capable.

The capability of the pigs, and their management, is reflected in the success of the farm: There is no wastage, no stealing. It is the biggest harvest in the farm's history; in addition, though the animals work hard, there is no leisure. Each animal works "according to his capacity." The Marxian slogan at the base of the success of the farm seems to me to prove conclusively

that Orwell does not question socialistic ideology. He does question the failure of ideology to accommodate human variety, implicit in the missing half of the quotation. At this point, Orwell specifically avoids mention of what goes *to* each animal: The irony of "need" is already apparent in what the pigs have taken and will be reinforced by the future miniscule gains of the other animals.

Orwell further stresses the human variability which undermines the best—or the worst—of systems in the character of Mollie, the vain mare more interested in ribbons than in harvests, and in the description of the cat, who disappears when there is work to be done. It is important that these animals are portrayed kindly and humorously: The cat, for example, "always made such excellent excuses, and purred so affectionately, that it was impossible not to believe in her good intentions." We soon learn the real nature of these "good intentions." The cat is spied one day talking to some sparrows who were "just out of her reach. She was telling them that all animals were now comrades and that any sparrow who chose could come and perch on her paw; but the sparrows kept their distance." We are reminded again of the natural, biological basis of the revolution—and remembering this we cannot blame the cat. If this attempt by the cat is at one level an ironic mirror of the pigs' later, horrifying "education" of the puppies into vicious trained killers, it is simultaneously natural—which the pigs' deed is not. Orwell reminds us of natural instinct and its inevitable conflict with political absolutism. It is to the point that Mollie soon leaves the farm. She is seen one day being stroked by a human on the outskirts of the farm; Clover finds sugar and several ribbons hidden under the straw in her stall. And so Mollie disappears, to be seen pulling a cart, her coat "newly clipped and she wore a scarlet ribbon around her forelock. She appeared to be enjoying herself, so the pigeons said." In political terms, she is, of course, a heretic, and her selfish behavior is inconsistent with selfless social ideals. But there is no intention on Orwell's part to criticize her. He rather suggests that too strict attention to the harsh, social demands of life obscures the love of beauty in the world. Any criticism seems rather to be directed at a political norm which makes the esthete the apostate.

For political and social demands do dominate life at Manor Farm; and the demands become more complex. Pilkington and Frederick spread stories about horrible conditions on the farm, stories which are contradicted by rumors among their animals about the wonderful paradise that exists on Animal Farm. Neither set of rumors is true, of course, and Orwell develops the consequences of such misrepresentation. The Farmers' animals begin to revolt in varying degrees—"bulls which had always been tractable suddenly turned savage, sheep broke down hedges and devoured the clover . . . ," while the humans, hearing in the song of Animal Farm "a prophecy of their future doom," invade the farm. It is not the social situations or conflicting ideologies that Orwell concerns himself with, but the misrepresentations, the falsification and distortion of fact, which he indicates leads ineluctably to disaster and misery. Falsification is at the heart of the main internal struggle on the farm, and the way fact is distorted and misrepresented is graphically pictured in the rivalry between Snowball and Napoleon over the construction of the windmill.

Snowball (who is a brilliant orator, compared with Napoleon, who was "better at canvassing support for himself in between times") conceives of a plan for a windmill, which Napoleon graphically disdains (he urinates on the plans). At the meeting in which the final vote for approval is to be taken, nine enormous dogs, "as ferocious as wolves," suddenly appear and chase Snowball off the farm; the dogs return and sit by Napoleon, wagging their tails, "as the other dogs had been used to do with Mr. Jones." And it is just a short time until Squealer appears to announce blandly that Napoleon, "who had advocated it from the beginning," himself proposes the building of the windmill. More is suggested here than the simple power struggle attendant on all revolutions, or the more specific overthrow of Trotsky, the party theoretician and planner, by calculating Stalin. The symbol of the windmill suggests much about Orwell's complex attitudes toward the political concepts within the story well beyond the primary irony of the pigs' manipulation of the hopes of Animal Farm's animals. The windmill has Quixotic overtones: Orwell suggests that the way the animals focus all their efforts on building it is a false and deluded if heroic struggle. The windmill becomes the means by which Napoleon controls deviation; he uses it to direct the animals' attention away from the growing shortages and inadequacies on the farm, and the animals ignorantly concentrate all their efforts on building the windmill—but its symbolic nature suggests an empty concentration, a meaningless, unheroic effort, for the idea is literally misguided.

At the same time the symbol works in other directions. The windmill is analogous in the political allegory to the New Economic Policy. As such, it functions in much the same way as do other symbols of secular paradise in twentieth-century writing. Dams and bridges replace churches as representations of man's hopes for eternity; the windmill becomes a symbol of "secular heaven," placed in the future, but now in a temporal sense. (pp. 104-18)

The construction of the windmill, its subsequent destruction in a storm (during which the hens hear a gun go off in the background; the allusion is probably to World War I), and its rebuilding provide the linear movement of the plot in the rest of the book. The thematic development is centered on the progressive alteration of the Seven Commandments. Two monstrous indignities are suffered by the animals, but even these are thematically secondary. There is a bitter winter on the farm and rations become scarce: "starvation seemed to stare them in the face." A scapegoat is needed, and Snowball is conveniently used by Napoleon—who blatantly tells the other animals that not only is Snowball responsible for all the mysterious destruction that suddenly begins to occur on the farm, but that his brave actions in fighting the humans at the Battle of the Cowshed, *which all the animals witnessed,* had never happened. This is, of course, a direct prevision of the rewriting of history in *1984.* "Four days later," after being warned by Napoleon that Snowball's secret agents are still among them, the animals are ordered to assemble in the yard. Suddenly the dogs attack four of the other pigs and Boxer; but Boxer easily fights them off.

> Presently the tumult died down. The four pigs waited, trembling, with guilt written on every line of their countenances. Napoleon now called upon them to confess their crimes. They were the same four pigs as had protested when Napoleon abolished the Sunday Meetings. Without any further prompting they confessed that they had been secretly in touch with Snowball ever since his expulsion, that they had collaborated with him in destroying the windmill, and that they had entered into an agreement with him to hand over Animal Farm to Mr. Frederick. They added that Snowball had privately admitted to them that he had been Jones's secret agent for years past. When

they had finished their confession, the dogs promptly tore their throats out, and in a terrible voice Napoleon demanded whether any other animal had anything to confess.

In an obvious parallel to the purge trials of the 1930's, three hens come forward and admit to having heard Snowball speak to them "in a dream"; they are slaughtered. A goose confesses to pilfering six ears of corn, followed by a sheep who, "urged to do this" by Snowball, had urinated in the drinking pool, in turn followed by two more sheep who had murdered a ram. "And so the tale of confessions and executions went on, until there was a pile of corpses lying before Napoleon's feet and the air was heavy with the smell of blood, which had been unknown there since the expulsion of Jones."

Orwell has managed to dramatize, in two short, terror-laden pages, the very essence of this strange psycho-political phenomenon of our times: the ritualistic, honestly believed but obviously spurious confession. The ramifications of the motif in contemporary literature are many: One is reminded of a parallel such as Rubashov in *Darkness at Noon* and that, in a political age which denies individual selfhood, the only way of asserting one's self may be through pain or its extension, death. Ontologically and eschatologically, it may be preferable to die horribly and perhaps anonymously than to live as a cipher. However, I wish to consider the relative *insignificance* of the horrors that have passed, as physical terror becomes thematically subsidiary to the falsification of history and the denial of objective reality. Following this scene, the animals

Cover of the 1947 Ukrainian translation of Animal Farm.
George Orwell Archive, University College London.

leave, led by Boxer and Clover. Boxer, unable to understand, thinks it "must be due to some fault in ourselves. The solution, as I see it, is to work harder." And so he trots up to the windmill to resume dragging loads of stone to it. The other animals huddle about Clover on the hillside.

> It was a clear spring evening. The grass and the bursting hedges were gilded by the level rays of the sun. Never had the farm—and with a kind of surprise they remembered that it was their own farm, every inch of it their own property—appeared to the animals so desirable a place.

Clover, looking down on this scene, remembers the promise and the hope of the revolution on the night she heard Major's speech, and her thoughts sum up the earlier images of the strong mare protecting the ducklings and recall the maxim at the base of the society, "Each working according to his capacity, the strong protecting the weak." Even here, she has "no thought of rebellion or disobedience," for the fundamental value of the revolution is reasserted: "Even as things were, they were far better off than they had been in the days of Jones." But the phrase "even as things were" implies too much, and so Clover, trying to somehow reestablish her continuity with that now quickly changing past, "feeling this to be in some way a substitute for the words she was unble to find," begins to sing the song, *Beasts of England,* which epitomized the egalitarian ideals Major expounded. The animals are singing the song when Squealer appears to announce that "by a special decree of Comrade Napoleon, *Beasts of England* had been abolished." Squealer tells the astonished animals that the reason is that "in *Beasts of England* we expressed our longing for a better society in days to come. But that society has now been established. Clearly this song had no longer any purpose."

The irony is of course the claim for a "better society," as the animals sit in the shadow of the heap of freshly slaughtered corpses. But the implications are more profound. Terror, bestiality, senseless death are all dreadful and shattering experiences; but they are at least comprehensible and do not radically alter the conceptualized values of the survivors. Far more terrifying is the overt alteration of consciousness which follows the slaughter, the blatant misrepresentation of the past, *which goes unchallenged.* The animals can only "sense" that the new song ("Animal Farm, Animal Farm / Never through me shalt thou come to harm") is different from *Beasts of England.* Squealer's pronouncement that the "better society" has now been established is uncontroverted. The commandments, which have begun to be altered recently, are now more rapidly and unquestioningly changed—and change pervades Animal Farm. A proposed timber deal vacillates between Pilkington and Frederick until the animals are forced to admit "a certain bewilderment, but Squealer was soon able to convince them that their memories had been at fault." Ironically, one of Major's prescriptions had been not to indulge in trade with the humans. Here the animals are not even sure whom the trade is with, much less can they remember past dogma.

The animals can no longer recognize reality, but they somehow manage to finish the windmill, concurrent with Napoleon's double-dealing with Pilkington and Frederick. We see the simultaneous strength and weakness, the goodness and corruption, that has evolved from the original rebellion. Despite all, the animals finish the windmill—they can accomplish a nearly impossible task—but at the same time, Napoleon, cheating and being cheated in his dealing, precipitates an attack upon the farm by Frederick and his followers (World War II, in the allegory). Though the animals win the battle, many are griev-

ously injured and the windmill is destroyed. But Squealer declares that they have a "victory," "we have won back what we had before." And so the animals celebrate—each is given an apple, two ounces of corn for each bird, and three biscuits for each dog—while Napoleon gets drunk. The mere inequity, the surface irony is compounded by the inevitable falsification of fact. The next morning the animals discover that the fifth commandment did not read, as they had thought, "No animal shall drink alcohol," but instead "No animal shall drink alcohol *to excess.*"

It is not the threat of violence, even the radically inexplicable self-violence which the deracinated individual must, ironically, bring upon himself for his own secular salvation in a wholly political world, nor the war, nor the social injustice that man is suffering that is the cancer of our times, but the loss of "objective truth." Choices vanish in a society which has no bases for choice.

The most darkly pessimistic aspect of **Animal Farm** is that the animals are unable even to recognize their new oppression, much less combat it. The difference is that the pigs control language; Mr. Jones controlled only action—not thought. Orwell portrays at least three animals as being potentially able to stand up to the state (in an admittedly limited yet meaningful way), yet each is inadequate in a vital respect. Boxer has probably enough power and strength to overthrow Napoleon's regime. When Napoleon's vicious dogs attack him, Boxer simply "put out his great hoof, caught a dog in midair, and pinned him to the ground. The dog shrieked for mercy and the other two fled with their tails between their legs." But Boxer is stupid; he cannot comprehend the present, much less conceptualize the past. He ingenuously looks to Napoleon to see whether or not he should let the dog go; when the slaughter is over, he retreats to work, thinking the fault must lie within the animals. Thus, his fate is not as pathetic, as some critics read the scene in which he is taken away, kicking in the truck, as it is the inevitable fate of utter stupidity. The most complex thought that Boxer can express is "if Comrade Napoleon says it, it must be right," in the face of blatant, gross falsification. Boxer's basic goodness, social self-sacrifice, and impressive strength are simply inadequately used; the stupidity which wastes them suggests interesting qualifications about Orwell's reputed love of the common man, qualifications which become even stronger when considered in light of the descriptions of the proles in *1984.*

Clover is more intelligent and perceptive than is Boxer, but she has a corresponding lack of strength. Her "character" is primarily a function of her sex: Her instincts are maternal and pacifistic. She works hard, along with the other animals, but there is no picture of any special strength, as there is with Boxer. And even with a greater intelligence, her insights are partial. Things may indeed be better than they "had been in the days of Jones," but, in the context of the slaughter of the animals, "it was not for this that she and all the other animals had hoped and toiled." Both perceptions are right, but both are incomplete. In both cases, Clover senses that there is something further to be understood, but just as Boxer uncomprehendingly moves to toil, so does Clover wistfully retreat to song—only to have this articulation of the past's ideals suddenly changed, without her dissent. A paradigm appears: Boxer is marked by great strength and great stupidity; Clover has less physical power but has a corresponding increase in awareness; the equation is completed with Benjamin, who sees and knows most—perhaps all—but is physically ineffectual and socially irresponsible.

Benjamin, the donkey, "was the oldest animal on the farm, and the worst tempered. He seldom talked, but when he did, it was usually to make some cynical remark. . . ." As archetypal cynic, Benjamin remains aloof and distant, refusing to meddle in the farm's affairs, but seeing all. He expresses no opinion about the rebellion; he works on Animal Farm "in the same slow, obstinate way" that he did on Manor Farm; he only remarks enigmatically that "Donkeys live a long time." Beneath the surface cynicism, he is, almost predictably, blessed with a heart of gold: He is devoted to Boxer, and it is he who discovers the plot to deliver Boxer to the glue-maker. But Benjamin is essentially selfish, representing a view of human nature that is apolitical, and thus he can hardly be the voice of Orwell within the book, as some readers hold. To Benjamin, the social and political situation is irrelevant: Human nature suffers and prospers in the same degree, no matter who is the master. He believes "that things never had been, nor ever could be much better or much worse—hunger, hardship, and disappointment being, so he said, the unalterable law of life." We know too much about Orwell's social beliefs from other contexts to assume that Benjamin speaks for Orwell here. Yet it is only fair to note that Benjamin sees most, knows most, is obviously the most intelligent and perceptive of all the animals on the farm, including the pigs. To a certain extent, he represents intelligence without the effectuating and necessary strength; perhaps more profoundly, he demonstrates the Orwellian heinous sin of irresponsible intelligence. The posture of assuming that only the very worst is inevitable in life, that change for the better is a delusion, and that the only alternative is a retreat into a social self-pity is exactly the posture from which Orwell presumptively jerks Gordon Comstock in *Keep the Aspidistra Flying*.

With the means of opposition to Napoleon's totalitarian rule so portrayed, there is little suspense in the outcome of the situation the novel describes. Years pass. Jones dies in an inebriates' home; Boxer and Snowball are forgotten by nearly all, for a new generation of animals has grown up. The situation on the farm is unchanged for most of the animals. The farm is more prosperous now, but the fruits of prosperity never pass beyond Napoleon and his comrades. And the attempt to judge whether the present situation is better or worse than it had been under Jones is fruitless.

> Sometimes the older ones among them racked their dim memories and tried to determine whether in the early days of the Rebellion, when Jones's expulsion was still recent, things had been better or worse than now. They could not remember. There was nothing with which they could compare their present lives: they had nothing to go upon except Squealer's lists of figures, which invariably demonstrated that everything was getting better and better.

Again, the condition itself is not as depressing as the loss of the rational criteria which allow evaluation. The denial of memory enables control of the present, and hence of the future.

"And yet the animals never gave up hope." For they do retain one ineradicable achievement: equality. "If they went hungry, it was not from feeding tyrannical human beings; if they worked hard, at least they worked for themselves. No creature among them went on two legs. No creature called any other 'Master.' All animals were equal." The social and economic hopes of the revolution may have become lost in the actualities of history, but the primary political gain of the revolution remains valid for the animals. Orwell articulates this one, final achievement of the animals. But within a page Squealer and Napoleon

appear, walking on their hind legs. Yet even this sight is not the final violation of hope. Clover and Benjamin walk around to the barn to read the seventh commandment:

ALL ANIMALS ARE EQUAL
BUT SOME ANIMALS ARE MORE EQUAL THAN OTHERS

After this, "it did not seem strange" that the pigs take the humans' newspapers, that the pigs dress like humans, invite neighboring humans in to feast and drink, that the name of the farm is changed back to Manor Farm, and that, in the final image of the book, the pigs become indistinguishable from the humans. The book has come full circle, and things are back as they were. If this is so, Benjamin's judgment becomes valid: Things do remain the same, never much worse, never much better; "hunger, hardship, and disappointment" are indeed the "unalterable law of life."

Power inevitably corrupts the best of intentions, apparently no matter who possesses the power: At the end, all the representatives of the various ideologies are indistinguishable—they are all pigs, all pigs are humans. Communism is no better and no worse than capitalism or fascism; the ideals of socialism were long ago lost in Clover's uncomprehending gaze over the farm. Religion is merely a toy for the corrupters, neither offensive nor helpful to master or slave. But perhaps more distressing yet is the realization that everyone, the good and the bad, the deserving and the wicked, are not only contributors to the tyranny, but are not only powerless before it, but are unable to understand it. Boxer thinks that whatever Napoleon says is right; Clover can only vaguely feel, and cannot communicate, that things are not exactly right; Benjamin thinks that it is in the nature of the world that things go wrong. The potential hope of the book is finally expressed only in terms of ignorance (Boxer), wistful inarticulateness (Clover), or the tired, cynical belief that things never change (Benjamin). The inhabitants of this world seem to deserve their fate.

One must finally ask, however, with all this despair and bleakness what are the actual bases for the tyranny of Animal Farm. Is the terrorism of the dogs the most crucial aspect? Is it this that rules the animals? Boxer's power is seen as superior to this violence and force. Is the basis of the tonal despair the pessimistic belief in the helplessness of the mass of the animals? Orwell elsewhere states again and again his faith in the common people. It seems to me that the basis of this society's evil is the inability of its inhabitants to ascertain truth and that this is demonstrated through the theme of the corruption of language. So long as the animals cannot remember the past, because it is continually altered, they have no control over the present and hence over the future. A society which cannot control its language is, says Orwell, doomed to be oppressed in terms which deny it the very most elemental aspects of humanity: To live in a world which allows the revised form of the seventh commandment of Animal Farm is not merely to renounce the belief in the possibility of human equality, but in the blatant perversion of language, the very concept of objective reality is lost.

The mode by which the recognition of reality is denied is the corruption of language. When a society no longer maintains its language as a common basis by which value, idea, and fact are to be exchanged, those who control the means of communication have the most awful of powers—they literally can create the truth they choose. *Animal Farm,* then, seems to be in one respect only an extension of *Burmese Days*—the common problem is the failure of communication and its corollary, community. But if in *Burmese Days* their failure was contingent, in *Animal Farm* it is brought about by willful manipulation. The next logical step is seen in *1984,* where the consequences press to the premonition of apocalypse. (pp. 118-27)

> *Robert A. Lee, in his* Orwell's Fiction, *University of Notre Dame Press, 1969, 188 p.*

ALEX ZWERDLING (essay date 1974)

[*Zwerdling is a German-born American educator and critic. In the following excerpt, he contends that Orwell intended* Animal Farm *to demonstrate in fable form the pattern formed by the predictable stages of revolution.*]

Much of Trotsky's book [*The Revolution Betrayed*] expounds a theory of the inevitable *stages* of revolution, a subject that haunted Orwell's imagination and was finally to produce *Animal Farm.* Trotsky constantly compares the Russian and French revolutions, and finds many similarities in their development. Nor is he averse to generalization: "It is sufficiently well known that every revolution up to this time has been followed by a reaction, or even a counter-revolution. This, to be sure, has never thrown the nation all the way back to its starting-point, but it has always taken from the people the lion's share of their conquests. The victims of the first reactionary wave have been, as a general rule, those pioneers, initiators, and instigators who stood at the head of the masses in the period of the revolutionary offensive." A pessimistic observer might modify Marx's theory that revolutions are the engines of history by commenting that some of the trains seemed to shuttle back and forth between two fixed points. But Trotsky insists that even in the inevitable counter-revolution, the nation is never brought *all* the way back to its starting point.

In Orwell's speculations about revolution as a method for achieving socialist goals, this was one of the major points at issue. He became far less confident than Trotsky that real progress was achieved through revolution, and his own view at times approaches Lord Acton's gloomy conviction that every revolution "makes a wise and just reform impossible." As early as 1938, the central idea of *Animal Farm* was running through Orwell's mind: "It would seem that what you get over and over again is a movement of the proletariat which is promptly canalised and betrayed by astute people at the top, and then the growth of a new governing class. The one thing that never arrives is equality. The mass of the people never get the chance to bring their innate decency into the control of affairs, so that one is almost driven to the cynical thought that men are only decent when they are powerless." Clearly Orwell still hesitates to accept this idea: he says he is "almost driven" to it. It remained an unresolved issue in his mind for years, and one can see why. His socialist faith made him need to deny it; his temperamental pessimism must have found it congenial. He could neither resolve the question nor forget it—perhaps the ideal condition for the creation of a vital literary work.

Orwell's uncertainty about revolution eventually produced *Animal Farm* and was responsible for the considerable ambiguity of the book. An ironic allegory is bound to mystify many of its readers, no matter how easy it is to identify the historical parallels on which it is based. We know that Orwell had a great deal of difficulty getting *Animal Farm* into print, and it is generally assumed that publishers rejected it because they did not want to publish an anti-Soviet satire in the middle of the war. Yet T. S. Eliot's letter of rejection from Faber makes it clear this was not the only problem the book raised. Eliot complains that "the effect is simply one of negation. It ought

to excite some sympathy with what the author wants, as well as sympathy with his objections to something: and the positive point of view, which I take to be generally Trotskyite, is not convincing." He goes on to suggest that Orwell "splits his vote" by refusing to confirm any of the standard Western attitudes toward the Soviet Union.

Eliot's argument suggests a thoroughly confused sense of Orwell's purpose. If *Animal Farm* can be said to have a "positive point of view" at all, it is certainly not Trotskyite: Snowball is hardly its tragic hero. The difficulties of understanding *Animal Farm* largely stem from its interpretation as an exclusive attack on the Soviet Union. Orwell's purpose, however, is more general: he is interested in tracing the inevitable stages of any revolution, and he shapes his fable accordingly. This is not to deny that the literal level of the story is almost exclusively based on Soviet history. But although Russia is his immediate target, Orwell says the book "is intended as a satire on dictatorship in general." He was faithful to the details of Soviet history, yet he did not hesitate to transform some of its most important elements.

The most striking of these is the omission of Lenin from the drama. Major (the idealist visionary who dies before the revolution takes place) is clearly meant to represent Marx, while Napoleon and Snowball act out the conflict in the postrevolutionary state between Stalin and Trotsky. Lenin is left out, it seems to me, because Orwell wants to emphasize the enormous disparity between the ideals of the revolution and the reality of the society it actually achieves. Lenin was the missing link in this process, both visionary and architect of the new state, but from Orwell's longer historical perspective, his brief period of power must have seemed like an irrelevant interlude in the stark drama that was unfolding. The heirs of Lenin had in fact begun to transform him into a myth even before he was dead; they legitimized their power by worshipping at his shrine. In order to demythify the Russian Revolution and present the Bolshevik leaders as they really were, Orwell must have felt compelled to eliminate the mythical hero altogether.

Such radical departures from history are of course Orwell's prerogative in constructing a story intended to have more general significance. He says in a preface to *Animal Farm* that "although the various episodes are taken from the actual history of the Russian Revolution, they are dealt with schematically and their chronological order is changed; this was necessary for the symmetry of the story." One might add that it was also necessary in order to achieve Orwell's purpose in writing it. This raises the question of how the topical and generic levels of satire in the book are related, and one might clarify the issue by citing the case of Swift, who was in some sense Orwell's model.

When *Gulliver's Travels* was first published, many read the book as an essentially partisan political document, a propaganda piece for the opposition party. Yet Swift himself wrote to his French translator that, if *Gulliver's Travels* could only be understood in England, it was a failure, for "the same vices and the same follies reign everywhere . . . and the author who writes only for a city, a province, a kingdom, or even an age, deserves so little to be translated, that he does not even deserve to be read." In the same way, *Animal Farm* is concerned both with the Russian Revolution and, by extension, with the general pattern of revolution itself. As the Stalinist period recedes into the distant past, Orwell's book (if it survives as a literary work) will more and more be appreciated as generic rather than topical satire, just as *Gulliver's Travels* has come to be.

Orwell chose to write his book in the form of a fable partly to give the pattern of historical events permanent mythic life, to emphasize that he was dealing with typical, not fortuitous, events. He is interested in constructing a paradigmatic social revolution, and the pattern that emerges is meant to apply to the Spanish Civil War and to the French Revolution (the main character, after all, is named Napoleon) as well as to the Russian one. Orwell's story suggests that revolutions inevitably go through several predictable stages. They begin with great idealistic fervor and popular support, energized by millennial expectations of justice and equality. The period immediately following a successful revolution is the Eden stage. There is a sense of triumphant achievement; idealistic vision is translated into immediate reality; the spirit of community and equality are everywhere apparent. Old law and institutions are broken and replaced by an inner, yet reliable, concern for the common good. The state has, for the moment, withered away.

Slowly the feeling of freedom gives way to the sense of necessity and bondage, "we" becomes "I-they," spirit turns into law, improvised organization is replaced by rigid institutions, equality modulates to privilege. The next stage is the creation of a new elite which, because of its superior skill and its lust for power, assumes command and re-creates the class structure. Its power is first universally granted but gradually must be upheld against opposition by terror and threat. As time goes on, the past is forgotten or expunged; the new elite takes on all the characteristics of the old, prerevolutionary leadership, while the rest of the society returns to the condition of servitude. The transition is too gradual to be dramatic, although it has its dramatic moments, and it is constantly presented in the guise of historical inevitability or as a necessary response to conspiracy or external danger. A scapegoat is found to explain the disparity between ideal and actual. The exploited class remains exploited basically because of its doggedness and stupidity but also because, having no taste for power, it is inevitably victimized by the power-hungry. In every new society—even if it consists exclusively of those without previous experience of power—some will rise above their fellows and assume the available positions of authority. When their power and privileges are consolidated, they will fight to keep them. The only surviving vestiges of revolution will be its rhetoric and its (conveniently altered) history. The reality of "equality" and "justice" will have withered away, to be replaced by the state.

"The effect," Eliot had said, "is simply one of negation." His objection raises the question of whether *Animal Farm* should be considered in moral terms at all. At this point in his career Orwell's mind had begun to work in an increasingly analytic way. He was interested in understanding the structure of revolution rather than in proposing a better way to achieve social goals. Eliot complains that the book fails to "excite some sympathy with what the author wants." Yet great satire has often been written out of the despairing sense that "what the author wants" may be unattainable. Orwell's socialism is not an act of faith. If he has a "positive point of view" at all in writing *Animal Farm,* it is the hope that socialists will be able to face the hard truths he presents rather than continue to accept the various consoling illusions their movement has generated to account for its disappointments.

And yet realism is not his only goal; he is also finally a moralist. In the essay on Dickens, Orwell makes an important distinction between the moralist and the revolutionary, which I take to be crucial for an understanding of his purpose in *Animal Farm.*

Dickens, he says, is a moralist: "It is hopeless to try and pin him down to any definite remedy, still more to any political doctrine. . . . Useless to change institutions without a 'change of heart'—that, essentially, is what he is always saying." Orwell realized that the need for a "change of heart" has been used as "*the* alibi of people who do not wish to endanger the *status quo,*" but he insists, that this does not make Dickens a reactionary apologist. The paradox can only be explained by understanding the writer's relation to the moment in which he writes:

> I said earlier that Dickens is not *in the accepted sense* a revolutionary writer. But it is not at all certain that a merely moral criticism of society may not be just as "revolutionary"—and revolution, after all, means turning things upside down—as the politico-economic criticism which is fashionable at this moment. Blake was not a politician, but there is more understanding of the nature of capitalist society in a poem like "I wander through each charter'd street" than in three-quarters of Socialist literature. Progress is not an illusion, it happens, but it is slow and invariably disappointing. There is always a new tyrant waiting to take over from the old—generally not quite so bad, but still a tyrant. Consequently two viewpoints are always tenable. The one, how can you improve human nature until you have changed the system? The other, what is the use of changing the system before you have improved human nature? They appeal to different individuals, and they probably show a tendency to alternate in point of time.

The passage is remarkable for the sense it gives of Orwell's long historical perspective and his ability to see a particular artistic choice (Dickens's and, at this point, his own) as being in perpetual conflict with its equally legitimate opposite. The attitude could be described as dialectical, except that Orwell does not stress the synthesis which grows out of each clash. Rather, he sees the conflict as eternal: the point of view is far from the ultimate optimism of Hegel and Marx. At a particular moment in time, then, the moralist who voices his outrage at what is accepted, even though he has no idea how things might be changed, is more of a revolutionary than the "revolutionary" writer who endorses the most advanced form of social engineering. Most revolutionaries, as Orwell also points out in the Dickens essay, "are potential Tories, because they imagine that everything can be put right by altering the *shape* of society; once that change is effected, as it sometimes is, they see no need for any other."

It is at this moment—when a given revolution has more to preserve than to transform—that it is ripe for the moralist's exposé. Orwell felt that Soviet society had reached this stage, although most of the socialist camp still saw in it only its earlier, triumphant achievement. In performing this task, he hoped he might also make his audience aware that the illusion they cherished was only a particular example of a temptation they would meet again—the habit of substituting wish for reality.

It is, finally, impossible to talk about the political or moral purpose of *Animal Farm* without considering its tone. If the book is an exposé, it is certainly a remarkably unindignant one. Critics have praised its detachment, economy, and tight formal control; yet in a work with a serious political purpose, these qualities may not be as desirable as they are in purely aesthetic terms. There is truth in Mark Schorer's objection that *Animal Farm* "undid its potential gravity and the very real gravity of its subject, through its comic devices." From the first page, Orwell's fable is marked by a sense of acceptance and composure. The satire is benevolent, the ridicule affectionate, the ingenuity and sophistication very far from impassioned preaching. It is as though the story of *The Revolution Betrayed* were retold a century later by a specialist in the ironies of history. Far more than *Nineteen Eighty-Four, Animal Farm* is written for posterity. The surprising thing is that it should have been the earlier book.

To describe the tone of *Animal Farm* in a few phrases is to suggest that it is consistent. Yet there are important moments in the book when Orwell's comic perspective is quite clearly abandoned. For example: "Napoleon stood sternly surveying his audience; then he uttered a high-pitched whimper. Immediately the dogs bounded forward, seized four of the pigs by the ear and dragged them, squealing with pain and terror, to Napoleon's feet. The pigs' ears were bleeding, the dogs had tasted blood, and for a few moments they appeared to go quite mad." The passage stands at the beginning of the scene meant to parallel the Stalinist purge trials, and it is typical of the tone of gravity Orwell employs to describe the reign of terror that now begins at Animal Farm. The purge trials are the first events in Soviet history that Orwell considers tragically. Although terror was not, of course, invented by Stalin, there is something about the Moscow Trials which Orwell cannot treat as a predictable part of his paradigmatic revolution, something new in human history. It is, perhaps, the triumph of the big lie in Napoleon's justification for this slaughter of the innocents, the false confessions and abandonment of objective truth it involves. Here was something Orwell could not treat with composure and ironic detachment.

Orwell's tone in both *Animal Farm* and *Nineteen Eighty-Four* is determined by his sense of the uniqueness or typicality of the events he records. As long as he describes what he considers an inevitable stage of revolution, he can allow himself the long, detached historical perspective and the ironic tone that is its aesthetic correlative. When, on the other hand, he senses that some new, unexpected, and therefore perhaps avoidable form of tyranny has appeared, his response is very different: he permits himself the indignation of first discovery. *Nineteen Eighty-Four* . . . is different in tone from *Animal Farm* primarily because it is a reaction to certain terrifying events in modern history that could not have been foreseen in the first years of the century in which they occurred. (pp. 88-96)

> *Alex Zwerdling, in his* Orwell and the Left, *Yale University Press, 1974, 215 p.*

RICHARD I. SMYER (essay date 1979)

[*In the following excerpt, Smyer contends that in* Animal Farm *Orwell is primarily concerned with presenting his view that the integrity of the lower, governed classes is preserved through their lack of ambition for political power.*]

As a number of critics have noted, the basic assumption of *Animal Farm* is that revolutions are bound to fail, merely replacing one group of oppressors with another. The ideals of equality and justice cannot be actualized because the existence of the liberated farm demands a continuous interaction with the surrounding world of humanity, which, in terms of the allegory, stands for oppression and exploitation. Paradoxically, the need to maintain an economically and politically viable society, a need that can be met only be reinstituting a hierarchical order and by trafficking with human beings, inevitably leads to the subversion of the beasts' utopian aims.

The action of *Animal Farm* takes place between two poles: at one extreme is the condition of animality, representing loyalty, decency, and a mode of existence untouched by the evil associated with the wielding of political power. At the other end is the immoral behavior of the animals' human masters, whose ways Old Major warns them against adopting. The tale records the unavoidable deterioration of the farm as the utopian dream transforms itself into the ugly reality of another tyranny.

However, we should remember that if this political fable has a tragic quality, it also has a comic dimension. This becomes clearer if we bear in mind that the basic design of the work is the innocence-guilt polarity. The problem implied by this tension has to do with morality rather than political practicality: the central concern is the preservation of innocence, not the success or failure of revolutionary activity. The essential action is a movement either toward or away from one pole or the other. The comic aspect of *Animal Farm* derives from the fact that for some of the animals the movement toward immoral humanity is no sooner begun than it is reversed, and their innocence is left intact.

A key factor in this pattern is that of intellectual superiority. "Generally recognised as being the cleverest of the animals," the pigs "naturally" become the teachers and organizers in the farm community. Because the pigs are the only animals able to substitute long-range planning for mere impulse, they are destined to lead the revolution, a role that unavoidably exposes them to moral corruption. The outward signs of their lost innocence start to appear during the second revolutionary stage (after the forcible ouster of Farmer Jones) when, as a result of their expanded awareness, they develop a historical consciousness. It is the descendants of Old Major who transform, and in effect pervert, his simple teachings into a "complete system of thought." As leaders the pigs must articulate goals and implement them by means of specific programs entailing institutionalized duties and restraints. In so doing, they are led to embrace the world of men with its brutality and double-dealing. The pigs, whose increased self-consciousness quickly turns to selfishness, are the first to betray communal solidarity by their cunning theft of milk intended for all the animals. And Napoleon's slaughter of animals that are guilty of petty offenses represents the appearance in their midst of cruelty, heretofore a uniquely human quality. Thus the development of political cunning, the end result of the pigs' innate intellectual capacity, involves an exodus from the innocence and stasis of the old farm and a wandering in the spiritual wilderness of political activism, in the unregenerate world of history.

Remembering Orwell's disinclination to attribute revolutionary power hunger to the lower classes, we need not be surprised that for the humbler beasts the failure of the revolution is closely linked to the fact that their garden has not been lost. Before they can be defiled by the taint of humanity, the humbler beasts are saved by a series of fragmentations. The physical movement of the pigs toward the farmhouse, where they take up residence, outwardly expresses the unbridgeable moral gulf that Orwell needs to place between rulers and ruled. And not only must the guilty be segregated from the innocent but also guilt-provoking knowledge must be fragmented from consciousness. The humanoid animals must be shown wholly cut off from the other beasts, and the minds of the latter must remain inviolate from even the awareness of evil. Because their violent overthrow of Farmer Jones springs from impulse and not from ideological formulations—"with one accord, though nothing of the kind had been planned beforehand, [the animals] flung themselves upon their tormentors''—their innocence is not imperiled by power hunger and the moral ambiguities associated with the assumption of a politico-historical identity. The humbler beasts are not guilty, indeed, cannot be guilty, of the premeditation of the political ideologist: " . . . almost before they knew what was happening, the Rebellion had been successfully carried through.''

Sheer mental incapacity preserves the animals' minds and spirits from the consciousness of evil. Because their memories are short, the humbler animals are not sure whether or not they earlier had passed a resolution against trade. Consequently Napoleon's proposal to begin commercial relations with the outside world gives them only a vague discomfort. For the same reason, the animals need feel no uneasiness about the breakdown of their social experiment after the pigs selfishly alter the wording of the commandment against sleeping in Jones's bed; and the rulers' slight rewording of the prohibition against killing sets the minds of the naive beasts at rest over the execution of supposedly disloyal comrades.

Since revolution implies change, the revolutionary identity is rejected when change is denied. While Napoleon physically reorganizes the old farm and Snowball puffs an electrification program to produce a technologically sophisticated utopia, something entirely new in animal experience, their ignorant subjects feel that life is no better now than before. The humbler beasts prefer the song "Beasts of England," which expresses their longing for a utopia vaguely situated in the future, to the recently adopted hymn celebrating the existence of a new order in the present. It is a sign of the animals' relatively untainted consciousness that they finally forget Snowball's vision of luxury, and even the rebellion itself becomes "only a dim tradition.''

If the general action of *Animal Farm* is so structured as to express Orwell's need to see the common people uncorrupted by revolutionary ambitiousness, the career of Boxer exemplifies the ruinous effects of upward leveling. Boxer is an emblem of the old-style working class, and throughout most of the fable he is one of the least human members of the community. By nature he is a beast of burden, and it is his basically worker-animal role of tireless drudge that earns him the admiration of his comrades. In fact, it is just this predilection for mindless toil that, in making him ignorant of the leaders' wickedness, renders his spirit immune (at least in the beginning) from the revolutionary urges triggering the pigs' latent viciousness: "His two slogans, 'I will work harder' and 'Napoleon is always right,' seemed to him a sufficient answer to all problems.''

At first Boxer's innocence and goodness are not affected by the rebellion. Jones's stable boy, whom Boxer fears he has slain during the fighting, suddenly comes to life; and later the horse, as though disclaiming any impious desire to benefit personally from the installation of an electricity-generating windmill, wishes only that it may be "well under way" before his retirement.

In time, however, we see signs of an ominous change in Boxer. During the fray that is almost fatal for the stable boy, the ordinarily gentle Boxer, as though mimicking his human oppressors, becomes bipedal, a gesture releasing a savagery alien to his normal behavior: " . . . the most terrifying spectacle of all was Boxer, rearing up on his hind legs and striking out with his great iron-shod hoofs." Significantly Boxer's eventual doom is described in terms of an inner pollution, symbolized by the ingestion of medicine taken from Jones's bathroom and ad-

ministered by the pigs. With this potion, this "human" element, inside him, Boxer shows the first signs of consciously giving up his identity as a worker and moving toward an upper-class (porcine-humanoid) status: he begins to look forward to retirement when he will have the "leisure to study and improve his mind" by learning the alphabet. It is consistent with Orwell's apprehensions that Boxer, thinking that his entry into the world of humanity will bring him renewed vitality (he is supposedly being taken to a veterinary surgeon), is actually being shipped off to a horse slaughterer.

If Boxer's fate indicates his creator's alarm at those forces eating away the class identity of the common people, the final state of the pigs expresses Orwell's certainty that political ambition has a morally destructive effect on the leadership. The two aces of spades that the porcine and human card players simultaneously throw down at the end of the fable symbolize both the pigs' ethical decay and, given the deadly significance of the ace of spades, the passing away of their working-class identities.

In the world of *Animal Farm,* revolution becomes a matter of good lost and evil got. Because it involves a development in the direction of "humanity," of evil, revolutionary activity is the greatest threat to the animals' spirit. But as I have already indicated, the farm is a split world: one region in which the knowledge of evil and change cannot thrive and another in which baseness and mutability cannot be denied. In the end, the humble and ignorant beasts are still victims. Yet as the story of Boxer reveals, this is the necessary condition for the preservation of their innocence, their group identity. If they are still oppressed, they are also still untainted, still the communal embodiment of the socialist ideals of brotherhood and equality.

Animal Farm is, in effect, a fairy tale, a mixture of fantasy and harshness, of mysterious dangers happily overcome by some characters and terrible punishments falling on the heads of others. The subject animals exist in a comic world, their goodness and simplicity magically protected from the witch's brew of politics and revolution. But their leaders are captives in a world of fearful transformations—where the Circe of awareness turns pigs into men.

There is another transformation that bears on Ben's second reading aloud. During the narrative appear signs that Boxer and Ben are doubles, and as such they dramatically express the conflict in the mind of their creator, Orwell the writer-intellectual trapped in an age of political madness. Like Orwell, suffering from a lung ailment, Boxer is the enthusiastic true believer who becomes involved heart and soul in the revolution, working year after year to turn the old farm into a brave new utopia. If Boxer is sheer energy and commitment, Ben, the friend and constant companion with whom Boxer hopes to share his retirement, is the horse's prudential self, his knowing half. It is a mark of his freedom from dangerous ambition that in contrast to Boxer, who marvels at the windmill, Ben remains unenthusiastic. Because he rejects progress, he feels confident of being immune to the fearful changes occurring on the farm: "Donkeys live a long time," he asserts. "None of you has ever seen a dead donkey.''

Yet there is something disturbingly ambiguous about Ben, who occupies an indefinite position between the porcine state of cunning, immorality, and historical awareness, and the ahistorical animal world of impulse, ignorance, and innocence. His class identity is uncomfortably vague. Lacking the selfishly humanoid wiliness of the pigs, he is not a leader; however, his mental capacity—he can "read as well as any pig"—keeps him from being wholly within the realm of the humbler animals. We might regard him as a representation of the disillusioned intellectual of the 1940s who, unlike his less perceptive compatriots, is cursed with the dispiriting awareness of the inevitable degeneration of revolutionary idealism into power worship. Figuratively as well as literally he can read the handwriting on the wall.

To repeat my earlier observation, twice, not once (as Orwell erroneously states), Ben has read, has broken his rule. That is, more than once, and more than the narrator cares to admit, Ben has revealed an affinity with the porcine condition of intelligence, and therefore, evil. To add to the ominous significance of this second transgression, the exercise of this humanoid skill involves the pronunciation of words that themselves represent the breaking of a rule, the subversion of the seven commandments established to keep the animals free from the corrupting effects of humanization.

Ben's fate is rather curious. Soon after reading aloud a second time, the donkey simply drops out of the narrative, even though he is one of the more important and more fully developed characters. One explanation for this abrupt and puzzling disappearance is that Orwell—too intimately acquainted with the intellectual's inner complexity to leave Ben in the thoughtlessly innocent realm of the humbler animals, yet morally repelled by the other alternative—allows the donkey to vanish into a limbo apart from either polarity. This turn of events underscores Orwell's view regarding the moral vulnerability of the intellectual unprotected by the mental limitations that make the lower animals, the common folk, resistant to inner contamination. The intellectual cannot combine escape with self-preservation. It is through a blind, instinctive assertion of their original collective identity that the animals remain inviolate. The intellectual's only refuge entails a self-negating loss of identity.

Because Ben's dilemma is so close to that of Orwell, the latter has failed to treat this character with the same artistic objectivity as he has done with the others. This need not, however, be the last word on the matter, for Ben's vanishing act calls attention to some interesting technical and thematic developments in *Animal Farm.* For one thing, since Ben is defined in terms of an inner tension between the desire to participate in the innocence of the humbler beasts and an effort to suppress the humanoid-porcine qualities that prevent this, he is a more complex and, therefore, more realistic character than the others, even Boxer, who unself-consciously play out their two-dimensional allegorical roles of goodness and villainy, naive enthusiasm and single-minded cunning.

In **"Inside the Whale,"** Orwell predicts that the "autonomous individual is going to be stamped out of existence" with the advent of totalitarianism, a warning reiterated several years later in "Literature and Totalitarianism." A few months after the publication of *Animal Farm,* he explained why under a tyranny the idea of personal autonomy was illusory. To be autonomous one had to be "free *inside,*" but in a totalitarian society even one's thoughts were controlled by the state. In fact, with the loss of free expression the mind itself becomes torpid, for it is "almost impossible to think without talking."

Ben is the autonomous individual caught in a double bind. The refusal to voice an opinion about the animals' utopian experiment is supposed to insure his moral survival as well as his physical safety, yet his reluctance to speak out makes him in effect a silent partner to the pigs' conspiracy and gradually erodes his autonomy. His disappearance from the narrative suggests that he has been "stamped out of existence."

There may be an emblematic connection between the disappearance of this relatively complex character and Zwerdling's observation [in *Orwell and the Left,* 1974] that during the forties Orwell was consciously attempting to abandon the conventions of the realistic novel, which, because of its documentary specificity and thematic obliqueness, was not flexible enough to satisfy Orwell's artistic needs or to deliver a direct message within the context of an enlarged historical perspective. By employing the fable, Orwell could invest *Animal Farm* with "permanent mythic life" and set forth the basic pattern of social revolution.

The transparency of the fable, its ability to convey meaning directly and with a minimum of authorial intrusion, makes the withdrawal of Ben appropriate, since he lacks the allegorical simplicity of the other figures. In *Coming Up for Air,* Tubby Bowling, the passive common man, fades away into a state of potentially self-destructive apathy; whereas the other Bowling, Bowling the author's mouthpiece, has, as the observer and recorder of his alter ego's decline into quietism, the last word. This, however, is not the case in *Animal Farm,* where Ben, as much the judgmental Orwellian persona in his silences as in his speech, is not allowed to outlast the narrative. This circumstance hints at Orwell's willingness to draw back from the events, to let the story (the final half dozen pages, at least) tell itself. The impression we are left with is that in the world of the forties there are no safe heights from atop which an author or his persona can calmly survey the violence below and formulate grand generalizations.

The withdrawal of the authorial commentator from the dramatized narrative action may also indicate a change in Orwell's relationship to the modernist tradition. The Orwell of the thirties often was making a forced march to join ranks with the moderns. Partly to achieve his childhood goal of literary fame, partly to expand his intellectual and imaginative horizons, Orwell chose as models those writers generally considered most sensitive to the moral and psychological ambiguities of contemporary man. From *Burmese Days* to *Coming Up for Air,* the Orwellian voice is noticeably derivative, and at times we feel that Orwell's admiration for such writers as Eliot and Joyce has outstripped his ability to adapt their imaginative worlds to his own creative aims. . . . [During] the forties Orwell turned his attention to other literary models better suited to the atmosphere of the age, with its technologically sophisticated barbarism, its tyrants able to mesmerize whole populations, and its rejection of the idea of individual freedom.

Finally, it is worth noting that in exposing the savagery concealed behind the official ideology of revolutionary activism, Orwell has chosen a relatively primitive literary form, the animal tale. Whether or not [Orwell's childhood friend] Jacintha Buddicom is correct in claiming that the original source of *Animal Farm* is Beatrix Potter's *The Tale of Pigling Bland* (which the young Blair read to her), the decision to examine social conflict "from the animals' point of view" suggests Orwell's willingness to experiment with a view of reality normally associated with a child's perspective and attitudes, his and ours. Although such an approach is obviously useful in creating ironic and satiric effects, we should be aware of the dangerous game Orwell the fabulist is engaged in when he blurs the distinction between man and animal to reveal the viciousness of the former. For the adult, the animal is something to be used as physical or literary beast of burden, as a source of amusement, as prey, or as object of scientific examination. But for the child—and this includes the child within the adult—the animal is a marvel, a source of wonder, perhaps even a magical being. In exploiting this creature for adult ends (for example, sociopolitical commentary), the writer has risked violating the sacred grove of his own childhood world. What remains of the child's primal response to life may wither away if yoked to the adult's moralistic or political obsessions. (pp. 104-10)

> *Richard I. Smyer, in his* Primal Dream and Primal Crime: Orwell's Development as a Psychological Novelist, *University of Missouri Press, 1979, 187 p.*

SANT SINGH BAL   (essay date 1981)

[*In the following excerpt, Bal discusses* Animal Farm *as an obvious satire of Soviet history that also applies to all revolutionary societies, and as a successful animal fable.*]

Through *Animal Farm,* which treats of events that are, in many ways, similar to those in which the writer himself had participated in Spain, Orwell satirizes the Russian totalitarianism. It is a devastating attack on Stalin and on his betrayal of the Russian Revolution. In fact, to write this novel at a time when everyone around him was glorifying Russia, was an act of courage and integrity for Orwell. The clouds of false propaganda and political expediency failed to darken his moral vision; and his righteous indignation turned against the Soviet totalitarian methods. In Stalin, he found the latest personification of political evil. Orwell was familiar with the work of European writers who had written books against totalitarianism. Of these writers, he was most interested in the themes of *Darkness at Noon.* He had also read *The Life and Death of Stalin* by Louis Fischer and *The Real Soviet Russia* by David J. Dallin (both critical of the Soviet Union). As an anti-totalitarian novel, *Animal Farm* will be Orwell's lasting achievement. He said about it that *Animal Farm* was the only one of his books he really "sweated over," and "the first book in which I tried, with full consciousness of what I was doing, to fuse political purpose and artistic purpose into one whole." (p. 121)

For understanding the deeper issues involved, it will be relevant to refer to the allegorical scheme of *Animal Farm.* The major events and characters in this book have a broad similarity with the events and personages of the Russian history from 1913 to 1943. The war of intervention, the New Economic Plan, the First Five-year Plan, the expulsion of Trotsky and the seizing of supreme political power by Stalin, the Great Purge Trials, the Hitler-Stalin Pact and the invasion of Germany are fully and clearly reflected. Again, while Old Major represents Karl Marx, Snowball and Napoleon represent Trotsky and Stalin respectively [the critic adds in a footnote that "I feel that Lenin is left out deliberately because he is not relevant in the context of the recession of the Russian Revolution"]. To quote Jeffrey Meyers: "The name Snowball recalls Trotsky's white hair and beard, and the fact that he melted before Stalin's opposition." Squealer is Napoleon's apologist, or Public Relations Officer and editor of "Pravda." The three dogs stand for the O.G.P.U. or the Cheka under Djerdjinsky and Yagoda, and the two cart-horses, Boxer and Clover, are the loyal proletariat. Benjamin, the donkey, is a cynic who is found in all times and in all societies. For him, there is hardly any difference between the

pre-revolution days and the post-revolution golden age. He believes that life has always been hard. He is sceptical of all promises of improvement. Moses, the raven, as his name suggests, symbolizes religion. He claims to know the existence of a mysterious country called "Sugarcandy Mountain" to which all animals go after death. Moses stands in contrast to Squealer, and specializes in the Kingdom of Heaven. His references to the "Sugarcandy Mountain" where "it was Sunday seven days a week, clover was in season all the year round, and lump sugar and linseed oil grew on the hedges," remind us of the tempting pictures of heaven painted by men of religion in order to divert the attention of the working classes from their exploited plight, and thus make them accept their earthly existence as a kind of preparation for tasting the eternal joys of heaven. Thus, although the jobs of Squealer and Moses are quite different, the final effect of the two coalesces, for if one asks the animals to work hard on earth, the other assures them that their labours will be rewarded in heaven. Moses is also the secret service agent of Mr. Jones. Furthermore, the quarrel between Napoleon and Snowball over the issue of windmill represents the rift between Stalin and Trotsky.

The two human farms, Pinchfield and Foxwood, in the neighbourhood of the Animal Farm, symbolize the two groups of non-Communist powers—the forces of Capitalism and Fascism. Pilkington is Churchill—England, while Frederick represents Hitler—Germany. The agreement between Frederick and Napoleon symbolizes the Hitler-Stalin pact of 1939: "Then came the eye-opener of the Hitler-Stalin pact. Suddenly the scum of the earth and the blood-stained butcher of the workers (for so they had described one another) were marching arm in arm, their friendship 'cemented in blood,' as Stalin cheerily expressed it" [the quote is from Orwell]. The basis of this fact was implicit in the betrayals and reversals that had characterized the working of the two regimes throughout the thirties.

The final scene of Animal Farm, *in which the animals "looked from pig to man, and from man to pig . . . but already it was impossible to say which was which." Illustrated by Joy Batchelor and John Halas. Secker and Warburg, 1954. Reproduced by permission of Martin Secker & Warburg Limited.*

In the last scene when the pigs have become "human," the wheel comes full circle; and the revolution ends where it had begun. The revolutionaries who had started with the dream of total liberation, in practice herald the return of the outworn ideals of despotism. It is the "human nature" of the animals that defeats them. The model workers' republic becomes a model of the exploited labour. The final identification of the pigs with humans (who essentially have something of the pigs about them) shows that the new privileged class has replaced the old privileged class represented by Mr. Jones. This new privileged class elbows its way into power by the methods Orwell marks in an essay on James Burnham: "All talk about democracy, liberty, equality, fraternity, all revolutionary movements, all visions of Utopia, or 'the classless society' or 'the Kingdom of Heaven on Earth,' are humbug (not necessarily conscious humbug) covering the ambitions of some new class which is elbowing its way into power." Another way of making this point is to compare *Animal Farm* with *Darkness at Noon* where also we see that the pig scores over the good. Orwell shows the end of Communism under Stalin as a replica of its beginning under the Czar, for the Communism in that period developed into a permanent ruling caste or oligarchy, recruited not by birth, but by adoption. I may point out that Kingsley Martin betrays a lack of understanding of the real issues when he says: ". . . the surface moral of his story is that all would have gone well with the revolution if the wicked Stalin had not driven the brave and good Trotsky out of Eden" [see Additional Bibliography]. The fact, however, is that the driving out of Trotsky is as much a part of the process of the recession of the revolution, as the purges are. Again, Martin's argument may be met with the following view of Orwell himself: "Trotsky, in exile, denounces the Russian dictatorship, but he is probably as much responsible for it as any man now living, and there is no certainty that as a dictator he would be preferable to Stalin. The essential act is the rejection of democracy."

The scene of confessions and executions of animals in *Animal Farm* is modelled on the Russian trials under Stalin's regime, and reminds us of Koestler's *Darkness at Noon*. Many of Lenin's old comrades and other innocent people were subjected to physical and psychological torture to confess to crimes which they had not committed; crimes which were sometimes pure invention. In July, 1938, in a review of Eugene Lyon's *Assignment in Utopia,* Orwell wrote of the Moscow treason trials of 1936-37 with a directness and courage quite rare at that time. Comparable to the trials of the Inquisition, they reveal the dangers of political orthodoxy by highlighting the heresies.

Thus, the Russian experiment has been beautifully worked out. In fact, simple considerations of political expediency are at the root of the sordid drama of the trials—the desire to convince the masses that the opposition is composed of people who stop at nothing in order to satisfy their hatred or ambition, that the Capitalist powers are conspiring against the fatherland of the workers, that the difficulties of building up the socialist state are attributable to the misdoings of its enemies. When the heroes of yesterday admit that they have plotted against the party, planned or committed acts of sabotage and terrorism, the cause of the revolution and the cause of the fatherland become finally and firmly identified with Stalin and his henchmen.

In the distortion and corruption of the Seven Commandments, we can clearly see the recession of the revolution, and the creation of many "cunning passages" and "contrived corri-

dors" in history. This act of the pigs results in the disintegration of the collective consciousness of the animals. Robbed of their memory of the glorious days of the revolution and of their ability to judge, they are unable to ascertain truth and penetrate to the immediate source of the evil in their social and political set-up, which is Napoleon's desire for power and privilege. Since the animals cannot remember the past, because it is continuously and systematically altered, they cannot have any control over the present and hence over the future. Clearly, Orwell believes that the really frightening thing about totalitarianism is not that it commits atrocities, but that it destroys the concept of objective truth; it claims to control the past as well as the future. The totalitarian rulers create their own "truth" to meet the new situations and safeguard their personal interests. Every change in policy demands a corresponding revaluation of prominent historical figures. Thus, Snowball's heroism at the Battle of the Cowshed is later condemned as cowardice. Sudden reversals of policy are bad enough not only in themselves, but they are also bad because they lead to an even greater crime, which is the re-writing of history. I may point out that history is not simply a store-house of juxtaposed facts, of individual decisions and adventures, ideas and interests and institutions; it is a totality, a sum of collective experience moving towards a state which will give meaning to the whole. But in a totalitarian state, history belongs to the most unscrupulous; they distort it through organized lying, and thus create a false sense of history which breeds only political evil and fanaticism. Commenting on the totalitarian regime of Russia, Orwell says: "Russia since 1928 shows distinctly similar reversals of policy, always tending to keep the ruling clique in power. As for the hate-campaigns in which totalitarian regimes ceaselessly indulge, they are real enough while they last, but are simply dictated by the needs of the moment. Jews, Poles, Trotskyists, English, French, Czechs, Democrats, Fascists, Marxists—almost anyone can figure as public Enemy No. 1. Hatred can be turned in any direction at a moment's notice, like a plumber's blow-flame."

In the light of the authenticity of Orwell's allegory, I cannot accept Kingsley Martin's view that Orwell's novel "is historically false and neglectful of the complex truth about Russia." Orwell has demonstrated that after the proletarian revolution succeeds, one privileged minority is replaced by another. In what way do the masses benefit? He denounces the Communist regime under Stalin as a total tyranny inspired and justified by a philosophy.

But although the literal level of the story is based on Soviet history, Orwell's purpose is more general. He says, the novel "is intended as a satire on dictatorship in general." *Animal Farm* is a study in the development of the totalitarian state. Orwell suggests that revolutions begin with great moral fervour and popular support. The masses are led on by promises and ideals of human brotherhood, equality and universal happiness. With collective effort, the idealistic dream is translated into reality. Old laws and institutions which symbolize fraud and tyranny are overthrown. The state virtually withers away for the moment. But when the new ruling class has entrenched itself in power, the feeling of freedom gives way to the sense of necessity and bondage. Thus, after they have done their job, the masses are again thrust into servitude, because they are enslaved by new masters. The ruling class re-creates the class structure once again. History repeats itself. In fact, as pointed out by E. H. Carr [in *Socialism in One Country: A History of Soviet Russia* (1958)]: ". . . no change, however, violent and abrupt in appearance, wholly breaks the continuity between past and present."

The truth is that the day when society as a whole becomes comparable to a single gigantic enterprise, there is surely an irresistible temptation for the men at the top to be totally indifferent to the sentiments and views of the masses below. They repudiate all moral values which transcend the class struggle; they sacrifice living men at the altar of abstract rules and principles framed and modified for maintaining the citadel of their personal power and glory. Criticizing the theme of Koestler's novel, *The Gladiators* (1939), Orwell rejects his view that the failure of revolutions is to be attributed to the incompetence or petty selfishness of the masses. He points out that the struggle for power among the leaders, not the "hedonism" of the masses, wrecks a revolution. Again, Orwell believes that it is not merely that "power corrupts;" the ways of attaining power also corrupt. He tells us that "the desire for pure power seems to be much more dominant than the desire for wealth. This has often been pointed out, but curiously enough the desire for power seems to be taken for granted as a natural instinct, equally prevalent in all ages."

Thus, *Animal Farm* is concerned with political evil and with what Orwell describes in his essay on Koestler as the impossibility of combining power with righteousness. Obviously, he points out the disparity between certain predictions contained in Karl Marx's works and the subsequent course of events. It may be pointed out that the analysis of the totalitarian regime of the Left offered by Orwell is not contestable on several points. His account of the revolution is not "over simplified" or "facile" as Alldritt feels. Alldritt further argues that "we cannot but be aware that the crises of a society are much more complex than Orwell is here able to suggest" [see excerpt dated 1969]. I may say that a work of art is not history, and an artist is not a social historian in a narrow sense. It is through certain images and symbols that he achieves the final effect. Thus, through the image of the pigs, Orwell successfully conveys the idea that an optimistic and positive interpretation of history with the liberation of humanity as the ultimate goal is replaced by a pessimistic and negative version according to which totalitarianism is the inevitable result of a movement which begins with the abolition of ancient wrongs and ends with the destruction of every human liberty. In fact, the totalitarian mentality dehumanizes the rulers. (pp. 125-30)

The moral that we draw from *Animal Farm* is that totalitarianism of the Left suffers from the same evils as the totalitarianism of the Right, namely that power inevitably corrupts and that revolutions, therefore, inevitably fail of their purpose, and that history is a record of the overthrow of old tyrants in order that new tyrants may be put in their place. Instead of being what Tennyson calls "the locomotives of history," revolutions generally are bogged down in the desert of the immoral consciousness of the new rulers. It is this plague which Orwell draws our attention to. Thus, Keith Alldritt's view that "today it is very difficult to share the admiration with which *Animal Farm* was received when it first appeared," is not convincing. If Swift's *Gulliver's Travels* can be enjoyed as an authentic work of literature, without a detailed knowledge of the eighteenth-century politics, why can't we enjoy *Animal Farm* for the deeper ethical issues which have a universal appeal? The author, in this novel, has adopted one of the classical formulas of satire on the pattern of Swift's *Tale of a Tub*—the corruption of principle by expediency. And Brander is right in observing: "There is a mocking similarity between what the pigs say and

what politicians say . . . *Animal Farm* has the Swiftian indictment of the offending race of human kind" [see excerpt dated 1954]. *Animal Farm* is a bitter comment on all totalitarian claims. In fact, the tragedy of all revolutions is that idealism and communal energy that inspire them are a transitory period in the overall history of the revolution. No political party is honest for more than a few months at a time, and those few months represent its heyday. The selfish and unscrupulous politicians take over, and re-establish the same kind of evil and tyrannical political system which the revolution had overthrown. [In *On Revolution* (1973)] Hannah Arendt has rightly pointed out: "Revolutions always appear to succeed with amazing ease in their initial stage, and the reason is that the men who make them first only pick up the power of a regime in plain disintegration; they are the consequences but never the causes of the downfall of political authority."

It may, at the same time, be pointed out that Orwell is not against revolution. Revolution as such is not worthless. In fact, Orwell spent his life in trying to show how conservative values in politics involved a denial of the right of fulfilment to a large section of society. He says that "all revolutions are failures, but they are not all the same failures." What he means to suggest is that certain kinds of revolutions are fated to result in a worse type of slavery for the masses than the ones they overthrow. Instead of bringing the promised Utopia of freedom and equality any nearer, they snuff out even such freedoms as existed before. He believes that it is only through a strictly ethical interpretation of events that the ideal emancipation of humanity can be made to appear the *sine qua non* of all progress and the first step towards redemption. The proletarians who are the real soldiers of revolution—a personification of ethical judgement and values—must not, under any circumstances, compromise with the "pigs" who are confident of the strength of their vested interests. The animals have tremendous strength. This is proved by the fact that they are able to defeat human beings. This same power can be used against their new oppressors. It may not be possible to change human nature through revolution, but it is possible for human beings to continue moving towards the land of their dreams. Thus, Orwell has not lost faith in mankind.

To sum up, *Animal Farm* is more than a mere animal fable for the amusement of children. It is a novel in which the obvious satire against the Communist Russia is applicable to all revolutions at another level, and to human government in general. The symbolic design itself suggests the universality of the theme. The fact that Orwell satirizes the fate of Soviet revolution gives his subject a definite historical context and validity. (pp. 131-32)

> *Sant Singh Bal, in his* George Orwell: The Ethical Imagination, *Arnold-Heinemann, 1981, 254 p.*

STEPHEN SEDLEY   (essay date 1984)

[*In the following excerpt, Sedley assesses* Animal Farm *as unsound both ideologically and as a work of literature.*]

Imaginative literature does not have to justify itself politically. On the contrary, part of its value may be to enhance or modify its readers' political comprehension. Marx's well-known preference for Balzac, a royalist, over Zola, a socialist, makes the point well enough, but it is or ought to be the experience of every socialist that it is not shared assumptions but shared experience that makes good literature a humanising and encouraging force.

Re-reading *Animal Farm* a generation after I first encountered it—as you my reader probably did—on the school curriculum, I am struck by its distance from any of these considerations. It lacks, deliberately, any effort to draw the reader into a convincing fiction, to invite a willing suspension of disbelief. Instead it demands assent to its major premiss that people in their political lives can be equated with domesticated animals, and to its minor premiss that civil society, like a farm, will be run for better or for worse by those who by birth or force inherit power. From these premisses the story and its moral follow; without them there is neither story nor moral.

The book is still required reading in most schools. Its presence on the curriculum does not disturb Sir Keith Joseph, Dr Rhodes Boyson or the *Daily Mail* in their crusade to eradicate political bias from the classroom, but I was interested that my eldest child, a good reader who was given it at the age of thirteen, was bored stiff by it. The reason, it turned out, was that she was too new to political ideas to have any frame of reference for the story: she literally couldn't see what it was about. There was no invitation to enter into the fiction, no common point of departure for reader and writer.

This is certainly not a necessary condition of political allegory or satire: one has to go no farther than Orwell's next major work, *Nineteen Eighty-Four,* to see that. Nor is it a necessary condition of animal fables: our literature is rich in examples. It is an abdication of imaginative art, and one which makes the critical and pedagogic success of *Animal Farm* a sobering example of the substitution of political endorsement for critical appraisal (a vice of which the political right does not have a monopoly).

Orwell's lineage from Swift is frequently spoken of. In background and personality there are similarities, and in some of their writings too, but not in *Animal Farm.* It is not only that Swift has humour as well as passion, which Orwell does not. Swift's satirical method is practically the reverse of Orwell's. Through the picaresque fantasy of *Gulliver's Travels* or the solemn reasoning of *A Modest Proposal* Swift draws the reader down a convincing false trail. The fiction stands, as his contemporaries would have said, on its own bottom. It is only when his readers have passed the point of no return that they realise that they are reading about themselves. But you cannot get into the fiction of *Animal Farm* at all without accepting as your starting point the very thing that Orwell has to prove—that in politics people are no better than animals: their traditional rulers may be feckless but ungovern them and a new tyranny will fill the place of the old. Naturally if you are prepared to accept that conclusion as your premiss, the story follows. You can demonstrate that the earth is flat by a similar process.

The use of animals to make a point about people is as old as art itself. Folk literatures abound in animals which are not only human but superhuman. Through them the human endeavour to understand and control the natural and social environments is expressed and developed. You find it in English folk tradition in the ballad of the *Cutty Wren,* the hedge-king; in Irish tradition in *Reynardine,* the man-fox; in Scots tradition in the *Grey Selchie,* the man-seal. In modern English literature we have at least two exponents who show up the poverty of Orwell's creativity, Beatrix Potter and Kenneth Grahame. The best of Beatrix Potter's stories are so well made that it is easy to lose critical perspective in evaluating them. It is enough perhaps to observe how meticulously she invests her animals with sufficient human qualities to enable them to be real char-

acters without ceasing to be animals. Mr. Jackson is a revolting old toad with a toad's predilections in food, but he mimics human character in ways which wryly enlarge your appreciation of human character. The quiet analogy between the amphibious and the human Mr. Jackson neither demands assent to the proposition that there is not much to choose between people and toads nor invites that conclusion. In its small way it is a piece of humane imaginative literature, drawing on the links between human and animal life without straining them.

Perhaps the most indicative contrast is between Potter's and Orwell's versions of the scatter-brained and least rational members of their animal societies—in Potter's books the ducks and rabbits, in Orwell's the sheep. The puddleducks, especially Jemima Puddleduck who nearly gets eaten by the fox in her desire to establish her independence (an interesting parallel with the *Animal Farm* story), are again small mirrors of humanity, pompous and opinionated in proportion to their foolishness. The extended rabbit family is what Beatrix Potter's successors would have regarded as a problem family, delinquents and all, held together by a long-suffering mother. The human presence, Mr. McGregor the grumpy old market gardener, is simply another element of risk in their world: they eat his lettuces and, when he can, he eats them.

In Orwell the silliest of the animals are the sheep. They are the essential and unwitting allies of the tyrant pigs, endlessly bleating the slogan "Four legs good, two legs bad" in any controversy and drowning all serious discussion. They have no reality as characters, but they do represent the British upper class's opinion of the working class: mindless creatures who do what others direct and bleat what others devise. The remaining farm animals, apart from the pigs, are more or less stupid and more or less good natured. The pigs are cunning and evil.

It is in the pigs that the political allegory takes its most precise form. The dream of revolution is dreamt by the old pig Major, who dies before it happens. His manifesto speech to the animals is couched in terms of self-evident absurdity:

> Man is the only real enemy we have. Remove Man from the scene, and the root cause of hunger and overwork is abolished for ever . . . No argument must lead you astray. Never listen when they tell you that Man and the animals have a common interest, and that the prosperity of the one is the prosperity of the others. It is all lies.

So it is, we are to understand, with civil society: only a fool could talk like this. (The sidelight this passage throws on Orwell's brand of socialism is interesting.)

To Major's Marx, Napoleon plays Stalin and Snowball Trotsky: the allegory becomes a simple set of personal disguises. The brightest of the other animals, the dogs, are finally bribed and bred into a private army at the pigs' service. The rest, from the willing cart-horses to the fecund hens, are put upon endlessly to keep the pigs in idle comfort.

No honest socialist or communist ignores or underrates the structural and political problems and distortions which have characterised the Soviet Union and other states that have taken a similar path. "More equal than others" is a barb which has stuck painfully in the consciousness of the left, for the existence of a privileged élite in any socialist state is a fundamental contradiction in political terms. For some on the left it argues that Marxism is not the way to socialism; for some, that Marxism has been betrayed; for some, that Marxism has been vindicated by the state's survival. Not one of these viewpoints, nor any variant of them, is explored or enriched by *Animal Farm*. Orwell's argument is pitched at a different level: it is that socialism in whatever form offers the common people no more hope than capitalism; that it will be first betrayed and then held to ransom by those forces which human beings have in common with beasts; and that the inefficient and occasionally benign rule of capitalism, which at least keeps the beasts in check, is a lesser evil. That proposition is Orwell's alpha and his omega.

So it is that the allegories of Soviet history in *Animal Farm* are just that—translations of the fall of Trotsky, the failure of the electrification programme, the enforcement of collectivisation; of a ruling élite looking for scapegoats for its own errors or for other catastrophes. Nothing in the use of an animal society as the vehicle of allegory particularly illuminates or enhances it or the points it seeks to make. It certainly does not make the case against Soviet socialism any more convincing. In fact it appears to confirm the underlying hostility of its opponents to any suggestion that the working class can emancipate itself. It does nothing to cast light on what for any socialist is the real question: what has gone wrong and why? If anything it has tended to fix the left in its own errors by aversion.

Is this essay then a criticism of *Animal Farm* for what it is not, for lacking a stance which was never Orwell's anyway? It would be less than candid to deny that both its assumption that people and animals are alike in their social or political existence, and its use of that assumption to insult the belief that ordinary people can put an end to want and privilege, make *Animal Farm,* to this writer at least, a pretty unattractive book. But that is not what makes it a poor piece of literature.

To take a second contrast from modern animal fiction, *The Wind in the Willows* is redolent of a particular social and political philosophy, all of it growing into and out of a beautifully told tale. Enough has been written about the class microcosm which contains the aristocratic playboy Toad, his yeoman friends Rat, Mole and Badger, and the feared (because unknown) Wild Wooders—the commoners, rogues and vagabonds. One can see and appraise Grahame's thoughts and feelings about class society and the stratum in which alone he feels secure, and one can have one's own views about them and him, without ever falling out with the fiction through which his idyll of contemplation and loyalty is conveyed.

The same is true of the misanthropy with which *Gulliver's Travels* is shot through. More to the point, both stories, because they work as stories, earn a measure of understanding for their authors' viewpoints. They enlarge intellectual as well as emotional horizons. For similar reasons more socialists have probably been made in Britain by *The Ragged Trousered Philanthropists* than by the *Communist Manifesto*.

Between its covers *Animal Farm* offers little that is creative, little that is original. Those who are interested in the links between politics and literature have far more to learn from the circumstances of the book's success. It is an extraordinary fact that it was written in the latter part of the Second World War, when the defeat of Nazism depended upon the Soviet Union's survival and military victory, and published (after three rejections) in the year of Labour's historic electoral victory. It was therefore certainly out of joint with its time, and it was no doubt in keeping with Orwell's penchant for heresy. But it was admirably in line with what rapidly became the political mode of government and press—a virulent and often unreasoning anti-communism. The prophet, to his own surprise, rapidly achieved honour in his own country.

When in 1947 Orwell wrote the preface to a Ukrainian edition of *Animal Farm* he explained that his aim had been to disabuse "the workers and intelligentsia in a country like England" of their naïve notions about the USSR (his Ukrainian readers were not there). He blamed their naïvety on the relative liberality of English political life:

> Yet one must remember that England is not completely democratic. It is also a capitalist country with great class privileges and (even now, after a war that has tended to equalise everybody) with great differences in wealth. But nevertheless it is a country in which people have lived together for several hundred years without knowing civil war, in which the laws are relatively just and official news and statistics can almost invariably be believed, and, last but not least, in which to hold and to voice minority views does not involve any mortal danger. In such an atmosphere the man in the street has no real understanding of things like concentration camps, mass deportations, arrests without trial, press censorship etc. Everything he reads about a country like the USSR is automatically translated into English terms, and he quite innocently accepts the lies of totalitarian propaganda.

This view of English political life in the mid-1940s does not now simply appear breathtakingly foolish; nor does it simply betray Orwell's socialism as a pose unsupported by analysis, experience or comprehension: it underscores *Animal Farm*'s message that ordinary people are too simple-minded to appreciate about Russia what is appreciated by a man who a page earlier has written:

> I have never visited Russia and my knowledge of it consists only of what can be learned by reading books and newspapers.

He goes on in the preface to explain how, years after Spain, his thoughts were crystallised by seeing a small boy driving a huge cart-horse with a whip:

> It struck me that if only such animals became aware of their strength we should have no power over them, and that men exploit animals in much the same way as the rich exploit the proletariat.

> I proceeded to analyse Marx's theory from the animals' point of view. To them it was clear that the concept of a class struggle between humans was pure illusion, since whenever it was necessary to exploit animals, all humans united against them: the true struggle is between animals and humans. From this point of departure, it was not difficult to elaborate the story.

The muddle is remarkable. Where, for instance, does Marx argue that there is a class struggle between members of the ruling class ("a class struggle between humans")? More important, whether the idea that "the true struggle is between animals and humans" is being attributed to the animals or to Orwell himself, the book begins and ends by debunking it, as of course it asks to be debunked. I have mentioned Major's fatuous early speech to this effect. The book goes on to argue that through revolution a human (that is a capitalist) oppressor will simply be replaced by an animal (that is a proletarian) oppressor. And remember how it ends?

The creatures outside looked from pig to man, and from man to pig, and from pig to man again; but it was already impossible to say which was which.

If Orwell in his preface is trying to say simply that human beings, however divided among themselves, are united in their exploitation of animals, this is *not* the point of departure of *Animal Farm.* Its point of departure, like its conclusion, is the proposition that human beings and beasts share characteristics of greed and ruthlessness towards their own kind.

Orwell concluded his preface:

> I do not wish to comment on the work; if it does not speak for itself, it is a failure.

He was of course right: but it is an interesting comment on the ideological argument of *Animal Farm* that its author was so unable to give an intelligible account of it. (pp. 155-62)

> Stephen Sedley, "An Immodest Proposal: 'Animal Farm'," *in* Inside the Myth: Orwell, Views from the Left, *edited by Christopher Norris, Lawrence and Wishart, 1984, pp. 155-62.*

ADDITIONAL BIBLIOGRAPHY

Aickman, Robert Fordyce. "*Animal Farm.*" *The Nineteenth Century and After* CXXXVIII, No. 826 (December 1945): 255-61.
Commends the pointed satire of *Animal Farm* and describes Orwell as "a man of the Left whose eye can leave the party line" and search for truth in individual integrity, noting how unusual any criticism of Soviet Russia is from the political Left.

Atkins, John. "*Animal Farm.*" In his *George Orwell,* pp. 221-32. 1954. Reprint. London: Calder & Boyars, 1971.
Praises *Animal Farm* as highly successful on many levels: as a children's story, an attack on Stalinism, and as an assessment of the failure of ideals.

Brown, Spencer. "Strange Doings at 'Animal Farm': A Case Study in Cultural Hocus-Pocus, New York, 1954-55." *Commentary* 19, No. 2 (February 1955): 155-61.
Severely criticizes reviewers of the full-length animated film version of *Animal Farm* for failing to identify Soviet Russia as the chief target of Orwell's satire.

Crick, Bernard. *George Orwell: A Life.* Boston: Little, Brown, 1980, 473 p.
The authorized biography. Crick was the first biographer granted access to private papers held by Orwell's widow.

Davis, Robert Murray. "Politics in the Pig-Pen." *Journal of Popular Culture* II, No. 2 (Fall 1968): 314-20.
Suggests that the American children's book *Wiggins for President* by Walter R. Brooks influenced Orwell to write his satire of Soviet Russia in the form of an animal fable.

Frye, Northrop. "Turning New Leaves." *The Canadian Forum* XXVI, No. 311 (December 1946): 211-12.
Early review of *Animal Farm* criticizing Orwell for not exploring the reasons why Soviet revolutionary principles failed.

Glicksberg, Charles I. "George Orwell and the Morality of Politics." In his *The Literature of Commitment,* pp. 289-318. Lewisburg, Pa.: Bucknell University Press, 1976.
Considers *Animal Farm* Orwell's devastating indictment of fascism on either end of the political spectrum.

Hammond, J. R. "Animal Farm." In his *A George Orwell Companion: A Guide to the Novels, Documentaries, and Essays,* pp. 158-68. New York: St. Martin's Press, 1982.

Interprets *Animal Farm* as "a profoundly pessimistic fable" that embodies universal truths about the nature of political revolution in its satirical and allegorical treatment of the Russian Revolution.

Hopkinson, Tom. *George Orwell.* Rev. ed. London: Longmans, Green, 1962, 36 p.
Describes *Animal Farm* as Orwell's masterpiece, a successful satire of dictatorship written with unaccustomed good humor and detachment.

Hunter, Lynette. *George Orwell: The Search for a Voice.* Stony Stratford, England: Open University Press, 1984, 242 p.
Examines Orwell's narrative voice in his major works.

Kalechofsky, Roberta. "Fables for Our Time: *Animal Farm* and *1984.*" In her *George Orwell,* pp. 99-136. New York: Frederick Ungar, 1973.
Considers *Animal Farm* an allegorical examination of why the Russian Revolution failed that questions whether any revolution can sustain its early ideals.

Karel, Thomas A. "George Orwell: A Pre-1984 Bibliography of Criticism, 1975-1983." *Bulletin of Bibliography* 41, No. 3 (September 1984): 133-47.
Extensive bibliography covering Orwell criticism published from 1975—the cutoff date for material listed in the Jeffrey Meyers and Valerie Meyers 1977 bibliography—through 1983.

Karl, Frederick R. "George Orwell: The White Man's Burden." In his *A Reader's Guide to the Contemporary English Novel,* rev. ed., pp. 148-66. Farrar, Straus and Giroux, 1972.
Briefly mentions *Animal Farm* as a satire that fails because of its predictability, and attributes the book's success to the time of its publication.

Kubal, David L. "Dilemma and Conclusion: 1939-1950." In his *Outside the Whale: George Orwell's Art and Politics,* pp. 115-48. Notre Dame, Ind.: University of Notre Dame Press, 1972.
Discusses *Animal Farm* as an expression of Orwell's belief that although natural instincts possess inherent virtues that could form the basis of a moral life, such instincts are readily perverted by those who seek power. Kubal maintains that the novel's artistic power lies in Orwell's skillful handling of the animal fable form and his use of metaphor.

Lall, Rama Rani. "George Orwell: *Animal Farm.*" In her *Satiric Fable in English: A Critical Study of the Animal Tales of Chaucer, Spenser, Dryden, and Orwell,* pp. 116-32. New Delhi: New Statesman Publishing Co., 1979.
Discusses *Animal Farm* within the context of classic beast fables, finding that Orwell fulfilled his satiric intent by presenting a deliberate simplification of complex events.

Leif, Ruth Ann. *Homage to Oceania.* Columbus: Ohio State University Press, 1969, 162 p.
Study of Orwell's political beliefs as evinced in his writing.

Lewis, Anthony. "T. S. Eliot and *Animal Farm.*" *The New York Times Book Review* (26 January 1969): 14, 16.
Discusses the circumstances under which T. S. Eliot, as a reader for Faber & Faber, turned down *Animal Farm* for publication. Lewis prints the text of Eliot's letter to Orwell explaining the reasons for his refusal.

Leyburn, Ellen Douglass. "Animal Stories." In her *Satiric Allegory: Mirror of Man,* pp. 57-70. 1956. Reprint. Archon Books, 1969.
Finds that the social satire of *Animal Farm* is successful because of the skillful drawing of the animal characters, each one "absolutely real as animals," yet embodying and satirizing a single distinct human characteristic.

Martin, Kingsley. "Soviet Satire." *The New Statesman and Nation* XXX, No. 759 (8 September 1945): 165-66.

Early review praising *Animal Farm* for its satiric view of Russia, finding that the novel displays the cynicism born of Orwell's disillusioned idealism.

Meyers, Jeffrey. "Orwell's Bestiary: The Political Allegory of *Animal Farm*." *Studies in the Twentieth Century*, no. 8 (Fall 1971): 65-84.
Attributes "complex satirical allegory of Communist Russia" to nearly every narrative detail of *Animal Farm*.

———, ed. *George Orwell: The Critical Heritage*. London: Routledge & Kegan Paul, 1975, 392 p.
Collection of reviews and critical studies with an excellent introduction by Meyers discussing Orwell's career and the dominant themes of Orwell criticism.

———, and Meyers, Valerie. *George Orwell: An Annotated Bibliography of Criticism*. New York: Garland Publishing, 1977, 132 p.
Thorough bibliography of Orwell criticism through 1975.

Oxley, B. T. "Two Histories of His Time." In *George Orwell*, pp. 66-82. 1967. Reprint. London: Evans Brothers, 1970.
Finds that "in the idea of a revolution carried out by farm animals Orwell found a kind of extended metaphor (technically, a fable) by which he could embody his first-hand experience of Spain and what he had read about Soviet Russia, and by which he could symbolize the tyrannous possibilities inherent in any revolutionary seizure of power." Oxley cautions against a close allegorical reading of the book "in which everything has to stand for something else," saying that to do so is to miss the universal application of Orwell's satire.

Patai, Daphne. "Political Fiction and Patriarchal Fantasy." In her *The Orwell Mystique: A Study in Male Ideology*, pp. 201-18. Amherst: University of Massachusetts Press, 1984.
Criticizes "Orwell's satire of a Marxist ('Animalist') revolution" for failing to discuss sexual inequality both before and after the revolution.

Rees, Richard. "Things to Come." In his *George Orwell: Fugitive from the Camp of Victory*, pp. 81-101. Carbondale: Southern Illinois University Press, 1961.
Considers *Animal Farm* a masterpiece of form and style, but contends that the book contains the awkward implication that in comparing the working classes to animals, Orwell "implies that they are at an irremedial disadvantage in the class struggle."

Rosenfeld, Isaac. "A Barnyard History." *The Nation* 163, No. 10 (7 September 1946): 273-74.
Early review calling *Animal Farm* an oversimplified fable that sheds no new light on revolutionary history.

Small, Christopher. "The Moral Pigsty." In his *The Road to Miniluv: George Orwell, the State, and God*, pp. 101-16. Pittsburgh: University of Pittsburgh Press, 1976.

Stresses that the satiric intent of *Animal Farm* is to show "political activity of any kind and in pursuit of any ostensible aim as ridiculous, base in motive, and of disastrous consequence."

Sperber, Murray. "The Author as Culture Hero: H. G. Wells and George Orwell." *Mosaic* XIV, No. 4 (Fall 1981): 15-29.
Overview of Orwell's life, career, and reputation, giving some reasons why he has attained an extraliterary status as a major twentieth-century figure.

Stansky, Peter, and Abrahams, William. *The Unknown Orwell*. New York: Alfred A. Knopf, 1972, 316 p.
Biography of Orwell's first thirty years. This is the first volume of a proposed three-volume biography.

———. *Orwell: The Transformation*. New York: Alfred A. Knopf, 1980, 302 p.
Biography of Orwell from the publication of his first novel to his involvement in the Spanish Civil War. This is the second volume of a proposed three-volume biography.

Sutherland, James. "Prose Satire." In his *English Satire*, pp. 79-107. Cambridge: Cambridge University Press, 1962.
Characterizes *Animal Farm* as "Orwell's one unique and perfect work," a relevant satire conveyed with literary finesse.

Thomas, Edward M. "Politics and Literature." In his *Orwell*, pp. 65-77. New York: Barnes & Noble, 1967.
Considers that Orwell "succeeded perfectly" in fusing political and artistic purpose in *Animal Farm* because of the suitability of animal allegory to Orwell's theme of moral decisions in political life.

Voorhees, Richard J. "Rebellion and Responsibility." In his *The Paradox of George Orwell*, pp. 15-74. Lafayette, Ind.: Purdue University, 1961.
Interprets *Animal Farm* primarily as an expression of Orwell's inherent mistrust of authority.

Warburg, Frederic. "*Animal Farm*." In his *All Authors Are Equal: The Publishing Life of Frederic Warburg, 1936-1971*, pp. 35-58. London: Hutchinson, 1973.
Account of Warburg's acquaintance with Orwell, events surrounding the writing of *Animal Farm*, and Warburg's decision to publish the controversial novel after it had been turned down by several other publishers because of its political content.

Webb, Tim. "Orwell: *Animal Farm*." In *European Patterns: Contemporary Patterns in European Writing*, edited by T. B. Harward, pp. 44-8. Dublin: The Dolmen Press, 1964.
Discusses *Animal Farm* as general commentary upon the methods of totalitarianism.

Wilson, Edmund. Review of *Animal Farm*, by George Orwell. *The New Yorker* XXII, No. 30 (7 September 1946): 97-8.
Early review calling *Animal Farm* first-rate satire, worked out with simplicity and dry wit.

George (Edward Bateman) Saintsbury

1845-1933

English critic, essayist, and biographer.

During the late nineteenth and early twentieth centuries Saintsbury was widely considered the greatest literary critic of the time. Interested exclusively in matters of literary form, he was able to appreciate the artistic value of a great variety of works, including many whose underlying ideologies conflicted with his strongly held conservative beliefs. A prolific author who wrote in an informal and often meandering style, Saintsbury has been praised for the enthusiasm and insight he brought to the study of literature.

Born in Southampton, Saintsbury was educated at King's College School in London and at Merton College, Oxford. After failing four times to obtain a fellowship to Oxford University, he took up teaching at a grammar school in Manchester and later at colleges in Guernsey. Saintsbury eventually left the teaching profession to become a journalist, writing literary and political columns for such magazines as the *Academy,* the *Manchester Guardian,* and the *Saturday Review.* The views he expressed throughout his life remained constant and extreme: concerning literature, he was a dogmatic aestheticist; concerning religion, a High Church Anglican; and concerning politics, a monarchist very critical of democracy. As a literary critic, he soon earned a reputation for his great erudition and informal, though at times distractingly parenthetical, writing style. In 1880 Saintsbury published his first volume of criticism, *A Primer of French Literature,* for which he prepared by reading an entire French novel every morning for several years. Saintsbury continued to write critical works and literary histories, and in 1895 became Professor of Rhetoric and English Literature at Edinburgh University, a position he held until he reached the mandatory age of retirement in 1915. During his years at Edinburgh he wrote prolifically and produced his most important works, including *A Short History of English Literature, A History of English Prosody,* and *A History of Criticism and Literary Taste in Europe* which encompassed ancient Greek, Latin, German, French, English, Russian, Spanish, Italian, and Icelandic literatures. Saintsbury continued to write after his retirement, but he increasingly turned away from the multi-volume literary histories for which he had become famous, producing collections, or "Scrap Books," of essays, as well as extended critical studies of single authors. He died in 1933.

One of the most distinctive qualities of Saintsbury's works is the profound love for literature they convey. "Reading," he said, "is to me like mental breathing." The achievement to which this love led him is legendary: Saintsbury read all of the major and many of the minor creative writers of Western civilization from the Homeric era to his own time, most in their native languages. In his *History of English Prosody,* he makes a startling claim: "I believe I have read nearly all the printed stock of English verse before 1600; and I know that I have read every poet of the slightest repute since that date, and a great number of poets who neither have nor deserve any," adding in a footnote that "this is not in the least a boast, but merely a guarantee" of his competency to judge the works under consideration in the volume. Few critics have disputed the extent of Saintsbury's reading, although some have objected

that his knowledge was too inclusive to be very penetrating in any single area, and that his criticism exhibits only surface concerns. Defenders of Saintsbury maintain that he chose to restrict himself to the role of a literary historian who was concerned purely with the aesthetic quality of a work, rather than its subject matter.

Although Saintsbury was never officially associated with the aestheticist or "art for art's sake" movement that developed around such figures as Walter Pater and Oscar Wilde, he espoused the essential philosophy of this movement: that the value of literature lay in its artistic form and not in its moral, political, psychological or philosophical significance. Saintsbury was one of the most outspoken defenders of the concept of separating a work's style from its content, a critical stance which enabled him to praise works that clashed violently in their political or religious implications with his unyielding conservatism. For example, he championed the works of Percy Bysshe Shelley, which proclaimed their author's atheism and progressive ideology. Saintsbury also refused to rate writers as superior or inferior based on the type of writing they practiced. One of his most famous axioms states that "B is not bad because it is not A, however good A may be." A result of this literary catholicity was Saintsbury's frequent celebration of minor authors, although his praise was always judiciously qualified. In this way, Saintsbury attempted to inspire interest in neglected writers whose works he considered worthy of attention.

While Saintsbury attached great importance to an author's style, he has frequently been criticized for stylistic flaws in his own writing. His style has been especially derided for its overuse of parenthetical structure, which often becomes so involved that essential points are obscured. An extreme example of this tendency occurs in the section on Shakespeare in *A Short History of English Literature*, where he writes, "But while none, save these, of men living, had done, or could have done, such things, there was much here which—whether either could have done it or not—neither had done." Those who knew Saintsbury contend that he wrote not in an artificially difficult style, but rather transcribed his manner of speech, in which qualifications and asides often intruded and became a part of his train of thought. Saintsbury himself never made any apologies for or defenses of his style. Although modern critics sometimes dismiss him as a somewhat antiquated figure, his literary histories remain unequalled in scope, and he is considered important for the insight his works afford into nineteenth-century literary attitudes.

(See also *Dictionary of Literary Biography*, Volume 57: *Victorian Prose Writers after 1867*.)

PRINCIPAL WORKS

A Primer of French Literature   (criticism)   1880
Dryden   (biography)   1881
A Short History of the Life and Writings of Le Sage
   (biography)   1881
A Short History of French Literature   (criticism)   1882
Marlborough   (biography)   1885
A History of Elizabethan Literature   (criticism)   1887
Manchester   (travel essay)   1887
Essays in English Literature: 1780-1860   (criticism)   1890
Essays on French Novelists   (criticism)   1891
The Earl of Derby   (biography)   1892
Miscellaneous Essays   (essays)   1892
Corrected Impressions   (criticism)   1895
Essays in English Literature: 1780-1860, Second Series
   (criticism)   1895
A History of Nineteenth Century Literature: 1780-1895
   (criticism)   1895
Inaugural Address   (speech)   1895
The Flourishing of Romance and the Rise of Allegory
   (criticism)   1897
Sir Walter Scott   (biography)   1897
A Short History of English Literature   (criticism)   1898
Matthew Arnold   (biography)   1899
A History of Criticism and Literary Taste in Europe. 3 vols.
   (criticism)   1900-1904
The Earlier Renaissance   (criticism)   1901
A History of English Prosody. 3 vols. [unabridged edition]
   (criticism)   1906-1910; also published as *An Historical
   Manual of English Prosody* [abridged edition]   1910
A History of English Criticism   (criticism)   1911
The Historical Character of English Lyric   (criticism)
   1912
A History of English Prose Rhythm   (criticism)   1912
The English Novel   (criticism)   1913
A First Book of English Literature   (criticism)   1914
The Peace of the Augustans   (criticism)   1916
A History of the French Novel. 2 vols.   (criticism)
   1917-19

Notes on a Cellar-Book   (nonfiction)   1920
Some Recent Studies on English Prosody   (criticism)   1920
A Scrap Book   (essays)   1922
Collected Essays and Papers. 4 vols.   (criticism and essays)
   1923-24
A Second Scrap Book   (essays)   1923
A Last Scrap Book   (essays)   1924
A Consideration of Thackeray   (biography)   1931
Prefaces and Essays   (criticism and essays)   1933
Shakespeare   (criticism)   1934
A Golden Book   (criticism)   1937
George Saintsbury: The Memorial Volume   (criticism and
   essays)   1945; also published as *A Saintsbury
   Miscellany: Selections from his Essays and Scrap
   Books*, 1947
French Literature and Its Masters   (criticism)   1946
A Last Vintage   (essays)   1950

THE NATION, NEW YORK   (essay date 1880)

[*In the following review of* A Primer of French Literature, *the critic praises the work as a whole but criticizes errors of fact and questions Saintsbury's judgment on specific writers.*]

The readers of Mr. Saintsbury's admirable sketch of French literature in the ninth edition of the *Encyclopaedia Britannica* will be glad to have their attention drawn to this shorter and more general outline, which should be in the hands of every French student. In the brief compass of one hundred and thirty-eight 16mo pages the author has, in his own words, "set before the learner such a general view of the outline of French literary history as he may best be able to fill up for himself afterwards. No writer of importance has been omitted, and the literary tendency of all such persons has been indicated, though of necessity in a kind of shorthand." This task has been very satisfactorily accomplished; the older literature has been fairly dealt with, and in spite of its necessary condensation the work has a literary value of its own, being singularly free from the perfunctory tone of such manuals. We have noticed an occasional slip of the pen, as on p. 18, where *Le Castoiement d'un Père* is spoken of as translated or adapted from the Arabic, whereas it is a translation of the Latin *Disciplina Clericalis*, which was compiled from Oriental sources; and we cannot agree with all the author's judgments, that on George Sand, for example, hardly laying emphasis enough on her style. Indeed, the final chapter on "Contemporary French Literature" is much the weakest, and if it were not that its predecessor on the "Romantic Movement" is one of the best, we should be inclined to think that Mr. Saintsbury had tired of his task toward the end. His treatment of the drama is at all times a little inadequate (excepting only the clear and simple and altogether admirable account of its genesis), and especially unsatisfactory is his criticism of the dramatists of our own day. To describe Scribe as "the most prolific of recent French dramatic authors, but distinguished from the Romantic school by a loose and careless style and by vulgar and unpoetical thought," is to miss entirely the characteristics of the man who first made play-making as easy and as intricate as watch-making. The two or three lines given to M. Émile Augier, the foremost French dramatist of our generation, and to M. Sardou, the most popular, are in the first case insufficient and in the second inaccurate. And quite out of proportion is the space given to the patriotic but feeble dramas of M. Henri de Bornier. The entire absence of bibliographical references is to be regretted. (pp. 468-69)

A review of "Primer of French Literature," in The Nation, *New York, Vol. XXXI, No. 809, December 30, 1880, pp. 468-69.*

THE NATION, NEW YORK   (essay date 1881)

[*In the following essay, the critic reviews* Dryden, *disparaging it for outmoded critical criteria and comparing it unfavorably with Samuel Johnson's study of John Dryden.*]

Mr. Saintsbury's [**Dryden**] coming as it does immediately after Mr. Ward's anthology, is something of a surprise. The "General Introduction" to that work asserted that "there are many signs to show that the eighteenth century and its judgments are coming into favor again," but the work itself did so much to render such signs insignificant as to lead one to believe the day of eighteenth-century judgments about poetry definitively past. This book, however, essays a rehabilitation of them and may count as one of the signs aforesaid. But no rehabilitation can be more than transitory, and must soon become discredited, for the reason that the mass of both expert and popular criticism is arrayed so decisively on the other side as to make it a more or less factitious work of literary *dilettanti*. Mr. Saintsbury is one of these, and, many as are his merits, the circumstance is fatal to the enduring value of a work in which he humors his natural inclination. To describe as *dilettanti* the small but alert and industrious body of English critics of whom he is one of the ablest may appear at first thought misleading, they have such a pungent tincture of Philistinism. It is true that nothing in Mr. Saintsbury's outward manner suggests the usual qualities we associate with dilettantism. Nothing, for example, could be more business-like than his style. It is rapid without great vivacity, curt rather than concise, peppery at times rather than animated, and has the air of a brisk young lawyer dispelling the cobweb mistiness of a fogy opponent before a jury of practical men. In controversy it is especially at home, and has a knack of converting criticism into controversy with great cleverness and promptitude, and thereupon displaying resources of intolerance, summariness, and surprised contempt that are considerable and effective, being in general judicial and deserved and the reverse of urbane. The conscious absence of nonsense is, perhaps, its main characteristic; its allusions are pat, its statements direct, its inferences plain, and, to be logical, you feel as if the party of the other part must be either incredibly ignorant or incredibly absurd. So far it is evident enough to whom belongs the credit of its invention. It is, however, an evolution rather than an imitation of Lord Macaulay's style, and though there is rarely absent from the latter a sound of the "rattling of dry bones" which in criticism was a favorite occupation of Macaulay, it has a rhetoric of its own so marked as to captivate the imagination of the hundreds of thousands in whose breasts it awakens a responsive thrill. Rhetoric is a stranger to the style of Mr. Saintsbury and his "set." It is as foreign to it as poetry or pliant grace. Straightforwardness is pursued to the verge of sterility, and the only affectation that remains is the "affecting to be unaffected"—as Congreve happily phrased it, Mr. Saintsbury might himself observe.

Affectation, nevertheless, owing to the constitution of the human mind and heart, is a constant peril; no sooner has a writer whose disposition inclines towards it freed himself from its more familiar manifestations than in subtler disguises it attacks

him anew, and perhaps at the present day it is in its paradoxical and disarming semblance of unconsciousness that it is most insidiously dangerous. In this form it overlays the most forbidding foundation with an incrustation of dilettantism. Mr. Saintsbury's manner has often behind it matter whose superficial and whimsical character is precisely what it is because of an ingrained dilettantism, apparently unlike what we usually mean by the term, but unlike only in appearance. It is, no one can dispute, competent and respectable. That, indeed, is its distinguishing mark. Its criticism lacks no qualification of excellence, except a fundamental sincerity obtainable by no study and the reward of no direct research.

> He drain'd from all, and all they knew,
> His apprehensions quick, his judgment true,
> That the most learn'd with shame confess
> His knowledge more, his reading only less,

Dryden says of Charles, and, as Johnson justly remarks, the praise might be transferred to himself. This is, to be sure, high praise only when the quality eulogized is contrasted with the "reading" that is not accompanied by "judgment true." And even then it is a commonplace, as Mr. Saintsbury, whose reading, in *belles-lettres* at least, is great, very well knows. But, unhappily, it is not yet a commonplace that a fundamental sincerity is the one thing that can unite mere erudition with soundness and a sure discrimination; otherwise the pedantry which is out of date, and which Mr. Saintsbury would blush to be guilty of, only gives place to the new dilettantism he frequently illustrates. The superficial faults of this book may nearly all be traced up to this mistake. The abundance of literary slang, much of which is as unfamiliar to "those who have to run as they read" (for whom, as Mr. Morley announced, the series to which the work belongs was designed) as it is hackneyed in the author's "set" of littérateurs; the similar assumption of familiarity upon the part of the reader with a score of allusions whose labels are a part of the writer's stock in trade; an air of wearing better apparel than one's neighbors, as it were, satisfied with the circumstance that it is real and not pinchbeck; in fine, the attitude of addressing esoterically the few people whose sympathies and accomplishments are also one's own—all these symptoms of a provincialism not the less unmistakable because it is intelligent are to be ascribed to an unconscious affectation, to be found only in the recent high development of the journey work of English literature. To the same cause also are attributable the vital blemishes of the work. Mr. Saintsbury observed recently that the essence of criticism was "to be able to appreciate what you don't like." A better way of formulating the theory of his practice could not be imagined. It is a statement which has certainly a taking sound, though one cannot fail to remark on reflection how little valuable criticism has been written upon this plan. But the truth is that the essence of criticism is to see that what you like is worth liking, which is not the converse but another plan altogether. It is difficult, doubtless, and often impracticable, and rather deficient in explicitness; sometimes, too, it involves a humiliating self-effacement, a "getting one's self out of the way and letting humanity judge," very different from the straightforward plan of appreciating what you don't like; but if one thinks of it a moment, almost all the criticism that is worth having will be found to proceed in this way, because it is the only way in which one can be quite sure of really meaning what he says.

This is why, to take the specific matter in hand, Johnson's life of Dryden is a better work than Mr. Saintsbury's. Of course Johnson owes his reputation as "the greatest power in English letters in the eighteenth century" to a natural tact and discernment in criticism which any one who is born without them can never supply, and in this respect it would be needless and ungracious to say whether the comparison is fair or unfair to Mr. Saintsbury. But whether the peculiarities that mark the work of the latter are the cause or effect of natural equipment, which is apt to be an idle question in most cases of the kind, it remains true that whereas we are sure of Johnson's sincerity we are in doubt as to Mr. Saintsbury's, and that this makes an important difference between them. Does Mr. Saintsbury like Dryden, or is he only endeavoring to appreciate him? is a question that occasionally recurs and mars the effect of his criticism. Does he really think Dryden the great poet he argues him to be, and is he really disgusted with the definition of poetry "which regards it wholly or chiefly from the point of view of its subject-matter," as he seems to suppose some persons do? Or did he perceive in his task opportunity for a *tour de force* in which he might rescue Dryden from the slight esteem in which as a poet he is sometimes held, and, by the arts of literary discussion so familiar to him, make a brilliant plea in a case in which a less clever writer would hesitate to accept a brief? This, at all events, is what he has accomplished; and he seems to acknowledge as much in concluding: "This general estimate, as well as much of the detailed criticism upon which it is based, . . . will no doubt seem exaggerated to not a few persons, to the judgment of some of whom I should be sorry that it should seem so." The book reads throughout like an apology; and as, in our opinion, the case is desperate, we cannot speak too highly of the accomplishment of the writer in making so ingenious a showing. The case is, however, hopeless, except in certain generally undisputed details which it seems to us the advocate wins with, after the manner of advocacy, a little unnecessary ostentation—Dryden's moral hypocrisy, for example; and for primer purposes the ingenious defence of a hopeless case is wholly unfitted. Indeed, the more ingenious it is the more out of place is it. For example, Mr. Saintsbury says that "when we want to see whether a man is a great poet or not let us take him in his commonplaces," and he selects four of Dryden's lines which he thinks "any poetical critic worth his salt" would "without knowing who wrote them, but merely from the arrangement of the words, the rhythm and cadence of the line, and the manner in which the images are presented," ascribe to "a poet, and probably a great poet"; finding "the same touch" almost invariably present in works by the same author, he would "be justified in striking out the 'probably.'" The verses are the following:

> O daughter of the rose, whose cheeks unite
> The differing titles of the red and white,
> Who heaven's alternate beauty well display,
> The blush of morning and the milky way!

Now, "any poetical critic worth his salt" might say in regard to this that a great poet's greatness is not usually to be argued from his commonplaces; but that this is a particularly favorable way of judging Dryden; that these verses are not especially commonplace as conceits go in the ten-syllable couplet order of poetry; that the lines are the expression of a pretty fancy by a skilful versifier; and that, finally, this "same touch" is by no means either almost invariably present in Dryden or even so much so as to be called characteristic, whereas the particular "touch" which marks his poetry at its best—*i.e.*, dignity combined with flexibility—Mr. Saintsbury nowhere remarks. But among those who have to run as they read, a poetical critic worth his salt is, as Mr. Saintsbury would say, "a rare animal." The majority of these are in no way benefited by dialectics of

the kind to which a poetical critic, whether he is worth his salt or not, has to resort in order to appreciate what he does not like and convince himself as well as his readers that "the poetical virtue which is present in Dryden is the same poetical virtue that is present in Lucretius and in Æschylus, in Shelley and in Spenser, in Heine and in Hugo," and that "Dryden's peculiar gift, in which no poet of any language has surpassed him, is the faculty of treating any subject which he does treat poetically." What this means, if it has any precise meaning, it is difficult to see. To find it in the work of a poetical critic who is at the same time an enthusiastic admirer of Mr. Swinburne and Mr. D. G. Rossetti and Walt Whitman is at least confusing. But when we get this explanation—

> My natural man may like "Kubla Khan," or the "Ode on a Grecian Urn," or the "Ode on Intimations of Immortality," or "O World! O Life! O Time!" with an intenser liking than that which it feels for anything of Dryden's. But that arises from the pure accident that I was born in the first half of the nineteenth century, and Dryden in the first half of the seventeenth—

it becomes clear that the critic is in pursuit of catholicity of judgment, and so enamored of the ability to transport everything of himself but his "natural man" into the seventeenth century by the sheer force of erudition, that the feat itself enthralls all his attention and transforms the critic into the dilettante. We cannot do better than to advise the reader of Mr. Saintsbury's critique to re-read the essay on Dryden in his Johnson's *Lives*, where he will, at least, be able to appreciate, even if he does not like, the "natural man" of the critic. (pp. 337-38)

> *"Saintsbury's Dryden," in* The Nation, *New York, Vol. XXXII, No. 828, May 12, 1881, pp. 337-38.*

WALTER PATER (essay date 1886)

[*An essayist, novelist, and critic, Pater is one of the most famous proponents of aestheticism in English literature. Distinguished as the first major English writer to formulate an explicitly aesthetic philosophy of life, he advocated the "love of art for art's sake" as life's greatest offering, a belief which he exemplified in his influential* Studies in the History of the Renaissance (1873) *and elucidated in his novel* Marius the Epicurean (1885) *and other works. In the following excerpt, from an essay originally published in 1886, Pater offers a positive review of* Specimens of English Prose Style, *an anthology edited by Saintsbury.*]

The making of an anthology of English prose is what must have occurred to many of its students, by way of pleasure to themselves, or of profit to other persons. Such an anthology, the compass and variety of our prose literature being considered, might well follow exclusively some special line of interest in it; exhibiting, for instance, what is so obviously striking, its imaginative power, or its (legitimately) poetic beauty, or again, its philosophical capacity. Mr. Saintsbury's well-considered ***Specimens of English Prose Style, from Malory to Macaulay,*** a volume, as we think, which bears fresh witness to the truth of the old remark that it takes a scholar indeed to make a good literary selection, has its motive sufficiently indicated in the very original "introductory essay," which might well stand, along with the best of these extracts from a hundred or more deceased masters of English, as itself a document or standard, in the matter of prose style. The essential difference between poetry and prose—"that other beauty of prose"—in the words of the motto he has chosen from Dryden, the first master of the sort of prose he prefers:—that is Mr. Saintsbury's burden. It is a consideration, undoubtedly, of great importance both for the writer and the critic; in England especially, where, although (as Mr. Saintsbury rightly points out, in correction of an imperfectly informed French critic of our literature) the radical distinction between poetry and prose has ever been recognized by its students, yet the imaginative impulse, which is perhaps the richest of our purely intellectual gifts, has been apt to invade the province of that tact and good judgment, alike as to matter and manner, in which we are not richer than other people. Great poetry and great prose, it might be found, have most of their qualities in common. But their indispensable qualities are different, or even opposed; and it is just the indispensable qualities of prose and poetry respectively, which it is so necessary for those who have to do with either to bear ever in mind. Order, precision, directness, are the radical merits of prose thought; and it is more than merely legitimate that they should form the criterion of prose style, because within the scope of those qualities, according to Mr. Saintsbury, there is more than just the quiet, unpretending usefulness of the bare *sermo pedestris*. Acting on language, those qualities generate a specific and unique beauty—"that other beauty of prose"— fitly illustrated by these specimens, which the reader needs hardly be told, after what has been now said, are far from being a collection of "purple patches."

Whether or not he admits their practical cogency, an attentive reader will not fail to be interested in the attempt Mr. Saintsbury has made to give technical rules of metre for the production of the true prose rhythm. Any one who cares to do so might test the validity of those rules in the nearest possible way, by applying them to the varied examples in this wide survey of what has been actually well done in English prose, here exhibited on the side of their strictly prosaic merit—their conformity, before all other aims, to laws of a structure primarily reasonable. Not that that reasonable prose structure, or architecture, as Mr. Saintsbury conceives it, has been always, or even generally, the ideal, even of those chosen writers here in evidence. Elizabethan prose, all too chaotic in the beauty and force which overflowed into it from Elizabethan poetry, and incorrect with an incorrectness which leaves it scarcely legitimate prose at all: then, in reaction against that, the correctness of Dryden, and his followers through the eighteenth century, determining the standard of a prose in the proper sense, not inferior to the prose of the Augustan age in Latin, or of the "great age in France": and, again in reaction against this, the wild mixture of poetry and prose, in our wild nineteenth century, under the influence of such writers as Dickens and Carlyle:—such are the three periods into which the story of our prose literature divides itself. And Mr. Saintsbury has his well-timed, practical suggestions, upon a survey of them. (pp. 3-6)

> Walter Pater, "English Literature," in his Essays from "The Guardian," *Macmillan and Co., Limited, 1901, pp. 1-16.*

WILLIAM WATSON (essay date 1893)

[*Watson was an English poet and critic who maintained that a writer should be an integral part of the social and intellectual life of an era and contribute to decisions of public policy. One of his primary aims as a poet was to elucidate current affairs; for that reason, he wrote much occasional poetry. He was alien to the aesthetic temper of the 1890s and in fact held more imaginative realms of poetry to be the province of the second-rate. Selected to compose the official elegy for Tennyson, "Lacrimae Musarum" (1892), he appeared to be Tennyson's successor to* the position of poet laureate. However, Watson's strong anti-imperialist views, expressed in particular in The Purple East (1889), and his numerous denunciations of the Boer War were probably responsible for his being passed over for that position. Although knighted in 1917, Watson died an impoverished and embittered man. In the following excerpt, Watson praises Saintsbury's style of literary criticism.]

The terms "author" and "critic" used to represent a distinction so pointed as almost to be antithetical. At present they shade into each other imperceptibly. The critic becomes more and more his own topic, and the reader sometimes vaguely wonders whether criticism any longer implies the existence of something criticised.

It is always good to be with Mr. Saintsbury, for he at least is a critic who keeps his object clearly in view, by taking care never to be preoccupied with a sense of his own clarity of vision. And he is so pleasantly free from nervous airs of responsibility. Without exactly having that "light touch," which is perhaps as much over-valued just now as a ponderous ceremoniousness of literary manners was over-valued by our forefathers, he always avoids taking either his subjects, himself, or, one may add, his readers too seriously, and whatever faults he may be chargeable with, that of dull decorum certainly cannot be numbered amongst them. We have a feeling that if (say) the Archangel Gabriel had occupied his doubtless ample leisure with writing and publishing poetry, and Mr. Saintsbury had undertaken to review it, his criticism would have betrayed no sign of his being in the least degree awed by the very exalted rank of the author. And while his attitude towards the writers whom he discusses may be described as one of easy yet respectful familiarity, his style is felicitously in accord with his attitude. It is a style which clearly pays no heed to dignity, yet we should hesitate to call it an undignified style, in any sense implying disparagement. Now such a style as Leigh Hunt's does really strike us as undignified in that sense, but the source of the impression is his loquacity, his prattling and fussing ways, not his contempt for starch and buckram. Beneath his jaunty, skittish airs there is some want of true inbred ease. In his light holiday attire he does not look a whit more really comfortable than does Sir Thomas Browne in his trailing cloth of gold, starred with antique gems, and overwrought with cabalistic symbols. Mere ease of style often gets more credit than is its due. It is ease with power, or ease with splendour that is the valuable thing. Anybody can be at ease in a shooting jacket and knickerbockers, but to look comfortable in court-dress is distinction. Besides, after all, writing and talking are two quite distinct arts, and a chatty style is no more truly appropriate to literature than a literary style is to conversation. Starch and buckram are as foreign to Mr. Saintsbury's wardrobe as to Hunt's; but Hunt, in eschewing stiffness, constantly falls into slatternliness, and goes about with hose down at heels, while Mr. Saintsbury's arm-chair negligence of pose is at worst an agreeable mannerism, which pleasantly invites the reader to make himself similarly at home. (pp. 84-6)

> William Watson, "Critics and Their Craft," in his Excursions in Criticism: Being Some Prose Recreations of a Rhymer, *Elkin Mathews and John Lane, 1893, pp. 81-8.*

C. H. HERFORD (essay date 1898)

[*Herford was an English educator, translator, and critic. In the following review of A Short History of English Literature, he praises the breadth and uniqueness of the work.*]

Professor Saintsbury, if not actually the creator, is a past-master of the Short History; and what he has done with admitted success for another literature, it was hardly likely that either public or publishers would permit him to leave undone for his own. Let it be said at once that he has produced a book which accomplishes something for English literary history not altogether achieved, nor indeed precisely attempted, before on the same scale and over so wide a range. Large tracts of the subject he had no doubt himself already handled: Elizabethan and Nineteenth Century Literature, the Middle English Romances, Dryden and other single lives. The student of these books will take up this Short History with tolerably well-defined expectations. He will look for certain peculiarities of method and foibles of manner, and will not fail to find them. The winds of conflict still at times blow aside the mantle of the literary historian, and expose the flashing armour of the militant reviewer; ignorant inquirers about a work A are still often put off with the information that it is good, or better than a work B, notwithstanding a too frequent opinion that it is bad, or worse than a work C; the page is still continually adorned with notice-boards giving warning that certain topics often found in literary histories are trespassers there and will find no quarter; and a peculiarly aggressive bitterness is still reserved for the great aggressors of literature—the iconoclasts who had the bad taste to make poetry the instrument of their iconoclasm. But with all this, there are still all the old atoning and more than atoning merits: immense reading, a quick vitalising touch, complete indifference to conventions, an unfailing freshness and individuality of criticism which makes the book, for the knowing and the unknowing alike, highly stimulating, and, *qua* literary history, very real.

The reader of Mr. Saintsbury's previous work will turn with special curiosity to see what he has made of the "origins",— the "Preliminaries of English Literature," as he calls the Anglo-Saxon period. His First Book is an excellent review of the extant monuments of Anglo-Saxon literature, recording with admirable point and precision the impression which each in turn has made upon a critic of fine and catholic sensibility, trained in another school. It is in so far comparable in kind— Mr. Saintsbury will not resent the comparison—with Hazlitt's lectures on the Elizabethan dramatists; though their discovery naturally struck out in Hazlitt critical raptures far unlike the sober joys which *The Ruin* and parts of *Beowulf* evoke in Mr. Saintsbury. But in the one work as in the other the appreciation is a little hard and external; it has not the intimacy which comes of habitual converse and many-sided approach. If the students of Edinburgh have heard him lecture upon *Beowulf,* they have certainly enjoyed no small privilege; but we question whether they were ever tempted, as was said of their *commilitonen* at Strassburg under Ten Brink, to imagine that some old Germanic bard in person was thrilling them with the tale of the hall-joys of Heorot or the wrath of Grendel. The comparison with Ten Brink's own First Book is inevitable, but perhaps scarcely just if we have regard to the divergent conceptions of literary history on which it is founded. Still, for better or worse, it is as well to make clear that where Ten Brink gave a sketch, as full and as penetrating as our knowledge then permitted, of the upgrowing of literature in the various provinces of the English-speaking folk, Mr. Saintsbury has in the main simply assessed the product, as an item in the later developments which more seriously interest him—somewhat in the manner of a steward counting up the rent which each tenant contributes to the estate, but not greatly concerned whether the rent is the produce of corn or cabbages, so long as it is paid. The opening sentences of the two books mark pretty incisively their different points of view. "A long interval had passed since the first settlement of English tribes upon British soil before English literature began to unfold." So Ten Brink. "The oldest document which has a possibly authentic claim to be English literature, if but English literature in the making and far off completion, is . . . *Widsith.*" So Mr. Saintsbury.

The early Middle English period, here called specifically "The Making of English Literature," seems to promise less to the severely literary historian. But Mr. Saintsbury has given a real freshness and zest to his treatment of it by grouping it about the history of the development of verse. "Metrik" is a valuable meeting-ground for the literary and the philological historian, where neither can dispense with the other's aid. Mr. Saintsbury's theories on metre are of value, as they could not fail to be; but they are advanced with too lofty a contempt for historical phonetics, and one listens with scepticism to a theorist who appeals for judgment upon an ancient metre to the ear of "every intelligent reader," and warns off a Ten Brink as "a foreigner" from the discussion of "a prosody not his own." In dealing with early English verse we are all foreigners; and if anyone is more a foreigner than the rest, it is the modern Englishman who approaches it armed with a serene confidence in the immediate inspiration of his ear instead of with the tools of science. Mr. Saintsbury dwells, with justice, upon the value for English verse of the principle of "syllabic equivalence," or "the possibility of substituting everywhere with due precautions, dactyl or tribrach or anapaest for iamb or trochee." But his gratitude for this "blessed result" leads him to hail every apparent premonition of it rather too hastily as a sign of technical advance; and altogether to conceive the early history of English metres as a much simpler and more continuous process than it really was. Throughout the mediæval division of the work he takes far too little account of the provincial distribution of literary groups which modern scholarship has worked out with so much fine discrimination; as with the Anglo-Saxons, so here (where the omission is of still more moment), we do not see the English folk feeling its way towards literature in scattered and remote districts with all manner of cross purposes and conflicting aims, but a series of literary monuments which are expected to illustrate a tolerably continuous progress. Yet the quasi-"anapaestic" treatment of the octosyllable, for instance, is largely a matter of local variation. It prevails, in various degrees, in a number of works of the 13th and 14th centuries—in the Genesis and Exodus, the Surtees Psalter, the "Prick of Conscience," "Havelok,"—all of Northern or North-eastern England; while the simpler "iambic" treatment of it predominates in another group covering the greater part of the same period, but extending beyond it, chiefly in the North or South—the "Owl and Nightingale," the "Cursor Mundi," the "Brus," the "Confessio Amantis." On the whole, the direction of artistic growth was towards a suppression of the freer in favour of the severe and simpler form. It would hardly be necessary to urge this point if Mr. Saintsbury had not somewhat peremptorily disturbed the accepted chronology of the "Poema Morale" (in the last half of the 12th century) on the ground of its "metrical maturity" compared with Layamon's "Brut," where "metrical as opposed to rhythmical scansion is barely struggling in." The solution rather is that the earlier writer was imitating a popular Latin verse of the day—the swinging *septenarius* of (*e.g.*) Map's famous

> Mihi est propositum in taberna mori—

though his imitation was tempered by traditional habits imperfectly overcome; while the later clung to the archaic English alliterative verse, though his conservatism was coloured by impulses towards rhyme and metre imperfectly resisted.

We have preferred to deal mainly with the portions of Mr. Saintsbury's book least likely to be taken for granted. But the chapters which cover ground previously trodden by him are far from being mere epitomes of the earlier books. The section on Shakspere, for instance, is now no mere critical summing-up, but a fresh and stimulating sketch, luminous with ideas and bristling with gibes. An important feature of the book, finally, is the striking and detailed account of the Scottish contributions to English literature. It would be absurd to suggest that to so ripe a critic the literature of Scotland looms larger when contemplated from Calton Hill than it did from Fleet Street; still, there is no mistaking the gain in sympathetic touch, if not in critical penetration, which is the proverbial fruit (in a fit nature) of "going into the poet's land." The book is in many ways a masterpiece, and we wish it all success. (pp. 45-6)

> C. H. Herford, "Professor Saintsbury's Short History of English Literature," in The Bookman, London, Vol. XV, No. 86, November, 1898, pp. 45-6.

JOHN CHURTON COLLINS (essay date 1901)

[*Collins was an English essayist, biographer, and critic who successfully crusaded for the establishment of a department of English at Oxford University. In the following excerpt, he denounces* A Short History of English Literature *for flagrant errors of fact and flawed critical judgement.*]

[*A Short History of English Literature*] is evidently designed for the use of serious readers, for the ordinary reader who will naturally look to it for general instruction and guidance in the study of English Literature, and to whom it will serve as a book of reference; for students in schools and colleges, to many of whom it will, in all likelihood, be prescribed as a textbook; for teachers engaged in lecturing and in preparing pupils for examination. Of all these readers there will not be one in a hundred who will not be obliged to take its statements on trust, to assume that its facts are correct, that its generalizations are sound, that its criticisms and critical theories are at any rate not absurd. It need hardly be said that, under these circumstances, a writer who had any pretension to conscientiousness would do his utmost to avoid all such errors as ordinary diligence could easily prevent, that he would guard scrupulously against random assertions and reckless misstatements, that he would, in other words, spare no pains to deserve the confidence placed in him by those who are not qualified to check his statements or question his dogmas, and who naturally suppose that the post which he occupies is a sufficient guarantee of the soundness and accuracy of his work. But so far from Professor Saintsbury having any sense of what is due to his position and to his readers, he has imported into his work the worst characteristics of irresponsible journalism: generalizations, the sole supports of which are audacious assertions, and an indifference to exactness and accuracy, as well with respect to important matters as in trifles, so scandalous as to be almost incredible.

Sir Thomas More said of Tyndale's version of the New Testament that to seek for errors in it was to look for drops of water in the sea. What was said very unfairly of Tyndale's work may be said with literal truth of Professor Saintsbury's. The utmost extent of the space at our disposal will only suffice for a few illustrations. We will select those which appear to us most typical. In the chapter on Anglo-Saxon literature the Professor favours us with the astounding statement, that in Anglo-Saxon poetry "there is practically no lyric." It is scarcely necessary to say that not only does Anglo-Saxon poetry abound in lyrics, but that it is in its lyrical note that its chief power and charm consists. In the threnody of the *Ruin,* and the *Grave,* in the sentimental pathos of the *Seafarer,* of *Deor's Complaint,* and of the remarkable fragment describing the husband's pining for his wife, in the fiery passion of the three great war-songs, in the glowing subjective intensity of the *Judith,* in the religious ecstasy of the *Holy Rood* and of innumerable passages in the other poems attributed to Cynewulf, and of the poem attributed to Cædmon, deeper and more piercing lyric notes have never been struck. Take such a passage as the following from the *Satan,* typical, it may be added, of scores of others:—

> O thou glory of the Lord! Guardian of Heaven's hosts,
> O thou might of the Creator! O thou mid-circle!
> O thou bright day of splendour! O thou jubilee of God!
> O ye hosts of angels! O thou highest heaven!
> O that I am shut from the everlasting jubilee,
> That I cannot reach my hands again to Heaven,
> . . . Nor hear with my ears ever again
> The clear-ringing harmony of the heavenly trumpets.

And this is a poetry which has "practically no lyric"! On page 2 the Professor tells us that there is no rhyme in Anglo-Saxon poetry; on page 18 we find him giving an account of the rhyming poem in the *Exeter Book.* Of Mr. Saintsbury's method of dealing with particular works and particular authors, one or two examples must suffice. He tells us on page 125 that the heroines in Chaucer's *Legend of Good Women* are "the most hapless and blameless of Ovid's Heroides." It would be interesting to know what connexion Cleopatra, whose story comes first, has with Ovid's Heroides, or if the term "Heroides," be, as it appears to be, (for it is printed in italics) the title of Ovid's Heroic Epistles, what connexion four out of the ten have with Ovid's work. In any case the statement is partly erroneous and wholly misleading. In the account given of the Scotch poets, the Professor, speaking of Douglas' translation of the *Æneid,* says, he "does not embroider on his text." This is an excellent illustration of the confidence which may be placed in Mr. Saintsbury's assertions about works on which most of his readers must take what he says on trust. Douglas is continually "embroidering on his text," indeed, he habitually does so. We open his translation purely at random; we find him turning *Æneid* II. 496-499:—

> "Non sic, aggeribus ruptis cum spumeus amnis
> Exiit, oppositasque evicit gurgite moles,"
> Fertur in arva furens cumulo, camposque per omnes
> Cum stabulis armenta trahit.

> Not sa fersly the fomy river or flude
> Brekkis over the bankis on spait quhen it is wode.
> And with his brusch and fard of water brown
> The dykys and the schorys betis down,
> Ourspreddand croftis and flattis wyth hys spate
> Our all the feyldis that they may row ane bate
> Quhill houssis and the flokkis flittis away,
> The corne grangis and standard stakkys of hay.

We open *Æneid* IX. 2:—

> Irim de cœlo misit Saturnia Juno
> Audacem ad Turnum. Luco tum forte parentis
> Pilumni Turnus sacratâ valle sedebat.
> Ad quem sic roseo Thaumantias ore locuta est.

We find it turned:—

> Juno that lyst not blyn
> Of hir auld malyce and iniquyte,
> Hir madyn Iris from hevin sendys sche

To the bald Turnus malapart and stout;
Quhilk for the tyme was wyth al his rout
Amyd ane vale wonnder lovn and law,
Syttand at eys within the hallowit schaw
Of God Pilumnus his progenitor.
Thamantis dochter knelys him before,
I meyn Iris thys ilk fornamyt maide,
And with hir rosy lippis thus him said.

We turn to the end of the tenth *Æneid* and we find him introducing six lines which have nothing to correspond with them in the original. And this is a translator who "does not embroider on his text"! It is perfectly plain that Professor Saintsbury has criticised and commented on a work which he could never have inspected. (pp. 93-8)

Turn where we will we are confronted with blunders. Take the account given of Shakespeare. He began his metre, we are told, with the lumbering "fourteeners." He did, so far as is known, nothing of the kind. Again: "It is only by guesses that anything is dated before the *Comedy of Errors* at the extreme end of 1594." In answer to this it may be sufficient to say that *Venus and Adonis* was published in 1593, that the first part of *Henry VI.* was acted on 3rd March, 1592, that *Titus Andronicus* was acted on 25th January, 1594, and that *Lucrece* was entered on the Stationers' books 9th May, 1594. This is on a par with the assertion, on page 315, that Shakespeare was traditionally born on 24th April! On page 320 we are told that *Measure for Measure* belongs to the first group of Shakespeare's plays, to the series beginning with *Love's Labour's Lost* and culminating with the *Midsummer Night's Dream*. It is only fair to say that the Professor places a note of interrogation after it in a bracket, but that it should have been placed there, even tentatively, shows an ignorance of the very rudiments of Shakespearian criticism which is nothing short of astounding. Take, again, the account given of Burke. Our readers will probably think us jesting when we tell them that Professor Saintsbury gravely informs us that Burke supported the American Revolution. Is the Professor unacquainted with the two finest speeches which have ever been delivered in any language since Cicero? Can he possibly be ignorant that Burke, so far from supporting that revolution, did all in his power to prevent it? The whole account of Burke, it may be added, teems with inaccuracies. The American Revolution was not brought about under a Tory administration. What brought that revolution about was Charles Townshend's tax, and that tax was imposed under a Whig administration, as every well-informed Board-school lad would know. Burke did not lose his seat at Bristol owing to his support of Roman Catholic claims. If Professor Saintsbury had turned to one of the finest of Burke's minor speeches—the speech addressed to the electors of Bristol—he would have seen that Burke's support of the Roman Catholic claims was only one, and that not the most important, of the causes which cost him his seat. Similar ignorance is displayed in the remark (p. 629) that "Burke joined, and indeed headed, the crusade against Warren Hastings, in 1788." The prosecution of Warren Hastings was undertaken on Burke's sole initiative, not in 1788, but in 1785. A few lines onwards we are told that the series of Burke's writings on the French Revolution "began with the *Reflections* in 1790, and was continued in the *Letter to a Noble Lord,* 1790. *A Letter to a Noble Lord* had nothing to do with the French Revolution, except collaterally as it affected Burke's public conduct, and appeared, not in 1790, but in 1795. (pp. 99-101)

The Professor's critical dicta are as amazing as his facts. . . . Cowley's *Anacreontics* are "not very far below Milton" (!)

Dr. Donne was "the most gifted man of letters next to Shakespeare." Where Bacon, where Ben Jonson, where Milton are to stand is not indicated. Akenside's stilted and frigid *Odes* "fall not so far short of Collins." We wonder what Mr. Saintsbury's criterion of poetry can be. But we forget, with that criterion he has furnished us. On page 732, speaking of "a story about a hearer who knew no English, but knew Tennyson to be a poet by the hearing," he adds that "the story is probable and valuable, or rather invaluable, for it points to the best if not the only criterion of poetry." And this is a critic! We would exhort the Professor to ponder well Pope's lines:

But most by numbers judge a poet's song,

* * * * *

In the bright muse, tho' thousand charms conspire,
Her voice is all these tuneful fools admire,
Who haunt Parnassus but to please their ear.

On page 734 we are told Browning's *James Lee*—the Professor probably means *James Lee's Wife*—is amongst "the greatest poems of the century." On Wordsworth's line, judged not in relation to its context, but as a single verse—"Our birth is but a sleep and a forgetting"—we have the following as commentary: "Even Shakespeare, even Shelley have little more of the echoing detonation, the auroral light of true poetry"; very "echoing," very "detonating"—the rhythm of "Our birth is but a sleep and a forgetting." Mr. Saintsbury's notions of what constitutes detonation and auroral light in poetry appear to resemble his notions of what constitutes eloquence in prose. Nothing, we may add in passing, is more amusing in this volume than Mr. Saintsbury's cool assumption of equality as a critical authority with such a critic as Matthew Arnold, whom he sometimes patronises, sometimes corrects, and sometimes assails. The Professor does not show to advantage on these occasions, and he leaves us with the impression that if "Mr. Arnold's criticism is piecemeal, arbitrary, fantastic, and insane," the criticism which appears, where it is not mere nonsense, to take its touchstones, its standards, and its canons from those of the average Philistine is, after all, a very poor substitute. But enough of Mr. Saintsbury's "criticism," which is, almost uniformly, as absurd in what it praises as in what it censures.

The style, or, to borrow an expression from Swift, what the poverty of our language compels us to call the style, in which this book is written, is on a par with its criticism. We will give a few examples. "It is a proof of the greatness of Dryden that he knew Milton for a poet; it is a proof of the smallness (and mighty as he was on some sides, on others he was very small) of Milton that (if he really did so) he denied poetry to Dryden." "What the *Voyage and Travaile* really is, is this—it is, so far as we know, and even beyond our knowledge in all probability and likelihood, the first considerable example of prose in English dealing neither with the beaten track of theology and philosophy, nor with the, even in the Middle Ages, restricted field of history and home topography, but expatiating freely on unguarded plains and on untrodden hills, sometimes dropping into actual prose romance and always treating its subject as the poets had treated theirs in *Brut* and *Mort d'Arthur,* in *Troy-book* and *Alexandreid,* as a mere canvas on which to embroider flowers of fancy." Again, "With Anglo-Saxon history he deals slightly, and despite his ardent English patriotism—his book opens with a vigorous panegyric of England, the first of a series extending to the present day (from which an anthology *De Laudibus Angliæ* might be made)—he deals very harshly with Harold Godwinson." "He had a fit of stiff

Odes in the Gray and Collins manner.'' ''*The Hind and Panther* (the greatest poem ever written in the teeth of its subject).'' ''His voluminous Latin works have been *tackled* by a special Wyclif Society.'' These are a few of the gems in which every chapter abounds.

Of Professor Saintsbury's indifference to exactness and accuracy in details and facts we need go no further for illustrations than to his dates. Such things cannot be regarded as trifles in a book designed to be a book of reference. We will give a few instances. We are informed on page 238 that Ascham's *School-master* was published in 1568; it was published, as its title-page shows, in 1570. Hume's *Dissertations* were first published, not in 1762, but in 1757. Bale's flight to Germany was not in 1547, when such a step would have been unnecessary, but in 1540. Pecock was, we are told, translated to Chichester in 1550, exactly ninety years after his death! As if to perplex the readers of this book, two series of dates are given; we have the dates in the narrative and the dates in the index, and no attempt is made to reconcile the discrepancies. Accordingly we find in the narrative that Caxton was probably born in 1415—in the index that he was born in 1422; in the narrative that Latimer, Fisher, Gascoign and Atterbury were born respectively in 1489, in 1465, about 1537 and in 1672—in the index that they were born respectively in 1485, 1459, 1525 and 1662; in the narrative Gay was born in 1688—in the index he was born in 1685. In the narrative Collins dies in 1756, and Mrs. Browning is born in 1806—in the index Collins dies in 1759, and Mrs. Browning is born in 1809. The narrative tells us that Aubrey was born in 1626, and John Dyer *circa* 1688—in the index that Aubrey was born in 1624 and Dyer *circa* 1700. In the index Mark Pattison dies in 1884—in the narrative he dies in 1889. In Professor Saintsbury's eyes such indifference to accuracy may be venial: in our opinion it is nothing less than scandalous. It is assuredly most unfair to those who will naturally expect to find in a book of reference trustworthy information.

We must now conclude, though we have very far from exhausted the list of errors and misstatements, of absurdities in criticism and absurdities in theory, which we have noted. Bacon has observed that the best part of beauty is that which a picture cannot express. It may be said, with equal truth, of a bad book, that what is worst in it is precisely that which it is most difficult to submit to tangible tests. In other words, it lies not so much in its errors and inaccuracies, which, after all, may be mere trifles and excrescences, but it lies in its tone and colour, its flavour, its accent. Professor Saintsbury appears to be constitutionally incapable of distinguishing vulgarity and coarseness from liveliness and vigour. So far from having any pretension to the finer qualities of the critic, he seems to take a boisterous pride in exhibiting his grossness.

If our review of this book shall seem unduly harsh, we are sorry, but a more exasperating writer than Professor Saintsbury, with his indifference to all that should be dear to a scholar, the mingled coarseness, triviality and dogmatism of his tone, the audacious nonsense of his generalisations, and the offensive vulgarity of his diction and style—a very well of English defiled—we have never had the misfortune to meet with. Turn where we will in this work, to the opinions expressed in it, to the sentiments, to the verdicts, to the style, the note is the same,—the note of the *Das Gemeine* [''vulgarity'']. (pp. 104-09)

John Churton Collins, ''Our Literary Guides: Part I,'' in his Ephemera Critica; or, Plain Truths about

Current Literature, Archibald Constable and Co. Ltd., 1901, pp. 93-109.

J. B. PRIESTLEY   (essay date 1924)

[*A highly prolific English man of letters, Priestley is the author of numerous popular novels that depict the world of everyday, middle-class England. In this respect, Priestley has often been likened to Charles Dickens, a critical comparison that he dislikes. His most notable critical work is* Literature and Western Man *(1960), a survey of Western literature from the invention of movable type through the mid-twentieth century. In the following excerpt, Priestley counters negative criticism of Saintsbury, discussing his critical theory, critical practice, and literary style.*]

When Mr. Saintsbury remarks in Hazlitt's criticism ''the *gusto*, the spirit, the inspiriting quality'' . . . ''that amorous quest of literary beauty and rapturous enjoyment of it. . .'' he is, I think, saving us the trouble of finding words to describe the essential quality of his own criticism. And though this central flame burns less brightly in the modern critic, the fact of its being there at all is certainly more to be wondered at. For Hazlitt, like some other of our great critics, was a desultory reader, who browsed where he pleased and followed his nose in criticism. It is true that he gave certain courses of lectures—the English Poets, the Comic Writers, the Dramatic Literature of the Age of Queen Elizabeth, which are among the happiest things in English criticism: but they are not literary history. In them Hazlitt does not map the country, but contents himself, and us too, with describing, with his singular felicity, the towering peaks and various great landmarks. That he could do this with such astonishing sureness of touch without knowing much or anything of minor persons is proof enough of his critical genius, but it does not give us much cause to wonder at his retaining that enthusiasm which has been remarked in him. No one who has read widely in critical literature can have failed to notice that the literary historian, who has ''to read everything,'' to devour methodically great masses of literature, to bring order into a bewildering array of names and dates, usually shows us little of this gusto, this ''amorous quest of literary beauty.'' The dead weight of books is usually too much for him. In the end the method remains; there is order where before there was chaos; but alas! the spirit has long since fled, and what we finally receive are the cold judgments of a man who has substituted a formula for a critical palate, a day's duty for a delicate but insatiable appetite. This in part explains why there has been such a gulf between our great critics, supremely felicitous in judgment, and our literary historians. Of the latter it would be foolish to speak slightingly, for they have done some wonderful pioneer work; but how many have given us the things, perhaps only phrases, that are keys to new treasure-chambers of literature?

Now, the great, and perhaps peculiar, glory of Professor Saintsbury is that he has retained this gusto, this central flame of literary enthusiasm, throughout a long career (be it noted that he is treated here as a writer) devoted to the chronicling of literary history and similar ventures. Note, first, the sheer bulk of his work: several volumes of essays on individual writers, periods, styles, and what not; anthologies and various editing work; biographies; histories of English, French, European literatures; histories of criticism, English prosody, English prose rhythm; the novel, English and French; and so forth. The list is amazing: the mere sight of it intimidates one and makes the more indolent of us wonder what we do with our time. But mere bulk tells us comparatively little. As some ubiquitous contemporaries have shown us, it is not difficult to suggest solid achievement, at least in the catalogues, by dint of hashing and rehashing. I have heard of a certain tradesman, now dead, who had a passion for collecting execrable verse and making books of it, until at last he took up more space in the literary reference books than almost any living writer. But if we examine some of the volumes in this list, and think of what went to the making of them, our wonder and admiration can only grow. To say, as Professor Saintsbury himself does somewhere, that he has "undertaken some tough literary ventures" in his time is only to understate the matter. With the audacity of an Elizabethan sea-captain, he has put out his cockle-boats into vast uncharted oceans of literature, and returned triumphant, laden with glittering spoil and odorous with strange spices.

Consider the three-volume *History of English Prosody,* the *History of English Prose Rhythm,* and, greatest of all, the immense *History of Criticism,* that epic of literary taste. Labours as vast (Courthorpe's *History of English Poetry,* for example) have been successfully accomplished even with us; Germany and, latterly, America have been prolific of such things and can show us bibliographies of an incredible size. But where else can we find, going along with these things and leavening them, raising them to a higher power, that unflagging spirit which we have already remarked in Professor Saintsbury, that keen savouring of literature, that enthusiasm, with its train of half-humorous and wholly admirable hyperboles, which never deserts him even in his most herculean labours? Throughout he never declines from the critic proper, apt to appreciate and compare, to the mere recorder with his blunted palate and lack-lustre eye. Hardly ever do we meet with the weary gesture, so familiar elsewhere, that directs the author and his work to their appointed pigeon-hole, the particular kind. Notwithstanding the vast scope of his research, the book never becomes to him merely a thing to be classified; it is always a prospective source of delight; and it is in that spirit, the only one for a critic to work in, that we see him approach book after book, writer after writer, in all that great mass of literature through which he has guided us. And it is this almost unique combination of extraordinarily wide reading and research and unflagging appreciation, gusto (call it what you will), that makes him so rare a critic, so delightful a guide and companion in letters, for these and any other times. There is such a brave and human spirit shining through everything that he has written that one is stupefied at the queer epithets—"academic," "pedantic," and the like—that have been hurled at him by novelists turned critics and others; until one remembers that to such persons, he has had the pedantry, the pedagogical insolence, to prefer Shakespeare and Fielding, Thackeray and Shelley, Dryden and Swift, to them and their friends.

It is easier to say—off-hand—what Professor Saintsbury's critical position is not than what it is. His criticism is known to us as it should be known—by its fruits. But if it is its roots that we wish to disentangle, one or two passages from his *History of Criticism* may be of some service. Replying to those who pronounced him wanting in philosophy in his *History of Criticism,* he wrote:

> I hold that the province of Philosophy is occupied by matters of the pure intellect: and that literary criticism is busied with matters which, though not in the loosest meaning, are matters of sense. I do not know—and I do not believe that anyone knows, however much he may juggle with terms—why certain words arranged in certain order stir one like the face of the sea, or like the face of a girl, while other arrangements leave one absolutely indifferent or excite boredom or dislike. I know that we may generalize a little; may "push our ignorance a little farther back"; may discover some accordances of sound, some rhythmical adjustments, some cunning and more or less constant appeals to eye and ear which, as we coolly say, "explain" emotion and attraction to some extent. But *why* these general things delight man he knows no more than, in his own more unsophisticated stage, why their individual cases and instances do so. I do not think that my own doctrine of the Poetic (or the literary) Moment—of the instant and mirific "kiss of the spouse"—is so utterly "unphilosophical": but I do know that that doctrine, if it does not exactly laugh to scorn theories of æsthetic, makes them merely facultative indulgences. And just as physiology, and biology, and all the 'ologies that ever were 'ologied, leave you utterly uninformed as to the real reason of the rapture of the physical kiss, so I think that æsthetics do not teach the reason of the amorous peace of the Poetic Moment.

As a pendant to this, particularly to the "matters of sense" part of it, we may add an earlier passsage from the Tennyson essay in *Corrected Impressions*:

> Readers, and I hope they are many, of Maginn's *Story without a Tail* will remember the various reasons assigned for taking a dram, until the candid narrator avowed that he took it "because he liked a dram." It is undoubtedly natural to humanity to disguise to itself the reasons and nature of its enjoyments; but I do not know that it exhibits this possibly amiable and certainly amusing weakness more curiously or more distinctly in any matter than in the matter of poetry. Men will try to persuade themselves, or at least others, that they read poetry because it is a criticism of life, because it expresses the doubts and fears and thoughts and hopes of the time, because it is a substitute for religion, because it is a relief from serious work, because and because and because. As a matter of fact, they (that is to say, those of them who like it genuinely) read it because they like it, because it communicates an experience of half-sensual, half-intellectual pleasure to them. *Why* it does this no mortal can say, any more than he can say why the other causes of his pleasures produce their effect. *How* it does, it is perhaps not quite so hard to explain; though here also we come as usual to the bounding-wall of mystery before very long. And it is further curious to note that the same kind of prudery and want of frankness comes in here once more. It often makes people positively angry to be told that the greatest part, if not the whole, of the pleasure-giving appeal of poetry lies in its sound rather than its sense, or, to speak with extreme exactness, lies in the manner in which the sound conveys the sense. No "chain of extremely valuable thoughts" is poetry in itself: it only becomes poetry when it is conveyed with those charms of language, metre, rhyme, cadence, what not, which certain persons disdain.

Here we have the doctrine of literature for our good pleasure's sake, of omnific form and its peculiar emotion, stated with a vengeance. Innumerable idols are tumbled down that the Word itself, mysterious, imperishable, may be throned on high. And throned with it, or above it, is the omnicompetent and omnipotent personal taste, from whose judgment there is no appeal. Some there may be who doubt whether actual practice in criticism can go very far on the lines we have seen laid down. If so, let them read in Professor Saintsbury's unnumbered volumes and decide for themselves. But they must not, of course, expect that cast-iron consistency from which our best English critics—happily, I think—have always been free. I can at least save such doubters and scoffers some trouble by taking them straight to a very promising little battleground, cleared and ready for the drums and tramplings of critical battalions; it is a passage from his *History of Nineteenth Century Literature,* and it runs as follows:

> But the Ode (Wordsworth's *Intimations of Immortality*) remains not merely the greatest, but the one really dazzlingly, supremely great thing he ever did. Its theory has been scorned or impugned by some; parts of it have been called nonsense by critics of weight. But, sound or unsound, sense or nonsense, it is poetry, and magnificent poetry, from the first line to the last—poetry than which there is none better in any language, poetry such as there is not perhaps more than a small volume-full in all languages.

It is not, of course, the judgment itself that will sound the trumpet-call to arms, but the cool "Sense or Nonsense—this is great poetry!"

Turning again to the *History of Criticism,* we may note, with approval, disgust, or mere amusement, a very characteristic passage expressing the critic's distrust of the definition:

> The port was the Fair Haven of Romanticism, and the purpose was to distinguish "that which is established because it is right from that which is right because it is established," as Johnson himself formulates it. And now, of course, the horse-leeches of definition will ask me to define Romanticism, and now, also, I shall do nothing of the sort, and borrow from the unimpeachable authority of M. Brunetière (*quoted in note*) my reason for not doing it. What most of the personages of this book sought or helped (sometimes without at all seeking) to establish is Romanticism, and Romanticism is what they sought or helped to establish. In negative and by contrast, as usual, there is, however, no difficulty in arriving at a sort of jury-definition, which is perhaps a good deal better to work to port with than the aspiring but rather untrustworthy mast-poles of "Renascence of Wonder" and the like. We have indeed seen, throughout the last volume, that the curse and the mischief of Neo-classicism lay in the tyranny of the Definition itself. You had no sooner satisfied yourself that Poetry was such and such a thing, that it consisted of such and such narrowly delimited Kinds, that its stamped instruments and sealed patterns were this and that, than you proceeded to apply these propositions inquisitorially, excommunicating or executing delinquents and nonconformists.

A further danger of the definition in criticism, a danger from which Professor Saintsbury has naturally been free, but one that has ensnared not a few critics of the last century, is that it tends to push the actual work into the background and itself into the foreground. Thus a body of work is given, perhaps for the sake of mere convenience, a certain label—romantic, neo-classical, realistic, naturalistic, or the like. Before long the "horse-leeches" are attracted by the label, and one or more definitions are fastened to it. From now on critics begin to batten on the definitions or quarrel about them and, all the while, the work itself, the only real thing and the only thing that matters, is fading further and further into the background. The ordinary reader begins to peer through the spectacles of definition, and risks losing whole periods of literature that would normally have proved a delight to him.

Another danger, one that is not so pressing now, though still liable to threaten from unexpected quarters, and one against which Professor Saintsbury has ever been careful to guard himself, is the critical fallacy of "This is beautiful but not to be tolerated." There is a characteristic explosion against this doctrine of monstrous beauty in the *History of English Prose Rhythm,* which may be quoted as an example of many things. It follows the quotation of a very beautiful passage in Ruskin's most opulent and puissant style:

> Now, of course, it obviously may be said, and probably has been said a hundred times, that this is illegitimate, a "monstrous beauty," something that "you *ought not* to like." Well, this is the seventh vial-volume (I blush for it) that I have opened in hope of pouring contempt and destruction on the doctrine of monstrous beauties. It is impossible that beauty should be monstrous; and if I met a monster that pretended to be one and was beautiful, I should, like Prince Seithenyn, tell it to its beautiful face that it was no monster. But *is* this beautiful? There of course we come to the old flaming walls of the world of taste. I can only say that if it is not, I do not know where beauty of prose is to be found.

As yet, however, we have seen more of the negative than the positive side of his theory and practice. But there is a passage in the conclusion of the *History of Criticism,* the result perhaps of the expansive mood that often comes at the end of a long labour, in which he proclaims the critical faith that is in him:

> But it may fairly be asked, How do you propose to define *any* principles for your New Critic? And the answers are ready, one in Hellenic, one in Hebraic phraseology. The definition shall be couched as the man of understanding would define it: and if any will do the works of the New Criticism he shall know the doctrine thereof. Nor are the works themselves hard to set forth. He must read, and, as far as possible, read everything—that is the first and great commandment. If he omits one period of a literature, even one author of some real, if ever so little, importance in a period, he runs the risk of putting his view of the rest out of focus; if he fails to take at least some account of other literatures as well, his state will be nearly as perilous. Secondly, he must constantly compare books, authors, literatures indeed, to see in what each differs from each, but never in order to dislike one because it is not the other. Thirdly, he must, as far as he possibly can, divest himself of any idea of what a book *ought to be,* until he has seen what it is. In other words, and to revert to the old simile, the plate to which he exposes the object cannot be too carefully prepared and sensitised, so that it may take the exactest possible reflection: but it cannot also be too carefully protected from even the minutest line, shadow, dot, that may affect or predetermine the impression in the very slightest degree.

Now, it is not so much his critical theory as his practice that we are concerned with here. With any born critic, I maintain, the two are never quite the same: his practice is always wider, deeper, more embracing than his theory. There is certainly nothing that Professor Saintsbury lays down above that he has not put into his own practice. No one can deny the scope of his reading, and few can be blind to his extensive use of the comparative method. This last is, I think, the source of one of his weaknesses, one chiefly to be found in his histories of special periods, where it may be partly excused by the lack of space. The weakness in question is a tendency to emphasize the continuity and development of the literature itself at the expense of the individual writers who compose that literature; a habit of explaining everybody in terms of everybody else, so that while one learns that B. (that great genius) is better than A., who paved the way for him, but not so wonderful as C., who followed after, one still feels uncomfortably ignorant about B. But when this is said, it is only fair to add that the literary historians on the other side, the "Forces," "Tendencies," "Spirit of the Time" mongers, are as a rule infinitely more unjust to their individual authors. Still there must be a good many of Professor Saintsbury's readers (and those not the least enthusiastic) who have been impressed by a certain lack of finality about his treatment of individual writers. This is in part also due to what appears to be his dislike of pushing an analysis very far. Often he leaves the lemon before he has squeezed it dry; after indicating a few well-marked characteristics, he is apt to take refuge too quickly in one of the innumerable terms, beginning, say, at the "je ne sais quoi" and ending somewhere near that mysterious verb "fondoos," he uses to describe the mystery of personality and genius. But if the method has sometimes left him weak where a few—a very few—other critics are strong, it has also made his stronghold of taste, comparison, and estimate impregnable when so many critical fortresses have been tumbling about their captains' ears. It has given him a sureness of touch in handling large masses of literature, the history of whole periods or special kinds, that is the admiration of students and the despair of critics who follow in his wake. Further, combined with certain innate qualities of mind, it has made him the best critic of critics, the best historian of books about books, in our literature. The humorless and timid academic may be alienated by certain peculiar—but, I think, delightful—idiosyncrasies of style and manner; other persons, who have axes to grind and are secretly afraid of his wide reading and hatred of fashionable literary cant, may pretend a great disdain; but those readers who have followed in his tracks find themselves turning again and again to his innumerable felicitous judgments with ever-increasing admiration and gratitude.

He has, of course, his limitations, most of them the natural limitations for which experienced readers are able to allow. I for one do not think that he shows the same extraordinary sureness of touch in dealing with literature produced, say, since 1850 that he does in dealing with work of an earlier date: it is not to be expected. He always shows, too, a tendency to react overmuch against current enthusiasms, against writers whom it is the fashion to praise. This, however, is not very deplorable, nor very unnatural; it comes from the desire, deep-seated in every true critic, to adjust the balance, to throw some weight into the lighter scale. Thus, when every one is clustered about the swings, Professor Saintsbury does not hesitate to come forward and praise the exquisite and delectable roundabouts. He has, as his readers know, some strong opinions and his fair share of rather Peacockian crotchets. He professes a creed of Toryism so extreme, so fantastic, that it probably has no fellow in these islands. He can take a strongly partisan interest in our politics up to 1832, but after that it is simply a matter of our going to the dogs at varying rates of speed. For the rest, he can still call Cambridge "the Whig University," and he may, for all I know to the contrary, be the last of the Jacobites. His attitude is so astonishing and puts him, for most of us at least, so far beyond the pale of controversy that one could no more quarrel with him about it than one could with Peacock's delightful Doctor Folliott, with whom he has much in common. Anyone who wishes to see the crotchets bristling has only to

turn to his invaluable *Peace of the Augustans,* and in particular to a passage on Johnson. But even in this volume, where he makes very unfair though entertaining comparisons between an eighteenth century that he clearly understands and loves and a twentieth century that he plainly does not care to understand and love—even here he performs his task supremely well; it is his business to comment upon the literature of the older century, and this he does magnificently. Crotchets or no crotchets, not once does he play the traitor to his love of letters; not once does he deny the Muse and conceal his delight or find none, because of extra-literary considerations. On the other hand, there are not a few writers whose characters are the very ones with which he is least likely to have any sympathy, whose views and aims must be abhorrent to him, to whom he has been one of the first to do full justice. No one, for example, has given Shelley a higher place among our poets. And no one has recognized more justly and generously the amazing critical genius of Coleridge, who has been so seriously underestimated by more than one critic of our time.

Again, no one has been bolder in speaking out when such a thing has been necessary. We must make no mistake about this. It is easy enough to speak out or to play the part of *l'enfant terrible* in criticism if one has no critical conscience and is a devotee of mere impudence in literary judgment, or addicted to what Professor Saintsbury himself calls the practice of "ragging." But for a critic who knows the English, nay, European tradition of literary judgment, and is himself working in that tradition, it requires no little courage and honesty to speak out against a weight of great authority. There was weight enough on the side of Byron as a great poet when the following passage, one example out of many of "speaking out," was written by Professor Saintsbury nearly thirty years ago. The passage is not quoted, be it understood, as a final estimate of Byron, for its purpose is simply to show what Byron is *not*:

> Byron, then, seems to me a poet distinctly of the second class, and not even of the best kind of second, inasmuch as his greatness is chiefly derived from a sort of parody, a sort of imitation, of the qualities of the first. His verse is to the greatest poetry what melodrama is to tragedy, what plaster is to marble, what pinchbeck is to gold. He is not, indeed, an imposter; for his sense of the beauty of nature and of the unsatisfactoriness of life is real, and his power of conveying this sense to others is real also. He has great, though uncertain, and never very *fine*, command of poetic sound, and a considerable though less command of poetic vision. But in all this there is a singular touch of illusion, of what his contemporaries had learnt from Scott to call gramarye. The often cited parallel of the false and true Florimels in Spenser applies here also. The really great poets do not injure each other in the very least by comparison, different as they are. Milton does not "kill" Wordsworth; Spenser does not injure Shelley; there is no danger in reading Keats immediately after Coleridge. But read Byron in close juxtaposition with any of these, or with not a few others, and the effect, to any good poetic taste, must surely be disastrous; to my own, whether good or bad, it is perfectly fatal. The light is not that which never was on land or sea; it is that which is habitually just in front of the stage: the roses are rouged, the cries of passion even sometimes (not always) ring false. I have read Byron again and again; I have sometimes, by reading Byron only and putting a strong constraint upon myself, got nearly into the mood to enjoy him. But let eye or ear once

catch sight or sound of real poetry and the enchantment vanishes.

(pp. 144-58)

It is possible, nay, probable, that I have been parting company with not a few well-disposed persons all along the route up to this point. I shall probably part company with many more from now onwards, for we have come inevitably to some discussion of Professor Saintsbury's style, that famous style over which so many people, themselves not likely to figure in any anthologies of prose, have made merry. Like most styles that are truly styles and native to their users, it has been largely conditioned by the work it has had to perform. The sort of style that will do admirably for little meditative essays on Love and Death will be little use for the writing of literary histories, in which an immense array of facts and a prodigious number of opinions have to be presented in the smallest possible space. Our prettiest stylists have usually kept clear of such roughhewing work. In his *History of English Prose Rhythm* Professor Saintsbury is very depreciatory and humorous about his own powers: in the preface he quotes with emphasis Diderot's epigram on Beccaria's "ouvrage sur le style où il n'y a point de style," and in the text there are, for the purpose of comparison, numerous references to "Cluvienus and myself." But elsewhere in the volume . . . the curious may find a spirited defence of the neologist and the parenthetic writer against the charges of slovenliness and bad grammar put forward by "half-educated critics" and others. So here are clues, if anyone should be blind and deaf enough to need them. The two most characteristic features of his style are, of course, his extraordinary use of parenthesis, clause within clause like the carven globes in the Oriental toys, and his uncommon use of literary allusion. He quotes widely, of course, but is much more given to allusion, ranging from the stock things of literature to rather obscure college jests, all natural enough in a man soaked in letters and of some humour, and eager to lighten his page and pass on good things, or recall them, to his readers. Of the two well-known dangers of allusion and quotation—first, that of being trite and boring; second, that of being obscure and teasing—he completely escapes the first to fall a victim to the second. There must be a good many people, of whom I am one, who profess to have read and remembered a little, but to whom more than a few of his allusions are still mysteries. His parenthetic manner is simply the result of a full mind, anxious to leave nothing unsaid on the subject in hand, working with little space at its command. There is, too, to be observed in it an entertaining duality in the writer, so that as we read we hear two persons addressing us. Mr. George Saintsbury, the enthusiastic lover of letters, begins the sentence with a smashing hyperbole, but is immediately checked by Professor Saintsbury, the scholar, who points out some exception, a reservation, or what not; the enthusiast promptly shakes off his interrupter, and gives a side-cut at those for whom it should be necessary to state such reservations, etc.; so the scholar immediately hints that there is something to be said for them; and so it goes on. Style and manner are, of course, so personal that we can only draw nearer and nearer to "the old flaming walls of the world of taste." Doubtless there are many readers who are only irritated by his repeated side-cuts at "critics of worship," "persons who shall be nameless," and the rest; but in its suggestion of a scholarly pugnacity dashed with oldfashioned courtesy this polemical manner of his has always given me, for one, more than a little delight. I have always found some entertainment, too, in his habit of not merely saying that a thing is good or excellent, but of applying to it a whole host of metaphors drawn from precious metals and stones and

(better) eating and drinking. Surely a man has a right to let off steam somewhere in a literary history! There is much to be said for the hyperbole, judiciously used, even though Macaulay has made it so unpopular in most quarters. There may be persons who really dislike an outburst like the following when they encounter it in a learned handbook; but I for one cannot join them: "To Dr. Brandes, Scott is an author 'whom no grown-up person reads'—a generalization perhaps the rashest, except Tolstoi's, that 'all prostitutes and madmen smoke,' which, in the course of a large experience of books, the present writer has registered." As for his style in general, although I have found it sometimes clumsy and altogether unlovely, at others irritating and positively obscure, nevertheless I hold that there is much to be said in its favour. It suits the matter (difficult as that usually is to cope with), and it suits the man. Because it is not a pastiche of the styles usually held up for imitation, its good qualities are, I fancy, apt to be overlooked. It is not for nothing that this style belongs to the man who has written so much and so well on English prose style and its rhythm in particular. The quotations I have given are mostly in one "key," and more fully representative of opinion than style; but even in them one can mark a certain felicity of rhythm and cadence, a certain crisp ring that falls easily and pleasantly upon the ear, and, of itself, tends to carry conviction. He has, too, some cunning in the long falling close, in which the pace gradually slackens and phrase after phrase goes ebbing out. And when occasion calls for a change of tone, demands that the loose easy style shall be raised into something more closely knit, more dignified and weighty, it does not call in vain, as many fine passages can testify. One such passage there was, that concluding one on Johnson in *The Peace of the Augustans,* I could have wished to quote, but I have quoted enough: let it remain with its fellows, ready to give the lie to those who have spoken hastily and unjustly. To any reader at all disposed to be friendly, this style of Professor Saintsbury's soon ceases to be a trick of assembling words and becomes the fit expression of a strong and winning personality: it becomes a voice. And it is a voice that lures us into places of enchantment, and tells of things infinitely beguiling, and thus earns for ever our gratitude; while we, on our part, can but stammer our thanks in some such poor way as this, and so remain for ever fathoms deep in debt. (pp. 161-64)

J. B. Priestley, "Mr. George Saintsbury," in his Figures in Modern Literature, *1924. Reprint by Books for Libraries Press, 1970, pp. 144-64.*

STEPHEN POTTER   (essay date 1937)

[*An English humorist, nonfiction writer, and critic, Potter is best known for his series of mock-instructional books on the art of "one-upmanship." In his study of education,* The Muse in Chains *(1937), Potter examined what he termed "the racket, the flummery, the techniques and the gambits of English Literature teaching." In the following excerpt from that work, Potter discusses Saintsbury's career as a critic and teacher.*]

1895 saw the coming of George Edward Bateman Saintsbury. (p. 126)

[Tradition], in even a narrow sense, was everything to him: he belonged to the age when one was born conservative or liberal, he felt himself to be born conservative, and that was that: at the age of ten he wrote a prize poem on Sicily which contained a denunciation of Garibaldi (Gladstone at the Speechday distribution said that he was "afraid he could not agree with the sentiments"). But Saintsbury is a power, an emblem, because though he followed the eighteenth-century rhetoricians in concentrating on the outward appearances of writing and never on what or who was being expressed; he did this consciously, from a motive, as part of a belief.

His rise to imperial rank may have been helped by what must have seemed an unlucky accident. As a young man, Saintsbury, his genial capacities for savouring literature and learning already developed, his love of tradition already marked, seemed cut out for a comfortable Oxford Fellowship. But here was an unexpected hitch. He took what was then called a ''smash''— a second class—in Greats. Saintsbury felt this deeply. ''A second always *hurts* so abominably,'' he said. Literary men feel, probably with justice, that Keats or Shakespeare, if they took a literary school, would be most likely to get a Fourth; just conceivably they might get Alpha plus plus plus on every paper: but never by any possible chance could they get a Second.

The Fellowship did not come. But this reverse was to call up new and unexpected qualities. Saintsbury felt the need to justify himself, and the necessity of earning his living.

For a time he taught, rather miserably, at a school in Guernsey. Then he returned to London.

Since the war, Saintsbury has been less recommended to students. A temporary thing. . . . Saintsbury is not what they call ''minute'' enough for current ideals of scholarship. But all servants of literature know and consult Saintsbury, know that pages of every library catalogue are pasted with his name, and have heard the legend of Saintsbury in retirement in Bath, where stands the Crescent in a bay window of which Saintsbury's white beard was to be seen, in the mornings, still prodigiously active over his typewriter. We know at any rate his portrait, of an old man with book-quenched eyes. What we forget is the gusto, the excitement, with which a Saintsbury younger than it is possible for us to imagine him seized on the great virgin field of Literature. The feverishness of gold-rush days was in the air then. On the one side were new veins of Middle English Literature, recently opened by Skeat and the philologists. On the other were the delicious tracts of unedited English classics. To start with, Saintsbury had to be content with articles and reviews—from first to last he reckoned that he had filled 100 volumes octavo with these alone. But soon the reprints began. ''Edited, with an introduction and notes by G.E.B.S.'' turned up year after year, quarter after quarter. Swift, Montaigne, Herrick, Fielding, *Sir Charles Grandison*, Sterne (6 vols.), Smollett, Peacock, *Pride and Prejudice*—and then, after the editions, the histories. It is in these histories that the unique Saintsbury attitude to literature appears. It is virgin country to be fenced; it is an unmapped waste, every outpost of which there is some compulsion to visit. Not only the whole of English, and all the details of its periods separately, but the framework of French Literature is here as well, and there are prolonged raids on the Italians (the Flourishing of Romance) and a complete conspectus of Spain (the rise of Allegory). English Prosody is brought under the flag, and the furthest margins of English Prose Rhythm.

The specialist had become the generaliser—and yet, by an extraordinary self-discipline, he had managed to remain a specialist at the same time. Rival editors began to complain. Churton Collins, especially, accused him of ''commenting on works which he could not even have inspected'' [see excerpt dated 1901]. No criticism could be more off the mark. Saintsbury made a special point of touching, opening, and at any rate reading *in* works to which he only refers in a footnote. He would be worth post-mortem examination if only because it is

certain that he read more than any man who has ever lived. When he says, dealing with the three-thousand-four-hundredth name in his *History of Criticism* (Chapter *Later German* Subsection *Heine* Intersubsection *Heine's Followers*) that Grillparzer's ''natural limitations appear to have been further tightened by his playwrightship and by the influence of Joseph Schreyvogel, a sort of Austrian Nisard, of whom I do not know so much,'' readers will realise that Saintsbury is at least as familiar with Schreyvogel as they are with, say, *Paradise Regained,* if not *Samson Agonistes*. Reading was the chief labour of his enormous life. It is recorded, for example, that for 18 years he *started the day* by reading a French novel (in preparation for his history of them)—an act so unnatural to man as almost in itself to amount to genius. And the notion that any one who wrote so much criticism could not possibly have done his proportion of reading is ludicrously anthropomorphic judgment. For Saintsbury in his powers of work was godlike.

Late in the 'nineties, even his scholastic reputation was beginning to grow high. He was chosen to succeed Masson in what was still far the most important of the Literature Chairs.

The question must now be asked, was Saintsbury as successful as a teacher as he was in those other fields in which we know him so much better?

It would be foolishly unjust to his reputation to say that he was. As a teacher in Edinburgh, he was suspect from the start, because he had not been born in Scotland. Needless to say, he had written the best monographs on Wilson, Jeffrey and Lockhart. He was working on Scott. He was able, also, to appreciate the Edinburgh knowledge of claret. But he came from the South.

Horrible things sometimes happen to lecturers who come from the South. The students may take a dislike to you. Not long before Saintsbury's time, a literary lecturer at Glasgow, a Southerner who had just been appointed, delivering his Inaugural to an audience who prevented him from once hearing the sound of his own voice, went straight back to London, wrote a letter to *The Times* about ''Scottish barbarians,'' and was never heard of again. Nothing comparable to this happened to Saintsbury. But the lectures to the big Edinburgh Pass classes are trying affairs. Aliens from other faculties drift in. Literature was still thought of as rather a freak subject—almost a comic subject. There were interruptions. There were times when Saintsbury became as irritated as his interrupters hoped he would.

Saintsbury continued to be irritated, but he stuck most conscientiously to his work. Later, it is possible to trace a slight increase of impatience in the growing sarcasm of his examination questions:

> *Without* remarking that the thing became a trumpet
> in his hands, say something relevant about Milton's
> Sonnets. . . .

His attitude to the average student became one of slightly sarcastic tolerance.

Saintsbury never completely fitted in to these academic surroundings. A kind of A, B, C, clarity is necessary to get the better of classes of this kind: and Saintsbury was the most indefinite of lecturers. He spoke from skeleton notes only, from little cards, with rather indecipherable headings written across them. It is said that there was ''some terrible disorder in the talk, with loose ends, pick-ups, recoveries, allusive asides.'' He was not impressive, nor was he precise. The whole was delivered in a level, high-pitched voice, a continuous stream, "unemphatic and unpausing." Yet with individuals, with small groups of Honours students, he was very good. These students now praise him high. To them he was a personality—even vigorous, anti-academic, half-swashbuckling, almost Elizabethan, anti-pedant.

But there is another characteristic of Saintsbury, more fundamental than his lack of Literature Lecturer's tricks, to account for this partial failure—his attitude to his subject.

Younger, post-war students, to whom "Saintsbury" was a name from the past, were surprised to see that only a few years before his death his name appeared attached to articles in a young intellectual Monthly *The Dial.* But there was no inconsistency whatever. Young intellectual magazines devoted to Art usually, in the twenties at any rate, followed Yellow Book principles: they concerned themselves with Art for Art's Sake; for them "treatment" was the thing, never the subject, nor the man: and this Art *pour l'Art* was precisely the concern of Saintsbury. If he would never have accepted himself as a typical production of the Wilde era, he preached the same doctrines. In a paper of 1926 on **"Technique"** he claims that "for more than half a century he has done his little best to accentuate the importance of treatment over that of mere subject." What a book is *about* means for him something as trivial as *what bedside motto does it contain.* Saintsbury, in fact, is the literary professor of the Æsthetic Period, standing out above the rest because in his case there is no slipping into littish talk about treatment to conceal a barbarous knowledge of man, life, and the motives of Genius: he writes thus because he has chosen to do so. His **History of Criticism,** though everybody is put in, is really a history of taste, of *what* people thought *what* "good" or "bad" *when:* it is not, and never could have been, an account of the men who re-created past writers for their own generation, as Coleridge re-created Shakespeare. In the preface to this almost incredibly ground-covering work, Saintsbury sets down his beliefs, defending himself against a friend who had accused him of "treating literature as something by itself":

> I hastened to admit the impeachment, and to declare that this is the very postulate of my book. That literature cannot be *absolutely* isolated, I agree.... But in that *comparative* isolation and separate presentation which Aristotle meant by his caution against confusion of kinds I do thoroughly agree.

But Saintsbury carried impersonality even further than this. Not only the motives of writers ought to be ignored, he says, but the principles on which their art is grounded. He is scornful of enquiries into the basis of things because, he says, such enquiries are mechanical. To seem more in a work of Art than its form, its characteristics, is to Saintsbury "Metaphysics"— always for him a Pity—and such attempts make him think sympathetically of a favourite quotation from Dr. Johnson about a set of men "who account for everything systematically. For instance, it has been a fashion to wear scarlet breeches; these men would tell you that according to causes and effects no other wear could at that time have been chosen."

Saintsbury, in a word, is the Apostle of Taste, stands for taste: and the question arises—can you *teach* taste? The answer seems to be, on the whole, that Yes, you can. But whether you can *examine* in taste—that is another matter altogether. Apparently experiments are now being made; but broadly speaking, the only examinable facts of Literature are dates, personal characteristics of writers, and dicta on the subject of How it Works. A, B, C, dates and doctrines is what the poor literature student

must, therefore, have, and what he therefore, with stern pencil pointed over his open notebook, demands from his teacher. This was exactly the kind of information which Saintsbury refused to give. It must have been as impossible to make note material out of his lectures as it is out of his books. He was always actually attacking what he called the "horse-leeches of definition," and the one rule of art he was anxious to impart was that there was no rule.

The pros and cons of this important and ancient question could not be adequately summarised in a volume. But in my opinion, so far as Saintsbury is concerned, this stern rejection of his, which makes him as narrow in his judgment of criticism as he is satisfyingly catholic in his criticism of art, is a limitation.

This subjugation of the personal element seems to have been carried even against himself. In some ways, despite all his informality, he seems to be one of the most intangible writers that ever lived. It is impossible to say, in his criticism, which are his favourite authors. The novelists?—but then his major work was on prosody and criticism. The writers of the eighteenth century—but what of his two books on the nineteenth? And so on. Has he no gaps? If he has a preconception it is, I think, that poetry should be Wordsworthian, Romantic, of high seriousness. This would make him antipathetic to Byron, and in fact it does; but even with Byron he performs astounding feats in the concealing of the pre-judgment. "I have read Byron again and again," he writes, "and I have sometimes, by reading Byron only and putting a strong constraint upon myself, got very nearly in the mood to enjoy him."

This personal ghostliness helps, I think, to account for his style, which, since the style is the man and in this case there is no man, is a non-style. No literary device of any kind, hackneyed or otherwise, is used.

The same explanation, I think, will account for the difference between Saintsbury criticising—all sensitive vitality, humour, shrewdness—and Saintsbury writing on his own, in a **Scrap Book,** for instance. Here, all the Saintsburian wealth seems to depart. It is strange, because his tone of voice is then more robust than ever—quite Falstaffianly jolly. Turning through **Scrap Book** pages I see almost at once a sentence which may explain what I mean—a note on H. D. Traill:

> He had a most agreeable laugh for other people's jokes as well as his own. And I always like to think of him as I once saw him, then perhaps the most formidable of all-round fighters in the Press in English journalism, sitting cross-legged in flannels, at his wife's feet on their lawn at Putney—just after a set at tennis, and discarding, with his laugh, a finished joram of lemon squash.

The description is cheerful, the use of the anti-cliché word "joram" is at least characteristic. Yet what has been said? It gives almost no picture. Saintsbury seems to be *refusing* to give a personal impression.

And this deficiency of course impedes his criticism. There is no actual Saintsbury against which he can measure all these writers. There is nobody there to catch fire, nor be quenched, nor feel strongly one way or the other.

I often think, when I contemplate Saintsbury, of Bacon's essay where he says "Reading maketh a full man." What does Bacon mean? Is it a compliment? Saintsbury is, must have been, full. Yet to those who never saw him this wealth seems unreal. True one can see even a sort of Elizabethanism in his style— it is like Nash: but some clue seems to be missing. Saintsbury was full: he knew the good things of these writers he had loaded himself with: he could even well over with a fine thought. But one cannot feel, distinctly, that it is Saintsbury who has spoken. If there are riches within, their texture seems to be as unaltered by what he reads as the texture of the cistern by its contents. There is no incorporation. His eagerness is equally measured whether he is talking about Wordsworth or Stephen Duck, the criticism in a minor Puritan pamphlet, or in Matthew Arnold. He writes even of the greatest with amiable connoisseurship, as if humorously apologising for his collector's mania. The possibility that the reading of books may result in a personal influence; that, to use a trite phrase, by the satisfaction of the desire for beauty individuality may be enriched—this does not seem to have occurred to him. I am *not* suggesting that individuality may be enriched by new political views—but it may be that Saintsbury was permanently affected by the shock of having once heard Rossetti say that a certain rather bad volume of poems ought to be praised "because it was on the right side." Well, that kind of criterion was never to be his. The great English writers are on the whole in the liberal tradition. Saintsbury must have read nearly 500 Sonnets to Liberty, 600 Odes on the Emancipation of Slaves, and about 7000 different kinds of eloquent condemnation of Church and State. Yet with the most amiable recognition of the literary qualities of these pieces, he remained to the end of his life a Tory of the kind that was always expecting, as soon as the right kind of government came along, a repeal of the Reform Bill of 1832.

Arnold Bennett often used to scratch his head over the problem of Saintsbury. Here I read these little introductions of his to the Balzac novels, he would say, and *every one* hits the nail on the head. It is impossible. It is not right that he should be familiar with such secrets—because the man was not a writer himself. This genial mock-criticism gives rather a true picture. Though by himself Saintsbury may have been a ghost, Saintsbury became exquisitely alive in the context of somebody else. Early in life it was borne in on him, he says, that he was not meant to be a creative writer. He very calmly and unswervingly determined to be the next best thing.

The power of Saintsbury is in these moments of perception, in these sensations. His reading was in advance of his experience. This prevented him from being a creative artist—from being a creative critic, even. But he *was* this next best thing, an apprehender of, and a pointer towards, the beauty created by others. Perhaps we ought to be glad, instead of sorry, that finding himself not to be one of those few elect capable of founding a philosophy on their own experience, he refused to re-arrange his judgments to pattern with the metaphysics of others. Here, I think, Saintsbury might be allowed his own, more eloquent, last word. I will quote from a passage in which he defends himself from the charge of not having made enough use of Æsthetics in the *History of Criticism:*

> I do not know, and I do not believe that any one knows, however much he may juggle with terms— why certain words arranged in a certain order stir one like the face of the sea, or like the face of a girl, while other arrangements leave one absolutely indifferent or excite boredom. . . . And just as physicists and biologists, and all the 'ologies that ever were 'ologised, leave you utterly uninformed as to the real reason of the rapture of the physical kiss, so I think that æsthetics do not teach the reason of the amorous peace of the Poetic Moment.

(pp. 126-39)

Stephen Potter, "Youth: Scotland," in his The Muse in Chains: A Study in Education, *Jonathan Cape, 1937, pp. 104-39.*

DOROTHY RICHARDSON   (essay date 1944)

[*Richardson was an English novelist who was among the principal authors to conceive and practice the literary technique of stream of consciousness. In the twelve volumes of her major work,* Pilgrimage (1915-35), *she explored the impressions of her fictional alter-ego, Miriam Henderson. Richardson's intention, as she stated, was to find "a feminine equivalent of the current masculine realism." Her method was to chart what she considered insights and perceptions specific to feminine consciousness. In the following excerpt, Richardson compares Saintsbury's critical theories to those which served as the basis for the art-for-art's-sake movement in England during the late nineteenth century.*]

The aestheticism of the 'nineties and of the two preceding decades in England has not been fully studied. As with most movements, attention has been focused chiefly upon its leaders. Among the minor figures—one who joined the movement in the early 'seventies—is George Saintsbury . . . , the ponderous but venerable historian of criticism. I wish, by analysis of his early writings in particular, to show his close relation to the movement and to point out that he was a remarkably consistent advocate of certain basic aspects of aestheticism—an advocate who has had some harmful effects upon the development of modern criticism.

Saintsbury's reputation rests primarily upon his voluminous literary histories and upon his position as for several decades "almost the official critic of England." The advent of scientific techniques and ideals of literary scholarship has not helped his reputation; he is now often dismissed, with some justice, as "a great connoisseur . . . but not a great critic."

Saintsbury's connection with the aesthetic group in England and his devotion to its ideals, though generally overlooked in scholarly studies of the movement, did not go unnoted by his contemporaries. In 1881, when he had been a reviewer only seven years, a critic charged him with dilettante insincerity and linked him with the aesthetic group [see excerpt from the *Nation* dated 1881]. In 1892 an anonymous reviewer found in his work "the nearly obsolete cant of the Boulevards during the Second Empire," and "an indifference to the underlying unity of art and morals." At the turn of the century these charges reappeared: "A formalist in the garb of an aesthete," a defender of "the moribund heresy of art for art's sake." In 1923 Saintsbury admitted that he was one of the early "apostles" of Art for Art's Sake and stated that he "got it 'over the face and eyes' from proper moral men for [such] delinquencies . . . when writing on Baudelaire in 1875 and Gautier some three years later."

Definition of the Art for Art's Sake concept, which is essential to this investigation, is difficult because "failure to define is . . . [its] first and essential manifestation." Saintsbury's definition is wholly negative: it is "partly a reaction from the excessive subject-worship . . . partly a revolt against the commercial and materialist tendencies of the mid-nineteenth century." In brief, one may expect to find in the Art for Art's Sake devotee: 1) Emphasis upon form and technique, and upon conscious artistry (this may lead to a view of form and matter as separable and as capable of separate valuation); 2) the rejection of all but artistic aims and the insistence upon beauty as an end in itself; 3) emphasis upon the sensuous, the emotional, and the exotic elements in art with the individual reaction as a standard and as the basis of impressionistic criticism—"the adventures of the soul among masterpieces"; 4) concern for and emphasis upon highly conscious artistic prose; 5) a tendency to aristocratic sentiment, a kind of aesthetic snobbery often linked with political conservatism; 6) a view of life as an art (this may become a view of art as a refuge or escape from life); 7) perhaps most familiar is the derivative attitude of moral defiance, of immorality as revolt or protest ("life for art's sake"); 8) in quite a different category is the eventual union of Art for Art's Sake with science which occurred in a few cases, and 9) the not infrequent melancholy or cynical tone of disillusionment.

The practical hallmark of the movement in England was not so much any theory but rather simply an interest in the new French school, in the art and the art theories of Gautier, Flaubert, Baudelaire, Banville, and Leconte de Lisle,—in the Parnassians with many of whom the ideas above first found expression. Most of the young Englishmen who pursued this interest were in revolt against Victorian prudery and bourgeois materialism, against the demand for "high seriousness" and "purpose" in art; they sought escape in aestheticism. There is evidence of this throughout Saintsbury's writing. (pp. 243-45)

When Swinburne's *Poems and Ballads* burst upon the world with all the attendant furor in 1866, Saintsbury, an undergraduate at Oxford, was, like many of his fellow students, deeply stirred by this revolt of the daring poet whose *Atalanta* they were already chanting devotedly. Saintsbury recalls that they waited impatiently after the spring announcements of the new volume, through the long summer which saw John Morley's violent attack upon Swinburne in August, until the fall when the book finally appeared. Saintsbury tells how he purchased three copies in London, and how next day they sat at Merton from luncheon till chapel time, "reading aloud by turns in a select company "Dolores," and the "Triumph of Time," "Laus Veneris" and "Faustine", and all the other wonders of the volume." Here in the 'sixties which Edmund Gosse calls "the most quiescent, the most sedate . . . the least effective and efficient period of our national poetry," was Young Oxford carried away by the daring and sensuality of Swinburne, and, as a result, sent searching for similar thrills abroad—"exploring through Gautier and Baudelaire and Flaubert," as Saintsbury later recalls. Saintsbury's own first copy of Baudelaire was brought to him from Paris by a friend in 1866.

When Saintsbury left Merton in 1868 for a short career of schoolmastering, he was already "indoctrinated" with the cause which he championed the rest of his life. From 1866 until 1876, while teaching at Manchester, in Guernsey, and at Elton, he was reading widely in French literature. He had time, which he did not have later as London journalist (1876-95) or Edinburgh Professor of English Literature (1895-1915), for thorough reading and digestion. That he read both the new and the old French writers is evidenced by a series of essays on French contemporaries in the *Fortnightly Review* (1876-78) and by his *Primer* and *Short History of French Literature*. His first published writings were reviews of French authors for the *Academy,* in which there is ample evidence of the taste acquired at Oxford and of the new critical attitude.

Saintsbury's first review, on Théodore de Banville's *Idylles Prussiennes* (July 1, 1873), strikes the true aesthetic note in its predominant concern for form:

> . . . here we have the poet struggling with, and in a degree mastering an unpromising, uncongenial, but inevitable subject. . . . In the whole volume . . . the

form is incomparably superior to the matter and this fact, which is not likely to render it popular with the average reader, must always give it a special interest in the eyes of the instructed and critical lover of poetry.

Banville chooses strange and grotesque subjects in order "to prove the omnipotence and omnipresence of his art and its fitness at all times and all places for making the common as it were uncommon." A month later Saintsbury condemns Lamartine because "he is satisfied with ordinary and accepted vehicles for his thought." Lamartine fails because too often "the formal beauty . . . is not sufficient to arrest the attention of those to whom his matter is commonplace and unattractive." In a more controversial tone the reviewer adds, "It is this fact which is overlooked by those critics who . . . object to 'cette importance exclusive donnée à la forme aux depens de la pensée' ['this exclusive importance given to form at the expense of thought']." Thus Saintsbury plunged into the battle that Swinburne had begun.

What do these terms—form, matter, manner, subject—mean to Saintsbury, and what for him is the relation of this element "form" to subject or matter? Too often in critical writing these terms are elusive because loosely used or ill defined, but they cannot be given a single precise definition here without doing violence to Saintsbury's loose and varying use. One thing can be said, however: Saintsbury's concept is mechanical. Art is the sum of two elements—a body of material which all artists draw upon and a manner or style or form of experience imposed upon that material by the artist. Two passages will illustrate this tendency which is present in all his thinking. In 1895 he writes, "Practically everything has been said . . . the only question is whether the present sayer and thinker has shown due skill and originality in his manner of thought and expression." Later he states, "The style—the form—is that which the author adds to the matter; it is that inseparable but separably intelligible element which cannot be transferred, taken away or lost."

Three effects of this oddly simple mechanical concept will be noted in Saintsbury's thinking. First, it does a real injustice to the creative process. Anyone who thinks of that process as an organic one does not speak of adding up style and meaning or matter like a mathematical sum. Second, given such a mechanical concept, the temptation is to narrow the terms and the focus of attention until manner or treatment, which can mean all that the artist contributes when he puts life into a poem, novel, or play, comes to mean only arrangement of words, sentences, phrases, rhythm, and image—style in the narrowest sense. A third effect of this concept is really a result of these other two. Usually, as in the reviews quoted above, not only is Saintsbury preoccupied with form, but also he thinks of it as a separate and distinct element, capable of being separately enjoyed and evaluated. Of many possible illustrations of this the most fantastic occurs in the *History of Prosody.*

> What does meaning matter when you have such verse as "A Death Song"? It must be a singularly feeble intellect which cannot perform the easy dichotomy of meaning and metre . . . you pour the poison or the ditch water out; you keep and marvel at the cup. You can refill it as far as meaning goes, at your pleasure, with the greatest things. . . .

Such thinking almost defies serious critical comment (by anyone with this "feeble intellect") but it is frequent enough in Saintsbury so that it must be taken seriously.

To return to the early reviews—in Banville Saintsbury found "art militant" mastering the uncongenial subject; in Lamartine he regrets the absence of "beauty of form" which is independent of the casual influences of time and place to which beauty of thought is subject. This is the evidence for 1873. In the next year Saintsbury was treating the poetry of Bryant, Whitman, and Blake with the same emphasis. Discussing Bryant, he declares his impatience with critics who confuse appreciation of poetry with "a mere feeling of gratification at seeing thoughts and feelings" which are congenial to them given expression. Such critics are "at 5 and 40 indignant at praise of Mr. Swinburne or Charles Baudelaire." Saintsbury offers a cure for such prejudice in his comment on Whitman: "Fortunately admiration for a creed is easily separable from admiration for the utterance and expression of that creed." He likes Whitman's style but not his message; the latter affords slight inconvenience if one is capable of the "easy dichotomy."

Though addressed to the critic or reader rather than the artist, this last sentiment is very close to Flaubert's famous expressed desire to write about nothing. And indeed Saintsbury is not to be outdone, as he reveals in discussing a new edition of William Blake. He argues that Blake in his later years was "overcome by the detestable heresy of instruction." The effect was disastrous, for

> when a man is once affected, whether the instruction he gives be moral or immoral, orthodox or unorthodox, it is almost hopeless thenceforward to expect perfect work to be produced by him. He becomes careful of what he says, instead of being careful how he says it; anxious to say something in any manner, rather than anxious to say everything (or it may be nothing) in the best manner possible.

Here the demand for perfect form is linked with the moral issue. The phrase "heresy of instruction" descended from Poe's "Poetic Principle" and Baudelaire ("Hérésie de l'enseignement") through Swinburne (who speaks also of "the great moral heresy"). Its implications are clear: the artist must look to form though he write about nothing; the critic must judge in terms of form; literature must be free from any but a pure artistic purpose. "The whole end, aim, and object of literature . . . as of all art . . . is beauty," as Saintsbury says simply in 1895.

This assumption of pure aesthetic standards is significant, but the far more heretical underlying assumption of the separation of form and matter deserves more analysis. This "heresy of the separable substance," as A. C. Bradley calls it, is something not paralleled in the French exponents of *l'art pour l'art*. Gautier says plainly, "Nous n'avons jamais pu comprendre la séparation de l'idée et la forme" ["We have never been able to understand the separation of idea and form"]. Both Flaubert and Pater also deny it vigorously. To discover where Saintsbury derived these extreme notions other than from his own temperament might be useful but is beyond the range of this paper.

It is more important here to note that while this heresy of separation is *not* a necessary concomitant of Art for Art's Sake, nevertheless it derives logically from an extreme emphasis upon form. The reasoning is this: if form is all-important, it must be tangible, real, and hence "separably intelligible." The next step is to regard style as something separately aimed at, to be achieved even with inferior or uncongenial matter, and therefore almost an entity in itself. Form thus becomes a pure aesthetic value and the primary value of art. This simple process of deduction is superficial and erroneous, no doubt, but plau-

sible to a mind which lacks a conception of the creative process as truly organic. In this way, I believe, Saintsbury reasoned—he who at the close of life still protests,

> Few things have surprised me more . . . than the objection of some who are not fools, to the separation of Form and Matter in Literature . . . what seems, to me at least, to be one of the necessary axioms of the study of Art and especially of literature.

Saintsbury is the most consistent and extreme practitioner of this theory in the history of criticism. While most critics are content to call attention to form, he endows it with an almost mystical existence. Herein lies his main exaggeration—or distortion—of the Art for Art's Sake theory. (pp. 245-49)

The final stage of the Art for Art's Sake attitude is the application of the aesthetic view to life, the "doctrine of the moment" which was the theme of the famous Conclusion to Pater's *Studies*. The general effect which was produced by this utterance in 1873, the concern Pater felt for the dangers of its influence, and his withdrawal of it in the second edition (1877) are familiar facts. Humphrey Ward (who entered Oxford in 1865) says that his generation received their first understanding of Art for Art's Sake from Pater's essays. Saintsbury knew Pater personally before and after the *Studies* appeared, but he holds that his sympathetic understanding of Pater was facilitated chiefly by their common Oxford background. They met first at the Oxford home of Mandell Creighton who "had considerable sympathy for the aesthetic movement" though "it was to him neither a gospel nor a fashion." Clearly parts of it were a gospel to Saintsbury.

His actual pronouncements on Pater's philosophy of sensation appeared in an essay entirely devoted to Pater in 1906. Here he asserts that Pater's attitude and method may well be applied "in almost the widest ranges of thought and life," with no danger and with "an infinite gain of satisfaction to the soul as well as the senses." This "Paterism" Saintsbury defines as "the perfecting, refining, illuminating of interest in things, . . . an intelligent, but not merely intellectual, *enjoyment* of them all, or as many . . . as your nature makes it possible for you to enjoy." One may exaggerate, caricature, or degrade the idea but in itself it is "a highly respectable, as well as attractive creed." You should have many interests, and they should be

> intensified, purified, ennobled . . . to clear the mind in regard to them of convention and cant; to clear it of confusion and commonplace; to make the flame (in that famous epithet which, with its context, I think he rather unwisely cut out) "gemlike," the essence quintessential, the gold free from alloy.

This philosophy reappears in an unpublished lecture by Saintsbury entitled **"The Sure Foundation"**:

> You will always have, with regret to leave some things untasted; but as long as the Upper Powers permit, you can go on tasting; And if you have prepared yourself properly, your taste will refine and strengthen from year to year and from day to day. The whole world of speech and thought is your province.

In the same spirit Saintsbury modified Arnold's definition of criticism to read "Criticism is the endeavour to find, to know, to love, to recommend, not only the best, but all the good, that has been known and thought and written in the world." Finally this literary epicure elsewhere admits that for him literature is the best means of satisfying the desire "to live with as great and varied an amount of pleasure as possible."

That Saintsbury never carried the "life for art's sake" idea beyond these mild statements is clear. He did not apply it to his conduct and he did not approve the extravagant gestures of the decadents. He was concerned with it as a guide to artistic experience not as a measure of behavior. He failed to see its inadequacy as a philosophy of life. This failure is one with his failure to see the need for some organic relation between one's aesthethic and the rest of one's philosophy. Both things are reflected in his refusal to treat literature as anything but 'pure' art. Its relation to politics, religion, economics, sociology, and so forth, he excluded from his sphere as a historian; as a result he has lost favor and respect as a literary historian. For many judges he fails likewise as a critic because in his desire for beauty of form he often made no demand for greater meaning or wider relevance. He usually praised the best books but often for what seem inadequate reasons or on an inadequate philosophical basis.

The projection of the "life for art's sake" attitude into the decadent "flare" and defiant "pose" of the 'nineties has one convenient symbol, *The Yellow Book*. In 1894 Saintsbury contributed to this periodical an innocuous sketch, **"A Sentimental Cellar."** This apparent identification with the decadents is misleading because Saintsbury suspected the young aesthetes, their extravagance, their paradoxes and posing, and his expressed attitude toward them reveals the limits of his own aestheticism. He had been identified with the movement many years when Wilde's moral perversity brought it into disrepute, and in 1895, the year of Wilde's trial and sentence to Reading Gaol, Saintsbury was in print defending the aesthetic view against a moralistic attack made by Churton Collins:

> . . . the doctrine of art-for-art's sake is neither more nor less cant, or liable to cant than any other doctrine . . . which is capable of being overstrained and misapplied, but which rightly held and intelligently limited contains like most doctrines its portion of truth.

This defense is a qualified one, probably because Saintsbury was now aware of a need to defend the theory not only against the moralist but also against those of its adherents who became its worst enemies. Wilde and his followers had passed the intelligent limits which seemed to him inherent in Pater's conclusion, "the reasonable bounds" within which he believed both Pater and Gautier held it.

Above all Saintsbury demanded sincerity and he saw the 'nineties riddled with literary affectation which is the kiss of death. "We are sitting at the deathbed of one of the great periods of European literature," he says. The symptoms of the fatal disease are:

> the pose of naughtiness . . . the pose of violence; the pose of neo-Bohemianism; the pose of platitude inverted; the pose of distorted form; the pose of attempted mixture of science and literature; the pose of cosmopolitanism. . . .

Recognizable in this list and its context are not merely Wilde and the other English decadents but also Zola, Ibsen, Tolstoi, and Nietzsche, far more important intellectual leaders. The intolerance Saintsbury felt for them shows that his judgment is of little value on any figure belonging to a generation later than his own. It also suggests that he had a very confused notion of what the *fin de siècle* really was and that he thought of it as something quite different from Art for Art's Sake as he meant it. He never followed the theory to its logical conclusions.

But what did he consider to be the "reasonable bounds" of aestheticism? He is never quite explicit, and from the great mass of his work it is possible to produce evidence of almost any kind. Since he wrote so often for the moment, it is perhaps surprising that we find as much consistency as we do. To set over against extreme statements quoted above, there are others less extreme. He says, once, for example, that "art for art *only*" is "at best but a half truth;" again, that the idea of "the moral irresponsibility of the artist" is an "error and a curse"; and, furthermore, that, while purpose may blind an artist, and a quest for "criticism of life" rather than beauty may produce bad poetry or make for its popularity, denial of *all* subject values is worse because art is a means and "means for means' sake only,' if not nonsense, is at any rate sense very incomplete." In one passage he distinguishes between "those who look *first* to form and expression," and "those who look no further, if there be any such." The former group, having evaluated form, admit other values and will concede that "though all does *not* depend upon the subject, yet of two poems equally good in other ways, that which has the better subject will be the better"; that "the greatest poet must have the greatest knowledge of human nature."

These are clearly modifications of the extreme view which Saintsbury, the crusader, had made the almost exclusive theme of his early articles. They do not negate the fact that in his early work he did go the whole way in devotion to form, that he remained unashamed of it, boasted of it at the age of 80, and returned to it again and again. Thus vacillating between the extreme and a more moderate view, contradicting himself and sometimes hedging, he was always conscious of a critical battle into which he felt he must throw himself to uphold the purely literary against the subject-worshippers and ethical critics. He clung to this even in the face of the *fin de siècle* and to the end of his life. In this he is typical of many men of his generation who resented the practical moral Victorian aesthetic, who, when awakened to a new enthusiasm for art by Ruskin, went beyond him to declare the independence of art but who never accepted the "topsyturvification" that the 'nineties bred. Many men like Saintsbury and Pater, no doubt, remained loyal to the ideals of 1866 and 1873.

No limit of evidence could be offered to show that Saintsbury's Art for Art's Sake notions continue as the main tenets of his position, in spite of contradictions and inconsistencies. "Le gout immodéré de la forme" ["The immoderate taste for form"], as Baudelaire called it, mingles with other statements on every page Saintsbury wrote. In 1875 he saw "warrant for accentuating and insisting upon the dogma"; in 1888 he was writing, "If he is a good artist, it does not matter how bad the subject is: if he is a bad artist it does not matter how good the subject is. All ready depends of the treatment." In the light of all his other statements this is no mere aesthetic truism. In 1895 he asked only intelligent limits to the theory, and in 1904 he comments regarding the Art for Art's Sake doctrine:

> . . . it was necessary and it was almost desirable, that the exaggeration should be formulated, because of the incessant intrusion of the opposite theories, which are scarcely even *quarter*-truths, that all depends on the subject—and the like.

In 1926 he describes himself as a "critic who for more than half a century has done his little best to accentuate the importance of treatment over subject."

The three *Scrap Books* (1922-24), the reminiscent jottings of his last years, offer final evidence. Here he says, "We"—the disciples of Art for Art's Sake—praised Baudelaire and Flaubert and ''rejoiced in them because they had followed Art for Art's Sake,'' but ''at the same time because they followed life for life's sake *as well*.'' He is emphatic:

> What we fought against when we carried that banner was the meddling and muddling of the two, the inability to distinguish them. . . . Unless you train yourself to value the art and the form and the literature apart from, though by no means to the neglect of, the matter and the life, you are likely to fall, as the delightful phrase of the Articles has it, into ''wretchlessness of most unclean [critical] living.''

And the veteran critic adds ominously, ''. . . let no one suppose this danger has passed.'' Thus in 1923 the crusade was the same he had joined in 1873. Through fifty years and almost as many volumes runs the creed, at times personal, extreme, fantastic, yet rooted in the Art for Art's Sake Movement. When joined with his oft-repeated view that for poetry at least there is but one supreme criterion, the transporting thrill of pleasure, ''the poetic moment,'' this preoccupation with form marks Saintsbury as an aesthetic critic of an extreme kind. All the major points of the Art for Art's Sake position he maintained: 1) form and style are the primary literary values, the main concern of both artist and critic; 2) ''the kind of literature, as such, is not the kind of ethics,'' for art is an independent realm with its own ends; 3) a record of the individual's reaction or impression is the true criticism; 4) life may, through art especially, become a succession of pleasurable moments finely savored. Among the minor elements of the theory there is in Saintsbury a hint of only one, an aristocratic attitude compatible with the conservatism of a ''Tory-High-Church mind.'' He never embraced the moral revolt of a Wilde, the pessimism of a Baudelaire or a James Thompson, or the union of the aesthetic and the scientific. These are secondary matters. On the main points he spoke clearly, strongly, and often.

The creed of Art for Art's Sake, rooted in Saintsbury's temperamental preference for formal values, offers one sure path through the maze of his thinking. He had an unphilosophic mind and was often inconsistent; yet the creed is omnipresent and it helps make both the man and his influence more understandable. Analysis of it reveals how short was the distance the Victorian mind had to travel in revolt against itself and it shows up a few more landmarks on the road from Ruskin and Arnold through Pater to Wilde.

As for Saintsbury's influence, it may well have been greater and more harmful than has been recognized. Generations of students and readers have accepted his authority; few have paused to challenge his position and prestige, even among those who deplored his inaccuracies. No one has tried to state his position fully. He certainly helped to preserve the dichotomy of matter and form—and indeed widened it. Through the prestige of his unphilosophical appreciative criticism he may have helped to delay the general acceptance of more organic theories of literary aesthetics. His work also has helped pave the way for the acceptance of the dilettantism of Anatole France, Lemaitre, Huneker, Gates, Mencken, and indirectly left a fertile ground for the work of our contemporary formalists, Ransom, Allen Tate, Cleanth Brooks, Ivor Winter, and the rest—much as they would give a ''scientific'' shudder at the suggestion.

It is time to take Saintsbury seriously as a critical influence, to evaluate his inadequacies as well as his gifts. Admitting his contributions to critical literary history and appreciation, recognizing his good taste, commonsense, and buoyant enthu-

siasm, it is well to face the unsound elements of his aesthetic discussed above. Indeed, criticism may do well in 1944 to turn its back upon his method and his spirit, in a world where the roots of civilization are attacked; temporarily at least our world inspires a more functional, organic, even a more ethical attitude toward its arts. And the pendulum is swinging. ''A great writer is a great man writing,'' said Van Wyck Brooks to a Conference on Science, Philosophy, and Religion at Columbia University in September, 1941. ''The value of art is not beauty but right action,'' said Somerset Maugham in 1938. Nevertheless, it is well to examine again and understand our aesthetic forebears. (pp. 254-60)

> Dorothy Richardson, ''Saintsbury and Art for Art's Sake in England,'' in PMLA, Vol. LIX, No. 1, March, 1944, pp. 243-60.

EDMUND WILSON (essay date 1946)

[*Wilson, considered America's foremost man of letters in the twentieth century, wrote widely on cultural, historical, and literary matters. He is often credited with bringing an international perspective to American letters through his widely read discussions of European literature. Wilson was allied to no critical school; however, several dominant concerns serve as guiding motifs throughout his work. He invariably examined the social and historical implications of a work of literature, particularly literature's significance as "an attempt to give meaning to our experience" and its value for the improvement of humanity. Although he was not a moralist, his criticism displays a deep concern with moral values. Another constant was his discussion of a work of literature as a revelation of its author's personality. Related to this is Wilson's theory, formulated in* The Wound and the Bow *(1941), that artistic ability is a compensation for a psychological wound; thus, a literary work can only be fully understood if one undertakes an emotional profile of its author. Wilson utilized this approach in many essays, and it is the most-often attacked element of his thought. However, though Wilson examined the historical and psychological implications of a work of literature, he rarely did so at the expense of a discussion of its literary qualities. Perhaps Wilson's greatest contributions to American literature were his tireless promotion of writers of the 1920s, 1930s, and 1940s, and his essays introducing the best of modern literature to the general reader. In the following excerpt from an essay first published in 1946, Wilson evaluates Saintsbury as the best critic of his time.*]

Saintsbury, since his death, has come more and more to stand out as the sole English literary critic of the late-nineteenth early-twentieth centuries, the sole full-length professional critic, who is really of first-rate stature. He is perhaps the only English critic, with the possible exception of Leslie Stephen, whose work is comparable, for comprehensiveness and brilliance, to the great French critics of the nineteenth century. Unlike them, he has no interest in ideas. In religion he was Church of England and in politics an extreme Tory, but his prejudices were rarely allowed to interfere with his appetite for good literature, wherever and by whomever written. He was probably the greatest connoisseur of literature—in the same sense that he was a connoisseur of wines, about which he also wrote—that we have ever had in English. In this, he stood quite outside the academic tradition. Though he contributed to the *Encyclopaedia* and to *The Cambridge History of English Literature*, he has always more or less the air of a man who is showing a friend the sights of some well-studied and loved locality.

In his *History of English Prose Rhythm,* Saintsbury apologizes for his own prose style; but the truth is that his prose is excellent: the rhythm of his own writing never falters. He had, in fact, invented a style of much charm and a certain significance: a modern, conversational prose that carries off asides, jokes and gossip as well as all the essential data by a very strong personal rhythm, that drops its voice to interpolate footnotes without seriously retarding the current, and that, however facetious or garrulous, never fails to cover the ground and make the points. The extreme development of this style is to be seen in the *History of the French Novel* written in Saintsbury's later years and one of the most entertaining of books on literature. It is all a gigantic after-dinner talk with an old gentleman who, to his immense entertainment, has read through the whole of French fiction. The only other writer I know who has created a style similar to Saintsbury's is the late Ford Madox Ford. Both these men are worth attention as writers because they found out how to manage a fine and flexible English prose on the rhythms of informal speech rather than on those of literary convention.

The *History of the French Novel* could never have been written by a Frenchman, because the books and the writers it deals with have not been organized and grouped as would have been done by a French professor. The literature of France itself has always been so much guided and rationalized by a criticism that was an integral part of it that it falls naturally into a well-ordered historical picture. Saintsbury's critical method had been evolved in connection with English literature, which, with its relative indifference to movements and schools and its miscellany of remarkable individuals, does not lend itself to this sort of treatment. In consequence, he stops a good deal longer over somebody like Pigault-Lebrun or Restif de La Bretonne than the ordinary French historian would. He does not need to make them fit into a scheme; he simply likes to tell you about them; and, since you will probably never read them, you do not mind getting them thus at second hand. Now, with English writing, this leisurely method of merely showing a guest the sights succeeds where other methods are inadequate. It is inevitable for academic surveys, English as well as French, to attempt to systematize, and since the material with which the English ones deal has been produced with a minimum of system, a great deal that is important and valuable is invariably left out or slighted. English surveys are likely to be dull, where French surveys may be stimulating, and are nearly always readable. But Saintsbury is never dull, because he misses no point of interest. He is to be seen at his very best in his studies of the minor nineteenth-century writers in his *Collected Essays and Papers:* such people as Peacock, Crabbe, George Borrow, Hogg, Praed and Barham of *The Ingoldsby Legends*. It is impossible to take care of these writers by subsuming them under some bigger name. Each is unlike anyone else, unique and fully developed; each has to be explored for his own sake. And Saintsbury explored and appraised them as nobody else has done. Though more searching essays than Saintsbury's have been written on some of the greater nineteenth-century writers, it would be true in a sense to say that the full history of English nineteenth-century literature has never been written except by Saintsbury.

Nor did his relish for such lesser figures confuse his view of the greater. He made a few rather queer evaluations, as every good critic does—his almost unqualified enthusiasm for Thackeray and his contempt for *Liaisons Dangereuses;* and it is true, as has sometimes been said of him, that he does not plumb the deepest literature deeply. But at least he has arrived by himself at his reasons for the greatness of the greatest. He never takes merits for granted. If the relative amount of space assigned to the various subjects may not always, in a given book of Saints-

bury's, seem proportionate to their importance, it is likely to be due to the fact that he had, in his career as a journalist, to treat some of the great figures so many times. If you feel, say, that Shakespeare seems slighted in his *History of Elizabethan Literature,* you will find that he has done him magnificently in *The Cambridge History of English Literature;* if Bulwer-Lytton, in some other work, seems to command as much attention as Dickens, you will find Dickens studied on a larger scale and in a more serious way somewhere else.

He had for a long time had some prejudice against Dante and did not read him till rather late in life, when the tastes of many critics would have already formed a closed cosmos; but when he did sit down at last to *La Commedia Divina,* he conceded its greatness at once. It is curious to find this confession cropping up in the history of the French novel, and it is somehow characteristic of Saintsbury that he should be comparing Dante with some novelist of the nineteenth century, and mention incidentally that he puts him at the top of imaginative fiction. For, except in treating books chronologically, as he might arrange wines in his cellar, he has little real interest in history, and social changes tend merely to annoy him because they distract from the enjoyment of literature. The books are on his shelves like bottles, and it is the most natural thing in the world for him to take down a good medieval vintage made from astringent Italian grapes along with a good dry vintage of French nineteenth-century realism. (pp. 306-10)

Edmund Wilson, *"George Saintsbury's Centenary,"* in his Classics and Commercials: A Literary Chronicle of the Forties, *Farrar, Straus and Company, 1950, pp. 306-10.*

RENE WELLEK   (essay date 1965)

[*Wellek is an American critic whose* History of Modern Criticism *(1955-86) is a major, comprehensive study of the literary critics of the last three centuries. Wellek's critical method, as demonstrated in* A History *and outlined in his* Theory of Literature *(1949), is one of describing, analyzing, and evaluating a work solely in terms of the problems it poses for itself and how the writer solves them. For Wellek, biographical, historical, and psychological information is incidental. Although many of Wellek's critical methods are reflected in the work of the New Critics, he was not a member of that group, and rejected their more formalistic tendencies. In the following excerpt, Wellek discusses the merits and limitations of Saintsbury's criticism.*]

Saintsbury became by far the most influential academic literary historian and critic of the early 20th century. His reputation has declined in the decades since his death, but recently an eminent English professor, James Sutherland [see Additional Bibliography], could argue that he is among the four most characteristically English critics, with Dryden, Johnson, and Hazlitt, and a biographical memoir asserts, apparently without fear of contradiction, that "among critics *per se* it is with Sainte-Beuve, and no other that he must be matched" [see Webster entry in Additional Bibliography]. But I am not aware of any extended consideration of Saintsbury's work. What has been written about Saintsbury is either general appreciation by grateful pupils and admirers, who founded Saintsbury clubs even during his lifetime and hailed him as "King Saintsbury," or exasperated dismissals by specialists irritated by his errors and his manner. The sheer bulk and scope of his writings have prevented an adequate discussion. A complete bibliography of Saintsbury's writings buried in the files of periodicals (much of it political journalism and book-reviewing between 1875 and the end of the 19th century) would run to several thousand items. According to his own estimate, a reprint of his works would fill over 100 large volumes. (p. 416)

Saintsbury's enormous reading, the almost universal scope of his subject matter, the zest and zeal of his exposition, the audacity with which he handles the most ambitious and unattempted arguments should be recognized as a great achievement. Not much need be made of the lapses in accuracy and the lacunae in information inevitable in a work produced at such speed and with such amazing facility. It is best not to probe too closely into anything he wrote of Russian, Scandinavian, or even modern German and Italian literature. He wrote on such topics only because the scope of his surveys demanded that he do so. The frequent errors of dates and titles and his almost total neglect of "secondary literature" of a technical kind cannot surprise us. He could not have done what he did, nor have done it on such a scale, without exposing himself to criticism.

In spite of its variety and scope, Saintsbury's work is held together by a few simple principles. He has two very different sets of critical standards: one for poetry and one for the novel. The drama (including Shakespeare) is either assimilated to poetry or dismissed. Saintsbury considers drama only "accidentally literary" and "not, in absolute necessity or theory, a part of literature at all." He took little pleasure in the theater and confesses, late in his life, that "I should not be sorry if I never passed through its doors again . . . The better the play is as literature, the more I wish that I might be left to read in comfort and see it acted with my mind's eye only."

Saintsbury's theory of poetry is akin to Swinburne's and Pater's and their sources: Baudelaire, and possibly Leigh Hunt, De Quincey, Hazlitt, and Lamb. Here he is a radical formalist. He constantly asserts that in poetry "the so-called 'formal' part is of the essence," that subject does not matter much, "though it is all important in prose." He resolutely divorces form from content, manner from matter, and often roundly condemns the subject matter while loudly praising the form. Thus he speaks of the "rubbish and, what is worse, the mischievous rubbish of the meaning of Morris' 'political poems,'" but asserts that this is not the concern of the *literary* critic. He proposes a strange mental experiment: "It must be a singularly feeble intellect and taste that cannot perform an easy dichotomy of metre and meaning. . . . You pour the poison or the ditchwater out; you keep and marvel at, the golden cup. You can refill it, as far as meaning goes at your pleasure with the greatest things." Saintsbury occasionally seems to believe that poetry is pure sound. He tells a story from the *Life* of Tennyson of a "hearer who knew no English, but knew Tennyson to be a poet by the hearing," and calls it "probable and valuable, or rather invaluable, for it points to the best, if not the only true, criterion of poetry." He thus justifies his own interest in prosody, without regard to meaning, and in "style" in his special sense of "the choice and arrangement of language with only a subordinate regard to the meaning to be conveyed." Usually Saintsbury recognizes that form is not completely independent of the subject. But subject in poetry, he argues, is unimportant because it is always the same, a limited repertory of commonplaces: love and life, man's fate, the inevitability of death, the beauties of nature. "The human intellect and the human temper," Saintsbury believes, "reduce themselves to few varieties." Philosophy amounts to a recognition of *vanitas vanitatum*. Saintsbury, in spite of his bounce and breeziness, is at bottom a melancholy pessimist who admires *Ecclesiastes* as

"one of the very greatest books in the world's literature" and is profoundly moved by the "abysmal sadness" of Lucretius. At the same time he feels completely secure in High Church Anglicanism and Tory politics of the extreme Right. The dichotomy between variable form and monotonous content necessarily stunts his insight into the world of intellect and thought and his interest in intellectual history. "Human nature in general is always the same; that which hath been shall be, and the dreams of new worlds and new societies are the most fatuous of vain imaginations." This antihistorical creed goes badly with Saintsbury's great historical learning and tolerance.

In poetry Saintsbury looks always for the "poetic moment," the "single-instant pleasure of image and phrase and musical accompaniment of sound." What matters are "beautiful words," though Saintsbury "does not know and does not believe that anyone knows—however much he may juggle with terms— why certain words arranged in certain order stir one like the face of the sea, or like the face of a girl, while other arrangements leave one absolutely indifferent or excite boredom or dislike." Poetry is ultimately inexplicable, unaccountable, and momentary. That is why he prefers the "multiple, atomic, myrioramic style" of a Tennyson to the "old substantive or structural kind," why he considers Shelley the greatest of lyrical poets and Poe a poet of the very first order. "Perhaps the best and certainly the most compendious definition of poetry" is its success in "making the common as though it were not common." He chides the French for lacking "a sense of the vague, of imagination which goes to make the very highest poetry" and can approve of a saying of John Wilson that "it is not necessary that we should understand fine poetry in order to feel and enjoy it, any more than fine music." The essence of poetry is "in form and colour, suggestion of sound rather than in precise expression and sense."

For a time, in essays on Dante, Milton, and Shakespeare, Saintsbury discussed the "grand style" in an effort to make his poetic theory more precise. But the "grand style" is merely another term for the poetic moment, that "perfection of expression in every direction and kind" which "transmutes the subject and transports the hearer or reader." It is as mysterious as poetry. "You cannot tell how it arises . . . it is truest, precisely because it is the most irresponsible, of the winds of the spirit." In Shakespeare it includes anything which can be picked out as striking, beautiful, and grand: all the *Sonnets* and all the poems, even *Venus and Adonis*, which might seem to us burlesque and sensual rather than grand. In Shakespeare the grand style is ubiquitous though intermittent; in Dante it is "pervading everything and affecting grotesque, extravagance, pedantry"; in Milton it is affectation, though "affectation transcendentalized and sublimed." The "grand style" seems quite unnecessary as a term: we are where we were before. Poetry "communicates an experience of half-sensual, half-intellectual pleasure." "*Why* it does this no mortal can say."

Though Saintsbury wrote the first universal **History of Criticism,** there is, it seems, little room for criticism in his scheme. He comes very near the view that taste is completely personal— as unarguable as the taste in wine or food which he often uses for comparison. Saintsbury appeals to the image of the hydrometer: in poetry we are ourselves the hydrometer and "consequently it is exceedingly difficult to refer matters to any common standard." "This is this to me and that to thee." The reader and the critic decide that a "thing is either poetry or it is not," and there is an end of it. In constant variations Saintsbury defends this retreat to the fortress of personal pleasure, the unpredictability and inexplicable impact of literature. He has no use for the attempts to make criticism science or philosophy. He rejects all theories of causal explanation, all social or political determinism. He laughs that in his youth everything used to be explained by association while today everything is explained "by selection and heredity, evolution and crossing." He disbelieves in "any easily calculable *ratio* of connection between national and literary idiosyncrasy, between political and literary events," and constantly denies that politics mean anything to literature except some excitement in the air or that there is any explanation for the flowering of a particular literature or genre at a particular time. Things literary "move in an orbit of their own" in which there are no predictable laws, continuities, or regularities. There is no decadence, "no death, no cessation in literature. Here the sadness and decay of certain periods is mere fiction." In Saintsbury's favorite quotation, "the wind of the spirit blows where it lists" and "mocks all attempts to foretell the times and seasons of its blowing or to discover the causes why it has blown."

Still, the critic can improve his own sensibility. Though his standard of poetry is obscurely personal and criticism seems to end with a "catalogue of likes and dislikes," Saintsbury sometimes objects to "arbitrary enjoyment and liking" or "mere caprice." Criticism is "an endless process of correcting impressions—or at least of checking and auditing them till we are sure that they are genuine, co-ordinated, and (with the real if not the apparent consistency) consistent." Certain tools for the critic help in elaborating this consistent taste and certain signs warn against aberrations and temptations. Saintsbury demands, first of all, catholicity of knowledge and taste. "The study of widely differing periods, forms, manners, of literature itself" leads to universal tolerance. He constantly rejects the view that there is "something insincere, unnatural, impossible almost in a liking for opposites and things different from each other. I have never been able to share the notion myself or to know why I may not admire A, because I admire B." Complacently, Saintsbury proclaims himself a "critical Pangloss" who has "hardly the slightest desire to alter . . . the literary course of the world," an optimist in literature (though not, we have seen, in life) who takes a "certain delight in reading even the worst books," a veritable library cormorant, a *helluo librorum* who welcomes and accepts almost everything with "an enormous fatalism."

Still, this universal reading cannot be merely passive: it must lead to "comparison" which for Saintsbury is "the one gate and highway to really universal criticism of literature, . . . the strongest, the safest, the best engine of literary criticism altogether." We must cultivate "the constant habit of looking at everything and every writer in conjunction with their analogues and their opposites in the same and other literatures." Saintsbury summarizes his creed in the Conclusion of the *History of Criticism:* the critic "must read, and, as far as possible, read everything—that is the first and great commandment . . . Secondly, he must constantly compare books, authors, literatures indeed, to see in what each differs from each, but never in order to dislike one because it is not the other. Thirdly, he must, as far as he possibly can, divest himself of any idea of what a book *ought to be,* until he has seen what it is." Saintsbury's ultimate critical goal is "an art of appreciation—a reasoned valuing and analysing of the sources of literary charm." He sometimes adds, however, the necessity of judging and ranking the "reasonable distribution of [literary work] into good, not so good, and bad." The final judgment will always

be "enthusiastic appreciation," a criticism of beauties, since negative and positive judgments are set off as

> utterly different in weight and scope. The negative is final as regards the individual; he has a right to dislike if he does dislike, though there may be subsequent questions as to his competence. But it is not in the least final as to the work in question. It is (let it be granted) not good for *him;* it does not follow that it is not good in itself. Now the affirmative carries with it results of a very different character. *This* is final in regard to the work as well as to the reader. That which should be delectable has delighted in one proven and existing case: and nothing—not the crash of the world—can alter the fact. It has achieved— though the value of the achievement in different cases may be different.

In this late passage a recognition of objective value is implied: Saintsbury seems to have abandoned his total impressionism but does not pursue the matter and does not see the consequences of his own position.

Saintsbury believes that all this—universal reading, comparison, appreciation, ranking, and judging—can be accomplished without any recourse to theory. He not only condemns neoclassical rigidity, rules and regulations, principles of kinds, and decorum, but argues in the *History of Criticism* in favor of complete freedom. He not only exalts Longinus' *On the Sublime* as "the greatest critical book of the world" because it takes "the true and only test of literary greatness" to be "the 'transport,' the absorption of the reader," but also avows that there can and should be "critical reading, without theory or with theory postponed." He exposes throughout the *History [of Criticism]* "the error of wool-gathering after abstract questions of the nature and justification of poetry, of the *a priori* rules suitable for poetic forms, of Unities, and so forth," the whole "Laputan *meteorosophia* of theories of poetry." This antitheoretical argument becomes particularly violent when Saintsbury, in his historical context, is compelled to deal with the rise of aesthetics. "Literary criticism," he asserts, "has not much more to do with aesthetics than architecture has to do with physics and geology—than the art of the wine-taster or the tea-taster has to do with the study of the papillae of the tongue and the theory of the nervous system generally."

When the first two volumes of the *History of Criticism* were censured by Croce and Spingarn for neglecting theory and aesthetics, Saintsbury defended himself merely by reasserting his position and defining, too modestly, his own aim. He wanted to give a "simple survey of the actual critical opinions," an "atlas of the actual facts." "The complement of Theory I do not pretend to supply, and I cannot see that anybody has a right to demand it." Croce easily replied that there are no "actual facts" in criticism and quoted *Bouvard et Pécuchet*, whose two doubtful heroes thought it sad that the "historians who pretend only to narrate, actually make choices." But one should recognize that the issue is by no means as clear-cut as the contrast between facts and philosophy would indicate. Saintsbury stumbled into a defense of mere facts; much later he complained that he was not, as Croce charged, "barren of philosophy," but had studied the subject in Oxford, had taken a fancy to scholasticism, and wanted to write a book about it. In practice, Saintsbury surely has a theory and principles of selection, and in the *History of Criticism* is not concerned merely with specific critical opinions. He does not worry about general aesthetics and ignores the implications of literary theories in philosophical attitudes and points of view; but he does constantly discuss theory of literature, poetics, rhetoric, and metrics, and generalizes very freely about periods, trends, schools, and movements in literary history.

The main objection to Saintsbury's work is not his neglect of philosophy or abstract theory or even the extreme individualism of his taste, but the poverty and haziness of his concepts and criteria of genres, devices, style, composition—of all the tools of analysis on the level with which he is professedly concerned. The blatant reliance on moods, whims, and crotchets vitiates such enormous, grandly conceived projects as *The History of English Prosody, The History of English Prose Rhythm,* and, to a lesser extent, *The History of the French Novel.*

The History of English Prosody has no clearly defined premises. Saintsbury speaks for instance, of "longs" and "shorts" but cannot make up his mind whether these terms refer to distinctions in duration or stress. He declares even that "shorts" and "longs" may as well have been called "abracadabra" and "abraxas," though at a later point he admits that his book "(as far as it is not a pure record of the facts) is written against the heresy of making stress the sole and single secret of meter." Saintsbury's convictions on metrical theory are all negative. He rejects the musical prosody of Sidney Lanier and William Thomson as well as the phonetic methods of Verrier, because they have "nothing, or next to nothing to do with those on which we are engaged" but deal with the "raw material only." He objects to Edwin Guest's old *History of English Rhythms* (1838) for denying the foot and worshiping the old Germanic accent. He sees nothing in the concept of counterpoint in metrics, of "an antinomy or antimachy of accent and quantity, of thought-movements and rhythms of language and verse." With these exclusions he is reduced to juggling scansions, agreeing with Swinburne that English is "a language to which all variations and combinations of anapaestic, iambic, or trochaic meter are as natural and pliable as the dactylic and spondaic forms of verse are unnatural and abhorrent." Nothing can be done, even by Saintsbury, with such a loose net of questions except to comment on a series of discontinuous scansions by introducing all kinds of extraneous considerations, which make these three volumes a disguised history of English poetry with special reference to versification, stanza forms, and metrical theories.

The History of Prose Rhythm is equally arbitrary in "granting length sometimes to stress, sometimes to positions and sometimes to other causes still." Saintsbury emphasizes that prose-rhythm consists in "variety" and "divergence" but leaves its essence as obscure as that of meter. If Saintsbury's principle of "variety" were correct, there would be no rhythm at all. But doubtless he was only warning us against the danger of having prose rhythm fall into exact metrical patterns. He can do little more than display hundreds of examples of scansion which assume some meaning only from his marginal comments on style and general tone—matters loosely related to the central topic of prose rhythm.

The History of the French Novel, Saintsbury's last extended work, is generally superior because in writing of the novel he moves beyond his basic poetic theories of the charm of the moment, the glow of individual words, and the sheer music of meter. *The History of the French Novel* is only the highpoint of his voluminous writings on the novel, which from the very beginning of his career applied standards totally different from those with which he judged poetry. "The novel is while the poem is not, mainly and firstly a criticism of life." Saintsbury even admitted that "some of the greatest novels of the world, are, as no one of the greatest poems of the world is, or could possibly be, written anything but well." The novel has "four wheels": "Plot, Character, Description, and Dialogue: Style being a sort of fifth." Saintsbury ordinarily disapproved of ideological intrusions in fiction. "The novel has nothing to do with any beliefs, with any convictions, with any thoughts in the strict sense, except as mere garnishings. Its substance must always be life not thought, conduct not belief, the passions not the intellect, manners and morals not creeds and theories." "The hand of any *purpose*," he repeats in the *History of the French Novel,* "Religious, Scientific, Political, what not, is apt to mummify story." But he is no longer sure that "story" means romance, adventure, and plot. In his earlier writings on the novel Saintsbury had usually sided with the romance, which is "of its nature eternal," while the novel of manners seemed to him "of its nature transitory and parasitic on the romance." He therefore argued against naturalism both in theory and in practice and welcomed enthusiastically the revival of romance late in the 19th century, when Robert Louis Stevenson seemed to promise a return to the adventure story. Saintsbury's enthusiasm for *Morte d'Arthur,* chivalric romances, pastorals, and historical novels à la Dumas père could not be greater. But in some early essays and in the *History of the French Novel* he admits the ideal of realism as "a completed picture of real human life" and contrary to his old rejection of any kind of progress in literature tries to trace the advance of realism from the *fabliaux,* which deserve "the immense praise of having deliberately introduced ordinary life," through the 17th and 18th centuries to Stendhal and Balzac. He even pays some attention to technical matters in the novel, to the relation of *récit* and dialogue, though on the whole he is again unable to analyze what he professes to be concerned with—plot, character, description, dialogue.

The odd result of this inability to use any tools of analysis is that Saintsbury's *History of the French Novel* contains much moralistic comment about the characters in the novels treated as figures in real life and often in deliberately comic or violent terms. Saintsbury would "very much like to have shot Julien Sorel" (in a proper duel, of course). He tells us: "I don't want to meet anybody in (Maupassant's) *Bel-Ami;* in fact, I would much rather not." He calls Emma Bovary "scum of womanhood," and Blanche Amory in Thackeray's *Pendennis* "extremely nice—one would not, I think, marry her except in polygamous and cloistral countries, but that is about all that can be said against her." Saintsbury is indignant about Choderlos de Laclos' *Liaisons dangereuses,* which he calls "prosaic and suburban," though he is not otherwise squeamish and prudish in a Victorian way. He admires Diderot's *La Religieuse* and many things in Crebillon and Restif de la Bretonne. *The History of the French Novel* has been almost completely neglected, even in England, though it contains much knowledge, truthful observation, good description, and some sensitive criticism. The fault is largely Saintsbury's. Like all of his longer histories, the book goes to pieces: it dissolves into an agreeable commentary of an enormously well-read man, sitting in his library, pulling books from his shelves, commenting on this or that passage or character, ranking and grading the books, haphazardly comparing them with others, suggesting historical relationships, and actually stimulating interest, conveying something of his own zest, luring the reader to share in his own enjoyment. Tastes will differ as to the allusive, whimsical style, the funny ferocities, and personal remarks: requesting, for instance, the British Museum to give him one of its three copies of Capriano's *Della Vera Poetica* (Venice, 1555), or pretending that he cannot recognize the gate of Trinity College,

Cambridge ("I cannot tell, I am an Oxford man"). One doubts whether the frequent comparisons with wine and food mean very much. "Charles de Bernard may but stand to Balzac and George Sand as champagne stands to Romanee Conti and to Chateau Yquem," tells us little even if we knew as much about wine as the author of the *Cellar Book* did. Still, Saintsbury achieves his purpose: even in the dull and dreary stretches on ancient or neoclassical criticism and the 17th-century French novel the personality of the speaker, his particular voice, comes through. The image of a fatherly authority, of an omniscient reader, a somewhat crotchety but amiable connoisseur, and a John Bullish, no-nonsense Englishman is established. All this may not have furthered the cause of criticism in the abstract, but it secured Saintsbury a place among the English essayists and the taste-makers.

In spite of his professions of complete catholicity, Saintsbury's taste has well-defined limitations and preferences. There never was so resolutely bookish a critic: he does not care for drama, for painting, or even for music. Poetry, the novel, and criticism are his concern. To list his enthusiasms would be to list almost all of Western literary history. But one should recognize that Saintsbury, for his time, had some unusual preferences: he began in 1875 with an article on Baudelaire that praises the poet as "the most original, and within his limits, the most remarkable of modern French poets" and dismisses the charge of immorality by "deprecating entirely the introduction of such questions into matters of literature." Saintsbury shrewdly observes that "you may write about murder as often as you like, and no one will accuse you of having committed that crime. You may depict an interesting brigand without being considered a thief. Not in either case will you be thought an inciter to either offence. But so soon as you approach the other deadly sin of Luxury in any one of its forms, instantly it appears self-evident that you not only take pleasure in those who do these things but also do them yourself." The actual analysis of Baudelaire's writings falls short of doing more than quoting and selecting, mainly from the *Poems in Prose*. The essay, courageous and lively as it was, also established the pattern of Saintsbury's shortcomings.

Saintsbury's taste for what today would be called baroque is much more clearly defined. In an introduction to an edition of the *Poems* (1896) he concretely describes Donne's "spiritualized worldliness and sensuality . . . the strange regions where sensuality, philosophy and devotion meet," and the characterization of Donne in the *Short History of English Literature* (1898) resumes the theme. "Behind every image, every ostensible thought of his, there are vistas and backgrounds of other thoughts dimly vanishing, with glimmers in them here and there, into the depths of the final enigmas of life and soul. Passion and meditation, the two avenues into this region of doubt and dread, are tried by Donne." The comment on the other metaphysical poets is equally appreciative and well-phrased, and with his edition of the *Minor Poets of the Caroline Period* (3 vols. 1905-21) Saintsbury made accessible a body of difficult and extravagant texts totally condemned by conventional 19th-century taste.

It will be shorter to list some of Saintsbury's exclusions from his Noah's Ark. They are largely confined to modern realism and naturalism, particularly outside of England. He detests the Goncourts but more rationally depreciates Zola. The condemnations of Ibsen and the Russians are quite sweeping and undiscriminating. He recommends "hanging" for Nekrasov, tells us that Dostoevsky is "such as one could have done without,"

and asserts that Tolstoy's novels are "hardly works of art at all," though he makes an exception for "The Death of Ivan Ilyich." At the same time, he praises Thackeray as "the greatest master of artistic realism," professes not to know "a greater novel than *Esmond*," and does not find any *longueurs* in *The Newcomes*.

Saintsbury does not succeed in strictly separating his artistic judgment from ideological or national prejudices and in achieving his ideal of universal learning and personal impression. But one should recognize his great merits as a mapmaker in the *History of Criticism* and as a lively commentator and surveyor of modern literary history, at least of England and France. His influence in the English-speaking academic world has been enormous. His insistence on comparison, on the broad map of Western literatures, on the comparative isolation of literary history from social history, on the necessity of judging is wholly admirable. On the other hand, he strengthened unfortunate tendencies in English criticism of the time: the contempt for theory, the pose of dilettantism, the indulgence in moral, political, religious, and national prejudice. He helped to bring about the situation that reached its nadir before the advent of T. S. Eliot: the loss of standards, coherence, penetration, and critical tools. (pp. 417-28)

> *René Wellek, "The Other English Critics," in his* A History of Modern Criticism, 1750-1950: The Later Nineteenth Century, *Vol. 4,* Yale University Press, *1965, pp. 400-32.*

WALTER LEUBA   (essay date 1967)

[In the following excerpt, Leuba discusses four of Saintsbury's most important works.]

Saintsbury's four major historical works are, in the order of publication, *A History of Criticism and Literary Taste in Europe from the Earliest Texts to the Present Day,* three volumes; *A History of English Prosody from the Twelfth Century to the Present Day,* three volumes; *A History of English Prose Rhythm,* one volume; and *A History of the French Novel,* two volumes. The first of these works is on the largest scale in both substance and time and is, perhaps, his masterpiece; the second, the most instructive, is a detailed application of the great principles of criticism analyzed in the first; the third is the most controversial; and the fourth, the most entertaining. Together, these books are a unique performance in both volume and quality, in the breadth and clarity of the writer's perspective, in the vast range of firsthand experience of the materials dealt with, and in the verve and variety of the presentation. These major works are broadly planned, carefully organized, fully documented, and written in a manner as far from the academic as the writings they discuss. They are written not as projects in research and study, nor as industrious compilations; but, from a full experience of life, they are books to be read and relished. They are intended to stimulate, as much as to satisfy, curiosity; and in no sense do they avoid giving occasion for controversy when such seems fitting to the writer. Saintsbury had sufficient reason to trust his judgment, and his manner made it clear that he did so.

The more than 1,700 pages of the *History of Criticism,* "that epic of literary taste," or "that encyclopaedic work in which the great critics of the past lie embalmed in academic pedantry," published between 1900 and 1904 by William Blackwood of Edinburgh, were the product of Saintsbury's full maturity. Fifty-five in 1900, he had already been professor of rhetoric and English literature for some time; and he also had behind him long years of experience in criticism; in literary and other historical studies; in biography, translation, and editing; in political and other journalism; in reviewing; and in school-mastering. The work considers historically all those writers who have either expressed formally or informally principles or theories of criticism, or have by their practice of criticism implied principles or theory.

In the preface to Volume I, Saintsbury acknowledged the project to the audacious and described it as "an attempt to supply for others," on the basis of more than thirty years of exploration, "the Atlas of which the writer himself so sorely felt the need." Oliver Elton described it as an "immense chronicle, embracing hundreds of authors famous and obscure, classical, French, Italian, German, and English. . . ." Saintsbury had no predecessor in the field as he defined it; and his definition itself not only is unexceptionable but is of the utmost interest to those who prefer reading to more popular kinds of activity. "The Criticism which will be dealt with here," he says on his opening page, "is the function of the judgment which busies itself with the goodness or badness, the success or ill-success, of literature from the purely literary point of view."

> In other words, the Criticism or modified Rhetoric, of which this book attempts to give a history, is pretty much the same thing as the reasoned exercise of Literary Taste—the attempt, by examination of literature, to find out what it is that makes literature pleasant, and therefore good—the discovery, classification, and as far as possible tracing to their sources, of the qualities of poetry and prose, of style and metre, the classification of literary kinds, the examination and "proving," as arms are proved, of literary means and weapons, not neglecting the observation of literary fashions and the like.

And, in the preface to Volume III, he adds:

> A friend who is at once friendly, most competent, and of a different complexion in critical thought, objected to me that I "treat literature as something by itself." I hastened to admit the impeachment, and to declare that this is the very postulate of my book. That literature can be *absolutely* isolated is, of course, not to be thought of; nothing human can be absolutely isolated from the general conditions of humanity, and from the other functions and operations thereof. But in that *comparative* isolation and separate presentation which Aristotle meant by his caution against confusion of kinds, I do thoroughly believe.

These ideas and the implied approach to literature are central to Saintsbury's histories and to his writing generally. He was clearly aware of the risks. In the second volume in the final chapter, in which he reviews "The Balance-Sheet of Neo-Classicism," he said that "it is still (1902) the very rarest thing to find a critic who, by equipment or even by inclination, is himself disposed to take a really catholic view of literature; and those who do endeavour to take such a view are constantly regarded with distrust by the general, and with a rather comic rancour by specialists." "In approaching a critic," Elton wrote, "Saintsbury asks what are his working principles, or *media axiomata,* what light they throw on literature, and how literature itself confirms or refutes them." Such is Saintsbury's position; and nothing in his entire work, apart from his manner of writing or "style," has been the source of more objection.

Two formidable critics, both otherwise favorable, must be mentioned. Joel E. Spingarn found Volume II of *History of Criticism* "an important contribution to modern scholarship in the field of critical history." He noted Saintsbury's "impressionistic method and his keen personal prepossessions" and his "aggressively romantic" sympathies. Yet, he added, in the "lack of philosophic unity and co-ordination, and in its neglect of recent research in the same field—it [the work] misses the touch of finality." I would guess that this "touch of finality," whatever it may be in anything but the very highest ranges of verbal expression, is still far to seek. Benedetto Croce discovered Saintsbury to be "equally skilled in literature and innocent of philosophy," and he characterized the three volumes of the *History of Criticism* as "instructive in many ways but [as] wholly deficient in method and definite object." The point is that Saintsbury deliberately excluded any discussion of "metaphysical aesthetic and other manifestations whose interaction and development are the fabric of history itself."

Saintsbury was "innocent of philosophy" only in the sense that George Berkeley was. His mind worked on the data furnished by his senses and on nothing else. As to deficiency in method, it is enough to point out that his methods, clearly described in prefaces and elsewhere, always included, or directed the reader to, the evidence for his assessments. This practice is not always that of theorists. And what Croce meant by "definite object" was known only to himself.

In 1944 Dorothy Richardson was echoing the same or similar complaints [see excerpt above]. Saintsbury "had an unphilosophic mind." But how do we determine the presence or absence of a philosophic mind, which I take to be something different from being a philosopher, a title Saintsbury never claimed? There is plenty of evidence in his work, certainly, that he had read and comprehended the philosophers from Plato to Nietzsche. There must, therefore, be something more to this term. Miss Richardson ws reasonably clear as to what she desiderated in the historian of literature, for she said of Saintsbury that the relationship of literature "to politics, religion, economics, sociology, and so forth, he excluded from his sphere as a historian; as a result he has lost favor and respect as a literary historian." I assume that the presence of these "relativities" in his work makes a writer acceptably philosophic.

What really troubles the experts and the philosophers is Saintsbury's ubiquitous "pleasure principle"—it would seem that the serious intellectual world, then and still, is more puritanical than it knows. What is it that makes literature pleasant, and therefore good? I, too, take it to be the purpose and the whole purpose of the criticism of literature to provide the answer to this question in each specific instance under consideration. To believe this aim in no way minimizes the value—the varied values—of a book. There is doubtless much else besides pleasure to be found in books, even in books that are literature; but, in the long run, nothing matters but the delight they continue to give. If the vitality of delight fades from them, what is left is food for worms, real or analogical.

Volume I of the *History of Criticism* deals with Classical and medieval criticism; Volume II, with the Renaissance "to the decline of eighteenth century orthodoxy"; and Volume III, with modern criticism; "present day" in the general title is taken to mean "to 1900." The volumes are broken down into books and the books into chapters; and the books themselves are followed by an interchapter in which the writer surveyed and commented upon general aspects of the material in the preceding book. As may be deduced, the *History [of Criticism]* "was a task of unimaginable difficulty, long neglected and often shirked, on a subject not in favour, anything but promising, and largely unexplored. It involved Greek, Latin, Italian, French, Spanish, and German as well as English." As A. Blyth Webster has said, quoting W. P. Ker: "there are hardly words available to praise the heroism of the undertaking" [see Additional Bibliography].

Most readers, those who have read rather than "examined" or used these volumes, have formulated similar impressions; and they have also found, as Webster did, that the work "cleared up large parts of the past, brought light to dark places of literature, and supplied some chapters of the *History of Human Error.*" [see Additional Bibliography]. And it proved, once and for all, Saintsbury's scholarship; however "apt to be cavalier" was his attitude to "ancillaries and to other aims," his scholarship was far broader and sounder than could be found elsewhere among his generations of contemporaries. Elton called the work "his widest and lengthiest contribution to learning" and added that, though it is "indeed, on the lengthy side" and "has had many critics . . . no one has tried to do the work again."

In the course of the three volumes Saintsbury considers chronologically each Classical and European critic of literature and each theorist of literary criticism. He summarizes and illustrates, by paraphrase and quotation, their views, judgments, and basic position in the history of criticism. These views, judgments, and theories he assesses historically in the light of the critic's experiences and times and in the context of their relevance to the literature from which they were derived, indicating the "taste" upon which they were founded or which they originated or encouraged. Each critic's relative contribution to the history of criticism is appraised, and his work is compared in its validity and influence with that of his predecessors and contemporaries. For the first time, a vast body of critical thinking is organized chronologically, placed in historical perspective, and judged. The major critics, from Aristotle to Coleridge and beyond, gain by this long historical perspective and by the careful analysis of the many minor figures who preceded, accompanied, or followed them. The result is a panoramic view of Western criticism and taste that is enlivened by copious and diverting allusion and reflection. Primary and secondary sources are carefully documented.

The *History [of Criticism]* remains a magnificent one; not, perhaps, in its language, though that is always fresh and idiosyncratic, but certainly in its ordering and presentation of a tremendous amount of detailed information, and in its analysis, comparison, and estimate of this information by an independent, sensitive intelligence. The reading may be "rough going" to some tastes, but anyone who notices the title pages should be aware that he is not embarking on a simple voyage and that the material itself will require serious, though far from deadly serious, attention. A faithful reading of the entire work gives the reader at least one unmatched perspective on what is civilized in Western civilization.

At the request of his publishers, Saintsbury later prepared a revision, adaptation, and supplementation of the English chapters of the *History of Criticism* that was published as a single volume in 1911. Another outgrowth of the larger history was, through the suggestion of Charles Mills Gayley, then of the University of California, the provision for an American publisher of a volume of serviceable extracts in English from the critics themselves. With the exception of those from Aristotle, which Saintsbury adapted from existing translations, all the translations from Classical and foreign authors were his own.

In a passage in his *Short History of English Literature,* discussing the work of Henry Hallam, one of his few predecessors in English, Saintsbury remarked "the strange slowness . . . with which English criticism mastered the comparative method" and the consequent limitations of Hallam's literary criticism, particularly in his *Introduction to the Literature of Europe.* And he went on to say: "For Hallam came a little too early to avail himself of that rediscovery of its earlier treasures which every nation in Europe made as a consequence of the Romantic movement; he was very partially in sympathy with that movement; and though he could understand he could not love—a nearly fatal disqualification for a literary critic or even a literary historian." The next big work Saintsbury produced, the three volume *History of English Prosody,* is incontrovertible evidence that he himself had no such disqualification.

The [*History of English*] *Prosody* reviews historically the prosodists and the prosodic practice of poets writing in English, relates theory and practice to the character of English verse, and assesses the comparative contribution of each. Though Saintsbury could not write a line of poetry himself and knew it, of all literatures it was the poetry, of which he was "an unsatiated and insatiable lover," that enraptured him most; and he had a flawless ear for its presence in six or more languages. Further, as a critic, he could account for the operations of poetry on the mind and on the imagination without in any sense pretending to account for its creation in the first place.

George N. Shuster's observation that "it is true that the author of *A History of English Prosody* has a good many blind spots, that his system of scansion is a bit elementary, and that he can be willful, careless, and eccentric," is almost a stereotype of the "qualified" appreciation of Saintsbury's work. Yet Shuster is eminently right despite his vocabulary when he proceeds to say: "yet it seems to me that nobody else has sensed so well the marvelous unity of English verse or has been so willing to objectivize his own responses to the beauty of a line or image."

The *History of English Prosody,* is, therefore, a brilliant record of Saintsbury's lifelong delight in the English Muse. His was love at first sight and love lasting, and nothing if not critical. The volumes almost burst with life and learning, but the detailed perceptions and discriminations, the analyses of specific phrases, lines, and passages, the glosses, and the comparative assessments of each poet's prosodic practice give the *History* its irresistible interest for every reader to whom poetry is, as it was to Saintsbury, Parnassus itself. Poetry is not for those who can "take it or leave it," nor has it ever been anything but an uncomfortable subject of instruction or research. Self-important critics and readers have always been a little ill at ease with Saintsbury's eclecticism and immediate embrace; they have found in these volumes much to quibble about, object to, disagree with, and regret. They are protected from Saintsbury's contagious delight and annoyed by his oceanic knowledge.

Amy Lowell, an intensely "prosy" poet, faced with the [*History of English*] *Prosody,* illustrated the extreme form of this rejection by describing Saintsbury as academic and unintelligent. Saintsbury was unduly modest and he would probably have agreed "that there are many things about poetry which the eminent professor had not plumbed." Miss Lowell, however, *had* plumbed; and she is unlikely to return to the surface. But George Sampson briefly expressed a far more reasonable and typical view in his *Concise Cambridge History of English Literature.* He called the [*History of English*] *Prosody* "the standard and necessary treatise, delightful to read and delightful even to differ from . . . with its wealth of illustration and *obiter dicta*.'' And it *was* differed from, though chiefly on the technical side, in the matter of prosodic systems.

The two previous attempts at a history of English prosody—one by William Mitford in 1774 (much expanded in 1804), and the other by Edwin Guest in 1836-38—were both generously dealt with in the *History of English Prosody*. Neither work bears, however, the least resemblance to the book Saintsbury produced. His purpose was to examine ''through at least seven hundred years of verse, what the prosodic characteristics of English have actually been, and what goodness or badness of poetry has accompanied the expression of those characteristics.'' He went on to say: ''I believe I have read nearly all the printed stock of English verse before 1600; and I know that I have read every poet of the slightest repute since that date, and a great number of poets who neither have nor deserve any.'' And he added in a footnote: ''As these statements are sometimes misunderstood, I may perhaps be allowed to say that this is not in the least a boast, but merely a guarantee. That it should be superfluous, I quite admit: whether it is, I leave those who know to judge.''

The book is ''a history of prosodic study as well as of prosodic expression.'' On the technical subject of prosody, Saintsbury not only took issue with most of his predecessors, who generally applied theory to convenient verse rather than derived theory from available verse; but Saintsbury found that a great many of his contemporaries and successors just as emphatically took issue with him. What to me is most curious is that, though the subject of prosody is, as Saintsbury himself acknowledged, a ''fair field full of *fighting* folk,'' there should be so much argumentative interest in the technical aspects of verse and in theories of meter, stress, quantity, etc. Saintsbury, to the annoyance of almost all prosodic specialists, took as usual a common-sense view of the matter: he trusted his ear; and he never forgot that ''the Rule comes from the Work, not the Work from the Rule.''

There is no mystery to Saintsbury's view; he did not explain the inexplicable: ''the central idea'' of the book was ''that feet or 'spaces' are the integers, the grounds, the secret, of English prosody.'' And as he proceeded to deal, in 1,548 pages, with the whole of English verse from the Canute Song to Walt Whitman and Robert Bridges, it was the ''foot'' all the way, with, finally, at the end of the third volume, a solid defense of his findings in a series of appendices, the first of which answered clearly and explicitly the question ''What is a Foot?'' (pp. 29-37)

Saintsbury's book is called, and it is, a *History of English Prosody*; but it is also the most encompassing and penetrating kind of history of English poetry itself because of its multitude of representative quotation and because of the comparative prosodic analyses of them. It is regrettable if the word *prosody* in the title holds off any reader, for in these volumes the actual treasures of English verse themselves show forth the prosody; and the theorists who accompany these treasures are for the most part, in the light cast by Saintsbury's wit and enthusiasm, both amusing and instructive.

Saintsbury had produced, in addition to his professional work at Edinburgh and much miscellaneous editing and prefacing, one volume of a major work every two years since 1900. *A History of English Prose Rhythm* in 1912 was the seventh, and there were three more volumes to come—one on the eighteenth century and two on the French novel. In a note to the preface

of the *Prose Rhythm*, Saintsbury emphasized that ''this attempts only to be a *History of English Prose Rhythm*, illustrated by examples from writers greater and lesser—not a *History of English Prose Style* generally.'' And, as in his earlier histories, he disclaimed any consuming interest in theory, wishing ''chiefly to bring out the *facts* of this interesting and much neglected matter; and to indicate the additional delectation which attends the study of them.'' He proposed to proceed ''by the application of the foot-system—that is to say, by studying the combinations of the two great sound-qualities which, for my part, I call, as my fathers called them from the beginning, 'long' and 'short,' but which you may call anything you like, so long as you observe the difference and respect the grouping. . . .''

Although the actual foot-scansion in the *Prosody* stimulated considerable controversy and much downright disagreement as to the nature of English verse, it nevertheless had a traditional basis that made it generally acceptable to the majority of readers, even without Saintsbury's technical defenses of it both in the history and in the prosodic [one-volume version, *An Historical Manual of English Prosody*]. The application of foot-scansion to English prose, however, was far more of a novelty; and although its logic and reasonableness, its consonance with the facts, were brilliantly demonstrated, there were few among those interested who could accept Saintsbury's method of analyzing how the effects of characteristic prose specimens were achieved. There was some quarrel with, and much gratitude for, the many actual examples contained in the book and for the sensitive characterizations of styles.

''The first history of the theme,'' Elton wrote of the [*A History of English*] *Prose Rhythm*, ''it furnishes a multitude of scanned and commented examples, and of nice analyses and judgments.'' But, he added, ''it is a history and a body of criticism rather than a theory. . . .'' In the same essay Elton pointed out that ''Professor Saintsbury, like many others, uses quantity-marks in scanning English, though he carefully avoids dogmatizing on the physics or physiology of the question.'' And again: ''Can we thus throw light on the special rhythm, the distinctive beauty or pleasure, furnished by different writers or by different sorts of prose? Professor Saintsbury's *History* is one long effort to discriminate such effects and to find words for them. He has much that is new to teach, and he will sharpen many impressions that were dim before, if indeed they were present to us at all.''

The ''physics or physiology of the question'' has occupied many critics and investigators before and since; but deeper, more perspicacious insights into English prose have been lacking. ''The scientific study of English prose rhythm, despite the very complete and provocative history devoted to it by Professor Saintsbury,'' wrote Herbert Read, ''is still very much in its infancy.'' ''What is a complete rhythm,'' he asks, ''what constitutes its essence, why once begun does it continue for a definite course and come to an appointed end? This is the question which Professor Saintsbury did not ask himself, and it is, indeed, perhaps the most difficult question in the whole complex of English prose style.''

These are the kinds of questions Saintsbury avoided as he avoided fools, for they are not even ''scientific.'' He had no quarrel with, though he had little admiration for, the ''scientific'' investigation itself of such matters, so long as no claims were made to explain the inexplicable, or to recommend measurements and formulas as substitutes for ears and eyes. With respect to ''sound-photography'' and other mechanical devices and gadgets for investigating prose and poetry, the procedure, he says,

> may tell us something about the physical-psycholog-
> ical characteristics of the individual experimenting,
> or being experimented upon. It may provide fresh
> material for that individual's dossier, to be registered
> and stored by a new Government Department. But
> on no passage of Chaucer or of Swinburne, of Malory
> or of Ruskin, can it shed the very dimmest light as
> to its structure, arrangement, or rhythmical quality.
> The results of the machinery remain as remote from
> literature as the machinery itself; while, even as re-
> gards these results, the tyranny of individuality re-
> tains its scornful predominance. Each intelligent ob-
> server, patient, subject, or whatever he is to be termed,
> can whisper to himself, "At the next examination,
> if I choose, I can upset my record utterly."

What the senses, controlled and cultivated by mind and ex-perience, tell us may be, after all, false; but it *can* be true. When science validly contradicts experience, the senses will, if we are not idiotic, adjust accordingly, but science cannot tell us *what* to experience.

Further, the flaw in all mechanical attempts to analyze the prose rhythms of English writers by vocalizing their words lies in the fact that writing and speech are not identical; and, whereas a good piece of written prose is unlikely to make any voice worse than it is, the human voice can rarely do even approx-imate justice to such prose as delights the inner ear directly from the printed page. Neither rhythm nor the silent sounds of words can be transferred into the audible without the destruc-tion of the subtleties proper to them, although by means of trained voices *other* subtleties proper to speech may take their places.

The main objections to **Prose Rhythm** stemmed not only from the absence in the book of any recognition of the value of other possible approaches to the subject, but also from Saintsbury's considered rejection of existing differences of approach. He proclaimed merely that "as the essence of verse-metre is its identity (at least in equivalence) and recurrence, so the essence of prose-rhythm lies in variety and divergence." And again: "As in reference to *Prosody,* so in reference to *Prose Rhythm,* I disclaim, detest, abominate, and in every other English and classical form renounce, the attempt to show how a prose-harmonist should develop his harmony. But I hope that I may perhaps have shown, and may now show farther, how the harmonists of the past have developed theirs." That aim was his full purpose. He staunchly refused to recognize a "scien-tific" examination of *literature as literature,* or any other ex-amination that by-passed or ignored the principal reason for its existence: its appeal to the mind and the emotions of a reader, whatever his interests, stands on the basis of a shared humanity. Saintsbury by no means dismissed the use of lit-erature as material for the exploration of non-literary elements, sociological, historical, psychological, or philological; he drew the line only when the discoveries of such explorations were used to *explain,* or even to *describe,* the literature. Since Saints-bury's day this procedure has become, as he foresaw, more and more common, more and more *de rigueur;* and the public that reads the Classics has dwindled until it consists mainly of students upon whom they are imposed and of the tyrants them-selves, the teachers, the scholars, the experimenters, and the theses-writers. The question as to who benefits from this ap-proach remains unanswered, unless we accept the fact that the beneficiary is that amorphous and less and less culturally sig-nificant *recitativo secco* called "the world of learning."

Some critics have preferred exclamation over the indisputable quantity of Saintsbury's reading to a recognition of his obvious, unique mastery of his subjects. That mastery is nowhere more evident than in the histories we have been considering and in the ones to come.

The Peace of the Augustans, A Survey of Eighteenth Century Literature as a Place of Rest and Refreshment is usually included with the previously discussed histories as the penultimate of Saintsbury's major works. Major it is, but it is not a history in the sense that the other books are, nor does Saintsbury call it one. It is what the title and subtitle imply: an extended and completely idiosyncratic survey of eighteenth-century English writers in their time and place, and in their roles as contributors to the rest and refreshment of a thoroughly independent scholar now in his seventies. Saintsbury himself modestly says in the preface that "he has given the usual *History of Eighteenth Century Literature* with a difference." And this *difference* is unique. It is an unusual book, unlike any other of his own or other men's. It bulges with the kind of enthusiasm that is rare even in youth, with unexpected judgments favorable and un-favorable, and with infinite sidelights, digressions, and reflec-tions on "matter and thought and temperament." A beautiful book, it is by far one of the best works extant about a century that has interested modern writers as much as any. Originally published by George Bell & Sons in 1916, in 1946 it was thought worthy of inclusion in the Oxford World's Classics where it carries a curiously qualified "Introduction" By H.J.C. Grierson, who took over from Saintsbury at Edinburgh in Oc-tober, 1915, the date affixed to Saintsbury's original preface.

Grierson is far from unappreciative of his predecessor—"for no critic was ever more human, less pedantic," he says; and "the book has all the characteristics of Saintsbury's literary criticism—the extraordinary gusto with which he wrote of whatever gave him pleasure, unabated by years and indeed brought into clearer relief from the fact that he is dealing with a period some aspects of which he thoroughly enjoyed while of one of its special glories in its own eyes he was, with the best will in the world, *not* a whole-hearted admirer." Yet Grierson spends most of the space at his disposal in drawing the prospective reader's attention to Saintsbury's limitations, to "two characteristics which explain its [Saintsbury's criti-cism] attractiveness to many readers and to some indicate cer-tain limitations." It is difficult to see that the first of these indicates "certain limitations": "literature was for him one, if poetry perhaps the chief, of the good things this world has to give us. He judged it simply and frankly by the pleasure which it gave him, as he judged of wine and food." That estimate sounds a bit as if Grierson were addressing a seminary.

The second characteristic, "Saintsbury's doctrine of the form, and the form only," although Grierson holds it to be "in the main incontestable," is, at length, oddly misrepresented in this Introduction. In the first place, Saintsbury neither believed in nor exemplified in actual practice any doctrine of "the form, and the form only." What Saintsbury reiterates throughout his critical work is merely that form is *primary;* that it clothes substance and makes it art; that the appreciation or disapproval of substance is irrelevant to the consideration of the quality of literature *as* literature, of the quality of poetry *as* poetry; and that it is the *form* the substance takes, or is given, that reveals the quality, if any, of the work under consideration. "Art for art's sake," as a notion, may have sheltered disorganized minds and small abilities at one time or another. That is no reflection on the viewpoint itself, which is the only possible one even for propaganda, even for didacticism and polemic, if it is to be art. Such a viewpoint is *necessary,* moreover, to the critical mind. The writer may completely reject it, or he may be quite unconcerned with or unconscious of it in his preoccupation with entirely other purposes and objects. To judge what he accomplishes *as a writer,* however, it does not do merely to be in or out of sympathy with his purpose or object. The form of his accomplishment is primary to the judgment, and it must be examined and assessed. In the process, substance or subject matter is *not* excluded, as any page of Saintsbury's will demonstrate; it is simply kept separate to whatever extent is possible. In the greatest art, the union of form and substance is perfect and absolute. *The Peace of the Augustans* is a superb illustration of this critical process; and there again Saintsbury in his Preface, explains what should be self-evident—were critics not so often more interested in theory than in fact. Eight years later he once more touches upon the subject briefly in an essay on **"Early Twentieth Century Literature":** "When the force is only in the matter it may not exactly lose all its power, but certainly finds that power what the financial people call 'a wasting asset'."

That the idea of "art for art's sake" can still produce exercises in muddled pedantry and passionate protest is evidence that the genuine artist is still an unwelcome phenomenon. Perhaps the confusion will never be cleared, though it is hard to see that there is a real problem here. We know, surely, that the artist is in one or another position with regard to his materials; they compel him, or he compels them. In the first case, he cannot be said to have any purpose beyond obedience to the mute demands of the substance with which he works: ideas, words, sound, movement. Whatever the realized quality and the fate of his work, this situation is plainly "art for art's sake." In the second case, we have to ask the artist *why* he is imposing himself on the materials, and to this question there can be many answers. He may like the struggle: this may be called pedantry. He may be bent on making himself feel important, victorious: this is vanity, and dangerous. Or he may wish to impress his friends or the public: this, at one end of the scale, is compromise; at the other, degradation.

Or to state the case another way: to the best of our insights and abilities, we show our respect for all that is external to us by careful and accurate recognition of it in its character and particularities, by an honorable confrontation of the world that has made and is making us. And we then respond boldly, freely, and securely to its demands. This is the artist's view, whether conscious or instinctive; and his art is consequently for "art's sake." For the rest of us, his art is merely there, a voluntary offering. The contrary view supports the inordinate cherishing of ourselves to the exclusion of all that might disturb us; so that what we do, as artists, is for our own comfort, prestige, and success. This is art for our own sakes, however it may be disguised as for the sake of others.

The Peace of the Augustans remains a constant delight to anyone interested in the great figures of eighteenth-century literature; and, along with the great, the reader's appetite is whetted for a host of minors of whom he may have known only what held him off from them. "The mood is given," wrote A. Blyth Webster, by, among other things, "the fact that for combination of humour, wisdom, melancholy, and manliness his absolute admiration and whole-hearted assent go to Swift, to Fielding, to Johnson, and to them alone. . . ." (pp. 39-46)

If Saintsbury was not "a wholehearted admirer" of the eighteenth century, the reader is scarcely aware of it. There were in its writers an astonishing variety of achievements to excite his enthusiasm—and innumerable corners from which his exploring mind brought forth delightful, amusing, and curious material. And, when it was necessary to condemn, he did it with a vigor, grace, and justness that made it as stirring in its way as his praise. On the great figures—Johnson, Fielding, Swift, and Pope—Saintsbury exhibited at its best that at once delicate and robust skill perfected by a lifetime of practice. He had a ranging splendor of recognition and appreciation that speaks of these men as they are and extenuates nothing. The most disagreeable of critics would find it hard to justify any serious disagreement, and only a sluggish mind could fail to enjoy the book and benefit by the enjoyment.

That once wicked phenomenon with a thousand-year history, the French novel, provided Saintsbury with the substance of the last of his big works, *A History of the French Novel (to the Close of the 19th Century)*. It came out in two volumes in 1917-19, and it was his "farewell to literary history, and a superbly generous installment, and sample of his method." Saintsbury was in his seventies, and his subject was "one with which I can at least plead almost lifelong familiarity." He opens his preface as follows:

> In beginning what, if it ever gets finished, must in all probability be the last of some already perhaps too numerous studies of literary history, I should like to point out that the plan of it is somewhat different from that of most, if not all, of its predecessors. I have usually gone on the principle (which I still think a sound one) that, in studying the literature of a country, or in dealing with such general characteristics of parts of literature as prosody, or such coefficients of all literature as criticism, minorities are, sometimes at least, of as much importance as majorities, and that to omit them altogether is to risk, or rather to assure, an imperfect—and dangerously imperfect—product.
>
> In the present instance, however, I am attempting something that I have never, at such length, attempted before—the history of a Kind, and a Kind which has distinguished itself, as few others have done, by communicating to readers the *pleasure* of literature. I might almost say that it is the history of that pleasure, quite as much as the history of the kind itself, that I wish to trace. In doing so it is obviously superfluous to include inferiorities and failures, unless they have some very special lesson or interest, or have been (as in the case of the minorities on the bridge of the sixteenth and seventeenth centuries) for the most part, and unduly, neglected, though they are important as experiments and links. We really do want here—what the reprehensible hedonism of Mr. Matthew Arnold, and his submission to what some one has called "the eternal enemy, Caprice," wanted in all cases—"only the chief and principal things." I wish to give a full history of how what is commonly called the French Novel came into being and kept itself in being; but I do not wish to give an exhaustive, though I hope to give a pretty full, account of its practitioners.

Saintsbury took "novel" to include "not only the prose books, old and new, which are more generally called 'romance,' but [also] the verse romances of the earliest period." He began with the *Chanson de Geste* and closed, more than a thousand generous pages later, with Catulle Mendès. And throughout most of the first volume he provided his own translation of illustrative passages from the verse and prose romances and novels under consideration.

The result is, to some tastes, the most delightful of his books. The critical and comparing eye is as watchful as ever, and "that enthusiasm, with its train of half-humorous and wholly admirable hyperboles," is more richly present than ever before. Elton called the *History* a "commentary upon the French genius that is not excelled in its union of range with flexible sympathy." One might like to know in what book or books it is even remotely equaled.

Few of us could possibly read the library of French literature with such relish as Saintsbury read it, yet the pleasure in what of it is read is immeasurably increased and heightened, both in retrospect and in anticipation, by his lavish historical and comparative account of the total. The *French Novel* is the sole comprehensive resource for English readers interested in the subject. A critical reader of "fiction" in a foreign language, from the *fabliau* to Zola, with such an appetite as Saintsbury's is unlikely to have a successor; and he had no predecessor. Such a reader would be even more unlikely to have Saintsbury's astonishing grasp of comparison and contrast in half a dozen literatures and languages. This detailed acquaintance with all varieties of French writing, together with comparable familiarity with Classical and other modern literatures, gives the *History of the French Novel* its interpretive depth along with its obvious surface vivacity and extraordinary range of reference and allusion. I know of few books more amusing to read, and the reader who wants a controlled and intelligible perspective on the kinds of "fictions" produced by the imagination of man has no other equally instructive and delightful source to go to.

The work met with the usual criticism from both specialists and cranks and, of course, there were those occasional errors of fact, omissions, and confusions which, in such herculean in-gatherings, Saintsbury himself—and every reasonable person—expected. The ability to correct mere error of fact is in everyone's hands. Saintsbury wrote no books of reference, although most of his larger works were constantly used as such. But what is more to the point, he was rarely, if ever, wrong in his descriptions and assessments; and he himself freely admitted reasonable differences of opinion in areas of taste and preference. With his own eye on the subject, he was content to invite the reader's eye to it.

In the *French Novel* Saintsbury gave more than six detailed pages to the brothers Goncourt, and he selected *Germinie Lacerteux* for a brief summary of the story. His conclusions, based on the novels, the brothers' theories of Naturalism, and their *Journal* were negative. He found *Germinie* "untouched and unconfirmed by the very slightest art; as destitute of any aesthetic attraction, or any evidence of artistic power, as the log-books of a common lodging-house and a hospital ward could be." He cited a few details from the *Journal* and described it as "being saturated, larded, or whatever word of the kind be preferred, with observations on the taste, intellect, and general greatness of the MM. de Goncourt, and on the lamentable inferiority of other people, etc., etc. If it could be purged of its bad blood, the book would really deserve to rank, for substance, with Pepys's diary or with Walpole's letters."

This estimate is cited at some length because it is dismissed by a partisan writer in these words: "Even in Professor Saintsbury's enormous and catholic survey of the French novel," Ernest Boyd wrote of the Goncourts, "they receive a few intolerant paragraphs, in which indignation takes the place of criticism and historical perspective." This statement is not so; the clash is one of taste, not of judgment. Saintsbury saw more

or less just what Boyd saw in the Goncourts. The difference is that, with a genuine "historical perspective," Saintsbury did not regard their work as literature. Boyd's perspective was that of 1925—and since then far grubbier works than those of the Goncourts have been celebrated.

There were numerous other criticisms of a similar kind: writers such as Hugo who were held in disesteem in some quarters were therefore overrated by Saintsbury; and there were writers who had come into temporary fashion to whom Saintsbury inexcusably did not do justice. Despite such expected carping, the *French Novel* was more widely read than the earlier histories; the subject was of more general interest, and there was no competitive treatment in either French or English.

Saintsbury also wrote a book on *The English Novel,* an historical study of its development from its "foundation in romance" to William Morris. It preceded the volumes on the *French Novel* and appeared in 1913 in a series, "The Channels of English Literature," in which that literature is treated by categories: epic and heroic poetry, lyric poetry, essays and essayists, historians and schools of history, etc., each by a different authority.

Saintsbury's volume, oddly enough, was the first in English to deal with such a subject and, as good a book as it is, one may regret that he did not have the freedom to deal, as he wished, with the English novel at length and in the manner in which he was subsequently to deal with the French. As it is, in addition to fulfilling its purpose admirably, the book is full of the expected good things. This one, for example: "just as the excessive desire to be *like* all the best models is the note of Classical decadence, so the excessive desire to be *unlike* everything else is the note of Romantic degeneration." Or, from among many others, is this statement about Jane Austen: "The value of her, artistically, is of course in the perfection of what she did; but the value of her historically is in the way in which she showed that, given the treatment, any material could be perfected." (pp. 48-52)

Walter Leuba, in his George Saintsbury, *Twayne Publishers, Inc., 1967, 129 p.*

HAROLD OREL   (essay date 1984)

[*Orel is an American educator and critic. In the following excerpt, he presents an overview of Saintsbury's critical precepts.*]

[The] charge of writing too much and of being too copious in his literary productions can be levied only by those who have not sampled a true cross-section of Saintsbury's wares. It is impossible to read any essay or book-chapter by Saintsbury that does not contain some characteristic, well-turned observation. In his essay **"Oxford Sights and Scenes"** he recorded Southey's remark that he never dreamt of Oxford, and added, within parentheses, "It was the only bad thing that he ever said of himself or that is ever said of him on good authority." The editors and publishers to whom Jeffrey sought to introduce himself in 1798—and who rebuffed his efforts to become a professional man of letters—"were either inaccessible or repulsive." Saintsbury admired Donne's satires, for their brilliant employment of intellect:

> It is a constant fault of modern satirists that in their just admiration for Horace and Juvenal they merely paraphrase them, and, instead of going to the fountainhead and taking their matter from human nature, merely give us fresh studies of *Ibam forte via sacra*

or the Tenth of Juvenal, adjusted to the meridians of Paris or London.

A comparison of Voltaire and Rabelais turns out very much to the former's disadvantage: Voltaire "believes in nothing, wishes for nothing very much, can excite himself about nothing. With Rabelais, on the contrary, the steam is not only always up, as modern slang says, but up with a full head, and escaping through every safety valve." There has never been a more vigorous defence of Malory's principles of editing his materials than that which Saintsbury records in *The English Novel:*

> It is what the artist does with his materials, not where he gets them, that is the question. And Malory has done, with *his* materials, a very great thing indeed. He is working no doubt to a certain extent blindly; working much better than he knows, and sometimes as he would not work if he knew better; though whether he would work as well if he knew better is quite a different point. Sometimes he may not take the best available version of a story; but we must ask ourselves whether he knew it. . . . A very remarkable compiler! It is a pity that they did not take him and cut him up in little stars for a light to all his brethren in compiling thereafter.

Saintsbury admired Macaulay, and appreciated particularly the author's habit of checking impressions by visiting the actual sites where history had taken place; but Macaulay, who never told a falsehood, "not seldom contrives to convey one," a judgement that many readers of Macaulay's historical essays have uneasily shared. In speaking of the notorious unequalness of Hazlitt's writings, Saintsbury argues that the inequality is

> due less to an intellectual than to a moral defect. The clear sunshine of Hazlitt's admirably acute intellect is always there; but it is constantly obscured by driving clouds of furious prejudice. Even as the clouds pass, the light may still be seen on distant and scattered parts of the landscape; but wherever their influence extends, there is nothing but thick darkness, gusty wind and drenching rain.

Saintsbury did not care for *Gorboduc,* which (with the exception of the choruses) "is couched in correct but ineffably dreary decasyllables, in which the sense usually lapses with the line, and the whole stumps on with a maddening, or rather stupefying, monotony." Reviewing Prévost's life as a hack writer in an effort to understand whence came the moment's flash of genius that produced *Manon Lescaut,* he pointed out that Prévost undoubtedly imitated not only his own countrymen Marivaux and Crébillon, but two English writers as well, Defoe and Richardson, the latter of whom he actually translated; and then, with irresistible puckishness, Saintsbury felt compelled to add, within parentheses, "Fancy translating Richardson!" He admired Dickens, but shuddered at the excesses of idolators of Dickens; he cited as one example the statement made "in a most respectable book of reference," that "Agnes is perhaps the most charming character in the whole range of fiction." He exploded, "*Agnes!* No decent violence of expletive, no reasonable artifice of typography, could express the depths of my feelings at such a suggestion." And in his Inaugural Address at the University of Edinburgh, when he sketched in masterly fashion his ambitions as a professor of English literature for the coming years, he said what most lovers of literature have doubtless felt, and seldom expressed as cogently:

> It has been complained of modern geography and travel by the fanciful, that the nice blank spaces, so comfortable to imagination, are being too fast filled up. There is no danger of that in literature, even in a single one. There are plenty of things that you can never find out at all—plenty of them that in the conditions of time and space there is no chance of finding out. But you can always be finding out something, and always, as you find it, the old things that you knew have fresh light shed on them—the old enjoyment that you felt acquires a fresh keenness.

If the true test is a reader's ability to enjoy a novel, poem or play—a test that Saintsbury, in the same address, admitted was "rebelliously simple"—the professional study of literature had to beware lest it take guidance from the pernicious example of German universities, and encourage the cataloguing of syllabic lengths in lines of poetry or the analysing of sex in animals in Shakespeare. Saintsbury's exuberant self-confidence, his relating of specific insights to a more generalised sense of the value of his own responses to literature, could not convert all readers; the scoffing at the possibility of absolute standards whereby a genre or a literary school might be judged led inevitably to the counter-reaction of new styles in literary analysis.

It is not unexpected, therefore, that Saintsbury should have enjoyed his own century (the nineteenth much more than the twentieth) fully as much as any previous one. True that he could not remember clearly details about the publication of Dickens's novels of the 1850s, and true that much of what he wrote about the first six decades of the century was based on what he had read in the study rather than on what had come to him in the reviewer's way. One would give much to have Saintsbury's comments on some of the greatest Victorians, written not after their death, but while they still lived and their works were most controversial. The reasons for his reluctance to discuss living authors—which, at a later time, included his reluctance to seem to be making judgements *ex cathedra* from his Chair at Edinburgh—have already been mentioned, and do him credit; but Saintsbury's relationship to his century was, in some respects, affected by both this chronological remoteness from the events of the first half of the century, and—in the final decades—by an understandable unwillingness to interpose himself between a reader and a living writer whose work could not yet be judged in relation to what Dryden had called the "firm perspective of the past."

Nevertheless, Saintsbury's observations about nineteenth-century English writers are expressed with an idiosyncratic pungency. He regarded Matthew Arnold—whose career he had followed with interest—as the best critic of his century, and admired him as one who knew what he meant, and who meant something not anticipated by any earlier critic. But Arnold's faults, as enumerated by Saintsbury, are quite serious. Arnold was given to formulas, and to repetition of phrases such as "criticism of life," "lucidity" and "grand style" ("misleading and snip-snap phrases," Saintsbury wrote with some exasperation). Arnold's arrogance in believing that what he did not like no person of taste could like either, originated in a narrow, crotchety personality. Moreover, Arnold frequently violated his own canons: "At least," said Saintsbury, "I am myself quite unable to reconcile that doctrine of confining ourselves to 'the best,' which it seems rules out the *Chanson de Roland* and makes Shelley more remarkable as a letter-writer than as a poet, with the attention paid to Sénancour and the Guérins." Arnold contributed greatly to the awakening of the Victorian sense that appreciation might justifiably precede codification (the doctrine was novel in his time), but his criticism suffered because he admired classical literature so highly that to be un-Greek was to follow inferior gods. "Now I will yield to no man in my respect for the classic," said Saintsbury; "and I do not think that, at least as far as the Greeks are concerned, anyone will ever do better the things that they did. But it is absurd to suppose or maintain that the canon of literary perfections was closed when the Muses left Philemon's house."

Arnold suffered from an unhistorical attitude toward Celtic literature, and worked with a limited number of translations and undated works as if they justified very large generalisations about "melancholy," "natural magic" and so forth. Saintsbury disdained "theory divorced from history." Arnold's later work, with notable exceptions, was inferior because much of the ebullience had "frothed and bubbled itself away"; because his critical views had matured, but not altered. Moreover, Arnold's dedication to the Poetic *Subject* rather than to the Poetic *Moment* was sometimes inconsistent with his admiration of such lines as *"In la sua volontade è nostra pace,"* quoted to demonstrate Dante's greatness, and to serve "as an infallible touchstone for detecting the presence or absence of high poetic quality in other poetry."

Arnold at the top; the others, lamentably farther down the mountain's side. Froude's criticism was damaged by political and philosophical prejudices; it had been tainted by Froude's admiration of Carlyle. Ruskin talked poetically, but was given to paroxysms of unreason: "You may admire the budding of a flower, but not a display of fireworks." George Henry Lewes may have been important as George Eliot's mentor and companion, and he wrote some decent dramatic criticism; but to perpetrate upon the public a work entitled *The Principles of Success in Literature* was to confess the existence of an ingrained vulgarity. "Fame may be the last infirmity of noble minds; Success is but the first and last morbid appetite of the vulgar." Everywhere, even in his best essay, "The Inner Life of Art," "the stamp of the Exhibition of 1851 is upon him also." Bagehot, praised for sanity, sense, and good humour, spread himself wide and thin, though his "odd moments were far from unprofitable." Richard Holt Hutton, on the other hand, hated criticism as criticism, and always allayed or sweetened its bitter cup "by sentimental, or political, or religious, or philosophical, or anthropological, or pantopragmatic adulteration." Saintsbury harbours a rather curious disapproval of Hutton's approach to Carlyle (Hutton persists in thinking of Carlyle as a man, teacher, philosopher, moralist, not as a writer); after all, Carlyle entertained a savagely low opinion of most writers, and did not wish to be regarded primarily as a writer, since he dealt with Truths; and Hutton's treatment was in line with Carlyle's own wishes. Pater could not be considered less than a second-rank Coleridge or Arnold, and might have been treated as their equal if he had not been trite in his championing of the pleasure-giving quality of literature, and if it were not that his style had been a little precious and his facility had interfered with the reader's appreciation of the importance of his subject-matter. Saintsbury gives full marks to Pater's emphasis on the definition of feeling, however, and adds, after quoting Pater's remarks on Amiel, "Indeed, I really do not know that to 'define feeling' is not as good—it is certainly as short—a definition of at least a great part of the business of the critic as you can get."

Saintsbury's attitude toward English critics of the second half of the nineteenth century is distinctly unsatisfactory, since he deals with broken lights. Pater, who comes closer to being an ideal appreciator of moments of pleasure than a fussy, patronising Arnold could, is not Arnold's equal in comprehensiveness

of interests, and his disciples, though fierce in adoration, were fewer in number, and more narrowly selective in the kinds of literature that they would willingly endorse. It may be that Saintsbury was justified in his refusal to group *kinds* of critics, since they had stubbornly refused to form schools, as in the eighteenth century, or for that matter as in the first half of the nineteenth; but the net impression after reading Saintsbury's brusque treatment of dozens of late Victorian critics is that he saw their occupation as harried, and the essays that they churned out, on demand, in the crowded periodical world to which he himself had belonged was—on the whole—an uninspiring business.

With the Victorian novel Saintsbury was more at ease, and his appreciation of that particularly productive period from 1845 to 1855 was very enthusiastic. Thackeray then wrote his best, and *David Copperfield* came out in 1850; Lever, Kingsley and Trollope were all publishing major works; there was "a stirring of the waters, a rattling among the bones, such as is not common in literature." Saintsbury did not want to attribute this flowering to the simple fact that good novelists were mature, and enjoying their camaraderie, in the same decade. The examples set by the works of Scott and Jane Austen had been studied, and assimilated. England had triumphed in the Napoleonic Wars; travels of both the aristocracy and the middle class were becoming more extensive; people were better educated; the change in manners and society by mid century affected all branches of creative endeavour, and the novel especially. The domestic novel, artistically treated, became the new favourite of both writers and readers. Scattered throughout *The English Novel* are brief analyses (less than 500 words) of specific examples of the craft that, for good sense and straightforward communication of one reader's "pleasure," can hardly be bettered. In his chapter "The Mid-Victorian Novel" (a subject that he kept treating in a surprisingly large number of essays and other books), he offers a concise statement of the reason why Mrs Gaskell so often disappoints midway through a narrative such as *North and South:*

> Mrs Gaskell seems to me one of the chief illustrations of the extreme difficulty of the domestic novel—of the necessity of exactly proportioning the means at command to the end to be achieved. Her means were, perhaps, greater than those of most of her brother-and-sister novelists, but she set them to loose ends, to ends too high for her, to ends not worth achieving. . . . She "means" well in Herbert's sense of the word: but what is meant is not quite done.

Of a minor writer as Elizabeth Sewell, Saintsbury could say, in a judgement that remains final,

> Though she wrote good English, [she] possessed no special grace of style, and little faculty of illustration or ornament from history, literature, her own fancy, current fashions, even of the most harmless kind, and so forth. The result is that her books have a certain dead-aliveness—that her characters, though actually alive, are neither interestingly alive nor, as Miss Austen had made hers, interesting in their very uninterestingness.

Happily, the need to set individual novels within a frame of generalisations does not prevent Saintsbury from remarking on several important aspects of literary history: the way in which "a sort of cheap machine-made" grand manner spread through the entire novel instead of being reserved for grand occasions; the temptation to make the second volume of a three-decker a convenient location for mere padding; the significant role played by circulating libraries in setting standards of content and morality for the kinds of novels they were willing to purchase from publishers; the importance of magazines in the evolution of the late Victorian novel (piecemeal production of a long work of fiction, Saintsbury maintained, was a mixed blessing for both the reading public and the novelist); and the growing perception among readers and critics that the novels of 1845-70 were, taken as a whole, as extraordinary a literary phenomenon as the drama of 1585-1625 and the poems of 1789-1825. Saintsbury believed that the note of perversity in the novels of the two most important late Victorians—George Meredith and Thomas Hardy—came from a determination to be "peculiar" in thought, style, choice of subject, handling of subject; yet he admired their refusal to change sail in order "to catch the popular breeze." Meredith, from one angle of vision, belonged with Cervantes, Shakespeare, Molière, Swift, Fielding and Thackeray (and "well above Dickens"), because he "undoubtedly enlarge[d] humanity's conscious knowledge of itself in the way of fictitious exemplification." No book by Meredith, however, was a masterpiece, and most of his work failed to convey the sense of inevitability in the writing: "after all, *Ich kann nicht anders* must be to some extent the mood of mind of the man who is committing a masterpiece."

There was little to be said in favour of most of Meredith's competitors. Scott wrote some four novels in one year, "and the process helped to kill him"; but Mrs Oliphant, who equalled the feat "over and over again," "only killed her novels." James Payn's novels might be readable a second time, but, as Saintsbury delicately put it, "I have seldom come across a novelist with whom I was so little inclined to try it." William Black began with problem novels and rapidly declined; his later work "was not up to a very good average." Walter Besant turned out machine-made novels, first with the collaborator James Rice, then by himself, and it made no difference one way or the other: "the system of novel-production *à la douzaine*" encouraged the writing of tales of brick. Wilkie Collins often made the reader "angry with him for his prudish poetical or theatrical justice, which is not poetical and hardly even just."

If Saintsbury's great love for French literature was based largely on his conviction that it was romantic, the high praise given to Robert Louis Stevenson, toward the conclusion of his chapter "The Fiction of Yesterday," becomes more understandable as a cry from the heart: "His style is of less importance" than the fact that he applied it almost wholly to the carrying out of a "rejuvenescence of romance." The novels of the second half of the century included some "very great things," though, after Scott and Jane Austen, the ordinariness of the talents of many novel-writers was all the more vividly exposed; and the appearance of Stevenson reminded Saintsbury that the novel, as a genre, did not suffer from terminal illness.

In 1923, Saintsbury took one of his final looks at the novel, and sniffed disapprovingly of books written "in accordance with a definite scheme," inasmuch as "the best stories of the past have not as a rule been constructed in such a fashion." There is an endearing crustiness to the plea Saintsbury addressed to the novelist who tried to beguile him with some "plan" or "purpose." "Never mind your significance, old man! . . . Give us story! Give us character!"

Those who regard Saintsbury as hopelessly old-fashioned, however, would do well to take a look at the chapter "The Second Poetical Period" in *A History of Nineteenth Century Literature (1780-1895)*. Its ordering of poets was exceptionally

perceptive for the time of its writing. It was based on enormously wide and intelligent reading of minor poets as well as in the total work of all the major ones (Saintsbury treated, with his usual zest, the humorists, the Spasmodics, the London Bohemian school, and a crocodile of women poets); and practically all its judgements have been accepted as the common wisdom of modern anthologies. It is true that the basis of judgement keeps shifting, and that he is sometimes particularly severe on a transgression in one poet that he has no time to annotate in the case of another; but there is little doubt at any given moment what Saintsbury is reacting to, or why. The number of illustrations that he provides of Mrs Browning's wilful and "tastelessly unusual vocabulary," careless rhymes, and tendency to run on and on, is, to say the least, generous. He has little patience with the argument that Martin Farquhar Tupper was, in private life, "an amiable and rather accomplished person," though he writes it down as a fact worth noting; he feels constrained to add, "But *Proverbial Philosophy* remains as one of the bright and shining examples of the absolute want of connection between literary merit and popular success." While conceding the unsettled condition of the merits of Lord Lytton, he encapsulates a later generation's disdain: "Though he frequently rewrote, it seemed impossible for him to retrench and concentrate."

Saintsbury never doubted that Tennyson was the best poet not merely of his generation, but of the entire second half of the century. In some respects Tennyson exceeded Keats, for he had "a wider range of interest and capacity," "the enormous advantage of thorough and regular literary training," and the capacity for taking infinite pains with editing of his own work. This did not mean that Tennyson's mannerisms were dismissed as trivial interferences with a reader's enjoyment. *In Memoriam* probably talked too much about the ineffable and the unprovable; what Saintsbury, in another context, called "the *Schwatzerei*, the endless, aimless talkee-talkee about 'thoughtful' things in which the nineteenth century has indulged beyond the record of any since what used to be called the Dark Ages." He conceded merit to the charge that Tennyson's dandyism (also called "finicalness" or "*mignardise*") produced over-rhetorical passages and manifested itself in a tendency to pile up tribrachs in his blank verse. *Maud* dragged in too many casual things such as "adulteration, popular politics, and ephemera of all kinds"; while *Idylls of the King* ran on too long, and belonged neither to the medieval nor to the modern period. But Tennyson was important not merely because of the breathtaking variety of his poems, or because he had come before the public with a great volume of such work, but because he had dominated his contemporaries longer than any other poet of the century: "The influences of Pope and Dryden were weak in force and merely external in effect, the influence of Byron was short-lived, that of Wordsworth was partial and limited, in comparison with the influence of Tennyson."

Next to Tennyson, Browning's work, for all its virtues, shone palely. Saintsbury, while not dismissing the charge of obscurity, termed the problem one of "breathlessness," or the expression "of a man who either did not stop at all to pick his words, or was only careful to pick them out of the first choice that presented itself to him of something not commonplace." Browning's masterpieces were "Christmas Eve and Easter Day" (1850) and *Men and Women* (1855), though *Bells and Pomegranates* and *Dramatis Personae* (1864) contained some fine poems, too. His dramas were involuted and uneven, his Greek translations indulged "a sort of hybrid and pedantic spelling of proper names," and his later works, from *The Ring and the*

Book onwards, were riddled by "an eccentric and almost burlesque phraseology." What Lang had disliked in Dickens's admirers, Saintsbury found particularly repellent in the Browning Society, to which, he said sternly, the poet had allowed "a kind of countenance which would certainly not have been extended to it by most English men of letters." Handbooks and the *Browning Dictionary* provided "for his disciples something to make up for the ordinary classical and other dictionaries with which, it seemed to be presumed, their previous education would have made them little conversant."

It may reasonably be concluded, therefore, that Saintsbury rated the Victorian novel more highly than the Victorian poem. But he sought diligently for shards of talent or promise in the disappointing poetry that duty compelled him to review. He believed that Arnold's genius—like that of most poets in the last two-thirds of the century—expressed itself best in shorter pieces; Rossetti's *The House of Life* was not (despite contemporary reactions) an indecent sonnet sequence; O'Shaughnessy lacked originality and human interest, and suffered from morbidity, but he had the *unum necessarium,* "the individual note of song"; Thomson suffered from "a monotonous, narrow, and irrational misery," but his stately verse contained splendid passages; Clough's work suffered from that brand of scepticism which had "neither the strength to believe nor the courage to disbelieve 'and have done with it'." The end of the century was notable, among other things, for a flagging of energy among the poets, and Saintsbury gloomily contemplated the growth in popularity of free verse: "It is quite clear that this kind of freedom is certain to indulge itself in mere anarchy at first. As to what some people seem still to think and do more than seem to say—that metre and rhyme will be superseded—one may be rash enough to pronounce this impossible. . . ."

Saintsbury's sympathy with literary effort of almost all varieties was, somewhat curiously, limited in so far as drama was concerned. He did not attend the theatre, preferring his study; and there are some indications that, given choices of how to pass his reading time, he preferred almost anything to a play. He certainly never speaks of the printing or the production of a new drama with the same enthusiasm that led him to bring home, along with a first-edition copy of Swinburne's *Poems and Ballads* (1866), "divers maroons" for accompaniment. Verse dramas had proved disastrous. Talfourd's *Ion* enjoyed what little success it had because of Macready's popularity and skill. Browning's plays continually raised the question, "Why are all these people behaving in this way?" As for Knowles, he was "content to dwell in decencies forever," a damning encomium. Perhaps the drama suffered because those who wrote the most ambitious plays for the nineteenth-century theatre were, in one sense, play-acting; their primary artistic interests did not lie in the writing of dramas so much as in acting, producing, the law, poetry or the novel. Saintsbury's final judgement is completely negative: "In this period the dramatic work of those who have been really men and women of letters is generally far inferior to their other work, and . . . with the rarest exceptions, the dramatic work of those who have not excelled in other kinds of literature is not literature at all."

It is not necessary to consider, in this context, Saintsbury's views on nineteenth-century historians, journalists, theologians and philosophers, beyond marvelling again at how much of the printed product turned out by men and women of fundamentally non-belletristic bias Saintsbury had taken some effort to master. But Saintsbury's feeling about the nineteenth century was intensely positive. *Bliss was it in that dawn to be alive:*

for Saintsbury is really saying that after the giants—after the Romantics, who benefited from the renewal of interest in medieval and foreign literature, the excitement of the French Revolution and its aftermath, and the growing conviction that theirs would be an age of "Progress"—came a sequel scarcely less interesting than the original renaissance between 1798 and 1824. A brief period of imitation ("school work"), and an undeniable falling-off; but Hood, Praed, Macaulay, Taylor, Darley, Beddoes, Hartley Coleridge and Horne had "singular excellence," and an eccentric and spasmodic orginality; and after them, of course, Tennyson, Browning, Arnold, and all the others who made poetry so watchable a profession fully half a century. "For total amount, total merit, total claims of freshness and distinctness, no period of poetical literature can much, if at all, exceed the ninety years of English verse from *The Ancient Mariner* to *Crossing the Bar.*"

Thus, unlike Lang, whose strictures against almost anything new became more severe as the century ended, Saintsbury looked back on what he considered to be an extraordinary period of talents, enthusiasm and achievement, and his "Huzzah!" could be heard everywhere. It may be argued that Saintsbury, who outlasted Lang by a full two decades, simply took longer to agree with Lang that English literature had exhausted itself, and was enduring a period of transition while a new yeast prepared to work itself out in the later years of the twentieth century. Saintsbury was well aware that the end of the Victorian Age was also the end of a number of literary movements. Saintsbury underestimated the merits of Yeats, Eliot, Pound, Joyce and a number of other modernists; he entertained more nostalgia than was necessary for the three-decker novel, an art form that had collapsed by the early 1890s; and dark suspicions that the kinds of periodicals for which he had laboured so valiantly over a twenty-year period had vulgarised everyone's reading-tastes.

Novels had become the only books for many men and women, who assumed that it was legitimate to adopt the standards found therein as the standards of both nature and life. The authors of these novels, in turn, had frequently imitated what they had found in earlier novels. There was, in brief, a second-hand look to ideas that Saintsbury found disconcerting, even distressing; and literary craftsmanship, or over-abundance of information about the "past and present of literature", did not compensate for the public's strong demand for quantity rather than quality, and for its willingness to pay handsomely for reading-pleasure of an inferior variety.

But Saintsbury believed in change, not only in its certainty, but also in its desirability, and he was willing to entertain the proposition that a new *Lyrical Ballads* might appear at any moment; that after Stevenson a new master of the romance might begin to publish; and that public taste might improve if genuine artists came forward to treat nature again at first-hand. The nineteenth century, which had ended on a note of diminuendo, might well be followed by stronger and newer chords played by a master musician, and, though Saintsbury saw few or none on the immediate horizon when he came to the end of his lengthy and productive life, he never forgot that English literature—if only the record could be trusted—continually renewed itself. The point, of course, is that he did trust the record, and in his own way had done a great deal to make journalistic and academic criticism respectable elements of that record.

At least one master-work deserves a closer look before we conclude this discussion of Saintsbury's work: *A History of Criticism,* which appeared in three volumes. It is both magisterial and surprisingly diffident. As Saintsbury indicated in his Preface to volume I, such a review had not been undertaken by anyone else on quite the scale that Saintsbury believed essential for a judicious consideration of the subject-matter. Dr Johnson had intended to write a *History of Criticism, as it related to Judging of Authours,* but never proceeded to do more than collect notes. B. Mazzarella's *Della Critica* (1866) "seems to be merely a torso" (though Saintsbury had not seen it personally); Théry's *Histoire des Opinions Littéraires* (c. 1830) dismissed too many important subjects too swiftly, in a page or a paragraph, and knew nothing about English criticism after Campbell and Blair. Forced to identify the major critics of European tradition and to trace their doctrines for himself, Saintsbury decided to put together the atlas that he himself had needed. "He may have put elephants for towns, he may have neglected important rivers and mountains, like a general from the point of view of a newspaper correspondent, or a newspaper correspondent from the point of view of a general; but he has done what he could."

Saintsbury did not disguise his disdain of attempts of critics to smash literary works which did not live up to theoretical laws that they had themselves devised; such critics hammer home the dubious propositions that this poem will not do because it fails to resemble the ideal epic, or that that poem, a romance, is too loose to be accounted an epic, and hence is barred altogether. Not too long ago one form of tragedy became the only permissible form; lyric "became a mere appendage to Tragedy," and history was relegated to "a sort of baggage-waggon to oratorical Rhetoric." The critics of antiquity—Aristotle followed by Dionysius of Halicarnassus and Longinus—began this notion of hierarchies of genres. Saintsbury did not much like the direction in which the rhetoric of classical times was moving, and he spoke often in terms such as "the bread-winning chicanery of forensic" and "the desert and chaos of wasted industry" that stretched in an "endless procession of some fifty generations." Aristotle, Plato, Plutarch, all had their eyes "mainly off the object," which means, essentially, that reading and examining a text in an untiring quest after "the secret of its charms" were seldom, if ever, regarded as worth the trouble until Longinus.

Latin literature, Saintsbury claimed, benefited from being able to refer its standards to the language and literature of the Greeks. The Greeks had had to evolve their own standards, and their diagnosis of the qualities that made a literary work distinctive suffered accordingly; but comparative techniques afforded the Roman critics an opportunity to see both the degree of originality and the acceptable variations in form of a given creative work. They were men of letters "almost always by accident, and on the way to being something else." Moreover, they kept fastening down upon themselves hard and fast rules.

If Saintsbury detested the false claims for the virtues of oratory made by the Greeks, he was driven to distraction by the even more exaggerated claims made by Romans for orators whose speeches survive only in fragments, or not at all. Rhetoricians who insisted on classifying the speeches of Virgil demeaned the greatness of their best poet; the emphasis on figures (antiphrasis, hyperbole, and so on) was "topsy-turvy" and, muttered Saintsbury ominously, could "come to no good end." Latin grammarians knew a great deal about metre, metrical quantity, and metrical quality; but they stopped short before coming to a consideration of the "higher criticism of literary form and charm," as if they feared being forced to render judgement on "the *poetical* quality of the Ennian, the Lucre-tian, and the Virgilian hexameter." A summing-up attempts to be generous, but succeeds primarily in reminding us how strenuously Saintsbury fought clear of restrictive rules and models meant to inspire awe rather than love: "A literature like classical Latin, which is from first to last *in statu pupillari,* which, with whatever strength, deftness, elegance, even originality at times, follows in the footsteps of another literature, must for the very life of it have a critical creed of order, discipline, moderation." Latin literature got the criticism it deserved. Served in good stead by these carefully defined rulings of grammar and rhetoric, worked out over a period of centuries, that literature led ultimately to the development of the Trivium and the Quadrivium, legacies of the classics. Anything more, and the Middle Ages would have been unable to accomplish its own work; critical appreciation of literary texts was not part of its self-assigned business.

Saintsbury was unimpressed by the literary criticism of the medieval period; but in *De Vulgari Eloquio,* presumably by Dante (though there has been considerable debate over the question), he found "such a diploma-piece as has been scarcely half-a-dozen times elsewhere seen in the history of the world." Not merely because Dante's authorship provides evidence of the links between the creative and critical faculties, but because Dante wrote without indebtedness to Aristotle or to Longinus, and without being tainted by overdependence on the figures and other kinds of rhetorical jargon; with due respect to questions of "form," with knowledge and appreciation of various prose fictions, a subtle and sophisticated awareness of the merits of literatures in other tongues, and anticipations of modern attitudes toward style. (Chaucer's efforts at literary criticism, Saintsbury maintains, are moral, and scarcely deserve the name. Only in Chaucer's discussion of Sir Thopas is there a "crystallised" opinion as to the difference between genuine and meretricious literature.)

Saintsbury admired the originality of much medieval literature, because authors then observed only "formal restrictions of the minor kind" which came naturally, and were of their own devising; but medieval authors, in general, rejected restrictions of literary theory. The Muse of an author of the Middle Ages "will wear no stays, though she does not disdain ornaments." Thus, the invention of story, the development of romance as a genre, the new understanding of the love motive, the cultivation of the short tale, and the originality of the medieval drama, made possible for later generations of critics the hammering-out of an entirely new calculus of critical variations. The signal contribution of the Middle Ages to the Renaissance grew out of two facts: "the immense provision of new kinds of literature by the Middle Age, side by side with its almost total abstinence from criticism," which, Saintsbury concludes, "was the best thing that could have happened."

Renaissance criticism, understandably, becomes a class of literary endeavour. Besides its ancient books, of the law (the Greek and Latin authorities are generally recognised to have survived because of their intrinsic quality), this body of criticism now has "quite a library of modern prophets, commentators, scribes." The sixteenth century brought together in recognisable form "the dogmas of the Neo-Classic creed, its appeal to the ancients and its appeal to Reason or Nature or Sense, its strict view of Kinds, its conception of Licence and Rule, its Unities," and the business of the seventeenth century was to "codify precedent case-law" rather than do anything new. Saintsbury notes that Renaissance criticism limits itself, rather surprisingly, to poetry, and more than compensates for those earlier times when oratory took precedence; but it also slights the prose romance, the essay, and other departments that now justify careful consideration. In addition, Ronsard, Du Bellay, Tasso, Sidney and Ben Jonson are not the great critics that earlier or later ages produced, so that the whole critical system came into existence "by a process of haphazard accretion."

As Saintsbury reviews "the crystallising of the Neo-Classic creed," his disapproval of pedantry, absurdities, literary history reshaped to fit a critic's preconceptions, and overdogmatic assumptions affect what he wants to say about Malherbe, Chapelain, Malebranche, La Bruyère, Fénelon and Boileau; Spanish writers never "kept creation and criticism separate" and had no critic of "real authority" to keep them honest; the Germans did not know enough about other cultures to develop "the comparative stimulus"; and intellects such as Milton, Cowley, Davenant and Hobbes served primarily to prepare the way for one greater than themselves in the field of English criticism.

Dryden (there is an almost audible sigh of relief) was never afraid to ask "Why?" He asked "not whether he ought to like such and such a thing, but whether he does like it, and why he likes it, and whether there is any real reason why he should not like it." Dryden, of course, was not perfect, but he was a genuine and catholic critic, and his interest in discovering for himself the reasons why he enjoyed a particular literary work was the very interest that Saintsbury declared every critic should cultivate. A critic (so Saintsbury concluded in his final chapter, "The Present State of Criticism")

> must read, and, as far as possible, read everything—that is the first and great commandment. If he omits one period of a literature, even one author of some real, if ever so little, importance in a period, he runs the risk of putting his view of the rest out of focus; if he fails to take at least some account of other literatures as well, his state will be nearly as perilous. Secondly, he must constantly compare books, authors, literatures indeed, to see in what each differs from each, but never in order to dislike one because it is not the other. Thirdly, he must, as far as he possibly can, divest himself of any idea of what a book *ought to be,* until he has seen what it is.

On these grounds the critics of the Neo-Classic period, however meritorious their individual insights might be, failed to satisfy Saintsbury. They were too ready to accept unquestioningly the authority of an ancient, of Aristotle or Horace; they believed too slavishly in the need of a drama to observe the "Unities" and in the indisputable greatness of the "Heroic Poem." Nor did Saintsbury accept the conventional view of the unbridgeable chasm between the Ancients and the Moderns, despite their notorious quarrel:

> The Moderns were, as a rule, just as "classical" in their ideas as the Ancients. They were as incapable of catholic judgment; they were even more ignorant of literature as a whole; they were at least as apt to introduce non-literary criteria; they were as much under the obsession of the Kind, the Rule (cast-iron, not leaden), the sweeping generalisation.

Hence, it was not surprising that the eighteenth century, with its hardening orthodoxy, neither deserved nor received the praise that Saintsbury felt more properly due to the succeeding century. But English criticism, at least, was saved from the worst excesses of the school of "correctness" by the fact that Dryden had championed Shakespeare and Milton, and Englishmen who

took an intelligent interest in poetry had already agreed that Chaucer and Spenser were great practitioners of the craft. Pope was succeeded by Dr Johnson, and both were humane and liberal enough to admit the difficulties that prevented them from issuing categorical imperatives. Saintsbury noted that Dr Johnson had refused to "judge genius merely by the event," and had said, in reference to Shakespeare, that, "if genius succeeds by means which are wrong according to rule, we may think higher of the genius but less highly of the work." To which Saintsbury replied that, if Shakespeare showed genius in neglecting the Rules, the inexorable voice of Logic was bound to point out that the Rules were evidently not necessary.

A History of Criticism reviewed, with enormous authority, the critical judgements of eight cultures and more than two thousand years. But Saintsbury's criteria for judging the worth of a critic, no matter where or in which century he lived, are no more complicated than has already been indicated. He opposed schematic criticism. The more rigorously a writer insisted on ignoring any possible exceptions to a morphology and a set of precedents that he had adopted, the less reliable would he be whenever he came to treat a fellow author whose work transcended predefined categories. Saintsbury maintained consistently that a critic must never neglect the artistic criterion, even if it suggests the existence of more things in heaven and earth than are dreamed of in his philosophy; even if it unnerves his self-confidence. Thus, while repudiating much of Dr Johnson's argument about the relative worth of English poets, Saintsbury conceded that Dr Johnson had "kept in constant touch with life," and that he easily passed the test of a great critic. With generosity, he speaks of the fact that Johnson's critical opinions were formed quite early in life: it is not necessarily true that regarding everything as an open question, or being willing to change any opinion "at a moment's notice," is worthy of praise. "As a matter of fact, we have record of not many men who have proceeded in this way; and it may be doubted whether among them is a single person of first-rate genius, or even talent." This is sensible stuff; the fact that Saintsbury, personally more rabidly Tory than Dr Johnson ever was, appreciated the conservative politics of Dr Johnson does not take away from the well-turned piquancy of the observation.

Criticism, as Saintsbury outlines its history, is not as ancient or as honourable a profession as its practitioners sometimes pretend. There have not been many good critics over the centuries; fortunate the nation that can boast, as Italy does, of a poet who also had original and useful things to say about the nature of his art.

> No Muse, or handmaid of the Muses (let it be freely confessed) has been less often justified of her children: none has had so many good-for-nothings for sons. . . . The purblind theorist who mistakes the passport for the person, and who will not admit without passport the veriest angel; the acrid pedant who will allow no one whom he dislikes to write well, and no one at all to write on any subject that he himself has written on, or would like to write on, who dwells on dates and commas, who garbles out and foists in, whose learning may be easily exaggerated but whose taste and judgment cannot be, because they do not exist;—these are too often justified patterns of the critic to many minds. The whole record of critical result, which we have so laboriously arranged and developed, is a record of mistake and of misdoing, of half-truths and nearly whole errors.

So stern a summing-up would be depressing save that, again, Saintsbury admits the delights inherent in the quest; and what has been known once and appreciated for what it is in all its splendour can never be less than what it was then seen to be. If Saintsbury expands Arnold's notion of the goal of criticism from an endeavour to know and recommend "not only the best, but all the good, that has been known and thought and written in the world," the enthusiasm is not unbecoming to a critic who has obviously read more and written more than practically all his contemporaries; and it is a truism throughout this enormous study that the best critic is one who first satisfies himself as to why he likes a work before he attempts to expand its reading audience.

To be a modern critic, one must disregard the precedents established by either the ancients or our contemporaries who assume, with some dogmatism, to speak for the ancients. Saintsbury's position is that "the most modern of works is to be judged, not by adjustment to anything else, but on its own merits." A critic, we are told, "must always behave as if the book he takes from its wrapper might be a new *Hamlet* or a new *Waverley*,—or something as good as either, but more absolutely novel in kind than even *Waverley*,—however shrewdly he may suspect that it is very unlikely to be any such thing." To some extent this argues with another proposition that one should know as much about the literary past as possible, and thus be able to judge on the basis of an awareness of the heritage of any new literary work. We can hardly evaluate intelligently the new *Hamlet* unless we know the old *Hamlet*. Saintsbury never satisfactorily reconciled these two positions, and his neglected law of criticism, that "B is not bad because it is not A, however good A may be," would be more widely accepted if one remembered Saintsbury's corollary law, that B and A must be compared and contrasted before the singularity of B may be established.

Perhaps Saintsbury stressed, more than most twentieth-century critics, the importance of the critic's response. His own appetite being omnivorous, he could read swiftly through enormous quantities of material (reading was not work, he once said, but writing criticism was), and decide which works were worth thinking about, and which could be safely discarded. An analogy with tasting grew naturally from consideration of such an image. The classic formulation by Bacon as to how books are to be digested must have been what Saintsbury had in mind when, in his book for all enthusiasts of drink, *Notes on a Cellar-Book,* he repeatedly linked his love of spiritous liquors with his love of literature. One learns to trust the critic when his appetite has been proved sound, and his ability to discriminate between tastes has been demonstrated.

No Victorian critic exposed himself more often or willingly to the kind of scrutiny that precedes trust than Saintsbury did. *A History of Criticism,* despite its 1800 pages, fulfils its author's claim that here, for the first time, the major critical texts have been reviewed to discover what, in fact, their authors had to say. Saintsbury has little patience with the notion that one must review what critics of the critics have had to say before one can estimate fairly what poems, plays, and novels are driving at; there is no fussing with Victorian views of what Dr Johnson meant when he wrote about Milton's opinions on the epic. Saintsbury's footnotes record aperçus and afterthoughts rather than citations to the secondary and tertiary literatures that have grown up around, and sometimes over, the critical texts. Saintsbury is not a technical critic in the modern sense, yet René Wellek's *A History of Modern Criticism 1750-1950* is highly respectful of Saintsbury's "atlas of the actual facts," even as Wellek measures its limitations [see excerpt dated 1965]. Like

Croce and Spingarn, Wellek disliked Saintsbury's neglect of theory and aesthetics, his occasional errors in dates and titles, his treatment of poetry as more sound than sense, his dismaying tendency to discuss form independently of the subject, his vagueness whenever he uses the term "grand style," his subjective readings, "the poverty and haziness of his concepts and criteria of genres, devices, style, composition," and his near-total impressionism. But Wellek concedes that Saintsbury, for all his faults, was a map-maker in the *History of Criticism*; his influence on academics has been not only "enormous" but also, we gather, helpful in the encouragement Saintsbury gave to those interested in comparative literary studies, including Wellek himself; and he was, throughout, a "lively commentator." (pp. 156-76)

Harold Orel, "George Saintsbury," in his Victorian Literary Critics: George Henry Lewes, Walter Bagehot, Richard Holt Hutton, Leslie Stephen, Andrew Land, George Saintsbury and Edmund Gosse, *St. Martin's Press, 1984, pp. 151-76.*

ADDITIONAL BIBLIOGRAPHY

Babbitt, Irving. "Are the English Critical?" *The Nation* (New York) Nos. 2438 and 2439 (21 and 28 March 1912): 282-84, 309-11.
Reviews *A History of English Criticism* and compares English literary criticism unfavorably with French literary criticism.

Buchan, John. "Professor Saintsbury and European Literature." In his *Comments and Characters,* pp. 217-22. Freeport, N.Y.: Books for Libraries Press, 1940.
Laudatory review of *The Later Nineteenth Century.*

Chapman, J. A. "Dr. Saintsbury's Heresy." In his *Papers on Shelley, Wordsworth, & Others,* pp. 103-14. Freeport, N.Y.: Books for Libraries Press, 1929.
Disputes Saintsbury's contention that the material of poetry is "invariable."

Chrystal, Sir George. "George Saintsbury, 1845-1933." *The London Mercury* XXVII, No. 161 (March 1933): 434-41.
Obituary of Saintsbury by one of his former students.

Review of *Dryden. The Dial* II, No. 13 (May 1881): 17.
Early, positive review of Saintsbury's work on Dryden.

Elton, Oliver. "George Saintsbury." In his *Essays and Addresses,* pp. 239-49. New York: Longmans, Green & Co., 1939.
Genial survey of Saintsbury's career.

Freeman, John. Review of *A Last Scrap Book. The London Mercury* XI, No. 66 (April 1925): 662-63.
Favorably appraises *A Last Scrap Book.*

Gosse, Sir Edmund. "Mr. Saintsbury." In his *Silhouettes,* pp. 213-18. London: William Heinemann, 1925.
Reviews *Collected Essays and Papers* and comments favorably on Saintsbury's range of learning, comparative method, and critical objectivity.

Hostettler, Gordon F. "George Saintsbury's View of Rhetoric." *Western Journal of Speech Communication* 41, No. 4 (Fall 1977): 210-20.
Summarizes Saintsbury's rhetorical theories as propounded in *A History of Criticism and Literary Taste in Europe.*

Lewisohn, Ludwig. "Saintsbury." In his *Cities and Men,* pp. 43-49. New York and London: Harper & Brothers Publishers, 1927.
Praises Saintsbury's critical acumen while disagreeing with his politics.

Lubbock, Percy. "Three Evenings with a Critic." *The Nation and The Athenaeum* XXXIV, No. 4 (27 October 1923): 156.

Predominantly affirmative review of *Collected Essays and Papers*.

Lynd, Robert. "Two English Critics." In his *The Art of Letters*, pp. 172-83. New York: Charles Scribner's Sons, 1921.
Includes a review of *Peace of the Augustans* praising Saintsbury's enthusiasm for eighteenth-century literature while questioning his critical judgment of the relative value of various works written during that period.

Moore, Marianne. "'Literature the Noblest of the Arts.'" In her *Predilections*, pp. 122-25. New York: Viking Press, 1955.
Review of *Collected Essays and Papers*. Moore writes, "These essays have a wing, a grace that recalls the Bible, Cicero, the seventeenth century, and 'the engaging idiom of the Gaul'."

Ralli, Augustus. "England 1910-1911." *A History of Shakespearian Criticism, Vol. II*, pp. 278-312. New York: Humanities Press, 1959.
Includes a summary of Saintsbury's judgments of the plays and sonnets of Shakespeare.

Read, Herbert. "George Saintsbury." In his *A Coat of Many Colours*, pp. 199-202. London: Routledge & Kegan Paul, 1945.
Criticizes Saintsbury for indiscriminate enthusiasm and for ignoring moral values in literature.

Richardson, Dorothy. Review of *A Saintsbury Miscellany*. *Modern Language Quarterly* 9, No. 1: 112-13.
Considers the essays reprinted in *A Saintsbury Miscellany* to include "all the best" that he wrote.

Roberts, R. Ellis. "George Saintsbury." *The Bookman* LXIX, No. 409 (October 1925): 20-21.
Appreciation written for Saintsbury's eightieth birthday.

Shapiro, Karl. *English Prosody and Modern Poetry*. Baltimore: Johns Hopkins Press, 1947, 16 p.
Includes a summary of Saintsbury's views on poetic form and meter as put forth in his *History of English Prosody*.

Strachey, Lytton. "Forgotten Poets." In his *Spectatorial Essays*, pp. 97-103. New York: Harcourt, Brace & World, 1964.
Reprint of Strachey's 1906 review of *Minor Poets of the Caroline Period*. Strachey criticizes the four writers included in Saintsbury's work.

Sutherland, James R. *The English Critic*. London: H. K. Lewis & Co., 1952, 19 p.
Inaugural lecture discussing John Dryden, Samuel Johnson, William Hazlitt, and Saintsbury as a succession of outstanding critics in the mainstream of English criticism.

Thompson, Francis. Review of *Minor Poets of the Caroline Period*. In his *The Real Robert Louis Stevenson and Other Critical Essays*, pp. 59-63. New York: University Publishers Incorporated, 1959.
Ambivalent review originally published in the *Athenæum* in 1905.

Webster, A. Blyth. *George Saintsbury*. Edinburgh and London: Oliver and Boyd, 1933, 47 p.
Biographical and critical study.

Ernest Thompson Seton

1860-1946

(Born Ernest Evan Thompson; also wrote under the pseudonym Ernest Seton-Thompson) English-born American novelist, short story writer, nonfiction writer, and autobiographer.

Renowned as one of the founders of the Boy Scouts of America, Seton was a respected naturalist and author whose primary goal was "to stop the extermination of harmless animals." Influenced by the writings of Charles Darwin, Seton viewed animals as the forbears of humankind and therefore deserving of more respect than they were generally accorded. He deplored mistreatment of animals, and in his fiction, often written from an animal's point of view, he exposed the needless suffering inflicted upon wild creatures by human beings. Similarly, Seton published his nonfiction works, which are thorough and painstaking records of his own wildlife observations, in the hope that wider knowledge of animals' lives would lead to increased respect for their rights. Often described as a Renaissance man, Seton was also a talented painter, an architect, a carpenter, an experienced woodsman, and an expert on native American cultures. As S. E. Read has written of Seton: "His success came from his extraordinary ability to fuse into a unified and an artistic whole his manifold gifts."

Seton was the eighth of ten sons born to an English family of Scottish descent. His father, Joseph Thompson, had amassed considerable wealth in the shipping trade, enabling Seton to enjoy a comfortable existence during the first five years of his life. However, when a series of financially disastrous maritime accidents partially consumed Thompson's fortune, he hurriedly liquidated the remainder of his assets and emigrated to Canada with his wife, ten sons, and an adopted daughter. Hoping to establish himself as a gentleman farmer, Thompson bought a large, partially cleared tract of land in Ontario. Even though the family relocated to the city of Toronto only a few years later, Seton's encounter with the Canadian wilderness during this period inspired the fascination with nature that shaped the rest of his life. His first response to nature was an attempt to capture its beauty in drawings; possessed of much innate talent, he rapidly became an adept wildlife artist. At the age of sixteen, he began working as an artist's apprentice, and shortly thereafter he enrolled at the Ontario School of Art. Four years later, convinced that he needed European training to complete his art education, Seton persuaded his father to send him to the Royal Academy in London.

Returning to Canada in 1881, Seton settled in Manitoba and began work on a study of Canadian birds, which he planned to write and illustrate. In order to support himself, he submitted portions of the incomplete manuscript for publication as essays; the first of these appeared as "The Life of the Prairie Chicken" in the *Canadian Journal*. Nevertheless, Seton soon realized that such random submissions would provide insufficient income, and late in 1883 he moved to New York City, where he secured a position as an illustrator. In 1887, he also began to write stories based on his experiences with wild animals. The immediate popularity of these stories resulted in frequent speaking invitations, and Seton soon became known as an expert on North American wildlife. The financial success of

his lecturing, writing, and illustrating endeavors thereafter enabled him to spend much of his time in the wilderness.

Seton's career as a naturalist was not, however, unmarred by controversy. In 1898 he collected several of his most popular animal stories in the volume *Wild Animals I Have Known*, a book that was denounced as "nature-fakery" by another leading naturalist, John Burroughs. Burroughs doubted whether Seton had witnessed the events depicted, noting that in his own vast experience of nature he had never seen or heard of such events and denouncing what he considered Seton's misrepresentations. In a later essay, Burroughs modified his position somewhat, conceding that for those who could separate the fact from the fiction, Seton's stories provided harmless entertainment. Yet Seton, who believed strongly in the scientific value of his stories, was much distressed by Burroughs's criticism. Biographer H. Allen Anderson has suggested that Seton's subsequent completion of the nonfiction study he had begun in 1881, which was published in 1909 as *Life-Histories of Northern Animals*, may have been an attempt to dispel any doubt about his qualifications as a scientist. In any case, questions of accuracy did not diminish the wide popularity of Seton's fiction, and he continued to publish animal stories throughout his lifetime.

Closely tied to Seton's respect for nature was his reverence for North American Indians, and he gradually came to believe that children growing up in an industrial society would benefit greatly from exposure to the healthful and highly moral Indian way of life. As a result, on an April weekend in 1901, Seton invited a group of neighborhood boys to his estate near Greenwich, Connecticut, to practice Indian ways and learn about Indian cultures. The experiment was a huge success: Seton's own "Woodcraft Indian" group grew rapidly, while other chapters sprang up across the country, inspired by Seton's column for boys in the *Ladies' Home Journal*. A few years later, when Seton's groups were supplanted by the Boy Scouts of America (whose founder, Robert Baden-Powell, had in fact appropriated Seton's ideas), Seton was invited to serve as Chief Scout. Although he objected to the quasi-military nature of Baden-Powell's Scouts, Seton agreed, and he continued to be associated with the group for the next several decades.

In 1930, Seton's interest in Indians led him to New Mexico, where remnants of Indian culture had survived the encroachment of European civilization. There, in an endeavor to preserve knowledge of North American native cultures, he established the Seton College of Indian Wisdom, which included a residential area known as Seton Village, an authentic Indian village, the naturalist's large retirement home, called Seton Castle, an 11,000 volume library, and a natural history museum. Although the college retained a staff of professional and native Indian instructors, Seton and his wife, Julie, taught many classes and served as administrators and support personnel. At the same time, Seton continued to write and conduct lecture tours, remaining actively involved in his various pursuits until his death at the age of eighty-six.

In his animal stories, Seton sought to provide a corrective to the concept of wildlife expressed in nineteenth-century anthropomorphic tales, in which animals spoke, wore clothing, and generally behaved like human beings. Finding the reality of animal existence more compelling and dramatic than any fictional treatment could be, he attempted to describe simply and accurately the phenomena he had observed during his years in the wilderness. As a result, Seton favored a genre he called the animal biography, which recounted the life of an individual animal from birth to death, thus enabling the author to include comprehensive information about the behavior, development, and social interactions of a given species. While he generally focused on wild creatures, as in the two renowned tales "Lobo, King of the Currumpaw" and *The Biography of a Grizzly*, he also wrote a number of stories about more domesticated species, including dogs and cats. Contemporary naturalists agree that while Seton no doubt witnessed many of the behaviors he described, he erred in assigning complex motivations such as greed, pride, remorse, and passion to the actions of animals. For example, in *The Biography of a Grizzly*, Seton correctly noted that bears frequently leave markings on the trunks of trees in their individual territories. However, surmising that they did so as a warning to other bears to avoid the territory, an assumption not generally accepted by modern naturalists, he created the improbable episode of a small bear marking a tree high up on its trunk in order to alarm others, who would assume that a huge bear had established residence in their area; critics agree that this episode represents a major flaw in an otherwise realistic and compelling work. Nevertheless, Fred Bodsworth has argued that in light of the traditional animal

story as practiced before Seton, his work was a "monumental step toward realistic animal portrayal," and further contends that "the anthropomorphic flaws are more than offset by the sound scientific realism that characterizes most of Seton's work."

Seton's varied talents and concerns naturally produced a multi-faceted lifetime achievement. His fiction, though not as widely read today as during his lifetime, continues to entertain and is particularly popular with children. His three highly respected nature studies—*Life-Histories of Northern Animals, The Arctic Prairies*, and *Lives of Game Animals*—remain valuable sources of information. In addition, although his participation in the Boy Scouts was limited by his disagreements with Baden-Powell, he did write the Scouts' manual, thus influencing the philosophy of the organization, particularly regarding conservation and forest skills. One of Seton's most enduring legacies has been Seton Village, which, while no longer serving as an institution of higher learning, continues to welcome visitors and to disseminate knowledge of Indian cultures. Finally, through his widely read stories, Seton increased public awareness of the true nature of animals and in so doing helped to initiate contemporary concern for wildlife conservation and animal rights.

(See also *Contemporary Authors*, Vol. 109 and *Something about the Author*, Vol. 18.)

PRINCIPAL WORKS

Studies in the Art Anatomy of Animals   (nonfiction)   1896
Wild Animals I Have Known   (short stories)   1898
The Trail of the Sandhill Stag   (novel)   1899
The Biography of a Grizzly   (novel)   1900
Lives of the Hunted   (short stories)   1901
Krag, and Johnny Bear   (novellas)   1902
Two Little Savages   (novel)   1903
Monarch, the Big Bear of Tallac   (novel)   1904
Animal Heroes   (short stories)   1905
Woodmyth and Fables   (short stories)   1905
The Birch-Bark Roll of the Woodcraft Indians   (handbook)
     1906; also published as *The Book of Woodcraft and
     Indian Lore*, 1912
The Natural History of the Ten Commandments
     (nonfiction)   1907
The Biography of a Silver Fox   (novel)   1909
Life-Histories of Northern Animals. 2 vols.   (nonfiction)
     1909
Boy Scouts of America   (handbook)   1910
The Arctic Prairies   (nonfiction)   1911
Rolf in the Woods   (novel)   1911
Wild Animal Ways   (short stories)   1916
The Preacher of Cedar Mountain   (novel)   1917
Woodland Tales   (short stories)   1921
Bannertail: The Story of a Gray Squirrel   (novel)   1922
Lives of Game Animals. 4 vols.   (nonfiction)   1925-28
The Biography of an Arctic Fox   (novel)   1937
*The Trail of an Artist-Naturalist: The Autobiography of
     Ernest Thompson Seton*   (autobiography)   1940
Santana, the Hero-Dog of France   (novel)   1945

THE NATION, NEW YORK   (essay date 1898)

[*In the following review of* Wild Animals I Have Known, *the critic praises the stories and illustrations presented in that volume.*]

The motive of [*Wild Animals I Have Known*] reminds us of the more formal treatise on the personality of animals by Prof. Shaler . . . , though the method is entirely different. Both books bear upon the kinship of man with other animals; bespeak kindly, sympathetic feelings towards our fellow-creatures of a lower order than ourselves; and dwell upon the marked individuality or personal peculiarities which every beast will be found to possess when studied closely enough. Prof. Shaler gave us the more scientific aspect of the theme which Mr. Thompson now presents from a more artistic point of view. The latter strikes his keynote in these passages of his preface:

> The fact that these stories are true is the reason why all are tragic. The life of a wild animal *always has a tragic end.*

> We and the beasts are kin. Man has nothing that the animals have not at least a vestige of, the animals have nothing that man does not in some degree share. Since, then, the animals are creatures with wants and feelings differing in degree only from our own, surely they have their rights.

By way of pointing out an extreme case of human possibility in the brutes, let us ask, who would imagine a Jekyl and Hyde dog? But there are such. Mr. Thompson tells us the story of Wully, the mongrel sheep-dog, and elsewhere speaks of another case—

> a similar yaller dog who long lived the double life— a faithful sheep-dog by day, and a bloodthirsty, treacherous monster by night. Such things are less rare than is supposed, and since writing these stories I have heard of another double-lived sheep-dog that added to its night amusements the crowning barbarity of murdering the smaller dogs of the neighborhood. He had killed twenty and hidden them in a sand-pit, when discovered by his master. He died just as Wully did.

One can never be indifferent to tragedy, and Mr. Thompson holds our unflagging interest in his stories. He knows his animals as individual characters, and sets forth their lives vividly, making us feel for and with them, through all their vicissitudes to the appointed death by violence. Not that these lives are all sad—on the contrary, there is plenty of fun, and keen enjoyment of living, and development of all sorts of traits; it is the inevitableness of fate that lends a sombre undertone to the whole recital. The treatment of these themes is not less artistic with the pen than with the pencil, in both of which modes of expression Mr. Thompson shows himself easily master of his subject.

The eight stories are of Lobo the wolf, "King of Currumpaw"; Silverspot the crow; Ruggylug the cottontail rabbit; Bingo the dog; the Springfield fox; the pacing mustang; Wully the "yaller" dog above mentioned; and Redruff the partridge. Each is illustrated with one or more full-page plates, which merit more than a mere word of praise. Mr. Thompson is now drawing the best mammals of any American artist; from a strictly technical or zoölogical standpoint they surpass his birds, in fact, and in the present case he has been able to give his fancy free play in depicting the sentiments and passions of animals, and the shifting scenes in their personal lives, as true to nature as their mere forms. (pp. 454-55)

A review of "Wild Animals I Have Known," in The Nation, *New York, Vol. LXVII, No. 1746, December 15, 1898, pp. 454-55.*

JOHN BURROUGHS   (essay date 1903)

[*Burroughs was a prominent American poet and naturalist whose name is often linked with those of the American Transcendentalists Henry David Thoreau and Ralph Waldo Emerson. In the following excerpt, he expresses disapproval for what he considers Seton's blending of fact and fiction in* Wild Animals I Have Known.]

[In] Mr. Thompson Seton's *Wild Animals I Have Known . . .* I am bound to say that the line between fact and fiction is repeatedly crossed, and that a deliberate attempt is made to induce the reader to cross, too, and to work such a spell upon him that he shall not know that he has crossed and is in the land of make-believe. Mr. Thompson Seton says in capital letters that his stories are true, and it is this emphatic assertion that makes the judicious grieve. True as romance, true in their artistic effects, true in their power to entertain the young reader, they certainly are; but true as natural history they as certainly are not. Are we to believe that Mr. Thompson Seton, in his few years of roaming in the West, has penetrated farther into the secrets of animal life than all the observers who have gone before him? There are no stories of animal intelligence and cunning on record, that I am aware of, that match his. Gilbert White, Charles St. John, Waterton, Wallace, Darwin, Jefferies, and others in England,—all expert students and observers; Bates in South America, Audubon roaming the whole country, Thoreau in New England, John Muir in the mountains of California and in the wilds of Alaska have nothing to report that comes within gunshot of what appear to be Mr. Thompson Seton's daily experiences. Such dogs, wolves, foxes, rabbits, mustangs, crows, as he has known, it is safe to say, no other person in the world has ever known. Fact and fiction are so deftly blended in his work that only a real woodsman can separate them. For instance, take his story of the fox. Every hunter knows that the fox, when pursued by the hound, will often resort to devices that look like cunning tricks to confuse and mislead the dog. How far these devices are the result of calculation we do not know, but hunters generally look upon them as such. Thus a fox hotly pursued will run through a flock of sheep. This dodge probably delays the hound a little, but it does not often enable the fox to shake him. Mr. Thompson Seton goes several better, and makes his fox jump upon the back of a sheep and ride several hundred yards. Of course no fox ever did that. Again, the fox will sometimes take to the railroad track, and walk upon the rail, doubtless with the vague notion of eluding his pursuers. Mr. Thompson Seton makes his fox so very foxy that he deliberately lures the hounds upon a long trestle where he knows they will be just in time to meet and be killed by a passing train, as they are. The presumption is that the fox had a watch and a time-table about his person. But such are the ways of romancers. The incident of the mother fox coming near the farmhouse at night to rescue her young, and, finding him held by a chain, digging a hole and burying the chain, thinking she had thus set him free, is very touching and pretty, and might well be true. It shows how limited the wit of the fox really is. But, finding herself unable to liberate her offspring, that she should then bring him poison is pushing the romantic to the absurd. In all the animal stories of Mr. Thompson Seton that I have read the same liberties are taken with facts. In his story of the rabbit, Raggylug, he says: "Those who do not know the animals well may think I have humanized them, but those who have lived so near them as to know something of their ways and their minds will not think so." This is the old trick of the romancer: he swears his tale is true, because he knows his reader wants this assurance; it makes the thing taste better. But those who know the animals are just the ones Mr. Thompson Seton cannot fool. Any country boy knows that the rabbit takes no account of barbed wire fences or of briers and brambles as a means of punishing the dog that is pursuing him. If these things were universal, it is possible that in the course of long generations rabbits might learn to interpose them between themselves and their enemies,—possible, but not probable.

Or take his story of the crow—Silver Spot; how truthful a picture is this? how much of the real natural history of the crow is here? According to my own observations of more than half a century, there is very little. In the first place, that these natural leaders among the fowls of the air ever appear I have no evidence. I have known crows almost as intimately as I have hens from by boyhood, and I have seen no evidence of it with them. For forty years I have seen crows in winter, in different parts of the country, passing to and fro between their rookeries and their feeding grounds, and I have never seen anything like leadership among them. They leave their roosting places at daybreak and disperse north and south or east and west to their feeding grounds, going in loose, straggling bands and silently, except in early spring and when they first leave their rookeries; and they return at night in the same way, flying low if it is stormy and windy, and high if it is calm, rising up or sheering off if they see a gunner or other suspicious object, but making no sound, uttering no signal notes. They all have eyes equally sharp and do not need to be warned. They are all on the alert. When feeding, they do post a sentry, and he caws when danger approaches, and takes to wing. They do not dart into a bush when pursued by a kingbird or a purple martin; they are not afraid of a hawk; they cannot count six, though such traditions exist (Silver Spot could count thirty!); they do not caw when you stand under them in winter to turn their course; they do not drill their young; they do not flock together in June; they cannot worry a fox into giving up half his dinner; they do not, so far as we know, have perpetual sentries; they have no calls that, we can be sure, answer to our words, "Mount," "Bunch," "Scatter," "Descend," "Form line," "Forage,"—on these and other points my observations differ radically from Mr. Thompson Seton's.

Crows flock in September. Through the summer the different families keep pretty well together. You may see the old ones with their young foraging about the fields, the young often being fed by their parents. It may be permissible to say that the old are teaching the young how to forage; they are certainly setting them an example, as the mother hen or mother turkey is setting her brood an example when she leads them about the fields. The cat brings her kitten a mouse, but does she teach him how to deal with the mouse? Does he need to be *taught?* (pp. 300-02)

It is always an artist's privilege to heighten or deepen natural effects. He may paint us a more beautiful woman, or a more beautiful horse, or a more beautiful landscape, than we ever saw; we are not deceived even though he out-do nature. We know where we stand and where he stands; we know that this is the power of art. But when he paints a portrait, or an actual scene, or event, we expect him to be true to the facts of the case. Again, he may add all the charm his style can impart to the subject, and we are not deceived; the picture is true, perhaps

all the more true for the style. Mr. Thompson Seton's stories are artistic and pleasing, but he insists upon it that they are true to the fact, and that this is the best way to write natural history. "I believe," he says in his preface, "that natural history has lost much by the vague general treatment that is so common." Hence he will make it specific and individual. Very good; but do not put upon our human credulity a greater burden than it can bear. His story of the pacing mustang is very clever and spirited, but the endurance of the horse is simply past belief. What would not one give for the real facts of the case; how interesting they would be, no matter how much they fell short of this highly colored account! There should be nothing equivocal about sketches of this kind; even a child should know when the writer is giving him facts and when he is giving him fiction, as he does when Mr. Thompson Seton makes his animals talk; but in many of the narrations only a real woodsman can separate the true from the false. (p. 303)

> *John Burroughs, "Real and Sham Natural History,"* in The Atlantic Monthly, *Vol. XCI, No. 3, March, 1903, pp. 298-309.*

THE NATION, NEW YORK (essay date 1909)

[*In the following excerpt, the critic assesses the scientific importance of* Life-Histories of Northern Animals.]

To the American and English publics, Mr. Seton is very much *persona grata;* and [*Life-Histories of Northern Animals*] is his monumental work. Its scope is suggested by the sub-title: *An Account of the Mammals of Manitoba;* but it is by no means bounded by it. The first volume is devoted to "The Grass-eaters," and it includes not only the hoofed animals, but also the rodents, to a total of twenty-nine species. The second volume is given up to "The Flesh-Eaters," and it embraces the true carnivora, the shrews, the moles, and the bats—thirty species in all. These species do indeed inhabit Manitoba; but all of them inhabit regions far beyond the borders of that province, and therefore the author's results cover animals that are quite as much at home in the United States as in Canada. Indeed, if a balance were to be struck, it is probable that the greater part of Mr. Seton's discourse would be found to apply southward of the international boundary.

It is quite impossible to give within available limits anything more than a bird's-eye view of this really great and also delightful work. First of all, the reader must be assured that it is a serious, scholarly, exact, and at times almost painfully conscientious work of science, yet made clear and "popular" for the benefit of the reading multitude and having also the most understandable and charming dissertations on the various habits of wild animals that have ever been laid before the public under the rules of science. (pp. 548-49)

Each of the fifty-nine species included is admirably handled, and with satisfactory fulness of detail. There are no long and tiresome lists of synonyms, descriptions of characters already well known, and anatomical details that are interesting only to the comparative anatomist. Whenever a species is thrown upon the screen, the author plunges at once into a consideration of the facts regarding it that are most interesting, most valuable, and freshest to the reader. Each species is considered systematically under thirty distinct heads; but the author is "shocked to find in how many cases the heading is missing, because there are no facts available for classification under it." With the smaller forms, and especially the earth-dwellers, this is not at all surprising.

It is interesting to note in detail the sub-heads under which this lover of wild animals classifies his knowledge. First of all, it is to be remarked that, contrary to the custom of those scientific writers who use Latin names only, Mr. Seton gives English names the important place, and treats the ever-changing Latin terms as the by-product that they really are. His descriptions aim to give "the impression that the animal makes when seen alive," and "the points that will distinguish it from its nearest relatives." The measurements given are only those that are of prime importance. His facts and figures relating to the speed of animals are new and most welcome; and so are the many admirable illustrations of tracks and feet. As an authority on tracks, Mr. Seton's book will be welcomed by thousands of persons who are seriously seeking to become skilled in wood-craft.

The subject of scatology—the droppings of animals—is here treated in *extenso* for the first time; and the publishers have courageously, and in the true scientific spirit, published Mr. Seton's very illuminating drawings in excellent form. Every outdoorsman who goes into the haunts of wild animals will gladly certify to the value of this section, and thank the author for the first information of importance, so far as we are aware, ever published in English on this subject.

The mind of the animal, its environment, geographic range, home range of the individual, migrations, numbers, food, property rights, storage habits, social habits, language, senses, amusements, mating habits, and mental and moral traits generally—all have been set forth for each animal, so far as knowledge was available. To many readers, the most interesting and valuable side of this work will be found in the observations of the author on the mental and moral life of wild animals.

In elucidation of the geographic ranges of his fifty-nine species, Mr. Seton has with great labor wrought out sixty-eight maps, nearly all of them of full-page size. Only those who make such maps can appreciate the amount of research that they cost. As a rule, the maps show not only the geographic range of the species specially considered, but also that of each of its nearest relatives. For example, the caribou map shows not only the range of the woodland caribou, but also the ranges of the entire nine other species found in North America; and they are now mapped in detail for the first time. It is noticeable that in the map of the author's own working range, his red line of travel goes up to the barren grounds of Canada, north of Great Slave Lake; but we regret the absence of the musk-ox from the life-histories. We do not place high value on the map of the faunal areas of North America. Like every map of its kind, it is too elaborately complicated, too much like a geographic puzzle, to be of great use. The impression that it leaves upon the mind is distinctly chaotic; but that is not the fault of the author.

The most important animals treated in the 1267 pages before us are the Canadian elk, white-tailed deer, mule-deer, moose, woodland caribou, prong-horned antelope, bison, grizzly bear, and black bear. In space and attention all these are treated liberally. The text brings each species squarely down to date, although it is to be noted as an exception that the moose recently introduced in the Adirondacks, to restock the northern wilderness, are all dead, and that this very commendable effort has ended in failure. The mountain sheep, mountain goat, and musk-ox have not been included, because they are not found in Manitoba. Among the smaller mammals treated are seven species of the squirrel family, the woodchuck, beaver, the muskrat, twelve species of mice and voles, the gray gopher, Canadian porcupine, and three rabbits and hares. All these are

in the first volume. The second volume contains the Canada lynx, four wolves and foxes, ten valuable fur-bearers of the marten family, the raccoon, two bears, six shrews and moles, and six bats. Incidentally, we do not subscribe to the author's new notion of writing the English name of *Ursus americanus* as "blackbear."

One of the most novel and interesting features is the wealth of new information, set forth with the aid of many plans and drawings, illustrating the underground life of the burrowing animals. All this is absolutely original and reveals years of painstaking observations. In this field Mr. Seton's pencil has given him an advantage over the ordinary naturalist, and he has used it to the utmost.

As might be expected of Mr. Seton, the illustrations of this work are well-nigh all of them by his own hand, the two volumes containing, in fact, 560 drawings by the author. In this day of many camera pictures of young wild animals in captivity, and of other photographs that fail to illustrate thoroughly their subjects, it is a pleasure to open a book liberally supplied with well-executed drawings that show precisely what the reader wishes to see. (p. 549)

> "Seton's Animal Book," in The Nation, *New York, Vol. LXXXIX, No. 2318, December 2, 1909, pp. 548-49.*

LAWRENCE J. BURPEE   (essay date 1910)

[*A prominent Canadian statesman and historian, Burpee was the author of several volumes on the early exploration of the Canadian wilderness. In the following excerpt, he praises the comprehensive nature of* Life-Histories of Northern Animals, *noting Seton's important additions to the corpus of knowledge about wildlife species.*]

Mr. Ernest Thompson Seton entered the world of letters in 1883 with an article on the Striped Gopher. Three years later he read a paper before the Historical and Scientific Society of Manitoba, on the Mammals of Manitoba. This modest little article formed the nucleus of the . . . magnificent work, *Life Histories of Northern Animals.* (p. 271)

In addition to his own personal observations, covering nearly every State in the Union, and most of the Canadian Provinces, Mr. Seton has gathered together from widely-scattered sources the evidence of hundreds of other students of the animal life of the continent, the result forming a most remarkable series of animal biographies. For some years past Mr. Seton has been widely known as a writer of entertaining stories of animal life. Some readers, judging the form rather than the substance, and with very limited knowledge of the facts of wild animal life, have assumed a rather patronizing attitude toward these tales, and jumped to the conclusion that they were founded on nothing more substantial than the vivid imagination of a clever maker of fiction. Not the least important feature of the present work is the testimony it affords, in clear and scientific terms, as to the substantial accuracy of these animal stories. Here, as in so many other cases, the fact is shown to be often more wonderful than fiction.

Another important result of Mr. Seton's work is the correction of many popular misconceptions. One of these concerns the speed of wild animals. We have all heard marvellous stories as to the phenomenal speed of the coyote, the antelope, and several other animals. After gathering all the available data on the subject, Mr. Seton has reached the deliberate conclusion that the horse still holds his own. "There seems no good reason," says he, "for supposing that any creature on legs—two, three, or four—ever went for any distance faster than a blood race-horse. Salvator's mile in 1 minute 35 1/2 seconds is the fastest pace reliably recorded for anything afoot." Tabulating the evidence, Mr. Seton puts the fastest four-footed animals in the following order: Race-horse, best speed for a mile at the rate of 34 miles an hour; Prong-horned antelope, 32 miles an hour; Greyhound, 30 miles; Texan Jackrabbit, 28; Common Fox, 26; Northern Coyote, 24; Foxhound, 22; and American Gray-wolf, 20. It is interesting to note that a man's best speed for a mile is at the rate of 14 miles an hour.

A number of ancient errors concerning the Beaver are also exposed. It cannot and does not drive stakes; it never plasters the lodge with mud outside—all beaver-lodges are finished outside with sticks; it does not use its tail as a trowel; it does not suck the air out of sticks to make them stay down; it does not cut or carry large logs or use them in the dam; when caught in a steel trap it does not deliberately amputate the foot, but twists about and pulls until it is torn off. On the other hand, Mr. Seton, in his very readable chapter on the Beaver, does much to rehabilitate the character of this sagacious animal. Time was when the Beaver was popularly endowed with almost superhuman intelligence. Of late years we have been inclined to rush to the opposite extreme, and deny it even moderate sagacity. The truth lies between. The facts here presented, and amply substantiated from the works of such careful observers as Lewis H. Morgan, Audubon, Bachman, and other naturalists, including the author, place the Beaver in the first rank among four-footed artisans. (pp. 271-72)

One is tempted to quote some of the many interesting bits of animal biographies found everywhere between the covers of these two substantial volumes, but limits of space make this impossible. It is sufficient to assure the reader that he will find here an immense amount of trustworthy information on each of the animals whose life-histories are given; and the whole is presented in such fascinating form, and so attractively illustrated, that he will find it impossible to skip a single page. (p. 272)

> Lawrence J. Burpee, "Biographical Studies of Wild Animals," in The Dial, Vol. 48, No. 572, April 16, 1910, pp. 271-72.

THE SPECTATOR   (essay date 1910)

[*In the following review of* Life-Histories of Northern Animals, *the critic notes the unique quality of Seton's wildlife descriptions.*]

The main lines of Mr. Thompson Seton's [*Life-Histories of Northern Animals*] are, as might be expected, a little different from those of other natural histories. The author of *Wild Animals I Have Known* and *The Biography of a Grizzly* would not be likely to cast a *magnum opus* into a shape already familiar; he would leave his own character scored deep on any subject he chose to treat. And here we have, in two large volumes, natural history as Mr. Thompson Seton thinks it should be written and illustrated. He has taken the mammals of Manitoba for his particular study, which means, practically speaking, the animals of the United States, for his sixty species exclude only about a dozen of those which belong to North America; and he has endeavoured to show these animals to his readers as the animals have shown themselves to him during thirty years of personal observation. In addition, he has collected the observations of others, always with the view of adding further

Self-portrait done by Seton in 1879.

information about the living animal rather than biological or anatomical detail. To some naturalists, as he puts it, wild animals are mere living targets. They have seen in the wild life round them "nothing but savage or timorous creatures, killing or escaping being killed." They quite forget that animals "have their homes, their mates, their problems and their sorrows—in short, a home life that is their real life, and very often much larger and more important than that of which our hostile standpoint has given us such fleeting glimpses."

We need not reargue here the question of how far we are justified in reading into the lives of animals the hopes and fears and loves and hates which belong to the thought of mankind. We may merely take Mr. Seton's facts as trustworthy data, and build upon them his own theory or any other theory we please. For himself, he sees his conclusions, or the general direction to which his facts will carry him, clearly enough. He finds that his observations fit in with a theory of evolution which derives the mind of man as well as his body from the animals below him, and so, in looking at animals in their home life, he expects to see at work the same tendencies and possibilities which have reached their fulfilment in the human intellect as we know it. He finds the beginnings of all sorts of human manners and capabilities; the rudiments of speech, of musical sense, of the making of a home, decoration and amusements, elementary systems of sanitation, the adoption of laws of marriage and of property, and the bases even of the morality which found its eventual expression in the Ten Commandments. In the range or home-region of an animal he sees parallels with the growth of territorial law among mankind. In the choice and persistent selection of food is the beginning of all property rights. The habit of storing food which belongs to most animals except the horned ruminants comes from the same origin as human frugality. The community of the beaver is "patriarchal rather than domestic." In the home-life, again, of animals the relation to that of human beings offers resemblances which could hardly be mere coincidences; the higher in the scale of creation, the stronger the tendency to monogamy and to the maintenance of a family circle. The more elaborate the home, the greater the necessity for keeping it clean; hence the strict cleanliness of the badgers, the gophers' dry earth-closets, and the communal middenheaps of other animals, such as voles. Vice, crime, and the idea of suicide are even further developments of the "little mind" along parallels with human morality; the main instances which Mr. Seton chooses are the killing of their young by parents, self-mutilation by monkeys and parrots, and breaches of laws of honour among animals which human beings might think of as thieves, such as rats. And so on; we may not follow Mr. Seton in all his deductions, but he is careful to keep facts and theories apart, and we can sift his evidence as we please.

But the main part of the two volumes, of course, consists of the setting down of actually recorded observation of the sixty different species of Manitoban mammals, from the wapiti and the moose to the smallest of pigmy shrews. We turn to the moose, and find records of migrations apparently regular, but never yet wholly explained; we read of rats and mice, and learn what may be news to some, that the common rat (*Mus Norvegicus*) has not yet succeeded in establishing itself in Manitoba. Some very interesting pages are devoted to the disappearance of the buffalo from the American prairies; the short answer to all lamenting over the destruction of those noble herds is that "it was absolutely inevitable." The buffalo occupied the plains which were needed by the overcrowded humanity of Europe. "Producing buffalo was not the best use to which those plains could be put." But it is interesting to note the order in which Mr. Seton classifies the enemies which as a fact brought about the extermination of the great herds. In inverse order of importance, the natural enemies of the buffalo were "blizzards, wolves, prairie fires, bogs, the Indian, and rivers." Even the Indian, driving the herds before him over precipices, did not destroy them as the rivers melting from solid ice to a breaking surface destroyed them every spring. In the opening years of the nineteenth century the traveller would meet a drowned herd which "formed one continuous line in the current for two days and nights"; and that drowning by tens of thousands happened year after year. The advent of the rifle merely hastened the end; but would it be logical, after all, to regard the process by which the Indian arrow and the rifle ended the buffalo as anything else but the working of a law of Nature? We are too much inclined, perhaps, to connect the workings of laws of Nature with processes which seem to be, but are not, more "natural," such as extermination by disease. Disease, for instance, ended the rabbits which swarmed in the south-western half of Winnipeg in 1886. To so astonishing an extent had rabbits multiplied in that summer that farmers began to wonder whether their future was to be that of the Australian farmer. A moderate calculation assessed the rabbit population at a hundred millions. And then, in a single winter, plague flecked the countryside white with dead bodies; the entire "population" vanished. Yet which is the more natural,—the extinction of numbers by diseases of overcrowding, or by the simple but inexorable law of the survival of the fittest?

It would be strange if a book such as this, containing the personal experience of thirty years, did not chronicle some queer incidents and ask some puzzling questions. If any nat-

uralist wished to select a test case to measure the qualities of animal reasoning, could he do better than choose the custom of the coyote when hunting antelope, which is to take up the chase by relays of two coyotes at a time, stationed at intervals on the probable line of flight? Or what could begin a new American *Jungle Book* better than the story told by Mr. Seton of a friendship between a Manitoban badger and a lost boy? The boy, seven years old, somehow found his way into a badger-hole; the badger fought him for the occupation of it, could not turn him out, and eventually brought him food which it shared with him in the hole. The boy was rescued after two weeks, much scratched, but alive, and he wept bitterly at being separated from his savage friend. . . .

It is difficult to conceive of a task of thirty years more admirably carried out than this natural history of the animals of North America. . . .

"Animals of North America," in The Spectator, *Vol. 105, No. 4292, October 1, 1910, p. 488.*

CHARLES G. D. ROBERTS   (essay date 1913)

[*Roberts was an esteemed Canadian poet, short story writer, and critic. Known for his Romantic verse, he was also the author of numerous stories featuring animals as protagonists, and these latter have been favorably compared to those of Seton. In the following excerpt, Roberts praises the realism of Seton's stories and notes the importance of his contributions to the knowledge of animal behavior.*]

If there be one man, since St. Francis of Assisi, whom all the kindreds of the wild have cause to bless, it is Ernest Thompson Seton. It is he who is chiefly responsible for the vogue of the modern "Animal Story." The effect of the modern animal story has been to persuade people that the wild creatures are of interest in their personalities, in their psychology, and not merely as things to be shot or put in shows. This has resulted in a more sympathetic and understandingly humane attitude toward our inarticulate kin.

When I credit the vogue of the modern animal story to Ernest Seton, I am not unmindful, needless to say, of the inimitable Mowgli. But those unrivalled creations of Kipling's are, obviously, of quite another species. They derive from the old fabliaux and from the folk-lore tales. Their natural history may be sound enough, as far as it goes, but it is incidental, and concerns us only so far as it helps along the story. The tales of Seton and his disciples, on the other hand, derive directly from the work of such close and loving observers of nature as Richard Jeffries and John Burroughs. They aim to present carefully observed fact. But to give it wider currency and more concrete personal interest, they present it in the form of fiction. They individualise the bird, beast, fish, or insect with which they deal. But, unlike the old fabliaux and their kind, they are careful not to humanise their subjects. They are either fragments of animal biography, or they are formally developed *nouvelles,* each with a central figure, about which gather the experiences which observation has shown appropriate to its kind. On the material side, such nature stories are fact disguised as fiction.

But there is another side to these stories, and it is the pre-eminently distinctive side. They aim above all to get at the psychology of their subjects. They are not content to deal with the skins of the wild creatures, but they seek to get inside those skins. From observed actions they strive to deduce motives and emotions. They are based on the conviction—shared by practically all experienced hunters and successful keepers or tamers of animals, and denied chiefly by closet theorisers—that there *is* an animal psychology. The old animal stories, if they went beyond mere external incident or adventure, simply humanised their subjects, ascribing emotions and motives that would be proper, in like circumstances, to human beings. Seton has taught us to expect, in the animal story, a psychology immeasurably simpler, to be sure, than that of man, a psychology to the last degree limited, indeed, but none the less real and worthy of investigation. He spurns the theory that all animal life below the human plane is the blind and helpless slave of reflex action.

As spokesman of the inarticulate kindreds, Ernest Seton is uniquely qualified. He approaches them from so many points. He knows them in so many ways. And he is untainted by that excess of sentimentality towards them which too often perverts the view of the sympathetic nature-lover. As a country boy in Canada he began their acquaintance very early, and found it so much to his taste that he has been following it up and extending it diligently ever since. He is an expert with gun, trap, and camera. Cunning as an Indian to unravel the tangled trails, and patient as a lynx in watching, he has been able to spy upon the wild things when they least suspected it, and so get at the intimate side of their lives. He has *seen* more than other men. And he has seen with such discriminating, accurate, and conscientious eyes, that I should be inclined to doubt the evidence of my own eyes, if I found it conflicting with that of his. I might, perhaps, join issue with him in a matter of the psychology at work behind the facts; but as to the facts themselves, gathered by his own observation, I would never regard them as open to question.

Having gained, as hunter and naturalist, so close an acquaintance with the creatures of the wilderness, Seton's first thought was to depict them as a painter, as a draughtsman. In the classrooms of the Royal Academy he trained his native aptitude for the brush and the pencil, and became a skilful artist—needless to say, not of the Post-Impressionist school. There is never any likelihood, for instance, of one of Seton's grizzlies being mistaken for a view of St. Paul's in a rainy sunrise. The product of his pencil is always so definitely and distinctively what it sets out to be, that the most austere of scientific naturalists may accept it as a label. At the same time we nature-lovers, who care more about the personal characteristics of a beast than about the number and configuration of his molars, are given that intimate individual touch which we are always seeking.

But when Ernest Seton undertook to convey his rich knowledge and fine enthusiasm, he found he had much more to say than brush and pencil could express. His own pictures drove him to writing about them. With the true instinct of the story-teller, his funds of authentic and verified material fall naturally into the form of fiction. The result was that fresh, vital book, **Wild Animals I Have Known.** To the credit of the popular taste be it said, this pre-eminently sane and convincing book won instantly a success as emphatic as that of the most sensational novel. It was no mere "boom" success, however, but an enduring one. His other books in the same vein drove home the triumph; and the modern Nature tale was established in a popularity which neither travesty nor attack has been able to undermine.

But to the temperament of this vigorous nature-lover even the pen and the pencil together did not seem to offer outlet enough. He had mimetic and dramatic faculty, a powerful and flexible voice accustomed to carrying across the wooded valleys, and the gift of telling a story vividly beside the camp-fire. These gifts he impressed to the task of interpreting his shy wilderness friends to the public. He went on the lecture platform; and hundreds of thousands who had been left cold by the printed page were reached and roused to interest by his magnetic personality. With his tall, lithe form, sinewy from much following of the trails, his lean and swarthy face, his wavy black hair worn rather longer than convention prescribes, his dark and watchful eyes, his head held somewhat up as if to sniff the air and search the hillsides, he looks his part as interpreter of the wilds. And when he adds to the convincing force of his narration his amazingly accurate mimicries, reproducing the calls of the beasts, the pipings and the cries of birds, the spell is so strong that the lights and the intent audience fade away, and once more one goes furtively with alert eyes and restrained breath, through the transparent but confusing shadows of the ancient forest. (pp. 147-48)

Charles G. D. Roberts, "Ernest Thompson Seton," in The Bookman, *London, Vol. XLV, No. 267, December, 1913, pp. 147-49.*

THE TIMES LITERARY SUPPLEMENT (essay date 1916)

[*In the following review of* Wild Animal Ways, *a collection of Seton's animal stories, the critic suggests that, while Seton's stories are not without literary merit, they are seriously flawed by anthropomorphism.*]

If you like animal stories told in this form, then you will like [**Wild Animal Ways**].That is not the mere truism that it may sound. The stories are in substance good, the narrator thoroughly knows his heroes and heroines and villains—the razorback, or wild boar, the wild geese, Way-Atcha, the racoon, and the rest of them. And they make good drama; their doings are interesting, full of movement; but is this the most satisfactory way of telling us about them? The way may be described very shortly; it is this: to make the animals think very human thoughts, and to tell the tale of their doings as if they were ordered by very human motives. In our opinion this is a mode which gets the whole psychology of the animals wrong, and so sets all in an unreal atmosphere. A tinted, artificial light is thrown on it, quite unlike the open-air sunshine or natural gloom of cloud. . . .

Here and there we meet some very charming passages. It is something of a triumph to make a reader's eyes grow a little misty over the death of a young porker. Mr. Seton achieves it.

> And Runtie [Runtie was a little wild pigling, slain by the wild cat—a death gloriously avenged by Foam, his father], he was lying deep in the brush on the other side of the stump. His mother came and nosed him over, and nudged him gently, and came again to nudge. But the brothers were lively and thirsty; she must go on with them. She raged against the fierce brute that had killed her little one. She lingered about, then led the others to the brook. Then they all came back. The little ones were once more merry and riotous. The mother came to nudge and coax the limp and bloody form, but its eyes had glazed. The father tossed the furry trash aside, and then all passed on. . . .

There is so much that is pleasant and true in this, as in the other books of Mr. Seton's, that it seems niggardly to deal it out such grudging praise as the above. They may indeed be taken as a type. Of their own sort they are very good. But is it the right sort? Is it the best way of telling animal stories? That is the question, and it is largely a question of taste. The present writer has to confess it not entirely to his taste. Tales of the talking animals—folklore and the "Jungle Book"—are one thing. Frankly, we are in the atmosphere of fiction, of poetry, or whatever you please to call it. It is an atmosphere that has its own truth to nature for all that. But here, where are we? In an atmosphere in neither sense real, scarcely quite honest, neither frankly fictitious and poetic nor severely true to fact. It is just a little too theatrical for the one and not quite candidly enough imaginative for the other. But there are many whom it pleases, and to those who like the form the substance here given us may be commended unreservedly.

> *"Wild Animal Ways," in* The Times Literary Supplement, *August 31, 1916, p. 411.*

MICHEL POIRIER   (essay date 1927)

[*In the following excerpt, Poirier examines the development of Seton's portrayals of animals.*]

A perusal of Thompson Seton's earliest writings clearly shows that his . . . conception of the animal story did not come to him of a sudden but was the result of attempts made in various directions by a man who, all his life, had been passionately interested in natural history. The first of these, **"A Carberry Deer Hunt,"** appeared in 1886 in *Forest and Stream,* a magazine for hunters and fishermen. Dealing with his experiences in the hunting of his first deer, it is, in his own words, "a strictly truthful diary," a record told in the first person, aiming above all at accuracy and giving lengthy particulars of his doings, interesting to no others but sportsmen. The second original variety of Thompson Seton's stories is exemplified for the first time by **"Why the Chickadee goes Crazy once a Year"** (1893). Mother Carey warns the little birds that live in North America that, as cold weather is coming, they should fly southwards. Most of them follow that advice but the chickadees think it is sheer nonsense. When the cold does come, they are out of their wits for a few days, during which "they look for the Gulf of Mexico in squirrels' holes, but finally make the best of it and resume their singing." A little later, in **"Rag-gylug,"** Thompson Seton explains that the roses once armed themselves with thorns in order to be protected against the animals that used to ill-treat them. These stories belong to the same vein as etiological Indian folk-tales and may have been inspired by them. That hypothesis appears most probable when one recalls that Thompson Seton knows and admires Indian life, from which he has borrowed many features in the organization of his scouting league.

From mere diary notes, the record of actual observations on one hand, from stories partaking of the nature of folk-tales on the other, Thompson Seton passes to a more polished and more realistic form. It is uncertain whether that change is the result of his own thoughts or is to be attributed to the influence of [Charles G. D.] Roberts' early stories, at that time not numerous and published only in magazines. **"Lobo,"** the tale of a wolf (1894), is his first attempt at a more ambitious treatment of his material. It seeks to entertain rather than to present a minute record of events; it is more carefully written and contains less precise details than the **"Carberry Hunt"**; notwithstanding a certain romantic tendency, it is on the whole far more realistic than **"Why the Chickadee . . ."** Since that time, he has endeavoured in many stories to make others share his

conviction that killing beautiful creatures solely for one's pleasure is unworthy of civilized men.

Thompson Seton is to be considered primarily as a naturalist. An examination of his methods of composition will demonstrate this, his stories being built in the very manner one might expect from a student of nature. He watches animals, notes down little facts about their appearance, customs, tastes, etc., then attributes many of these, observed in various individuals of the same species, to a single one. This perfectly legitimate device, by means of which the story remains scientifically true, is justified by the desire of giving a full presentation of a wild animal's life, from which the most eager naturalist can only hope to witness fragments. Consequently, most of Thompson Seton's narratives are told in what may be called the subjective manner: while the tale as a whole is the author's invention, it is nothing but a mosaic composed of facts that have either been witnessed directly by himself or related by other observers or again surmised from the traces they left. The animals in his works are always seen through the eyes of the writer, who appears as the direct follower of the nineteenth century tame animal story writers, enlarging their field but retaining their method. In particular, he shows, like them, a marked partiality to his heroes, due to his sympathy for animals and also to his desire of increasing the interest of his tales; he rejoices at their triumphs, bewails their sufferings, calls the impassible forces of nature to their help.

His stories may be divided into two groups. Some relate an animal's life and adventures, during a certain period, more especially its relations with men, relations that may be caused by the fact that the animal is domesticated (dog in **"Wully,"** pigeon in **"Arnaux"**), by a man's wish to destroy a beast that tries to escape, often by accomplishing extraordinary exploits (**"Lobo"**), or again by the naturalist's desire to take observations and gain a more intimate knowledge of wild life (*Johnny Bear*). His more elaborate tales are biographies, partial, i.e. stopping before the animal's death to avoid a tragical ending, more frequently complete, and of which an important part is devoted to attempts at killing the hero. The biography, the favourite form of story for a naturalist, enables him to convey more information about animals since they can be shown at all the stages of their development with all the habits and tendencies particular to these respective stages.

Not content to show animals in action, Thompson Seton cannot always refrain from adding comments and general considerations: his desire to teach is manifested in a number of short didactic passages scattered in his writings. **"Krag,"** for instance, is interspersed with paragraphs on social conventions among animals, on the qualities required from the leader of a herd or pack, the advantages of zigzag bounding, and so forth. This tendency concurs with the juxtaposition of small facts to impair the unity of the tales. In some of the shorter stories, such as **"Lobo,"** a number of brief episodes are discreetly inserted in the main plot, but the difficulty is greater in biographies. Mr. Seton made some attempts to obviate this. Monarch, the Bear's life is compared to a river, flowing down from a mountain, the birthplace of both, leaping over or breaking all the barriers or obstacles it encounters until it reaches the plain where it ends, landlocked; Wabb's life appears as a period of strength between two ages of weakness; again, the sentimental climax at the end of other stories may help to give a feeling of completeness. None the less, the reader too often feels that the tale is a "plotless," inorganic succession of small incidents.

Realizing that such tales would appeal especially to children, Thompson Seton has written many of them in the manner of juvenile books. Truly, most animal stories are well suited to children, although some have a genuine interest for adult readers. Besides their usefulness due to the information they convey about creatures that often capture youth's fancy, the simplicity of the psychological processes described and the brisk succession of events make them better suited for young readers than many other forms of fiction. In some of Thompson Seton's tales, the language is excessively simple, the vocabulary very limited, the animals shown as thinking, feeling and acting like men; these stories give information by means of questions and answers, display a constant care to avoid all unpleasant incidents and contain a tendency to moralize which, for instance, transforms some episodes in *Bannertail* into veritable Esopic fables. Such tales, which however form only a portion of his work, can appeal only to young children and remain outside the sphere of literature.

Thompson Seton belongs to a school of nature study that looks upon animals not as mere automata, led blindly by their sole instincts, but as creatures enjoying the faculty of reasoning, of course to a lesser degree than man. "We and the beasts are kin. Man has nothing that the animals have not at least a vestige of; the animals have nothing that man does not in some degree share."

Although he may believe in a closer resemblance between man and beasts than many, this interpretation, which underlies all the tame animal stories that preceded his, is a condition *sine qua non* of realistic representation of animal life. Creatures entirely governed by instinct may be the objects of the most fascinating observations, but they present no purely human and therefore no literary interest. Thompson Seton often chooses as his heroes unusual, exceptional individuals, i.e. animals endowed with a particularly large share of strength and intelligence. Their remarkable features make them easier for the naturalist to distinguish from their fellow-creatures in the wilderness; above all, they enable the writer to attribute uncommon performances or exploits to them and thus create admiration and amazement in the reader. He presents a series of animal heroes, of "animal great men" who improve the physical condition of their descendants, transmit new methods of defence and livelihood to them and thus have a most beneficial influence on their species.

Probably because of the exceptional endowments of Thompson Seton's animals, instinct, presented chiefly as a warning sent by nature to her children or as a sure means of recovering impaired health, plays a very small part in their lives. The knowledge that guides their actions originates from their own personal experience, Thompson Seton assuming that they have the faculty of generalizing, or from the teaching of their parents, whom he repeatedly shows performing certain acts referring to hiding, scenting, or hunting, in the presence of their young, in order that they may repeat and learn them. It must be confessed that Thompson Seton seems too ready to call upon intelligence to explain the different habits and actions of animals. One instance will suffice to illustrate this: noticing that big animals such as bears stamp their claws on some trees, he surmised that this marking is either a declaration that they consider the surrounding district as their own private range or a means of exchanging information with other animals who recognize the various impressions and smells. Upon that theory is built an important episode in *The Biography of a Grizzly:* a small bear, seeing Wahb's mark, rolls a log under the tree and,

standing upon it, imprints his claw much higher, thus terrorizing Wahb who is convinced that a bear of monstrous size inhabits the same region. . . . Again, Thompson Seton describes some schemes imagined and carried out by animals and so ingenious as to be hardly credible. His animals can also exchange ideas between themselves. His anthropomorphic tendency is in a few cases so strong as to make his heroes appear as actual men in disguise. The old Wahb, weary of an existence embittered by enemies and disease, deliberately shambles to a crevice whence poisonous gas emanates and thus commits a sort of suicide. It is hardly conceivable that man's hobbies, derived from his sense of property, should be shared by an animal like Silverspot, the crow, who owns a collection of shells and bits of earthenware which he digs up and handles in his leisure moments.

The relative importance to be given to the above remarks should not however be exaggerated; it is only fair to add that, in spite of an incredible fact here and there, the general impression left by Thompson Seton's tales is one of satisfactory verisimilitude. Most actions attributed to animals are in perfect keeping with the amount of intelligence commonly ascribed to them; nay, some clearly illustrate intellectual limitations. Thus a captured bear buries the trap that holds him, believing that he will thus no longer be tied.

Although not proportionally numerous, the passages tainted with anthropomorphism brought disapproval from a few competent naturalists and were the cause of what is known as the "nature-fakers controversy." John Burroughs opened the campaign in 1903 with an article on "Real and Sham Natural History" [see excerpt dated 1903]; a strong opponent of instinct, he refused to admit that Thompson Seton's stories are composed of true facts: "True as romance, true in their artistic effects, true in their power to entertain they certainly are, but true as natural history they as certainly are not," and he supports this affirmation by an examination and refutation of a few characteristic episodes. Some years passed, during which Thompson Seton's success encouraged others to follow him in the new path of the animal story. In his turn, President Roosevelt censured those writers who present fiction labelled as fact, thus starting a polemic which was to rage during many months in American periodicals. "Mr. Thompson Seton," he said, "has made interesting observations of fact and much of his fiction has a real value. But he should make it clear that it is fiction and not fact." While this controversy had disastrous effects on the reputation of other nature writers, in particular on that of the Rev. W. J. Long, it left Thompson Seton's almost undamaged as his works contain but a small proportion of incredible incidents. It can hardly be denied that occasionally, carried away by his desire of making a captivating tale, he oversteps the limits of scientific truth. Nevertheless, we subscribe to President Roosevelt's statement: there would be no cause for such discussions if authors of animal stories, and Thompson Seton in particular, instead of boasting of the absolute truthfulness of their books, would acknowledge that they use natural history just as some novelists use history, not primarily to teach but to entertain. No one denies all merit to Sir Walter Scott's and Alexandre Dumas' novels because of the inaccuracies they may contain, but when historical facts are required, more reliable authorities should be consulted.

It remains true that the great danger that besets the animal story writer is the tendency to humanize too much—for, up to a certain degree, humanization is permissible, nay desirable, in modern as well as in Esopic fiction. Thompson Seton has not always avoided that danger: carried away by his admiration of animal nature, he has occasionally attributed incredible exploits to his heroes, not frequently enough to impair the value of his stories materially.

It is astonishing to notice that he has failed to perceive how descriptions of nature, provided they were discreetly inserted into the stories, would have heightened the interest and beauty of those. With the exception of a page at the beginning of "**Krag**" and a shorter fragment in *The Sandhill Stag,* the scenes of the dramas are never described. Yet, nature has a place in Thompson Seton's works, not as the scenery but as a powerful deity, a protecting mother who sometimes listens to her children's prayers and intervenes on their behalf, to avenge them as in "**Krag,**" or to save them as in *Silver Fox.* When, at the end of a long hunt, Domino the fox is brought to bay on a spit of land jutting into a river and dives into the water, Thompson Seton, in the manner of a Greek chorus commenting upon the drama and entreating the gods, addresses the river, in whose power the fox's fate now lies:

> O River, flashing the red and gold of the red and golden sky, and dappled with blocks of sailing ice! O River of the long chase that ten times before had saved him and dashed red death aside! This is the time of times! Now thirty deaths are on his track and the track is of feebling bounds. O River of the aspen dale, will you turn traitor in his dire extremity, thus pen him in, deliver him to his foes?

We are next told that the fox successfully swims across, in spite of the strong current which engulfs his fiercest enemy, the cruel hound Hekla.

Writing most frequently in a simple and straightforward style, Thompson Seton sometimes excels in the humorous presentation of facts, the accurate and original rendering of some scenes. Yet in his descriptions, too often abstract and dry, we miss the numerous and vivid details with which Roberts composes his pictures and which make them so easy for the imagination to visualize. A distinguished naturalist but not a born writer, he falls short of the artistic standard attained by [Charles G. D. Roberts]; if the reader contrasts their respective treatment of the same subject, namely the description of a forest on fire and of its various dwellers taking shelter in a pond (*Monarch,* ch. IX, and *Red Fox,* ch. XIV), he cannot fail to come to that conclusion.

If we now seek what is the author's aim in composing his stories, we find that, besides the desire of amusing by means of tales of adventures, a desire which he shares with most authors of imaginative literature, Thompson Seton writes with several objects in view. In the first place, he wishes to convey to his readers his admiration of wild animals, his keen sense of the glory of life, his almost pagan love of physical strength and beauty.

> There is no greater joy to the truly living thing than the joy of being alive, of feeling alive in every part and power. It was a joy to Krag now to stretch his perfect limbs in a shock of playful battle with his friends . . . it was a joy to press his toes on some thin ledge, then sail an impossible distance across some fearful chasm to another ledge . . .

Also, Thompson Seton eagerly desires to preserve wild life threatened with complete destruction by the daily holocausts of hunters; "My chief motive, my most earnest underlying wish has been to stop the extermination of harmless animals; not for their sakes but for ours, firmly believing that each of

Seton with one of his taxidermy specimens. Courtesy of the Seton Memorial Library, Philmont Scout Ranch.

our native wild creatures is in itself a precious heritage that we have no right to destroy or put beyond the reach of our children." In order to stop that work of destruction, he has more confidence in appeals to sympathy than to reason: hence the sentimental element, either under the form of direct addresses to his readers or, more frequently, of touches inserted in the narrative and designed to create pity for suffering animals.

A third object impels him to write animal stories, namely his desire to popularize natural history, to present scientific facts in the most attractive form. Repeatedly, this study has shown that he is a naturalist first and foremost. Hence the great stress he lays on the scientific aspect of his work and the corresponding neglect of its literary side which displays no very great inborn gifts. Nevertheless, while appraising the value of his work, it must be borne in mind that he had the boldness to devoting much energy to the animal story at a time when that literary form was not highly appreciated; he proved that there was a "demand" for tales of animals and induced others to deal with the same subject. (pp. 304-12)

> Michel Poirier, "The Animal Story in Canadian Literature: E. Thompson Seton and Charles G. D. Roberts," in Queen's Quarterly, Vol. 34, No. 3, January, 1927, pp. 298-312.

FRED BODSWORTH (essay date 1959)

[*Bodsworth is a Canadian naturalist and author. In the following excerpt, he contends that, despite their flaws, Seton's animal stories were an important contribution to the development of animal fiction.*]

In *Wild Animals I Have Known,* Seton originated a strikingly new literary form known now as the "realistic" animal story. In all previous fiction of this type the animals talked and thought like humans, but Seton tried to show animal lives and personalities as they are in nature. Many biologists today, viewing Seton in the sharper light of modern biological knowledge, claim he fell short of depicting animals as they actually are; but sixty years ago *Wild Animals I have Known* was a new and monumental step toward realistic animal portrayal. It revealed to millions of readers that animals have loves and tragedies not unlike our own. It started a whole generation looking with new understanding at the world of nature. It was the real beginning of the movement which grew into today's vigorous conservation crusade.

Probably a majority of today's naturalists and biologists had their interest sparked first by Seton's stories, for he turned thousands of boys to the outdoors. I remember vividly the impact of Seton on my own generation—the classroom in tears as the teacher read **"Raggylug"** or **"Lobo, King of the Currumpaw"**; the library waiting list for *Two Little Savages,* which most boys reread religiously each year; the hours in the woods trailing animals, building Indian tepees, with a Seton woodcraft book as our Bible and constant guide. Seton is still in demand, I hear, holding his own despite the Lone Ranger and Wyatt Earp. It was a moving and reassuring thing recently to lift a tattered copy of *Two Little Savages* from a library shelf and find a bundle of dried pine needles in its pages—evidence that Seton is still going into the woods with boys. I hope that, like Tennyson's brook, he goes on forever, and he shows good signs of doing so. Recent paperback editions have pushed Seton book sales to three million. The Seton message—"We and the beasts are kin"—lives on.

But Seton has a special significance to Canada other than the fact that he has kept three generations of us animal-conscious. Our homegrown belittlers of Canadian art and culture, who bemoan that Canada has originated nothing of artistic merit, overlook that Seton's wildlife fiction was an original Canadian literary form that was quickly imitated by Kipling and other literary greats throughout the world. Though he was born in England and lived most of his life a U.S. citizen, Ernest Thompson Seton wrote his first stories in Canada, and most of his wildlife characters were animals he studied here. Because of this, and because another Canadian, Charles G. D. Roberts, followed quickly along the literary trail that Seton blazed, the realistic animal story is now recognized as a Canadian contribution to world literature.

Seton had three careers—art, science and writing—and he won recognition in all of them. But his fiction writing, the career that interested him least, was the one that brought him wealth and fame. He had begun it merely as a hobby, as an expression of his love for nature, and even after it had thrust him into world prominence he still wished to be known first as a scientist. The recognition he gained in scientific circles as a competent, self-taught biologist he prized more than all the fame and wealth he won as a teller of animal tales. Of his forty-two books, he was proudest of his huge four-volume *Lives of Game Animals,* a scientific work to which he devoted ten years of his life. He obtained a wry satisfaction from the fact that his *Lives,* though it established him as a scientist, sold only twenty-six hundred copies while his animal fiction sold millions and made him a millionaire. Today, almost fifty years later, Seton's

Lives is still a must for every mammalogist's library and second-hand copies are in demand at five times the original price.

But despite his reputation as a scientist, there are glaring scientific flaws in his popular fiction. Some of Seton's stories show a fallacy common for his time—the error of anthropomorphism, or unduly humanizing of animals. Modern biologists contend that Seton's animal heroes are too liberally endowed with human emotions like love, grief and hate. Some possess too much reasoning power to be acceptable as animals today. There is the small bear in *Biography of a Grizzly,* for example, which rolls a log up to a tree and stands on it so that it can reach up and leave a higher claw mark in the bark, hoping to make other grizzlies believe there is a monstrous bear inhabiting the region. Modern authorities on animal behavior say this and other episodes imply a degree of intelligence that animals just don't possess. But the anthropomorphic flaws are more than offset by sound scientific realism that characterizes most of Seton's work. (pp. 22, 32)

Fred Bodsworth, "The Backwoods Genius with the Magic Pen," in Maclean's Magazine, Vol. 72, No. 12, June 6, 1959, pp. 22, 32, 34, 38-40.

S. E. READ (essay date 1962)

[*In the following excerpt, Read provides an assessment of Seton's writings and literary talents.*]

[Ernest Thompson Seton] started in a modest way with articles and short stories, but eventually he wrote more than thirty volumes, ranging from scientific and semi-scientific works to the vast bulk of his writing, which is specifically directed towards the younger reader. In all his works, however, Seton centres his interest on one focal point—the world of nature.

From the moment he bought Ross's *Birds of Canada* (he was then thirteen), he was well on his way to becoming a self-taught naturalist. Early in his career he published scientific articles on birds and animals, and in 1909 he produced his *Life-Histories of Northern Animals: An Account of the Mammals of Manitoba.* Not until some nineteen years later, however, when he was approaching seventy, did Seton complete his most ambitious work, his *Lives of Game Animals.* This vast work, originally published in four volumes, immediately brought him recognition as an outstanding naturalist. Professor McTaggart Cowan, himself a wild life specialist of international reputation, tells me that the *Lives* still stands as an invaluable reference work in its field, in spite of errors and unscientific observations and of its anecdotal passages and personal reminiscences. For Seton, even in his scientific garb, could never get far away from the technique of the tale, nor from the personal approach he exhibited with such skill in his more popular writings.

In some ways Seton was actually in revolt against the scientific method. To him the type of natural history then current was too general, too vague, to be effective. Scientists, he said, placed their emphasis on the species. For him a true understanding of animals and birds came through a study of the individual. To him each animal was different, possessing its own particular characteristics, its own special profile of behaviour. Moreover the line of demarcation setting man apart from animal was a slight one. He even endowed his heroes and heroines with human virtues—dignity, sagacity, mother-love, love of liberty, obedience, fidelity—and encouraged man to look closely at the beasts of the fields and the birds of the air so that he, man, might learn from them ways to a better life.

At times, especially in his early stories, he so humanized his figures as to strain the credulity of his more critical readers and to antagonize the scientifically minded. At first, he even made his animals talk, not as the animals of Aesop talked, but as human beings talk when caught in situations that arouse such emotions as terror, love, or pity. He translates the single "thump" of a rabbit into "look out" or "freeze" and the triple "thump, thump, thump" into "run for dear life." In his later stories, however, he declared this conversational technique to be "archaic", but he never ceased to endow his heroes with human characteristics far beyond the accepted reaches of instinct. In **"The Springfield Fox"**, for example, his heroine, Vix, leads the pursuing hounds across a railway trestle just in time to have an engine overtake and destroy them. And Wahb, the aging and heroic figure in *The Biography of a Grizzly,* is given a truly Roman end when, worn out and burdened by a sense of defeat, he courageously enters a cave filled with fumes he knows to be lethal.

It was, I believe, because of this same stress on the importance of the individual, with its consequent narrowing of the gap between animal and man, linked of course with his ability to tell a good tale, that Seton as a wild life biographer was from the first successful. He started in a modest way with such tales as **"The Story of a Little Gray Rabbit,"** which appeared in that grand old magazine for children, *St. Nicholas,* in October, 1890, and he was soon in full flight as a writer of animal fiction. With the great success of *Wild Animals I Have Known* (it was published in 1898 and ran through four editions in two months) his fame was firmly established.

It would be a mistake to suppose that Seton's path to fame was completely smooth. Naturalists especially regarded his works with scepticism. Foremost among them was the famous and formidable John Burroughs, who turned his sharp pen against Seton in "Real and Sham Natural History", in the *Atlantic Monthly* [see excerpt dated 1903]. The attack opened obliquely and ended frontally. Early in the article Burroughs warmly praises [Charles G. D.] Roberts' most recent work, *Kindred of the Wild,* a volume in which "one finds much to admire and commend, and but little to take exception to . . . in many ways the most brilliant collection of animal stories that has appeared." This was a bitter dose for Seton to swallow, but more bitter was the one given a page later. "Mr. Thompson Seton says in capital letters that his stories are true, and it is this emphatic assertion that makes the judicious grieve. True as romance, true in their artistic effects, true in their power to entertain the young reader, they certainly are; but true as natural history they are not."

Seton was deeply hurt. He was, if one can judge by his writings, a self-centred man—opinionated and sincerely convinced of the validity of his techniques. He was also sensitive, especially to this unfavourable criticism from a man he had long admired. His autobiography bears witness to his distress. He devotes a full chapter to the Burroughs affair. He refused, he says, to answer the attack publicly, waiting, rather, like a clever hunter until he could meet his antagonist face to face. The chance soon came, for the two men were brought together at a dinner given by the fiery little Andrew Carnegie, who not only loved wealth but also worshipped famous authors. With Boswellian glee, and with considerable gloating, Seton records his conversation with the older naturalist. Burroughs, he says, was awkward and ill at ease. He, on the contrary, was self-pos-

sessed and quickly took full control of the situation. It was he who chose the subject of conversation—wolves, his favourite topic. With barrage-like intensity he covered Burroughs with probing questions about his first-hand knowledge of these animals. Had he ever seen even *one* wild one? Under the attack, says Seton, all that "poor old John" could answer was "No", "No", and "No", until finally, after a further scattering of shots, he completely "broke down and wept".

If the incident is accurately recorded the evening must have been far from a jolly one, but I am moved to doubt by what follows in a subsequent paragraph. Burroughs, says Seton, quickly made a public apology in the *Atlantic* for July, 1904, by lauding Seton in these words: "Mr. Thompson Seton, as an artist and a raconteur, ranks by far the highest in this field; he is truly delightful." But a glance at the actual article bears interesting fruit. Entitled "The Literary Treatment of Nature" it really continues Burroughs' early attack, though perhaps with slightly less acidity. "I do not expect my natural history to back up the Ten Commandments," wrote Burroughs, "or to be an illustration of the value of training-schools and kindergartens, or to afford a commentary upon the vanity of human wishes." And, most significant: "We have a host of nature students in our own day, bent on plucking out the heart of every mystery in the fields and woods. Some are dryly scientific, some are sensational, and a few are altogether admirable. Mr. Thompson Seton, as an artist and *raconteur*, ranks by far the highest in this field, *and to those who can separate the fact from fiction in his animal stories*, he is truly delightful." As I have indicated by the last italics, old John's public apology was limited, to say the least. I still wonder a bit if he really did break down and weep before Carnegie and his assembled guests.

Yet this brief encounter has its points of interest. The soundness of Burroughs' position is obvious, but so, too, is the deep faith that Seton had in himself. The modern naturalist still looks on the Seton stories as a strange mixture of fact and fiction. But the young reader is not a trained naturalist, and willing to suspend disbelief, if any exists, he reads the biographies as written, feels the full impact of their conflicts and tragedies, and obtains much factual information about the world of wild life.

Standing quite aside from all of Seton's other works are two books that demand special comment—*Rolf in the Woods* and *Two Little Savages*. The first is nominally an historical novel for the young; the second a rich brew in which are mixed nearly all the ingredients found in varying degrees elsewhere in his writings. It is the quintessence of Seton.

I first read *Rolf* shortly after it appeared in 1911. In the half-century that had slipped away since then the details of the yarn had disappeared beyond recall, but the general impact of the book still lingered. When I re-read it recently I could easily see why. Set in the era of the border war of 1812-14, the story revolves around its two central figures—Rolf Kittering, a desolate, insecure white orphan, and Quonab, a noble Indian, with whom Rolf seeks refuge and through whom he learns the ways of life in the woods, and the values of a simple and primitive religious faith. The inherent didacticism in the work is not repulsively obvious, for both preaching and teaching are well blended with the exciting events of the narrative itself, including Rolf's escape from the combined tyranny of a besotted uncle and a rigid New England society, the struggle for survival in the deep woods of the Green Mountains, and the dangers of acting as scout and guide for American forces along the Canadian border.

The actual war, with its causes, events, and attendant horrors, is carefully kept in the background, for Seton hated war and the military mind. Only towards the conclusion of *Rolf* does he allow the excitement of armed combat to creep in at all; he prefers—and in this he is consistent—to concentrate on the more peaceful thrills of camping, canoeing, hunting, trapping, and learning the Red Man's way of living. It all makes for good reading, and inasmuch as there is something of a plot with considerable suspense it is a good yarn, too. Seton wrote nothing else quite like it.

But another work also stands by itself—the classic in the Seton canon—*Two Little Savages*. It contains the essence of all of the beliefs that Seton held so dear. It is also the best and most evenly written of his works, evidencing not only his superb knowledge of animal life, but also his ability to tell a good story, to handle dialogue and to catch the sounds and accents of dialects, to write clear expositions, to preach unobtrusively, a good sermon, and to create convincing characters. It has been, I would guess, the most widely read of his books, and it is the book, I believe, that will last the longest.

Basically the ingredients are autobiographical. In the summer of 1875 the fifteen-year-old Thompson was seriously ill, and, under the doctor's orders, he was sent to Lindsay to live with the Blackwell family, who had moved into the large house formerly owned by Mr. Thompson when he was attempting, without success, to be a "gentleman farmer." William Blackwell, the head of the household, was a practical, hard-working, hard-bargaining man. Superficially he was tough and severe, but under the surface he was kindly and understanding. To Ernest he was a better man by far than his own father. As for Mrs. Blackwell, she was a fountain of motherly sympathy. Quickly the lonely, sickly boy became a member of the family group. In *Two Little Savages* the Blackwells become the Raftens, and one of the Blackwell boys is transformed into the second little savage—Sam. As for Ernest himself, he is given the name of Yan—his favourite nickname from his Toronto days. Even the minor characters are drawn from the folk of the village and its neighbouring farms—dirty, snivelling Guy; old Caleb, wise in woodcraft and Indian lore; and the Sanger (Lindsay) Witch, the ageless Granny de Neuville, who, though a repulsive crone, proves an unending source of folklore and herbal knowledge, which she transmits to Yan in a thick Irish accent. Around these characters the plot is formed, and thin though it is, it is sufficient to hold most readers to the end. The vicious three-fingered tramp is duly caught and subdued, and the evidence extracted from him is enough to terminate the bitter quarrel between Raften and old Caleb, and to restore that poor but dignified ancient to his rightful place in the community.

The obvious plot, however, is really a subsidiary affair. The real purpose of the work is to show how Yan, the insecure, sensitive, unhealthy boy, achieves status among his fellows. This he does through his unremitting study of nature, through practical camping, through learning *and* using Indian woodcraft lore, and through his willingness to venture into the dark and mysterious recesses of the forest and to face danger.

To Sam and Yan achievement brought excitement. It was exciting to make a tepee—not any old tepee but a real Indian tepee. It was exciting, too, to make a fire with rubbing-sticks, to cook, Indian fashion, to listen to the strange night noises,

to track animals (even the family cat), to trap, to hunt, to kill—not a coon but a spitting, vicious lynx. It was exciting for these two little savages to do all these things for the very reason that in such things Seton himself found his own particular, exciting way of life. He knew of what he wrote and was able to convey that knowledge with enthusiasm to the millions who were to read the work.

Thus far I have said nothing about his ability as a writer in the more limited sense of that word. To avoid some comment on him as a literary person would be a continuation of the silence with which he has been generally treated by literary historians and critics. But to separate his skill as a stylist from the other ingredients that he poured into his moulds is not an easy task. Perhaps he did not even regard himself as a literary figure. His writings indicate little interest in the great works of literature and he seldom refers to other writers. Yet he did formulate for himself a simple theory of composition from which he seldom wavered. It is found in an interesting passage in *Rolf*, and, reduced to its fundamentals, is this: follow the practice of Wordsworth and write of what you know and of the times in which you live. To do otherwise is folly. In following this theory Seton placed severe limits on himself, but it may be said that it was partly through his limitations he achieved success. He knew of what he wrote; he knew for whom he wrote; and what he said was generally stated with apparent simplicity, and effective lucidity.

I at one time thought that Seton was not really interested in writing as an art. But I am now convinced that he was a conscious stylist, quite willing to alter and to prune in order to produce the effects he desired. As a writer of expository passages he was a master; he could handle dialogue with an easy naturalness (this is especially evident in the *Two Little Savages*); and in his best descriptive passages he writes with sensitivity and poetic feeling. Take, for example, this description of a marten, from *Rolf in the Woods:*

> Into a thicket of willow it disappeared and out again like an eel going through the mud, then up a tall stub where woodpecker holes were to be seen. Into the largest so quickly Rolf could scarcely see how it entered, and out in a few seconds bearing a flying squirrel whose skull it had crushed. Dropping the squirrel it leaped after it, and pounced again on the quivering form with a fearsome growl; then shook it savagely, tore it apart, cast it aside. Over the ground it now undulated, its shining yellow breast like a target of gold. Again it stopped. . . . Then the snaky neck swung the cobra head in the breeze and the brown one sniffed, and sniffed, advanced a few steps, tried the wind and the ground. Still farther and the concentrated interest showed in its outstretched neck and quivering tail.

This, which is not atypical, illustrates Seton's competence as a writer. The structural quality of the sentences is such as to produce impressions of rapid motion and of tension. The language, basically simple, is precise and concrete, and appeals to the multiple senses of the reader. And the well controlled occasional metaphor or simile adds a touch of poetic magic to the overall effects.

But Seton nods much more frequently than Homer. His punctuation can be not only erratic but erroneous; his grammar is by no means always precise; and when sentimentality or moralizing overpowers his judgment he produces bathos of the worst order. This will serve to make the last point. It comes from the story of Tito, the wily coyote. She is quietly approaching a prairie-dog, just before the kill:

> She soon cut the fifty yards down to ten, and the ten
> to five, and still was undiscovered. Then, when again
> the Prairie-dog dropped down to seek more fodder,
> she made a quick dash, and bore him off kicking and
> squealing. Thus does the angel of the pruning-knife
> lop off those that are heedless and foolishly indif-
> ferent to the advantages of society.

It should be evident from the quotations above that no valid claim can be made for Seton as a great writer; but it can be argued that, within his limitations and for his particular purposes, he was usually competent, and at times good. But—and again it must be said—he cannot be finally judged solely as a writer. His success came from his extraordinary ability to fuse into a unified and an artistic whole his manifold gifts—his wide and deep knowledge as a naturalist, his skill as an artist, and his competence as a writer, especially for the young.

Today the success that he first achieved some seventy years ago has been reaffirmed by the myriads of people who have read, and loved, and remembered his works. His brilliant successors, such as Williamson, Gerald Durrell, and Haig-Brown, all of whom write with deep insight of the animal world, have not driven the ancient Nimrod off the stage, nor have the radical changes that have occurred in our own civilization; a brief bibliographical excursion reveals that at least twelve of his volumes are in print and that a limited number of his works are being translated abroad.

Some day, perhaps, old Seton Thompson—or Thompson Seton—will be forced into the limbo where dwell forgotten authors. But for the moment he sits securely on his small throne in the hierarchy of the living. And I believe that he will continue to hold his place so long as the young pitch tents (even backyard, drugstore tents), or gather around camp fires with the gloom of the forests as a backdrop, or look with inquiring eyes into the world of nature. (pp. 50-7)

> *S. E. Read, "Flight to the Primitive: Ernest Thompson Seton," in* Canadian Literature, *No. 13, Summer, 1962, pp. 45-57.*

MARGARET ATWOOD (essay date 1972)

[*Atwood is a Canadian poet, novelist, short story writer, and critic. Internationally known for her poetry and fiction, most notably the novels* Surfacing *(1972) and* The Handmaid's Tale *(1985), she has also been instrumental as a critic in defining the identity and goals of contemporary Canadian literature. In addition, her exploration of women's issues in her fiction has earned her a distinguished reputation among feminist writers. In the following excerpt from* Survival, *her seminal study of attitudes in Canadian literature, Atwood discusses Seton's identification with animal victims as a significant feature of Canadian culture.*]

You'd think that the view of Nature as Monster so prevalent in Canadian literature would generate, as the typical Canadian animal story, a whole series of hair-raising tales about people being gnawed by bears, gored to death by evil-eyed moose, and riddled with quills by vengeful porcupines. In fact this is not the case; fangs and claws are sprouted by mountains and icebergs, it's true, but in stories about actual animals something much more peculiar happens, and it's this really odd pattern I'd like to pursue. . . . In the course of the hunt I hope to demonstrate that the "realistic" animal story, as invented and developed by Ernest Thompson Seton and Sir Charles G. D.

Roberts, is not, as Alec Lucas would have it in *A Literary History of Canada,* "a rather isolated and minor kind of literature," but a *genre* which provides a key to an important facet of the Canadian psyche. Those looking for something "distinctively Canadian" in literature might well start right here.

The Canadian *genre* and its approach to its subject are in fact unique. It is true that stories ostensibly about animals appear in British literature; but as anyone who has read Kipling's Mowgli stories, Kenneth Grahame's *The Wind In The Willlows,* or Beatrix Potter's tales can see, the animals in them are really, like the white rabbit in *Alice in Wonderland,* Englishmen in furry zippered suits, often with a layer of human clothing added on top. They speak fluent English and are assigned places in a hierarchical social order which is essentially British (or British-colonial; as in the Mowgli stories): Toad of Toad Hall is an upper-class twit, the stoats and ferrets which invade his mansion are working-class louts and scoundrels. The ease with which these books can be—and have been—translated into plays, ballets and cartoon movies, complete with song, dance, speech and costume, is an indication of the essentially human nature of the protagonists. Of note also are the invariably happy endings.

Animals appear in American literature minus clothes and the ability to speak English, but seldom are they the centre of the action. Rather they are its goal, as these "animal stories" are in fact hunting stories, with the interest centred squarely on the hunter. The white whale in *Moby Dick,* the bear in Faulkner's "The Bear," the lion in Hemingway's "The Short Happy Life of Francis Macomber," the grizzlies in Mailer's *Why Are We In Viet Nam?,* the deer glimpsed by the narrator in James Dickey's *Deliverance*—all these and a host of others are animals endowed with magic symbolic qualities. They are Nature, mystery, challenge, otherness, what lies beyond the Frontier: the hunter wishes to match himself against them, conquer them by killing them and assimilate their magic qualities, including their energy, violence and wildness, thus "winning" over Nature and enhancing his own stature. American animal stories are quest stories—with the Holy Grail being a death—usually successful from the hunter's point of view, though not from the animal's; as such they are a comment on the general imperialism of the American cast of mind. When Americans have produced stories which superficially resemble those of Seton and Roberts, they are likely to be animal success-stories, the success being measured in terms of the animal's adjustment to people—as in Jack London's *White Fang,* where the wolf-dog, mistreated in youth, begins by hating men but ends up loving them, saving them and living in California.

The animal stories of Seton and Roberts are far from being success stories. They are almost invariably failure stories, ending with the death of the animal; but this death, far from being the accomplishment of a quest, to be greeted with rejoicing, is seen as tragic or pathetic, *because the stories are told from the point of view of the animal.* That's the key: English animal stories are about "social relations," American ones are about people killing animals; Canadian ones are about animals *being* killed, as felt emotionally from inside the fur and feathers. As you can see, *Moby Dick* as told by the White Whale would be very different. ("Why is that strange man chasing me around with a harpoon?") For a Canadian version of whale-meets-whaler, see E. J. Pratt's *The Cachalot,* in which it's the whale's death—not the whaler's—that we mourn. (The whaler, incidentally, is from New England. . . .)

"The fact that these stories are true is the reason why all are tragic. The life of a wild animal *always has a tragic end*," says Seton in the Preface to *Wild Animals I Have Known.* He's defending his position as a realist, a purveyor of truth. However, "realism" in connection with animal stories must always be a somewhat false claim, for the simple reason that animals do not speak a human language; nor do they write stories. It's impossible to get the real inside story, from the horse's mouth so to speak. "Animal" stories must be stories written by people *about* animals, just as "Indian" stories have until very recently been stories written by white people *about* Indians. In the latter case the Indian tends to be made into a symbol; onto him the white man projects his own desire or fear. And so with the animal. "We and the beasts are kin," says Seton, all but acknowledging this connection.

The world of Nature presented by Seton and Roberts is one in which the animal is always a victim. No matter how brave, cunning and strong he is, he will be killed eventually, either by other animals (which these authors don't seem to mind too much; it's part of the game) or by men. Seton, especially, reverses the Nature-as-Monster pattern in stories such as **"Lobo," "The Springfield Fox"** and **"Redruff."** Here it is man who is the threat and the villain: the animals suffer much more through men, with their snares, traps, chains and poisons, than they would through other animals, who are at least quick. The amount of elegiac emotion expended over the furry corpses that litter the pages of Seton and Roberts suggest that "tragic" is the wrong word; "pathetic" would be a better one. Tragedy requires a flaw of some kind on the part of the hero, but pathos as a literary mode simply demands that an innocent victim suffer. Seton and Roberts rarely offer their victims even a potential way out. As James Polk says in his essay "Lives of the Hunted: The Canadian Animal Story and the National Identity" [see Additional Bibliography],

> These doleful endings and the number of stoic moose, tragic bears, grouse dying in the snow, woodchucks devoured, salmon failing to make it upstream, grief-stricken wolves and doomed balls of fur, feathers or quills squealing for dead mothers tend to instill a certain fatalism in the reader. . . .

If animals in literature are always symbols, and if Canadian animal stories present animals as victims, what trait in our national psyche do these animal victims symbolize? By now that should be an easily-guessed riddle. . . . (pp. 73-5)

[In] Canada it is the nation as a whole that joins in animal-salvation compaigns such as the protest over the slaughter of baby seals and the movement to protect the wolf. This could—mistakenly, I think—be seen as national guilt: Canada after all was founded on the fur trade, and an animal cannot painlessly be separated from its skin. From the animal point of view, Canadians are as bad as the slave trade or the Inquisition; which casts a new light on those beavers on the nickels and caribou on the quarters. But it is much more likely that Canadians themselves feel threatened and nearly extinct as a nation, and suffer also from life-denying experience as individuals—the culture threatens the "animal" within them—and that their identification with animals is the expression of a deep-seated cultural fear. The animals, as Seton says, are us. And for the Canadian animal, bare survival is the main aim in life, failure as an individual is inevitable, and extinction as a species is a distinct possibility. (p. 79)

> Margaret Atwood, "Animal Victims," in her Survival: A Thematic Guide to Canadian Literature, Toronto: Anansi, 1972, pp. 69-86.

PATRICIA MORLEY (essay date 1973)

[Morley is a Canadian author, editor, and critic. In the following excerpt, she discusses the importance of Seton's work in furthering the cause of animal rights.]

"How many of us have ever got to know a wild animal?" Not in a cage, Seton continues in the opening paragraph of the story of Silverspot, but in its natural state and over a continued period of time? We know the answer only too well. Very few. Very few indeed. If we choose to make their acquaintance via the art of Seton, Roberts, Fraser and Saunders, we may end up with an unexpected bonus—namely, knowledge of ourselves. The realistic animal story is a peculiarly Canadian genre and serves to hold a mirror up to certain aspects of the national psyche.

Conservationist John Livingston believes that Western society is, and traditionally has been, indifferent to the rights of non-human nature: "Perhaps this is because we cannot conceive of having any ethical responsibility to that which is not capable of reciprocating. Ethics, morals, fitness and propriety of behavior—these are human attitudes." Western society is a big subject, and it's not mine, here. But the point is of interest because, while this exploiting attitude towards the natural world may be typical of Western technology, it is emphatically not the attitude of many Canadian writers of both the last century and the present one.

In the preface to **Wild Animals I Have Known,** Seton writes that his stories emphasize "a moral as old as Scripture—we and the beasts are kin." Animals, he insists, are creatures with wants and feelings differing from our own only in degree, and hence they have *rights;* Moses knew this, as did the Buddhist of two thousand years ago. As Redruff, the Don Valley partridge, hangs in the air in a snare, "slowly dying; his very strength a curse," Seton asks: "Have the wild things no moral or legal rights? What right has man to inflict such long and fearful agony on a fellow-creature, simply because that creature does not speak his language?"

Seton's interest in animals as in men lay not in the species but in the individual, the individual hero. It is a romantic bias, and Seton was a romantic by temperament and by choice. He was in search of the picturesque, and he regretted that he had not lived in the wilderness or on the frontier during an earlier epoch, before the natural glories of lakes and woods were forced to give way before "progress" and "the higher beauties of civilization and art." He believed that man's great work is to develop and know himself, and that in order to know himself he must study all things to which he is related: "Each animal is in itself an inexhaustible volume of facts that man must have in order to solve the great problem of knowing himself."

Animal Heroes, the title of one of Seton's books, is the constant theme of his stories about individual animals. In the prefatory note to this collection of eight tales, Seton writes: "A Hero is an individual of unusual gifts and achievements. Whether it be man or animal, this definition applies; and it is the histories of such that appeal to the imagination and to the hearts of those who hear them." The sub-title of **Wild Animals I Have Known** declares the book to be the Personal Histories of Lobo, Silverspot, Ruggylug, Bingo, the Springfield Fox, the Pacing Mustang, Wully, and Redruff. The prefatory note to this first book of Seton's refers to the high degree of heroism and personality in these animals, and the author emphasizes that his theme is "the real personality of the individual, and his view of life" rather than the ways of the species.

Most animals of one species all look alike to human beings, as Seton acknowledges at the beginning of his story of Silverspot the crow: "But once in awhile, there arises an animal who is stronger or wiser than his fellow, who becomes a great leader, who is, as we would say, a genius, and if he is bigger, or has some mark by which men can know him, he soon becomes famous in his country, and shows us that the life of a wild animal may be far more interesting and exciting than that of many human beings."

Julia Seton's biography of her husband includes the text of an early poem by Seton called **"The Kingbird."** He greatly admired this little bird for its ability to defy and repel birds many times its own size. The concluding lines of his poem describe the kingbird as a sparrow in size, an eagle in spirit. Mrs. Seton acknowledges that **"The Kingbird"** is not great poetry, and we can only agree. But she tells us that Seton himself considered it to be the beginning and foundation of all his work as a writer of wild animal stories. The poem celebrates the courage and individuality of the tiny hero-bird. (p. 195)

Seton's attitude towards his writings, and towards his vocation as an artist-naturalist, reflects his basic religious orientation. He shows the Victorian preference for truth over art or beauty, and his primary intention is to write what is true, edifying, and moral. His Note to the Reader in *Wild Animals I Have Known* begins, "These stories are true." Seton admits to often leaving "the strict line of historical truth" and to having "pieced together" some of the characters, while noting that in some of the stories there is "almost no deviation from the truth." The preface to *Animal Heroes* reveals the same preoccupations. While the stories are admitted to be "more or less composite," they are founded on "the actual life of a veritable animal hero." Seton duly records which tales are the most and which the least "composite," preferring this strangely technical or scientific word to any reference to imagination or art.

Critics have taken Seton at his word and seen his animal stories as the simple case-histories of a naturalist. In his 1958 Introduction to the New Canadian Library edition of Charles G. D. Roberts' *The Last Barrier and Other Stories,* Alec Lucas states: "Roberts wrote as a creative artist and Seton as a naturalist, and one dependent on his imagination and the other on his powers of observation to give his natural-history meaning, or, more briefly, for Roberts it was art first; for Seton it was science." Seton, had his opinion been asked, might well have agreed. But should we? Certainly I have no quarrel with the view that Roberts is a creative artist, and never more so than in the best of his animal stories. Seton's tales, however, have a unique strength and beauty. The animal protagonists are living personalities who hold the reader's attention throughout. Our interest in their fate is reinforced by the fine sense of detail, the delightful humour, the simple yet vivid language and, occasionally, the perceptions of a mystic. In these "composite" portraits, the artist in Seton worked better than he knew.

Julia Seton notes that a previously unpublished Seton manuscript reveals her husband's single-minded intention to record the truth. Seton's article refers to the fairy tale and its near kinsman, the romantic animal story. A few of these tales retain a permanent hold on old and young alike: "Their strength lies in this: THEY ARE TRUE. They may be mixed with error, they may be disguised by the fanciful . . . But still, in the main they are true . . . As with all lasting work, they are *the truth from the heart through the head* of a man of genius."

Aesop's Fables, Seton writes, humanize the animals in order to exemplify a moral truth, thereby "creating a false picture on the whole." St. Francis of Assisi struck a new note in the twelfth century with the gospel that the animals were meant to share with man in the benefits of Christian charity. In the middle of the nineteenth century, the evolutionists preached that animals are not simply our spiritual breathren but our blood kin. These are the literary and philosophic antecedents which Seton sees for the new type of animal story which begins to appear in the late nineteenth century. It differed from the fable chiefly in the degree of sympathy evoked for the animal hero. In crediting the evolutionists with the view that the animals are our kin, Seton ignores for the moment the fact that he had ascribed this knowledge, in his 1898 preface, to Moses and the ancient Buddists.

The truth, then, was Seton's touchstone. While remaining faithful to what he saw as the truth, Seton felt free to choose unusual individuals (animal *heroes*), to ascribe to them the adventures and attributes of several of their race (his "composite" method), and to allow them to do things, which although never observed were completely possible and even probable. To the anticipated criticism that he has added a human atmosphere, a sensibility foreign to his animal subjects, Seton replies: "No man can write of another personality without adding a suggestion of his own. The personal touch may be the poison of science, but may also be the making of literature, and is *absolutely inevitable*." All fiction, Seton implies, is a kind of autobiography.

Seton's autobiography is entitled, significantly, *Trail of an Artist-Naturalist.* While seton may not have thought of himself as an artist in words, he was also the illustrator of his own books. He studied art in Toronto (winning a gold medal at the Ontario College of Art in 1879) and in Paris, Seton was a man of diverse talents: practical architect, sculptor, portrait painter, graphic artist. He worked in many mediums including pencil, charcoal, ink, wash and water colour. Julia Seton writes that her husband "never thought of his work as art presentation— although he knew it was good. Each delineation was to him merely a documentary record of what he had seen, but each an authoritative portrait of an experience in his life." Merely? This may be Julia Seton's view and now Seton's; or perhaps Seton undervalued the artistic element in his visual art as in his written tales, in his effort to honour the "truth."

However that may be, Seton's sketches and paintings speak for themselves. I came to them first at the age of twelve, and both drawings and stories remained vividly in my mind. The stories in *Wild Animals I Have Known* each begin with an illustrated capital letter, as in medieval manuscripts. These depict, often with whimsical humour, the hero of the tale or some aspect of his story. Miniature sketches of plants and animals enliven the margins of many pages. Four foxcubs polishing off a too-curious squirrel are tagged "And the little ones picked his Bones e-oh!" Along with these numerous small drawings are thirty full-page illustrations: "There she had lain, and mourned;" "Frank retreated each time the world turned;" "No chance to turn now;" "The hound came sniffing along the log." Seton's ability to depict animal movement is remarkable, his sense of composition authoritative, and he includes the telling detail while suggesting vast space.

His drawing, like his writing, testifies to his imagination and humour. Seton illustrated his *Life Histories of Northern Animals* with 1500 illustrations. These included not only scientifically accurate drawings but others that Seton called his synoptic drawings. These sketches caught the life and character of the animal, its very essence. The publisher was horrified to find humorous and imaginative sketches in "'an otherwise erudite book'" and attempted to persuade the author to remove them, but Seton held firm and won out.

His illustrations are also comments on his philosophical and religious concepts. A small two-inch square drawing on the title page of *Wild Animals I Have Known* depicts the Peaceable Kingdom. A man, seated at the foot of a giant tree, is surrounded by birds and animals: a horse, two foxes, a rabbit, dog, wolf, partridge, crow—a Canadian version of the lion lying down with the lamb. The final sketch in this volume shows a naked man flanked by a large bird and a dog or wolf. A flaming sun encircles the trinity of creatures and this mandala is placed at the centre of a double-spiralling "eye."

Seton's love for his animal heroes is one of the most striking features of his tales. In his outline of the historical development of the animal story, he characterized the late nineteenth-century animal story by the sympathy it evokes for the animal hero. This sympathy takes two forms: firstly, an interest in the doings of creatures whose lives, as Seton claims, are often more dramatic and exciting than those of many human beings; and secondly, pity for their fate. In the Note to Wild Animals, Seton writes: "The fact that these stories are true is the reason why all are tragic. The life of a wild animal *always has a tragic end.*" In the story of Silverspot, Seton observes that there are no hospitals for sick crows.

When Lobo, the "grand old outlaw" and King of the Currumpaw range, has finally been trapped through his love for his mate, Seton eulogizes the fallen king in a passage of great tenderness: "Poor old hero, he had never ceased to search for his darling, and when he found the trail her body had made he followed it recklessly, and so fell into the snare prepared for him." Lobo is staked out with a collar and chain. He refuses food and water, and dies of a broken heart; "A lion shorn of his strength, an eagle robbed of his freedom, or a dove bereft of his mate, all die, it is said, of a broken heart; and who will aver that this grim bandit could bear the three-fold brunt, heartwhole? . . . his spirit was gone—the old King-wolf was dead."

Seton admires courage, and also commonsense, which he describes as a thousand times better than the reckless courage of the bulldog. The Springfield foxes know better than to try to dig for a woodchuck: "hard work was not their way of life; wits they believed worth more than brow-grease."

Seton describes in detail the social organization of the band of crows who made their headquarters near Castle Frank in Toronto's Don Valley. He says the crow organization is admitted by the bird kingdom to be the best that there is, and that crows, "though a little people, are of great wit, a race of birds with a language and a social system that is wonderfully human in many of its chief points, and in some is better carried out than our own." Since it is essentially a benevolent monarchy where the leader and his lieutenants are the oldest, wisest and bravest, and since this form of government obviously evokes the author's admiration at the time he wrote *Wild Animals I Have Known,* it is surprising to discover that in later years Seton declared himself to be "deeply in sympathy with the American ideal of government." (pp. 195-97)

How many of us have ever had the chance to know a wild animal? But we can know Seton's. Conrad, in his Preface to *The Nigger of the 'Narcissus'*, says that the task of the artist is, before all, to make us *see*. And that is exactly what Seton does. His vision is leavened with humour, as in the picture of Slum Cat, held against her will in an antiseptic house and a garden *polluted* with roses: "The very Horses and Dogs had

the wrong smells; the whole country round was a repellent desert of lifeless, disgusting gardens and hayfields, without a single tenement or smoke-stack in sight . . . altogether it was the most unlovely, unattractive, unsmellable spot she had ever known."

He moves easily between homely comparisons (it is as impossible for the crows to protect their spoil from kingbirds as it is for the fat apple-woman to catch the small boys who have raided her basket) and poetic descriptions such as that of the barren uplands where battles of sun and frost have split the grey-green rocks and exposed "their inner fleshy tints." From time to time an incident will suggest a parallel between animal and human experience: "The life game is a hard game, for we may win ten thousand times, and if we fail but once our gain is gone." The Bible supplies some of his metaphors: the mourning Vixen watches over her dead cubs "like Rizpah" (Saul's concubine); and the little mare used to snare the Pacing Mustang is tagged Delilah.

Seton, whose long life-time spanned two eras, was one of our first conservationists. Was it necessary to agriculture that the wonderful things of the wilderness be exterminated? Certainly not, he told the Canadian Club in 1924: "We have desolated our heritage, absolutely devastated these wonderful wilds. We have robbed our children. We have robbed our country."

The naturalist and the artist were wonderfully complementary in this man. One thinks of Frederick Philip Grove, whose *Over Prairie Trails* exhibits this same combination of scientific detail and artistic vision; or Henry Jackson, Ottawa mycologist and watercolourist, whose technically accurate paintings of mushrooms are at the same time works of beauty. Woodcraft is the oldest of all sciences. Art's lineage is equally ancient. In Seton's work, they make a good team. (p. 198)

Patricia Morley, "Seton's Animals," in Journal of Canadian Fiction, *Vol. II, No. 3, Summer, 1973, pp. 195-98.*

PATRICIA MORLEY   (essay date 1977)

[*In the following excerpt, Morley discusses the stories collected in* Selected Stories of Ernest Thompson Seton *(1977).*]

Talent is always sufficiently rare to command our attention. Most people's talents, moreover, lie in one particular direction. Now and again there comes an individual whose gifts are so diversified that we hardly know what to call him. Ernest Thompson Seton was such a man. To many, he is the writer of animal stories beloved in youth and age alike. To others, he is an artist and illustrator. To still others, a naturalist, a scientist of international repute whose four-volume work, *The Lives of Game Animals,* was awarded the most honoured scientific prizes when it was published in the 1920s. There is little point in debating the problem of which of Seton's gifts predominated. Surely the genius of the man lies in this very combination of gifts: the scientific interests, the warmth, wit, humour, and imagination. It was opportune that conditions in Canada and the United States during his lifetime conspired to encourage the flowering of those gifts. And peculiarly fit that his view of animals and our relationship to them should become a part of our heritage.

Late in the nineteenth century, the impact of the Canadian wilderness upon sensibilities which were by education largely British or European led to the formation of a new and unique genre, the realistic animal story. Formal education in Canada at this time was largely British. Canadian writers were subject to cultural influences which included Burke's idea of Nature's sublimity, Wordsworth's faith in Nature's goodness and maternal aspect, and Darwin's hypothesis of natural selection and the survival of the fittest. They were also subject to a climate and landscape radically different from that of Britain. There were, then, two prominent influences: a wilderness environment, and an educational system that was largely European.

It may be an illustration of the famous Canadian capability for compromise, but whereas Darwin's theories had caused a furor in the English academic community, they were absorbed relatively quietly in Canada. Scientists such as Sir William Dawson, an ardent Presbyterian, led the way in reconciling Darwinian concepts with religious faith. Writing in 1926, Lionel Stevenson assessed the peculiar combination of forces which helped to prepare for the realistic animal story. The wilderness, and the forms of life found there, impressed Canadian writers as something to be feared, respected, and loved. Here was an intricately related world which fostered a sense of equality and kinship. Wilderness conditions reinforced the evolutionary concept of the common origin of man and beast. "We and the beasts are kin," Seton writes in his first and best-known collection of short stories, *Wild Animals I Have Known:* "Man has nothing that the animals have not at least a vestige of, the animals have nothing that man does not in some degree share." (pp. 9-10)

Both Seton and [Charles G. D.] Roberts outline, in various prefaces and journals, the literary antecedents of the realistic animal story. Interestingly, they connect the various literary forms with stages in human development, placing the hunting story as chronologically first and ethically lowest. Roberts describes fabulists such as Aesop and La Fontaine, who humanized the animals for didactic and satiric purposes and compelled the beasts to serve as concrete types of virtue and vice, as exhibiting an "unsophisticated ethical sense." Seton links Kipling's *Jungle Book* with the evolutionists, "who preached that the animals are not simply our spiritual brethren but actually our bloodkin," and sees his own type of animal story as the latest development in the form. Roberts, in his Preface to *Kindred of the Wild*, also links the development of the animal story to Darwinian theory. Roberts connects a revival of interest in "the lower kindreds" with the general intellectual interest of the time. After criticizing Kipling's animal stories as frankly humanized, Roberts praises the work of Seton, selecting **"Krag, the Kootenay Ram"** for special mention. Seton's combination of scientific accuracy with sympathetic understanding seems to Roberts to represent the ultimate development of the genre: "there would seem to be no further evolution possible, unless based upon a hypothesis that animals have souls . . . Such a development would seem to be at best merely fanciful." (pp. 10-11)

Seton's autobiography, *Trail of an Artist-Naturalist,* and posthumously published journals, *By A Thousand Fires,* reveal his early and lasting passion for woodcraft and his burning desire to pursue what he called "the oldest of all sciences." Of his competence as a scientist there can be no doubt. This competence was seriously questioned only once, in a famous controversy from which Seton emerged victorious. John Burroughs, poet and amateur naturalist, attacked *Wild Animals I Have Known* in an article in *The Atlantic Monthly*, calling Seton a fraud, a faker, and a sham naturalist [see excerpt dated 1903]. In his autobiography, Seton described Burroughs' article as bitter, unfair, reeking of jealousy. He encountered Burroughs

Seton in his lecture costume, 1917. Public Archive of Canada Photograph. Reproduced by permission of Dee Seton Barber.

at a dinner party given by Andrew Carnegie for fifty New York writers, and good-naturedly joshed him about the attack. Later, Seton invited the critic home to show him his library of five thousand volumes, his collection of two thousand animal photographs taken by himself, his museum with thousands of bird and mammal skins collected and skinned by himself, and his dozens of fat journals, the record of over thirty years of observation. According to Seton, the astonished and contrite Burroughs subsequently made a recantation. There is evidence, however, that Seton exaggerated the extent of this apology. It may be that Burroughs chose to modify in print the generosity of his oral remarks. In "The Literary Treatment of Nature," Burroughs praises Seton as artist and *raconteur* but warns the reader against his "romantic tendencies." The general tone of Burroughs' article does not support Seton's version in *Trail of an Artist-Naturalist.*

Despite his scientific training, Seton's consuming interest in his stories lies in *the individual hero*. It is a romantic bias, and Seton is a deeply romantic and idealistic artist. Burroughs is right in this regard. In the Preface to **Animal Heroes,** Seton defines a hero as "an individual of unusual gifts and achievements." More than one preface emphasizes that his theme is the real personality of the individual animal and its view of life rather than the ways of the species. *Wild Animals I Have*

Known is sub-titled "the Personal Histories of Lobo, Silverspot, Raggylug, Bingo, the Springfield Fox, the Pacing Mustang, Wully, and Redruff," while the prefatory note refers to the high degree of heroism and personality in the animals. Seton was convinced that the life of a wild animal may be far more interesting and exciting than that of many human beings. His readers are likely to agree.

It has been suggested that Seton's stories support the theory that Canadians are victims and losers. It is true that his animal characters usually die. Seton notes in the preface to his first collection: "The fact that these stories are true is the reason why all are tragic. The life of a wild animal always has a tragic end." To this may be added an observation from "Silverspot": "There are no hospitals for sick crows." Certainly there are victims in his stories, such as the baby foxes of Erindale. It would be folly to forget, however, that Seton places his focus upon animal heroes, creatures who excite our admiration in the highest degree. A hero, whether dead or alive, is neither victim nor loser. The Winnipeg Wolf leaves "a deathless name," and Krag's horns hang enshrined on a palace wall, a treasure among treasures. (pp. 12-13)

"Silverspot," a story to which Burroughs took particular exception, is of interest not only as an individual portrait but also for its portrayal of the social organization of a band of crows. Seton describes crow customs at some length, calling them the best in the bird kingdom. He praises their wit, their language, and their "wonderfully human" social organization. Their system is essentially a benevolent aristocracy or meritocracy, where the leader and his lieutenants are the oldest, wisest and bravest of the band. Training supplements instinct. As chieftain and educator, Silverspot's eulogy is given a communal slant: "His long life of usefulness to his tribe was over—slain at last by the owl that he had taught so many hundreds of young crows to beware of." One of the distinctive techniques in the story are the crow calls, in the form of musical scores. An engaging episode shows the old crow as miser among the docks and skunk cabbages of Rosedale Ravine, gloating over his treasures. These include the handle of a china cup, the gem of the collection. "Silverspot" illustrates Seton's belief that knowledge of the creatures to which we are related is the beginning of self-knowledge.

In "Raggylug, the Story of a Cottontail Rabbit," Seton allows his animals to talk. While explaining that rabbits convey ideas by a system of sounds, scents, and movements, he insists that his free translation includes *nothing that they did not say*. The story was written in 1888; in 1901, Seton referred to this early technique as an archaic method that he had dropped in favour of a more scientific one. However the romantic heroism, comedy and suspense in "Raggylug" appeal to the adult as much as to the child. The drawings are particularly good. One tends to remember the fascinating details of Rag's education, the beautiful nemesis of the bully's death, and the pathos of Molly's fate. Above all, the story is marked by a pervasive humour.

Humour is also characteristic of "**Bingo, the Story of My Dog.**" The quietly ironic and amused narrative voice is one of the attractive features of Seton's stories. When Bingo's fondness for herding the old yellow cow becomes an obsession, the dog is drily described as "this energetic cowherd"; attempts to make him "more moderate in his pleasures" are unsuccessful; and when the narrator enters the dog in a herding contest at the local fair, it is on the advice of "a false friend." The story also illustrates Seton's loose but generally effective episodic structure, and the range in mood within one story from the

comic to the horrific. The scene where the narrator lies staked out on the ground in the grip of two wolf traps while a wolf pack draws relentlessly closer is full of suspense. The closing scene, where the poisoned dog seeks the aid of his first and lasting master "in the hour of his bitter extremity," demonstrates the heroic virtue of loyalty that Seton so admires.

"**The Springfield Fox**" is set in the pine woods of Erindale near Toronto. Like "**Silverspot,**" it illustrates Seton's claim that animals depend as much on parental training as on instinct. The reader, in company with the concealed narrator, is privileged to observe the early lessons in woodchuck, squirrel, and mice: "Old Vixen was up in natural history—she knew squirrel nature and took the case in hand when the proper time came." Initially, the story is a battle of wits between the narrator (a reluctant hunter conscripted by a wrathful relative) and the foxes. With the death of old Scarface, the end is near for the brood and the den laid bare. The imprisonment of the last little fox, the mother's frantic efforts to free him, and her final choice of death over captivity is dramatic and moving writing.

The ending of "**Redruff**" makes a point that Seton emphasizes in his prefaces and journals: animals are creatures with wants and feelings differing from our own only in degree, and hence they have *rights*. As Redruff hangs in the air in a snare, with his own strength prolonging his agonizingly slow death, the narrator asks: "Have the wild things no moral or legal rights? What right has man to inflict such long and fearful agony on a fellow-creature, simply because that creature does not speak his language?" In the Preface to *Lives of the Hunted,* Seton pleads for a policy of intelligent conservation, since "each of our native wild creatures is in itself a precious heritage that we have no right to destroy or put beyond the reach of our children." In Redruff, the moral is driven home by the interest and beauty of the partridge's life, and the villainy of old Cuddy, the out of season hunter. The Darwinian concept of kinship reinforces the humanitarian conviction that the animals have rights.

Most of the stories in *Wild Animals I Have Known* end on an elegiac note which suggests the end of a golden era. After Redruff's death, no partridges come to Castle Frank and the old pine drumming log has rotted silently away. The Erindale woods are empty of foxes. The crows of Castle Frank are dwindling, "and soon they will be seen no more about the old pine-grove in which they and their forefathers had lived and learned for ages." Implicit is the idea that with the death of the heroic leader, an entire society has passed away.

"**The Winnipeg Wolf**" begins with a dramatic scene glimpsed from a train in 1882. The narrator's heart goes out to "the lonely warrior," a great grey wolf facing a rabble of dogs in the snow near St. Boniface. From this point, the narrative moves backwards and forwards in time to complete the story of the strange wolf who preferred the city to the country, always hunted alone, hated men smelling of whisky, and loved children. The wolf has been taken alive as a cub. His hatred and his love stem from his mistreatment at the hands of the saloonkeeper and his customers, and his friendship with little Jimmy, the saloonkeeper's son. Seton's humour in this story ranges from the broad farce of the child's remark as, threatened by Fiddler Paul, he struggles with the wolf's chain ("Wolfie; back up just a little, and you shall have him") to the black humour of the conclusion reached by Nanette's father—by eating Fiddler Paul, the wolf has saved his little girl from a bad marriage: "He always was good to children." Melodrama is currently out of fashion, despite its perennial popularity. But fashion is an unreliable arbiter of taste. This story has realistic features but is obviously more romantic than the stories in *Wild Animals I Have Known*. Its action depends more upon human characters and the inter-relation of man and beast. Romantic elements include little Jimmy's death and the wolf's inconsolable grief, his continuing attachment to the woods about the church cemetery, the half-breed beauty and planned elopement, the horror of the huskies returning bloodied and unhungry, the detective work of tracing events from the tracks in the snow, the wolf's last stand, and the legend that the wierd and melancholy wolf-cry sounds each year from the wooded graveyard when the tolling Christmas Eve bell marks the anniversary of the death of little Jim, "the only being on earth that ever met him with the touch of love."

The importance of obedience is one of Seton's recurring themes. Creatures obedient to parental training live longer, in Seton's observations. Even the mate must sometimes defer. In **"The Wild Geese of Wyndygoul,"** the mother bird leads while the father, "born a fighter, follows—yes, obeys." When the parents are unable to fly with clipped wings, the young choose to winter with them in the northern lake: "It was a conflict of their laws indeed, but the strongest was, *obey,* made absolute by love." By the second autumn, the mother's wing feathers have grown so that she can fly with her double brood. The gander is deserted, apparently for life, since wild geese mate but once. But the thirteen geese return in spring for a triumphal reunion, an ending uncommon among Seton's stories. Obedience to inscrutable laws gives them a long and happy life. The circular design of the beautiful semi-abstract sketch suggests not only the unity of love but also a clock face, symbolizing the passage of days and seasons which regulates the life of the wild creatures.

"Krag" is a strange and haunting tale of obsession, madness, and grandeur. The antagonists, Scotsman and ram, seem to have been bound together by fate. They meet first before Krag is an hour old. The bond is irrational but, in Seton's handling, absolutely credible. Scotty is cast as the infernal Hound of Hell, and his character and ancestry support the role: "For added to his tireless strength was the Saxon understreak of brutish grit, of senseless, pig-dogged pertinacity—the inflexible determination that still sticks to its purpose long after sense, reason, and honor have abandoned the attempt, that blinds its owner to his own defeat . . ."

The early life of Krag permits a panoramic view of the life of the mountain sheep and their social organization. As with the crow band, the wisest leads. The leader is slowly selected by unanimous consent as the one safe to follow. Seton emphasizes that social rules are not nonsensical tyrannies but important natural laws like those of physics. The days of Krag's prime include a dramatic fight with a band of wolves on a narrow pass, and an incredible escape down a five hundred foot canyon. Led by Krag, the sheep ricochet down the cliffs from side to side while the pursuing dogs fall to their deaths. The superb melodrama of Scotty's demonic twelve-week pursuit is capped by the suggestion of supernatural vengeance wreaked by the ram after his death. Seton leaves us in no doubt as to who is the victor. The "wonderful horns," which compose a yearly record of Krag's long and glorious life, survive unharmed amid the ruins of Scotty's cabin, atop the shredded remains of his killer. The man is forgotten while the ram has joined the immortals.

"My theme," Seton writes in the Preface to *The Life-Histories of Northern Animals,* "is *the living animal.*" In the service of this theme, Seton employed what he called a composite method. His stories, he insists, are true, although the animal characters have been pieced together from the actual lives of several of their kind. While he tended to disclaim any literary pretensions, the artist in Seton worked better than he knew. His animal protagonists are dramatically rendered with a fine sense of detail, delightful humour, and simple yet vivid language. His imaginative drawings catch the very essence of a character or a situation.

The man will be remembered as a forceful, highly talented, uncompromising and idealistic personality. Along with Leacock and Montgomery, for example, Seton was among the very few Canadian writers known in Japan in the 1960s and 70s. It is clear from his writings that Seton truly *loved* the animal creation and its natural terrain. He attempted to penetrate the intimate side of the animals' lives and to understand their psychology. At the same time he was, from earliest childhood, in the grip of something he described as knowledge-hunger. He killed and dissected animals in the service of this passion. In his autobiography, he speaks of the loneliness which resulted from such interests. And he refers to his sense of mission, his desire "to be the prophet of outdoor life." Seton was true to that vision throughout a long and very full life. The naturalist and the artist are wonderfully complementary in this man. (pp. 13-17)

> *Patricia Morley, in an introduction to* Selected Stories of Ernest Thompson Seton, *edited by Patricia Morley, University of Ottawa Press, 1977, pp. 9-17.*

ALEC LUCAS   (essay date 1977)

[*Lucas is a Canadian critic and biographer who has edited numerous volumes of Canadian short stories. In the following excerpt, he assesses the importance of* Wild Animals I Have Known.]

In all probability *Wild Animals I Have Known* has outsold any other book by a Canadian author. It was an instant success, reaching its twentieth reprinting within eight years of publication. Four stories from it—**"Lobo," "Redruff," "Raggylug,"** and **"The Springfield Fox"** went almost at once into a separate book, *Lobo, Rag, and Vixen,* and also later into braille. It has never been out of print and has, moreover, appeared in at least fifteen English-language and fifteen foreign-language editions.

The importance of *Wild Animals I Have Known* rests on more than continuing popularity, however significant that may be, for the book established, if it did not originate, a new literary genre, the realistic animal story. It is not possible to give entire credit to Seton for originating the genre, since, on the one hand, he cites Brown's "Rab and His Friends" (1861) and Warner's "A-Hunting of the Deer" (1878) as very strong influences and since, on the other hand, Roberts had published a story of the kind, "Do Seek Their Meat From God," in 1892. Seton had, however, produced much of *Wild Animals I Have Known* long before 1898. He had written **"Bingo"** as a note-book account in 1882 and had published **"The True Story of a Little Gray Rabbit"** (renamed **"Raggylug"**) in 1890 and **"Lobo,"** "the turning point" in his career, in 1894. (Seton gives 1890 as the date of publciation of both **"Raggylug"** and **"Silverspot,"** although the latter first appeared in February, 1898, and asserts that Kipling admiringly informed him of their strong influence on the Jungle Books.)

Whatever bearing these facts may have on the origin of the realistic animal story, they are significant in its development. Whereas **"Bingo"** was never intended for publication, **"Raggylug"** was, and has, in its sentimental didacticism and animal conversations, some resemblance to Kingsley's, Gatty's, and Traill's animal stories and perhaps even to Gosse's *The Canadian Naturalist*. Significantly (and thankfully) though, Seton's story omits the eagerly curious child and, in addition, presents the animals' point of view. **"Lobo,"** too, was written for publication, but for adults and in the style and manner of the notebooks. It was eminently successful and prompted Seton to adhere from them on to "the more scientific method" in writing of animal life. All the stories, whatever their dates, treat animals as animals and not as human beings in disguise, as in the fable and the fairy story, and not as mouthpieces for propaganda, as in such books as *Black Beauty* and *Beautiful Joe*. Furthermore, wild creatures fascinated Seton, and he wished to depict them as living individuals, to preserve them from *belles-lettres* refinements, Thoreauvian transcendentalism, and the lifeless cataloguing of the nature study guide, and to replace life histories of species with specific biographies of animals he had known.

Seton came to his task well prepared, for, by the time he published *Wild Animals I Have Known,* he was a member of the American Ornithologists' Union, Government Naturalist to the Government of Manitoba, and the author of several scientific papers and *The Birds of Manitoba*. Yet Seton was more the naturalist than scientist. His studies were often personal, anecdotal, and conjectural. Objectivity came hard for him, and recasting his "scientific" records into stories gave him no particular difficulty. As a result Seton's realism came under attack for alleged inaccuracy of fact and for falsification of animal behaviour by imposing human thought and feeling on creatures largely of habit and instinct. Seton denied the first charge on the basis of his work as field observer. These stories are true, he proclaimed, and he was right about much of his natural history, including such tricky woodlore as the behaviour of newly-hatched grouse and the manner in which the male bird produces his mating "drum-roll." He argued, too, that one may legitimately ascribe to one creature the attributes and adventures of several of the species and even "make it do" what the species has never been known to do, "provided the case is completely hedged round with probabilities."

As for the criticism that he unduly humanized his animals, he held that there is also a truth that comes from the "heart through the head" and that "interpreting" their behaviour was valid, since man and animal differ only in degree. He was on thin ice here, since animal motivation and reaction can be read in different ways. Perhaps he did know, as he said he knew, of a vixen that poisoned a cub that it might "die rather than live in captivity." That aside, could he have proved the existence of Silverspot's school for crows, or has he confused folklore with woodlore? Or could he have learned Raggylug's thump-language? And can foxes really learn train timetables?

Undoubtedly Seton's stories are "flawed" in this way, but the question of their anthropomorphism seems of much less moment to critics now than formerly. Krutch argues that since no one really knows how animals think and feel, Seton's interpretation is as good as any other. Polk [see Additional Bibliography] and Atwood [see excerpt dated 1972] also accept the impossibility of getting inside the animal world (even though "the stories are told from the point of view of the animal"), but make a case that Seton's animals are symbolic of the Ca-

nadian psyche inasmuch as Canadians see themselves as a people struggling for survival, victims of powerful and inimical forces. Morley agrees that Seton's animals derive from the psyche of disturbed colonials, but goes one step further and suggests that they may stem from Seton's unhappy childhood relationships with his father. As further evidence of this kind of "Canadianism" in Seton's stories, these writers hold that his and American animal stories differ significantly. The latter are man, not animal, centred and are stories of success, not failure, as they see them, and, to substantiate their point, compare Seton's work with *Moby Dick*, "The Bear," and similar American fiction.

These attempts to see Seton's (and the Canadian) animal story in such a single perspective have led to some distortion. In many of Seton's stories, the animal protagonists do not fail, and, in a total of sixteen stories in *Lives of the Hunted* and *Animal Heroes* the two books that followed *Wild Animals I Have Known,* only five end in death. Again, many animal stories by Seton's American contemporaries—Long, Hawkes, and Bull—in the early twentieth century have animal victims as protagonists. Besides, to give some kind of balance to these appraisals of the place of the animal in Canadian and American literature, not Seton's stories but Callaghan's *They Shall Inherit the Earth*, Roberts's *The Heart of the Ancient Wood*, Bodsworth's *The Strange One*, and similar novels should be set off against the American works mentioned above. Seton recognized that any animal story must inevitably be humanized to a point, since authors are not robots, but he and Roberts believed sincerely they were writing about animals. To see Seton's animals as symbolic of Canadianism is to convert his stories to beast fables and, in the way in which this Canadianism is interpreted, into expressions of national self-pity.

An additional and related point here is that Seton avowedly wrote his stories in the name of conservation and, accordingly, to win sympathy for his animal heroes he far more often presented them as victims of man's inhumanity than as prey of their natural "enemies." If they found little protection in their own world, man, the superior animal (as Seton is careful to explain in *The Natural History of the Ten Commandments,* was duty bound to proffer protection in his. Although in many fairy stories, animals had for long received sympathetic treatment, it was not until the nineteenth century that man got round to recognizing the barbarous cruelty they suffered in actuality.

To try to right this wrong, The Royal Society for the Prevention of Cruelty to Animals was founded in 1824. The movement spread and finally gave rise in literature to such famous pleas for the rights of animals as *Black Beauty* and *Beautiful Joe*, but, except for the protection of game in England by game-keepers and the passing of a few feckless game laws in North America, no significant steps were taken on behalf of wild creatures in either Britain or America. In the United States, however, market gunning, the feather trade, and the terrible slaughter of the bison and the passenger pigeon in the late nineteenth century finally awakened man to the urgent need for the conservation of wildlife. As a result protective legislation was greatly increased, a national parks system was set up in both Canada and the United States and two very important groups for the cause of conservation, the Boone and Crockett Club and the Audubon Society came into being; and on this wave of enthusiasm (and the great vogue of the short story), Seton rode to fame and fortune. Although he wrote of "Canadian" animals in the stories of Silverspot, Raggylug, Vixen, and Redruff, he wrote for an American public, and it was the

Americans who read him, out of a sense of national guilt it might be argued, and made him popular. Seton's motive resembled Sewell's and Saunders'. His subject and method differed from theirs, but his purpose on one level was the same. Consequently few of his stories centre on animals alone. In *Wild Animals I Have Known,* for example, seven of the eight stories focus on relationships between man and animal, and three, despite the name of the book, concern dogs and a feral horse.

Seton's attitude toward wildlife is, however, sometimes ambivalent. He describes the gruesome cruelty of the killing of Blanca without a flinch and yet concludes the story with an elegy on the dead Lobo, an "inconsistency" that an American version of **"Lobo"** remedies by omitting its conclusion, though the change alters the whole thrust of the story. By and large Seton seems to have thought of conservation in terms of game birds and game animals. Several species he therefore categorized as vermin to be dealt with by means of a gun. For all his laments over the deaths of his heroes, he did not wish to denounce the hunter or the trapper out-of-hand, so long as each disclosed a "fellow feeling" for wild creatures. Cuddy, that Canadian equivalent to an English poacher, and those who participate "in the lawful murder season," are damned because they have no such saving grace, but the narrator of **"Lobo"** readily atones for his actions with his eulogy of the dead wolf.

Wild Animals I Have Known is more than a plea for conservation; it is a statement of Seton's philosophy of nature, which, like Roberts', revolves around Darwin's theory of evolution, and which, in part, also helps explain Seton's interest in victims. But Seton was only a half-hearted Darwinian. The squirrel that attempted to prey on Redruff's brood was not an animal living according to the natural order of its world, but a "red-haired cutthroat" with a "strange perverted thirst for birdling blood." Seton found it hard to accept the fact that the existence of foxes and owls presupposes the existence of rabbits and crows. He was generally too involved with his protagonists to allow them to die to demonstrate a theory, though his reactions vary from the matter-of-fact comments on the deaths of Redruff's brood—indeed so casual is he that he loses count—to the sentimental tribute to Molly Cottontail.

For Seton nature was red in tooth and claw, yet moral; a kindly old nurse, yet "inexorable law" that destroyed the weakest. He saw no contradictions in his attitudes and even posited a theory of moral evolution in which Moses and Darwin stood together. "The Ten Commandments were not," he asserted, "arbitrary laws given to man, but fundamental laws" drawn from "highly developed animals," and *Wild Animals I Have Known* was meant to demonstrate something of this theory. Lobo, according to Seton, embodies dignity and love constancy; Silverspot, sagacity; Vixen and Molly Cottontail, mother love; Redruff, obedience; Bingo, fidelity; and the Pacing Mustang, love of liberty. Though not so categorized, Wully is surely an embittered Bingo, a study of canine fidelity destroyed by human infidelity. Yet all these animals have such vitality as animals (even Raggylug, who almost falls prey to didacticism) that they seldom seem devices in moral fables.

Darwin's theory may have provided a "philosophic" basis for *Wild Animals I Have Known,* but it contributed little to whatever dramatic tension the stories may have. **"Silverspot"** and **"Raggylug"** centre on the struggle for surival among animals, but the rest, even the animal biography, **"Redruff,"** deal with the struggle between man and animal, whereby man denies his superior place in the evolutionary pattern (which Seton considered teleological though a closed system) and his consequent moral responsibility. A story that depends on the relationship between man and animal often has a plot drawn from stories about people. Probably no fox ever performed such a deed as Vixen's. Probably no wolf ever died of a broken heart as Lobo died, though Seton is careful only to suggest that as the cause. The classical and biblical overtones of the tearful mustang and Turkeytrack's horse, **"Delilah,"** tend to make the story seem fabricated and the ending, consequently, theatrical. Generally Seton avoids "fictional" plots and, in contrast to Roberts, those involving the powerful primal instincts, sex and hunger. Even **"Raggylug"** and **"Silverspot,"** although almost exclusively stories about animals, contain little of the violent and sensational.

Aside from considerations of plot and of narrative interest, Seton chose heroic protagonists because they are the fittest— the strongest, bravest, wisest—and because of his romantic bent. A hero, however, presupposes a villain, a role that usually falls to man in Seton's stories. The mustang's beauty and love of freedom stand out boldly against the "ugly little crooked form" and trickeries of Turkeytrack, and Seton himself has to resort to remorse and eulogy to save face in **"Lobo."** If, however, an animal is a villain in a story, it can be a hero in the next, as in **"Raggylug"** and **"The Springfield Fox."** If one owl murders Silverspot, another mercifully kills Redruff and atones for a man's cruelty. Seton considered his protagonists tragic heroes. "The life of a wild animal *always has a tragic end*," he declares, though Raggylug disproves him, and, as regards *Wild Animals I Have Known* at least, he ought to have added "thanks to man." Since, moreover, his protagonists are unflawed, "pathetic" has been suggested as more appropriate than "tragic." Yet there is something of the tragic about them, victims as they are, not of a flaw in thesmelves but in mankind.

Straight-forward accounts, each loosely held together by an interesting central character and written in clear-cut prose, Seton's stories reveal the art of the story-teller *vis-à-vis* that of the short story writer. Seton's originality may not now be obvious (although **"Wully"** is a pleasant relief to the ubiquitous boy-dog story), but his imaginative sympathy with characters is, for it makes them—even Cuddy and Turkeytrack—living beings. His illustrations may have helped popularize his animal heroes, but they have need of no such aid, for they themselves are memorable tributes to Seton as both naturalist and writer. (pp. vii-xii)

> Alec Lucas, in an introduction to Wild Animals I
> Have Known *by Ernest Thompson Seton, McClelland
> and Stewart Limited, 1977, pp. vii-xii.*

ROBERT H. MacDONALD   (essay date 1980)

[*In the following excerpt, MacDonald examines Seton's rejection of instinct as the primary motivation for animal behavior, comparing Seton's attitudes with those of his colleague and contemporary Charles G. D. Roberts.*]

In his introduction to *Kindred of the Wild*—a chapter that stands as a succinct apologia for the animal story—Sir Charles Roberts in 1902 explained the particular inspiration of the new genre practised by Ernest Thompson Seton and himself. Animals and men, he said, were not so separate as had been supposed, for animals, far from being mere creatures of instinct, could and did reason, and what is more, frequently displayed to the discerning observer signs not only of their psychologies, but also of something which might appeal to man's spiritual self. "We have come face to face with personality, where we were blindly wont to predicate mere instinct and automatism." The animal story, Roberts concluded, was thus a "potent emancipator," freeing us from "shop-worn utilities" and restoring to us the "old kinship of earth," a spiritual and uplifting union with nature.

These statements can be labelled "romantic," or "transcendental," and dismissed as a rather sentimental defence of the "inarticulate kindred" of the wild, who are distinguished from Black Beauty and Beautiful Joe only by the fact that they live in the woods. I propose, however, to take Roberts at his word, and to examine his and Seton's stories in the light of his crucial distinction between instinct and reason. The animal story, I shall show, is part of a popular revolt against Darwinian determinism, and is an affirmation of man's need for moral and spiritual values. The animal world provides models of virtue, and exemplifies the order of nature. The works of Seton and Roberts are thus celebrations of rational, ethical animals, who, as they rise above instinct, reach towards the spiritual. This theme, inspired as it is by a vision of a better world, provides a mythic structure for what is at first sight, realistic fiction.

At the popular level, the chief implication of Darwin's theories of evolution and the principle of natural selection had been to diminish the distinction between man and the animals. We were descended from the apes, and if the apes were mere brutes, could we be very much different? All creatures, it seemed, owed their present form to certain inherited characteristics, which together with environmental influences, dictated their ability to survive. Nature was amoral; life was a power-struggle in which only the fittest survived. Instinct, to a large extent, seemed to govern animal behaviour; there was little place in nature for ethics or spirituality. Though man traditionally had been separated from the animals by his unique power of reason, could it not now be that man himself was little more than a brute beast?

By 1900 one of the most important controversies in the biological sciences was the question of animal behaviour: did animals act instinctively, or were they capable of learning? What was the nature of an animal's knowledge: was it inherited, or was it acquired? Were animals capable of reason? Did they learn from experience, did they teach each other? The weight of opinion, at least from the biologists, seemed to favour instinct and inheritance. In their reaction to this controversy (and in a larger sense to the whole impetus of Darwinism), Seton, Roberts and their fellow nature writers rescued their public from the awful amorality of Darwinian nature. They reassured their readers, not so much that man was superior to animals, but that animals were superior in themselves, that they could reason, that they could and did educate their young, and that they possessed and obeyed laws of their own. Judging by the commercial success of their stories, this was a popular and much-needed antidote to Darwinian pessimism.

"The life of a wild animal," said Seton in *Wild Animals I Have Known*, *"always has a tragic end."* By that he meant that all animals die, and since most of them prey upon each other, they frequently die violently. Both Seton and Roberts refused to evade this unpleasant fact: kill or be killed is the natural law. To this extent they were both Darwinians: nature was indeed red in tooth and claw, and only the best escaped for a time. Thus "Kneepads," the mountain ewe who took to kneeling as she grazed, was an easy prey for the mountain lion, and Red Fox's weaker and stupider siblings met an early death. Survival does indeed go to the fittest.

In their biographies of animal heroes, both men repeatedly illustrate this central fact of the evolutionary theory. Their animals are not ordinary animals, but superior animals, distinguished by their size, skill, wisdom and moral sense. These animals have all learned to cope with a hostile environment; they endure. They are the leaders of their kind. Thus Wahb is the largest and most intelligent grizzly, Krag the noblest mountain sheep, Lobo a giant among wolves, Raggylugs a most sagacious rabbit, and so on. From the first Red Fox is the pick of his litter, larger, livelier, more intelligent, and, curiously, redder. Seton's comment on the old crow, Silverspot, will serve to characterize all these heroes: "once in awhile there arises an animal who is stronger or wiser than his fellow, who becomes a great leader, who is, as we would say, a genius, and if he is bigger, or has some mark by which men can know him, he soon becomes famous in his country, and shows us that the life of a wild animal may be far more interesting and exciting than that of many human beings."

Both Seton and Roberts took pains to establish that everything they wrote was within the bounds of truth. Their animal biographies were frequently "composite" biographies; that is, they included everything that had been done, or might have been done, by a crow, or a wolf, or a fox, but they contained nothing that was not possible. Thus Seton, in his preface to *Wild Animals I Have Known,* acknowledges having "pieced together some of the characters," but claims that there was, in at least three of the lives, "almost no deviation from the truth." Roberts, introducing Red Fox, makes the same point saying that in the life of his hero, "every one of these experiences has befallen some red fox in the past, and may befall other red foxes in the future." He has been, he assures his readers, "careful to keep well within the boundaries of fact." We may take these statements at face value: by and large, both men were astute and careful observers of nature, and in most of their writing give realistic, though fictionalized, descriptions of animal life. Both also claim that though they have given their animals language and emotions, these are, within the demands of the genre, realistic, and not anthropomorphized.

However it is not realism that entirely inspires the art of Seton and Roberts, whatever strength that lends to their work, but certain ideas which frame and condition the realism, and which give to it symbolic form. The animal heroes may live and die in the wild, being only interesting specimens of their race, but their biographies, as literature, belong in the world of myth. What matters is not that everything that is told *could* have happened to a fox, or a grizzly, but that it *did* happen, and that, for the author, the life of the animal was organized according to certain basic ideas, and that in its living it demonstrated certain fundamental truths. At the heart of the myth that gives structure to the work of both Seton and Roberts is their belief that animals are rational and ethical beings, and that they rise above instinct. This is demonstrated most clearly in the ways the animals train their young to survive, and the ways in which their young respond to the challenge.

Seton's story of the cottontail rabbit, Raggylugs, will serve to illustrate. The young rabbit Raggylugs is "unusually quick and bright as well as strong," and he has in his mother Molly an extremely intelligent and valiant tutor, a "true heroine," a devoted mother who finally gives her life so that her son may survive. Here, as we might expect, are the superior animals, models of intelligence and mother love. Molly's first duty is to train her son, to educate him in the skills of life. His first duty, as a successful and superior animal, is to obey. "Molly was a good little mother and gave him a careful bringing up . . . he did as he was told." Rag learns the essential rabbit lessons, to "lay low," to "freeze," and to regard the briarbush as his best friend. "All the season she kept him busy learning the tricks of the trail, and what to eat and drink and what not to touch. Day by day she worked to train him; little by little she taught him. . . ." In some of his lessons he shows himself "a veritable genius," and he even goes on to take a "post-graduate course" in how to use water. On the one occasion he is disobedient—he sits up to watch his mother lose a dog—he is severely punished, being cuffed and knocked over by Molly.

Throughout this story Seton's emphasis is on the intelligence and skill of the successful animal, the "tricks" it uses to outwit its enemies, and the way in which it is able to educate its young. Molly shows her son how to run a dog into a barbed-wire fence, how to avoid snares, and how to use water as a last resource. Animals are not mere creatures of instinct, behaving according to a set of inherited responses, but capable, within their own terms, of intelligent reasoning, of teaching and learning, and of knowing right from wrong. Rabbits, for instance, have their own language: they "have no speech . . . but they have a way of conveying ideas by a system of sounds, signs, scents, whisker-touches, movements, and example that answers the purpose of speech. . . ."

It is worth pausing here to answer some questions: is Seton not right—do animals not have some very definite ability to communicate in a language of their own, and are they not capable of some kind of inductive reasoning? Do they not, in fact, educate their young, and is there not more to animal behaviour than a set of instinctive reactions?

The modern ethologist would almost certainly approach these problems with caution, for the whole question of animal behaviour has become one of immense complexity. In 1900 there seemed to be a straightforward contrast to be made between instinctive and learned behaviour; now the first point to be made is that rigid alternatives are simplistic. Even the terms have changed. The "nature or nurture" controversy has been replaced by a discussion of innate or acquired characteristics, and behaviour is now classified as "environmentally stable" or "environmentally labile." The discovery of imprinting, the process by which certain animals when young respond as a species to certain stimulae, has been contrasted to "adaptive" learning. The mental processes of animals are not simple, but they are clearly not always automatic, or mechanical, or, in the old sense, simply instinctive. Apes have been taught to communicate with humans using the American Sign Language: the higher mammals, it has been argued, have mental experiences and probably even a conscious awareness.

In spite of the complexity of the problems, certain generalizations may be made. Many animals are able to learn from experience. Many animals do teach their young, chiefly by example. Some animals are capable of inductive reasoning. Some other animals may be able to adapt their behaviour, by a process of trial and error, and though it might appear that they act rationally, they do not always seem to comprehend what they are doing. Considered in general terms, however, the observations and speculations of the nature writers are closer in many ways to current scientific thinking than those of their more sceptical, behaviourist contemporaries. Animals have complex means of communicating with one another: Seton's description of rabbit language, a "system of sounds, signs, scents, whisker-touches" and so on, is not fanciful, though modern naturalists might argue with the details. What matters

is not the scientific accuracy of Seton's nature stories—although that itself is an interesting question—but the ideas which give his work symbolic form. By the lights of his day he played down instinct; his animals are rational creatures who educate their offspring to be obedient and successful. As such, they are intended to be models for human edification, and nature, though full of sudden and "tragic" death, is an ordered and in many ways superior world.

Seton, as a careful naturalist, frequently describes instinctive (or innate) behaviour in animals. In most cases, he regards it as an inherited substratum, a built-in defence against the early dangers of life. He speaks of an animal's "native instincts," which are supplemented by the twin teachers of life, experience and the example of fellow animals. The little mountain lambs in *Lives of the Hunted,* surprised and chased by a hunter just after birth, are able to dodge and escape, for "Nature had equipped them with a set of valuable instincts." Instinct, however, takes an animal only just so far. Its role in survival is subsidiary to reason. In the story of the Don Valley partridge, for instance, Seton tells us that the partridge chicks soon graduate from instinctive to rational behaviour: "their start in life was a good mother, good legs, a few reliable instincts, and a germ of reason. It was instinct, that is, inherited habit, which taught them to hide at the word from their mother; it was instinct that taught them to follow her, but it was reason which made them keep under the shadow of her tail when the sun was smiting down. . . ." And, Seton concludes, "from that day reason entered more and more into their expanding lives." (pp. 18-22)

The intelligent young animal is also the obedient young animal. In the School of the Woods, obedience is a primary virtue. The child must obey the parent. "For a young animal," Seton said, "there is no better gift than obedience," and he demonstrated this again and again by showing us the fate of the disobedient, the young lambs who do not come when they are called, and are caught and killed, or the foolish partridge chicks who refuse to stay close to mother. (p. 23)

The essential argument of this article should be clear by now: the fiction of both Seton and Roberts is inspired by their desire to present a moral and coherent order in the life of the wild, which is part of the greater order of the cosmos. That many of their observations of animal life are accurate is undeniable—animals do learn, they are intelligent in their way, and they are probably even capable of reason. Yet what is important in Seton and Roberts is the way the details are presented. Animals, we are told, are very much like ourselves. They obey certain laws, they demonstrate qualities we would do well to admire, they are our own kin. They inhabit what is often clearly a mythic world; they are symbols in our own ontological system. Nowhere is this more obvious than in the context of morality.

Each animal, first of all, must learn to obey the laws of its kind. Morality is not a human invention, but an integral part of all nature. "It is quite common," says Seton in *Lives of the Hunted,* "to hear conventionality and social rules derided as though they were silly man-made tyrannies. They are really important laws that, like gravitation, were here before human society began, and shaped it when it came. In all wild animals we see them grown with the mental growth of the species." The higher the animal, the more clearly developed the moral system. The better the animal—the more successful, or superior specimen—the more moral the animal. Thus superior animals fight fair, but the weak, the cowards, and the mean may well resort to dirty tricks. Krag the mountain sheep, whose strength, and size, and curling horns make him appear like a "demi-god" to his ewes, has to beat off two other rams to defend his rights to his harem. One ram fights fair and meets Krag horn to horn; the other fights foul, and attacks from the side. It is important that in this moral world the immoral ram "works his own destruction," running himself over a two hundred foot cliff to his death.

These animal laws would appear to be somewhat flexible, coloured as they are by the vision of the human observer, since occasionally even a "good" animal will break the rule of his kind to preserve himself or another. This is always done for a reason: the law may be broken in the name of the higher good. We are told, in **"Raggylugs,"** that "all good rabbits forget their feuds when their common enemy appears." Rag's rival, the stranger, ignores this basic rule of rabbit society, trying to drive Rag into the reach of a goshawk. This is bad. Yet one sentence later we find Rag playing the same game to save himself and his mother, as he successfully lures old Thunder the hound into the nest of "the stranger." This, we infer, is good.

It is at moments like this that it is most evident that the animal story belongs not to the world of natural science, but to the world of literature. There are good animals and bad animals, and we, as readers, are always expected to be on the side of morality. Seton, however, is usually careful not to denigrate a species: each animal, of whatever kind, has some quality that a man might admire. Even the hated rat is courageous. Roberts, on the other hand, lets his sympathies show: there are some species who exhibit only the worst. Such are lynx. In "Grey Lynx's Last Hunting" we are shown a portrait of animal cruelty, selfishness and marital hatred, whose appropriate outcome is the sordid death of the male, killed by his savage and mad mate. Both writers, in their desire to make a moral point, cross from realism into romance. Seton has a story of wolves who lynch an apparent cheat and liar, and Roberts the fanciful tale of a society of animals who voluntarily resolve not to kill "within eyeshot" of a sensitive and disapproving child.

Throughout Roberts' work there is an insistence on the meaning, the vitality, the harmony and the morality of the struggle of life, and in Seton, of the fairness and ultimate order of nature. Perhaps the most dramatic illustration of their essentially similar moral philosophy is Seton's short *The Natural History of the Ten Commandments,* in which he finds that the Mosaic laws are not "arbitrary laws given to man, but are fundamental laws of all highly developed animals." Animals, in their own way, observe the last six of the ten commandments, and in their occasional willingness to "throw themselves on the mercy of some other power," manifest the beginnings of a spiritual life. Man, obeying the first four commandments, acknowledges the Deity; the higher animals acknowledge man.

This is an idea which, in its implications of a natural cosmic order, testifies to the true symbolic role of the animals. There is an obvious correspondence here to the writing of Seton's contemporary, Kipling, and especially to the society of *The Jungle Books* (1894-95). Roberts, in his preface to *The Kindred of the Wild,* praised the Mowgli stories, though, noting that the animals were "frankly humanized," distinguished them as a different and a separate kind of fiction from Seton's and his own. Yet the difference is one of degree, rather than kind: Kipling's jungle animals are also rational creatures, who live in a balanced and reasonably harmonious society, provided they obey the rules of their kind. There are good and superior animals such as Bagheera the panther and Baloo the bear, and

evil animals such as Shere Khan the tiger and the whole tribe of monkeys. The evil are punished and the good survive. The laws of the jungle must be obeyed. Man, in the shape of Mowgli himself, is superior to all the other animals.

In their insistence on certain social principles—for instance the all-important rule that the young must obey the old, and that obedience is both a necessity and a duty—Seton, Roberts and Kipling all use their animal stories to exemplify clear and precise morality. The first law an animal learns, Seton tells us, is obedience, and it is with the Fifth Commandment, "Against Disobedience," that he begins his examination of the Mosaic code of nature. This is the law "which imposes unreasoning acceptance of the benefits derivable from the experience of those over us." We remember from *Red Fox* "how sternly Nature exacts a rigid observance of her rules," and how Red Fox himself is always obedient to his mother, for "it was no small part of his intelligence that he knew how much better his mother knew than he." Obedience for Kipling is the first law of the jungle; every cub of the wolf pack must learn it:

> "Now these are the Laws of the Jungle, and many and mighty are they;
> But the head and the hoof of the Law and the haunch and the hump is—Obey!"

It could be argued that the evidence for the success of this moral philosophy, and the public acceptance of an anti-Darwinian optimism, can be found in the popularity of the nature writers. Both Seton's and Roberts' nature stories went through edition after edition at the beginning of the century, and one would suspect that Kipling's *Jungle Books* were read to generations of young listeners. All three writers supported the status quo; a child, if he paid attention to the moral lessons, would surely be improved. There is, however, one other means of estimating the popular encouragement given the nature writers, and that in a surprising though socially significant place— the Boy Scouts. The Scouts were also trained to be superior animals, to be brave, helpful, and especially, obedient. The third and most important part of the Scout Promise was obedience to the Scout Law. Curiously, their founder, General Robert Baden-Powell, used the work of the nature writers, and of Kipling, when he came to write the manual for his movement, *Scouting For Boys.*

"Any naturalist," Baden-Powell told his scouts, "will tell you that animals largely owe their cleverness to their mothers." Older animals taught younger animals, and they taught them to obey. Instinct was not half as important as training. Seton was closely associated with the scouting movement from the first, having in fact organized a "woodcraft" group for the boys of America, and in *Scouting For Boys,* Baden-Powell used many of his ideas. Baden-Powell also recommended several of Seton's books to his readers, but when it came to the crucial questions of education, of training and obedience, and the naturalists' models of good conduct, he turned not to Seton or Roberts but to the American writer, William Long. Long's work has now sunk without trace; reading him one can see why he would appeal to a straightforward moralist like Baden-Powell. Much more sentimental and didactic than his contemporaries, and, one would guess, a less careful observer of animal life, Long made no pretense at Darwinism, but preferred to see in the school of the woods "no tragedies or footlight effects of woes and struggles, but rather a wholesome, cheerful life to make one glad and send him back to his own school with deeper wisdom and renewed courage." He was quite clear on the unimportance of instinct, and he had no doubt at all about the necessity for obedience: "when one turns to animals, it is often with the wholesome, refreshing sense that here is a realm where the law of life is known and obeyed. To the wild creature obedience is everything. It is the deep, unconscious tribute of ignorance to wisdom, of weakness to power."

In *Scouting For Boys* Baden-Powell quoted Long at some length. "The Old Wolf" himself was a military man, and he believed in old-fashioned virtues; the scouting movement, though encouraging individual initiative, was authoritarian, its aim to turn out patriots and model citizens. It was important that boys be well trained, and if, in the stories of the nature writers, they had models of good behaviour, these were models that would naturally appeal to boys. Even the scout patrols were named after animals. When it came time to form the junior organization, Baden-Powell went to Kipling, and with his permission took his inspiration from *The Jungle Book*. Significantly, the first "law" of the Wolf Cubs was "the Cub gives in to the old Wolf."

We have in this last detail the clue to the stories of animal heroes. Animals are not so much animals as emblems, symbols of a more perfect world. Baden-Powell called himself the "Old Wolf," and Seton used the wolf paw mark as his signature. To each, the wolf was a superior creature, a star in an ordered and moral universe. The animal stories thus are best considered mythopoeically: Old Silverspot, Seton's crow, drilling his troops and training his youngsters, could well be a model for General Baden-Powell. Red Fox, in his bravery and intelligence, might stand as a shining example to any young scout.

Seen in this light, the lives of the animals resemble, in their structure, the life of the mythic hero: they are born, go through early trials, win their kingdom and die. Some, like Seton's Krag, who returns after death to haunt his murderer, even have an apotheosis. Fate in the shape of a Darwinian catastrophe ensures in the evitable death of the hero a technical tragedy, though the prevailing note in both Seton and Roberts is one of life ever renewed. Man, especially in Seton's stories, may be part of a corrupt and decadent postlapsarian world. In Roberts, man's ignorance and callousness are crimes against nature, though innocence and goodness are often represented by a child or youth, the sensitive girl or boy who knows and loves the creatures of the woods. In Roberts also, the landscape is often magical or enchanted.

In all these details it is clear that the animal tales of both Seton and Roberts take their inspiration and structure as much from literature as from life. In their use of the conventions of the romance, in their echoing of a mythic pattern, and in their quite definite symbolic treatment of animal character, both men translate the indiscriminate facts of nature into the ordered patterns of art. At the centre of their fiction is their belief in moral and rational animals, which in its extensiveness and pervasive force, takes on the quality of an organizing myth. It is ironic that at a time when the forces of instinct, intuition and the unconscious were being rediscovered in man, the power of the Logos was found in the kingdoms of the brute beasts. (pp. 24-8)

> Robert H. MacDonald, "The Revolt against Instinct: The Animal Stories of Seton and Roberts," in Canadian Literature, *No. 84, Spring, 1980, pp. 18-29.*

WAYLAND DREW   (essay date 1986)

[*In the following excerpt, Drew places Seton's animal stories in historical perspective and assesses their impact.*]

Seton wrote about the wilderness and its inhabitants at a significant time. Darwinism, exactly as old as Seton himself, had encouraged thoughtful writers to look more inquiringly at their fellow-creatures and their environments. The impact of industrialization and expansionism on wild nature was apparent everywhere; some species had already been eradicated. A new respect for the complexity of ecological checks and balances was spreading. In the United States, new definitions of "progress" were taking shape. Americans had already achieved an imaginative containment of their land, and had begun a bureaucratic process of redefining wilderness in terms of national parks. Looking northward across the expanses of Canada, they were ready for Seton's stories of wild, stately creatures free in their natural settings. The identification of Canada with immensities, generative immensities beyond human control, had begun. It is that identification which continues today to sell Seton's books by the thousands in Europe and Japan.

In the first Boy Scout *Handbook,* published in 1910, Seton identified an "unfortunate change" and a "degeneracy" growing from urbanization, and he urged a return to nature and to "primitive" honest skills. The *Handbook* is reputed to have sold seven million copies in the U.S., outsold only by the Bible.

But what does a modern reader find if he skirts the mass of critical writing on Seton . . . and comes fresh to his stories themselves? First, although Seton is frequently given credit for writing some of the first "natural" animal stories, equally free of propaganda and anthropomorphism, all of these stories are in some degree anthropomorphic and the early ones cloyingly so. However, one feels that this is less the result of any exploitative motive than of Seton's honest, intense and emotional identification with his animals. Detached observer though he was, he was bewitched often into seeing animals as just cute little folks after all. In **"Raggylug, The Story of a Cottontail Rabbit,"** for example, he drifts from the perfectly sound observation that rabbits "have a way of conveying ideas by a system of sounds, signs, scents, whisker touches, movements, and example," to the embarrassing claim, "I freely translate from rabbit into English, *I repeat nothing that they did not say*" (italics his). Inevitably, Molly Cottontail becomes "a good little mother" who in death "was a true heroine . . . the stuff that never dies." Seton explained: "I have tried to stop the stupid and brutal work of destruction by an appeal—not to reason: that has failed hitherto—but to sympathy, and especially the sympathies of the coming generation."

Of course one can argue that such anthropomorphism is acceptable and even desirable if it leads children to appreciate and to protect wild creatures. Ultimately, however, its very selectivity is harmful because it militates against the ecological outlook. Readers who sympathize with the "good" animals of these early Seton stories and who learn to hate and fear the "bad" (predatory) species are in danger of becoming bigots who lobby for the extermination of the wolf. Seton seems to have recognized this fact fairly early, and in his more mature stories, examples of which are to be found in *Selected Stories,* there are fewer references to "murderous" owls, squirrels, mink, and so on. The sense of wilderness *as a whole* increasingly asserts itself.

The second thing that will impress a modern reader is Seton's scrupulously detailed and often lyrical descriptions. Consider this, for example, from **"Redruff":**

> The wind blew down the valley from the north. The
> snow-horses went racing over the wrinkled ice, over

the Don Flats, and over the marsh toward the lake, white, for they were driven snow, but on them, scattered dark, were rainbow ruffs. And they rode on the winter wind that night, away and away to the south, over the dark and boisterous lake. . . .

And this, from **"Krag, The Kootenay Ram"**:

All that day the White Wind blew, and the snow came down harder and harder. Deeper and deeper it piled on everything. All the smaller peaks were rounded off with snow, and all the hollows of the higher ridges levelled. Still it came down, not drifting, but piling up, heavy, soft, adhesive—all day long, deeper, heavier, rounder. As night came on, the Chinook blew yet harder. It skipped from peak to peak like a living thing—no puff of air, but a living thing, as Greek and Indian both alike have taught, a being who creates, then loves and guards its own.

Finally, Seton's very readability is impressive. These are rather simple, straightforward stories, sometimes even pedestrian, but they are very much worth reading, even after the work of much more sophisticated nature writers like Fred Bodsworth and Allan Eckert. It would be unfair to fault Seton because early in his career he had not achieved their cool, committed effectiveness. In later stories like **"The Winnipeg Wolf"** and **"Krag, The Kootenay Ram"** he examined the interaction of man and wild beast with depth, control, compassion. There are no caricatures, feral or tamed, bestial or human, in these stories. The great advantage of *Selected Stories* over the reprinted *Wild Animals,* Seton's first book, is that the former includes all the tales mentioned above and thereby permits the reader to appreciate Seton's development as a story-teller, besides making available once again two haunting and genuinely moving pieces of fiction. Both of these late stories are dominated by the image of a lone, stately creature, the typical Seton hero, full of disdain, implacably facing enemies diminished by hapless antagonisms. (pp. 183-85)

Wayland Drew, "Seton: Selected & Reprinted," in Journal of Canadian Fiction, Nos. 35/36, 1986, pp. 183-85.

H. ALLEN ANDERSON (essay date 1986)

[*Anderson is an American historian and the author of* The Chief: Ernest Thompson Seton and the Changing West. *In the following excerpt from that work, Anderson examines Seton's fiction, focusing in particular upon the ways in which the naturalist's animal stories reflect his concern for the demise of the frontier way of life and the disappearance of those values it inspired.*]

The predominant assumption in Western thought at the turn of the century was that all life, whether human or animal, was more or less predetermined. Many upper-class Americans embraced the theories of Herbert Spencer, who argued that free competition and the survival of the fittest were just as basic for society as they were for nature. However, there were others who envisioned a universe in which almost everything could be challenged and changed by human reason. Pragmatists like William James and John Dewey argued that though there were natural laws for animals and plants that could not be broken, man, on the other hand, could shape his society and environment to suit his interests.

These clashing streams of thought were reflected in the authors of the so-called "new literature." Compared with previous literary trends, the works of authors like William Dean Howells, Frank Norris, Jack London, and Theodore Dreiser tended to be more urban-centered, less limited to middle-class characters and themes, and more consciously environmental. Their characters were early "anti-heroes" rather than prime movers, and their determinism veered away from that of the nineteenth century. Quantitatively, the new literary movement showed an attitude of indignation as its authors delved into such touchy themes as politics, religion, and science. Few of the great writers readily accepted Hamlin Garland's notion that fiction should reflect life and show its unpleasant sides in order to transform society; however, a host of lesser talents eagerly plunged in and added their voices and pens to the spirit of reform. Thus Alfred Kazin could call this spurt of literary realism "a history of grievances."

Ernest Thompson Seton was a bright star among these "lesser talents." He had attracted a large enough reading audience to become a best-selling author, and his lectures helped all the more in that respect. Indeed, Seton's writings contained elements of the two underlying Progressive streams of thought, enabling him to attract both mainstream and outlying regionalist (sometimes radical) authors. He was a great believer in Dewey's "perpetual open frontier," with its emphasis on creativity. He embraced the new "social gospel," which preached that men were basically more alike than different and were by nature inherently good. He was anti-Spencerian in his belief that unmitigated competition, rather than rewarding the best, might select the least ethical. Overall, Seton supported the popular belief that science itself was the ultimate in self-government and that the scientific spirit, in the words of Walter Lippmann, was "the discipline of democracy, the escape from drift, the outlook of a free man." Yet throughout his animal stories, Seton's retention of traditional determinist-environmentalist thought clearly shows. Man's presumed dominion over nature was, in his eyes, clearly illusory.

The publication of *Wild Animals I Have Known* helped establish the realistic animal story as a new literary form. Ever since his first nature essays for *St. Nicholas* in 1887, Seton had gradually shifted his style from mere fable and folklore to a biological, deterministic stance. In so doing, he adopted the standard Canadian approach of attempting to view life from the animal's perspective. While he considered his stories scientifically accurate, he did mix fact and fiction in order to give his reading audience dramatic introductions to particular animals. Essentially, his main message was that man had a special kinship with the beasts; therefore, the latter should be enjoyed and respected, not destroyed. On his wilderness field trips, Seton recorded precise details of animal appearance and behavior. Previously, however, the naturalist had found it difficult to restrain the artist, who wanted to dramatize an animal's "heroism," or the moralist, who sought to interpret wildlife behavior. His quasi-factual stories proved to be the perfect vehicle for all three concerns. In developing his style, Seton frequently tended to push beyond the limits of scientific accuracy and embellish details for the sake of his art. While the scientist uses a word to mean only one thing, the artist uses a word as a symbol with many meanings. In this use of language, both artistically and scientifically, Seton may be seen as a sort of historian, recording accurate details about animals but placing his facts in a pattern to suggest interpretation. Yet he denied writing fiction or moral parables, insisting in his prefaces that his stories were "literally true." Seton was soon to discover that certain of his scientific colleagues were unprepared to grant such poetic license.

The question of how much Seton "humanized" his animal heroes has been a subject of debate among literary analysts in recent years. Critics have either praised or belittled his works, with no apparent middle ground. The secret to his hybrid of literature and natural history, however, lies in the simple fact that Seton was well aware of the contemporary literary trends. In several instances he simply borrowed the styles of his peers and applied them to his own.

Seton's dog stories, for example, emphasize the standard themes of the dog's faithfulness to its master and its role as a "middleman" between the wild and tame aspects of nature. In the story of **"Bingo,"** the dog hero seems to be degenerating into a wolfish lifestyle when he joins a pack. Yet he remains true to his master and keeps the wolves away when the narrator (who is Seton himself) is caught in the traps. The dog-master relationship is further exploited in the story of **"Chink."** Here, the master's first love is his "pard," despite the dog's foibles, but the price of that loyalty is Old Aubrey's job in Yellowstone Park, for in helping Chink he breaks a man-made law. Seton's experience with the Eaton brothers' bull terrier inspired in part at least two well-known tales. **"Snap"** represents animal nature harnessed by man to help him subdue his environment. Although the ferocious Snap seems unmanageable at first, he proves useful when given a wolf-hunting job for which his breed was meant, and he loyally follows that job to his death. In the tale of **"Billy, the Dog That Made Good,"** Seton plays with the Tolstoyan theme of destiny and circumstance producing the hero. At the most critical moment, Billy shows "the stuff that a good bear dog is made of," while the Terrible Turk, a pit bulldog, proves "a bully, a coward, a thing not fit to live." Both Snap and Billy have proved themselves good bull terriers, earning love and respect from their masters. Unlike Jack London, Seton neither evades tragedy nor slips into "a celebration of the hunter's world." **"Wully"** is the exact opposite of London's "White Fang": because of human neglect after his separation from old Robin, Wully degenerates into a Jekyll-Hyde sheep killer and dies violently after his last owners uncover his double life.

Although not all of Seton's animal tales are set in the West, much of his style is strongly influenced by the literary images of the West prevalent during that time. Occasionally, he uses wild animals as villains: the "Mephistophelian" coyote of **"Chink"**; Old Reelfoot of **"Billy, the Dog"**; and the Kogar Bear of **"Foam."** More often, however in attempting to illustrate man's conflicts with nature, he characterizes such carnivores like formula western outlaw heroes. For instance, while carrying a personal admiration for Lobo, whom he lauds as a "grand old reprobate," Seton realizes that the wolf's destructive habits are detrimental to the ranchers' means of livelihood and thus seeks to end his marauding ways. Such conflicting viewpoints reflect, to some extent, his own persecution complex. These animals are outlaws because man, by his paradoxical mixture of cruelty and kindness, made them that way; thus, conflict is inevitable. Some of these outlaw heroes, like Tito, Domino, and Badlands Billy, ultimately win their battle against man and his dogs. Others, like Lobo and Garou, the Winnipeg Wolf, die fighting for their freedom. Monarch, because of his weakness for honey, ends up a caged prisoner. Vixen, the devoted mother of **"The Springfield Fox,"** gives her captive pup poisoned bait to save it from a "fate worse than death" before departing for parts unknown. Wahb, plagued most of his life by unfriendly animals, hard winters, and man's traps and rifles, becomes a sullen loner "with neither friendship nor love." Afflicted in his old age by rheumatism and tricked by a lesser bear into giving up his territory, he chooses a classical "Roman" death by asphyxiation when he walks into

Yellowstone Park's Death Gulch. Whatever their end, Seton is clearly in sympathy with his animal outlaws, who are seen as victims of circumstance and their very natures. They, like their "West," die out.

The familiar Western themes of the chase, confrontation, and retribution are also frequently used by Seton. Examples include the "barbarous" fox hunt, in which the heroic Domino makes his escape, while the sheep-killing mastiff, Hekla, floats off to a well-deserved end. King Ryder, the wolfer in **"Badlands Billy,"** gets his just deserts when the wolf he had orphaned sends his pack of hounds over the cliff to their doom. The most graphic example of a Western-type "showdown" is the last stand of Garou, the Winnipeg Wolf, at the slaughterhouse; the telephone, representing civilized man's technology, proves the key factor in enabling the "posse" of men to locate the outlaw and turn the dogs on him. Surrounded at last, Garou heroically battles his howling adversaries before falling to the hunters' guns.

Not all of Seton's dramatic confrontations end so violently. This is particularly true of his treatment of certain herbivorous mammals, some of which are almost redemptive "cosmic beasts." In *The Trail of the Sandhill Stag,* when Yan finally confronts his intended quarry face to face, he realizes that he cannot kill this harmless, glorious creature. Love and respect for nature triumph over the hunting instinct; his inner conflict is resolved, and he accepts the limitations of his intimate knowledge fatalistically. Unlike Yan, Scotty MacDougall in **"Krag, the Kootenay Ram"** is crazed by his lust for the hunt and its trophies as he stalks the bighorn. But after he succeeds in killing his prey, Scotty's overwhelming guilt leads to his destruction at the hands of the "Mother White Wind" in the form of an avalanche. Such stories contain a spiritual and mystical quality. Like Herman Melville's *Moby Dick,* they are effective in driving home the theme of nature's uncompromising aspects, something Seton earlier expressed in his painting, *Awaited in Vain.*

Most of Seton's human characters are undesirable types, and their world is anathema to animals. Wolfer Jake, the tipsy cowboy of **"Tito,"** is a far cry from Wister's or Remington's noble knights of the Western ranges; so is "Wild Jo" Calone, who sets the story of the Pacing Mustang in motion with his cowboy dialogue. Both Jake and Jo have a weakness for whiskey and thus squander their pay on a good time with the boys. Certain ethnic stereotypes also appear throughout Seton's works. Fiddler Paul in **"The Winnipeg Wolf"** is representative of the brutal, villainous Métis so common in Canadian literature, while Pedro and Faco Tampico in *Monarch* reflect the cowardly, shiftless "greaser" image of Mexican-Americans. The cockney Jap Malee and his cohort Negro Sam, in **"The Slum Cat,"** are urban versions of the Duke and the Dauphin, Mark Twain's conniving river rascals in *The Adventures of Huckleberry Finn.*

Through such degenerate folk, Seton expresses his contempt for the prevalent attitudes of his time. These personifications of materialism and industrialism seek to devour the pristine wilderness and the natural order of things that his animal heroes represent. The cattle and the sheep of the Western range are seen merely as "four-legged cash," and the men who herd them as vanguards of the urban-industrial society, with all its ills, soon to follow. Because of his high connections, Seton often found it better to express his opinions through "conventional" attitudes, such as the traditional Westerner's view of sheep, animals which he once called "grumbling hoofy locusts." Yet his underlying motives are evident; he once stated:

"I am not a sheep owner and I do not love sheep. My sympathies are all with the forest." Sometimes he purposely assumed the role of the civilizer: the first-person narrator of **"Snap"** is a barbed-wire salesman. Whatever position he took, however, Seton always emphasized the Westerner's homespun philosophy. He never failed to express the outdoorsman's appreciation for his domestic animals and their importance to his occupation. At the burial of Snap, who is fatally wounded by the wolf he has slain, the dog's rancher owner remarks: "By jingo that was grit—c'lar grit! Ye can't raise cattle without grit."

Double meanings and symbolism are evident. The horns of Krag, the Kootenay Ram, are not merely a prized hunting trophy; they may also represent the vast wealth and innumerable secrets of the natural world which humanity so greedily attempts to exploit. **"The Slum Cat"** is not just the tale of an ordinary stray cat (the conglomeration of Seton's cat observations in Toronto and New York) who makes it by sheer pluck and luck; it is a lighthearted commentary on American society, particularly on the gullibility and shallowness of the rich and their failure to understand the masses. Outwardly, the cat becomes a pedigreed "Royal Analostan" and is thus admitted to the elite rank of "patrician" cats that get the first pickings from the liver man. But at heart, she is still a slum cat, and nothing can ever change that.

The truly outstanding human characters in Seton's tales are the children and young people, whose impressionable minds and love for mystery allow them to enter part of the natural world. Little Jimmy Hogan, the abused son of the saloon owner, is the only friend of the Winnipeg Wolf. Likewise, Lizette Prunty is the only human who can touch the usually ferocious razorback boar, Foam. Sometimes such youngsters are instrumental in winning certain of their adult peers over to their side. Bob Yancey's little daughter prevents her frustrated father from getting rid of Silly Billy, thus enabling the pup to prove his mettle later. An extreme example of child-animal unity is the story of a seven-year-old boy who becomes lost on the prairie and survives for three weeks by sharing a den with a badger. In the tale of Domino, young Abner Jukes is at first overcome by his desire for the chase, but after he witnesses the fox's dramatic escape and begins courting the gentle Garden-girl (who has earlier saved Domino from the horde of hounds and hunters), the "shadow" is removed; no longer does he see the silver fox merely as a valuable pelt.

Occasionally, Seton plays with the Progressive-Turnerian themes of patriotism and free individualism. In one scene, the Garden-girl lovingly prevents Domino from raiding a wild turkey's nest by surrounding it with metal objects, which the fox associates with traps. The objects she uses are chain links, a broken plowshare, and a horseshoe—symbolizing friendship, labor, and luck, all essential ingredients of the American dream. The clearest reference to these themes appears in the story of **"Little Warhorse."** After the jackrabbit hero is captured in a rabbit drive and sent to a coursing park, he gains the admiration of Mickey Doo, an Irish-born jack trainer. With the boss's consent, Mickey vows to set Warhorse free after he outshines the greyhounds thirteen times. To show this, the Irishman uses a gatekeeper's punch to stamp the rabbit's long ears with stars, one for each achievement. "He is won his freedom loike every Amerikin done," he quips. However, the boss reneges for monetary reasons and persuades Mickey to run Warhorse once more against two new hounds. Just as the exhausted rabbit is about to be done in, Mickey intercedes and turns Warhorse

loose on the prairie. The trainer's closing remark, "Shure an its ould Oireland that's proud to set the thirteen stars at liberty wance more," reflects the fierce patriotism of both Irish and Americans.

Seton makes widespread use of local color, and many of his characters are based on real people whom he met during his travels. Colonel Pickett, for example, is instrumental in setting the story of Wahb in motion and remains a prime mover throughout the action. Frequently, Seton changes or plays around with names: the Penroof brothers in the narratives of Snap and Badlands Billy are the Eatons; the Chimney-pot Ranch, which figures prominently in **"Tito,"** is Roosevelt's Chimney Butte; Lan Kellyan and Lou Bonamy, the captors of Monarch, are Allen Kelly and Louis Ohnimus.

Seton was always interested in what finally became of the heroes of his tales. In 1902, he learned that Mountain Billy's pelt was finally taken near Sentinel Butte by Montana cattleman G. W. Myers. Three years later, on a return visit to the zoo at Golden Gate Park, Seton was pleased to find that Old Monarch, whose frustrated desires for freedom he had compared to a dammed-up river's flow, had mated and sired two healthy cubs. Admittedly, Seton was not always historically accurate as to the real fate of some of his animal outlaws; old Wahb, for instance, was finally shot by A. A. Anderson, who displayed the carcass in his studio.

While Seton borrowed heavily from European classical and romantic genres, one outstanding feature of conventional western lore was popularized in his story, **"The Pacing Mustang."** The hero is a wild black stallion who makes himself a nuisance by running off several mares belonging to area ranches in eastern New Mexico. The conflicts between man and nature come into play as "Wild Jo" Calone and his fellow cowboys, stimulated by a five-thousand-dollar reward offer in Clayton, seek to either kill or capture the Pacer and stop him from adding to his "harem." They finally manage to retrieve the mares by "walking" them to exhaustion, but the Pacer, like so many outlaw stallions of lore, seems possessed of supernatural stamina. The honor of capturing the mustang falls to an unlikely old saddle tramp, Tom "Turkeytrack" Bates, who ingeniously snares his quarry at a water hole by using his brown mare as bait. But the Pacer, like Lobo, will not give up his freedom and chooses a suicidal death by leaping off the wall of Piñabetitos Canyon. In a later version of the tale, the stallion takes his captor with him. As Seton explained: "At this, the close of the great heroic age of the West, it seemed the proper ringdown for the last great scene—the magnificent horse, the peerless old horseman, the symbols of their kind meeting in heroic and final stance, in tragic double sacrifice." While Seton was certainly not the originator of wild mustang lore, his **"Pacing Mustang"** probably influenced Zane Grey and other writers to use the theme.

Although his animal tales are not true "formula" westerns, Seton in his own way sought to preserve for his readers one aspect of the West that by 1900 was rapidly dying. He knew that technological changes were inevitable, but because of them, his beloved natural world was in danger of vanishing for good. Along with the lone mountaineers and gunmen of other western authors, Seton's animal outlaws have emerged as larger-than-life heroes of a bygone era. (pp. 94-101)

H. Allen Anderson, in his The Chief: Ernest Thompson Seton and the Changing West, *Texas A&M University Press, 1986, 363 p.*

ADDITIONAL BIBLIOGRAPHY

Burroughs, John. "The Literary Treatment of Nature." *Atlantic Monthly* 94 (July 1904): 38-43.

> Discussion of the works of various nature writers in which Seton is briefly mentioned. Burroughs modifies his earlier opinion of Seton's work (see excerpt dated 1903), noting: "We have a host of nature students in our own day, bent on plucking out the heart of every mystery in the fields and woods.... Mr. Thompson Seton, as an artist and *raconteur*, ranks by far the highest in this field, and to those who can separate the fact from the fiction in his animal stories, he is truly delightful."

"The Animal Story." *Edinburgh Review* CCXIV, No. CCCCXXXVII (July 1911): 94-118.

> Examines the evolution of the animal story from ancient to modern times. The critic praises Seton's departure from the ancient style of depicting animals as representatives of individual human qualities.

Keller, Betty. *Black Wolf: The Life of Ernest Thompson Seton*. Vancouver: Douglas & McIntyre, 1984, 240 p.

> Sympathetic, noncritical biography.

Lilliard, Charles. Review of *Selected Stories of Ernest Thompson Seton*, edited by Patricia Morley. *Malahat Review*, No. 49 (January 1979): 128-29.

> Welcomes the republication of Seton's stories.

Peattie, Donald Culross. "Nature and Nature Writers." *Saturday Review* XVI, No. 18 (28 August 1937): 10-11.

> Negative review of *Great Historic Animals*, a compilation of several of Seton's more popular animal stories. Peattie states, "I am going to burn Ernest Thompson Seton's *Great Historic Animals* because I don't believe in its sincerity, because its style is extremely mawkish, because the morals of it are . . . wrong."

Polk, James. "Lives of the Hunted." *Canadian Literature*, No. 53 (Summer 1972): 51-9.

> Contrasts the attitudes toward animals reflected in American, Canadian, and British fiction, noting that Seton and other Canadians consistently identify with the hunted rather than with the hunter.

Rohrbough, Malcolm J. "A Dedication to the Memory of Ernest Thompson Seton." *Arizona and the West* 28, No. 1 (Spring 1986): 1-4.

> Biographical sketch.

Shi, David E. "Ernest Thompson Seton and the Boy Scouts: A Moral Equivalent of War?" *South Atlantic Quarterly* 84, No. 4 (Autumn 1985): 377-91.

> Discusses Seton's role in formulating the philosophy of Scouting.

"The Cunning of Criminal Animals." *Spectator* 81, No. 3674 (26 November 1898): 780-81.

> Review of *Wild Animals I Have Known*, which the critic judges "a well-written and well-illustrated book."

"Wild Animal Ways." *Spectator* 117, No. 4604 (23 September 1916): 345-46.

> Review of *Wild Animal Ways* in which the critic commends Seton's concern for the welfare of animals.

Wiley, Farida A. Introduction to *Ernest Thompson Seton's America*, edited by Farida A. Wiley, pp. xv-xxiii. New York: Devin-Adair, 1954.

> Biographical essay which focuses on Seton's early years and formative influences.

Edith (Irene) Södergran

1892-1923

Finland-Swedish poet.

Södergran is recognized as one of the chief precursors of Finland-Swedish literary Modernism. In her works she combined a familiarity with turn-of-the-century European literary movements—particularly German Expressionism and Russian Symbolism—with aggressively frank language and subjects that reflect her personal idiosyncrasies. Her innovative verses are considered a distinguished achievement in modern Finnish literature, and critic George C. Schoolfield has hailed her work as "a major liberating force" in Scandinavian poetry of the twentieth century.

Södergran was the only child born to a wealthy Finland-Swedish couple living in St. Petersburg, Russia. For several centuries, a period that ended in the early nineteenth century, Finland was a part of Sweden, and the Södergrans were among a large group of Swedish-speaking Finns descended from the former rulers of Finland. Shortly after her birth the family moved to Raivola, a provincial town near the Russian border in southeastern Finland. Södergran returned to St. Petersburg to attend school, where she gained a knowledge of European languages and literature, most notably German, the language of instruction at the school and the language of her first verses. In 1907 her father died of tuberculosis, a disease which she developed the following year and which overshadowed the rest of her life. From the time of her diagnosis in early 1909 to her death in 1923, Södergran divided her time between Raivola and treatment centers in Finland and Switzerland. Many biographers have noted the importance to her literary development of her visits to Nummela, a sanatorium near Helsinki. At Nummela, Södergran belonged to a predominately Finland-Swedish community for the first time in her life. Previously she had spoken Swedish only at home, but at the sanatorium she gained greater familiarity with the language and literature of her ancestors. It was also at Nummela that she developed an unrequited passion for a member of the medical staff, which biographers view as one manifestation of a tendency in Södergran to associate illness and eroticism. In 1914 and 1915 this pattern culminated in a disappointing love affair with a married physician who lived in a Russian coastal resort near Raivola. Many critics maintain that this unhappy romance was the inspiration for many of the poems in Södergran's debut collection, *Dikter*.

In 1917 and 1918 Södergran's comfortable domestic life in Raivola ended unexpectedly: the family's fortune, invested chiefly in Russian interests, was lost as a result of the Bolshevik Revolution, leaving Södergran and her mother virtually destitute; then, in 1918, the Finnish Civil War brought violence to Raivola as military skirmishes and political executions occurred in the district. These events, along with her avid study of the writings of Friedrich Nietzsche, are considered significant to a period of intense poetic creativity in September 1918, during which she produced the works collected in *Septemberlyran*. In the following years, restricted by poverty and illness and depressed by critical disregard of her writing, she turned from writing poetry and from her studies of Nietzsche to the anthroposophy of Rudolf Steiner, and eventually to Christi-

anity. Her newfound faith in Christianity brought renewed interest in writing; however, her health deteriorated steadily in the 1920s, and she died at Raivola in 1923.

Modern critics have called *Dikter* Södergran's most accessible collection, but at the time of its publication it was controversial for its rejection of traditional rhyme and meter and its undisguised revelations of personal traumas. Generally perceived as a response to her failed love affair, *Dikter* is remembered for its confessional tone and unique expression of feminine longing. Melancholy lyrics expressing erotic disappointment or describing dreamlike landscapes are characteristic of the volume. These richly symbolic works display Södergran's knowledge of the themes and techniques of German Expressionism, as well as those of other movements current in European literature, and critics recognize their importance in introducing modern innovations to Finland-Swedish poetry. The sexual frustration expressed in her earlier verses deepens in *Septemberlyran* into a desire for erotic revenge; many of the poems also serve as records of her spiritual development. Written during the chaotic period of the Civil War, this collection expresses Södergran's exultation in her newly acquired Nietzschean vitalism. According to critics, she presents herself as a priestess of Nietzschean philosophy and repeatedly proclaims her vocation to convert humanity to her beliefs. In later collections, Södergran continued to present her philosophical beliefs in emotional poems characterized by vivid imagery. Explaining the nature of her verses, she wrote: "I do not write poems, I create myself, my poems are for me the way to myself." According to critics, Södergran seems spiritually exalted in her later works, many of which focus on her search for self-knowledge and contemplation of death.

Considered a daring and controversial poet by most critics during her lifetime, Södergran has achieved a distinguished reputation in Finland-Swedish literature. According to Gurli Hertzman-Ericson: "So strongly individual and vital is the personality revealed in the five collections of verse which she has left behind that not even her opponents can pass her by with indifference."

PRINCIPAL WORKS

Dikter (poetry) 1916
Septemberlyran (poetry) 1918
Broikiga iakttagelser (aphorisms) 1919
Rosenaltaret (poetry) 1919
Framtidens skugga (poetry) 1920
Landet som icke är (poetry) 1925
Min lyra (poetry) 1929
Edith Södergrans dikter (poetry) 1940
   [*The Collected Poems of Edith Södergran*, 1980]
Samlade dikter (poetry and aphorsims) 1949
Ediths brev (letters) 1955
Dikter 1907-1909. 2 vols. (poetry) 1961
We Women (poetry) 1977
Love and Solitude: Selected Poems, 1916-1923 (poetry)
   1981
Poems (poetry) 1983
Complete Poems (poetry) 1984

GURLI HERTZMAN-ERICSON (essay date 1933)

[*In the following excerpt, Hertzman-Ericson praises the vitality and individuality of Södergran's poetry.*]

With Edith Södergran a new epoch was inaugurated in Finnish poetry. She is above all the pioneer who scorns the old familiar paths and enters in upon strange and unknown ways where the traditional no longer counts. Many of her followers have been nothing more than mere formalistic seekers after effect, but in her lyrics there burns a pathos which even in its occasionally obscure expression yet bears the stamp of artistry. It is a strange and tragic fate which meets us in this young woman who was snatched away at the early age of thirty-one. So strongly individual and vital is the personality revealed in the five collections of verse which she has left behind that not even her opponents can pass her by with indifference. (p. 426)

We do not know exactly when Edith Södergran began to write, but her first collection of poems appeared in 1916. It did not pass unremarked. It contained new notes which gave rise both to enthusiasm and scorn, according as people reacted to it. She wrote freely out of her own heart, now with strains of tremulous longing, now with a bold recklessness. She is a young woman who, reaching longingly out towards life, bursts out:

> The day cools towards evening . . .
> Drink warmth from out my hand,
> my hand has the same blood as the Spring.
> Take my hand, take my white arm,
> take the longing of my narrow shoulders . . .
> It would be wonderful to know,
> a single night, a night like this
> thy heavy head against my breast.

But disillusionment does not tarry:

> You sought a flower
> and found a fruit.
> You sought a fountainhead
> and found a sea.
> You sought a woman
> and found a soul—
> You are betrayed.

A year or two later *September Lyre* came out, followed by *Altar of Roses* and *Shadow of the Future*. The feminine accent of her first collection of verse yields here before a stronger and more violent pulse. She desires to burst all bounds, to raise herself up above suffering, and her poetry takes on an aspect of greatness and of exultant defiance.

> What do I fear? I am part from out infinity.
> I am a part of the great might of the All,
> a lonely world within a million worlds,
> like a star of the first rank, extinguished last.
> What triumph to feel time ice-cold run through one's veins
> and hear the silent flood of night
> and stand upon the mount beneath the sun.

She repudiates suffering and rises to mighty heights of exaltation:

> What is pain to me, misery?
> the whole world burst asunder with a crash:
> I sing.
> Then pain's great hymn arises from a happy heart.

In every strophe she writes one feels the confession of her heart and perceives something of her radiant vision of eternity. She desires to go up herself on to the high mountains and to lead thither those who are wandering in the depths and the darkness. She casts off everyday existence and her poetry rises towards the cosmos. She knows her power, and if her visions be mingled with the heat of fever and the heart's panting beat, they nevertheless possess something of the splendor of eternity and of a never-ceasing quest.

Those poems which were published after Edith Södergran's death are perhaps the most beautiful she wrote. The first years of her life were bound up with the old orchard, and when the circle is completed, it is childhood's peace in nature, its intimacy with flowers and animals, which again sinks down upon her. She lives upon the border of eternity, but it is her firm conviction that

> We should love life's long hours of illness
> and stifled years of yearning
> As those brief moments when the desert blooms.

The bond which still binds her to things temporal becomes ever more tenuous, the life flame languishes, thought no longer wrestles with cosmic visions, and there is a quiet resignation in these rarely beautiful strophes:

> I long for the land that is not,
> for all that which is I am tired of desiring.
> The pale moon tells me in silvery runes

of the land that is not.
The land where all our desires are wondrously fulfilled,
the land where all our chains drop off,
the land where we cool our lacerated brows
in the dew of the moon.
My life was a hot illusion.
But one thing I have found and that I have really won—
the road to the land that is not.

Although Edith Södergran was early marked by the illness which caused her death, she preserved to the last the noble stamp of a brave and proud soul. Her poetry was never marred by weariness or exhaustion, but rather had that peace which passeth all understanding. She achieved only five collections of verse, but these have assured her a distinguished place in Finnish literature. (pp. 427-28)

> Gurli Hertzman-Ericson, "Poetic Profiles in Finland," in The American-Scandinavian Review, Vol. XXI, Nos. 8 & 9, August & September, 1933, pp. 423-28.

ROSS SHIDELER (essay date 1977)

[In the following excerpt, Shideler discusses Södergran's influence on modern Swedish poetry.]

The quality of [Edith Södergran's poetry] . . . that made her the forerunner of modernism in Sweden is a visionary realism. Ironically, many of the critics who reviewed her first volume spoke of the dreamlike quality of her poetry, yet we now perceive this quality as a personal realism. The dreams in Edith Södergran's poetry are of three kinds: first, childhood sagas, simpler, but not wholly unlike Rimbaud's; second, prophetic visions of the future; and third, realistic poems that seem like dreams. The poems in the last group had the greatest influence, although many of her poems contain a startling imagery of dreams and, until her final years, a pessimistic, hard view of life.

[Biographer Gunnar Tideström] comments that a large portion of Södergran's early poems, up until 1916, fall into the nature-lyric category of Vilhelm Ekelund. He describes one poem:

> Everything here is seen with the eye: the light of the air, the water reflections, the gray and silver-white colors. . . . No detail is symbolic. Nevertheless, the picture is transformed. . . .

Though nature, as Tideström suggests, was the source for much of both Ekelund's and Södergran's poetry, each of them transformed what was seen and felt into a personal expression that at times appears unrealistic. Ekelund gave symbolic dimensions to the scenes he saw. Södergran often used dreams as simple fantasies, but her poetic imagery conveys that sharp and startling focus on reality which characterizes literature arising from the unconscious and from dreams. She suggests the power of dreams in her early poem **"Dangerous Dreams."**

> Don't go too near your dreams:
> they are smoke and could be stolen—
> they are dangerous and could endure.
>
> Have you looked your dreams in the eye:
> they are sick and understand nothing—
> they have only their own thoughts.
>
> Don't go too near your dreams:
> they are lies, they should go—
> they are madness, they want to stay.

Even in this simple poem we see a surprising and unfamiliar vocabulary for dreams. The dreams themselves are given strange powers that are focused inward, on themselves. One feels, because of the opening admonition, that the madness of dreams may be extremely valuable to the narrator. Södergran's more famous poems combine vivid imagery and personal emotion in a way which makes them dreamlike.

> My soul was a light blue dress the color of the sky:
> I left it on a cliff by the sea
> and I came to you naked looking like a woman
> And like a woman I sat at your table
> and drank a toast of wine and breathed the odor of roses.
> You found I was beautiful and resembled something you had
>   seen in dreams.

This excerpt from one of Södergran's best-known poems ("**Love**") demonstrates the imagery and subjectivity which had so much influence on Ekelöf and modern Swedish poetry. (p. 531)

> Ross Shideler "'The Glassclear Eye of Dreams' in Twentieth-Century Swedish Poetry," in World Literature Today, Vol. 51, No. 4, Autumn, 1977, pp. 530-34.

GLADYS HIRD (essay date 1978)

[In the following excerpt, Hird discusses prominent symbols, themes, and subjects of Södergran's poetry.]

Dogged by ill-health, made worse by abject poverty during the latter years of her short life, Edith Södergran published only four slender volumes of verse and a collection of aphorisms. The first two volumes, **Dikter** (**Poems**) and **Septemberlyran** (**September Lyre**), were edited in a manner which caused her considerable distress. Poems were rearranged or excluded, her dating was ignored and the sense was distorted by misprints. A crueller blow, however, was the derisive criticism of the reviewers. The revolutionary style was too much for the taste of critics unfamiliar with pre-Expressionist and Futurist movements elsewhere in Europe. . . . In culturally isolated Finland only a few choice spirits dared to stand up in her defence. Of these, two kindred souls, Elmer Diktonius and Hagar Olsson—the latter soon to become Edith Södergran's dearest friend and "sister"—offered her the support necessary for her survival as one of the greatest literary phenomena in Finland since Runeberg. Edith Södergran's poetry is confessional. "I do not write poems," she said, "I create myself, my poems are for me the way to myself." An understanding of many of the poems depends on some knowledge of their personal setting. . . .

In 1908 she contracted the disease which had killed her father and although she was successfully treated in Switzerland she found on her return to Finland in 1914 that the cure was not complete. Henceforth she was to be haunted by the fear of death and her life was to be a constant, hopeless struggle to remain alive and to find "happiness." (p. 5)

Her first volume of verse is regarded as the most accessible. **Dikter** was written by a woman who still dreamed of leading a normal life. They express her conflicting feelings in the face of her situation: despondency, joy, humility, arrogance, love, hate. A brief love affair with a married man some sixteen years her senior lies behind the intense disappointment expressed in her best-known poem **"Dagen svalnar"** . . . (**"The Day Cools. . ."**). It encapsulates Edith Södergran's experience of the traditional male and female roles, of arrogant dominance and humiliating submission. The tough, masterful lover who abandons his proud mistress when he discovers she is not just a sex object is bitterly characterized in the epigrammatic final lines:

> You sought a woman
> and found a soul—
> you are disappointed.

Although the imagery in this first collection appeared novel, a closer examination of the symbolism reveals a strong traditional element. Passion is red, innocence and inexperience are white, happiness is yellow. One of the most beautiful and enigmatic poems, **"Den speglande brunnen"** (**"The Reflecting Well"**) uses colour symbolism to describe the tension between Edith Södergran's awareness of death and her desire to live a full life:

> Fate said: white you shall live or red you shall die!
> But my heart resolved: red I will live.

It has been said that this poem is about resignation, death and the waiting for death. The poet imagines herself resting by a well. She gazes at the mirror-image of herself, an image which lives in a country which knows nothing of death. Passers-by ask her if she is happy, but happiness in terms of husband and children is not to be hers. Red roses, the symbols of beauty and transience, in bloom round the well in the last lines of the poem suggest that her "red life," her decision to dedicate herself to the cult of beauty will, as Fate predicted, lead only to a "red death."

The Russian October Revolution in 1917, although welcomed by the anti-tsarist Edith, left the Södergrans penniless. During the ensuing Finnish Civil War the Karelian Isthmus became a scene of fighting in the struggle between Finnish Whites and Russian and Finnish Bolsheviks. Brought close to starvation Edith Södergran suffered a rapid deterioration of health and a severe lung haemorrhage. This is the backcloth to the wave of inspiration she experienced in September 1918 which resulted in *Septemberlyran*. Nourished on Nietzschean vitalism she felt she had survived the chaos and misery around her only through her art. The fact that she had been able to keep alive reinforced her belief that she belonged to a future type of human being. Her poems were exalted, prophetic, heroic, "My self-assurance," she wrote in the preface, "springs from the fact that I have discovered my dimensions. It does not become me to make myself less than I am." The critics were sceptical. The poet's "culte du moi" gave some of them cause to wonder whether she was mentally ill.

The obscure **"O mina solbrandsfärgade toppar"** (**"O My Peaks Tinged with the Sun's Fire"**) can be taken as an example of the kind of lyric which became the subject of scathing remarks. Here Edith Södergran assumes the role of the poet-seer who will redeem the world. Her gospel is the Nietzschean will to power. The alpine peaks are symbols of the power and ecstasy she is striving for. Her imagination transports her to the mountain tops and she is reborn. Divorced from reality, however, she wonders whether she is justified in abandoning the world in exchange for boundless strength. The answer is a firm yes. In finding a way to overcome her earthly ordeals she can help others:

> If I heal myself,
> this drop is enough for all that breathes.

The incident which inspired **"Månens hemlighet"** (**"The Moon's Secret"**), a grimly haunting poem in this collection, was the execution of some Reds by the White forces near the Södergrans' house. A full moon was shining. Edith later expressed disapproval of the piece, speaking of a "furtive attraction for the smell of corpses." Suggestive as the poem is of Baudelaire, there is something repellent in its aesthetic enjoyment of the slaughter, but Edith Södregran's beautifying of death can perhaps be explained by her need to overcome her own fears.

The anti-Christian view of life expressed in *Septemberlyran* grew more pronounced in the next volume. *Rosenaltaret* (*The Rose Altar*). From being the symbol of sensual love in **"Dagen svalnar . . ."** the rose has now become the symbol of beauty. The poet is the priestess who has consecrated her life to beauty and her poems take on cosmic dimensions reminiscent of German pre-Expressionism. Her companions and equals are the sun, space and the stars. A short visionary lyric, **"Till fots fick jag gå genom solsystemen"** (**"I Had to Tramp through Solar Systems"**), describes her search for self-knowledge and enlightenment which are symbolized by her "red attire." Her identity towards which she is walking is her heart hanging somewhere in space and the sparks it is emitting will ignite other great spirits. This theme of the missionary is also evident in **"Jorden blev förvandlad till en askhög"** (**"The Earth Was Transformed into an Ash-Heap"**). Edith Södergran had sometimes wondered whether she was capable of enduring the deep suffering necessary to become the superman, but her struggle with death the previous autumn had provided her with proof enough. "Death—I faced you, I held the the scales against you," she chants. Suffering has made her strong, she is now able to impart joy to the world.

The poems which make up the last published collection, *Framtidens skugga* (*Shadow of the Future*), stood beneath the shadow of Edith Södergran's awareness of approaching death. In it her aesthetic preoccupations and her exaltation surpass everything in her earlier writing.

Hagar Olsson had confirmed her belief in the visionary nature of her poetry, and she rejoiced in her task of moulding the masses for the brave new world. But she is also aware that she will not live to witness it. In the opening poem, **"Mysteriet"** (**"The Mystery"**) she is the knight who slays the dragon that prevents humanity from partaking of the new vision of the future. Her task is to reveal to mankind the "mystery" of achieving superhuman power through the experience of beauty. Some poems in the collection do, however, indicate that Edith Södergran was entering on a new emotional crisis which was eventually to lead her via anthroposophy to Christ. One of these poems is entitled **"Materialism"** (**"Materialism"**). It speaks of the chemical composition of her body forever struggling against decomposition. Since there is and never has been any soul, was, she asks, her "game of games"—the role of superman—only an illusion?

The unfavourable reviews of *Framtidens skugga* strengthened her growing resolve to abandon her art; her progress towards peace of mind is recorded in poems published posthumously under the title *Landet som icke är* (**"The Land That Is Not"**). The title poem, found shortly after her death, expresses in simple, refreshing language her readiness to leave this earth to meet her loved one. "Who is my beloved? . . . What is his name?" The answer "Christ" has been assumed by many scholars, but there is no certain answer. Intensely jealous of privacy during her lifetime, Edith Södergran remained private also beyond her death. (pp. 5-7)

Gladys Hird, "Edith Södergran: A Pioneer of Finland-Swedish Modernism," in Books from Finland Vol. XII, 1978. pp. 4-7.

HELMER LÅNG (essay date 1980)

[In the following excerpt, Lång discusses Expressionism in Södergran's verses.]

In 1916 Modernism made its appearance in Scandinavian poetry. There had been sporadic attempts at a new style earlier, at the turn of the century—in Norway with Sigbjørn Obstfelder, in Sweden with Vilhelm Ekelund, and with Fröding in the poems from his illness—but Modernism first became really widely known and discussed when Pär Lagerkvist published his volume *Angest* (*Anguish*), and Edith Södergran her first book *Dikter* (*Poems*). Lagerkvist had prepared the public for a shock in his polemical essay "Ordkonst och bildkonst" ("The Art of Words and the Art of Images") in 1913, when he drew attention to the expressionism or "cubism" he had met with in France (Jacob, Apollinaire). But the poems of Edith Södergran struck down like a bomb in the duck pond of the Finnish bourgeoisie, where only nationalistic poems attacking Russification could be approved as exceptions from well-groomed idealism.

By and large, Edith Södergran's first volume of poems was received with indifference or ridicule; this was also true of her following books. One critic later hinted that she was mentally deranged. The accusation caused a serious debate in the press, in which the roses she was offered by her defenders could not remove from her sensitive soul the cruel wounds of her enemies. Today's readers find her first book—and most of her later work—simple, natural, and straightforward. It is free verse, a parlando vibrating with emotion, where one is always aware of the cadence of her voice.

In some strange way the style of Södergran is intimately connected with her illness—tuberculosis—although, quite naturally, she also had formal models, first and foremost Vilhelm Ekelund, but also German and Russian expressionism. She had made the acquaintance of Walt Whitman, and admitted to a feeling of kinship with him, rather than influence: both poets share a strong self-assertion and a feeling of sympathy for the smallest phenomena of nature. Even as regards their form one may sometimes observe similarities (repetitions, the "cataloging" technique). But liberation from the fetters of form is, with Edith Södergran, a natural part of the therapeutic action of the poetic process. In 1909, at the age of sixteen, she wrote a poem where the diction is already strikingly personal, and the imagery very concrete. A few months earlier she had been told that she suffered from tuberculosis, the dread disease which had taken the life of her father. Her long stays at various sanitariums now commenced. She rejects joy as superficial, an earthbound butterfly, while sorrow is symbolized as a bird with great strong wings which carries it high above ordinary mortals. The poems already possess the cosmic perspective which we find in many of her most perfect later poems.

> Joy is a butterfly
> fluttering low above the ground
> but sorrow is a bird
> with big, strong, black wings,
> they carry you high above life
> which flows down there in sunlight and greenery.
> The bird of sorrow flies high
> where the angels of pain stand guard
> by the bed of death.

From her suffering and sickness springs the fresh fountain of her poetry. Her first poems are full of melancholy or resignation, expressed in open and translucent imagery. "**The Days of Autumn**" is a symbolic poem. Autumn is decay, winter is death. But there is also a complication: the wreath, which stands for suffering, love, and death. Such imagery can be readily understood by everyone; in her later poems she uses it with even greater mastery and beauty.

Already in her first book Södergran showed that she was conscious of the revolutionary form of her language. Her poem "**Beauty**" contains a new esthetic program: "Beauty is not the thin sauce in which the poets serve themselves up." What she wants is an expressionism after her own style, a very personal expressivity where she can speak straight from her heart to the reader. She returns again to the same demand on form (which excludes neither rhyme nor a firm rhythm, alternating with free verse). In "**My Hope**" (*The Land That Is Not*) she exclaims:

> I want to be free and easy—
> that's why the noble styles mean nothing to me
> and I roll up my sleeves.
> The dough of poetry is fermenting . . .

These demands are also found in American Modernism, and Elmer Diktonius voices them in Finland. But from the very first moment she also shows her own elevated tone, her striving for excellence, her over-weening aspiration. She tells us proudly: "Before I die I will bake a cathedral" ("**My Hope**").

The second phase of Södergran's poetry is less easily accessible. She reacted with provocative self-assertion against incomprehension and indifference, e.g. in the preface to *The September Lyre:*

> My self-assurance depends on the fact that I have discovered my own proportions. It behooves me not to make myself smaller than I am.

(pp. 7-9)

In so far as we may perceive traces of external reality in Södergran's poetry they are nearly always connected with Raivola and its garden and surrounding village. There stood the tall trees which she climbed in order to sight "the smoke from the chimneys of my country" (the reference is to St. Petersburg, where she went to school), there was the grass and the raspberry patch, there was the cemetery opposite the Södergran villa. This is the setting for the poem "**The Secret of the Moon**," a bloody drama from the revolution and the Finnish civil war, 1918:

> corpses will lie on a beach of marvelous beauty.

In this poem the poet, oppressed by illness and poverty, turns herself into a superior, triumphant being. She derives strength from the philosophy of Friedrich Nietzsche, and his work inspires her images and figures:

> O, my peaks, tinted by the glow of the sun

or the dionysically intoxicated horsemen—

> the unknown, lighthearted, strong

in "**The Creators**." *The September Lyre, The Rose Altar,* and *The Shadow of the Future* were all fertilized by Zarathustra and the philosophy of the Superman.

But the heightened ardor and intensity of Södergran's new poetry is also directly connected with the Russian revolution. While Professor Gunnar Tideström, who wrote the standard work on Edith Södergran, called her early poetry "a late autumn flower of ego-contemplating symbolism,'' we find her later poems full of pathos and enthusiasm for reforms. It is true that the Reds soon led the revolution into terror and a revolting dictatorship, but at the outset Edith Södergran and other liberals who were hostile to the Czar experienced the change as a liberation. She felt that the air of the Finland of her time was too stuffy, and she expresses this feeling in the 1917 poem **"Grimace d'artiste"** with an effective artist's grimace and a repetition of the political slogan "red":

> All that I possess is my luminous mantle,
> my red daring.
> My red daring seeks adventures
> in mean lands.

She extends her adventures to the cosmos. While *The September Lyre* describes how humanity hears the voice of the Creator, and is united with the cosmos at his bidding, Södergran turns herself into the Creator in *The Rose Altar*. It is she, not God, who kindles the stars and illumines every "midnight farmstead in the Alps," in the landscape of Nietzsche and the Superman. In **"Scherzo"** she speaks to the glorious starry night as to an equal ("We are one"):

> Do I not sit trembling on a string of stars . . .

But her Dionysian arrogance carried in itself the seed of contrition and renewed self-appraisal, and already in *The Shadow of the Future* we sense a feeling of poetical insufficiency:

Here, in **"The Star"** the speaker is no longer creative lordship, but humility:

> Before my star, which stands there threateningly,
> I feel my own inadequacy.

And in **"Tantalus, Fill Your Cup"** (Tantalus being, of course, a classical symbol of the vanity of all human efforts) she exclaims:

> Are these poems? No, they are rags, little bits,
> everyday scraps of paper.

Although she knows the consolation that composing poetry can give, she confesses her resolve "never to write a poem again" (**"Resolve"**):

> Every poem shall be the tearing up of a poem,
> not poetry, but claw marks.

This sounds more like Diktonius, the author of the programmatic poem "The Jaguar," than Södergran—but the strange thing is that she really does stop publishing poetry. At the same time the Zeitgeist has caught up with her, and a lively lyrical modernism grows up round Diktonius as its central figure, followed by several successors (Gunnar Björling, Rabbe Enckell, and others).

Her last poems were published posthumously in *The Land That Is Not*. Some of these poems had appeared shortly before her death in *Ultra*, the magazine where the modernists joined forces in an attack on traditional poetry in Finland.

If the second phase of Södergran's poetry was written under the signum of Nietzsche, the third phase is equally clearly stamped by another and different Superman: Christ. He is her beloved in **"The Land That Is Not,"** and He may also appear as Death, the singing Liberator in **"Arrival in Hades."** Both these poems, the poet's last, were found by her pillow after her death by her mother.

Total humility before the miracles of God and nature is the most striking feature of the new poems:

The key to all secrets lies in the grass at the raspberry patch.

But she never abandoned her enthusiasm. There is something passionate, almost erotic, in Edith Södergran's relation to Christ. "Can one dance with Christ?" she asks provocatively in a letter to her friend Hagar Olsson, who has showed us the poet's naked face in her book *Edith's Letters*. And if we were to look for a single formula which would encompass the whole of Edith's poetry, it must surely be this, which includes both love, Nietzsche, and Christ: *lyrical ecstasy*. (pp. 9-11)

> *Helmer Lång, "The Lyrical Poetry of Edith Södergran," in* The Collected Poems of Edith Södergran, *translated by Martin Allwood with Cate Ewing and Robert Lyng, Anglo-American Center, 1980, pp. 7-11.*

GEORGE C. SCHOOLFIELD   (essay date 1983)

[*An American educator and critic specializing in German and Scandinavian language and literature, Schoolfield is one of the foremost English-language authorities in his field. He has translated the works of several Finland-Swedish writers, including Hagar Olsson and Edith Södergran. In the following excerpt, Schoolfield discusses Södergran's response to criticism of her second collection,* Septemberlyran.]

On the day before Christmas 1918, Edith Södergran complained to Runar Schildt [the house literary advisor of her publisher]; he (or someone else) had left out several poems, as well as the dates of composition which she had wished to have included [in her second collection, *Septemberlyran*], eager to call attention to her development as a poet: "May I be allowed to say that the book would not have appeared in this condition, in the event I had been able to participate in the final decision?"

It would have been wiser if Edith Södergran had left her regrets to the privacy of the correspondence with Schildt. Instead, she wrote an open letter, **"Individual Art,"** to *Dagens Press*, which the paper printed on December 31:

> This book is not intended for the public, scarcely even for the higher intellectual circles, only for those few individuals who stand closest to the boundary of the future. A circumstance has caused me not to be able to be involved in the final decision regarding the choice of the poems, and I did not read proof either. As a result, certain important poems are missing, and superfluous ones have been included. This gives a certain air of trumpery to the book, which already, in itself, stands under the sign of carelessness and is, in fact, nothing more than an intimate sketchbook. The dates have also disappeared, and poems are intermingled between which a chasm lies, as great a chasm as between my first collection and the present one. What makes many of these poems precious is that they come from an individual of a new sort . . . A loftier flame streams from these poems, a mightier passion than not only [*sic*] from the art work of my past. I cannot help the person who fails to feel that the wild blood of the future courses through these poems. . . .
>
> I sacrifice every atom of my strength to my lofty goal, I live the life of a saint, I lose myself in the highest productions of the human spirit, I avoid all influences of a baser kind. I regard the old society as a mother cell which ought to be sustained until the individuals [*sic*] erect the new world. I admonish the individuals to work only for immortality (an erroneous expression), to make the highest thing pos-

sible out of themselves, to place themselves in the service of the future . . . I hope that I shall not be alone with that greatness which I have to bring.

This statement caused an unprecedented uproar in Finland-Swedish letters; experienced newspapermen could sense good copy here. *Dagens Press* carried a *causerie*, by a "Pale Youth," where the poems were called "thirty-one laughter-pills" and where **"Tjuren" ("The Bull,"** a verse-attack by Edith Södergran on her critics) was parodied as **"Kossan" ("Bossy"**); in *Hufvudstadsbladet*, an article by "Jumbo" (Gustaf Johansson, a friend of the late Mattsson, whose lightly derisive style he tried to imitate) talked about "Nietzsche-crazed women-folk." Indignant, the poet and artist Ragnar Ekelund sent a letter to *Dagens Press*, praising Södergran's "ruthless honesty" but admitting that both the open letter and the introduction to the volume betrayed an astounding naïveté; Johansson retorted with words that expressed what many readers of the open letter may have thought—that Edith Södergran had been "infected by the same intellectual disease which in the political field is called bolshevism." His remark seemed by no means as farfetched in the Finland of 1918 as it does today. (pp. 91-2)

George C. Schoolfield, "A Life on the Edge," in *Books from Finland, Vol. XVII*, No. 3, 1983, pp. 86-92.

GEORGE C. SCHOOLFIELD (essay date 1984)

[*In the following excerpt, Schoolfield offers a chronological survey of Södergran's major works.*]

At first glance, *Dikter* may seem to be inchoate; after further readings, its structure will become apparent—a suite of landscapes, into which four sets of thematically related lyrics are woven: reflections on the enigma of the poet's self, a tale of unhappy love, variations on a central myth borrowed from antiquity, and a series of instructions for survival.

The landscape, naturally enough, is most apparent in the collection's earlier pages; the poet wants her audience to behold her world, a surprisingly lush and southern one, shot through with dreaminess and melancholy. Here, before the book's overriding theme of erotic disappointment is introduced, the melancholy arises from the encroachments of industrialization, or the metropolis, on old places, old houses, old beauties; it is a sadness familiar to the reader . . . *Dikter* repeatedly reflects literary concerns, and techniques, of the turn-of-the-century. In **"Det gamla huset" ("The Old House"**), Edith Södergran says: "I live on in the dearness of old days, / amidst strangers who build their cities here / on bluish hillocks up to the heavens' rim / while I speak gently with the prisoner trees / and sometimes placate *them*." (For much of this mood-music, Edith Södergran uses the poetic devices of the German poetry of *Jugendstil*, regular rhythmic patterns and occasional rhyme, e.g., "himlens rand / ibland.") The gentle melancholy of **"Nocturne"** comes from a different Neo-Romantic source, and is a response to the "Moonlit evening, sheer with silver": "Shadows fall across the pathway, / gently, at water's edge, the bushes weep, / black giants by the edge's silver keep / their watch. Deep silence in summer's midst." A similar sweet sadness clings to **"Höstens dagar" ("The Autumn's Days"**): "It is so sweet without a wish to dream / Sated with flowers and grown tired of green, / with the vine's red wreath at pillowside." Languor may be ruffled by longing ("Have you ever stood at the iron gate and yearned / and seen how on dreaming pathways / the evening to blueness was turned?"); and there

is a mild regret at passion untasted ("a blood-red sun disappeared"), as in the poem, **"Du som aldrig gått ut ur ditt trädgårdsland" ("You Who Never Left Your Garden-Land"**), or a mild anxiety at winter's coming, as in **"Höstens dagar"** or **"Höst" ("Autumn"**): "A child still plays in the autumn's greyish haze, / a girl walks forth with flowers in her hand, / and on the horizon's band, / birds all silver-white ascend." (pp. 35-6)

Stock elements of the continental lyric of Neo-Romanticism are adduced, . . . reminiscent of Rilke or Maurice Maeterlinck: the haze, the solitary girl, the high-flying birds; and further poems—for example, **"Skogs sjön" ("The Forest Lake"**) or **"Irrande moln" ("Wandering Clouds"**)—have more elements of nature as viewed by the lyricists of the preceding decades: "the clouds wait for the wind which will carry them over the plain," the "sweetness of summer" drips slowly from the forest's trees by the lake; vague anticipation—of a seasonal transformation, of an erotic adventure, of an end to the idyll—is the key signature of such poetry. There is even a suggestion of a favorite deity of the late nineteenth century's arts-and-letters, Pan: "The sick god lies in the shadows, and dreams his malicious dreams" (**"Skogsdunkel" ("Forest Darkness"**). (It should be noted that the *fin-de-siècle's* concern with enervation or illness plays a significant role in *Dikter*; here, literary custom went in tandem with Edith Södergran's own physical condition.) Yet the world of these poems is by no means a literary construction; Raivola is its source, with Lake Onkamo, the great forest, and the Södergrans' garden—the magical place of **"Tidig gryning" ("Early Dawn"**): "Spread over the lake, a silence rests, / There lies a whisper in wait among the trees, / my old garden listens with half an ear / to the breathing of night, that soughs across the path." As these whisperings become more audible, their emotional burden becomes clear; the garden and the trees speak, as they would again in the final poems of Edith Södergran. In consequence of her isolation, the objects around her must have voices; and it is this almost childlike ability to bring her surroundings to life that distinguishes her from the poets of the Bethge and Benzmann anthologies she had studied and imitated. (p. 36)

Had Edith Södergran produced still more pleasantly melancholy lyrics, and included them in *Dikter*, it could have increased the book's chances for wholehearted approval by Finland-Swedish criticism; the verse offered a home-grown form of a recent and altogether acceptable foreign fashion, and, in Finland, the way had been prepared by the popular collections of Hjalmar Procopé and Bertel Gripenberg. . . . The fatally original and upsetting element in *Dikter* was Edith Södergran's mythologizing of herself. (p. 37)

In **"Jag" ("I"**), the poet—the title can be taken as a bald statement of autobiography—is held captive by the pressure of the sea. Its waters admit swirls of sunlight, and become, all of a sudden, air that "flows between my hands." The vague melancholy of the mood-poems turns to impatience, the garden and the forests become a prison, and the city, whose expansion was hateful to the poet in **"The Old House,"** becomes a "homeland"—as in the **"Fragment"** of *Septemberlyran*, where St. Petersburg is called the place of her "childhood's enchanted banner," of her "youth's glow."

I am a stranger in this land,
which lies deep beneath the pressing sea,
the sun looks in with swirling beams
and the air flows between my hands.

> They told me that I was born in imprisonment—
> there is no face that would be known to me.
> Was I a stone that they cast to the bottom here?
> Was I a fruit, too heavy for its branch?
> I lie in wait here at the soughing tree's foot,
> How can I climb up the slippery trunks?
> Up there, the waving crowns meet,
> I shall sit there and look out
> for the smoke of my homeland's chimneys . . .

The thought of imprisonment in a strange, submarine world (where a human being cannot, in fact, survive) is followed by dreams of anticipation again ("I lie in wait"), and of yearning for escape. . . . The poem is more vivid, certainly, thanks to its striking metamorphoses, than a thematic companion, **"En fången fågel"** (**"A Captive Bird"**), where the sea-depths (or the forest) have been exchanged for an ideal landscape, the almost feral ego for a captive bird, which sits "imprisoned in a gilded cage beside a deep-blue sea." The site of the imprisonment is altogether lovely; the castle is surrounded by "yearning roses which / promise pleasure and happiness"; but the bird sings of an Alpine world where "the sun is king and silence queen," and where "sparse little flowers in shining colors / bear witness to life which offers defiance and persists." The Raivola world softens and stultifies with its beauty, the harder Alpine world [of the Sanatorium at Davos] had been life-giving. The poem's teaching—that hardship is better than pleasure—will be offered again in the later pages of *Dikter*. (pp. 38-9)

One of the most frequently discussed poems in *Dikter* is **"Den speglande brunnen"** (**"The Mirroring Well"**). It has structural features . . . [similar to those of **"Färgernas längtan"** (**"Longing for Colors"**)]—color symbolism, apparent pronominal confusion, repeated self-injunction—but, unlike that poem, it offers a picture; an artist, illustrating *Dikter*, would have no difficulty in making a vignette from it:

> Fate said: white you shall live, or red you shall die!
> But my heart said: red I shall live.
> Now I dwell in the land where all is yours,
> death never enters this realm.
> I sit the whole day long with my arm resting on the well's
>   edge,
> when they ask me if happiness has been here,
> I shake my head and smile:
> happiness is far away, there a young woman sits, sewing a
>   child's blanket,
> happiness is far away, there a man walks in the forest and
>   builds himself a cabin.
> Here red roses grow around bottomless springs,
> here beautiful days mirror their smiling features
> and great flowers lose their fairest petals. . . .

(p. 45)

As Gunnar Tideström has argued, the poet casts a backward glance at the Hobson's choice which fate—a kind of brutal physician—appeared to offer her, as a fragile tubercular: to live ascetically, or to die while partaking of the fullness of life; she decided to defy "fate," to attempt to live "red," fully, as long as she could. (In a later poem, **"Eros hemlighet,"** she says: "I live red, I live my blood.") But the decision, bravely taken, could not be put into effect; against her will, she was consigned to the contemplative and inactive realm of "the mirroring well." (p. 45)

The collection's striking overture, **"Jag såg ett träd"** (**"I Saw a Tree"**) has been seen by Tideström as a retelling of the story [of Södergran's affair with a man from Terijoki], by means of carefully chosen detail: "I saw a tree which was taller than all the others / and hung full of inaccessible cones; / I saw a great church with open doors / and all who came out were pale and strong / and ready to die; / I saw a woman who, smiling and painted, / cast dice for her happiness / and saw that she lost." In this, Tideström has detected the Raivola scene: the great trees, the community's Orthodox church, Edith Södergran herself as the woman who has lost; yet it may be asked if the poem, instead is not a kind of preparatory life-review. The first of the anaphoric "I saw" constructions may be a reference to the experience with Muralt (the might tree of other poems, with its genuine inaccessibility); the second "I saw" may refer to her violent rejection of Christianity, the faith which gave strength and certainty with regard to death, but abhorred life's pleasures (near the end of *Dikter*, there is the parody on a hymn, **"Kristen trosbekännelse"** (**"Christian Confession of Faith"**): "happiness is not in our longing's song"); and the third "I saw" arrives at the situation of the disappointed woman of Raivola—the audience, thus, is brought up to date. In the poem's conclusion: "A circle was drawn around these things / which no one crosses," the idea of the encircling and imprisoning ring is posited. One of the themes in this overture to *Dikter*—the celebration of Muralt—is only sparsely represented in the book proper, another, the attack upon Christianity, is oblique here, and becomes patent only in *Rosenaltaret*; the other two themes, however, that of the woman who seeks happiness (and fails), and of the imprisoning ring, are repeatedly to be found. Throughout the collection, the poet presents her *personae*, again and again, as both the one and the other, the disappointed woman and the prisoner. Plainly, these are the thoughts that most obsess the poet, and about which she wishes to speak. Yet the overture's conclusion may have another sense, as well; these are secrets which the outsider may not approach: the ring may not be crossed from within or from without. The reader is warned, in effect, that he will confront hermetic structures—and so is lured into paying them close attention. **"Longing for Colors"** asks: "What is greater than meeting an unsolved riddle with strange features?" Yet the teller of mysteries, even as she warns against the solving of them, also wants them to be solved.

Immediately upon the heels of the *caveat*, there follows **"Dagen svalnar"** (**"The Day Cools"**), the four-part suite that is the most translated of all the poems of Edith Södergran. Plainly, it is a little love-story, and not a happy one, for it ends (by the poet's own concluding word) in the narrator's disappointment. In the first part of the suite, a multiple invitation is extended: "Drink warmth from my hand . . . / Take my hand, take my white arm, / take my slender shoulders' longing . . ." But we are directly made aware of an incommensurability between the lovers: we learn that his head is "heavy" while, as we have seen, she is frail, and, as she speaks of the night of love ("a single night, a night such as this"), she offers an example of what will be one of her favorite rhetorical devices, the *aprosdoketon*, the unexpected word: "It would be *strange* to feel . . . your heavy head against my breast." Instead of "underligt," we might have looked for "underbart," "wonderful." In the pause between parts one and two, the invitation to love has been accepted, and the female partner makes a brief description of what has happened, of her loss of virginity ("red rose / white lap") and of the quick disappearance of his passion (a *double entendre*—the "daughter of the forest" said she was "shameless"): "You cast your love's red rose / into my white lap— / In my hot hands I hold tight / your love's red rose which quickly withers . . . / Oh, you ruler with cold eyes, / I receive the crown you hand me, / which bends my head down toward my heart." The sexual allusions of the section's opening are clear enough; the remainder is a little less transparent. He has become her ruler . . . but he is a ruler who directly shows his coldness; he crowns her as his beloved (or, as we might say, sentimentally "the queen of his heart"), but his affection is a heavy crown which, quite literally, pulls her head, the seat of reason, down toward her heart, the seat of emotion. She is not wholly overwhelmed, however, for at the opening of the third part she is able to indulge in cutting word-plays (at the same time putting the lover into the third person, thus at a distance): "I saw my lord for the first time today, / trembling I immediately recognized him, / Now I already feel his heavy hand on my light arm . . ." For the first time, she has seen him for what he really is; the term she applies to him, "min herre," "my lord," has a second sense: it is the formally humble and oblique way in which shopgirls once addressed male customers who were patently "gentlemen." The gentleman's behavior is demanding or peremptory, as though toward a prostitute, and the adjectives "heavy" and "light" continue the comparison made in the suite's first part. She reacts with amazement at her degradation: "Where is my ringing maiden laughter, / my woman's freedom with high-borne head? / Now I already feel his tight grasp around my quaking body, / now I hear reality's hard sound / against my fragile, fragile dreams." Verbal intensification shows what has become of her ("heavy" becomes "tight") and describes her reaction ("trembling" becomes "quaking"); the full perception of the brutality of her lover (of the "real" state of things, unadorned) shatters her dreams, dreams as frail (repeated for emphasis) as she is.

The poem's last section is an epilogue, a reflection, with shorter lines than those in the body of the narration: the romance is over, and the disappointment which she, in her heavy irony, attributes to him, is in fact hers. He sought a flower (or, we may say, his rose sought a sexual respondent), he sought a source of refreshment, he sought (literally) a woman, and, in each case, found something more mature, larger, more intangible: "You sought a flower / and found a fruit. / You sought a spring / and found a sea, / You sought a woman / and found a soul— / you are disappointed." The story is over, the man condemned. Edith Södergran has been a strikingly clever advocate of her own cause; the selfish male never has the chance to speak in his defence. (pp. 46-8)

Much of . . . [Södergran's] "romantic" poetry is directly anti-romantic, prescribing a proud self-control, for example, the untitled **"Låt ej din stolthet falla": "Do Not Let Your Pride Fall"**—as though it were clothing—"do not go naked, sweetly into his arms." The erotic experience is denigrated, and Paul's injunction ("it is better to marry than to burn") is turned around: "For him who has seen the filth in joy's short spring / nothing remains save hotly freezing"—passion cannot be rooted out, but it must be controlled, at whatever emotional cost. The word "filth" ("smuts") comes back in **"Två vägar" ("Two Ways")**, a poem of self-instruction, again with echoes of scriptural commonplace ("put off the old man, put on the new"). "You must abandon your old way, / your way is filthy / there men walk with lustful glances, / the word 'happiness' is heard on all lips, / and farther along the way a woman's body lies / and vultures tear it apart": the woman has succumbed to the seducers, has thought she found happiness, and has been destroyed. The new way, of the second strophe, is "pure"—but it leads again to a land of quieter unhappiness, where children's lives are stunted, and where they play with the flower of sleep and death, where women mourn, and where the dragon of sensuality is slain, but at what cost to the slayer! Purity prepares a place where "motherless children walk and play with pop-

pies, / where women walk in black and speak of sorrow, / and farther along a pale saint stands with a foot on a dead dragon's neck." It is an insight which takes us back . . . to Södergran's ["Till Eros"] "To Eros." (p. 49)

There are indications that Edith Södergran took some care in arranging the parts of **Dikter** in an approximate sequence; **"Kärlek" ("Love")** follows directly after ["Sorger"] **"Cares"** and ["Min själ"] **"My Soul"** in a triptych of uneasiness. It is one of the finest of her love poems, a confession of a loss of personal freedom, of betrayal of commitments, of fears about sexual abnormality (or "incompleteness") and physical disease:

> My soul was a bright blue dress of the sky's color;
> I left it on a rock beside the sea
> And naked I came unto you and resembled a woman.
> And as a woman I sat at your table
> and drank a toast with wine and breathed in the smell of some roses.
> You found that I was beautiful and resembled something you had seen in a dream,
> I forgot everything, I forgot my childhood and my homeland,
> I only knew that your caresses held me prisoner.
> And smiling you took a mirror and asked me to see myself.
> I saw that my shoulders were made of dust and crumbled,
> I saw than my beauty was sick and had no will than—to disappear.
> Oh, hold me closed in your arms so tightly that I need nothing.

With what borders on satirical art, Edith Södergran suggests the classical seduction scene of late nineteenth-century literature: the *chambre separée*, wine, roses, the lover's flattering remarks, his smiling efforts to get her to admit that she is beautiful; this seducer's strain, composed of the expressions of practiced insincerity, runs in contrast to her uncertainty, her surrender, and finally her desperation. The concluding outcry is almost unbearably poignant; in her mortal terror at what her lover has shown her, albeit half-realizing his unworthiness (was there a trace of cruelty in his offer of the looking-glass?), she calls for the passing security of his embrace. (pp. 53-4)

She is also a traditionalist as she fills her collection out with specimens of the catalogue poem (which, in Edith Södergran's practice, is customarily a catalogue of definitions, the stating of various and sometimes mutually contradictory meanings for a word or concept), a structure to which she often gives, by implication, a didactic content. . . . **"Vierge moderne"**. . . is an example of her practice, defining and instructing; in its thirteen anaphoric lines (or fourteen: the first line is comprised of two sentences), it tells the "modern virgin" how to use her manifold strengths. Still another example is **"Livet" ("Life")**. "Life is the narrow ring which holds us prisoner / . . . Life is scorning one's self / and lying unmovable on the bottom of a well"—existence must be perceived as imprisonment; here, the anaphoric structure is less faithfully observed but still discernible. (p. 57)

The poems [in **Septemberlyran**] from 1916-1917 would . . . be quite at home in **Dikter**—**"Skymning" ("Twilight")** is a mood-poem with an attractively childlike touch ("The night comes large in his woolly beard"), and the unhappy love-affair can be discerned behind several of the poems. **"Upptäckt" ("Discovery")** has the often quoted lines: "Your hand is lust—my hand is longing"; the "Young Woman" is told that, after listening to the man's many promises and clinging to him as "a flower does to its stalk," she will discover that ". . . he lives only from your purity's white bread / and that his blood merely streams in your motherly tenderness' *basin*,'' the last formulation particularly bold if one remembers that "bäcken" also means "pelvis." Otherwise, the story not of woman's submission but of her superiority reappears, quite plainly, in the discarded ["**Dianas körer**" ("**Diana's Choruses**")] and more cryptically in ["**Starka hyacinter**" ("**Strong Hyacinths**")], contemporaneous, it should be remembered, to the lost prose-tale, "Princess Hyacintha," whose heroine (or so Hagar Olsson recalled) lived in a shining castle surrounded by four islands, among them an "isle of maidens." The "disgusting flies" of the poem are human triviality in general. . . ; but the triumphant and pure flowers of the poem, the hyacinth and the lily, can be associated with Diana's aggressive purity: "They won't get me to believe in disgusting flies / —revenge and small desires. / I believe in strong hyacinths which drip primal juice. / Lilies are healing and pure as my own sharpness." The speaker of these poems of chastisement and rebuke would seem to threaten the addressee of the poem ["**Vad är i morgon?**"] "**What is Tomorrow?**" with a kind of haunting; the reader will recognize the familiar anaphoric style of *Dikter*, as well as the intention of revenge on the man: "I shall go from you with a *certainty* which is like no other: / I shall come again as a piece of your own pain . . ." The speaker gives herself animal attributes; she will turn the recipient's former "barren" passion into the scene of something new, wild, and (for him) frightening: "I shall come to you strange, *angry* and faithful / with a wild animal's step from your heart's desert homeland." But then a final degradation of the man is threatened, using especially "feminine" imagery (threads, yarn, dress) to humiliate him: "I shall smile and twist silken threads around my finger / And I'll hide your fate's little ball in a fold of my dress." (pp. 63-4)

Beyond erotic disappointment, another wound dealt Edith Södergran also got a poetic response, the critical reception accorded *Dikter*. ["**Jungfruns död**" ("**The Maiden's Death**")] was written, as Tideström says, directly after the somewhat chilly review of the debut book by Holger Nohrström:

> The tender maiden's soul never made a mistake,
> she knew everything about herself,
> she knew still more: about others and the sea.
> Her eyes were blueberries, her lips raspberries, her hand wax.
> She danced for the autumn on yellowed carpets,
> She shrank and whirled and sank—and was extinguished.
> When she was gone, no one knew that her corpse was left in
>   the forest . . .
> Long she was sought among the maidens on the beach,
> they sang of small mussels in red shells.
> She was sought among the men who were drinking,
> they fought for shining knives from the duke's kitchen.
> She was sought in the field of lilies of the valley,
> where her shoe was left since last night.
>
>   (p. 64)

Other poems in *Septemberlyran* also respond to the critical reception which Edith Södergran had been accorded. "**Tjuren**" ("**The Bull**") was regarded by Elmer Diktonius . . . and by Hagar Olsson as a statement on the indifference of Swedish Finland's reviewers to the splendid novelty of *Dikter*. Critics themselves missed this point, the infamous "Jumbo" implying that the poem was an erotic wish-dream on the poet's part: "Why does the bull hesitate? / My character is a red cloth," and even Sten Selander, a Swedish poet and critic of considerable stature, took the poem to be an erotic statement, saying that it "only apparently" deals with the indifference which met her "proclamation," while its "unconscious and thereby primary content is surely disappointment that men have not

conquered her.''. . . Even when she spoke consciously about criticism, her erotic urges revealed themselves: "**Lillgubben**" ("**Little Old Man**") in *Septemberlyran* is incontestibly an epigram aimed at those pedantic critics who "count eggs" and thereby reduce the value of a poet's work. But, in its manner and its main figure, it resembles "**Ur 'Liliputs saga'**," one of the poems on erotic revenge in *Dikter*. Later on, Edith Södergran became quite aware, as we know, of the erotic force's permeation of the whole of life.

Yet in the more self-conscious "**Grimace d'artiste**" from September, 1917, there is very little, save the word "red" itself, which could lead the mind back to the erotic world of *Dikter*. (p. 66)

The title, "**Grimace d'artiste**," has an air of wryly smiling at the poem's melodrama; and Hagar Olsson attested frequently to her friend's fluctuation between good-humored common sense and quite unreasoning exaltation; there is plenty of evidence in the poetry written before the marvelous September that the one side of her personality viewed the other with considerable skepticism. The opening poem of *Septemberlyran* is the jubilant "**Triumph of Existing**," the title of which has become a motto for Södergran enthusiasts, since it captures that affirmation of existence which is basic to her poetic world; two selections from her poetry bear the poem's name. It's principle theme is a Zarathustran celebration of the sun ("Truly, like unto the sun, I love life"): "I walk on sun, I stand on sun, / I know of naught else than sun." The quiet hint in "**The Maiden's Death**"—the girl is like a leaf (or a star) that is extinguished—turns, here, into a full and victorious metaphor: "What do I fear? I am a part of infinity. / I am a part of the cosmos' great strength, / a lonely world among millions of worlds, / like unto a star of the first power which is extinguished last . . ." (p. 67)

[The] poems from the spring of 1918—"**Stormen**" ("**The Storm**"), "**Aftonvandring**" ("**Evening Promenade**"), "**Månens hemlighet**" ("**The Moon's Secret**"), "**Visan från molnet**" ("**The Song from the Cloud**")—bear the marks of Finland's own chaos. Long before Raivola was taken by the Whites [during the Finnish Civil War], there had been fighting in its vicinity; on March 10, the Reds, who held Viborg, had advanced on the White position at Antrea, and, later in the month, Russian forces from St. Petersburg had gone up the second of Karelia's railroad lines to a station called Rauta, where bloody fighting took place at the end of March and the beginning of April. Tideström suggests that "**The Storm**" contains an allusion to the approach of the White army, whose general, Mannerheim, had suddenly taken the destiny of Finland into his hands: "Where will he strike, / the one come from the heights, unconquered, future-winged," and he precedes his suggestion with the thought (in which he is seconded by Enckell) that there is a strong echo of Nietzsche here, of the salute to those beings for whom Zarathustra waits in the mountains: "I wait for others here in these mountains—for higher, stronger, more victorious, happier-hearted ones"; it is a message Zarathustra gives his strange company of guests, themselves "higher men" but not lofty and strong enough for the task. The poem ends with: "Guests seat themselves again at toppled tables / Unknown ones steer the world . . . / Higher, fairer, like unto gods." Certainly, Edith Södergran and her mother looked forward to the coming of the Whites; but it was the mythical aura of the victorious general (who, as it were, had come out of nowhere) which charmed her—a year later, she dreamed that Mannerheim embraced her. The storm, "carried up to imperishable heights by eagles," is clearly masculine, called "han" ("he"); and there is an army with him: "Do you not hear voices in the storm? / Mars-helmets in the mist . . ." (pp. 69-70)

The probability of the poet's imminent death comes up several times amidst the ecstasies of the September-poems, in every case in lyrics dealing principally with poetic creation; much of this verse offers special problems of interpretation, probably because of its mixture of bliss, willingly proclaimed, and fear, severely repressed. ["**Min lyra**" ("**My Lyre**")] begins *in medias res:* "I abhor (the) thought . . . / Where is my beloved giant lyre? / Sunshine-stringed, fairy-tale-like, hanging from the clouds. / O my giant lyre, / you hang above the world like a question mark." Olof Enckell argues that the mysterious first line should be taken as an attack on "dry intellectualism," rational thought in general, to be contrasted with the mighty lyre of poetry, which has never paid heed to logic, and which appears to the world as a question mark, variously baffling or challenging. The strophe is followed by a string of dashes, a device which Edith Södergran often uses to indicate work of a fragmentary nature. The second strophe begins as abruptly as the first, with a vision of the poet's death: "When I die, / I shall cast myself unconcernedly into your strings . . . .". Two spirits, "arising from the unknown," will carry the singer and her instrument out over the seas of the world, stopping in the midst of the Atlantic. There, after a second line of dashes, they disappear: "And we are both vanished from the world, / my beloved lyre!" Is the surprising adverb, "unconcernedly," a sign that the singer (like the girl of the cloud, dropping her bombs) no longer cares about the world, and goes willingly into death? And is the final pair of lines to be read as a somehow contemptuous valedictory to the world, which does not know what it has lost (or what it may unwittingly have gained: in ["**Gryningen**" ("**Dawn**")], the Atlantic is the "birthplace of the future"). Or is the conclusion to be read as an outcry of despair, at ceasing to exist? In such case, the poem's opening line, "I abhor (the) thought," might be a specific statement, of abhorrence of a specific thought, that of her personal annihilation, and with her, the lyre's. Thus the poem, made up of three clearly delineated fragments, is the record of an inner argument, the voice of terror, followed by the voice of lofty unconcern, followed again by fear: "And we are both vanished from the world." (pp. 77-8)

As it first was printed, *Septemberlyran* closed with two poems which . . . are a solemn probing of the poet's self. One is the three-strophed question, "**Varför gavs mig livet?**" ("**Why Was I Given Life?**"), in which she asks whether she was intended to be a victor ("to flash past all the people in a triumphal chariot"), or a priestess ("to seize the glimmering bowl in ring-adorned hands") or a magic book ("to pass from hand to hand, / burning through all souls")—roles all indicated by the September poems; but the key to the poem lies not in the catalogue (which can be reduced to the question: has she in fact been born to dazzle, to lead, to inspire?), but in the refrain about her driving force, "longing for more" and, twice, "thirsting for more." It is that measureless urge for something higher and beyond human power which is the main urge of the September poetry and, in fact, of the whole of Edith Södergran's works. The second "autobiographical" reflection, however, begins with a disgusting shock. After two lines of dashes, once again indicative of the visionary nature of the work, the "**Fragment**" which is the longest of Edith Södergran's extant works begins as follows: "Life's bacteria flourish on your mucous membrane.". . . Forced to observe her own body's functions and malfunctions closely, she felt no embarrassment

at putting such observations into her work—it was an old practice of hers: the adolescent verse says: "Today, the cosmos is menstruating." (pp. 79-80)

The "**Fragment**" is one of the great visionary poems in a Northern literature. It is odd that her contemporary critics noted neither the poem's extravagances nor its grandeur in their reviews; perhaps they were put off by the poem's very length, and the difficulty of its allusions. Yet it may have been to Edith Södergran's advantage, in post-Civil War Finland, that the poem went unnoticed; for, of all her works, it could most convincingly—if quite incorrectly—be interpreted as a call for political revolution from the left. Perhaps Jumbo was thinking of it as he wrote about "literary Bolshevism." Evidently, she was quite oblivious to this danger; as Nietzsche said, Dionysian emotions encroach upon the political instincts. Dionysian emotions . . . play a large role in the fragment, her proclamation, she liked to think, to the world, and, at the same tiime, a chronicle of the stages on her own life's way. (pp. 82-3)

The completion of *Rosenaltaret* only four months after the publication of *Septemberlyran* may be attributed in part to Edith Södergran's sense that she was still possessed by her "September-rapture"; her message had to be brought to the world a second time and, perhaps, clarified. (p. 84)

The choice of "**Rosenaltaret**" as the title poem of the new volume is a challenge thrown in the face of the critics; it states once again the tenets of the September poetry and, rather pathetically, tries to recruit followers for the new faith, of which the poem's speaker will be the priestess: "In the twilight I am / (a) temple priestess, / initiate, guarding / the future's fire." There are sideswipes at Christianity: "I step forth to you / with a glad message" (the tidings of great joy in Luke 2:10)— "God's kingdom begins, / Not Christ's dwindling empire, / No, higher, brighter human forms / step forward to the altar," which is crowned with roses, "a mountain of beauty." Here, discounting the past, "Lightly / the spirit of the moment will sit / drinking / a toast to the moment / from a fragile golden glass." The "higher beings," the worship of beauty, the denial of the past, and the implied fragility of the beautiful dream, are all the elements quite familiar from what has gone before; Hagar Olsson was correct in her opinion about the lack of novelty.

The recruitment, and the exhortations, continue in poem after poem. "The strong" are told that they should flee into isolation ("Be men! / Do not remain dwarfs with shrunken limbs") and follow "the stars' unwritten laws." Or "human beings" are instructed to bow before those powers, "the gods," so that they may be lifted up (["**Gudarna komma**"] "**The Gods Are Coming**"); that the gods are products of the human spirit, however, is clear enough from the second line: "Kneel, oh humans. The gods are coming. / The gods arise from dust-weighted brows," and the old-fashioned sublimity of this poetry is signalled not only by the "biblical imperative" in *-en (knäböjen)* but by Edith Södergran's use of the poetic word "änne" ("brow"). She admonishes mankind (or the candidates for "God's realm," at any rate) again and again; in ["**Besvärjelsen**" ("**Conjuration**")] she tries to bend her audience to her will, in order that they may receive a higher and wilder strength: "I would wish that you grow weak from my will, / I would wish that you tear apart your hearts, / and that the demons would find a place in your limbs, / wild, inhuman, bursting all life asunder." (p. 85)

[In] the closing poem of the collection's first part, "**Martyren**" ("**The Martyr**"), the poet sees herself as a proud victim. The martyr speaks, looking pityingly and not a little scornfully at the crowd which watches his death: "What do you / who swarm back and forth / with ugly movements, / know of your well-being or woe, (or) how it feels to lift one's head *freely*." With a play on words (from "fritt" to "frikänd"), the martyr welcomes the hemlock: "He whom the whole world condemned / is *spoken free*. / The black beaker / is purest sun." If the mode of the martyr's death suggests Socrates, his dress suggests the *sanbenito* in which the victim of the auto-da-fé was traditionally clad or, simultaneously, a jester's hood; Tideström has proposed that the poem was written at the time when the furor concerning *Septemberlyran* was at its cruellest. The martyr falls silent while he is described: "Lightly he takes upon his shoulders / the victim's many-colored cloak," and then he speaks again, gladly accepting his fate, in which he is sustained by his will: "you caress like velvet, like softest velvet— / my will's raiment." The purple cloak of the "artiste," the velvet dress of the "triumfator," has undergone another transformation: it has become the Nietzschean garment *par excellence*.

The claims of the priestess-poetess are made again and again. . . . In **"Vägen till Elysium och Hades"** (**"The Road to Elysium and Hades"**), she will ascend "a mountain of fate," while men "wander below, in the midst of clouds"; somewhat more modestly, the speaker of **"På Himalayas trappor"** (**"On the Himalayas' Staircase"**) makes another mountain ascent in order to address the solar deity Vishnu, offering "to sacrifice my life for a single moment of your dreams." Conversely, in [**"Jorden blev förvandlad till en askhög ("The Earth Was Transformed into an Ash-Heap")**)], the speaker has faced down death. (pp. 87-8)

Nonetheless, the priestess is beset by an enormous longing; seven poems in the first part of *Rosenaltaret* have "my heart" as their central image, a replacement of the lyre of *Septemberlyran*. But "heart" is a more emotionally charged word than "lyre"; implications of poetic inspiration (and poetic technique) give way to implications of sheer affective power: in **"Förvandling"** (**"Transformation"**), she addresses herself, "Fortunate fairytale princess, / your heart storms harder than the oceans," and in **"Conjuration"** she asks: "How shall I speak to you from my deepest heart?" The heart is an instrument of communication, seeking contact with others like itself, and the journey to find this mighty heart has been an overwhelmingly long one. (p. 88)

"Fantastique" was called the "sister-cycle" by Edith Södergran in an accompanying letter to Hagar Olsson: "Are you satisfied with it?". It begins with **"Vårmysterium"** (**"Spring Mystery"**), which Edith Södergran said was not "a strong poem, but it belongs to the whole, it has the aroma of violets and gracefulness and the same delicious, burning atmosphere." (pp. 92-3)

"Jag tror på min syster" (**"I Believe in My Sister"**), the longest of the poems in the cycle, is misleadingly titled; or, rather, the title makes an assertion which the body of the poem disputes. . . . [The] sister is described by means of Edith Södergran's fairytale apparatus: "The elves wove her silken dress / The moon-maid sprinkled dew upon her breast." These allusions are apt enough here, for it is the intention of the two to tell "fairytales to one another, / unending fairytales for a thousand years" until one day "the dawn will come, our new dawn." The prediction is not fulfilled, however; the very outset of the poem has shown that all is not well: "I walk in the wilderness and seat myself alone in the mountain, / on the devil's stone, / where cares have waited / a thousand years,"

a period corresponding exactly to that allotted to the happy telling of fairytales. No doubt unintentionally, Edith Södergran uses time-honored material from European love poetry—the Petrarchan topos of the lover alone and wretched, in a desert place—which she combines with a vague Scriptural memory, the temptation of the hungering Christ in the wilderness, where the devil challenges Him to change stones into bread (Matthew 4:3). In her emotional starvation, the poet succumbs to the temptation to doubt her beloved, and so sets free the army of cares that wait in the stone; the poem's third section (after the predictions of happiness) is one of the most painfully melodramatic outbursts in her poetry: "My sister . . . / Has she betrayed me? / Does she bear the dagger in her bosom—the lightfooted one? / Answer me—laughing eye," and the answer is the "No, a thousand times no." . . . "I do not believe it, / though angels wrote it with unerring styluses / on the sheets of time." (pp. 93-4)

The cycle's last poems—**"Gudabarnet"** (**"The Divine Child"**) and **"Syster, min syster"** (**"Sister, My Sister"**) betray a growing resignation or hopelessness. In **"The Divine Child,"** the disposition of tenses is once again noteworthy; the first two lines have the past: "The divine child sat with me. / The golden lyre sang from my hands," but the two middle lines are in the present: "the divine child stares out into endless twilights. / The song circles over her head with broad wings," in what may well be valedictory benediction. Then (another of the many queries put to the "sister" in the cycle), the question is asked: "What do you see in the song?," and the reply, moving into the future, is frightening: "It is your own future which rises (there) / from the icy twilights, / your own future, admonishing, calling, waiting." (p. 95)

The third section of *Rosenaltaret* is given over to several figures from Edith Södergran's actual life or from her mythology. The elegy on the death of Ludwig von Muralt, **"Fragment av en stämning,"** (**"Fragment of a Mood"**), repairs what Edith Södergran seems to have regarded as her failure to estimate the physician properly when he was alive; "It happens at times that one neglects to express one's entrancement (hänryckning) in relation to someone. That is what happened to me, for example, with Muralt." In *Septemberlyran* she had included a brief poem on Muralt's passing, **"Trädet i skogen"** (**"The Tree in the Forest"**), which builds upon the topos of the mighty tree struck down by the tempest, or, in this case, by lightning— a tree ascending, of course, toward the Södergranian heights: "It rose above the mists of the depths to the peaks of the earth in lonely splendor." In the elegy, the Alpine background is given in more detail, and the subject of the poem is the "son of the high land" ("höglandets son") whose memory is illuminated by the "high land's sun" ("höglandssolen"), while the "summer of the high land" ("höglandets sommar") looks forth from the forest, and the "gods of the high land" ("höglandets gudar") play their melancholy pipes. The poem is unabashedly confessional about Edith Södergran's experiences at Davos, and equally unabashed in its dramatization of the events: "If I love mountains, the love of my youth lies in them. / Over tender, green crocus, over my first budding love / memory walks with triumphant feet. / Thus one pulls along, reluctantly, a young / barbarian prisoner, with flashing yellow locks." The prisoner is the Alpine spring, come violently and against his will; at the same time the prisoner is the speaker herself, the unwilling captive from the North in the sanatorium. It is impossible to miss this self-identification: early in the poem, she has referred to the "high land's sun shining wildly in my locks" and, then, to "my wild longing," and says finally (after the description of the springtime's coming) that: "Was I not young in those days with flashing yellow locks." The idea is broken off, and four lines of dashes ensue; then a statement is made about the happy result of the captivity: "It happens at times that the briar-rose blooms / that the briar's dry tangle is covered with rosy wonders. / That is what befell me, too- - -." More dashes follow. (p. 97)

The last poem in *Rosenaltaret* is "**Roses,**" the statement of the artist who "loves each marble ear which perceives his words." In "**The Martyr,**" the crowd, with its ugly movements, had not comprehended the martyr's calling; the "marble ear" is, we assume, a beautiful one, that can hear beauty. That poem, put at the end of the collection's first section, was a jab at uncomprehending critics, and a praise of the poet's difficult task; this one is the *envoy* for those who have ears to hear—or who are worthy of worshipping at the rose-altar. As for the poet, or the priestess at the altar, she survives—or, indeed, overcomes: "What are pain and misery to me? / Everything collapsed with a crash: / I sing. / Thus pain's great hymn ascends from a happy breast." Haranguing Hagar Olsson, Edith Södergran said that she herself had been "un-liberated" ("oförlöst") until she was "able to begin to create from my fullest heart . . . I am become bliss and the light itself." (p. 100)

An aggressive tone prevails in the . . . first part [of *Framtidens skugga*], "Planeterna stiga" ("The Planets Ascend"). The speaker of the opening poem, "**Mysteriet**" ("**The Mystery**"), announces that she will "convert everyone to a more holy god, / sweeping away all superstition with a soundless broom; / slaying all pettiness with mockery." The Nietzschean tone is unmistakable, but the culmination, from medieval legend, is what made Hagar Olsson call the time of *Framtidens skugga* the "Saint George period" in Edith Södergran's life: "I will climb up onto your mighty serpent. I will pierce his head with my sword. / Oh my good sword which I have got from heaven, I kiss you." The poem is not a rose, as before, but a weapon. (p. 101)

These poems are often minatory, for example, "**Tolerans**" ("**Tolerance**"), whose title is utterly misleading; it demands tolerance for its own supreme intolerance, the intolerance of the chosen one, "the star which climbs toward the heights / can you measure its flight? / Do not stop it from climbing." The star has a color which could have made the anxious Finland-Swedish reader of the early 1920's (with Bolshevism just next door) wonder about Edith Södergran's political views; its "redder shine," however, only signifies preternatural vitality: it tells others, literally, to get out of the way ("ur vägen"), it is "a hand which follows its own law, / (and) will topple what others preserve. / A victor comes, inaudible lips speak the forcer's name." The victor (and "forcer") is then defined more closely in the aptly named "**Makt**" ("**Power**"): "I am commanding strength . . . I follow no law. I am law in myself. / I am the human being who takes."

All these unvarnished praises of arrogant strength and power—recalling Edith Södergran's several aphorisms on Napoleon from the same time—are interwoven, nonetheless, with worry: how can a star be sure that it has pre-eminence? This is the problem of "**Fientliga stjärnor**" ("**Hostile Stars**"), where no solution is found; a long anaphora tells us that: "Every star has an icy glance. / Every star is proud and lonely in its strength . . . / Every star comes marching like a red shine from afar / in order to destroy, devour, consume, exercise its power." But, in their rivalry, they bring—as "**Stjärnorna vimla**" ("**The Stars Abound**") says—a "golden madness" to man who, hear-

kening to a voice that sings on high, forgets all else: "With a bold hand, every star casts its mite onto the earth: ringing coin. / From every star infection comes over creation: the new sickness, the great happiness." (It is characteristic that Edith Södergran describes even the spread of her teachings in pathological terms.) These stars, teeming as a bedazzled mankind stares at them, are creative intellects, each making exclusive claims ("Every star wishes to seduce one into believing that *she* (sic) is all"), each wishing to set the world afire, each preparing the future: "The stars ascend. The stars abound. Strange evening. / A thousand hands lift the veil from the countenance of the new age." In reading this pair of star poems, we must remember not only the doubts which beset Edith Södergran about her own calling, but her transference of allegiance from one star, one teacher, to another. Nonetheless, her hesitations are put aside in the finale of the book's opening suite, the grandiose "**Planeterna**" ("**The Planets**"). In its feat of the imagination, it is comparable to the ode of Klopstock, "An die nachkommenden Freunde" ("To the Friends Coming After"), which tries to capture the sensations of a planet as it hurtles through the cosmos; "**The Planets,**" in fact, represent the apotheosis of Edith Södergran's poetic athleticism: "Wild earth that rolls forward in burning, smarting space, / blissful that the air strikes against your cheek, / blissful that the speed makes you turn. / The planets wish naught else but swiftness in their course." Beauty has been forgotten, as have the lyre and the heart; instead, as poetry's symbol, the pitiless sword has been joined by the equally pitiless planet, "swifter, quicker, more merciless."

The euphoria of imaginary action ends quickly. The book's next section, which gave the collection its title, "The Shadow of the Future," suggests that the shadow is a first sign of the happiness which Edith Södergran insists will fall to mankind's lot, if it will listen to her; but the title also has an ominous personal note. In a letter of July 22, 1919, Edith Södergran complains to Hagar Olsson that she has lost her poetic gift: "I have no inspiration. I hear wonderful tones within me, but have nothing which lifts them forth," a writer's block for which she seems to blame her friend: "You put a mute (en sordin) on me." After another appeal for friendship, she alludes to the title of her new book: "They say that coming things cast their shadow, is it true?—you are familiar with the dark." . . . (pp. 102-03)

The initial poem of the series, "**The Shadow of the Future,**" tries bravely to the confront the inevitability of death, stated in its first line: "I sense the shadow of death." Some amelioration, or consolation, is sought in the customary anaphoric catalogue, with a reference to the Nordic fates (an isolated example in Edith Södergran's work) and then the fatedness, and so the importance, of all deaths; "I know that our fates lie piled upon the table of the Norns, / I know that not a drop of water is sucked into the earth / which is not written into the book of eternal times." However, the last item in the catalogue is, in fact, a cry of anguish: "I know as certainly as the sun rises / that I shall never behold the endless moment when it is at the zenith." The adduction of the sun, though, affords the chance to make death's prospect bearable, at least for the Dionysian: it will be a death in exaltation. (The source is . . . from the vadecum, *Also sprach Zarathustra*—Zarathustra's vision of his own end, "a star, ready and mature in its zenith, glowing, pierced, blessed by destructive arrows of the sun.") "The future casts its blessed shadow upon me; / it is nothing other than the streaming sun: / pierced through by light I shall die, / when I have trampled all chance with my foot, I shall turn away smiling from life.'' The thought that mankind is at the mercy of forces quite beyond its control had been brought up by Edith Södergran in **"The Storm"** in *Rosenaltaret,* where it ''is driven like cattle from dark corners''; now, she convinces herself that she can rise above life's accident and death's necessity by the very act of willing an acceptance of death—actively, in exaltation, not in resignation or despair. (p. 105)

The first of the two erotic hymns in ''The Shadow of the Future,'' called **"Du store Eros"** (**"Thou Mighty Eros,"**) is a proclamation; mankind has known this force, that ''breathes of marriage,'' since time's beginning; but, thus far, lust has merely joined two bodies together. The erotic drive has not yet reached the mind of mankind: ''the lightning has not yet attained man's forehead.'' **"Eros tempel"** (**"The Temple of Eros"**) continues the complaint—Eros' power has not yet been understood: ''No one knows what his lips offer, / No one knows what his innermost thoughts are; / His glance merely whips those carelessly youthful bodies / which play with one another. / We do not know his pleasure--------------'' (Edith Södergran uses her interruptive device: a second full line of dashes ensues.) Those who are ''Eros' comrades in play'' (to be contrasted to the bodies which ''play with one another'') have but a single wish, readily connected with the wish for death ''pierced by the sun'': ''we wish but one thing: / to become flame of your flame, and to be consumed.'' The Finnish poet Aale Tynni says that ''Edith Södergran's Eros arises from the bosom of her Dionysus''; both divinities require a dissolution of the individual, but a dissolution in what is a highly individualistic way, even a theatrical one. Edith Södergran may hint, or assert, that her concept of eroticism is novel, something not yet understood; however, it can be easily connected with her favorite myth from antiquity, that of Ariadne, and with a favorite myth of the nineteenth century, the Wagnerian love-death—save that in Edith Södergran's case, the love-partner is imaginary.

The cycle, ''The Shadow of the Future,'' ends with a melodramatic ''occasional poem'' (in Edith Södergran's subtitle), **"Uppståndelse-mysterium"** (**"Resurrection Mystery,"**) about a dead woman, around whose bier great candles burn, and ''on whose face there is a lust for Life.'' Heavenly choruses summon her, and she replies: ''Yes, Lord, I come.'' The imagery and language seem patently Christian, but we must wonder if the poem perhaps makes a blasphemous point not unlike that of D. H. Lawrence's ''The Man Who Died'': there, Christ, taken from the cross, is aroused by the Priestess of Isis, here, the summoning lord is the male lover. This bizarre work (''Suddenly, a fire flames over the dead woman'') is directly followed by the most bizarre of Edith Södergran's necrophiliac visions, **"Älvdrottningens spira"** (**"The Elf-Queen's Wand"**). . . . The fragment opens with a series of questions, a search for the lover: ''Where is he, whom I have beheld in an ecstatic dream . . . / Where is he / who lifts up a tired flower from the road / and shrouds her in transparent silk / and wraps veils around her feet / and watches her for a long time, wondering: how did you die, child?'' Then the speaker of the poem (on whose forehead it is written: ''She is sleeping'') begins the poem's second section, a series of admonitions to the man who found her in the dream, and who has vanished: ''Your tears will fall upon my feet / they will trickle between my knees / as though they would cause an awakening unto life.'' The phantasy substitutes tears for semen; instructions are supplied, one after another, by the girl (dreaming a continuation of the ''ecstatic dream'') to the imaginary savior: ''You will arrange the golden locks on my forehead, you will smooth the silk on

my belly.'' . . . The erotic imaginings grow still more detailed: the mourner will play with the girl's hair and brush her lips with a duster of silver-down, place her in the grass, and, taking a diamond ring from her finger, press it into the flesh of her upper arm. She bleeds: ''Through red veils you see that I still live.'' The instructions given to the mourner now are unambiguous: ''And you unlace my dress / and you put your hand on my heart to listen. / You disrobe me, / the silk falls from my shoulders.'' But all the mourner's efforts are in vain; the dreamer, albeit alive, sleeps on, and her ''marvelous head'' falls back ''lifelessly.'' Still, the lover will not give up: ''Yet, you have more courage,'' and he plays with her fingers ''as with a child's.'' (pp. 107-08)

There is a sharp break in tone between **"The Elf-Queen's Wand"** and the poems about Eros which follow it. The language is often more brutal, sometimes more elevated and more proclamatory; Eros appears as a simple force: this is, in fact, **"Eros hemlighet"** (**"Eros' Secret"**): ''You are not man and not woman. / You are the force / which sits squatted in the temple, in order then, rising up, wilder than a moan, / more violent than a cast stone / to cast out the striking words of the message across the world . . .'' The linguistic devices are of the elementary nature; the single semi-rhyme (''skrän / sten,'' ''moan / stone'') calls attention to the violence of the act, as do the repetition of the verb, ''slunga,'' ''to cast'' (''slungad sten / slunga ut,'' ''cast stone / cast out'') and the implication that ''striking'' modifies ''stone'' as well as ''words.'' Just so, the poem's first lines have blared out the poem's message: ''I live red. I live my blood. / I have not denied Eros.'' It is not a long way from the overwhelming and humiliating Eros of 1916 to the new standpoint—save that now the force has been accepted without reserve, just as a death in ecstasy has been. Variation after variation is made on the theme. **"Eros skapar världen ny"** (**"Eros Makes the World Anew"**) emphasizes the potentiality of the force, as yet unrealized: ''in his hand the earth is filled with *miracles*'' and ''on (his) forehead great *wonders* are already dawning''—a play on the Swedish ''under'' and ''underverk.'' **"Vattenfallet"** (**"The Waterfall"**) opens with a description of the ''creative anguish'' around the speaker's heart, and after a middle section of doubt (''I will go to a fortune teller''), comes to a joyous acceptance: ''Oh you thundering waterfall of pleasure.'' In ''its thundering, plunging rush,'' the cascade is filled with surety; like Eros, like poetic inspiration (which are equated here), it cannot be resisted, nor can the lightning (in the poem of that name, **"Blixten"** be turned aside. ''My body lies like a rag / in order one day, seized by electric hands, / more firmly than all the ore of earth / to send the lightning.'' The speaker's very person will become a transmitting agent, more dependable than metal, to convey to lightning's force onward—the poem does not say toward what goal. (pp. 109-10)

Long ago, the critic Bengt Holmqvist expressed a not unreasonable fear—that Edith Södergran would fall into the hands of cultists or, at any rate, uncritical enthusiasts. The pathetic and yet exotic circumstances of her life, the efforts of some of her contemporaries to surround her earthly existence, and her production, with sanctity's odor, the strong emotional appeal some of her poetry makes (to such disparate groups as unhappy adolescents, radical feminists, and fundamentalist Christians), the visionary quality of many poems in the middle collections—it is readily understandable how, and why, a canonization may occur. But we have seen what damage the cultic approach did to the study of Rainer Maria Rilke, obscuring his place in literary history, diverting his audience's attention from his remarkable poetic means to his several "philosophies," and, what was worst, driving away potential readers who were unprepared for full enlistment among his worshippers. It is to be hoped that, in the future, scholarship will grapple with Edith Södergran's language, in all of its aspects, with an expansion of our knowledge about the circumstances of her life (Tideström has had no successor thus far), and with the complex story of her reception in the North and abroad. (p. 133)

George C. Schoolfield, in his Edith Södergran: Modernist Poet in Finland, *Greenwood Press, 1984, 175 p.*

ADDITIONAL BIBLIOGRAPHY

Espmark, Kjell. "The Translantion of the Soul": A Principal Feature in Finland-Swedish Modernism." *Scandinavica,* supp. (1976): 5-27.
  Traces the influence of Alfred Mombert and Max Dauthendey on Södergran and discusses her career in the context of Finland-Swedish Expressionism, which flourished in the 1920s. According to Espmark: "*Septemberlyran, Rosenaltaret,* and *Framtidens skugga* show us the poetess in supreme possession of an idiom designed for the expression of extreme emotion. It is here that she appears to be in a secret pact with the contemporary avant-garde on the European continent."

Gustafsson, Lars. "Edith Södergran." In his *Forays into Swedish Poetry,* translated by Robert T. Rovinsky, pp. 99-106. Austin and London: University of Texas Press, 1978.
  Considers Nietzschean and biographical inspiration in "Mitt liv, min död och mitt öde" ("My Life, My Death and My Fate").

Lucas, John. "Translating Difficulties." *New Statesman* 107, No. 2771 (27 April 1984): 21.
  Includes an unappreciative review of *Complete Poems.* Lucas argues that while Södergran has gained a reputation as a visionary poet, David McDuff's versions "make her seem merely eccentric—even, dare it be said, mad." He concludes: "On the basis of these translations [Södergran] is less of a poet than a case."

Rossel, Sven H. Review of *Complete Poems,* by Edith Södergran, edited and translated by David McDuff. *World Literature Today* 59, No. 2 (Spring 1985): 280-81.
  Praises Södergran as Modernism's "first and finest representative" in Finland-Swedish literature and lauds her work for the uniqueness of its "existential tone and bold, visionary expressivity."

St. Germain, Sheryl. "Found in Translation." *Women's Review of Books* IV, No. 4 (January 1987): 14-15.
  Favorable review of *Love and Solitude.* According to St. Germain, the collection offers "a banquet of poems on which to feed."

Schoolfield, George C. "Edith Södergran's 'Wallensteinprofil'." In *Scandinavian Studies: Essays Presented to Dr. Henry Goddard Leach on the Occasion of His Eighty-Fifth Birthday,* edited by Carl F. Bayerschmidt and Erik J. Friis, pp. 278-92. Seattle: University of Washington Press, 1965.
  Considers the connections between Södergran's poetic portrait of the historical Austrian general Wallenstein and the twentieth-century Finnish general and statesman Mannerheim, whose leadership assured the independence of Finland.

Wrede, Johan. "The Birth of Finland-Swedish Modernism: A Study in the Social Dynamics of Ideas." *Scandinavica,* supp. (1976): 73-103.
  Places Södergran at the center of the Finland-Swedish Expressionist movement and discusses it in an ideological and social context.

Sully Prudhomme

1839-1907

(Pseudonym of René François Armand Prudhomme) French poet, philosopher, essayist, and diarist.

One of the most highly respected French poets of the late nineteenth century, Sully Prudhomme was the first recipient of the Nobel Prize in literature. He has earned particular esteem for the compassion and idealism of his work, as well as for the clarity and simplicity of his poetic style. In his early verse Sully Prudhomme combined the formal precision of the Parnassians with an emotional force reminiscent of the Romantics, while in his later writings he became a philosopher-poet, composing epic verses on scientific and metaphysical themes.

Sully Prudhomme was born into a middle-class Parisian family in 1839. Ill health, the early death of his father, and the somber home atmosphere resulting from his mother's grief are factors often cited by biographers to explain the air of melancholy that characterized both his personality and his writings. After graduating from the Lycée Bonaparte, where he excelled in both classics and science, Sully Prudhomme intended to study mathematics in preparation for a career as a scholar and teacher. However, he was forced to curtail his studies due to a chronic eye inflammation and went to work as a clerk in a foundry, and later as an apprentice in a law office, hoping eventually to take a degree in law. During this period he wrote his first poems, which were well received among his circle of literary acquaintances and soon began to be accepted by literary journals. After several of his poems were published in the influential journal *Le parnasse contemporain*, Sully Prudhomme became identified with the Parnassians, a group of poets who cultivated objectivity and precision in traditional verse forms as a reaction against the stylistic and emotional excesses of Romanticism. His first poetry collection, *Stances et poèmes,* was published in 1865 to popular and critical acclaim, winning him such distinguished admirers as the critic Charles Augustin Sainte-Beuve. Encouraged by this reception of his work, Sully Prudhomme resolved to discontinue his legal training in order to pursue a literary career; an independent income provided by his family enabled him to devote his time to writing.

During the 1870s Sully Prudhomme's depressive nature was exacerbated by several events: his traumatic experience as a member of the Garde Mobile during the Franco-Prussian War, the onset of a chronic paralytic illness, and a series of deaths among his relatives. For the remainder of his career he avoided the social and political activities of the Parisian literary world; however, this did not prevent his becoming one of the most well-known and respected writers of the era, hailed by some commentators as a successor to Victor Hugo. He was elected to the French Academy in 1881, and in 1901 was presented with the first Nobel laureateship for literature. The Swedish Academy announced that it bestowed the honor upon Sully Prudhomme "as an acknowledgment of his excellent merit as an author, and especially of the high idealism, artistic perfection, as well as the usual combination of qualities of the heart and genius to which his work bears witness." As his paralysis worsened in the final years of his life, Sully Prudhomme lived as a recluse, devoting himself to literature and philosophy until his death in 1907.

Throughout his career Sully Prudhomme employed the highly structured, traditional verse forms identified with the Parnassian movement. His early works, however, diverged from those of the Parnassians by focusing on human emotion and deeply personal subjects, especially romantic love. His poem "La vase brisé" from *Stances et poèmes,* with its metaphor of a broken flower vase as the embodiment of a shattered love affair, became a favorite among fanciers of sentimental poetry, to the bemusement of admirers of his more serious work. A number of his early verses, such as the group of poems titled "Jeunes filles," express the author's sorrow over a broken engagement. The themes of loneliness and sadness recur throughout the collections that followed *Stances et poèmes,* such as *Les épreuves, Les solitudes,* and *Les vaines tendresses*; at the same time, these works also express uplifting, altruistic sentiments, many of them relating to science and the wonders of the natural world. While rejecting Christian theology, Sully Prudhomme maintained a strong belief in a positive humanistic philosophy that celebrated human aspiration towards goodness, wisdom, and spiritual understanding.

According to commentators, Sully Prudhomme's illness and other personal tragedies moved him to turn away from confessional poetry to works that deal with profound universal themes. This change is reflected in poems such as *Les destins,* a meditation on the struggle between good and evil occasioned by a disastrous fire in a Spanish church, and *Le zénith*, an apotheosis of the quest for truth in the form of an elegy for a group of scientists killed in a ballooning accident. Influenced by the classical Roman poet and philosopher Lucretius, whose *De rerum natura* explains the scientific theories of Epicurus in verse, Sully Prudhomme also sought to use poetry to enlighten readers about recent scientific discoveries. He hoped to fuse the aesthetic and analytical functions of the human intellect in his poetry and establish an empirical foundation for the study of philosophy so that humanity's understanding of its spiritual condition could develop in the same progressive fashion as its comprehension of the physical world. The most noted products of Sully Prudhomme's middle period are two epic poems, *La justice* and *Le bonheur,* which implement this idealistic fusion of philosophy, poetry, and science. *La justice* is a series of dialogues between a protagonist identified as the Seeker, an intellectual who despairs of finding justice in nature or society, and a Voice which assures him that justice can be found within every human soul. *Le bonheur* follows the adventures of Faustus and Stella, two lovers who pass through death and the afterlife in pursuit of knowledge and happiness. While many commentators have admired Sully Prudhomme's accomplished mingling of lyricism and philosophical insight in these poems, others have found fault with their didactic tone. In the final years of his life, Sully Prudhomme devoted himself to literary theory and philosophy. In such works as *Testament poétique*, he set forth his theories of poetics, including his explanations of prosodic form in terms of the laws of physics. *Que sais-je?* is a philosophical work expounding his ideas about the natural sciences and metaphysics. His last work, *La vraie réligion selon Pascal,* concerns spiritual values in life and literature.

Sully Prudhomme made his greatest impact in his own lifetime, when his works and ideas had relevance to prevailing literary tastes and ideological fashions. Critics admired the tenderness and sincerity of his early lyric verses and the beauty and nobility of the ideas expressed in his later, more ambitious poems. Although little commentary on Sully Prudhomme has appeared in English since the 1920s, he remains a noted figure in French literary history.

PRINCIPAL WORKS

Stances et poèmes   (poetry)   1865
Les épreuves   (poetry)   1866
Les solitudes   (poetry)   1869
Les destins   (poetry)   1872
Les vaines tendresses   (poetry)   1875
Le zénith   (poem)   1876; published in journal *Revue des deux mondes*
La justice   (poem)   1878
Oeuvres de Sully Prudhomme. 8 vols.   (poetry and prose) 1883-1908
Le bonheur   (poem)   1888
Que sais-je?   (philosophy)   1896
Testament poétique   (essays)   1901
La vraie religion selon Pascal   (essays)   1905
Epaves   (poetry)   1908
Journal intime   (journal)   1922

EDWARD DOWDEN   (essay date 1877)

[*An Irish man of letters, Dowden was one of the foremost Shakespearean scholars of the Victorian era and an important literary biographer. His numerous books and essays on English literature and literary figures—including the influential* Shakspere: His Mind and Art *(1875) and* The Life of Percy Bysshe Shelley *(1886)—illustrate his conviction that interpretation of a literary work should be based on an understanding of the author's life and personality. In the following excerpt, Dowden discusses Sully Prudhomme's eclecticism.*]

Sainte-Beuve observed of M. Sully Prudhomme that he belonged to none of the schools of contemporary poetry. "His was rather the noble ambition of conciliating them, of deriving from them and reuniting in himself what was good in each. With much skill in the treatment of form, he was not indifferent to the idea; and among ideas, he did not adopt any group to the exclusion of the rest." This rightly defines the position of Sully Prudhomme. Like Leconte de Lisle, he is intellectual, but, unlike that master, he is tender; his intellect is not severe and haughty, but humane and sympathetic; and the sympathy which he gives is other than that which takes its origin from scientific curiosity. He does not traverse the world of ideas as an aristocrat who from his eminence of thought surveys and studies many things, of which none can succeed in mastering his reason or really gaining his affections. Rather he yields to this influence, and yields again to that, and is in danger of "losing himself in countless adjustments." He has perceptions of truth on one side and on the other, and can deny none of them. There is something in the pantheistic way of thinking which seems needful to his imaginative interpretation of the facts of consciousness; there is something in theism which corresponds with the cravings of his heart; yet he cannot deny a lurking doubt that after all the agnostic may be in the right. This is the burden which he bears, a divided intellect, for ever adapting itself to what appear to be diverse forms of truth. He is not angry with modern science or modern industry; he would, if possible, conciliate the real with the ideal. He loves the colour of Gautier's verse, the passion and vivid humanity of Musset, and can value the abstractedness, the aspiration, the Druidic nature-worship of Laprade; he would fain possess something of each; and his manifold sympathies leave him sad and restless.

Sully Prudhomme's unhappiness arises from the lack of a cause, a creed, a church, a loyalty, a love, to which he can devote his total being, knowing that such devotion is the highest wisdom. He is a born eclectic, and the only remedy he can apply to his malady is more eclecticism. He may serve as a pathetic witness to the truth that culture, as we too often conceive it nowadays, may lead to an issue less fortunate than that of asceticism. In Edgar Quinet's poetical romance *Merlin* the great enchanter traverses a vast desert to visit the abbey of the famous Prester John. The architecture of the abbey struck Merlin with astonishment. It was a composite style, formed on the pagoda, the Greek temple, the synagogue, the mosque, the basilica, the cathedral, without counting an almost innumerable number of marabouts, minarets, Byzantine and Gothic chapels. When Prester John appears, the magician beholds before him an august old man, with a beard of snow descending to his waist.

> Upon his head he wore a turban enriched with a sapphire cross. At his neck hung a golden crescent, and he supported himself upon a staff after the manner of a Brahman. Three children followed him, who supported each upon the breast an open book. The first was the collection of the Vedas, the second was

the Bible, the third the Koran. At certain moments Prester John stopped and read a few lines from one of the sacred volumes which always remained open before him; after which he continued his walk, with eyes fixed upon the stars.

Prester John was Quinet's type of the eclectic philosopher, and he may equally well represent the modern man of spurious culture. Prester John's architecture is not a true conciliation of styles, nor Prester John's faith of creeds.

M. Sully Prudhomme however, if he has dwelt for a while in the eclectic abbey, has not divided his heart between ideals of beauty and realities of shame. He is for ever returning to an aspiration after truth, after beauty, after simplicity of life, and yet he has never wandered far from these; and part of his moral perplexity arises from suggestions and checks to which a person of harder or narrower personality would have been insensible. There is in him something of feminine susceptibility and sensitiveness; and that a man should possess a portion of a woman's tenderness is not wholly ill. (pp. 424-27)

> *Edward Dowden, "On Some French Writers of Verse, 1830-1877," in his* Studies in Literature: 1789-1877, *fifth edition, Kegan Paul, Trench & Co., 1889, pp. 392-427.*

THE SPECTATOR   (essay date 1892)

[*In the following essay, the critic offers an admiring assessment of Sully Prudhomme's writings.*]

French verse is undoubtedly alien to English ears, perhaps from some physical diversity of æsthetic sense, as of historical association which has apparently increased since Lamartine, Victor Hugo, and Musset forced a hearing from the world. They belong to a past dimmed by the gloom of national disaster, and it is time that we should recognise in Sully Prudhomme's poetry of the present, the skill of language, the scientific thought, hereditary in the France of Descartes and of Voltaire, while in direct spiritual and poetical ancestry the poet can claim descent from Pascal and André Chenier. The first of living French poets, his song is in the key of Mr. M. Arnold, but, as we think, tenderer, more sincere, and wider in its reach. He is not content to suggest the problems that are most urgent in our conduct of the larger life; he faces them with the courage of one who leads a forlorn but undying hope in the siege of many-towered Truth. He recognises, but escapes from, the pessimism which saturates modern thought, and of which the note was sounded in literature by *Werther, René,* and *Manfred,* and since elaborated in full chord by so many lesser heroes. His sense of solitude in the evolution of forces outside himself, is deeper than theirs by all the century which seems to have cost us so many of the ideals on which we had relied.

M. Sully Prudhomme, in his prose work on *Expression in the Fine Arts,* and in his elaborate preface to the translation of the first book of *De Natura Rerum,* has written what are probably the most brilliant essays of philosophic thought which modern France has produced, essays that justify his right to teach in poetry the reconciliation of material fact and conscious aspiration, which is the object of his endeavour. To analyse the internal not less than the outward experiences of man; to seize on their relations in all the phases of life as in the historical sequence of philosophies and creeds; to link art and the material being of man; to find noble poetry in the prismatic changes of the simplest human life; to unify man and his environment, of which he is the only measure conceivable to our consciousness,

with rare analysis and perfection of poetry,—is M. Sully Prudhomme's title to the love and praise of his fellow-thinkers, if not to the applause of the street. His genius and training, perhaps, tend to a too logical analysis, but his verse so abounds in imagery, and his rhythm is so perfected, that by every right he is singer; and science but strengthens his flight into the æther he loves. Few poets have so deeply probed, and with so fine an instrument, the tragedy of our race, though not its individual tragedies. While it attains more physical comfort, it appears to suffer as never before by selfish egotism and blindness to the lights by which our fathers found their way. The poet's effort to escape the tyranny of laws beyond his grasp, and to stay the strife of man and circumstance, is perhaps all the finer because he has no ark of dogma in the deluge of cosmic forces. There is a religion, the mother of all creeds, the religion which confesses a power from which man would sometimes hide, but cannot conjure. In his keen consciousness of it, and his sensitiveness to the cry of those who are orphaned of the divine Father, M. Sully Prudhomme is the most modern of those whose office it is to make music alike for the intellect as for the senses. . . .

[His] first volume, *Stances et poemes,* earned Sainte-Beuve's admiration, and at twenty-five Sully Prudhomme produced some of his loveliest sonnets. His finished and tender lyric, **"Le vase brisé,"** became at once so popular, that it partly obscured the more serious poems which were in the same volume. . . . [It is] an example of slight fancy, expressing pain from which many have suffered, and of the perfected linguistic form which is seldom wanting to whatever height, and under whatever stress of thought the master attained in his longer poems. . . . (p. 16)

Few of us appreciate the finish to which French writers had brought the art of versification before the *décadente* school ravaged the fair vineyard, and called their license freedom. In a small treatise . . . , M. Sully Prudhomme expounds the real source and end of rhythm and rhyme as based on purely physical laws. It might be a chapter in his greater work on *Expression in Fine Art,* a careful study of which is necessary to full appreciation of his æsthetic standards. The emission of the breath, the quickening of utterance under emotion, the laws of proportionate number which govern vibration through the senses, excite our perception of far-reaching order. Centuries of elaboration have adapted French rhythm to French ears. We are not judges of it, except to feel its exact proportions and the repose gained by its simpler accents,—repose, which is the essential end of art, and art which is none the less noble because it more easily satisfies the sensuous memory, and because its surprises are ordered as are the lines of a French rather than of an English garden. M. Sully Prudhomme claims for his poetry that it can treat of all human interests. He holds with Pascal that he who knows most loves best, and therefore sings best. . . . Science and art equally beckon him on to the ideal which haunts him.

He has himself partly lifted the veil of his early love for a girl who withdrew from her engagement to him, in the group of poems entitled **"Jeunes filles,"** touched with delicate passion and sincere intensity, worthy of Mrs. Browning's *Sonnets from the Portuguese.* . . . The haunting sweetness of his first passion echoes throughout the five volumes of M. Sully Prudhomme's poetry, not as a grief, but as the dominant note of a self-sacrificing life. Only in one or two sonnets does he touch on the lower influences of women, and let us hasten to say that he is pure in imagination, in purpose, and in expression, as ever Wordsworth was.

In diction he uses no tricks of alliteration; words are to him rather symbolic than expressive of particular sounds; but he is keenly alive to the nobleness that words possess by association. It is difficult to overestimate the ease and finish of his style. His has the good sense and clearness of Boileau's rule; and his rhymes, if they are not a perpetual surprise, never influence his exactness of thought. He writes of the latest discoveries in biology and mechanics with scientific accuracy, yet in noble words, illustrated in every line by an imagination fed on truth.

While he was still attached to the Creuzot factory, he began his versified translation of the first book of Lucretius. The treatise prefixed explains the poet's mind, and it accounts for his not continuing his task. It attests his analytic power, as does his preface to his fine poem, *La justice,* and his essay on æsthetic science. The more salient of its points is that man must remain the measure of the beauty he conceives. To think adequately of the poet, his prose should be studied; and it will go far to justify that reading of his own emotions into his environment, which has been called the pathetic fallacy. In philosophy he inclines to Kant as his master; but as a poet he cannot content himself with the Deity offered by Kant:—

> Comme avec une image on console un enfant.

> ["As one comforts an infant with a picture"]

In him, as he says of Pascal, his faith is—

> qu'une agonie étrange,
> On croirait voir lutter Jacob avec son ange."

> ["a strange anguish,
> One could believe seeing Jacob wrestling with his angel."]

Meantime, M. Sully Prudhomme has given his great poetic gift to the reconciliation of that modern mental struggle induced by the pressure of natural forces and recognition of the still supreme human consciousness. He seeks for the concord of fact and aspiration. He beats his wings against human limitations, but he refuses religious dogma; yet his is not despairing complaint, and it may be that a nobler, certainly a more tragic intensity, rings in his poetry than could be attained by one who does not "beat his music out." (pp. 16-17)

We cannot pause to praise the many sonnets, probably the best in a language which is so well trained to chiselled thought and exact prosody. We pass by *Vaines tendresses,* graceful but enduring as the lace-work of the Taj Mahal, and the *Épreuves* of Doubt and Love and Dream and Action which are at the threshold of a man's career. In his verses written before the war of 1870, there is sometimes an over-strain of sentiment, as in the **"Rendezvous,"** musical as it is. The pain of solitude has often in it a tinge of sick self-love; but the disaster of that year roused in him a more serious effort to confront the problems of life. . . .

It was the suffering of France which begot the fine poem of *La justice.* Not able to find the personal God, the poet takes Justice as a power revealed to conscience, by which during the past she has been slowly evolved, and can alone be perfected by a fuller sympathy of mutual good-will. The sincerity of the long debate between hope and discouragement, aspiration and perplexed doubt, is as austere in form as are Dante's cantos. We wish we had space to quote the sonnet of the fifth "Watch," of which there are ten, each complete in question and answer.

La justice would be the finest of modern "questionings," if in 1888 *Le bonheur* had not been published. It is the sum of the ideas which from the first inspired M. Sully Prudhomme. In admirable poetry, he declares that as justice is a sublimated

love of our neighbour, so in this perfect charity is happiness. Faustus and Stella, who loved each other but had not been united on earth, awake in a paradise wherein human life and its powers are perfectly satisfied. In a procession, graceful as one in a Greek frieze, the triumphs of art, the teachers of philosophies old and new, and the heroes of science, masterpieces of drawing and epithet, are marshalled as discoverers of all known truth. . . . In the summary of modern science, perhaps the finest passage is the description of the sun as our life-sustaining star. While Faustus learns the limitations of knowledge, he hears the lamentations that rise from the planet he has left, which penetrate the universe with their faint clamour. That sense of ideal justice of which M. Sully Prudhomme is the prophet, impels Faustus, after a fine discussion with Stella, who unites her fate with his, to invoke Death,—

> la force qui fraye aux âmes leur chemin,
> Et les entraîne au but que l'Espérance indique.

> ["the power which opens to souls their way,
> And carries them to the destination shown by Hope"]

Death replaced them on the painful Earth, but there had been no sense of the lapse of time in Paradise, and the race of man had passed away to rise or fall elsewhere.

But having willed their sacrifice and proved their sympathy, Faustus and Stella are again rapt by Death to the highest heaven. There are few, if any, passages of greater beauty than the concluding lines of this fine poem. They describe a beatitude worthy of Dante's vision when Faustus and Stella arrive.

> Au port d'embarquement, à la source du Monde.

> ["At the port of embarkment, at the source of the World."]

Pain and death and love can alone open its gates and discover its secrets. And M. Sully Prudhomme leads us through all the mazes of intelligence to the foot of the Christian Cross, while refusing the Christian creed. His life illustrates his doctrines by its labour, its kindness, its purity of aim and nobleness of emotion. His fine achievement is the sincere reflection of himself, and his advanced post in the vanguard of modern thought should win for him, not only the honour due to a fine poet, but the admiration of all men of good-will, and perhaps most of those who, like the *pèlerin de l'idéal,* ["pilgrim of the absolute"], have been scared from the old paths by the clashing machinery of dogma. (p. 17)

"Sully Prudhomme," in The Spectator, *Vol. 69, No. 3340, July 2, 1892, pp. 16-17.*

MAURICE BARING   **(essay date 1900)**

[*An English man of letters, Baring was the author of over fifty books, including novels, dramas, poetry, essays, criticism, and travel narratives. During the early twentieth century he was known as one of the most important Catholic apologists in England, while today he is remembered primarily as a novelist. In the following excerpt from an essay written in 1900, he describes Sully Prudhomme's characteristic style and themes.*]

What strikes the reader first and foremost in Sully-Prudhomme's poetry is that he is a thinker, and, moreover, a poet who thinks, and not a thinker who turns to rhyme for recreation. What is most strikingly original in his work is to be found in his philosophic and scientific poetry. If he had not the scientific genius of Pascal, he had at least the scientific habit of mind, and found delight in the certainties of mathematics. He wrote before the days of relativity. In attempting to interpret the universe as it is revealed to man by science, he succeeded in creating a form of poetry which seemed to be new, and which was not without a certain grandeur. One of his most beautiful poems, **"L'idéal"** (*Stances et poèmes*) was inspired by the thought which is due to scientific calculations, of stars so remote from our planet that their light has been on its way to us for thousands of centuries and will one day be visible to the eyes of a future generation. Even if this is untrue, even if it is only one of the fairy tales of science, it is a good subject for a poem. The second chief characteristic of Sully-Prudhomme's poetry is the extreme sensibility and the profoundly melancholy note of his love lyrics and his musings. Sully-Prudhomme was above all things introspective; he penetrated into the hidden corners of his heart; he laid bare the subtle torments of his conscience, the shifting currents of his hopes and fears, belief and disbelieving, when faced by the riddle of the universe, in so poignant a manner as to be sometimes almost painful. To render the fugitive phases and tremulous adventures of his spirit, he lit upon incomparably delicate shades of expression and an exquisite and sensitive diction. In his poems there is a striking nobility in the ideas and a religious elevation like that of Pascal; and there is something of Lucretius as well. Yet he was neither an Epicurean nor a Jansenist; he was rather a Stoic to whom the disappointments of life brought pity instead of bitterness.

In Sully-Prudhomme's work all oratorical effect is conspicuous by its absence; it has an extreme simplicity and fastidious precision of diction. Other poets have had a more glowing imagination; his verse is neither exuberant in colour nor rich in sonorous combinations of sound. The grace of his verse is one of outline and not of colour; his compositions are distinguished by his subtle rhythm; his verse is as if carved in ivory, his music is like that of a unison of stringed instruments. His imagination is inseparable from his idea, and this is the reason of the extraordinary perspicuity of his poetic style. His poetry extends to two extreme limits: on the one hand, to the borderland of the unreal and the dreamlike, as in a poem such as **"Le rendezvous"** *(Vaines tendresses),* in which he seems to express the inexpressible; on the other hand, in his scientific poems he encroaches on the realms of prose. His poetry is plastic in the creation of forms which fittingly express his fugitive emotions and his lofty ideas. Both on account of the charm of his pure and perfect phrasing and by the consummate art and the dignity which informed all his work, Sully-Prudhomme deserved the rank which he held amongst the foremost French poets of the nineteenth century. (pp. 218-19)

> *Maurice Baring, "Sully-Prudhomme," in his* Punch and Judy & Other Essays, *Doubleday, Page & Company, 1924, pp. 216-19.*

E. PRESTON DARGAN   (essay date 1911)

[*Dargan is an American poet and critic who has written several studies of French literature and literary figures. In the following excerpt, he surveys Sully Prudhomme's poetry.*]

There are dozens of pieces in [the first volume of Sully Prudhomme's *Oeuvres*], expressing poignantly the whole gamut of disappointed passion from direct jealousy and baffled desire, through the mournfulness of memories, down to the more discreet though scarcely less moving hint of the happiness that might have been. Of bitter invective there is little; of resignation not a trace as yet. Especially in this first volume, there is occasional *mièvrerie* and infelicity. The lyrics are usually quite simple in form, of a few stanzas only. . . . (p. 197)

Other elements are the ever-defeated yearning to grasp and sympathize with all things; the powerlessness of the dream which yet remains a habit; the sharply snapped link between the ideals of youth and the facts of manhood; the disconcerted gaze over the domain of human action, producing already the unappeasable *cui bono* questionings; and chiefly that attachment of everything to the loved object, according to Stendhal's crystallization process, with the feeling that the loss of her meant the loss of all. There are many poems where these things are not directly considered, where they merely serve as a pensive background to some less intimate, equally poetic outburst.

To analyze his reveries is easier than to bring out, except by too frequent quotation, the great charm and delicacy of his treatment. It is the brush of a bee's wing, the coloring of a wild-flower. One striking technical point is the handling of the last stanza and the last line. It is generally conceded that the last line is what makes the modern sonnet. Therein lies the epigrammatic sting, like the closing sentence of one of Burke's paragraphs or of the Maupassantian short story. Sully Prudhomme applies this principle with a craftsmanship effecting rather more than a suspension of interest, a veritable revelation at the close. (pp. 197-98)

I find again and again poems of a Wordsworthian, almost a conversational phrasing, which lose nothing, for a foreigner at least, by their directness. Certainly poetic diction is less of an enclosed garden with the French than with us. At the same time, the Romanticists and the Parnassians have sufficiently shown that the cult of the fatal word can be extended, if not to the ornamental word, at least to the exotic, rare, subtly associative word, which seeks to reveal horizons. Sully Prudhomme too could do this on occasion—**"Le cygne"** is an example. Yet his talent was not really descriptive. He has, for instance, few landscape effects. Nature for him was mainly an enigma who vouchsafed symbols, and Zyromski notices particularly the lily, the star, the clear sky. But the poet's heart-throbs usually subsist by the force of their independent rhythm.

It should also be remarked that he naturally strengthened and sobered his vocabulary as he matured. Similes lost their occasional touch of the conceit, and the sonnets especially sweep to their close with a masterly impulsion of winged words. (pp. 198-99)

Passing from the strictly subjective lyrics, I will say at once that Sully Prudhomme's best work seems to me to lie in those fields where his personal melancholy is swayed to a larger expression, and his spirit, rising from its fruitless revery, comes into grave conscious strife with the ever-waiting problems. The philosophic *"méditation"* tempered with sentiment was his forte.

I have thought of him as a metaphysician *malgré lui* ["in spite of himself"], and he was that, inasmuch as love-poetry would have been his more natural utterance, had the inspiration for this been happy and durable. But contemning

> Ces deuils voluptueux des vaincus sans combats

> ["The voluptuous mournings of those conquered without a fight"],

he was forced by his "sublime stranger" to enter the cold repugnant halls of philosophy, and he came out, as he perfectly admitted twenty years later, by the same door wherein he went, as far as a thorough intellectual or scientific explanation of the universe is concerned. Yet it would be a mistake to imagine that his passage through is bare of interest and meaning.

Already in the poem called **"Intus"** of the first volume, there are heard the two warring voices, that of iconoclastic reason and that of love which cries, "Espère, ô ma sœur! . . . " ["Hope, O my sister!"] Later, the combat takes many forms.—Poetry is set against science in half-a-dozen pieces. Poetry is outwardly reconciled to science in the sonnets of *Les épreuves*, in *Le zénith*, which was inspired by a balloon ascension, and notably in one place where he divines that the great poetry of the future must grasp and go beyond scientific conclusions, must feel the symbolism of "many inventions," while ignoring their detail. He frequently apostrophizes the scientists—he seeks "a Newton of the soul." **"La beauté"** shows the joy of the plastic artist as opposed to the suffering of the man of letters, who must endeavor to set up the dream of his rigid goddess in the full tide of realities. Still another aspect of the strife appears in **"Sur un vieux tableau."** This is a poignant depiction of the death of Christ set off by the indifference of men, the banality of the day's work, the composure of earth and heaven. **"La Voie Lactée"** shows the loneliness of the stars, paralleling the loneliness of man. **"L'une d'elles"** declares that a soul isolated in its Palace of Art, surrounded by luxuries, is yet unsatisfied. The parable **"L'art et l'amour"** tells us that the wind of inspiration cannot linger with the flower of love which implores him, and that both die before evening. In **"Sur la mort"** bewildered by the riddles and crying out on dogmas, the poet abandons himself and a dead loved one to the laws of the universe—whatever they may be.

The best of these vital lyrics are the sonnets—the noble sequence called *La France*, where the poet tries to discover a future for his country—the moving intimate sonnets of *Les épaves*, and especially those of *Les épreuves*, where I think his most artistic mingling of thought and sentiment is to be found. As Lemaître has pointed out, nearly half of these are symbols or metaphors, with their application justly and grandly developed. In their four divisions of Amour, Doute, Rêve, Action, they include such masterpieces as the **"Inquiétude"** . . .; the familiar **"Danaïdes"**; **"Rouge ou noire,"** where he tosses on the *tapis* with Pascal for the chance of a divinity; **"Un bonhomme,"** a remarkable presentment of Spinoza; **"La fatalité,"** showing the necessity of the poet's love, the hopelessness of changing it for another happier one. Finally **"Un songe"** and **"Homo sum"** return to the sense of human fellowship, the rejoicing in labor, the call of action. As evincing his control of the form and as characteristic of his "âme en peine et de passage" ["soul in pain and in transition"], I would mention especially the sonnet styled **"La fontaine de jouvence."**

For his systematic conclusions in the matter of philosophy, we must turn to the two poems *La justice* and *Le bonheur*.

The purport of *La justice* is to ascertain whether there is a moral order in the universe—no less. Otherwise stated, it investigates whether the rhythm of nature accords with the aspirations of man, and seeks a higher harmony, an ultimate law. The argument unrolls itself in a series of eleven *veilles* ["vigils"], consisting of debates between the poet and certain "voices." The first half of the poem is an arraignment of nature as the enemy of justice, life and love. The evolutionary hypothesis, based on strife and tending to destruction, is adopted. In the soberest of styles, beautiful only with the cold beauty of thought, the poet tries to contemplate impassively a loveless world. The hard brilliant sonnets are answered by a voice which maintains more tenderly the value of dreaming, of a certain forgetfulness, and recommends an easy acceptation of love and of justice as a "cri du cœur" ["cry of the heart"]. But the poet will have

only the truth, and he finds it, following science, in the statement that death is the law of life between species. (pp. 201-03)

The world began in a state of war, as it was long ago declared by Hobbes. The first right of man is a "brevet de bourreau" ["executioner's license"]. Morality is a later compact, still for egoistic ends.

In the same species, the apparently finer impulses can all be traced to self-interest. Nature is prudent, cunning, uses even the ideal attraction of sexual love as a veil for her own purposes. (pp. 203-04)

Between governments, war is complicated with trickery and military honor is founded on murder. It is a false abstraction to speak of the brotherhood of man—men are often more remote from one another than from their dogs—and, who, pray, is my neighbor? The apparent reciprocity in cities continues to be based on need, and the strongest get what they can. In other planets, fatality points to like conditions merely more entangled by a possible divinity.

As I understand the second part of the poem, called "Appel au Cœur," the facts of science are not to be answered by a heavenly escape or by resort to a vaporous faith. The facts are very much as they have been stated. Granted the aloofness of Nature, the material strife-basis, the whole evolutionary doctrine—and in *Le bonheur* he even goes so far as to grant the annihilation of earth and its inhabitants—there remain the other facts, equally inexpugnable, that man has an inner order of his own which he has to some extent imposed upon his world, that mere intelligence, wrestling only with matter, leaves out of account one human specific difference, which is the persistent rule of conscience. It is very possible that Justice, outside of man, has no reason for being, and that we are foolish in applying human conceptions to God and Nature. But the evolutionary laws of the latter are none the less paralleled in the growth of the moral sense. Remorse is then the voice of this wider nature scolding her heir. . . . (p. 204)

Finally, the conscience working with the intelligence produces sympathy. Kindliness and co-operation rear up the City, which is the highest expression of humanity—and the concluding definition is:

> La Justice est l'amour guidé par la lumière.
>
> ["Justice is love guided by enlightenment."]

In order to compare this directly with *Le bonheur*, the content of the latter poem may also be briefly given. The scene is laid in some unknown Paradise. Faustus, the hero, awakens there and finds his earthly love, Stella, by his side. The first part, *Les ivresses*, is the apotheosis of "l'amour-passion." The lovers, as blessed as love can make them, wander through Elysian delights, which take the somewhat mundane manifestations of savors and perfumes, forms and colors, harmony and beauty. It is again a Palace of Art, where painters possess their ideal models and music soars unrestrained by sorrow. . . . This suggests what is the matter with it. The lovers are shrouded in a "linceul de joie" ["shroud of joy"]. Aspiration is the highest soul-expression, but this very beautiful love of two is not the perfect aspiration, since it has no *lendemain* ["tomorrow"] and hence no life. Desire and dreaming wear themselves out. The insistent Voix de la Terre, where mortals still suffer, comes as an interlude after every ecstasy.

The second part, *La pensée*, shows Faustus tormented by *le mal de l'inconnu* ["the evil of the unknown"]. The philosophers, ancient and modern, and the scientists speak; the whole parchment of human thought is unrolled. Pascal appears and seems to solve the unknown with the three key-words of charity, modesty before the first cause, and law. Stella, by some transfiguration, endues and symbolizes for Faustus these three attributes. Their love, crowned and fortified by knowledge, would now seem truly perfect.

Still the Voices of the Earth come nearer, individualized in their woe. The idea that "l'amour-sacrifice" is the only complete happiness, in that it contains no inquietude or aftermath, is exemplified by the descent of Faustus and Stella, after long hesitation, to relieve the world's burden. They tread upon an extinct earth, where "la Mort, l'aveugle Mort, l'infaillible Passeuse" ["Death, blind Death, the infallible ferry-woman"] has extended her reign and assures them that man has totally disappeared. The impressive description of this manless world, its effect on the would-be benefactors, are followed by Stella's determination to give birth to a new and more enlightened race. Thus brusquely *Le bonheur* ends.

One may well hesitate as to the absolute ranking of these cosmic epics, when Brunetière and Anatole France [see excerpt dated 1914], in reviewing them, have thought fit to abstain from a summarizing judgment. That they contain much deep thought, splendid lyrical interludes, some prosing and incoherence, and that they end in a fine faith may be granted. But *Le bonheur* is an epic drama of three hundred pages, on the same scale and dealing with the same matters as *Faust* or *Paradise Regained*. It falls below these, of course. Few men living can be prepared to decide whether it is a huge failure *per se*, whether it is a *succès d'estime*, what posterity will prefer to do about it. The long poem is the critic's bane, and still more frequently the reader's.

Happily, Sully Prudhomme's fame as a poet of meditation can rest on other evidence. At least one may say that before the magnificent range of thought and feeling developed in these poems, the insidious doubter had best bow his head. If he insists on raising it, perhaps he may question how far this man's failure to realize himself in "l'amour-passion" may have influenced his advocacy of "l'amour-sacrifice." It is really by the withering of the individual that the world is more and more? Again, he admits the reign of law and the *souffle* of aspiration. What if we aspire beyond the law?

That reverence before natural law, which seems to be his chief article of faith, finds manifestation as well in his *ars poetica* and his own technique. The *Testament poétique* contains first a noble view of the poet's function, declaring that he should be neither an egoistic whiner nor a mere entertainer, but that he must guide, philosophize and befriend. It contains also certain uncompromisingly conservative views on versification. He will have none of the innovations of the symbolists. Victor Hugo carried rhythm as far as it could possibly be carried, and later novelties simply invade illegitimately the realms of prose or of music. The physiological laws of hearing and the law of least effort must apply to the two kinds of rhythm, regular and irregular. In regular rhythm, where the lines are of an equal number of syllables, the cæsura must so fall that each line is divided either into two equal parts, or parts that shall be as little unequal as possible, having, that is, a greatest common divisor. In lines of an unequal number of syllables, the cæsura must fall as nearly as possible in the middle. These principles are elaborated with illustrations. Also he admits no *rime plus que suffisante* ["rhyme that is merely sufficient"]. He is willing to make some concessions about eye-rimes and hiatuses;

but as a whole his intransigent academic attitude is clearly shown.

He boasts that he himself has found "la vieille lyre" ["the old lyre"] capable of answering every vibration of his heart. Technically he has introduced nothing. He has given his individual note to certain forms, such as the sonnet and that swallow-flight of song which consists of a few quatrains.

This individual note is a quaver of hope over a ground-bass of defeat. Humanly speaking, as compared with most of his contemporaries of song, it would be narrow not to observe that he is cast in a finer mould, and that he has remained in the fight, keeping a larger sense of the world-struggle. Of what others can that be said? The Parnassians frankly represent the poetry of evasion, frequently obtaining thereby only an aggravated *Weltschmerz* to which they lost the antidote. Gautier and Théodore de Banville are incomparable artists—but are they good alike at grave and gay? Coppée, it is true, comes familiarly nearer the living heart of things. From the standpoint of pure beauty-worship, however,—and certainly, whatever may be said of the other sixty-eight, it is impossible to abjure this fundamental way of constructing tribal lays—Sully Prudhomme bows to several of the masters named as well as to Verlaine, who, purely as a matter of voice, seems to me decidedly the most exquisite French singer after Hugo.

But occasionally "the dominant's persistence" must make its sterner appeal. When we are in such moods, such plight, if you will, Sully Prudhomme may well be heard with his doctrine of aspiration beyond but for this world, a world frankly taken as not very satisfactory to the sensitive and the thoughtful. Leaving out of account improbable heavens, he holds that the idealizing function of man must call for some fulfillment. (pp. 205-08)

The doubts of this developed creed which I suggested a few pages back mean only that the poet has not finally fixed the individual in the cosmos. When that is done, we shall have no further need of philosophers, and every man can be his own poet. While waiting, in one and the other capacity, Sully Prudhomme may be commended to the youth of America as embodying in nobler fashion than many what it should be our chief "disinterested endeavor to learn and propagate"—the modern cultural ethos of Europe. (p. 208)

E. Preston Dargan, "The Poetry of Sully Prudhomme," in Studies in Honor of A. Marshall Elliott, *Vol. I by E. Preston Dargan and others, The Johns Hopkins Press, 1911, pp. 195-208.*

ANATOLE FRANCE   (essay date 1914)

[*A French novelist, short story writer, and essayist, France was widely regarded during his lifetime as his country's greatest author. In two diverse areas of literature—wistful storytelling and trenchant satire—his works embody what are traditionally considered the intellectual and artistic virtues of French writing: clarity, control, perceptive judgment of worldly matters, and the Enlightenment virtues of tolerance and justice. A persistent tone of irony is often considered the dominant trait of France's writing. In his critical works this ironic expression becomes an effective tool of literary analysis. In the following excerpt he discusses* Le bonheur. *Translations in brackets are by the critic.*]

Said Candide, "There are no longer any Manicheans," and Martin answered, "I am one." We say in the same way today that there are no longer poets who write long works, and

M. Sully-Prudhomme replies by publishing a philosophic poem in twelve cantos on "Happiness."

We must first of all admire the audacious novelty of the enterprise. Is it not, in truth, a singular and admirable effort to set out in verse an ample succession of thoughts, to forge in cadence a long chain of ideas, at a time when poetry, which seems to have definitely renounced the old heroic and didactic forms, has been satisfied, for the past three generations, with the ode and the elegy, and as regards epic poetry, willingly limited herself to experiments or fragments? The sonnet has again found the favour which it enjoyed in the days when the "Pléiade" shone. It is regarded as not offering too narrow a frame for the poet's thought, and M. Sully-Prudhomme has himself written a collection of sonnets of a beauty at once intellectual and concrete. Several of those little poems which compose the collection of *Épreuves* express the profoundest thought in the most fragrant language. Such undoubtedly are the sonnets on **"La grande ourse"** and on **"Les Danaïdes."** Such is the sonnet which begins with this delicious strophe:

> S'il n'était rien de bleau que le ciel et la mer,
> De blond que les épis, de rose que les roses,
> S'il n'était de beauté qu'aux insensibles choses,
> Le plaisir d'admirer ne serait point amer.

> ["If nothing were blue save the sky and the sea, were fair save the corn, or rose but the roses, if beauty were found only in inanimate things, the pleasure of admiring would not be a bitter one."]

It is above all by his little poems, by his stanzas and his elegies, that M. Sully-Prudhomme is widely known and deeply loved. His first long poem, *La justice,* added to the admiration with which so sincere a poet inspired those who care for literature, without greatly adding to the sympathy which flows on all sides from refined and gentle souls towards the author of *Solitudes.* It was for his elegies that M. Sully-Prudhomme was first of all loved and blessed. And what love and what blessings does he not deserve for having poured forth for us that balm, unknown before his time, that exquisite mixture, in which intelligence joins with feeling to refresh the heart and to fortify the mind? It was a miracle to find a poet at once so sensitive and so intelligent. As a rule, miracles last only for a short time. This one ended too soon. The perilous equilibrium of two contrary faculties which had astounded us was lost. In M. Sully-Prudhomme intelligence conquered feeling. The intellectual faculties, so rich in his nature, developed with a tyrannical power. To the poet of *Solitudes* succeeded the poet of *Justice.* To rapid and profound impressions, M. Sully-Prudhomme preferred pure thoughts linked in a long succession to one another. He ceased to be elegiac and became philosophical. I am far from rejoicing at this. But I cannot blame him for it. Even when one secretly prefers the delicious troubles of the first hour of the day to the serenity of evening, one should be silent about one's vain regrets, and cheerfully admit that if there is an end of smiles and tears, it is perhaps a good thing to meditate, and that in the end the kneeling Polymnia has also irresistible grace.

The poem of *Bonheur* is a philosophical poem. One learns in it the extra-terrestrial adventures of Faustus and Stella. Like the Eiros and the Charmion, like the Monos and the Una of the American visionary, Faustus and Stella form a couple set free by death. Together they enjoy, far from this humble and miserable earth, peace in desire and joy in immortality. When he evokes them, the poet adjures them to tell us what is ineffable. And that is a formidable adjuration. Faustus and his

gentle Stella return from the unknown, at the poet's command, only to make dark sayings clear to us, and to reveal to us those secrets that are buried deepest in our hearts. To tell the truth, this is a task in which your Faustus and your Stella will eternally fail. The poet knew it. He fell into no illusion for a single moment regarding the authority of his personages. He does not flatter himself that the speeches of Faustus will put an end to human uncertainty. If Faustus proclaims what is true, as he himself says in his preface, "if this dream borders upon reality, upright and steadfast hearts would have no reason to repine, but it is to chance above all that they should attribute the credit." Alas! it is then true, the adventure of Faustus and Stella is only a beautiful dream. This is that dream:

Faustus and Stella, who had loved one another on Earth without being able to be united, rediscover each other, after death, on a new planet. Faustus is welcomed there by Stella, who had died before him. In this planet, different from ours, the poet, as one might expect, shows us nothing that is not terrestrial. It is impossible, in truth, to invent anything. Our whole imagination is made up of memories.

We have even manufactured Heaven out of materials taken from earth. The myrtles of the Elysian fields are to be found in our gardens, and the angels' harps come from our lute-makers. The nameless planet to which the poet carries us is more beautiful and pleasanter than ours, but it contains nothing which Earth does not contain.

M. Sully-Prudhomme must at least be praised for not having peopled unknown worlds with incoherent visions as Swedenborg did. We do not know what the planets illuminated by Sirius and the Polar Star are like. We shall never know. We must content ourselves with knowing that the distant sun which gave them birth is composed of a gas that is known to us. The unity of the composition of the heavenly bodies is certain. It may well be that the universe is upon the whole monotonous enough, and that it does not deserve the insatiable curiosity with which it inspired us.

In the planet inhabited by Faustus and Stella, there are winged horses. It is true that none of these are found on Earth, but there are wings and there are horses, and without these the Greeks would not have formed the idea of Pegasus. A Pegasus, one of these horses of the air, carries the two restored lovers through the new world they inhabit, and deposits them at the entrance to an ancient forest. They plunge into it, and soon there opens before them a valley in which flowers and fruits of every species delight the taste and the smell. These flowers and fruits are the sole food of the inhabitants of this planet.

No being exists there to the detriment of others.

The struggle for life is unknown there. Murder not being the necessary condition of existence, the spirits there are naturally peaceable and kindly. Just as life is established on our earth in such a manner as constantly to engender crime and pain, existence in the nameless planet has nothing but gentle and lenient necessities. People are not wicked there, since they do not suffer, and wickedness is inconceivable without pain; but for the same reason they are unable to display their good qualities. For it is impossible to imagine beings possessing at the same time goodness and beatitude. Virtue necessarily supposes the faculty of sacrifice; a being that cannot cease to be happy is condemned to a perpetual moral mediocrity. That causes some embarrassment. When one thinks of it, one does not know what to desire, and one dare not wish for anything, not even universal happiness.

Faustus and Stella meet a numerous troop of cavaliers of all races, formerly slaves on the earth, but now free and enjoying their freedom with rapture. They admire in them the beauty of the different human types. And this is not without reason: liberty beautifies those strong enough to embrace it, and this natural truth has served as a foundation for the aristocratic prejudices so deeply rooted in all human societies. I shall only remark here that Faustus and Stella have still before their eyes the outward appearances of the earth, since they represent to themselves so vividly the image of liberty. For liberty could not exist in a world where servitude did not exist. The vision of the two lovers is, properly speaking, only a mirage. The planet of the happy cannot carry in its flowery bosom the warrior-maiden Liberty, the virgin with the blood-stained arms. She only reveals herself in combat: happy planets do not know her. The more I think of it, the more I am persuaded that happy planets know nothing.

In their new abode, Faustus and Stella are charmed by its sounds, its forms, and its colours. I should never have believed that, being immortal, they could enjoy the pleasures of sight and hearing. Is not to see, to hear, or to smell to use up something of one's self, is it not to die a little? And what is to live as we live on earth but to die continually and to spend every day a part of the totality of life that is in us? But the poet's vision is so pure and his art is so subtle that we are transported and delighted.

Stella reveals to Faustus the highest expression of music. He enjoys the charm of the voice in a happy ecstasy which makes him forget his past life. Stella, who had hitherto appeared to him in a terrestrial shape, assumes before him her perfect beauty. They exchange their love in a sublime communion.

That is their happiness! But how can they enjoy it if they are immortal? We have love on earth, but it is at the price of death. If we were not destined to perish, love would be something inconceivable. Scarcely has Faustus embraced Stella in his rejuvenated arms than he becomes abstracted and thoughtful. Has his happiness lasted a day or thousands of millions of centuries? We do not know, and he himself is equally ignorant. An unalloyed happiness cannot be measured. Even he who possesses it does not enjoy it or feel it. However this may be, curiosity, satiated for a moment by the delights of Paradisiacal life, awakens again in Faustus. He aspires to comprehend the nature he is enjoying. He wants to know. Immortal yesterday,

> Une vague inquiétude,
> Le souci de savoir, que nul front fier n'élude,
> Le mal de l'inconnu l'avait déjà tenté.

> ["A vague disquiet, the care to know, which no proud brow eludes, the misery of not knowing had already tempted him."]

By this sign also, I recognise him as one of our brethren. He has not put off the old man; he remains in mind a citizen of the little old planet on which some Latin schoolman once wrote this maxim: "We tire of everything except of understanding things."

Faustus evokes, in his disquiet, the distant memory of human knowledge. At first he recalls to his memory the philosophical systems of Greek antiquity; then he passes in review the Alexandrians and the schoolmen. At last he braves the moderns, Bacon, Descartes, Pascal, Spinoza, Leibnitz, Locke, Berkeley, Hobbes, Hume, Kant, Fichte, Hegel, Schopenhauer, Comte. . . . This latter stops him, forbids him metaphysical speculations, and imposes on him a general view of human knowledge. But

that philosophy does not lead to the knowledge of the origin and end of things; the resignation which it imposes on his unsatisfied curiosity is not less repugnant to him than the rashness of metaphysical conceptions. Faustus, despairing of finding the truth in the teaching of terrestrial thinkers, abandons their deceptive aid.

He has thenceforth exhausted the joys of feeling and those of intelligence. Now, whilst he was enjoying his unconscious felicity, the chorus of human lamentation, incessantly growing larger since the most distant ages, was going up from earth to Heaven. It at last reaches the planet inhabited by Stella. Faustus hears those laments, recognises them, and feels awakening within him the consciousness and sympathy of brotherhood.

Oh! what a dolorous eloquence swells the voice of Earth!

> Lamentable océan de douleurs, dont la houle
> Se soulève en hurlant, s'affaisse et se déroule,
>   Et marche en avant sans repos!
> N'est il donc pas encore apparu sur ta route
> Un monde fraternel où quelque ami t'écoute:
>   N'auras-tu nulle part d'échos?

> ["Lamentable ocean of griefs, whose waves uplift themselves in moans, subside and fall, and onward press unresting! Has there not yet appeared upon the way any fraternal world in which some friend may listen to thee: shalt thou know no echo?"]

Faustus, as he listens to the cries, promises himself that he will descend again to the earth, to bring to men the resources of his knowledge; Stella will follow him and share his sacrifice. Obedient death will come to take them again.

How little man is made for immortality! Faustus and Stella seemed to breathe it as if it were a suffocating fluid. Their death has the joyous sweetness of a re-birth. One feels that it will give back to the lovers their true destiny. The poet has found rare and exquisite tones in which to sing it, something refined, flowing, subtle (one must recur to that word). (pp. 34-42)

Death has borne their unconscious forms to the earth. At the moment they touch the ancient planet whence there arose so great a cry of pain, the reanimated Faustus and Stella recognise their first home, but they perceive that there are no longer any men in it; the human species has long been extinct upon it. No matter; they will descend into this evil world. They will devote themselves to creating a happy race on the soil that formerly nourished so much suffering. Whilst they are making this decision, Death, obeying a Divine order, carries them towards the highest abode, which they have deserved by their incomparable devotion. Alas! what will they do in that glorious abode? Since we know, from their example, that even outside the earth there is joy only in sacrifice, we fear that in that seventh heaven where Death deposits them, they will enjoy but an insipid felicity. What is the true name of that sublime abode which the poet does not name? Is it not Nirvana that one finds there? And does not the poet's happy dream end with the irreversible absorption of the two souls in the Divine nothingness?

Such is the subject, or rather the bald argument, of this fine poem, at once one of the most audacious and agreeable of philosophic poems. (p. 43)

Anatole France, "'Happiness'," in his On Life & Letters, second series, *translated by A. W. Evans, John Lane, The Bodley Head Ltd., 1914, pp. 34-43.*

RENÉ LALOU   (essay date 1922)

[*French essayist and critic, Lalou was the author of a comprehensive history of modern French literature entitled* Histoire de la littérature française contemporaine *(1922; Contemporary French Literature). As a critic Lalou was noted for his impartiality and frankness (he had no strong ties to any literary movements), for his historical discrimination and perspective, and for the balance and clarity of his critical judgments. In English translation, his critical writings have been credited with introducing the works of leading modern French authors to the English-speaking world. Lalou also helped to make the works of numerous English authors accessible to the French through his translations of works by William Shakespeare, Edgar Allan Poe, and George Meredith, and through critical studies of modern English authors, most notably his* Panorama de la littérature anglaise contemporaine *(1927). In the following excerpt, he discusses the union of poetry and philosophy in Sully Prudhomme's work.*]

From Sully Prudhomme's first collection, **Stances et poèmes,** the public immediately adopted one piece, **"Le vase brisé"** which quickly became popular. While these charmingly playful, delicately sentimental stanzas were being recited in drawing-rooms, the author was preparing a translation of Lucretius the first volume of which he published with a preface revealing his veritable preoccupations. After discussing the graver questions of psychology and of scientific method, after questioning both outward and inward experience, he concludes: "The spiritualists are certainly justified in maintaining that moral phenomena do not spring from physical phenomena, though subservient to them; but the materialists are right in affirming that nothing authorizes a substantial distinction between the moral and the physical. . . . For our part, we are inclined to think that these two orders of phenomena are irreducible, one to the other, inasmuch as they depend upon two distinct moods of the universal being." We need then, he adds, "a theory of curiosity. We must incessantly multiply the results of the two experiences by analysing them more and more." In so doing, we come to "understand ourselves." In this fashion, philosophy, "instead of beginning over again in each mind, in every generation, will be able to hand on accepted results and to continue from century to century, which will be the certain sign of its scientific organization."

Thus love of poetry, belief in the value of poetical expression, reconciled two poets in Sully Prudhomme: the delicate successor of the confidential Musset, whose first appearance had been greeted by public opinion, and the philosophical, scientific mind, ambitious to "give some undisputed foundation to philosophy," to become the French Lucretius; and no doubt he esteemed the successes of the first only as they rendered ears attentive to the truths which were to be announced by the second.

For Sully Prudhomme is not alternately a poet and a philosopher. He is always a poet-philosopher. So that his work, so little autobiographical outwardly, retraces the history of his mind where the intelligence, daily more strengthened in its ideal of severe beauty, gradually dominates his sensibility, reducing its function to adorning with a new garment the truth bared by the patient seeker. In the first volume, on the contrary, he abandoned himself to the simple pleasure of feeling, which inspired him with rapid modern elegies such as **"La prière,"** or with pretty, delicate notations:

> Un voyage! telle est la vie
> Pour ceux qui n'osent que rêver . . .
>
> ["A voyage! Such is life
> For those who only dare to dream . . . "]

Already, however, he expressed his high conception of the poet's rôle:

> Car si l'humanité tolère encor nos chants,
> C'est que notre élégie est son propre poème;
>
> ["For if humanity still tolerates our songs,
> It is because our elegy is its own poem;"]

and this sense of duty, this perpetual recollection that *noblesse oblige,* explains the weakest poems—the too obvious glorification of material love, moral apostrophes to **"La vertu,"** the rather facile symbolism of **"L'etranger."** He still sang **Vaines tendresses**; but already he had taken up his position and, among the sonnets of **Les epreuves,** one reads a complete portrait of Spinoza in fourteen lines—a *tour de force* perhaps more to the honour of the critic than to that of the poet.

The most discreetly revealing evidence of this double inspiration was offered us by Sully Prudhomme when, in **Le prisme,** he brought together poems composed at different periods. When the occasional verses have been eliminated from it, each reader is free to prefer, according to his own taste, the charming society madrigals, like **"L'eventail,"** or the tenderly delicate reveries (**"Le soir"**), or the hymns to philosophical effort (**"Les chercheurs"**). Before **Le prisme,** Sully Prudhomme had published **Justice,** not without a certain apprehension. In the preface he declares that the events of 1870-71 have disturbed him and inclined him to pessimism; and then "a corner of azure and some white summits reappeared . . . it was impossible not to hope still." **Justice** is the story of a seeker who forced his heart to remain silent and wished to chart his course with his reason alone. In vain he seeks justice between species and between states, in the species and in the state. He finds it nowhere; but a voice in him forbids despair. He discovers that this voice is the heart's and decides to listen to it. In his conscience he finds, steadfast, the idea of justice bound up with the most intimate essence of humanity, the progress of which, slow but sure, is shown by the history of the city. This idea imposes itself upon the world as the true dignity proper to man, through the sympathy which unites beings progressively with the development of understanding and science; and he is justified in defining it as "the ideal goal of science closely united with love."

It is idle to deny that such a poem is difficult of access. Sully Prudhomme knew it, but he believed that in addition to all sentiments, "nearly all ideas can be confided to verse."

Sully Prudhomme was too loyal to force his convictions and to affirm poetically a faith which his philosophical thought had not discovered. After **Justice,** however, it seemed to him he could, without forfeiting his sincerity, openly express his hope in human destiny. Such is the subject of **Bonheur.** Faustus, after his death, awakes in another life where his earthly friend, Stella, greets him, inviting him to a delicious celestial banquet where she shows him the procession of the world's wise men and of the artists who have become blessed in pure beauty. The two lovers unite in a sublime, harmonious marriage; but this intoxication has not lulled thought in Faustus. Unsatisfied, he aspires to know the secret of Being. He questions antique, then modern philosophy, then the sciences, finally Pascal who drowns doubt in faith. Disappointed, he returns to Stella. However, the earth's voices, which have not ceased to accompany his anxious quest, reach him, like a goad. Stella refuses to abandon him. They decide to make the sacrifice and return to earth. The earth is empty. Death has killed man. Faustus and Stella offer to remake a humanity—to begin again the pathetic story. The divine will intervenes. An angel bears them away and brings them in triumph to the true paradise, to the world's source.

The same reasons which have discouraged many a reader of *La justice* repelled them from *Le bonheur* also; and it is fitting here moreover to make allowance for the somewhat arid dogmatic presentation as well as for the astral novel in the manner of Flammarion. Sully Prudhomme has not always avoided the two stumbling-blocks inherent in his subject. There is, however, in *Le bonheur,* over and above the qualities of philosophical precision noted in *La justice,* a more vibrating inspiration than in the preceding poem. The thought more readily leaves the abstract zone to incarnate itself in living portraits of philosophers. It lets itself swerve in fine appeals of human tenderness and chaste love. Up to the moment of the sacrifice, the earth voices support the journey of Faustus and Stella with their vibrant canticles. *Le bonheur* contains the pages in which Sully Prudhomme has best realized his ambition for a meditative fraternal poetry. (pp. 23-6)

> René Lalou, "Le Parnasse," in his Contemporary French Literature, *translated by William Aspenwall Bradley, Alfred A. Knopf, 1924, pp 17-27.*

ANNIE RUSSELL MARBLE (essay date 1925)

[*Marble was an American critic and literary historian. In the following excerpt she offers an overview of Sully Prudhomme's career.*]

René François Armand Sully-Prudhomme, the first author to win the [Nobel] prize in literature, in 1901, received adulatory comments from French journals and several pages of *personalia* and criticism in literary magazines of England, Germany, Scandinavia, and America. For more than forty years he had been recognized as one of the greatest living poets, the philosophical poet of the nineteenth century in France, about whose life and work there was inadequate information in English translations; the inadequacy is still apparent. The French Academy was happy that one of its members should have been chosen for this honor, the first on the list of international candidates. Born in Paris, May 16, 1839, this French poet evidently belonged to the nineteenth century, in its middle and later decades, rather than to the twentieth century and its productive or prophetic writers.

In the poetry of Sully-Prudhomme are found, almost always, two elements sometimes in conflict, wistful tenderness and serious, challenging reflection. (p. 22)

The first collection of his poems, *Stances et poèmes,* appeared when he was twenty-six years old. . . . In this collection is found **"Le vase brisé,"** one of the most familiar of his poems, with the extended analogy between the broken vase, the verbena, and the heart; here is the echoing refrain,

> Il est brisé, n'y touchez pas.

> ["It is broken, do not touch it."]

The next year *Les epreuves,* translated as *The Test,* was published, followed by *Les solitudes* three years later, and *Les vaines tendresses,* in 1875. In these poetic meditations he showed the conflict, ever present in his own nature, between the reason and the emotions. . . . Even more pronounced was this motif of disharmony in the two later poems, *La justice* and *Le bonheur.* . . . In the long and best known poem by Sully-Prudhomme, *La justice,* there are strong traces of the influence of Lucretius,

the classic poet whom he admired and translated with felicitous skill. A Prologue and an Epilogue and eleven "Vigils" comprise the structure of this poetic search for the element of *Justice.* There are two divisions; Part I is entitled "Silence au cœur," rendered into English as "Heart, Be Silent!" and Part II, "Appel au cœur." The chosen medium of expression is dialogue between two symbolic characters, "The Seeker," who analyzes all things with metaphysical exactness, and "A Voice" which proclaims the "divine aspect in all things." Justice cannot be located in the Universe; it may be found in the heart of man, "which is its inviolable and sacred temple."

As *La justice* exemplified the search for Justice in Universal Nature, so *Le bonheur,* the second long poem published in 1888, was a symbolic epic, a progress towards supreme Happiness by three routes—curiosity, sensuousness and science, virtue and sacrifice. The three Parts have been called, in one translation, "Intoxication," "Thought," "The Supreme Flight" ("Le suprême essor"). There are lines that are strained in effect, far less convincing and harmonious than the arguments in *La justice;* by contrast there are passages of poetic beauty. Faustus and Stella are the two seekers after Happiness. In a climax—which might be more dramatic—they "take flight" spiritually from the temptations and disillusionments of earth to seek, in sacrifice, their fruition of possible happiness. (pp. 23-5)

After the Franco-Prussian War, which was a great strain upon the physical and spiritual endurance of the poet, Sully-Prudhomme wrote *Impressions* that awakened political discussion and revealed his pervasive idealism. *Essays upon the Fine Arts, The Art of Versification* and *Le testament poétique* were expressions of his poetic studies and theories. On the other hand, *Que sais-je?* which appeared in 1896 was another index to his scientific inquiries into natural science, philosophy, and metaphysics. A commentator upon these queries, well entitled *What Do I Know?,* has said that his last words might be summarized as "peut-être" ["perhaps"]. Doubts, yet never bitterness of despair, characterize his speculative poetry. Four years after he received the Nobel prize and two years before his death, at the age of sixty-six, he wrote *La vraie religion selon Pascal,* a last record of his profound search for spiritual values in life and literature. (pp. 27-8)

> Annie Russell Marble, in "Poets of France and Provence," *in her* The Nobel Prize Winners in Literature, *D. Appleton and Company, 1925, pp. 21-41.*

MAX I. BAYM (essay date 1971)

[*A Lithuanian-born American poet, critic, and literary historian, Baym is the author of* A History of Literary Aesthetics in America (1973) *and* Let These Symbols Speak (1974). *He has written: "I am essentially a historian of ideas, with interdisciplinary orientation. My work in literary aesthetics has aimed to emphasize a monism which regards knowledge and sensibility as correlative aspects of the human spirit." In the following excerpt, he analyzes Sully Prudhomme's effort to establish unity between poetry, philosophy, and science.*]

The history of ideas reveals a tendency to propose man's nature as a central problem in the universe, and with this an implicit drive for Monism. This propensity has always been marked by a preoccupation with psychology; and we find a particular illustration of this fact in Sully Prudhomme whose *Journal intime* bristles with the subject long before it became a heavy assembly-line industry or, to use Wallace Stevens's phrase, "a mechanical and slightly detestable operandum.'' Intrigued by the hidden nexus between mind and the world it contemplates (psychology and physics), the young Prudhomme joined others in their passionate effort (as Whitehead has said somewhere) of ''piercing the blindness of activity in respect to its transcendental functions.'' In such a quest metaphysics was inescapable. To save himself from the feeling that alongside of the great ventures of science poetry was a puerile activity, he had to conceive of aesthetic experience as an integral part of ontology; and he also had to regard poetic expression as a means of easing the metaphysical malaise which accompanied the drive for a monistic view of mind and cosmos.

His *Journal intime,* better than any other document, affords us an insight into Prudhomme's inner chaos during his formative period. But as poet, he incorporates his spiritual and intellectual conflicts in lyrical symbols in which the adjective ''brisé'' occurs prominently. The fact that the poem **''Le vase brisé''** has, through wanton use, become a machine for the exudation of sentimentality, in no way obscures the psychodynamic factors which it re-represents: Eros, Alienation, Impotence *(Son eau fraîche a fui goutte à goutte)* [''Its fresh water has leaked out drop by drop''], and Death. In this chain of psychic events, thought or memory is, of course, present. But we recall with Freud that there is no thought without cathexis. The image or memory of gratification is always in the background, if indeed it is not in the very heart of thought. Another poem which is closely associated with the Broken Vase, through the common expression of fragmentation, is **''Le nid brisé.''** In the latter poem, the motherbird ventures away from her little ones to procure some food; but on returning, she finds a broken nest with a number of the fledglings—so many naissant ideas, you see, in aspirational flight—lying inert, with wings broken, some dead, some still breathing.—*Elle reviendra. . . .* Quel retour! [*''She had returned. . . .* What a homecoming!'']—All this is obviously related to the Broken Vase symbolism to which we shall return later.

The Journal makes clear the poet's vacillations. He asks himself: Am I a poet;—am I a philosopher? He thanks God for not having mutilated him in making him exclusively the one or the other. Philosophy, he says, enables him ''to plunge into vertiginous depths and poetry to feel there the horror of the infinite and the admiration for living nature.'' He takes flight, however, from metaphysical uncertainty to the algebra of series in order to enjoy certainty, as he says, and health of mind. It is as if he were applying a poultice to his soul when he asserts, ''However, I am happy with my psychologic meditation; there is no contradiction in man.'' Certainly, he knew better than that, as so many reflections in his journal show.

There was no escape from the fact that man's finite mind was impelled to dwell on its own most awesome creation, the infinite, in which (as William James has told us) man is not at home. For the poet, the concept of the infinite—and its source—is obviously of paramount importance; for it is this concept which is intimately associated with transcendence and universality by dint of which the imagination is validated as a binding and plastic force in the cauldron of multiplicity and the atomization of knowledge and experience. Yet the concept of the infinite is frightening and requires the counterbalacing effect of a ''living presence.'' Hence Prudhomme's ''admiration for living nature.'' The tension we witness here is an aspect of the continuing strife between the Romantic Imagination and Science.

We cannot agree with Zyromski that Prudhomme freed himself easily from the romantic spirit. If that spirit be defined by the intimate connection between poetic expression and personality, then our poet was never utterly divorced from the romantic frame of mind. His philosophic ardor is a direct indication of a desire to realize within himself the world as one. This is a form of anthropocentricity which Zyromski ascribes to the romantics from whose midst he would exclude Prudhomme. The latter's *analyse émue* relates him to Novalis whose interest in science and mathematics is commonly known. Did not Sully Prudhomme himself say that ''Romanticism is, at bottom, an insurrection against the boring style, the only evil according to Voltaire''? Of course, like Poe, he believes that the highest flights cannot—precisely because of their elevation—be sustained too long. The one error the poet must guard against is the notion that elevation can be sustained through sheer declamation. Again he must avoid this in order to avoid boredom.

Furthermore, if inspiration and intuition are aspects of the Romantic movement, then our poet is certainly part of it. For what is his cult of *aspiration* if not first cousin to *inspiration?* In his doctrine of the alliance of intuition and research—a truly romantic idea—he joins the great mathematicians of the nineteenth century and relates himself to Schelling (a forerunner of Bergson and Freud). The latter, as we know, emphasized the creative power of intuition and the role of the unconscious as a force that can reveal what philosophy cannot,—the original unity which eludes us in nature and in history. Prudhomme also joins Kant who held that it was impossible to draw an absolute distinction between the imagination and the understanding, because the two are continuous. Accordingly, we agree with Zyromski when he says that for Sully Prudhomme poetry is the art of interesting the heart in the problems of thought; but we must add to this the poet's own statement, ''Poetry is the universe put to music by the heart'' (*La poésie c'est l'universe mis en musique par le coeur*).

We return to the problem of the infinite. The so-called secular error (to which Zyromski refers) of confounding the hunger for the infinite with insatiable desire, may not be an error at all from the point of view of instinctual drive. Prudhomme himself asks a question which he answers only in part:—''Why does Descartes insist that man not look within himself for the idea of the infinite?'' The reply, we believe, may be found in the historic circumstance that the seventeenth-century orientation was a physico-mathematical one instead of psycho-biological, as was becoming the case more and more in the nineteenth century. The poet does argue that it is precisely because of man's limitations that he is led to imagine that which he does not possess;—a proof that he can derive from his own nature the idea of the infinite. He does, in fact, conceive of its existence without precisely comprehending its extent. And this imperfect intelligence of the infinite is proof enough for Prudhomme that man has it within himself. In our present terms, then, the poet would relate the conception of the infinite to the subconscious. The quest for the infinite is an adventure in depth.

In **''La pensée,''** the flower which is about to open is the symbol of nascent thought. Here again Zyromski sees an instance where our poet differs from the Romantics who looked at nature passionately because it mirrored them. The argument is that Prudhomme, by contrast, detaches himself from himself in order to belong entirely to the flower, which presumably symbolizes his thought.

> Elle voulait s'ouvrir
> Et moi je me sentais mourir;
> Toute ma vie allait en elle.

["She wanted to open
And I felt myself dying;
All my life was going into her"]

As we see it, the poet is enunciating the primal truth that the creative process is like the love-making sexual process—a passion which is the source of life and at the same time the kiss of death; life for that which is about to be generated and death for the generator. The creator dies unto himself and survives in what he creates. The consciousness of that fact, even by way of shadowy intimation, brings a sense of panic experienced as pain and fear, as anxiety. Actually, we have here an early instance of what we find later in Ponge,—the projection of existentialist tension unto the realm of things. We mentioned earlier Sully's admiration for living nature. But as a student of Lucretius, he feared it while loving it. And like many of the Romantics, far from possessing the *aequanimitas* of Spinoza, he—as a critical reader of that philosopher—was torn between *natura naturata* and *natura naturans;* or, as Muirhead puts it, between Nature as a dead mechanism and Nature as a force related to the creative spirit of man.

On the question of Prudhomme's separation from the Romantics, then, we may make this summary remark: However much he might have tried to eliminate the *lament* of Lamartine, the violin sobbing of Musset, the oratorical recitative of Hugo, he never freed himself from those sensibilities which are associated with romanticism and which remain persistent aspects of the human spirit:—the hunger for the infinite, the simultaneous fear and love of nature, and the desire to transcend the tumult of opposites in one's own mind and soul (the quest for Unity).

It is high time to realize that the sentimental phase of Romanticism does not correctly define all of it; just as the time is ripe to understand that the cult of the impersonal is not the invention of the Parnassians. Taking Shakespeare as the great exemplar—the model and source of so much romantic poetry—Keats had already spoken, in one of his letters, of the *impersonality* ("it has no self") of the true poet. Prudhomme did well to free himself from his Parnassian friends. No philosopher-poet can remain satisfied with the idea that a poem is composed of words only and that it has fulfilled its highest function in mere representation. We grant that at times Sully Prudhomme's philosophic scruples overpower his poetic sensibility; then his speech, while still important in content, is without the wingedness of music. His imagination is energized by the flight of his own thought in infinite space among the populous stars. This affords him a *frisson esthétique* ["aesthetic thrill"]. At the same time he admires "the intuition of Shakespeare when, in a word, he reveals to us the secret recesses of the heart." But, he adds, "if the heart is an abyss, Heaven is another, and the finger of Le Verrier pointing in the sky, on the strength of his own calculations, to the precise place of an unknown planet, fills me with a sublime astonishment which no less stirs the poet within me."

It does not make sense to say (as Zyromski does) that Prudhomme added Truth to Poetry. If poetry is a lie, why should adults ever pay any attention to it? It is not that the poet preferred the anguish of research and scientific quest to the enchantment of art; it is rather that he moved in a realm where thought was melodied by poetry and poetry was substantiated by knowledge. He moved towards something at once speculative and emotional, namely, metaphysics. "Metaphysics," he said, "is a speculative and emotional thing."

When Sully Prudhomme returns to the subject of the infinite, our attention is drawn again to the symbol of the *vase*. He tells us that the philosophers seemed to consider the spirit or the mind as a vase with limited capacity. According to "the axiom that the container ought to be greater than the contained,—the finite understanding of man cannot embrace the infinite." If the mind, however, cannot contain the infinite as a concretion, it can do so as a metaphor or enter its domain on the wings of music. When we combine Prudhomme's philosophy of aspiration with the musicality which he ascribes to all transformations that the spirit of man can effect, we become aware of his inner *conatus* at once to preserve the integrity of the *vase* and to transcend its limitations. As Sully Prudhomme puts it, "L'homme conçut alors que l'esprit porte une aile / Qui devance tourjours lex yeux." ["Man understands in the flight of the spirit / Which always goes before the eyes"]. The principle of musicality, in the poet's estimation, vouchsafes an intimate connection between sensations and feelings, which are related to intuitive knowledge.

Clearly, in keeping with a general tendency in the nineteenth century, Prudhomme was preoccupied with the linkage of ideas and with the inherent dialectic of thought itself. He asserts, for instance, that two contrary and disparate thoughts could be reconciled by an intermediate idea. Ultimately, his dialectic has as its background the aesthetic realm where physics and psychology coalesce within the aesthetic experience. "For me," he writes, "aesthetics is an integral part of ontology. . . ." From a careful reading of his **Journal intime** one may gather the catenation of his ideas: psychology—a concern with the operations of the mind and the heart; music—the aesthetic notion of pure sensibility unencumbered by facts and details; the poetry-science tension—a variation on the Pascalian *esprit de finesse—esprit de géométrie* polarity; the inevitability of Metaphysics; the overall question of the need to overcome the incommensurability of thought, feeling, and language. The *enchaînement des idées* ["association of ideas"] also receives some attention in his thinking on **Final Causes**. There he indicates the fundamentally substantial identity of the physical and the psychologic. He arrives at this connection through his study of the phenomenon of expression, in which he finds that movements of the body and movements of the soul are two aspects of the same activity.

Do what he will, conflict was raging within him,—a conflict between intuition which affirmed and deduction which denied. Since for him the aesthetic was an integral part of ontology, he was under compulsion to find a definition of the Beautiful. To accomplish this, he found that his quest would take him among the manifestations of necessary Being, the substratum and principle of all constitutive forms of organic life and the expression of the psychic life. "Is it possible," he asked hopelessly, "that necessity can engender the superior ideal, the music of Beethoven, for example?" Or that "the position and value of a word be fatalistically prefixed, like the position and mass of a star?" It strikes us that the poet was lost in the penumbra of Spinoza and was frightened by the aspect of determinism even as William James was, though both were scientists and poets enough to have been impressed by the philosopher's metaphor of a stone being asked, in the course of describing a certain trajectory, whether it was its will to travel in that path.

Prudhomme ponders the elements of his conflict. "On the one hand, there is the satisfaction afforded to my understanding by the fundamental concept of metaphysics, the idea of necessary Being from which are logically derived the ideas of the Eternal, the Absolute, the Infinite. On the other hand, there is the inexpressible delight engendered by lofty music, by a musical phrase unaccompanied by any word, but which nevertheless speaks to man and transports him into an indescribable beyond.'' These two moral states—the one confining, the other liberating—represented the opposite poles of his psychic life. "You can imagine," he says, "what an abyss I had to cross to go from one to the other. The aesthetic delight is not purely passive: it is an enthusiasm which makes one *aspire* towards an ideal;—it is, in short, a flight *(essor).* A hopeless flight, alas!—but all the more active for its being restricted, like the energy furnished by transformed heat in a locomotive ready to start, which is the more intense the more it encounters resistance in the closed boiler.'' He realizes that his metaphor spells out *mechanical necessity,* whereas he likes to think of his mental activity or potential as free. Petulantly, he concludes: "Well, right or wrong, I believe myself free because I feel free.'' But he does feel trapped, as he goes on to remark: "Here I am, then, obliged—for better or worse—to explain the existence of Free Will in the chain of events engendered by necessary Being,—the unique origin of the universal process. . . . I feel that moral value cannot be reduced to values measured by the dynamometer. . . . Free Will is the foundation of such value, even if Free Will is presented to me as absurd by my own reasoning.'' Thus we see that the conflict within him was pervasive. He seemed to be caught in a sort of existentialist crisis with its attendant hysteria which he tried to shake off in his writing. He had turned to Plato and found the "Philebus'' especially striking, since the question of happiness was posed there in a masterful way. This fact has been overlooked by writers on Prudhomme. In his reading of this dialogue we have the crux of the whole matter: the seesawing of a sensitive spirit between γενεσις ("process of becoming''), which pleasure is, and ουσια, stable, determinate being or "natural state.'' In the "Philebus,'' the metaphysics of pleasure is involved in the problem of intellectual value.

We see him torn, in 1876, between poetry and science, still characterizing the latter as the highest *materia poetica.* "One must be completely puerile to place poetry above science. That is hardly worth discussing, especially when one considers that science opens horizons essentially poetic.'' Yet, he declares (in a manner reminiscent of Pascal whom he admired): "The heart is an instrument of knowledge whose instructions ought to be considered as of the same value as those of reason, although intuitions be irreducible to those of reason.'' At the same time he finds in philosophy the plastic means of imposing form on that which has been fragmented by scientific analysis. Whereas the sciences deal with parts, philosophy deals with the whole. In this respect, it is closer to poetry than to science. But in so far as philosophy courts system and intelligibility, it partakes of the nature of science while bringing poetry into it. Prudhomme might have found comfort in Emerson (whose work was highly appreciated in France) when the latter declared: "The Universe is the externization of the soul. . . . Therefore science always goes abreast with the just elevation of man, therefore keeping step with religion and metaphysics; or, the state of science is an index of our self-knowledge. . . . *The world being thus put under the mind for verb and noun, the poet is he who can articulate it.''* As one who was under

pain to give semantic unity to the syntax of the sentence called the world, Prudhomme certainly was "the poet.''

If we grant with Sully Prudhomme that the genesis of rational categories finds its poetic expression in metaphysics, then poetry becomes a fundamental statement which embraces the relationship of subject and object, and, as such, a *scientia universalis.* Whereas ontologic inanity may be crouching in metaphysics *tout court,* on the wings of poetry there is at least the reality of mobility as undeniable as the motion of wind upon water. The poet as metaphysician looks at the broken vase as a fragmentation of the whole which begs to be restored,—and that in the interest of aesthetic wholeness. (pp. 29-37)

Max I. Baym, "On Mending the Broken Vase: Sully Prudhomme's Aspiration to a Unifying Aesthetic," in The French Review, *Vol. XLIV, No. 2, December, 1971, pp. 29-37.*

ADDITIONAL BIBLIOGRAPHY

France, Anatole. "Three Poets: Sully-Prudhomme—François Copée—Frédéric Plessis.'' In his *On Life & Letters,* first series, translated by A. W. Evans, pp. 134-45. London: Dodd, Mead and Co., 1911.
> Praises the nobility and sincerity of Sully Prudhomme's poetry and predicts that *Le bonheur* will be more popular than *La justice* because of the greater appeal of its subject.

Grierson, Francis. "Sully Prudhomme and the French Academy.'' In his *Parisian Portraits,* pp. 66-80. London: John Lane, The Bodley Head, 1913.
> Biographical sketch by an acquaintance, focusing on Sully Prudhomme's membership in the Academie française.

May, James Lewis. *Anatole France: The Man and His Work,* p. 75. Port Washington, N.Y.: Kennikat Press, 1924.
> Reprints the following sketch of Sully Prudhomme by France: "Sully Prudhomme. 36. Former student of the Ecole Polytechnique. Has remained mathematical and geometrical even in his sonnets. Given to love-making and algebra. Solves problems of passion by means of equations. Intellectual and profound, but losing his bloom. Has suffered from ill-health. Rich and handsome. Finds life a bore.''

Roz, Firmin. "Sully-Prudhomme.'' In *Library of the World's Best Literature,* Vol. XXIV, edited by Charles Dudley Warner, pp. 14209-211. New York: J. A. Hill & Co., 1896.
> Brief biographical and critical sketch. Maintaining that *La justice* and *Le bonheur* contain "incomparable beauties, truly new,'' Roz writes that "never has philosophic poetry been more rigorous, while retaining more of beauty; never has the fusion been so close between the thought, the sentiment, and the image.''

Thieme, Hugo Paul. *The Technique of the French Alexandrine: A Study of the Works of Leconte de Lisle, Jose Maria de Heredia, François Coppée, Sully Prudhomme, and Paul Verlaine.* Ann Arbor: Inland Press, 1897, 68 p.
> Technical analysis demonstrating to what extent the poets studied adhered to the principles of versification practiced by the Classical, Romantic, Parnassian, and Symbolist schools of poetry.

Federigo Tozzi

1883-1920

Italian novelist, short story writer, poet, critic, and dramatist.

Tozzi is considered one of the most distinctive Italian novelists of the early twentieth century. In contrast to the elegant diction and aesthetic formalism that characterized much Italian literature of his time, Tozzi wrote in colloquial language and disregarded formal narrative structure, an approach which he found best suited the rendering of lower-class life in his native Tuscany. Most of Tozzi's works are based on episodes from his emotionally troubled youth and express an anguished, nihilistic sensibility which has been compared to that conveyed by the writings of Franz Kafka and Luigi Pirandello.

Tozzi was born in Siena, a provincial capital in central Italy. His father, an illiterate peasant who had earned respectability as a restaurant owner, subjected his son to physical and emotional abuse. After Tozzi's mother died when he was twelve, this mistreatment by his father worsened. Biographers have concluded that it was because of the traumatic conditions of his early life that Tozzi suffered from chronic anxiety and other psychological problems. He was expelled from several schools because of his disruptive behavior and refusal to study; with difficulty, he managed to earn a degree from a technical academy. Despite his limited educational background and habitual self-denigration, Tozzi believed in his own intellectual gifts, and resolved to become a writer. In 1907, he went to Rome in an attempt to establish his independence from his father, but was soon forced to return to Siena after failing to find work. The next year, he left home again to take a job as a railway clerk, only to be recalled a few months later when his father died. Inheriting his father's restaurant business and two farms, Tozzi now had the financial security that enabled him to marry his fiancée, Emma Palagi, and biographers credit their marriage with greatly improving his emotional stability. He divided his time between Siena and their apartment in Rome, managing his properties, writing fiction and poetry, and pursuing other literary endeavors such as co-editing the short-lived journal *Torre*. As a writer, Tozzi remained relatively obscure until 1917, when the critic Guiseppe Borgese arranged for a major publisher to bring out a collection of his short stories, *Bestie*. This work, which earned few but positive notices, inaugurated a period in which Tozzi produced a number of works including fiction, plays, and criticism. When he died of pneumonia in 1920 at the age of 37, he had completed, or was in the process of completing, several novels which were later released to considerable acclaim.

Tozzi's first published works, *La zampogna verde* and *La città delle Vergine*, comprise poetry written in the elegant manner of Gabriele D'Annunzio. In subsequent works of poetry and prose, however, Tozzi strove to adapt his style to his subject—life in rural Tuscany—by ignoring traditional rules of composition and writing in a rough, plain idiom meant to mirror the local dialect. Critics have often compared him to such Italian Naturalists as Giovanni Verga for his starkly realistic portrayals of country life and his use of colloquial Italian rather than formal literary language. Although Tozzi admired Verga and other Naturalists, he did not adhere to their view of life as a set of processes understandable by scientific theories.

Tozzi saw existence as a random succession of meaningless events, with all living beings at the mercy of malevolent, destructive forces. While the Naturalists cultivated objectivity, Tozzi indulged in unrestrained expression of his deepest emotions. He developed a deliberately unstructured, often awkward prose style that alienated many readers, as did the neurotic, self-centered attitude behind his writings. The collection *Bestie* is representative of his pessimistic worldview, with the cruelty inflicted on helpless animals in such stories in "Ozio" and "Il ciuchino" symbolizing the fate humanity is subject to in an unjust universe. This analogy between humans and suffering beasts is also a recurrent motif in Tozzi's novels.

Commentators have compared Tozzi to Kafka, noting their mutual predilection for creating fictional surrogates to embody their feelings of personal inadequacy. The anti-heroes of Tozzi's fiction, usually thinly disguised portraits of his younger self, are frustrated misfits who are unable to achieve satisfaction in work or in love. Four novels in particular contain such self-abasing, semi-autobiographical portraits. *Con gli occhi chuisi*, for instance, bitterly recounts his worshipful infatuation with a young peasant woman and his disillusionment when he discovered she was pregnant by another man. *Ricordi di un impiegato (Journal of a Clerk)* uses the months he spent employed as a railway clerk as the basis for a dreary, Kafkaesque depiction of alienation. *Il podere* draws upon the problems he experienced in managing his father's estate, enlarging them to tragic proportions. The novel's protagonist ruins his property through incompetence, fights a losing battle with creditors, and is finally murdered by a disgruntled farmhand. *Gli egoisti*, a novel left unfinished at Tozzi's death, focuses on a character who, like the young Tozzi, failed dispiritingly in his first attempt to escape provincial life by establishing himself as an artist in Rome.

Tozzi died just as he was reaching what appeared to many critics to be the most fruitful period in his career, turning from self-contemplation to a more objective authorial viewpoint. This stylistic maturation, evident in *Gli egoisti*, had fully emerged in his last complete novel, *Tre croci (Three Crosses)*. Rather than drawing directly from his own experience, he based the novel on a news item about three brothers who committed forgery in order to save their bankrupt family business. Tozzi told the story of the crime by presenting a detailed psychological profile of each brother, revealing the stupidity, greed, and ineptitude that led to their self-destructive actions.

Most English-language criticism on Tozzi focuses on his novels and, to a lesser degree, the stories in *Bestie*, while his poetry and plays are regarded as relatively inconsequential. Excepting the support of Borgese and a few others, Tozzi received little appreciation from critics during his lifetime. His reputation was established after the release of his last novels, however, and reaffirmed in the period following World War II, when he became a significant influence on the Italian Neorealists. As a seminal figure of the Modernist period, he has been cited as an inspiration by such contemporary Italian writers as Alberto Moravia.

PRINCIPAL WORKS

La zampogna verde (poetry) 1911
La città della Vergine (poem) 1913
Bestie (short stories) 1917
Con gli occhi chiusi (novel) 1919
L'amore (short stories) 1920
Ricordi di un impiegato (novel) 1920
  [*Journal of a Clerk,* 1964]
Tre croci (novel) 1920
  [*Three Crosses,* 1921]
Il podere (novel) 1921
Gli egoisti (unfinished novel) 1923
L'incalco (drama) 1923
Novale (letters) 1925
Realtà di ieri e di oggi (criticism) 1928
Opere. 5 vols. (novels, short stories, drama, and poetry)
  1961-81

THE TIMES LITERARY SUPPLEMENT (essay date 1920)

[*In the following excerpt, the critic reviews* Con gli occhi chiusi *and* Tre croci.]

Last March, a citizen of Siena, a humble railway official, arrived in Rome with a bag stuffed full of manuscripts and proofs, and his head still more crowded with far-reaching ideas. Men like Borgese, Papini, Prezzolini, Tonelli, and other notable writers had already recognized his value, and rejoiced that his books, too big to win the public at the first appearance of their "dolce stil' nuovo," had found an appreciative publisher. When the young novelist died that very month of Spanish fever in a back street in Rome, just as Fame stood on his threshold, Borgese wrote in *I Libri del Giorno* that "the greatest force which had hitherto sprung up out of the rough tangle of modern literature in Italy was spent." He wept because Federigo Tozzi was dead. And people asked, and perhaps still ask, "Who is Federigo Tozzi?"

The general lamentation by other writers at this loss to literature is chiefly caused by the limitless possibilities they saw in the work of Tozzi, who in three books, written within three years— *Bestie,* made up of brilliant fragments; *Con gli occhi chiusi,* mainly autobiographical; and *Tre croci,* a masterpiece—developed an individual art with astonishing rapidity and an ever-increasing depth of feeling and understanding. There is a natural inclination to pigeon-hole Tozzi as an Italian Balzac or Tchehof; and it is, perhaps, idle to speculate what ultimately he would have done with his great gifts; but this much is certain—that Italy has lost a man who could have altered the course of novel-writing for those who had the wit to follow him. He was driven to utterance as the traveller to the wayside fountain; and instinctively he knew that some day he would write a book quite different from anything which he had read. In his novel *Con gli occhi chiusi* he was feeling his way; and much strength and pure beauty are shown in the delineation of character, together with knowledge of emotion in the study of the chaste yet ardent lover Pietro, who is captivated by Ghisolda, the peasant girl, so full of naïve witchery and animal spirits. He loves her "con gli occhi chiusi" ["with closed eyes"] until disillusionment opens his eyes. Although in human interest and as a picture of Italian farm life the book gains from being autobiographical, it loses as a work of art in unity and detachment.

It is in *Tre croci* that we must look for the real Tozzi; for out of it something strange and beautiful would have grown. Here, defying convention and popular taste, he writes a novel without a love story, without an unnecessary adjective, and practically without a plot. He expects us to take an interest in the sordid lives of three greedy and gouty brothers, who in order to keep their bookshop going forge on a bill of exchange the name of a friend who has already lent them a considerable sum. They await inevitable disaster while they talk of food, as only the Latin can do with success, buy false antiques, and discuss Sienese pictures with a French art critic who comes to buy Berenson's latest article in the *Burlington*. At first we are outraged; but as the book unfolds a tale of human frailty and sorrow, with the mystical gospel of atonement, and the truth so clearly shown that human sorrow cannot be thrown into the scale of social progress, we are drawn within the magic circle of the old Sienese bookshop, and we look with pity on the shipwreck of lives.

"An Italian Master," in The Times Literary Supplement, *No. 966, July 22, 1920, p. 468.*

MARIO PRAZ (essay date 1920)

[*A noted art and literary critic, Praz is remembered as an authority on the baroque and romantic periods, a reviewer of English and American fiction, and the author of* La carne, la morte e il diavolo nella letteratura romantica *(1930;* The Romantic Agony*), a pioneering study of the macabre in Romantic literature, art, and music. In the following excerpt from a letter written to the* London Mercury *in December 1920, he describes the characteristic style and themes of Tozzi's fiction.*]

Among the Italian writers of to-day an eminent position is held by the Tuscans, men who have in common not so much that country as a particular quality which, though it recurs among them with various degrees of intensity, differentiates them as a body from other Italian authors.

When one wishes to define this Tuscan spirit one thinks back to Dante's *Inferno*; to some of the old anonymous lyrics—for example, the song which begins, "Cosi nel mio parlar voglio esser aspro"; to Michelangelo's *Last Judgment*, and his poems whose hardness, intractability, and despair are already the expression of a spirit more modern, more tormented than Dante's; to the disdainful, cruel, mocking, and gloomy breed which produced a Filippo Argenti, a Vanni Fucci, and a Cecco Angiolieri.

This Tuscan spirit I speak of is quite different from that of a Boccaccio or a Politian, authors more superficial, more bourgeois, whose ornate and redundant style of writing (which is the Saxon for literature) gives the whole world ready access to them. Nor is it the Tuscany that Leigh Hunt saw, that Keats imagined, a suburban Arcadia echoing with song and dance in sunny vineyards. It is another Tuscany—profounder, rougher, less cultivated, one whose secret it is more difficult to penetrate.

One has glimpses of this Tuscany in the works of Ardengo Soffici. It is the motive of many of Giovanni Papini's pages, especially in *Uomo finito*. But Soffici lived long in Paris, and Papini is a man of enormous reading, so that a certain bookishness has permeated their primitiveness.

It is not, therefore, surprising that the characteristic appears more clearly in Federigo Tozzi, who has lived entirely at his birthplace, Siena, an old provincial capital which obstinately retains its mediæval character in its quaint streets, steep twisting, grassgrown, almost without passengers; in its huge lonely churches, lit only by the sad smile of some Madonna standing out above an altar from her background of a heaven of faded gold. Siena, which seems built for war and civil strife, whose strong bastions, with their bare towers, never look more beautiful than when beneath a springtime sky dark with rainclouds.

Federigo Tozzi is, in truth, a fellow-citizen of the thirteenth-century poet, Cecco Angiolieri, who poured hatred on his own parents, addressed insulting poems to Dante, and composed that famous expression of inhumanity, the sonnet "S'io fosse foco arderei lo mondo"—"Were I a fire, I'd burn the world." Tozzi revived the ages of war and mysticism in one of his first works—the poem in fourteeners called *La città della Vergine* (that is to say, Siena, which is under her protection), a curiosity, written in thirteenth-century language recalling to mind both by subject and manner d'Annunzio's poems on *Città del silenzio*—cities of silence; especially that one on Perugia. But such barren archaism could not finally satisfy a modern man like Tozzi; and the poem remained an isolated attempt, a written proof of the strong fascination exercised on the author's mind by his country and his race.

In the works that followed, in the form of diaries, novels, short stories, Tozzi has recounted passages in his life and laid bare his bizarre and solitary spirit,

> Growing up in the still shadows of Siena, apart, without friendships, cheated every time it has tried to be understood.

His sad pages are truly dominated by the shadow of the masculine and naked towers of Siena. He has tried in a natural and perfect form what Georges Rodenbach tried in his novel *Bruges la morte,* to express the unseen presence of the spirit of the place in the thoughts and actions of his characters. But Rodenbach's novel suffers from an æstheticism entirely absent from the pages of Tozzi, who does not introduce the city in order to form a background with its immortal monuments and works of art like the Venice of d'Annunzio's *Fuoco.* But the crookedness of the Sienese streets, the houses one above the other, supported as if miraculously, clinging to precipitous cliffs, represent the author's attitude and express his feeling of vertigo before the spectacle of human life; the gloomy and claustral walls seem made of his own invincibly obstinate egoism; and the open spaces where the sun is as "ineffectual as water in a well" are symbols of the despair in the author's heart.

When confronted by other people Tozzi falls into a condition which one might call "moral vertigo." He finds it absolutely impossible to escape from the closed circle of his egoism, and sympathise with men's love and suffering. But he is not a self-satisfied egoist, contented with the world of his own sensations. He fully knows his terrible isolation; he feels the gulf that surrounds him; he is fascinated by the abyss and cannot withdraw his gaze from it. The spectacle of a suffering animal compels his attention, but he feels no pity for it, only sorrow sharpened by his inability to be moved by it. His condition is like that of Coleridge's Ancient Mariner, the curse is never lifted from his head. For example, it amuses him in *Bestie* to tell of some toads which he saw die martyred by peasants; not to describe their death with a realist's flat adherence to details

of every sort, whether beautiful or disgusting, but only to reproduce the scene.

And these pictures of his are more than the mere exhalation of confused sensuality which d'Annunzio throws off in many of his *Novelle della Pescara.* Tozzi's circumstances serve above all to exacerbate his loneliness, to make him feel more vividly the impossibility of sympathy, knowledge of which makes him pessimistic and miserable. It almost gives him bitter pleasure to see himself and others suffer. Thus his temperament is violently masculine; it is not content with vague melancholy, but becomes almost exalted by torturing itself. He has in him the making of a mystic, an ascetic. He is a true son of that Siena where, as Maurice Barrès says there are

> Peu de nuances, des couleurs fortes et quelque chose de l'âpre sensualisme dont l'Espagne est exaspérée.
>
> ["Few nuances, strong colors and something of the coarse sensualism with which Spain is exasperated."]

The characters in Tozzi's stories and novels are seen through this veil of terrible sorrow. Sons hate their fathers, brothers torture each other; husbands storm against their wives. Love, when there is any, brings with it the odour of death. The author describes in a pungent, blunt, and unpitying style the decay of families, the downfall of illusions, the turbulent passions of rough men, the melancholy that afflicts the more refined.

In this sort Tozzi has discovered how to make a masterpiece— his romance *Tre croci.* From this book the motive of love is entirely absent. Its argument is so simple that one can relate it in a few words.

There are in Siena three brothers called Gambi, who own an antiquity shop. Their business is falling away, and they have recourse to their friendship with a gentleman called Nicchioli, who consents to give them a bill of exchange. But this help is not enough, and Giulio, in agreement with the others, forges the signature of the guarantor and obtains a further loan from the bank. In the end the swindle is found out, and Giulio, who was guilty of it, hangs himself.

The plot is no more than this. But the book does not end with this tragedy. Tozzi knows that there is drama more profound and more afflicting than there is in any action concluded by a single deed of violence; namely, the drama of the gradual downfall of an individual, the progressive decay of a family, proceeding day by day amid the monotony of ordinary life. The suicide of Giulio is one of those actions that stir the crowd, but more tragical perhaps are the deaths of Niccolò and Enrico which, at a short interval, follow their brother's—one through overwork at his new business (after the bankruptcy he became an insurance agent), the other in the poorhouse, where he had taken refuge after months of drunkenness and mendicity. Niccolò's wife and his two nephews place three crosses of rough wood exactly alike on the brothers' graves, and with this act of pity the story ends.

The impression that this book leaves on one is as extremely powerful as the means employed to that end are simple. The Sienese author does not indulge in that subtle and frequent psychological analysis characteristic of the novels of the last ten years, but destructive of verisimilitude. In reality, our novel-writers have one and all brought the Psychological Novel to such a pitch that the palate is cloyed and exasperated by it, and a writer to-day who resolves to write a novel has only two possible courses: to use irony or to return to simplicity. Tozzi has chosen the latter. He draws his characters with the strength and certainty that reveal the great artist. They are often types of simple men like Niccolò or downright rude figures like Enrico; and even when they are more refined like Giulio their outlines are very firm.

But Tozzi is not one of those purely intellectual writers whom it amuses to consider the soul as a nest of boxes one inside the other, of which the insidemost contains nothing at all. His art has no commerce with what is fictitious, rhetorical, artificial—in a word, with all that is connoted by the word Literature in its worst sense.

Just as his Siena is no museum, set down in his novel merely to give it a connective theme, but a living creature, a sort of Greek Tragedy chorus that comments even by its silence on the actions and thoughts of the characters, even so are the characters themselves not wise and inhuman marionettes, but they are the men whom we meet everyday, and in this novel they are consecrated by art, we see in them what is eternal. We hear them in their brief conversations, speaking the language of everyday; we see them engaged in actions that are often trivial and seemingly insignificant (one must remember that in a sense one is reading in the story the author's own experiences), and yet from this background of vigorous simplicity the characters stand out as clear-cut and powerful as those towers of the Sienese land, which seem, in their hard angles and clean mouldings, to belong to an order above ours, to partake of immortality.

Tozzi's work is not to be mistaken for that of anyone else. His artistic method, already shown in *Bestie* in outline, had attained, in *Tre croci*, a very lofty expression; but even in his less successful works, like the novel *Con gli occhi chiusi* and in some volumes of short stories (*L'amore, Giovani*), he reveals the indisputable traces of a great writer. (pp. 321-23)

> Mario Praz, "A Letter from Italy," in The London
> Mercury, Vol. III, No. 15, January, 1921, pp. 321-23.

DOMENICO VITTORINI (essay date 1930)

[*Vittorini is an Italian-born American critic and biographer. In the following excerpt, he surveys Tozzi's novels.*]

As an artist, Tozzi makes one think of the old Sienese masters, woodcarvers or painters, who in the almost complete absence of technique are capable of conveying a strong impression of life. Tozzi has kept in his art the strength and simplicity of these ancestors who like him lived in the silent, austere and mediaeval city which is conducive to concentration and mysticism. (p. 211)

His art is, in general, gray and static. There is in it a fixity which can be explained only by the author's constant autoanalysis and by his feeling as if he were a ghost among real men, mostly of the peasant class, to whom he lends, by way of contrast, a granite hardness and well-defined contour. Occasionally a gentle note softens the cold melancholy which permeates his novels. It is the remembrance of his mother's quiet resignation and of the patient and intelligent devotion of his young wife.

Tozzi's first book was *Bestie* (*Beasts*), 1917, a kind of diary in which, day by day, drop by drop, he distills the gray monotony of his life in Siena. It is written in lyric prose and in an extremely personal tone, as Tozzi's dissatisfaction with his

life has not yet taken a concrete form in the character of a novel.

In *Con gli occhi chiusi* (*Blindfolded*), 1919, he lends his bitter loneliness to Pietro Rosi, a vacillating and misunderstood youth who lives in the country near Siena in his father's inn. There, among the girls who work on his father's farm, he meets Ghisola, a peasant girl.

Ghisola is instinctive to the point of being unmoral, and Tozzi in so presenting her breaks away from the usual theme that considers a woman the destruction of the hero's mysticism. He does not take sides either with the weak or against the strong. He does not judge. He merely observes what happens and from the day that Ghisola with a knitting-needle pricks the hand of Pietro, who was then a child, to the day that she tells him that she expects to become a mother, she is presented purely as a passive creature of instinct. As an instinctive being she is perfectly drawn, contrasted as she is with Pietro's sensitive nature.

Pietro, struggling against the primitive Ghisola and the Sienese peasants, suffers unspeakably. Lost in the haze of a platonic aspiration, he falls prey to his naïveté and feels his responsibility, even when he knows that Ghisola has belonged to others.

Although one is conscious of Tozzi's effort in breaking away from his own subjectiveness, the lyric motif of his isolation has taken a concrete form in the uncertainty of Pietro and in the directness of action and feelings of a finely etched throng of peasants. There are notations of this sort in the novel: "Pietro, then a little boy, was not listening, but it seemed to him that those around him acted as figures in his dreams." Or, following the introspection of the child as the latter grew into manhood: "He asked himself why people and things around him should appear to him only as an oscillating and heavy nightmare." "A feeling of annihilation took possession of his brain, like the icy water of a spring. It seemed to him strange to exist, he was frightened at himself, tried to forget himself, gazing for a long time at the palms of his hands until he saw them no longer." Pietro's mother dies: "He got down from his bed and, while dressing, pretended to imitate the gestures of grief that he had seen. In this manner he finally experienced a mute hilarity, mixed with terror. But when he was made to kiss his mother, before they put her in the coffin, he thought: 'Why do I not get into it too? Put me in there too.' " The book is a continuous flashing of strange lights that explore mysterious depths in Tozzi's heart. Heavy dark clouds hang over the slowly moving events that seem to stifle life and to make the world desolate and bleak.

Tozzi's best experiments at fiction are *Le tre croci* (*The Three Crosses*), 1920, and *Il podere* (*The Estate*), 1921. Austere and strong, having eliminated every superfluous detail, sure of his technique, or rather unaware of it, he concentrates his efforts on a study of life which is as objective as a writer like Tozzi can make it.

Le tre croci is the story of the three Gambi brothers who slowly deteriorate physically, financially, and morally to such a degree that death is the only solution. (pp. 211-13)

The slow process of disintegration of those uneventful existences is such as tests the skill of any artist, yet Tozzi, through his penetrating and tenacious art, has succeeded in differentiating very clearly the three brothers. He has carved out their ordinary profiles, tenaciously working until they have acquired the sharp relief of an etching. The passions here described, gluttony, apathy, passivity, are so common, so dull, that he is forced to insist on them in order to make them visible and vivid. They are vivid, however, with a cold light of their own; they are human and true.

In *Il podere* Tozzi returns to the autobiographical novel, and disguises himself in Remigio Selmi, a weak and pitiful man in his thirties, who inherits his father's farm and sees everybody and everything conspire against him. He appears to be unable to cope with the violence of nature, which destroys his crops, and with the dishonesty of his farmers, who steal everything from him until he is killed by one of them who hates him. Both in *Tre croci* and in *Il podere* Tozzi has reduced the number of his characters to the essential figures on whom he focuses all his attention. The central figure here is Remigio, a perfectly drawn character. Tozzi has searched into the heart of this weak man and has discovered tender feelings that no one appreciates. It is his own life and heart that he bares and his analysis has the pathos and warmth of real life. Around him move three farmers and their wives, clear-cut solid figures who press hard around the weak Remigio and finally destroy his farm and him, too. In the background, there are secondary figures, a lawyer, a business man, merely sketched, living in the light that Remigio sheds on them.

Tozzi has acquired a sureness of touch and a strength that heretofore he did not possess. We quote at random: "A filthy old man who wore an overcoat even in summer, with his mustache always dirty with saliva and tobacco." "Corrado Crestai was almost two metres tall, thin, and always yellow, with eyes that seemed made of lead, with fingers so thin that one could see the shape of the bones." He has purified his art by pruning away all that was not strictly necessary and by transfusing his lyricism into the acts and events that constitute life.

These novels of Tozzi express a sort of pitiless asceticism, an asceticism without heaven and without the stars. They are based on a negative point of view of man and of life, just as Tozzi's life at Siena was negative. With his visit to Rome, where he went to find work and a publisher, his constructive period begins. In *Gli egoisti* (*Egoists*), 1923, a novel left unfinished, he presents a new hero in Dario, a musician who has lost the passiveness of Tozzi's early characters, and a man of faith. Tozzi has emerged from his solitude. Indeed he looks upon it with a sense of friendliness. "He [Dario] wanted to understand his solitude: he wanted to understand it without hating it. He found in it that indefinable sense of things which remain unknown even to our soul—solitude was good." Dario is now amenable to love, and he falls in love with Albertina, a girl who understands his struggles and his art. He acquires through her a new sense of purity. One day a harlot tempts him. The temptation seems to him absurd and repugnant. "He felt sure and tranquil, as vast as the night, lost in the softness of the stars, that are always alike."

Dario's life is not barren like that of Pietro or Remigio. He has his affection for Albertina, he has his music, he has faith in God. These states of mind are not prosaically static; they are vivified by sudden reactions that give life to them. Here is Dario in a religious mood: "He felt the need of expressing his thankfulness, to thank *someone*. He would have liked to see God immediately." He goes to an old church in Rome, the Ara Coeli. "Dario did not remember any prayer, but he concentrated his thoughts and tried to pray until it seemed to him that he and the whole church had merged into one feeling.

Then he asked whether that would be enough for the Lord. But when he stood up he was no longer capable of believing."

Albertina, his music, God, are the constructive elements out of which Tozzi fashions his new hero's life. As in the case of Moretti, of Pirandello, and of Borgese, we find here a solution, a synthesis in a sort of spiritual program. "Those who succeed must continuously live by themselves and not give explanations to any one but themselves. Those who succeed in working are to be readily recognized from the mob of those who are boastful, stupid, and perverse." These are the "egoists" and Dario has been one of them. Now he leaves for the country and there he expects to find "a certitude which would have formed the sentiment of his conscience." Tozzi, too, had reached his unity in the harmony of his intellect and of his sentiment, but the span of his life was too short to express it in full. (pp. 213-16)

> Domenico Vittorini, "*The Novel of Humility and Uncertitude: 'I Crepuscolari' or 'Twilight Writers'*," in his *The Modern Italian Novel*, University of Pennsylvania Press, 1930, pp. 201-23.

BEN JOHNSON (essay date 1959)

[*In the following excerpt, Johnson characterizes Tozzi's writing and place in literary history.*]

[Tozzi], with Svevo and Verga, must be accounted one of the three masters of Italian narrative writing since the unification of Italy.... Tozzi was a kind of Tuscan Verga who, like Svevo, reacted vigorously against the effeteness and floweriness of D'Annunzio and D'Annunzio's imitators—and for this was roundly maligned and derided by critics and writers of the Fascist era, whether they were party members or simply heeders of Croce's 1925 Manifesto which cautioned intellectuals not to "contaminate literature with politics" (implicit in politics is taking a stand, just as it is implicit in writing honestly). With a touch, or, actually, with rather more than a touch, of madness, Tozzi's vision of the world, of the high drama in the lives of the plainest people is convincing because of his deep-rooted belief in the absurd and inexplicable at the base of human existence. Tozzi sees life as though it is reflected in a shattered mirror, whose pieces somehow can't be fitted together, and his stories (unlike his novels, *Con gli occhi chiusi, Tre croci*, and *Il podere*) fail only infrequently, and then only when, in his lunacy, he seems to sense that at some point his narrative has led him off the deep end and, in trying to recompose matters, falls back on Roman Catholic mysticism to explain the absurd and inexplicable.

From the dates of Tozzi's novels and finest short stories, one sees that he burned himself out in a few short seasons, like a hard white magnesium flame. He has had an influence on many writers, some of whom, like Pratolini, own up to it, although others, like Moravia, don't. As a writer, no Italian has been so Dostoievskian as Tozzi, but it is not so much his personality as a man, and its reflection on his works, that has counted with writers who have come after him, as the influence he has had upon the Italian written language. Every great writer rapes the language he is given to use, bending it to his own ends, and Tozzi did just that. If in some stories he anticipated Kafka, whose works he could not possibly have known, in the same way he anticipated the Imagists: in the last couple of years of his life he expunged from his writing all verbiage, stripped it to the essentials, to the neglect even of grammar and syntax—and to the horror of purists. (pp. xviii-xix)

Ben Johnson, in an introduction to Stories of Modern Italy: From Verga, Svevo and Pirandello to the Present, *edited by Ben Johnson, The Modern Library, 1960, pp. xiii-xxv.*

GIACOMO DEBENEDETTI (essay date 1969)

[In the following excerpt, Debenedetti offers a psychobiographical explication of Tozzi's fiction.]

The short stories of Tozzi—those we knew, those we never thought to find again, and a large number hitherto unpublished, all gathered together in a collection [*Opere: Le novelle,* Vols. I-II] which seems, for the present, to be definitive—raise once again the whole problem of his fiction. Indeed, Tozzi's narrative work is now shown to be so much more prolific than he had previously appeared, revealing an originality which we had never suspected, even after we have read so many other books, listened to other music, and looked at other paintings.

The point of departure for our evaluation might be a review Pirandello wrote in 1919, immediately after the appearance of the pregnant, labyrinthine, inexorable masterpiece of the novel *Con gli occhi chiusi* (*With Closed Eyes*). With its involution and intuition, we might say that it was written in invisible ink, which only the passage of time could bring to light, especially when we see it run up against the criticism that such a narrative method "might be called naturalistic but actually is not." Pirandello, too, from the very beginning, had taken up naturalism as an optical device in order to lend credibility and acceptability to characters and events which had lost all civic rights in the world in which they continued to trespass; his was a naturalism, in short, that laid charges of dynamite in its own path. In his review, whether he knew it or not, Pirandello offered Tozzi a testimonial to the congeniality between them. Actually, both contributed to the portrayal of the "new man" of modern art, a man animated by reasons of his own, who continues to be ignored by accredited and traditional reason that still claims a monopoly of the rational. They did this by quite different means, but their breaks with the past eventually converge. Pirandello is more demiurgic, more aggressive and autocratic in the manipulation of his material; to use an expression familiar to those who look at contemporary art, his narrative might be called "squared." Tozzi is more unaware; his subject leads him to results whose existence he ignored, and perhaps would not choose to follow; but on the other hand, he is more of a poet, more of an artist, in the classical and still persuasive and moving sense of the word.

"Il faut être absolument moderne" ["It is necessary to be absolutely modern"], Rimbaud once said. But for readers and critics like ourselves can modernity be the criterion of excellence? Perhaps not, we agree. Nor should I like to give the impression that an attack upon naturalism is today the essential, even if not the complete ground for being taken seriously as a writer. We continue, to be sure, to admire the achievements of the great naturalists—of Zola, for instance. If we couldn't do so, we should feel like orphans. But when we tell of ourselves, of people of our own time, then the naturalistic point of view no longer satisfies us. What was this point of view, anyway?

A well-known epigram of Svevo, only superficially cynical, says: "It's not so much that I enjoy eating a steak as the fact that I'm eating it and others aren't." Naturalism took for granted a public of steak-eaters. The pleasure, edification, and participating, the satisfying compassion, the life-giving intellectual gain, registered by its reading public were to be found precisely in the feeling of superiority on the part of conventional, successful men who, by following the rules of the game, had won their steak while the heroes of the novels were starving or else eating the bread of affliction. Indeed, the greatest novels of the period presented stories that were implacably bound to end in catastrophes. And even those with happy endings pointed up the difficulties which the hero had to overcome in order to win his steak, beyond which he no longer appeared worthy of interest.

We can extricate ourselves from these metaphors by clarifying our parallels. A beefsteak stands for worldly goods, or, more abstractly, possession. It is not by chance that Giovanni Verga has been demoted to a mere leader of *verismo*. His masterpieces have been interpreted as being about things, and their psychological correlative, possession. The identification of personality with worldly goods or things is particular to the man of the middle class, the capitalist. Even in the realm of feeling the bourgeois is a capitalist and owner; he is the one who defines as possession his most ardent and purposeful relationship with a woman. And naturalist novels that deal with love are novels of possession. The pathos of the hero betrayed by his wife or mistress is that of the dispossessed man or, more precisely, of the man who has been robbed of his belongings. Marcel Proust, who, with a blunted ax and melancholy mildness, dealt the hardest blows to the naturalist novel, did not realize that he was epitomizing his objections to this genre when, in one of the love episodes of *A la recherche du temps perdu,* he declared that the word "possession" is absurd, that it mythologizes the impossible. Actually the loves which he narrates are for the most part explicitly or implicitly homosexual in character, which means that they reduce the idea of possession to absurdity, since such possessions are of a kind considered illicit and out of order.

Indeed, the society which was coming to birth with our century, through a travail whose upheavals we are still experiencing, was moving toward the elimination of Svevo's steak-eaters, at the cost of bringing everyone—as long as it was really everyone—down to the level of eating from a can. Now it happens that Tozzi won a name with *Tre croci* (*Three Crosses*) and *Il podere* (*The Farm*), that is, with two novels that seem concerned with *things* but actually deny the capitalistic *fetishism* of worldly goods, or possession. By using traditional, apparently conservative plots, he upset the mechanisms and the motivations and broke the springs of the positivistic, deterministic, middle-class novel. Of course, in spite of his youthful anarchistic socialism and his enduring Christian anarchism, he did not write, or even attempt to write, a novel of social protest. But his development as an artist can be deciphered here and now—far better than yesterday, far better than when he was alive, and a great deal better than he ever suspected it would be—under the discernable content of his short stories and novels.

We know that the first boost to Tozzi's fame—which thereafter marked time—was given by Giuseppe Antonio Borgese, a critic generally considered more of a special pleader than a man distinguished for his sensitivity and intuition. In the case of the campaign he waged for Tozzi the opposite turned out to be true. Intuition told him that he had come upon a writer who upset customary perspectives, while his gift for special pleading counseled him to base his advocacy on backward-looking reasoning. It was sufficient for him to recognize that, with Tozzi, there was an end to the rule of impressionistic fragmentation in the tradition of *La voce* and *Lacerba,* that it was once more ''a time for building,'' that narrative form was freed from its enslavement to frivolity and raised to an artistic genre of the highest artistic importance. And he pointed out as a model the well-built, concise, splendid and tragic perfection of *Tre croci,* in which he saw a brilliant ''return to the past,'' understandable only in terms of naturalism. He did not use this word, but he proclaimed that, after the toilsome and admirable apprenticeship of the ''autobiographical trilogy''—*Ricordi di un impiegato (Diary of a Clerk), Con gli occhi chiusi,* and *Il podere*— Tozzi had finally attained, in *Tre croci,* such an impersonal material that it opened up to him the ''broader road'' that was unfortunately cut short by his death. We need not add that impersonality was the criterion of excellence of the naturalistic novel.

The proof of this misunderstanding, which was, at that time, perhaps, providential in winning Tozzi his rightful place in the history of the Italian novel, was made evident when Borgese, as literary executor of his friend's unpublished work, mutilated the first and posthumous edition of *Ricordi di un impiegato.* Only in 1960, when Tozzi's son brought out the complete text of this very early (1910) work, was it clear that the figure of the supposedly naturalistic Leopoldo grew out of a ganglion of obscure and untamable motives, of amorphous and unassimilated matter, of existential bewilderment strangely evasive in relation to the role which he plays under the spotlight of the stage. It would take a long time of citing passages which may seem, as they did to Borgese, parenthetical and digressive, with no bearing upon the plot, to analyze the perturbatory function exercised upon the outward development and coherence of the story and upon the plausibility of the *tranche de vie* [''slice of life'']. I am reluctant to speak in terms of music when our discourse is of literature, but I might briefly say that here is a case where the insertion, here and there, of a few bars of atonal notes makes us realize that the whole composition is written without the harmonical and accoustical conventions to which our ears are soothingly accustomed. These create in us a state of alarm and tension which cannot be calmed by the satisfyingly familiar cadences, the succession of notes and chords with a reassuring pattern of cause and effect that follow.

We need only look at the episodes of the apparitions, mentioned here not merely as an example but, rather, as the indispensable evidence for the point I am making. Up to this point the hero, Leopoldo, may have seemed the product—however unhappy— of a legitimate union with so-called natural reality and average experience. Now, all of a sudden, he appears as the son of an as yet nameless chaos, in which ordinary classifications do not hold sway. We have a stage crowded with flesh-and-blood presences of reincarnated memories, which push their way, confusedly, to the foreground, without any rationale of time, space, or causality, bound together only by their power of vexation and evil. Their impellent was fear, as we may see from the declaration that precedes their entrance: ''Every time that I am approached by someone I don't know I am afraid; and sometimes even a friend affects me the same way. I'm not afraid, actually, of him, but of the consequences which I may suffer when he starts talking.'' What consequences? What harm can Leonardo suffer from the unknown farmer whom he evokes as one of the many maleficent figures?

> I remember how, outside of Florence, just beyond the suburbs, I had to pass by the green wooden gate of a farmer. Every time, as I drew near and saw the farmer standing at the open gate, I either turned back or crossed over to the other side of the road, in order not to meet him face to face.

It is understandable that, in the same place, Tozzi says in the words of his mouthpiece, Leopoldo: ''I never wanted to be brought close to certain people.'' *Brought close,* he writes, rather than *bring myself close,* as if he were at the mercy of unknown impersonal and deplorable forces that control him. His way of avoiding the farmer has on the one hand, something of a superstitious ritual, and on the other hand something of a fear of the watchdog, of fierce and noxious beasts, of the dragon at the gate. Both fears have the same root, since superstition is always linked to a taboo, to a feeling of guilt and the fear of punishment by something that cannot be concretely foreseen but only guessed at by virtue of certain flashing and impenetrable signs. Animal fear is born of the presence of a living creature, similar to us inasmuch as he is alive, but giving out an alien and incomprehensible message, foretold yet not concretely stated.

If we are to come out with the whole point, let us say that Tozzi's characters are born in the same way as the apparitions to which Leopoldo is enslaved. We know this from a passage written several years later, when Tozzi was even more strongly driven by his storyteller's vocation. This is in that chapter of *Bestie* where he recalls how, as a boy, he watched a craftsman put red lead paint on the wheelspokes of peasant wagons, set them out to dry in the sun and then remove, with the handle of his brush, any fly that got stuck in the paint. The boy enjoys the sight of this simple, unproblematical work, deriving from it a feeling of physical well-being which makes him first hungry and then sleepy. In this euphoric condition, he is led to mull over his dreams and ambitions as an aspiring artist. ''I thought how, when I was grown, I would write a book different from any I knew: an ingenious and tragic story like one of the vineleaves that the wind blew down between my knees; yes, my book would be just like one of these vine-leaves.'' Then, suddenly the space around him is filled with characters invisible to the kindly craftsman: ''The whole road was filled with people, with a light, transparent nightmare which stirred, like my soul, at the least breath of wind. Eventually I had to ask them to let me off; I felt them cluster around my youth like insects around a newly-lit lamp.'' Surely a crystal-clear allegory, with many facets, with responding echoes and understanding nods exchanged between inspiration and professionalism, between the sure hand of the craftsman and the anxious bewilderment of the artist. At the center there is the peremptory image of people seen as insects or animals, *Bestie,* as they are called in the title of the book, which is the most seminal work of Tozzi's entire literary production.

So preoccupied a vision of his characters has something obsessive about it, and indeed Tozzi speaks of a nightmare. It is as if he had to defend himself against them before putting them down on paper. We are brought into the realm of the unhealthy, the threatening, the evil which is to be averted. Yet it would be a mistake and an oversimplification to attribute this artistic dilemma to a pathological condition. Alfredo Gargiulo tried something of the sort, on the basis of shaky clues in both style and content and of literary associations. The result was an offkey hatchet job, which does not add to his critical glory even if, among those who put him on the wrong track, we must include Tozzi himself, with his fear of illness, particularly mental illness, which he makes quite explicit in his *Diary of a Clerk* and elsewhere. With quite different intentions, and in spite of the affectionate tone of his portrayal, even Borgese seems to make us suspect that there was something morbid about him, when he says: "He used to walk close to the walls, like a man who thinks he is being followed." If we are to bring pathology into it at all, then we must remove it from a clinical angle and consider it in relation to certain spiritual ills to which we are condemned in our century, thanking Tozzi for having sublimated them in his art and, where his personal life is concerned, thinking of them insofar as he is concerned as painful tricks played upon him by Providence.

Let us look again for a moment at Leopoldo, in *Diary of a Clerk.* If he makes his job as a railway employee so tormenting and unbearable, it is because he sees in it the external, concrete, perhaps still curable evidence of a *mal de vivre* so deeply ingrained that it is inseparable from his personality. In reality Leopoldo is a perpetual employee, an employee of life, which to him is an incessant rain of orders, unspoken but inescapable, of orders and threats on the part of a boss who is no one in particular, but everyone and everything and everywhere. There is another such figure in literature: Gregory Samsa, the petty employee who is the protagonist of Kafka's *Metamorphosis.* We see how this fellow wakes up one morning to find himself transformed into a centipede. This disgusting insect is the symbolical incarnation of his true identity as a humiliated underling, condemned to blind obedience by a world which dominates and despises him and continually makes him feel that it can get along without him. Gregory, too, was an employee of life. Tozzi's very personal anxiety caused him to discover, in the everyday figure of Leopoldo, a character of the most revealing and symptomatic family of man that has appeared in contemporary fiction.

For Kafka, the insect was the final metamorphosis, on its way to a tragic and liberating end. For Tozzi it would have been, rather, the symbol for a point of departure, which he must make into a man, while preserving the alarming stigmata of his previous animal existence. If we go beyond the borders of the literary and artistic Italy of Tozzi's day, we shall find even more striking parallels and analogies. In the early years of the century the German painter Franz Marc, a friend of Klee and one of the most convincing practitioners of expressionism and abstraction, wrote an essay entitled *Constructive Ideas of Modern Painting,* in which he systematically demolished naturalism, from the end of the Renaissance to, and including, the impressionists. The seed of his argument was the need "to return by another path to the images of spiritual life, which does not follow the laws of a world conceived on a scientific basis." (We may say, parenthetically, that Tozzi too was to speak of "new intimate and spiritual perceptions.") For Marc it was a question of releasing the latent forces behind matter, that worn object of copying and photography, of "tearing off the mask," as one of his critics puts it, "from the superficial image of nature, in order to reveal the powerful laws that hold sway behind its bland appearance." But these theoretical premises are less important than the remedy which Marc sought to pit against "naturalizing," and which he called "animalizing."

Thus Tozzi's most keen-minded contemporaries consciously and theoretically formulated his earlier, spontaneous, and inevitable vision. For him, other men and the other self were "animalized" from the start, as we have seen in the hallucinatory and prophetic passage—a passage which dispenses us from quoting numerous other examples drawn not only from the metaphorical *Bestie* but also from *Con gli occhi chiusi,* where even the physical aspects of inanimate nature are animalized. How, then, does Tozzi react to what he calls this "insidious animation"?

Fiction seemed to him the only way to assimilate, by portraying them, the live beings and things so tightly closed and so reluctant to communicate to him the reasons for their existence. His isolation turned into a potential springboard for storytelling on the day when he said to himself that "any *mysterious* [his italics] human action," however apparently insignificant, (for instance, that of a man "who at a certain point on the road stoops down to pick up a stone and then goes on his way"), is of deeper interest than the most remarkable fictional invention. The words just quoted are from Tozzi's volume of collected essays *Realtà di ieri e di oggi* (*Realities of Yesterday and Today*). Here we may see another amazing parallel, this time with Joyce's theory of the "epiphany." But we shall more profitably read into such essays the fact that for Tozzi to write meant to capture these mysterious actions and their inexpressible mystery. His was to be a narration not of cause and effect but of inexplicable patterns and ways of appearance and being. Hence Tozzi's innate antinaturalism. Naturalism narrates by virtue of explaining, whereas Tozzi narrates inasmuch as he cannot explain.

An animalizing vision, with the superstitious uneasiness and terror that it entails, illuminates the essence of Tozzi's novel of behavior from within. The way of looking at things that imposed itself upon him goes back to remote antiquity, indeed to the prehistoric cave-drawing. Our primitive ancestors, fearful of animals and dependent upon them, sought from them fertility and the capture and death of their enemies by painting these acts on the walls of their caves for purposes of imitative magic. Diggers have discovered the preparatory sketches for some of the wall paintings, from which it is clear how meticulously the artist studied his model in order to ensure the accuracy of its reproduction, and hence its efficacy, as an instrument of magic possession and deliverance from fear. Tozzi, too (I hope the reader will forgive the ingenuousness of the phrase), tormented himself in order to make things come out as he saw them. This, of course, is true of any artist; but in him there was a strong element of craftsmanship, which drove him to make the best possible rendition of the mysterious actions which he portrayed. Besides the practical results which primitive man set before him there was the reward, the compensation, the triumphal transfer of the actions and powers of the portrayed subject to the portrayer, who with his own hands reproduced them. Thus he redeemed his condition of succubus, becoming master of the man of whom he had formerly been the slave and establishing a *modus vivendi* between himself and his fears.

The reader may ask what connection there is between this archaic and pagan process and the art of a Tozzi who, under his hard-won status as a self-taught man, preserved the heritage of Tuscan and Christian culture. The fears, nightmares, and feelings of dependency and persecution to which he was prey dwelled deeply within him and worked upon elementary levels of his psychic makeup, levels which are primitive and react in a primitive manner. By a coincidence which gives further proof of Tozzi's accord with the time in which he lived, these were the years when the great art centers of the world went in for discovering the artefacts of primitive man; there was a special enthusiasm for African art, stemming largely from Paris and the studio of Pablo Picasso. This art (and here lies the reason for our mentioning it) permitted the reintegration with the cultivated ego of Western man of a baggage of long-lost, censored, in short, "savage" notions which for some time had indicated that they would no longer tolerate the psychological colonialism by which they had been checked. Picasso and his friends worked from ethnological documents and artefacts; they adopted and stylized the original signs and language that they found therein. Tozzi, on the other hand, ingeniously repeated the basic processes of what was described by an ethnology being imported in Europe—an ethnology he himself ignored. Once more, by virtue of a wonderful coincidence of fate and vocation, which became, in him, a dramatic daimon, he instinctively followed the path of modern art, while fundamentally expressing his own personal makeup and attempting—with a boldness which he often deemed insufficient and unsuccessful—to absorb the signs and language of a national illustrious and homely native tradition. He was an isolated, suffering, unconscious, yet eloquent guinea pig, involved in a crisis which was far more widespread than he imagined and was being experienced, at the same time, by artists more sophisticated than he, who handled it with greater awareness and managed to give names to phenomena which he confusedly and anxiously adumbrated truly "with closed eyes."

In order to understand how all this came about and reconstruct the human model from which Tozzi's poetry sprang with an impulse even more overwhelming than that of the creative will, we must turn to psychology. And this, to purist critics, is the most corrupt, sinful, and, in short, inadvisable of tools. But whether or not it is acceptable, there are times when nothing but psychology will do, and in this case we have ready proof that we are not calling upon it in vain, or without an enrichment of understanding. We have already seen that something, undefined, persecuted Tozzi to the point of obsession, producing images, resentments, and a whole chain of coercive reactions. Psychology would call these manifestations of the unconscious. But we have already noticed—indeed, Tozzi has told us so himself—that they were accompanied by another symptom, that of fear. With such a complete picture we might expect a classical picture: a youthful trauma which caused a chronic inhibition of his freedom to choose his own repressions or to cope with those to which he gives way. All this could well amount only to a psychological conjecture, called upon in order to reinforce a dangerous critical scaffolding. And if by any chance the trauma cannot be found, then the whole theory falls apart. Without wishing to sound overdramatic, I must confess that it was with considerable trepidation that I searched for the unknown factor that would confirm my theory.

A superfluous search, the reader may say, since a father complex is shouted out by Tozzi's life story and his major works, in every one of which there is an inhibited son. Yes, but all this is too generic, it is a plight shared by millions of other men and perhaps by dozens of great artists. Besides, Tozzi would be wasted as a mere case history in one of the lesser manuals of psychoanalysis. There must be something more personal, capable of explaining why his protagonist is condemned to live "with closed eyes," without the power to open them to everyday reality which, indeed, appears to him through a veil of apprehension, in both the physical and the spiritual sense of the word, as an agglomeration of monsters. Closed eyes, blindness to life, here is Tozzi's central myth, the open or secret connecting theme that runs through all of his most important fiction.

And it is in the novel *With Closed Eyes* that the trauma which we postulated is revealed in the course of a scene that seems to reproduce, in a terrifyingly realistic and at the same time symbolic condensation, the event that started the whole thing. This scene is not necessary to the plot; to a highly aesthetic critic it may seem merely picturesque, reminiscent of the rustic

and bloodthirsty D'Annunzio, of whom the young Tozzi was a fanatically enthusiastic reader. Indeed, it breaks into the fabric of the book like an extraneous body, propelled by a sudden necessity that knows no law. In other words, it has the character of an involuntary confession. Briefly, the young hero Pietro looks on, stunned, at the general, almost indiscriminate castration of all the animals of the farm, in the presence of his father who has ordered it. It is hardly necessary to add, by way of explanation, that the idea of having to submit to a mutilation of this kind, willed by a father, is one of the basic features of the Oedipus complex. Pietro has visual evidence that his father is capable of such a gesture. What relation, we may ask, is there between this episode and the loss of sight, of the ability to look at things as they are, that is, the specific and quite different lesion from which Tozzi himself suffered? We ask this rhetorical and naive question in order to recall that Oedipus, the youth who bears the name of the complex, when he wants to atone for the murder of his father, that act of unconscious revenge and reconquest of his own destiny, blinds himself. He perpetrates upon himself, with his own hands, the mutilation which his father, anxious to preserve his life, his wife, and his kingdom, had inflicted upon him when he was a babe in swaddling clothes, hanging him up by his feet and leaving him to be found and brought up by shepherds, ignorant of his identity and his right to the throne. Here, from the very beginning of the myth, we have the connection between the loss of sight and the terrifying castration operation.

The letters collected in the volume entitled *Novale* show that Tozzi's demandingly affectionate father insisted that he make his way in the world, in compliance with a model which his father had set up but did not follow, preferring to indulge in all the pleasures to be had from life without ever paying for them. The mutilation has altered the son's initiative; it blocked the confrontation with reality which could have opened his eyes. He begins to vegetate like a blind man, both in real life and in the novel *With Closed Eyes*. To begin with, he was lazy and did badly both in and out of school, as if he were making a sort of negative affirmation in order to reproach his father for having forbidden him a positive posture. We have already said that the Leopoldo of the *Diary of a Clerk* was an "employee of life." When his father forces him to submit to the frustrating ordeal of a competitive examination for a petty government job, his bitter revenge is to wear his sleeves rolled up, as emblems of what his father has done to him, of the incurable incapacity to which he has been reduced. Once his father is dead, he leaves his job and takes over the administration of the family property. Now that his father is not there to make demands on him, there is no longer any reason for him to protest by refusing the task.

But the lesion still hurts, and calls for destructive compensations. *With Closed Eyes* is essentially the story of a willful failure in love, with which Pietro tries to punish the person who has made him psychologically impotent. *The Farm* and *Three Crosses* retell the drama of mutilation in an apparently more detached and objective guise.

In *The Farm* the protagonist, Remigio Selmi, quits his job in a small-town railway station (as did Tozzi) in order to go look after the farm left to him by his father. With a sort of passive rage and guile he lets himself fall into the hands of cheats and vultures; he is caught up in devious lawsuits and evasions that bring him close to outright violation of the law; he turns to dishonest or inept lawyers and signs promissory notes, perhaps for the very purpose of losing his newly acquired property.

This property is, of course, the symbol of his father's power, and he must destroy it in order to obtain a morbid enjoyment out of the impotence to which his father had condemned him. As we read his story we want to tug at his sleeve, to save him, and yet every time we are disarmed by his stubborn and shapeless ingenuousness, by the innocence of his distraught face and wide-open, unseeing eyes. After the court has sentenced him for the shady dealings into which he had entered on the fundamentally hypocritical basis of saving his financial situation, the book closes in a poetical key: "A few hours later there was a hailstorm. Grape-leaves and green grapes were scattered over the ground together with pelted vine shoots and branches." Natural destruction is added to financial and moral ruin, and yet the impression left with us is one of brightness and shining. The havoc wrought by the storm, following upon the loss of Remigio's case in court, seems to release a feeling of peace and catharsis. Under the tarpaulin which the peasants hold over his head Remigio appears finally relieved. He has put down his father with an act of vengeance as irreparable as the lesion which his father had inflicted upon him.

Three Crosses repeats the same tale, against a different background—this time an antique shop which, if things were to go well, could produce material wealth. The wounded, antiheroic protagonist of Tozzi is this time split into the three Gambi brothers, owners in partnership of the bookshop. In the book there is not even a mention of their father. But his mute presence is immanent in the brothers' relationship. He left them the small estate which enabled them to make a living and go into business, and his presence endures in a thousand underlying ways. The novel tells how, by means of a false promissory note, the brothers go bankrupt. A lawsuit, financial ruin, and moral disgrace, and at the end three crosses which rise one beside the other in the cemetery of Siena.

In Tozzi's time, and in the social class to which he belonged, the promissory note was, to the older generation, a symbol of dishonor. By borrowing money against a promissory note, the Gambi brothers were, indirectly, fighting the memory of their father. But this was not enough. They had to destroy his power, and even his survival, by completely wasting his substance. These three characters, whom Tozzi, by anecdotes and description, makes into separate entities, are actually fragments of a single mirror, all of them reflecting the same view of life, each projecting a ray of light on the same psychological situation, that of a man who has been deprived of his power of getting his teeth into reality. And for this they substitute something as obvious and miserable as the joys of the table, striving to compensate their impoverished existences by orgies of greed and, through them, attaining a perverse euphoria and a physical enhancement like that of lovers' orgasm. They bleed themselves financially in order to buy the best fish, meat, chickens, and fruit on the market. With ribald arrogance they display their gastronomic satisfaction in the same way that a Don Juan brags of his sexual prowess; the table overflowing with delicacies is an assertion of virility, expressed by the liberal devouring of their possessions. Their daily banquets are grim and tedious affairs, intended to damage the good name and reputation of their father, eliminating his enduring presence, incarnate in material things.

It has been said that the heroes of Tozzi's novels are inept and incapable of living. But the inept man is doomed from the start and cannot develop in a novel. The assertion holds true only if Tozzi is branded as a naturalist. But his novels are irresistibly dramatic; they are concerned not with an inept hero caught up in some kind of action, but with the origin and development of that mortal illness, the inability to live or, rather, to adapt to life. Naturalism examined what has been called psychology without a psyche, seen in the broad light of day. The contemporary novel, such as Tozzi wrote before its time, has a nocturnal point of view; it operates in a zone where there are no worldly explanations, no cut-and-dried solutions, in the true realm of the psyche, where chance cannot be abolished by a throw of the dice.

Tozzi thought, and stated quite clearly, that art should turn "toward the summits of more modern psychological components." He told stories that smacked of those of the preceding generation, hoping that the cases he described were exceptional and that other men would not have the same fate as that of his lonely heroes. Yet, unwittingly, he created a character who, with his "more modern psychological components," could not live in the way that had been taught him. The conflict between his inner being and his outward appearance takes place below the surface of the novel, and here is the unconscious and far-reaching secret of Federigo Tozzi.

Moved by impulses which caused him to be at war with himself and with his immediate artistic demands, his human desire for recognition, Tozzi portrayed a lost, suffering hero, a frail runner in life's race. A brother, this hero, to the passersby whose strained expressions and rude, alienated behavior mirror the travail of the man of today, trying to adapt himself to the incognita which he has discovered within, to find a meaning in the new structure of his future, which history still pushes away as if it were arbitrary and premature. Under a burden such as would have crushed many another artist, Tozzi found the courage, patience, and humility to go about his work with all the devotion of a scrupulous craftsman, like the wagoner of his youthful memory or dream who, with the handle of his brush, removed from the wheelspokes any fly that got stuck in the paint. (pp. 102-19)

> Giacomo Debenedetti, "Federigo Tozzi: A Psychological Interpretation," *translated by Frances Frenaye, in* From "Verismo" to Experimentalism: Essays on the Modern Italian Novel, *edited by Sergio Pacifici, Indiana University Press, 1970, pp. 102-19.*

GIOSE RIMANELLI (essay date 1971)

[*In the following excerpt, Rimanelli discusses the figure of the* antipatico, *or individual alienated from society, in Tozzi's novels.*]

Tozzi is an autobiographical writer. He is the Pietro of *Con gli occhi chiusi* who loves the rather paltry mother and who trembles for her, but who shuns his choleric father; the Pietro who is apathetic, indolent, bustling with a morbid sensibility to whom, nevertheless, he securely entrusts himself because it partakes of that of himself about which he knows most. And he is the Giulio of *Tre croci,* overwhelmed by the misfortune and incapable of struggling with the brothers. He is the Remigio of *Il podere,* a man outside the real, incapable of defending himself against the basenesses that life reveals everyday and who in himself perceives and fears—an inexplicable fundament of turbidness, but who nevertheless saves himself when he raises his eyes and in his faculty of exaltation finds the courage still to be able to look at the sky and nature. And he is Leopoldo Gradi, the unpleasing stranger of *Ricordi di un impiegato.*

But this figurative autobiographism would signify nothing if Tozzi had not stamped his writings with the profound conviction of his no exit existential situation. When Tozzi tries to objectify himself in the real that he "sees," the preference goes to humble individuals and to the washed-out characters "of everyday," those who are of no importance. And it is always from them that he starts out for his escape into mystery. Reading him, one quickly notes that, for him, any human act whatsoever is a mysterious act. At times these acts . . . generate the temporariness of the individual and the absurdity of living. The Tozzian point is the inexplicability of existence, which always seems to be characterized by unmotivated motives. The unmotivated is in many episodes of *Bestie*, as also in the finale of *Il podere,* in which the "salaried worker" mortally fells Remigio, and that which is done has the fatal sense of a pre-destination.

The unmotivated is everywhere in *Ricordi di un impiegato,* and it seems all the more absurd in that every described and living thing is in its proper, exact, ineluctable, irrational place. Tozzi's observation is also precise, violent, wounding. His eye is brought to bear on the abnormality of the normal, wherever it is found. Why, in the last analysis, do Tozzi's eyes rest upon crippled persons, stabbings, asymmetrical roofs, the deformations of the landscape? Because the inadequacy of his physical state finds a bearing only in an external inadequacy. The external abnormality is nothing else but a reflex of an interior situation: that paradoxical one of the spiritual isolation in which every human being finds himself in the middle of the crowd of other beings, all of whom are more or less spiritually isolated like himself. What emerges therefrom is the concept of man-prison with which a great part of European literature enriches itself.

In one of my books many years ago I noted that certain Tozzian images are transpositions and refractions of feelings, as we often come upon them in Kafka or in Henri Barbusse. And I noted that in the Tozzian unmotivatedness there already exists, and well defined literarily, that which in the 50's and 60's was denominated the spontaneous irrationality of the outsider, in addition to that feeling of feeling oneself to be uprooted and at the same time the "victim" of an impersonal mechanism which constitutes the core of Kafkian reason.

In Tozzi the concept of not-belonging and of irrationality in a world governed only apparently by rational motives or laws engendered the dialectic of the Antipatico.

The Antipatico (or the unpleasing one) is the individual who does not belong, of whom one speaks behind his back, who is avoided, who is rejected, who is attacked often for unmotivated motives. The Antipatico is the loner, the anti-social one, the person out of step, the mouse in his hole, the earthworm. He is the man who maybe sees too many things all too thoroughly, but who does not succeed in coexisting with others. The Antipatico is the one at whom the finger of scorn is pointed for faults that often are not his.

Here is a singular passage from *Ricordi di un impiegato.* We are in a restaurant of Pontedera, which is usually frequented by railroad employees. Today a new employee has also shown up there, Leopoldo Gradi, whom his colleagues eye diffidently and with provocation. The proprietress says:

> "Do you wish a bowl of soup, a couple of eggs, a beefsteak. . ."

> "A beefsteak."

> She does not hide her offended air from me.

> "Don't you want a bowl of soup?"

> "No."

> "But we have an excellent broth today!"

> And she darts a look at the engine driver so that he will side with her.

> Nevertheless I remain firm:

> "I want a beefsteak."

> Then, with an unforgiving contempt, she replies: "Yes, sir!"

> But it takes little to see that I am very displeasing, and the engine driver demonstrates it to me most evidently with his looks.

This quality of being displeasing circulates throughout the book. The red-nosed porter Drago is even more explicit than the others. "Drago, who is passing outside the windows, spits the moment he sees me." But it is the displeasing one, being almost always the one offended against, who is the one who finally chooses. He is the rebel, he is the one who ends up by preferring his corner of the wall instead of the crowded public square. (pp. 52-5)

[On] December 28, 1902, Tozzi writes in *Novale:* ". . . I had no friends because I did not like all those whom I had an opportunity to approach. . . ." Thoughts of this kind ultimately rooted themselves so deeply in Tozzi's personality that, in the end, they assumed the status of literary principles and speculations, even despite his effort to avoid being autobiographical. *Tre croci,* in fact, aims at being, or seeming to be, an objective novel. Yet Tozzi, from his first poetic stammerings, delineates himself in his fixed metaphor. *La zampogna verde,* of clear d'Annunzian derivation, however, contains some singular poems. With them he had tried to identify the nature of his "excellency" which is a loudly voiced and melancholy separation, now united in comradeship with Cecco Angiolieri and now with Edgar Allan Poe, that is to say with the idols of memory, not of the real. (p. 55)

In *Bestie* there are numerous examples of the author's isolation from society. "My soul has grown in the silent shadow of Siena, apart, without friendship, deceived each time that it has asked to be known. Thus many times I went out alone at night, avoiding even the street lamps." And in the same passage he adds: "Since I managed to live this way, separated from everybody, every time somebody looked at me with his sharp curiosity that offended me, I became sadder, and took the shortest route possible."

As is characteristic of Tozzi's first works, the theme of the Antipatico is not presented as a central, unifying or unified motif. Rather, it is expressed in a minor key, on dissonant modulations. In another passage of the same book the author inserts himself in an arcadian background of verdant meadows and men at work. "I am suffocated by the world; and when I speak it seems that my soul succeeds in getting out of it." In another passage Tozzi is even more closely reminiscent of Kafka.

> One morning I got up with the desire to kill myself: from the window it seemed that my field overturned like myself in the wind, as if it wanted to carry off all the olive trees with it. The walls of the room increasingly narrowed, drawing toward each other, and my breath mixed with theirs. I felt the taste of the mortar. Suddenly, right in front of my mouth, I saw a tiny, almost transparent, cobweb, attached to its thread like a weight.

Bestie, composed by Tozzi in 1915 and published by Treves in 1917, is the ideal continuation of *Novale.* But it could represent the literary systematization of the displeasing one's observations on nature and of his psychic states. The prose works stand by themselves and they fit like pieces of mosaic into the figurative cartoon which the writer has imagined to draw. Only this cartoon, after all the individual pieces have found their place in it, does not offer a concrete image of the landscape because it has been distorted by them, a little like that which happens in Cubist composition. Even when Tozzi tries to objectify and to get out of his "I" he never succeeds in bracketing a scene with the minuteness of details, in the naturalistic manner. He is interested only in a foreshortening of it and his play hinges upon it.

Here are some examples:

> He is tubercular with a yellow and hollow-cheeked face. Only the tip of his nose is purplish, with small warts. He wears glasses, and it seems that ashes fall inside his eyes.
>
> They got to know each other one Sunday in an ale house next to the public promenade: the small, round stone tables, the stoves of varnished iron, the orchestra, directed by the bald headed maestro, playing out of tune.
>
> They got married.
>
> They hardly ever go out together.

(pp. 56-7)

With *Ricordi* Tozzi took a long step forward in presenting us the dialectic of the Antipatico for the reason that, aside from *Il podere,* no other of his lengthy works rests almost exclusively on this theme. From the beginning to the end of the narration the protagonist is confronted by a series of situations in which his isolation is rendered practically inevitable. The atmosphere that surrounds him is of an abject solitude, interrupted only here and there by unpleasant contacts with society. As is known, Tozzi could not have known Kafka. Tozzi died in 1920, Kafka in 1924. Almost all of Kafka's work, save for some long short stories, (*The Metamorphosis,* for example, published in 1915) saw light between 1925 and 1931. Nevertheless the similarities between the two writers are striking. Often they adopt the same images, and that of the mouse often recurs in both. ". . . I am only a mouse in the corner of a very large house," Kafka writes of himself. And Tozzi, precisely in the beginning of *Ricordi,* writes: "My feeling resembles a tiny mouse caught by surprise in a room which has been filled with people before it has had time to find its hole again."

The ambience of Pontedera serves only to increase the awareness of the employee Gradi-Tozzi that he does not belong. He is the mouse who has not had time to find his hole again.

> On the streets I am stared at by everybody. The girls returning to work in the industrial plants laugh over me. One of them says out loud: "How ugly he is! He looks like a priest."

(pp. 57-8)

The Antipatico is displeasing not only because he is ugly and looks like a priest. The Antipatico is displeasing because everybody would like to take possession of him in the false man-in-the-street assumption that "here, we are equal." Finding himself in a tavern with his colleagues of the station, the porter Drago

> has a great desire to pick a quarrel with me, and he seeks all pretexts to drag me into a conversation.

Before leaving, he says, "I can't stand men without moustaches!" And Brilli asks me: "Why don't you grow one? Do you know that you're a strange type? Or do you wish to be without a moustache? Here in Pontedera they will all take a dislike to you." "I've noticed that, but I won't give in!" The manager then feels compassion for me. "You'll be sorry!" Capri, instead, wants to make light of the matter, and relates that even the assistant-manager wants to advise me to shave nothing by my beard. To boot, the proprietress asks me: "Why didn't you want to eat in my place the first night? Perhaps because my place seems too modest to you? One can quickly see that you have acquired bad habits. But you must also adjust yourself. Signor Brilli eats here more gladly than in any other inn. And you are less than he!" The manager laughs saying: "Perhaps, inside himself, he considers himself more than me." Marcello Capri adds: "I've noticed that, too. You don't know how to treat us as equals. Why? Here we are all equal." I ask: "Why do you stuff your heads with such ideas?" The Brilli reproaches me rudely: "It's true, and you would not permit yourself to talk this way with your superiors!"

These notes serve to illustrate that the Antipatico not only knows that he is different from others, but thinks and believes that others consider him different. Nevertheless the hostile attitude taken by Tozzi's acquaintances in Pontedera does not only represent the characteristic reaction of everyone to the intruder. The psychic complex of the Antipatico is not subject to geographic deviations, as he himself observes.

> Every time a man whom I do not know approaches me, I am afraid, sometimes even if it's a friend. I am not afraid of him in particular, but of the consequence that can derive from it to my mind when he may begin to talk. For this reason I never wanted to draw near certain persons. I remember that, once, finding myself on a street outside Florence, beyond the houses of the suburb, I had to pass before the green gate of a garden. Each time, before nearing it, I saw the gardener standing by the open gates either I turned back or passed from the door opposite the street, thereby avoiding turning towards him.

Inasmuch as the Antipatico has pushed away from himself all society, his values are exclusively intrinsic: "I feel, instead, the regret of so many good things which come spontaneously, by themselves."

The author withdraws behind a closed door, and observes reality through the peep-hole of his soul. "It is I who has closed my soul forever, like when, as a boy, I wanted to be alone and spied from the half-opened door on those who were talking in the room."

If we had to determine phases of development of the Antipatico, we would have to examine the Tozzian novels following only this intuitive thread, leaving aside the many other items of information which they also offer us. We therefore should say that in *Novale,* Tozzi's autobiography, there is *in nuce* the portrait of man-prison, that is to say of the Antipatico, in diverse varied aspects. With it, however, we remain only in the field of the diary, of confession which concerns the personal history of the man Tozzi, stranger par excellence.

But in his novels and stories this man becomes a literary vehicle, perhaps a message. The various aspects of the Antipatico, therefore, are developed from work to work. And, in our opinion, the first phase seems to begin with the novel *Con gli occhi chiusi.*

Discussing the significance of the title *Con gli occhi chiusi* [which can be translated as "With Closed Eyes"], Borgese observes that it "alludes frankly to a method of austere introspection, to a pitiless examination of conscience in which it involves the other characters and the landscape with himself." (pp. 58-61)

Unfortunately this interpretation, albeit in part, does not correspond with our way of reading Tozzi. The indication that Tozzi himself gives us of that title, when he observes that Pietro "was comfortably on the bed, with his eyes closed" (and parenthetically this indication is a typical Tozzian way of situating his Antipatico), suggests a more indigenous interpretation. Tozzi tells us that among some companions there was a young man, Pietro, who had lived too long with them. For this reason Pietro refers to the others, the companions, as though they were boys. He disapproves of their acquiescent conduct toward the instructors, nor can he laugh at what they laugh about. Often they annoy him and he reproves them for this. Nevertheless he tried to win their affection, but in vain. His indifference towards some of them is, by degrees, transformed into open hostility and enmity. He particularly dislikes the boys coming from well-to-do or rich families, who consider him a socialist. And Tozzi adds: "In the last days he felt, with anxiety, but also with pleasure, increasingly different from the others. And he could not explain to himself how the others could study without being forced to do like himself. And he was ever in a greater hurry to leave."

In this light the closing of the yes becomes a symbol of Pietro's spiritual isolation, but also of his difference from others, of his "outsiderdom," so to speak, of his exclusion from society. Pietro closes his eyes not to examine himself from a social point of view, nor for the purpose of involving characters and landscape, even though he often asks himself why he is so different from others, and "why try vainly to be like others?"

Con gli occhi chiusi is a reflection on the imponderable, on the alienable, but also on the vice of growth. Once his eyes are opened Pietro reflects on the same question, "why vainly try to be like the others?" But now he finally notices that he must necessarily, albeit painfully, abandon his search in the direction of sentimental knowledge because "the things and the person around him can appear to him only as an oscillating and heavy incubus."

Con gli occhi chiusi is a dictionary of poetical speculations and of real dolorous and irreplaceable facts. For Pietro opening his eyes signifies naught else but the admission of his and their failure in the search to effect at least a cohesion with others, if not love. In short, summarizing the book, we must say that the Antipatico has a name, and he is called Pietro, an adolescent. In the beginning Pietro is presented to us like a young man, the same as the others. In fact, we quickly come to know that he has friends and that he often talks and plays with them. For him, the friends are society, the external world, the world of everybody, also accepted by him. But it is in this point of realization that the fracture occurs in him, in that he detaches himself from them voluntarily, because "he felt different." It is at this point that he is no longer able to enjoy their enjoyments and their conversations, perhaps because he feels himself to be more mature than the others, as one who is living among persons who are not his chronological peers, but children. The superman insidiously arouses himself in Pietro, and it is this realization that induces him to retire into himself, into his immobility. Hence the separation has been promoted by him,

and it is his responsibility. The first phase is simply called incommunicability.

The second phase is amply illustrated in *Ricordi di un impiegato,* which has already been mentioned. In this book is depicted the effort of the stranger, now an adult, to be accepted or at least tolerated by society. However, it is society, now, that rejects him. He is *antipatico.*

The third phase is marked by *Il podere.* In this novel *l'Antipatico*—burdened now with a responsibility which he cannot, nor wished to bear—ends up by consuming himself in the intolerable tangle of his own solitude, even though, often, he does naught else but invoke the solitude. Here the Antipatico is externally in action, laboriously engaged in worldly affairs from which he later emerges completely defeated. He has little time to reflect, or to indulge himself in his condition of endemic outsiderdom. It is because of this urgency that Tozzi now prefers to write in the third person. Yet Tozzi, although using the third person as a device, merely constructs a whole novel on a single particular psychic state, without, however, burdening it with uselessly explicit words or expressions. De Michelis understands this aspect when he writes: "The drama is born precisely from the feeling that he is condemned to remaining uncomprehended and uncomprehending even more deeply mired in the incubus of his solitude, despite every effort he makes to break through it." And when certain existential definitions are born from Tozzi's pen in order ethically to reinforce his protagonist's position vis-à-vis with the absurd world outside, fashioned of clerks and tribunals, they cannot but have a definitive character. "All of his life seemed closed within a sack, from which there was no way of putting forth his head." The Antipatico discovers the moments of intimate, intense passion only when he gives a moral consciousness to his own solitude, when breathing freely as though liberating himself from an extremely heavy burden, he can exclaim: "Alone! He was alone! His heart beat as when, as a boy, he was in love."

The excitement of being alone before the universe, comes to represent the ultimate assertion of the only happiness granted to the Tozzian alienated person. And this is also his redemption, the realization of his destiny as an outsider after his many attempts to effect an opening towards the external world. The final tragedy, the blow of the axe administered by Berto, is unmotivated on the theoretical plane. "Remigio continued to walk ahead. Then, maddened, Berto landed the axe on his neck." The integral absurdity of the situation is that the assassin is as much as an outsider as his victim. This final act is also liberation from the absurd, since assassin and assassinated have sinned with the same sin: to defend the terms of their own destiny.

Summing up we will say that with *Il podere,* the Antipatico immobilizes himself. Having failed to insert himself in the world of others, he no longer feels anxiety or remorse. Indeed he is suffused with a strange fear in the state of isolation, which for him now is the only state that becomes him. He does not keep others at a distance, but neither does he seek them. To the extent that he is compelled to act by purely external, utilitarian factors, he is secure only in his hole, on the farm. Nevertheless it is a security that is an illusion, since his death sentence is decreed precisely on the farm, and by one who is as much an outsider as himself, an Antipatico like himself, Berto, who finds the rebellion against his fate only through violence.

Berto rebels in the name of human sorrow, his sorrow. It is that which generates the unmotivated, the absurd and which, at the same time, resolves it in that Berto—as men often do—refuses to be what he is. True, he strikes one of his breed. But this necessity to kill that he feels is nothing else but the necessity to assert himself and his identity. It is a revolt against creation and submission to fate. And because of this refusal he destroys himself and Remigio, feeling himself unconsciously justified by his innocence.

The fourth phase is constituted by the novel *Gli egoisti.* Here all the preceding themes are reexamined, and exacerbated by boredom to boot. Dario Gavinai, a young musician, loses himself in Rome in a series of impossible encounters. He tries to avoid boredom, but in vain. He intuits that only an acquaintanceship with Albertina might be able to resolve his problem of a rootless being who has lost contact with reality. Everything around him is incomprehensible, abstract. Only Albertina is real. But Albertina is elusive; and his state of death, boredom, unreality devours him to the extreme of the most inane fits of madness. (pp. 61-5)

The Tozzian Antipatico, however, has found his way out, constituted by love, in this last phase. Love is transcendental and here it signifies the re-discovery of hope in life after having cancelled the terms of boredom and separation. Here the Antipatico re-enters into the crowd, or gives us to understand that now he is mature enough to effect this re-entry. "Their love was to be born in that very moment; and, in the end, gazing into each others eyes, they understood that they truly loved each other for the first time."

The last two years of Tozzi's life were feverishly intense. And *Gli egoisti,* a novel which in many respects is highly elaborated, constitutes the book of catharsis in the Tozzian thematic of the Antipatico. Begun in Rome (August-September 1917), according to the author's son, Glauco Tozzi, it was interrupted for the composition of *Il podere* (finished in July 1918) and for the composition of *Tre croci* (October-November 1918). In this period Tozzi also busied himself with polishing other minor works, and with the revision for the last time of *Ricordi di un impiegato* which, according to Borgese, Tozzi finished shortly before falling ill, that is to say between the end of 1919 and the beginning of 1920. *Gli egoisti,* which reflects the Rome of 1917-1919, was terminated (between corrections of the typed manuscript and additions) in January of 1920. Therefore *Gli egoisti* falls into place as the key novel in the development of Tozzian thought. More probably, however, the book that convinced Tozzi to find a way out of his thematic of the Antipatico is the novel *Tre croci.*

Tre croci exhibits only an angular aspect of this thematic, but the author does not dwell on it. The Gambi brothers belong to the world of the many, or at least they belonged to it at one time. They are forced to remove themselves from it not because of intellectual awareness or because of inability to adapt to it, but because they have betrayed the laws and the morality of society. It is in fact their financial bankruptcy that reduces them to a situation where they close themselves up in their own hole. But the external world continues to treat them normally, as before, as always. This external world is symbolized by the art critic Nisard, by the friend Vittorio Corsali, by the landowner Riccardo Valentino, by the chevalier Orazio Nicchioli, by the accountant Bruno Pallini who would like to be affianced with one of the nieces of the three brothers, Chiarina.

Nisard represents the detached cordiality and the culture of this external world, consequently civility and good manners; Cor-

sali the gossipy and pretentious friendship, that borders on stupidity; Valentino the intruding business man; Nicchioli, spurious charity, masked avarice, the sentimental, and finally, justice; Pallini, the repetition of a conventional rite, that of a bloodless and lukewarm betrothal, without the flame of love. Pallini represents absolute mediocrity.

But when they are forced to crawl into their hole, the relation of the three brothers with the outside world is set afire by Niccolò; "Between us and the others there is something that nobody will forgive us for. Therefore we, too, should not have any tender feelings for others." Their position consciously becomes one of offense and defense. The upshot is the conclusion that this society, to which they have ceased to belong, after all is not worth much more than they are. (pp. 66-8)

It is a society of betrayed and betrayers, dissolute, licentious, inept individuals, contented idiots and deluded beings. There is no order, no morality, or sincerity, or love. Niccolò describes it in order to condemn it, but by so doing he knows very well that he condemns himself; consequently he laughs over the whole spectacle. He too forms a part of this society. Thus with the Gambi brothers the condition of the Antipatico is turned upside down. Giulio will kill himself not as an act of rebellion against this society, because he feels his guilt. Hence it is not a revolt, but a punishment. And when the other two brothers die, they will not be forsaken. This society has never abandoned them. And, in fact, it re-accepts them and absolves them, by erecting on their graves those pitiful crosses, placed there by the nieces Lola and Chiarina.

The intimate tragedy of the Gambi brothers is born of the dualization that they have made of their body and mind. On the one hand the mind, the conscious motor center, feels the suffering of the isolation and the universal bankruptcy; on the other hand the body, a dead weight, that no longer responds to commands, that impedes every activity and that succeeds in enjoying only putting the mind to sleep before fanciful foods, the extreme refuge. The mind is the cross of doubt and of fear, the body the escape from the real. Laziness and spleen are connected to fear and sorrow. Often it is the mind that weakens the body in them, and at other times it is the body that puts the mind to sleep. The mind suffers and sees, the body revenges itself taking refuge in the lust for food. The game is clear. (pp. 68-9)

There is no symbolism in this novel, if we except the reference to gout with which all three brothers are afflicted. It, however, is not there to symbolize a material and spiritual situation of isolation, because it does not make them feel different from others, thereby increasing their solitude. The gout is attributed to them like a stain or sin, something impure, a destructive element characteristic only of their person.

Esthetically this novel would be referred to as realist. All of Tozzi's books, for that matter, have a realistic form. But there is a new element in this book: Tozzi has attempted an ambitious literary effort: to escape subjectivism, in order to objectify. *Tre croci* made the Tozzi "case" explode. And the critics found it opportune to link him once more with the Verghian tradition. But *Tre croci* is not a "choral" novel, as there was a will to believe, nor the best orchestrated one. The more intimate and authentic Tozzi is the one that we have seen come out from his other books, now tender and now violent, frightened and frightening, the outsider who finally succeeds in climbing the slopes of purgatory, opening himself to the calls of love, after having passed through the hell of doubt and of voluntary negation. Federigo Tozzi is an opaque pearl in twentieth century Italian literature. But indisputably he is rising in all his fullness and importance from the shadows from which he has been retrieved and cast back from time to time. His solitary and dogged work, as Debenedetti has already reminded us [see essay dated 1969], is a highly moral teaching towards the courage to live, which is the courage to create, especially for those who, at one moment or other of their own human and intellectual history have felt the cruel blows of despair and failure, negation and exile, and who have renounced surrender notwithstanding. Writing, at bottom, is nothing else but living with oneself in all the latitudes. But the pang that this sacrifice involves is warmed by the hope that, perhaps, it may be justified with the satisfaction that attends and ensues from significant accomplishment. (pp. 69-70)

> *Giose Rimanelli, "Federigo Tozzi: 'Misfit and Master'," in* Italian Quarterly, *Vol. XIV, No. 56, Spring, 1971, pp. 29-75.*

SERGIO PACIFICI (essay date 1973)

[*Pacifici is an American critic who has written extensively on Italian literature. In the following excerpt, he analyzes theme and technique in Tozzi's fiction.*]

The seriousness of Tozzi's fiction, the depth of his insights, his sober style through which he so brilliantly translates onto the written page the schizophrenic or paranoiac temperament of his characters, more than amply compensate for what some may call a limited vision. Seldom before him has the Tuscan countryside been painted in such splendid and yet foreboding ways, and even more rarely have Italian novelists succeeded in recapturing the violence, the squalor, and the loneliness of existence in a provincial town as successfully as he. The reader ready not to be dismayed by the singularly awkward and ungrammatical style of Tozzi, with its special Sienese words and expressions carefully reproduced in their spelling, will find his fiction rewarding for the completeness in which his statements on life are articulated.

Comparisons and parallels with other writers are frequently, if not irrelevant, invidious. Yet, there is much that Tozzi has in common with such contemporaries as Verga, Svevo, and Pirandello, whose work he admired and by whom he was respected. With Verga, Tozzi shares a realistic, unpretentious style as well as a brutally honest manner of looking at life; with Svevo, he shares not only a defiance of *il bello scrivere,* but a commitment to explore the psyche of his characters, giving their actions a psychological justification; and, finally, with Pirandello he shares considerable skepticism vis-à-vis human nature: "I do not believe any other writer feels as much as Pirandello that evil and meanness [are] natural conditions that cannot be abolished," he wrote about the Sicilian master. A careful reading of Tozzi's work bears out how much such a comment is pertinent to his own vision of the world. (pp. 137-38)

The world of Federigo Tozzi is already and unmistakably sketched out in many of the short stories he began writing as early as 1908, a full decade before the completion of the bulk of his novels. Beyond any question, his is a sensual, highly volatile, proud, and, above everything else, violent world, where men and women fall victims of their passionate desires, have their share of erotic or tragic adventures, and frequently long, or so it seems, to fulfill their death wish. In **"Assunta"** (1908), for example, we confront a woman who has many of the typical traits of Tozzi's heroines: she is beautiful, amoral, sensual, totally incapable of stop dreaming of being physically possessed by as many men as possible. Understandably enough, Marco is extremely jealous of his bride-to-be, all the more since he suspects, with ample justification, that she is carrying on with Domenico, the son of a moderately well-to-do family of farmers. His suspicions proved to be well-founded: when Assunta does not deny that she and Domenico have been together, he strikes her. When Domenico suddenly arrives on the scene and attempts to free Assunta from Marco's grip as he is trying to strangle her, Marco stabs him in the heart and kills him.

Violence of another sort prevails in yet another story, **"Il ciuchino"** (**"The Little Donkey,"** 1908), the tale of a new-born donkey that is forced to die by its mother, who refuses to nurse it. Set for the most part in a humble stable, it is a striking tale bound to recall a similar and well-known story by Giovanni Verga, "Storia dell'asino di San Giuseppe." But while Verga's tale is one of exploitation (the donkey passes from one owner to the next, always decreasing in value as its health deteriorates, always doomed to harder and more miserable work until, one day, it drops dead on the road, at which point his carcass is sold for the price of its hide) Tozzi's is one of alienation, of total rejection by the very creature that has given birth to the protagonist of the *racconto*. The rejection is unexplained, mysterious, but just the same tragic, a source of misery and of death. The estrangement of Roberto Falchi, the hero of another story, **"Musicomane"** (**"Musicmaniac,"** 1908), is certainly more understandable, if only because his mental retardation is caused by an acute case of meningitis. After his illness, Falchi abandons his studies that will prepare him for a professional career, and spends his time meandering all over the town, prey of an illness that knows no cure, object now of pity, now of jest on the part of the passersby.

The texture of Tozzi's tales is a strange mixture of the pathetic and the sarcastic, the haunting and the hallucinatory; the author's attitude shifts nervously from hostility to a Christian resignation and warm compassion for the victims of life. The tension created in his tales is electric, much like that of two wires always exposed to and eventually touching each other, thus setting off the spark that sets off the sound and fury of the action.

Death is also the culmination of another short story, **"Ozio"** (**"Idleness,"** 1910), revolving around the visit paid to a farm by two city dwellers, Gastone and his wife, Giovacchina, to Enrico, his wife Gemma, and her stepmother. After a rather gluttonous repast, they all decide to take a nap on the grass, under the shade of a large chestnut tree. The chirping of a bird awakens their interest, and they begin a short chase to capture the little thing. Having caught it at last, they first wonder whether they should release it from its brief captivity; then Gastone takes its little head between his index finger and his thumb and squashes it.

Adulteresses, idiots, paralytics, peasants doomed to a wretched existence, brothers and sisters alienated from one another to the point of driving each other relentlessly to the grave, menial clerks, gross, insensitive farmers—such are the characters that live in the pages of Tozzi's short stories. The prevailing mood is somber, frequently morbid, and bordering on a kind of despair a human being experiences when, for some mysterious reason, he has lost the will to live. "I have a desire to cry [so strong] that it upsets me. I feel my heart so sad and so tired, that I do not know how I am capable of living," confesses the protagonist of another of Tozzi's early short stories, **"Un ra-**

gazzo'' ("A Boy," 1914?). Once again, his tale of sad events is narrated both simply and detachedly. He feels unwanted and hated by his father, whose affection he desperately needs now that his mother has passed away. His father, instead, maltreats him, demeans and beats him constantly, making him pay physically for his shortcomings and for what he sees as unbearable ignorance and arrogance. He is finally disowned by his father, who names his servant Giulia who has become his mistress, the heiress of his property.

Such and other short stories by Tozzi reveal some of his early preoccupations and prepare us for his novels. Indeed, it comes as no surprise to us to find that the hero of *Ricordi di un impiegato* (*Journal of a Clerk*) shares much of the same temperament of his predecessors. But the links go even further: Leopoldo Gradi, such is the name of the protagonist of Tozzi's novella, lives out a life not of action but of feelings: his relationship with his father, marked by misunderstandings, his paranoiac sense of being threatened by the town where he has moved, his loneliness, and his general fear of life. Written in the form of a diary irregularly kept between one January 3 and one April 22, the work has hardly a plot. The simple story it tells, however, has a Kafkaesque quality about it. Leopoldo is practically forced by his father to accept a post with the state railroad at Pontedera. Accepting the job means to leave his family and his fiancée Attilia, who in the diary appears less a real person than a transparent symbol of the tranquility for which Leopoldo yearns. Once in Pontedera, Leopoldo finds it difficult to adjust himself to the new milieu. One day, quite unexpectedly, he receives a letter informing him that Attilia is seriously ill. His request for a short leave is approved, and he sets off for Florence in time to see his newly born sister while finding his fiancée Attilia dead. "The desolation of the scene," writes F. N. Cimmino, "has a reflection of the same intonation on the face of his mother, who has recently given birth to a baby girl; life and death run after each other; they remain naturally different, but have the same flavor." Now that life has taken such a different turn, Leopoldo begins wishing that he would not have to go back to Pontedera. With his father's approval, his wish is fulfilled. Leopoldo's tormented diary ends with this laconic note: "I am staying in Florence."

Much like the bulk of Tozzi's literary production, the novella is to some extent autobiographical less because of the obvious parallels with the private events of its author, than for the sense of estrangement and isolation its protagonist experiences. (pp. 141-45)

It should be noted that the figure of the clerk is a popular one with naturalism. To limit ourselves to the Italian scene, the most obviously similar character is to be found in Svevo's novels *Una vita* (1892) and *Senilità* (1898). But the comparison between Leopoldo and his counterparts Alfonso Nitti and Emilio Brentani cannot be pressed too far: Svevo's characters entertain dreams that prove to be unrealizable because of their ineptness, their lack of initiative, their incapacity to exploit those opportunities that could easily change the course of their lives. Svevo's irony is possible precisely because of such a contrast, as well as a persistent inability to read life realistically, as it were. On the other hand, Leopoldo only senses a secret hostility toward him, which becomes a barrier that is all but unsurmountable. There cannot be any rapport between himself and the people whom he meets but who immediately repel him. Incapable of relating to anyone, Leopoldo withdraws to his little "hole," resigned to be inescapably unhappy. He is, of course, trapped in a situation which is not of his own making

and over which, as a mere clerk, he has no control: he has an insignificant job in an alien environment, victim of the manipulations first of his father, then of his supervisor. "The remedy [for his infected personality, his wrong behavior]," observes Debenedetti [see essay dated 1969], "consists precisely in avoiding finding a remedy: Leopoldo's human definition is all here." It is here that Tozzi offers us more than a glimpse of the changing technique of the novel. Plot is subjugated to character study, dialogue gives way to monologues, reality is seen with the distorted lenses of a neurotic or a psychological misfit. Man no longer has the upper hand on life, by which he is emotionally and psychologically subdued. The crudest scenes, the most trivial incidents, arc magically transformed into extremely effective tools to illuminate man's character. At one point, Leopoldo counts his shorts, his underwear, and his socks as though he were actually attempting to take stock of what he is. Tozzi's characters think very little or too highly of themselves, and much of their time is actually spent in tormenting themselves, gnawing, and even physically destroying each other. "So I have alienated myself from this kind of reality," confesses Leopoldo. "Why, why? Why have I shut my soul like this? Even when I was a boy I liked to be alone; I used to like standing at a half-open door watching the people in a room talking. I regret what I do and yet I keep on doing the same thing. I am hungry, but I don't eat; yet I like this sense of kindly reality that always returns as though it were in love with me."

In the novels, as in many of his short stories, Tozzi's heroes are by necessity always engrossed in some sort of money-making activity in which they fail miserably. We see them, small merchants or farmers, living comfortably or even beyond their means, intent on making sure that their bellies are full even if they cannot satisfy their emotional needs. Losers in what they do and failures in what they are is their common denominator. Because they are bent on a senseless self-destruction, they deny themselves the air they need, the bread they must eat to survive, the love and compassion for which they frequently yearn. Fate inexorably denies them both peace of mind and compassion for human suffering. Seldom are Tozzi's characters granted a respite for the anguish of living or the chance to communicate to others their inner torment. There is no way to work out problems, and even when a dialogue begins it soon degenerates into an angry confrontation.

If *Ricordi di un impiegato* succeeds in setting up the general climate of mistrust and dishonesty that prevails in much of Tozzi's fiction, *Con gli occhi chiusi* provides the key to the fundamental theme of his novels. The story the book tells is definitely drawn from its author's life. The locales, Siena and Florence, were places where he had spent much of his youth; the characters are modeled upon people he had known firsthand. Pietro, the main character, is Tozzi himself; Ghísola (after whom the novel was originally entitled) is Isola, the author's first love; Domenico and Anna (Pietro's parents) bear much more than a casual resemblance to Domenico and Annunziata, right down to their occupation. But there is something far more central to our understanding of Tozzi's novels that finds its proper place in *Con gli occhi chiusi*, and it has to do with the complicated, tortuous relationship between Pietro and his father with the element that sets it on its course. Everything else in the book is subordinated to such a relationship and overshadowed by it.

When the book opens, the protagonist is a mere thirteen-year-old boy; his mother, whose previous seven children have died at various times shortly after birth is an epileptic; his father is the proprietor of a modest but highly renowned restaurant in Siena, the "Pesce Azzurro." Anna's health, already precarious, deteriorates after an accident at the restaurant (when her husband narrowly escapes being stabbed to death by a drunk customer), and on the advice of her doctor, she goes to live in their nearby farm, together with Rebecca (Pietro's wet nurse and Domenico's mistress), her parents Giacco and Masa, and, a few years later, their niece Ghísola.

For a number of reasons, some of them having to do with his health, Pietro's studies do not proceed well at the local seminary, and eventually he is asked by the principal to leave the school. His friendship with Ghísola is at least a modest consolation for his loneliness and general unhappiness; his mother, feeling guilty for her illness, barely manages to talk with him; Domenico, contemptuous toward education, disappointed and even angered by his son's poor scholastic record, is hardly a father to him. With his mother's permission, Pietro enrolls in a technical school of fine arts. Just when his mother decides to take him to the parish priest to discuss their plan, she dies quite suddenly and Pietro's situation worsens considerably. Domenico now finds himself entirely responsible for his son's upbringing and his education. The two have preciously little in common: Pietro lacks his father's aggressiveness, his ambition, his toughness of manners and living, and is therefore ill-suited for the sort of job his father has in mind for him as the manager of the family's inn. What at first appeared as a simple difference of temperament soon explodes into an open antagonism and even hostility when Domenico realizes that his son will have no part of his plans and will not accept the task of managing the inn. Even three years later, when Pietro has finally achieved his degree, Domenico finds him "useless to [his] interests, like any other idiot!" His spirit undampened, Pietro continues studying on his own for a year, having already been accepted by a technical school in Florence. This time, however, the event marks "the total disappearance of any tie between the father and his son. More and more, they treated one another like two strangers forced to live together." Unable to bear the sense of guilt and shame for still being considerably behind in his studies, and not wishing to live near a person who rejects him, Pietro takes a room in Florence. His situation, however, is hardly one conducive to a tranquil existence, and he begins brooding over his past, full of sorrow and neglect, his lonely present, and his uncertain future. Those who live around him cannot change his predicament: "He realized that he had tried, in vain, to become closer to his friends; his indifference toward some changed into hostility and enmities; he felt an aversion toward everyone, especially those who were rich and who esteemed him very little because he was a Socialist. Most people thought he was crazy; but almost everyone was fond of him."

After some years spent away from the farm at Poggio de' Meli, Ghísola returns and has an affair first with one of Pietro's boyhood friends, Borio, then with his overseer, and with other men. In order to avoid a scandal, Ghísola is persuaded to leave town and becomes the mistress of Alberto, a small merchant who is himself separated from his wife. Pietro, of course, cannot reconcile himself to the idea that the girl he thinks he loves has left him. After taking his exams, he goes to the farmhouse where Ghísola is kept by her lover. Alberto, realizing that he is much older than his mistress and that his precarious financial situation has deteriorated substantially (he files for bankruptcy before too long), suggests that Ghísola exploit Pietro's naïveté and make him believe that he is the

father of the child she is bearing. When Pietro refuses to make love to her, she becomes terrified by the prospect of having to account for a child without a father and runs away to Florence. An anonymous letter informs Pietro of Ghísola's whereabouts. And it is in a house for expectant mothers and prostitutes that he finally finds her. At last Pietro understands the reality of the situation: the shock of seeing Ghísola pregnant is too much for him. He faints at her feet: he now knows that he no longer loves her.

As is frequently the case with Tozzi, the story of *Con gli occhi chiusi* is simple and linear. Yet, its simplicity does not make it an easy book; on the contrary, it serves as an effective contrast with the psychological complexity of the characters of the novel. The tensions at work begin in a low key and gain momentum as the morbid, murky story develops in its provincial setting. There are tensions everywhere: between Domenico and his customers and his employees, between father and son, between Pietro and his playmates and Ghísola herself. Each relationship carries within the possibility of psychological confrontations. The central point of the book and what turns out to be the leitmotif of Tozzi's novels, is to be found in the very title of the book—*Con gli occhi chiusi* (*Blindfolded*), a perfectly convincing emblem of his world view. Borgese, reviewing the novel, spoke of its being "too autocritical," alluding "frankly to a method of austere introspection, a relentless examination of conscience, in which the author implicates the other characters and landscapes with himself." Actually, as Debenedetti has brilliantly shown, Tozzi's novels are the extensions and dramatizations in a psychological key of a single theme, the traumatic conflict between a neurotic human being and his intolerant, unsympathetic, and insensitive father.

It is in this context that we begin to realize how Tozzi, himself an admirer and a perceptive reader of Giovanni Verga, offers a modern treatment of the ancient question of *la roba*, property. While in Verga's masterpieces *I Malavoglia* and *Mastro-don Gesualdo* the drive to improve one's own economic lot inevitably leads to their ultimate defeat all those ready to forsake the "religion of the home" and the "ideal of the oyster" (and its tenacious attachment to its shell), in Tozzi's novels property is shown as no longer acceptable as a valid yardstick of man's real worth. Quite the opposite: material possessions, far from being an asset, are actually a detriment for they obfuscate the real issue of how man can be socially and morally defined. As such, property must be rejected, refused, and denied if one is to find one's own identity in a confused and confusing world. Thus, years before the school of the Absurd, Tozzi was writing novels whose climate and themes are distinguished by a willful and pronounced lack of commitment to a life of property, by an estrangement from middle-class values. Time and again, Pietro is depicted as being "absent," "distracted," disinterested, as it were, from accepted standards of social worth, an attitude that reflects a peculiarly contemporary uneasiness in living in a world that has mysteriously ceased to have much attraction to man. Like Pietro, most of Tozzi's characters behave strangely or erratically, leading an existence that, for all its realism, is often incomprehensibly cut off from the ordinary ways of men. Indeed, it is even possible for some readers to sympathize (although the term is not appropriate from a moral position) with Pietro's father, who does not hesitate to beat his son, scold him, and insult him, according to the circumstances, hoping that he might succeed in bringing him back to the world of money, sex, and violence in which he thrives with considerable success.

The figure of the father, with his propensity to castrate his son most likely to usurp his power, is very central in Tozzi's major novels, particularly *Con gli occhi chiusi*. But even when he is not there physically, he is nevertheless ever-present like a curse one cannot forget, a part of the past one cannot eradicate from his memory—a symbol of what must ultimately be destroyed, at whatever cost, if one is to become liberated from the nightmares of one's youth.

The protagonist of *Il podere* (*The Farm*), Remigio Selmi, is coming home, unexpectedly and urgently summoned to the bedside of his moribund father Giacomo. In Tozzi's fiction, the theme of the return to the homestead assumes a special meaning, for it is a return to a home that has always lacked its traditional security and its association with the warmth of love and happiness. One returns home, an empty, desolate, forbidding shell, not to live but to die. And Remigio will die, in the very last paragraphs of the book, at the hand of a discontented farmhand, Berto, in what is yet another of a numerous list of incomprehensible, absurd facts that take place in the tale.

The "odor" of death and of decay, already present in the opening scene of the book, permeates the entire work. Summoned home from his post at the Campiglia railroad station (we are never told specifically what his functions there are), Remigio sneaks into his father's bedroom, and is at once scolded by two of the farmhands for the manner in which he has chosen to arrive. Death and hostility, humiliation and incomprehension will remain, throughout the story, recurrent motifs and attitudes. Like Pietro's father (in *Con gli occhi chiusi*), Giacomo, too, is a well-to-do farmer who has succeeded not only in tripling the estate he inherited upon his father's death, but in commanding the respect of those who work for him. After the death of his first wife (Remigio's mother), Giacomo took a country hick, Giulia, as his mistress. Soon afterward, wishing to stop once and for all local gossiping, he married Luigia. For all practical purposes, their marriage ends when Luigia's place in the matrimonial bed is usurped by Giulia. Giacomo is now at the end of his life: a gangreneous infection in his foot is rapidly spreading throughout his blood, and he is beyond help. Doctor Umberto Bianchini, a local surgeon, is asked to intervene. He, too, however, like the rest of the characters in the story, turns out to be just another exploiter of human misery, who does not hesitate to look out for his interests by prescribing medicines he knows to be useless and making frequent calls on his patient only to pad his already high bill for services rendered.

Immediately after Giacomo's death, the schemes to cheat Remigio begin. People furiously demand that their accounts be settled, their bills rendered, their back salaries paid, even though there is no possible way to check the legitimacy or veracity of their claims. Giulia herself, banned from the farm, seeks revenge with the help of Boschini, a lawyer of dubious reputation. With the assistance of two false witnesses who wish to engage in a personal vendetta against Giacomo's son only because of their personal grudge against the dead man, Giulia demands payment of a large sum of money, eight thousand liras, she claims represents a loan extended to her lover several months before his death plus six years of back pay. The scheme is obviously fraudulent, but without documents or witnesses to disprove the claim, Remigio is forced into an untenable legal situation. Luigia, a vulgar and insensitive woman, looks upon him with increasing suspicion, despite the fact that there is absolutely nothing in what Remigio does or says to justify even

remotely the dishonesty of which she accuses him. Clearly Remigio is inept, he is incompetent in the devious ways of the business world. His naïveté makes him an easy prey of all those who try to persuade him that they are on his side, eager to help him get out of his predicament, while in effect conspiring to destroy him. He never succeeds in understanding the incomprehensible, nasty, and hostile world into which he has been thrust. He never succeeds in establishing a meaningful rapport either with the people who work for him and who resent him, or his relatives who mistrust him, or even his own lawyer, Neretti, charged with the responsibility of protecting his rights and safeguarding his interests. Remigio seems to be perennially, literally and metaphorically, on trial, always at a loss to provide the documents and witnesses any court of law requires or the confidence in his integrity without which no human bond can be established. Remigio is as incapable of penetrating the secret that has contributed to the success of his father as he is of grasping the puzzling laws inexorably turned against him. He is ridiculed by his own attorney, antagonized by his farmhands, suspected by those who should have a measure of faith in his decency. His predicament is summed up in an observation the author makes shortly before most of his disasters fall upon him: "His whole life seemed shut in a sack, from which there was no way to pull his head out."

As the study unfolds and the complexities unravel one after the other, we see that an extra element, this time totally independent from human machination, is unleashed with all its furies against Remigio. The weather has now joined those men and women who are conspiring to deny Remigio a bare moment of well-being, at least a glimpse of contentment and serenity. Whether by thievery, or spite, or natural causes, all prospects of a good harvest are cancelled. First a small crop of cherries suddenly vanish from the tree that stands right in front of Remigio's bedroom window; then a violent rainstorm damages the haystacks and rots half of the crop; then the already critical situation is worsened when a fire, apparently mysteriously started by an unknown person (we discover that the culprit is another of Remigio's enemies, Chiocciolino), burns a good part of the harvest of wheat. A small calf, purchased at the monthly fair in Siena at the insistence of Picciòlo, almost dies, while a cow miscarries, thus extending the initial preoccupation with death. Without the affection of whatever family Remigio has left, constantly harassed in the courts by his father's mistress and by one of her false witnesses who tries to extort two hundred liras for two pigs he claims Giacomo never paid for, the protagonist slowly realizes that he has no one in whom to confide. Riddled by debts and by the promissory notes he is forced to sign in order to have the necessary cash to meet his increasingly longer list of obligations, Remigio loses heart. His farm, poorly cared for by the farmhands, parched by the sun, falls into neglect and becomes an intolerable burden.

All throughout the unfolding of the story, the reader is bound to ask whether there is indeed a reason for the inequities and injustices victimizing Remigio. The answer, or at least *an* answer, is provided by something that Dr. Bianchini tells Giulia, who is asking him for help. The doctor speaks in harsh terms about Remigio: "For me," he says, "a son who goes away from his home, whatever his reasons may be, must be punished. His duty was to remain in the family and obey his father, because he would have been better off that way. He had no right to go against his father's will." The statement has Verghian overtones: leaving one's home is equivalent to betraying the ideals of the family, the legacy of values of our forefathers. By departing, man breaks the continuity and the order of the *casa*, becoming uprooted and eventually estranged not merely from the world about him, but from his very self. "I believe," affirms Berto at one point, "that [all] these things never happen without God's wishes." A kind of a curse seems to hang over Remigio's life, made wretched by circumstances he cannot control and by a sin he must expiate by his sufferings and his eventual death, anticipated by a stark passage notable for its gloom and sadness:

> This time, however, he could not hope in anything; and he abandoned himself to his own feelings. Why had he not fled that night when his farm was burning? Why had he returned to Siena, if his father wanted to die without letting him know it? Why had he become the owner of the Casuccia [estate] almost by subterfuge? He feared something unknown, more consistent than his own soul. But, although he had not thought of God for many years, he could not believe that God wanted to annihilate him in that way. What had he done wrong? Why could not his will exist? . . . He thought also of all the people he knew who had died without his caring. He too could now die, and no one would mourn him.

It is Remigio's fate to exist in a world beyond his rational, or emotional comprehension, in an incoherent, tragic world of discord, anger, and hatred. It is hatred, indeed, that eventually causes the hero's downfall, a hatred that is traceable to nothing more than envy, resentment, and arrogance. It is no wonder then why, to the very end of his drama, Remigio's important question, "Why does he [Berto, his future murderer] hate me?" should go unanswered: there is no rational explanation to the chain of misfortunes that fall upon him. The mystery of fate defies penetration, just as there is no escape from such a sordid, hopeless world. Much like the work of Beckett, the tension of Remigio's drama lies precisely in his feeling of impotence, of powerlessness in finding a reason for his futile existence. Evil is heaped upon evil, wrong upon wrong, and there is no end to it: for there is evil not only among the creditors, the notaries, the lawyers, the farmhands who take an active role in the systematic destruction of Remigio, but there is evil in his own intense desire to destroy the inheritance left to him by his father: the land, the house, the animals—the things, *la roba* that rather than making his life easier make it monstrously unbearable. Once again, Tozzi's private trauma finds its expression in the novel: the denial of those values based upon a system of possessions is effectively turned into a denial of what they represent, a paternal power that destroys rather than builds the ego of the son. It matters little whether the relentless destruction that erodes Remigio's power is self-imposed or brought on by inexplicable forces. The defeat to which he seems doomed from the very beginning is traceable to his inability to surrender what he has not really earned. And it is precisely in such a struggle, which will climax with Remigio's death, that we see mirrored the sociopolitical battle that was to intensify after the end of World War I. The farmhands emerge as a force opposing and eventually fighting a bourgeois system of values they consider unjust and abhorrent. As Tozzi presents his story, we know that the theme will be developed in a vertical manner. The conflict will not follow a linear development: it will only be intensified, worsening the already poisonous air everyone breathes. Remigio must go down to defeat without uttering a single word: he never understood, much less developed a capacity to rebel against his fate, and it is therefore natural that he should be unable to perceive the reason for the chain of disasters that eventually wreck his life. Like Remigio, most of Tozzi's characters in the novel are failures because, in the

words of Ferruccio Ulivi, they have displayed an "inability to catch by surprise, and bend adroitly and cunningly" the land itself, the soil that can yield its harvest only when it is mastered by man. "When nature, the soil, is confronted by someone who is timid or inexperienced, it reacts like human society ruining even its best harvest."

Il podere tells the tale of the wretched existence of a young man whose ineptness causes his downfall, but whose sudden death can be ascribed only to the inexorable, inexplicable laws of fate. *Tre croci* (*Three Crosses*), certainly the most objective novel Tozzi wrote, is linked to the earlier narratives through the theme of failure. This time, however, the heroes—all failures—are three, and the story of their ruin begins as all of them rapidly approach their end. The violent, primitive world of the farm, the wrath and contempt of the farmhands, the ignoble machinations of lawyers, notaries, and false witnesses, give way to a more bourgeois, but equally sordid world of the Gambi brothers. This time the tables are turned: it is no longer a secret conspiracy that drives the three brothers to their ignoble and miserable death, but themselves. Their characters prove to be their fate. We now find ourselves not in the farms of Sienese country, but in the city of Siena itself, almost always in a somber, depressing bookshop that has become a sort of trap from which there is no escape. For some time prior to the opening of the book, the protagonists have been leading a life riddled with debts, cheating, and supreme indifference. Much like other Tozzian heroes, Giulio, Niccolò, and Enrico Gambi seem to be bent upon destroying the little shop they have inherited from their father, and, by so doing, wipe out the last vestige of his memory.

Their incredibly poor management and business practice have forced them to borrow money from a kind friend, the Cavaliere Orazio Nicchioni, who has signed a promissory note for them. For several months, they have forged his signature on additional notes, promptly cashed by the bank, and their debt has now mounted to fifty thousand liras, a sum of money they can conceivably repay only at the cost of extraordinary sacrifices. Yet, while on the one hand they appear to be indifferent to their disastrous financial affairs, squandering their money on refined and expensive fruits and meats, they also dread the coming of the day of reckoning—the moment when they shall be forced to give a public account of their fraudulent scheme. The greater part of the book is given over to creating the special atmosphere in which the three brothers live, their fears, and their gluttonous pleasures. Visitors to the bookshop are few and customers even fewer. The sporadic visits of their friends have the functional role of allowing the personality of the three brothers to become more sharply delineated. The insularity of their lives, their unwillingness to confront realistically their irresponsible fiscal situation, becomes more clearly understandable in the light of their incredible vanity and egocentricity. The voice of their conscience turns out to be a faithful friend, Nisard, a student of art, a scholarly bibliophile and historian: it is he who makes them realize the opportunities they have missed to lead a meaningful and productive existence.

The drama of the Gambi brothers explodes suddenly one day when, quite accidentally, their fraudulent scheme is uncovered by one of the bank's tellers. The three brothers find themselves with the prospect of a trial they cannot possibly win and the inevitable loss of their reputation that will write them off, once and for all, from their community. The possibility of being found guilty proves to be too hard to bear for Giulio, who commits suicide by hanging himself in the dark bookshop. His brother Niccolò sets himself to restore a minimum of integrity to his name so that he might earn a livelihood without leaving his native city. He is helped by a favorable judgment of the court that has found him and Enrico innocent of the charge of fraud. With the assistance of his wife and of a few generous friends, he begins a new life as an insurance agent. But his dishonest past weighs heavily on his conscience, all the more since he and Enrico have placed the entire blame for their fraud on their dead brother. Niccolò begins suffering first from insomnia then from deliriums and, after a brief illness, dies of rheumatic apoplexy.

A similarly unhappy fate awaits the last surviving member of the unhappy trio, Enrico. After the death of his two brothers, Enrico rapidly sinks into a degrading kind of life, drinking and begging, spending his nights in public parks, in the streets, or wherever else he happens to find himself. He is finally taken to a local sanitarium where a short time later he dies of a blood infection caused by a serious case of gout which has afflicted him for some years.

As with his earlier works, *Tre croci* is less a novel of plot than one of characters masterfully and soberly created by Tozzi: the three brothers, with all their idiosyncracies, their human flaws, are portrait studies of unusual depth. Their gluttonous feasts, their eruptions of rage, their irresponsible behavior hardly conceal and much less alleviate their unconscious fear, a kind of subterranean dread that their existence will no longer provide them with pleasures they enjoy at a heavy price. They are doomed to wait, with all the anxiety and trepidation of a human being expecting his final confrontation with truth, for the ruin and shame they know they justly deserve. They exist only to allow their inevitable tragedy to take place and run its course, and their expectation is subtly deepened by the somber descriptions of Siena, their prison. In the words of Giorgio Luti, "Siena itself, which is the only background of the novel, lives of its own autonomous life, first among [its] personages." Siena is, indeed, the hostile and inclement city "Tozzi knew in the years of his 'pathological' youth." Its inhabitants are the characters peopling the novel, "absurd personages of a ghostlike humanity," prisoners of a human condition one can escape only at the end of one's life. The gloomy stillness of the city, its dark, labyrinthine, narrow streets weigh heavily upon the action of the book. By contrast, the vibrant sunsets and the descriptions of the lovely countryside surrounding Siena serve as apt contrasts to the predicament of the three brothers, whose existence has become as twisted as the streets of their city. The setting becomes an integral part of the narrative, a kind of musical background to a symphony of despair and desolation.

"Niccolò: wake up!" shouts Giulio at the opening of the novel. His cry is a plea replete with anticipatory signals whose full significance will not be understood until the story has had the chance to unfold, gaining its momentum despite the slow, deliberately monotonous pace of the novel. Here as well as elsewhere in Tozzi's fiction, to wake up means to open our eyes to a dreadful reality in which we find ourselves, the reality of a life made squalid and hopeless not merely by its incongruity, but by a painfully obvious lack of love and companionship. Without them, life becomes but a series of meaningless and purposeless grotesque acts: the hours spent sleeping when there is work to do; the idle talk about a good table; the non-action of the three brothers, content to pursue the easy and yet fatal path that can only lead to disaster; the constant bickering

and arguing that goes on between them, are yet other reflections of the uneasiness of their own lives.

Invariably in a narrative where the action, or the plot, plays a lesser role, as in the case of *Three Crosses,* the writer works through different structures to achieve the desired effects. The drama of the protagonists unfolds not through descriptions, which could easily have damaged the impartiality of the narration, but through the heated, often depressing and bizarre conversations they have with each other and with their few friends. Tozzi's language is scabrous, excited—with all its curses, its dire predictions of impending disasters, its numerous outbursts of anger and boredom—and as such it effectively reflects the neuroses of the book's central personages. Even their common illness, the gout, becomes symbolic of the sickness that pervades and eventually infects not only their blood but their very souls. Unlike their predecessors, the characters of *Three Crosses* are not humiliated and insulted, nor much less are they victims of an enigmatic destiny. They know beforehand and almost wait anxiously for the disaster that will conclude their preposterous schemings. The promissory note, the famous *cambiale* that is at the center of ever so many feverish conversations and reflections that animate the book, is turned into a tangible sign of the evil that just *is* in their lives, the reminder of a shame that is upon them, a sin they must expiate. It may also be, as Debenedetti persuasively sustains in his essay, "an indirect aggression against their father's memory."

Of the three protagonists, Giulio, presented as "the most melancholy of the Gambi brothers, but also the strongest," remains to the end the most acutely aware of what they have become. He is also, however, the most tragic figure because of his failing to harness whatever strength there was in him to bring about a change to their situation. Indeed, since he engineered the fraudulent scheme of forging the Cavaliere's signature, Giulio must live more intensely than his two brothers in the drama of the dishonesty of which they are guilty and the loneliness to which they are condemned. He has lived, as he acknowledges in a moment of extreme lucidity, "a kind of regularity that seemed to me to be just and appropriate. Now I realize," he continues, "how I have been living only provisionally, until one day some decisive event, such as that of the promissory note, should come along, transforming into weakness whatever had formerly seemed strong and well chosen." His freedom, as he sees it, is in his choice to live or coexist with his fears in a silence that allows him to suffer for himself and for others as well. His loneliness is his meager achievement, the only one his pride can yield. But pride is also what causes him to assume an arrogant, immoral stance that only hastens the end of his miserable existence. "Debts and [promissory] notes," as Giorgio Luti underscores, "are symbols of a provincial society that grants no freedom to the individual, no possible choice, leaving no room to the dream in the increasingly more restless relation between past and present."

It befalls on Giulio, the real protagonist of the tragedy of the Gambi brothers, to articulate through his reflections shortly before he commits suicide, the nature of their predicament, the very reason why life can no longer be understood neither as a challenge, nor as a source of pleasure:

> He felt that the act of living had become for him a
> totally involuntary matter. He no longer cared about
> anything, and the voices of the others speaking in
> the next room seemed as though checked by some
> obstacle, which prevented them from reaching him
> or including him in their circle. . . . He could not

even be sad or worried; an unchanging and fatal clarity in a medley of recollections and thoughts reminded him that he could do nothing to change the state of affairs. He felt that all around him was crumbling and he could find no solid basis in which to take a decision. He even felt that it would always be impossible for him to account for this conscious silence and emptiness that overwhelmed him.

Passages such as the one just quoted give us at least a feeling of the modernity and relevance of a writer whose work, seemingly written in the conventions of *verismo*, could easily be mistaken for regionalistic. A more careful analysis of the book quickly dispels such a notion. True enough, judging at least from his setting, Tozzi was indeed a provincial. But the real reason for his insistence upon locating most of his fiction in Siena had less to do with prevailing fashions at that time (one thinks here of Fogazzaro, Deledda, Pirandello, d'Annunzio, and a score of other contemporaries of his) than with his determination to write from his own experience. He was less interested in giving us yet another believable tableau of life in the provinces—although judging from his work he eminently did succeed in this—than in creating a world riddled by violence and haunted by dark fears. He accepted the gamble of being classified as just another regionalistic writer in an era when Italian culture was striving to shed its provincialism and insularity and insert itself in the mainstream of European letters, by creating characters and landscapes that were nothing if not universal symbols of the suffering and estrangement of the whole of mankind. Thus, for all the deceptive realism of his fiction, Tozzi was hardly interested in reality as such. Depicting life on the farms, or in a small bookshop in the silent, sleepy, and yet terrifying city of Siena, was for him but a way to descend into the mysterious regions of private consciousness and explore its fragility. "Our sweetest and tenderest feelings must go through a fatal necessity which completely disregards them. In Pirandello there is laughter, but never joyfulness. . . . next to goodness, there is always the threat of evil and meanness," so Tozzi wrote about one of the writers he held in great esteem. Pirandello's "human world is conceived as a kind of punishment, which often forces it to become twisted and limited." These accurate insights apply as much to Tozzi as they were meant to apply to Pirandello.

While to some extent the problem of good and evil is most central in his stories, it is the manner in which it is worked out in the world of the human heart, rather than in the world of action, that matters. And that world, as Tozzi rightly perceives, never yields easy answers to troublesome and complex problems. Unlike the masters of *verismo* whose work he admired, he did not attribute the defeat and eventual destruction to which his characters are inexorably doomed to economic, and much less, to religious causes. Unlike the naturalists, he did not believe in and was therefore incapable of dramatizing the connection between cause and effect. Instead, he contented himself with painting the fragmentation of human life whose pieces, like those of a shattered mirror, "can't be fitted together," as Ben Johnson notes [see excerpt dated 1959].

In the area of language Tozzi left his unmistakable mark on contemporary Italian literature. "It is not so much his personality as a man, and its reflection on his works," continues Johnson, "that has counted with writers who have come after him, as the influence he has had upon the Italian written language. Every great writer rapes the language he is given to use, bending it to his own end, and Tozzi did just that. . . . in the last couple of years of his life he expunged from his writings all verbiage, stripped it to its essentials, to the neglect even of grammar and syntax and to the horror of purists." In a manner not at all dissimilar from Verga's and Svevo's, Tozzi set for himself the task to create—there is no better term for it—a language through which he could give life to the sordid, sensual, and violent collection of Sienese peasants and small merchants that people his world. Through what eventually became his style, he succeeded in conjuring up the stifling, alienated vision that emerges bit by bit from the haunted novels of a haunted man. Confronted by an existence deprived of all traditional logic, Tozzi's characters must sit, like Beckett's heroes, waiting not for Godot, but for a death that will free them from their anxieties and dread. "The new novel, discovered and at once realized by Tozzi,"concludes Debenedetti in his essay, "looks at psychology from a nocturnal side, in a zone that affords no mundane explanations, does not conceive of problems that may be explained with a ruler and a compass, a zone that is more precisely called the psyche." Unlike Svevo, whose major novel *The Confessions of Zeno* was to appear barely three years after the death of the Sienese, Tozzi never found in irony or humour the element that would enable him to resolve the tensions of his tales. Gloomy, somber almost to excess, the characters of Tozzi's world live out the consequences of an alienated existence, and in this sense they have at least something in common with the creations of Luigi Pirandello. . . . [However], Pirandello's characters come forward to the center of the stage to argue out their case, and attempt to resolve their predicament by a deceit that becomes a kind of *modus vivendi*, an arrangement that will permit them to make peace with their situation. Not so in Tozzi's case: his characters are destined to live an existence that both psychologically and physically constitutes a rejection of an unhealthy family bond. "We have," writes Debenedetti, "a stage crowded with flesh-and-blood presences of reincarnated memories, which push their way, confusedly, to the foreground, without any rationale of time, space, or causality, bound together only by their power of vexation and evil." It ultimately matters little, in the context of the attitude of Tozzi's characters, whether society expects them to be proficient students, successful farmers and overseers, or astute businessmen. Inevitably they are asked to accept a legacy of mores and values they find, in the depth, to be thoroughly repulsive.

Everywhere, in the private life as well as in the artistic world of Federigo Tozzi, there are tangible signs of an estrangement that has chocked off the possibility of happiness as well as the impelling need of human companionship and communion. Lonely, alienated, wretched, the heroes of Tozzi truly live, *ante litteram*, the ordeal of contemporary man, looking everywhere for answers to the riddle of existence. Their drama is ours: and our responsiveness to it is what ultimately cancels the chronological distance that separates us from him. (pp. 145-64)

Sergio Pacifici, "Federigo Tozzi: The Novel Reborn," in his The Modern Italian Novel from Capuana to Tozzi, *Southern Illinois University Press, 1973, pp. 136-64.*

PETER N. PEDRONI   (essay date 1983)

[*In the following excerpt, Pedroni examines the autobiographical nature of Tozzi's works and their dissimilarity to works of the Naturalist school.*]

L'incalco, Federigo Tozzi's final work, adds nothing to his status as a writer, but it is an essential document for whoever wishes to understand fully the man and his novels. Tozzi nurtured ambitions of becoming a successful dramatist and used his budding reputation as a novelist to gain acceptance for his plays. He did enjoy some limited success in Florence with a series of brief comedies, but a more ambitious comedy titled *Le due mogli* was a failure in Milan.

L'incalco was an attempt at serious drama, a kind of contemporary middle class tragedy based on the classic Greek model. As such it admirably respects the Aristotelian unities of time, place, and action. The entire play takes place in two rooms of the family villa. The third act takes place several years after the first two, but the duration of all three acts is a matter of hours. The characters are limited to six. Enzo and Flora Poggi are domineering parents who expect their children to fit into the mold that they have created for them. The children, Virgilio and Silvia, however, rebel against the mold. Virgilio wants to leave his family and home even at the risk of losing his inheritance. Silvia, to the dishonor of her parents, wants to leave her husband, Guido Bardi, in order to live with Mario Girelli, Virgilio's friend who is in love with her. Nevertheless, after many brave speeches on the part of Virgilio, Mario and Silvia, all three quickly capitulate and the third act seems to serve as a rebuttal to the first two. The tragic element is supplied by the death of Enzo, provoked by the bitter frustration caused by Virgilio's rebellion, Flora's suicide resulting from a bitter argument with Virgilio, and Virgilio's incipient insanity, a consequence of the remorse felt for Enzo's death without fulfillment and the shock of Flora's suicide. (p. 10)

The most obvious defect of *L'incalco* is that it has the appearance and tone of a caricature. The contradicting sentiments of the two generations are too extreme and rigid and expressed too heroically to be taken seriously in the context of middle class mediocrity. The characters seem to be reciting rehearsed speeches rather than living their emotions. One could argue to Tozzi's defense simply that the author died before he had an opportunity to rework the play properly. What is clear is that through *L'incalco* he wished to express in artistic, but unequivocal, terms the deep remorse that he felt for his own youthful rebellion against his father and the determining effect that this remorse had on his life. (p. 11)

[As] much as the young Tozzi loved to strike the pose of a Cecco Angiolieri, the reality of his father's death and the apparent satisfaction of his egotistical desires caused in him a morbid awareness of death and natural destruction and a deep sense of guilt and remorse toward his father. This bitter feeling is expressed throughout his short stories, which are characterized by unexplained lost opportunities, wasted existences, and death. In *Bestie,* a collection of prose fragments, Tozzi's animals are generally small silent creatures that live and die without any apparent purpose or reason and in whom are reflected the generic suffering of man and the inexplicability of the human condition. In *Ricordi di un impiegato,* the young author's first attempt at a novel, Leopoldo Gradi, the autobiographical protagonist, suffers from an identity crisis and an inability to communicate. His parents do not understand him or appreciate him. He perceives himself as intelligent, sensitive, and romantic and yet is forced by circumstances to accept the mental and material drudgery of the life of a clerk. He simply cannot cope with such a banal atmosphere and, because of his apparent snobbery, is disliked and ridiculed by his colleagues and others with whom he must associate. Underlying the general sense of sadness that pervades Leopoldo's spirit is his awareness of and concern with the useless passing of his youth, the unrelenting consumption of his existence, and inevitable and unexplained death. After contemplating the mysteries of existence and being unable to rationalize death, Leopoldo reacts by closing his mind to it. . . . (pp. 12-13)

This rejection of reality is reflected in the title of Tozzi's first major novel, *Con gli occhi chiusi,* in which he expresses the rebellion of a son against his father. Domenico Rosi incarnates the traditional hero of "la roba," that is, the man who by virtue of his hard work and sacrifice has achieved material well-being, a condition which he expects his children to increase or at least maintain, and in any case, to appreciate. Pietro, the beneficiary of this well-being, to the exasperation of Domenico, has no interest in any of this. This problematic relationship is simple and well known. The successful older generation presumes to have found the correct way of living and expects the younger generation to live in the same way. However, the younger generation feels a need to distinguish itself and cannot accept this preestablished mold. For Tozzi, to accept the form of life preestablished for him by his father was tantamount to not living. In order to live he had to establish an identity completely distinct from that of his father. Since Pietro is overpowered by his father and therefore basically weak, his attempt to be different is more negative than positive and takes the form of rejection. Pietro consistently rejects whatever his father stands for, and does whatever will offend him, not out of hatred, but out of a need to be different. That is why, to Domenico's great frustration, Pietro is completely incompetent for working in his father's restaurant. It also explains why their personalities are so different. While Domenico is aggressive, talkative, joyful, and emotional, Pietro is withdrawn, taciturn, sad, and apparently emotionless. To make the distinction complete, Tozzi, who in reality inherited his father's physical strength and stature, created Pietro with a weak and fragile body.

Pietro fails in school in order to displease his father and becomes a socialist for the same reason. But more significantly, he falls in love with and wants, against his father's wishes, to marry a poor peasant girl who is reputed to have already made love with several men. Domenico, of course, had always enjoyed sexual relations with women, including peasant women, but had always been properly discreet, had never become emotionally involved, and had never allowed these relationships to affect his family's well-being. And he would have had no objection to Pietro enjoying sexual relations in the same way. Thus for Pietro to have simply taken sexual advantage of Ghisola would have been following the father's pattern. It is for this reason that Pietro resists any temptation for sexual relations with Ghisola and instead courts her with maximum respect and wishes to marry her.

Ghisola is an illiterate peasant girl endowed with natural beauty and a thirst for life. Based on the real-life Isola with whom the young Tozzi was in love, she is the least complex and the most innocent of the principal characters inasmuch as she lives according to her natural impulses and instincts. She is corrupted only when the taboos of society incite her to attempt to trick Pietro into thinking that he is the father of her expected child. Pietro's complex character and his "blindness" to reality render him unattractive to Ghisola. She would prefer that he recognize her for what she really is so that she could live with him according to her natural instincts. It is interesting to note that while Tozzi the person and Pietro the autobiographical protagonist idealize and thereby fail to respect the real Ghisola,

Tozzi the author understands and admires her. That is because Ghisola serves two functions in the novel. First she serves as a means for Pietro to rebel against his father's reality. Furthermore, Tozzi expresses through her his wish for a free and individual life. Ghisola does what Pietro cannot do. While Pietro simply acts to displease his father, but remains dependent on him, Ghisela makes a positive attempt to live according to her natural impulses. She is, of course, defeated. Society will undoubtedly condemn her to a life of prostitution and misery.

Pietro is also defeated. The "opening of his eyes" is not a cure. Rather it is the violent destruction of his hope for individuality, freedom, and life. Now he is forced to see and accept his father's reality, a reality that condemns him to an existence that is a denial for real living. These two defeats, which are really one defeat in the author, manifest the decidedly tragic character of the novel.

In the simplest sense of the word, *Con gli occhi chiusi* is an autobiographical novel. That is to say that the plot is based on the author's true life experiences. It is important to observe, however, that the plot is a relatively minor element of the total structure of the novel. Nevertheless, the novel is autobiographical in a much more significant sense. Pietro's way of observing the world around him is really Tozzi's way of observing the world around him. For this reason and not for the more or less autobiographical plot, Pietro is truly an autobiographical character. Through Pietro, Tozzi expresses his view of reality, which is a rejection of normally accepted reality.

In the same spirit and to express better his rejection of standard reality, Tozzi discarded the traditional structure and form of the novel, the most obvious manifestation of which is the elimination of the division of the novel into chapters. For Tozzi, chapter divisions were at best an unnecessary attempt to categorize and at worst the enforcement of an external order. Instead, the narrative proceeds freely and with no apparent order, the frequent breaks in the narrative identified only by a short blank space. Tozzi was, after all, a lyricist, which is to say that he wrote to express his own feelings, emotions, and ideas generally indirectly through dialogue and narration. Rejecting the naturalists' principle of the impersonality of the author, Tozzi also exercised occasionally the freedom to intervene directly to express himself. (pp. 13-15)

Although it was interrupted for the writing of the major novels *Il podere* and *Tre croci*, the first novel that Tozzi started after *Con gli occhi chiusi* was *Gli egoisti*. As the former was a novel of youthful rebellion, so the latter was intended as a novel of mature resignation. The importance that the author attached to the work is demonstrated by the fact that he returned to it and attempted to finish it during the last year of his life. Like *L'incalco*, *Gli egoisti* betrays an unfinished quality that adds little or nothing to Tozzi's status as a writer, but is essential for a clear understanding of the man and his major novels. The material for *Gli egoisti* was Tozzi's 1907 sojourn in Rome, his failure to find work as a journalist, and his return to his father in Siena. Dario Gavinai, the clearly autobiographical protagonist, is a would-be musician who has come from provincial Pistoia to Rome in search of a career. He survives on the small sum of money that an aunt sends him each month and the occasional charity of two friends he has made in Rome. In the dichotomy Rome/Pistoia (Siena), Rome represents the opportunity to break the mold, to experience the unusual, to live life to its fullest, and, in short, to satisfy the demands of the ego. Pistoia (Siena) represents security, normality, mediocrity, and the acceptance of the mold. Dario's determination to stick it

out in Rome is put to the test by Carraresi, a fictionalized version of Tozzi's friend Domenico Giuliotti, who attacks the evils of the capital and praises the virtues of provincial life.

Far more important in the intentions of the author, however, is the influence of Albertina, a fictionalized version of Emma Palagi. Although *Gli egoisti* is a novel of resignation, in it the author wishes to demonstrate the positive influence and the curative power of the love that Dario (Tozzi) finds in Albertina (Emma). Unfortunately, Tozzi was hardly more successful in depicting Emma through Albertina than he had been with Attilia, who in *Ricordi di un impiegato* remains little more than a concept that helps Leopoldo to keep faith in himself despite the mental drudgery of his life as a railroad clerk and the misunderstanding of his parents and colleagues. (pp. 15-16)

In the final analysis, the importance of Emma's role in Tozzi's life is best expressed by her absence in the two major novels, *Il podere* and *Tre croci*, in which a son or sons are punished for sins against their father or against society. *Il podere* is based on the period following Tozzi's father's death and the inheritance of the family farms. The protagonist, Remigio Selmi, is the spiritual continuation of Pietro Rosi and Leopoldo Gradi. However, in the case of *Il podere*, the fundamental difference between the protagonist and the author is that Remigio has no Emma. In fact, *Il podere* can be read as a tribute by Tozzi to Emma Palagi, inasmuch as this novel represents the imagined life of the author without the loving support of his wife. Remigio is utterly alone as he confronts the problems of the farm and the inheritance, just as Tozzi would have been were it not for Emma. Remigio's problems begin the day he comes home to his father's deathbed and continue unrelentingly until he is murdered by Berto, a farmhand. It is as though Remigio were condemned from the outset. His tragic end is inevitable and he will live just long enough to witness the destruction of his inherited material well-being. (pp. 16-17)

Tre croci is also a story of destruction. On a visit to Siena from Rome in 1918, while walking home from the station, an acquaintance told Tozzi the latest news of Siena including the demise of the Torrini brothers whom Tozzi had known as the proprietors of a local book store. The author was so impressed by the story and the material that it provided that he decided to use it for a novel. Back in Rome he interrupted his work on *Il podere* and wrote *Tre croci* with one burst of enthusiasm between October 25 and November 9.

In the story of the three brothers and their bookstore, Tozzi saw the opportunity to move away from the autobiographical material that he had been using exclusively in his novels until then, and to universalize the expression of his ideas and emotions through someone else's story. Nevertheless he surely was attracted by a certain affinity between their story and his own life. They, like him, had inherited their father's business for which they had little ability or desire. Tozzi either knew or imagined that they felt confined by Siena as he had. Thus, the novel provided for him the vehicle with which to express his own love/hate relationship with Siena.

The atmosphere in which Giulio, Niccolò, and Enrico Gambi live is very similar to the atmosphere depicted in *Bestie*. While they struggle and squirm to satisfy their physical urges, the rest of the world seems to wait like scavenger birds for their collapse. Niccolò imagines the satisfaction others will get from their failure. Enrico's friends tell him that they will celebrate the day he dies. Just before hanging himself, Giulio imagines "un branco di gente" ["a crowd of people"] trying to knock down the door to get to him. Shortly before being taken into a home for the poor, Enrico is described as envying a stray dog that finds a bone to lick in a pile of trash. This image of Enrico's desperate hunger is an ironic reference to the importance that he and his brothers had given to the pleasures of eating. It is in large part the expense of satisfying their mutual gluttony that causes their downfall. They do not appear to have other vices. They do not gamble and they do not squander money on women, both of which vices are peculiar to human beings. Instead their vice is one that they have in common with animals, the only distinction being their more sophisticated tastes.

Most of the novel takes place inside the Gambi brothers' bookstore or in their home. Even when the characters are out of doors the scenes seem to be internal because they are closed within the confines of the narrow winding streets of Siena. The few descriptions of the surrounding countryside are a view from a window or from the city walls as though from within a prison. Whenever there is a description of the countryside it is in association with one of the characters who are outside the Gambi family or with the young and innocent nieces, Chiarina and Lola, and with their aunt Modesta. For the three Gambi brothers, Siena has the characteristics of a confining antagonist. The Sienese are characterized as nosy and gossipy and the Gambi brothers are no exception to the rule. Niccolò entertains himself by commenting on the people who pass by the bookstore, each of whom, according to Niccolò, has something embarrassing to hide. Enrico specializes in pointing out the married men that he believes are cuckolds. In turn, however, it is this same nosiness on the part of other people that causes Giulio, Niccolò, and Enrico to put up a false front of prosperity when in reality their business is failing rapidly. . . . Even when they are alone they have difficulty in admitting the truth to each other. In effect they are forced to play roles, like actors on a stage. This atmosphere of suffocating inquisitiveness and falseness that Tozzi associated with Siena was one of the principal influences on Tozzi's life and one which he successfully expressed in *Tre croci.*

One of the problems that the author confronted was that he had to deal with three brothers rather than with a single protagonist as he had in his previous novels. He had to be able to depict three distinguishable personalities and to assign a significant role to each. Enrico is the least developed, at least until the final chapter, which is devoted to him. He is also the least responsible, the most insensitive, and the crudest of the brothers. Niccolò is lazy, impolite, and demanding, but capable of an occasional show of emotion. Except for his lack of industriousness, he has much in common with Tozzi's father. Giulio is the most conscientious of the three and the only one who really works. His existential concerns make him the most autobiographical of the three and the one to whom Tozzi devoted the most attention. (pp. 19-20)

Although this least autobiographical of Tozzi's novels has been compared to Verga's *I Malavoglia* for its apparent naturalism, there is in reality little similarity. Whereas Verga's novel is rich in plot and vicissitudes and takes place over a period of several years, in *Tre croci* the important events have already taken place before the novel begins and, except for the final two chapters which serve as a kind of epilogue, the novel takes place during a very brief period of time. The Gambi brothers had inherited their father's bookstore, but apparently because of a decrease in business and because they have been living beyond their means, it was necessary to take out a loan. Their trusting friend, the Cavaliere Nicchioli, signed the loan as guarantor. When a subsequent loan became necessary Giulio forged Nicchioli's signature. These antecedent facts are all revealed in the first pages of the novel as we see Giulio forging Nicchioli's signature again. At that point it is already clear that there is no possibility that they will ever be able to repay the loans and it is only a question of time before their business will fail and their fraud will be discovered. In short, their tragic ending is inevitable. In contrast to what would be expected in a naturalistic novel, there is no discussion of cause and effect. There are no clear reasons why the book business is bad or why the Gambi brothers are the way they are. Nothing is said about their father or any other family member that might have influenced their character. They exist as in a vacuum and the reader is simply expected to accept the given facts. Indeed, *Tre croci* has more in common with classic Greek tragedy than it does with Verga's novel or with the naturalist school. After the initial revelation of facts and events the author's interest focuses on the reaction of the characters to their inevitable fate.

However, the hope of Christian salvation is expressed in the final scene when Chiarina and Lola place three crosses on their uncles' graves. The young and innocent nieces serve to offset what is otherwise an atmosphere of complete corruption and pessimism in the novel. One of the most beautiful scenes is dedicated to a walk in the country that they take with Modesta, during which, with great trepidation, the girls reveal that Chiarina has a boyfriend and wants to become engaged. The episode is virtually superfluous to the plot, but its atmosphere of innocence and optimism serves perfectly to highlight the dominant atmosphere of corruption and pessimism. The insertion of this episode is another example of Tozzi's antinaturalism.

None of the three brothers believes in God, but Giulio envies those that do. He would like to believe but cannot, and therefore cannot be saved. Giulio, like Remigio and like Tozzi, is guilty of a sin against society and is therefore liable for a punishment from which he can be saved only by a reconciliation with God. But that reconciliation is impossible without the loving guidance of an Emma Palagi. As in the case of Remigio in *Il podere,* Tozzi imagined through Giulio what might have happened to himself without Emma's love. *Tre croci,* like *Il podere,* is a tribute to the saving influence of Emma Palagi on Federigo Tozzi.

Tozzi's existential crisis is least artistically but most clearly stated in *L'incalco.* His thirst for life, which meant complete freedom to manifest his individuality, was impeded by his father's desire to perpetuate himself through his son. His father's death gave him his freedom, but also caused him to realize that his egotism had caused his father's existential defeat. The irreconcilable conflict between competing egos and the inexplicability of the determination of one's destiny turned him against positivism and naturalism and towards a vague belief in a supreme being. Emma Palagi led him to a firm belief in God and a sincere faith in a superior, but inexplicable, order.

It is exactly this inexplicability that in turn determined Tozzi's antinaturalistic style. Since the reality of the world around him revealed no discernible order, he made no effort to impose an external order or symmetry on his novels. Instead he felt completely free to devote large amounts of detail to brief time periods and then to summarize with a few short sentences the apparently important events of a year. His vocation was lyric, not narrative. He did not write to tell a story, but rather to express his view of reality. When the story offered him the kind of material through which he could express his ideas and emotions, he developed it fully; when it did not, he merely reported the facts. In other words, Tozzi wrote only when he had something significant to express; otherwise he cut the discussion short and went on to something else, often with little care for what might be considered smooth transition.

Furthermore, Tozzi felt no compulsion to justify psychologically or rationally the actions of his characters. On the contrary, he rejected the positivistic notion that everything is explainable. In contrast to naturalists like Verga and Zola, who wrote with a spirit of confidence in the explicability of man's behavior, Tozzi wrote to express the complete lack of such explicability. If Tozzi had understood the events about which he wrote, he would not have written about them. He wrote about them because he did not understand them. Since he perceived almost nothing in life as absolute, he consistently avoided absolute expressions and preferred instead indirect and ambiguous expressions like "sembrava," "come se fosse," and "una specie di" ["seems like," "as if it were," and "sort of like"], which conveyed a lack of precision, creating for the reader a vaguely uncomfortable feeling that nothing really *is*, but only seems to be. That is, of course, the way that Tozzi viewed life, and it is that view that he wished to express in his novels. (pp. 19-23)

Peter N. Pedroni, "Federigo Tozzi: Autobiography and Antinaturalism," in Italica, *Vol. 60, No. 1, Spring, 1983, pp. 10-23.*

ADDITIONAL BIBLIOGRAPHY

Klopp, Charles. "Federigo's Ark: Beasts and Bestiality in Tozzi." *Italian Quarterly* XXI, No. 81 (Summer 1980): 55-62.
   Examines the narrative function of animals in Tozzi's fiction and the significance of animals in the expression of his worldview.

————"Metaphor and Psychology in Tozzi's *Gli egoisti.*" *Italian Culture* V (1984): 141-55.
   Analyzes Tozzi's attempt to express "aspects of the inner life . . . through metaphor and other figures of comparison."

Pacifici, Sergio. Introduction to *From Verismo to Experimentalism: Essays on the Modern Italian Novel,* edited by Sergio Pacifici, pp. xv-xxxvi. Bloomington: Indiana University Press, 1970.
   Discusses Tozzi's critical reputation, ranking him among "that small group of artists who . . . revolutionized the traditional concept of the novel."

Wilkins, Ernest Hatch. *A History of Italian Literature,* p. 486. Cambridge, Mass.: Harvard University Press, 1954.
   Brief commentary on *Tre croci* and *Il podere.*

Thorstein (Bunde) Veblen

1857-1929

American economist and social philosopher.

Veblen was an economic and social theorist whose works severely criticized the dominance of capital in American society. In numerous books and articles, most prominently in *The Theory of the Leisure Class,* he detailed the manners and morals of wealthy society, the fundamental incompatibility of business and industrial interests, and the natural tendency of finance capitalism to generate policies of war and imperialism. Veblen's method was to pose as a dispassionate, scientific observer while satirizing the values of the wealthy and the classical economic theories which justified their ascendancy. He is especially known for his scholarly, polysyllabic prose style and his use of irony to conceal his bias against his subject.

Veblen was born in Wisconsin to Norwegian immigrant farmers who had arrived in the United States in 1847. Norwegian was the language of the Veblen household and of the culturally isolated communities where the Veblens resided. Consequently, Veblen learned English as a second language and this, combined with the deep distrust that the Scandinavians felt for the Anglo-Saxon culture that dominated the Midwest, cultivated in Veblen feelings of being an outsider and a dissident. Veblen's father moved the family to Minnesota in 1865, where he acquired 290 acres of rich farmland. A precocious child, Veblen was often exempted from the usual farm labor because his parents recognized and wanted to encourage his intellectual development. Veblen attended local schools and then, like his brothers and sisters, went to Carleton College, a small, religiously based liberal arts college. There Veblen excelled in philosophy and studied under John Bates Clark, who later at Columbia University became recognized as America's leading economist.

After graduating from Carleton in 1881, Veblen began to study philosophy at Johns Hopkins University, but he soon transferred to Yale. At Yale, Veblen studied under William Graham Sumner, a social Darwinist and exponent of the philosophy of Herbert Spencer, and after two and a half years he obtained his doctorate in philosophy. Unable to secure a teaching position at a university, partly due to the fact that he was not a subscribing Christian, he returned to the family farm, where he remained for the next seven years. In 1891 he married Ellen Rolfe, the daughter of an affluent midwestern family, and resumed his studies at Cornell as a student of economics. There Veblen's dedication and intelligence impressed one of his professors, J. Laurence Laughlin, who two years later was named head of the Department of Economics at the newly instituted University of Chicago. Laughlin gave Veblen a position at the university, where among other subjects Veblen taught a course on the history of socialism. During this time he also published numerous articles, many of which contained the theoretical bases of his later books. In 1899, Veblen published what was to become his best known work, *The Theory of the Leisure Class,* and he soon became one of the most controversial thinkers of his day.

Controversy surrounded not only Verblen's works, in which he challenged many fundamental values of American society,

but his personal life as well. He was perpetually unable to resist the advances of the numerous women he infatuated, and his disregard for social norms and penchant for exhibitionism kept him from making any effort to conceal his dalliances. After being dismissed from the University of Chicago in 1906 for taking a transatlantic journey with the wife of a fellow professor, he accepted a position at Stanford. In California, Veblen resided at times with his wife, at times with other women, and the scandal created by his living arrangements resulted in his dismissal from Stanford three years after his appointment. Joseph Dorfman wrote that Veblen's "interest in a woman was usually only a passing desire for amusement and diversion, but their interest in him was often so tenacious that for him the affairs became baffling and in some cases even appalling." Concerning his domestic habits, Veblen once remarked, "What is one to do if the woman moves in on you?" Veblen eventually found another teaching position at the University of Missouri, divorced his first wife, and married Anne Fessenden Bradley. In 1917 he left for Washington to assist in wartime administration, but soon went on to New York to become an editor of the *Dial* and a professor at The New School for Social Research. Anne died in 1920, and several years later Veblen retired to California, where he lived in semi-seclusion and finished a translation of the *Laxdaela Saga* from the Icelandic. He died in 1929.

Max Lerner has written that, in *The Theory of the Leisure Class,* Veblen "took as his theme the unproductiveness and inutility which become the ideals of a leisure class, and their psychological effects upon the whole of a society." Veblen used not only economic, but also anthropological, historical, and psychological data to explore how the pursuit of capital affected human behavior. One of the most controversial aspects of the book was the comparison of modern to primitive cultures; for example, Veblen maintained that the acquisitive behavior of the leading industrialists was virtually identical to that of a Papuan chieftain. Veblen's basic argument was that the primary motive that the rich have in acquiring and using their wealth is not to enjoy the goods they acquire, but rather to show off their wealth and foster "invidious distinctions" between themselves and others in order to increase their own social prestige. Veblen further maintained that the only effective way of acquiring this prestige is to spend wealth on useless ostentation, which he termed "conspicuous waste." Ruthlessly satirizing their behavior, Veblen discussed the wealthy as anthropological specimens: he assigned derogatory terms to their behavior, such as calling their consumption of luxury goods "waste," while at the same time declaring that these terms were used in a non-critical and purely descriptive sense. He thus claimed for himself "scientific objectivity" while lambasting the manners of the leisure class. Veblen's prose style complements this guise of objectivity, particularly in its elevated scientific tone and recondite technical vocabulary. Some critics have called this style a parody of the wasteful ostentation of scholarly prose, while others, noting that it is characteristic of all of Veblen's works, argue that it is Veblen's natural voice. In an 1889 review of *The Theory of the Leisure Class,* W. D. Howells praised the passionless analysis of the leisure class, detecting no animus in Veblen for his subject and noting that a dramatic treatment of the circumstances that Veblen described would be "the supreme opportunity of the American novelist." By contrast, H. L. Mencken ferociously attacked Veblen's works for "the astoundingly grandiose and rococo manner of their statement, the almost unbelievable tediousness and flatulence of the gifted headmaster's prose, his unprecedented talent for saying nothing in an august and heroic manner." Some critics have emphasized Veblen's satire and have compared him to Jonathan Swift; Lewis Mumford, for example, called Veblen not only the foremost economist in America but also the most important satirist. Others have commented on the application of Veblen's ideas about conspicuous waste and invidious distinction to linguistic theory, theories of fashion, and to the class-determined nature of taste.

In the works that followed *The Theory of the Leisure Class,* Veblen explored various social and economic subjects. *The Theory of Business Enterprise* focused on the conflict between business and industry. Business, Veblen asserted, is primarily interested in making profits, while the interest of industry is to manufacture products. Veblen believed that maximum production should be the primary economic goal and noted that business interests should not be allowed to direct industry because their main goal was optimum profits, which could only be achieved by limiting production in order to artificially increase prices, thus causing the whole economy to suffer. In *An Inquiry into the Nature of Peace and the Terms of Its Perpetuation,* written during World War I, Veblen sought to outline terms "on which peace at large may be hopefully installed and maintained." He supported the American war effort, arguing that the absolute defeat and dissolution of the German imperial coalition was necessary for any sustained peace, since Germany (and Japan) had a need for warlike en-terprise to attain their goal of dynastic ascendancy. At the same time, Veblen argued that the status of the wealthy in England and the United States, and the established patriotic order of things, were also incompatible with any lasting peace, and he called for the neutralization of all citizenship in order to subdue the patriotic fervor that would lead to another war. This aspect of Veblen's book engendered harsh criticism and lead to its suppression by the government.

In 1918, Veblen published *The Higher Learning in America: A Memorandum on the Conduct of Universities by Business Men,* which he had written several years earlier but had withheld from publication, possibly to avoid any occupational discrimination which this attack on the university system might have engendered. Veblen was concerned with the dominance of capital in the university community, a situation which he regarded as detrimental to the pursuit of higher learning. As Joseph Dorfman explains, Veblen contended that pecuniary motives in universities fostered "a competitive seeking of endowments and an increase of students from among the reputable, so that life and substance may be expended for a further accumulation of funds and immature students." Accumulation of capital becomes the primary objective, and stands in the way of freedoms of inquiry and criticism that are fundamentally necessary to education. Veblen called presidents of universities "captains of erudition," who worked in the interests of such patrons of higher education as Andrew Carnegie, Cornelius Vanderbilt, and John Rockefeller. Veblen's later works, *The Vested Interests and the State of the Industrial Arts, The Engineers and the Price System,* and *Absentee Ownership and Business Enterprise in Recent Times: The Case of America* advanced his views on the management of the economy. Central to Veblen's economic philosophy was the proposition that engineers, rather than businessmen, were most fit to run industry, since they could assure maximum production and technological development. Under the direction of a "soviet of technicians," Veblen believed that the planned economy would most efficiently use resources and labor, resulting in a more equitable distribution of goods. Veblen recognized that his plans for social reform had as little chance of application as had his plans for peace; his criticisms of the existing political, economic, and social orders, however, altered the way that the manners of the rich were perceived.

While many of Veblen's theories have become dated, he remains esteemed for the unique perspective he introduced in examining the workings of society and human behavior. Attesting to Veblen's wide ranging influence, Jerry L. Simich and Rick Tilman have written that the "writings of Thorstein Veblen brought forth enthusiastic responses from many and diverse fields of interest. Not only did Veblen spark controversy in economics, his primary interest, but in sociology, politics, literature, anthropology, journalism, and other fields as well. The number and quality of the responses to his ideas remain testimony to his insight and originality."

PRINCIPAL WORKS

The Theory of the Leisure Class   (treatise) 1899
The Theory of Business Enterprise   (treatise) 1904
The Instinct of Workmanship and the State of the Industrial Arts   (treatise) 1914
Imperial Germany and the Industrial Revolution   (treatise) 1915

W. D. HOWELLS   (essay date 1899)

[*Howells was the chief progenitor of American Realism and the
most influential American literary critic during the late nineteenth
century. He successfully weaned American literature away from
the sentimental romanticism of its infancy, earning the popular
sobriquet "the Dean of American Letters." Through Realism, a
theory central to his fiction and criticism, Howells sought to
disperse "the conventional acceptations by which men live on
easy terms with themselves" that they might "examine the grounds
of their social and moral opinions." To accomplish this, according to Howells, the writer must strive to record detailed impressions of everyday life, endowing characters with true-to-life motives and avoiding authorial comment in the narrative.* Criticism
and Fiction *(1891), a patchwork of essays from* Harper's Magazine, *is often considered Howells's manifesto of Realism, although, as René Wellek has noted, the book is actually "only a
skirmish in a long campaign for his doctrines." In addition to
his perceptive criticism of the works of his friends Henry James
and Mark Twain, Howells reviewed three generations of international literature, urging Americans to read the works of Emile
Zola, Bernard Shaw, Henrik Ibsen, Emily Dickinson, and other
important authors. In the following excerpt, he praises Veblen's
insight into the habits and manners of the American leisure class.*]

One of the most interesting books which has fallen in my way
since I read *The Workers* of Mr. Wyckoff is Mr. Thorstein
Veblen's ***Theory of a Leisure Class.*** It does for the Idlers in
terms of cold, scientific analysis the office which Mr. Wyckoff's book dramatically performs for the Workers; and I think
that it is all the more important because it deals, like that book,
with a class newly circumstanced rather than newly conditioned. The workers and the idlers of America are essentially
the same as the workers and the idlers of occidental civilisation
everywhere; but there is a novelty in their environment peculiarly piquant to the imagination. In the sociological region
the spectacle has for the witness some such fascination as
geological stratification would have for the inquirer if he could
look on at its processes; and it is apparently with as strong a
zest as this would inspire that Mr. Veblen considers the nature
and the growth of the leisure class among us.

His name is newer to me than it should be, or than it will
hereafter be to any student of our status; but it must be already
well known to those whose interests or pleasures have led them
into the same field of inquiry. To others, like myself, the clear
method, the graphic and easy style, and the delightful accuracy
of characterisation will be part of the surprise which the book

has to offer. In the passionless calm with which the author
pursues his investigation, there is apparently no animus for or
against a leisure class. It is his affair simply to find out how
and why and what it is. If the result is to leave the reader with
a feeling which the author never shows, that seems to be solely
the effect of the facts. But I have no purpose, as I doubt if I
have the qualification, to criticise the book, and it is only with
one of its manifold suggestions that this notice will concern
itself.

The suggestion, which is rather a conclusion, is the curious
fact, noted less securely and less scientifically before, that the
flower of the American leisure class does not fruit in its native
air, and perhaps cannot yet perpetuate itself on our soil. In
other words, the words of Mr. Veblen, "the English leisure
class being, for purposes of reputable usage, the upper leisure
class of this country," the extraordinary impulse among us
toward the aristocraticisation of society can as yet fulfil itself
only in monarchical conditions. A conspicuous proof of this
is the frequent intermarriage of our moneyed bourgeoisie with
the English aristocracy, and another proof, less conspicuous,
is the frequent absenteeism of our rich people. The newspapers
from time to time make a foolish and futile clamor about both
these things, as if they were abnormal, or as if they were not
the necessary logic of great wealth and leisure in a democracy.
Such things result as infallibly from wealth and leisure as in-
digence and servility, and are in no wise to be deprecated.
They are only representations on a wider stage of the perpetual
and universal drama of our daily life. The man who makes
money in a small town goes into the nearest large town to
spend it—that is, to waste it; waste in some form or other being
the corollary of wealth; and he seeks to marry his children there
into rich and old families. He does this from the instinct of
self-preservation, which is as strong in classes as in individuals;
if he has made his money in a large town, he goes to some
such inland metropolis as Chicago to waste his wealth and to
marry his children above him. The Chicago, and San Francisco,
and St. Louis, and Cleveland millionaires come to New York
with the same ambitions and purposes.

But these are all intermediate stages in the evolution of the
American magnate. At every step he discovers that he is less
and less in his own country, that he is living in a provisional
exile, and that his true home is in monarchical conditions,
where his future establishes itself often without his willing it,
and sometimes against his willing it. The American life is the
life of labor, and he is now of the life of leisure, or if he is
not, his wife is, his daughters and his sons are. The logic of
their existence, which they cannot struggle against, and on
which all the fatuous invective of pseudo public spirit launches
itself effectlessly, is intermarriage with the European aristocracies, and residence abroad. Short of this there is no rest,
and can be none for the American leisure class. This may not
be its ideal, but it is its destiny. (pp. 361-62)

• • • • •

Mr. Thorstein Veblen does not evolve his Theory of a Leisure
Class from his knowledge of that class in America alone. Until
very lately we had no such class, and we rather longed for it.
We thought it would edify us, or, if not that, at least ornament
us; but now that we have got it, on certain terms, we can hardly
be sure that it does either. The good things that we expected
of it have not come to pass, and perhaps it is too soon; but in
Mr. Veblen's analysis our leisure class does not seem essentially different from any of the older aristocracies, which seem
not to have brought to pass the good things expected of them

and often attributed to them. As with these, "pecuniary emulation" and "conspicuous leisure" are the first evidences of its superiority, and "conspicuous consumption," direct or delegated in the splendid apparelling and housing of its women and its dependents, is one of the gross means of striking the popular imagination. The "pecuniary standard of living" is really the only standard, and the "pecuniary canons of taste" are finally the only canons; for if the costly things are not always beautiful, all beautiful things which are cheap must be rejected because they are not costly. "Dress as an expression of pecuniary culture" is left in our day mostly to women by the leisure class; but the men of that class share in it at least as fully as in the "devout observances" and "the higher learning." Both sexes in our leisure class, as in the European aristocracies, are distinguished by the love of sport, in which they prolong their own childhood and the childhood of the race, and they are about equally devoted to the opera and the fine arts, as these minister to their magnificence. It would be hard, in fact, to draw the line between our leisure class and any aristocracy in the traits of piety, predacity, courage, prowess, charity, luxury, conservatism, authority, and the other virtues and vices which have characterised the patricians in all times.

The most notable difference, and the difference which would most invite the study of the novelist, is that hitherto our leisure class has had no political standing. It has had no place in the civic mechanism; but we seem to be at the moment when this is ceasing to be less apparently so. It is idle to suppose because the leisure class, which with us is the moneyed class, does not hold public offices that it does not control public affairs; and possibly it has always controlled them more than we have imagined. The present proof is in the fact that the industrial classes, with all the means of power in their hands, are really powerless in any contest with a group of rich men; it is almost impossible for the people to balk the purpose of such a group; to undo what money has done has been so impossible, with all the apparatus of the elections, the legislatures, the courts, that there is hardly yet an instance of the kind in our history.

All this, however, makes the situation the more attractive to a novelist of imaginative force. This is the most dramatic moment, the most psychological moment which has ever offered itself to fiction; this is the supreme opportunity of the American novelist. Hitherto our politics have repelled the artist by their want of social complexity, by their rude simplicity, as a fight between parties. But if he can look at the situation from the point of view suggested, as an inevitable result from the nature of the class which Mr. Veblen has studied, I believe he will find it full of charm. If he is psychologist enough he will be fascinated by the operation of the silent forces which are, almost unconsciously, working out the permanency of a leisure class, and preparing for it in our own circumstance the ultimation it now seeks elsewhere.

But I should be content if he would portray the life of our leisure class without an eye to such implications, with an eye merely to its superficial facts. If he did this he would appeal to the widest general interest in our reading public. Our appetite for everything that relates to the life removed from the life of work, from the simple republican ideal, is almost insatiable. It strives to satisfy itself, in plays and romances, with the doings of princes and nobles in realms as surely fictitious as Lilliput and Brobdignag; it gluts itself, in the newspapers, with fables almost as gross as Gulliver's concerning the social affairs of our leisure class.

Seen truly and reproduced faithfully these would be extremely interesting, and the field they offer to inquiry is almost wholly unexplored. Our fiction has brought pretty fully into literature the country and village life of the Americans of all sections. We know this through our short stories in New England, in the South, in the middle and farther West, and on the Pacific Slope; and in a certain measure our novels have acquainted us with the lower and upper middle-class life in the minor and even the greater cities. But the attempts to deal with the life of fashion, of luxury, of leisure, have been so insufficient that they cannot be considered. This life can hardly be studied by one who is a part of it, not merely because that sort of life is not fruitful in talent, but because the procession cannot very well look on at itself. The observer must have some favorable position on the outside, and must regard it neither "with a foolish face of praise," nor with a satiric scorn. Like every other phase of life, it has its seriousness, its importance, and one who studies it rightly will find in it the old elements of interest so newly compounded that they will merit his most intelligent scrutiny, often his most sympathetic scrutiny. It would be easy to burlesque it, but to burlesque it would be intolerable, and the witness who did this would be bearing false testimony where the whole truth and nothing but the truth is desirable. A democracy, the proudest, the most sincere, the most ardent that history has ever known, has evolved here a leisure class which has all the distinguishing traits of a patriciate, and which by the chemistry of intermarriage with European aristocracies is rapidly acquiring antiquity. Is not this a phenomenon worthy the highest fiction?

Mr. Veblen has brought to its study the methods and habits of scientific inquiry. To translate these into dramatic terms would form the unequalled triumph of the novelist who had the seeing eye and the thinking mind, not to mention the feeling heart. That such a thing has not been done hitherto is all the stranger, because fiction, in other countries, has always employed itself with the leisure class, with the aristocracy; and our own leisure class now offers not only as high an opportunity as any which fiction has elsewhere enjoyed, but by its ultimation in the English leisure class, it invites the American imagination abroad on conditions of unparalleled advantage. (pp. 385-86)

> *W. D. Howells, "An Opportunity for American Fiction: First Paper" and "An Opportunity for American Fiction: Second Paper," in* Literature, *n. s. Nos. 16 and 17, April 28 and May 5, 1899, pp. 361-62; 385-86.*

A. M. DAY (essay date 1901)

[*In the following essay, Day discusses the major theses of* The Theory of the Leisure Class.]

"The emergence of a leisure class," says Professor Veblen [in *The Theory of the Leisure Class*], "coincides with the beginning of ownership." As industrial activity displaces predatory activity, "accumulated property more and more replaces trophies of predatory exploit as the conventional exponent of prepotence and success." Later, "the possession of wealth, which was at the outset valued simply as an evidence of efficiency, becomes, in popular apprehension, itself a meritorious act." Then, as "esteem is awarded only on evidence," abstention from labor "comes to be a requisite of decency." And so it happens that "in itself and in its consequences the life of leisure is beautiful and ennobling in all civilized men's eyes."

The term "leisure," according to the author's usage, "connotes nonproductive consumption of time"; and the leisure class, (1) "from a sense of the unworthiness of productive work, and (2) as an evidence of pecuniary ability to afford a life of idleness," devotes itself to such accomplishments as "do not conduce directly to the furtherance of human life."

> So, for instance, in our time there is the knowledge of the dead languages and the occult sciences; of correct spelling; of syntax and prosody; of the various forms of domestic music and other household art; of the latest proprieties of dress, furniture and equipage; of games, sports and fancy-bred animals—

all of which commend themselves to the leisure class as "serviceable evidence of an unproductive expenditure of time."

The conspicuous consumption of valuable goods is an approved method by which the gentleman of leisure may put his opulence in evidence, but here he is obliged to exercise much ingenuity. After expanding his personal expenditures as far as possible, he imposes upon his wife the "duties of vicarious leisure and consumption" and finds guests to consume vicariously for him. The principle of conspicuous, honorific waste forms his canons of beauty, until "the cheap coat makes the cheap man" and costliness is a full equivalent for beauty; it leads him to foster sports, as satisfying the requirements of substantial futility, together with a colorable pretense of purpose; it shapes his educational ideals, so that he causes his children to spend years in getting "substantially useless information"; it even turns his religion mainly into a "devout consumption of goods and services," which means "a lowering of the vitality of the community."

All this is, of course, a study of motives; and the author's main thesis is that the motive of ownership is emulation—that wealth, as a proof of the owner's prepotence, is purely an invidious distinction. Though he admits that there are non-invidious motives, and one in particular—the "instinct of workmanship"—which is often opposed to the motive of conspicuous consumption; and although he concedes that the latter is in many cases not directly in the consumer's mind, but is only indirectly present, in the desire of that individual to conform to the standard of living in his class, still he contends that the dominant canons of conduct are "the principles of waste, futility and ferocity." "Waste" he defines as that expenditure which "does not serve human life or human well-being on the whole"; and the test of all expenditure, he asserts, is "the question whether it serves directly to enhance human life."

Obviously, in judging so radical a thesis, based only on personal interpretation of facts of everyday life, readers will easily find reasons for dissenting from parts, or even all, of the doctrine. Some such reasons are: The author's failure to make clear the limits of the leisure class, his questionable estimates of the force and value of various motives and, perhaps most of all, his neglect to explain why his, rather than another's, "dispassionate common sense" should decide for us whether a given expenditure results in a "net gain in comfort or in the fulness of life."

Better worthy of discussion, from some points of view, is Professor Veblen's thesis that the leisure class, preserving traditions because of its sheltered position, not only lowers efficiency but retards functional adaptation—as witness our apologetic defense of "institutions handed down from a barbarian phase of life" and the "reluctant tolerance" in the universities of new views of human relations. In particular, our author points out that

the relation of the leisure (that is, propertied, non-industrial) class to the economic process is a pecuniary relation—a relation of acquisition, not of production; of exploitation, not of serviceability.

Living by, rather than in, the industrial process, in a parasitic way, this class gives to the growth of economic institutions a bent of considerable industrial importance. It

> hinders cultural development immediately (1) by the inertia proper to the class itself, and (2) through its prescriptive example of conspicuous waste and of conservatism, and (3) indirectly through that system of unequal distribution of wealth and sustenance on which the institution itself rests.

Furthermore, "the accumulation of wealth at the upper end of the pecuniary scale" not only "involves privation at the lower end," but also, as an essential factor in the process of exploitation, the conservation of the barbarian temperament, with the substitution of fraud for force. "The interest of the community no longer coincides with the emulative interests of the individual"; only "within narrow limits, and then only in a Pickwickian sense," is honesty the best policy; "freedom from scruple, from sympathy, honesty and regard for life" further the success of the individual; the captain of industry is "an astute man rather than an ingenious one." Thus—albeit with some counter-tendencies which cannot be developed in a brief exposition—the dominance of leisure class ideals leads to the prevalence of predatory practices.

Here again we have to note that everyday facts are interpreted from the point of view of a single individual. Few will agree with the author's analysis of the facts, and many will dissent vigorously from his conclusion as to the tendencies of the competitive régime. Just at this point, moreover, a careful reader will realize the defect in method involved in the subtitle, "An Economic Study of the Evolution of Institutions," and in the sweeping statement that "the collective interests of any modern community center in industrial efficiency." Any such attempt to gauge the functions of a social institution by its results upon economic welfare alone must be unsuccessful or un-"economic." Even though the given institution were as harmful, in its effects on industrial efficiency, as the author alleges, it might yet be a most useful social agent.

Attention should, furthermore, be directed to the keenness of much of the analysis, to the masterful ways in which the author has presented his case and to the humor with which he has illumined his exposition—as in his discussion of conventions of dress, of the vicarious life of women, of "costliness masquerading under the name of beauty," of our exaltation of the defective in book-making and of our standards of taste in general. Some of his phrases are admirable, as when he says that, by shrewd mimicry and systematic drill, "a syncopated evolution of gentle birth and breeding is achieved." In some cases, however, it is to be regretted that his love of phrase has led him into that wasteful use of "archaic idiom" which he derides and even into the gratuitous making of enemies. Thus, he speaks of the lawyer as having "no taint of usefulness," of the scholar as spending more than others in conspicuous waste, of "clergymen and other pillars of society," of the devout as "low in economic efficiency, or in intelligence, or both." Yet every one of these and other similar phrases has its sting because it conveys an unpleasantly large amount of truth. And of the book it may honestly be said that practically every page forces the reader to consider anew, while smarting under a phrase, the real value of some cherished habit or ideal, and once more to remember that, as the author insists, rationality is of supreme importance in modern society. Professor Veblen has not presented *the* theory of the leisure class, but a *part* of *one* theory; and his success in stimulating the reader, at least, is beyond dispute. (pp. 366-69)

A. M. Day, in a review of "The Theory of the Leisure Class: An Economic Study in the Evolution of Institutions," in Political Science Quarterly, *Vol. XVI, No. 2, June, 1901, pp. 366-69.*

WINTHROP MORE DANIELS   (essay date 1905)

[*In the following excerpt, Daniels criticizes* The Theory of Business Enterprise *as presenting an imbalanced and pessimistic portrait of business and industry.*]

The social prophet, like the poor, is with us always, and possibly the most striking Jeremiad of the year comes in the guise of an estimate of our industrial system. *The Theory of Business Enterprise,* by Professor Veblen, is a singular instance of how economic philosophy is sometimes infected by tendencies rife in widely separated fields of thought. Through the transparent veil of this sociological essay one gets many a glimpse of the cosmic irony of Ibsen and the nihilistic doctrine of Nietzsche. A very readable quality is thus imparted to the speculation by the author, but at the cost of a most unenviable frame of mind. Professor Veblen has a preternaturally vivid insight into the pathological side of business and society; and he follows remorselessly the poisoned tract which his critical scalpel has discovered. But his exploratory incision suggests nothing for "the healing of the nations," and from his lips there falls only the thinly disguised irony which mocks the misery of them that perish. The morbid element in economic life has for him so great a fascination that it blinds him to the normal and healthful aspects of industry, and the business world in his apprehension becomes but a congeries of "embossed sores and headed evils."

And yet, despite the fact that the author's attitude renders the highest approval from either the scientific or the ethical standpoint impossible, the book is an uncommonly suggestive one. The penetrating glance into certain broad and seamy aspects of our industrial life prompts to a reflective testing of one's social beliefs and ideals.

The heart of the book centres in the analysis of modern business enterprise. The author contends that it is no longer the making of a livelihood, but the accumulation of profits, which motives the direction of modern enterprise. Industry is carried on for "business," not "business" for industry. Pecuniary gain is, on the whole, frequently associated with industrial disturbance, not with industrial welfare. The old-fashioned Captain of Industry has therefore become a wrecker of trade. The business man of to-day directs his attention, not to the surveillance of processes, but to the "alert redistribution of investments." Only rarely does the entrepreneur cumber himself with "the coördinating of industrial processes with a view to economics *(sic)* of production and heightened serviceability." The loan market is a sphere of pecuniary legerdemain, for "funds of whatever character are a pecuniary fact, not an industrial one"; nor do they "increase the aggregate industrial equipment." The remuneration of business services bears "no determinable relation to the services which the work in question may render the community," but represents only "parasitic income." Hence the "traffic in vendible capital (that is, securities) is the pivotal and dominant factor in the modern situation of business and industry." Business depression is to-day primarily "a malady

of the affections" of the business man, not a dearth in the output of consumable goods "except as measured in price." "The persistent defection" in hoped-for profits must become a "chronic depression . . . under the fully developed régime of machine industry." For this "persistent defection" of profits there are but two remedies: "an increase in unproductive consumption," or a curtailed output. "Wasteful expenditure" on war and armaments by governments in their "policy of emulative exhaustion" may help; but, "barring providential intervention *(sic)* the only refuge from chronic depression is thorough-going coalition" of industry (that is, trusts). But even this in the course of the Great Year is unavailing, for the "cultural incidence of the machine process" has eradicated from the wage-earning class all reverence for "natural rights" and all belief in the philosophy of private property, in both of which modern capitalism is rooted. This cultural growth of the machine-tender is necessarily "of a skeptical, matter-of-fact complexion, materialistic, immoral, unpatriotic, undevout." While "business discipline" therefore tends to conserve "the bourgeois virtues of solvency, thrift, and dissimulation," and tends to maintain among wage-earners the useful sense of "status or fealty involved in the concept of sin," it stands to lose at the last, although for a time, by playing on "the happy knack of clannish fancy," called patriotism, it may prolong its dominion by using the military power of governments to open wider markets in lands now "pecuniarily unregenerate."

The sting of this indictment of the industrial world lies not in its novelty nor in its finality, but in its partial truth. The doctrine that the pursuit of business affords the frequent opportunity of undeserved gain, and that, among a society where mutual service is the rule, a clever scamp may live by his wits, is as old as Aristotle. Retail trade, it may be remembered, was condemned by that philosopher, as an unnatural art of money-making. Professor Veblen would exonerate the retailer, but fears for the social welfare when entrusted to the corporate directorate.

Professor Veblen's wholesale cheapening of the operations of the workaday world, veiled though it be by frequent protestation of conformity to the conventional industrial creed, is bound after all to prove a boomerang. Its paradoxes may awake the reader from dogmatic slumbers, its epigrams may tickle his ears with their mordant cynicism, but neither his heart nor head will respond to its skepticism or its pessimism. "A conscientious person," says Burke, "would rather doubt his own judgment, than condemn his species. . . . He will grow wise, not malignant, by his acquaintance with the world. But he that accuses all mankind of corruption, ought to remember that he is sure to convict only one." (pp. 558-59)

Winthrop More Daniels, "Significant Books on Politics and Economics," in The Atlantic Monthly, *Vol. 95, No. 4, April, 1905, pp. 549-64.*

FRANCIS HACKETT   (essay date 1917)

[*Hackett was a respected Irish-American biographer, novelist, and literary critic during the first half of the twentieth century. His reviews appeared in the* New Republic, *the* Saturday Review of Literature, *and other prominent American periodicals. In the following essay, he praises* An Inquiry into the Nature of Peace and the Terms of Its Perpetuation.]

Comparatively few people know the work of Thorstein Veblen. Some thousands have read his best-known book, the brilliant, drastic *Theory of the Leisure Class;* but only a few hundred have read his *Theory of Business Enterprise,* his *Instinct of Workmanship* and his *Imperial Germany.* So little is he known that a pretentious man the other day met my mention of *The Nature of Peace* by saying: "Ah, of course, a new translation." He did not know that Thorstein Veblen was an American, was graduated from an American university, in the eighties, and has been teaching in American universities ever since. Mr. Veblen is an American writer but the kind of American writer whose merit is rather more clearly recognized abroad than at home, an American who ought to have been a foreigner to be appreciated in America.

To read Mr. Veblen is not and cannot be an entertainment. There is a kind of fashionable lady who knows precisely when a literary Paquin has ceased to be the thing, and who twitters as unfailingly as any bird at the first breath of another master's dawn. For all this turn for novelty, few ladies have twittered much or are ever going to twitter much about Mr. Veblen's performance. He is too difficult to understand. It is hard intellectual labor to read any of his books, and to skim him is impossible. He is not a luxurious valley of easy reading, a philosophic Tennyson. He is a mountain—stubborn, forbidding, purgatorial. There is no funicular to bring him under subjection of the indolent, and sometimes there is barely a foothold even for the hardy amid the tortuosities of his style. But the reward for those who do persist in reading him is commensurate with the effort. No mountain pierces to heaven, not even Mr. Veblen's, but the area that he unrolls is strategically chosen and significantly inclusive. Part of the reward of reading him may be like the reward of mountain-climbing itself, the value of tough exercise for its own sake, but unless Mr. Veblen created the conviction that his large purposes did reasonably necessitate intricate and laborious processes of thought and that such processes had to be followed in detail in order that his argument might be mastered, no one would be quite satisfied to take the pains he exacts. The greatest justification of such pains is the final sense conveyed by him that he has had a singular contribution to make, and has made it with complete regard to the formidable requirements of responsible unconventional utterance.

The responsible unconventionality of Mr. Veblen has never been better exemplified than in this new book of his, finished February, 1917, on the nature of peace. It is, so far as I know, the most momentous work in English on the encompassment of lasting peace. There are many books that aim to give geographic domicile to the kind of tinkered peace that is likely to come out of this war, but I know of no book that gives so plain and positive account of the terms "on which peace at large may be hopefully installed and maintained," and I know of no discussion so searching as to "what if anything there is in the present situation that visibly makes for a realization of these necessary terms within a calculable future." Those who are acquainted with Mr. Veblen's work are aware of the ironic inscrutability of his manner, the detachment that is at once an evidence of his impartiality and an intimation of his corrosive skepticism. It may no longer be said, with *The Nature of Peace* under examination, that either impartiality or skepticism induces Mr. Velben to withhold his preference, to conceal his bias, in the present contingency. That bias, however, does not lead him into any of the current patriotic extravagances. If critical acid can corrode the patriotic conceptions of "democracy" and "liberty" that are now so familiar, Mr. Veblen makes no attempt to keep such fancies from being eaten into. What is left, however, is sufficiently substantial to give him the issue that abides in the war, and its bearing on peace, and

it provides him with his clue to the great eventuality, "the consequences presumably due to follow."

It would be wrong in any review of Mr. Veblen to give a mere bald outline of the work that is so full of his manifold mind. There are so many "patent imbecilities" (like the protective tariff), so many current egregious practices (like business men's sabotage), that receive characteristic illumination in transit, the bare colorless statement of his conclusions would completely leave out the poignancy that accumulates as he proceeds. His conclusions are, on the other hand, impressive enough to indicate the importance of the argument back of them, and if only for their suggestion of the massive argument they need to be reported. Defeat for the German-Imperial coalition, not victory for the Entente belligerents, is the first step toward lasting peace that he recognizes, because of the decisive difference "between those people whose patriotic affections centre about the fortunes of an impersonal commonwealth and those in whom is superadded a fervent aspiration for dynastic ascendancy." Peace on terms of Germany's unconditional surrender is not discussed by Mr. Veblen on the basis of likelihood but on the basis of its desirability in relation to the chances for peace, and the unlikelihood of lasting peace in its absence. But this is not the ordinary orgiastic contemplation of an enemy destroyed. The elements in Germany that conspire against lasting peace are carefully computed, and the terms of their disintegration discussed in every detail. It is by no means forgotten that if the victorious side is not "shorn over the comb of neutralization and democracy" there can in any event be no prospect of perpetuating peace.

The present unfitness of Germany (or Japan) for lasting peace is ascribed by Mr. Veblen to the essential dynastic need for warlike enterprise, but he has no hesitation whatever in declaring in regard to the Allied Powers that peace in general demands the "relinquishment of all those undemocratic institutional survivals out of which international grievances are wont to arise." This is not the customary emphasis of goodwill pacifists. They are fain to propose peace on the present basis of "national jealousies and discriminations" and what Mr. Veblen in his highly personal jargon calls "discrepancies." Mr. Veblen alludes to the League to Enforce Peace as a movement for the "collusive safeguarding of national discrepancies for force of arms." This toleration of existing nationalisms Mr. Veblen plainly regards as an insuperable obstacle to peace. He exposes in every detail the predisposition to war that inheres in nationalisms. "What the peace-makers might logically be expected to concern themselves about would be the elimination of these discrepancies that make for embroilment."

The military defeat of Germany seems to the author a requisite step on the direct path to peace. This is only because Germany is dynastic, however, and the German people subservient to the dynasty. One of the issues most thoroughly debated by Mr. Veblen is the pregnant issue of German democratization, and while he lays great stress on the necessity for military defeat as a first requirement of democratization he does not believe the disintegrating of Germany's dynastic "second nature" is of so hopeless a character as its historic persistence might imply. There is no complacency in the attitude that leads him to regard imperial Germany (or imperial Japan) as a stumbling-block in the road to lasting peace. It is an attitude founded on a strict and even solicitous estimate of the patent German and Japanese aims. And in so far as a peace policy involves treatment of the German people Mr. Veblen is quite certain that no trade discrimination against them, necessarily bound to re-coil on the common people, would be pacifically effective or justifiable. The persecution of the German common people could take no form that would conceivably advance the cause of peace, and Mr. Veblen is careful to dissociate his belief that Germany should be beaten from the belief that the people of Germany should be made to suffer for their differentiation after the war.

Where *The Nature of Peace* seems to me to rise far and away above the current discussions of supernationalism is in its comparative freedom from unanalyzed conceptions. There is nothing sacred to Mr. Veblen in the conception of patriotism, of property, of success, of manliness, of good breeding, of national honor, of prestige. The notion of nonresistance has no terrors for him—he writes a chapter on its merits. But so dry is he that it is only one reading him attentively who will gather his extraordinarily subversive character, his invincible mind. The blessedness of this unsparing intelligence is so great that one has a constant acute pleasure in pursuing Mr. Veblen's argument. If one had long perceived for oneself, for example, that "business" means waste and inefficiency, it is pleasant to have Mr. Veblen introduce the same perceptions, but when he proceeds to locate them in his spacious understanding of the whole international problem, and to reveal their unquestionable bearing on the alternatives of war and peace, one has a happy consciousness of coming honestly to a wider and deeper view of realities. This is the supreme gift of Mr. Veblen's disinterested inquiry.

The notion that a lasting peace is compatible with the established patriotic order of things, with the status of the gentleman in England or the business man in the United States, is not entertained for one moment by Mr. Veblen, and regardless of the "maggoty conceit of national domination" which demands "the virtual erasure of the Imperial dynasty," he sees an impediment to peace in the dear establishments of "upperclass and pecuniary control" in the allied commonwealths. Chief and foremost in the pacific arrangement must come "a considerable degree of neutralization, extending to virtually all national interests and pretensions, but more particularly to all material and commercial interests of the federated peoples; and, indispensably and especially, such neutralization would have to extend to the nations from whom aggression is now apprehended, as, e.g., the German people." All manner of trade discrimination has to be abolished—"import, export and excise tariff, harbor and registry dues, subsidy, patent right, copyright, trade mark, tax exemption whether partial or exclusive, investment preferences at home and abroad." Besides this prescription for "the elimination of discrepancies that make for embroilment," a neutralization of citizenship is also indicated, the common man standing to lose nothing by these revisions. But Mr. Veblen is frank to say that "this prospect of consequences" points to a general revolution.

> It has appeared in the course of the argument that the preservation of the present pecuniary law and order, with all its incidents of ownership and investment, is incompatible with an unwarlike state of peace and security. This current scheme of investment, business, and sabotage, should have an appreciably better chance of survival in the long run if the present conditions of warlike preparation and national insecurity were maintained, or if the projected peace were left in a somewhat problematical state, sufficiently precarious to keep national animosities alert, and thereby to the neglect of domestic interests, particularly of such interests as touch the popular

well-being. On the other hand, it has also appeared that the cause of peace and its perpetuation might be materially advanced if precautions were taken beforehand to put out of the way as much as may be of those discrepancies of interest and sentiment between nations and between classes which make for dissension and eventual hostilities.

The weight of these phrases it is not easy to catch in passing, but nothing more significant has been written since the outbreak of war. One has only to go back to *The Theory of Business Enterprise,* published in 1903, to learn how Mr. Veblen foresaw this war, and America's participation in it. The same rigor of intellectual standard that gave him a command of the situation at that time is discernible in this present volume, and gives him dominance now. Such severity of mind as Mr. Veblen exhibits is not likely to win him many readers, but the recommendation of Mr. Veblen is not merely the recommendation of a great philosopher of industrialism. It is not his relentless logic alone that elevates him. It is the democratic bias which *The Nature of Peace* indicates. (pp. 345-52)

> *Francis Hackett, "The Cost of Peace," in his* Horizons: A Book of Criticism, *B. W. Huebsch, 1918, pp. 345-52.*

BRANDER MATTHEWS   (essay date 1919)

[*An American critic, playwright, and novelist, Matthews wrote extensively on world drama and served for twenty-five years at Columbia as professor of dramatic literature, the first to hold such a position in an American university. He was also a founding member and president of the National Institute of Arts and Letters. Matthews, whose criticism is both witty and informative, has been called "perhaps the last of the gentlemanly school of critics and essayists" in America. In the following excerpt, he harshly criticizes* The Higher Learning in America.]

One thing is obvious even to the casual and cursory reader of Mr. Thorstein Veblen's *Higher Learning in America:* it is a most unusual book. And it is unusual in half a dozen different ways. It is unusual in the first place because of the illiteracy of the author—or, if this is putting it too discourteously, because the author is deficient in the craftsmanship of writing. His opinions are doubtfully weighty, but his pages are undoubtedly heavy. His style is painfully awkward, and his phrasing is painfully slovenly. He writes English as if it were a foreign language which he had acquired late in life. His vocabulary is limited and he indulges in a fatiguing repetition of a dozen or a score of adjectives. His grammar is woefully defective, and in fact, as we turn Mr. Veblen's pages we have a feeling that we are at last entering into the grammatical millennium, foretold many years ago by the late George T. Lanigan, "when the plural noun shall lie down with the singular verb and a little conjunction shall lead them."

On Page 28 Mr. Veblen asserts that "the material so made use of for technical ends *are* taken over and turned to account without afterthought," and on Page 32 he tells us that "within the university precincts any aim or interest other than those of irresponsible science and scholarship—pursuit of matter-of-fact knowledge—*are* to be rated as interlopers." Surely, it is not too much to ask that when a man invites us to consider what he has to say about the Higher Learning he shall first of all equip himself with the Lower Learning—at least, with the elementary grammar of the English language. Before he attempts to climb the lofty steps that lead to the university he ought to be able to prove that he has passed through the portals of the grammar school. So frequent and so flagrant are Mr. Veblen's violations of accepted usage that I was moved to look him up in "Who's Who," and I was astonished to learn from the autobiography he contributed that he is not only a college graduate, but that he is even a Doctor of Philosophy. It may be possible that, with a humor unrevealed elsewhere in his pages, he desires to proffer himself as a Horrible Example of the deficiencies of our university instruction.

Nor is his rhetoric any less at fault than his grammar. It is evident enough that Mr. Veblen does not write cleanly, because he does not think clearly. His presentation of the results of his cogitation is so vague and so vaporous that the reader is often left in doubt as to what it is that the author believes he believes. He is verbose and repetitious, tautological and entangled, cumbrous and hazy. He ties himself in knots and trips over them. Words are his masters and not his servants. His metaphors play tag with one another. (p. 125)

In the second place, this book is unusual in its tone of condescensions, in its attitude of impregnable superiority, in its toplofty contempt for all men and for all things. From a contributing editor to one or another of the subsided weeklies, which vaunt themselves as the friends of the New Freedom and as the organs of the Uplift, we have no right to expect the persuasive urbanity which characterized every page of Newman's *Idea of a University;* but we are justified in looking for that respect for others which is a necessary companion of self-respect. Apparently Mr. Veblen has not taken to heart Robert Louis Stevenson's suggestive assertion that the pleasures of condescension are curiously one-sided. Mr. Veblen does not argue with his readers; he tells them. He demands compliance like one who has come down from the mountain with the tables of stone in his hand. He is like the bust of Molière in Bunner's little lyric:

> Yet high his haughty head he heaves.

The gentle reader is also the humble reader, but, however gentle or humble, he does not like to be trampled in the dust. We cannot help wondering what warrant Mr. Veblen believes himself to have for his arrogant assumption of the right to look down on the rest of mankind. In fact, one reader, in spite of the gentleness of his humility, was reminded of the protest of the British barrister to the brow-beating Judge before whom he was trying a case: "Your lordship seems to forget that I am after all a vertebrate animal, whereas your lordship's tone to me would be unbecoming in God Almighty to a black beetle!"

In the third place, Mr. Veblen's book is unusual in its disclosure of its author's absolute ignorance of the institution he has taken for his topic. He does not understand the organization of a univeristy—or, if he does, he misrepresents it completely. He does not perceive the interrelation of its several parts, nor the reasons for these interrelations, nor the manifold advantages of them. He imputes motives to boards of trustees, to university presidents, and to college professors—motives which are so absurd that they can only be termed grotesque. Mr. Veblen's typical trustee, his typical president, his typical professor, cannot even be accepted as a caricature, because a caricature, however willfully distorted, must be drawn from an actual original; and it is evident that Mr. Veblen has evolved out of his inner consciousness his idea of the trustee, the president, and the professor. His types are as unrelated to any possible originals as though Mr. Veblen had spent his life in a vacuum. His vision of the American university is not what he calls it "something of a fancy sketch"; it is something altogether fantastic.

It would be fatiguing to catalogue all the stark misstatements of fact made by Mr. Veblen; but a few of them must be set down here. He says that the graduate school and the college "are still commonly coupled together as subdivisions of a complex whole; but this holding together of the two disparate schools is at best a freak of aimless survival." The fact is that this coupling is advantageous to both partners, and especially—as I can testify from nearly thirty years' experience—to the professor who is fortunate enough to teach both in the college and the graduate school. He says that "the technologist and the professional man are, like other men of affairs, necessarily and habitually impatient of any scientific and scholarly work that does not obviously lend itself to some practical use." The fact is that nearly all the leaders in the professions, like many leaders among the men of affairs, have a very high regard for "work that does not lend itself to some practical use."

He says that the professional and technical schools are now "autonomous and academically self-sufficient," (whatever that may mean,) and that "their connection with the university is superficial and formal at the best, so far as regards any substantial control of their affairs and policy by the university authorities at large." The fact is exactly the contrary; medical and law schools which used to be autonomous and even proprietary are now integrally connected with the university, to which they often owe the enlargement of their aims and the reinvigoration of their teaching. He says that "poor men and men without large experience in business affairs are felt to have no place" on Boards of Trustees. The fact is that such men are frequently elected as Trustees and are often among the most useful members of their boards.

He says that "under the stress of businesslike management in the universities the drift of things sets toward letting the work of science and scholarship to the lowest bidder, on a roughly applicable piece-wage plan." The fact is—well, the fact is that this assertion is simply silly. But it is not sillier than a host of other assertions which companion it in Mr. Veblen's volume. Indeed, I cannot now recall that I have ever read any book on any subject in which there is amassed such a mess of miscellaneous misinformation.

Fourthly and finally—for this Catalog of the Slips must not be allowed to become as fatiguing as its text—this book is unusual in its bad manners and perhaps, I should say, in its bad morals. There is a discourtesy very close to dishonesty in slandering by insinuation. The man who comes straight at us with a bowie knife in his hand may be dangerous, but he is not despicable, like the creature who creeps up stealthily with a stiletto to deal a stab in the back. On Page 67 and on Page 70 Mr. Veblen seems to suggest that there are Boards of Trustees whose members make a personal profit out of the funds intrusted to them; the insinuation is hedged about with weasel words—i.e., "instances of the kind are not wholly unknown, though *presumably* (!) exceptional." Mr. Veblen is ready to believe the worst about all college Trustees, since they are likely to be business men, and he holds that "the spirit of American business is a spirit of quietism, caution, compromise, *collusion,* and *chicane,*" and that "success in business affairs . . . comes only by getting something for nothing."

We all know that the university President is an important figure in American public life and without exact parallel in European public life. No one would decry the high ability and the lofty character of Eliot of Harvard, Gilman of Johns Hopkins, White of Cornell; and every one recognizes the scholarly equipment of Butler of Columbia, Hadley of Yale, and Lowell of Harvard.

But Mr. Veblen does not hesitate to declare it "a safe generalization that in point of fact the average of university Presidents fall short of the average of their academic staff in scholarly or scientific attainments." He asserts also that "as to the requirements of scholarly or scientific competency, a plausible speaker with a large gift of assurance, a businesslike educator or clergyman, some urbane pillar of society, some astute veteran of the scientific *demi-monde* will meet all reasonable requirements." On Page 269, but more or less diminished in prominence by the finer type of a foot note, may be found what we must regard as Mr. Veblen's most characteristic utterance:

> A person widely conversant with current opinion and
> its expression among the personnel of the staff . . .
> might unguardedly come to the persuasion that the
> typical academic head, under these latter-day con-
> ditions, will be a *feeble-minded rogue.*

The President of Mr. Veblen's vision is naturally uncomfortable in the presence of a real scholar, and he is swift to oust any such person who has obtruded himself into the Faculty. On Pages 172-3 we are warned that "it is not an easy or a graceful matter for a businesslike executive to get rid of any undecorative or indecorous scientist whose only fault is an unduly pertinacious pursuit of the work for which alone the university claims to exist." But on Pages 178-9 we are informed how the scientist whose only fault is that he is truly a scientist may be crowded out: "By a judicious course of vexation and equivocation, an obnoxious scientist may be manoeuvred into such a position that his pride will force a voluntary resignation. Failing this, it may become necessary, however distasteful, delicately to defame his domestic life."

These quotations must suffice to prove how truly unusual Mr. Veblen's book is; indeed, I like to hope that it is not only unusual, but actually unique, in the exact sense of that abused word. "None but itself can be its parallel." (pp. 125, 127, 138)

> Brander Matthews, "Mr. Veblen's Gas Attack on
> Our Colleges and Universities," in The New York
> Times Book Review, *March 16, 1919, pp. 125, 127,
> 138.*

H. L. MENCKEN   (essay date 1919)

[*From the era of World War I until the early years of the Great Depression, Mencken was one of the most influential figures in American letters. His strongly individualistic, irreverent outlook on life and his vigorous, invective-charged writing style helped establish the iconoclastic spirit of the Jazz Age and significantly shaped the direction of American literature. As a social and literary critic—the roles for which he is best known—Mencken was the scourge of evangelical Christianity, public service organizations, literary censorship, boosterism, provincialism, democracy, all advocates of personal or social improvement, and every other facet of American life that he perceived as humbug. In his literary criticism, Mencken encouraged American writers to shun the anglophilic, moralistic bent of the nineteenth century and to practice realism, an artistic call-to-arms that is most fully developed in his essay "Puritanism as a Literary Force," one of the seminal essays in modern literary criticism. Another important polemic, "The Sahara of the Bozart"—considered a powerful catalyst in spurring realism in Southern literature—attacked the paucity of* beaux arts *in Southern culture as well as the tendency in the region's literature toward romanticizing the Old South as a land of latter-day knights and fair ladies. A man who was widely renowned or feared during his lifetime as a would-be destroyer of established American values, Mencken once wrote: "All of my*

work, barring a few obvious burlesques, is based upon three fundamental ideas. 1. That knowledge is better than ignorance; 2. That it is better to tell the truth than to lie; and 3. That it is better to be free than to be a slave." In the following excerpt, he ridicules Veblen's ideas as unoriginal or irrational and his prose style as impenetrable.]

Ten or twelve years ago, being engaged in a bombastic discussion with what was then known as an intellectual Socialist (like the rest of the *intelligentsia,* he succumbed to the first fife-corps of the war, pulled down the red flag, damned Marx as a German spy, and began whooping for Elihu Root, Otto Kahn and Abraham Lincoln), I was greatly belabored and incommoded by his long quotations from a certain Prof. Dr. Thorstein Veblen, then quite unknown to me. My antagonist manifestly attached a great deal of importance to these borrowed sagacities, for he often heaved them at me in lengths of a column or two, and urged me to read every word of them. I tried hard enough, but found it impossible going. The more I read them, in fact, the less I could make of them, and so in the end, growing impatient and impolite, I denounced this Prof. Veblen as a geyser of pishposh, refused to waste any more time upon his incomprehensible syllogisms, and applied myself to the other Socialist witnesses in the case, seeking to set fire to their shirts.

That old debate, which took place by mail (for the Socialist lived like a munitions patriot on his country estate and I was a wage-slave attached to a city newspaper), was afterward embalmed in a dull book, and made the mild pother of a day. The book, by name, *Men vs. the Man,* is now as completely forgotten as Baxter's *Saint's Rest* or the Constitution of the United States. I myself, perhaps the only man who remembers it at all, have not looked into it for six or eight years, and all I can recall of my opponent's argument (beyond the fact that it not only failed to convert me to the nascent Bolshevism of the time, but left me a bitter and incurable scoffer at democracy in all its forms) is his curious respect for the aforesaid Prof. Dr. Thorstein Veblen, and his delight in the learned gentleman's long, tortuous and (to me, at least) intolerably flapdoodlish phrases.

There was, indeed, a time when I forgot even this—when my mind was empty of the professor's very name. That was, say, from 1909 or thereabout to the middle of 1917. During those years, having lost all my old superior interest in Socialism, even as an amateur psychiatrist, I ceased to read its literature, and thus lost track of its Great Thinkers. The periodicals that I then gave an eye to, setting aside newspapers, were chiefly the familiar American imitations of the English weeklies of opinion, and in these the dominant Great Thinker was, first, the late Prof. Dr. William James, and, after his decease, Prof. Dr. John Dewey. (pp. 59-61)

I myself greatly enjoyed and profited by the discourses of this Prof. Dewey and was in hopes that he would last. Born so recently as 1859 and a man of the highest bearable sobriety, he seemed likely to peg along until 1935 or 1940, a gentle and charming volcano of correct thought. (pp. 62-3)

Then, of a sudden, Siss! Boom! Ah! Then, overnight, the upspringing of the intellectual soviets, the headlong assault upon all the old axioms of pedagogical speculation, the nihilistic dethronement of Prof. Dewey—and rah, rah, rah for Prof. Dr. Thorstein Veblen! Veblen? Could it be—? Aye, it was! My old acquaintance! The *Doctor obscurus* of my half-forgotten bout with the so-called intellectual Socialist! The Great Thinker *redivivus!* Here, indeed, he was again, and in a few months—almost it seemed a few days—he was all over the *Nation,* the *Dial,* the *New Republic* and the rest of them, and his books and pamphlets began to pour from the presses, and the newpapers reported his every wink and whisper, and everybody who was anybody began gabbling about him. The spectacle, I do not hesitate to say, somewhat disconcerted me and even distressed me. On the one hand, I was sorry to see so learned and interesting a man as Dr. Dewey sent back to the insufferable dungeons of Columbia, there to lecture in imperfect Yiddish to classes of Grand Street Platos. And on the other hand, I shrunk supinely from the appalling job, newly rearing itself before me, of re-reading the whole canon of the singularly laborious and muggy, the incomparably tangled and unintelligible works of Prof. Dr. Thorstein Veblen. . . .

But if a sense of duty tortures a man, it also enables him to achieve prodigies, and so I managed to get through the whole infernal job. I read *The Theory of the Leisure Class,* I read *The Theory of Business Enterprise,* and then I read *The Instinct of Workmanship.* An hiatus followed; I was racked by a severe neuralgia, with delusions of persecution. On recovering I tackled *Imperial Germany and the Industrial Revolution.* Malaria for a month, and then *The Nature of Peace and the Terms of Its Perpetuation.* What ensued was never diagnosed; probably it was some low infection of the mesentery or spleen. When it passed off, leaving only an asthmatic cough, I read *The Higher Learning in America,* and then went to Mt. Clemens to drink the Glauber's salts. Eureka! the business was done! It had strained me, but now it was over. Alas, a good part of the agony had been needless. What I found myself aware of, coming to the end, was that practically the whole system of Prof. Dr. Veblen was in his first book and his last—that is, in *The Theory of the Leisure Class,* and *The Higher Learning in America.* I pass on the good news. Read these two, and you won't have to read the others. And if even two daunt you, then read the first. Once through it, though you will have missed many a pearl and many a pain, you will have a fairly good general acquaintance with the gifted metaphysician's ideas.

For those ideas, in the main, are quite simple, and often anything but revolutionary in essence. What is genuinely remarkable about them is not their novelty, or their complexity, nor even the fact that a professor should harbor them; it is the astoundingly grandiose and rococo manner of their statement, the almost unbelievable tediousness and flatulence of the gifted headmaster's prose, his unprecedented talent for saying nothing in an august and heroic manner. There are tales of an actress of the last generation, probably Sarah Bernhardt, who could put pathos and even terror into a recitation of the multiplication table. The late Louis James did something of the sort; he introduced limericks into *Peer Gynt* and still held the yokelry agape. The same talent, raised to a high power, is in this Prof. Dr. Veblen. Tunnel under his great moraines and stalagmites of words, dig down into his vast kitchen-midden of discordant and raucous polysyllables, blow up the hard, thick shell of his almost theological manner, and what you will find in his discourse is chiefly a mass of platitudes—the self-evident made horrifying, the obvious in terms of the staggering. Marx, I daresay, said a good deal of it, and what Marx overlooked has been said over and over again by his heirs and assigns. But Marx, at this business, labored under a technical handicap: he wrote in German, a language he actually understood. Prof. Dr. Veblen submits himself to no such disadvantage. Though born, I believe, in These States, and resident here all his life, he achieves the effect, perhaps without employing the means, of thinking in some unearthly foreign language—say Swahili, Su-

merian or Old Bulgarian—and then painfully clawing his thoughts into a copious but uncertain and book-learned English. The result is a style that affects the higher cerebral centers like a constant roll of subway expresses. The second result is a sort of bewildered numbness of the senses, as before some fabulous and unearthly marvel. And the third result, if I make no mistake, is the celebrity of the professor as a Great Thinker. In brief, he states his hollow nothings in such high, astounding terms that they must inevitably arrest and blister the right-thinking mind. He makes them mysterious. He makes them shocking. He makes them portentous. And so, flinging them at naïve and believing minds, he makes them stick and burn.

No doubt you think that I exaggerate—perhaps even that I lie. If so, then consider this specimen—the first paragraph of Chapter XIII of *The Theory of the Leisure Class:*

> In an increasing proportion as time goes on, the anthropomorphic cult, with its code of devout observances, suffers a progressive disintegration through the stress of economic exigencies and the decay of the system of status. As this disintegration proceeds, there come to be associated and blended with the devout attitude certain other motives and impulses that are not always of an anthropomorphic origin, nor traceable to the habit of personal subservience. Not all of these subsidiary impulses that blend with the bait of devoutness in the later devotional life are altogether congruous with the devout attitude or with the anthropomorphic apprehension of sequence of phenomena. Their origin being not the same, their action upon the scheme of devout life is also not in the same direction. In many ways they traverse the underlying norm of subservience or vicarious life to which the code of devout observances and the ecclesiastical and sacerdotal institutions are to be traced as their substantial basis. Through the presence of these alien motives the social and industrial régime of status gradually disintegrates, and the canon of personal subservience loses the support derived from an unbroken tradition. Extraneous habits and proclivities encroach upon the field of action occupied by this canon, and it presently comes about that the ecclesiastical and sacerdotal structures are partially converted to other uses, in some measure alien to the purposes of the scheme of devout life as it stood in the days of the most vigorous and characteristic development of the priesthood.

Well, what have we here? What does this appalling salvo of rhetorical artillery signify? What is the sweating professor trying to say? What is his Message now? Simply that in the course of time, the worship of God is commonly corrupted by other enterprises, and that the church, ceasing to be a mere temple of adoration, becomes the headquarters of these other enterprises. More simply still, that men sometimes vary serving God by serving other men, which means, of course, serving themselves. This bald platitude, which must be obvious to any child who has ever been to a church bazaar or a parish house, is here tortured, worried and run through rollers until it is spread out to 241 words, of which fully 200 are unnecessary. The next paragraph is even worse. In it the master undertakes to explain in his peculiar dialect the meaning of "that non-reverent sense of aesthetic congruity with the environment which is left as a residue of the latter-day act of worship after elimination of its anthropomorphic content." Just what does he mean by this "non-reverent sense of aesthetic congruity"? I have studied the whole paragraph for three days, halting only for prayer and sleep, and I have come to certain conclusions. I may be wrong, but nevertheless it is the best that I can do.

What I conclude is this: he is trying to say that many people go to church, not because they are afraid of the devil but because they enjoy the music, and like to look at the stained glass, the potted lilies and the rev. pastor. To get this profound and highly original observation upon paper, he wastes, not merely 241, but more than 300 words! To say what might be said on a postage stamp he takes more than a page in his book!. . .

And so it goes, alas, alas, in all his other volumes—a cent's worth of information wrapped in a bale of polysyllables. In *The Higher Learning in America* the thing perhaps reaches its damndest and worst. It is as if the practice of that incredibly obscure and malodorous style were a relentless disease, a sort of progressive intellectual diabetes, a leprosy of the horse sense. Words are flung upon words until all recollection that there must be a meaning in them, a ground and excuse for them, is lost. One wanders in a labyrinth of nouns, adjectives, verbs, pronouns, adverbs, prepositions, conjunctions and participles, most of them swollen and nearly all of them unable to walk. It is difficult to imagine worse English, within the limits of intelligible grammar. It is clumsy, affected, opaque, bombastic, windy, empty. It is without grace or distinction and it is often without the most elementary order. The learned professor gets himself enmeshed in his gnarled sentences like a bull trapped by barbed wire, and his efforts to extricate himself are quite as furious and quite as spectacular. He heaves, he leaps, he writhes; at times he seems to be at the point of yelling for the police. It is a picture to bemuse the vulgar and to give the judicious grief.

Worse, there is nothing at the bottom of all this strident wind-music—the ideas it is designed to set forth are, in the overwhelming main, poor ideas, and often they are ideas that are almost idiotic. One never gets the thrill of sharp and original thinking, dexterously put into phrases. The concepts underlying, say, *The Theory of the Leisure Class* are simply Socialism and water; the concepts underlying *The Higher Learning in America* are so childishly obvious that even the poor drudges who write editorials for newspapers have often voiced them. When, now and then, the professor tires of this emission of stale bosh and attempts flights of a more original character, he straightway comes tumbling down into absurdity. What the reader then has to struggle with is not only intolerably bad writing, but also loose, flabby, cocksure and preposterous thinking. . . . Again I take refuge in an example. It is from Chapter IV of *The Theory of the Leisure Class*. The problem before the author here has to do with the social convention which frowns upon the consumption of alcohol by women— at least to the extent to which men may consume it decorously. Well, then, what is his explanation of this convention? Here, in brief, is his process of reasoning:

> 1. The leisure class, which is the predatory class of feudal times, reserves all luxuries for itself, and disapproves their use by members of the lower classes, for this use takes away their charm by taking away their exclusive possession.

> 2. Women are chattels in the possession of the leisure class, and hence subject to the rules made for inferiors. ''The patriarchal tradition . . . says that the woman, being a chattel, should consume only what is necessary to her sustenance, except so far as her further consumption contributes to the comfort or the good repute of her master.''

> 3. The consumption of alcohol contributes nothing to the comfort or good repute of the woman's master, but ''detracts sensibly from the comfort or pleasure'' of her master. *Ergo*, she is forbidden to drink.

This, I believe, is a fair specimen of the Veblenian ratiocination. Observe it well, for it is typical. That is to say, it starts off with a gratuitous and highly dubious assumption, proceeds to an equally dubious deduction, and then ends with a platitude which begs the whole question. What sound reason is there for believing that exclusive possession is the hall-mark of luxury? There is none that I can see. It may be true of a few luxuries, but it is certainly not true of the most familiar ones. Do I enjoy a decent bath because I know that John Smith cannot afford one—or because I delight in being clean? Do I admire Beethoven's Fifth Symphony because it is incomprehensible to Congressmen and Methodists—or because I genuinely love music? Do I prefer terrapin à la Maryland to fried liver because plowhands must put up with the liver—or because the terrapin is intrinsically a more charming dose? Do I prefer kissing a pretty girl to kissing a charwoman because even a janitor may kiss a charwoman—or because the pretty girl looks better, smells better and kisses better? Now and then, to be sure, the idea of exclusive possession enters into the concept of luxury. I may, if I am a bibliophile, esteem a book because it is a unique first edition. I may, if I am fond, esteem a woman because she smiles on no one else. But even here, save in a very small minority of cases, other attractions plainly enter into the matter. It pleases me to have a unique first edition, but I wouldn't care anything for a unique first edition of Robert W. Chambers or Elinor Glyn; the author must have my respect, the book must be intrinsically valuable, there must be much more to it than its mere uniqueness. And if, being fond, I glory in the exclusive smiles of a certain Miss— or Mrs.—, then surely my satisfaction depends chiefly upon the lady herself, and not upon my mere monopoly. Would I delight in the fidelity of the charwoman? Would it give me any joy to learn that, through a sense of duty to me, she had ceased to kiss the janitor?

Confronted by such considerations, it seems to me that there is little truth left in Prof. Dr. Veblen's theory of conspicuous consumption and conspicuous waste—that what remains of it, after it is practically applied a few times, is no more than a wraith of balderdash. In so far as it is true it is obvious. All the professor accomplishes with it is to take what every one knows and pump it up to such proportions that every one begins to doubt it. What could be plainer than his failure in the case just cited? He starts off with a platitude, and ends in absurdity. No one denies, I take it, that in a clearly limited sense, women occupy a place in the world—or, more accurately, aspire to a place in the world—that is a good deal like that of a chattel. Marriage, the goal of their only honest and permanent hopes, invades their individuality; a married woman becomes the function of another individuality. Thus the appearance she presents to the world is often the mirror of her husband's egoism. A rich man hangs his wife with expensive clothes and jewels for the same reason, among others, that he adorns his own head with a plug hat: to notify everybody that he can afford it—in brief, to excite the envy of Socialists. But he also does it, let us hope, for another and far better and more powerful reason, to wit, that she intrigues him, that he delights in her, that he loves her—and so wants to make her gaudy and happy. This reason may not appeal to Socialist sociologists. In Russia, according to an old scandal (officially endorsed by the British bureau for pulling Yankee noses) the Bolsheviki actually repudiated it as insane. Nevertheless, it continues to appeal very forcibly to the majority of normal husbands in the nations of the West, and I am convinced that it is a hundred times as potent as any other reason. The American husband, in particular, dresses his wife like a circus horse, not primarily because he wants to display his wealth upon her person, but because he is a soft and moony fellow and ever ready to yield to her desires, however preposterous. If any conception of her as a chattel were actively in him, even unconsciously, he would be a good deal less her slave. As it is, her vicarious practice of conspicuous waste commonly reaches such a development that her master himself is forced into renunciations—which brings Prof. Dr. Veblen's theory to self-destruction.

His final conclusion is as unsound as his premises. All it comes to is a plain begging of the question. Why does a man forbid his wife to drink all the alcohol she can hold? Because, he says, it "detracts sensibly from his comfort or pleasure." In other words, it detracts from his comfort and pleasure because it detracts from his comfort and pleasure. Meanwhile, the real answer is so plain that even a professor should know it. A man forbids his wife to drink too much because, deep in his secret archives, he has records of the behavior of other women who drank too much, and is eager to safeguard his wife's self-respect and his own dignity against what he knows to be certain invasion. In brief, it is a commonplace of observation, familiar to all males beyond the age of twenty-one, that once a woman is drunk the rest is a mere matter of time and place: the girl is already there. A husband, viewing this prospect, perhaps shrinks from having his chattel damaged. But let us be soft enough to think that he may also shrink from seeing humiliation, ridicule and bitter regret inflicted upon one who is under his protection, and one whose dignity and happiness are precious to him, and one whom he regards with deep and (I surely hope) lasting affection. A man's grandfather is surely not his chattel, even by the terms of the Veblen theory, and yet I am sure that no sane man would let the old gentleman go beyond a discreet cocktail or two if a bout of genuine bibbing were certain to be followed by the complete destruction of his dignity, his chastity and (if a Presbyterian) his immortal soul. . . .

One more example of the Veblenian logic and I must pass on: I have other fish to fry. On page 135 of *The Theory of the Leisure Class* he turns his garish and buzzing search-light upon another problem of the domestic hearth, this time a double one. First, why do we have lawns around our country houses? Secondly, why don't we employ cows to keep them clipped, instead of importing Italians, Croatians and blackamoors? The first question is answered by an appeal to ethnology: we delight in lawns because we are the descendants of "a pastoral people inhabiting a region with a humid climate." True enough, there is in a well-kept lawn "an element of sensuous beauty," but that is secondary: the main thing is that our dolicho-blond ancestors had flocks, and thus took a keen professional interest in grass. (The Marx *motif!* The economic interpretation of history in E flat.) But why don't *we* keep flocks? Why do we renounce cows and hire Jugo-Slavs? Because "to the average popular apprehension a herd of cattle so pointedly suggests thrift and usefulness that their presence . . . would be intolerably cheap." With the highest veneration, Bosh! Plowing through a bad book from end to end, I can find nothing sillier than this. Here, indeed, the whole "theory of conspicuous waste" is exposed for precisely what it is: one per cent. platitude and ninety-nine per cent. nonsense. Has the genial professor, pondering his great problems, ever taken a walk in the country? And has he, in the course of that walk, ever crossed a pasture inhabited by a cow (*Bos taurus*)? And has he, making that

crossing, ever passed astern of the cow herself? And has he, thus passing astern, ever stepped carelessly, and—

But this is not a medical work, and so I had better haul up. The cow, to me, symbolizes the whole speculation of this laborious and humorless pedagogue. From end to end you will find the same tedious torturing of plain facts, the same relentless piling up of thin and over-labored theory, the same flatulent bombast, the same intellectual strabismus. And always with an air of vast importance, always in vexed and formidable sentences, always in the longest words possible, always in the most cacophonous English that even a professor ever wrote. One visualizes him with his head thrown back, searching for cryptic answers in the firmament and not seeing the overt and disconcerting cow, not watching his step. One sees him as the pundit *par excellence,* infinitely earnest and diligent, infinitely honest and patient, but also infinitely humorless, futile and hollow. . . .

So much, at least for the present, for this Prof. Dr. Thorstein Veblen, head Great Thinker to the parlor radicals, Socrates of the intellectual Greenwich Village, chief star (at least transiently) of the American *Athanæums.* I am tempted to crowd in mention of some of his other astounding theories—for example, the theory that the presence of pupils, the labor of teaching, a concern with pedagogy, is necessary to the highest functioning of a scientific investigator—a notion magnificently supported by the examples of Flexner, Ehrlich, Metchnikoff, Loeb and Carrel! I am tempted, too, to devote a thirdly to the astounding materialism, almost the downright hoggishness, of his whole system—its absolute exclusion of everything approaching an aesthetic motive. But I must leave all these fallacies and absurdities to your own inquiry. More important than any of them, more important as a phenomenon than the professor himself and all his works, is the gravity with which his muddled and highly dubious ideas have been received. At the moment, I daresay, he is in decline; such Great Thinkers have a way of going out as quickly as they come in. But a year or so ago he dominated the American scene. All the reviews were full of his ideas. A hundred lesser sages reflected them. Every one of intellectual pretentions read his books. Veblenism was shining in full brilliance. There were Veblenists, Veblen clubs, Veblen remedies for all the sorrows of the world. There were even, in Chicago, Veblen Girls—perhaps Gibson girls grown middle-aged and despairing.

The spectacle, unluckily, was not novel. Go back through the history of America since the early nineties, and you will find a long succession of just such violent and uncritical enthusiasms. James had his day; Dewey had his day; Ibsen had his day; Maeterlinck had his day. Almost every year sees another intellectual Munyon arise, with his infallible peruna for all the current malaises. Sometimes this Great Thinker is imported. Once he was Pastor Wagner; once he was Bergson; once he was Eucken; once he was Tolstoi; once he was a lady, by name Ellen Key; again he was another lady, Signorina Montessori. But more often he is of native growth, and full of the pervasive cocksureness and superficiality of the land. I do not rank Dr. Veblen among the worst of these haruspices, save perhaps as a stylist; I am actually convinced that he belongs among the best of them. But that best is surely depressing enough. What lies behind it is the besetting intellectual sin of the United States—the habit of turning intellectual concepts into emotional concepts, the vice of orgiastic and inflammatory thinking. There is, in America, no orderly and thorough working out of the fundamental problems of our society; there is only, as one

Englishman has said, an eternal combat of crazes. The things of capital importance are habitually discussed, not by men soberly trying to get at the truth about them, but by brummagem Great Thinkers trying only to get *kudos* out of them. We are beset endlessly by quacks—and they are not the less quacks when they happen to be quite honest. In all fields, from politics to pedagogics and from theology to public hygiene, there is a constant emotional obscuration of the true issues, a violent combat of credulities, an inane debasement of scientific curiosity to the level of mob gaping.

The thing to blame, of course, is our lack of an intellectual aristocracy—sound in its information, skeptical in its habit of mind, and, above all, secure in its position and authority. Every other civilized country has such an aristocracy. It is the natural corrective of enthusiasms from below. It is hospitable to ideas, but as adamant against crazes. It stands against the pollution of logic by emotion, the sophistication of evidence to the glory of God. But in America there is nothing of the sort. On the one hand there is the populace—perhaps more powerful here, more capable of putting its idiotic ideas into execution, than anywhere else—and surely more eager to follow platitudinous messiahs. On the other hand there is the ruling plutocracy—ignorant, hostile to inquiry, tyrannical in the exercise of its power, suspicious of ideas of whatever sort. In the middle ground there is little save an indistinct herd of intellectual eunuchs, chiefly professors—often quite as stupid as the plutocracy and always in great fear of it. When it produces a stray rebel he goes over to the mob; there is no place for him within his own order. This feeble and vacillating class, unorganized and without authority, is responsible for what passes as the well-informed opinion of the country—for the sort of opinion that one encounters in the serious periodicals—for what later on leaks down, much diluted, into the few newspapers that are not frankly imbecile. Dr. Veblen has himself described it in *The Higher Learning in America;* he is one of its characteristic products, and he proves that he is thoroughly of it by the timorousness he shows in that book. It is, in the main, only half-educated. It lacks experience of the world, assurance, the consciousness of class solidarity and security. Of no definite position in our national life, exposed alike to the clamors of the mob and the discipline of the plutocracy, it gets no public respect and is deficient in self-respect. Thus the better sort of men are not tempted to enter it. It recruits only men of feeble courage, men of small originality. Its sublimest flower is the American college president, well described by Dr. Veblen—a perambulating sycophant and platitudinarian, a gaudy mendicant and bounder, engaged all his life, not in the battle of ideas, the pursuit and dissemination of knowledge, but in the courting of rich donkeys and the entertainment of mobs. . . .

Nay, Veblen is not the worst. Veblen is almost the best. The worst is—but I begin to grow indignant, and indignation, as old Friedrich used to say, is foreign to my nature. (pp. 63-82)

H. L. Mencken, "Professor Veblen," in his Prejudices, *first series, Alfred A. Knopf, 1919, pp. 59-82.*

WESLEY C. MITCHELL   (essay date 1929)

[*Mitchell was an American economist who studied under Veblen. In the following excerpt, he describes Veblen's contribution to economic theory.*]

[Veblen, an] offshoot of Norwegian culture, reared in an American environment of farm life and conventional schools, had disconcerting ways. He observed the tamest acts and com-

monest opinions of those about him with narrowed eyes, as if they were curious phenomena which called for an explanation. Now and then he would drop a quizzical comment, which came from outer space like a meteor, shocking some bystanders and amusing others. He had extraordinary notions about what was relevant to the subjects he was supposed to teach. Students who enrolled in his courses on agricultural economics and socialism heard as much about the practices of the Hopi Indians, the Samurai, the Hebrews of the Old Testament, the Andaman Islanders, and the trading pirates of the North Sea as they did about populism and Karl Marx. They were puzzled to find their own convictions and loyalties analyzed and accounted for on evolutionary grounds. The plainer was a piece of commonsense, the more universally accepted, the more curious did Veblen find it, and the farther back in human culture did he go for an explanation.

But the most disconcerting thing to students properly brought up was that Veblen never denounced nor commended anything. That tingling psychological reaction known as righteous indignation seemed lacking in his make-up—though he would inquire why different people get morally indignant with each other. Even about intellectual matters he was singularly unexcited. If an ingenuous student waxed enthusiastic about the passion for research, Veblen's temperature did not rise a degree. The root of scientific inquiry is "idle curiosity"; indulging this propensity has led successive generations of men to the quaintest of notions about the world; the stock of scientific ideas on which we now plume ourselves is blood-brother of the cosmologies which satisfied savages; that the current notions give us better control over natural forces is interesting and has significant cultural consequences; but in due time these notions will come to seem as quaint as any that are now out of date.

Small wonder that students over whose minds the "cake of custom" had formed solidly put Veblen down as a profane juggler with the verities. Others less well protected did not know what to think; but at least they began to wonder about many things they had always taken for granted—opinions other people held, even opinions they caught themselves expressing. They felt uncomfortably sophisticated, as if they had lost their mental innocence and were no longer quite respectable.

When Veblen published his first book, *The Theory of the Leisure Class,* in 1899, those of us who had been in his classes watched excitedly to see how the reading public would react. There were protests as we expected; but there were also warm praises from men of letters. William Dean Howells, in particular, smiled benignly. Veblen was classified as a social satirist—"the most powerful since Swift." That classification was a shield against attacks by the deadly serious. A satirist is permitted to speak freely, because he is not supposed to mean quite what he says. Readers are expected to chuckle; they are likely to be laughed at if they boil over with indignation. All Veblen's elaborate explanations of social foibles, professedly based upon anthropological and historical evidence, were taken as literary machinery for producing effects—an equivalent for the empire of Lilliput.

There was justification for this interpretation of the book. Veblen loved producing literary effects. He was an arch phrasemaker. He took a naughty delight in making people squirm. His aloofness, his objectivity were partly stage make-up. He did not want anyone to be quite sure when he was indulging his peculiar sense of humor at the expense of the public. He liked to feel sophisticated and to smile at the simple critics who frothed over his jibes. But, though these dispositions colored everything he ever wrote, no matter how technical, Veblen was genuinely interested in the explanations he sketched. Human behavior was to him the most fascinating puzzle in the world, and he thought he had clues to the solution—clues which the social scientists had missed, though they were suggested by writers so well known as Darwin and William James.

Accepting the current opinion of biologists that the human species has undergone but slight physical change since neolithic times at any rate, Veblen held that the gulf which yawns between the lives of modern communities and the lives of cave dwellers has been bridged; or created, by the evolution of culture. Culture is substantially a complex of widely prevalent habits of thought. Mass habits are determined primarily by the way men and women spend their time. By all odds the most time-consuming occupation of mankind is making a living. Therefore the economic factor has been most potent in shaping culture. It is primarily economic necessity that has forced us into new ways. Whenever changes in the physical environment, the dwindling of a staple food supply, migration to different habitats, or any other cause, threw their traditional methods of getting a living out of gear, men were forced to alter their practices or succumb. The new ways of working, developed through trial and error, modified old habits of thinking and added to the stock of commonplace information. In their turn these results reacted upon methods of getting a living, thereby modified habits afresh, and so on indefinitely. Thus human culture has evolved under pressure, through an age-long process of cumulative changes in standard ways of thinking by creatures with non-evolving brains.

It follows, according to Veblen, that the only explanation in harmony with modern science, of how men have behaved at any stage in their checkered career, is an account of the evolution of social habits of thought in the given community up to the given date. To be sciences at all, anthropology, economics, sociology, and politics must be evolutionary sciences on the pattern of Darwinian biology. Properly conceived, these social disciplines trace the descent of culture from the point where Darwin ended his account of the descent of man. But is that the program on which economists and their cousins are now working?

The patent answer to this question is Veblen's fundamental criticism of economic theory. In its best formulations, this body of speculations is a beautifully articulated set of doctrines, logically consistent with the preconceptions from which they are derived, and convincing to anyone who shares the view of human nature which prevailed in Western Europe shortly before and shortly after 1800. That view of human nature is still tacitly accepted by many contemporary economists, and they are content to walk a little further in the paths marked out by Adam Smith, Ricardo, and John Mill. There is no need to controvert these estimable logicians. Rather, one should inquire into the causes which have preserved economic theory from infection by latter-day science. And Veblen proceeded to explain his colleagues to themselves with all the arts he had employed in explaining leisure-class institutions. Economists were used to being criticized by each other; but they did not know what to make of this person who took them apart to show how they worked.

More important was the task of rebuilding economics upon modern lines. At this task of reconstruction Veblen worked in the unsystematic fashion congenial to him. His books are all monographs, devoted to the genetic explanation of certain institutions—that is, habits of thought which have prevailed in various times and places. What particularly fascinated him in the contemporary field were the relations between making goods and making money, between the machine process and business enterprise, engineers and absentee owners. Material well-being depends upon the steady operation of our industrial plants under the direction of scientifically trained engineers. But these plants are run for profit, by business men, in the interest of security holders who typically take no share in the work. Making money depends upon the prices paid for commodities and services used in industry and upon the prices received for the output. Business managers are concerned to keep the profit margins at the maximum-net-revenue point. They are advisedly fearful lest an increase in current supply may force sellng prices so low that the larger turnover will be no comfort. Hence they habitually keep production below the point which engineering skill makes practicable with existing plant capacity. That is, the business man's chief contribution to welfare now consists in practicing "capitalistic sabotage." Given a free hand, Veblen guessed that, by reorganizing industry on a continental scale, the engineering profession could double the national income of consumable commodities without increasing working hours. But in the process they would smash myriads of independent business enterprises. So society is gestating a conflict of interests between business men and absentee owners upon the one side, and engineers and the mass of the "underlying population" upon the other.

How long this conflict of interests can be kept from becoming a conflict of classes is the leading problem of current civilization. Veblen argued, in 1904, that business enterprise cannot run a long career under our present economic institutions. For the discipline of daily work in the factory, which is the lot of an increasing number of men, breeds a practical habit of mind, which makes it increasingly difficult for the factory hand to see what right absentee owners have to an appreciable part of what he and his mates produced. Engineers, brought up on mathematics and the physical sciences, harbor similar doubts about the legitimacy of "unearned incomes." Let this habit of thought develop somewhat further, as develop it must unless the machine process is checked, and business enterprise will go the way of feudalism and slavery. After the War, Veblen seemed for a time to hope that the change might come, and come quickly. In the articles he wrote for the *Dial*, and allowed to be reprinted as books, his bland tone became strident; his analysis suggested a problem of action; he repeated his favorite phrases like an agitator. But that was a passing phase. ***Absentee Ownership***, the last of his books save for the translation of an "Icelandic Saga," regains much, though not all, of the elfish aloofness which marked *The Theory of Business Enterprise* and *The Instinct of Workmanship*.

Veblen's contribution to economics consisted in replacing the hedonistic conception of human nature by the instinct-habit psychology. That shift allied economics to biology rather than to mechanics. It brought new problems to the fore and relegated old problems to the background. It suggested a close working agreement between economists and the other students of human behavior—historians, psychologists, anthropologists, political scientists and sociologists. It was a service the full value of which has yet to be grasped. But like other intrepid explorers of new lands, Veblen made hasty traverses, seeing what appealed to him. His sketch maps are enormously suggestive, but not accurate in detail. For example, he looked at the "vested interests" and at the machine-tender from too far away with the eyes of a farmer. He credited the first with more singleness and more clarity of purpose than the miscellaneous and changing aggregate of the rich can claim. He saw the machine-tender as a standardized product, which machine-tenders are far from being. More at large, Veblen let his saturnine humor color his scientific analysis. Like earlier economists, he paid too little attention to checking his conclusions by patient observation, he paid too little attention to what did not harmonize with his favorite patterns. Yet, when all detractions are made, he remains the most interesting economist of his generation, and the one who is provoking most thought in others. (pp. 66-8)

> *Wesley C. Mitchell, "Thorstein Veblen: 1857-1929,"*
> in The New Republic, *Vol. LX, No. 770, September 4, 1929, pp. 66-8.*

MAX LERNER (essay date 1931)

[*Lerner is a political scientist, educator, author and nationally syndicated columnist. His career as a social commentator began in 1927 as an editor for the* Encyclopedia of Social Sciences; *from 1936 to 1939 he served as editor of the* Nation; *and since 1949 he has worked as a columnist for the* New York Post. *Throughout his career, Lerner has also interspersed academic work with his writing. Of his political philosophy, he states: "My political convictions are on the left, although I belong to no party. I feel that my energies must lie with the movement toward a democratic socialism." Lerner's numerous works include the popular* It Is Later Than You Think *(1938), a study of contemporary politics, and what he considers his most ambitious work,* America As a Civilization: Life and Thought in the United States Today *(1957). In the following essay, originally published in 1931, Lerner discusses Veblen's contribution to economics and social theory.*]

By some strange mutation there emerged out of the arrested energies of the nineties the most considerable and creative mind American social thought has yet produced. It belonged to Thorstein Veblen, whose paradox it was that, himself a product of Scandinavian stock which had for generations fought with the soil for life, he became absorbed with the surpluses of a leisure-class civilization; that, starting to reform professional economic theory, he made Americans aware of the wasteland of their contemporary social institutions.

After some *Wanderjahre* as a student and further years spent in desultory callings, Veblen came finally in 1892 to the glittering new University of Chicago as an instructor in economics. Into the group there—the first body of autonomous economic teaching in America—Veblen threw his startling generalizations about society, quarried from ethnological writings dusted off in the dark corners of the university library, or fashioned from a hint derived from conversations with John Dewey about philosophy or with Jacques Loeb about tropisms. But always, more coercive of his thought than anything else, there was Chicago itself, pressing its bulk and growth and tinsel wealth into his consciousness. Scarcely mentioned in his writings, it nevertheless polarized his thought and became a symbol of the society toward which his curious indirections were directed. And when on a battered Blickensderfer he had pounded out night after night the amazing pages of *The Theory of the Leisure Class* that society was for the first time made disquietingly aware of itself.

Veblen took as his theme the unproductiveness and inutility which become the ideals of a leisure class, and their psychological effects upon the whole of a society. He showed how, in such a society, prestige depends upon the flaunting of superfluous wealth through "conspicuous consumption" and "conspicuous waste," and through the "vicarious consumption" and "vicarious leisure" of the lady of the house and the corps of servants. He showed how the pecuniary values that dominated such a social structure informed every phase of life—religion, art, government, education; and in the tracing of the ramifications of leisure-class ideals through the whole of bourgeois culture he fulfilled the subtitle of the book—"An Economic Study of Institutions." Although his argument was unlocalized, we applied the moral to ourselves—to our *parvenu* millionaires and the ostentations of the gilded age—to the "common man" whom the previous decades had discovered and made a symbol of, and whom Veblen now showed to be exploited, accepting his status cringingly, subservient to those in whose pecuniary glory he hoped some day to participate.

With the writing of the **Leisure Class,** Veblen's energies were liberated and his thought flowed strongly into the channels of significance that he found in modern life. He had waited for maturity to write his first book (he was forty-two when it appeared) and had in the interim crammed his mind full of hypothesis and conjecture about social institutions. Now in ten books, in the space of two decades, he poured forth this stream of ideas, spilling over each theme he treated; for he could never prune his thought or narrow his emotion to his specific subject. The argument is considerably repetitive and far from clear-cut. Veblen's writing is obscure, mannered, baffling; as Mr. H. L. Mencken has pointed out in one of his wittiest and least sympathetic essays [see excerpt dated 1919], it wastes much effort in labored explanation of the obvious. But it encompasses the most important body of social analysis in modern American thought.

Veblen's principal motivation lay probably in making economic thought congruous with the conditions and spirit of latter-day economic activity. His brilliant series of essays on method, *The Preconceptions of Economic Science,* in a manner which exasperated because it was at once summary and elegiac, rejected not only the prevailing economic doctrines but the unconscious premises behind them. These premises had emerged from the intellectual temper of their day, but they were out of accord with ours. Their world had vanished. In its place there was a new world whose principal economic outlines Veblen sought to sketch in *The Theory of Business Enterprise.* The small-scale entrepreneur had been replaced by an absentee-owned corporation, the thrifty captain of industry by the financier, the isolated machine by a well-knit and exacting machine process, the higgling of the market by an all-pervading price system, and competition by a set of refined and ingenious devices for price control.

But the most important change of all was the broadening cleavage, in economic activity, between industry and business. Industry was the thing-technique; it worked with things to produce things. But at the helm, directing industry to its own purposes, was business, which worked with intangibles to produce money-values. This dichotomy fascinated Veblen. It became for him something closely symbolic of Balder and Loki—a dualism which in spite of his detestation of moral valuations he could not help viewing morally. His quest for the springs of human motive behind these two strains led him to write *The Instinct of Workmanship,* at once the most searching and perplexing of his books. It is an ambitious affair, full of provocative blind alleys, and at least half a splendid failure. Plunging morass-deep into "instinct" psychology, it emerges with the thesis that the "instinct of workmanship," deeply ingrained in man since savage times, has impelled him always not to waste his resources on alien and irrelevant purposes, but that it has been thwarted throughout human history by the piling-up of institutions which have run counter to it.

Veblen tended more and more to dwell on this monstrous conflict. As the steady pressure of science and technological advance beats the conditions of life mercilessly onward, and keeps forever changing the economic landscape and with it the contours of society, man finds himself ever farther away from the sense of economy and workmanship and social order that his primitive instincts called for. And as if to deepen the irony of his position, every attempt that he makes to adjust himself rationally to the new conditions of life is doomed by the nature of his own institutions. For an institution, while Veblen often thought of it merely as a pattern of social life—an organized way of doing things—was much more essentially for him the common way of thinking implied by it and growing out of it. And these ways of thinking—the belief, for example, in the "natural rights" of the individual—exercise their most tyrannical power when the patterns of life to which they were attached have been superseded. Out of their phantasmal world they reach the "dead hand of the past" to paralyze any attempt man might make to come to terms with his new world.

Inducted into a group of academic theorists who had exhausted themselves in warfare between rival camps, such an economics as this, with its airy rejection of all the stakes of conflict and its amazing vitality of thought, had an element of the grotesque, as if it were some exotic growth transplanted into dour and barren ground. Like all new doctrine, it had its trials at first. It was not even dignified by being called a heresy, but was dismissed as, whatever its merits, something other than economics—sociology, perhaps. But rapidly the younger scholars, those with energy and eagerness and a glimmer of daring, clustered around it. They became a school—the "institutionalists," from the conspicuous place in economic study that they give to the institutional patterns. And so Veblen's doctrine had its triumphs as well; and if it has not yet become orthodox, it ranks at least as a respectable heresy.

The generation which thus welcomed Veblen had been nurtured on a body of thought whose informing principle was that of a neatly arranged universe. In economics, physics, psychology, in art, morality, religion, political and legal theory, the prevailing attempt was to cling to a rapidly slipping sense of order. Veblen's principal achievement lay in his summary rejection of these dreams of social order. He saw a world in which the accumulated technical knowledge of generations of scientists and craftsmen—the current "state of the industrial arts"—was turned to the uses of an indifferent and even hostile system of business enterprise; a world in which there was a continuous "sabotaging" of industry by business whenever the aims of production threatened to clash with those of profit-making; and in which the natural resources of a country such as America had been squandered and exploited because, by our system of economic individualism, haste is especially profitable when it is accompanied by waste. In the realm of business he saw the growth of huge corporations under an "absentee ownership," where the most valuable arts were the refinements in manipulating items on a balance-sheet. He saw the incrustation of the "haves" into "vested interests" with a heavy stake in the maintenance of things as they are; and, exploited by them and subservient to them, an "underlying population" whose function as producers was to feed the "machine process," and as consumers to pay for their commodities a price of which the larger part went to items such as advertising and salesmanship

and marketing. He saw in religion that the churches had become infected with commercialism, and in education that men had almost given up their strange task of domiciling the ideals of a disinterested "higher learning" in a society at the mercy of pecuniary values.

From what obscure impulsions in his brain Veblen's chugging polysyllables took their perverse direction can be left only to conjecture. But we do know that the advancing *Zeitgeist* was on his side. His thought, judged cynical and pessimistic by the generation that saw the publication of the **Leisure Class,** struck an accord with the mood of the generation that read T. S. Eliot. In its essential symbols Veblen's wasteland of social institutions corresponded with the world as it revealed itself to the more sensitive post-War poets and novelists. If Veblen in some respects anticipated their notation of the modern spirit it was because, while they had needed the personal experience of War to impress upon them the plight of the individual in a disintegrating society. Veblen had sensed this plight more easily because his mind was not turned in upon itself, but was always directed toward the volcanic play of social energies. His greatest appeal was to those for whom the neat garden-walks and trim hedges of contemporary social thought contained fictitious patterns, clipped of all emotional evocation and unfruitful of any satisfying analyses.

In a sense Veblen helped tide American social thought over a period of desperate transition. The optimistic world of the early stages of industrialism, in which the machine had been accepted as an absolute boon, was behind us. A not impossible world in which we shall have learned what to do with the things that the machine has put within our reach is still to come. In the confusion between these two certitudes it was Veblen's achievement to make articulate the desolateness of our position. He has shown us by what impalpable puppet-strings we are tied to our racial and cultural past, and yet how uniquely our economic institutions differ from any the world has seen. The fierceness of his intellectual processes was combined paradoxically with an unimpassioned appraisal of all our bigness and shrillness and showiness. By insisting on a realistic picture of our economic society, by himself isolating and analyzing the economic changes which were cutting away the ground under established ways of living and orderly habits of thought, he revealed transitional America to itself.

How efffectively he did this is attested by the rapidity with which his analyses have become the customary and slightly worn currency of our thinking. Walton Hamilton has remarked that practically every vein of importance that is being explored today in economic thought may be traced back to Veblen. Not alone in the technical literature of economics but in so influential a lay theorist as Stuart Chase and so appreciable a figure in fictional social criticism as Sinclair Lewis, the influence is unmistakable. Known first as an eccentric who spun out labored ironies on what the reviewers were pleased to call our "social foibles," Veblen has suffered the most consummate compliment that can be paid to any thinker: in a few decades his ironies have become the basic material of economic discussion. (pp. 123-29)

Max Lerner, "Thorstein Veblen: Veblen and the Wasteland," in his Ideas are Weapons: The History and Uses of Ideas, *The Viking Press, 1939, pp. 123-29.*

EDGAR JOHNSON   (essay date 1941)

[*Johnson is an American biographer, novelist, and critic who is best known for his studies of Charles Dickens. In the following essay, he examines Veblen's use of satire.*]

Satire has various devices for overcoming our hatred of hearing ourselves criticized. Sometimes, to be sure, when it speaks outright, truth alone seems its sufficient sword and shield; more often, it disarms us by aping the sacred madness of Don Quixote or by masquerading as fool and jester. The ironical satirist, on the other hand, dupes our resistance by a pretense of innocence. He disguises himself as our defender, or, at the very least, as a disinterested arbiter judiciously weighing the pros and cons of a problem. Instilling the narcotic of a false security, he thus subtly undermines our defenses, imperceptibly crumbles them away.

Thorstein Veblen as satirist remarkably combines some of these methods. In part he is the remote scholar, the skeptical scientist subjecting everything to the test of his laboratory apparatus and the tribunal of reason. In part he is a growling and surly old Norwegian uncle whose smelly pipe and acid home-truths we wonder at ourselves for putting up with. But this very harshness is in fact an ingratiatory device; the truculence of the critic convinces us of his honesty and courage. It arises only out of the ironic understatements that dissimulate his aims and enable him to imply that satire was far from being his purpose. So handled, the unveiling achieved seems less of his engineering than inherent in the circumstances themselves, the facts constituting, as it were, their own satire.

Little attention has been paid to Veblen as a satirist. Economists have been concerned chiefly with a factual appraisal of Veblen's ideas and have almost ignored the satiric animus glinting through them. Literary critics, misled by his purely technical reputation, have for the most part left his work unanalyzed; and when H. L. Mencken once attempted it, he came the ludicrous cropper of reading Veblen's stylistic ironies as mere professorial verbosity [see excerpt dated 1919]. Veblen's rhetoric, his mingling of anthropological, sociological and economic analysis, and the oblique insights of his thought were all so novel that criticism has been slow to deal with him, and slow to comprehend his remarkable exploitation of the devices of skepticism and irony.

Skepticism and irony were for Thorstein Veblen instruments of an elaborate strategy. They were both elephantine armorplate and tremendous tonnage of heavy guns combined. From behind the device of the Persian visitor and the Chinese sage, Montesquieu and Goldsmith had projected their satire on eighteenth-century Europe. Veblen magnified the trick to an unbelievable remoteness and abstraction. Not using any overt fiction, characterizing himself only by manner, he put on the insuperable detachment of a Martian observer: he was an inhabitant of another world curiously describing and analyzing the habits of an alien form of existence. Constantly he repeated disclaimers of any "intention to find fault," or to be speaking "by way of praise or blame," or to imply "anything discreditable or immoral." Almost as often he made ironical show of commendation, "these wise measures of restraint and incitement," "this straight and narrow path of business integrity." Both serve to maintain his complicated masquerade of scientific dissection.

But Veblen is more than an interplanetary traveler from Mars. He is a Martian professor, couching his comments in a grotesquely sesquipedalian vocabulary that is a parody of all the pedantic jargon that ever obscured meaning. This solemn and ludicrous style has a triple function. It underlines the grave and scholarly disinterestedness we are supposed to believe behind Veblen's statements; it helps protect the author from censorial indignation by obscuring for many people his subversive meaning; and it makes subtly absurd the very institutions it pretends to handle with such pompous reverence. Veblen's style, in fact, which has seemed to hasty critics a weakness, is one of his greatest claims to respect. It is idiosyncratic, deliberately. But it is no harder to grow accustomed to than the styles of Meredith or Henry James. And once assimilated, its seeming ponderousness turns out to be rich in delicate malice and destructive sarcasms.

Veblen's whole career is a perfect illustration of Kenneth Burke's suggestion that in satire "the artist is seeking simultaneously to take risks and escape punishment for his boldness." Veblen's work was a detailed and devastating criticism of finance-capitalism, a withering analysis of business civilization; and yet his livelihood lay in an academic career carried on in universities endowed and dominated by business men. Veblen said ten times over and ten times more damagingly the things that Sinclair Lewis sketched in the flaring caricature of *Babbitt* and *Arrowsmith*. But Veblen was careful to say them in scholarly books on abstract topics written in a polysyllabic style both repellent and, often, incomprehensible to the bankers, business men and corporation counsel who made up the personnel of most boards of trustees. Even so, in the end his ambiguities caught up with him. He found it increasingly difficult to obtain scholarly posts to which his eminence entitled him, and was able to hold them only during steadily decreasing periods of time. At last nowhere but in the New School for Social Research was academic freedom broad enough to harbor him.

What were these subversive doctrines that made Veblen both satirist and suspect revolutionary? All their main tenets appear in his most brilliant work of satire, *The Theory of the Leisure Class;* although he examines in greater detail now one and now another facet of his general thesis in a cluster of further books including *The Instinct of Workmanship, The Theory of Business Enterprise, The Engineers and the Price System* and *The Higher Learning in America.* All these purport to be, and are in fact, serious contributions to economics and sociology, but their force as satire lies in their deep undercurrent of sardonic implication. (p. 121)

[Veblen] draws upon the evidence of anthropology to support that view of the origin of property that Anatole France displayed in the hilarious mythological chapters of *Penguin Island.* He shows the consistent principle behind that chaos of chicane, mendacity and exploitation that Wells drew in *Tono-Bungay.* Distinguishing between business and industry, he suggests cogent reasons for identifying business and the business temperament with the predatory and aggressive, using a "conscientious withdrawal of efficiency" to sabotage social welfare. In the very spirit of *Jonathan Wild* he writes that "the gifts of good-nature, equity and indiscriminate sympathy" impede, whereas "freedom from scruple, from sympathy, honesty and regard for life . . . further the success of the individual in the pecuniary culture."

Sinclair Lewis often seems to be nothing but dramatized Veblen. Pecuniary emulation is shown multiplying useless needs in the gadget-ridden world of *Babbitt;* and the domination of business men smothering and prostituting genuine science and scholarship, which Veblen analyzed in *The Higher Learning in America,* Lewis narrowed down to the realm of medicine alone and mirrored in *Arrowsmith.* The acrimonious tirades of Tolstoy's *What Is Art?* Veblen subjects to measured insight in his elucidation of how pecuniary snobbery imposes itself imperceptibly but pervasively even within the realm of esthetic judgment. This whole range of observation and judgment—

both in those who wrote before him and in later writers, some of whom indubitably lean on him—Veblen integrates into a penetrating intellectual system.

Veblen's sardonic paradoxes are almost unexampled in their power to startle. The involved and painstakingly equivocal sentences uncoil their tortuous syllables interminably in a parody of academic stodginess, and then the legerdemain that was preparing is accomplished, the heavy abstractions concentrate themselves into a weighty epigram as incisive as an axe, and the slaughter is done. The annihilating force of Veblen's blows is derived, of course, from their intellectual unity and strength; there are no scattered strokes; every one is in the same direction, and every one strikes home. But it would be an error to overlook Veblen's ability to sharpen their cutting edge by devices of style.

The device he chiefly uses is a deliberately planned incongruity. We have already seen it in some of his epithets, "conspicuous consumption," "conspicuous waste," "vicarious leisure," "*the performance* of leisure," "conscientious withdrawal of efficiency," where the mere crackle of the syllables implies an ironic derision sometimes reinforced by the unexpectedness of the thought relationships. The same qualities can be seen in such combinations as "reputable notoriety," "genteel solemnities" (academic ceremonies), "captains of erudition" (university presidents), "reputable waste of time and means," "politely blameless dissipation." They appear in his description of the erection of churches as a "devout consumption of sacred edifices," and of their characteristic architecture as an "austerely wasteful discomfort." Sometimes they concentrate themselves into phrases discreetly mordant, as when he outlines the qualifications in those who would find favor with university presidents as a "ready versatility of convictions, and a staunch loyalty to their bread," or remarks that the endowment of cultural institutions has "the character of an investment in good fame." Not infrequently he coins an epigram: "Conservatism, being an upper-class characteristic, is decorous;. . . innovation, being a lower-class phenomenon, is vulgar." "Gentle blood is blood which has been ennobled by protracted contact with accumulated wealth or unbroken prerogative."

Two things are noteworthy about this technique. One is its elaborately innocent use of planned incongruity, expressions whose sober dignity is jarred by a qualification that seems out of tone or contradictory, but that turns out to have an esoteric and wounding appropriateness. The other is that the wounds so inflicted are almost invariably mortal, so that his epithet remains in memory as a derogatory monument to the concept it has slain. First he twists his description into a distortion of the conventional that is discovered to have a lethal truth; with it he crushes the life from a deluded idea, and leaves it beneath his own ponderous phrase transformed now into the headstone on a malefactor's grave. This is indeed, not only in the sense originally intended by Mrs. Malaprop, but in the literal application of that lady's words, "a nice derangement of epitaphs."

That his epithets were epitaphs, however, is not at all a product of the manner. Veblen carried irony to the point where it became a burlesque of itself, but he did so to conceal a genuine anger and to protect himself in a dangerously radical undertaking. When his irony seems on occasion the most ludicrous farce, the farce is really more often in the facts from which his probing sentences have stripped their masks. His pretense of a positively inhuman detachment enables him to engage in his suspect enterprise of eliciting the satire intrinsic in our pecuniary standards. A trace of indignation and Veblen would

have been labeled a fanatic; but that lunar irony of his ranges over delusions and leaves devastation behind. (pp. 122-23)

Edgar Johnson, "Veblen: Man from Mars," in The New Republic, *Vol. 105, No. 4, July 28, 1941, pp. 121-23.*

ALFRED KAZIN (essay date 1942)

[*A highly respected American literary critic, Kazin is best known for his essay collections* The Inmost Leaf (1955) *and* Contemporaries (1962), *and particularly for* On Native Grounds (1942), *a study of American prose writing since the era of William Dean Howells. Having studied the works of "the critics who were the best writers—from Sainte-Beuve and Matthew Arnold to Edmund Wilson and Van Wyck Brooks" as an aid to his own critical understanding, Kazin has found that "criticism focussed many—if by no means all—of my own urges as a writer: to show literature as a deed in human history, and to find in each writer the uniqueness of the gift, of the essential vision, through which I hoped to penetrate into the mystery and sacredness of the individual soul." In the following excerpt, he describes Veblen's tragic worldview.*]

In 1919, when he had come to New York to lecture at the New School for Social Research and to write editorials for the *Dial*, Thorstein Veblen published a characteristic little essay in a professional journal in which he expressed the hope that the Jews would never form a nationalistic movement of their own, since that would be a loss to world culture.

> It appears to be only when the gifted Jew escapes from the cultural environment created and fed by the particular genius of his own people, only when he falls into the alien lines of gentile inquiry and becomes a naturalized, though hyphenate, citizen in the gentile republic of learning, that he comes into his own as a creative leader in the world's intellectual enterprise. It is by loss of allegiance, or at the best by force of a divided allegiance to the people of his origin, that he finds himself in the vanguard of modern inquiry.

For the first requisite for constructive work in modern science, Veblen continued, is skepticism; the Jew, lost between the native tradition he has discarded and the Gentile world he can never fully accept,

> is a sceptic by force of circumstances over which he has no control. . . . He becomes a disturber of the intellectual peace, but only at the cost of becoming an intellectual wayfaring man, a wanderer in the intellectual no-man's-land, seeking another place to rest, farther along the road, somewhere over the horizon.

It was one of Veblen's rare self-portraits. He put the matter a little portentously, as he did everything, half in jest, half because he could not help it (a later generation, discovering that he often affected a witty pomposity, would think his prose nothing but elaborate impersonation); but he exposed the austerity and poignance of his intellectual career as few of his exegetes and literary admirers ever have. He was, in truth, an "intellectual wayfaring man and a disturber of the intellectual peace." His own generation thought him ridiculous or vaguely dangerous, when it did not ignore him; a later generation, having heard that his economic heresies have become commonplace, thinks of him chiefly as an economist who spent most of his time parodying the official prose of other economists and designing lugubrious epigrams for clever intellectuals. As a phrasemonger for critics of the established order, Veblen has become a hero of the intelligentsia. As a Cassandra foretelling the collapse of the economic order in 1929, a satirist of the status quo and the conduct of the middle class, he has even appeared to be one of the most substantial figures in the development of a native radicalism. But that is another phase of Veblen's public reputation and the public legend which delights in his domestic eccentricities and has forgotten that he was one of the most extraordinary and tragic figures in the history of the American imagination.

Professionally Veblen was a leading figure in the destruction of classical economics in America and a post-Darwinian who adapted evolutionary insights and methods in every available social study to institutional economics. But he was also a Western writer with an agrarian background who belonged to Hamlin Garland's generation and shared the problems of Theodore Dreiser's. He was a Norwegian farmer's son who, like so many of his background, was half-destroyed by the struggle to attain self-liberation in the endless conflict with the hostile dominating culture. Veblen was an alien twice over, for he was by every instinct estranged not only from the "pecuniary culture" of the East, but also from the native tradition and speech of his neighbors. He was not Norwegian, but his imaginative sympathies were linked to the parental culture; he was an American scholar and trained exclusively in America, but he spoke English always with a slight accent and wrote it always with more difficulty than his subsequent literary admirers were to know. Until he went to school English had been a foreign language, and the young Norskie who scandalized the denominational world of Carleton College, Minnesota, in the eighties by championing Björnson and Ibsen (and the Greenbackers) spent a good part of his life pottering at a translation of the great Norwegian Laxdaela Saga. (pp. 131-33)

Significantly [*The Theory of the Leisure Class*] was immediately picked up by literary people; it was Howells who wrote the review that helped to make it famous [see excerpt dated 1899]. No other economist would have thought of writing the book; not too many economists at the moment troubled to read it. Yet for all its rhetorical tricks and ambitious literary manner, it was a purely professional work from Veblen's own point of view. In his earliest essays, notably, **"Why Is Economics Not an Evolutionary Science?"** he had attacked classical economics on the ground that it was pre-evolutionary in its method, artificial in its logic, and a "system of economic taxonomy." Drawing upon the radical psychological studies of William James, Jacques Loeb, and John Dewey, which had already destroyed the mechanical antiquated psychology that buttressed classical economics, Veblen had become the principal exponent of a modern and genetic economics. Economics had too long been a pseudo-metaphysical study of Manchester "natural law." At this time he wrote:

> In so far as it is a science in the current sense of the term, any science, such as economics, which has to do with human conduct, becomes a genetic inquiry into the human scheme of life; and where, as in economics, the subject of inquiry is the conduct of man in his dealings with the material means of life, the science is necessarily an inquiry into the life-history of material civilization, on a more or less extended or restricted plan. . . . Like all human culture this material civilization is a scheme of institutions—institutional fabric and institutional growth.

It was this insight into the need for an economics that would constitute an "inquiry into the life-history of material civilization" that gave a design to *The Theory of the Leisure Class* and suggested the imaginative range and depth of Veblen's

mind. He had always been an omnivorous student of anthropology and social psychology, of folk habit and language (he had once seriously thought of devoting himself to philology). As an evolutionary economist, a student of contemporary material civilization in all its complexity, he could now freely study the bourgeois Americanus with impunity and in the interests of a modern institutional economics. For as an anthropologist of the contemporary, an anatomist of society, an evolutionist who had synthesized the social studies, he could now legitimately describe his interpretation of the history of civilization—in his eyes a history of predation, conquest, and ostentatious leisure. Later, in books like *The Theory of Business Enterprise* and *The Instinct of Workmanship,* this theory would develop into his famous doctrine that the industrial skill that runs modern technology is opposed to those who draw their profits from it; that there is an inveterate conflict between engineers and businessmen, efficiency and the profit system, the Veblens of this world and university trustees in general.

The Veblen who had always been the great outsider, who as a cultural and social alien had always been obsessed by cultural differences, now found that he could investigate them with propriety. The Veblen who "loved to play with the feelings of people not less than he loved to play with ideas" [Wesley Mitchell] could now adapt his contempt and hatred for the pecuniary culture to a playful "scientific" scrutiny. As an evolutionist, Veblen could now prove, as Alvin Johnson once put it, that "the pirate chieftain of one epoch becomes the captain of industry of another; the robber baron levying upon peaceful trade becomes the financial magnate." The introduction to *The Theory of the Leisure Class* featured a solemn study of leisure-class habits among Eskimos and Japanese and Pacific islanders; the subject was Dreiser's Cowperwood and Norris's Octopus and David Graham Phillips's Reign of Gilt.

Veblen was, at bottom, not an anthropologist at all, and possibly not as learned as his display of neolithic data seemed to indicate; but he could use anthropology as a form of malicious genealogy, and ethnology as a medium of "protective coloration." He had no direct interest in the past; he always despaired of the future; but the material civilization of the present was his subject, even his obsession, and he made the most of it. His great insight, and the one on which he literally deployed his fantastic erudition, was the realization that in the process of human evolution the businessman had become the archetype of modern Christendom. His learning became a series of illustrations by which to "prove" that the warrior of barbarism had given way to the priest and noble of feudalism only to yield in turn to the trader, the financier, and the industrialist. Beneath the ferocious solemnity of manner and the humor that was only an exaggeration of a psychic habit, Veblen could now vent his hatred of modern capitalism on a study of the materialism that sustained it and the elaborate pattern of manners, dress, ritual, education, that illustrated its vulgarity and its greed.

The satiric element in Veblen's book is almost pyrotechnical in its elaboration; but the art in his prose has often been exaggerated. The Veblen legend of a great prose craftsman stems from the fact that Veblen wrote a prose esthetically more interesting than most economists in America (not to forget literary historians, political scientists, and philosophers) have ever written or seem likely to; it has even thrived on the delightful irony that he must always seem imaginatively superior to many American novelists and critics. But the fact remains that he was as much the victim of his material as he was the master of it, and that the pains he took with his prose should not obscure the pain he can still inflict on his readers. If he sought at times to outrage deliberately, he succeeded too often without premeditation; though he loved to parody academic solemnity, it was his natural element. For though Veblen was an extraordinary phrase-maker and even an epigrammatist of superb wit, he was, as John Chamberlain once said, not a good sentence-maker. The peculiar quality of his prose lies, like Dreiser's, in the use he made of a naturally cumbersome and (despite its polysyllabic sophistication) primitive medium. The ironist in Veblen, occasionally mad and often delightful, was always a little ponderous. He succeeded too often, as in his famous passage on "the taxonomy of a monocotyledonous wage-system," by wringing academic jargon to death; but the humor was monstrously grotesque. Veblen's trickery as a writer lay in his use of the "grand" style, but he did not choose it; it chose him.

For Veblen *was* an alien; and like so many alien writers, he had a compensatory need (as he would have said) for formality. The deracinated always exaggerate the official tone of the race among whom they are living at the moment, and to no one could dignified circumlocutions have been so natural in the nineties as to a Norwegian farmer's son moving in the company of academic intellectuals who did not accept him. Veblen had that certain pompousness of style, largely undeliberate, which has not yet ceased to be the mark of the professional scholar in America; in his early years it was an article of clothing like the Prince Albert coat, and in many respects resembled it. In a day when wild-eyed Populists wrote like Senators, and Senators talked like Shakespeare's Romans, purity of style demanded a compelling direct interest in diction and rhythm which Veblen did not have. He often parodied the academic style, but with a suffering mischievousness that betrays the intensity of his exasperation. His leading ideas were brilliant intuitions, but he developed their implications slowly, so that the quality of his prose is often characterized by insensitiveness to proportion. Every style is an accumulation of psychic habits and records some organic personal rhythm; the Veblen who mumbled in the classroom those "long spiral sentences, reiterative like the eddas," as John Dos Passos called them [see Additional Bibliography], also mumbled in his book.

From this point of view Veblen's celebrated irony and prose devices do not appear any less skillful and amusing than worshipful admirers of his style have claimed them to be; they are merely one phase of his temperament and his powers as a writer. He used devices and played with grotesque phrases; he startled the reader into an awareness of the ties that exist everywhere in modern "material civilization" between new institutions and the use men make of them, between habits of work and prejudices of thought. But his style was not, as such, a pullover satiric style like Swift's or the one Goldsmith employed in his Chinese letters. A satiric style is a dramatic characterization, an impersonation; Veblen's verbosity was often painfully ingenuous. When he was ironic, as in a famous passage in *The Theory of the Leisure Class* in which he disclaimed any invidious use of the word "invidious," the humor was almost too palpable for comfort. "In making use of the term 'invidious,' it may perhaps be unnecessary to remark, there is no intention to extol or deprecate, or to commend or deplore. . . . The term is used in a technical sense as describing a comparison of persons with a view to rating and grading them in respect of relative worth or value . . . ." and so forth. This type of bearish pleasantry appeared in his definition of leisure as connoting "non-productive consumption of time," which

was a hit, a very palpable hit indeed at the jargon of economists, and one that pointed up his satiric interpretation of leisure in modern bourgeois society.

It may be true that Veblen's solemnity of style was a medium of concealing his contempt for the pecuniary culture; but he did not conceal it, and it is an extremely simple and even sentimental criticism which can suppose that Veblen did nothing but play the comedian for thirty years in a world that he found excruciatingly wretched. He had, admittedly, a masquerade; but it was a projection of desperation as well as a disguise. The native self, and the native prolixity, often stole through. For all his labor, he seems to have had a lurking cynicism toward his own work, as if it were only another aspiration that had been disappointed. Veblen's view of the world was not only mordant, it was densely, even profoundly, tragic. As a satirist in *The Theory of the Leisure Class* he could write with almost cheerful irony of the "peaceful," the "sedentary," the "poor," whose "most notable trait" was a "certain amiable inefficiency when confronted with force or fraud"; but his obsession with the forms and honors of property did not, in later books, conceal his despair at their supremacy.

No one before Veblen had realized with such acuteness the monstrous conflict between what he called the instinct of workmanship and the profit motive; the conflict became the design he saw in modern life. In his mind the conflict was not between capital and labor, but between capital and the intellectual élite which ran the profit system for capital and sacrificed itself for capital. He was never interested in the Marxian dream of a revolution by the working class; he had a certain contempt for Marxism, and thought of it as romantic and, in one sense, even unintelligible. The tragedy of that other class struggle, as Veblen saw it, was that it could never be resolved. The engineers, the symbolic protagonists of a harmonious new world, could do nothing about it. In Veblen's view, as Max Lerner has expounded it, "man finds himself ever farther away from the sense of economy and workmanship and social order that his primitive instincts called for. And as if to deepen the irony of his position, every attempt that he makes to adjust himself rationally to the new conditions of life is doomed by the nature of his own institutions" [see excerpt dated 1931]. This dilemma had the ruthless severity of Greek tragedy, in which man, like Prometheus, has brought light to the world but must suffer for it. The interests of profit and the community, of industry and business, of skill and greed, were diverse. "Gain may come to" the business classes, Veblen wrote in *The Theory of Business Enterprise,* "whether the disturbance makes for heightened facility or for widespread hardship." Modern life had become petrified in institutional habits of waste and greed. Like Henry Adams, Veblen had a bitter respect for the machine process; but he did not regard it as a literary symbol; it had become the focus of the modern tragedy. The machine, as Veblen was among the first to show, had its own rhythm which it dictated to men and compelled them to live by. The will rebelled, the machine persisted; the critical mind might quarrel with it, the body acquiesced.

Only a thinker who had so pressing a need of social change could have brought so much passion to the doubt of its realization. Veblen's distinction as an American writer of his time was thus uniquely tragic. He saw what so few in his generation could ever see; yet he affirmed nothing and promised nothing. Lonely all through a fairly long life plagued by poverty, alienation, ill-health, he suffered even more deeply from the austere honesty of his vision. Applauded by Marxists for his attacks upon the status quo, he laughed at their optimism; he threw the whole weight of his life into his examination of the pecuniary culture, but bolstered its institutional vanity. He was a naturalist, a more tragic-minded and finely conscious spirit than any American novelist of the naturalist generation; his final view of life was of an insane mechanism, of a perpetual and fruitless struggle between man and the forces that destroy him. Yet though he had what Dreiser and Crane and Norris seemed to lack, he was not their equal as an artist. He knew the rationale of everything where Dreiser, for example, has known only how to identify all life with the poignant gracelessness of his own mind; but he did not have the ultimate humility or enjoy the necessary peace. Veblen was an alien to the end, and the torment of his alienation is forever to be felt in his prose. (pp. 136-41)

> Alfred Kazin, "Progressivism: Some Insurgent Scholars," in his On Native Grounds: An Interpretation of Modern American Prose Literature, Reynal & Hitchcock, 1942, pp. 127-64.

PAUL M. SWEEZY (essay date 1946)

[*Sweezy is an American economist. In the following excerpt from an essay originally written in 1946, he reviews* The Nature of Peace *and notes theoretical shortcomings of Veblen's works.*]

Veblen's *The Nature of Peace,* which first appeared early in 1917, has now very appropriately been reissued. In it, he set down his thoughts on the war which was raging about him and on the prospects of the peace to come. The work as a whole, however, is not dated by the particular circumstances of the day; Veblen was really writing about a whole historical period from which we are only now beginning to emerge, and the reader today will find the book as stimulating and absorbing as he would have on the morrow of its publication.

The historical period about which Veblen was writing began roughly in the last quarter of the ninteenth century with the emergence of Germany and Japan as unified imperial states. He saw clearly that these two nations, preserving intact their feudal-dynastic political institutions and appropriating the most modern techniques of production and warfare, had come to dominate the international scene, and that they would continue to do so until their entire social structure had been radically and permanently transformed. "The upshot of all this recital of considerations," he says at one point, and the idea frequently recurs, "appears to be that a neutral peace compact may, or it may not, be practicable in the absence of such dynastic states as Germany and Japan; whereas it has no chance in the presence of these enterprising national establishments." This analysis led Veblen to advocate—usually he wrote specifically of Germany with an addendum to the effect that the same applies to Japan, "only more so"—the "disestablishment of the Imperial dynasty and the abrogation of all feudalistic remnants of privilege in the Fatherland and its allies, together with the reduction of those countries to the status of commonwealths made up of ungraded men." Thereafter, there would have to be a long period of surveillance during which the defeated country would be kept strictly disarmed—a period, he warned, much longer than the time required to prepare a new campaign of conquest. Eventually, however, he believed the German people would slough off their aggressive inclinations and acquire the matter-of-fact and essentially peaceful outlook which is fostered by the discipline of modern machine industry.

Generally speaking, Veblen was not very sanguine about the Allies' willingness to go as far as this, and the German revolution of 1918, which accomplished at one stroke much of what he advocated, must have come as a pleasant surprise to him. Nevertheless, his pessimism turned out in the long run to be fully justified. The German revolution, unlike its Russian counterpart, failed to make a clean sweep of the old order; the forces of reaction simply bided their time and eventually, with Allied connivance, returned to power in the doubly vicious and aggressive form of the Hitler dictatorship. Had he lived to see it, Veblen would undoubtedly have been profoundly depressed, for he would have immediately understood the full meaning of the event. At the same time, however, it can hardly be maintained that he would have been surprised. (pp. 295-96)

While history has fully vindicated Veblen's analysis of the role of Germany and Japan, I think one must nevertheless adopt a critical attitude toward much of the reasoning which underlies that analysis and which has a direct relevance to a wide range of vital problems of the day. (In this connection, one must not be misled into supposing that a correct conclusion proves the correctness of the reasoning by which it is reached.) Veblen takes his departure from a theory of nationalism or patriotism—he uses the terms interchangeably—which is very one-sided and, despite appearances to the contrary, unhistorical. According to this theory, the prehistoric forerunner of modern patriotism was a sense of group solidarity which served the utilitarian purposes of survival. Later on, however, when society had become differentiated into classes, there were no longer interests common to the group at large. Nevertheless, the ruling classes fostered the traditional sense of group solidarity which now became essentially a device for hiding real conflicts of interest within the group. During feudal tmes, this sense of group solidarity became fixed in the form of the loyalty of the subject to his ruler, and it is in this form that it has come down to modern times. In the case of such countries as imperial Germany and Japan, Veblen considers the relationship to be direct and obvious, while in the case of the democratic countries he asserts that their "patriotism" or "national spirit" is "after all and at best an attenuated and impersonalized remnant of dynastic loyalty."

Now of course there is much truth in the view that patriotism, especially in its more extreme forms, provides a cover for class, as opposed to general, interests. But to suggest, as Veblen does, that nationalism is nothing but a hangover from feudal times, and that it constitutes a purely negative and destructive force in the modern world, is to leave out one whole epoch of history and to forget that we are passing through another. In the formative stages of modern society, it was bourgeois nationalism which carried the banner against feudal separatism and obscurantism; and in the very country which Veblen often picks out as the only one devoid of a spirit of patriotism—China—we have been witnessing the growth of a nationalism that extends to nearly all classes and basically reflects a desire for independence and social reform. Similarly, in the Soviet Union a new sense of patriotism has grown up in recent years which embraces not only Great Russians, in whose case it might be supposed to be a carry-over from prerevolutionary times, but also peoples who were previously among the most backward in the world. Thus one cannot avoid the conclusion that Veblen's theory, while it happens to work well in the case of contemporary Germany and Japan, is at best a half-truth which can easily lead to false diagnoses of existing social situations.

The treatment of nationalism is only one example of theoretical inadequacy in Veblen's work. Despite the fact that he is commonly rated as an economist, it must be said that his economic analysis is usually weak and often misleading. He regards capitalism—for which he has a variety of designations, among the most frequent of which are "business enterprise" and "the price system"—in a wholly negative light and thus sees only one side, historically the least important side, of its nature. In Veblen's view, the capitalist operates purely in the realm of finance, and his only relation to production is one of sabotage and obstruction; his object is to mulct the underlying population to the maximum possible degree and to waste the proceeds in ostentatious display. Meanwhile, despite the obstruction of capitalists, mechanical industry expands and becomes increasingly productive. This view leads Veblen to regard the industrial engineer as the truly progressive factor in the modern economy and to postulate the existence of a basic conflict between the capitalist and the engineer. There are four main weaknesses in this theory: (1) it ignores, or at best slurs over, the capitalist's fundamental urge to add to his wealth as distinct from consuming it; (2) it entirely fails to see that accumulation by the capitalist can take place only through the steady expansion of the means of production and employment of more labor; (3) consequently it fails to see that the capitalist in effect calls into existence the industrial engineer, pays him, and gives direction to his work; and finally, (4) it inverts the relationship of engineer to capitalist, which is in reality one of dependence of the former on the latter, and makes it appear as a relation of conflict. It is not hard to understand how this theory of Veblen's became the basis of a variety of crackpot and even semifascist schemes in the hands of "followers" who totally lacked his deep historical knowledge and insight.

But the theory also had unfortunate consequences for Veblen's own work. Because he ignored the accumulation process—what modern economists would call the problem of savings and investment—he was debarred from developing an adequate theory of employment and of business fluctuations in general. (What he had to say on these subjects, chiefly in *The Theory of Business Enterprise,* is obscure and seems to center largely on expansion and contraction of the debt structure.) And without such a theory, his views on the economic functions and policies of the state were necessarily one-sided and frequently have a strong air of unreality about them. Indeed, what Veblen wrote on these questions often seems as though it could have come from the pen of a nineteenth-century Manchester liberal who had acquired his economics at second hand from Adam Smith. Tariffs, encouragement of exports, conquest of colonies, and so on, are all lumped together as patent economic absurdities which benefit only a few people directly concerned and cause damage and loss to everyone else. In a world of full employment and extreme mobility of productive resources, this would be largely true; but this is just another way of saying how far from true it was in the real world about which Veblen was writing. Since Veblen regarded practically all government economic policies as absurd and harmful, he was forced to assume that they must be linked up with the competitive struggle for prestige which, like its twin brother patriotism, is a carry-over from the feudal period. Thus in Veblen's treatment, many of the most important phenomena of modern social life have the character of an elaborate make-believe centering around the beliefs and customs of the feudal period and having nothing whatever to do with the real interests of living people.

The weaknesses of Veblen's economic analysis show through repeatedly in the book under review, but most clearly in the final chapter entitled "Peace and the Price System." This chapter may be taken as typical of most of Veblen's economic

writings: full of brilliant perceptions and insights but based on a theory which is always threatening to put him off the track and not infrequently leads up a blind alley.

For all the criticisms that can be made against it, however—and there are many that cannot be included in a brief review—it must nevertheless be said that *The Nature of Peace* is a great book which stands head and shoulders above the innumerable contributions to the subject which have flowed in a steady stream from the pens of respectable authorities during the period of the two world wars. That is because Veblen, unlike the respectable authorities, had a profound understanding of history and was able to see the present not as an epoch of anarchy and unreason but as a stage in a long-run process of social change.

Here we have the key, I think, to one of the most puzzling things about Veblen, namely, that the so-called "institutionalist" school which he inspired disintegrated rapidly and never produced anything of lasting value. He was a great man, and he attracted followers because of it. But he was greater than his own theories; and unfortunately greatness cannot be passed on, while theories can. (pp. 297-301)

> Paul M. Sweezy, "Thorstein Veblen: Strengths and Weaknesses," in his The Present as History: Essays and Reviews on Capitalism and Socialism, *Monthly Review Press, 1953, pp. 295-301.*

DANIEL AARON   (essay date 1951)

[*In the following excerpt, Aaron explores Veblen's major theories, maintaining that, while Veblen's posthumous renown is due to the relevance of his social and economic ideas, "his general and more enduring appeal lies in his power as a moralist, satirist, and rhetorician."*]

Irascible, dour, and sardonic, living precariously along the fringes of the American university world he anatomized so mercilessly, Veblen remained during his lifetime a kind of academic rogue, admired by an increasing number of discriminating disciples but never winning the kudos handed out to his less able but more circumspect colleagues (p. 212)

Almost from the beginning of his career, however, the virus of Veblen's thought infected a handful of scholars and writers, and during the ensuing years these ideas were introduced into ever widening circles. Events themselves seemed to justify his most heretical opinions and to confirm his seemingly far-fetched prognostications, and it was natural for men watching the fascinating convolutions of American business during the late 'twenties and early 'thirties to discover new insights in Veblen's caustic reflections.

Why has Veblen's influence been so pervasive and far-reaching? He was by no means the first American to find fault with business enterprise and its cultural ramifications; the criticism of money-makers and money-making is as old as the country. Radicals of every description assailed the activities of the entrepreneur with greater fury and eloquence. There is nothing in Veblen, for instance, to match the invective of Theodore Parker's tirade against the merchants, or Thoreau's cutting references to the slaves of property. Other investigators, such as Henry Demarest Lloyd, dealt more exhaustively with specific examples of capitalistic chicanery; socio-religious writers, muckrakers, and progressives exposed the gross inequalities of our society with greater passion.

Veblen's current popularity must be attributed in part to the relevance of his social and economic ideas (his views on war, religion, education, business, and manners are as pertinent today as when he first expressed them), but his general and more enduring appeal lies in his power as a moralist, satirist, and rhetorician. Critics of Veblen have pointed out, and with justification, that he was careless in acknowledging his intellectual debts and given too much to unsupported generalizations. Such accusations are becoming less and less important as Veblen's contemporaries fade into the past. It was Veblen's talent for making the usual unusual and illuminating the commonplace, his gift for stating thinly veiled value-judgments in a startling and provocative manner that make his writing perennially interesting. In spite of his academic trappings, his conspicuous erudition, and his ostensibly scientific predisposition, it is Veblen the moralist setting out quite deliberately to destroy national myths and unsettle time-honored conventions who will continue to delight and to exasperate future readers.

Veblen's writings must therefore not be judged simply as a critical appraisal of a particular economic system or as a detached and informative analysis of a culture. Had this been true, he might never have inspired his assiduous cult. Far from being an aloof and disembodied intelligence benignly contemplating the antics of earth-dwellers, he was, like most great satirists, a fierce hater who tried but failed to conceal his ethical preconceptions. "We are interested in what is, not what ought to be," he would tell his students, but the venom and anger frequently discernible in his works belied his feigned neutrality. America, in Veblen's eyes, was a land full of Yahoos, and the beneficiaries of our business civilization, the "kept classes," became for him the quintessence of all the human ineptness, stupidity, cruelty, self-delusion, and credulity that satirists have jeered at for centuries.

This critical spirit, this inability to adjust himself to the views of the workaday world have been attributed in part to his Norwegian family background and in part to his personal idiosyncrasies. Had he been a more normal person, more at ease in Zion, his enemies have charged, he would have been less disgruntled with what he saw. But the *ad hominem* argument which imputes Veblen's bitterness to his poverty and dismisses him as a crank whose "sense of inferiority caused him to withdraw within himself . . . and sneer at American life and American business" is beside the point. By the same kind of logic college professors would be less radical if their salaries were higher and Jews would never be communists if they were not snubbed at summer resorts. No matter what prompted Veblen to become a renegade, immune, as he described another kind of renegade, "from the inhibitions of intellectual quietism," it does not lessen the accuracy of his observations or blur the truths that his biased perspective enabled him to discern. All radicals, in one sense, are out of step with their times. The psycho-neurotic or racial factors that alienate a man from the majority will sometimes clarify his vision. Veblen's characterization of Marx as "a theoretician busied with the analysis of economic phenomena" while "at the same time, consistently and tenaciously alert to the bearing which each step in the process of this theoretical work has upon the propaganda," might just as well apply to himself.

By setting himself, as it were, upon another planet, Veblen saw an America that differed sharply from the picture in the eyes of the uncritical majority. It was deluded topsy-turvy America, illogical, irrational, vainglorious, superstitious. Veblen was realistic enough to see that this state of affairs could not be attributed solely to the machinations of an unscrupulous

elite, and he had no formula to bring about the Golden Day. The perpetuation of decrepit institutions, whose only function was to keep a parasite class in the ascendancy, simply illustrated man's reluctance to forsake outmoded ideas and adjust himself to new ones.

He made much of the ludicrous paradox of deluded men cheerfully acting against their own best interests, bolstered in their irrationality by the resurgence of old superstitions, clannishness, and national conceit. The common man, swayed by "imponderables" (by "imponderable" he meant "an article of make-believe which has become axiomatic by force of settled habit"), was forever befuddled by his "picturesque hallucinations." The retention of obsolescent beliefs in the workings of business enterprise, education, and politics, beliefs "so at variance with the continued life-interests of the community," tended to enhance Veblen's instinctive skepticism about the possibility of a future millennium. Sometimes, he admitted, the instincts of workmanship and efficiency were powerful enough to break through the dams of prescription and precedent and permit "the current of life and cultural growth" to flow again. But episodes of this kind were rare. In general, he concluded, "history records more frequent and more spectacular instances of the triumph of imbecile institutions over life and culture than of peoples who have by force of instinctive insight saved themselves alive out of a desperately precarious institutional situation, such, for instance, as now faces the peoples of Christendom."

But because Veblen's belief in the thickheadedness of the human race existed side by side with a generous awareness of man's potentialities, he could never maintain the godlike scorn that marks the true misanthrope. The possibilities of human progress were as evident to him as the failure thus far to achieve them. One might almost say that the intense bitterness with which he analyzed human error revealed an inner concern for his fellow men that all his icy disdain could not conceal.

His conception of human nature was essentially utopian and very similar to the notions of the other progressive reformers, despite the anthropological vocabulary with which he encased his sometimes unscientific assumptions. Even if he did not sentimentalize about an ideal state of nature, he expressly repudiated the naïve ideas about primitive society espoused by nineteenth-century ethnologists and denied the political and social conclusions of the Hobbists. If the selfishness and egotism everywhere present in pecuniary society rested on deep-seated human traits, so did the ideals of friendliness and brotherly love, the "Christian morals," as Veblen called them, which actually antedated the Christian era and were not vouchsafed to man through divine grace. "And in an obscure and dubious fashion," Veblen wrote of brotherly love, "perhaps sporadically, it recurs throughout the life of human society with such an air of ubiquity as would argue that it is an elemental trait of the species, rather than a cultural product of Christendom."

One can detect behind Veblen's scientific pose a view of man and society which links him with the middle-class reformers he patronizingly disregarded. Thus he could speak of institutions diverting the "genius of the race from its natural bent" and anticipate the time when human nature, no longer savagely repressed, would once more take on its mild and pacific character. The competitive way of life, of comparatively recent out-growth and coinciding with radical economic transformations, did not encourage Christian forbearance, mutual aid, or "the ties of group solidarity." In the competitive society all "social and civil relations" are formed "for pecuniary ends, and enforced by pecuniary standards." Yet, Veblen observed, even in a business-minded society, the "savage spiritual heritage" of brotherly love could not be extinguished: "this principle is forever reasserting itself in economic matters, in the impulsive approval of whatever conduct is serviceable to the common good and in the disapproval of disserviceable conduct even within the limits of legality and natural right." In the fight between business as "an impersonal, dispassionate, not to say graceless, investment for profit" and "the impulsive bias of brotherly love," he believed that ultimate victory lay with the latter.

The ideas of Veblen, then, despite their outmoded and mechanistic features, were not merely destructive and negative. He was no reformer with a systematic program, to be sure, but he at least held forth the prospect of a rational and orderly economic life once mankind had freed itself from "prehensile ideas." Less evangelical than most American nineteenth-century reformers, more dubious about the inevitability of a foreordained progress, he kept his eyes fixed on the world around him and on the problems of the men who inhabited it.

There was something comforting in Veblen's serene naturalism, even though it explains some of his shortcomings. He too was aware of the failure of nerve that followed in the wake of the First World War, the "maggoty conceits" of the supernaturalists, and he scornfully assailed the "same fearsome credulity . . . running free and large through secular affairs as well." He offered no positive remedy, only suggestions. He remained honestly skeptical. But if he did not encourage his readers to dream visions, at least he rid their minds of cant. (pp. 212-16)

Veblen . . . was not only an astute diagnostician of economic institutions; he was also a kind of splenetic prophet. Like Marx, he attracted disciples by his startling insights and remorseless logic, but his appeal was not limited to the reason. He quite consciously overemphasized and oversimplified. He was fond of dramatic dichotomies, or what the semanticists call the two-valued orientation. He juxtaposed "business" and "industry," the entrepreneur and the engineer, the instinct of predation and the instinct of workmanship, the absentee owner and the "underlying population." These distinctions, more ethical perhaps than scientific, carry an emotive appeal and imply unstated preconceptions. They offer further proof that Veblen was quite capable of deliberate distortion and bias despite his pose of Olympian detachment.

What Veblen did was to destroy holy shibboleths by means of a language ordinarily identified with ritualistic or pedantic expression; he was, in other words, reverently irreverent. His technique, useful as a kind of protective coloration to misdirect potential enemies, suggested the outrageous solemnity of Swift's *A Modest Proposal* and the weightiness and aloofness of Gibbon's chronicle of Rome.

In his best writing he demonstrated both his bias and his artistry and turned ideas made blunt by excessive handling into sharp-cutting instruments. For style is more than embellishment and contributes immeasurably to the total impression; shreds of additional meaning cling to the apt metaphor, and the bald informative statement is not necessarily the most accurate. Veblen announced his message (men are potentially decent damned fools who honor their oppressors and habitually act against their own best interests) in a series of amusing paradoxes. His strong personal feelings he conveyed through the use of a loaded diction.

Most critics when they praise Veblen's style are thinking primarily of his talent as a phrasemaker. Such unusual but now familiar collocations as "conspicuous consumption," "trained incapacity," "business sabotage," "sagacious restriction of output," "collusive sobriety," and "blameless cupidity," have become the well-known hallmarks of Veblenese. This device of balancing opposites, the arbitrary linking of words with respectable and dishonorable connotations, is a literary expedient not usually employed by scientific writers. It resembles the oxymoron, or the conceit used by the metaphysical poets in the seventeenth century to achieve a new and shocking perspective. Veblen's readers, trained to the automatic response, were sometimes puzzled by the seeming incongruity of his phrases. Does not "business" suggest efficiency, honesty, respectability, practical results? Is not "sabotage" associated with anarchy, waste, treachery? In joining the meritorious with the blameworthy, Veblen was of course making a value judgment and imprisoning a whole philosophy in a single phrase.

By using language in this way, he reduced the prestige of business, contemplating it, as it were, through the wrong end of a telescope. The words *petty, nugatory, conciliatory, reliable, cupidity,* when applied to businessmen, are less pejorative and picturesque than *pirate* or *robber baron* or *Titan* or *tycoon,* but they strip away the romance and glamour that so frequently has mitigated dishonesty on a grand scale. The businessman, Veblen is saying, is not an audacious and genial freebooter, a gambler, an unscrupulous but God-struck empire builder. He has none of the larger wisdom. He is small, mean, circumspect, and useless—a creature formed by the price system and victimized by the values of his own pecuniary culture.

As a more specific illustration of Veblen's artifice, consider the sentence with which Veblen winds up his discussion of the similarity between religious and business institutions. The very fact that he identifies the Church with Big Business is significant, if not original, but the sentence itself deserves closer analysis:

> All told—if it were possible—it will be evident that the aggregate of human talent currently consumed in this fabrication of vendible imponderables in the nth dimension, will foot up to a truly massive total, even after making a reasonable allowance, of, say, some thirty-three and one-third per cent., for average mental deficiency in the personnel which devotes itself to this manner of livelihood.

Here the language of economics, morally toneless, is applied to a subject that is not ordinarily associated with the market places. The conceit ("fabrication of vendible imponderables") not only puns on the word "fabrication" but relates in a particularly insulting manner the tricks of salesmanship with spiritual salvation. Veblen, in an earlier passage, had been admiring the "perseverance, tact, and effrontery" of the propaganda of the faith, that "magnificent" institution whose "enterprise in sales publicity" makes "the many secular adventures in salesmanship" seem raw and crude by comparison. Now, in the sentence quoted above, he joins the most material and the most spiritual of institutions, identifying them both with mumbo jumbo and deceit. Business and the Church, exploiting the credulity of the "underlying population," take on the "same air of stately benevolence and menacing solemnity." Disarming, insolent, or official—always ostensibly neutral—Veblen can slant his judgments without explicitly committing himself.

Much may be said in jest that would be intolerable if uttered with perfect seriousness, and Veblen is apt to adopt the character of the playful satirist when he is being the most subversive. His humor is very largely the humor of incongruity, the grotesque or willful rearrangement of conventional word patterns into droll and unusual combinations: business schools specialize in ''widening the candidates' field of ignorance''; academic opportunists succeed by virtue of a ''ready versatility of convictions and a staunch loyalty to their bread.'' But Veblen also likes to embellish his writing with witty epigrammatic touches. Illegitimate births ''may be rated as an undesigned triumph of the hormones over the proprieties.'' The ''watchful waiting'' policy of the cautious entrepreneur is likened to ''a toad who has reached years of discretion and has found his appointed place along some frequented run where many flies and spiders pass and repass on their way to complete that destiny which it has pleased an all-seeing and merciful Providence to call them.'' The captain of industry, he continues, is motivated by the same ''safe and sane strategy'' of ''sound business principles'' that governs the toad. ''There is a certain bland sufficiency spread across the face of such a toad so circumstanced, while his comely bulk gives assurance of pyramidal stability of principles.''

Veblen's dead-pan manner, according to some critics, places him in the same tradition as the frozen-faced humorists of the frontier and the ''cracker barrel'' school, but this resemblance is only superficial. As a general rule American humorous writers (the more consciously ''literary'' and popular ones, at any rate) have ridiculed the aberrations from the norm and indirectly supported national prejudices. Primarily they are the amiable guardians of the middle classes. Veblen made use of the stock American trick of being seriously unserious, but instead of jesting at the deviations from conventional behavior, he flouted the unquestioned beliefs of bourgeois folkways.

He is, in fact, much closer to Thoreau than, let us say, to Artemus Ward. Both Thoreau and Veblen, diametrically opposed in so many ways, announced ideas outrageous to their contemporaries; both, to borrow Emerson's description of Thoreau, resembled ''some philosophical woodchuck or magnanimous fox''; both, if we are to believe the accounts of their friends, were reserved and antisocial; both, in their principal works, revealed the craziness of everyday life and exposed the conspiracy of institutions; and both—the one directly and the other by implication—advocated the drastic simplification of living and the stripping away of unessentials. All of these attitudes and characteristics were incorporated in the sardonic jokes they made at the expense of moldy cultural hangovers and established patterns of conduct. Unlike the majority of American humorists, folksy and homely, Thoreau and Veblen were the queer ones who stood beyond the pale and made fun of the solid citizens.

When a man feels strongly about the bad state of the world and wants to put his feelings into words, he can convey his disapproval and his suggestions for amendment in an infinite number of ways. He can spoof and debunk. He can expatiate warmly and tolerantly. He can fume, tabulate, preach, lament. The vehicle he chooses for self-expression will depend partly upon his personal make-up and partly, perhaps, on the degree of concern he feels for the situation he wants to remedy.

Thoreau, hostile to the values of his generation and holding fast to what his contemporaries (had they read him) would have regarded as an incomprehensible position, spoke with measured force and insolent assurance. Obligated to no one and unintim-

idated by a public opinion he habitually disregarded, he affronted his world with impunity; requiring no elaborate subterfuges, he subverted society in broad daylight.

Veblen could not afford to make the frontal assault. As the angry recluse and mocking Prometheus, he required a style and vocabulary that would muffle his rage and allow him to stalk his victims without their being conscious of his intentions. His milieu was the university, ostensibly dedicated to the quest for truth but guided in actuality by a ''meretricious subservience'' to the Philistines. Veblen may be said to have betrayed the betrayers by thinking unholy thoughts on holy ground and by using the ritualistic paraphernalia of scholarship—ordinarily employed in buttressing the social order and impressing the gullible—for profoundly subversive purposes. Had he been a cynic or debunker, content to shock and to smash images, he could have been dismissed as a troublesome smart-aleck. But Veblen was too much of a moralist and a conspirator. He diverted his readers while he systematically undermined their social order. He attacked the institutions and culture of capitalism while at the same time laying the foundations for a more humane and natural way of life. (pp. 238-42)

> *Daniel Aaron, ''Thorstein Veblen: Moralist and Rhetorician,'' in his* Men of Good Hope: A Story of American Progressives, *1951. Reprint by Oxford University Press, 1961, pp. 208-42.*

C. WRIGHT MILLS   (essay date 1953)

[*Mills is an American sociologist whose best-known work is* White Collar, *an analysis of American middle-class mores. In the following excerpt from his introduction to a reprint of* The Theory of the Leisure Class, *Mills discusses various aspects of Veblen's writings.*]

Thorstein Veblen is the best critic of America that America has produced. His language is part of the vocabulary of every literate American; his works are the most conspicuous contribution of any American to American studies; his style, which makes him the only comic writer among modern social scientists, is an established style of the society he dissected. Even the leisure class, which has now been reading Veblen for more than a generation, talks a little like him.

Veblen would have appreciated the fate his work has suffered. An unfashionable mind, he nevertheless established a fashion of thinking; a heretic, his points of view have been received into the canon of American social thought. Indeed, his perspectives are so fully accepted that one is tempted to say there is no other standard of criticism than the canon which Veblen himself established. All of which seems to prove that it is difficult to remain the critic of a society that is entertained by blame as well as praise.

Veblen is still read, not only because his criticism is still plausible, but because his style makes it so, even when the criticism is not taken seriously. Style is not exactly a strong point of American social science; in fact, most sociologists avoid style, even as some historians cultivate it. And, in this respect, Veblen is more historian than ''social scientist.'' At any rate, it is his style that has kept this rather obscure and unsuccessful sociologist of the ''Progressive Era''—he died in 1929—alive, after the immediate scene he anatomized has become history.

George Bernard Shaw, in his Preface to *Man and Superman*, remarks that ''. . . he who has something to assert will go as far in power of style as its momentousness and his conviction will carry him. Disprove his assertion after it is made, yet his style remains. Darwin no more destroyed the style of Job or Handel than Martin Luther destroyed the style of Giotto. All the assertions get disproved sooner or later; and so we find the world full of a magnificent debris of artistic fossils, with the matter-of-fact credibility gone clean out of them, but the form still splendid."

That is true of Veblen—although in his case we cannot say that all "the matter-of-fact credibility" in his works has "gone clean out of them."

In a grim world, Veblen's style is so hilarious that one would wish to see it left intact as a going force for sanity. One may not always be sure of his meaning today, but his animus remains unmistakable and salutary. Whether or not his style in this, his first book, is his best, Veblen's books as a whole do constitute a work of art, as well as a full-scale commentary on American life.

As works of art, Veblen's books do what all art properly should do: they smash through the stereotyped world of our routine perception and feeling and impulse; they alert us to see and to feel and to move toward new images, many of them playful and bright and shrewd.

Veblen creates a coherent world in which each part is soon understandable and which is peopled by fascinating types of men and women who are soon though newly recognizable. We might learn from him that the object of all social study is to understand the types of men and women that are selected and shaped by a given society—and to judge them by explicit standards. Much of Veblen's comedy comes simply from his making his fresh standards explicit.

The form of Veblen's books and their content are one. It is as much the exact way he says things as what he says that one appreciates in his work. His phrases stick in the mind, and his insights, if acquired early, often make a difference in the quality of one's life. No, his thought could not properly be expressed in any other form than the form which he gave it. And that is why, like all works of art, you must "read" his work for yourself.

Thorstein Veblen realized that the world he lived in was dominated by what one might call "crackpot realism." This was, and one must use the word, Veblen's metaphysic—his bone-deep view of the nature of everyday American reality. He believed that the very Men of Affairs whom everyone supposed to embody sober, hard-headed practicality were in fact utopian capitalists and monomaniacs; that the Men of Decision who led soldiers in war and who organized civilians' daily livelihoods in peace were in fact crackpots of the highest pecuniary order. They had "sold" a believing world on themselves; and they had—hence the irony—to play the chief fanatics in their delusional world.

No mere joke, however, but a basic element of his perspective caused Veblen to write in 1922 what might with equal truth be written today: "The current situation in America is by way of being something of a psychiatrical clinic. In order to come to an understanding of this situation there is doubtless much else to be taken into account, but the case of America is after all not fairly to be understood without making due allowance for a certain prevalent unbalance and derangement of mentality, presumably transient but sufficiently grave for the time being. Perhaps the commonest and plainest evidence of this unbalanced mentality is to be seen in a certain fearsome and feverish credulity with which a large proportion of the Americans are affected."

The realization of this false consciousness all around him, along with the sturdiness of mind and character to stand up against it, is the clue to Veblen's world outlook. How different his was from the prevailing view is suggested by his utter inability to be "the salesman." (pp. vi-viii)

Two schools of sociological study have flourished in America since Veblen's time. One of them makes a fetish of "Method," the other of "Theory." Both, accordingly, lose sight of their proper study.

The Higher Statisticians break down truth and falsity into such fine particles that we cannot tell the difference between them; by the costly rigor of their methods, they succeed in trivializing man and society, and in the process their own minds as well.

The Grand Theorists, on the other hand, represent a partially organized attempt to withdraw from the effort plainly to describe, explain, and understand human conduct and society: they verbalize in turgid prose the disordered contents of their reading of eminent nineteenth-century sociologists, and in the process mistake their own beginnings for a finished result.

In the practice of both these leading schools, contemporary Social Science becomes simply an elaborate method of insuring that no one learns too much about man and society, the first by formal but empty ingenuity; the second, by formal but cloudy obscurantism.

The work of Thorstein Veblen stands out as a live protest against these dominant tendencies of the higher ignorance. He always knew the difference between the trivial and the important, and he was wary of the academic traps of busywork and pretension. While he was a man at thought, he kept the bright eye of his mind upon the object he was examining. Veblen was quite unable to be a specialist. He tried philosophy and he was trained as an economist, but he was also a sociologist and a psychologist. While specialists constructed a world to suit only themselves, Veblen was a professional anti-specialist. He was, in short, a social thinker in the grand tradition, for he tried to do what Hegel and Comte and Marx and Spencer and Weber—each in his own way—had tried to do:

> To grasp the essentials of an entire society and epoch,
> To delineate the characters of the typical men within it,
> To determine its main drift.

The results of Veblen's attempt to do these things exist in some ten books. His first attempt, published in 1899, is [*The Theory of the Leisure Class*]. . . . Five years later he published *The Theory of Business Enterprise,* and then, in 1914, *The Instinct of Workmanship.* When World War I occurred, naturally Veblen turned to it, publishing *Imperial Germany* in 1915, and *The Nature of Peace* in 1917. After that, published a few years apart, he produced *The Higher Learning* and *The Vested Interests;* his more technical essays were collected in *The Place of Science in Modern Civilization.* He wrote *The Engineers and The Price System,* published as a book in 1921, and *Absentee Ownership*—which many consider his best single volume—in 1923. After his death, *Essays in Our Changing Order* was published. These constitute the heritage Veblen left for the use of the human community. There is no better set of books written by a single individual about American society. There is no better inheritance available to those who can still choose their own ancestors.

Since the intelligentsia, just now, are in a conservative mood, no doubt during the nineteen-fifties Veblen, when he is not ignored, will be re-interpreted as a conservative. And, from one rather formal viewpoint, Veblen was a profoundly conservative critic of America: he wholeheartedly accepted one of the few un-ambiguous, all-American values: the value of efficiency, of utility, of pragmatic simplicity. His criticism of institutions and the personnel of American society was based without exception upon his belief that they did not adequately fulfill this American value. If he was, as I believe, a Socratic figure, he was in his own way as American as Socrates in his was Athenian.

As a critic, Veblen was effective precisely because he used the American value of efficiency to criticize American reality. He merely took this value seriously and used it with devastatingly systematic rigor. It was a strange perspective for an American critic in the nineteenth century as it would be in our own. One looked down from Mont St. Michel, like Henry Adams, or across from England, like Henry James. With Veblen perhaps the whole character of American social criticism shifted. The figure of the last-generation American faded and the figure of the first-generation American—the Norwegian immigrant's son, the New York Jew teaching English literature in a midwestern university, the southerner come north to crash New York—was installed as the genuine, if no longer 100 per cent American, critic.

If Veblen accepted utility as a master value, he rejected another all-American value: the heraldry of the greenback, the world of the fast buck. And since, in that strange institution, the modern corporation, the efficiency of the plain engineer and the pecuniary fanaticism of the business chieftain—are intricately confused, Veblen devoted his life's work to clarifying the difference between these two types and between their social consequences.

The America Veblen saw seemed split in two. Running through everything Veblen wrote was the distinction between those activities and moods that are productive and useful and those that are ostentatious and honorific, workmanlike as against businesslike, industrial and amiable in contrast to pecuniary and predatory.

In the course of history, his account ran, material labor had become unworthy; predatory exploit had become the very essence of high dignity. Labor, Veblen believed, became irksome because of the indignity imputed to it; it had not become undignified because it was irksome. By "leisure" Veblen really meant everything that is not of the world of everyday, productive work and of the workmanlike habit of mind.

The key event in the modern history of the leisure class was its involvement with private ownership. Originally, Veblen tells us, predatory warlords seized property—especially the women—of an enemy, and hence their ownership of the booty revealed their prowess. This was of course honorific, because it was an assertion of superior force. In due course, the struggle for existence became a competition for pecuniary emulation: to own property was to possess honor; it was to set up an invidious distinction, a better-than-thou feeling on the part of absentee owners: those who own more than they could personally use, against those who did not own enough for their livelihood.

Popular esteem thus came to be based upon property, and accordingly became the basis for "that complacency which we call self-respect." For men judged themselves favorably or unfavorably in comparison to others of their general class in point of pecuniary strength, and this led to an insatiable, restless straining for invidious distinction.

But would not such a pecuniary struggle lead men to industrious and frugal lives? Perhaps for the lower classes, but not for the higher. Being useless in the struggle for status that had succeeded the struggle for existence, productive work was held to be unworthy. The better classes abstained from it while at the same time they emulated one another. It was not enough to possess wealth in order to win esteem; one had to put it into evidence; one had to impress one's importance upon others. Conspicuous leisure, according to Veblen, did just that—it put one's wealth and power on social display. That was the value of leisure for this pecuniary society. When one's group was compact and all its members intimately known, either leisure or consumption served to demonstrate one's wealth. But when one moved among wider circles of urban strangers, it became necessary to advertise one's wealth. Conspicuous consumption was then needed as a means of ordinary decency. With what was obviously expensive and wasteful one could impress all transient and anonymous observers.

So mere idleness was not enough: it had to be the idleness of expensive discomfort, of noble vice, and costly entertainment. It had, in short, to be conspicuous consumption: the obvious waste of valuable goods as a means of gaining reputability.

Opposed to all this, there stand in Veblen's world the industrial interests of the modern community, and the honest, prosaic man who would serve these industrial interests. But such peaceable men, having a "non-emulative, non-invidious interest in men and things" lack what passes for initiative and ingenuity, and end up as amiable good-for-nothing fellows. For what is good for the community is, of course, in a regime of crackpot realism, "disserviceable to the individual."

By his master split, with businessmen on the pecuniary side, Veblen linked the theory of the leisure class with the theory of business enterprise. For ownership and acquisition belonged to the pecuniary range of employments, to the moneyed life. And the "captain of industry" was misnamed, for his was a pecuniary rather than an industrial captaincy.

"All this is incredible," Veblen suddenly remarks in the middle of one of his books, "but it is everyday fact." Veblen has made Alices of us all, and dropped us through the looking glass into the fantastic world of social reality.

What Veblen said remains strong with the truth, even though his facts do not cover the scenes and the characters that have emerged in our own time. He remains strong with the truth because we could not see the newer features of our own time had he not written what and as he did. Which is one meaning of the fact that his biases are the most fruitful that have appeared in the literature of American social protest. But all critics are mortal, and some parts of Veblen can no longer live for us. In the criticisms of Veblen which follow, I shall examine only his theory of the leisure class.

Veblen's theory is not "The Theory of the Leisure Class." It is *a* theory of a particular element of the upper classes in one period of the history of one nation. It is a criticism of the *nouveau riche*, so much in evidence in Veblen's formative time, the America of the latter half of the nineteenth century, of the Vanderbilts, Goulds, and Harrimans, of Saratoga Springs and Newport, of the glitter and the gold.

Moreover, what he wrote about was mainly Local Society and its Last Resorts, and especially the women of these worlds. He could not of course have been expected in the eighteen-nineties to see the meaning for the *national* status system of the professional celebrities, who have risen as part of the national media of mass communication and entertainment, nor the major change in national glamour, in which the debutante is replaced by the movie star, and the local society lady by the military and political and economic managers—the power elite—whom crackpot realists now celebrate as their proper chieftains.

The spleen of Veblen is due to the assumption, in his own words, that "the accumulation of wealth at the upper end of the pecuniary scale implies privation at the lower end of the scale." He tended always to assume that the pie was of a certain size, and that the wealthy class withdraws from the lower classes "as much as it may of the means of sustenance, and so reducing their consumption, and consequently their available energy, to such a point as to make them incapable of the effort required for the learning and adoption of new habits of thought." Again, the moral edge of the phrase, "conspicuous consumption" lies in the fact that it tends "to leave but a scanty subsistence minimum . . . to absorb any surplus energy which may be available after the pure physical necessities of life . . ." All this, strangely enough, was a sort of survival in Veblen's thought of classic economic conceptions of scarcity, and betrays a lack of confidence in technological abundance which we cannot now accept in the simple terms in which Veblen left it.

Veblen, thinking of the immigrant masses of his time and of the enormously unequal distribution of income and wealth, did not leave enough scope for the economic pie to expand—and what has happened, especially since the second World War, has meant that the majority of the U.S. population can consume conspicuously. In fact, in the absence of "lower classes on a scanty subsistence," the term "conspicuous consumption" becomes a somewhat flat description of higher standards of living because the invidious element is lacking. Of course the æsthetics of Veblen's case remain applicable.

In depicting the higher style of life, Veblen seemed to confuse aristocratic and bourgeois traits. Perhaps this is a limitation of his American viewpoint. He did this explicitly at one or two points: "The aristocratic and the bourgeois virtues—that is to say the destructive and pecuniary traits—should be found chiefly among the upper classes . . ." One has only to examine the taste of the small shopkeeper to know that this is certainly not true.

Conspicuous consumption, as Veblen knew, is not confined to the upper classes. But today I should say that it prevails *especially* among one element of the new upper classes—the *nouveau riche* of the new corporate privileges—the men and women on the expense accounts, and those enjoying other corporate prerogatives—and with even more grievous effects on the standard and style of life of the higher middle and middle classes generally. And of course among recent crops of "Texas millionaires."

The supposed shamefulness of labor, on which many of Veblen's conceptions rest, does not square very well with the Puritan work ethic so characteristic of much of American life, including many upper class elements. I suppose, in the book at hand, Veblen is speaking only of upper, not middle classes—certainly he is not writing of wealthy Puritan middle classes. He did not want to call what the businessman does "work,"

much less productive work. The very term, leisure class, became for him synonymous with upper class; but, of course, there is and there has been a *working* upper class—in fact, a class of prodigiously active people. That Veblen did not approve of their work, and in fact refused to give it that term—work being one of his positive words—is irrelevant. Moreover, in this case it obscures and distorts our understanding of the upper classes as a social formation. Yet for Veblen fully to have admitted this simple fact would have destroyed (or forced the much greater sophistication of) his whole perspective and indeed one of the chief moral bases of his criticism.

Veblen was interested in psychological gratification; he tended to ignore the social function of much of what he described. He would not, in fact, have liked the term "function" to be used in this way, because, given his values, the solid word "function" is precisely the sort he would have reserved for workmanlike men and forces. Consider merely as illustrations three close to hand:

Many of the social scenes with which Veblen had so much fun were, in fact, meeting places for various elite of decision, for prestige behavior mediates between various hierarchies and regions. Hence prestige is not merely social nonsense that gratifies the individual ego: it serves a unifying function; leisure activities are one way of securing a coordination of decision between various sections and elements of the upper class.

Such status activities also coordinate high families; they provide a marriage market, the functions of which go well beyond the gratifications of displayed elegance, of brown orchids and white satin: they serve to keep a propertied class intact and unscattered; by monopoly of sons and daughters, anchoring the class in the legalities of blood lines.

And "snobbish" exclusiveness, of course, secures privacy to those who can afford it. To exclude others enables the high-and-mighty to set up and to maintain a series of private worlds in which they can and do discuss issues and decisions and in which they train their young informally for the decision-making temper. In this way they blend impersonal decision-making with informal sensitivities, and so shape the character structure of an elite.

There is another function—today the most important—of prestige and of status conduct. Prestige buttresses power, turning it into authority, and protecting it from social challenge.

"Power for power's sake" is psychologically based on prestige gratification. But Veblen laughed so hard and so consistently at the servants and the dogs and the women and the sports of the elite that he failed to see that their military, economic, and political activity is not at all funny. In short he did not succeed in relating their power over armies and factories to what he believed, quite rightly, to be their funny business. He was, I think, not quite serious enough about prestige because he did not see its full and intricate importance to power. He saw "the kept classes" and "the underlying population," but he did not really see the power elite.

Perhaps Veblen did not pay appropriate attention to the relevance of status to power because of his theory of history. The members of his "leisure class" are no history-makers; in fact, they have no real function in history. For in modern societies, Veblen held, industrial forces are the motors of history, and the leisure class is a survival and a lag, an anachronism or a parasitical growth. In fact, Veblen explicitly believed that "they are not in the full sense an organic part of the industrial community.'' For in that matter-of-fact community, it is the innovator who counts, and in the leisure class the innovator is vulgar, and innovation, to say the least, bad form.

Technological innovators are the history makers, and next to them, according to Veblen, those who are forced to change their ways in order to meet new technical conditions. Today, we cannot go along with what seems to us this over-simple view of the relations of technology to the institutions and the men who adapt and guide its developments and uses. This is one of the several Marxist overtones in Veblen, the assumption that those who are functionally indispensable to the community are the men who count and that those who are parasites are doomed. In our time, of course, we have seen too many technically parasitic men gain power and hold it with authority to believe in this rational, optimistic theory of history.

Veblen had an inadequate view of the effect of industrial efficiency upon the rationality of the men close to the machine process. He failed to recognize the terrible ambiguity of rationality in modern man and his society. He assumed that the skilled workmen and the engineers and the technicians would increasingly come to embody mater-of-fact rationality—as individuals and as strata. It was, in fact, upon these strata that he rested as he lectured about the "leisure class." And this, again, is a result of his over-simple split between the honorific and the workmanlike.

Veblen failed to appreciate that the increasing rationality of the efficiency-machines does not at all mean that the individuals who are linked together to run these machines are personally more rational or intelligent—even inside the fabulous engine room itself, and certainly not inside the mass society of which it is a part. In fact, the judgment of "the technicians" and their capacity for general intelligence, especially in social and political affairs, often seems quite paralyzed and is no better than that of the pecuniary fanatics. The rational apparatus itself has expropriated the rationality of the individual to the point where we must often assume that those in charge of the big institutions are normally quite stupid. Moreover, the few key individuals who are able rationally to understand the structure of the whole are no more likely to be engineers than workingmen.

What Veblen called industrial efficiency, "the opaque run of cause and effect," does not necessarily increase the substantive rationality of independent judgment. Nor does close contact with the big machine increase in men any of those amiable, sane traits that Veblen stuffed into his "instinct of workmanship." For in truth, Veblen's "workmanship" is an ideal set forth by a man afraid to set forth ideals, and it is more socially at home in some simple artisan society than in the modern social disorder we are trying to live in and understand.

Just what does all the pretentious monkey business about status, which Veblen analyzed so well, have to do with the operations of the political economy? I have intimated that the local society of the very rich—about which Veblen wrote—turned out to be too economically unstable and too politically weak to become an enduring center for a national system of prestige. The professional celebrities of the mass media are without power of any stable sort and are in fact ephemeral figures among those we celebrate.

And yet there is an upper-class demand for some sort of organization of enduring and stable prestige, which Veblen's analysis somehow misses. It is a "need" quite consciously

and quite deeply felt by the elite of wealth and especially the elite of power in the United States today.

During the nineteenth century neither the political nor the military elite were able to establish themselves firmly at the head or even near the head of a national system of prestige. John Adams's suggestion—in his *Discourses on Davila*—which leaned in that direction, was not taken up. Other forces and not any official system of distinctions and honors have given such order as it has had to the polity. The American economic elite—and for this very reason it is uniquely significant—rose to economic power in such a way as to upset repeated attempts to found national status on enduring family lines.

But in the last thirty years, with the managerial reorganization of the propertied class, and the political roles assumed by the managerial elite, there have been signs of a merger of economic, political, and military elite in a new corporate-like class. Together, an as elite of power, will they not seek, as all-powerful men everywhere have always sought, to buttress their power with the mantle of authoritative status? Will they not consolidate the new status privileges, popularized in terms of the expense account but rooted deeply in their corporate class? And in view of their position in the cultural world of nations—as they come more fully to realize it, will they be content with the clowns and the queens—the professional celebrities—as the world representatives of their American nation?

In due course, will not those we celebrate come to coincide more closely with those who are the most powerful among us? In due course, will not snobbery become official, and all of us startled into our appropriate grade and rank? To believe otherwise, it seems to me, is to reject all that is available and relevant in our understanding of world history.

We must remember that we could not entertain, at least not so easily, such criticisms and speculations had Veblen not written. And that is his real and lasting value: he opens up our minds, he gets us "outside the whale," he makes us see through the official sham. Above all, he teaches us to be aware of the crackpot basis of the realism of those practical Men of Affairs who would lead us to honorific destruction. (pp. x-xix)

> *C. Wright Mills, in an introduction to* The Theory of the Leisure Class: An Economic Study of Institutions *by Thorstein Veblen, 1953. Reprint by New American Library, 1959, pp. vi-xix.*

BERNARD ROSENBERG (essay date 1956)

[*In the following excerpt, Rosenberg contrasts Veblen's social philosophy with Marxism.*]

"I say," declared Matthew Arnold, "the critic must keep out of the region of immediate practice in the political, social, humanitarian sphere if he wants to make a beginning for that more free speculative treatment of things, which may perhaps one day make its benefits felt even in this sphere, but in a natural and thence irresistible manner."

Veblen, who did not always take this cautious Victorian advice, made a few editorial forays into the "real" world toward the end of his career. He was impressed with the urgency of improving social and economic conditions and as a contributor to *The Dial* magazine he tried to assume unbecoming pedestrian tones. But Veblen was not a propagandist or a demagogue and his efforts to reach the common man whom he sometimes exalted were futile. Of the two books which have been compiled from this period, one is by far the weightier.

The Vested Interests and the Common Man is a forceful but unfortunately repetitious, garrulous, and bitter restatement of Veblenism. Its analogies are overdrawn: business is simply reduced to blackmail or ransom, but the worker is represented as an exemplar of honesty and industry. Here the schism between Veblen and Marx narrows, as it was to widen again and for good in ***The Engineers and the Price System***.

At the outset of this book Veblen reiterates his conviction that sabotage is the prime strategy of business management. By sabotage he means surreptitious and/or peaceable restriction, delay, withdrawal, and obstruction. The strike is one form of sabotage; the lockout is another—and although the one is denounced by Substantial Citizens, the other is ordinarily judged a legitimate maneuver. If capitalists were other than saboteurs most of the time, they could not survive. The present industrial system can hardly be allowed to work at full capacity for any appreciable length of time. If it did there would be business stagnation.

In 1919 Veblen is able to write, not without justice, that "The common man has won the war and lost his livelihood." There was in that year an acute state of distress, "an altogether unwholesome pitch of privation for want of the necessary food, clothing, and shelter." Yet it is perfectly clear to Veblen that while so many people are being deprived of the bare necessities man's ability to produce goods and satisfy his wants has been immeasurably enhanced. Nearly forty years later, with potential productivity at an unprecedented peak, another post-war generation is in still worse straits. Western democracy and Russian Bolshevism have won a great victory, and three years after the Second World War more masses are starving than before it was waged. Little has been done to palliate this crisis and a great deal has been done to perpetuate it.

It is a matter of common knowledge that after every modern war a grave emergency sets in, but this seems exceptional to Veblen and the Veblenians only in its magnitude and severity. The same kind of thing goes on as a matter of course in what are euphemistically labeled normal times. This fact is illustrated by protective tariffs which are hateful to Veblen from first to last because their effects are to keep the supply of goods down and thereby to keep prices up.

Veblen reasons that there will never cease to be deprivation of the many who serve the few so long as plenary discretion in industrial matters remains with those least able to understand it. It is still so in America that the financier, who is seldom more than a routine administrator, has final authority. He is supposed to direct a technology that has grown into the most diversified, specialized, extensive, and difficult process yet created by man. The cash nexus is evidently not a strong enough link to bind his concerns with the ones he is called upon to guide.

Now the engineer, according to Veblen, is as knowledgeable as the businessman is ignorant. The organization of mechanical power and material demands what it does not get: systematic control under the direction of skilled technologists. It is the heart of Veblen's destructive argument . . . that business is a parasitic supernummerary, and that those individuals who fall into the merely commercial class have outlived their historical welcome. So far as there is no great incompatibility with Marxism. But Veblen does not at all favor the establishment of a classless society, whether or not it is ushered in by the dictatorship of the proletariat. (pp. 111-12)

The first tenet of Marxism is a Hegelian dialectic through which the resolution of opposites is reached in a continuous spiral leading to the empyrean. Capitalism must lose out in the struggle with beneficent socialism. The wicked institutions will be replaced by good ones. Behind this magnificent change are the material forces of production, the state of the industrial arts. It is this frame of reference that must be remembered when we reflect upon what Veblen does in his study of American education.

The United States is in an advanced state of technological development. If there were but one irreducible cause that shaped the social situation, our universities would be much better than those of Europe and they would inevitably improve. However Veblen thinks the movement is toward complete abandonment of reason in American education. He hopes that some palliative will help and faint-heartedly proposes the establishment of shelters where scholars might carry on their inquiry in academic quarantine. Veblen does not believe that such shelters will be found, for "a seminary of higher learning, as distinct from an assemblage of vocational schools, is not a practicable proposition in America under current conditions." And current conditions stand every chance of prevailing or deteriorating for an incalculable period of time.

It is inconceivable that Marxists should be so thoroughly disheartened about anything as Veblen came to be about almost everything. In ***The Higher Learning*** this difference is fully apparent and may in part account for its neglect. In other books Veblen will equivocate and vacillate. In this book he does neither and is therefore able to see the social complex as one in which simultaneity may be granted to a rationalism which is minimal and an irrationalism which is maximal. In other words, the maturation of Veblen's thought leads him to note two forces of unequal magnitude whose coetaneous presence acts first in the promotion of reason and then in its derangement. As for bureaucratized institutions of learning, they will not be freed—they will be further bureaucratized.

Bureaucratism is the main datum with which Veblen works, when he notes its presence in American universities, when he refers to trained incapacity as a trait of business administrators, and when he forsees cultural configurations to come. The bureaucratization of society was a side issue to Marx; it is a central and decisive one to Weber and Veblen. But because Marx hovers over us as a specter, we are too much inclined to accept his formulations.

Even conservatives believe that what lies before the world is a choice between Marxist socialism and free enterprise capitalism. Veblen is the first important social scientist to deny this choice and to detect the emergence of a new class whose dominance is *de facto* already and may soon become *de jure* as well. James Burnham has pushed Veblen's analysis to its political extreme: the societal form now universalizing itself is neither socialism nor capitalism but bureaucratic collectivism. Everywhere capitalism is dead except in its last great fortress (the U.S.A.) where it appears to be dying. It would be pointless to argue about this. However, critical differences arise over what will, and over what should, take place in the future.

Both normatively and descriptively Veblen's stand diverges from that of Karl Marx. Like Weber, he neither especially wants nor in any sense predicts a classless society—and his negative vision is being borne out all over the world. Society has not ceased to be stratified (least of all where lip-service is paid to Marxism); it is merely stratified in a new way. This is an age that calls for the specialist, the expert, the technician, the engineer. It can literally be said that bureaucratism and not egalitarianism is inevitable. Short of dismantling industry and putting our modern tools to rest in a museum, like Butler's Erewhonians, short, in other words, of reverting to a simple precapitalist state of barbarism, it is certain that the bureaucrat will rule us. Marx did not even reckon with such a leader except as the transient figure who lived in a kind of hazy prehistory that would presage the socialist dream. In Veblen's work he is the main character. The industrial specialist and his scientific compeers are a real General Staff in an economic army that cannot do without them.

Veblen explains how the engineers could take power by declaring a general strike. It is true, he says, that they might be no more than a fraction of one percent of the total population. But if they withdrew it would precipitate the speedy collapse of a timeworn system. Any moment, a Council of Technological Workers could be organized whose purpose would be the discontinuance of existing industrial conditions. That such a turn of events might develop is suggested by the fear into which capitalists have been thrown by Bolshevism. However, Veblen tells them, in effect, that they may breathe easily for their fears are not justified—as yet. The forces of unreason, of reaction, of tradition are too great.

Radicalism is certainly no menace to the vested interests in America. *The necessary class consciousness* which a few technologists feel in their common distaste for inefficiency is wholly lacking among the workers in America. A revolution of any kind could scarcely be instigated by the stodgy directors of unions organized not for optimum production but for advantageous bargaining. No guardian of the price system need worry about trade unionism in a country where that institution actually helps to suppress revolt.

It is true, Veblen observes, that the Russian people have succeeded in effecting a revolutionary change, but for the very reason Marx least suspected: their industrial backwardness. America, on the other hand has an advanced technology, which is precisely what will prevent the revolution Marx envisioned. There might be riotous disorder in the United States, for a time, "but it would come to nothing, however substantial the provocation." True, there is growing unrest in America: some are surfeited with the prevarications of advertising; others are outraged at the inequities of commerce. But the underlying population is still very credulous about business, so that whatever the degree of discontent there need be no apprehension of mutinous outbreak.

Nor is there any present promise of a breakdown in business. To Veblen, a visibly sufficient reason for revolution already exists—which by no means insures its development. Business has been irresponsible with the delicately balanced and highly complex mechanism of industry and by obstructive tactics it has imposed a tremendous handicap on the economy. The margin for error is nevertheless so great that a decent modicum of productivity suffices to save the whole structure from collapsing.

The present state of the industrial arts is such that if we were to have anything like a Soviet in America it would be a Soviet of Technicians, but Veblen writes this off as a remote contingency. Chances are much greater of continued and increasing

shame, confusion, hardship, waste and insecurity. Veblen knows that the technicians are by settled habit a harmless and docile sort who derive contentment from the full dinner pail and work tirelessly for vested interests which he feels they should overthrow. Veblen certainly does not expect this commercialized élite to use its knowledge for the common good.

It is typical of the man that his "constructive" ideas should have been compressed into a brief chapter entitled: "A Memorandum on a Practical Soviet of Technicians." Its suggestions are quite hypothetical. They are not, as a blurb writer says on the dust jacket of this book, "to the engineers what the Communist Manifesto purported to be for the proletariat," but this construction was popularly put upon it. Subsequently, when Veblen's proposals had been sufficiently distorted, they led to Technocracy. The most apparent of a dozen essential programmatic differences between Veblen and Marx is that Veblen does not forecast a forceable dispossession of the capitalists. Whereas Marx had said, wisely enough, that no ruling class ever willingly abdicates, Veblen allows himself to believe that the capitalists will one day, reluctantly but voluntarily give up their positions of supremacy. Then, he conjectures, an industrial directorate could be formed with a large ramification of subcenters and local councils, whose main duty would be to avoid, "all unemployment of serviceable equipment and manpower on the one hand, and all local or seasonal scarcity on the other." Veblen advises the mythical board to make full use of consulting economists who might occupy a place analogous to that of the legal counsel among statesmen.

This plan can only succeed if it rigidly excludes businessmen from all positions of trust. There is the rub. Americans fundamentally trust no other group but businessmen—the very group, and the only one Veblen regards as completely unqualified. He imagines that if there were a great deal of cooperation between engineers and economists, one could be more hopeful, but teamwork appears to be lacking and there is no reason to anticipate a reversal so great that it will provoke the liquidation of absentee ownership.

The revolution could be accomplished peacefully, but Veblen doubts that it will be accomplished at all. By themselves, the technicians can effectually incapacitate the country's industrial system and take it over. But without what Veblen calls the tolerant consent of public opinion, backed by aggressive support from below, they will be practically helpless to institute an organization on the new footing. To conclude, he summarizes his viewpoint, "There is nothing in the situation that should reasonably flutter the sensibilities of the Guardians or of that massive body of well-to-do citizens who make up the rank and file of absentee owners just yet." (pp. 113-17)

If a balance sheet were to be drawn up, the disinterested critic [of Veblen] would have to admit some seriously faulty thinking, some second hand ideas that are worn out altogether, and a quantity of vagueness and haziness. When all this is cut away, if one juxtaposes the main lines of Veblen's theory next to what social science tells us today, with due regard for the transitorinesss of hypotheses—this conglomeration of hunches, insights, philosophies, and impressions that we have examined stands up remarkably well.

Many of the incidental ideas do not bear scrutiny at all. An outmoded racial theory strikes the modern reader as simply bizarre, but it is obliterated in his mind's eye by the sound prediction of a Second World War, what forces are at work to guarantee it and who the combatants will be. There is an astonishing predictive value in Veblenism which the new social scientist would scarcely expect from the flimsiness of its empiricism.

Robert Redfield, an anthropologist who has spent much time in "the field" has recently classed Veblen with De Tocqueville and Sumner as a social scientist who teaches us very little about research methods but whose books are "important, influential, and meritorious." Redfield advises the contemporary sociologist to emulate men of Veblen's character. He remarks that "one may be taught how to pursue a course of questioning, how to map a neighborhood, or how to tabulate and treat statistically the votes cast in an election; but to know how to do these things is not to be assured of meaningful conclusions. Besides these skills, one needs also the ability to enter imaginatively, boldly, and at the same time self-critically into that little fraction of the human comedy with which one has become scientifically concerned." He continues, "To train a man to perform a technique may result in making him satisfied with mastery of the technique . . . Proficiency is excellent, but it must be combined with imaginative dissatisfaction."

The revival of interest in Veblen points to a growing awareness that proficiency is not enough, and this is the great methodological lesson social scientists have begun to learn. It may be that they will also recapture a degree of imaginative dissatisfaction. (p. 117)

Bernard Rosenberg, in his The Values of Veblen: A Critical Appraisal, *Public Affairs Press, 1956, 127 p.*

ERNEST W. DEWEY (essay date 1959)

[*In the following essay, Dewey examines Veblen's views on the development of values as evidence of his essentially conservative social philosophy.*]

Veblen's biting satire and uninhibited criticism of all that has been held economically holy, and his frank doubt of almost all else held holy, has led to a popular view of him as a pessimistic iconoclast and bombastic academic radical. Such a view oversimplifies and generally obscures the basic and positive contributions of Veblen's thought to the interpretation of social phenomena. In seeking to point out some of the often slighted contributions of Veblen to general value interpretation, I propose to show that Veblen was philosophically an optimist and, while perhaps a radical in his hopes for some fundamental changes in social institutions, nevertheless one of history's most sincere and sound apologists of the extrinsic value of the conservative's role in society.

Veblen saw the basic struggle of man as a struggle for tools; tools which may be physical instruments to do things or abstract principles to explain things. In either case they are the means of extending man's power over his environment and reducing the power of his environment over him. Men call successful principles true, good, trustworthy, pleasant, etc. These add practical certainty to problems of logic, ethics, epistemology, and psychology. And although tools solve problems of a practical nature, in reality these are problems of value or types of value. The interpretation of these problems involves a general theory of valuation. Whatever else Veblen was doing, he was considering man's struggle for values as a general struggle, and Veblen's study of social trends, institutions, and idiosyncrasies is based on a general theory of valuation. I use the term "valuation" rather than "value" for two reasons: first, to indicate Veblen's emphasis on the active process of value for-

mation or creation and its immanence in human activity; and second, to show that Veblen did not believe in the transcendency of values, but rather that he held them to be immanent and impermanent. In short, Veblen conceived of philosophy primarily as the study of values and the process of valuation. Moreover, Veblen's basic philosophical commitments are not only logically prior, but systematically underlie his economic evaluations and criticisms.

The extraction of Veblen's general theory of value might seem to be made difficult by his writing from, rather than about, his more general philosophic position; but, such extraction is not particularly difficult, for although statements of his philosophical position are scattered through his writings, they are quite explicitly stated. Moreover, Veblen's general approach is always primarily theoretical rather than descriptive. Even his celebrated attack on hedonistic psychology is directed more at demonstrating hedonism's inadequacies in fulfilling the need for a universal human psychology than in proving its inadequacy in explaining economic behavior.

Veblen believed that the success or failure of man's search for truth would be determined by the answer to this basic question: how shall man conceive of his experience? The answer finds its resolution in the conflict between superstition and science, between the animistic approach to mystical or supernatural powers and the toughminded, matter-of-fact approach dictated by a world of cause and effect relationships.

Veblen sees human nature as the product of a long evolutionary development, but something which has reached a relative stability. Man's past has conditioned or selected those traits which enable him to survive in his present environment. Veblen believes man has become an efficient organism. The central drive in man is the instinct of workmanship, a constructive bent with an aversion to waste motion, and a desire for the peaceful environment necessary to pursue his creative impulses uninhibited. But today, it is the social environment which determines to a great extent how these general instincts common to all men shall manifest themselves in social action.

Despite the inherent propensity for flexible efficiency in the human personality, Veblen points out that mankind has created for himself an environment of social and cultural pressures embodied in institutional traits which remain rigid and inflexible. Truth defined with reference to inflexible institutions is transcendent, absolute, and ineffectual in the long run. Fundamentally, such an interpretation of truth makes us force our problem to fit the tools rather than devise tools to fit problems. It is here that one of the most interesting and significant innovations in Veblen's thought arises. Essentially, his view is that such transcendent and inflexible principles are impossible of human verification and thus, as absolutes, are retardative and worthless as categories of evaluation. Nevertheless, he holds that what might be called immanent but impermanent absolutes are essential for the process of postulation, prediction, and action.

The phrase "immanent but impermanent absolutes" may cause discomfort at first reading, but I believe it is well chosen in expressing Veblen's position. Veblen is saying that there is an opinion which correctly or accurately describes, conforms to, or encompasses any situation whatever. Such an opinion is an absolute to which our opinion may conform in many varying degrees. Practically, there are "betters" or "truers" but logically, Veblen would say, there must be a "true" or absolute. It is an impermanent absolute, fleeting and transitory because the particular situation or particular type of situation or phenomenon is impermanent. Nevertheless, it is *the accurate opinion* in that particular case. This accurate opinion or truth is what contributes significance, order, and meaning to tangible data. Significance, order, and meaning are instruments of telelogy, and man alone is teleological.

Only men give direction and order to the neutral forces of a "colorless" world of cause and effect relationships. The world is rational because man gives it rationality by making the neutral causes and effects into means and ends. Man is no longer merely a product of his environment; he is the active factor of control by which the factors of environment are given direction, and changed into a course of progress. Man makes process synonymous with progress. Man's choice of neutral causes makes goals of resultant effects. Prediction is not part of the nature of things; it is meaning given by man to the relation of things. Thus the interpretation of human activity is the description of how man individually and socially gives meaning to his environment, and how, in doing so, he modifies and recreates that environment. Veblen's position is a rejection of that conception of reality which holds the world to be a given, fixed, and determined moral and social order to which man should conform.

Veblen is advocating an approach in the interpretation of human activities in the field of values and, especially, in the realm of economic study, which has been basic since the time of Darwin. This approach deals with phenomena as connected parts of a process and explains that process in the "matter-of-fact" terms of cause and effect relationships.

According to Veblen, if we are to understand the individual and society, we must understand the relationship of each to the process-continuum which results in progress. By progress Veblen means the increasing advantage gained by man in relation to his environment. But society is not the *sum* of acting, responding individuals; it is not the individual "writ large." Nor is the individual a mere reflection of the social order. Both the individual and the social order perform a distinct function in the role of progress; each is causally determinative in the environment; yet, each conditions the other without exposing either to the metaphysical morass of solipsism or determinism.

Veblen sees society or the community at large as the carrier or vehicle of progress. The organized structure of society, together with its institutional parts, is a going concern maintaining a body of principles which represent established responses to the varying conditions of life, and embodying a common measure of truth and sufficiency which are accepted as final and self-evident at any given time and place. These established principles of good, truth, and beauty represent an habitual body of rules for action which have reached a degree of poise and consistency:

> It is only because there is such a degree of consistency and such a common measure of validity among the commonly accepted principles of conduct and belief today, that it is possible to speak intelligently of the modern point of view, and contrast it with any other point of view which may have prevailed earlier or elsewhere, as *e.g.*, in the Middle Ages or in Pagan Antiquity.

The process of cultural adaptation is a fact of group life, not the creative achievement of individuals working in isolation. The common body of accepted principle for conduct and belief is always a heritage from past group experience, the substantial body of which is "knowledge" handed down from previous generations. This body of principle is always in the process of change and the learning process of a society is a process of cumulative causation, causation which must realize itself in a community of individuals by achieving group assent. It is a rehabituation of attitudes at the collective level and is necessarily a slow and irresolute growth. The acceptance of a new theory or principle of action on the part of a community must be based on a definite need of changing the old norm plus accepted evidence that the new theory or norm affords a more satisfactory principle of action. Both the need for change and the satisfactoriness of the new principle must be established in a community-awareness by experience; hence the gradual and protracted character of social change.

> Veblen recognizes the individual as the source of innovation and insight: Each successive move in advance, every new wrinkle of novelty, improvement, invention, adaptation, every further detail of workmanlike innovation, is of course made by an individual and comes out of individual experience and initiative, since the generations of mankind live only in individuals.

But, Veblen points out, the basis of any new approach or principle by the individual is that store of knowledge common to the individual's social environment:

> A new departure is always and necessarily an improvement on or alternation in that state of the industrial arts that is already in the keeping of the group at large; and every expedient or innovation, great or small, that is so hit upon goes into effect by going into the common stock of technological resources carried by the group.

Although it is the individual that exercises that reflective judgment which results in insight into new efficiency, new harmony between man and his environment, it is society which judges that contribution and determines whether it shall be significant to progress and whether it shall be a determinative factor in process. That common stock of knowledge or belief belonging to a social group at any particular time represents the accumulated acceptances of previous generations and times.

The approach of the individual and likewise the attitude of society as a whole in the process of adaptation rests on one of two distinct types of response to the universe, or a combination of them. The first type of response is the approach of "mythology," "animism," "magic," "superstition," "sentimentalism," or "theology." Veblen sees this as falsely attributing a teleological structure and order to the universe. It presupposes either that physical objects think and act as we do, or that their actions are determined by some intelligent transcendent force, which acts like man, sets up goals or ends, and chooses means.

The second type of response Veblen calls "scientific," "technological," or "matter-of-fact." It is this latter approach that Veblen sees as "true." But despite the assertion that "Modern Civilization is peculiarly matter-of-fact," Veblen points out that virtually all social and individual thought, even in our modern culture, is a combination of these two approaches to experiential-phenomena.

Institutions, then, are principles of adaptation or rules of action which have received a general and uncritical acceptance by the social group. They represent the habitual responses to environment sanctioned by the social order as true, right, or good. They may have as their origin or fundamental apology either the "supernatural" or the "matter-of-fact" approach to the phenomena of experience; but their uncritical acceptance and embodiment into norms of belief, conduct, or law is an act of human nature whereby men respond collectively. There has been the tendency in the institutionalist approach to economics and in the instrumental theory of value to view the phenomena of social institutions, because of their conservative character, as essentially ceremonial, unscientific, and unhealthy. Veblen, however, saw the institution as a functional social instrument which, though retardative in many instances, represents the means by which society preserves what it believes to be the best principles of individual and social adaptation.

In all lines of human activity, man tends to perpetuate habitual modes of behavior in an institutional framework, sometimes in the ceremonial forms of religious sects, sometimes in the combined forms of political apology for governmental theory, or sometimes in the technological forms of academic disciplines. Veblen believes that such a framework of institutionalized habitual modes of behavior provides the stable social environment in which problems can be met and solved, even to the extent that a society's own stability may provide the fulcrum for replacing its own foundational principles. The totality of environment cannot be held in question nor responses determined as if all events and phenomena were novel. To do so would destroy the basis of social order and even individual response.

> If the contrary were true, if men universally acted not on the conventional grounds and values afforded by the fabric of institutions, but solely and directly on the grounds and values afforded by unconventionalized propensities and aptitudes of hereditary human nature, then there would be no institutions and no culture.

The transition from the supernatural and mystical interpretation of the world in the Middle Ages to the "modern point of view" took several centuries and is by no means complete. The gradual disintegration of the medieval position has been the result of the cumulative and gradually increasing awareness of its inadequacies as the foundation for principles of action, together with an increasing awareness of the "success" resulting from the matter-of-fact approach.

To be sure, by the time a new principle of explanation or value becomes socially accepted, it may no longer be the best explanation available or the highest value that might be realized. But, despite the obvious fact that such "cultural lag" exists, resulting in an imperfect adjustment between the material basis of life and the social institutions which describe, direct, and choose the ends or goals of life, Veblen sees this as a fundamental part of the phenomenon of progress. Obviously, it would be to the advantage of society to work consciously toward reducing this lag to a minimum; but according to Veblen, there would be some lag because of the very nature of the process. Moreover, the fact that the new idea must always traverse the filter of social inertia if it is to become a moment in the social process, acts virtually to guarantee that the social process will be progressive.

The nature of this guarantee is found in Veblen's conception of the role of institutions as prescribed norms. Institutions, he points out, exert their influence on two levels, the first of which is the source and foundation of the second. The first of these two levels of institutional discipline comprises those principles of knowledge and belief which define actuality and credibility. These principles tell us what is, what society regards as ascertained fact or the realm of truth. The second consists of principles which serve as canons of conduct, defining law,

custom, tradition, and morals. These tell us what society regards as proper ends or goals of action, what ought to be, or the realm of values.

It is the first of these levels that defines the limits within which the alternative ends or goals of action must be found, and so it is this level which conditions and serves as a foundation for the second.

> It is by use of their habitual canons of knowledge and belief that men construct those canons of conduct which serve as guides and standards in practical life.

Value and the process of valuation are to be defined with reference to these two levels.

The nature and function of values for society and for the individual is the capstone of Veblen's approach to human activity as a peculiar phenomenon in a universe of material causation. Individuals and society as a whole participate in the prophecy of, and response to, possible or probable "futures." The fact that man can act in a manner other than as a mere moment in a determined universe is due to his novel position and characteristics.

> Like other animals, man is an agent that acts in response to stimuli afforded by the environment in which he lives. Like other species he is a creature of habit and propensity. But in a higher degree than other species, man mentally digests the content of the habits under whose guidance he acts, and appreciates the trend of these habits and propensities. He is in an eminent sense an intelligent agent. By selective necessity he is endowed with a proclivity for purposeful action.

His thinking must be in terms of the means and conditions that can be utilized in his actions because his principles of adaptation are rules of action, and his rules of action are the meaning and order which he gives to his world of experience. Those principles of action which "prove" themselves by subsequent experience to be satisfactory—that is, foreseen events or desired results predicted and realized—become established patterns of individual behavior and response. After successful and general usage, these principles become the commonly accepted measure of truth and validity.

In turn, this measure of the actual serves to define the means and conditions available to society for achieving goals. These limits indicate possible goals, but the choice of ends by the social group is a matter of habituation, not of reflective intelligence. The accumulated knowledge of society or the accepted principles of adaptation are the final product of progress at any particular time; but, this structure of community judgments assumes the rationality of the individual. It is in his acts, his awareness, his frustration, and reflection, that old principles are first questioned and begin their descent into oblivion, and new principles are formulated, tested, and begin the ascent to social acceptance. The individual is the condition for society, but it is the social organization into which man is born and reared which preserves the successful generalizations of prior experience, and thereby furnishes that general body of knowledge and belief which is the basis of the individual's reflective approach to the novel situation or event. When the individual questions ends or goals, he is questioning society's definitions of "right," "proper," or "good" action. But in the examination of values, as in the formation of values, man does not simply put one value or end over against another. He tries to preserve, as far as possible, that which has been accepted.

Short of social disintegration, the overthrow of a whole system of beliefs and values can come about only over a long period of time and piecemeal. Such canons of conduct as are sanctioned by society and preserved in our systems of custom, law, tradition, and morals represent tested responses to recurring situations. These values come about through the active process of value formation or creation which begins in individual awareness of the novel, and spreads to a group awareness of a problem. The dissatisfaction of the group becomes significant only when a parallel process of attempted solutions furnishes a more satisfactory basis of response than the established pattern which has been questioned.

Veblen, however, expresses little doubt that in the gradual process of readjustment and re-evaluation of man's principles of adaptation, the cultural scheme is definitely becoming more matter-of-fact. He sees this is not as a result of mere chance, but a virtually inevitable process. This is because the matter-of-fact approach is "true": that is, it corresponds to the actual world of material causation. The fact that modern society is more matter-of-fact in its approach than previous cultures is both evidence of, and cause for, its progress. Many of its values are still institutional habits of primarily ceremonial origin, but the dynamic character of the valuation process and the greater "serviceability" of the matter-of-fact approach constantly tends to undermine these beliefs and goals. The result is an increasingly scientific civilization of means with an accumulatively more satisfactory set of values, that is, goals or ends in harmony with means. (pp. 171-80)

Ernest W. Dewey, "Thorstein Veblen, Radical Apologist for Conservatism," in The American Journal of Economics and Sociology, *Vol. 18, No. 2, January, 1959, pp. 171-80.*

STEPHEN S. CONROY (essay date 1968)

[*In the following excerpt, Conroy analyzes Veblen's prose style.*]

Economics formerly was called "The Dismal Science" by its professors because they believed it to be the science of the distribution of scarce products. What more tragic study could there be than one based on the pessimistic premise that there simply was not enough of anything to go around, that supply could never equal demand? However, most American students, raised in an economy of abundance, are soon convinced that the adjective "dismal" applies to the quality of economic prose, and generally speaking they are correct. Thorstein Veblen was an orthodox economist, at least to the extent that he believed in an economy of scarcity, but his use of the English language would not normally be characterized as dismal, although his style is puzzling and at times even misleading. One who seems to have been misled was the usually astute H. L. Mencken. Mencken heartily detested Veblen, his economics and especially his prose style. To him the only remarkable things about Veblen's ideas were "the astounding grandiose and rococo manner of their statement, the almost unbelievable tediousness and flatulence of the gifted headmaster's prose, his unprecedented talent for saying nothing in an august and heroic manner" [see excerpt dated 1919].

Although quite a few people share Mencken's view, many more, it would seem, are delighted by Veblen's provocative treatment of institutions and by his unique and ironic style. A generation raised on Veblenian echoes finds it difficult to imagine his prose causing as much difficulty as it did to earlier readers. Veblen's purpose and his manner were widely mis-

apprehended, so much so that when *The Theory of the Leisure Class* appeared in 1899 it was frequently misread as a *literary* satire of the *nouveaux riches* of the period. Even so sophisticated a critic as William Dean Howells, writing one of the few friendly reviews of the work [see excerpt date 1899], made the error of taking it solely as literary satire, and failed to take adequate notice of the serious intent of Veblen's social and economic criticism.

In our comparatively enlightened age the moderately educated reader is in little danger of overlooking Veblen's serious theoretical points; on the contrary, some modern readers profess to see little or no satire in *The Theory of the Leisure Class*. A few students feel that Veblen's elaborate disclaimers of animus are sincere, that he is merely examining institutions from a scientific point of view, making no judgments of them. Others remark that a puzzle exists about whether he knew his language was "loaded." David Riesman [see Additional Bibliography], for example, says that Veblen presents his assumptions in such a way that:

> We do not know where he stands and hence how literally to take him. Could he be writing a fairy story, as grim as such tales usually are, as a form of reporting his personal terrors and doubts? . . . His repeated insistence that he is a value-free, "opaque" scientist, his contempt for his colleagues who allowed reformism to show, leave the answer in doubt.

Nor is Riesman alone in his position; even so serious a student of Veblen's thought as Joseph Dorfman [see Additional Bibliography] tends to deny Veblen's use of satire. He writes:

> Thorstein Veblen's *Theory of the Leisure Class* has customarily been viewed as a satire. . . . No one would consider Herbert Spencer's work satire. Yet what Veblen did in *The Theory of the Leisure Class* was to use Spencer's material, particularly his *Principles of Sociology*, to reverse Spencer's position.

Dorfman goes on to show quite clearly that Veblen owed a heavy debt to Spencer for material he used in his first book, but he does not demonstrate that *The Theory of the Leisure Class* is not satirical.

There are also those who believe that Thorstein Veblen wrote the way he did because English was not his native language—that somehow the fact that he was raised in a Norwegian-speaking community caused him not to understand that English words have connotations as well as denotations. According to this theory, he used words solely for their denotative value and was unaware that one term (hoarding) could have a pejorative implication while another (saving) could be fairly neutral. If this idea is correct, then Veblen's "elaborate disclaimers of animus" must be sincere and not ironical. But this position involves a logical absurdity, for if Veblen were unaware of connotation, why would he deny that his usage was slanted? His denial certifies his awareness.

Furthermore, and in direct contrast to the above theory, there are those who say that Veblen wrote his characteristic involuted, polysyllabic prose because he was afraid to come straight out and say what he meant. He was, after all, a penniless scholar who owed his professorial existence to the very capitalistic system he was attacking. In order not to be discharged, the logic goes, he camouflaged his ideas in ornately academic verbiage. This conclusion is based on a low opinion of both Veblen and capitalists, and is not completely justified by the facts.

All the above theories concerning the rhetoric of Thorstein Veblen are quite erroneous. Joseph Dorfman denies that *The Theory of the Leisure Class* is satiric because all Veblen did was use the materials of *Principles of Sociology* to reverse Herbert Spencer's position. Such a reversal is, of course, the essence of satire. Furthermore, only a person utterly lacking a sense of humor could possibly miss the ironical outlook which pervades every page of a work like *The Theory of the Leisure Class.* And to intimate that Veblen's prose style was what it was because he was somehow deficient in his knowledge of the English language is also patently absurd. He may have been raised in a Norwegian-speaking community, but his command of the English language enabled him to earn a doctorate from Yale, to write several books and innumerable articles, to translate one of the Icelandic sagas from Old Norse into modern English, and to edit the *Journal of Political Economy* for several years. No one of these accomplishments by itself would indicate special competence, but taken together they suggest that Veblen must have had some mastery of English, including its nuances.

Remaining to be dealt with is the criticism that Veblen's style was a defense, hiding his economic theories from the eyes of the very class he was satirizing. Thorstein Veblen's whole life belies this picture of him as a Machiavellian Milquetoast. Veblen was not afraid to speak out in a fashion that could not be misunderstood, and he often did so. The concluding sentences of *The Higher Learning in America,* although mixing a few metaphors, openly state his somewhat radical solution to the problems of American university education as he saw them:

> ... as seen from the point of view of the higher
> learning, the academic executive and all his works
> are anathema, and should be discontinued by the
> simple expedient of wiping him off the slate; and ...
> the governing board, in so far as it presumes to ex-
> ercise any other than vacantly perfunctory duties, has
> the same value and should with advantage be lost in
> the same shuffle.

At all times Veblen was an outspoken opponent of what he called predatory capital and made no attempt to hide this opposition. We may be sure that the people he attacked knew that they were being attacked, and by whom. To say that Thorstein Veblen used his style as this sort of disguise is to underestimate the quality of Veblen and also to underestimate the quality of those he opposed.

The only logical conclusion that can be reached is that Veblen wrote the way he did because he wanted to write that way; in other words, he was a conscious stylist who chose his method and manner of writing for reasons of his own. We cannot be completely sure just what those reasons were, although undoubtedly he felt that his style was the most effective way of presenting his material. However, it is possible to point out some reasons why he might have chosen to write in the fashion that he did. In the first place, it should be remembered, he was dealing largely in abstractions. He was the father of the institutional school of economics, and he defined an institution as a habit of mind. Habits of the mind, it will be granted, are rather abstract conceptions. But Veblen carried the process of abstraction even further, for he was not only dealing with abstract institutions, but he was dealing with them in the process of change. His method was to examine a contemporary institution in the light of its origin and to predict from this double vantage point what its future development would be. J. A. Hobson seems to think that the ironic attitude of *The Theory of the Leisure Class* was not a conscious stylistic device.

Rather, says Hobson, "It was inherent in the social situation as he saw it." Granting that Veblen is correct in his conjectures about the origins of the leisure class, Hobson's statement is true enough, though somewhat exaggerated. There *is* an inherent irony in the thought that the elegant and cultured aristocrat is a direct descendant of the fierce and cunning barbarian.

There exists the possibility that Veblen was trying to reinforce his position as an authority by adopting a tone of academic detachment. In this view Veblen is seen essentially as a reformer. As a reformer one of the principal things he must do is to insist upon and strengthen his position as one who presumably knows what the situation is and how it should be dealt with. Finally, it is to be noted that this sense of detachment which Veblen strives to achieve is most necessary for maintaining a tone of irony. The rhetoric cannot reveal that the author's emotions are involved if the irony is to be effective. There may be passion and fury seething beneath the surface, but the outward manner must always be as calm as it is in Swift's *A Modest Proposal,* for instance.

A writer must work within a certain vocabulary, the limits of which are set by such incidentals as the intelligence, education and taste of the author, and what he conceives to be the level of the audience which he wishes to reach. The basic building materials of a style, then, are words. As Richard Teggart noted [see Additional Bibliography], Veblen's diction has a surprising range. His words are gathered from the most learned discourse as well as from the most slangy, but he is especially fond of using polysyllables and of constructing sentences of many words. The word stock of Professor Veblen's vocabulary is overwhelmingly Latinate; a review of the origins of words in a sample list of favorites reveals that about 85 per cent of them are of Latin origin, although many of them came into English through French. Although two of Veblen's favorite words, *barbarian* and *stratagem,* are of Greek origin, the majority of his favorites (*conspicuous, vicarious, consumption, instinct,* etc.) come from the Latin. Veblen's sentences are so long and his vocabulary so obviously polysyllabic that anything more than a cursory word count or a casual search of word origins is an unnecessary endeavor. But any such sample serves as a rough indicator that the obvious conclusions about Veblen's prose are not mistaken.

Perhaps Veblen will be remembered longest as a phrase-maker, since many of the phrases he coined have become an integral part of the vocabulary of educated America. *Conspicuous consumption* is probably his most widely circulated coinage, although he originated many others which are almost as familiar: *vicarious leisure, conspicuous waste, instinct of workmanship, invidious emulation, peaceable savagery, higher barbarism.* The list could be made much longer, of course; almost everyone could add a favorite phrase or two to it. Veblen makes phrases like these memorable in a number of ways. First among his devices is the poetic one of alliteration: *conspicuous consumption, persistent and pervading, acquisition and accumulation, proximate purposefulness, disinterested and dispassionate, science and scholarship.* It is to be noted that many of the above pairs of words are separated from one another by "and," giving an occasional Biblical flavor to Veblen's prose. Rather than alliterating only two words, as in the examples above, Veblen sometimes gives a whole series of words the same initial sound or letter. The connoisseur of Veblenese finds the alliteration of the following sentence delightful: "The spirit of American business is a spirit of quietism, caution, compromise, collusion and chicane." To prove that Veblen was a self-conscious stylist it is only necessary to point out the modulation of the ''k'' sound alliteration with *chicane* as well as the progressive strengthening of the pejorative implications of the words from the fairly neutral *quietism* to the heavily derogatory *chicane.*

Veblen's phrases are also memorable because of his trick of using adjectives which are heavily pejorative while insisting that he is using them only in their most restricted sense. The famous phrase *conspicuous consumption* is the most obvious example of this usage. As Max Lerner notes, ''Presumably he means 'conspicuous' only in the sense of 'open' or 'manifest.' Yet in his use it takes over all the emotionally loaded meaning of 'ostentatious' that it has in common speech. . . .'' Another of Veblen's favorite terms, *conspicuous waste,* is even more heavily loaded, for the term *waste* is also negatively charged. Veblen does not fail to indicate this:

> The use of the term ''waste'' is in one respect an unfortunate one. As used in the speech of everyday life the word carries an undertone of deprecation. It is here used for want of a better term that will adequately describe the same range of motive and phenomena, and it is not to be taken in an odious sense, as implying an illegitimate expenditure of human products or of human life.

Veblen nowhere writes with more ironic intent. It seems certain that he desires his readers to come to the exact conclusions against which he warns. By calling attention to the pejorative connotation of the word *waste* he makes sure that its derogatory sense will not be overlooked. In addition, the fact that both terms of *conspicuous waste* have a pejorative element makes the condemnatory nature of the phrase much stronger. The sly technique of calling attention to the usage desired by denying the term is used in the obvious sense reaches some sort of a climax in *The Theory of the Leisure Class* when Veblen explains that he is using *invidious* in a non-invidious manner!

> In making use of the term ''invidious,'' it may perhaps be unnecessary to remark, there is no intention to extol or depreciate, or to commend or deplore any of the phenomena which the word is used to characterize.

Much of the effectiveness of Veblen's prose is a cumulative one; his favorite phrases are repeated again and again. And just as he repeats phrases he also repeatedly denies, especially in *The Theory of the Leisure Class,* any bias on his part. His denial that he meant anything deprecatory by the use of the word *invidious* is only one of many disclaimers of the same sort sprinkled throughout this work:

> All this, of course, has nothing in the way of eulogy or deprecation of the office of the leisure class. . . . ''Right'' and ''wrong'' are of course here used without conveying any reflection as to what ought or ought not to be. . . . The exigencies of the language make it impossible to avoid an apparent implication of disapproval of the aptitudes, propensities, and expressions of life here under discussion. It is, however, not intended to imply anything in the way of deprecation or commendation of any one of these phases of human character or of the life process.

The disclaimers are most emphatically not exhausted by the above list. And anyone who thinks they are to be taken seriously does not remember his Shakespeare, for to paraphrase Hamlet's mother, ''The gentleman doth protest too much, methinks.''

Veblen occasionally restates what has gone before in an ironic fashion, or rephrases earlier statements in a more derisive way. For instance, in *The Theory of the Leisure Class* he writes, ''So soon as the possession of property becomes the basis of popular esteem, therefore, it becomes also a requisite to that complacency which we call self-respect.'' A few pages later the reader finds the term ''self-complacency'' being used rather than the more normal ''self-respect.'' Somewhat akin to this sort of shift of statement is Veblen's use of a rhetorical device which might be called ''transference.'' Transference involves the shifting of terms from one area of society to another. For instance, in *The Higher Learning* Veblen speaks of the ''inmates'' of colleges. It is more usual to call the inhabitants of prisons or insane asylums ''inmates''; what Veblen is doing, of course, is intimating that there is some similarity among the environments of college students, criminals and the insane. In the same work the author refers to a degree granted to a graduate of a college as an ''honorable discharge.'' Here Veblen is implying a similarity between the bureaucratic organization and the coercive discipline of the armed forces, and the organization and discipline of the undergraduate college.

The satirist who is also a scholar must always be tempted to insert ironic footnotes into his writings, and Veblen sometimes gave in to this temptation. David Riesman does not think very highly of Veblen's use of the footnote, which he believes indicates a lack of the ability to organize material. Veblen, he says, ''cannot decide . . . what is central, what peripheral; a footnote is as likely as the text to contain crucial matter inserted as a seeming afterthought.'' It is quite true, as Riesman says, that a footnote is liable to contain crucial matter, but he overlooks the fact that Veblen seldom uses footnotes; therefore the few that he does use call special attention to themselves, and thus serve as an effective means of emphasis. In a long footnote Veblen reveals how the board of trustees of a university managed a thirty million dollar endowment so ''efficiently'' that there was almost no money available for the legitimate ends of the university. This footnote is more than a mere afterthought; it is central to the thesis of *The Higher Learning.* It makes Veblen's point quite explicitly: men of affairs are not competent to manage the activity of a community of scholars. In a footnote placed much later in the same book he makes a searing attack on a ''typical'' university president of his day (based on William Rainey Harper of the University of Chicago). And this footnote too is central to his thesis, for it emphasizes his second main point: the proper functioning of a university is sabotaged by its president. Although both examples cited here are quite central to the work involved, it is not suggested that all of Veblen's footnotes are so important to the text, nor that they are always ironic, for that matter. But the majority of his footnotes are ironic and to the point, so that they are tremendously effective in emphasizing what Veblen wants to emphasize.

In the bag of tricks of the satirist, one device goes under the name of the great English satirist, Jonathan Swift—the Swiftian miscellaneous catalogue. In one such catalogue, Veblen cites articles of conspicuous waste such as ''carpets and tapestries, silver table services, waiter's services, silk hats, starched linen, many articles of jewelry and of dress.'' Later he lists the consumption of such ceremonial paraphernalia as ''shrines, temples, churches, vestments, sacrifices, sacraments, holiday attire.'' Again, calling the southern way of life barbarian, he points out that compared to northern society it has more ''duels, brawls, feuds, drunkenness, horse-racing, cock-fighting, gambling, male sexual incontinence.'' The articles in these catalogues are not all of the same order; thus their juxtaposition introduces an element of incongruity. By making it clear that he considers carpets as wasteful as silk hats, that shrines and temples and churches are of no more utility than holiday attire, and that horse-racing and cock-fighting are of equal cultural value, Veblen gives his readers a new perspective on the institutions represented in the quoted word clusters.

With a humor not entirely dependent on satire or irony, Veblen could be quite genuinely funny. He was at his most amusing when he was examining with eagle eye certain customs and habits of fairly minor importance in human behavior. Two examples of his lighter side are his treatment of the origins of the gaits and accouterments of the riding horse, and the origin of the customs surrounding Labor Day. He concludes his examination of horseback riding by saying, "A person of decorous tastes in horsemanship today rides a punch with a docked tail, in an uncomfortable posture and at a distressing gait, because the English roads during a great part of the last century were impassable for a horse traveling at a more horse-like gait. . . ." Later, in three sardonic sentences, he succeeds in making what was in his day the new institution of the Labor Day holiday seem ridiculous:

> A day of vicarious leisure has in some communities been set apart as Labor Day. This observance is designed to augment the prestige of the fact of labor, by the archaic, predatory method of a compulsory abstention from useful effort. To this datum of labor-in-general is imputed the good repute attributable to the pecuniary strength put in evidence by abstaining from labor.

Veblen could of course wield the axe as well as the rapier—perhaps even better. However, it would not do to leave Veblen accused of cruelty without pointing out that he was unsparing in his satire—he did not even spare himself.

The wry self-portraiture of Veblen's picture of the scholar or scientist (his amiable incompetence in dealing with men of affairs; his idle curiosity, etc.) has been noticed by most perceptive readers. The point of view which does not spare the author himself is most apparent in *The Higher Learning,* and has often been commented on by readers. But no one has pointed out the lengthy self-satire which Veblen includes in *The Theory of The Leisure Class.* Veblen ends the book with a long attack on the prose style of the leisure class, but he is obviously describing, to some extent at least, his own use of the English language.

> The archaic idiom of the English language is spoken of as "classic" English. Its use is imperative in all speaking and writing upon serious topics. . . . Elegant diction, whether in writing or speaking is an effective means of reputability. . . . A discriminate avoidance of neologisms is honorific, not only because it argues that time has been wasted in acquiring the obsolescent habit of speech, but also as showing that the speaker has from infancy habitually associated with persons who have been familiar with the obsolescent idiom. . . . A breach of the proprieties in spelling is extremely annoying and will discredit any writer in the eyes of all persons who are possessed of a developed sense of the true and beautiful. English orthography satisfies all the requirements of the canons of reputability under the law of conspicuous waste. It is archaic, cumbrous, and ineffective; its acquisition consumes much time and effort; failure to acquire it is easy of detection. Therefore it is the first and readiest test of reputability in learning, and

> conformity to its ritual is indispensable to a blameless scholastic life. . . . It is contended, in substance, that a punctilious use of ancient and accredited locutions will serve to convey thought more adequately and more precisely than would the straightforward use of the latest form of spoken English. . . . Classic speech has the honorific virtue of dignity; it commands attention and respect as being the accredited method of communication under the leisure-class scheme of life, because it carries a pointed suggestion of the industrial exemption of the speaker. The advantage of the accredited locutions lies in their reputability; they are reputable because they are cumbrous and out of date, and therefore argue waste of time and exemption from the use and the need of direct and forcible speech.

[It] is suggestive that Veblen reserves the final pages of his book for a discussion of certain qualities of English prose as it is used by the leisure class. It is, he says, obsolescent, given to the use of words which are difficult to spell, and full of cumbrous locutions. The possession of all these qualities in one's prose proves that one has been exempt from work, and is, in fact, a member of the leisure class.

The main quality of leisure-class prose which Veblen attacks is its "archaic idiom," as he calls it. The style of Thorstein Veblen, in the above passage as well as in other places, is closer to that of the 18th century essayists, Swift say, than it is to his contemporaries, the 19th century American muckrakers. In other words, his own idiom is slightly obsolescent or archaic; there is about his style, as Max Lerner points out, an air of controlled quaintness. Veblen continues his discussion by emphasizing the necessity of avoiding neologisms, an avoidance which in itself tends to reinforce the use of the "archaic idiom." It is true that Veblen himself very occasionally makes use of a neologism, a slangy word or phrase; but the very effectiveness of this device depends to a great extent on the incongruity between the word from the marketplace and the rather mannered and elegant diction which precedes it. He goes on to treat the importance to the reputability of a scholar of an easy knowledge of English orthography. It is impossible to know whether or not Veblen spelled perfectly, but possibly his addiction to the use of polysyllabic words was in part at least an amused and self-conscious attempt to insinuate a virtuosity in this area, not to hide his criticism from the leisure class but to insure that it would be "reputable" enough to gain a hearing from them.

Veblen believed that the leisure-class usage was a positive hindrance to free and effective communication, but he also realized that for his work to get any kind of hearing at all his style would have to conform, at least on the surface, to the leisure-class style. As a matter of fact, a concise enumeration of the elements of Thorstein Veblen's prose would parallel his description of leisure-class usage. Veblen uses a polysyllabic stock of words, and his rhetoric is quaintly archaic and full of circumlocutions. But it is more than that; it is a baroque overelaboration, a self-conscious exaggeration, of the leisure-class style—in many ways a parody of itself. Strangely enough then, with a double irony, the critics of 1899 who thought *The Theory of the Leisure Class* a literary satire were only partly mistaken. They felt the satire, but they did not see the serious economic ideas underlying it nor did they recognize the self-parody of Veblen's prose. And as William Dean Howells would have admitted, self-parody is surely one form of satire. (pp. 605-15)

Stephen S. Conroy, "Thorstein Veblen's Prose," in American Quarterly, *Vol. XX, No. 3, Fall, 1968, pp. 605-15.*

JOHN KENNETH GALBRAITH   (essay date 1973)

[*Galbraith, one of the most influential modern American economists, is known for his pragmatic approach to economic problems and his witty, epigrammatic prose style. In the following excerpt from his preface to a reprint of* The Theory of the Leisure Class, *he evaluates Veblen's major work.*]

The nearest thing in the United States to an academic legend—the equivalent of that of Scott Fitzgerald in fiction or of the Barrymores in the theater—is the legend of Thorstein Veblen. The nature of such a legend, one assumes, is that the reality is enlarged by imagination and that, eventually, the image has an existence of its own. This is so of Veblen. He was a man of great and fertile mind and a marvelously resourceful exponent of its product. His life, beginning on the frontier of the upper Middle West in 1857 and continuing, mostly at one university or another, until his death in 1929, was not without adventure of a kind. Certainly by the standards of academic life at the time it was nonconformist. There was ample material both in his work and in his life on which to build the legend, and the builders have not failed.

There is, in fact, a tradition in American social thought which attributes all contemporary comment and criticism of American institutions to Veblen. As with Marx to a devout Marxist, everything is there. The Marxist, however, is somewhat more likely to know his subject. It is possible, indeed, that nothing more clearly marks an intellectual fraud in our time than a penchant for glib references to Veblen, particularly for assured and lofty reminders, whenever something of seeming interest is said, that Veblen said it better and first. (p. v)

[Veblen's] life was richly interesting; his boyhood, if much less grim than commonly imagined, had a deep and lasting effect on his later writing. Veblen is not a universal source of insight on American society. He did not see what had not yet happened. Also, on some things, he was wrong, and, faced with a choice between accuracy and a formulation that he felt would fill his audience with outrage, he rarely hesitated. He opted for the outrage. But no man of his time, or since, looked with such a cool and penetrating eye not so much at pecuniary gain as at the way its pursuit makes men and women behave.

This cool and penetrating view is the substance behind the Veblen legend. It is a view that still astonishes the reader with what it reveals. While there may be other deserving candidates, only two books by American economists of the nineteenth century are still read. One of these is Henry George's *Progress and Poverty;* the other is *The Theory of the Leisure Class.* Neither of these books, it is interesting to note, came from the sophisticated and derivative world of the Eastern seaboard. Both were products of the frontier—reactions of the frontiersman, in the one case to speculative alienation of land, in the other to the pompous social ordinances of the affluent. But the comparison cannot be carried too far. Henry George was the exponent of a notably compelling idea; his book remains important for that idea—for the notion of the terrible price society pays for private ownership and the pursuit of profit in land. Veblen's great work is a wide-ranging and timeless comment on the behavior of people who possess or are in pursuit of wealth and who, looking beyond their wealth, want the eminence that, or so they believe, wealth was meant to buy. No one has really read very much if he hasn't read *The Theory of the Leisure Class* at least once. Not many of more than minimal education get through life without adverting at some time or another to "conspicuous consumption," "pecuniary emulation" or "conspicuous waste" even though they may not be quite certain whence these phrases came. (pp. vi-vii)

There is little that anyone can be told about *The Theory of the Leisure Class* that he cannot learn better by reading the book himself. It is a marvelous book; it is also, in its particular way, a masterpiece of English prose. But the qualification is important. Veblen's writing cannot be read like that of any other author. Wesley C. Mitchell—regarded, though not with entire accuracy, as Veblen's leading intellectual legatee—once said that "One must be highly sophisticated to enjoy his [Veblen's] books." All who cherish Veblen would wish to believe this. The truth is simpler than that. One needs only to realize that, if Veblen is to be enjoyed, he must be read very carefully and slowly. He enlightens, amuses and delights but only if he is given a good deal of time.

It is hard to divorce Veblen's language from the ideas it conveys. The ideas are pungent, incisive and insulting. But the writing itself is also a weapon. Mitchell noted that Veblen normally wrote "with one eye fixed on the squirming reader." Veblen also startles his reader with an exceedingly perverse use of meaning. This meaning rarely varies from that sanctioned by the most precise and demanding usage. But in the context it is often, to say the least, unexpected. This Veblen attributes to scientific necessity. Thus, in his immortal discussion of conspicuous consumption, he notes that expenditure, if it is to contribute efficiently to the individual's "good fame," must generally be on "superfluities." "In order to be reputable it [the expenditure] must be wasteful." All of this is quite exact. The rich do want fame; reputable expenditure is what adds to their repute or fame; the dress, housing, equipage, that serve this purpose and are not essential for existence are superfluous. Nonessential expenditure is wasteful. But only Veblen would have used the words *fame, superfluity, reputable* and *waste* in such a way. In the case of *waste* he does decide that a word of explanation is necessary. This is characteristically airy and matter-of-fact. In everyday speech he says, "the word carries an undertone of deprecation. It is here used for want of a better term . . . and it is not to be taken in an odious sense. . . ."

And so he continues. The wives of the rich forswear useful employment because "Abstention from labor is not only an honorific or meritorious act, but it presently becomes a requisite of decency." *Honor, merit* and *decency* are all used with exactness but they are not often associated with idleness. A robber baron, Veblen says, has a better chance of escaping the law than a small crook because "A well-bred expenditure of his booty especially appeals . . . to persons of a cultivated sense of the proprieties, and goes far to mitigate the sense of moral turpitude with which his dereliction is viewed by them." One does not ordinarily associate the disposal of ill-gotten wealth with good breeding.

Thus the way *The Theory of the Leisure Class*—or anything by Veblen—must be read. If one goes rapidly, words will be given their ordinary contextual meaning—not the precise and perverse sense that Veblen intended. Waste will be wicked and not a source of esteem; the association of idleness with merit, honor and decency will somehow be missed as also that between the crook and his expenditure. . . . The writing is clear and lucid. It is only that the words must be weighed. The book yields its meaning, and therewith its full enjoyment, only to those who too have leisure. (pp. xiv-xv)

The thesis of *The Theory of the Leisure Class* can be rather quickly given. It is a tract, the most comprehensive ever written, on snobbery and social pretense. Some of it has application to American society at the end of the last century—at the height of the gilded age of American capitalism—but more is wonderfully relevant to modern affluence.

The rich have often been attacked by the less rich for enjoying a superior social position that is based on assets and not moral or intellectual worth, for using their wealth and position to sustain a profligate consumption of resources of which others are in greater need, and for defending the social structure that accords them their privileged position. And they have been attacked for the base and wicked behavior that wealth sustains and that their social position sanctions. In all this the attackers, in effect, concede the rich their superior power and position; they deny them their right to that position or to behave as they do therein. Usually the denial involves a good deal of righteous anger or indignation. The rich have been thought worth the anger and the indignation.

Here is Veblen's supreme literary and polemical achievement. He concedes the rich and the well-to-do nothing; and he would not dream of suggesting that his personal attitudes or passion are in any way involved. The rich are merely anthropological specimens whose behavior the possession of money and property has made more interesting and more visibly ridiculous. The effort to establish precedence for one's self and the yearning for the resulting esteem and applause are the most nearly universal of human tendencies. Nothing in this respect differentiates a Whitney, Vanderbilt or Astor from a Papuan chieftain or what one encounters in "for instance, the tribes of the Andamans." The dress, festivals or rituals and artifacts of the Vanderbilts and Whitneys are more complex; that does not mean that their motivation is in any way different from their barbarian counterparts.

Indeed, it is inconceivable that the affluent should be viewed with indignation. The scientist does not become angry with the primitive tribesman because of the extravagance of his sexual orgies or the sophistication of his self-mutilation. Similarly with the social observances of the American rich. Their banquets are equated in commonplace fashion with the orgies; the self-mutilation of the savage is on all fours with the painfully constricting dress in which (at that time) the well-to-do bound up their women or their women corseted themselves.

It is well to remember that Veblen wrote in the last years of the last century—before the established order suffered the disintegrating onslaught of World War I, V. I. Lenin and the leveling oratory of modern democratic politics. It was a time when gentlemen still believed they were gentlemen and—in the United States at least—that it was wealth that made the difference. And, by and large, the rest of the population still agreed. Veblen calmly identified the manners and behavior of these so-called gentlemen with the manners and behavior of the people of the bush. Speaking of the utility of different observances for the purpose of affirming or enhancing the individual's repute. Veblen notes that "Presents and feasts had probably another origin than that of naive ostentation, but they acquired their utility for this purpose very early, and they have retained that character to the present. . . . Costly entertainments, such as *the potlach or the ball,* are peculiarly adapted to serve this end." The italics equating the potlach and the

ball are mine; Veblen would never dream of emphasizing so obvious a point.

The book is a truly devastating put-down, as it would now be called. But much more was involved. *The Theory of the Leisure Class* brilliantly and truthfully illuminates the effect of wealth on behavior. No one who has read this book ever again sees the consumption of goods in the same light. Above a certain level of affluence the enjoyment of goods—of dress, houses, automobiles, entertainment—can never again be thought intrinsic as, in a naive way, the established or neo-classical economics still holds it to be. Possession and consumption are the banner which advertises achievement—which proclaims, by the accepted standards of the community, that the possessor is a success. In this sense—in revealing what had not hitherto been seen—*The Theory of the Leisure Class* is a major scientific achievement.

It is also true, alas, that much of the process by which this truth is revealed—by which Veblen's insights are vouchsafed—is scientifically something of a contrivance. There is no doubt that before writing *The Leisure Class* he had read widely on anthropology. He has a great many primitive communities and customs at his finger tips, and he refers to them with a casual insouciance that suggests—and was probably meant to suggest—that he had much more such knowledge in reserve. But the book is wholly devoid of sources; no footnote or reference tells on what Veblen relied for information. On an early page he explains that the book is based on everyday observation and not pedantically on the scholarship of others. This is adequate as far as Fifth Avenue and Newport are concerned. Accurate secondhand knowledge can be assumed. But Veblen had no similar opportunity for knowning about the Papuans.

In fact Veblen's anthropology and sociology are weapon and armor rather than science. He uses them to illuminate (and to make ridiculous) the behavior of the most powerful class—the all-powerful class—of his time. And since he does it in the name of science and with the weapons of science—and since no overt trace of animus or anger is allowed to appear—he does it with nearly perfect safety. The butterfly does not attack the zoologist for saying that it is more decorative than useful. That Marx was an enemy whose venom was to be returned in kind, capitalists did not doubt. But not Veblen. The American rich never quite understood what he was about—or what he was doing to them. The scientific pretense, the irony and the careful explanations that the most pejorative words were being used in a strictly nonpejorative sense put him well beyond their comprehension. (pp. xv- xviii)

The last chapter of *The Leisure Class* is on "The Higher Learning as an Expression of the Pecuniary Culture." It anticipates a later, much longer and much more pungent disquisition by Veblen on the influence of the pecuniary civilization on the university (*The Higher Learning in America: A Memorandum on the Conduct of Universities by Businessmen* published in 1918). In this chapter Veblen—though also concerned with other matters—stresses the conservative and protective role of the universities in relation to the pecuniary culture. "New views, new departures in scientific theory, especially new departures which touch the theory of human relations at any point, have found a place in the scheme of the university tardily and by a reluctant tolerance, rather than by cordial welcome; and the men who have occupied themselves with such efforts to widen the scope of human knowledge have not commonly been well received by their learned contemporaries." No one will be in doubt as to whom, in the last clause, Veblen had in mind.

Elsewhere he notes that "As further evidence of the close relation between the educational system and the cultural standards of the community, it may be remarked that there is some tendency latterly to substitute the captain of industry in place of the priest, as head of seminaries of the higher learning."

Given such an environment, and given also his subject, it will be evident that Veblen needed the protection of his art. On the whole it served him well. In the course of his academic career he was often in trouble with academic administrators—but mostly on personal and idiosyncratic rather than political or ideological grounds. He was not understood or appreciated by his more pedestrian, if often more fashionable, academic colleagues. A man such as Veblen creates problems for such people. They accept the established view, rejoice in the favor of the Establishment. Anyone who does not share their values is a threat to their position and self-esteem, for he makes them seem sycophantic and pedestrian as, indeed, they are. Veblen, throughout his life, was such a threat. But the rich, to whom ultimately he addressed himself, never penetrated his defenses. (pp. xix-xx)

In the years following the publication of *The Leisure Class* Veblen turned to an examination of the business enterprise in its social context—an interest that is foreshadowed in the distinction early in this volume between *exploit*, which is such of business enterprise as is devoted to making money, and *industry*, which makes things. (In a characteristically matter-of-fact assertion of the shocking, Veblen notes that "employments which are classified as exploit are worthy, honourable, and noble," others involving a useful contribution to product being "unworthy, debasing, ignoble.") In 1904, Veblen developed this point (and more) in *The Theory of Business Enterprise*. That Veblen's books had yet to attract an audience is indicated by the fact that, out of his meager income, he was required to pay a good part of the bookmaking cost himself.

In introducing a recent (and best-selling) French edition of *The Theory of the Leisure Class* Raymond Aron gives the opinion that Veblen was better in his social than in his economic perception. With this I agree. The basic idea of *The Theory of Business Enterprise* is a plausible one—I can still remember my excitement when I first read the book while a student at Berkeley in the thirties where the Veblen influence was still strong. There is a conflict between the ordered rationality of the machine process as contrived by engineers and technicians and the pecuniary context in which it operates. The latter in its competition and interfirm aggression, and the resolution of the latter by consolidation and monopoly, sabotage the possibilities inherent in the machine process. But—though some will still object—the idea has been a blind alley. Organization and management is a greater task than Veblen implies; so is the problem of accommodating production to social need. And so is that of motivation and incentive. This has become evident in the socialist economies where far more problems have been encountered in translating the rationality of the machine process into effective economic performance than Veblen would have supposed. In the thirties after Veblen's death the political movement (perhaps more properly the cult), "technocracy" was founded on these ideas by Howard Scott. For a while it flourished. The technocrats, had they been given a chance, would have faced the same problem as the socialists. Though much read in the first half of the century, *The Theory of Business Enterprise*, unlike *The Theory of the Leisure Class*, has not quite survived. (pp. xxii-xxiii)

John Kenneth Galbraith, "Introduction: Thorstein Veblen and 'The Theory of the Leisure Class'," in

The Theory of the Leisure Class *by Thorstein Veblen, Houghton Mifflin Company, 1973, pp. v-xxv.*

JOHN P. DIGGINS (essay date 1978)

[*Diggins is an American critic specializing in the history of ideas. In the following excerpt, he assesses the future prospects of society and social theory in the light of Veblen's works.*]

Bourgeois society has enjoyed few friends among the intelligentsia, and capitalism, its lifeblood, has usually been analyzed by means of gloomy metaphors having to do with pathology, decay, and inevitable demise. Though they flourish best precisely in capitalist society, intellectuals may be justly charged with having harbored a death wish for capitalism. So frequently have they proclaimed its impending collapse that its perverse ability to survive disaster, and to thrive anew, must seem to them little less than miraculous, like the spontaneous remission of symptoms by a terminally ill patient.

The latest in a long line of grim prognoses is that of Daniel Bell, who is too sophisticated to succumb to the one-dimensional analysis—Marxist or otherwise—but whose recent study of the "modalities" of capitalism, its expressive and symbolic forms, is nearly as doom-laden as that of the Marxists who focus on the mode of production. Bell is convinced that contemporary industrial society is in the grip of grave "cultural contradictions" chiefly because the bourgeois ethos which fueled its rise has given way to the "sensate" culture of modernism.

> The bourgeois world-view—rationalistic, matter-of-fact, pragmatic; neither magical, mystical, nor romantic; emphasizing work and function; concerned with restraint and order in morals and conduct—had by mid-nineteenth-century come to dominate, not only the social structure (the organization of the economy), but also the culture, especially the religious motivation in the child. It reigned triumphant everywhere, opposed only in the realm of culture by those who disdained its un-heroic and anti-tragic mood, as well as its orderly attitude toward time.

Bell laments the passing of this world we have lost. This triumphant outlook succumbed in the twentieth century to a culture of freedom and pleasure, a life-style that made the mystique of self-realization tantamount to an inalienable right, and a mass consumption economy of unlimited gratification. The value system of capitalism, Bell concludes, is at last experiencing a fundamental crisis of legitimacy.

Significantly, both Marxist writers and anti-Marxists (in some cases ex-Marxists themselves) are willing to grant capitalism its ascetic, rationalistic world-view that was first formulated by Max Weber. Yet such a world-view cannot explain how modern capitalist society is possible. If early capitalism has its genesis in the ethic of self-restraint, mature capitalism has come to be, as Weber himself acknowledged, the rational systematization of irrational needs, an enslavement to the sovereignty of desire. Seen from this perspective, we may better understand why capitalist culture retains its legitimacy and hegemony and seemingly absorbs all challenges, turning crises and conflicts into further evidence of an all-pervasive consensus.

The problem of hegemony, man's subjugation to ideas and not only to force alone, could very well be the future reality of bourgeois society. If so, it is necessary to add another dimension to the anguished speculations of Daniel Bell. The present "cultural contradictions" of capitalism may derive not only from the disjunction between its work ethic and its pleasure principle. On the contrary, ever since the philosophy of property received its classical liberal formulation in the writings of Locke one may discern a central paradox: labor is considered to have value as a source of wealth, but the laborer himself is regarded as cursed with the burden of work; the more the principle of labor is praised economically, the more the activity is denigrated socially. It would be facile to dismiss such attitudes as an aspect of "alienation" or a species of "false consciousness." Indeed Veblen's analysis suggests that the distinction between the fruits of labor and the acts of workmanship, between the esteem for the product and the disesteem for the producer, is reified thinking experienced as anthropomorphism, and that therefore alienation itself may have its roots in the sphere of consumption rather than in production. In our age, when fewer and fewer people are engaged in industrial labor, and when technology and affluence have enabled more people to engage in the "pursuit of happiness" in leisure activities, it would seem that we need to turn our attention from the "productive forces" to the commodity culture, perhaps the crucial formative element in the development of modern popular consciousness. Veblen's writings may serve as a starting point for a study of the anthropological ties which bind the "civilized" present to the "barbaric" past.

Veblen's writings may also illuminate a new dimension in the contemporary debate between the consensus scholars and the conflict or coercion theorists of modern society. Representatives of both schools are interested primarily in the Hobbesian question: How does social order exist? In the consensus model, first articulated by Alexis de Tocqueville, and in our time by Seymour Martin Lipset and Talcott Parsons, a society exists because the mass of citizens share common norms, ideas and beliefs, a value system and structure of organizing principles that function to hold together the social order. In the conflict school, first put forward systematically by Marx, and in contemporary thought revised by non-Marxists like Ralf Dahrendorf and Lewis Coser, social phenomena are explained by either the interaction of class interests or the reality of authority relations, and hence the social system is perpetuated not by norms but by power.

Veblen's position bears similarities to both schools of thought yet is distinct from each. The America that he described at the turn of the century appears as a class society in which the workers suffered not so much from economic misery as from status deprivation, a phenomenon that indicated the pervasiveness of the capitalist norms of pecuniary achievement. But it is also a society in which the values of the dominant industrial class prevail because of its prior success in the struggle for power. The captain of industry is admired for much the same reason that primitive man stood in awe of the warrior: he is "gifted with ferocity." The persistence of such deferential attitudes toward personal force is the result both of biological evolution and ideological coercion. "This effect," wrote Veblen in reference to leisure-class hegemony,

> is wrought partly by a coercive, educational adaptation of the habits of all individuals, partly by a selective elimination of the unfit individuals and lines of descent. Such human material as does not lend itself to the methods of life imposed by the accepted scheme suffers more or less elimination as well as repression. The principles of pecuniary emulation and of industrial exemption have in this way been erected into canons of life, and have become coercive factors of some importance in the situation to which men have to adapt themselves.

To Veblen the structure of power is the basis from which social attitudes evolve. The ideas and culture of the victorious class take on a life of their own and give modern capitalist ideology the same reified status that previous ruling-class ideologies enjoyed in the past. In one respect Veblen offers a synthesis of the consensus-conflict debate: the history of society is the history of power struggles that issue in a culture of status fetish, a cult of masculine triumph around which a consensus is formed and through which society itself is sustained. It is no coincidence that Veblen discerned in capitalist ideology what other philosophers like George Sanytayana and William James saw as the curse of American culture itself: the worship of "the bitch-goddess of success."

Had Veblen merely demonstrated nothing more than the authority which the strong acquire over the weak, he would have asserted nothing more than a variation of nineteenth-century Social Darwinism. Yet by grounding his analysis in the anthropomorphic nature of cultural phenomena, Veblen's approach to attitude formation not only absorbed the distinction between norms and power that divide the consensus and conflict theorists, it also called into question an assumption shared by liberals and Marxists as well as Social Darwinists—the assumption of historical progress. Where the theorists of progress saw change, he saw only continuity; where they saw man's increasing rationality and mastery of the environment, he observed man acting out in symbolic forms of animistic behavior the residues of his barbaric nature; and where they looked either to "intelligence" or to "class consciousness" in order to undermine the old order and produce a new society and perhaps even a "new man" (Trotsky's phrase), he looked to the "discipline of the machine" to liberate man from his archaic traits by restoring almost intact his productive, wholesome nature that had supposedly flourished in the early stage of "primitive savagery."

Veblen's ultimate hope has always seemed "paradoxical" to intellectual historians; and one must say that the idea that the machine, a product of modern man, could revitalize the healthy primal instincts of human nature does seem a dubious proposition. Yet viewed in historical perspective the liberating power of science and technology cannot be denied. What, after all, is more threatening to false social distinctions than a "machine process" that makes no cultural distinctions? What is more revolutionary than an impersonal mode of cognition which has a logic and independent reality apart from the user? What is more democratic than an empirical enterprise that has no higher obligation than to the practical and useful? The problem, as Lewis Mumford astutely observed, is that in western culture the machine emerged purely as an "external instrument" for the conquest of the environment rather than as an extension of man's intellectual powers; and thus as modern life became more mechanized, and work dull and alienating, civilization assimilated the objects that technology brought forth rather than the "spirit" that had produced them. Mumford deserves to be quoted at length since he has expressed the Veblenian promise of the machine "aesthetic" more lucidly than Veblen himself:

> The possibility that technics had become a creative force, carried on by its own momentum, that it was rapidly ordering a new kind of environment and was producing a third estate midway between nature and the human arts, that it was not merely a quicker way of achieving old ends but an effective way of expressing new ends—the possibility in short that the machine furthered a new mode of *living* was far from the minds of those who actively promoted it. The

industrialists and engineers themselves did not believe in the qualitative and cultural aspects of the machine. In their indifference to these aspects, they were just as far from appreciating the nature of the machine as were the Romantics: only what the Romantics, judging the machine from the standpoint of life, regarded as a defect the utilitarian boasted of as a virtue: for the latter the absence of art was an assurance of practicality.

If the machine had really lacked cultural values, the Romantics would have been right, and their desire to seek these values, if need be, in a dead past would have been justified by the very desperateness of the case. But the interests in the factual and the practical, which the industrialists made the sole key to intelligence, were only two in a whole series of new values that had been called into existence by the development of the new technics. Matters of fact and practice had usually in previous civilizations been treated with snobbish contempt by the leisured classes: as if the logical ordering of propositions were any nobler a technical feat than the articulation of machines. The interest in the practical was symptomatic of that wider and more intelligible world in which people had begun to live, a world in which the taboos of class and caste could no longer be considered as definitive in dealing with events and experiences. Capitalism and technics had both acted as a solvent of those clots of prejudice and intellectual confusion; and they were thus at first important liberators of life.

One suspects that Marx would immediately have agreed with Mumford's assessment of the liberating role of capitalism and science. But what went wrong? How did the acquisitive culture of capitalism gain ascendancy over its rationalized system of production? Against the objectivity of the machine, why does the subjectivity of man continue to prevail? How did ideology come to triumph over technology? In Veblen's writings, where capitalism is not so much a definitive break with the past as a continuation, in modified form, of feudal status relations and barbarian survivals of prowess and esteem, where the market economy did not so much "tame the passions" of glory and power as rechannel them, we may find a compelling answer to this problem in contemporary social theory. (pp. 227-31)

In some deep personal sense [Veblen's] life remains as interesting as his ideas. Yet any attempt to assess Veblen in relation to his writings leads only to a plethora of baffling paradoxes which reveal the man as: an empiricist who derided the value of literature and art but who spent his last years translating Icelandic poetry; a social philosopher who denounced leisure as wasteful and who yet wrote an essay to prove that idleness was the highest state of knowing; a radical who attacked property and absentee ownership but who fought fiercely for possession of his own land and cabin; a feminist who championed the liberation of women but who allowed his own wives and mistresses to wait upon him hand and foot; an inveterate seducer who developed a theory of human nature that was coldly indifferent to the sex instinct so crucial to Freud; a technocrat who called upon the engineers to take power while declining the presidency of the American Economic Association; and a social scientist who looked forward to modern technology and backward to primitive harmony. One may well wonder whether such contradictions ever bothered Veblen. Perhaps he merely agreed with Emerson that a probing mind cannot permit itself to be vexed by the bugaboo of consistency.

No less enigmatic were Veblen's last days in California. Who can surmise what thoughts must have occupied him as he sat in his cabin in the hills outside of Palo Alto, staring into space as a stray wood rat or skunk brushed up against his baggy trousers? Did he succumb, in his final mood of elegiac resignation, to some secret suspicion that capitalist society had eluded the powerful net of his analysis? One thing is certain: the dynamics of Veblen's personality still elude the intellectual historian, even as they baffle the psychohistorian. Perhaps this is as it should be. He gave us the ideas and insights with which we now know better the subtle cultural forces, social pressures, and power realities of modern industrial society. He made the invisible world of values, habits, and customs seem real and tangible, and even a little silly. Indeed, he not only succeeded in adding comic relief to the "dismal science" of economics but endured the absurdities of social existence while keeping his own individuality stubbornly intact. What more can one ask of life? Should we trouble ourselves over the enduring "mystery" of his personality? Apparently it did not trouble him. Must we analyze the sources of his "discontent," or should we accept his alienation as the necessary condition of consciousness in the act of perception? "The world owes its onward impulses," advised Nathaniel Hawthorne, "to men ill at ease." (pp. 231-32)

> *John P. Diggins, in his* The Bard of Savagery: Thorstein Veblen and Modern Social Theory, *The Seabury Press, 1978, 257 p.*

ADDITIONAL BIBLIOGRAPHY

Adorno, Theodor W. "Veblen's Attack on Culture." In his *Prisms,* pp. 73-94. Cambridge, Mass.: MIT Press, 1982.
    Explores Veblen's critique of consumption and his theories about human adaptation and adjustment to changes in the social and cultural environment.

Bates, Ernest Sutherland. "Thorstein Veblen." *Scribner's Magazine* XCIV, No. 6 (December 1933): 354-60.
    Biographical study of Veblen and discussion of his "prophetic" economic analyses.

Bell, Daniel. "Veblen and the Technocrats." In his *The Writing Passage: Essays and Sociological Journeys, 1960-1980,* pp. 69-90. Cambridge, Mass.: ABT Books, 1980.
    Reprint of a 1963 essay summarizing Veblen's efforts to promote the idea of a ruling class of engineers.

Bell, Quentin. "Sartorial Morality" and "Deviations from Veblen." In his *On Human Finery,* pp. 15-24 and 179-85. New York: Shocken Books, 1976.
    Contends that Veblen's analysis of conspicuous display is the true manner to approach the phenomenon of fashion.

Brooks, John. "Veblen's Cow." In his *Showing Off in America,* pp. 74-83. Boston: Little, Brown and Company, 1979.
    Invokes Veblen's theories to explain the place of lawns and lawn care in American life.

Brooks, Van Wyck. "Chicago: Four Writers." In his *The Confident Years: 1885-1915,* pp. 185-200. London: J. M. Dent and Sons, 1952.
    Discusses Veblen's literary efforts in the context of his times.

Burke, Kenneth. "The 'Invidious' as Imitation in Veblen." In his *A Rhetoric of Motives,* pp. 127-32. New York: George Braziller, Inc., 1955.
    Examines the terminology that Veblen employed to describe the motivations for human behavior.

Commager, Henry Steele. "Veblen and the New Economics." In his *The American Mind: An Interpretation of American Thought and Char-*

acter Since the 1880's, pp. 227-46. New Haven: Yale University Press, 1950.

Analyzes Veblen's major ideas.

Cummings, John. "The Theory of the Leisure Class." *The Journal of Political Economy* 7, No. 4 (September 1899): 425-55.

Critiques the economic theory presented in *The Theory of the Leisure Class*.

Daugert, Stanley Matthew. *The Philosophy of Thorstein Veblen*. New York: King's Crown Press, 1950, 134 p.

Studies the origin and development of "Veblen's critical and theoretical views in philosophical analysis and speculation."

Dell, Floyd. "Peace?" *The Masses* IX, No. 9 (July 1917): 40-1.

Review of *An Inquiry into the Nature of Peace and the Terms of Its Perpetuation*. Dell calls Veblen "the most brilliant and perhaps the most profound of American scholars."

Diggins, John P. "Dos Passos and Veblen's Villains." *The Antioch Review* XXIII, No. 4 (Winter 1963-64): 485-500.

Traces themes in several of John Dos Passos's novels to Veblen's social and economic theories.

Dobriansky, Lev E. *Veblenism: A New Critique*. Washington, D.C.: Public Affairs Press, 1957, 409 p.

Argues that Veblen's ideas, when stripped of the style in which he presented them, are essentially akin to modern pragmatism and are not especially profound.

Dorfman, Joseph. *Thorstein Veblen and His America*. New York: Augustus M. Kelley, 1961, 572 p.

Standard biography of Veblen.

Dos Passos, John. "The Bitter Drink." In his *U.S.A.: The Big Money*, pp. 93-105. New York: Harcourt, Brace & Co., 1930.

Impressionistic description of Veblen's life and influences, noting that he "suffered from a constitutional inability to say yes."

Dowd, Douglas F., ed. *Thorstein Veblen: A Critical Reappraisal*. Ithaca: Cornell University Press, 1958, 328 p.

Collection of retrospective essays by Joseph Dorfman, Walton Hamilton, C. E. Ayres, Norman Kaplan, Morris A. Copeland, Lawrence Nabers, Melvin D. Brockie, Forest G. Hill, Allan G. Gruchy, Paul M. Sweezy, Joel B. Dirlam, Leslie Fishman, Philip Morrison, Muron W. Watkins, Carter Goodrich, Douglas F. Dowd, and G. W. Zinke.

Duffus, Robert L. *The Innocents at Cedro: A Memoir of Thorstein Veblen and Some Others*. New York: Macmillan Co., 1944, 163 p.

Recounts his experiences with Veblen while he was living with him in 1907-08.

Dugger, William M. "Veblen and Kropotkin on Human Evolution." *Journal of Economic Issues* XVIII, No. 4 (December 1984): 971-85.

Argues that whereas Kropotkin's human evolutionary theory mainly tried to show the importance of group-seeking behavior, Veblen's theory tried to explain how both group-seeking and self-seeking behavior influenced human evolution.

Galbraith, John Kenneth. "The American Mood." In his *The Affluent Society*, pp. 48-63. Boston: Houghton Mifflin Company, 1958.

Discusses Veblen's iconoclastic position in economics.

Hall, Robert A. "Thorstein Veblen and Linguistic Theory." *American Speech* XXXV, No. 2 (May 1960): 124-30.

Examines the chapter "Usage, Spelling, and Conspicuous Waste" in *The Theory of the Leisure Class*.

Harris, Abram L. "Thorstein Veblen: Toward a Soviet of Technicians." In his *Economics and Social Reform*, pp. 156-213. New York: Harper and Brothers, 1958.

Analyzes Veblen's social philosophy, noting that the popularity of "the idea of substituting a system of planning by technical experts for management by businessmen" is "traceable directly to the influence of Thorstein Veblen."

Heilbroner, Robert L. "The Savage World of Thorstein Veblen." In his *The Worldly Philosophers: The Lives, Times and Ideas of the Great Economic Thinkers*, pp. 181-213. New York: Simon and Shuster, 1961.

Emphasizes Veblen's importance as an economist and social philosopher.

Hobson, John A. *Veblen*. New York: John Wiley & Sons, 1937, 227 p.

Examines Veblen's attitudes on economics, Karl Marx, and socialism.

Homan, Paul T. "Thorstein Veblen." In *American Masters of Social Science*, edited by Howard W. Odum, pp. 231-70. Port Washington, N.Y.: Kennikat Press, 1927.

Argues that Veblen, while criticizing orthodox economic theory, supplied an institutional theory based on human instincts and habits of thought which "served to jar the younger generation of economists out of the rut of traditional habits of thought before they were deeply settled in them."

Lapham, Lewis H. "Veblen Revisited: A Theory of the Leisure State." *Harper's* 255, No. 1530 (November 1977): 8, 12, 15.

Describes modern American society in terms of Veblen's explanation of conspicuous waste.

Mitchell, Wesley C. Introduction to *What Veblen Taught*, pp. vii-xlviii. New York: The Viking Press, 1936.

Discusses Veblen's major ideas, his worldview, and his "characteristic animus."

Mumford, Lewis. "A Stick of Dynamite Wrapped Like Candy." *The Saturday Review of Literature* XI, No. 26 (12 January 1935): 417, 421-22.

Argues that Veblen is America's outstanding social scientist and satirist.

Noble, David W. "Dreiser and Veblen: The Literature of Cultural Change." *Social Research* 24, No. 3 (Autumn 1957): 311-29.

Compares Veblen's ideas about human progress to those of Theodore Dreiser.

————. "Thorstein Veblen: The Economist as Scientist and Prophet." In his *The Paradox of Progressive Thought*, pp. 199-227. Minneapolis: University of Minnesota Press, 1958.

Discusses Veblen's views on the relationship of science to social progress.

Pluta, Joseph E. and Leathers, Charles G. "Veblen and Modern Radical Economics." *Journal of Economic Issues* XII, No. 1 (March 1978): 125-46.

Traces the similarities and differences between the theories of modern radical economists and those of Veblen.

Riesman, David. *Thorstein Veblen: A Critical Interpretation*. New York: Charles Scribner's Sons, 1953, 221 p.

Explains Veblen's theories with reference to his background and personality, emphasizing the ambiguity and contradictions of Veblen's thought.

Rosenberg, Bernard. *The Values of Veblen: A Critical Appraisal*. Washington, D.C.: Public Affairs Press, 1956, 127 p.

Assesses Veblen's contribution to the social sciences, classing him with De Tocqueville and William Sumner as a social scientist "who teaches us very little about research methods but whose books are 'important, influential, and meritorious'."

Schlesinger, Arthur M., Jr. "The Philosophy of Liberalism." In his *The Age of Roosevelt, Vol. 1: The Crisis of the Old Order, 1919-1933*, pp. 13-44. Boston: Houghton Mifflin Co., 1957.

Discusses how Veblen's work helped establish the liberal ideas that "classical economics was fundamentally wrong" and that "intelligent planning could abolish the nonsense of scarcity."

Schneider, Louis. *The Freudian Psychology and Veblen's Social Theory*. Westport, Conn.: Greenwood Press, 1974, 270 p.

Analyzes the connections between Freudian psychology and Veblen's theories of social behavior.

Seckler, David. *Thorstein Veblen and the Institutionalists: A Study in the Social Philosophy of Economics*. Boulder: Colorado Associated University Press, 1975, 190 p.
    Analyzes major aspects of Veblen's work, noting that his general theorizing is out of vogue and that his contributions both to economics and to social philosophy are no longer highly valued.

Simich, J. L. "Thorstein Veblen and his Marxist Critics: An Interpretive Review." *History of Political Economy* 14, No. 3 (Fall 1982): 323-41.
    Discusses the attitudes of various Marxist theorists to Veblen's ideas.

————and Tilman, Rick. "Critical Theory and Institutional Economics: Frankfurt's Encounter with Veblen." *Journal of Economic Issues* XIV, No. 3 (September 1980): 631-48.
    Examines similarities and differences between the Frankfurt School of Economics and Veblen, noting how the ideas of both might be synthesized to obtain a better understanding of contemporary social problems.

————and Tilman, Rick. *Thorstein Veblen: A Reference Guide*. Boston: G. K. Hall & Co., 1985, 217 p.
    Annotated bibliography of writings on Veblen from 1891 to 1982.

Teggart, Richard Victor. *Thorstein Veblen: A Chapter in Economic Thought*. Berkley: University of California Press, 1942, 125 p.

Studies the cultural and intellectual influences on Veblen's life and writings, his critical approach to the problems of economics, and his technique of social criticism.

Tilman, Rick. "Some Recent Interpretations of Thorstein Veblen's Theory of Institutional Change." *Journal of Economic Issues* XXI, No. 2 (June 1987): 683-90.
    Reviews recent scholarship on Veblen's theory of institutional change.

Vining, Rutledge. "Suggestions of Keynes in the Writings of Veblen." *The Journal of Political Economy* 47, No. 5 (October 1939): 692-704.
    Compares the economic theories of Keynes and Veblen.

Ward, Lester F. Review of *The Theory of the Leisure Class*, by Thorstein Veblen. *The American Journal of Sociology* V, No. 6 (May 1900): 829-37.
    Defends the basic arguments of *The Theory of the Leisure Class*.

Wells, B. W. Review of *The Theory of the Leisure Class*, by Thorstein Veblen. *The Sewanee Review* VII, No. 3 (July 1899): 369-74.
    Maintains that *The Theory of the Leisure Class* is worth reading not for its serious contribution to economic theory but for the amusement that its social satire affords.

Wells, D. Collin. Review of *The Theory of the Leisure Class*, by Thorstein Veblen. *The Yale Review* VIII, No. 2 (August 1899): 213-18.
    Hostile review, calling the book "pretentious" and not founded upon economic data.

William Butler Yeats

1865-1939

(See also *TCLC*, Vols. 1, 11, and 18.)

Irish poet, dramatist, essayist, critic, short story writer, and autobiographer.

Yeats is considered one of the greatest poets in the English language. Although his interest in Irish politics and his visionary approach to poetry often confounded his contemporaries and set him at odds with the intellectual trends of his time, Yeats's poetic achievement stands at the center of modern literature. His poetry evolved over five decades from the vague imagery and uncertain rhythms of *The Wanderings of Oisin, and Other Poems,* his first important work, to the forceful, incantatory verse of the *Last Poems.* His remarkable creative development in his final years illustrates a lifelong determination to remake himself into his ideal image of the poet: a sacerdotal figure who assumes the role of mediator between the conflicting forces of the objective and subjective worlds. Yeats was devoted to the cause of Irish nationalism and played an important part in the Celtic Revival Movement, founding an Irish literary theater, the Abbey, with the help of Lady Augusta Gregory and J. M. Synge. Yeats also promoted the literary heritage of Ireland through his use of material from ancient Irish sagas in his poems, dramas, and short stories. Desiring to recapture the Ireland of heroic times, he believed that only by "expressing primary truths in ways appropriate to this country" could artists hope to restore to modern Ireland the cultural unity that he felt was needed to bring an end to his country's internal division and suffering. In addition to the myths and history of Ireland, magic and occult theory were also important elements in Yeats's work. Yeats viewed the poet as kindred to the magician and the alchemist, and he was deeply interested in spiritualism, theosophy, and occult systems. Many of the images found in his poetry are derived from Rosicrucianism and his own occult researches as described in the prose work *A Vision.*

Yeats was born in Dublin. His father, J. B. (Jack) Yeats, was the son of a once-affluent family whom Oscar Wilde's father, Sir William Wilde, described as "the cleverest, most spirited people I ever met." For as long as he lived, Jack Yeats, himself an artist, exercised an important influence on his son's thoughts about art. Yeats's mother, Susan Pollexfen, was the daughter of a successful merchant from Sligo in western Ireland. Many of the Pollexfens were intense, eccentric people interested in faeries and astrology. From his mother Yeats inherited a love of Ireland, particularly the region surrounding Sligo, and an interest in folklore.

Yeats received no formal education until he was eleven years old, when he began attending the Godolphin Grammar School in Hammersmith, England. He continued his education in Ireland at the Erasmus Smith High School in Dublin. Generally, he was a disappointing student—erratic in his studies, prone to daydreaming, shy, and poor at sports. In 1884, Yeats enrolled in the Metropolitan School of Art in Dublin, where he met the poet George Russell (A.E.). Russell shared Yeats's enthusiasm for dreams and visions, and together they founded the Dublin Hermetic Society for the purposes of conducting

magical experiments and promoting their belief that "whatever the great poets had affirmed in their finest moments was the nearest we could come to an authoritative religion and that their mythology and their spirits of water and wind were but literal truth." This event marked the beginning for Yeats of a lifelong interest in occult studies, the extent of which was only revealed by the examination of his unpublished notebooks after his death. Following his experience with the Hermetic Society, Yeats joined the Rosicrucians, the Theosophical Society, and MacGregor Mathers's Order of the Golden Dawn. He frequently consulted spiritualists and engaged in the ritual conjuring of Irish gods. Yeats found occult research a rich source of images for his poetry, and traces of his esoteric interests appear everywhere in his poems. "The Rose upon the Rood of Time," for example, takes its central symbol from Rosicrucianism, and "All Soul's Night" describes a scrying, or divination, ceremony.

In 1885, Yeats met the Irish nationalist John O'Leary, who was instrumental in arranging for the publication of Yeats's first poems in *The Dublin University Review* and in directing Yeats's attention to native Irish sources for subject matter. Under the influence of O'Leary, Yeats took up the cause of Gaelic writers at a time when much native Irish literature was in danger of being lost as the result of England's attempts to anglicize Ireland through a ban on the Gaelic language. O'Leary's ardent nationalism and resolute opposition to violence also impressed Yeats and were instrumental in shaping political views that he held for the rest of his life. Perhaps the most fateful day in Yeats's life was January 30th, 1889, when he met the actress Maud Gonne, an agitator for the nationalist cause whose great beauty and reckless destructiveness in pursuit of her political goals both intrigued and dismayed him. He began accompanying her to political rallies, and though he often disagreed with her extremist tactics, he shared her desire to see Ireland freed from English domination. During this period he wrote the drama *Cathleen ni Houlihan* for Gonne, and she was featured in the title role in its initial production. Yeats considered the play, which is about a noblewoman who sells her soul to the devil in order to save starving peasants, as appropriately symbolic of the activities to which Gonne had dedicated her life. Although Gonne's repeated refusals to marry Yeats brought him great personal unhappiness, their relationship endured through many estrangements, including her brief marriage to Major John MacBride, and nearly all of the love poetry that Yeats wrote during his career is addressed to her. In his verses she is associated with Helen of Troy, whose capriciousness led to the destruction of a civilization. To Yeats she represented an ideal, and throughout his life he found the tension between them, as well as their friendship, a source of poetic inspiration.

It was not until 1917, when he was fifty-two years old, that Yeats married. On their honeymoon his young wife, Georgiana Hyde-Lees, discovered that she had mediumistic abilities and through the technique of automatic writing could receive communication from a supernatural realm. Her efforts over many months produced the notes and materials on which Yeats based the text of *A Vision*—his explanation of historical cycles and a theory of human personality based on the phases of the moon. Late in his life, when decades of struggle by the Irish nationalists had finally culminated in the passage of the Home Rule Bill, Yeats became a senator for the Irish Free State. He left the senate in 1928 because of failing health, intending to devote his remaining years to poetry. He died in 1939.

In his earliest poetic works, such as *Mosada*, Yeats took his symbols from Greek mythology; however, after meeting John O'Leary, he turned instead to Irish mythology as a source for his images. The long narrative poem, "The Wanderings of Oisin" was the first he based on the legend of an Irish hero. In spite of its self-consciously poetic language and immature imitations of Pre-Raphaelite poetic technique, the poem's theme—the disagreement between Oisin and St. Patrick—makes it important to an understanding of the later Yeats. The sense of conflict between vision and corporeal realities, as symbolized by the saint and the hero, is the essential dichotomy in Yeats's poetry. Throughout his poetic career Yeats's chief concern was to resolve the disparity between the imaginative individual's need to seek immortality through renunciation of the world of "mire and blood," and the instinctive human love of what perishes. He believed such a resolution was necessary because the world of pure forms was impotent without its connection to life, but he also recognized that only through imagination could the raw materials of life be transformed into something enduring. For Yeats, the role of the artist was the same as that of the alchemist: he must effect a transformation that obscures the distinction between form and content, between "the dancer and the dance." This theme is most effectively expressed in the later poems "Sailing to Byzantium" and "Byzantium."

As Yeats grew older and more sure of his themes, his approach to the techniques of poetry changed. Recognizing that faerie songs were less suited to the tragic themes that preoccupied him than were more realistic narratives, he began, with the poems of *In the Seven Woods*, to write verses describing actual events in his personal life or in the history of Ireland. One of his most famous lyrics, "Easter 1916," about a rebel uprising that resulted in the martyrdom of all who participated, belongs to this latter group. In his maturity, Yeats wrote little narrative poetry. Instead he adopted the dramatic lyric as his most characteristic form of expression. Influenced by Ezra Pound, he simplified his diction and modified his syntax to more closely reflect the constructions of common speech, and in works such as *Responsibilities, and Other Poems, The Wild Swans at Coole,* and *Michael Robartes and the Dancer,* his verses began to take on the rhetorical, occasionally haughty tone that readers today identify as characteristically Yeatsian. Critics agree that Yeats's poetic technique was impeccable. It was this mastery of technique that enabled him to perfect the subtle, forceful, and highly unusual poetic meter that he used to create the effect of a chant or an incantation in such poems as "The Tower."

Yeats considered his dramas an aspect of his plan to revitalize Irish culture. He wanted to create dramas that were symbolic and austere—a reflection not of life, but of "the deeps of the mind." However, the form that such dramas should take and the manner in which they should be staged eluded him for many years. In his early works, such as *The Shadowy Waters* and *The Land of Heart's Desire,* he found that conventional stage techniques and realistic characters were not suited to the poetic portrayal of spiritual truths and psychological realities. It was not until Pound introduced him to the ancient Nō plays of Japan that he found a form he felt was suited to the heroic and tragic subjects that he wished to depict. In *Four Plays for Dancers,* as well as in subsequent works such as *Purgatory,* Yeats experimented with techniques borrowed from the Nō, such as ritualized, symbolic action and the use of masks. These plays contain some of his most highly regarded verse, and critics now believe that Yeats's approach to drama in many ways anticipated later developments in modern theater.

Yeats's most important prose writings are his *Autobiographies* and *The Celtic Twilight*. A source of controversy among critics, Yeats's *Autobiographies* provides a sensitive, if sometimes ironic, view of his age while revealing little about his own life and thoughts. Even his close friend George Russell, in reviewing the *Autobiographies*, criticized Yeats for these omissions. Nonetheless, these memoirs are a valuable source of information about Yeats's views on art and his theories of personality. In *The Celtic Twilight,* his collection of Irish folktales, Yeats endeavored to record the folk legends of Irish peasants in a simple and dignified manner, rather than in the patronizing and comic way such materials were often treated by English writers. Yeats not only wished to preserve these legends, he also wanted to make them more widely available to the Irish people, who had lost touch with ancient Irish traditions. He sought in this way to promote the "unity of culture" that he believed could only be achieved in modern Ireland through an increased awareness of Ireland's heroic past.

Yeats was awarded the Nobel Prize in literature in 1923. However, for many years his intent interest in subjects that others labelled archaic and perceived as an affront to their modernity delayed his recognition among his peers. At the time of his death in 1939, Yeats's views on poetry were regarded as eccentric by students and critics alike. This attitude held sway in spite of critical awareness of the beauty and technical proficiency of his verse. Yeats had long opposed the notion that literature should serve society. As a youthful critic he had refused to praise the poor lyrics of the "Young Ireland" poets merely because they were effective as nationalist propaganda. In maturity, he found that despite his success, his continuing conviction that poetry should express the spiritual life of the individual estranged him from those who believed that a modern poet must take as his themes social alienation and the barrenness of materialist culture. As Kathleen Raine wrote of him: "Against a rising tide of realism, political verse and University wit, Yeats upheld the innocent and the beautiful, the traditional and the noble," and in consequence of his disregard for the concerns of the modern world, was often misunderstood. As critics became disenchanted with modern poetic trends, Yeats's Romantic dedication to the laws of the imagination and art for art's sake became more acceptable. Indeed, critics today are less concerned with the validity of Yeats's occult and visionary theories than with their symbolic value as expressions of timeless ideals, considering his interest in arcana as a manifestation of the truth of Wallace Stevens's statement that "poets are never of the world in which they live."

(See also *Contemporary Authors*, Vol. 104; *Dictionary of Literary Biography*, Vol. 10: *Modern British Dramatists, 1900-1945;* and Vol. 19: *British Poets, 1880-1914*.)

PRINCIPAL WORKS

Mosada (poetry) 1886
The Wanderings of Oisin, and Other Poems (poetry) 1889
The Countess Cathleen, and Various Legends and Lyrics (poetry) 1892
The Celtic Twilight (folklore) 1893
The Land of Heart's Desire (drama) 1894
Collected Poems (poetry) 1895
The Secret Rose (short stories) 1897
The Wind among the Reeds (poetry) 1899
The Shadowy Waters (drama) 1900
Cathleen ni Houlihan [with Lady Gregory] (drama) 1902
The Hour-Glass [with Lady Gregory] (drama) 1903
Ideas of Good and Evil (essays) 1903
In the Seven Woods (poetry) 1903
The King's Threshold [with Lady Gregory] (drama) 1903
On Baile's Strand (drama) 1904
Stories of Red Hanrahan (short stories) 1904
Deirdre [with Lady Gregory] (drama) 1906
Discoveries (essays) 1907
The Unicorn from the Stars [with Lady Gregory] (drama) 1907
The Golden Helmet (drama) 1908
Poetry and Ireland [with Lionel Johnson] (essays) 1908
The Green Helmet, and Other Poems (poetry) 1910
Responsibilities, and Other Poems (poetry) 1914
At the Hawk's Well (drama) 1916
The Wild Swans at Coole (poetry) 1917
Per Amica Silentia Lunae (essay) 1918
The Player Queen (drama) 1919
Michael Robartes and the Dancer (poetry) 1920
Four Plays for Dancers [first publication] (dramas) 1921
Four Years: 1887-91 (memoir) 1921
Later Poems (poetry) 1922
The Cat and the Moon, and Certain Poems (poetry) 1924

A Vision (essay) 1925; also published as *A Vision* [enlarged edition], 1937
*Autobiographies (memoir) 1926; also published as *The Autobiography of William Butler Yeats* [enlarged edition], 1938
The Tower (poetry) 1928
The Winding Stair (poetry) 1929
The Dreaming of the Bones (drama) 1931
Words for Music Perhaps, and Other Poems (poetry) 1932
The Collected Poems of W. B. Yeats (poetry) 1933
The Collected Plays of W. B. Yeats (dramas) 1934; also published as *The Collected Plays of W. B. Yeats* [enlarged edition], 1952.
The King of the Great Clock Tower (poetry) 1934
Wheels and Butterflies (drama) 1934
A Full Moon in March (poetry and dramas) 1935
The Herne's Egg (drama) 1938
New Poems (poetry) 1938
Purgatory (drama) 1938
Last Poems and Two Plays (poetry and dramas) 1939
On the Boiler (essays and poems) 1939
Last Poems and Plays (poetry and dramas) 1940
The Death of Cuchulain (drama) 1949
The Letters of W. B. Yeats (letters) 1954
W. B. Yeats: Essays and Introductions (essays) 1961
The Poems: A New Edition (poetry) 1983

*This work includes the memoirs *Reveries over Childhood and Youth* and *The Trembling of the Veil*. The enlarged edition of 1938 also includes the memoirs *Dramatis Personae, Estrangement, The Death of Synge,* and *The Bounty of Sweden*.

EZRA POUND (essay date 1914)

[*Pound, an American poet and critic, is regarded as one of the most innovative and influential figures in twentieth-century Anglo-American poetry. He was instrumental in obtaining editorial and financial assistance for T. S. Eliot, Wyndham Lewis, James Joyce, and William Carlos Williams, among others. His own* Cantos, *published throughout his life, is among the most ambitious poetic cycles of the century, and his series of satirical poems* Hugh Selwyn Mauberly (1920) *is ranked with Eliot's* The Waste Land (1922) *as a significant attack upon the decadence of modern culture. In the following excerpt, Pound considers with what success Yeats recast his poetic style in* Responsibilities.]

I live, so far as possible, among that more intelligently active segment of the race which is concerned with today and tomorrow; and, in consequence of this, whenever I mention Mr. Yeats I am apt to be assailed with questions: "Will Mr. Yeats do anything more?", "Is Yeats in the movement?", "How *can* the chap go on writing this sort of thing?"

And to these inquiries I can only say that Mr. Yeats' vitality is quite unimpaired, and that I dare say he'll do a good deal; and that up to date no one has shown any disposition to supersede him as the best poet in England, or any likelihood of doing so for some time; and that after all Mr. Yeats has brought a new music upon the harp, and that one man seldom leads two movements to triumph, and that it is quite enough that he should have brought in the sound of keening and the skirl of the Irish ballads, and driven out the sentimental cadence with memories of **"The County of Mayo"** and **"The Coolun"**; and that the production of good poetry is a very slow matter, and that, as touching the greatest of dead poets, many of them could easily have left that *magnam partem,* which keeps them with us, upon a single quire of foolscap or at most upon two; and that there is no need for a poet to repair each morning of his life to the *Piazza dei Signori* to turn a new sort of somersault; and that Mr. Yeats is so assuredly an immortal that there is no need for him to recast his style to suit our winds of doctrine; and that, all these things being so, there is nevertheless a manifestly new note in his later work that they might do worse than attend to.

"Is Mr. Yeats an Imagiste?" No, Mr. Yeats is a symbolist, but he has written *des Images* as have many good poets before him; so that is nothing against him, and he has nothing against them (*les Imagistes*), at least so far as I know—except what he calls "their devil's metres."

He has written *des Images* in such poems as **"Braseal and the Fisherman"**; beginning, "Though you hide in the ebb and flow of the pale tide when the moon has set"; and he has driven out the inversion and written with prose directness in such lyrics as, "I heard the old men say everything alters"; and these things are not subject to a changing of the fashions. What I mean by the new note—you could hardly call it a change of style—was apparent four years ago in his **"No Second Troy,"** beginning, "Why should I blame her," and ending—

> Beauty like a tightened bow, a kind
> That is not natural in any age like this,
> Being high and solitary and most stern?
> Why, what could she have done being what she is?
> Was there another Troy for her to burn?

I am not sure that it becomes apparent in partial quotation, but with the appearance of *The Green Helmet, and Other Poems* one felt that the minor note—I use the word strictly in the musical sense—had gone or was going out of his poetry; that he was at such a cross roads as we find in

> *Voi che intendendo il terzo ciel movete.*

> ["O you whose intellects turn the third great wheel"]

And since that time one has felt his work becoming gaunter, seeking greater hardness of outline. I do not say that this is demonstrable by any particular passage. **"Romantic Ireland's Dead and Gone"** is no better than Red Hanrahan's song about Ireland, but it is harder. Mr. Yeats appears to have seen with the outer eye in **"To a Child Dancing on the Shore"**. . . . The hardness can perhaps be more easily noted in **"The Magi."**

Such poems as **"When Helen Lived"** and **"The Realists"** serve at least to show that the tongue has not lost its cunning. On the other hand, it is impossible to take any interest in a poem like **"The Two Kings"**—one might as well read the *Idyls* of another. **"The Grey Rock"** is, I admit, obscure, but it outweighs this by a curious nobility, a nobility which is, to me at least, the very core of Mr. Yeats' production, the constant element of his writing.

In support of my prediction, or of my theories, regarding his change of manner, real or intended, we have at least two pronouncements of the poet himself, the first in **"A Coat,"** and the second, less formal, in the speech made at the Blunt presentation. The verses, **"A Coat,"** should satisfy those who have complained of Mr. Yeats' four and forty followers, that they would "rather read their Yeats in the original." Mr. Yeats had indicated the feeling once before with

> Tell me, do the wolf-dogs praise their fleas?

which is direct enough in all conscience, and free of the "glamour." I've not a word against the glamour as it appears in Yeats' early poems, but we have had so many other pseudo-glamours and glamourlets and mists and fogs since the nineties that one is about ready for hard light.

And this quality of hard light is precisely what one finds in the beginning of his **"The Magi"**:

> Now as at all times I can see in the mind's eye.
> In their stiff, painted clothes, the pale unsatisfied ones
> Appear and disappear in the blue depth of the sky
> With all their ancient faces like rain-beaten stones,
> And all their helms of silver hovering side by side.

Of course a passage like that, a passage of *imagisme,* may occur in a poem not otherwise *imagiste,* in the same way that a lyrical passage may occur in a narrative, or in some poem not otherwise lyrical. There have always been two sorts of poetry which are, for me at least, the most "poetic"; they are firstly, the sort of poetry which seems to be music just forcing itself into articulate speech, and, secondly, that sort of poetry which seems as if sculpture or painting were just forced or forcing itself into words. The gulf between evocation and description, in this latter case, is the unbridgeable difference between genius and talent. It is perhaps the highest function of art that it should fill the mind with a noble profusion of sounds and images, that it should furnish the life of the mind with such accompaniment and surrounding. At any rate Mr. Yeats' work has done this in the past and still continues to do so. (pp. 64-8)

> *Ezra Pound, "The Later Yeats," in* Poetry, *Vol. IV, No. 11, May, 1914, pp. 64-9.*

LUDWIG LEWISOHN   (essay date 1915)

[*A German-born American novelist and critic, Lewisohn was considered an authority on German literature, and his translations are widely respected. In 1919 he became the drama critic for* The Nation, *serving as its associate editor until 1924, when he joined a group of expatriates in Paris. After his return to the United States in 1934, Lewisohn became a prominent sympathizer with the Zionist movement, and served as editor of the Jewish magazine* New Palestine *for five years. Many of his late works reflect his humanistic concern for the plight of the Jewish people. In the following excerpt, Lewisohn objects to the neo-romanticism of Yeats's dramas.*]

So much has recently been written of the Irish movement by people who understand it well, that I shall let my own account of it be quite brief. And I am the more impelled to such brevity by the suspicion that I look upon these Irish plays with the eyes of a stranger who, though most eager to understand and to sympathise with the latest productions of a brave and charming race, feels his eyes dimmed by these infinite patterns in faintest green and grey and silver, and his ears dulled by the endless and endlessly subdued murmur of these

> Old, unhappy, far-off things
> And battles long ago.

My vision is at the breaking point for a note of colour, my hearing for a tone of passion. In vain. When her beloved dies without a glance for her and Grania turns to Finn in the wild bitterness of her grief, her speech remains like an exquisite decorative pattern in style. And indeed I think it is meant to be so from two passages I find in Mr. Yeats' *Ideas of Good and Evil.* "I would like to see a poetical drama which tries to keep at a distance from daily life that it may keep its emotion untroubled, staged with but two or three colours.'' And further on in the same remarkable book he confesses his conviction that ''the hour of convention and decoration and ceremony is coming again.'' Reading these sentences and thinking of Mr. Yeats' *The Shadowy Waters* or Lady Gregory's *Dervorgilla*, I see that this art intentionally approaches a decoration and a ceremony, in the mystical and religious sense, and thus deliberately, from my point of view, renounces the vitality and meaningfulness reserved for art that grows from the immediate experience of the impassioned soul. I can understand a drama that would ''keep at a distance from daily life''; but a drama that would thereby ''keep its emotion untroubled,'' that is to say the emotion (if I understand rightly) it is trying to express, is frankly lyrical or decorative and not dramatic at all.

Behind these theories of art there hovers, of course, a vision of the world. When Mr. Yeats writes,

> How shall I name you, immortal, mild, proud shadows?
> I only know that all we know comes from you,
> And that you come from Eden on flying feet,

I am aware of that joy which is the perception of beauty. For this verse is like the swaying of roadside grasses and there is a faint, wild, inimitable pathos in its uncertain cadences. But, unless I stupidly misunderstand, Mr. Yeats expresses here what is to him not a sentiment but a conviction. He really believes that the legends of Celtic antiquity contain a mystic truth which is the key to the door of the world's secrets. In other words his art is based upon a vision of things which is not only unreal but, if one must be frank, puerile.

In addition, there is in Mr. Yeats' work a kind of wild logic, like the logic of mad people. That quality may be illustrated by the play in prose *Where There Is Nothing*. At the opening of the play Paul Ruttledge is overtaken, like most of us in our more illuminated moments, by a sense of the utter triviality of practical things, of possessions and conventions and laws. So he joins the tinkers and there is some very excellent description of the roadside life. Interesting, too, and humorous is the trial of the Christians in the fourth act, though it is based upon an obviously unfair assumption. But Paul is unaccustomed to exposure and must leave the road to take refuge in a monastery. Here he develops his early rebellion against a worldly and materialistic life into a heresy for which he and his adherents are driven out. And the apparently logical but quite mad conclusions to which he has come, are summed up thus: ''We must destroy all that has law and number!'' ''Where there is nothing, there is God!'' Now it is obvious that law, in the sense of natural law, and number, do not inhere in things at all, but are the human mind's really very mysterious way of dealing with things and subduing them into order and helpfulness. You cannot destroy law by destroying things, but only by destroying physicists; you cannot destroy number except by destroying mathematicians. In brief, Mr. Yeats not only believes like a child, he also reasons like a child. And that is bound to vitiate a work of art the main business of which is to reason about life and things.

Mr. Yeats' plays in verse are always sustained as literature, if not as drama, by the enchanting beauty of their medium, by that ''speech, delighted with its own music,'' though even here one often yearns for emphasis, concentration, density. Some of these plays, moreover, are no less exquisite for their meaning than for their form. I am not thinking of *The Countess Cathleen* which carries but a commonplace moral in the end, but of *The Land of Heart's Desire* in which the old Pagan world of visible charm and brightness and beauty captures the Irish lass, and

pre-eminently of that pregnant poem *The King's Threshold* with its fine protest against the least compromise on the supreme and eternal issues; with its great reply of the poet Seanchan to his beloved:

> If I had eaten when you bid me, sweetheart,
> The kiss of multitudes in time to come
> Had been the poorer;

and with its brave emphasis upon the arts which are the light of the world:

> Comparing them to venerable things
> God gave to men before he gave them wheat.

In these plays Mr. Yeats has seen ''the world as imagination sees it'' and that, indeed, as he says, is ''the durable world.'' But very often he and his fellow workers in the Irish movement have described a world which only their very special kind of imagination has seen at all, and it is then that their art seems fragile and evanescent and a little empty. (pp. 267-72)

> *Ludwig Lewisohn, ''The Irish Movement,'' in his* The Modern Drama: An Essay in Interpretation, *B. W. Huebsch, Inc., 1915, pp. 265-74.*

J. MIDDLETON MURRY   (essay date 1919)

[*Murry is recognized as one of the most significant English critics and editors of the twentieth century. Anticipating later scholarly opinion, he championed the writings of Marcel Proust, James Joyce, Paul Valéry, D. H. Lawrence, and the poetry of Thomas Hardy through his positions as the editor of the* Athenaeum *and as a long-time contributor to the* Times Literary Supplement *and other periodicals. In his early exposition on literary appreciation,* The Problem of Style *(1922), Murry espoused a theoretical premise that underlies all his criticism: that in order to fully evaluate a writer's achievement the critic must search for crucial passages which effectively ''crystallize'' the writer's innermost impressions and convictions regarding life. In the following excerpt, Murry examines Yeats's use of myth and imagination in* The Wild Swans At Coole, *concluding that the allusive style of that work masks a profound lack of substance.*]

In the preface to *The Wild Swans at Coole,* Mr. W. B. Yeats speaks of ''the phantasmagoria through which alone I can express my convictions about the world.'' The challenge could hardly be more direct. At the threshold we are confronted with a legend upon the door-post which gives us the essential plan of all that we shall find in the house if we enter in. There are, it is true, a few things capable of common use, verses written in the seeming-strong vernacular of literary Dublin, as it were a hospitable bench placed outside the door. They are indeed inside the house, but by accident or for temporary shelter. They do not, as the phrase goes, belong to the scheme, for they are direct transcriptions of the common reality, whether found in the sensible world or the emotion of the mind. They are, from Mr. Yeats's angle of vision (as indeed from our own), essentially *vers d'occasion* [''occasional verses''].

The poet's high and passionate argument must be sought elsewhere, and precisely in his expression of his convictions about the world. And here, on the poet's word and the evidence of our search, we shall find phantasmagoria, ghostly symbols of a truth which cannot be otherwise conveyed, at least by Mr. Yeats. To this, in itself, we make no demur. The poet, if he is a true poet, is driven to approach the highest reality he can apprehend. He cannot transcribe it simply because he does not possess the necessary apparatus of knowledge, and because if he did possess it his passion would flag. . . . Therefore the poet turns to myth as a foundation upon which he can explicate his imagination. He may take his myth from legend or familiar history, or he may create one for himself anew; but the function it fulfils is always the same. It supplies the elements with which he can build the structure of his parable, upon which he can make it elaborate enough to convey the multitudinous reactions of his soul to the world.

But between myths and phantasmagoria there is a great gulf. The structural possibilities of the myth depend upon its intelligibility. The child knows upon what drama, played in what world, the curtain will rise when he hears the trumpet-note: "Of man's first disobedience. . . ." And, even when the poet turns from legend and history to create his own myth, he must make one whose validity is visible, if he is not to be condemned to the sterility of a coterie. The lawless and fantastic shapes of his own imagination need, even for their own perfect embodiment, the discipline of the common perception. The phantoms of the individual brain, left to their own waywardness, lose all solidity and become like primary forms of life, instead of the penultimate forms they should be. For the poet himself must move securely among his visions; they must be not less certain and steadfast than men are. To anchor them he needs intelligible myth. Nothing less than a supremely great genius can save him if he ventures into the vast without a landmark visible to other eyes than his own. Blake had a supremely great genius and was saved in part. The masculine vigour of his passion gave stability to the figures of his imagination. They are heroes because they are made to speak like heroes. Even in Blake's most recondite work there is always the moment when the clouds are parted and we recognise the austere and awful countenances of gods. The phantasmagoria of the dreamer have been mastered by the sheer creative will of the poet. (pp. 39-41)

The effort which such momentary victories demand is almost superhuman; yet to possess the power to exert it is the sole condition upon which a poet may plunge into the world of phantasms. Mr. Yeats has too little of the power to vindicate himself from the charge of idle dreaming. He knows the problem; perhaps he has also known the struggle. But the very terms in which he suggests it to us subtly convey a sense of impotence:—

> Hands, do what you're bid;
> Bring the balloon of the mind
> That bellies and drags in the wind
> Into its narrow shed.

The languor and ineffectuality of the image tell us clearly how the poet has failed in his larger task; its exactness, its precise expression of an ineffectuality made conscious and condoned, bears equal witness to the poet's minor probity. He remains an artist by determination, even though he returns downcast and defeated from the great quest of poetry. We were inclined at first, seeing those four lines enthroned in majestic isolation on a page, to find in them evidence of an untoward conceit. Subsequently they have seemed to reveal a splendid honesty. Although it has little mysterious and haunting beauty, *The Wild Swans at Coole* is indeed a swan song. It is eloquent of final defeat; the following of a lonely path has ended in the poet's sinking exhausted in a wilderness of gray. Not even the regret is passionate; it is pitiful. (pp. 41-2)

It is pitiful because, even now in spite of all his honesty, the poet mistakes the cause of his sorrow. He is worn out not with dreams, but with the vain effort to master them and submit them to his own creative energy. He has not subdued them nor

built a new world from them; he has merely followed them like will-o'-the-wisps away from the world he knew. Now, possessing neither world, he sits by the edge of a barren road that vanishes into a no-man's land, where is no future, and whence there is no way back to the past.

> My country is Kiltartan Cross,
> My countrymen Kiltartan's poor;
> No likely end could bring them loss
> Or leave them happier than before.

It may be that Mr. Yeats has succumbed to the malady of a nation. We do not know whether such things are possible; we must consider him only in and for himself. From this angle we can regard him only as a poet whose creative vigour has failed him when he had to make the highest demands upon it. His sojourn in the world of the imagination, far from enriching his vision, has made it infinitely tenuous. Of this impoverishment, as of all else that has overtaken him, he is agonisedly aware.

> I would find by the edge of that water
> The collar-bone of a hare,
> Worn thin by the lapping of the water,
> And pierce it through with a gimlet, and stare
> At the old bitter world where they marry in churches,
> And laugh over the untroubled water
> At all who marry in churches,
> Through the white thin bone of a hare.

Nothing there remains of the old bitter world, which for all its bitterness is a full world also; but nothing remains of the sweet world of imagination. Mr. Yeats has made the tragic mistake of thinking that to contemplate it was sufficient. Had he been a great poet he would have made it his own, by forcing it into the fetters of speech. By re-creating it, he would have made it permanent; he would have built landmarks to guide him always back to where the effort of his last discovery had ended. But now there remains nothing but a handful of the symbols with which he was content:—

> A Sphinx with woman breast and lion paw,
> A Buddha, hand at rest,
> Hand lifted up that blest;
> And right between these two a girl at play.

These are no more than the dry bones in the valley of Ezekiel, and, alas! there is no prophetic fervour to make them live.

Whether Mr. Yeats, by some grim fatality, mistook his phantasmagoria for the product of the creative imagination, or whether (as we prefer to believe) he made an effort to discipline them to his poetic purpose and failed, we cannot certainly say. Of this, however, we are certain, that somehow, somewhere, there has been disaster. He is empty, now. He has the apparatus of enchantment, but no potency in his soul. He is forced to fall back upon the artistic honesty which has never forsaken him. That it is an insufficient reserve let this passage show:—

> For those that love the world serve it in action,
> Grow rich, popular, and full of influence,
> And should they paint or write still it is action:
> The struggle of the fly in marmalade.
> The rhetorician would deceive his neighbours,
> The sentimentalist himself; while art
> Is but a vision of reality. . . .

Mr. Yeats is neither rhetorician nor sentimentalist. He is by structure and impulse an artist. But structure and impulse are not enough. Passionate apprehension must be added to them. Because this is lacking in Mr. Yeats those lines, concerned though they are with things he holds most dear, are prose and not poetry. (pp. 43-5)

J. Middleton Murry, "Mr. Yeats's Swan Song," in his Aspects of Literature, W. Collins Sons & Co. Ltd., 1920, pp. 39-45.

SEÁN O'FAOLÁIN (essay date 1935)

[*Generally considered one of the greatest Irish short story writers of the twentieth century, O'Faoláin has also earned a wide reputation as a novelist, biographer, dramatist, editor, and critic. An active nationalist, he has often used his fiction as a forum for social criticism, while rendering Irish subjects and characters with compassion, humor, and irony. In the following excerpt, O'Faoláin discusses Yeats's poetic self-image and examines the evolution of his presentation of conflict.*]

> The statues of Mausolus and Artemesia at the British Museum, private, half-animal, half-divine. . . . became images of an unpremeditated joyous energy that neither I nor any man, racked of doubt and enquiry, can achieve, and that yet, if once achieved, might seem to men and women of Connemara or Galway, their very soul.

In *Four Years.*

> We were the last romantics, chose for theme
> Traditional sanctity and loveliness.
> Whatever written in what poet's name
> The book of the people. . . .
> But all is changed, that high horse riderless. . . .

In *The Winding Stair, and Other Poems.*

That conflict and that desire is all over Yeats from his childhood on. It is part of him, as it was part of his father John Yeats, before him—a desire for "the abounding glittering jet," and a conflict with everything that in disintegrating the soul—character, intellect, speculation—prevents spontaneous and instinctive vision.

"It is always to the Condition of Fire where emotion is not brought to any sudden stop, where there is neither wall nor gate, that we would rise," he said in *Per Amica Silentia Lunæ,* and we remember that Luna means to him the occult way to all generation, as on his ring the butterfly contrasts with the hawk which is the straight road of logic for which he has small liking. But then he goes on:—

> When I remember that Shelley calls our minds "mirrors of the fire for which all thirst," I cannot but ask the question, as all have asked, "What or who has cracked the mirror." I begin to study the only self that I know, myself, and to wind the thread upon the perne again.

He wishes the condition of fire, and he begins therefore to speculate on himself!

So, from the beginning to the end he winds and unwinds his thread, out and in, from his isolated self—"for triumph can but mar our solitude"—out to the triumph of the world, and back from all human preoccupations, even the preoccupations of sexual desire or patriotic avocations, into his own bowel. "Innocence!" he seems to cry. "Where shall I find innocence again? Hero and saint and fool have had it. But not I—The Janus poet—caught between two shapes of myself."

For Yeats has never been content to be a merely lyric poet; he has been trying always to purify himself, as a saint might, to reach that condition of fire in which the Holy Ghost would

light upon him and he speaks in divers tongues the wonders of God. For no other reason, I feel, was he so much attracted by Shelley, as a young man, than because he felt that the Intellectual Beauty contained all beauty; to the hocus-pocus of Blavatsky, but because he felt her spirits, allied to the faery world of Sligo would link him with the Great Memory that contains all truth; to Blake but because his Divine Passion kills the reason and generates the imagination which is the "first emanation of divinity"; to Symbolism, but because it "entangles a part of the Divine essence." So his loyalties are the passionate man, the imaginative man, the man fused into an unity with himself and with Being by a traditional faith or a mood or an ecstacy, until his characteristics fall away and his naked personality becomes more symbol than man, an Alastor, an Axel, a Manfred, an Ahasuerus, "half-animal, half-divine."

It is a romantic's desire, a Celt's reaching out for the Star of Indefinite Desire. And in a world which had long since broken down into fragments from a condition of common faith and hopes still existed, to a dream of creating a new Prometheus Unbound, with Columcille or Patrick for Prometheus, and Croagh Patrick or Ben Bulben for the Caucasus. Then at last life might become whole again and he, as part of that wholeness, see "artist and poet, craftsman and day-labourer" accept a common design.

Life, and particularly life in so poor a country as Ireland, had other ambitions, however, and yet she seduced him from his heights. He came, sadly, though I think, prematurely, to confess his folly. "That a modern nation can return to Unity of Culture is false; though it may be we can achieve it for some small circle of men and women and these leave it till the moon bring round its century." He left his plays and his committees—"a curse on plays"—that had kept him busy from 1902 to 1912, and he returned to a deeper and more persistent study of this matter of Unity of Being. But he who had betrayed the Intellectual Beauty and the Divine Passion, spent nearly fifteen years in cleansing himself for readmission to the temple. *The Wild Swans at Coole,* is the mark of his return to the fold, and no study of the essential Yeats but must begin at that date, or somewhat before, for the reasons implicit in what I have said about these secret and deepest desires of his heart.

One may attempt to trace this in his poetry, keeping to his poems alone; but sooner or later one comes on this internal conflict, and is obliged to declare that though much of it is more personal to the man than to the poet, it is, from 1900 on, more and more essential to him *as artist.*

What had been his course before, roughly, 1912, as seen in his verse? He had begun in the Ivory Tower, and his genius made of it *The Wanderings of Oisin.* But he needed more than that, and needed to enlarge his personal world to do more than that. He was interested in the occult from, at least, '85, in Blake and Symbolism from '90—though he did not meet Verlaine until '94, and Symons probably not until about '96; but symbolism was at its height, in any case, from 1890 to, say, 1910. Had it not been for Ireland he might have petered out (or come sooner up against himself) with the petering out of the shallow inspiration of the Yellow Book period, or the exhaustion of the symbolist impulse. *The Wind among the Reeds* marks, in fact, the last wine he sucked from the symbolist flagons, and he had exhausted even Ireland—in so far as it meant only the Celtic Twilight kind of thing—by 1900. Then he got new lease of life from Ireland, and was vitalized by Synge and the theatre, so that we find him by 1903 saying that he is trying to put a "less dream-burdened will" into his work, and by 1906, driving out of his cocoon of self, delighting in "the whole man, blood, intellect and imagination running together." It was as if his will then said to him: "Well, are you always going to be just a lovely lyric poet? Finding stimulus here, there and everywhere, from Florence Farr and the psaltery, or theosophical maunderings about the Infinite, or spooks in Soho? When are you going to make something out of your own guts?"

He did not need to reply. He was come, by the very act of leaving his own self behind, into this conflict of which I have spoken; found his naked personal self engaged in a war with his anti-self. He had gone too far. Bitterly he reveals it in *The Green Helmet,* a slim volume that is all he can show of verse for the six years before 1910, where he rails at all that has been distracting him, the day's war, plays, management of men; he is still railing in *Responsibilities* four years later, at the nationalists, the realists, the haters, the miserly Paudeens, the men who damned the "Playboy," and who would not help Hugh Lane, and who not only embittered him and wasted his time, but stole him from the Eternal Beauty. He is eager, it is clear, to fly back to the Ivory Tower. But there is the crux; other selves have been born within him in the meantime, shell within shell, and whether he knew it or not that twin and triplet birth was to bring him his finest verse of all. For, after all, conflict *is* "spontaneous energy," and breeds without thought. (pp. 680-83)

So he wrote in 1916:

> I would be ignorant as the dawn,
> That has looked down
> On that old queen measuring a town
> With the pin of a brooch,
> Or on the withered men that saw
> From their pedantic Babylon
> The careless planets in their courses,
> The stars fade out where the moon comes,
> And took their tablets and did sums;
> I would be ignorant as the dawn
> That merely stood, rocking the glittering coach
> Above the cloudy shoulders of the horses;
> I would be—for no knowledge is worth a straw—
> Ignorant and wanton as the dawn.

It is an Elegy for Innocence, and it goes rightly with **"Lines Written in Dejection,"** where, under the symbolism of sun and moon—the moon being the obscure and shadowy cave of generation—he sighs that being come to fifty years he must endure the timid sun—the timid, objective, unmysterious sun.

I do not see that it matters if Yeats really does not wish to be ignorant as the dawn, or if he knows well that his complex and arrogant and coloured nature could never conceivably have any bridge across to these who are really ignorant and innocent and simple and spontaneous. Indeed, if one even said, "It is all a great pose," I do not see that that matters a pin. . . . Something had been felt by him, even if felt no more deeply than a great actor feels a part, and it had helped him, so feeling, to dramatize himself out of the Anima Mundi into a symbol.

Thereby, then, so curiously, by 1919, comes the finest of Yeats' verse. See a poem like **"Ego Dominus Tuus,"** in *The Wild Swans at Coole,* too long to quote, or the magnificent:

> There is a queen in China or maybe it's in Spain,
> And birthdays and holidays such praises can be heard
> Of her unblemished lineaments, a whiteness with no stain
> That she might be that sprightly girl trodden by a bird;

> And there's a score of duchesses, surpassing woman kind,
> Or who have found a painter to make them so for pay
> And smooth out every blemish with the elegance of his mind;
> I knew a phœnix in my youth, so let them have their day. . . .

That is the poetry of a personality self-dramatized with arrogance, moving towards the creation of a new Beatrice. Again and again he beats out that deeper and more vibrant note of a Narcissus-Faustus:—

> Never until this night have I been stirred.
> The elaborate starlight throws a reflection
> On the dark stream,
> Till all the eddies gleam,
> And thereupon there comes a scream,
> From terrified invisible beast or bird:
> Image of poignant recollection.

Or it is heard again in:

> Turning and turning in the widening gyre
> The falcon cannot hear the falconer;
> Things fall apart; the centre cannot hold;
> Mere anarchy is loosed upon the world,
> The blood-dimmed tide is loosed and everywhere
> The ceremony of innocence is drowned;
> The best lack all conviction, while the worst
> Are full of passionate intensity. . . .

Or in that lovely, lovely poem, **"A Prayer for My Daughter"**. . . . (pp. 684-85)

After that comes *The Tower* and *The Winding Stair,* where his verse becomes so powerful and so evocative and so tragic that one who did not know the sequence of his work, or the sequence of his life, or have the key to his internal conflict, could never have thought it possible for the rather feminine poet of *The Wanderings of Oisin,* to write:—

> It is time that I wrote my will;
> I choose upstanding men
> That climb the streams until
> The fountain leap, and at dawn
> Drop their cast at the side
> Of dripping stone: I declare
> They shall inherit my pride
> The pride of people that were
> Bound neither to Cause nor to State
> Neither to slaves that were spat on,
> Nor to the tyrants that spat,
> The people of Burke and of Grattan,
> That gave, though free to refuse—
> Pride, like that of the morn,
> When the headlong light is lose,
> Or that of the fabulous horn,
> Or that of the sudden shower
> When all the streams are dry,
> Or that of the hour
> When the swan must fix his eye
> Upon a fading gleam,
> Float out upon a long
> Last reach of glittering stream
> And there sing his last song.
> And I declare my faith:
> I mock Plotinus' thought
> And cry in Plato's teeth,
> Death and life were not
> Till man made up the whole,
> Made lock stock and barrel
> Out of his bitter soul,
> Aye, sun, moon, and star, all,

> And further add to that
> That, being dead, we rise
> Dream and so create
> Translunar Paradise. . . .

I wish I could quote it all, but the quality of it is apparent, and it is a quality of poetry that is clearly driven up out of a man preoccupied with self, yet rising out of the bonds of self. He has not unified himself, he never could have unified himself, but he has not corroded within himself as all men do who vainly eat their own hearts, feed on and feed their own dreams.

I am a young man, and my generation in Ireland sometimes finds it hard to make a bridge across to the generation of Yeats. We find a lack of widsom in it, of humanity, and of sincerity. We feel we are of the age of steel and that these last romantics are of the age of gold, to use his imagery again. Though what one really means by "lack of sincerity" is, no doubt, that our values differ, and our insistence on intellectual sincerity and his insistence on emotional sincerity must both of them be tested by time; since there is, no doubt, in both, equal room for self-deceit.

That preoccupation of Yeats with his own conflicts is, I think, dangerous and seductive, and I feel that wherever, in that poetry of conflict, one is aware, not of the conflict, but of Yeats, as in a drama one might suddenly become aware not of the theme but the author, his poetry is at its weakest. Graceless though it be, I close with a poem of that sort, a section in a long poem called "**Vacillation**," beginning:—

"Between extremities man runs his course. . . ." it says:—

> Must we part, Von Huegel, though much alike, for we
> Accept the miracles of the saints and honour sanctity?
> The body of Saint Teresa lies undecayed in the tomb,
> Bathed in miraculous oil, sweet odours from it come,
> Healing from its lettered slab. Those self-same hands perchance
> Eternalised the body of a modern saint that once
> Had scooped out Pharaoh's mummy. I—though heart might find relief
> Did I become a Christian man and choose for my belief
> What seems most welcome in the tomb—play a predestined part,
> Homer is my example and his unchristened heart.
> The lion and the honeycomb, what has Scripture said?
> So get you gone, Von Huegel, though with blessings on your head.

Conflict on conflict! Yeats was born in 1865, seventy years ago this month, and has been wavering ever since, between that romanticism and this realism, between that traditionalism and this revolt, that prettiness and this ugliness, that loyalty to the *moi* ["me"] and this loyalty to the *nous* ["we"] that inwardness and this outwardness, that picturesque Ireland and this raw Ireland, that kind of truth and this. "We were the last romantics" . . .

> But all is changed, that high horse riderless,
> Though mounted in the saddle Homer rode
> Where the swan drifts upon the darkening flood.

He has lived long enough to see a world go and a world come, and he is so vigorous and so alive and so emotionally intact that he cannot deny the validity of either of them. Which may explain why neither generation trusts him, and each claims him, and both give him the fullness of their admiration for the loveliness he has taken—I might even say, robbed without payment from each time. (pp. 686-88)

Seán O'Faoláin, "W. B. Yeats," in The English Review, *Vol. LX, No. 6, June, 1935, pp. 680-88.*

ARTHUR MIZENER (essay date 1941)

[*Mizener is an American educator and critic who is recognized chiefly for his biographies of F. Scott Fitzgerald and Ford Madox Ford. In the following excerpt, he examines the essential Romanticism of Yeats's poetry.*]

There seems to be pretty general agreement among critics that the later poetry of Yeats is superior to the kind he was writing at the turn of the century. But the tendency has been to analyze the difference between the two either in terms of the change in Yeats's style, of the development of what [Louis] MacNeice thinks "we might call the neo-classic beauty" of the later poetry, or in terms of the part played in this change by Yeats's commitment to magic and the system set forth in *A Vision*. It seems to me possible that the points aimed at by these analyses can be made clearer if we are willing to recognize that Yeats was, to the end of his career, a poet of the romantic '90's and that the greatness of the later poetry is a kind of greatness inherent in the '90's attitude.

No one, I suppose, will wish to argue that the style of the later poems is not different from the style of the earlier ones, but it is a curious fact that Yeats remained all his life devoted to the idea of Style in the 1890's sense, scoring, as he must have supposed, some of his most telling points off George Moore, for instance, with anecdotes which demonstrated Moore's inability to write like Pater. And late in *Dramatis Personae* he is still talking, with all the lack of historical perspective which characterized the '90's on this point, of "style, as it has been understood from the translators of the Bible to Walter Pater" as distinguished from "a journalistic effectiveness." Yeats's own conception of his later style was that he had cunningly used "occasional prosaic words" because "if we dramatise some possible singer or speaker we remember that he is moved by one thing at a time, certain words must be dull and numb." The achievement of the end suggested by these quotations was, I think, very near the heart of Yeats's astonishing success in the later poems. But that success did not consist in making "something memorable and even sensuous out of ordinary words, austere rhythms and statements bleakly direct," or at least this is a distorted account of both the means and their result.

If we are to talk of style in the abstract, as both Yeats and Mr. MacNeice are inclined to, it would be better to say that Yeats, retaining to the end an 1890's conception of style, learned to use for the purpose of style a much larger vocabulary and a number of colloquial—though never either loose or simple—rhythms; that above all he learned to give an impression of the "active man" speaking, to dramatize the speaker of the poem, by a cunning mixture of the "dull and numb" words and the colloquial rhythms with the romantic diction and rhythms of his earlier poetry. But he never sought to write verse that was "journalistically effective," and the result of supposing so is the notion that in Yeats's later poetry there is "an almost Wordsworthian simplicity"—a somewhat curious gloss on "neo-classic beauty." This is a description patently inappropriate to Yeats's great symbolic poems, for these poems are as exotic in their splendor as anything well could be. And it is a description equally if perhaps less obviously inappropriate to the great poems of meditation. I think Yeats would not forgive us for so describing these achievements of what he believed the "calm . . . of ordered passion.". . .

The difference between a poem by the early Yeats and the late Yeats is not the difference between a rhetorical poem and a poem of Wordsworthian simplicity. It is the difference between a poem where rhythm and vocabulary are obvious and conventional, because the poet has deliberately eliminated from it the dramatic and the concrete, and a poem where neither is obvious or conventional—in either the bad or the good sense—because the poet is bent on including both.

What happened to make Yeats's later poetry different from his early poetry was that he came to feel the early poetry unsatisfactory, not because its theme was unsatisfactory, but because its manner of realizing its theme was. He wanted not only to present his theme but to present it in terms of the "real" world; he wanted his poems to be true not only to the dreams where his responsibility began but also to the facts; he wanted, when he wrote, to hold not only justice but reality in a single thought. This is a development rather than a conversion, a technical change rather than a substantial one. And it is the development of something present in Yeats from the start, for he was a very young man on that occasion when he walked down the street eying himself in the shop windows and wondering why his tie did not blow out in the wind as Byron's did in the picture.

The obvious moral of this incident is that Yeats was not satisfied simply to dream the pictures in which his desires were realized; he wanted to realize them in fact. It is, if less obviously, also its moral that the picture he dreamed was always a romantic one and that it never occurred to Yeats to modify it at any point in order that it might conform with the demonstrable habits of the wind. Yeats could not change the habits of the wind, nor could he ever quite bring himself to leave the miraculous intervention to which he was committed in other hands than his own. What he could do was his best always to stand on corners where the wind was most likely to blow to his satisfaction; and he tried hard to believe that the ensuing flutter of tie-ends was the result of the wind's ordinary habits, not the result of his careful selection of corners. As a consequence his poetry and, I suspect, his life were, when the wind came up to snuff, intensely dramatic, if they were also sometimes merely theatrical.

Yeats was, as he knew, a man with a "faint perception of things in their weight and mass" as such, who nevertheless had a desire for the world of these things, the world where men were "almost always partisans, propagandists and gregarious." He therefore sought, as he says in *A Vision* men of his phase must, "simplification by intensity." For he knew himself also one of those who define themselves "mainly through an image of the mind," and he was too much of a romantic ever to believe the task of defining the world of weight and mass could be anything like of equal importance with the definition of self:

> I turn away and shut the door, and on the stair
> Wonder how many times I could have proved my worth
> In something that all others understand or share;
> But O! ambitious heart, had such a proof drawn forth
> A company of friends, a conscience set at ease,
> It had but made us pine the more. The abstract joy,
> The half-read wisdom of daemonic images,
> Suffice the ageing man as once the growing boy.

Speaking in *The Autobiography* of the early career here referred to Yeats said that he "overrated the quality of anything that could be connected with my general beliefs about the world";

and, he might have added, was willing to use almost any ingenuity of interpretation in order to connect what he found moving with these general beliefs. He was, as Rothenstein remarked, "too easily impressed by work which showed a superficial appearance of romance or mysticism." He never wholly conquered this habit; it sufficed the aging man as once the growing boy. It is a result of this fact that Yeats's later poetry never has a consistently representational surface, never represents the shows of things. What it does have is a marvelous concreteness and immediacy which is the result of Yeats's presenting with the maximum specification of sensuous detail a startling variety of objects which were attached, by some more or less obscure implication which Yeats found in them, to his general beliefs; it is here, and here only, that they find their unity and value for Yeats.

The later Yeats, then, desired what he called "reality," that is simplicity, order and concreteness; and in this sense it is true, as Mr. Reed Whittemore has said, that Yeats was a romantic who did not want to be one; not, however, because he wanted to be something different, but because he wanted to be something more. He wanted reality, but only on his own terms, and the main requirement of these terms was that particular version of the romantic objective on which the '90's concentrated: intensity of feeling. In desiring reality only on his own terms, Yeats was of course desiring something he could not get, since this pragmatical, preposterous pig of a world, its farrow that so solid seem, have a certain stubborn independence of the mind's theme, in spite of God-appointed Berkeley, whom Yeats seems to have thought God appointed to prove He does not exist rather than that He does. Imagination, by which he meant emotion, he thought "is always justified by time, thought hardly ever. It can only bring us back to emotion." This devotion to imagination in the sense of emotion, to what the heart says, was for Yeats, as for all romantics, the defining characteristic of the artist. "Since Phase 12," he wrote in *A Vision* "the *Creative Mind* has been so interfused by the *antithetical tincture* that it has more and more confined its contemplation of actual things to those that resemble images of the mind desired by the *Will*. The being has . . . been more and more the artist."

The 1890's, in their reductio ad absurdum way, were prepared to sacrifice "reality" altogether ("as for living . . .") to the aesthetic expression of the passionate self, for "to maintain this ecstasy is success in life." But Yeats, knowing the lives of Johnson and Wilde, knew that one could not live wholly in the imagination. It was plain from the experience of the '90's that to refine ecstasy to perfection, to a purely aesthetic and contemplative thing, was self-defeating. It was self-defeating because life will have its revenge; it was self-defeating because, since passion and energy were physical things, to have them only in contemplation, or in the ritual of manners and the ancestral houses out of which the "bitter and violent" living had passed, was not to have them.

> O what if gardens where the peacock strays
> With delicate feet upon old terraces,
> Or else all Juno from an urn displays
> Before the indifferent garden dieties;
> O what if levelled lawns and gravelled ways
> Where slippered Contemplation finds his ease
> And Childhood a delight for every sense,
> But take our greatness with our violence?

It was, then, in life, with its bitterness and violence, its fury and mire, and not in the contemplative peace of the imagination, that ecstasy could be realized. In one sense it was an intolerable insult that this should be so, an insult to the doll-gods, the Magi in their stiff painted clothes, the lifeless but beautiful gods of the poet's imagination. For it was in the Great Memory, that conglomeration of all that men with high imaginations like Yeats's had dreamed, that ecstasy was perfectly conceived, and to such, mere human love was "A noisy and filthy thing." Always Yeats found it "a poor and crazy thing that we who have imagined so many noble persons cannot bring our flesh to heel." On the other hand, it was precisely in what was temporal and evanescent, in the unaesthetic mess of physical life, that ecstasy had its realized being.

It was thus that Yeats came to think of life as at once a horror and a glory:

> Why must those holy, haughty feet descend
> From emblematic niches and what hand
> Ran that delicate raddle through their white?
> My heart is broken, yet must understand.
> What do they seek for? Why must they descend?
> For desecration and the lover's night.

It was thus that he came to dream of a paradise where ecstasy could disdain ("distain," as Yeats first wrote it, free itself from the stain of and so be free to scorn)

> All that man is,
> All mere complexities,
> The fury and the mire of human veins. . . .

Here ecstasy would achieve perfection and permanence of simplicity and intensity, though at the terrible cost of not being able really to burn at all:

> Where blood-begotten spirits come
> And all complexities of fury leave,
> Dying into a dance,
> An agony of trance,
> An agony of flame that cannot singe a sleeve.

In such a paradise one could burn with this hard gem-like flame, could maintain this ecstasy, eternally; here "religious, aesthetic and practical life were one" and "the strain one upon another of opposites," the conflict of desires for the subjective and objective lives, was resolved. Yet Yeats so loved the flame that can singe a sleeve, that all his poems which describe this paradise are prayers that he may be relieved of that love:

> O sages standing in God's holy fire . . .
> Consume my heart away; sick with desire
> And fastened to a dying animal
> It knows not what it is. . . .

For all his conviction that

> He who can read the signs nor sink unmanned . . .
> Has but one comfort left: all triumph would
> But break upon his ghostly solitude;

for all this conviction, he could not forget the ecstasy of the heart:

> But is there any comfort to be found?
> Man is in love and loves what vanishes,
> What more is there to say?

Sometimes, for a moment, Yeats was able to visualize a romanticized version of some actual life which approached what he wanted. This privately mythologized version of actuality he could give his heart to because it seemed actually to realize his heart's desire, a life of that "calm which is . . . an ordered passion." "Yet is not ecstasy," he wrote, speaking of the proper end of tragedy, "some fulfillment of the soul in itself, some slow or sudden expansion of it like an over-flowing well?

Is not this what is meant by beauty?" And precisely this same metaphor he applied, conditionally, to the life of the Irish gentry:

> Surely among a rich man's flowering lawns,
> Amid the rustle of his planted hills,
> Life overflows without ambitious pains;
> And rains down life until the basin spills,
> And mounts more dizzy high the more it rains
> As though to choose whatever shape it wills
> And never stoop to a mechanical
> Or servile shape, at others' beck and call.

But the mood of romantic irony follows quickly upon this always.

So long as Yeats had remained in the strict sense a poet of the '90's he had been able to rely on that vague, traditional order which the conventional romantic metaphors and symbols had acquired through constant use, and this was adequate for his purposes. But when he began to draw for symbols and metaphors not merely on the supply of conventional ones but also on the world of his personal and felt experience, he lost even that minimum support. It is clear enough when the moon, rather vaguely, symbolizes emotion, dreams, imagination; we are all at home with such a symbol because it is held down by the many previous contexts which constitute its traditional meaning. But when Yeats tells us by the use of this symbol the familiar story of how the romantic imagination scorns the limitations and complexities of ordinary life, we are likely to be in difficulties. For instead of using the traditional impedimenta of the moon, he entirely re-equips her with such startling armor as the domes of St. Sophia and, by adducing starlight, adds, to his own satisfaction at least, that the lowest state of being, the state of "complete Plasticity," shares with the high state of pure imagination, the state of "complete Beauty," this scorn.

> A starlit or a moonlit dome disdains
> All that man is,
> All mere complexities,
> The fury and the mire of human veins.

Yeats realized this difficulty quite clearly himself. "It is not," he said, "so much that I choose too many elements, as that the possible unities themselves seem without number." It was his hope that *A Vision* would remedy this situation.

So far as it goes to provide enough logical content to give his poems that amount of "thought" required by the romantic poem, *A Vision* is perfectly satisfactory. But this is a much smaller achievement than Yeats aimed at. Always Yeats's primary concern with an account of the world, an experience or a story, was that it should satisfy what he called the imagination, his feelings. But always also a part of him desired to believe that what did so satisfy him was not only satisfactory to the imagination, but true in fact, that it belonged not only to the soul but to history. So he sought to produce in *A Vision* "a system of thought that would leave my imagination free to create as it chose and yet make all it created, or could create, part of one history, and that the soul's." Without doing violence in any way to what his heart felt to be right and just, he was going to produce an account of the phenomenal world which would be systematic and inclusive. By this means he would make it possible for himself "to hold reality and justice in a single thought," for "he has best imagined reality who has best imagined justice." This is a large order; it requires that observation, analysis and feeling shall be unified, not with due respect for all, but by an absolute subordination of observation and analysis to feeling. This is the same Yeats who had such trouble with his tie, still quite unrepentant, "Still," as Matthew Arnold wrote of the romantics,

> bent to make some port he knows not where,
> Still standing for some false, impossible shore.

For Yeats, though he refused to restrain its freedom to bulge in whatever direction it would, still hoped that his "hands" might have the power to

> Bring the balloon of the mind
> That bellies and drags in the wind
> Into its narrow shed.

A Vision inevitably disappoints this hope, and I think Yeats knew it did. (pp. 601-09)

At a sufficient remove of generalization it was of course possible to state the pattern of Yeats's feelings, for those feelings responded most positively to whatever seemed to represent life lived for ecstasy, and most negatively to what seemed to represent life lived merely for practical ends, the life of submission not to the "sense of glory" but to the facts. This was the pattern Yeats felt in his own life and it was the pattern his imagination sought to impose on all life. Men and history would satisfy his sense of justice only if it could be made true that they were in reality instances of this conflict between the desire to live the subjective life or—as Yeats (who did not love the "dull and numb words") liked to call it—the *antithetical* life, and the desire to live the objective or *primary* life.

But Yeats does not appear to have been able—and certainly did not choose—to develop, by a process of strict definition and consistent logical elaboration, this initial insight into a complete and self-contained system of thought. "I had never put the conflict in logical form, never thought with Hegel that the two ends of the see-saw are one another's negation, nor that the spring vegetables were refuted when over." Yeats has his right, of course, to disagree with Hegel, though it is a little ironic to remember that Hegel, in principle if not always in practice, agreed with Yeats that a contrary was not a contradictory and that negation is a refutation of a thing only in so far as that thing claims a false absoluteness. But surely this is a curious confession for one who is producing a "system of thought." Whether reality is logical or not (and it is hard not to feel that Yeats denied it was only because he did not realize the full possibilities of logic), a system of thought must be, if it is to be a system at all. Nor was Yeats, with a lifetime's cultivation of the habit of treating the observable world selectively and of getting hold of such objects as he grasped by the most convenient handle, able to make a systematic examination of men and history in terms of this insight.

What *A Vision* does is to set up this insight as a general framework and to improvise around it the consequences which Yeats "felt" must follow, that is, which he connected to it by the rather vague use of one or another of the possible ways of looking at things, of the "possible unities . . . without number" which he was so unhappily—from the point of view of system—aware of. He strove to give these improvisations the authority which they could not gain from logic by claiming they were revelation, though he was shrewd enough—or *antithetical* enough—to make it part of his theory that revelation was really the "playing back" to us, as it were, of our communal dreams, "that the communicators are the personalities of a dream shared by my wife, by myself, occasionally by others." (Yeats qualifies this belief somewhat to the advantage of the supernatural.) Which is after all only to elevate to the status of dogma a familiar enough romantic fancy which must, I suppose, go back to the influence on nineteenth-century thought of the anthropological theory that the gods are merely the projections of man's hopes and fears.

Such a "system" does not give us much help toward finding for Yeats's poems what Mr. Winters would call "a paraphrasable content"of any great precision, and in so far as Yeats longed to write poems like Dante's ("We can (those hard symbolic bones under the skin) substitute for a treatise on logic the Divine Comedy."), he failed. For behind the *Divine Comedy* is a logical, self-contained system of thought which accounts completely for the observable world. Dante, by disciplining his feelings until they felt the world to be arranged exactly as it was by this system, could describe the world he saw as it was, and feel the justice of its being so; he could describe the world his age knew literally and yet find that world allegorically and anagogically explicable at every point. But what is under the skin of Yeats's poems is at best gristle. They realize with immense eloquence and concreteness Yeats's rather specialized kind of justice, the 1890's vision of a ritually ordered life of ecstatic joy, and its contrary. But they achieve their concreteness by an eclectic and sometimes anarchic interpretation of "reality," which it is impossible to systematize. In so far, then, as Yeats was trying to produce a *Summa* in *A Vision,* he failed. From this point of view it is a ha'penny worth of bread for the mind to live by to an intolerable deal of sack of the very best quality.

For if it was the unachievable secondary need of Yeats's temperament to produce a completely logical poetry like Dante's, it is not necessary to our admiration for him that we should claim he did so. *A Vision* gives us a general notion of what Yeats's major symbols mean, which is probably as precise an intellectual content as they had for Yeats himself. And this is a great help, for it is hardly to be expected that one man, however visionary, will produce a revelation universally recognizable and wholly without its private eccentricities. And Yeats was in fact a mystic only in so far as any lifelong romantic is. Wordsworth, Keats and Tennyson, none of whom appears to have been a congenital mystic, had similar visions, though they did not insist on the absolute authority of these visions, did not

> . . . mock Plotinus' thought
> And cry in Plato's teeth,
> Death and life were not
> Till man made up the whole,
> Made lock, stock and barrel
> Out of his bitter soul. . . .

For these early romantics had not yet had completely destroyed in them their ability to believe that something beside their own imaginations had made the universe, nor were they so hard pressed by the complete unwillingness of the scientific thought of their day to lend itself to their purposes. It may even, indeed, be that they were somewhat better advised than Yeats of the difficulties of solipsism, out of which Yeats was constantly struggling, only to slip back again at the thought that he might be depriving the mind of some of its freedom to change its theme. Beyond this, *A Vision* gives sometimes very moving and always, in their '90's way, rhetorically very distinguished displays of that clustering of emotive images around a tenuous "paraphrasable content" which is characteristic of Yeats's poetry. (pp. 609-12)

The later poetry of Yeats is far finer than the poetry he wrote for the '90's, and it is finer because in it he sought to shape life to his heart's desire not merely in fancy but in fact. But it remains the poetry of a man committed to the heart's desire, a romantic poetry. As such it is at once colloquial and orotund, straightforward and full of astounding, "irrelevant" implications. As such it is full of enthusiastic and crochety extremes which are forever on the verge of destroying its coherence of statement or its unity of style. It knows neither decorum of idea ("For love has pitched its mansion in / The place of excrement") nor decorum of vocabulary ("perne in a gyre"). This is not the logical, decorous, "neo-classical" poetry so many of Yeats's critics appear to be trying to make it out, and it is not because it rests on that conviction which Hulme the neo-classicist was at such pains to deny: that the divine is life at its intensest. Mr. Winters's low opinion of it is a perfectly logical judgment from his point of view, and I do not see how we are to dissent from his account of Yeats's procedure, however much we may disagree with his evaluation of its results. The poetry of **The Tower** is not harder and drier and more logical than the poetry of **The Rose**; it is only more concrete, more skilful in rhetoric, and more crowded with what Yeats found solid in life. (pp. 622-23)

Arthur Mizener, "The Romanticism of W. B. Yeats," in The Southern Review, *Louisiana State University, Vol. VII, No. 3, Winter, 1941, pp. 601-23.*

R. P. BLACKMUR   (essay date 1942)

[*Blackmur was a leading American literary critic of the twentieth century. His early essays on the poetry of such contemporaries as Yeats, T. S. Eliot, and Ezra Pound were immediately recognized for their acute and exacting attention to diction, metaphor, and symbol. Consequently, he was linked to the New Critics, who believed that a literary work constituted an independent object to be closely analyzed for its strictly formal devices and internal meanings. Blackmur distinguished himself from this group of critics, however, by broadening his analyses through discussions that explored a given work's relevance to society. In the following excerpt, Blackmur discusses Yeats's method of poetic composition, paying particular attention to the translation of his belief system into concrete imagery.*]

It may be risked that in dealing with the structure of poetry thought may be taken as felt assertion, irrelevant to critical analysis, but open to discussion with regard to what it permitted the poet to discover in his poems. Thought becomes metaphor, if indeed it was not already so; from a generalized assertion it becomes in each poetic instance an imaginative assertion that has to do with identity, the individual, the rash single act of creation. We seek to recover the generalized form of the assertion as a clue to what happened to it in the poetry, to find, that is, the spur of the metaphor: an operation which even if failure is an aid to understanding. It gives us something we can verbalize.

So in Yeats, we can detach certain notions which we call basic—though we may mean only that they are detachable—as clues to better reading. At the end of the first version of **A Vision**, Yeats suggests the need of putting myths back into philosophy, and in the "Dedication to Vestigia" in the same version, there is the following sentence: "I wished for a system of thought that would leave my imagination free to create as it chose and yet make all that it created, or could create, part of the one history, and that the soul's." If we take these two notions as sentiments, as unexpanded metaphors, we can understand both what drove Yeats to manufacture his complicted abstract system and the intensity of his effort to make over

half of the consequent poetry as concrete as possible. He knew for himself as a poet that the most abstract philosophy or system must be *of* something, and that its purpose must be to liberate, to animate, to elucidate that something; and he knew further that that something must be somehow present in the philosophy. His system, if it worked, would liberate his imagination; and if it worked it must put those myths—the received forms, the symbolic versions of human wisdom—which were its object concretely into his system. A philosophy for poetry cannot be a rationale of meaning, but, in the end, a myth for the experience of it.

I should like to put beside these two notions or sentiments, two more. At different places in his autobiographies and in his letters to Dorothy Wellesley, Yeats quotes one or another version of Aristotle's remark that a poet should "think like a wise man, yet express himself like the common people." It should be insisted that this is a very different thing from what has been lately foisted on us as a model in the guise of Public Speech. To turn poetry into public speech is to turn it into rhetoric in the bad sense or sentimentality in the meretricious sense.

> The rhetorician would deceive his neighbors,
> The sentimentalist himself; while art
> Is but a vision of reality.

If we keep these lines—from one of Yeats's more esoteric poems—well in mind, they will explain for us much of what Yeats meant by the desire to express himself like the common people. He wanted to charge his words to the limit, or to use words that would take the maximum charge upon themselves, in such a way that they would be available to the unlearned reader, and demand of him all those skills of understanding that go without learning. We shall come to an example shortly.

The fourth sentiment that I want brought to mind here is again one found in many places in both prose and verse in Yeats's work. This is his sentiment that a poet writes out of his evil luck, writes to express that which he is not and perforce, for completion or unity, desires to be. Dante required his exile and beggary, the corruption of the Church, the anarchy of Florence, in order to write *The Divine Comedy,* with its vast ordering of emotion, its perspicuous judgment of disorder and corruption. Villon needed his harlots and his cronies at the gibbet. "Such masters—Villon and Dante, let us say—would not, when they speak through their art, change their luck; yet they are mirrored in all the suffering of their desire. The two halves of their nature are so completely joined that they seem to labour for their objects, and yet to desire whatever happens, being at the same instant predestinate and free, creation's very self." So Yeats in his chapter of autobiography called **Hodos Chameliontos**—the path of muddlement, of change, of shift from opposite to opposite. And he goes on, in language characteristic elsewhere of his regard both for his own life and his own works. "We gaze at such men in awe, because we gaze not at a work of art, but at the re-creation of the man through that art, the birth of a new species of man, and it may even seem that the hairs of our heads stand up, because that birth, that re-creation, is from terror." Lastly, in the next paragraph, there is a declaration of exactly what I want to make manifest as the effort in the dramatically phrased poems of the later years. "They and their sort," he writes, and it is still Dante and Villon, "alone earn contemplation, for it is only when the intellect has wrought the whole of life to drama, to crisis, that we may live for contemplation, and yet keep our intensity."

Now I do not believe Yeats felt all these sentiments all the time, for a man is never more than partly himself at one time, and there is besides a kind of outward buoyancy that keeps us up quite as much as the inward drive keeps us going—but I believe that if we keep all four sentiments pretty much consciously in mind we shall know very nearly where we are in the simplest and most dramatic as in the most difficult and most occult of Yeats's poems. With these sentiments for landmarks, he is pretty sure to have taken a two- or a three- or even occasionally a four-point bearing, in setting the course of a particular poem.

To say this smacks of instruments and tables, of parallel rules and compass roses. But only when the waters are strange and in thick weather are thoughts taken as instruments necessary or helpful. With familiarity the skill of knowledge becomes unconscious except in analysis, running into the senses, and all seems plain sailing. As with sailing so with poetry, the greatest difficulties and the fullest ease lie along known coasts and sounds; there is so much more in the familiar to work on with the attention, whether conscious or not. The object of these remarks is to suggest why it is appropriate to research, so to speak, the original perils of certain poems of Yeats—those in which one way or another the intellect has wrought life to drama—and thereby to jolt the reader's attention, on as conscious a level as possible, back to those aids to navigation which long practice safely ignores but which alone made the passage, in the beginning, feasible. In this figure it is the intellect, the imagination, the soul that is sailed. The poem is not the ship, the poem is the experience of sailing, the course run, of which it is possible to make certain entries. It should be insisted, though, that these entries in the log only recount and punctuate the voyage, and in no way substitute for it. The experience of sailing cannot be put in any log, in any intellectual record. There is the sea, and there is language, experienced; there is the sailing and the poetry: there are not only no substitutes for these, there is nothing so important as getting back to them unless it be to begin with them.

Let us begin then, and it is quite arbitrary to begin in this way, and to many minds will seem extreme, by conceiving that there is a play of words in the composition of poetry, which the conscious mind cannot control but of which it must take continuous stock, and which, by holding itself amenable, it can encourage or promote. Let us insist, further, that to equip himself with conscious amenities of this order is the overt training of a poet: remarking that this is one way to consider the acquisition of habits of meter, pattern, phrase, cadence, rhyme, aptitude for trope and image: adding, that without such intellectual training the poet will be quite at a loss as to means of taking advantage of the play of the words as it begins and will write wooden of demeanor, leaden of feet. Let us insist on this because Yeats himself insisted on it. Aubrey Beardsley once told Yeats—and Yeats liked to repeat it—that he put a blot of ink on paper and shoved it around till something came. This is one routine hair-raising practice of the artist of any sort: to invoke that which *had been* unknown, to insist on the apparition, to transform the possible into a vision. The artist poaches most on his resources when ad libbing, when he meets, and multiplies, his perils with, as Yeats said, nonchalance. The rest is cribbing or criticism.

To crib is to find something from which to start—some system, some assumption, some assertion; and to criticize is only to spot the connections, to name the opposite numbers. To crib and criticize together is to get the whole thing back on a con-

crete or actual basis where it is its own meaning. It is in this sense that art is a realized, an intensified (not a logical or rhetorical) tautology. Art declares its whatness, its self, with such a concreteness that you can only approach it by bringing abstractions to bear, abstractions from all the concrete or actual experience you can manage to focus. That is how art attracts richness to itself and reveals its inner inexhaustibleness; that is how art becomes symbolic, how it lasts, how it is useful, how it is autonomous and automotive—how it puts its elements together so as to create a quite unpredictable self. (pp. 106-09)

Yeats, as he grew older, wrote a good many of his most effective poems by ad libbing around either some fragment of his "system" or some free assumption or assertion. Often these *donnée's* turn up as refrains. For example, the poem called **"The Apparitions"** works around the refrain lines:

> Fifteen apparitions have I seen;
> The worst a coat upon a coat-hanger.

The whole poem is made of three stanzas, of three couplets each, with the refrain added. The first stanza is "about" talking vaguely, implausibly, untrustingly of an apparition. The second is "about" the pleasure of talking late with a friend who listens whether or not you are intelligible. There is no "poem," there is nothing made, so far; the refrain with one repetition seems to hang fire, but there is a sense of fire to come. The blot of ink is beginning, after a move this way and that, after just *possible* movements, to turn itself into a vision; and indeed the third stanza shows itself as the product, backed or set by the first two stanzas, of the vision and the refrain. Put another way, the possible is pushed over the edge and into the refrain, so that the refrain is, for the instant, the limit of meaning.

> When a man grows old his joy
> Grows more deep day after day,
> His empty heart is full at length,
> But he has need of all that strength
> Because of the increasing Night
> That opens her mystery and fright.
> Fifteen apparitions have I seen;
> The worst a coat upon a coat-hanger.

The scarecrow hangs in that closet for good; nobody knows how or why, unless we say by ad libbing around the refrain. That the refrain may in fact have come earlier and required the stanzas, or that the stanzas may in fact have searched for the refrain, makes no difference. Something has been done to the refrain by the progressive interaction between it and the stanzas that has built up a plurisignificance (to borrow Philip Wheelwright's substitute for the Empsonian term Ambiguity) that has not stopped when the poem stops. The astonishing thing is that this plurisignificance, this ambiguity, is deeper than the particular words of the poem, and had as well been secured by other words at the critical places, indeed by the opposite words, so far as superficial, single meanings go. I do not mean to rewrite Yeats; I mean to take a slightly different tack on the course he himself set, and with the same wind in my tail. Ignoring the exigences of rhyme, let us ad lib the stanza quoted above so that instead of joy growing more deep it grows less, so that the full heart grows empty, and remark that he has need of all that room—the room of emptiness, it will be—precisely

> Because of the increasing Night
> That opens her mystery and fright.

But let us not stop there. Could not the night diminish as well as increase; could it not, for the purposes of the achieved poem, close as well as open? One tends to let poems stay too much as they are. Do they not actually change as they are read? Do they not, as we feel them intensely, fairly press for change on their own account? Not all poems, of course, but poems of this character, which engage possibility as primum mobile and last locomotive? Is not the precision of the poem for the most part a long way under the precision of the words? Do not the words involve their own opposites, indeed drag after them into being their own opposites, not for contradiction but for development? After such queries we can return to the poem as it is, and know it all the better so, and know that we have not altered, even tentatively, anything of its actual character by playing with what is after all merely its notation. We have come nearer, rather, to the cry, the gesture, the metaphor of identity, which as it invades the words, and whichever words, is the poem we want.

I bring up this mode of treating a poem, because Yeats more than any recent poet of great ability has written many of the sort that invite the treatment, and because it is that class of his poems which this paper proposes to treat. In these poems he is dealing with a kind of experience which is understood by the unlearned better than, as a rule, by the learned; for the learned tend to stick to what they know, which is superficial, and the unlearned, who should ideally be, in Yeats's phrase for his own ambition, as ignorant as the dawn, have their own skills of understanding immediately available.

That this race of the unlearned, these common readers every poet hopes for, cannot be found in a pure state, whether under the apple tree or the lamplight, is not relevant beyond first thought. There are no poems, only single lines or images, entirely fit for this kind of common reading. There are only poems which move in the direction of such reading—such hearing, I would rather say; and, similarly, there are only readers sufficiently able to rid themselves of their surface, rote expectations to get down to their actual abiding expectations about poetry. It was such readers as well as such poetry that Yeats had in mind when he ended his verses rejecting the embroidered brocade of his early work with the lines:

> For there's more enterprise
> In walking naked.

And it was the poetry which came out of that enterprise made him put this in a letter to Dorothy Wellesley: "When I come to write poetry I seem—I suppose because it is all instinct with me—completely ignorant." The excitement and the difficulty of the enterprise show in another letter: "I have several ballads, poignant things I believe, more poignant than anything I have written. They have now come to an end I think, and I must go back to the poems of civilisation." (pp. 110-12)

Yeats as a poet was . . . a double man and the drive of one half was always encroaching upon the drive of the other half, the one richening, quickening, anchoring, disfiguring the other, as the case might be. The one half was always, to come back to our poem, infecting the other with the violence and inevitability of an apparition, proof, as he wrote in **"Under Ben Bulben,"**

> Proof that there's a purpose set
> Before the secret working mind:
> Profane perfection of mankind.

Let these lines be an example as well as a commentary; and let the example, before we are done, flow back into the whole poem with a kind of extra resilience for our having pulled it out taut. The lines have their prose meaning clear and immediate enough for the purposes of quotation, a meaning that brings up as something of a puzzler only, at first sight, on the word profane. Just what that word signifies here I don't know in any sense that I can communicate. But I am certain that its meanings are plural, and that neither Yeats nor his poem may have intended to apply all of them. It is one of those words which, looked at, gets ahead of all its uses and makes something unexpected of its context, as words in poetry should. As it seems to have in it the theme—that which is held in tension—of the poems I want to discuss, some of the meanings may be elaborated a little.

There are meanings over the horizon, meanings that loom, and meanings that heave like the sea-swell under the bows, and among them, when you think of them all, it is hard to say which is which, since any one gradually passes through the others. There is the traditional association of profane with Sacred and Profane Love. There is profane in the sense of violated, of common in the good sense, of racy rather than austere, of instinctive or passionate rather than inspired. There is profane in the sense of known to everybody, to the uninitiate, known in ignorance without articulation. And there is also profane in the etymological sense, still thriving in Donne, the sense which the other senses only get back to, the sense which has to do with that which is outside or before the temple; and this suggests, of course, profane in the senses of the impious, the disorderly, the random, even the wicked, the lustful: all that is anathema to the absolute or obsessed mind. To elaborate further is vain waste, for with what we have the context begins to draw the meanings in, and begins to illustrate, too, in passing, to what degree the poet using this mode of language cannot help ad libbing, playing, with his most inevitable-seeming words: he cannot possibly control or exclude or include all their meanings.

But to return to the text. Wondering a little whether profane is not alternatively both verb and adjective, we attach it to the word perfection, enhanced or confused as we may have rendered it. Profane perfection! what is that but man's perfection outside the temple of his aspiration, the perfection from which his aspiration sprang, and yet a perfection which cannot be felt except in apposition to the temple. Let all the meanings of profane play in the nexus, here surely is the madness of vision, the "sense of the relation of separated things that you cannot explain," into which, with his double view, Yeats felt he had plunged. But we are not finished; we are not yet concrete enough. If we go back a little in the poem, and remind ourselves that Yeats is only developing his admonition to the sculptor and poet to

> Bring the soul of man to God,
> Make him fill the cradles right,

then the relatedness between profane and perfection becomes almost a matter of sensation; and indeed does become so if we now at last take the lines as they come. We see, as in the Apparitions poem, how the ad libbing of notions and images finally works full meaning out of the final reading of profane perfection.

> Measurement began our might:
> Forms a stark Egyptian thought,
> Forms that gentler Phidias wrought.
> Michael Angelo left a proof
> On the Sistine Chapel roof,
> Where but half-awakened Adam
> Can disturb globe-trotting Madam
> Till her bowels are in heat,
> Proof that there's a purpose set
> Before the secret working mind:
> Profane perfection of mankind.

It should be noted that we have deliberately begun with two poems where the ad libbing is for the most part done with material that may well have been derived from Yeats's system; at least it may all be found outlined in *A Vision* or in the *Autobiographies*. We have plain examples of the system affording the poet's imagination the chance to create what it chose: it gave backing, movement, situation to the intuitive assertions, and the intuitions, working backward, make the rest seem concrete. The reader will not now object, I think, if I insist that here as in the other poem all except the lines quoted separately could have as well been different, most of all could have been their own opposites without injury to the meaning which is under the lines. I believe that this is one of the freedoms of imagination consequent upon having a sufficiently complex system of reference, though I know, as Yeats knew, that there are other ways of securing similar freedom. There is that freedom, for example, which would have come had Yeats set the course of his poem according to the first of the four bearings mentioned above: had there been enough mythology put into this particular patchwork of his system to keep his invention a little nearer the minimum. Thus we can say that as it stands there is a little too much tacking to the poem. The famous sonnet to **"Leda and the Swan"** gives us the nearly perfect example of the fusion of mythology and system and intuitive assertion so dramatized in crisis as to provide an inexhaustible symbol in contemplation without loss of intensity. [In this poem] . . . the circulating presence of the myth, like the blush of blood in the face, brings the underlying richness of meaning nearer the surface, and nearer, if you like, too, to the expectations of the learned reader, than the poems we have just examined. There is less in the meanings but curiously more in the words themselves that could have been different; which is witness that the reality of myth is much further beneath the words in which it happens to appear than mere unmoored philosophy can be.

An example halfway between the two comes to hand in the short poem called **"Death,"** which had it been given but a situation, a place in history, and the man in it a name, would have been a myth in little.

> Nor dread nor hope attend
> A dying animal;
> A man awaits his end
> Dreading and hoping all;
> Many times he died,
> Many times rose again.
> A great man in his pride
> Confronting murderous men
> Casts derision upon
> Supersession of breath;
> He knows death to the bone—
> Man has created death.

Here lines five to nine provide out of Yeats's system the *necessary* stuffing to complete the interval between dread and hope and the supersession of breath; they both could be too readily something else and too much invite expansion in terms of Yeats's known field of reference. Yet the splendid word supersession almost makes up for them, almost removes from them their murk of facileness; for supersession, mind you, means both plain stoppage and the condition (here death) of having become superfluous. As it stands, I think it is one of those poems that tremble between on the one hand collapse and on the other hand supreme assertion. It depends on what voice you hear or say the poem in. It allows but does not itself release a great gesture.

The trouble is, generally, that not all a man wishes to write always finds for itself bodily support in existing myth, and that, too, even if it did, most readers would be insufficiently familiar with the machinery of the myth used to understand the development to which it had been pushed without the use of reference books. This has been my experience in a practical way with readers of **"Leda and the Swan."** The skill of nearly instinctive, deposited understanding of the classic myths has become either mechanical or muddled where it has not disappeared; and without such a skill in his reader the poet cannot use his own, and is driven inward. Specifically, the trouble with Yeats was that the system that he had been driven to invent in despite of both Christianity and rationalism, did not in actuality leave him free to create what he chose more than, say, half the time. Thus as a poet he was left in the dubious position of being unable to believe in his own system more than half the time; he was constantly coming on things which his system could not explain, and which he was yet compelled to turn into poetry.

Yeats's solution was to wipe out of his consciousness the whole middle class, the educated class, the Christian class, the rationalist class, both as subject matter and for direct audience, and write poems addressed to a double-faced class of his own creation, which luckily includes a part of us all, half peasant or fisherman or beggar, half soldier or poet, half lord and half lout. It was as if, groping for Dante's luck he had come suddenly on Villon's, but with the knowledge of Dante in his blood beating in furious aspiration and with the burning indignation of Swift blinding his eyes with light: Dante the "chief imagination of Christendom" and

> Swift beating on his breast in sibylline frenzy blind
> Because the heart in his blood-sodden breast had dragged him
>   down into mankind.

Villon's luck was enough as Yeats used it in the poems I think of—the best of the Crazy Jane poems and the best of his other three groups with a similar ballad-like surface and subterranean symbolism—Villon's luck was enough to make the hair stand up cold on end. This quality is present only in the best of these poems; in others there is a deal of aimless and irredeemable violence, or worst of all an aimlessness without violence. One can say immediately, with this discrepancy in mind, that in the successful poems the machinery is fused in the dramatized symbol, and that in the worst there is not enough machinery—whether from Yeats's system or from the general machinery of the tradition—to bring the symbolism to light, let alone dramatize it. (pp. 113-18)

There is a kind of general fact involved when in the phrase above the hair is said to stand up *cold* on end; there is a kind of coldness in the sense of remoteness about the best Yeats that we do not find either in Dante or Villon or Swift; the kind of coldness which we associate with the activities of a will incapable of remorse or compunction or humility: the kind of coldness that reverses itself only as the heat of a quarrel, the violence of assault, the fire of the merely tumescent emotions. I do not speak of the man but of the poetry, which he made, as he said, out of his antithetical self: the self which in his old age he called old Rocky Face, that *other* self for which he wrote this epitaph in a moment of rage against Rilke's warmer ideas about death—

> Cast a cold eye
> On life, on death.
> Horseman, pass by!

The coldness of this created self shows most, I think, in the fact that none of the human figures in his poems—most of them nameless, for to name, he thought, was to pin the butterfly—are created as individuals. They are rather types dramatized as if they were individuals. They move as all that is typical must in a separated space. There is a barrier between them and wholly individual being which is set up by the fact that they cannot ever quite overcome the abstractions from which they sprang. Thus when Yeats pushed furthest to escape from his system he was in most peril of collapsing into it, which is what fills his figures—his Crazy Jane, his Bishop, his men and women Young and Old—with the focusing force of dramatic crisis. It is his system precariously dramatized, the abstract felt as concrete: the allegorical simulacrum churned with action. The point is, the system *is* dramatized, the typical figures *are* liberated into action, however precariously, which we can and do experience as actual within their limited focus. And the curiosity is, they are liberated most, seem most nearly individuals crying out, when inspection shows they are in fact most nearly commentaries upon some notion or notions taken out of Yeats's system. Man being man and in his senses, right or wrong, even as a poet, there is vertigo in wondering whether Yeats at bottom is giving us "felt thought" or is giving us a generalized version of what he could grasp of certain fundamental, self-created symbols of love and death. Is it insight or experience that is invoked, or a third thing which is neither but reveals both?

I do not mean to be mystifying—there is enough of that in Yeats—but I find it difficult to ascribe the right quality to such lines as come at the end of the seventh poem in **"A Woman Young and Old."** It is a dialogue between lovers in three quatrains and a distich called "Parting," and the first ten lines in which the two argue in traditional language whether dawn requires the lover to leave, are an indifferent competent ad libbing to prepare for the end. The stable element or symbol is the singing bird, and it is almost a version of "The bird of dawning singeth all night long," which indeed as a title would have strengthened the poem. It ends:

> SHE. That light is from the moon.
> HE. That bird . . .
> SHE.   Let him sing on,
>   I offer to love's play
>   My dark declivities.

Declivities—my dark downward slopes—seems immediately the word that clinches the poem and delivers it out of the amorphous into form, and does so as a relatively abstract word acting in the guise of a focus for the concrete, delicately in syllable but with a richness of impact that develops and trembles, a veritable tumescence in itself of the emotion wanted. Call it lust and you have nothing, certainly not lust; call it as the poem does and you do have lust as a theme, and life caught in the theme. But the last two lines do not perform that feat by themselves; the situation is needed, the bird, the dawn, the song, and the moon, perhaps the moon most of all. The moon is all machinery, and very equivocal machinery out of Yeats's system. To use John Ransom's terms, does the moon supply structure to the declivities, or does the word declivities supply texture to the moon? Or is there a kind of being set up between the two, a being which is the created value of both? If so, and I think that this is one way of putting it, can we not say that Yeats has created a sort of rudimentary symbol, nameless but deeply recognizable, good in any apt repetition? Is not that what this sort of poetry is for? In what else does its immanent richness consist?

Yeats did the same thing again in **"The Lover's Song"** from *Last Poems.*

> Bird sighs for the air,
> Thought for I know not where,
> For the womb the seed sighs.
> Now sinks the same rest
> On mind, on nest,
> On straining thighs.

The illuminating, synergizing word here, without which the rest is nothing but maundering, is of course the word sighs; but I am afraid it will not take analysis. (pp. 118-20)

In comparing this poem with "Parting," there is the important difference that here the symbolic line could ride by itself, so that if it were plausible in English to have poems of one line, "For the womb the seed sighs" would be enough, and would make its own work of application wherever apt. English poetry being what it is, we say rather that the line infects the rest of the poem with its symbolic richness. But in saying that, it should not be forgotten that it is not a situation but something as primitive as a pulse that the poem dramatizes.

If the reader objects to the ascription of such qualities as rudimentary and primitive to the symbols in these two poems, I mean them so only relatively and do not at all mean that they lack complexity. Primitive symbols like primitive languages are likely to be more complex than those in which the mind has a longer history at work. This will be clear I think if we look now at the poem called **"Crazy Jane Talks with the Bishop"** (the second, not the first of that name). In this poem the Bishop tells Crazy Jane she is old enough to die and had better leave off the sin of flesh, but she answers him valiantly in the flesh, ending:

> "A woman can be proud and stiff
> When on love intent;
> But love has pitched his mansion in
> The place of excrement;
> For nothing can be sole or whole
> That has not been rent."

This is like the "torn and most whole" symbolism of Eliot's *Ash Wednesday* and of much other religious poetry, but it is also like the sexual symbolism in *Lear* and in Swift's poems, and again is like some of the "lighter" sexual poems of Blake, where the lightness of the verse forms covers profound observation; indeed, it is a fusion, with something added, of all three. Beyond that, as a trope it is an enantiosis, which includes as well as expresses its own opposite. Further, and in fact, it is an enantiodromia, the shocked condition, the turning point, where a thing *becomes* its own opposite, than which there is no place at once more terrifying and more fortifying to find oneself in. Feeling and sensation and intuition and thought are all covertly at work here, and what we see is the sudden insight at the end of a long converging train.

It may be risked that this insight, this symbol, cannot be as easily "used" as those of the two poems just discussed. As there is a great deal more development of all kinds behind this stanza, so a greater stature of response is required of the reader. At first it merely makes the hair stand on end; only later it reveals itself as an object of contemplation. Neither the terror nor the strength will show, nor will they resolve themselves in full symbolic value, unless the reader gets over the shock of the passage and begins to feel, even if he does not analyze, the extraordinary plurisignativeness of the words of the verses, taken both separately and together. I doubt if even in **"Sailing to Byzantium"** Yeats ever packed so much into the language of his poetry. The words are fountains of the "fury and the mire in human veins." Yet none of the meanings are abstruse or require a dictionary; none of them are derived directly from Yeats's system, but come rather from the whole history of the common language of the mind, or as Yeats calls it of the soul. The reader has been long at home with all these words, yet as he reflects he will perceive that he has never known them in this particular completeness before. It was only the convention of this poem that Yeats invented; the rest was discovery of what had long since been created. The terror is in recognition, the strength in the image which compels assent: a recognition and an assent which it is the proper business of the symbolic imagination to bring about, whether as philosophy or as myth, or as the poetry of either.

Yeats commonly hovered between myth and philosophy, except for transcending flashes, which is why he is not one of the greatest poets. His ambition was too difficult for accomplishment; or his gift too small to content him. His curse was not that he rebelled against the mind of his age, which was an advantage for poetry, considering that mind, but that he could not create, except in fragments, the actuality of his age, as we can see Joyce and Mann and it may be Eliot, in equal rebellion, nevertheless doing. Yeats, to use one of his own lines, had "to wither into the truth." That he made himself into the greatest poet in English since the seventeenth century, was only possible because in that withering he learned how to create fragments of the actual, not of his own time to which he was unequal, but of all time of which he was a product.

To create greatly is to compass great disorder. Yeats suffered from a predominant survival in him of that primitive intellect which insists on asserting absolute order at the expense of the rational imagination; hence his system, made absolute by the resort to magic and astrology, which produced the tragic poetry appropriate to it. But hence, too, when the system failed him, his attempt to create a dramatic, concrete equivalent for it. If the examples we have chosen are fairly taken, he found himself ad libbing—as most poets do—most of the time. But his ad libbing was in the grand manner and produced passages of great and luminous poetry. (pp. 121-23)

> *R. P. Blackmur, "W. B. Yeats: Between Myth and Philosophy," in his* Language as Gesture: Essays in Poetry, *Harcourt Brace Jovanovich, 1952, pp. 105-23.*

L. C. KNIGHTS (essay date 1946)

[*Knights was a renowned English Shakespearean scholar and critic. Along with F. R. Leavis and Q. D. Leavis, he was part of a group of critics who, during the 1930s, sought to emphasize social setting and close reading as ways to develop a complete response to a given work. In the following excerpt, Knights assesses the importance of social criticism in Yeats's poetry.*]

In the section of *Autobiographies* headed *Four Years: 1887-1891* Yeats has recorded the "monkish hate" that, as a young man, he felt for the world of thought corresponding to the world of nineteenth-century mechanical progress. His youthful objection to Huxley, Tyndall, Carolus Duran and Bastien-Lepage (he invested the quartet with a sort of symbolic significance) was never merely the aesthetic objection of the Nineties, but it rested on rather dimly grasped feelings, and in his poetry of that period simply prompted withdrawal and immersion in the pre-Raphaelite dream. When, in the first decade of this century, he began with such admirable vigour to work his way out of the Romantic manner a change in the subject-matter of his verse was no less apparent than the change in idiom. With the increasingly sinewy and "unpoetical" quality of his diction and rhythms went an increasing preoccupation with "public" themes, and at the same time his objections to the modern world took a more substantial form. What I wish to suggest in this essay is that Yeats's developed "social criticism"—scattered throughout his essays and autobiographical writings—illuminates the task that he set himself as a poet, and so helps to clarify the standards by which his poetry must be judged.

We can begin by noticing those features of "an age like this" that roused his most vigorous protests. From about the time of *The Green Helmet* onwards he protested emphatically and continuously against democratic vulgarity ("all things at one common level lie"), middle-class caution (". . . the merchant and the clerk breathed on the world with timid breath"), and ready-made newspaper notions and sentiments ("a mill of argument"); against violence of opinion ("an old bellows full of angry wind") issuing in physical violence and cruelty ("Nothing but grip of claw, and the eye's complacency"); against, in short, the related symptoms of a social, political and cultural disintegration summed up in the well-known lines from **"The Second Coming"**:

> Things fall apart; the centre cannot hold;
> Mere anarchy is loosed upon the world,
> The blood-dimmed tide is loosed, and everywhere
> The ceremony of innocence is drowned;
> The best lack all conviction, while the worst
> Are full of passionate intensity.

To these features of a chaotic democratic world Yeats came to oppose the idea of an aristocratic *order*. His belief in an aristocracy contained a streak of snobbery, and occcasionally it led him into absurdity, as when he declared that King George V should have abdicated as a protest against the dethronement of his cousin the Czar. It was nourished by his preoccupation with the Irish past, particularly the eighteenth century, and it took small account of the actual conditions of an industrialized world in which aristocracy merges into plutocracy. Louis MacNeice, remarking that in his later years Yeats considered the possibility of a new aristocracy developing from the Irish bureaucrats of the present, says: "In pre-War years, however, before the Irish burnings, he was still pinning his faith to the Big House, and preferring to ignore the fact that in most cases these houses maintained no culture worth speaking of—nothing but an obsolete bravado, an insidious bonhomie and a way with horses.". . . Yeats's predilections for an aristocracy had decidedly their weak side, but it is only possible to speak of him as a "Fascist" or social reactionary by ignoring the reasons—or perhaps one should say, the intuitions—that led him to put such stress on the aristocratic life. It is these that are most relevant here.

At first sight it is easier to distinguish the negative aspects of Yeats's code than to grasp its positive implications. The aristocratic banner was his red flag—something with which he could make offensive gestures. "By aristocracy," says Dorothy Wellesley, "he meant the proud, the heroic mind. This included a furious attitude towards the cheap, the trashy, the ill-made. And he certainly deplored the passing of the stately houses, and the gradual effacement of the well or highly born." To exalt the aristocracy was one way of expressing his "passion of hatred against the vulgarity and materialism whereon England has founded her worst life and the whole life that she sends us." More positively, he valued the aristocratic life because it seemed to him to make possible the free play of instinctive energies which the mill of modern materialism ground into inert uniformity. Trying, for example, to account for the power of Lady Gregory's translations of the Irish heroic tales, he says: "I can see that they were made possible by her past; semi-feudal Roxborough, her inherited sense of caste, her knowledge of that top of the world where men and women are valued for their manhood and their charm, not for their opinions." And in his **Diary Kept in 1909** he writes: "I see that between *Time*, suggestion, and *Crossroads*, logic, lies a difference of civilization. The literature of suggestion belongs to a social order when life conquered by being itself and the most living was the most powerful, and not to a social order founded upon argument. *Leisure, wealth, privilege were created to be a soil for the most living* [my italics]. The literature of logic, the most powerful and the most empty, conquering all in the service of one metallic premise, is for those who have forgotten everything but books and yet have only just learnt to read." But it is a metaphor from his poetry that best expresses the essentially humane longing that prompted him to indulge in his aristocratic myth.

> Surely among a rich man's flowering lawns,
> Amid the rustle of his planted hills,
> Life overflows without ambitious pains;
> And rains down life until the basin spills,
> And mounts more dizzy high the more it rains
> As though to choose whatever shape it wills
> And never stoop to a mechanical
> Or servile shape, at others' beck and call.

This comes from a distinguished poem in which desire is balanced by a keen sense of reality; the resulting irony—

> And maybe the great-grandson of that house,
> For all its bronze and marble, 's but a mouse

—acts as a purifying agent so that what is valid in Yeats's feelings about aristocratic life is revealed with uncommon clarity.

> Mere dreams, mere dreams! Yet Homer had not sung
> Had he not found it certain beyond dreams
> That out of life's own self-delight had sprung
> The abounding glittering jet; though now it seems
> As if some marvellous empty sea-shell flung
> Out of the obscure dark of the rich streams,
> And not a fountain, were the symbol which
> Shadows the inherited glory of the rich.

The image of the fountain of life, "the abounding glittering jet"—here explicitly associated with the "dream" inspired by Ancestral Houses—provides the criterion by which Yeats makes his most significant judgments of human values. He held, with one of the greatest of his masters, that "Everything that *lives* is holy," and those he condemns are those who refuse to live freely and fully—the men of mere opinion, mere intellect or mere will. If, then, Castiglione's Court of Urbino is a recurring symbol in his verse and prose, it is because in his eyes it stood for a civilization based on respect for the essential energies of the individual, for "the natural impulses of the mind, its natural reverence, desire, hope, admiration, always half-unconscious, almost bodily," as opposed to the modern democratic substitute, "self-improvement." Aristocracy, he thought, was the form in which natural vitality might combine with civilized ease, and if the development of his theories blinded him to some of the social realities of the present we can at least respect the intuitions that prompted his thinking. Before considering the relation of those intuitions to his literary criticism and his poetry we may remark that his idea of an aristocracy may perhaps be best regarded as a myth, complementary in some respects to the greater modern myth of a classless society. Its

value lies in its assertion of those living energies without which equality will be worthless. (pp. 170-74)

"Life" is a key-word in Yeats's literary, as it is in his social, criticism, and for definition we cannot do better than turn to *Discoveries* and some other essays in which his own thought is beginning to emerge from the received ideas of his generation. Life is, in the first place, the instinctive life of the body. In a passage on **"The Thinking of the Body"** that deserves to be famous he wrote: "Art bids us touch and taste and hear and see the world, and shrinks from what Blake calls mathematic form, from every abstract thing, from all that is of the brain only, from all that is not a fountain jetting from the entire hopes, memories, and sensations of the body." But it is "the personality as a whole," not merely "the tumult of the blood" that informs the greatest poetry. He saw clearly that the divorce between "higher" and "lower" faculties was a symptom of the disease which had afflicted the post-Renaissance world, so that by the beginning of the nineteenth century, "the highest faculties had faded, taking the sense of beauty with them, into some sort of vague heaven and left the lower to lumber where they best could." In literature, therefore (and Yeats touches here the now familiar contrast between the poetry of the seventeenth and the poetry of the nineteenth century), "partly from the lack of that spoken work which knits us to normal man, we have lost in personality, in our delight in the whole man—blood, imagination, intellect, running together." When, consciously and deliberately, he broke with his pre-Raphaelite past—abandoning "that conventional language of modern poetry" which, he said in 1905, "has begun to make us all weary"—it was in an attempt to develop "a technique sufficiently flexible for expression of the emotions of life as they arise," for the expression, that is, of energies which a decadent literary tradition had excluded from poetry. The results were remarkable, and for many years now it has been a critical commonplace that the verse of Yeats's middle and later years has a vitality not found in that of his early manhood. Whether he actually achieved that highest kind of poetry which he set as his own standard—poetry expressing the life of "the personality as a whole"—is a question that the very greatness of his qualities forces us to ask. In some important ways, it seems to me, he remained a Romantic to the end.

Romanticism in literature, we may say, is the expression of a sensibility deliberately limited, both as regards it objects of interest and the modes of consciousness that it employs. In Yeats's early verse, for example, a narrow range of uncomplicated emotional attitudes is expressed in a technique incapable of variety, force or subtlety. What is less obvious is that even when in the interests of a fuller and more abounding life he had developed a technique of flexible and forceful speech, persistent habits of Romantic simplification remained. An example of what I mean can be found in his use of figures from heroic legend. Instead of impossible heroes and languishing queens with cloud-pale eye-lids and dream-dimmed eyes, we now have "Helen and her boy," Solomon with Sheba "planted on his knees," and Leda, "that sprightly girl was trodden by a bird." At first reading it seems that the purpose served by these and similar phrases is the recreation of the heroic world in modern idiom, the ironic application—in Elizabethan fashion—of old fable to contemporary needs. That perhaps was the intention, but the references also serve a deeper need, a nostalgia for an imagined past in which painful complexities are evaporated. Mr. MacNeice says rightly that Yeats "was orientated . . . towards a simplified past"; and it is significant that in the poem **"Ancestral Houses"** the irony relies on an absolute acceptance of the past—"a haughtier age"—and is directed solely against the present: there is no suggestion of the two-way irony which in *The Waste Land* sets present *and* past in a clearer light. To romanticize *any* element in a given situation is to admit an inability to deal with it completely and with a full awareness of all that is involved; and Yeats, even in his middle and later periods, continued to use Romantic glamour as an escape from difficult or painful problems. The poem, **"No Second Troy,"** opens in the tones of straightforward speech:

> Why should I blame her that she filled my days
> With misery, or that she would of late
> Have taught to ignorant men most violent ways,
> Or hurled the little streets upon the great,
> Had they but courage equal to desire?

But from the sixth line the poem draws largely on romantic idealization:

> What could have made her peaceful with a mind
> That nobleness made simple as a fire,
> With beauty like a tightened bow, a kind
> That is not natural in an age like this,
> Being high and solitary and most stern?

And in the end a woman with whom only difficult relations were possible is transformed into that Helen who exists only for the imagination:

> Why, what could she have done being what she is?
> Was there another Troy for her to burn?

In **"Easter, 1916,"** the refrain—

> All changed, changed utterly:
> A terrible beauty is born

—represents an escape from full realization. Sometimes, as in the instances just quoted, the nature of the transformation is indicated by a change in diction, a lapse into something like Yeats's earlier manner. At other times it is half concealed by the assured use of an idiom professedly non-Romantic. Yeats in fact uses his later colloquial technique with such self-confident swagger that often one gives him credit for doing all that he merely claims to do. The speech of "My Self" which ends **"A Dialogue of Self and Soul"** (*The Winding Stair*) has a sinewy vigour:

> I am content to live it all again
> And yet again, if it be life to pitch
> Into the frog-spawn of a blind man's ditch,
> A blind man battering blind men.

But when the poem ends,

> I am content to follow to its source
> Every event in action or in thought;
> Measure the lot; forgive myself the lot!

we have no warrant that "follow to its source," "measure" and "forgive myself" stand for explorations actually undertaken. And if the poems dealing explicitly with contemporary chaos are, in the long run, disappointing, it is for a similar reason. In **"Meditations in Time of Civil War"** and **"Nineteen Hundred and Nineteen"** (*The Tower*) there are memorable lines and striking images:

> Nothing but grip of claw, and the eye's complacency,
> The innumerable clanging wings that have put out the moon.

> Violence upon the roads: violence of horses. . . .
> Herodias' daughters have returned again,
> A sudden blast of dusty wind and after
> Thunder of feet, tumult of images,
> Their purpose in the labyrinth of the wind;

but if the success of the poems seems partial and fragmentary it is because "the half-read wisdom of daemonic images" (which, we are told, "suffice the ageing man as once the growing boy") is made to take the place of a deeper understanding.

Perhaps the best way of defining the disappointment that one feels on returning to so many of Yeats's poems that had previously seemed deeply moving is to say that they fail to "gather strength of life, with being," to grow, that is, with one's own developing experience,—unlike so much of Eliot's poetry where each fresh reading brings fresh discovery. For not only does Yeats tend to simplify his problems, there is in much of his poetry a static quality which can be traced to the adoption of certain fixed attitudes in the face of experience. "There is a relation," he said, "between discipline and the theatrical sense. . . . Active virtue as distinguished from the passive acceptance of a current code is therefore theatrical, consciously dramatic, the wearing of a mask." But his preoccupation with the mask was not merely a search for a discipline: sometimes it seems like the rationalization of a self-dramatizing egotism which made him feel happier if he could see himself ("Milton's Platonist") in an appropriate light. Consider, for example, his attitude of pride. One can relish his criticism of those who "long for popularity that they may believe in themselves" and of poets who "want marching feet," and at the same time recognize a danger to sincerity in a too persistent assertion of "something steel-like and cold within the will, something passionate and cold." There is a smack of the Nineties here; and one remembers his fondness for Dowson's lines,

> Unto us they belong,
>   Us the bitter and gay,
> Wine and women and song.

"'Bitter and gay,' that is the heroic mood," he wrote in 1935. Like the aristocratic order that he imagined, pride is valued as an assertion of the living spirit confronted with democratic commonness; but there is something unliving in the use he makes of "cold" and "bitter" and "proud"—adjectives that tend to appear with the same regularity as the "emblems" which, in his later poetry, too often take the place of living metaphor. There is no doubt that the sap flows most freely when the conscious pride is forgotten, remaining only as a temper of mind that is sufficiently assured not to insist on its own firmness. The pose that results from over-insistence is most obvious in admittedly minor poems, like the short sequence **"Upon a Dying Lady"** and those verses that celebrate "the discipline of the looking-glass," which he seems to have continued to regard as the appropriate discipline for beautiful women; but it also betrays itself in work of greater power. In the third section of the title poem of *The Tower* he writes of "upstanding men,"

>   I declare
> They shall inherit my pride,
> The pride of people that were
> Bound neither to Cause nor to State,
> Neither to slaves that were spat on,
> Nor to the tyrants that spat,
> The people of Burke and of Grattan
> That gave, though free to refuse. . .

The rhythm of these lines seems almost mechanical when compared with the vigorous protest against old age with which the same poem opens. The pride, in short, sometimes seems like another form of the escape from complexity. Referring, once more, to the mask, he wrote: ''I think all happiness depends on the energy to assume the mask of some other self; that all joyous or creative life is a re-birth as something not oneself. . . . We put on a grotesque or solemn painted face to hide us from the terrors of judgment, invent an imaginative Saturnalia where one forgets reality, a game like that of a child, where one loses the infinite pain of self-realization.'' Yeats knew as well as anyone that ''the infinite pain of self-realization'' is the price paid for ''life''; and in the lines that he wrote for his epitaph there is a deep and unintended pathos:

> Cast a cold eye
> On life, on death.
> Horseman, pass by.

This account, I know, ignores many fine poems—poems on ''that monstrous thing, returned yet unrequited love,'' and on the encroachment of age, some satiric pieces, and some others—and where much remains it must seem peculiarly ungrateful to insist on inadequacies and disappointments. But I hope I have made it plain that it is precisely because of his great qualities that one must judge Yeats's work, not simply in relation to the poetry of the late nineteenth century (his own included) but in the light of his own conception of the poet's function. That conception is not only defined in the prose criticism, it is embodied in two poems which, without any qualification, deserve the title of ''great poetry.'' I refer to **''Sailing to Byzantium''** and **''Among School Children.''** These poems have been often and justly praised, and all I wish to do here is to suggest how magnificently they enforce the central doctrine of Yeats's criticism: that the higher forms of vitality (unlike gusto, swagger or self-assertion) are a function of the personality as a whole, ''blood, imagination, intellect, running together.'' There is no doubt of their vitality, but the sense of ''joyous energy'' that they release is not purchased at the price of exclusion; there is, instead, a remarkably clear-eyed acceptance of things as they are. The opening of **''Among School Children''** has a cool, prose-like clarity:

> I walk through the long schoolroom questioning,
> A kind old nun in a white hood replies;
> The children learn to cipher and to sing,
> To study reading-books and history,
> To cut and sew, be neat in everything
> In the best modern way—the children's eyes
> In momentary wonder stare upon
> A sixty-year-old smiling public man.

The sight of the children calls to mind the childhood and youth of the woman he loved, and then, contrasting her youthful beauty with ''her present image''—

> Hollow of cheek as though it drank the wind
> And took a mess of shadows for its meat

—the poet is led to question the values which, men believe, give meaning to life:

> What youthful mother, a shape upon her lap
> Honey of generation had betrayed,
> And that must sleep, shriek, struggle to escape
> As recollection or the drug decide,
> Would think her son, did she but see that shape
> With sixty or more winters on its head,
> A compensation for the pang of his birth,
> Or the uncertainty of his setting forth?

Philosophy and poetry (verse vi)?—''Old clothes upon old sticks to scare a bird''; religion (verse vii) is born of man's need and can answer no questions; and the painful antinomy of desire and frustration is felt as rooted in experience. But this is to paraphrase too crudely; for just as elements which, in a lesser poem, might appear Romantic are balanced by a sober grasp of reality, as strong personal emotion (''my heart is driven wild'') is blended with a play of mind, witty and ironic, so in the consideration of the satisfactions that life has to offer there is a similar firm poise. The ''honey'' of verse v is not merely ''the 'drug' that destroys the 'recollection' of pre-natal freedom'' (see Yeats's note); it invokes a ''positive'' attitude to experience which is explicit in the wit and the lovely singing movement of the succeeding verse:

> Plato thought nature but a spume that plays
> Upon a ghostly paradigm of things;
> Solider Aristotle played the taws
> Upon the bottom of a king of kings;
> World-famous golden-thighed Pythagoras
> Fingered upon a fiddle stick or strings
> What a star sang and careless Muses heard:
> Old clothes upon old sticks to scare a bird.

And in verse vii the ''images'' of religion may be ''self-born mockers of man's enterprise,'' but they are also

> Presences
> That passion, piety or affection knows,
> And that all heavenly glory symbolize,

and the human emotions that inform them are real and valuable. It is this fine and complex balance of varied recognitions and energies that lies behind and justifies the final verse, which in one sense provides an answer to the questions and in another sense supersedes them.

> Labour is blossoming or dancing where
> The body is not bruised to pleasure soul,
> Nor beauty born out of its own despair,
> Nor blear-eyed wisdom out of midnight oil.
> O chestnut tree, great rooted blossomer,
> Are you the leaf, the blossom or the bole?
> O body swayed to music, O brightening glance,
> How can we know the dancer from the dance?

At the level of prose and logic the last four lines may be taken to imply the futility of dissecting life which is growth and movement in order to find its values; but the poetic force of the imagery conveys a triumphant affirmation of wholeness and spontaneity which is no less ''real'' for existing only in the form of a symbol of possibilities perpetually unfulfilled.

''Sailing to Byzantium'' reveals a similar ''reconciliation of opposite or discordant qualities'' as the source of its power. It opens with a richly concrete evocation of instinctive life:

> The young
> In one another's arms, birds in the trees,
> —Those dying generations—at their song,
> The salmon-falls, the mackerel-crowded seas. . . .

When the poet turns from ''that sensual music'' towards the unchanging world of art and contemplation, imagery and movement—''as though mere speech had taken fire''—continue to express a positive vitality.

> O sages standing in God's holy fire
> As in the gold mosaic of a wall,
> Come from the holy fire, perne in a gyre,
> And be the singing masters of my soul.
> Consume my heart away; sick with desire

And fastened to a dying animal
It knows not what it is; and gather me
Into the artifice of eternity.

There is a steady recognition of what is now, for the poet, unattainable, but not only is "Byzantium" itself alive (for images of spontaneous movement and delight qualify the deliberately chosen "monuments" and "mosaic"), the theme of its mediation and its song is "what is past, or passing, or to come"; and the function of the "artifice of eternity" is to celebrate that living world of the first stanza in which the stress falls equally on dying and generation.

These two poems seem to me to represent the high peaks of Yeats's poetic achievement. In them the "life" so ardently pursued is revealed as wholeness, integrity, with no surreptitious finger on the balance; and they set a standard. Even that striking poem, **"Byzantium,"** has a less rich and complex organization than **"Sailing to Byzantium."** "The unpurged images of day recede," but not into that "more powerful life" revealed in the earlier poem. Common life—now represented simply by "the fury and the mire of human veins"—is rejected in favour of an art that has nothing to do with humanity:

> . . . by the moon embittered, scorn aloud
> In glory of changeless metal
> Common bird or petal
> And all complexities of mire or blood.

It is the "embittered" note that predominates in many of the latest poems, both in *The Winding Stair* and *Last Poems and Plays*. The pride tends more and more to narrowness and assertion ("A proud man's a lovely man"); poems such as **"A Dialogue of Self and Soul"** and **"Vacillation"** represent a recognition of the need for integration rather than achieved wholeness; talk about sex is, too often, offered as a substitute for vitality; and although the lechers and drunkards are *personae* deliberately adopted as a protest against "Whiggery"—

> A levelling, rancorous, rational sort of mind
> That never looked out of the eye of a saint
> Or out of drunkard's eye,
>
> **("The Seven Sages")**

they are but fragmentary embodiments of a personality richer than any one of them can suggest. For a poet so gifted as Yeats, Crazy Jane—even at her haunting best—was an admission of failure.

> A strange thing surely that my heart when love had come
>   unsought . . .
> Should find no burden but itself and yet should be worn out.
> It could not bear that burden and therefore it went mad.
>
> **("Owen Ahern and His Dancers")**

Measured by potentiality, by aspiration, and by the achievement of a few poems, it is as an heroic failure that one is forced to consider Yeats's poetic career as a whole. The causes were complex. Something, no doubt, must be attributed to defects of "character"; and a very great deal must be attributed to the literary tradition of the nineteenth century which, as he came to see so clearly, offered the very opposite of an incitement to maturity. But, since "the death of language . . . is but a part of the tyranny of impersonal things," that tradition itself appears as the symptom of a deeper disease. Yeats wrote of W. E. Henley: "He never understood how small a fragment of our nature can be brought to expression, nor that but with great toil, in a much divided civilization"; and of himself as a young man, already half-conscious that "nothing so much matters as Unity of Being": "Nor did I understand as yet how

little that Unity, however wisely sought, is possible without a Unity of Culture in class or people that is no longer possible at all." These passages, representative of many others, are part of a diagnosis that is valuable not merely for the light that it throws on Yeats's poetry. For those who would understand our divided and distracted civilization, in which the "passionate intensity" of partial men offers itself as a substitute for the vitality that springs from the whole consciousness, few things are more profitable than a study of Yeats's·poetry and prose together. "The mischief," he said, "began at the end of the seventeenth century when man became passive before a mechanized nature." (pp. 174-85)

> *L. C. Knights, "Poetry and Social Criticism: The Work of W. B. Yeats," in his* Explorations: Essays in Criticism Mainly on the Literature of the Seventeenth Century, *Chatto & Windus, 1946, pp. 170-85.*

FRANK KERMODE   (essay date 1957)

[*Kermode is an English critic whose career combines modern critical methods with expert traditional scholarship, particularly in his work on Shakespeare. In his critical discussions of modern literature, Kermode has embraced many of the conceptions of structuralism and phenomenology. Kermode characterizes all human knowledge as poetic, or fictive: constructed by humans and affected by the perceptual and emotional limitations of human consciousness. Because perceptions of life and the world change, so does human knowledge and the meaning attached to things and events. Similarly, for Kermode, a work of art has no single fixed meaning, but a multiplicity of possible interpretations; in fact, the best of modern writing is constructed so that it invites a variety of interpretations, all of which depend upon the sensibility of the reader. True or "classic" literature, to Kermode, is thus a constantly reinterpreted living text, "complex and indeterminate enough to allow us our necessary pluralities." In the following excerpt, Kermode discusses Yeats's concept of the artist as a tragic figure.*]

No one has written better than Yeats about that generation of poets who "had to face their ends when young"—about Wilde, who so admired **"The Crucifixion of the Outcast,"** about [Ernest] Dowson, and [Lionel] Johnson, who was to become crucial to Yeats's own developing idea of isolation. When the outcast counts on being crucified, indeed savours the prospect; when, bitter and gay, he abstains from morality for fear, as Yeats put it in a late letter, of losing the indispensable "heroic ecstasy," then we know we are dealing with a tradition which has become fully, not to say histrionically, self-conscious. (p. 22)

[That] art exhausts life was a notion that haunted Yeats: "Exhausted by the cry that it can never end, my love ends," he says magnificently in *A Vision*; and the song in *Resurrection* says the same thing. Johnson drained his life away into art, looking forward, with a kind of tragic irony, to ten years on when he would be ruined, begging from his friends; but he fell once too often before the time was up. What of the artist who continues to exist, preying gloomily upon the substance of his own life? Age merely confirms his abstraction, his exclusion from ordinary vitality, by turning him into a scarecrow. Age is as hateful as the headache and the cough, the inky laborious craft—Adam's curse—whether the artist be young or old. "My first denunciation of old age," said Yeats, "I made before I was twenty." Indeed the antithesis of living man and creator was one of the root assumptions of his life and work; he drew the artist as a tragic hero, proving life by the act of withdrawing from it. He was of the great conspiracy of contemplative men, and had made his choice of "perfection of the work"; but he retained and developed a harrowing sense of the goodness of life and action, and a conviction that "real success was to resemble *that*."

"Art is solitary man," wrote J. B. Yeats to his son, in the midst of their rich wartime correspondence. At that time, the poet was obviously unhappy about his abstinence from the exceptionally violent contemporary life of action; he had a taste for such violence, satisfied later when affable irregulars frequented Thoor Ballylee, and gunfights went on round the offices of Dublin, but in the English war he could not even play a poet's part. At such a time his father's emphasis on the proper detachment of the artist must have been agreeable. "All art is *reaction from life*," said J. B. Yeats, "but never, when it is vital and great, *an escape* . . . In Michelangelo's time it was not possible to escape for life was there every *minute* as real as the toothache and as terrible and impressive as the judgment day." This is a very Yeatsian formula. Yet, whatever the quality of life he has to deal with, "the poet is the antithesis of the man of action." He does not "meddle in ethics"; he is a magician, "his dreams shall have a potency to defeat the actual at every point"—this is the poet *versus* the universe of death, the world of reason.

> Art exists that man cutting himself away from nature may build in his free consciousness buildings vaster and more sumptuous than these [the "habitations of ease and comfort"] built by science; furnished too with all manner of winding passages and closets and boudoirs and encircled with gardens well shaded and with everything he can desire—and we build all out of our spiritual pain—for if the bricks be not cemented and mortised by actual suffering, they will not hold together. Those others live on another plane, where if there is less joy there is much less pain . . . The artist . . . out of his pain and humiliations constructs for himself habitations, and if she [Nature] sweeps them away with a blow of her hand he only builds them afresh, and as his joy is chiefly in the act of building he does not mind how often he has to do it.

Here, apart from the dubious connotations of the architectural analogy, we have something close to the essence of the younger Yeats's résumé of the tradition. What, after all, is the *Vision*, but a blueprint of a palace of art, a place in the mind where men may suffer, some less and some more, where the artist explains his joy in making at the cost of isolation and suffering? The joy of building is the same thing as Yeats's brief victory, the creation of an antithesis for fate. The father admitted his intellectual debt to his son; but nobody could have restated the Romantic case so suitably to the son's purposes.

The free, self-delighting intellect which knows that pain is the cost of its joy; the licence to look inward and paint, as Blake and Palmer painted, a symbolic world; to make a magical explanation of a divine order—all this represents the victory of Coleridge, of Blake and the French; it is the heritage, delightful and tragic, to which Yeats was born. Much in his own life made him kick against the pricks; his love of aristocratic skills, of the achievements of others in the sphere of action, of his own successes in the active life. Out of this oscillation between the two states of life came the desire, natural to a magician, to tame by explaining, to answer the question, why are men different, and why are men divided? But long before Yeats ventured on his schematic explanations he had been concerned in a more general way with the justification of the ways of the artist and the defence of poetry.

The development of Yeats's cluster of ideas about the status of the artist in life is complex. . . . So certain was he that art

was not "escape" that he thought of the situation the other way round: art was what you tried to escape from. The failure of Wilde to understand this was, for Yeats, something to be explained only by taking Wilde out of the ranks of the artists altogether. It was because he hated the conventional notion of "escape" that Yeats was early troubled by that dreaminess, that conscientious lack of actuality, which prevailed when he made his début; he was trying to shake it off much earlier than is usually supposed, trying to get strong, living rhythms and a language "as subtle, as complex, as full of mysterious life, as the body of a flower or of a woman." He grew suspicious of a kind of covert sensuality in this Romantic dream. We may be grateful that he did; the extension of his range, the cult of a language of organic rhythms and of great rhetorical variety, are what made him a great poet. But for all that, he never ceased to subscribe to the old doctrine that art is a kind of dream, and that to dream it well is the most difficult and exhausting of all callings. (pp. 24-7)

In *A Vision*, Yeats wrote of "an early conviction of mine that the creative power of the lyric poet depends upon his accepting some of a few traditional attitudes, lover, sage, hero, scorner of life"; and as early as *The Celtic Twilight* he describes a Symbolist vision, of apes eating jewels in hell, which contains the elements of what later became a powerful and immediate impulse. "I knew that I saw the Celtic Hell, and my own Hell, the Hell of the artist, and that all who sought after beautiful and wonderful things with too avid a thirst, lost peace and form, and became shapeless and common." Here, in embryo, is the story of the cost to the artist of what Yeats, in an early essay entitled **"Poetry and the Tradition,"** calls his unique "continual and self-delighting happiness"; it turns the dedicated, however pretty their plumage, into old scarecrows, and excludes them from life. Hanrahan, of whom the poet was to speak again in the isolation of the Tower,—"leave Hanrahan, For I need all his mighty memories"—is tricked into leaving the dance of life, just as he was coming to where comfort was. Later he composed a great curse on old age; he had been touched by the Sidhe—a Yeatsian figure for the dedication, voluntary or no, of the artist—and had to pay the cost. The poet is not like the others. Joy makes him free for his task of stitching and unstitching, of labour at the higher reality of the imagination. But this labour is what ruins life, makes the body shapeless and common. Solitude grows with what Yeats calls the growing absorption of the dream; the long series of indecisive victories, "intellectual recreations of all that exterior fate snatches away," increase it further and torment the poet. His fate is a ruined life, intermittently illuminated by the Image. Poets and artists, says Yeats in *Per Amica Silentia Lunae,* "must go from desire to weariness and so to desire again, and live for the moment when vision comes life terrible lightning, in the humility of the brutes." Tormented by the necessary failure of his life, appalled in conscience or in vanity, he can say, "I suffered continual remorse, and only became content when my abstractions had composed themselves into picture and dramatisation." This content is impermanent; the poet is thus perpetually divided against himself. Hence the distinction Yeats makes "between the perfection that is from a man's combat with himself and that which is from a combat with circumstance." Behind it lies the hopeless anger of an artist in love with action, with life. This occupied Yeats incessantly, and it is hardly too much to say that it informs most of his later poetry as well as his universal history, which is, virtually, an attempt to make all history an explanation of why the modern artist is isolated.

A young poet, encountering for the first time the *fertilisante douleur* [''fruitful pain''] and the massive indifference of the public, might be aware of the pressure of problems similar to his own in the poetry of Yeats without grasping the fullness of Yeats's statement, the institutional—one might almost say apostolic—quality of this poet, which places the enthusiastic anti-Romanticism of a Hulme as a heresy, the sad heresy of the slightly misinformed, who seek a primitive purity with eyes blinded by tradition. The modern truth about the poet's difference, about that stern injunction, ''No road through to action,'' about the problem of communication—how and to whom?—is in Yeats, in a rich and perfected context. He is the poet in whose work Romantic isolation achieves its full quality as a theme for poetry, being no longer a pose, a complaint, or a programme; and his treatment of it is very closely related to his belief in what Pater called ''vision'' and the French called Symbol. He does not deny the pain that is terminated momentarily by the daily victory, permanently by death; indeed the fascination of this last, fierce solution was as apparent to him as to Moritz and some of the French writers. He simply understands it more fully than anybody else, in its relation to the Image. (pp. 27-9)

Frank Kermode, ''The Artist in Isolation,'' in his *Romantic Image*, *The Macmillan Company, 1957, pp. 1-29.*

NORTHROP FRYE (essay date 1965)

[*Frye has exerted a tremendous influence in the field of twentieth-century literary scholarship, mainly through his study* Anatomy of Criticism *(1957). In this seminal work, Frye argues that judgments are not inherent in the critical process and asserts that literary criticism can be ''scientific'' in its methods and its results without borrowing concepts from other fields of study. For Frye, literature is schematic because it is wholly structured by myth and symbol. The critic becomes a near-scientist, determining how symbols and myth are ordered and function in a given work. The critic need not, in Frye's view, make judgments of value about the work; a critical study is structured by the fact that the components of literature, like those of nature, are unchanging and predictable. In the following excerpt, Frye examines the cosmology of Yeats's* Vision *and notes the function of that cosmology in Yeats's poetry. In an introductory statement to the essay from which this excerpt is taken, Frye concedes: ''Yeats's* Vision *has baffled and exasperated me for many years: this essay is by no means completely successful in laying a . . . haunting ghost to rest, but it supplies some analogical context for Yeats's schematisms which may be useful.''*]

There are two great rhythmical movements in all living beings: a movement towards unity and a movement towards individuality. These are opposed and contrasting movements, and are symbolised in Yeats by a double gyre, a movement in one direction which, as it grows more pervasive, develops the counteracting movement within itself, so that the apex of the next gyre appears in the middle of the base of the preceding one and moves back through it. The simplest way to represent the entire double-gyre rotation is by a circle. Because of its traditional association with the moon, this circle has twenty-eight phases, and the twenty-eight-phase cycle exists, Yeats says, in every completed movement, whether it takes a moment or thousands of years to complete itself. But, of course, it is in the larger rhythms of history that the detail is easiest to see. Yeats sees history as forming a series of cycles, each lasting about two thousand years, with each cycle going through twenty-eight parallel phases. The conception is similar in many ways

to that of Spengler's *Decline of the West,* and Yeats often remarks on the similarity of his views to Spengler's.

In Spengler, who is most rewarding when he is read as a Romantic and symbolic poet, each historical cycle or ''culture'' exhibits the rhythms of growth, maturation and decline characteristic of an organism, though Spengler also uses the metaphor of the four seasons. There were, for instance, a Classical and a Western cycle, each having a ''spring'' of feudal economy and heroic aristocracy, a Renaissance ''summer'' of city-states, an ''autumn'' in Periclean Athens and the eighteenth century, when the cultural possibilities of the cycle were exhausted, and a ''winter,'' ushered in by Alexander and Napoleon respectively, when a ''culture'' changes to a technological ''civilisation'' of huge cities, dictatorships and annihilation wars. In between comes a Near Eastern or ''Magian'' culture, with its spring at the birth of Christ and its later stages in the period of Mohammedanism, the religion of the crescent moon. In each cycle the period of highest development is the period of greatest individuality in both art and political life, and both the early and the late stages are marked by a strong sense of communal or mass-consciousness.

In Yeats this communal consciousness is part of the drive toward unity. It is the primitive mentality in which all historical cycles begin, and the decadent mentality in which they end, hence it is the ''primary'' rhythm of existence. Over against it is an ''antithetical'' development of individuality, which reaches its greatest height in the hero. In primitive society the communal consciousness is so strong that there hardly seems to be any real individuality, as we know it, at all. Those who show signs of individual consciousness often have simply a different kind of unity, with animals or with the fairies and other spirits of the invisible world, like the inspired fools who haunt romantic literature (Phase 2). The types from Phase 2 to about Phase 6 are intellectually simple and self-contained: Phase 6 is the phase of Walt Whitman, who never quite distinguished individual from communal well-being. Individuality begins in the unhappy and tormented souls who are aware of a double pull within them around Phase 8. As we cross the quadrant of Phase 8 we begin to move into the antithetical area, beginning with intense and withdrawn figures like Parnell (Phase 10) or Nietzsche (Phase 12). Individuality then advances to heroic proportions, and we have ''sensualists'' so complete that they represent a kind of antithesis to sanctity (Phase 13), artists of tempestuous passion, women of fully ripened physical beauty, and heroes of arrogant pride like the heroes of Shakespeare's tragedies.

At the point of highest development represented by Phase 15 the counter-movement back to communal consciousness begins. Artists become less embodiments of passion and more intellectualised (Phase 21), or technicians (Phase 23); heroes come to think of themselves as servants of impersonal force, like Napoleon (Phase 20), or the money-obsessed characters in Balzac; women come to be guardians of a generally accepted morality like Queen Victoria (Phase 24). The ''personality,'' which is the fully developed individuality, becomes the ''character,'' a subjective conception implying that something objective to it is greater. Yeats speaks of the antithetical types as subjective, too, but their subjectivity creates its own world, whereas primary subjectivity first separates itself from the objective world, then is increasingly drawn to it as a unity destined to absorb all subjects. These two aspects of subjectivity are symbolised in Yeats by two expressions of the eye: the stare, which sees nothing but expresses an inner consciousness, and the glance, the subject looking *at* a reality set over against it. At later primary stages personality becomes more fragmented, this fragmentation being represented by the physical deformity of the hunchback (Phase 26), and the mental deformity of the fool (Phase 28). What Spengler calls the "second religiousness" comes into society in the forms of spiritualism, theosophy, and various forms of revived occultism, seeking the same kind of kinship with the invisible world, at the other end of the social cycle, that primitive societies show in their myths and folk-tales and so-called superstitions. Yeats often recurs to the similirity between the primitive and the sophisticated conceptions of unseen beings, the legendary rumour in remote cottages and the seances in suburban parlours. The entire cycle describes a progression through the four elements of earth, water, air and fire, each quadrant having a particular relationship to each element.

The conception on which the whole of *A Vision* turns is the contrast of antithetical and primary natures, which is part of a dichotomy that runs through Yeats's writing and thinking. In an early letter he says: "I have always considered myself a voice of what I believe to be a greater renaissance—the revolt of the soul against the intellect—now beginning in the world," and this involves a preference of the swordsman to the saint, of the aristocratic to the democratic virtues, of the reality of beauty to the reality of truth, of (to use categories from Eliot's "Burnt Norton") the way of plentitude to the way of vacancy. The contrast is so far-reaching that it may be simplest to set all its aspects out at once in a table, though many of them will not be intelligible until farther on in this essay.

ANTITHETICAL	PRIMARY
individuality	unity
Leda and Swan	Virgin and Dove
Oedipus	Christ
son kills father	son appeases father
incest with mother	redemption of mother and bride
drive toward nature	drive toward God
tragic	comic
master-morality	servant-morality
aristocratic	democratic
discord	concord
quality	quantity
freedom	necessity
fiction	truth
evil	good
art	science
ecstasy	wisdom
kindred	mechanism
particularity	abstraction
lunar	solar
natural	reasonable
war	peace
personality	character
Michael Robartes	Owen Aherne
Oisin	St. Patrick
(Eros)	(Agape)
(Chinese Yang)	(Chinese Yin)
(Nietzsche's Apollo)	(Nietzsche's Dionysus)
(Blake's Orc, "Devils," Rintrah, "Science of Wrath")	(Blake's Urizen, "Angels," Palamabron,"Science of Pity")

(pp. 15-18)

The Apollonian and Dionysiac categories seem curiously placed, but Yeats thinks of Apollo as a creative force and of Dionysus as a transcendent one.

The drive to individuality is a drive toward nature, Yeats says, and has for its goal a complete physical self-fulfilment or "Unity of Being," which may be attained in the phases close to Phase 15, the phase of the full moon. Phase 15 itself realises this so completely that it cannot be achieved in human life at all. We thus arrive at the difficult conception of a creature which is superhuman because it is completely natural. We are not told much about these Phase 15 beings, beyond a mysterious passage in **"The Phases of the Moon,"** but, of course, a perfect human harmony could also be symbolised by perfect sexual intercourse, and we are told in that delightful poem **"Solomon and the Witch"** that a union of this kind would restore man to the unfallen world. Yeats strongly hints that Christ was a superhuman incarnation, a unique entry of Phase 15 into human life, though an explicit statement on this point would doubtless have annoyed his instructors. He often refers, for instance, to an alleged belief that Christ was the only man exactly six feet high. Why so arbitrary a measure as the foot should have been in the mind of the Trinity from all eternity is not clear, but the meaning is that Christ had the perfect "Unity of Being" which, Yeats tells us, Dante compares to a perfectly proportioned human body.

The opposite drive toward an objective unity is a drive toward "God," and has as its goal an absorption in God (Phase 1) which is similarly a superhuman phase of pure "plasticity." Hence the real direction of the attempt in the primary phases to subordinate oneself to objective powers is revealed in the religious leader (Phase 25) and most clearly of all in the saint (Phase 27). As far as this twenty-eight-phase cycle of being is concerned, "God" for Yeats appears to be a character like the button-moulder in *Peer Gynt,* pounding everything to dust with the pestle of the moon, a cosmic spider or vampire who swallows the Many in the One. In short, God occupies the place of Death, which makes Yeats's remark that he tends to write coldly of God something of an understatement.

We have spoken so far of a general social cycle from primitivism to decadence, but there are two more specific ones in Yeats, which correspond to the Classical and Western cycles in Spengler. Draw a circle on a page and mark its four cardinal points 1, 8, 15 and 22. These phases on Yeats's historical calendar (or at least the most important of several he uses) are a thousand years apart. Phase 1 is 2000 B.C.; Phase 8 is 1000 B.C.; Phase 15 is the time of Christ; Phase 22 is A.D. 1000; Phase 1 is therefore our own time as well as 2000 B.C., and Phase 8 is also a thousand years from now. Classical civilisation extends from Phase 8 to 22, 1000 B.C. to A.D. 1000, and Christian civilisation, which is our own, from A.D. 1000 to 3000, Phases 22 to 8. We are half-way through the latter now, at the same point Classical civilisation reached in the time of Christ. Phases 8 and 22 are represented by Troy and Byzantium, one an Asiatic city destroyed by Europeans and the other a European city captured by Asiatics, yet so close together that Byzantium, when it became a centre of Roman power, was thought of as a new Troy. Each civilisation is the opposite or complement of its predecessor. Classical civilisation was essentially antithetical, tragic, heroic and strongly individualised; Christian civilisation is therefore essentially primary, democratic, altruistic and based on a subject-object attitude to reality. Byzantium was the main source of early Irish culture, and its place in Yeats's thought gives a special significance to his allusions to people roughly contemporary with its golden age, such as Charlemagne and Harun Al-Rashid.

Half-way through, a civilisation generates the beginning of its counteracting movement, hence Christ, the presiding genius of the civilisation that began a millennium later, appears in the middle of the Classical cycle. "The Incarnation," says Yeats, "invoked modern science and modern efficiency, and individualised emotion." Thus a religious movement cuts the cycle of civilisations at right-angles, and Christianity as a religion extends from the time of Christ to about our own day. It follows that a similar Messianic figure announcing Classical civilisation must have appeared around 2000 B.C., and that another, announcing a second antithetical civilisation of the future, is to appear somewhere around our own time. Yeats speaks of an antithetical influx setting in "a considerable time before" the close of its predecessor, perhaps to get it more exactly into his own time. In 2000 B.C., in the middle of a pre-Classical culture associated vaguely by Yeats with "Babylonian starlight," the annunciation of the Greek culture pattern was made, in what way we do not know, but surviving in two myths. One is the myth of Leda and the swan, the divine bird impregnating the human woman, the fulfilment of their union being, eventually, the fall of Troy, which began Greek history, properly speaking. The other is the myth of Oedipus, whose parricide and mother-incest set the tragic and heroic tone of an antithetical culture. The complementary myths appear with the birth of Christ, the myth of the dove and the Virgin and the myth of the son appeasing his father's wrath and redeeming his mother and bride. Our own day is the period of the annunciation of a new Oedipus and Leda mythology, heralding the tragic and warlike age of the future and ushering in a religion contrasting with Christianity. The Messiah of our day is an Antichrist, that is, an antithetical Christ, the terrible reborn Babe of Blake's "Mental Traveller." As Christ's mother was a virgin, so the new Messiah's mother, in **"The Adoration of the Magi,"** is a harlot and a devotee of the Black Mass, resembling the Virgin only in being rejected by the society of her time. In *The Herne's Egg* the new Messiah is to be born in Ireland, the Judea of the West, the offspring of a heron and his fanatical priestess. What this Messiah has to announce, of course, is the future age when "another Troy shall rise and set."

In Spengler each culture has a "prime symbol" expressing its inner essence, which is a Doric column for the Classical, a cavern for the Magian, a garden for the Chinese, and so on. For some reason he gives no primary symbol for Western culture, saying only that it is characterised by a drive into the infinite. Yeats, learning from Pound that Frobenius found two major symbols in Africa, a cavern and an altar with sixteen roads leading from it, suggests that Spengler took his Magian cavern from Frobenius and should have provided us with the altar for the Western symbol. In Yeats the middle "Magian" cycle is replaced by the conception of a religious cycle cutting the historical one midway, but Yeats resembles Spengler in associating Christ, who was born in a manger and rose from a tomb, with the cavern. Hence "At or near the central point of our civilisation must come *antithetical* revelation, the turbulent child of the Altar." Yeats, however, does not use the altar as a symbol for our own time in his poetry, though the cavern appears as an image of the passage from death to rebirth (Phase 1, more or less) in **"The Hour before Dawn."** The chief images he does use are those of birds and animals. The bird is often the swan, for obvious reasons, but with a whole parliament of fowls in addition. If we take three representative poems on this theme, **"The Second Coming," "Demon and Beast,"** and **"On a Picture of a Black Centaur by Edmund Dulac,"** we find a gyring falcon in the first, a gyring gull and a green-headed duck in the second, and "horrible green birds" in the third, accompanying the age in which the "demon" (not daimon, which is a quite different conception) of late phases

gives place to the "beast" of early ones, the "rough beast" of **"The Second Coming"** who modulates into the centaurs of the Dulac poem.

Everybody belongs fundamentally to one of the twenty-six human phases or types, but, of course, a man of any phase can be born at any time in history. If a social cycle has reached, say, Phase 22 (more or less the Victorian period in European culture), those who belong to phases near 22 will be typical of their time, and those of early phases (George Borrow and Carlyle in Phase 7, for example) have a more difficult adjustment to make. But a man may also be typical or atypical of his own phase, and Yeats begins many of his descriptions, very confusingly, by dealing with the "out of phase" variant of the type. Yeats further tells us that in practice he cannot point to historical examples of several of the phases, partly because many of the more primary ones do not produce types who make any impression on history.

For one reason or another, what Yeats calls in **"The Gift of Harun Al-Rashid"**

> Those terrible implacable straight lines
> Drawn through the wandering vegetative dream

turn out in practice to be nearly as accommodating as Baconian ciphers in Shakespeare. For instance, Yeats tells us that each millennium of the two-thousand-year cycle can be considered as a complete twenty-eight-phase wheel in itself, so that we are also near the Phase 1 end of the first millennium of our Christian civilisation, which adds to its chaos. This millennium reached its antithetical height of Phase 15 at the Quattrocento, when men attained to personality in great numbers," and when Europe was infused by the spirit of the recently fallen Byzantium. This curtailed millennial version of the rhythm of Western culture, which incidentally is much closer to Spengler, lies behind most of Yeats's references to Michelangelo and to one of his seminal books, Castiglione's *Courtier* (see, for example, **"The People"**). In the Renaissance there was also a kind of minor annunciation of the opposite kind of civilisation, and so Yeats has reasons (he tells us in a passage in *On the Boiler* . . .) both to "adore" and to "detest" the Renaissance.

Again, there are larger rhythms in history, obtained by adding a solar and zodiacal cycle to the lunar one. One of these is the "Great Year," traditionally formed by the precession of the equinoxes, and which lasts for twenty-six thousand years, a "year" of twelve "months" of two thousand odd years each. One of these Great Years ended and began with Christ, who rose from the dead at the "full moon in March" which marks that point. Caesar was assassinated at another full moon in March a few decades earlier. Yeats points out how contemporaries of Christ, such as Virgil in the Fourth Eclogue and Horace in the *Carmen Saeculare,* felt a peculiar cyclical significance about that time which Christianity itself, anxious as it was to get away from cyclical theories, ignored. The birth of Christ took place at a (primary) conjunction of Mars and Venus, and our new Messiah will be born at the opposite conjunction of Jupiter and Saturn, when the "mummy wheat" of the buried Classical civilisation will start to sprout.

The emotional focus of *A Vision* is also that of Yeats's life, the sense that his own time is a time of a trembling of the veil of the temple, eventually defined as a myth of a new religious dispensation announcing a new God to replace Christ and accompanied by the traditional signs of the end of the world. Yeats traces his sense of an imminent Armageddon back to such early poems as **"The Hosting of the Sidhe"** and **"The**

Valley of the Black Pig.'' A note to the former poem tells us that the sidhe or fairy folk of Ireland dance in gyres or whirlwinds which are called the dance of the daughters of Herodias: the last section of **"Nineteen Hundred and Nineteen"** applies this imagery to Yeats's own time. Although our own time is Phase 15 of the Christian era, it can be read in different ways on Yeats's various clocks, and Yeats tends to think of it primarily as a passing through Phase 1, when a great age has finally reached the crescent of the "fool" and hears the irrational cry ("the scream of Juno's peacock") of a new birth.

Yeats's treatment of the theme of contemporary annunciation exhibits a complete emotional range, from the most raucous nonsense to the most serene wisdom. We may divide his personal reactions to it into a cycle of six phases. First comes the phase of the deplorable if harmless rabble-rouser of *On the Boiler,* shouting for a "just war," hailing Fascism as the force that will restore all the traditional heroic dignities to society, and prophesying a new "science" compounded of spiritualism and selective breeding. Some of Yeats's instructors appear to have been incapable of distinguishing a lunar vision from a lunatic one, and this phase in Yeats seems to be part of the backwash from revising *A Vision* around 1937. In an early letter Yeats says: "Every influence has a shadow, as it were, an unbalanced—the unbalanced is the Kabalistic definition of evil—duplicate of itself." Fortunately this phase is not allowed to spoil much of his poetry, though it is creeping around the fringes of **"Under Ben Bulben."**

The second phase is that of the traditionalist who stresses the importance of convention and manners, "where all's accustomed, ceremonious," and sees the preservation of this as preliminary to developing a new aristocracy. Yeats's cabinet of great Irishmen, Swift, Burke, Berkeley and others, are called upon to endorse this attitude, which is also heard in a simpler form in the contented reveries emanating from Coole Park and Stockholm on the values of hereditary privilege. The third phase is that of the neo-pagan, the poet who celebrates a rebirth of physical energy and sexual desire, who insists on the sacredness of bodily functions, who helps Crazy Jane to refute the Bishop on the primacy of the life of the soul, and who asks the unanswerable question:

> If soul may look and body touch,
> Which is the more blest?

The fourth phase is that of the teacher, the author of the *Samhain* essays who stands out against a "primary" mob, assuming the role, in his own literary context, of

> A great man in his pride
> Confronting murderous men.

This is the critic who patiently points out to his Irish audience that no true patriotism can be built on the stock response and no true religion on the consecration of it; that the morality of art must always be liberal, and that the sectarian instinct, "a pretended hatred of vice and a real hatred of intellect," is always part of the mob, whether it expresses itself in politics, religion or art. The fifth phase is the prophet, the troubled visionary of **"The Second Coming"** and elsewhere, who sees and records but does not try to rationalise the horror and violence of his own time, who can understand the ferocity of "The weasel's twist, the weasel's tooth" without confusing it with heroism. Finally, there is the phase of the sage, the poet of **"Lapis Lazuli"** who can speak of the "gaiety that leaps up before danger or difficulty," and who understands that even horror and violence can inspire a kind of exuberance. We notice

that all these phases which are directly connected with literature are very precious attributes of Yeats, but that for the others the best we can do is to apply to Yeats what Yeats himself says of Shelley: "Great as Shelley is, those theories about the coming changes of the world, which he has built up with so much elaborate passion, hurry him from life continually."

Or, as Yeats also says, "All art is the disengaging of a soul from place and history." It has doubtless occurred to more than one reader of *A Vision* that Yeats might more easily have seen his cycle, not as the archetypal forms of human life, but of human imagination: in other words as a perfect circle of literary or mythical types, which is how Blake saw the pilgrims of Chaucer. Many of Yeats's examples are writers who, like Whitman at Phase 6, have made their lives conform to literary patterns, or who, like Shakespeare at Phase 20, are described by the kind of poetry they produced and not personally. The primitives of phases 2 to 7 are much easier to understand as archetypes of pastoral or Romantic conventions in literature; Dostoievsky's Idiot is the only example given of Phase 8; and Nietzsche's Zarathustra fits better into the "Forerunner" position of Phase 12 than Nietzsche himself. Phase 15 would then become intelligible as the phase of the poet's ideal or male Muse: the Eros of Dante and Chaucer, the "Ille" of **"Ego Dominus Tuus"**; the beautiful youth of Shakespeare's sonnets, and the like. The high antithetical phases would be much more clearly represented by characters in Shakespeare or Irish legend, and the high primary ones by characters in Balzac and Browning, than they are by Galsworthy or Lamarck or "a certain actress."

Such a rearrangement would bring out the real relation of the *Vision* cycle of types to Yeats's own characters. The fool and the blind man who remain on the stage at the end of *On Baile's Strand* symbolise the disappearance of the Cuchulain cycle (which is symbolically the Christian cycle, too, as Cuchulain was contemporary with Christ), the blind man representing the dark moonless night of Phase 1. The happy natural fool of *The Hour-Glass* is also a fool of Phase 28, with a Creative Mind from the **"Player on Pan's Pipes"** of Phase 2. In *Resurrection* a blind man and a lame man, the two together making up the physical deformity of the "hunchback," appear beside a saint, and in *The Player Queen* the opposition of Decima and the Queen she supplants is a burlesque illustration of the opposition of Phases 13 and 27, antithetical and primary perfection. The Queen in any case is a much better example of what Yeats appears to mean by sanctity than the historical examples he gives, which are Socrates and Pascal.

In the cycle of "The Mental Traveller" Blake symbolises the subjective and objective aspects of life as male and female. All human beings including women are symbolically male, part of the reborn "Boy," and nature, or the physical environment that is temporarily transformed into human shape by a culture, is what is symbolically female. Male and female cycles rotate in opposite directions, one growing older as the other grows younger. *A Vision* refers briefly to this symbolism, but *A Vision* says little about the objective aspect of civilisation. The conception of the individual is much more complicated. Here, as in Blake, there are subjective and objective factors, but there are two of each, making four "Faculties" in all. An individual may be thought of as acting man (Will) or as seeing, knowing or thinking man (Creative Mind). In so far as he thinks or knows or sees, man operates on a known or seen world, a set of *données* or given facts and truths and events that make up what Yeats calls the Body of Fate. In so far as he acts, he acts in the light of a certain vision of action, which Yeats calls the Mask, and which includes both what he wants to make of himself and what he wants to make of the world around him. In "antithetical" phases action is motivated by an "image" springing from the self which complements the Will: in "primary" phases, where man is more apt to say, with Hic in **"Ego Dominus Tuus,"** "I would find myself and not an image," it is motivated by a desire to act on the world as a separated or impersonal thing, and eventually by a desire to be absorbed in that world. Each man is defined by the phase of his Will, and his Mask comes from the phase directly opposite, fourteen phases away. The Body of Fate is similarly opposite the Creative Mind, and Will and Creative Mind are related by the fact that, like male and female principles in Blake, they rotate in opposite directions. The details are too complicated to go into here, but a man of Phase 23 is actually made up of a Will of Phase 23, a Mask of Phase 9, a Creative Mind of Phase 7, and a Body of Fate of Phase 21.

In the Platonic tradition the relation of Creative Mind and Will is differently conceived. There is a superior intelligible world and an inferior physical world. In the latter the body perceives and acts on the image; in the former the soul perceives the form or idea, not as an object, but as something ultimately identical with itself. The soul and the world of forms are imprisoned in the physical world and struggle to break out of it. For Yeats, too, there is another way of looking at the four Faculties we have just dealt with. If we think of man as actor and creator, we see his life as an interplay of action and thought; if we think of him as a creature, we see his life as a physical contact with objects out of which a higher kind of identity is trying to emerge. In this perspective the four "Faculties" become four "Principles." Will and Mask now become two lower Principles, Husk and Passionate Body, the physical subject and the physical object. Creative Mind and Body of Fate become Spirit and Celestial Body, the soul and the world of forms. This introduces a dialectical element into the cycle, a movement out of it into a world of changeless being.

From the beginning Yeats's poetic world comprised a state of experience and a state of innocence, the latter being associated with the Irish fairy world, a "land of heart's desire" where there was an eternal youth of dancing and revelry. In *The Celtic Twilight* this world is once described as the Paradise still buried under the fallen world, but its associations are usually more specific. Yeats quotes legends indicating that the seasons of this world are the reverse of ours, like the southern hemisphere, and, in the *Autobiographies,* a remark of Madame Blavatsky that we live in a dumbbell-shaped cosmos, with an antipodal world at our North Pole. This conception is most readily visualised as an hour-glass, the emblem of time and the basis of Yeats's "double gyre" diagrams, and in the play that is explicitly called *The Hour-Glass* we are told that "There are two living countries, the one visible and the other invisible; and when it is winter with us it is summer in that country." The fairy world has occasionally, according to legend and folk tale, caught up human beings, who found, when they returned to their own world, that time moves much faster here than there, and that a few days in fairyland had been many years of human life. As Yeats began to try to fit together what he knew of Irish legend with what he read in Swedenborg or learned at seances, he also began to think of his fairy world as complementary to our own in time as well as climate, and as moving from age to youth. He often refers to Swedenborg as saying that the angels move towards their youth in time, as we move towards age.

Yeats's doctrine of reincarnation eventually annexed this world and transformed it into the world that we enter at death and leave again at birth, which is also a rebirth. It lost most of its cheerfulness in this process and acquired many of the characteristics of a penal régime. Book III of *A Vision,* called "The Soul in Judgement," is supposed to tell us what his instructors knew about the antipodal world, but Yeats speaks of this section with some disappointment as more fragmentary than he hoped it would be. It uses a good deal of material from the earlier essay **"Swedenborg, Mediums, and the Desolate Places."** The discarnate soul is pulled in the ideal direction of Spirit and Celestial Body, and away from Husk and Passionate Body, by a series of spiritual or imaginative repetitions of the major emotional crises of its earthly life, which tend eventually to exhaust them, as the confessional techniques of psychology are supposed to do with neuroses. Yeats calls this the "dreaming back," the most important of several stages of the return to rebirth. A violent crime may be re-enacted for centuries in the same spot, a fact which accounts for many types of ghost story; brutal masters and submissive slaves may exchange rolls in a tenebrous saturnalia. Yeats suggests that our dreams, though they use our own experiences and desires as material, are actually part of the psychic life of the dead moving backwards to rebirth through us. The more fully a life has been lived, the less expiation is needed and the more successful the next life. Another life is, in fact, part of the whole "dreaming back" operation, so that every life is a movement from birth to death and simultaneously part of a purgatorial movement from death to rebirth. When a spirit is completely purified and ready for what in Christianity would be heaven, it may seek rebirth as an act of deliberate choice, like the Bodhisattva in Buddhism.

In the Eastern religions the cycle of life, death and rebirth is regarded as an enslavement, from which all genuine spiritual effort tries to liberate itself by reducing the physical world to unreality. The attitude of the Christian saint, even without a belief in reincarnation, is similar. Such a course is, according to some moods of Yeats, opposed to that of the poet and artist, whose function it is to show the reality incarnate in the appearance of the physical world and in the physical emotional life of man. The poet accepts the plenitude of the phenomenal world, and in the cycle of Faculties the most strongly "antithetical" types, heroes and beautiful women who are driven by the passions of a titanic ego, are the poet's natural subjects. Long before *A Vision* Yeats had written: "If it be true that God is a circle whose centre is everywhere, the saint goes to the centre, the poet and artist to the ring where everything comes round again." Hence his emotional preference of the "antithetical" to the "primary," of the way of the poet to the way of the saint, leads to a preference for cyclical and rebirth symbolism in contrast to the kind of symbolism that separates reality into an apocalyptic and a demonic world.

The conflict of the abstract vision of the saint and the concrete vision of the poet, one seeking deliverance from the wheel of life and the other ready to accept the return of it, is the theme of many of Yeats's best-known poems. The setting of such poems is some modification of the top of Dante's mountain of purgatory, a winding stair in a tower leading upwards to a point at which one may contemplate both an eternal world above and a cyclical world below. In **"A Dialogue of Self and Soul"** the Soul summons to an upward climb into the dark; the Self, preoccupied with the dying-god symbol of the Japanese ceremonial sword wrapped in embroidered silk with flowers of "heart's purple," looks downward into rebirth and maintains "I am content to live it all again." In **"Vacillation,"** where there is a similar dialogue between Soul and Heart, the opening image is the tree of Attis which stands between eternity and rebirth, and the final contrast is between the saint whose body remains uncorrupted and the poet who deliberately seeks the cycle of corruption in generation symbolised by Samson's riddle of the lion and the honeycomb. In **"Among School Children"** there is a similar antithesis between the nun and the mother, the former symbolising the direct ascent to eternity and the latter the cycle of generation. Here the tree, appearing at the end instead of at the beginning, seems a resolving or reconciling image rather than one of "vacillation," but the contrast remains in the poem's argument.

However much imaginative sympathy we may have with these poems as poems, they indicate a deficiency in *A Vision* as an expression of some of Yeats's more profound insights. Yeats speaks of Emerson and Whitman as "writers who have begun to seem superficial precisely because they lack the Vision of Evil," but his own lack of a sense of evil borders on the frivolous. Visions of horror and violence certainly haunt his poetry, but in *A Vision* and elsewhere in his later essays, even in much of the poetry itself, they are all rationalised and explained away as part of the necessary blood-bath accompanying the birth of his new and repulsive Messiah. The absence of any sense of a demonic world, a world of evil and tyranny and meanness and torment, such as human desire utterly repudiates and bends every effort to get away from, is connected with, and is perhaps the cause of, the absence in *A Vision* of the kind of dialectical imagery that appears in, say, **"The Two Trees,"** which in Blake would be the tree of life and the tree of mystery. Occasionally in earlier prose writings we get glimpses of a whole dimension of symbolism that seems to have got strangled in *A Vision*. Yeats says in an early essay: "To lunar influence belong all thoughts and emotions that were created by the community, by the common people, by nobody knows who, and to the sun all that came from the high disciplined or individual kingly mind." This imagery is repeated in **"A Dialogue of Self and Soul,"** but in *A Vision* the sun is "primary," and has been absorbed into the lunar cycle: the solar and zodiacal symbolism in *A Vision,* already glanced at, only extends the lunar cycle, and adds nothing new in kind.

What we miss in *A Vision,* and in Yeats's speculative prose generally, is the kind of construct that would correspond to such a poem as **"Sailing to Byzantium."** This poem presents an eternal world which contains all the concrete imagery and physical reality associated elsewhere with the cycle of rebirth, which is not a mere plunge into nothingness and darkness by an infatuated soul, and yet is clear of the suggestion that nothing really lasts except what Blake calls the "same dull round." Such a poem is apocalyptic, a vision of plentitude which is still not bound to time. *The Shadowy Waters,* also, differs from the later poems of the **"Vacillation"** group in that the chief characters go on to finish their quest and the subordinate characters (the sailors) return to the world. The goal of the quest is also described in apocalyptic terms:

> Where the world ends
> The mind is made unchanging, for it finds
> Miracle, ecstasy, the impossible hope,
> The flagstone under all, the fire of fires,
> The roots of the world.

For a theoretical construct to match this apocalyptic imagery we have to set aside the main body of *A Vision,* with its conception of unity and individuality as opposed and impossible ideals which only superhuman beings can reach, and look for another construct in which they are at the same point, and that point accessible to human life.

There are two apocalyptic symbols in *A Vision:* one is the "Record" or consolidated form of all the images of "ultimate reality," associated by Yeats, I think correctly, with Blake's Golgonooza. The other and more important one is the "Thirteenth Cone," which is not really a cone but a sphere, and which "is that cycle which may deliver us from the twelve cycles of time and space." We are further told, in what ought to be one of the key passages of *A Vision,* that this thirteenth cone confronts every cycle of life, large or small, as "the reflection or messenger of the final deliverance," and at the very end of the book it is said to exist in every man and to be what is called by man his freedom. There are also "teaching spirits" of this thirteenth cone who direct and inspire those who are in the cycle, and Yeats calls the thirteenth cone his substitute for God. He speaks of it as "like some great dancer," recalling the great last line of **"Among School Children"** which unites being and becoming, imagination and image.

The temporary mixture of four Faculties that constitutes what is ordinarily thought of as an individual is not final human reality. A poet discovers this, for example, when he realises that the images that great poetry uses are traditional, archetypal, conventional images, and that the emotions he employs to set these images forth are traditional and conventional emotions, representing states of being greater than himself. Thus the poet finds himself drawn out of his Husk into his Spirit, and thereby enters into much larger conceptions of what subject and object are. He is drawn up into a world in which subject and object become the human imagination and the human image, each being archetypes that recur in every individual man and poem. These great traditional states of being which the poet enters into and expresses are akin to the "giant forms" of Blake's prophecies, Orc, Tharmas, Los and the rest, and, more generally, to the "gods" of beauty and nature and war who inform so much of literature. Yeats sometimes calls them "moods," and speaks of them as divine beings whose dreams form our own waking lives. Thus in *The Shadowy Waters* the central characters discover that

> We have fallen in the dreams the Ever-living
> Breathe on the burnished mirror of the world.

In *A Vision* the poetic imagination begins in the self of the individual, but moves in the direction of identifying with a greater self called the "daimon," and the process of purgation between lives has for its eventual goal a similar identification.

Apart from the contrast of self and soul, there is also an abstract vision associated, not with sanctity, but with art itself. This is the vision linked with the name of Pythagoras, whose mathematical genius "planned" the art of exquisite proportion embodied in Greek sculpture and architecture. The role of art in imposing mathematical proportion on reality is connected by Yeats also with the geometrical diagrams of his own *Vision,* which he compares to the forms of Brancusi sculpture. Here we see how art, no less than sanctity, moves in the direction of a greater identity. In the poem **"To Dorothy Wellesley"** it is not the soul that climbs the stair towards darkness, but the poetic power, which ascends in search of identity with the greater forms and figures of existence represented by the "Proud Furies." Such identity is no loss of individuality; it is merely a loss of what we might call the ego. In Yeats's terms, it loses character and gains personality. The saint attains a powerful personality by forgetting about his ego; but the poet, too, as Yeats says, "must die every day he lives, be reborn, as it is said in the Burial Service, an incorruptible self.'' For the poet, Yeats also says, ''is never the bundle of accident and incoherence that sits down to breakfast: he has been reborn as an idea.''

''I think,'' says Yeats, ''that much of the confusion of modern philosophy . . . comes from our renouncing the ancient hierarchy of beings from man up to the One.'' The process of entering into a life greater than our ordinary one, which every poet knows, is a process of entering into this hierarchy, and of beginning to ascend the stair of life. The Thirteenth Cone, therefore, is a symbol of the way in which man emancipates himself by becoming part of Man, through a series of greater human forms. Here we move toward an existence in which Phases 1 and 15, unity and individuality, are the same point. It is therefore impossible that the ''One'' could be anything but Man, or something identical or identifiable with man. Yeats refers occasionally to the ''One'' as a sleeping giant like Blake's Albion or Joyce's Finnegan (**''The Mountain Tomb,'' ''The Old Stone Cross,''** etc.), but he is even nearer the centre of his own intuitions when he speaks of man as having created death, when he says that there is nothing but life and that nothing exists but a stream of souls, and that man has, out of his own mind, made up the whole story of life and death and still can

> Dream, and so create
> Translunar Paradise.

The Thirteenth Cone, then, represents the dialectical element in symbolism, where man is directly confronted by the greater form of himself which challenges him to identify himself with it. This confrontation is the real form of the double gyre. ''The repose of man is the choice of the Daimon, and the repose of the Daimon the choice of man . . . I might have seen this, as it all follows from the words written by the beggar in *The Hour-Glass* upon the walls of Babylon.'' He might also have seen that this conception of the double gyre reduces his twenty-eight-phase historical cycle to something largely useless as a commentary on his own poetry, except for the poems deliberately based on it.

Yeats often speaks of entering into these personal archetypes, daimons or moods as a process of literal or symbolic death. ''Wisdom is the property of the dead,'' he says, and his fascination with the remark in *Axël,* ''As for living, our servants will do that for us,'' is connected with the same conception. Yeats's own interpretation of the *Axël* passage is indicated in **''The Tables of the Law'':** ''certain others, and in always increasing numbers, were elected, not to live, but to reveal that hidden substance of God which is colour and music and softness and a sweet odour; and . . . these have no father but the Holy Spirit.'' Two of his poems describe the direct passage across from ordinary life to archetype, **''News for the Delphic Oracle''** and **''Byzantium.''** The latter poem is mainly about images, which are, as always in Yeats, generated in water and borne across water by dolphins into the simplifying and purgatorial world of fire. The former poem applies the same movement to human souls, and makes it clear that nothing of the physical or concrete world is lost, or even sublimated, by the kind of redemption here described.

These two poems, then, deal with the consolidation of imaginations and images, the true subjects and the true objects, into a timeless unity. But, of course, the image is a product of the imagination: in the imaginative world the relation of subject and object is that of creator and creature. In this perspective the whole cycle of nature, of life and death and rebirth which

Yeats in his later years. The Granger Collection, New York.

man has dreamed, becomes a single gigantic image, and the process of redemption is to be finally understood as an identification with Man and a detachment from the cyclical image he has created. This ultimate insight in Yeats is the one expressed in his many references (one of which forms the last sentence of *A Vision*) to a passage in the *Odyssey* where Heracles, seen by Odysseus in hell, is said to be present in hell only in his shade, the real Heracles, the man in contrast to the image, being at the banquet of the immortal gods. Here we come to the heart of what Yeats had to say as a poet. The vision of Heracles the man, eternally free from Heracles the shadowy image bound to an endless cycle, is nearer to being a ''key'' to Yeats's thought and imagination than anything else in *A Vision*. To use the phraseology of *Per Amica Silentia Lunae*, it is an insight he had acquired, not by eavesdropping on the babble of the *anima mundi*, but from his own fully conscious *anima hominis*, the repository of a deeper wisdom than the ghostly house of rumour ever knew. (pp. 18-32)

> Northrop Frye, ''The Rising of the Moon: A Study of 'A Vision','' *in* An Honoured Guest: New Essays on W. B. Yeats, *edited by Denis Donoghue and J. R. Mulryne, Edward Arnold (Publishers) Ltd., 1965, pp. 8-33.*

LEONARD E. NATHAN (essay date 1965)

[*In the following excerpt from Nathan's conclusion to* The Tragic Drama of William Butler Yeats, *Nathan assesses the degree to which Yeats realized his dramatic aims.*]

Yeats, in one of his last critical pronouncements, speaks of a perpetual war "where opposites die each other's life, live each other's death." This is no less than the war of "spiritual with natural order," the subject of *The Secret Rose* nearly forty years earlier—the war at the heart of human experience and therefore, so Yeats believed, the most serious subject for the drama. On the strength of that belief, he labored, often in bitterly discouraging circumstances, to find a dramatic form that would suit a living stage. The intensity of Yeats's desire to find a suitable embodiment for this chosen subject can be measured by his ruthless self-criticism; he was, both as poet and playwright, a constant and careful reviser. From the beginning he got little enough help from the English theatre where the only war was between the proponents of a dying traditional drama and the advocates of the realistic problem play. In this situation the temptation for a literary man, with an inclination for playwriting, would be closet drama or, perhaps, dramatic monologue. But Yeats wanted to write plays for a living theatre, "character in action," not "action in character"; the result was years of experiment that began in the shadowy precincts of Pre-Raphaelite moodiness and ended in the lucid depths of the individual mind, scene of a relentless but sometimes ennobling conflict between spirit and nature. (pp. 251-52)

[The] last period in the long search contains the best plays because in them Yeats had for the first time satisfied his own dramatic requirements. When the supernatural order appeared on stage in *The Only Jealousy of Emer* it could not by any rationalization be passed off as a symbol for psychological or sociological realities; the supernatural, in the last plays, is the supernatural or the spiritual reality either in the self or beyond it, no more and no less. This achievement cannot be claimed for the earlier plays.

It is perhaps indicative of their failure to offer a serious presentation of the supernatural that *The Land of Heart's Desire, The Countess Cathleen,* and even *On Baile's Strand* are so easily accepted into the traditional repertory. If *Purgatory* is also accepted, I think that must be laid to the fact that the play looks a little like *Waiting for Godot,* that is, seems to fit into the new fashion.

The question then is this: Do the last plays, understood as serious embodiments of spiritual reality, have any place in the tradition of plays that deserve a stage, or are they brilliant closet dramas at best, despite Yeats's intention? One easy answer is to "interpret" these plays in some way so that they do become psychological after all. Another such answer, a better one, is to invoke the "willing suspension of disbelief," to say, in substance, that in their own terms the plays are valid, as *The Divine Comedy* is valid for non-Catholics or unmedieval Catholics.

The first answer will not do; the second is somewhat evasive and fails to do justice to . . . Yeats's philosophical seriousness as a playwright. For Yeats demands belief, if not in his system, then in the reality the system names and orders. Just how much belief he demanded is indicated by the requirements for staging his dance plays: better than fair actors, unremitting adherence to the convention, and an audience that comes with no expectation of daily reality or some noble form of it. Yeats saw to it, in short, that his last words in the drama would not be easily domesticated to the modern stage. And naturally enough the reaction from those not willing to make concessions to so stubborn an eccentric has been indifference, baffled irritation, or patronizing dismissal. It is one thing to admit the "theatre of the absurd" into the repertory; it is quite another to admit

what looks very odd but lays claim to being just the opposite. Yeats is perhaps *too* clear to misinterpret on this score. So he can be safely left to the bravery of college theatres which may not be quite so devoted to fashion and so much the victims of box office. Or the plays can be studied in class as literature, an adjunct to the poems but less important than some of the secondary texts used.

Yeats understood the consequences of his position but was willing to take the risks. He never expected, at least in our era, that he would be regarded as another in a long line of tragic playwrights of the western tradition and that his last plays would be familiar to a wide audience, so perhaps any justification of these plays as part of the great tradition is beside the point. In *On the Boiler* he sums up his awareness with a fine clarity:

> The theatre has not . . . gone my way or in any way I wanted it to go, and often looking back I have wondered if I did right in giving so much of my life to the expression of other men's genius. According to the Indians a man may do much good yet lose his own soul. Then I say to myself, I have had greater luck than any other modern English-speaking dramatist; I have aimed at tragic ecstasy and here and there in my own work and in the work of my friends I have seen it greatly played. What does it matter that it belongs to a dead art and to a time when a man spoke out of an experience and a culture that were not of his time alone, but held his time, as it were, at arms length, that he might be a spectator of the ages.

Yet I think there is reason to regard the best of the last plays as fit for the modern stage, even if one grants their obvious and demanding limitations. *Purgatory* and *The Only Jealousy of Emer* are moving works not because they fit neatly into categories like the psychological or social that give moderns a way of interpreting even the strangest kinds of art but because they treat man's fate with the ruthless honesty and convincing dignity open to the tragic dramatist, more especially open, if history is any proof at all, to the tragic dramatist who is also a great poet. Nor are the honesty and dignity alien to moderns. Yeats's last plays restate, in a new way, the traditional position of tragedy: man, divided and complex, vulnerable both to the world and to himself, is forced to make choices that give him his destiny. Built into this very situation is the possibility—almost probability—that he will bring down suffering on his head and injure others in the process. The total reality of his condition compels him to make his choice; this reality involves a mystery that goes beyond the "natural" or the social, and one cannot account for this mystery by reducing it to psychological, sociological, or historical categories. It is a vital, sometimes terrible presence that man recognizes in moments when his passions seem to break out of the circle of the human. Call the presence anything you like, Apollo or daemon, it is a fact of experience and, in the drama, a fact that inspires belief. The hero is a man who draws this presence to him; it arouses him, by its opposition, to great passion and to action that leads to calamity and suffering in which he discovers his destiny and the wonder of his humanness. In this discovery there can be something like joy, or at least that high, resonant calm in which the whole being accepts what must be and finds its part in the nature of things. If, as in *Purgatory,* the passion falls back on itself without achieving the calm of acceptance, at least the

audience has been in the presence of an intensity that is a
revelation of one great human possibility.

> O bitter reward
> Of many a tragic tomb!
> And we though astonished are dumb
> Or give but a sigh and a word,
> A passing word.

(pp. 252-54)

Leonard E. Nathan, in his The Tragic Drama of
William Butler Yeats: Figures in a Dance, *Columbia
University Press, 1965, 307 p.*

WILLIAM H. O'DONNELL (essay date 1983)

[*In the following excerpt from his* A Guide to the Prose Fiction
of W. B. Yeats, *O'Donnell presents a survey of Yeats's early
short stories.*]

[Yeats's first short story, **"Dhoya,"**] is a poorly executed,
amateurish attempt at a Pre-Raphaelite folk tale. The young
author probably hoped to amaze his readers with a fantastic
plot and to delight them with poetic mannerisms. The style is
a compound of exaggerated, Pateresque, poetic effects flavored
with a sprinkling of Irish inversions, such as: "Human face
he never saw." While there are occasional poetic successes,
awkwardness is much more characteristic: "When his fury was
on him even the bats and the owls, and the brown frogs that
crept out of the grass at twilight, would hide themselves—
even the bats and the owls and the brown frogs."

This apprentice work is overloaded with gratuitous remarks,
such as "for dreams wander nearest to the grave and the cradle,"
which make it the least organically unified of his stories. Yeats
did not hesitate to insert a completely extraneous paragraph in
order to mention a deep spot in Sligo Bay known as Polly or
Pooldhoya. (p. 31)

Yeats's decision in 1886 to use Irish subjects and settings is,
of course, reflected in this story, whose Irishness is established
by use of a County Sligo setting and by direct mention of the
Donegal cotters who still hear the hooves of Dhoya's horse.
Furthermore, as Phillip Marcus has pointed out, the story is
analogous to the old Irish tale of King Eochaid and his fairy
bride, Edain, whom he lost in a chess game to Midhir, her
fairy husband. The possession of a fairy bride on earth by a
mortal husband is not an uncommon motif in Irish folklore.
(pp. 31-2)

Mortality or mutability provides the central theme of **Dhoya,"**
even though largely confined to the final two sections of the
story. Mortals enjoy a vigorous life which the pale, immortal
fairies envy. But mortal strength is necessarily accompanied
by mutability and death, which even the extremely powerful,
almost super-human Dhoya cannot escape. **"Dhoya"** contains
hints of many of the major themes used in *The Secret Rose,*
notably the war between mortal and immortal worlds, the vigor
of mortals in contrast to the shadowy immortals, the inhos-
pitality of the ordinary world toward mortals of great passion
or strength, and man's inevitable mortality. But this early story
fails to assemble the material into a cohesive pattern.

Much of the story is given over to demonstrations of the mortal
Dhoya's power and passions, which the supernal world envies.
The fairy woman tells him: "I have left my world far off. My
people . . . are . . . always happy, always young, always without change. I have left them for thee, Dhoya, for they cannot
love. Only the changing, and moody, and angry, and weary

can love.'' But Dhoya's passionate fits are patently unattractive. We find it difficult to admire a sullen, silent outcast whose
hatred of "placid and beautiful" things leads to the wanton
destruction of a kingfisher, the symbol of peacefulness. . . .
Then, during the term of his cohabitation with the fairy woman,
when his mortal passions are supposed to be an advantage, the
passionate fits disappear. There is thus a fundamental confusion
between the power of love to soothe an unattractive, sullen,
powerful mortal and the power of mortal passions to vivify
love. The attractiveness of mortal passion is further undermined
by the fairy woman's refusal to participate actively in mortal
love. Unlike Cleona, who in **"The Devil's Book"** (1892) takes
on mortality to enjoy the passions of love, Dhoya's fairy wife
is content merely to encourage and passively accept his love,
without giving love herself. She refuses to abandon her immortality. Amid this weakening and confusion of the story's
central themes, all we are left with is the inevitable frustration
of mortality.

The thematic chaos of the story results from the lack of organic
structure. Yeats put more, unrelated elements into this single
story than his apprentice skills could handle. (pp. 32-3)

["**The Devil's Book**"] opens at a shop in mid-eighteenth-cen-
tury Cork, where Hanrahan (called Owen O'Sullivan in the
text of 1892), a wandering Gaelic schoolmaster and poet, buys
an old book, *The Grimoire of Pope Honorius,* rumored to have
been written by the Devil. Hanrahan uses the book to reinforce
his wicked reputation among the peasantry, brazenly scorning
the local priest. One evening he employs the book to invoke
a fairy queen, Cleona of the Wave, but when she appears he
asks her only an unimportant question, which she laboriously
answers in the course of several nights. Finally she comes to
him in a mortal body and tells him that she has left the fairy
world to become his mortal lover, willingly forfeiting her immortality in exchange for the delights of his passionate love.
Hanrahan angrily tells her that he has desired her only because
she was immortal and that he does not love her now that she
has become mortal. After her departure, a fairy whirlwind
destroys his house. In the 1897 version, before leaving, Cleona
imposes a curse on Hanrahan that henceforth he will be tormented by seeing the ideal everywhere he looks in the real
world, but will not be able to attain that ideal:

> Owen Hanrahan the Red, you have looked so often
> upon the dust that when the Rose has blossomed there
> you think it but a pinch of coloured dust; but now I
> lay upon you a curse, and you shall see the Rose
> everywhere, in the noggin, in woman's eye, in drift-
> ing phantoms, and seek to come to it in vain; it shall
> waken a fire in your heart, and in your feet, and in
> your hands. A sorrow of all sorrows is upon you,
> Owen Hanrahan the Red.

The story has many parallels with **"Dhoya."** Both describe
encounters between a mortal man and a fairy woman. Dhoya
is a sullen, solitary outcast; Hanrahan says to the fairy woman
who has turned mortal: "I hate ye—for I hate everybody, and
I hate the world, and I want to be out o' it." Both Dhoya and
Hanrahan meet fairy women who desire the fierceness and
passion that only mortal lovers possess. Hanrahan's Cleona of
the Wave tells him: "I love ye, for ye are fierce and passionate,
now good and now bad, and not free and dim and wave-like
as are the Sheogues. I love ye as Eve loved the Serpent.'' The
fairy women in both stories enjoy their newfound physicality.
Dhoya covers his cave's floor with soft rugs for her to rub her
feet in; Cleona stands "looking at her own foot-marks in the
ashes." The significant difference between the two women is,

as we have noted in the discussion of "**Dhoya,**" that Cleona is willing to sacrifice her immortality in exchange for mortal love. That she should do so makes the attraction of mortal passion much more convincing than it was in the earlier story. (p. 34)

The emergence in 1897 of Cleona's curse, explicitly announcing Hanrahan's hopeless thirst for the supernal, might seem to be the most important difference between the 1892 and 1897 texts. Certainly his unquenchable desire for the immortal realms is a fundamental motif that runs through all the Hanrahan stories. But Cleona's curse is implicit in the 1892 version and was made explicit well before 1897 in subsequent Hanrahan tales. The original story has the fairies destroy Hanrahan's house and then sing about the inevitable failure of attempts, like that of Cleona, to "change the sowls [sic] that are in them to please another." But Hanrahan's dual thirst for mortal and immortal, which forms the basis of Cleona's curse of him, is present in the 1892 conflict between his recent affection for Molly Casey and his banishment of Cleona for having become mortal. Furthermore, Hanrahan's desire for both mortal and immortal worlds is apparent in "**The Twisting of the Rope,**" which was published one month after "**The Devil's Book**" and in which he dreams of taking a blushing young maiden along with him on an escape into the realm of timelessness. His failure in that venture and his announcements that there is a devil in the soles of his feet and that the winds that awakened the stars are blowing through his blood are all in consonance with Cleona's curse. (p. 35)

Hanrahan's duality of interest inmortal and supernal worlds, established in "**The Devil's Book,**" is extended in "**The Twisting of the Rope**" to incorporate a contrast of the ancient, heroic Irish life against that of the modern bourgeois. Hanrahan aligns himself with Irish legendary figures in "**The Devil's Book**" by saying, "Their way is my way." He repeats that allegiance in "**The Twisting of the Rope,**" where he pictures himself "the last of that mighty line of poets which came down unbroken from . . . Oisin." The modern bourgeois have expelled the Irish heroes from the real world and have forced them to exist only in a shadowy land between heaven and earth. Similarly, Hanrahan, who is hounded by "the priest and his angry neighbours," must flee to the remote West of Ireland where he hopes "the glory of the Gaelic poets was little faded." He passes "deeper and deeper into that great Celtic twilight, that shadowy sunset of the Gaelic world, in which heaven and earth so mingle that each one seems to have taken upon itself some shadow of the other's beauty." He visits places sacred to the legendary heroes and spends nights dreaming of them: "The immense shadows seemed to be taking him to themselves, unhumanising him away into the dim life of the Powers that have never lived in mortal bodies." But he always awakes to the mortal world as "a rough-clad peasant, shivering on the earthen floor."

When his sexual passions are aroused by the "soft dreamy-looking" young girl, he compares her beauty to Deirdre's and makes her feel as if she were "of the rank and lineage of the king's daughters of old and the ungainly dancers about her were shadows haunting the pathway of her banishment." All of this emphasis on the dreamy world of Irish heroes is punctuated by evidence of Hanrahan's inescapable mortal passions; his interest in the girl is sexual, not spiritual. His elaborate comparison of the conjunction of their souls to the celestial union of sun and moon cnds with a very unspiritual reference to "one long sweet dance of love," and the girl answers, "They say you have been very wicked." Like Dhoya, he dreams of

escaping to a remote place where death can find neither him nor his lover. Hanrahan soon remembers that mortal lovers cannot escape death, but grandly sweeps its threat aside as a trifling price to pay for the exquisite physical passion they will share. He has already rejected the only manifestation of supernal love that is available to him, and in the present story the girl's mother, representing the anti-heroic modern Irish spirit, insures that he will not be able to satisfy his mortal lust. The story is a demonstration of his allegiance to the passions that the modern world is unwilling to accommodate. Ancient Irish heroes had been able to act passionately in the real world, but their era has passed and Hanrahan, their lonely descendant, can join them only briefly in dreams. His attempt to consummate a heroic, passionate love with the girl is quickly frustrated by bourgeois who fear that his passion might disrupt their unheroic lives. (pp. 44-5)

The story's central image echoes [the] . . . lesson that in the modern world passion is a curse to those few who possess it. Hanrahan recognizes the "ever wandering serpentine passion" in the "swift serpentine motions" of an ancient dance. He enthusiastically endorses serpentine passion, but when he attempts to satisfy his lust for that passion in this unheroic, bourgeois world, the serpent changes into "the rope of human sorrows," which seems in a dream to be a "vast serpent coiling about him and taking him ever more closely in its folds; till it filled the whole earth and the heavens, and the stars became the glistening of its scales." Supernal forms fly round the serpent's coils singing Cleona's curse: "Sorrow be upon him who rejects the love of the spirits, for he shall seek in vain for the love of the children of men." The fairies punish him by simply heightening the heroic passion he already possesses as a descendant of Oisin. In the story, serpentine passion is simultaneously a heroic asset and, given the fallen condition of this world, an awful curse. (pp. 45-6)

"**The Heart of Spring**" is unusual among Yeats's stories because its first text . . . was left substantially unrevised in all later printings. It is also unique for its straightforward celebration of a magus who triumphs over mortality. Elsewhere in Yeats's work a magus is usually frustrated or at least mocked by some contrary force. Fergus learns that "great webs of sorrow" accompany his newly won Druidic wisdom, Oisin cannot forget the mortal world, and the narrator of "**Rosa Alchemica**" fails initiation. But Angus MacForbis, the old man in "**The Heart of Spring,**" has the necessary diligence and asceticism that eventually bring him success. His purity and gentleness contrast sharply with Hanrahan's passion and vigor. Hanrahan accepts mortality in order to enjoy passions, but the old man willingly denies himself those passions so that he can escape the penalty of mortality.

Mysticism becomes increasingly central in Yeats's stories. In 1892 he explicitly legitimizes the presence in Irish "ballad and story, rann and song" of mysticism's "red-rose bordered hem." "**The Heart of Spring**" is the first example of mysticism uncompromised by any interest in mortal passion. To call it a mystical story does not mean, however, that it is a roman à clef susceptible to detailed occult exegesis. In his public works, Yeats largely ignores the wealth of specific symbols available in occult lore. He strictly limits his use of mysticism to very elementary and generalized principles, while staying clear of specific details of doctrine. His description in "**The Heart of Spring**" of "a moment after the Sun has entered the Ram and before he has passed the Lion" is merely an elaborate way of saying "in spring." Readers need not trouble themselves to learn that occultists associate the Ram and the Lion with the south, where the old man's eternal kingdom lies, and with fire, which is the highest element and thus appropriate to a transcendence of earthly mortality. Yeats avoids technical references intelligible only to students of the occult. (pp. 47-8)

Although Hanrahan and the old man have very different views about the value of mortal passion, they can both endorse the rigorous condemnation of the boy's bourgeois mentality in **"The Heart of Spring."** This important theme centers on the contrast of the old man with the boy, whose only ambition is peaceful domesticity, who fears the fairies and the ancient gods, and who fails to comprehend the old man's triumph. At the end of the story, when the old man has achieved his spiritual victory, the boy comments, "It is better for him . . . to have said his prayers and kissed his beads!" The boy acknowledges the dissimilarity between his master's and his own beliefs, but rationalizes his five years of service to a heretic by invoking the comfortable doctrine that "God has made out of His abundance a separate wisdom for everything which lives." The notion that every creature has its own proper and separate law was endorsed a few years earlier in *John Sherman,* but it fails here to protect the bourgeois world from contemptuous attack: "Why . . . do you fear the ancient gods who made the spears of your father's fathers to be stout in battle, and the little people who came at night from the depths of the lakes and sang among the critics upon their hearths? And in our evil day they still watch over the loveliness of the earth."

"The Heart of Spring" represents a marked advance in craftsmanship over its loosely organized and clumsily worded predecessors. **"Dhoya"** is full of digressions, but this new story focuses sharply on the old man's triumph, a single action which vividly exemplifies his and the lad's differing ideals. (pp. 48-9)

In **"Out of the Rose,"** . . . Yeats portrays a knight who, as "doer and dreamer in one" is a unique and ideal figure. In **"Fergus and the Druid"** dreaming and doing are mutually exclusive; Fergus says: "A wild and foolish labourer is a king / To do and do and do and never dream." Normally in Yeats's works a character can either dream or do, but not both. . . . The knight is a man of action, but like the old man in **"The Heart of Spring,"** he is completely devoted to spiritual aims. Here then is a model that Yeats longed to emulate, a skilled warrior who "fought like the gods and giants and heroes" in the service of subjectivity. The knight's dedication to "the wayward light of the heart" and his opposition to the "mere external order and outer fixity" that are corrupting the fourteenth-century world of this story are parallel to the battle of the Theosophists and the Golden Dawn against the rising tide of materialism.

The knight differs fundamentally from the old knight in Yeats's 1885 poem, **"The Seeker,"** who dies at the end of a long quest begun when he heard a mystical voice. Both he and the knight of **"Out of the Rose"** are contrasted with local rustics, but the story knight, unlike his counterpart in **"The Seeker,"** pursues a valid quest and always acts courageously. In the story, his courage is preposterous and even pitiful, not because of any fault of his own, but because the world has shrunk around him during his long, and perhaps magically extended, lifetime. Externality and materialism so completely triumph that, as the prophetic vision announces, only the "innocent" lad, a "foolish good man who could not think," is left as a reminder of the once subjective world.

The knight's humiliating ineffectiveness in an alien, increasingly objective world demonstrates why "doing" and "dreaming" must remain separate in the modern world. By implication, the story acknowledges that the only solution would be a reversal of the gyres, the advent of a new subjective era. But the new cycle is not announced until **"The Adoration of the Magi"** in 1897; the present story rests with showing that Yeats's ideal figure would be absurd in the present, objective world. . . . Bound to "seek good causes, and die in doing battle for them," he must settle for aiding impious peasants whom he bribes to fight alongside him for his "pious" cause. After the knight is mortally wounded, they pray "to God and His Mother" that he will live long enough to pay them. In such a world only the "innocent" lad can be trusted not to steal money, but he is too stupid to comprehend the knight's story and eventually betrays him, when a cock crows, by leaving the knight's body unburied.

Not only does the prophetic vision foresee the eventual triumph of objectivity in the world, but it also correctly insists on death as the only escape from the objective world. A true opponent of materialism will regard death as the cessation of material existence and he must therefore desire bodily death. Both Hanrahan and Yeats stop short of the full commitment to anti-materialism that the old man of **"The Heart of Spring,"** the knight, and Angus in **"Where There Is Nothing"** all share. In addition to being a complaint against the overly materialistic world, the story, by mercilessly undercutting the knight's noble quest, is a powerful argument against embarking on such a quest.

"Out of the Rose" is superior to all of Yeats's earlier stories. He now handles the exposition of prior action much more adroitly than before. (pp. 49-51)

"The Curse of the Fires and of the Shadows" . . . is a simple wonder tale drawn from Sligo folk history, but endowed with elaborate unity by the dance motif. The Dominican or Black Friar Abbey at Sligo was attacked by Sir Frederick Hamilton and his Puritan troopers during the 1641 sack of Sligo. . . . **"The Curse of the Fires and of the Shadows"** is close enough to the traditional story that the *Academy*'s reviewer takes Yeats to task for departing from "tradition" by having a fairy, rather than "a simple peasant," lead the troopers over the precipice. (p. 52)

In view of Yeats's frequent complains about the difficulty of inventing plots, it is not surprising that he made extensive use of traditional stories or incidents. In 1897 one reviewer admired the strong story line of **"The Curse of the Fires and of the Shadows,"** while noting that the other *Secret Rose* stories were very weakly plotted: "Too often one feels that his story is incoherent and haphazard, making itself as it goes along." This charge reflects the critic's loyalty to the relatively strongly plotted stories of Stevenson and Kipling at the expense of a more modern emphasis on mood or symbolism instead of action. Even so, Yeats is always more comfortable with a lyric moment than with a narrative sequence, and he often takes over traditional plots. (pp. 52-3)

"The Curse of the Fires and of the Shadows" provides an excellent example of the subjective handling of traditional stories. He takes a ready-made plot, but gives it an elaborate, artistic structure by adding the dance motif. Sir Frederick and his troopers disturb the "peace upon earth and in the heavens" by troubling "the steady light of the holy candles" and by awakening the saints and martyrs "as from a sacred trance, into an angry and vehement life." The troopers call down upon themselves the curse of fires and shadows, which evidences itself in the dancing of their shadows and of flames on the abbey walls, the angry dance of the saints and martyrs, the forest shadows, and the dancing light of moon and stars. The alliance of heaven and earth to punish this disturbance of the steady light of God is aided by the fairies, who, after showing death to the troopers, lead them to their ungovernable fate. (pp. 53-4)

"Michael Clancy, the Great Dhoul, and Death" is an extravagant, humorous folktale which Yeats describes as a "little bit of fooling" and as "unlike the rest of my writings." (p. 54)

As the story opens, the Devil accidentally jumps into the tool bag of Michael Clancy, a Sligo tinker. Michael takes the bag to a forge and beats the bag with a heavy hammer until the Devil grants his request that anyone who touches his apple tree will stick to the tree for as long as Michael desires. Later Michael finds Death stuck to the apple tree and consents to free Death only in exchange for learning how to tell if a sick person is going to die or recover. Equipped with this skill, Michael becomes a doctor and, by refusing to accept any patient who is not going to recover, soon earns fame and wealth in his new profession. Finally, Michael becomes bored with life and asks Death to come to him. Turned away from the heavenly gates, he tries to enter hell, but the Devil remembers the heavy blows that Michael gave him and refuses to admit him. The fairies transform Michael into the wily, immortal salmon who lives in the river at Ballisodare, County Sligo.

"Michael Clancy" is an isolated experiment in humorous fantasy, a conventional variety of folktale. The story, according to its 1893 headnote, is founded on a legend that Yeats heard in Sligo. In his other stories, he at least attempts to transform the source materials into a higher form of art. But **"Michael Clancy"** is a simple, nonsymbolic tale that subscribes to the limits of its popular genre. (pp. 54-5)

"The Crucifixion of the Outcast" . . . is a bitter indictment of Irish Christianity's suppression of pagan, heroic ideals. Cumhal the gleeman, who alone has remained faithful to the old ways, shouts: "O cowardly and tyrannous race of monks, persecutors of the bard and the gleeman, haters of life and joy! O race that does not draw the sword and tell the truth! O race that melts the bones of the people with cowardice and with deceit!" In sharp contrast with the solid orderliness so dear to the abbot's heart, Cumhal delights in being known as "Lua Ech Ella, the swift, wild horse." The Christians believe "there is no steadfastness of purpose upon the roads, but only under roofs and between four walls." The lay brother boasts of a "decent and orderly" soul, but Cumhal wants to join birds flying to "the ungovernable sea."

Cumhal stands with Yeats's other famous antagonists of Christianity, Hanrahan and Oisin, both of whom practice the heroic passions and despise priests. . . . Cumhal, Hanrahan, Oisin, and Yeats share, in addition to anticlericalism, an affinity for the mystical world. Oisin enjoys a supernal lover, Niamh, for three hundred years. Yeats in **"To Ireland in the Coming Times,"** Hanrahan in **"The Devil's Book,"** and Cumhal each encounter a supernatural woman in a "rose-bordered dress."

Predictably, the story's pagan loyalties offended many Catholic readers and at least one reviewer, who wrote: "The old Irish monks stood for gentleness and peace in a cruel and savage age. There is wanton untruth in Mr. Yeats's presentation of them." (pp. 55-6)

"The Rose of Shadows" is a flaccid and hopelessly confused story. It was first published as **"Those Who Live in the Storm"**. . . . Oona, a young maiden, sits in an eighteenth-century Sligo cottage with her mother, father, and brother. A violent storm rages outside. Exactly one year earlier, her brother had murdered Michael Creed, her lover. . . . Oona announces that her dead lover came to visit her last night and told her to join him during a storm. Her family tries unsuccessfully to interest her in the material world: "Look, daughter, to the spinning wheel, and think of our goods that, horn by horn and fleece by fleece, grow greater as years go by, and be content." But she sings a song, written by Hanrahan after Cleona cursed him, which announces her readiness to flee the material world and join her lover. The fire goes out and, while the others freeze to death, Oona awaits her lover. . . . The roof is blown off by the storm and her lover descends amid unearthly flames: "His heavy and brutal face and his part naked limbs were scarred with many wounds, and his eyes were full of white fire under his knitted brows."

Oona's rejection of bourgeois materialism aligns her with Hanrahan, whom Cleona curses with the desire for a love that, in the words of Oona's mother, is "too great for our perishing hearts." Like Hanrahan and Proud Costello, Oona learns that death is a necessary preliminary for entering the spirit world and, like the old man in **"The Heart of Spring,"** she joyously accepts loss of the mortal world. . . . The ending is intentionally mysterious. Since we are not given any evidence to show that Oona's lover is not demonic, we are unable to tell if she errs in choosing to join him, despite the generally approving light in which Oona's decision is presented. (pp. 59-60)

In 1897 one reviewer, who believed that the Irish simplicity of many stories in *The Secret Rose* was ruined by over-elaboration, praised **"Red Hanrahan's Curse"** as an example of naive peasant humor. I would argue that both the original version [1894], and the Kiltartanese version of 1905 suffer from tiresome passages that destroy the effectiveness of much of the comedy. Yeats, however, transcends folk humor by giving the story a carefully elaborated theme of mutability.

Hanrahan confronts the fact of his old age in a scene set not only with May blossoms, a beautiful maiden, and schoolchildren, but also with old men and an aged trio of eagle, pike, and yew. His response is to curse mutability, even though he must curse himself to do so: "The poet, Owen Hanrahan, under a bush of may / Calls down a curse on his own head, because it withers grey." He wants to be young and beautiful forever, but cannot. The only example he discovers of life long youth and beauty is patently unsatisfactory: May blossoms which die very young. Hanrahan is left an old man raging against old age. (p. 62)

[**"The Wisdom of the King"**] is not a departure from the earlier stories, for it depicts the incompatibility of the natural and supernatural worlds, a theme that we have already seen in **"The Heart of Spring"** and **"The Rose of Shadows"** and that the 1897 preface to *The Secret Rose* asserts is present in all those stories.

We first see the king as the royal infant, still a mortal and still subject to the law of the natural world. But as soon as the mysterious, immortal crones transform him into a supernatural creature, he takes on immortal wisdom and ceases to be subject to mortal laws. His absolute difference from mortals is signalled by the feathers that begin to grow in his hair. As long as he is kept from discovering his own uniqueness, the king tragically and unsuccessfully attempts to combine the roles of dreamer and doer. When he discovers the truth, he abandons the mortal world and repeats the now familiar proclamation that there are separate laws for mortals and immortals: "Law was made by man for the welfare of man, but wisdom the gods have made, and no man shall live by its light, for it . . . follow[s] a way that is deadly to mortal things." His proper role is to be separate from mortals. . . . (p. 65)

Many of the important issues in this story have been obscured by revisions. As is typical of all except the Hanrahan stories, "The Wisdom of the King" was revised for the editions of 1897, 1908, 1914, and 1925. In each instance there are some verbal improvements, but in the revisions made for 1914 and, especially, 1925 so much explanatory material is deleted that the story shrinks to a relatively spare narrative whose symbolic import flirts with unintelligibility. (p. 67)

["The Old Men of the Twilight," first published as "St. Patrick and the Pedants,"] is a clear example of Yeats's penchant for taking a source plot, adding familiar Irish material, and then personalizing it by using a Sligo setting, as well as Yeatsian symbols and themes.

In an 1890 review of Lady Wilde's folklore collection, *Ancient Cures,* Yeats recounts his Irish folk source and characterizes it as being touched with the "very essence" of "our Irish sadness":

> At the grey of dawn an Irish peasant went out to the hills, to shoot curlew or what not. He saw a deer drinking at a pool, and levelled his gun. Now iron dissolves every manner of spell, and the moment he looked along the barrel he saw that the deer was really an old man changed by wizardry: then, knowing him for something wicked, he fired, and the thing fell, and there upon the grass, quite dead, lay the oldest man he ever set eyes on; and while he stood watching a light wind rose, and the appearance crumbled away before his eyes, and not a wrack was left to tell of what had been.

Many of the details of the struggle between King Laoghaire's Druids and Saint Patrick are traditional. Yeats personalizes the story by setting it at Rosses Point. He knew the old pilot house there from his visits at the Middleton's summer home, Elsinore, which was supposedly haunted by the ghosts of smugglers.

One of his most significant alterations of the source is the replacement of the deer by a heron. Yeats regards the lonely heron as a type of the subjective and solitary dreamer, the opposite of objective, active members of society: "Certain birds, especially as I see things, such . . . as the heron, hawk, eagle and swan, are the natural symbols of subjectivity, especially when . . . alighting upon some pool or river, while the beasts that run upon the ground, especially those that run in packs, are the natural symbols of objective man." Loneliness or exile from active society is an inescapable condition of subjectivity. The old man of "The Heart of Spring" chooses to renounce the world; Hanrahan, whether by choice or destiny, finds himself increasingly ostracized; and the Rhymers, who advocate purely personal poetry, are, in Yeats's view, representatives of subjective isolation. (p. 68)

[In] "The Old Men of the Twilight," Yeats's long standing dislike of Saint Patrick does not turn the subjective man of learning into an unblemished hero. In fact, there are extensive parallels between the man of learning, as he is when Saint Patrick arrives, and the rather unattractive old smuggler. Neither is physically active and each is a complacent follower of

a religion or set of ideals that has dwindled into moribundity. Christianity has become spiritually defunct and has survived only as an aid to material aspirations; the smuggler invokes Saint Patrick's help in hopes of getting a heron pie and a cloak. The men of learning or ollamhs are neither Druids nor poets and have drifted into a habitual and mindless acceptance of their comfortable position in the royal household. Their relationship with the ancient gods and the heroic ideals has become sterile. They are called pedants in the story's original title and, as Yeats makes quite clear in a 1915 poem "The Scholars," their lack of creative energy is unattractive. (p. 69)

These figures of the grey twilight represent the dangers of a too subjective life. "The Heart of Spring" is the single demonstration of a successful escape from the objective, material world. Hanrahan wrestles with simultaneous desires for subjective spirituality and the objective attractions of youthful maidens. "The Old Men of the Twilight," which is set, as is "The Heart of Spring," in the very early morning, establishes the solitary heron as a symbol of the sterile inaction that can accompany subjectivity. (pp. 69-70)

"The Binding of the Hair" is one of the weakest stories in the 1897 collection and has been (deservedly) described as "an overheated piece of Celtic legendry" and "overstuffed to the point of self-parody." (p. 70)

The story . . . is set in pre-Christian Sligo and opens with Aodh, the bard in the court of "the young and wise queen Dectira." He is reciting a martial tale to inspire her warriors for battle with "the races with ignoble bodies and ragged beards." One tress of Queen Dectira's hair falls down over her cheek and, "sighing a long, inexplicable sight," she binds the tress about her head and fastens it with "a golden pin." Aodh, in love with Dectira, is inspired by this act and prepares to sing a song of praise. At that moment, messengers burst into the hall with news of the enemy attack. Before Aodh goes out to fight, Dectira asks him to promise to sing the song before the morning. He answers, "There are two little verses in my heart, two little drops in my flagon, and I swear by the Red Swineherd that I will pour them out before the morning for the Rose of my Desire, the Lily of my Peace, whether I live or be with Orchil and her faded multitude!" He is killed in the battle, but before dawn Dectira finds his severed head hanging from a bush. The head sings the poem now titled "He gives his Beloved certain Rhymes," which begins: "Fasten your hair with a golden pin, / And bind up every wandering tress." Crows that have been eating the flesh of fallen warriors then knock the head from the bush and send it rolling to Dectira's feet. (pp. 70-1)

Aodh sums up nearly all of Yeats's ambitions of early manhood. . . . Yeats's conflicting desires to write dreamy, subjective poems and to be a vigorous man of action find expression in Aodh, who, according to his whims, is capable of being either a courageous warrior or a "dream distraught" lover. This alternation between anger and love is represented in the story by Aodh's shift from a fierce war tale to a gentle love song. The supernatural power displayed in his ability to keep the oath would have attracted both the magus and the heroic bard aspects of Yeats's personality. As we saw in "Red Hanrahan's Curse," Yeats prematurely regards himself as an old man. Aodh, suitably, has "grey hairs mingling before their time with the dark of his beard."

Hints of death envelop Aodh in the story, preparing for the tragic fulfillment of his love for Dectira. His tragedy demonstrates Yeats's melancholy opinion that perfect love is not possible in the mortal world, that death is the necessary price of ideal romance. (pp. 71-2)

"Where There is Nothing, There Is God" was first published in the *Sketch* for 21 October 1896. The heavy cuts that Yeats made for the 1914 edition seriously weaken the text printed in *Mythologies,* but earlier versions, to which he returned for the never-published 1932 *Mythologies,* make effective use of irony to indict clerical pride and materialism. The basis of that irony is the contrast of the proud monks with both Angus, the beggar-saint, and Olioll, the empty-headed boy. Angus, who deliberately chooses to protect himself from worldly pride by becoming a humble servant, and Olioll, whose stupidity preserves his simple innocence, represent the godliness from which the monks have exempted themselves by acquiring learning, riches, and material comfort. The monks, ruddy-faced from the heat of a large fire they keep for the comfort of their students, are making a jeweled case for a large, ornate book and are afraid to open their door to let in the starving, nearly frozen Angus. When Angus's identity is discovered, the abbot announces, "Let us go to him and bow down before him; for at last, after long seeking, he has found the nothing that is God; and bid him lead us in the pathway he has trodden." But the description, deleted in 1914, of their procession to Angus's quern-house exposes their hopeless distance from godly nothingness: "They passed in their white habits along the beaten path in the wood, the acolytes swinging their censers before them, and the Croab, with his crozier studded with precious stones, in the midst of the incense." (p. 75)

Although the story's central theme, that God dwells where there is nothing, is likely to have come from occult sources, the story can be easily understood without any occult knowledge. The elucidation of God's anti-materialism offered in the text is sufficiently detailed that an Irish Catholic reviewer complained of "over-much elaboration" that spoiled the story of Saint Angus. Yeats follows this Christian saint's legend very closely. According to Butler's *Lives of the Saints,* Saint Angus moved to a cell at Dysart-enos, several miles away from Clonenagh monastery, in order to continue unnoticed his famed austerities and mortifications, but that

> the fame of his sanctity soon attracted too many visitors, and the holy anchorite found his solitude invaded and his devotions disturbed. Fearing also the suggesions of vain-glory he resolved to seek some other shelter, and departed secretly from his hermitage.... He finally reached the great monastery of Tamlacht on Tallacht [often spelled "Tallagh"] Hill, three miles from Dublin, and asked to be received as a serving-man—concealing his name and scholarship. He was accepted by the abbot, St. Maelruain, and for seven years he was given the meanest and most labourious offices, but he was well satisfied because he found plenty of time to raise his heart and thoughts to heaven. His identity, however, was discovered....
>
> (p. 77)

"Where There Is Nothing, There Is God" shares part of its title with the 1902 play *Where There Is Nothing,* which was succeeded in 1908 by *The Unicorn from the Stars.* There is almost no similarity between the story and the plots of those plays, even though each includes a saintly character who scorns the worldly values of his fellows. In both plays the hero proclaims that materialism is evil and that "where is nothing, there is God." Further correlation between the story and plays

is limited to Paul Ruttledge in *Where There Is Nothing,* who, like Angus, "does not care what happens to his body." Both are contrasted with disciples who still have worldly pride, and both subscribe to an anti-materialistic "religion so wholly supernatural ... so [wholly] opposed to the order of nature that the world can never capture it." (p. 78)

[The plot of **"The Cradles of Gold"**] centers on the traditional belief that peasant mothers are, as Yeats says elsewhere, "sometimes carried off to nurse the children of the fairies." ... The specific folk-tale source of **"The Cradles of Gold"** is given in Yeats's folklore article of April 1898, **"The Broken Gates of Death"**:

> An old man at Lisadell, in county Sligo ... told me one tale, full of that courtesy between "the others" and the living which endures through all the bitterness of their continuous battles.... A woman died, and was taken by "the gentry," and her husband often saw her after she was dead, and was afraid to speak to her. He told his brother, and his brother said he would come and speak to her, and he came, and at night lay on a settle at the foot of the bed. When she came in, he laid hold of her and would not let her go, although she begged him to let her go because "she was nursing the child of the King." Twelve messengers came in one after the other, and begged him to let her go, but he would not; and at last the King came himself, and said that she had been always well treated, and let come and nurse her own child, and that if she might stay until his child was weaned, he would send her home again.... The man said, "Do you promise this on your honour as a King?" and the King said, "I do," and so the man let her go, and all happened as the King had promised.
>
> (p. 79)

Briefly summarized, **"The Cradles of Gold"** tells how Whinny Hearne, a young peasant mother whom the fairies have "taken" as a wet nurse, is allowed to return to her Lough Gill cottage each night to nurse her own infant. Whinny's husband is afraid of the fairies, but he enlists the aid of his brother Michael, a sturdy fellow renowned as a cudgel-fighter. Michael seizes Whinny when she enters the cottage that evening and refuses to let her return to nurse the child of Finivaragh, the fairy king, until Finivaragh has promised to return Whinny to the mortal world as soon as his child is weaned. Whinny comes back, a month later, remembering nothing of her experiences.

Like **"Michael Clancy,"** this story is a relatively straightforward folk tale that was excluded in 1897 from *The Secret Rose.* **"The Cradles of Gold,"** however, is much closer to the manner and the central themes of *The Secret Rose* than to the broadly humorous **"Michael Clancy."** The *Secret Rose*'s "war of spiritual with natural order" is embodied in Michael Hearne's successful struggle with Finivaragh. The melancholy gloom that follows Michael's victory shows the story's basic allegiance to the supernal world. His victory, because it frustrates Whinny's escape into the immortal world of the Sidhe, is viewed more as a defeat than as a triumph. Finivaragh is correct in saying that Whinny would have been better suited for the fairy life than for life in the mortal world: "There are those in the world for whom no mortal kiss has more than a shadowy comfort, nor the rocking of any mortal cradle, but a fragile music, and she is of them." If Michael had not interfered, Whinny would have become immortal, "a crowned flame, dancing on the bare hills and in the darkness of the woods." (p. 80)

Finivaragh, the traditional king of Irish fairies, is, like Cu-chulain and like Costello, in another of Yeats's stories from 1896, **"Costello the Proud,"** a proud and confident hero. . . . He announces in an "imperious voice": "I am Finivaragh, the King, and understand many things that even the archangels do not understand." This heroic figure's inability to overcome the physical strength of a mortal demonstrates the absolute incompatibility of immortal and mortal worlds, a lesson we have already learned from **"The Heart of Spring,"** Hanrahan's stories, and **"The Wisdom of the King."** Yeats may have dreamed of achieving the wisdom and immortality that Finivaragh possesses, but Yeats never deluded himself about the inherent limitations of the supernal world.

Finivaragh's defeat injures only Whinny. The fairies are already immortal and the failure of one mortal to escape mortality will not endanger their own status. Finivaragh is not, as some readers assume, "competing with the mortal child for what might appease the hunger of the [fairy] host and lessen their paleness." Whinny's milk would not alter the fairy child; fairy children are traditionally suckled by mortals and are not made any less immortal by that experience. Whinny's role as wet nurse is merely a conveniently traditional means for giving her access into the fairy world. She, not the fairy child, will be changed and she, not Finivaragh, is the victim of the story's melancholy defeat. (pp. 80-1)

In **"The Death of Hanrahan,"** . . . Hanrahan finally achieves eternal union with a perpetually beautiful woman. He escapes from mortality into the supernal condition described in the old hag's chant: "I am beautiful, I am beautiful. . . . I am young: look upon me, mountains; look upon me, perishing woods, for my body will be shining like the white waters when you have been hurried away." But, as we could expect from the previous *Secret Rose* stories, his spiritual marriage is necessarily accompanied by physical death. At the moment of his "wedding," Hanrahan sees that "the house" is "crowded with pale shadowy hands, and that every hand" holds what seems "sometimes like a wisp lighted for a marriage, and sometimes like a tall white candle for the dead." The incompatibility of supernatural and mortal worlds is further emphasized by housing this beautiful, unwearying female spirit in the ugly and decrepit body of Winny of the Cross-Roads:

> He saw Winny's withered face and her withered arms that were grey like crumbled earth. . . . And then there came out of the mud-stiffened rags arms as white and as shadowy as the foam on a river, and they were put about his body, and a voice that he could hear well but but that seemed to come from a long way off said to him in a whisper, "You will go looking for me no more upon the breasts of women."
>
> "Who are you?" he said then.
>
> "I am one of the lasting people, of the lasting unwearied Voices, that make my dwelling in the broken and the dying.

The spirit's explicit reference to Hanrahan's previous curse of seeing the eternal rose everywhere he looked in the mortal dust is one indication of the intricate unity of this story. As we might suspect in a story where Yeats has no sources upon which to draw, the plot contains very little action. Practically everything that happens is subordinate to the echoing of previous Hanrahan stories and to elaborate preparation for Hanrahan's impending death. (pp. 81-2)

William H. O'Donnell, in his A Guide to the Prose Fiction of W. B. Yeats, *UMI Research Press, 1983, 182 p.*

JOHN LUCAS   (essay date 1986)

[*Lucas is an English poet and critic who writes primarily on nineteenth- and twentieth-century fiction. In the following excerpt, he examines Yeats's attitudes toward twentieth-century Ireland as manifested in his poetry and prose.*]

[Yeats] is radically different from nearly all English poets of the twentieth century, simply because they lack his complex sense of responsibility. You cannot hope to be fully responsible to your art unless you know—or at least take into consideration—what art is for. For Yeats, poetry serves the profoundly critical and creative purpose of being both for and about a nation's culture. It is an intervention in the history of that culture, meant to contribute to it in crucial ways, to testify to its vitality, to modify the stance of others, to engage in what is seen as a living process. But if you live at what you conceive to be the end of a culture—and that is what the sense of being at the end of a tradition amounts to—you can have no such energy of purpose. [The best modern English poets]—Hardy, Thomas and Gurney—consider that they are at the end of the line. Their sense of the past includes a sense of its absolute uncoupling from the future. Whether they are correct is not my concern. Their conviction is. Their best poetry comes out of a last, desperate, deeply rooted wish to testify to the worth of what they are convinced is about to disappear. It is possible to say that there is nothing new in this, that it is in fact a strategy that had been employed by poets so otherwise different from each other as Pope and Wordsworth. But the difference is this: that none of these later poets has any sense of a fit audience, it is ever so few, to whom they can address their work, so that their producing poetry of worth is a triumph against the odds which they feel to be stacked against them. Pope had his circle, Wordsworth had his. But Hardy, Thomas and Gurney feel themselves to be living out on the end of an event. You may, if you like, argue that their sense of an ending is properly to be seen in terms of the end of particular class formations or of the role of the déraciné poet in an increasingly complex society; or you may say that all three of them are victims of the historical process which they lack the terms (or will) to understand. There is truth in all these contentions. But the fact remains that whatever the cause or the explanation, you come face to face with the inescapable truth that the best English poets [of the period] cannot feel themselves responsible to the kinds of large social issues that engage Yeats. (pp. 114-15)

It is this ability to intervene in current, critical issues which makes Yeats's poetry so different from and more valuable than contemporary English poetry. To say this is by no means to endorse all his positions. In what follows I shall offer reservations against some of his stances and I am even more critical of others. But this is possible—even necessary—just because Yeats's poetry occupies public space, as it were. This means that although much of it springs from deeply held or long-pondered convictions, it can come into being as a way of writing to the moment: it is occasional in the sense that a particular event requires Yeats to comment, and the comment is tested by and puts to the test the values, certainties, commitments, that he has fashioned out of his developing sense of responsibilities. Given this it is inevitable that Yeats is vulnerable to the charge of "getting it wrong" or of "misunderstanding"; or of an improper certainty. But this is what being his kind of poet necessarily entails. Yeats both takes away from poetry its Arnoldian "infallibility" and at the same time gives it a centrality which Arnold's way of thinking about the poet and poetry could never achieve. These comments bear particularly on the poems I am here considering.

According to [Elizabeth Cullingford in her study *Yeats, Ireland and Fascism*], Yeats thought that "the great man is genuinely the servant of his people, although he alone determines the form his service will take. For Nietzsche the "noble" man has rights but no obligations: for Yeats rights entail duties." Perhaps, but what I find in **"To a Wealthy Man"** is a rancorous contempt, even hatred, that cannot be fully explained or justified by the events of 1912/13. The events become somehow displaced by Yeats's determination to compare Lane with great Italian Renaissance princes:

> What cared Duke Ercole, that bid
> His mummers to the market-place,
> What th'onion-sellers thought or did
> So that his Plautus set the pace
> For the Italian comedies?
> And Guidobaldo, when he made
> That grammar school of courtesies
> Where wit and beauty learned their trade
> Upon Urbino's windy hill,
> Had sent no runners to and fro
> That he might learn the shepherds' will.

It would be absurd to deny the panache of these lines. If you except Tennyson's lovely, late poem to Edward FitzGerald you have to go back to Marvell before you will find the tetrameter better handled. Yet this panache comes near to, and occasionally topples into, posture. It is the posture of a snobbish ranter. "Onion-sellers," "shepherds"; aren't they the equivalent of that peasantry which Yeats is usually so keen to invoke as integral to his dream of an Ireland united in politics as well as culture?

There is an analogous problem about **"September 1913."** Here, Yeats's contempt for the prudential values of those who oppose him—Murphy and his ilk—leads him to contrast contemporary Ireland with a past rich with heroes whose "wasteful virtues" brought each of them a martyr's death.

> Was it for this the wild geese spread
> The grey wing upon every tide;
> For this that all that blood was shed,
> For this Edward Fitzgerald died,
> And Robert Emmet and Wolfe Tone,
> All that delirium of the brave?
> Romantic Ireland's dead and gone,
> It's with O'Leary in the grave.

It is difficult to read these lines without thinking that Yeats is recommending the blood sacrifice which had famously been at the heart of his play *Cathleen ni Houlihan*, set in 1798, the year of the uprising in which both Fitzgerald and Wolfe Tone died. When the play was performed at the Abbey in 1902 Cathleen, the spirit of Ireland, was played by Maud Gonne, and at one key moment in the play the heroine is made to say "They that have red cheeks will have pale cheeks for my sake, and for all that, think they are well paid." The words were greeted with ecstatic applause, as was the play's ending. A young man enters to announce the French have landed at Killala, come to help the rising. Has he seen an old woman—i.e. Cathleen—going down the path, he is asked. No, he answers, "but I saw a young girl, and she had the walk of a queen."

Two years after the staging of *Cathleen ni Houlihan,* Yeats gave a lecture on Robert Emmet to an American audience, in the course of which he imagined Emmet going to his death

> full of a kind of ecstasy of self-sacrifice. . . . And out of his grave his ideal has risen incorruptible. His martyrdom has changed the whole temper of the Irish nation. . . . In Ireland we sing the men who fell nobly and thereby made an idea mighty. When Ireland is triumphant and free, there will be yet something in the character of the people, something lofty and strange, which shall have been put there by her years of suffering and by the memory of her martyrs. Her martyrs have married her forever to the ideal.

"September 1913" is written out of an angry despair, a voiced belief that memory of the martyrs no longer holds good. Yeats cherished memory. In the dedicatory verses to *Responsibilities* he spoke of one of his "fathers" who was "A hundred-year-old memory to the poor"; and his intense concern for the sanctity of such memory means that he lashes out against those who have "come to sense" and who merely "fumble in the greasy till" rather than murmur name upon name: of Wolfe Tone, Fitzgerald, Emmet, O'Leary. The phrase "murmur name upon name," however, appears in **"Easter 1916,"** and that poem is about the extraordinary moment where the power of memory has shown itself in the most devastating way possible. For the new martyrs have indeed "risen incorruptible." Yeats is brought to face the full implications of that memory which in **"September 1913"** he had wholly celebrated, which undoubtedly is essential to a nation's sense of its identity, but which may turn out to be curse as much as blessing. It is not so much the attack on those who add "the prayer to the shivering prayer" that concerns me about **"September 1913."** Rather, it is the endorsement of the dream of "Romantic Ireland." For such a dream may carry with it a responsibility to accept the blood sacrifice, for oneself and for others. Can such a responsibility be justified?

The short answer is, no. This is what **"The Second Coming"** is about. The blood-dimmed tide that has been loosed on the world is not merely sweeping over Russia and mainland Europe; it is threatening to engulf Ireland. Seeing this, Yeats comes to understand the full implications of what memory may mean, of what the ecstasy of self-sacrifice may entail; and these things cause him to redefine his sense of responsibilities. He does not become any less of an Irish patriot. But the events of 1916 and the following years reveal the full horrors of entering history. It is a subject that preoccupies him in a number of great poems, including **"Easter 1916,"** **"Meditations in Time of Civil War,"** **"Leda and the Swan"** and, more problematically, **"In Memory of Eva Gore-Booth and Con Markiewicz."**

"Easter 1916" has often been compared to Marvell's Horatian Ode, and the comparison is just. Both poems try to keep a difficult balance while exploring and weighing the terrible complexities of recent events; neither is merely evasive or rhetorical, although because they resist the chance to make final judgements both have been seen—perhaps unfairly—as evasive. As is well known, the events of Easter 1916 took Yeats entirely by surprise. He had not known what was in the offing and he makes that much clear in the poem's opening section, whose typically anapaestic trimeter line implies the trivia of a Dublin existence where all are thought to wear "motley." Only at the end of the section do the anapaests disappear, with the hammer-blow of "All changed, changed utterly," which, while it can be read as a pure iambic line has, in its forced, shocked utterance the feel of a molossus (''All chánged, chánged utterly''). Yeats names and honours those who resigned their part in the casual comedy, but it is the problematic nature of their heroism that most concerns him. Their strong certainty of purpose both rebukes the casual flux of human affairs lived for the moment and gives those same affairs an allure that is new in his poetry. The paltriness of fumbling in a greasy till is, as it were, transmuted by events into instinctive acceptance of the living moment. Or rather, what Yeats had seen as living by prudential values becomes redefined: the commonness of life is now seen in terms that make it natural, unselfconscious, glad with movement:

> A shadow of cloud on the stream
> Changes minute by minute;
> A horse-hoof slides on the brim,
> And a horse plashes within it;
> The long-legged moor-hens dive,
> And hens to moor-cocks call;
> Minute by minute they live:
> The stone's in the midst of all.

And then follows the grieving recognition that ''Too long a sacrifice / Can make a stone of the heart.'' In **''September 1913''** Yeats had celebrated the ''wasteful virtues'' of Emmet and the others who had ''weighed so lightly what they gave.'' But now?

In his marvellous autobiography, *An Only Child*, Frank O'Connor writes of the time during the Civil War in Ireland when he fought on the Republican side. Taken prisoner by the Free Staters he spent much of his time reading Goethe's *Faust*. He also came to be increasingly suspicious of the notions of heroism and martyrdom that sustained the fighters on both sides. One line from *Faust* so impressed him that he wrote it out and pinned it over his bed. ''Grey is your theory, dear friend, and green is the golden tree of life.'' O'Connor had become sickened by the mystique of ''dying for the cause.'' He tells of his revulsion at the song made up to celebrate the death of one young soldier whom O'Connor had seen, minutes before his execution, sobbing and screaming in abject terror at what was to happen to him. According to the song the soldier went to his death gladly. O'Connor protested at the horror of it all. ''And did Pearse not want to die?'' he was asked. ''No,'' he replied, ''He awoke too late.''

Perhaps. Perhaps not. Yeats did not think so, but he did come to share O'Connor's fear of what sacrificial death might mean. In **''The Rose Tree,''** one of a group of poems written out of the Easter uprising, Yeats has Pearse and Connolly discuss how the Irish rose may bloom once more:

> ''But where can we draw water,''
> Said Pearse to Connolly,
> ''When all the wells are parched away?
> O plain as plain can be
> There's nothing but our own red blood
> Can make a right Rose Tree.''

The blood sacrifice is beyond reason. Or rather it is an expression of commitment immune to all feeling: so at least Yeats believed, and it explains why he places Con Markiewicz at the head of those whose sacrifice he celebrates and, at the same time, questions. As woman she is most cruelly the victim of the historical moment at which she chooses to act. The original sweetness of her voice has become shrill in argument. Her mind has become a ''bitter, an abstract thing'' (the phrase comes from *''On a Political Prisoner''*). Like Maud Gonne,

Con Markiewicz has destroyed herself for the cause. That, at least, is Yeats's view of the matter.

''O when may it suffice?'' Yeats asks in the last section of **''Easter 1916,''** and answers, ''That is heaven's part.'' I grant that to say this may seem evasive, but I do not think it is. What the phrase implicitly acknowledges is that once you have let violence loose you can't choose when to lock it up again. From the shocked awareness of this truth Yeats turns to the traditional role of poetry as consolation. The poet must

> murmur name upon name
> As a mother names her child
> When sleep at last has come
> On limbs that had run wild.
> What is it but nightfall?

But the murmured cadences of those lines are cut off by the insistent ''No, no, not night but death.'' The poet may not retreat from the actualities of what happened into the false consolation of lyricism. Yet these consolation seem to return with the litany of names:

> MacDonagh and MacBride
> And Connolly and Pearse
> Now and in time to be,
> Wherever green is worn,
> Are changed, changed utterly:
> A terrible beauty is born.

I have argued with more than one friend who thinks that these final lines are merely rhetorical and so constitute an evasion of responsibilities. Yeats, they say, is letting ''poetry'' win over hard thought. I can see the force of the argument but I cannot accept it. What else can he do? He has already explored the terrible beauty of the martyrs' act, of their being metamorphosed into stony certainty of purpose. To honour their achievement is not to underestimate its cost. Indeed, it seems to me that it is the cost which most engages him. Hence the importance of the poem's appearing in the same volume as **''The Second Coming''** and **''A Prayer for My Daughter,''** poems which brood on the terrors of history. Again, the contrast with English poets is instructive. There is only one English poet who even begins to approach Yeats's passionately intelligent concern with what he sees as the ''mere anarchy'' being loosed upon the twentieth-century world, and that is Auden.

Michael Robartes and the Dancer was published in 1921. By then Ireland had become, in Yeats's own phrase, ''a whirlpool of hate,'' and worse was to follow with the outbreak of the Civil War. In a letter of the time Yeats commented gloomily, ''Perhaps there is nothing so dangerous to a modern state, when politics take the place of theology, as a bunch of martyrs. A bunch of martyrs (1916) were the bomb and we are living in the explosion.'' In 1923 he wrote **''Meditations in Time of Civil War,''** and in the sixth section of that poem he speaks in anguish of how

> We had fed the heart on fantasies,
> The heart's grown brutal from the fare;
> More substance in our enmities
> Than in our love. . . .

''We'' honestly admits to the shared dream of an heroic past—*Cathleen in Houlihan*, **''September 1913''**—whose realization in the present has become terrifying.

The same year he composed his great sonnet **''Leda and the Swan.''** This poem has been the subject of a great deal of commentary, not all of it to the point; but its central meaning is clear enough. Yeats is writing here about the violence of entering history, and about how all, even the most innocent, are caught up in it. The rape of Leda becomes, in his imagination, an instance of the ways in which violence is both intoxicating and terrible. Moreover, as in **"Easter 1916"** so here: once you let violence loose you cannot decide when to lock it up again; its consequences are further violence, unpredictable, appalling, cataclysmic. From the rape of Leda came Helen and Clytemnestra, Castor and Pollux.

> Being so caught up,
> So mastered by the brute blood of the air,
> Did she put on his knowledge with his power,
> Before the indifferent beak could let her drop?

That brilliant pun on "Being so caught up" makes it inevitable, I think that the answer to the question in these lines is "yes."

And this explains why in **"Easter 1916"** Yeats sees Con Markiewicz as caught up by the events of her time and why in the elegy he composed for her and her sister he should see the girls as "dear shadows" who only in death come to "know it all, / All the folly of a fight / With a common wrong or right." But here we do come to a critical question. For all the tenderness with which Yeats here speaks of the girls, and for all the magnanimity he elsewhere displays toward Maud Gonne, the fact remains that he never swerves from his view of their "folly," he never thinks of them as other than victims, he never considers the possible justification of their "fight." Why not? The answer has to be that he is committed to a dream of Irish culture which W. H. Auden contemptuously called "the parish of rich women," and which, although it certainly amounts to more than that, is nevertheless not entirely or easily defensible. (Auden's phrase is more accurate about Yeats's image of Lady Gregory, and the Gore-Booth sisters, than it is about the women themselves.)

Yeats of course was too intelligent not to realize just how vulnerable was his dream of Anglo-Irish culture. In the first section of **"Meditations in Time of Civil War"** he writes magnificently about the failure of the country-house tradition in Ireland. It is not merely that "Maybe the great grandson of that house / For all its bronze and marble's but a mouse," where the angry splutter of the second line admits to a lost vitality of purpose. More radically, Yeats knows that violence and bitterness are inextricably present in the creation of the country-house tradition. For after all, the Anglo-Irish ascendancy got their houses by usurping the land. They ascended on the backs of others. Deep at the heart of the literature of the country house is and must be a sense of possible guilt. That is why Ben Jonson is so keen to insist that Penshurst is a model of social relations ("Thou art built with no man's ruin, no man's groan"); and it is why Jane Austen should wish to introduce Elizabeth Bennet and Fanny Price, among others, to the country house. Their marrying the heirs of such property will bring a much-needed flow of new blood as well as symbolizing those harmonious relationships which image social peace.

The Anglo-Irish poet faces even more acute problems when he comes to celebrate the country-house tradition. The taking of the land is not merely an act of appropriation by one class over another; it is imperialistic, the domination of one nation over another. Yet such houses, "where all's accustomed, ceremonious," symbolize Yeats's cultural, social and political ideal for Ireland. The ideal is most perfectly realized in Lady Gregory's house, Coole Park, and in two poems Yeats sets out his sense of its significance. As is well known, he had himself bought an old, broken-down tower on the edge of her estate.

It became both the artist's tower, image of a lonely search for truth, and the indication of how he placed his art at the service of the landed gentry, or more particularly, of Lady Gregory.

Perhaps the first important poem to make use of the tower is **"In Memory of Major Robert Gregory,"** and we need to note that Yeats writes this poem not merely to celebrate Gregory's life and mourn his death, but to affirm his commitment to values that are, so it seems, to become time's victims. For Gregory's death is, after all, one of millions that contribute to the "blood-dimmed tide." This does not necessarily mean that "Our Sidney and our perfect man" has died prematurely. Yeats implies that Gregory knew his work to be finished in one brief flaring of creative intensity and that he therefore chose death rather than wasting into unprofitable old age. (At the time of writing the poem Yeats, in common with others, had been led to assume that Gregory had killed himself. Only later was it discovered that he had been accidentally shot down.) In **"An Irish Airman Foresees His Death"** Yeats presents Gregory in the act of balancing all, seeing himself poised between "this life, this death." In the Elegy, Gregory is more mysteriously presented as Renaissance man born out of time: "What made us dream that he could comb grey hair?" But this is alluded to rather than paraded as fact, for the simple reason that Yeats needs to proceed tactfully. To celebrate an act of suicide is not easy; but on the other hand, it will hardly do to suggest that Gregory behaved irresponsibly. The solution Yeats fashions is to imply that the values by which Gregory lived or with which he associated are edging towards extinction. Hence the importance of the tower, which Gregory helped to decorate. It is an image of a way of life—service to high art, to the country-house ideal—whose day is nearly done.

> Now that we're almost settled in our house
> I'll name the friends that cannot sup with us
> Beside a fire of turf in th'ancient Tower,
> And having talked to some late hour
> Climb up the narrow winding stair to bed:
> Discoverers of forgotten truth
> Or mere companions of my youth,
> All, all are in my thoughts tonight being dead.

The country-house ideal takes for granted sociability, and the token for such sociability is eating. But in Yeats's house friends "cannot sup with us." The sense of living on into the fag-end of a tradition is implicit, it seems to me, in that deliberate antiquated "th' tower." In other words, the tower is self-consciously maintained as a symbol of a disappearing world. (In **"Meditations in Time of Civil War"** Yeats says that he has taken Thor Ballylee "that after me / My bodily heirs may find, / To exalt a lonely mind / Befitting emblems of adversity"). At the end of the Elegy, the poet's attention is called to the "bitter . . . wind / That shakes the shutter"; and this is the apocalyptic "roof-levelling wind" of **"A Prayer for My Daughter."** It is Shelley's wind of revolutionary change blowing in from the Atlantic, but bringing for Yeats the deadly energy of democratic vistas.

It is in this context that we need to consider the two poems in which Yeats celebrates Lady Gregory and her house. The first of these, **"Coole Park, 1929"** is an extremely beautiful poem, both decorous and passionate in its affirmation of the values which Yeats associates with his great friend; and the amplitude of its cadences finely tells of his and fellow-writers' gratitude for all that she meant to them:

> They came like swallows and like swallows went,
> And yet a woman's powerful character
> Could keep a swallow to its first intent;

And half a dozen in formation there,
That seemed to whirl upon a compass-point,
Found certainty upon the dreaming air,
The intellectual sweetness of those lines
That cut through time or cross it withershins.

But as that last line indicates, the house's accomplishments succeed almost in defiance of time; and time will have its way. The last stanza makes this abundantly clear:

Here, traveller, scholar, poet, take your stand
When all these rooms and passages are gone,
When nettles wave upon a shapeless mound
And saplings root among the broken stone. . . .

This is not empty fear. During the 1920s many great houses in Ireland were burnt down, others were abandoned; still others were falling into decay. Coole Park itself was no longer in Lady Gregory's ownership, although she continued to live there. But some years after her death in 1932 the house was pulled down.

It is Yeats's near certainty of the house's fate that makes him want to celebrate what it stands for. He is its elegist, and he returns to the role in **"Coole Park and Ballylee, 1931."** But here I am not so persuaded that all is as it should be. I baulk when I come to the insistent claim that Lady Gregory is "a last inheritor / Where none has reigned that lacked a name and fame / Or out of folly into folly came." What, *none*? And anyway, although the phrase "name and fame" may at first seem strikingly sonorous, isn't it rhetorical tat at best, and at worst shrilly snobbish? The same seems to me true of the moment where Yeats asks us to believe that "gardens rich in memory glorified / Marriages, alliances and families, / And every bride's ambition satisfied." Reading that, I recall Mr. Dombey reflecting that "a matrimonial alliance [with himself] *must,* in the nature of things, be gratifying and honourable to any woman of common sense. . . . That Mrs. Dombey must have been happy. That she couldn't help it." And what are we to make of the poem's conclusion?

We were the last romantics—chose for theme
Traditional sanctity and loveliness;
Whatever's written in what poets name
The book of the people; whatever most can bless
The mind of man or elevate a rhyme;
But all is changed, that high horse riderless,
Though mounted in that saddle Homer rode
Where the swan drifts upon a darkening flood.

I grant that the last line has a certain majesty in its dying fall, but the theme of "traditional sanctity and loveliness" which has on other occasions been treated with some scepticism (as in **"Ancestral Houses"**), is here made part of an uninflected threnody for past glories. Much the same thing happens in **"The Municipal Gallery Revisited,"** where Yeats announces of Lady Gregory, Synge and himself, that "We three alone in modern times had brought / Everything down to that sole test again, / Dream of the noble and the beggar man." You might say that Yeats is to be defended because he is speaking out of a proper deference to Lady Gregory's social standing. But when does such deference become servility? And yet even this isn't the point. For what Yeats ignores in these poems is Lady Gregory's own critical awareness of the culpability of the tradition in which he now uncritically places her. You have only to read her *Journals* of the 1920s to see how far he has mythicized her, just as he mythicized Hugh Lane, and in doing so has made a simplified and sentimentalized image out of someone who was far more complex than he wants to admit,

since to do so would upset his own dream of the country-house ideal.

My own view is that Yeats, a man of passionate intensity, increasingly convinced himself that what he read into local and world affairs spelled death, not only for his ideal, but for any worthwhile dream of Ireland.

This is why, I think, he turned to Byzantium, as a refuge of art and artifice against the cruelties and inadequacies of life. In **"Sailing to Byzantium"** he speaks of wishing to leave a country where "Caught in that sensual music all neglect / Monuments of unageing intellect." The country is not Ireland, perhaps, and yet in a way it is. For the monuments of unageing intellect—Coole Park, Thor Ballylee?—are clearly of no appeal to young Ireland, or so Yeats has come to feel. The country might of course stand more generally for the post-war world. In his very interesting essay, "Barbarism and Decadence," Renato Poggioli suggests that decadence in Yeats's poem is represented by the "modern and changing West," and that Yeats willingly exchanges it for the "eternal East." The decadence Poggioli has in mind is "the sickness of youth." Certainly, the cultivated cynicism of the 1920s amounts to a kind of decadence. But the passionate tone of **"Sailing to Byzantium"** suggests Yeats's need to save himself. The poem concerns more his desire to make his soul than the country he has left behind, but at the end he is returned to the flux of history, to "What is past or passing or to come."

This, I think, is where Yeats's responsibilities always lead him, and it is not perhaps to be wondered at that on occasions he should seem to be petulant or arrogant or shrilly venomous when speaking of them or on behalf of those to whom he feels most responsible. Yeats can be extremely, tediously snobbish. He can also be offensively harsh. But his intemperate manners and speech arise out of the inevitable vulnerabilities of a poet who sees himself enacting or speaking for large responsibilities. As such, he is a potent force in a way that no English poet of the twentieth century can match. . . . (pp. 117-28)

John Lucas, "W. B. Yeats: The Responsibilities of the Poet," in his Modern English Poetry—From Hardy to Hughes: A Critical Survey, *B. T. Batsford Ltd., 1986, pp. 103-29.*

ADDITIONAL BIBLIOGRAPHY

Adams, Hazard. *Blake and Yeats: The Contrary Vision.* Ithaca, N.Y.: Cornell University Press, 1955, 328 p.
    Extensive comparison of the symbolic systems of Blake and Yeats. Adams maintains that "the vortex and related images provide a main link between the poets."

Adams, Joseph. *Yeats and the Masks of Syntax.* New York: Columbia University Press, 1984, 111 p.
    Linguistic study focusing on Yeats's anamolous "syntactic masks." According to Adams: "The syntactic masks exemplify, for one thing, a shift in the relation of subjectivity to language, with the subject seen as a textual product or construct rather than a full center of consciousness expressing itself through languge. Syntactic masks also exemplify the role of 'difference' in language—a more familiar notion, especially in linguistic theory. Both these aspects link the masks with a larger cultural and philosophical shift that continues to be played out in modern language, literature, and thought."

Aldington, Richard. "W. B. Yeats." In his *A. E. Housman & W. B. Yeats: Two Lectures,* pp. 20-35. The Peacocks Press, 1955.

An informal tribute praising Yeats's early, romantic poetry and discussing his search for a substitute for religious devotion. According to Aldington: "I sometimes feel, in spite of all the beauty, a trace and even more than a trace of affectation in Yeats's poetry, just as I used to feel it in his manner and conversation. I don't doubt that on the whole the emotion of these poems was not unreal, but there is something of an air of unreality about them, just as there was in the ideas, the stories and the epigrams of Yeats's infinitely attractive talk."

Brunner, Larry. *Tragic Victory: The Doctrine of Subjective Salvation in the Poetry of W. B. Yeats.* Troy, N.Y.: Whitson Publishing Co., 1987, 184 p.

Maintains that "the failure of the subjective doctrine and Yeats's final rejection of knowledge as a means to truth point out the awful inadequacy of a philosophy which promised personal freedom and vital redemption but was unable to deliver them. In his wrestling with the ultimate significance and value of human life, Yeats entered into the abyss of himself and found there not victory but despair and desperation; his struggle finally epitomizes the terrible urgency of redemption and the utter inadequacy of subjectivity to attain it."

Byrd, Thomas L., Jr. *The Early Poetry of W. B. Yeats: The Poetic Quest.* Port Washington, N.Y.: Kennikat Press, 1978, 151 p.

Concentrates on Yeats's adaptation of the pastoral tradition and "an important theme or set of metaphors that not only is included in the pastoral but also serves to unify the early poetry: the figure of the poet-seeker and the poetic quest for truth."

Clark, David R. *Yeats at Songs and Choruses.* Amherst: University of Massachusetts Press, 1983, 283 p.

Interpretive analysis of manuscript versions of "Crazy Jane on the Day of Judgment," "Three Things," "After Long Silence," "Her Triumph," "Colonus Praise," "From *Oedipus at Colonus,*" and "From the *Antigone.*"

Croft, Barbara L. *"Stylistic Arrangements": A Study of William Butler Yeats's "A Vision."* Lewisburg, Pa.: Bucknell University Press, 1987, 196 p.

Studies form and content in Yeats's *A Vision,* comparing the 1925 and 1937 versions, and assessing the material and presentation from a modern viewpoint.

Donohue, Denis. "Yeats: The Question of Symbolism" and "On *The Winding Stair.*" In his *We Irish: Essays on Irish Literature and Society,* pp. 34-51, pp. 67-86. New York: Alfred A. Knopf, 1986.

Discusses the influence of the Symbolist movement on Yeats's poetry and examines antinomies in *The Winding Stair.*

Driver, Tom F. "The Search for Reality in Poetry and Irony." *Romantic Quest and Modern Query: A History of the Modern Theatre,* pp. 124-58. New York: Delacorte Press, 1970.

Presents a description of Yeats's dramatic style within a survey of modern drama. Driver concludes that "Yeats's approach to drama was utterly that of a poet whose exploration was inward. . . . In Yeats's plays imitation of life is subordinated to poetic imagination, narrative to the evocative power of symbol."

Ellman, Richard. *Eminent Domain: Yeats among Wilde, Joyce, Pound, Eliot, and Auden.* New York: Oxford University Press, 1967, 159 p.

Biographical and critical study by a noted Yeats scholar focusing on Yeats's literary relationships with other prominent writers of the era.

Engelberg, Edward. *The Vast Design: Patterns in W. B. Yeats's Aesthetic.* Toronto: University of Toronto Press, 1964, 224 p.

Charts the emergence of the "vast design" of Yeats's aesthetic as a synthesis of oppositions. According to Engelberg: "The argument of this study holds that the 'vast design' is balanced by the conception of the 'single image,' the design itself becoming that image and the image transcending, finally, the design itself."

Fletcher, Ian. *W. B. Yeats and His Contemporaries.* New York: St. Martin's Press, 1987, 224 p.

Study of the interrelation between Yeats's ideas and those of other early twentieth-century artists.

Freyer, Grattan. *W. B. Yeats and the Anti-Democratic Tradition.* Totowa, N.J.: Barnes and Noble Books, 1981, 143 p.

Traces "the evolution of Yeats's political ideas and their interplay in the intellectual climate of his age." Freyer concludes: "However we regard the various comments and excursions into other nations' affairs of the final years, Yeats's central preoccupation was with twentieth-century Ireland. He believed Ireland should look to modern materialist Britain for what to avoid; to early fascist Italy for certain things to learn from; and to Ireland's own eighteenth century for a foundation to preserve and to build on for the future. His aim was a well-governed nation, where Protestant and Catholic, planter and Gael, would find their place equally, drawing the imagination of the young to itself by a vigorous culture. His ideal state was one where able rulers led and where ordinary people lived a life of mental and physical adventure. For leaders, he looked to those ready to live with 'precision and energy,' capable of demonstrating in themselves 'character isolated by a deed.' He believed the 'levelling frenzy' of modern times would not in the end produce a happier society but one of money-grubbing boredom.'"

Good, Maeve. *W. B. Yeats and the Creation of a Tragic Universe.* Basingstoke, England: The Macmillan Press Ltd., 1987, 176 p.

Analyzes the creation of a tragic universe in Yeats's works.

Gwynn, Stephen, ed. *Scattering Branches: Tributes to the Memory of W. B. Yeats.* New York: The Macmillan Co., 1940, 229 p.

Personal reminiscences and tributes written on the occasion of Yeats's death. Gwynn's collection includes essays by Maud Gonne, William Rothenstein, Edmund Dulac, and C. Day Lewis, among others.

Harrison, John R. "W. B. Yeats." In his *The Reactionaries: Yeats, Lewis, Pound, Eliot, Lawrence—A Study of the Anti-Democratic Intelligentsia,* pp. 39-73. New York: Schocken Books, 1967.

Examines Yeats's social and political views and their presentation in his works. According to Harrison: "Yeats made practically no attempt to come to terms with twentieth-century society, and what attempt he did make failed. He is probably the last poet who could legitimately reject our modern civilization without being guilty of intellectual and moral evasion."

Hassett, Joseph M. *Yeats and the Poetics of Hate.* New York: St. Martin's Press, 1986, 189 p.

Considers "ways in which Yeats's preoccupation with hate illuminates particular poems and poetic themes."

Hoffman, Daniel. *Barbarous Knowledge: Myth in the Poetry of Yeats, Graves and Muir.* New York: Oxford University Press, 1967, 266 p.

Traces Yeats's career from his beginnings in the ballad tradition to his development of a mythological framework from which to draw subjects, characters, and imagery.

Hough, Graham. *The Mystery Religion of W. B. Yeats.* Totowa, N.J.: Barnes and Noble Books, 1984, 129 p.

Offers a simplified explanation of Yeats's belief system and places it in the context of occult literary tradition. Detailed difficulties of Yeats's philosophy are addressed in the final chapter.

Jeffares, A. Norman. *The Circus Animals: Essays on W. B. Yeats.* London and Basingstoke: Macmillan and Co., 1970, 183 p.

Contains essays on Yeats, his father, and his friend Oliver St. John Gogarty, including examinations of Yeats's "mask," Yeats as a critic, gyres, and women in Yeats's poetry.

———. *A New Commentary on the Poems of W. B. Yeats.* Stanford: Stanford University Press, 1984, 543 p.

Line by line explications of each poem in *The Poems: A New Edition* cross-referenced to the second edition of Yeats's *Collected Poems* (1950). Secondary material includes maps, index to titles, and index to first lines.

———, ed. *W. B. Yeats: The Critical Heritage.* London: Routledge & Kegan Paul, 1977, 483 p.

Reprints reviews, essays, and other critical assessments written between 1884 and 1939 by prominent commentators of the period.

Jochum, K. P. S. *W. B. Yeats: A Classified Bibliography of Criticism.* Urbana: University of Illinois Press, 1978, 801 p.
> Extensive, annotated bibliography listing more than 7,900 items.

Knowland, A. S. *W. B. Yeats: Dramatist of Vision.* Totowa, N.J.: Barnes and Noble Books, 1983, 256 p.
> Chronological survey of Yeats's dramas in which the works are viewed, "not as appendages to or extensions of his poetry, or as expressions of his 'philosophy', but as viable theatrical experiences, offering insights to audiences with and without previous acquaintanceship with his work."

Lerner, Laurence. "W. B. Yeats: Poet and Crank." *Proceedings of the British Academy,* XLIX (1963): 49-67.
> Questions how it is that Yeats, "the greatest poet of the century, a poet of wisdom and understanding of the heart, a sage as well as a singer . . . expounded in his poems such absurd, such eccentric, such utterly crackpot ideas" and determines that his system, "when turned into poetry, widens its significance and sheds its eccentricities: . . . the symbols, freeing themselves from an arbitrary and detailed magical meaning, become no more (and no less!) than the great universal symbols of the poetic tradition."

Levine, Herbert J. *Yeats's Daimonic Renewal.* Ann Arbor, Mich.: UMI Research Press, 1977, 169 p.
> Commentary focusing on the daimonic argument in *Per Amica Silentia Lunae* and Yeats's middle poetry.

MacGloin, T. P. "Yeats's Faltering World." *Sewanee Review* XCV, No. 3 (Summer 1987): 470-84.
> Discusses Yeats's role within the social context of late nineteenth- and early twentieth-century Ireland.

Martin, Heather C. *W. B. Yeats: Metaphysician as Dramatist.* Waterloo, Ontario: Wilfred Laurier University Press, 1986, 153 p.
> Traces Yeats's belief system as it is developed through metaphors, themes, symbols, and form in his dramas.

McNally, James. "Cast a Cold Eye on Yeats on Arnold." *Victorian Poetry* 25, No. 2 (Summer 1987): 173-80.
> Suggests that "Yeats's frequent putting down of Matthew Arnold may be attributed in part to 'anxiety of influence.' Yeats owed some poetic debts to Matthew Arnold, and like those of an aristocratic or imperious nature he had some difficulty in acknowledging debts or obligations."

Menon, V. K. Narayana. *The Development of William Butler Yeats.* Edinburgh and London: Oliver and Boyd, 1960, 92 p.
> Second edition of a study of the form and content of Yeats's poetry first published in 1942. According to Menon: "He was the last poet in the aristocratic tradition, and . . . with the bottom knocked out of his moral code, and unable to fully grasp the historical process, he fell back upon the pride and strength of the individual will, harping always on the type of nobility and greatness he had been brought up to accept. But his imaginative intensity never flagged, and everywhere his character and his personality stood out. Whatever the verdict of the future, his work will remain for ever the greatest personal document of our times."

Murphy, Frank Hughes. *Yeats's Early Poetry: The Quest for Reconciliation.* Baton Rouge: Louisiana State University Press, 1975, 172 p.
> Traces Yeats's "efforts toward an ultimate reconciliation of the contrary forces of human experience as they are reflected in the first eight groups of his lyric poetry, as arranged in *The Collected Poems.*"

Myles, Ashley E. *Theatre of Aristocracy: A Study of W. B. Yeats as a Dramatist.* Salzburg, Austria: Institut für Anglistik und Amerikanistik, Universität Salzburg, 1981, 124 p.
> Assessment of Yeats's career as a poet-dramatist. According to Myles: "Yeats's verse-plays have a charm and beauty of their own. He had a quintessential poetic power, strong dramatic perception and theatre-consciousness. The height attained by Yeats could not be achieved by any other poet-dramatist of his age. In addition to opening new and rich vistas into dramatic imagination, his plays offer a revaluation of the verse-form in drama."

Neuman, Shirley. *Some One Myth: Yeats's Autobiographical Prose.* Atlantic Highlands, N.J.: Humanities Press Inc., 1982, 160 p.
> Survey treating each of the major autobiographical works separately.

O'Donnell, William H. *The Poetry of William Butler Yeats: An Introduction.* Ungar: New York, 1986, 192 p.
> Chronological survey of Yeats's poetry. According to O'Donnell: "Yeats's masterful command of language and his willingness to face squarely the full complexity of life have deservedly won him permanent fame."

O'Faoláin, Seán. Review of *Selected Poems, Lyrical and Narrative,* by W. B. Yeats. *The Criterion* IX, No. xxxvi (April 1930): 523-28.
> Comments on Yeats's poetic strengths and weaknesses in a review of *Selected Poems,* which contains altered versions of many of Yeats's early works. In O'Faoláin's opinion: "One had rather on the whole that he left us the music of his youth as he originally gave it."

O'Neill, William. "Yeats on Poetry and Politics." *Midwest Quarterly* XXV, No. 1 (Autumn 1983): 64-73.
> Offers a discussion of Yeats's career in the context of Irish political and social events of the period.

Pack, Robert. "Yeats as Spectator to Death." In his *Affirming Limits: Essays on Mortality, Choice, and Poetic Form,* pp. 151-73. Amherst: University of Massachusetts Press, 1985.
> Examines the presentation of death in Yeats's poetry.

Parkin, Andrew. *The Dramatic Imagination of W. B. Yeats.* New York: Barnes and Noble Books, 1978, 208 p.
> Examines the nature of Yeats's imagination, concluding that "it is neither epic nor even wholly lyric, but essentially dramatic."

Porter, Katherine Anne. "From the Notebooks: Yeats, Joyce, Eliot, Pound." In her *Collected Essays and Occasional Writings of Katherine Anne Porter,* pp. 298-300. New York: Delacorte Press, 1970.
> Praises Yeats in an obituary tribute to James Joyce originally published in the *Southern Review* I, No. 3 (Summer 1965). In Porter's view: "Yeats was the greater imagination; Joyce did not have greatness in the grand manner, as Yeats did. . . . Yeats *grew* great, the only kind of greatness, really: as if all his life he was fulfilling some promise to himself to use every cell of his genius to its fullest power."

Raine, Kathleen. *Yeats the Initiate: Essays on Certain Themes in the Work of W. B. Yeats.* Mountrath, Ireland: The Dolmen Press, 1986, 449 p.
> Addresses various subjects of interest to Yeats scholars, including his use of Irish settings and folk subjects, his occult studies, and his debt to William Blake.

Rawson, Claude. "A Question of Potency." *Times Literary Supplement,* No. 4,399 (24 July 1987): 783-85.
> A review of several biographical and critical studies of Yeats. Rawson considers the effects of Yeats's vasectomy on his poetry and discusses Yeats's belief that a vital connection exists between "versemaking and lovemaking."

Regueiro, Helen. "Yeats." In her *The Limits of Imagination: Wordsworth, Yeats, and Stevens,* pp. 95-145. Ithaca and London: Cornell University Press, 1976.
> Dialectical criticism that sees Yeats's poetry as his quest for unity of being.

Ronsley, Joseph. *Yeats's "Autobiography": Life as Symbolic Pattern.* Cambridge: Harvard University Press, 1968, 172 p.
> Assesses the *Autobiography* as "one of the most important works of its kind in English." According to Ronsley: "Yeats's artistic pre-eminence and his participation in several cultural movements, the complexity of the book's form and the beauty of its style, and the part it plays in Yeats's intellectual framework, all contribute to its importance."

Seiden, Morton Irving. *William Butler Yeats: The Poet as a Myth-maker, 1865-1939*. East Lansing: Michigan State University Press, 1962, 397 p.

Examines Yeats's attempt in *A Vision* to create a "privately religious faith and simultaneously to write many poems—*the fragments of a great myth*—all based on that faith."

Shaw, Priscilla Washburn. *Rilke, Valéry and Yeats: The Domain of the Self*. New Brunswick, N.J.: Rutgers University Press, 1964, 278 p.

Comparative study utilizing Yeats's works as a norm "between the poetic extremes of Rilke and Valéry" because, according to Shaw, Yeats's poetry "communicates a more balanced awareness of self and world, in which the irreducible existence of each is made felt."

Thurley, Geoffrey. *The Turbulent Dream: Passion and Politics in the Poetry of W. B. Yeats*. St. Lucia, Australia: University of Queensland Press, 1983, 235 p.

Loosely chronological survey based on a dialectical structure. Thurley treats Yeats's career in three phases: (Early) "Thesis: Fantasy," (Middle) "Antithesis: Terror," and (Late) "Synthesis: Gaiety."

Ure, Peter. *Towards a Mythology: Studies in the Poetry of W. B. Yeats*. London: University Press of Liverpool, 1946, 123 p.

Assesses the role of mythology in Yeats's poetry, how he adapted Irish myths to his "developing concept," and how Yeats's "search for a mythology itself brought to birth a mythologizing process which in its turn evolved a new myth to fulfill the functions of the old."

Warren, Austin. "William Butler Yeats: The Religion of a Poet." In his *Rage for Order: Essays in Criticism*, pp. 66-83. Chicago: University of Chicago Press, 1948.

Traces prominent influences in Yeats's spiritual development, including Irish mythology, Theosophy, and others.

Webster, Brenda S. *Yeats: A Psychoanalytic Study*. Stanford: Stanford University Press, 1973, 246 p.

Argues that "the central thread of Yeats's life and work is his tireless, driven effort to 'remake' himself, to bring himself as man and artist into a satisfactory relationship both with his impulses and with a threatening reality. In this struggle, he was haunted by certain traumas from his childhood. He grappled with them in his everyday life as in his work, objectifying them in themes and symbols that he repeated obsessively in his writing."

Whitaker, Thomas R. *Swan and Shadow: Yeats's Dialogue with History*. Chapel Hill: University of North Carolina Press, 1964, 340 p.

Studies the dual perspectives of history in Yeats's works. According to Whitaker: "History was for Yeats a mysterious interlocutor, sometimes a bright reflection of the poet's self, sometimes a shadowy force opposed to that self. He conversed with it as with his double and anti-self. . . . This visionary and paradoxical dialogue—both strikingly individual and highly traditional—was a central fact underlying Yeats's complex and sustained growth. It led him beyond a facile subjectivism toward an awareness of his own more comprehensive nature and toward a passionate self-judgment that was also a judgment of the dominant qualities of his time."

Wright, David G. "Yeats as a Novelist." *Journal of Modern Literature* 12, No. 2 (July 1985): 261-76.

Discusses the autobiographical basis of characterization, structure, and text in Yeats's two early novels, *John Sherman* and *The Speckled Bird*.

Young, David. *Troubled Mirror: A Study of Yeats's "The Tower."* Iowa City: University of Iowa Press, 1987, 153 p.

Ranks Yeats among the greatest English poets based on a close reading of the poems in *The Tower*. Young argues that the greatness of that work "rests on the careful ordering of individual lyrics to make up an equivalent to a traditional long poem."

Zwerdling, Alex. "W. B. Yeats: Variations on the Visionary Quest." *University of Toronto Quarterly* XXX, No. 1 (October 1960): 72-85.

Discusses Yeats's conception of the visionary quest as a move toward the mortal, an idea directly opposed to the traditional notion of the visionary quest as a move by humans toward God.

Acknowledgments

The following is a listing of the copyright holders who have granted us permission to reprint material in this volume of *TCLC*. Every effort has been made to trace copyright, but if omissions have been made, please let us know.

THE COPYRIGHTED EXCERPTS IN TCLC, VOLUME 31, WERE REPRINTED FROM THE FOLLOWING PERIODICALS:

American Literature, v. XLIII, March, 1971; v. 53, January, 1982. Copyright © 1971, 1982 Duke University Press, Durham, NC. Both reprinted by permission of the publisher.

American Quarterly, v. XX, Fall, 1968 for "Thorstein Veblen's Prose" by Stephen S. Conroy. Copyright 1968, American Studies Association. Reprinted by permission of the publisher and the author./ v. X, Winter, 1958 for " 'My Antonia': A Frontier Drama of Time" by James E. Miller, Jr. Copyright 1958, renewed 1986 American Studies Association. Reprinted by permission of the publisher and the author.

The American Slavic and East European Review, v. VIII, 1949. Copyright 1949, renewed 1977 by American Association for the Advancement of Slavic Studies, Inc. Reprinted by permission of the publisher.

Books from Finland, v. XII, 1978 for "Edith Södergran: A Pioneer of Finland-Swedish Modernism" by Gladys Hird. Reprinted by permission of the Literary Estate of Gladys Hird./ v. XVII, 1983 for "A Life on the Edge" by George C. Schoolfield. Reprinted by permission of the author.

California Slavic Studies, v. X. 1977. © 1977 by the Regents of the University of California. Reprinted by permission of the publisher.

Canadian Literature, n. 13, Summer, 1962 for "Flight to the Primitive: Ernest Thompson Seton" by S. E. Read; n. 84, Spring, 1980 for "The Revolt against Instinct: The Animal Stories of Seton and Roberts" by Robert H. MacDonald. Both reprinted by permission of the respective authors.

Chicago Review, v. 27, Autumn, 1975. Copyright © 1975 by *Chicago Review.* Reprinted by permission of the publisher.

Colby Library Quarterly, series X, September, 1973. Reprinted by permission of the publisher.

The Commonweal, v. XLIV, September 13, 1946. Copyright 1946, renewed 1974 Commonweal Publishing Co., Inc. Reprinted by permission of Commonweal Foundation.

The French Review, v. XLIV, December, 1971. Copyright 1971 by the American Association of Teachers of French. Reprinted by permission of the publisher.

Italian Quarterly, v. XIV, Spring, 1971. Reprinted by permission of the publisher.

Italica, v. 60, Spring, 1983. Reprinted by permission of the publisher.

Journal of Canadian Fiction, v. II, Summer, 1973; n. 35/36, 1986. Both reprinted by permission from *Journal of Canadian Fiction,* 2050 Mackay St., Montreal, Quebec H3G 2J1, Canada.

Kentucky Romance Quarterly, v. XVII, 1970. © 1970 University Press of Kentucky. Reprinted by permission of the publisher.

The New York Times Book Review, October 24, 1915; March 16, 1919; June 12, 1921; October 29, 1922; March 13, 1932. Copyright 1915, 1919, 1921, 1922, 1932 by The New York Times Company. All reprinted by permission of the publisher.

Perspectives on Contemporary Literature, v. 5, 1979. Copyright © 1979 by The University Press of Kentucky. Reprinted by permission of the publisher.

PMLA, v. 84, March, 1969. Copyright © 1969 by the Modern Language Association of America. Reprinted by permission of the Modern Language Association of America.

Queen's Quarterly, v. LXXIX, Summer, 1972 for "Ralph Connor and the Canadian Identity" by Lee Thompson and John H. Thompson. Copyright © 1972 by the authors. Reprinted by permission of the authors.

Renaissance and Modern Studies, v. XXIV, 1980. Reprinted by permission of the publisher.

Review: Latin American Literature and Arts, n. 30, September/December, 1981. Copyright © 1981 by the Center for Inter-American Relations, Inc. Reprinted by permission of the publisher.

Shenandoah, v. 14, Autumn, 1962 for "Hope and Memory in 'My Antonia' " by Robert E. Scholes. Copyright 1962 by Washington and Lee University. Reprinted from *Shenandoah* with the permission of the Editor and the author.

Studies in the Novel, v. IV, Fall, 1972. Copyright 1972 by North Texas State University. Reprinted by permission of the publisher.

The Times Literary Supplement, n. 3171, December 7, 1962. © Times Newspapers Ltd. (London) 1962. Reproduced from *The Times Literary Supplement* by permission.

Western American Literature, v. II, August, 1967. Copyright, 1967, by the Western Literature Association. Reprinted by permission of the publisher.

World Literature Today, v. 51, Autumn, 1977. Copyright 1977 by the University of Oklahoma Press. Reprinted by permission of the publisher.

THE COPYRIGHTED EXCERPTS IN TCLC, VOLUME 31, WERE REPRINTED FROM THE FOLLOWING BOOKS:

Aaron, Daniel. From *Men of Good Hope: A Story of American Progressives.* Oxford University Press, 1951. Copyright 1951 by Oxford University Press, Inc. Renewed 1979 by Daniel Aaron. Reprinted by permission of the publisher.

Anderson, H. Allen. From *The Chief: Ernest Thompson Seton and the Changing West.* Texas A&M University Press, 1986. Copyright © 1986 by H. Allen Anderson, Jr. All rights reserved. Reprinted by permission of the publisher.

Alldritt, Keith. From *The Making of George Orwell: An Essay in Literary History.* Edward Arnold, 1969. © Keith Alldritt 1969. Reprinted by permission of the author.

Atwood, Margaret. From *Survival: A Thematic Guide to Canadian Literature.* Toronto: House of Anansi Press Limited, 1972. Copyright © Margaret Atwood, 1972. Reprinted by permission of the publisher.

Bal, Sant Singh. From *George Orwell: The Ethical Imagination.* Arnold-Heinemann, 1981. © Sant Singh Bal. Reprinted by permission of the publisher.

Balakian, Anna. From "A Triptych of Modernism: Reverdy, Huidobro, and Ball," in *Modernism: Challenges and Perspectives.* Edited by Monique Chefdor, Ricardo Quinones, and Albert Wachtel. University of Illinois Press, 1986. © 1986 by the Board of Trustees of the University of Illinois. Reprinted by permission of the publisher and the author.

Bitsilli, Peter M. From *Chekhov's Art: A Stylistic Analysis.* Translated by Toby W. Clyman and Edwina Jannie Cruise. Ardis, 1983. Copyright © 1983 by Ardis Publishers. All rights reserved. Reprinted by permission of the publisher.

Blackmur, R. P. From *Language as Gesture: Essays in Poetry.* Harcourt Brace Jovanovich, 1952. Copyright, 1935, 1936, 1940, 1942, 1943, 1945, 1946, 1948, 1950, 1951, 1952, by Richard P. Blackmur. Renewed 1980 by Elizabeth Blackmur. Reprinted by permission of Harcourt Brace Jovanovich, Inc.

Brown, E. K. From *Willa Cather: A Critical Biography.* Knopf, 1953. Copyright 1953 by Margaret Brown. Renewed 1981 by Margaret Brown and Leon Edel. All rights reserved. Reprinted by permission of Alfred A. Knopf, Inc.

Chandler, Frank W. From *Modern Continental Playwrights.* Harper & Brothers, 1931. Copyright 1931 by Harper & Row, Publishers, Inc. Renewed 1958 by Adele Walton Chandler. Reprinted by permission of Harper & Row, Publishers, Inc.

Costa, René de. From *Vicente Huidobro: The Careers of a Poet.* Oxford at the Clarendon Press, 1984. © René de Costa, 1984. All rights reserved. Reprinted by permission of Oxford University Press.

Debenedetti, Giacomo. From "Federigo Tozzi: A Psychological Interpretation," translated by Frances Frenaye, in *From "Verismo" to Experimentalism: Essays on the Modern Italian Novel.* Edited by Sergio Pacifici. Indiana University Press, 1970. Copyright © 1969 by Indiana University Press. All rights reserved.

Diggins, John P. From *The Bard of Savagery: Thorstein Veblen and Modern Social Theory.* The Seabury Press, 1978. Copyright © 1978 by John P. Diggins. All rights reserved. Reprinted by permission of the publisher.

Dyson, A. E. From *The Crazy Fabric: Essays in Irony.* Macmillan, 1965. Copyright © A. E. Dyson 1965. Reprinted by permission of Macmillan, London and Basingstoke.

Frye, Northrop. From "The Rising of the Moon: A Study of 'A Vision'," in *An Honoured Guest: New Essays on W. B. Yeats.* Edited by Denis Donoghue and J. R. Mulryne. Arnold, 1965. © Edward Arnold (Publishers) Ltd., 1965. Reprinted by permission of the author.

Galbraith, John Kenneth. From "Introduction: Thorstein Veblen and 'The Theory of the Leisure Class'," in *The Theory of the Leisure Class.* By Thorstein Veblen. Houghton Mifflin, 1973. Introduction copyright © 1973 by John Kenneth Galbraith. All rights reserved. Reprinted by permission of Houghton Mifflin Company.

Gerber, Philip. From *Willa Cather.* Twayne, 1975. Copyright 1975 by Twayne Publishers. All rights reserved. Reprinted with the permission of Twayne Publishers, a division of G. K. Hall & Co., Boston.

Glicksberg, Charles I. From *The Literature of Nihilism.* Bucknell University Press, 1975. © 1975 by Associated University Presses, Inc. Reprinted by permission of the publisher.

Greenblatt, Stephen. From *Three Modern Satirists: Waugh, Orwell, and Huxley.* Yale University Press, 1965. Copyright © 1965 by Yale University. All rights reserved. Reprinted by permission of author.

Guss, David M. From "Introduction: Poetry Is a Heavenly Crime," in *The Selected Poetry of Vicente Huidobro.* Edited by David M. Guss, translated by David M. Guss and others. New Directions, 1981. Copyright © 1976 by David M. Guss. All rights reserved. Reprinted by permission of New Directions Publishing Corporation.

Holmes, Henry Alfred. From *Contemporary Spanish Americans.* Crofts, 1942. Copyright 1942 by F. S. Crofts & Co., Inc. Renewed 1969 by J. W. Brown. Excerpted by permission of Prentice-Hall, Inc., Englewood Cliffs, NJ.

Huidobro, Vicente. From "Manifesto Perhaps," translated by Geoffrey Young, in *Relativity of Spring: Thirteen Poems by Vicente Huidobro*. Translated by Michael Palmer and Geoffrey Young. Sand Dollar Press, 1976. Copyright © 1976, 1981 by Michael Palmer. Copyright © 1976, 1977, 1981 by Geoffrey Young. Reprinted by permission of the publisher.

Huneker, James. From *Unicorns*. Charles Scribner's Sons, 1917. Copyright, 1917, by Charles Scribner's Sons. Renewed 1945 by Josephine Huneker. Reprinted with permission of Charles Scribner's Sons, an imprint of Macmillan Publishing Company.

Jackson, Robert Louis. From "Chekhov's 'Seagull': The Empty Well, the Dry Lake, and the Cold Cave," in *Chekhov: A Collection of Critical Essays*. Edited by Robert Louis Jackson. Prentice-Hall, 1967. Copyright © 1967 by Prentice-Hall, Inc. All rights reserved. Excerpted by permission of Prentice-Hall, Inc., Englewood Cliffs, NJ.

Jarrell, Randall. From "Chekhov and the Play" and "The Acts," in *The Three Sisters*. By Anton Chekhov, edited and translated by Randall Jarrell. Macmillan, 1969. Copyright © 1969 by Estate of Randall Jarrell. All rights reserved. Reprinted by permission of Mary Von S. Jarrell.

Johnson, Ben. From an introduction to *Stories of Modern Italy: From Verga, Svevo and Pirandello to the Present*. Edited by Ben Johnson. The Modern Library, 1960. © Copyright, 1960, by Random House, Inc. All rights reserved. Reprinted by permission of Random House, Inc.

Kazin, Alfred. From *On Native Grounds: An Interpretation of Modern American Prose Literature*. Reynal & Hitchcock, 1942. Copyright 1942, 1970, by Alfred Kazin. All rights reserved. Reprinted by permission of Harcourt Brace Jovanovich, Inc.

Kirk, Irina. From *Anton Chekhov*. Twayne, 1981. Copyright 1981 by Twayne Publishers. All rights reserved. Reprinted with the permission of Twayne Publishers, a division of G. K. Hall & Co., Boston.

Lalou, René. From *Contemporary French Literature*. Translated by William Aspenwall Bradley. Knopf, 1924. Copyright 1924, renewed 1952, by Alfred A. Knopf, Inc. Reprinted by permission of the publisher.

Lang, Helmer. From "The Lyrical Poetry of Edith Södergran," in *The Collected Poems of Edith Södergran*. Translated by Martin Allwood with Cate Ewing and Robert Lyng. Anglo-American Center, 1980. Copyright 1980 Martin Allwood. Reprinted by permission of Helmer Lang and Martin Allwood.

Lee, Robert A. From *Orwell's Fiction*. University of Notre Dame Press, 1969. Copyright © 1969 by University of Notre Dame Press; Notre Dame, IN 46556. Reprinted by permission of the publisher.

Leuba, Walter. From *George Saintsbury*. Twayne, 1967. Copyright 1967 by Twayne Publishers. All rights reserved. Reprinted with the permission of Twayne Publishers, Inc., a division of G. K. Hall & Co., Boston.

Lewisohn, Ludwig. From *The Modern Drama: An Essay in Interpretation*. Huebsch, 1915. Copyright 1915 by B. W. Huebsch. Renewed 1942 by Ludwig Lewisohn. Reprinted by permission of Viking Penguin Inc.

Lucas, Alec. From an introduction to *Wild Animals I Have Known*. By Ernest Thompson Seton. McClelland and Stewart, 1977. Introduction copyright © 1977 by McClelland and Stewart Limited. All rights reserved. Reprinted by permission of Alec Lucas.

Lucas, John. From *Modern English Poetry—From Hardy to Hughes: A Critical Survey*. B. T. Batsford Ltd., 1986. © John Lucas 1986. All rights reserved. Reprinted by permission of the publisher.

McCourt, Edward. From *The Canadian West in Fiction*. Revised edition. The Ryerson Press, 1970. © Edward McCourt, 1970. Reprinted by permission of the publisher.

Mencken, H. L. From "Willa Cather," in *The Borzoi 1920*. Edited by Alfred A. Knopf. Knopf, 1920. Copyright 1920, renewed 1947, by Alfred A. Knopf, Inc. Reprinted by permission of the publisher.

Mencken, H. L. From *Prejudices, first series*. Knopf, 1919. Copyright 1919 by Alfred A. Knopf, Inc. Renewed 1947 by H. L. Mencken. Reprinted by permission of the publisher.

Mills, C. Wright. From an introduction to *The Theory of the Leisure Class: An Economic Study of Institutions*. By Thorstein Veblen. New American Library, 1953. Copyright 1953, renewed 1981 by New American Library. All rights reserved. Reprinted by arrangement with NAL Penguin Inc., New York, NY.

Morley, Patricia. From an introduction to *Selected Stories of Ernest Thompson Seton*. Edited by Patricia Morley. University of Ottawa Press, 1977. © University of Ottawa Press, 1977. Reprinted by permission of the publisher.

Mulgan, Alan. From *Great Days in New Zealand Writing*. A. H. & A. W. Reed, 1962. © 1962 Alan Mulgan. Reprinted by permission of Heinemann Reed, a division of Octopus Publishing Group (NZ) Ltd.

Nathan, Leonard E. From *The Tragic Drama of William Butler Yeats: Figures in a Dance*. Columbia University Press, 1965. Copyright © 1965 Columbia University Press. Used by permission of the publisher.

O'Donnell, William H. From *A Guide to the Prose Fiction of W. B. Yeats*. UMI Research Press, 1983. Copyright © 1983 William Hugh O'Donnell. All rights reserved. Reprinted by permission of the publisher.

Twentieth-Century Literary Criticism

Cumulative Indexes
Volumes 1-31

This Index Includes References to Entries in These Gale Series

Contemporary Literary Criticism

Presents excerpts of criticism on the works of novelists, poets, dramatists, short story writers, scriptwriters, and other creative writers who are now living or who have died since 1960. Cumulative indexes to authors and nationalities are included, as well as an index to titles discussed in the individual volume. Volumes 1-51 are in print.

Twentieth-Century Literary Criticism

Contains critical excerpts by the most significant commentators on poets, novelists, short story writers, dramatists, and philosophers who died between 1900 and 1960. Cumulative indexes to authors, nationalities, and titles discussed are included in each new volume. Volumes 1-31 are in print.

Nineteenth-Century Literature Criticism

Offers significant passages from criticism on authors who died between 1800 and 1899. Cumulative indexes to authors, nationalities, and titles discussed are included in each new volume. Volumes 1-20 are in print.

Literature Criticism from 1400 to 1800

Compiles significant passages from the most noteworthy criticism on authors of the fifteenth through eighteenth centuries. Cumulative indexes to authors, nationalities, and titles discussed are included in each new volume. Volumes 1-9 are in print.

Classical and Medieval Literature Criticism

Offers excerpts of criticism on the works of world authors from classical antiquity through the fourteenth century. Cumulative indexes to authors, titles, and critics are included in each volume. Volumes 1-2 are in print.

Short Story Criticism

Compiles excerpts of criticism on short fiction by writers of all eras and nationalities. Cumulative indexes to authors, nationalities, and titles discussed are included in each new volume. Volumes 1-2 are in print.

Children's Literature Review

Includes excerpts from reviews, criticism, and commentary on works of authors and illustrators who create books for children. Cumulative indexes to authors, nationalities, and titles discussed are included in each new volume. Volumes 1-16 are in print.

Contemporary Authors Series

Encompasses five related series. *Contemporary Authors* provides biographical and bibliographical information on more than 90,000 writers of fiction, nonfiction, poetry, journalism, drama, motion pictures, and other fields. Each new volume contains sketches on authors not previously covered in the series. Volumes 1-124 are in print. *Contemporary Authors New Revision Series* provides completely updated information on active authors covered in previously published volumes of *CA*. Only entries requiring significant change are revised for *CA New Revision Series*. Volumes 1-24 are in print. *Contemporary Authors Permanent Series* consists of updated listings for deceased and inactive authors removed from the original volumes 9-36 when these volumes were revised. Volumes 1-2 are in print. *Contemporary Authors Autobiography Series* presents specially commissioned autobiographies by leading contemporary writers. Volumes 1-7 are in print. *Contemporary Authors Bibliographical Series* contains primary and secondary bibliographies as well as analytical bibliographical essays by authorities on major modern authors. Volumes 1-2 are in print.

Dictionary of Literary Biography

Encompasses three related series. *Dictionary of Literary Biography* furnishes illustrated overviews of authors' lives and works and places them in the larger perspective of literary history. Volumes 1-72 are in print. *Dictionary of Literary Biography Documentary Series* illuminates the careers of major figures through a selection of literary documents, including letters, notebook and diary entries, interviews, book reviews, and photographs. Volumes 1-5 are in print. *Dictionary of Literary Biography Yearbook* summarizes the past year's literary activity with articles on genres, major prizes, conferences, and other timely subjects and includes updated and new entries on individual authors. Yearbooks for 1980-1987 are in print. A cumulative index to authors and articles is included in each new volume.

Concise Dictionary of American Literary Biography

A six-volume series that collects revised and updated sketches on major American authors that were originally presented in *Dictionary of Literary Biography*. Volumes 1-3 are in print.

Something about the Author Series

Encompasses two related series. *Something about the Author* contains heavily illustrated biographical sketches on juvenile and young adult authors and illustrators from all eras. Volumes 1-53 are in print. *Something about the Author Autobiography Series* presents specially commissioned autobiographies by prominent authors and illustrators of books for children and young adults. Volumes 1-6 are in print.

Yesterday's Authors of Books for Children

Contains heavily illustrated entries on children's writers who died before 1961. Complete in two volumes. Volumes 1-2 are in print.

Literary Criticism Series
Cumulative Author Index

This index lists all author entries in the Gale Literary Criticism Series and includes cross-references to other Gale sources. For the convenience of the reader, references to the *Yearbook* in the *Contemporary Literary Criticism* series include the page number (in parentheses) after the volume number. References in the index are identified as follows:

AITN: *Authors in the News*, Volumes 1-2
CAAS: *Contemporary Authors Autobiography Series*, Volumes 1-7
CA: *Contemporary Authors* (original series), Volumes 1-124
CABS: *Contemporary Authors Bibliographical Series*, Volumes 1-2
CANR: *Contemporary Authors New Revision Series*, Volumes 1-24
CAP: *Contemporary Authors Permanent Series*, Volumes 1-2
CA-R: *Contemporary Authors* (revised editions), Volumes 1-44
CDALB: *Concise Dictionary of American Literary Biography*, Volumes 1-3
CLC: *Contemporary Literary Criticism*, Volumes 1-51
CLR: *Children's Literature Review*, Volumes 1-16
CMLC: *Classical and Medieval Literature Criticism*, Volumes 1-2
DLB: *Dictionary of Literary Biography*, Volumes 1-72
DLB-DS: *Dictionary of Literary Biography Documentary Series*, Volumes 1-5
DLB-Y: *Dictionary of Literary Biography Yearbook*, Volumes 1980-1987
LC: *Literature Criticism from 1400 to 1800*, Volumes 1-9
NCLC: *Nineteenth-Century Literature Criticism*, Volumes 1-20
SAAS: *Something about the Author Autobiography Series*, Volumes 1-6
SATA: *Something about the Author*, Volumes 1-53
SSC: *Short Story Criticism*, Volumes 1-2
TCLC: *Twentieth-Century Literary Criticism*, Volumes 1-31
YABC: *Yesterday's Authors of Books for Children*, Volumes 1-2

Adler, C(arole) S(chwerdtfeger)
1932-........................CLC 35
See also CANR 19
See also CA 89-92
See also SATA 26

Adler, Renata 1938- .... CLC 8, 31
See also CANR 5, 22
See also CA 49-52

Ady, Endre 1877-1919 .... TCLC 11
See also CA 107

Agee, James 1909-1955....... TCLC 1, 19
See also CA 108
See also DLB 2, 26
See also CDALB 1941-1968
See also AITN 1

Agnon, S(hmuel) Y(osef Halevi)
1888-1970............. CLC 4, 8, 14
See also CAP 2
See also CA 17-18
See also obituary CA 25-28R

Ai 1947-....................... CLC 4, 14
See also CA 85-88

Aiken, Conrad (Potter)
1889-1973.............CLC 1, 3, 5, 10
See also CANR 4
See also CA 5-8R
See also obituary CA 45-48
See also SATA 3, 30
See also DLB 9, 45

Aiken, Joan (Delano) 1924- ....CLC 35
See also CLR 1
See also CANR 4
See also CA 9-12R
See also SAAS 1
See also SATA 2, 30

Ainsworth, William Harrison
1805-1882................. NCLC 13
See also SATA 24
See also DLB 21

Ajar, Emile 1914-1980
See Gary, Romain

Akhmatova, Anna
1888-1966.................. CLC 11, 25
See also CAP 1
See also CA 19-20
See also obituary CA 25-28R

Aksakov, Sergei Timofeyvich
1791-1859.................. NCLC 2

Aksenov, Vassily (Pavlovich) 1932-
See Aksyonov, Vasily (Pavlovich)

Aksyonov, Vasily (Pavlovich)
1932-..................... CLC 22, 37
See also CANR 12
See also CA 53-56

Akutagawa Ryūnosuke
1892-1927.................. TCLC 16
See also CA 117

Alain-Fournier 1886-1914 .... TCLC 6
See also Fournier, Henri Alban

Alarcón, Pedro Antonio de
1833-1891.................. NCLC 1

Alas (y Urena), Leopoldo (Enrique Garcia)
1852-1901................. TCLC 29
See also CA 113

Albee, Edward (Franklin III)
1928-..... CLC 1, 2, 3, 5, 9, 11, 13, 25
See also CANR 8
See also CA 5-8R
See also DLB 7
See also CDALB 1941-1968
See also AITN 1

Alberti, Rafael 1902-..............CLC 7
See also CA 85-88

Alcott, Amos Bronson
1799-1888.................. NCLC 1
See also DLB 1

Alcott, Louisa May 1832-1888..... NCLC 6
See also CLR 1
See also YABC 1
See also DLB 1, 42
See also CDALB 1865-1917

Aldanov, Mark 1887-1957 .... TCLC 23
See also CA 118

Aldington, Richard 1892-1962......CLC 49
See also CA 85-88
See also DLB 20, 36

Aldiss, Brian W(ilson)
1925-.................. CLC 5, 14, 40
See also CAAS 2
See also CANR 5
See also CA 5-8R
See also SATA 34
See also DLB 14

Aleichem, Sholom 1859-1916...... TCLC 1
See also Rabinovitch, Sholem

Aleixandre, Vicente
1898-1984................. CLC 9, 36
See also CA 85-88
See also obituary CA 114

Alepoudelis, Odysseus 1911-
See Elytis, Odysseus

Aleshkovsky, Yuz 1929- ...... CLC 44 (29)
See also CA 121

Alexander, Lloyd (Chudley)
1924-.......................CLC 35
See also CLR 1, 5
See also CANR 1
See also CA 1-4R
See also SATA 3, 49
See also DLB 52

Alger, Horatio, Jr. 1832-1899..... NCLC 8
See also SATA 16
See also DLB 42

Algren, Nelson
1909-1981.............. CLC 4, 10, 33
See also CANR 20
See also CA 13-16R
See also obituary CA 103
See also DLB 9
See also DLB-Y 81, 82
See also CDALB 1941-1968

Allen, Heywood 1935-
See Allen, Woody
See also CA 33-36R

Allen, Roland 1939-
See Ayckbourn, Alan

Allen, Woody 1935-................CLC 16
See also Allen, Heywood
See also DLB 44

Allende, Isabel 1942-........ CLC 39 (27)

Allingham, Margery (Louise)
1904-1966...................CLC 19
See also CANR 4
See also CA 5-8R
See also obituary CA 25-28R

Allston, Washington
1779-1843.................. NCLC 2
See also DLB 1

Almedingen, E. M. 1898-1971......CLC 12
See also Almedingen, Martha Edith von
See also SATA 3

Almedingen, Martha Edith von 1898-1971
See Almedingen, E. M.
See also CANR 1
See also CA 1-4R

Alonso, Dámaso 1898-.............CLC 14
See also CA 110

Alta 1942-.......................CLC 19
See also CA 57-60

Alter, Robert B(ernard)
1935-................. CLC 34 (515)
See also CANR 1
See also CA 49-52

Alther, Lisa 1944- .... CLC 7, 41
See also CANR 12
See also CA 65-68

Altman, Robert 1925-.............CLC 16
See also CA 73-76

Alvarez, A(lfred) 1929-......... CLC 5, 13
See also CANR 3
See also CA 1-4R
See also DLB 14, 40

Álvarez, Alejandro Rodríguez 1903-1965
See Casona, Alejandro
See also obituary CA 93-96

Amado, Jorge 1912- .... CLC 13, 40
See also CA 77-80

Ambler, Eric 1909-.......... CLC 4, 6, 9
See also CANR 7
See also CA 9-12R

Amichai, Yehuda 1924- .... CLC 9, 22
See also CA 85-88

Amiel, Henri Frédéric
1821-1881................... NCLC 4

Amis, Kingsley (William)
1922-........ CLC 1, 2, 3, 5, 8, 13, 40,
                      44 (133)
See also CANR 8
See also CA 9-12R
See also DLB 15, 27
See also AITN 2

Amis, Martin 1949-.......... CLC 4, 9, 38
See also CANR 8
See also CA 65-68
See also DLB 14

Ammons, A(rchie) R(andolph)
1926-............ CLC 2, 3, 5, 8, 9, 25
See also CANR 6
See also CA 9-12R
See also DLB 5
See also AITN 1

Anand, Mulk Raj 1905-............CLC 23
See also CA 65-68

Anaya, Rudolfo A(lfonso)
1937-......................CLC 23
See also CAAS 4
See also CANR 1
See also CA 45-48

Author Index

Bunyan, John (1628-1688)..........LC **4**
See also DLB 39

Burgess (Wilson, John) Anthony
   1917-.....CLC **1, 2, 4, 5, 8, 10, 13, 15,
                                    22, 40**
See also Wilson, John (Anthony) Burgess
See also DLB 14
See also AITN 1

Burke, Edmund 1729-1797..........LC **7**

Burke, Kenneth (Duva)
   1897-....................CLC **2, 24**
See also CA 5-8R
See also DLB 45, 63

Burney, Fanny 1752-1840.......NCLC **12**
See also DLB 39

Burns, Robert 1759-1796............LC **3**

Burns, Tex 1908?-
See L'Amour, Louis (Dearborn)

Burnshaw, Stanley
   1906-.............CLC **3, 13, 44** (456)
See also CA 9-12R
See also DLB 48

Burr, Anne 1937-.................CLC **6**
See also CA 25-28R

Burroughs, Edgar Rice
   1875-1950...................TCLC **2**
See also CA 104
See also DLB 8
See also SATA 41

Burroughs, William S(eward)
   1914-..........CLC **1, 2, 5, 15, 22, 42**
See also CANR 20
See also CA 9-12R
See also DLB 2, 8, 16
See also DLB-Y 81
See also AITN 2

Busch, Frederick
   1941-.................CLC **7, 10, 18, 47**
See also CAAS 1
See also CA 33-36R
See also DLB 6

Bush, Ronald 19??-.........CLC **34** (523)

Butler, Octavia E(stelle) 1947-......CLC **38**
See also CANR 12
See also CA 73-76
See also DLB 33

Butler, Samuel 1835-1902........TCLC **1**
See also CA 104
See also DLB 18, 57

Butor, Michel (Marie François)
   1926-.............CLC **1, 3, 8, 11, 15**
See also CA 9-12R

Buzzati, Dino 1906-1972..........CLC **36**
See also obituary CA 33-36R

Byars, Betsy 1928-................CLC **35**
See also CLR 1, 16
See also CANR 18
See also CA 33-36R
See also SAAS 1
See also SATA 4, 46
See also DLB 52

Byatt, A(ntonia) S(usan Drabble)
   1936-......................CLC **19**
See also CANR 13
See also CA 13-16R
See also DLB 14

Byrne, David 1953?-..............CLC **26**

Byrne, John Keyes 1926-
See Leonard, Hugh
See also CA 102

Byron, George Gordon (Noel), Lord Byron
   1788-1824................NCLC **2, 12**

Caballero, Fernán 1796-1877....NCLC **10**

Cabell, James Branch
   1879-1958..................TCLC **6**
See also CA 105
See also DLB 9

Cable, George Washington
   1844-1925..................TCLC **4**
See also CA 104
See also DLB 12

Cabrera Infante, G(uillermo)
   1929-..................CLC **5, 25, 45**
See also CA 85-88

Cage, John (Milton, Jr.) 1912-.....CLC **41**
See also CANR 9
See also CA 13-16R

Cain, G. 1929-
See Cabrera Infante, G(uillermo)

Cain, James M(allahan)
   1892-1977..............CLC **3, 11, 28**
See also CANR 8
See also CA 17-20R
See also obituary CA 73-76
See also AITN 1

Caldwell, Erskine (Preston)
   1903-1987......CLC **1, 8, 14, 50** (298)
See also CAAS 1
See also CANR 2
See also CA 1-4R
See also obituary CA 121
See also DLB 9
See also AITN 1

Caldwell, (Janet Miriam) Taylor (Holland)
   1900-1985........CLC **2, 28, 39** (301)
See also CANR 5
See also CA 5-8R
See also obituary CA 116

Calhoun, John Caldwell
   1782-1850..................NCLC **15**
See also DLB 3

Calisher, Hortense
   1911-....................CLC **2, 4, 8, 38**
See also CANR 1, 22
See also CA 1-4R
See also DLB 2

Callaghan, Morley (Edward)
   1903-..................CLC **3, 14, 41**
See also CA 9-12R

Calvino, Italo
   1923-1985.......CLC **5, 8, 11, 22, 33,
                                    39** (305)
See also CA 85-88
See also obituary CA 116

Cameron, Peter 1959-........CLC **44** (33)

Campana, Dino 1885-1932......TCLC **20**
See also CA 117

Campbell, John W(ood), Jr.
   1910-1971...................CLC **32**
See also CAP 2
See also CA 21-22
See also obituary CA 29-32R
See also DLB 8

Campbell, (John) Ramsey
   1946-......................CLC **42**
See also CANR 7
See also CA 57-60

Campbell, (Ignatius) Roy (Dunnachie)
   1901-1957...................TCLC **5**
See also CA 104
See also DLB 20

Campbell, Thomas
   1777-1844..................NCLC **19**

Campbell, (William) Wilfred
   1861-1918..................TCLC **9**
See also CA 106

Camus, Albert
   1913-1960......CLC **1, 2, 4, 9, 11, 14,
                                    32**
See also CA 89-92
See also DLB 72

Canby, Vincent 1924-.............CLC **13**
See also CA 81-84

Canetti, Elias 1905-........CLC **3, 14, 25**
See also CA 21-24R

Cape, Judith 1916-
See Page, P(atricia) K(athleen)

Čapek, Karel 1890-1938.........TCLC **6**
See also CA 104

Capote, Truman
   1924-1984........CLC **1, 3, 8, 13, 19,
                                    34** (320), **38**
   ....SSC **2**
See also CANR 18
See also CA 5-8R
See also obituary CA 113
See also DLB 2
See also DLB-Y 80, 84
See also CDALB 1941-1968

Capra, Frank 1897-...............CLC **16**
See also CA 61-64

Caputo, Philip 1941-.............CLC **32**
See also CA 73-76

Card, Orson Scott
   1951-...... CLC **44** (163), **47, 50** (142)
See also CA 102

Cardenal, Ernesto 1925-..........CLC **31**
See also CANR 2
See also CA 49-52

Carey, Ernestine Gilbreth 1908-
See Gilbreth, Frank B(unker), Jr. and
   Carey, Ernestine Gilbreth
See also CA 5-8R
See also SATA 2

Carey, Peter 1943-................CLC **40**

Carleton, William 1794-1869......NCLC **3**

Carlisle, Henry (Coffin) 1926-......CLC **33**
See also CANR 15
See also CA 13-16R

Carman, (William) Bliss
   1861-1929..................TCLC **7**
See also CA 104

Carpenter, Don(ald Richard)
   1931-......................CLC **41**
See also CANR 1
See also CA 45-48

Dillon, Eilís 1920- ....CLC 17
See also CAAS 3
See also CANR 4
See also CA 9-12R
See also SATA 2

Dinesen, Isak 1885-1962...... **CLC 10, 29**
See also Blixen, Karen (Christentze
Dinesen)
See also CANR 22

Disch, Thomas M(ichael)
1940- .... CLC 7, 36
See also CAAS 4
See also CANR 17
See also CA 21-24R
See also DLB 8

Disraeli, Benjamin 1804-1881 ..... NCLC 2
See also DLB 21, 55

Dixon, Paige 1911-
See Corcoran, Barbara

Döblin, Alfred 1878-1957........ TCLC 13
See also Doeblin, Alfred

Dobrolyubov, Nikolai Alexandrovich
1836-1861..................... NCLC 5

Dobyns, Stephen 1941- ....CLC 37
See also CANR 2, 18
See also CA 45-48

Doctorow, E(dgar) L(aurence)
1931-...........CLC 6, 11, 15, 18, 37,
44 (166)
See also CANR 2
See also CA 45-48
See also DLB 2, 28
See also DLB-Y 80
See also AITN 2

Dodgson, Charles Lutwidge 1832-1898
See Carroll, Lewis
See also YABC 2

Doeblin, Alfred 1878-1957....... TCLC 13
See also CA 110

Doerr, Harriet 1910-........ CLC 34 (151)
See also CA 117, 122

Donaldson, Stephen R. 1947-.......CLC 46
See also CANR 13
See also CA 89-92

Donleavy, J(ames) P(atrick)
1926- .... CLC 1, 4, 6, 10, 45
See also CA 9-12R
See also DLB 6
See also AITN 2

Donnadieu, Marguerite 1914-
See Duras, Marguerite

Donnell, David 1939?-....... CLC 34 (155)

Donoso, José 1924- ....CLC 4, 8, 11, 32
See also CA 81-84

Donovan, John 1928- ....CLC 35
See also CLR 3
See also CA 97-100
See also SATA 29

Doolittle, Hilda 1886-1961
See H(ilda) D(oolittle)
See also CA 97-100
See also DLB 4, 45

Dorfman, Ariel 1942- ....CLC 48

Dorn, Ed(ward Merton)
1929-.................... CLC 10, 18
See also CA 93-96
See also DLB 5

Dos Passos, John (Roderigo)
1896-1970..... CLC 1, 4, 8, 11, 15, 25,
34 (419)
See also CANR 3
See also CA 1-4R
See also obituary CA 29-32R
See also DLB 4, 9
See also DLB-DS 1

Dostoevski, Fedor Mikhailovich
1821-1881..................NCLC 2, 7
.... SSC 2

Doughty, Charles (Montagu)
1843-1926................. TCLC 27
See also CA 115
See also DLB 19, 57

Douglas, George 1869-1902...... TCLC 28

Douglass, Frederick
1817-1895................. NCLC 7
See also SATA 29
See also DLB 1, 43, 50
See also CDALB 1640-1865

Dourado, (Waldomiro Freitas) Autran
1926-.......................CLC 23
See also CA 25-28R

Dove, Rita 1952- .... CLC 50 (152)
See also CA 109

Dowson, Ernest (Christopher)
1867-1900................... TCLC 4
See also CA 105
See also DLB 19

Doyle, (Sir) Arthur Conan
1859-1930............... TCLC 7, 26
See also CA 104, 122
See also SATA 24
See also DLB 18, 70

Dr. A 1933-
See Silverstein, Alvin and Virginia
B(arbara Opshelor) Silverstein

Drabble, Margaret
1939-........CLC 2, 3, 5, 8, 10, 22
See also CANR 18
See also CA 13-16R
See also SATA 48
See also DLB 14

Drayton, Michael 1563-1631 .... LC 8

Dreiser, Theodore (Herman Albert)
1871-1945............... TCLC 10, 18
See also SATA 48
See also CA 106
See also DLB 9, 12
See also DLB-DS 1
See also CDALB 1865-1917

Drexler, Rosalyn 1926-.......... CLC 2, 6
See also CA 81-84

Dreyer, Carl Theodor
1889-1968....................CLC 16
See also obituary CA 116

Drieu La Rochelle, Pierre
1893-1945................. TCLC 21
See also CA 117
See also DLB 72

Droste-Hülshoff, Annette Freiin von
1797-1848................. NCLC 3

Drummond, William Henry
1854-1907................. TCLC 25

Drummond de Andrade, Carlos 1902-
See Andrade, Carlos Drummond de

Drury, Allen (Stuart) 1918-........CLC 37
See also CANR 18
See also CA 57-60

Dryden, John 1631-1700 .... LC 3

Duberman, Martin 1930-..........CLC 8
See also CANR 2
See also CA 1-4R

Dubie, Norman (Evans, Jr.)
1945-......................CLC 36
See also CANR 12
See also CA 69-72

Du Bois, W(illiam) E(dward) B(urghardt)
1868-1963............... CLC 1, 2, 13
See also CA 85-88
See also SATA 42
See also DLB 47, 50
See also CDALB 1865-1917

Dubus, André 1936- .... CLC 13, 36
See also CANR 17
See also CA 21-24R

Ducasse, Isidore Lucien 1846-1870
See Lautréamont, Comte de

Duclos, Charles Pinot 1704-1772 ..... LC 1

Dudek, Louis 1918-........... CLC 11, 19
See also CANR 1
See also CA 45-48

Dudevant, Amandine Aurore Lucile Dupin
1804-1876
See Sand, George

Duerrenmatt, Friedrich 1921-
See also CA 17-20R

Duffy, Bruce 19??-........... CLC 50 (33)

Duffy, Maureen 1933-.............CLC 37
See also CA 25-28R
See also DLB 14

Dugan, Alan 1923-.............. CLC 2, 6
See also CA 81-84
See also DLB 5

Duhamel, Georges 1884-1966 ....CLC 8
See also CA 81-84
See also obituary CA 25-28R

Dujardin, Édouard (Émile Louis)
1861-1949................. TCLC 13
See also CA 109

Duke, Raoul 1939-
See Thompson, Hunter S(tockton)

Dumas, Alexandre (Davy de la Pailleterie)
(*père*) 1802-1870........... NCLC 11
See also SATA 18

Dumas, Alexandre (*fils*)
1824-1895.................. NCLC 9

Dumas, Henry (L.) 1934-1968.......CLC 6
See also CA 85-88
See also DLB 41

Du Maurier, Daphne 1907- ..... CLC 6, 11
See also CANR 6
See also CA 5-8R
See also SATA 27

Dunbar, Paul Laurence
1872-1906............... TCLC 2, 12
See also CA 104
See also SATA 34
See also DLB 50, 54
See also CDALB 1865-1917

Ellis, Bret Easton 1964- ...... CLC 39 (55)
See also CA 118

Ellis, (Henry) Havelock
1859-1939................. TCLC 14
See also CA 109

Ellison, Harlan (Jay)
1934-................. CLC 1, 13, 42
See also CANR 5
See also CA 5-8R
See also DLB 8

Ellison, Ralph (Waldo)
1914-................. CLC 1, 3, 11
See also CA 9-12R
See also DLB 2
See also CDALB 1941-1968

Ellmann, Richard (David)
1918-1987.............. CLC 50 (305)
See also CANR 2
See also CA 1-4R
See also obituary CA 122

Elman, Richard 1934-............CLC 19
See also CAAS 3
See also CA 17-20R

Éluard, Paul 1895-1952 .... TCLC 7
See also Grindel, Eugene

Elvin, Anne Katharine Stevenson 1933-
See Stevenson, Anne (Katharine)
See also CA 17-20R

Elytis, Odysseus 1911- .... CLC 15, 49
See also CA 102

Emecheta, (Florence Onye) Buchi
1944-................... CLC 14, 48
See also CA 81-84

Emerson, Ralph Waldo
1803-1882................. NCLC 1
See also DLB 1
See also CDALB 1640-1865

Empson, William
1906-1984.......... CLC 3, 8, 19, 33,
                              34 (335; 538)
See also CA 17-20R
See also obituary CA 112
See also DLB 20

Enchi, Fumiko (Veda)
1905-1986..................CLC 31
See also obituary CA 121

Ende, Michael 1930-..............CLC 31
See also CLR 14
See also CA 118
See also SATA 42

Endo, Shusaku 1923- .... CLC 7, 14, 19
See also CANR 21
See also CA 29-32R

Engel, Marian 1933-1985..........CLC 36
See also CANR 12
See also CA 25-28R
See also DLB 53

Engelhardt, Frederick 1911-1986
See Hubbard, L(afayette) Ron(ald)

Enright, D(ennis) J(oseph)
1920-................... CLC 4, 8, 31
See also CANR 1
See also CA 1-4R
See also SATA 25
See also DLB 27

Enzensberger, Hans Magnus
1929-.......................CLC 43
See also CA 116, 119

Ephron, Nora 1941- .... CLC 17, 31
See also CANR 12
See also CA 65-68
See also AITN 2

Epstein, Daniel Mark 1948-........CLC 7
See also CANR 2
See also CA 49-52

Epstein, Jacob 1956-..............CLC 19
See also CA 114

Epstein, Joseph 1937-....... CLC 39 (463)
See also CA 112, 119

Epstein, Leslie 1938-..............CLC 27
See also CA 73-76

Erdman, Paul E(mil) 1932- ....CLC 25
See also CANR 13
See also CA 61-64
See also AITN 1

Erdrich, Louise 1954-...... CLC 39 (128)
See also CA 114

Erenburg, Ilya (Grigoryevich) 1891-1967
See Ehrenburg, Ilya (Grigoryevich)

Eseki, Bruno 1919-
See Mphahlele, Ezekiel

Esenin, Sergei (Aleksandrovich)
1895-1925................... TCLC 4
See also CA 104

Eshleman, Clayton 1935-...........CLC 7
See also CAAS 6
See also CA 33-36R
See also DLB 5

Espriu, Salvador 1913-1985........CLC 9
See also obituary CA 115

Estleman, Loren D. 1952-.........CLC 48
See also CA 85-88

Evans, Marian 1819-1880
See Eliot, George

Evans, Mary Ann 1819-1880
See Eliot, George

Evarts, Esther 1900-1972
See Benson, Sally

Everson, Ronald G(ilmour)
1903-.......................CLC 27
See also CA 17-20R

Everson, William (Oliver)
1912-................... CLC 1, 5, 14
See also CANR 20
See also CA 9-12R
See also DLB 5, 16

Evtushenko, Evgenii (Aleksandrovich) 1933-
See Yevtushenko, Yevgeny

Ewart, Gavin (Buchanan)
1916-................... CLC 13, 46
See also CANR 17
See also CA 89-92
See also DLB 40

Ewers, Hanns Heinz
1871-1943................. TCLC 12
See also CA 109

Ewing, Frederick R. 1918-
See Sturgeon, Theodore (Hamilton)

Exley, Frederick (Earl)
1929-................... CLC 6, 11
See also CA 81-84
See also DLB-Y 81
See also AITN 2

Ezekiel, Tish O'Dowd
1943-................. CLC 34 (46)

Fagen, Donald 1948-
See Becker, Walter and Fagen, Donald

Fagen, Donald 1948- and
    Becker, Walter 1950-
See Becker, Walter and Fagen, Donald

Fair, Ronald L. 1932-.............CLC 18
See also CA 69-72
See also DLB 33

Fairbairns, Zoë (Ann) 1948- ....CLC 32
See also CANR 21
See also CA 103

Fairfield, Cicily Isabel 1892-1983
See West, Rebecca

Fallaci, Oriana 1930- ....CLC 11
See also CANR 15
See also CA 77-80

Faludy, George 1913-..............CLC 42
See also CA 21-24R

Fargue, Léon-Paul 1876-1947 .... TCLC 11
See also CA 109

Farigoule, Louis 1885-1972
See Romains, Jules

Fariña, Richard 1937?-1966 ....CLC 9
See also CA 81-84
See also obituary CA 25-28R

Farley, Walter 1920-..............CLC 17
See also CANR 8
See also CA 17-20R
See also SATA 2, 43
See also DLB 22

Farmer, Philip José 1918- ...... CLC 1, 19
See also CANR 4
See also CA 1-4R
See also DLB 8

Farrell, J(ames) G(ordon)
1935-1979....................CLC 6
See also CA 73-76
See also obituary CA 89-92
See also DLB 14

Farrell, James T(homas)
1904-1979............CLC 1, 4, 8, 11
See also CANR 9
See also CA 5-8R
See also obituary CA 89-92
See also DLB 4, 9
See also DLB-DS 2

Farrell, M. J. 1904-
See Keane, Molly

Fassbinder, Rainer Werner
1946-1982....................CLC 20
See also CA 93-96
See also obituary CA 106

Fast, Howard (Melvin) 1914-.......CLC 23
See also CANR 1
See also CA 1-4R
See also SATA 7
See also DLB 9

Faulkner, William (Cuthbert)
1897-1962...... CLC 1, 3, 6, 8, 9, 11,
                              14, 18, 28
.... SSC 1
See also CA 81-84
See also DLB 9, 11, 44
See also DLB-Y 86
See also DLB-DS 2
See also AITN 1

Author Index

Author Index

Martinson, Harry (Edmund)
1904-1978.....................CLC 14
See also CA 77-80

Marvell, Andrew 1621-1678 ....LC 4

Marx, Karl (Heinrich)
1818-1883.................NCLC 17

Masaoka Shiki 1867-1902.......TCLC 18

Masefield, John (Edward)
1878-1967................CLC 11, 47
See also CAP 2
See also CA 19-20
See also obituary CA 25-28R
See also SATA 19
See also DLB 10, 19

Maso, Carole 19??- ....CLC 44 (57)

Mason, Bobbie Ann 1940- .....CLC 28, 43
See also CANR 11
See also CA 53-56
See also SAAS 1

Mason, Nick 1945-
See Pink Floyd

Mason, Tally 1909-1971
See Derleth, August (William)

Masters, Edgar Lee
1868?-1950...............TCLC 2, 25
See also CA 104
See also DLB 54
See also CDALB 1865-1917

Masters, Hilary 1928-.............CLC 48
See also CANR 13
See also CA 25-28R

Mastrosimone, William 19??- ......CLC 36

Matheson, Richard (Burton)
1926-.......................CLC 37
See also CA 97-100
See also DLB 8, 44

Mathews, Harry 1930- ....CLC 6
See also CAAS 6
See also CANR 18
See also CA 21-24R

Mathias, Roland (Glyn) 1915-......CLC 45
See also CANR 19
See also CA 97-100
See also DLB 27

Matthews, Greg 1949-.............CLC 45

Matthews, William 1942-..........CLC 40
See also CANR 12
See also CA 29-32R
See also DLB 5

Matthias, John (Edward) 1941-......CLC 9
See also CA 33-36R

Matthiessen, Peter
1927-................CLC 5, 7, 11, 32
See also CANR 21
See also CA 9-12R
See also SATA 27
See also DLB 6

Maturin, Charles Robert
1780?-1824..................NCLC 6

Matute, Ana María 1925-..........CLC 11
See also CA 89-92

Maugham, W(illiam) Somerset
1874-1965.............CLC 1, 11, 15
See also CA 5-8R
See also obituary CA 25-28R
See also DLB 10, 36

Maupassant, (Henri René Albert) Guy de
1850-1893...................NCLC 1
.....................SSC 1

Mauriac, Claude 1914-...........CLC 9
See also CA 89-92

Mauriac, François (Charles)
1885-1970.................CLC 4, 9
See also CAP 2
See also CA 25-28

Mavor, Osborne Henry 1888-1951
See Bridie, James
See also CA 104

Maxwell, William (Keepers, Jr.)
1908-.......................CLC 19
See also CA 93-96
See also DLB-Y 80

May, Elaine 1932-.................CLC 16
See also DLB 44

Mayakovsky, Vladimir (Vladimirovich)
1893-1930...............TCLC 4, 18
See also CA 104

Maynard, Joyce 1953-.............CLC 23
See also CA 111

Mayne, William (James Carter)
1928-.......................CLC 12
See also CA 9-12R
See also SATA 6

Mayo, Jim 1908?-
See L'Amour, Louis (Dearborn)

Maysles, Albert 1926-
See Maysles, Albert and Maysles, David
See also CA 29-32R

Maysles, Albert 1926- and **Maysles, David**
1932-......................CLC 16

Maysles, David 1932-
See Maysles, Albert and Maysles, David

Mazer, Norma Fox 1931-..........CLC 26
See also CANR 12
See also CA 69-72
See also SAAS 1
See also SATA 24

McAuley, James (Phillip)
1917-1976..................CLC 45
See also CA 97-100

McBain, Ed 1926-
See Hunter, Evan

McBrien, William 1930-..... CLC 44 (431)
See also CA 107

McCaffrey, Anne 1926- ....CLC 17
See also CANR 15
See also CA 25-28R
See also SATA 8
See also DLB 8
See also AITN 2

McCarthy, Cormac 1933-..........CLC 4
See also CANR 10
See also CA 13-16R
See also DLB 6

McCarthy, Mary (Therese)
1912-....CLC 1, 3, 5, 14, 24, 39 (484)
See also CANR 16
See also CA 5-8R
See also DLB 2
See also DLB-Y 81

McCartney, (James) Paul
1942-......................CLC 35
See also Lennon, John (Ono) and
McCartney, Paul

McCauley, Stephen 19??-..... CLC 50 (62)

McClure, Michael 1932-........ CLC 6, 10
See also CANR 17
See also CA 21-24R
See also DLB 16

McCorkle, Jill (Collins) 1958-......CLC 51
See also CA 121
See also DLB-Y 87

McCourt, James 1941-.............CLC 5
See also CA 57-60

McCoy, Horace 1897-1955.......TCLC 28
See also CA 108
See also DLB 9

McCrae, John 1872-1918.......TCLC 12
See also CA 109

McCullers, (Lula) Carson (Smith)
1917-1967........ CLC 1, 4, 10, 12, 48
See also CANR 18
See also CA 5-8R
See also obituary CA 25-28R
See also CABS 1
See also SATA 27
See also DLB 2, 7
See also CDALB 1941-1968

McCullough, Colleen 1938?- ....CLC 27
See also CANR 17
See also CA 81-84

McElroy, Joseph (Prince)
1930-.....................CLC 5, 47
See also CA 17-20R

McEwan, Ian (Russell) 1948-......CLC 13
See also CANR 14
See also CA 61-64
See also DLB 14

McFadden, David 1940-...........CLC 48
See also CA 104
See also DLB 60

McGahern, John 1934-......CLC 5, 9, 48
See also CA 17-20R
See also DLB 14

McGinley, Patrick 1937-..........CLC 41
See also CA 120

McGinley, Phyllis 1905-1978.......CLC 14
See also CANR 19
See also CA 9-12R
See also obituary CA 77-80
See also SATA 2, 44
See also obituary SATA 24
See also DLB 11, 48

McGinniss, Joe 1942- ....CLC 32
See also CA 25-28R
See also AITN 2

McGivern, Maureen Daly 1921-
See Daly, Maureen
See also CA 9-12R

McGrath, Thomas 1916- ....CLC 28
See also CANR 6
See also CA 9-12R
See also SATA 41

McGuane, Thomas (Francis III)
1939-.................... CLC 3, 7, 18
See also CANR 5
See also CA 49-52
See also DLB 2
See also DLB-Y 80
See also AITN 2

McGuckian, Medbh 1950-........CLC 48
See also DLB 40

McHale, Tom 1941-1982 .... CLC 3, 5
See also CA 77-80
See also obituary CA 106
See also AITN 1

McIlvanney, William 1936-........CLC 42
See also CA 25-28R
See also DLB 14

McIlwraith, Maureen Mollie Hunter 1922-
See Hunter, Mollie
See also CA 29-32R
See also SATA 2

McInerney, Jay 1955-........ CLC 34 (81)
See also CA 116

McIntyre, Vonda N(eel) 1948-......CLC 18
See also CANR 17
See also CA 81-84

McKay, Claude 1890-1948........ TCLC 7
See also CA 104
See also DLB 4, 45

McKuen, Rod 1933- .... CLC 1, 3
See also CA 41-44R
See also AITN 1

McLuhan, (Herbert) Marshall
1911-1980...................CLC 37
See also CANR 12
See also CA 9-12R
See also obituary CA 102

McManus, Declan Patrick 1955-
See Costello, Elvis

McMillan, Terry 19??- .... CLC 50 (67)

McMurtry, Larry (Jeff)
1936-.....CLC 2, 3, 7, 11, 27, 44 (253)
See also CANR 19
See also CA 5-8R
See also DLB 2
See also DLB-Y 80
See also AITN 2

McNally, Terrence 1939- ..... CLC 4, 7, 41
See also CANR 2
See also CA 45-48
See also DLB 7

McPhee, John 1931- ....CLC 36
See also CANR 20
See also CA 65-68

McPherson, James Alan 1943- .....CLC 19
See also CA 25-28R
See also DLB 38

McPherson, William
1939-................... CLC 34 (85)
See also CA 57-60

McSweeney, Kerry 19??- .... CLC 34 (579)

Mead, Margaret 1901-1978........CLC 37
See also CANR 4
See also CA 1-4R
See also obituary CA 81-84
See also SATA 20
See also AITN 1

Meaker, M. J. 1927-
See Kerr, M. E.
See Meaker, Marijane

Meaker, Marijane 1927-
See Kerr, M. E.
See also CA 107
See also SATA 20

Medoff, Mark (Howard)
1940-.................... CLC 6, 23
See also CANR 5
See also CA 53-56
See also DLB 7
See also AITN 1

Megged, Aharon 1920-..............CLC 9
See also CANR 1
See also CA 49-52

Mehta, Ved (Parkash) 1934- ....CLC 37
See also CANR 2
See also CA 1-4R

Mellor, John 1953?-
See The Clash

Meltzer, Milton 1915-..............CLC 26
See also CA 13-16R
See also SAAS 1
See also SATA 1
See also DLB 61

Melville, Herman
1819-1891................NCLC 3, 12
.... SSC 1
See also DLB 3
See also CDALB 1640-1865

Mencken, H(enry) L(ouis)
1880-1956.............. TCLC 13
See also CA 105
See also DLB 11, 29, 63

Mercer, David 1928-1980..........CLC 5
See also CA 9-12R
See also obituary CA 102
See also DLB 13

Meredith, George 1828-1909 ..... TCLC 17
See also CA 117
See also DLB 18, 35, 57

Meredith, William (Morris)
1919-................. CLC 4, 13, 22
See also CANR 6
See also CA 9-12R
See also DLB 5

Merezhkovsky, Dmitri
1865-1941................. TCLC 29

Mérimée, Prosper 1803-1870...... NCLC 6

Merkin, Daphne 1954- .... CLC 44 (62)

Merrill, James (Ingram)
1926-.......... CLC 2, 3, 6, 8, 13, 18,
34 (225)
See also CANR 10
See also CA 13-16R
See also DLB 5
See also DLB-Y 85

Merton, Thomas (James)
1915-1968...... CLC 1, 3, 11, 34 (460)
See also CANR 22
See also CA 5-8R
See also obituary CA 25-28R
See also DLB 48
See also DLB-Y 81

Merwin, W(illiam) S(tanley)
1927-..... CLC 1, 2, 3, 5, 8, 13, 18, 45
See also CANR 15
See also CA 13-16R
See also DLB 5

Metcalf, John 1938-...............CLC 37
See also CA 113
See also DLB 60

Mew, Charlotte (Mary)
1870-1928................... TCLC 8
See also CA 105
See also DLB 19

Mewshaw, Michael 1943-...........CLC 9
See also CANR 7
See also CA 53-56
See also DLB-Y 80

Meyer-Meyrink, Gustav 1868-1932
See Meyrink, Gustav
See also CA 117

Meyrink, Gustav 1868-1932...... TCLC 21
See also Meyer-Meyrink, Gustav

Meyers, Jeffrey 1939-........ CLC 39 (427)
See also CA 73-76

Meynell, Alice (Christiana Gertrude
Thompson) 1847-1922 .... TCLC 6
See also CA 104
See also DLB 19

Michaels, Leonard 1933- .... CLC 6, 25
See also CANR 21
See also CA 61-64

Michaux, Henri 1899-1984...... CLC 8, 19
See also CA 85-88
See also obituary CA 114

Michener, James A(lbert)
1907-................CLC 1, 5, 11, 29
See also CANR 21
See also CA 5-8R
See also DLB 6
See also AITN 1

Mickiewicz, Adam 1798-1855 ..... NCLC 3

Middleton, Christopher 1926-......CLC 13
See also CA 13-16R
See also DLB 40

Middleton, Stanley 1919- .... CLC 7, 38
See also CANR 21
See also CA 25-28R
See also DLB 14

Miguéis, José Rodrigues 1901- .....CLC 10

Mikszath, Kalman 1847-1910 .... TCLC 31

Miles, Josephine (Louise)
1911-1985......CLC 1, 2, 14, 34 (243),
39 (352)
See also CANR 2
See also CA 1-4R
See also obituary CA 116
See also DLB 48

Mill, John Stuart 1806-1873 ..... NCLC 11

Millar, Kenneth 1915-1983
See Macdonald, Ross
See also CANR 16
See also CA 9-12R
See also obituary CA 110
See also DLB 2
See also DLB-Y 83

Pratt, E(dwin) J(ohn)
　　1883-1964.....................CLC 19
　　See also obituary CA 93-96

Premchand 1880-1936..........TCLC 21

Preussler, Otfried 1923-...........CLC 17
　　See also CA 77-80
　　See also SATA 24

Prévert, Jacques (Henri Marie)
　　1900-1977....................CLC 15
　　See also CA 77-80
　　See also obituary CA 69-72
　　See also obituary SATA 30

Prévost, Abbé (Antoine Francois)
　　1697-1763.....................LC 1

Price, (Edward) Reynolds
　　1933-....... CLC 3, 6, 13, 43, 50 (228)
　　See also CANR 1
　　See also CA 1-4R
　　See also DLB 2

Price, Richard 1949-...........CLC 6, 12
　　See also CANR 3
　　See also CA 49-52
　　See also DLB-Y 81

Prichard, Katharine Susannah
　　1883-1969...................CLC 46
　　See also CAP 1
　　See also CA 11-12

Priestley, J(ohn) B(oynton)
　　1894-1984...... CLC 2, 5, 9, 34 (360)
　　See also CA 9-12R
　　See also obituary CA 113
　　See also DLB 10, 34
　　See also DLB-Y 84

Prince (Rogers Nelson) 1958?-......CLC 35

Prince, F(rank) T(empleton)
　　1912-.......................CLC 22
　　See also CA 101
　　See also DLB 20

Prior, Matthew 1664-1721...........LC 4

Pritchard, William H(arrison)
　　1932-................... CLC 34 (468)
　　See also CA 65-68

Pritchett, V(ictor) S(awdon)
　　1900-................CLC 5, 13, 15, 41
　　See also CA 61-64
　　See also DLB 15

Procaccino, Michael 1946-
　　See Cristofer, Michael

Prokosch, Frederic 1908-....... CLC 4, 48
　　See also CA 73-76
　　See also DLB 48

Prose, Francine 1947-.............CLC 45
　　See also CA 109, 112

Proust, Marcel 1871-1922 ..... TCLC 7, 13
　　See also CA 104, 120

Pryor, Richard 1940- ....CLC 26

P'u Sung-ling 1640-1715.............LC 3

Puig, Manuel 1932-.......CLC 3, 5, 10, 28
　　See also CANR 2
　　See also CA 45-48

Purdy, A(lfred) W(ellington)
　　1918-.......... CLC 3, 6, 14, 50 (234)
　　See also CA 81-84

Purdy, James (Amos)
　　1923-.................CLC 2, 4, 10, 28
　　See also CAAS 1
　　See also CANR 19
　　See also CA 33-36R
　　See also DLB 2

Pushkin, Alexander (Sergeyevich)
　　1799-1837...................NCLC 3

Puzo, Mario 1920-.........CLC 1, 2, 6, 36
　　See also CANR 4
　　See also CA 65-68
　　See also DLB 6

Pym, Barbara (Mary Crampton)
　　1913-1980............. CLC 13, 19, 37
　　See also CANR 13
　　See also CAP 1
　　See also CA 13-14
　　See also obituary CA 97-100
　　See also DLB 14

Pynchon, Thomas (Ruggles, Jr.)
　　1937-........CLC 2, 3, 6, 9, 11, 18, 33
　　See also CANR 22
　　See also CA 17-20R
　　See also DLB 2

Quasimodo, Salvatore
　　1901-1968...................CLC 10
　　See also CAP 1
　　See also CA 15-16
　　See also obituary CA 25-28R

Queen, Ellery 1905-1982 .... CLC 3, 11
　　See also Dannay, Frederic
　　See also Lee, Manfred B(ennington)

Queneau, Raymond
　　1903-1976...........CLC 2, 5, 10, 42
　　See also CA 77-80
　　See also obituary CA 69-72
　　See also DLB 72

Quin, Ann (Marie) 1936-1973 ......CLC 6
　　See also CA 9-12R
　　See also obituary CA 45-48
　　See also DLB 14

Quinn, Simon 1942-
　　See Smith, Martin Cruz

Quiroga, Horacio (Sylvestre)
　　1878-1937.................TCLC 20
　　See also CA 117

Quoirez, Françoise 1935-
　　See Sagan, Françoise
　　See also CANR 6
　　See also CA 49-52

Rabe, David (William)
　　1940-................... CLC 4, 8, 33
　　See also CA 85-88
　　See also DLB 7

Rabelais, François 1494?-1553 .... LC 5

Rabinovitch, Sholem 1859-1916
　　See Aleichem, Sholom
　　See also CA 104

Rachen, Kurt von 1911-1986
　　See Hubbard, L(afayette) Ron(ald)

Radcliffe, Ann (Ward)
　　1764-1823...................NCLC 6
　　See also DLB 39

Radiguet, Raymond
　　1903-1923..................TCLC 29

Radnóti, Miklós 1909-1944 ...... TCLC 16
　　See also CA 118

Rado, James 1939-
　　See Ragni, Gerome and
　　Rado, James
　　See also CA 105

Radomski, James 1932-
　　See Rado, James

Radvanyi, Netty Reiling 1900-1983
　　See Seghers, Anna
　　See also CA 85-88
　　See also obituary CA 110

Raeburn, John 1941-....... CLC 34 (477)
　　See also CA 57-60

Ragni, Gerome 1942-
　　See Ragni, Gerome and Rado, James
　　See also CA 105

Ragni, Gerome 1942- and
　　Rado, James 1939-...........CLC 17

Rahv, Philip 1908-1973 ....CLC 24
　　See also Greenberg, Ivan

Raine, Craig 1944- ....CLC 32
　　See also CA 108
　　See also DLB 40

Raine, Kathleen (Jessie)
　　1908-.................... CLC 7, 45
　　See also CA 85-88
　　See also DLB 20

Rainis, Janis 1865-1929 .... TCLC 29

Rakosi, Carl 1903-.................CLC 47
　　See also Rawley, Callman
　　See also CAAS 5

Rampersad, Arnold
　　19??- .... CLC 44 (506)

Rand, Ayn
　　1905-1982.........CLC 3, 30, 44 (447)
　　See also CA 13-16R
　　See also obituary CA 105

Randall, Dudley (Felker) 1914-......CLC 1
　　See also CA 25-28R
　　See also DLB 41

Ransom, John Crowe
　　1888-1974........ CLC 2, 4, 5, 11, 24
　　See also CANR 6
　　See also CA 5-8R
　　See also obituary CA 49-52
　　See also DLB 45, 63

Rao, Raja 1909-..................CLC 25
　　See also CA 73-76

Raphael, Frederic (Michael)
　　1931-..................... CLC 2, 14
　　See also CANR 1
　　See also CA 1-4R
　　See also DLB 14

Rathbone, Julian 1935-............CLC 41
　　See also CA 101

Rattigan, Terence (Mervyn)
　　1911-1977....................CLC 7
　　See also CA 85-88
　　See also obituary CA 73-76
　　See also DLB 13

Raven, Simon (Arthur Noel)
　　1927-.......................CLC 14
　　See also CA 81-84

Rawley, Callman 1903-
　　See Rakosi, Carl
　　See also CANR 12
　　See also CA 21-24R

Author Index

Author Index

Smith, Martin William 1942-
 See Smith, Martin Cruz

Smith, Mary-Ann Tirone
 1944-................... **CLC 39** (97)
 See also CA 118

Smith, Patti 1946-................**CLC 12**
 See also CA 93-96

Smith, Pauline (Urmson)
 1882-1959.................. **TCLC 25**
 See also CA 29-32R
 See also SATA 27

Smith, Sara Mahala Redway 1900-1972
 See Benson, Sally

Smith, Stevie
 1902-1971...... **CLC 3, 8, 25, 44** (431)
 See also Smith, Florence Margaret
 See also DLB 20

Smith, Wilbur (Addison) 1933-.....**CLC 33**
 See also CANR 7
 See also CA 13-16R

Smith, William Jay 1918-..........**CLC 6**
 See also CA 5-8R
 See also SATA 2
 See also DLB 5

Smollett, Tobias (George)
 1721-1771...................... **LC 2**
 See also DLB 39

Snodgrass, W(illiam) D(e Witt)
 1926-...............**CLC 2, 6, 10, 18**
 See also CANR 6
 See also CA 1-4R
 See also DLB 5

Snow, C(harles) P(ercy)
 1905-1980....... **CLC 1, 4, 6, 9, 13, 19**
 See also CA 5-8R
 See also obituary CA 101
 See also DLB 15

Snyder, Gary (Sherman)
 1930-.............. **CLC 1, 2, 5, 9, 32**
 See also CA 17-20R
 See also DLB 5, 16

Snyder, Zilpha Keatley 1927-......**CLC 17**
 See also CA 9-12R
 See also SAAS 2
 See also SATA 1, 28

Södergran, Edith 1892-1923 ..... **TCLC 31**

Sokolov, Raymond 1941-...........**CLC 7**
 See also CA 85-88

Sologub, Fyodor 1863-1927....... **TCLC 9**
 See also Teternikov, Fyodor Kuzmich

Solomos, Dionysios
 1798-1857................ **NCLC 15**

Solwoska, Mara 1929-
 See French, Marilyn

Solzhenitsyn, Aleksandr I(sayevich)
 1918-.....**CLC 1, 2, 4, 7, 9, 10, 18, 26,**
           34 (480)
 See also CA 69-72
 See also AITN 1

Somers, Jane 1919-
 See Lessing, Doris (May)

Sommer, Scott 1951-..............**CLC 25**
 See also CA 106

Sondheim, Stephen (Joshua)
 1930-.............. **CLC 30, 39** (172)
 See also CA 103

Sontag, Susan
 1933-............ **CLC 1, 2, 10, 13, 31**
 See also CA 17-20R
 See also DLB 2

Sophocles c. 496-c. 406 B.C. .....**CMLC 2**

Sorrentino, Gilbert
 1929-............ **CLC 3, 7, 14, 22, 40**
 See also CANR 14
 See also CA 77-80
 See also DLB 5
 See also DLB-Y 80

Soto, Gary 1952-.................**CLC 32**
 See also CA 119

Souster, (Holmes) Raymond
 1921-..................... **CLC 5, 14**
 See also CANR 13
 See also CA 13-16R

Southern, Terry 1926-.............**CLC 7**
 See also CANR 1
 See also CA 1-4R
 See also DLB 2

Southey, Robert 1774-1843 .... **NCLC 8**

Soyinka, Akinwande Oluwole 1934-
 See Soyinka, Wole

Soyinka, Wole
 1934-....... **CLC 3, 5, 14, 36, 44** (276)
 See also CA 13-16R
 See also DLB-Y 1986

Spackman, W(illiam) M(ode)
 1905-.....................**CLC 46**
 See also CA 81-84

Spacks, Barry 1931-..............**CLC 14**
 See also CA 29-32R

Spanidou, Irini 1946- .... **CLC 44** (104)

Spark, Muriel (Sarah)
 1918-........**CLC 2, 3, 5, 8, 13, 18, 40**
 See also CANR 12
 See also CA 5-8R
 See also DLB 15

Spencer, Elizabeth 1921-..........**CLC 22**
 See also CA 13-16R
 See also SATA 14
 See also DLB 6

Spencer, Scott 1945-..............**CLC 30**
 See also CA 113
 See also DLB-Y 86

Spender, Stephen (Harold)
 1909-.............. **CLC 1, 2, 5, 10, 41**
 See also CA 9-12R
 See also DLB 20

Spengler, Oswald 1880-1936 ..... **TCLC 25**
 See also CA 118

Spenser, Edmund 1552?-1599....... **LC 5**

Spicer, Jack 1925-1965......... **CLC 8, 18**
 See also CA 85-88
 See also DLB 5, 16

Spielberg, Peter 1929-.............**CLC 6**
 See also CANR 4
 See also CA 5-8R
 See also DLB-Y 81

Spielberg, Steven 1947-............**CLC 20**
 See also CA 77-80
 See also SATA 32

Spillane, Frank Morrison 1918-
 See Spillane, Mickey
 See also CA 25-28R

Spillane, Mickey 1918-......... **CLC 3, 13**
 See also Spillane, Frank Morrison

Spinoza, Benedictus de 1632-1677 .... **LC 9**

Spinrad, Norman (Richard)
 1940-......................**CLC 46**
 See also CANR 20
 See also CA 37-40R
 See also DLB 8

Spitteler, Carl (Friedrich Georg)
 1845-1924.................. **TCLC 12**
 See also CA 109

Spivack, Kathleen (Romola Drucker)
 1938-.......................**CLC 6**
 See also CA 49-52

Spoto, Donald 1941- .... **CLC 39** (444)
 See also CANR 11
 See also CA 65-68

Springsteen, Bruce 1949-..........**CLC 17**
 See also CA 111

Spurling, Hilary 1940- ...... **CLC 34** (494)
 See also CA 104

Squires, (James) Radcliffe
 1917-.......................**CLC 51**
 See also CANR 6, 21
 See also CA 1-4R

Staël-Holstein, Anne Louise Germaine
 Necker, Baronne de
 1766-1817................... **NCLC 3**

Stafford, Jean 1915-1979 ..... **CLC 4, 7, 19**
 See also CANR 3
 See also CA 1-4R
 See also obituary CA 85-88
 See also obituary SATA 22
 See also DLB 2

Stafford, William (Edgar)
 1914-................... **CLC 4, 7, 29**
 See also CAAS 3
 See also CANR 5, 22
 See also CA 5-8R
 See also DLB 5

Stannard, Martin 1947- ..... **CLC 44** (520)

Stanton, Maura 1946-..............**CLC 9**
 See also CANR 15
 See also CA 89-92

Stapledon, (William) Olaf
 1886-1950.................. **TCLC 22**
 See also CA 111
 See also DLB 15

Stark, Richard 1933-
 See Westlake, Donald E(dwin)

Stead, Christina (Ellen)
 1902-1983.........**CLC 2, 5, 8, 32**
 See also CA 13-16R
 See also obituary CA 109

Steele, Timothy (Reid) 1948-.......**CLC 45**
 See also CANR 16
 See also CA 93-96

Steffens, (Joseph) Lincoln
 1866-1936.................. **TCLC 20**
 See also CA 117
 See also SAAS 1

Stegner, Wallace (Earle)
 1909-...................... **CLC 9, 49**
 See also CANR 1, 21
 See also CA 1-4R
 See also DLB 9
 See also AITN 1

Author Index

Su Man-shu 1884-1918 . . . . TCLC 24

Sudermann, Hermann
      1857-1928 . . . . TCLC 15
   See also CA 107

Sue, Eugène 1804-1857 . . . . NCLC 1

Sukenick, Ronald
      1932- . . . . CLC 3, 4, 6, 48
   See also CA 25-28R
   See also DLB-Y 81

Suknaski, Andrew 1942- . . . . CLC 19
   See also CA 101
   See also DLB 53

Sully-Prudhomme, Rene
      1839-1907 . . . . TCLC 31

Summers, Andrew James 1942-
   See The Police

Summers, Andy 1942-
   See The Police

Summers, Hollis (Spurgeon, Jr.)
      1916- . . . . CLC 10
   See also CANR 3
   See also CA 5-8R
   See also DLB 6

Summers, (Alphonsus Joseph-Mary Augustus)
      Montague 1880-1948 . . . . TCLC 16

Sumner, Gordon Matthew 1951-
   See The Police

Surtees, Robert Smith
      1805-1864 . . . . NCLC 14
   See also DLB 21

Susann, Jacqueline 1921-1974 . . . . . . CLC 3
   See also CA 65-68
   See also obituary CA 53-56
   See also AITN 1

Süskind, Patrick 1949- . . . . . . CLC 44 (111)

Sutcliff, Rosemary 1920- . . . . CLC 26
   See also CLR 1
   See also CA 5-8R
   See also SATA 6, 44

Sutro, Alfred 1863-1933 . . . . TCLC 6
   See also CA 105
   See also DLB 10

Sutton, Henry 1935-
   See Slavitt, David (R.)

Svevo, Italo 1861-1928 . . . . TCLC 2
   See also Schmitz, Ettore

Swados, Elizabeth 1951- . . . . CLC 12
   See also CA 97-100

Swados, Harvey 1920-1972 . . . . CLC 5
   See also CANR 6
   See also CA 5-8R
   See also obituary CA 37-40R
   See also DLB 2

Swarthout, Glendon (Fred)
      1918- . . . . CLC 35
   See also CANR 1
   See also CA 1-4R
   See also SATA 26

Swenson, May 1919- . . . . CLC 4, 14
   See also CA 5-8R
   See also SATA 15
   See also DLB 5

Swift, Graham 1949- . . . . CLC 41
   See also CA 117

Swift, Jonathan 1667-1745 . . . . LC 1
   See also SATA 19
   See also DLB 39

Swinburne, Algernon Charles
      1837-1909 . . . . TCLC 8
   See also CA 105
   See also DLB 35, 57

Swinfen, Ann 19??- . . . . CLC 34 (576)

Swinnerton, Frank (Arthur)
      1884-1982 . . . . CLC 31
   See also obituary CA 108
   See also DLB 34

Symons, Arthur (William)
      1865-1945 . . . . TCLC 11
   See also CA 107
   See also DLB 19, 57

Symons, Julian (Gustave)
      1912- . . . . CLC 2, 14, 32
   See also CAAS 3
   See also CANR 3
   See also CA 49-52

Synge, (Edmund) John Millington
      1871-1909 . . . . TCLC 6
   See also CA 104
   See also DLB 10, 19

Syruc, J. 1911-
   See Miłosz, Czesław

Szirtes, George 1948- . . . . CLC 46
   See also CA 109

Tabori, George 1914- . . . . CLC 19
   See also CANR 4
   See also CA 49-52

Tagore, (Sir) Rabindranath
      1861-1941 . . . . TCLC 3
   See also Thakura, Ravindranatha

Taine, Hippolyte Adolphe
      1828-1893 . . . . NCLC 15

Talese, Gaetano 1932-
   See Talese, Gay

Talese, Gay 1932- . . . . CLC 37
   See also CANR 9
   See also CA 1-4R
   See also AITN 1

Tallent, Elizabeth (Ann) 1954- . . . . . CLC 45
   See also CA 117

Tally, Ted 1952- . . . . CLC 42
   See also CA 120

Tamayo y Baus, Manuel
      1829-1898 . . . . NCLC 1

Tammsaare, A(nton) H(ansen)
      1878-1940 . . . . TCLC 27

Tanizaki, Jun'ichirō
      1886-1965 . . . . CLC 8, 14, 28
   See also CA 93-96
   See also obituary CA 25-28R

Tarkington, (Newton) Booth
      1869-1946 . . . . TCLC 9
   See also CA 110
   See also SATA 17
   See also DLB 9

Tasso, Torquato 1544-1595 . . . . LC 5

Tate, (John Orley) Allen
      1899-1979 . . . . . . CLC 2, 4, 6, 9, 11, 14,
                                                          24
   See also CA 5-8R
   See also obituary CA 85-88
   See also DLB 4, 45, 63

Tate, James 1943- . . . . CLC 2, 6, 25
   See also CA 21-24R
   See also DLB 5

Tavel, Ronald 1940- . . . . CLC 6
   See also CA 21-24R

Taylor, C(ecil) P(hillip)
      1929-1981 . . . . CLC 27
   See also CA 25-28R
   See also obituary CA 105

Taylor, Eleanor Ross 1920- . . . . CLC 5
   See also CA 81-84

Taylor, Elizabeth
      1912-1975 . . . . CLC 2, 4, 29
   See also CANR 9
   See also CA 13-16R
   See also SATA 13

Taylor, Henry (Splawn)
      1917- . . . . CLC 44 (300)

Taylor, Kamala (Purnaiya) 1924-
   See Markandaya, Kamala
   See also CA 77-80

Taylor, Mildred D(elois) 1943- . . . . . CLC 21
   See also CLR 9
   See also CA 85-88
   See also SATA 15
   See also DLB 52

Taylor, Peter (Hillsman)
      1917- . . . . . . CLC 1, 4, 18, 37, 44 (304),
                                                          50 (250)
   See also CANR 9
   See also CA 13-16R
   See also DLB-Y 81

Taylor, Robert Lewis 1912- . . . . CLC 14
   See also CANR 3
   See also CA 1-4R
   See also SATA 10

Teasdale, Sara 1884-1933 . . . . TCLC 4
   See also CA 104
   See also DLB 45
   See also SATA 32

Tegnér, Esaias 1782-1846 . . . . NCLC 2

Teilhard de Chardin, (Marie Joseph) Pierre
      1881-1955 . . . . TCLC 9
   See also CA 105

Tennant, Emma 1937- . . . . CLC 13
   See also CANR 10
   See also CA 65-68
   See also DLB 14

Teran, Lisa St. Aubin de 19??- . . . . . CLC 36

Terkel, Louis 1912-
   See Terkel, Studs
   See also CANR 18
   See also CA 57-60

Terkel, Studs 1912- . . . . CLC 38
   See also Terkel, Louis
   See also AITN 1

Terry, Megan 1932- . . . . CLC 19
   See also CA 77-80
   See also DLB 7

Tesich, Steve 1943?- . . . . CLC 40
   See also CA 105
   See also DLB-Y 83

Tesich, Stoyan 1943?-
   See Tesich, Steve

Tertz, Abram 1925-
   See Sinyavsky, Andrei (Donatevich)

Author Index

Verlaine, Paul (Marie)
1844-1896.................... NCLC 2

Verne, Jules (Gabriel)
1828-1905.................... TCLC 6
See also CA 110
See also SATA 21

Very, Jones 1813-1880 .... NCLC 9
See also DLB 1

Vesaas, Tarjei 1897-1970......... CLC 48
See also obituary CA 29-32R

Vian, Boris 1920-1959 .... TCLC 9
See also CA 106
See also DLB 72

Viaud, (Louis Marie) Julien 1850-1923
See Loti, Pierre
See also CA 107

Vicker, Angus 1916-
See Felsen, Henry Gregor

Vidal, Eugene Luther, Jr. 1925-
See Vidal, Gore

Vidal, Gore
1925-........ CLC 2, 4, 6, 8, 10, 22, 33
See also CANR 13
See also CA 5-8R
See also DLB 6
See also AITN 1

Viereck, Peter (Robert Edwin)
1916-....................... CLC 4
See also CANR 1
See also CA 1-4R
See also DLB 5

Vigny, Alfred (Victor) de
1797-1863.................... NCLC 7

**Villiers de l'Isle Adam, Jean Marie Mathias
Philippe Auguste, Comte de,**
1838-1889.................... NCLC 3

Vine, Barbara 1930-........ CLC 50 (262)
See also Rendell, Ruth

Vinge, Joan (Carol) D(ennison)
1948-....................... CLC 30
See also CA 93-96
See also SATA 36

Visconti, Luchino 1906-1976....... CLC 16
See also CA 81-84
See also obituary CA 65-68

Vittorini, Elio 1908-1966 ..... CLC 6, 9, 14
See also obituary CA 25-28R

Vizinczey, Stephen 1933- .... CLC 40

Vliet, R(ussell) G(ordon)
1929-1984.................... CLC 22
See also CANR 18
See also CA 37-40R
See also obituary CA 112

Voigt, Cynthia 1942-............. CLC 30
See also CANR 18
See also CA 106
See also SATA 33, 48

Voinovich, Vladimir (Nikolaevich)
1932-.................... CLC 10, 49
See also CA 81-84

Von Daeniken, Erich 1935-
See Von Däniken, Erich
See also CANR 17
See also CA 37-40R
See also AITN 1

Von Däniken, Erich 1935-.........CLC 30
See also Von Daeniken, Erich

Vonnegut, Kurt, Jr.
1922-......CLC 1, 2, 3, 4, 5, 8, 12, 22,
40
See also CANR 1
See also CA 1-4R
See also DLB 2, 8
See also DLB-Y 80
See also DLB-DS 3
See also AITN 1

Vorster, Gordon 1924- ...... CLC 34 (121)

Voznesensky, Andrei 1933- ..... CLC 1, 15
See also CA 89-92

Waddington, Miriam 1917-....... CLC 28
See also CANR 12
See also CA 21-24R

Wagman, Fredrica 1937-...........CLC 7
See also CA 97-100

Wagner, Richard 1813-1883 ...... NCLC 9

Wagner-Martin, Linda
1936-.................. CLC 50 (439)

Wagoner, David (Russell)
1926-.................. CLC 3, 5, 15
See also CAAS 3
See also CANR 2
See also CA 1-4R
See also SATA 14
See also DLB 5

Wah, Fred(erick James)
1939-.................. CLC 44 (323)
See also CA 107
See also DLB 60

Wahlöö, Per 1926-1975 ....CLC 7
See also CA 61-64

Wahlöö, Peter 1926-1975
See Wahlöö, Per

Wain, John (Barrington)
1925-................CLC 2, 11, 15, 46
See also CAAS 4
See also CA 5-8R
See also DLB 15, 27

Wajda, Andrzej 1926-.............CLC 16
See also CA 102

Wakefield, Dan 1932-.............CLC 7
See also CAAS 7
See also CA 21-24R

Wakoski, Diane
1937-........... CLC 2, 4, 7, 9, 11, 40
See also CAAS 1
See also CANR 9
See also CA 13-16R
See also DLB 5

Walcott, Derek (Alton)
1930-.......... CLC 2, 4, 9, 14, 25, 42
See also CA 89-92
See also DLB-Y 81

Waldman, Anne 1945- ....CLC 7
See also CA 37-40R
See also DLB 16

Waldo, Edward Hamilton 1918-
See Sturgeon, Theodore (Hamilton)

Walker, Alice
1944-.......... CLC 5, 6, 9, 19, 27, 46
See also CANR 9
See also CA 37-40R
See also SATA 31
See also DLB 6, 33

Walker, David Harry 1911-........CLC 14
See also CANR 1
See also CA 1-4R
See also SATA 8

Walker, Edward Joseph 1934-
See Walker, Ted
See also CANR 12
See also CA 21-24R

Walker, George F. 1947- .... CLC 44 (329)
See also CANR 21
See also CA 103
See also DLB 60

Walker, Joseph A. 1935- ....CLC 19
See also CA 89-92
See also DLB 38

Walker, Margaret (Abigail)
1915-...................... CLC 1, 6
See also CA 73-76

Walker, Ted 1934-................CLC 13
See also Walker, Edward Joseph
See also DLB 40

Wallace, David Foster
1962-.................. CLC 50 (92)

Wallace, Irving 1916- .... CLC 7, 13
See also CAAS 1
See also CANR 1
See also CA 1-4R
See also AITN 1

Wallant, Edward Lewis
1926-1962................. CLC 5, 10
See also CANR 22
See also CA 1-4R
See also DLB 2, 28

Walpole, Horace 1717-1797......... LC 2
See also DLB 39

Walpole, (Sir) Hugh (Seymour)
1884-1941.................... TCLC 5
See also CA 104
See also DLB 34

Walser, Martin 1927-............. CLC 27
See also CANR 8
See also CA 57-60

Walser, Robert 1878-1956....... TCLC 18
See also CA 118

Walsh, Gillian Paton 1939-
See Walsh, Jill Paton
See also CA 37-40R
See also SATA 4

Walsh, Jill Paton 1939-............CLC 35
See also CLR 2
See also SAAS 3

Wambaugh, Joseph (Aloysius, Jr.)
1937-..................... CLC 3, 18
See also CA 33-36R
See also DLB 6
See also DLB-Y 83
See also AITN 1

Ward, Arthur Henry Sarsfield 1883-1959
See Rohmer, Sax
See also CA 108

Ward, Douglas Turner 1930-.......CLC 19
See also CA 81-84
See also DLB 7, 38

Warhol, Andy 1928-1987.........CLC 20
See also CA 89-92
See also obituary CA 121

Wesley, Richard (Errol) 1945-.......CLC 7
See also CA 57-60
See also DLB 38

Wessel, Johan Herman
1742-1785......................LC 7

West, Anthony (Panther)
1914-1987............ CLC 50 (359)
See also CANR 3, 19
See also CA 45-48
See also DLB 15

West, Jessamyn 1907-1984...... CLC 7, 17
See also CA 9-12R
See also obituary CA 112
See also obituary SATA 37
See also DLB 6
See also DLB-Y 84

West, Morris L(anglo)
1916-...................... CLC 6, 33
See also CA 5-8R

West, Nathanael
1903?-1940............... TCLC 1, 14
See Weinstein, Nathan Wallenstein
See also DLB 4, 9, 28

West, Paul 1930-.............. CLC 7, 14
See also CAAS 7
See also CANR 22
See also CA 13-16R
See also DLB 14

West, Rebecca
1892-1983...... CLC 7, 9, 31, 50 (393)
See also CA 5-8R
See also obituary CA 109
See also DLB 36
See also DLB-Y 83

Westall, Robert (Atkinson)
1929-...........................CLC 17
See also CANR 18
See also CA 69-72
See also SAAS 2
See also SATA 23

Westlake, Donald E(dwin)
1933-...................... CLC 7, 33
See also CANR 16
See also CA 17-20R

Westmacott, Mary 1890-1976
See Christie, (Dame) Agatha (Mary Clarissa)

Whalen, Philip 1923-.......... CLC 6, 29
See also CANR 5
See also CA 9-12R
See also DLB 16

Wharton, Edith (Newbold Jones)
1862-1937.............TCLC 3, 9, 27
See also CA 104
See also DLB 4, 9, 12
See also CDALB 1865-1917

Wharton, William 1925-....... CLC 18, 37
See also CA 93-96
See also DLB-Y 80

Wheatley (Peters), Phillis
1753?-1784.....................LC 3
See also DLB 31, 50
See also CDALB 1640-1865

Wheelock, John Hall
1886-1978....................CLC 14
See also CANR 14
See also CA 13-16R
See also obituary CA 77-80
See also DLB 45

Whelan, John 1900-
See O'Faoláin, Seán

Whitaker, Rodney 1925-
See Trevanian

White, E(lwyn) B(rooks)
1899-1985......... CLC 10, 34 (425), 39 (369)
See also CLR 1
See also CANR 16
See also CA 13-16R
See also obituary CA 116
See also SATA 2, 29
See also obituary SATA 44
See also DLB 11, 22
See also AITN 2

White, Edmund III 1940-.........CLC 27
See also CANR 3, 19
See also CA 45-48

White, Patrick (Victor Martindale)
1912-........... CLC 3, 4, 5, 7, 9, 18
See also CA 81-84

White, T(erence) H(anbury)
1906-1964...................CLC 30
See also CA 73-76
See also SATA 12

White, Terence de Vere 1912-......CLC 49
See also CANR 3
See also CA 49-52

White, Walter (Francis)
1893-1955................. TCLC 15
See also CA 115
See also DLB 51

White, William Hale 1831-1913
See Rutherford, Mark

Whitehead, E(dward) A(nthony)
1933-.........................CLC 5
See also CA 65-68

Whitemore, Hugh 1936-..........CLC 37

Whitman, Sarah Helen
1803-1878................. NCLC 19
See also DLB 1

Whitman, Walt 1819-1892....... NCLC 4
See also SATA 20
See also DLB 3, 64
See also CDALB 1640-1865

Whitney, Phyllis A(yame)
1903-.........................CLC 42
See also CANR 3
See also CA 1-4R
See also SATA 1, 30
See also AITN 2

Whittemore, (Edward) Reed (Jr.)
1919-..........................CLC 4
See also CANR 4
See also CA 9-12R
See also DLB 5

Whittier, John Greenleaf
1807-1892................... NCLC 8
See also DLB 1
See also CDALB 1640-1865

Wicker, Thomas Grey 1926-
See Wicker, Tom
See also CANR 21
See also CA 65-68

Wicker, Tom 1926-...............CLC 7
See also Wicker, Thomas Grey

Wideman, John Edgar
1941-.............CLC 5, 34 (297), 36
See also CANR 14
See also CA 85-88
See also DLB 33

Wiebe, Rudy (H.) 1934-..... CLC 6, 11, 14
See also CA 37-40R
See also DLB 60

Wieland, Christoph Martin
1733-1813.................... NCLC 17

Wieners, John 1934-...............CLC 7
See also CA 13-16R
See also DLB 16

Wiesel, Elie(zer)
1928-................CLC 3, 5, 11, 37
See also CAAS 4
See also CANR 8
See also CA 5-8R
See also DLB-Y 1986
See also AITN 1

Wight, James Alfred 1916-
See Herriot, James
See also CA 77-80
See also SATA 44

Wilbur, Richard (Purdy)
1921-.................CLC 3, 6, 9, 14
See also CANR 2
See also CA 1-4R
See also CABS 2
See also SATA 9
See also DLB 5

Wild, Peter 1940-.................CLC 14
See also CA 37-40R
See also DLB 5

Wilde, Oscar (Fingal O'Flahertie Wills)
1854-1900.............TCLC 1, 8, 23
See also CA 104
See also SATA 24
See also DLB 10, 19, 34, 57

Wilder, Billy 1906- ....CLC 20
See also Wilder, Samuel
See also DLB 26

Wilder, Samuel 1906-
See Wilder, Billy
See also CA 89-92

Wilder, Thornton (Niven)
1897-1975....CLC 1, 5, 6, 10, 15, 35
See also CA 13-16R
See also obituary CA 61-64
See also DLB 4, 7, 9
See also AITN 2

Wiley, Richard 1944- .... CLC 44 (118)
See also CA 121

Wilhelm, Kate 1928-...............CLC 7
See also CAAS 5
See also CANR 17
See also CA 37-40R
See also DLB 8

Willard, Nancy 1936- .... CLC 7, 37
See also CLR 5
See also CANR 10
See also CA 89-92
See also SATA 30, 37
See also DLB 5, 52

Williams, C(harles) K(enneth)
1936-........................CLC 33
See also CA 37-40R
See also DLB 5

Author Index

TCLC Cumulative Nationality Index

Nationality Index

TCLC Cumulative Title Index

Title Index

Title Index

Title Index

Title Index

Title Index

Title Index

Title Index

Title Index

Title Index

Title Index

Title Index

Title Index

Title Index

Title Index

Title Index

Title Index

Title Index

Title Index

Title Index

Title Index

Title Index

Title Index

Title Index

Title Index

The Princess Casamassima 2:255, 269-70; 11:325, 327-29, 336-38, 342; 24:343
The Princess Far-Away
  See *La princesse lointaine*
Princess Ida; or, Castle Adamant: A Respectable Operatic Per-version of Tennyson's "Princess" 3:214, 216-17
The Princess Maleine (La princesse Maleine) 3:319
"Princess Mymra"
  See "Tsarevna Mymra"
The Princess Nobody 16:264
"A Princess of Egypt" 7:448
"The Princess of Kingdom Gone" 5:175
A Princess of Mars 2:77, 80
"The Princess of the Golden Isles" 8:346
"The Princess of the Sun" 8:346
Princess Russalka
  See *Fürstin Russalka*
The Princess Who Liked Cherry Pie 14:459
The Princess Zoubaroff 1:227
La princesse lointaine (The Princess Far-Away) 6:372-78, 380
La princesse Maleine (The Princess Maleine) 3:317, 319, 325
La princesse Phénissa 17:130-31
"Los principios de moral" 15:292
The Principles of Nationalities 16:461
The Principles of Psychology 15:139, 142, 178-80, 183-86, 188, 190, 192
"Prinkin' Leddie" 8:521
"Printemps et cinématographe mêlés" 6:198-99
"Printemps: Journal d'un convalescent" 21:456
"Prishchepa" 2:27; 13:21
Le prisme 31:306
"A Prisoner" 3:9
"Prisoner and Death"
  See "Gefangener und Tod"
Prisoner in Fairyland: The Book That "Uncle Paul" Wrote 5:70-1
Prisoner of Grace 1:140, 147-48; 29:68-9, 73, 76-8, 92, 96-9, 107, 109
"Prisoner of the Sands" 2:516
"A Prisoner Shakes Hands with Death"
  See "Gefangener reicht dem Tod die Hand"
Prisoners
  See *Rabock*
"The Prisoners of the Pitcher-Plant" 8:323
The Prisoners' Poems
  See *Gedichte der Gefangenen*
"The Prisoners' Songs"
  See "Lieder der Gefagenen"
La prisonnière 7:549
"A Private" 10:463
"Private Eye" 10:276
"A Private History of a Campaign That Failed" 6:466; 19:385-86
"Private Jones" 3:285, 288
Private Lives of Chinese Scholars
  See *Ju lin Wai Shih*
The Private Papers of Henry Ryecroft 3:224-26, 230, 232-33, 236-37; 24:218, 222, 226-27, 230, 249
Private Theatricals 7:383; 17:189
Private View 4:81
The Privateer 14:450, 460
"The Private's Story" 11:166
"Pro aris" 23:255

Pro aris et focis 6:154
Pro domo et mundo 5:291
"Pro domo suo" 10:81
"Pro eto" 18:257-58
"Pro patria" 25:145
"Pro rege nostro" 8:106
"The Problem of Cell Thirteen" 19:91-3, 95-7
The Problem of Cell Thirteen
  See *The Thinking Machine*
"A Problem of Life" 7:103
The Problem of Style 16:347, 348, 351, 355, 358
"The Problem of the Stolen Rubens" 19:96
"Probleme der Lyrik" (Problems of Lyrical Poetry) 3:105, 114
Probleme der Lyrik 3:111
Le problème du style 17:126-27, 130, 138, 142-43, 148, 150, 155
"Problems of Lyrical Poetry"
  See "Probleme der Lyrik"
The Process of Real Freedom 29:65
Processions 9:90-1
Le procuateur de Judée (The Procurator of Judea) 9:47-8, 52-4
"The Procurator of Judea"
  See *Le procurateur de Judée*
The Prodigal Parents 4:251; 13:350; 23:136
"The Prodigal Son" 19:220
"Proditoriamente" 2:541
"Proem" (Crane) 5:187-88
"Proem" (József) 22:160
"The Professional Instinct" 7:343
The Professor
  See *Professoren*
"The Professor and the Mermaid" 13:293, 295
Professor Bernhardi 4:387-88, 390, 397-98, 401
Professor Unrat (The Blue Angel; Small Town Tyrant) 9:322-25, 327, 329, 331
Professoren (The Professor) 5:279
The Professor's House 1:153-54, 156-58, 163; 11:95, 97-9, 102, 107, 109, 111; 31:26-7, 48-9, 54
"The Professor's Sister" 25:249
"Profit" 14:409
"Profit from My Experience" 17:458
"Progress" 19:104, 116, 129, 135
Progress 19:104, 119
"The Progress of the Gold Coast Native" 24:132
"The Progressive" 25:454
Lo prohibido (Forbidden Fruit) 27:250, 252, 257, 285
La proie et l'ombre 19:331, 338-43, 345
Proiskhozhdenie mastera (The Origin of a Master; Origins of a Master Craftsman) 14:409, 423
"Prolog"
  See "Gasnut rozovye kraski"
"Prolog for a Monument to Goldoni" 7:309
"Prologue" 8:110
A Prologue to "King Lear," Marshall, and The Violet
  See *Szinház: Elójáték Lear Királyhoz, Marshall, Az ibolya*
Prologues and Addresses-of-Mourning 11:294
"Prologues to What Is Possible" 3:450

Promenades littéraires 17:127, 130, 136, 138, 145-46, 148-50, 158
Promenades philosophiques 17:127, 130, 136
"La promesse du merle" 19:58-9
Le Prométhée mal enchaîné (Prometheus Illbound; Prometheus Misbound) 5:215, 235; 12:171-72, 178
Prometheus (Pramithas) 23:48, 50-2
Prometheus and Epimetheus
  See *Prometheus und Epimetheus*
Prometheus der Dulder 12:340, 349-50
Prometheus Illbound
  See *Le Prométhée mal enchaîné*
Prometheus Misbound
  See *Le Promfhée mal enchaîné*
Prometheus the Firegiver 1:124, 130, 132
Prometheus und Epimetheus (Prometheus and Epimetheus) 12:335-39, 342, 347-50, 352
Promethidenlos 4:205
"Promise" 3:6
"Promise and Fulfillment" 12:106
The Promise of Air 5:72
"The Promised Land" 11:210, 212, 214
The Promised Land
  See *Ziemia obiecana*
"The Promisers" 5:374
"Un pronóstico cumplido" 29:262
"Proof of the Pudding" 19:183
"Proofs of Holy Writ" 8:205
"Prophet" 21:254
The Prophet (Asch)
  See *Ha-navi*
The Prophet (Gibran) 1:325-29; 9:82-7, 89-94
"The Prophet and the Country" 8:202
"The Prophet Lost in the Hills at Evening" 18:41
The Prophet of the Russian Revolution 29:231
The Prophet Unarmed 22:376
"Propheta gentium" 19:243
"Prophets, Ancient and Modern" 7:359
"Die Prophezeiung an Alexander" 8:478
La propia estimación 3:94
"A propos de la campagne 'antisuperstitues'" 19:342, 346
Propos d'exil 11:353
"Propos sans suite" 19:340, 345
"Prosa fetida" 20:83
Prosa II 11:308
Prosas profanas, and Other Poems
  See *Prosas profanas, y otros poemas*
Prosas profanas, y otros poemas (Prosas profanos, and Other Poems) 4:57-63, 65
The Prose of Christopher Brennan 17:46
The Prose of Osip Mandelstam: The Noise of Time. Theodosia. The Egyptian Stamp 6:259
The Prose of Rupert Brooke 7:126
"Prosëlki" 23:211
Proserpina 20:312-15
Proses moroses 17:127
"The Prospector" 15:404
The Prospector 31:106-11, 114, 116
"The Protected"
  See "Pokrovennaia"
Protée 10:123, 127
"A Protegee of Jack Hamlin's" 25:203
Protesilaj umeršij 10:84

Title Index

Title Index

Title Index

Title Index

Title Index

Title Index

Title Index

Title Index

Title Index

Title Index

Title Index